Grade 1, Unit 3

Changes

PEARSON
Scott Foresman

scottforesman.com

Editorial Offices: Glenview, Illinois • Parsippany, New Jersey • New York, New York
Sales Offices: Boston, Massachusetts • Duluth, Georgia • Glenview, Illinois
Coppell, Texas • Sacramento, California • Mesa, Arizona

We dedicate Reading Street to
Peter Jovanovich.

His wisdom, courage,
and passion for education
are an inspiration to us all.

Cover Daniel Moreton

About the Cover Artist
Daniel Moreton lives in New York City, where he uses his computer to create illustrations for books. When he is not working, Daniel enjoys cooking, watching movies, and traveling. On a trip to Mexico, Daniel was inspired by all the bright colors around him. He likes to use those colors in his art.

ISBN-13: 978-0-328-24364-8

ISBN-10: 0-328-24364-7

8 9 10 V064 14 13 12 11 10 09

CC: N1

Reading STREET

Where the Love of Reading Begins

Reading Street Program Authors

Peter Afflerbach, Ph.D.
Professor, Department of Curriculum and Instruction
University of Maryland at College Park

Camille L.Z. Blachowicz, Ph.D.
Professor of Education
National-Louis University

Candy Dawson Boyd, Ph.D.
Professor, School of Education
Saint Mary's College of California

Wendy Cheyney, Ed.D.
Professor of Special Education and Literacy, Florida International University

Connie Juel, Ph.D.
Professor of Education, School of Education, Stanford University

Edward J. Kame'enui, Ph.D.
Professor and Director, Institute for the Development of Educational Achievement, University of Oregon

Donald J. Leu, Ph.D.
John and Maria Neag Endowed Chair in Literacy and Technology
University of Connecticut

Jeanne R. Paratore, Ed.D.
Associate Professor of Education
Department of Literacy and Language Development
Boston University

P. David Pearson, Ph.D.
Professor and Dean,
Graduate School of Education
University of California, Berkeley

Sam L. Sebesta, Ed.D.
Professor Emeritus,
College of Education,
University of Washington, Seattle

Deborah Simmons, Ph.D.
Professor, College of Education and Human Development
Texas A&M University
(Not pictured)

Sharon Vaughn, Ph.D.
H.E. Hartfelder/Southland Corporation Regents Professor
University of Texas

Susan Watts-Taffe, Ph.D.
Independent Literacy Researcher
Cincinnati, Ohio

Karen Kring Wixson, Ph.D.
Professor of Education
University of Michigan

Components

Student Editions (1–6)

Teacher's Editions (PreK–6)

Assessment
Assessment Handbook (K–6)
Baseline Group Tests (K–6)
DIBELS™ Assessments (K–6)
ExamView® Test Generator CD-ROM (2–6)
Fresh Reads for Differentiated Test Practice (1–6)
Online Success Tracker™ (K–6)*
Selection Tests Teacher's Manual (1–6)
Unit and End-of-Year Benchmark Tests (K–6)

Leveled Readers
Concept Literacy Leveled Readers (K–1)
Independent Leveled Readers (K)
Kindergarten Student Readers (K)
Leveled Reader Teaching Guides (K–6)
Leveled Readers (1–6)
Listen to Me Readers (K)
Online Leveled Reader Database (K–6)*
Take-Home Leveled Readers (K–6)

Trade Books and Big Books
Big Books (PreK–2)
Read Aloud Trade Books (PreK–K)
Sing with Me Big Book (1–2)
Trade Book Library (1–6)

Decodable Readers
Decodable Readers (K–3)
Strategic Intervention Decodable Readers (1–2)
Take-Home Decodable Readers (K–3)

Phonics and Word Study
Alphabet Cards in English and Spanish (PreK–K)
Alphabet Chart in English and Spanish (PreK–K)
Animal ABCs Activity Guide (K)
Finger Tracing Cards (PreK–K)
Patterns Book (PreK–K)
Phonics Activities CD-ROM (PreK–2)*
Phonics Activities Mats (K)
Phonics and Spelling Practice Book (1–3)
Phonics and Word-Building Board and Letters (PreK–3)
Phonics Songs and Rhymes Audio CD (K–2)
Phonics Songs and Rhymes Flip Chart (K–2)
Picture Word Cards (PreK–K)
Plastic Letter Tiles (K)
Sound-Spelling Cards and Wall Charts (1–2)
Strategies for Word Analysis (4–6)
Word Study and Spelling Practice Book (4–6)

Language Arts
Daily Fix-It Transparencies (K–6)
Grammar & Writing Book and Teacher's Annotated Edition, The (1–6)
Grammar and Writing Practice Book and Teacher's Manual (1–6)
Grammar Transparencies (1–6)
Six-Trait Writing Posters (1–6)
Writing Kit (1–6)
Writing Rubrics and Anchor Papers (1–6)
Writing Transparencies (1–6)

Practice and Additional Resources
AlphaBuddy Bear Puppet (K)
Alphasaurus Annie Puppet (PreK)
Amazing Words Posters (K–2)
Centers Survival Kit (PreK–6)
Graphic Organizer Book (2–6)
Graphic Organizer Flip Chart (K–1)
High-Frequency Word Cards (K)
Kindergarten Review (1)
Practice Book and Teacher's Manual (K–6)
Read Aloud Anthology (PreK–2)
Readers' Theater Anthology (K–6)
Research into Practice (K–6)
Retelling Cards (K–6)
Scott Foresman Research Base (K–6)
Skill Transparencies (2–6)
Songs and Rhymes Flip Chart (PreK)
Talk with Me, Sing with Me Chart (PreK–K)
Tested Vocabulary Cards (1–6)
Vocabulary Transparencies (1–2)
Welcome to Reading Street (PreK–1)

ELL
ELL and Transition Handbook (PreK–6)
ELL Comprehensive Kit (1–6)
ELL Posters (K–6)
ELL Readers (1–6)
ELL Teaching Guides (1–6)
Ten Important Sentences (1–6)

Digital Components
AudioText CDs (PreK–6)
Background Building Audio CDs (3–6)
ExamView® Test Generator CD-ROM (2–6)
Online Lesson Planner (K–6)
Online New Literacies Activities (1–6)*
Online Professional Development (1–6)
Online Story Sort (K–6)*
Online Student Editions (1–6)*
Online Success Tracker™ (K–6)*
Online Teacher's Editions (PreK–6)
Phonics Activities CD-ROM (PreK–2)*
Phonics Songs and Rhymes Audio CD (K–2)
Sing with Me/Background Building Audio CDs (PreK–2)
Songs and Rhymes Audio CD (PreK)

My Sidewalks Early Reading Intervention (K)

My Sidewalks Intensive Reading Intervention (Levels A–E)

Reading Street for the Guided Reading Teacher (1–6)

* 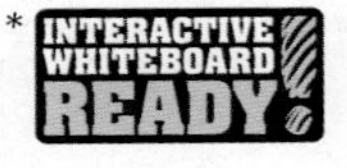

Grade 1

Priority Skills

Priority skills are the critical elements of reading—phonemic awareness, phonics, fluency, vocabulary, and text comprehension—as they are developed across and within grades to assure that instructional emphasis is placed on the right skills at the right time and to maintain a systematic sequence of skill instruction.

Key
● = Taught/Unit priority
◑ = Reviewed and practiced
❍ = Integrated practice

	Kindergarten Review	UNIT 1 Weeks 1–3	UNIT 1 Weeks 4–6
Phonemic Awareness			
Recognize and produce rhyming words	●		
Count words in sentences	●		
Segment, blend, or count syllables	●		●
Segment and blend onset and rime	●		
Identify sounds that are the same or different	●		
Identify and isolate initial, final, and medial sounds in spoken words	●	●	◑
Blend sounds orally to make words or syllables	●	●	●
Segment a word or syllable into sounds	●	●	●
Add, delete, or substitute phonemes		●	●
Phonics			
Know letter-sound relationships	●	●	●
Blend sounds of letters to decode			
Consonants		●	◑
Consonant blends and digraphs			●
Short Vowels		●	●
Long Vowels			
r-Controlled Vowels			
Vowel Digraphs			
Diphthongs			
Other vowel patterns			
Phonograms/word families			
Decode words with common word parts			
Base words and inflected endings		●	●
Contractions			
Compounds			
Suffixes and prefixes			
Blend syllables to decode words			
Fluency			
Read aloud with accuracy, comprehension, and appropriate rate		●	●
Read aloud with expression			
Attend to punctuation and use appropriate phrasing			●
Practice fluency in a variety of ways, including choral reading, paired reading, and repeated oral reading		●	●
Work toward appropriate fluency goals			

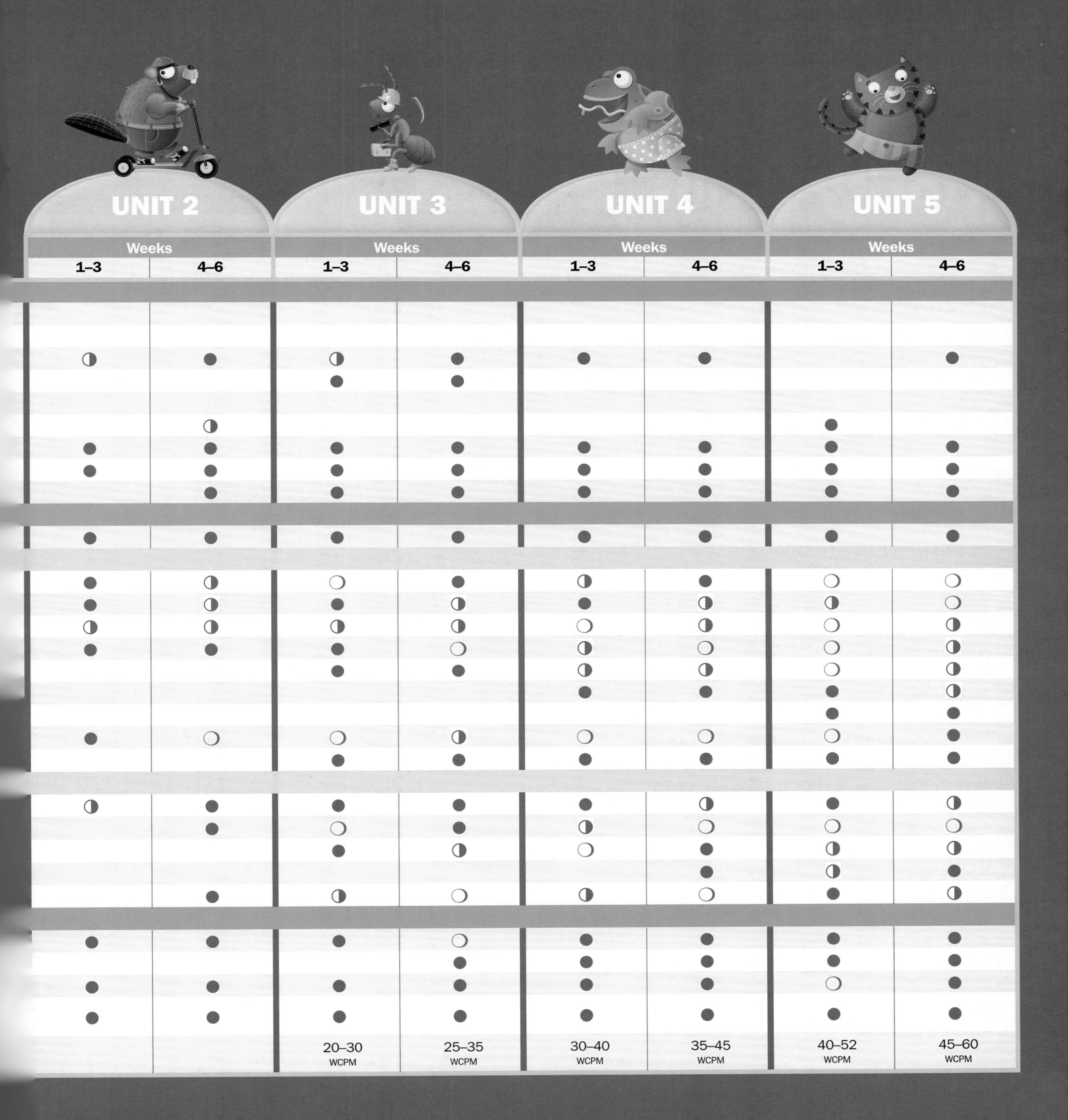

UNIT 2		UNIT 3		UNIT 4		UNIT 5	
Weeks		Weeks		Weeks		Weeks	
1–3	4–6	1–3	4–6	1–3	4–6	1–3	4–6
◑	●	◑	●	●	●		●
		●	●				
	◑					●	
●	●	●	●	●	●	●	●
●	●	●	●	●	●	●	●
	●	●	●	●	●	●	●
●	●	●	●	●	●	●	●
●	◑	○	●	◑	●	○	○
●	◑	●	◑	●	◑	◑	○
◑	◑	◑	◑	○	◑	○	◑
●	●	●	○	◑	○	○	◑
		●	●	◑	◑	○	◑
				●	●	●	◑
						●	●
●	○	○	◑	○	○	○	●
		●	●	●	●	●	●
◑	●	●	●	●	◑	●	◑
	●	○	●	◑	○	○	○
		●	◑	○	●	◑	◑
					●	◑	●
	●	◑	○	◑	○	●	◑
●	●	●	○	●	●	●	●
			●	●	●	●	●
●	●	●	●	●	●	○	●
●	●	●	●	●	●	●	●
		20–30 WCPM	25–35 WCPM	30–40 WCPM	35–45 WCPM	40–52 WCPM	45–60 WCPM

Grade 1
Priority Skills

Key
● = Taught/Unit priority
◑ = Reviewed and practiced
○ = Integrated practice

	Kindergarten Review	UNIT 1 Weeks 1–3	UNIT 1 Weeks 4–6
Vocabulary			
Read regular and irregular high-frequency words automatically		●	●
Develop vocabulary through direct instruction, concrete experiences, reading, and listening to text read aloud		●	●
Use word structure to figure out word meaning			
Use context clues to determine word meaning of unfamiliar words, multiple-meaning words, homonyms, homographs		●	○
Use grade-appropriate reference sources to learn word meanings			
Use new words in a variety of contexts		○	○
Use graphic organizers to group, study, and retain vocabulary		●	●
Classify and categorize words			●
Text Comprehension			
Strategies			
Preview the text		○	○
Set and monitor purpose for reading			
Activate and use prior knowledge		○	○
Make and confirm predictions			
Monitor comprehension and use fix-up strategies		●	●
Use graphic organizers to focus on text structure, to represent relationships in text, or to summarize text		○	○
Answer questions		○	○
Generate questions			●
Recognize story structure			●
Summarize text by retelling stories or identifying main ideas		●	○
Visualize; use mental imagery		●	○
Make connections: text to self, text to text, text to world		○	○
Skills			
Author's purpose			
Cause and effect			●
Compare and contrast			
Draw conclusions			◑
Main idea and supporting details			●
Realism/fantasy		●	●
Sequence of events		◑	○
Literary Elements			
Character		●	◑
Plot and plot structure			
Setting		●	◑
Theme			

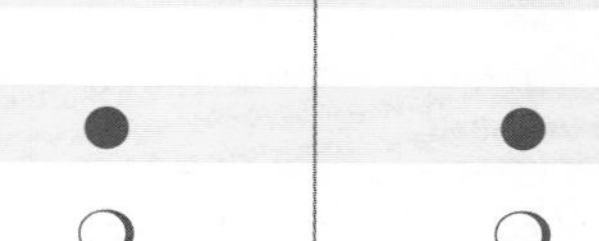

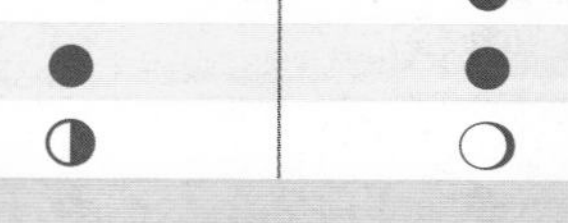

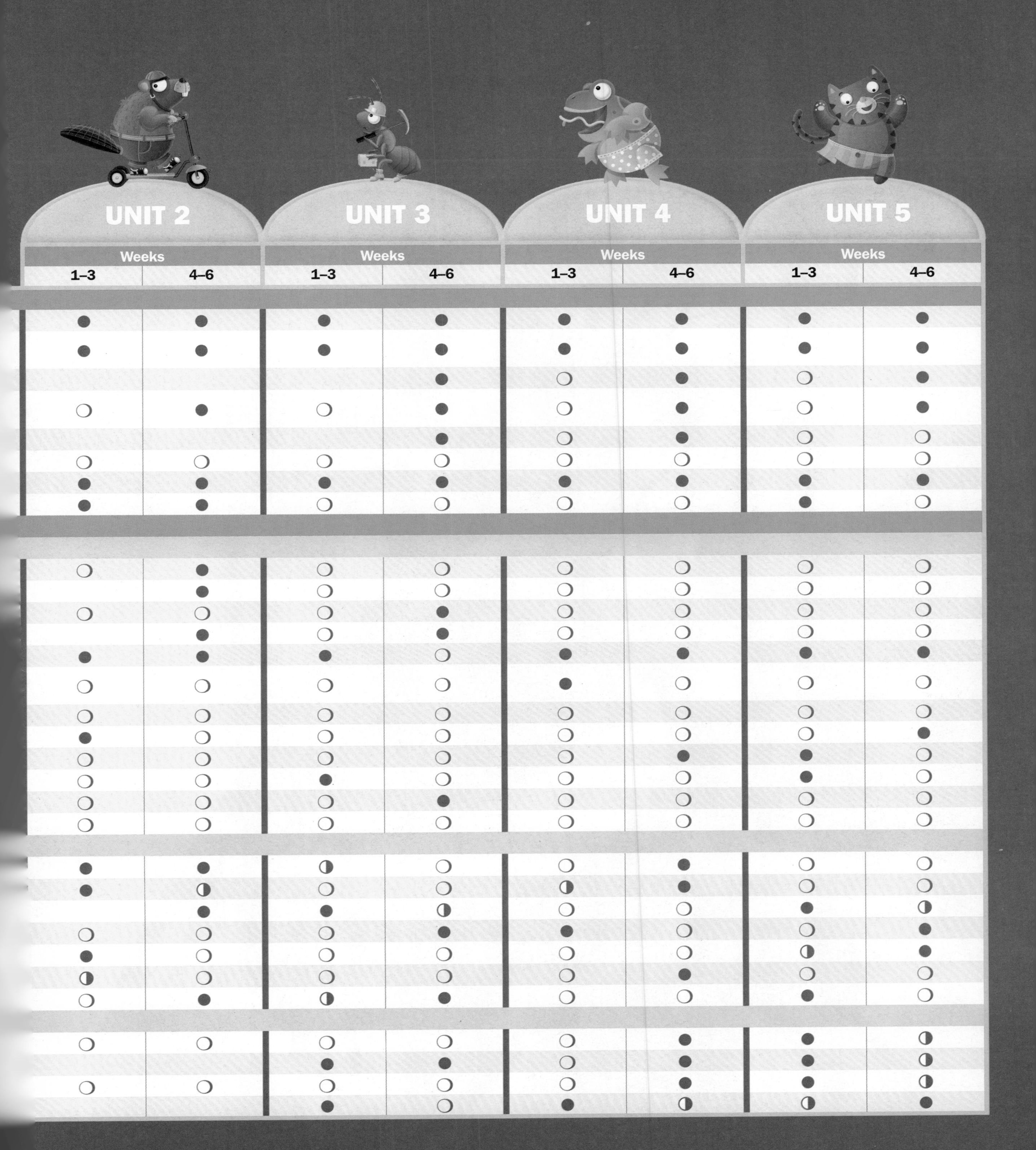

UNIT 2		UNIT 3		UNIT 4		UNIT 5	
Weeks		Weeks		Weeks		Weeks	
1–3	4–6	1–3	4–6	1–3	4–6	1–3	4–6
●	●	●	●	●	●	●	●
●	●	●	●	●	●	●	●
			●	○	●	○	●
○	●	○	●	○	●	○	●
			●	○	●	○	○
○	○	○	○	○	○	○	○
●	●	●	●	●	●	●	●
●	●	○	○	○	○	●	○
○	●	○	○	○	○	○	○
	●	○	○	○	○	○	○
○	○	○	●	○	○	○	○
	●	○	●	○	○	○	○
●	●	●	○	●	●	●	●
○	○	○	○	●	○	○	○
○	○	○	○	○	○	○	○
●	○	○	○	○	○	○	●
○	○	○	○	○	●	●	○
○	○	●	○	○	○	●	○
○	○	○	●	○	○	○	○
○	○	○	○	○	○	○	○
●	●	◐	○	○	●	○	○
●	◐	○	○	◐	●	○	○
	●	●	◐	○	○	●	◐
○	○	○	●	●	○	○	●
●	○	○	○	○	○	◐	●
◐	○	○	○	○	●	○	○
○	●	◐	●	○	○	●	○
○	○	○	○	○	●	●	◐
		●	●	○	●	●	◐
○	○	○	○	○	●	●	◐
		●	○	●	◐	◐	●

UNIT
3

Unit 3

Changes

Unit 4

Treasures

Unit 5

Great Ideas

Unit 1

Animals, Tame and Wild

Unit 2

Communities

UNIT 3

Read It Online
PearsonSuccessNet.com

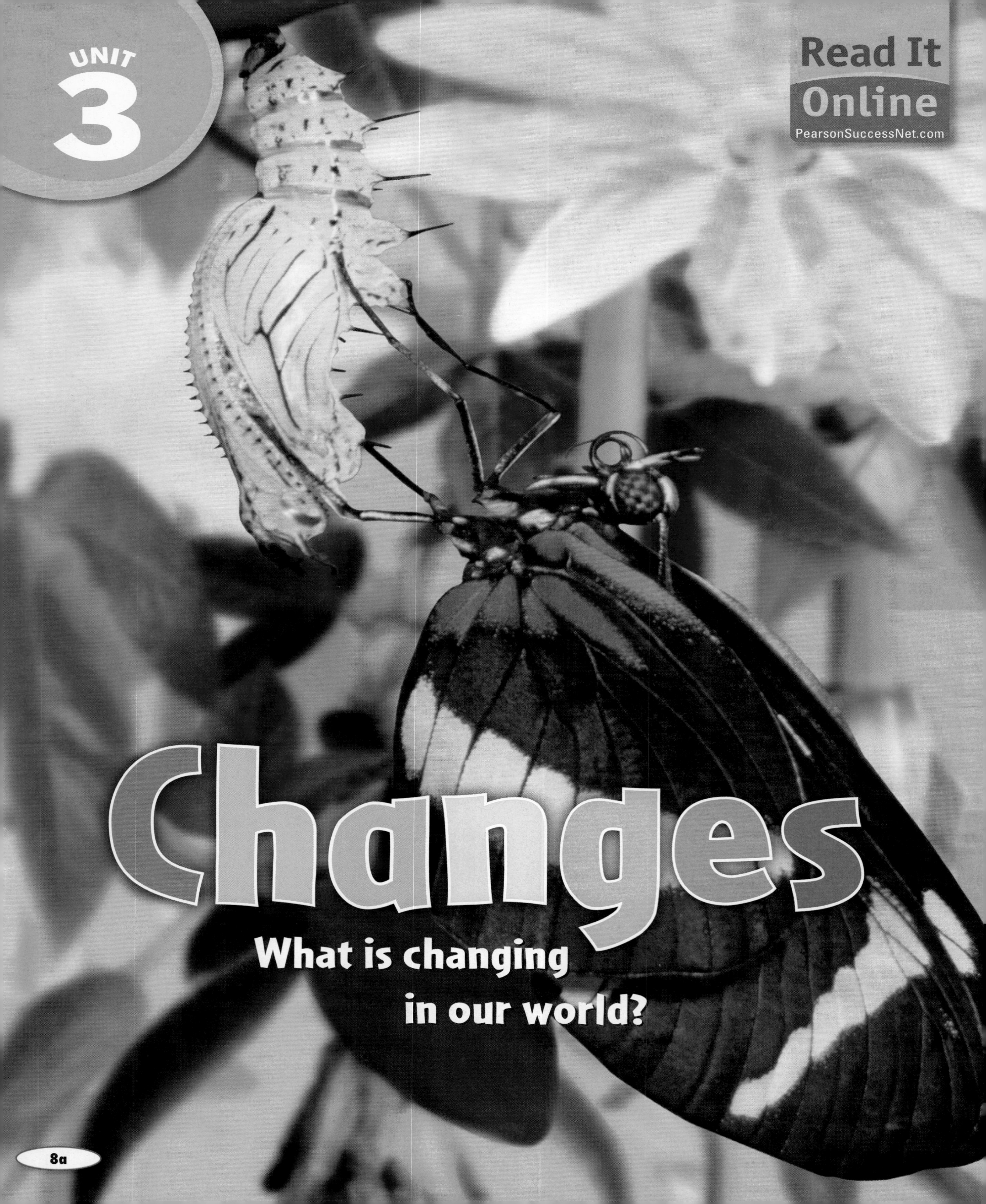

Changes

What is changing in our world?

An Egg Is an Egg

A boy describes changes in our world.

REALISTIC FICTION

connect to SCIENCE

Paired Selection

Nothing Fits!

FICTION

Ruby in Her Own Time

A young duckling grows and learns.

ANIMAL FANTASY

connect to SOCIAL STUDIES

Paired Selection

I'm Growing

FICTION

Jan's New Home

Moving is a difficult change for Jan.

REALISTIC FICTION

connect to SOCIAL STUDIES

Paired Selection

A Letter from Jan

LETTER

Frog and Toad Together

Toad sees his garden grow and change.

ANIMAL FANTASY

connect to SCIENCE

Paired Selection

Growing Plants

DIAGRAM

I'm a Caterpillar

A caterpillar changes to a butterfly.

NARRATIVE NONFICTION

connect to SCIENCE

Paired Selection

My Computer

NEW LITERACIES

Where Are My Animal Friends?

The seasons bring many changes to the forest.

PLAY

connect to SCIENCE

Paired Selection

"This Tooth," "Tommy," and "Where Do Fish Go in Winter?"

POETRY

Unit 3

Skills Overview

		WEEK 1	WEEK 2	WEEK 3
		14–33 **An Egg Is an Egg/ Nothing Fits!** REALISTIC FICTION	40–65 **Ruby in Her Own Time/ I'm Growing** ANIMAL FANTASY	72–89 **Jan's New Home/ A Letter from Jan** REALISTIC FICTION
Oral Language		*How do we change as we grow?*	*What do we learn as we grow and change?*	*Why are changes exciting?*
Word Work	**Phonemic Awareness**	Segment Phonemes	Blend and Segment	Add Phonemes /əz/
	Phonics	T Vowel Sounds of *y* T Long Vowels (CV) T REVIEW Long *e: e, ee*; Syllables VCCV	T Final *ng, nk* T Compound Words T REVIEW Vowel Sounds of *y;* Long Vowels CV	T Ending *-es*, Plural *-es* T *r*-Controlled *or, ore* T REVIEW Final *ng* and *nk;* Compound Words
	Spelling	T Long *e* and Long *i: y*	T Words with *ng* and *nk*	T Adding *-es*
	High-Frequency Words	T *always, become(s), day, everything, nothing, stays, things*	T *any, enough, ever, every, own, sure, were*	T *away, car, friends, house, our, school, very*
Reading	**Comprehension**	T **Skill** Compare and Contrast **Strategy** Predict REVIEW **Skill** Author's Purpose	T **Skill** Plot **Strategy** Summarize REVIEW **Skill** Sequence	T **Skill** Theme **Strategy** Monitor and Fix Up REVIEW **Skill** Plot
	Vocabulary	Antonyms	Synonyms	Descriptive Words
	Fluency	Accuracy/Appropriate Rate	Attend to Punctuation	Attend to Punctuation
Language Arts	**Writing**	**Weekly Writing** Steps, Journal Entry, Story Response, Math Story **Unit Process Writing**	**Weekly Writing** List, Poem, Story Response, Time Line **Unit Process Writing**	**Weekly Writing** Greeting Card, Letter, Story Response, Signs **Unit Process Writing**
	Grammar	T Action Verbs	T Verbs That Add *-s*	Verbs That Do Not Add *-s*
	Speaking, Listening, Viewing	Follow Directions	Give Directions	Making Introductions
	Research/Study Skills	Alphabetical Order	Glossary	Map
Integrate Science and Social Studies Standards		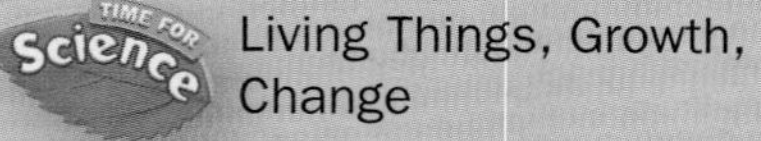 Living Things, Growth, Change	 Changes Over Time, Respecting Differences, Time Lines	 Geography, Place, Movement

Target Skill   T Tested Skill

Growing and Changing WEEKS 1–3
Changes in Nature WEEKS 4–6

WEEK 4	WEEK 5	WEEK 6
96–115 **Frog and Toad Together/Growing Plants** ANIMAL FANTASY	122–141 **I'm a Caterpillar/ My Computer** NONFICTION	148–171 **Where Are My Animal Friends?/ Poetry** PLAY
What changes happen in a garden?	*What changes can we observe in nature?*	*How does nature change during the year?*
Blend and Segment Syllables	Blend and Segment	Add Phonemes /er/, /est/
T Inflected Endings *-ed, -ing* T *r*-Controlled *ar* T REVIEW Ending *-es,* Plural *-es; r*-Controlled *or, ore*	T *r*-Controlled *er, ir, ur* T Contractions *'s, 've, 're* T REVIEW *r*-Controlled *ar;* Inflected Endings *-ed, -ing*	T Comparative Endings T *dge/j/* T REVIEW *r*-Controlled *er, ir, ur;* Contractions *'s, 've, 're*
T Adding *-ed*	T Words with *er, ir, ur*	T Adding *-er* and *-est*
T *afraid, again, few, how, read, soon*	T *done, know, push, visit, wait*	T *before, does, good-bye, oh, right, won't*
T **Skill** Plot **Strategy** Visualize REVIEW **Skill** Compare and Contrast	T **Skill** Draw Conclusions **Strategy** Text Structure REVIEW **Skill** Sequence	T **Skill** Sequence **Strategy** Prior Knowledge REVIEW **Skill** Compare and Contrast
Inflected Endings	Reference Source: Dictionary	Multiple-Meaning Words
Expression	Attend to Punctuation	Expression/Intonation
Weekly Writing Poem, List, Story Response, List **Unit Process Writing**	**Weekly Writing** Facts, Description, Story Response, Cycle Chart **Unit Process Writing**	**Weekly Writing** Song, Journal Writing, Story Response, Math Story **Unit Process Writing**
T Verbs for Now and the Past	*Am, Is, Are, Was,* and *Were*	Contractions with Not
Retell a Story	Summarize Information	Nonverbal Communication
Diagram/Scale Drawing	Technology: My Computer	Bar Graph
 Plant Needs, Parts of Plants, Life Cycle of a Plant	 Life Cycles, Adaptions	 Seasonal Changes, Animal Behavior, Weather

Unit 3

Monitor Progress

Predictors of Reading Success	WEEK 1	WEEK 2	WEEK 3	WEEK 4
Word Reading — **Phonics**	Vowel Sounds of *y* Long Vowels (CV)	Final *ng, nk* Compound Words	Ending *-es;* Plural *-es* *r*-Controlled *or, ore*	Inflected Endings *-ed, -ing* *r*-Controlled *ar*
WCPM — **Fluency**	Accuracy/Appropriate Rate 20–30 WCPM	Attend to Punctuation 20–30 WCPM	Attend to Punctuation 20–30 WCPM	Read with Expression 25–35 WCPM
High-Frequency Words — **High Frequency Words/ Vocabulary**	always become(s) day everything nothing stays things	any enough ever every own sure were	away car friends house our school very	afraid again few how read soon
Oral Vocabulary — **Vocabulary/ Concept Development** (assessed informally)	adult bounce crooked handsome healthy measurement shuffle teeter	attempt awkward correct event famous flatter lovely time line	arrive crumple depart location route stampede swoop tumble	blossom (n/v) destroy dim gardener humongous nature shade sprout
Retelling — **Text Comprehension**	**Skill** Compare and Contrast **Strategy** Predict	**Skill** Plot **Strategy** Summarize	**Skill** Theme **Strategy** Monitor and Fix Up	**Skill** Plot **Strategy** Visualize

Target Skill   SuccessTracker/Unit 3 Benchmark Tested Skills

Make Data–Driven Decisions

Data Management
- Assess
- Diagnose
- Prescribe
- Disaggregate

Classroom Management
- Monitor Progress
- Group
- Differentiate Instruction
- Inform Parents

Success Tracker™

ONLINE CLASSROOM

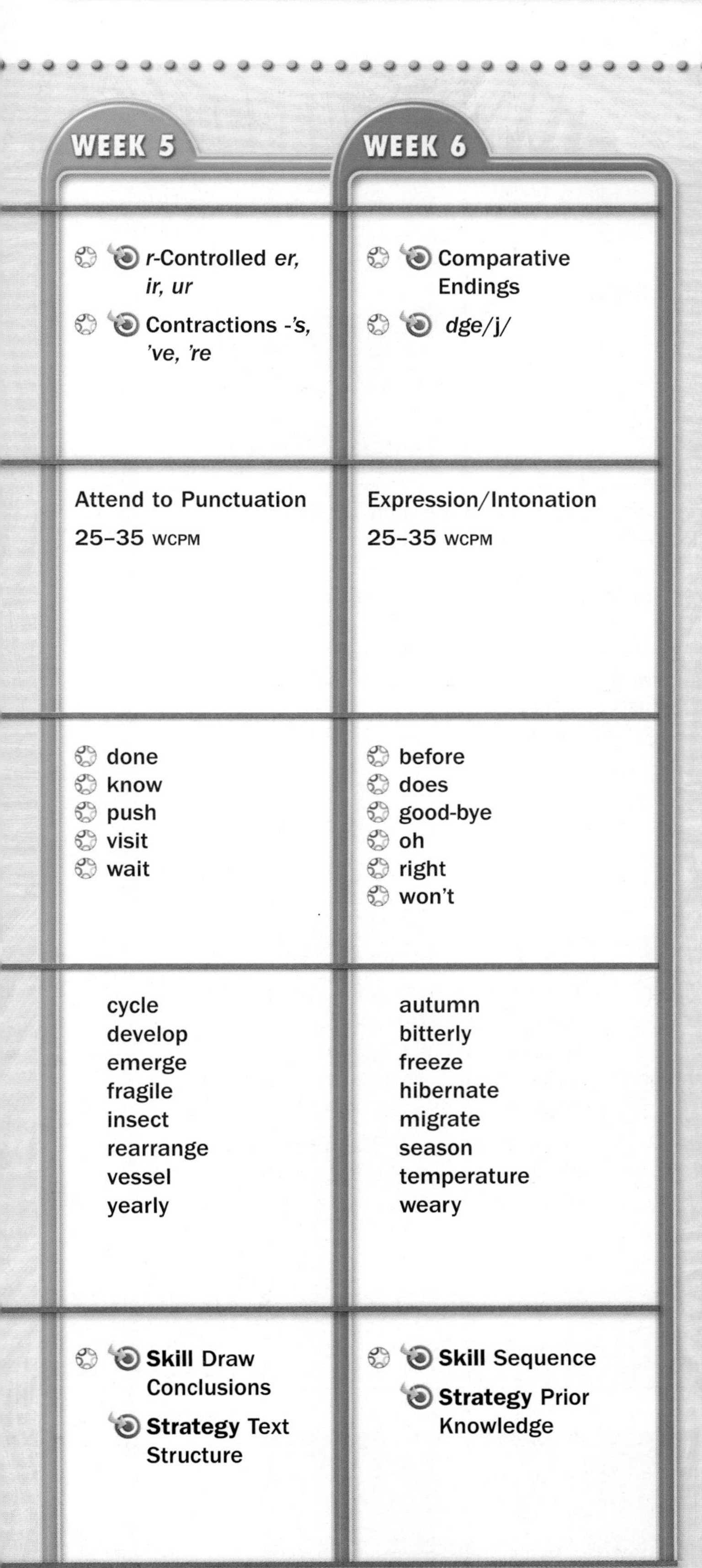

WEEK 5	WEEK 6
r-Controlled *er, ir, ur* Contractions *-'s, 've, 're*	Comparative Endings *dge/j/*
Attend to Punctuation 25–35 WCPM	Expression/Intonation 25–35 WCPM
done know push visit wait	before does good-bye oh right won't
cycle develop emerge fragile insect rearrange vessel yearly	autumn bitterly freeze hibernate migrate season temperature weary
Skill Draw Conclusions **Strategy** Text Structure	**Skill** Sequence **Strategy** Prior Knowledge

Manage Data

- Assign the Unit 3 Benchmark Test for students to take online.
- SuccessTracker records results and generates reports by school, grade, classroom, or student.
- Use reports to disaggregate and aggregate Unit 3 skills and standards data to monitor progress.
- Based on class lists created to support the categories important for AYP (gender, ethnicity, migrant education, English proficiency, disabilities, economic status), reports let you track adequate yearly progress every six weeks.

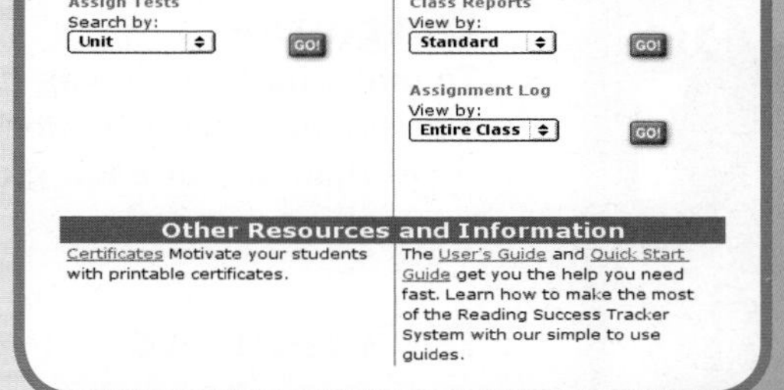

Group

- Use results from Unit 3 Benchmark Tests taken online through SuccessTracker to regroup students.
- Reports in SuccessTracker suggest appropriate groups for students based on test results.

Individualize Instruction

- Tests are correlated to Unit 3 tested skills and standards so that prescriptions for individual teaching and learning plans can be created.
- Individualized prescriptions target instruction and accelerate student progress toward learning outcome goals.
- Prescriptions include resources to reteach Unit 3 skills and standards.

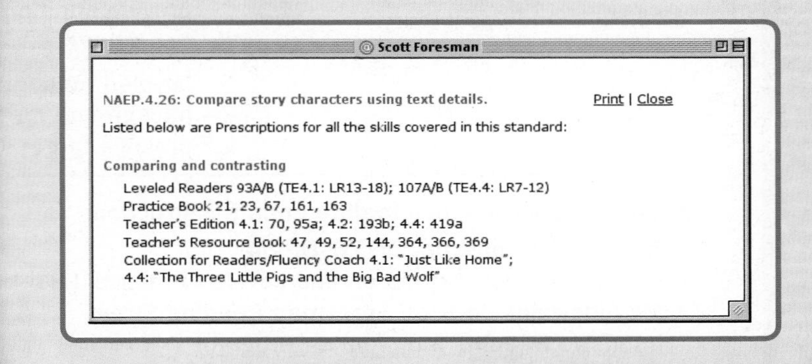

Scott Foresman

NAEP.4.26: Compare story characters using text details. Print | Close

Listed below are Prescriptions for all the skills covered in this standard:

Comparing and contrasting

Leveled Readers 93A/B (TE4.1: LR13-18); 107A/B (TE4.4: LR7-12)
Practice Book 21, 23, 67, 161, 163
Teacher's Edition 4.1: 70, 95a; 4.2: 193b; 4.4: 419a
Teacher's Resource Book 47, 49, 52, 144, 364, 366, 369
Collection for Readers/Fluency Coach 4.1: "Just Like Home";
4.4: "The Three Little Pigs and the Big Bad Wolf"

Unit 3

Grouping for AYP

STEP 1

Diagnose and Differentiate

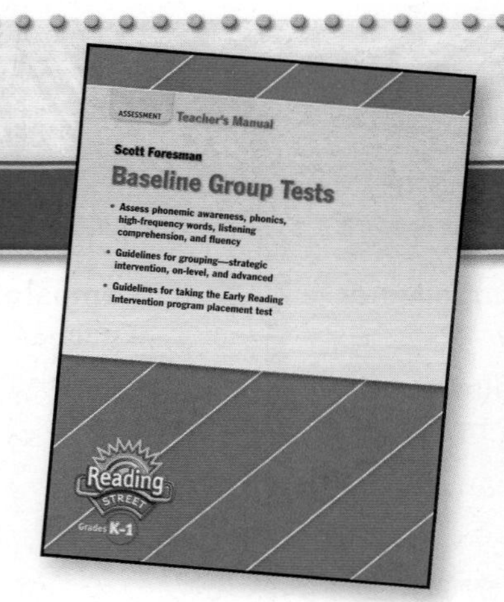

Diagnose

To make initial grouping decisions, use the Baseline Group Test or another initial placement test. Depending on children's ability levels, you may have more than one of each group.

Differentiate

If... a child's performance is	Below-Level	**then...** use the regular instruction and the daily Strategic Intervention, pp. DI•16–DI•74.
If... a child's performance is	On-Level	**then...** use the regular instruction for On-Level learners throughout each week.
If... a child's performance is	Advanced	**then...** use the regular instruction and the daily instruction for Advanced learners, pp. DI•10–DI•75.

Group Time

On-Level

- Explicit instructional routines teach core skills and strategies.
- Ample practice for core skills.
- Independent activities provide practice for core skills.
- Leveled readers (LR1–56) and decodable readers provide additional reading and practice with core skills and vocabulary.

Strategic Intervention

- Daily Strategic Intervention provides more intensive instruction, more scaffolding, more practice with critical skills, and more opportunities to respond.
- Decodable readers practice word reading skills.
- Reteach lessons (DI•76–DI•84) provide additional instructional opportunities with target skills.
- Leveled readers (LR1–56) build background for the selections and practice target skills and vocabulary.

Advanced

- Daily Advanced lessons provide compacted instruction for accelerated learning, options for independent investigative work, and challenging reading content.
- Leveled readers (LR1–56) provide additional reading tied to lesson concepts.

Additional opportunities to differentiate instruction:

- Reteach Lessons, pp. DI•76–DI•84
- Leveled Reader Instruction and Leveled Practice, LR1–LR56
- My Sidewalks on Scott Foresman Reading Street Intensive Reading Intervention Program

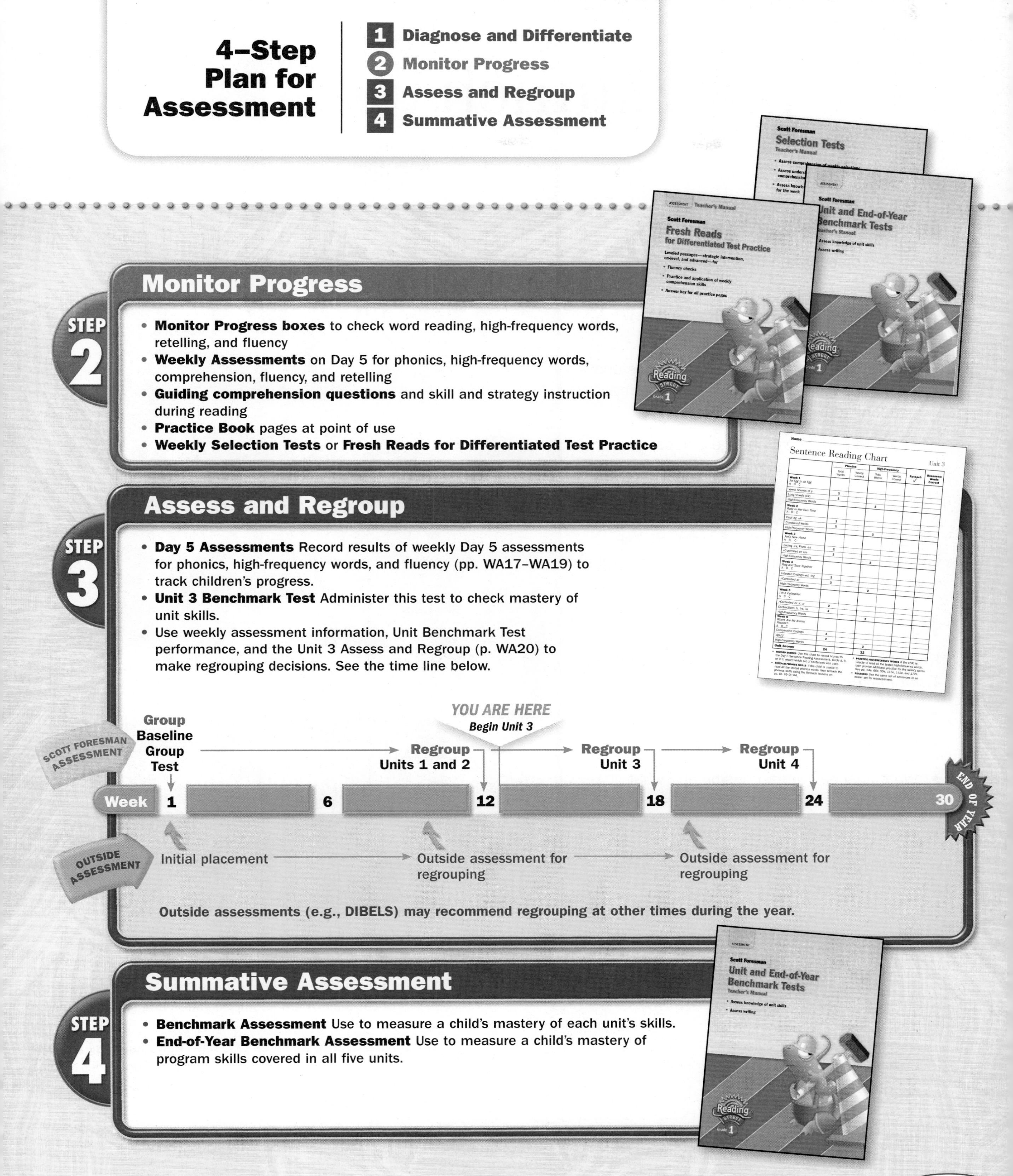

4–Step Plan for Assessment

1. Diagnose and Differentiate
2. Monitor Progress
3. Assess and Regroup
4. Summative Assessment

STEP 2 Monitor Progress

- **Monitor Progress boxes** to check word reading, high-frequency words, retelling, and fluency
- **Weekly Assessments** on Day 5 for phonics, high-frequency words, comprehension, fluency, and retelling
- **Guiding comprehension questions** and skill and strategy instruction during reading
- **Practice Book** pages at point of use
- **Weekly Selection Tests** or **Fresh Reads for Differentiated Test Practice**

STEP 3 Assess and Regroup

- **Day 5 Assessments** Record results of weekly Day 5 assessments for phonics, high-frequency words, and fluency (pp. WA17–WA19) to track children's progress.
- **Unit 3 Benchmark Test** Administer this test to check mastery of unit skills.
- Use weekly assessment information, Unit Benchmark Test performance, and the Unit 3 Assess and Regroup (p. WA20) to make regrouping decisions. See the time line below.

Outside assessments (e.g., DIBELS) may recommend regrouping at other times during the year.

STEP 4 Summative Assessment

- **Benchmark Assessment** Use to measure a child's mastery of each unit's skills.
- **End-of-Year Benchmark Assessment** Use to measure a child's mastery of program skills covered in all five units.

Unit 3

Theme Launch

Discuss the Big Idea

Read and discuss the theme question. Explain

- we are changing (growing, learning new things, getting new ideas)
- the world around us is changing (trees and plants, people and animals, weather and seasons, day and night)
- some things do not change unless we change them (chair, window, objects)

Have children use the pictures along the side of the page to preview the stories in this unit. Read the titles and captions together. Ask children what they think each story might tell about "change."

Read Aloud

Read the Big Books *Mr. George Baker* and *What Makes the Seasons?*

- What changes are in the books?
- How do these things change?
- What changes are surprising and what changes are expected?
- What does not change? Why?

For more read alouds related to the theme, see the *Read Aloud Anthology.*

CONNECTING CULTURES

You can use the following selection to help children learn about their own and other cultures and explore common elements of culture.

Jan's New Home Children who have moved can tell some of the changes that they experienced. Children from other regions can share changes that they noticed in their moves.

An Egg Is an Egg

A boy describes changes in our world.

REALISTIC FICTION

connect to SCIENCE

Paired Selection

Nothing Fits!

FICTION

Ruby in Her Own Time

A young duckling grows and learns.

ANIMAL FANTASY

connect to SOCIAL STUDIES

Paired Selection

I'm Growing

FICTION

Jan's New Home

Moving is a difficult change for Jan.

REALISTIC FICTION

connect to SOCIAL STUDIES

Paired Selection

A Letter from Jan

LETTER

Frog and Toad Together

Toad sees his garden grow and change.

ANIMAL FANTASY

connect to SCIENCE

Paired Selection

Growing Plants

DIAGRAM

I'm a Caterpillar

A caterpillar changes to a butterfly.

NARRATIVE NONFICTION

connect to SCIENCE

Paired Selection

My Computer

NEW LITERACIES

Where Are My Animal Friends?

The seasons bring many changes to the forest.

PLAY

connect to SCIENCE

Paired Selection

"This Tooth," "Tommy," and "Where Do Fish Go in Winter?"

POETRY

9

Unit Inquiry Project

Take a Closer Look

Children can take a closer look at things around them and keep a journal that documents the changes they see.

PROJECT TIMETABLE

WEEK	ACTIVITY/SKILL CONNECTION
1	**INTERVIEW** Children choose at least two objects to observe, and interview family members and teachers for ways to best observe them.
2	**GATHER INFORMATION** Children begin their journals by observing and, if appropriate, measuring their objects. Children make notes and pictures about the objects at this point.
3	**ORGANIZE INFORMATION** Children continue their journals by observing and measuring the objects. Children make new notes and pictures about the objects and order the new information next to the original information or devise a numbering system to keep notes in order.
4	**USE GRAPHIC SOURCES** Children continue to observe, measure, and record their observations. Children can chart the growth of objects they are measuring.
5	**DRAW CONCLUSIONS** Children observe, measure, and record their observations for the last time. Children comment in their journals on the changes they have observed.
6	**PUBLISH** Children publish the information in their journals by sharing them in a conference with their teacher.

An assessment rubric can be found on p. 174a. Rubric 4|3|2|1

CONCEPT DEVELOPMENT

Unit 3 Changes

CONCEPT QUESTION

What is changing in our world?

Growing and Changing

Changes in Nature

Week 1

Time for Science

Expand the Concept

How do we change as we grow?

Connect the Concept

Literature

Develop Language
adult, bounce, crooked, handsome, healthy, measurement, shuffle, teeter

Teach Content
Living Things
Growth
Change

Writing
Steps

Week 2

Time for Social Studies

Expand the Concept

What do we learn as we grow and change?

Connect the Concept

Literature

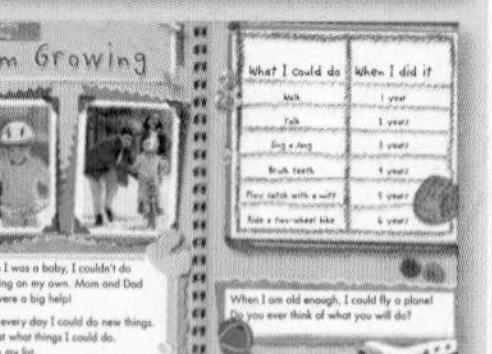

Develop Language
attempt, awkward, correct, event, famous, flatter, lovely, time line

Teach Content
Changes over Time
Respecting Differences
Time Lines

Writing
List

Week 3

Time for Social Studies

Expand the Concept

Why are changes exciting?

Connect the Concept

Literature

Develop Language
arrive, crumple, depart, location, route, stampede, swoop, tumble

Teach Content
Geography
Place
Movement

Writing
Greeting Card

Week 4

Time for Science

Expand the Concept

What changes happen in a garden?

Connect the Concept

Literature

Develop Language
blossom, destroy, dim, gardener, humongous, nature, shade, sprout

Teach Content
Plant Needs
Parts of Plants
Life Cycle of a Plant

Writing
Poem

Week 5

Time for Science

Expand the Concept

What changes can we observe in nature?

Connect the Concept

Literature

Develop Language
cycle, develop, emerge, fragile, insect, rearrange, vessel, yearly

Teach Content
Life Cycles
Adaptations

Writing
Facts

Week 6

Time for Science

Expand the Concept

How does nature change during the year?

Connect the Concept

Literature

Develop Language
autumn, bitterly, freeze, hibernate, migrate, season, temperature, weary

Teach Content
Seasonal Changes
Animal Behavior
Weather

Writing
Song

Unit 3
Changes

CONCEPT QUESTION
What is changing in our world?

Growing and Changing

Week 1
How do we change as we grow?

Week 2
What do we learn as we grow and change?

Week 3
Why are changes exciting?

Changes in Nature

Week 4
What changes happen in a garden?

Week 5
What changes can we observe in nature?

Week 6
How does nature change during the year?

Week 1

EXPAND THE CONCEPT
How do we change as we grow?

TIME FOR Science

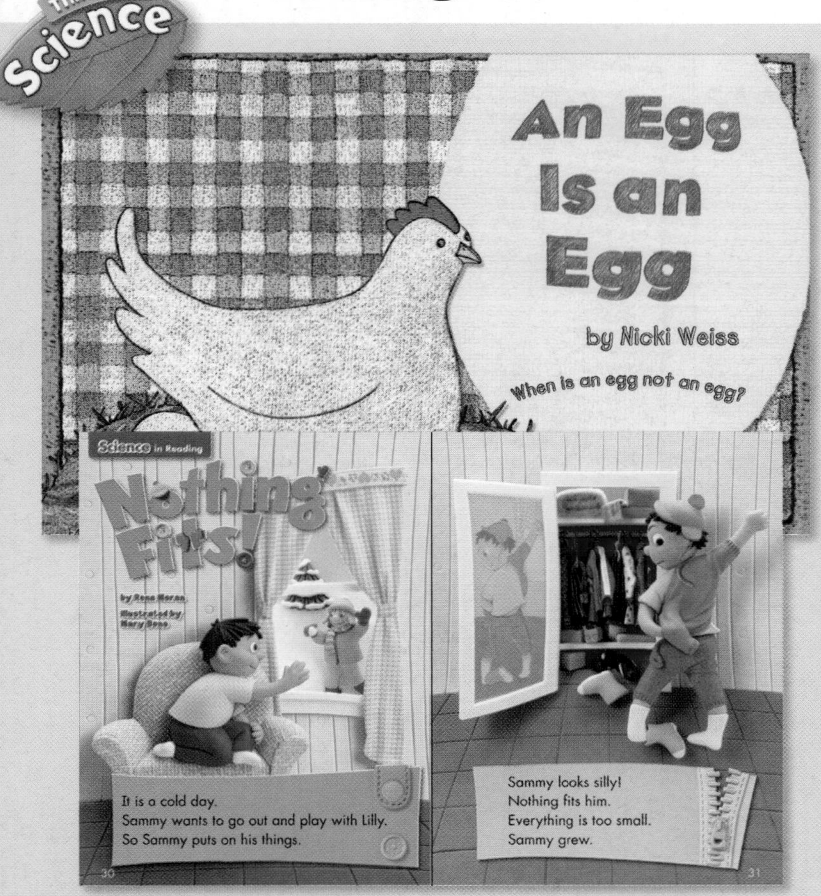

CONNECT THE CONCEPT

▶ **Build Background**

adult	*handsome*	*shuffle*
bounce	*healthy*	*teeter*
crooked	*measurement*	

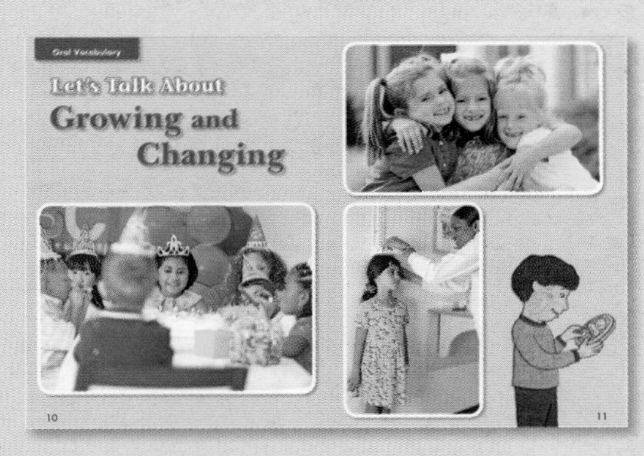

▶ **Science Content**
Living Things, Growth, Change

▶ **Writing**
Steps

Preview Your Week

How do we change as we grow?

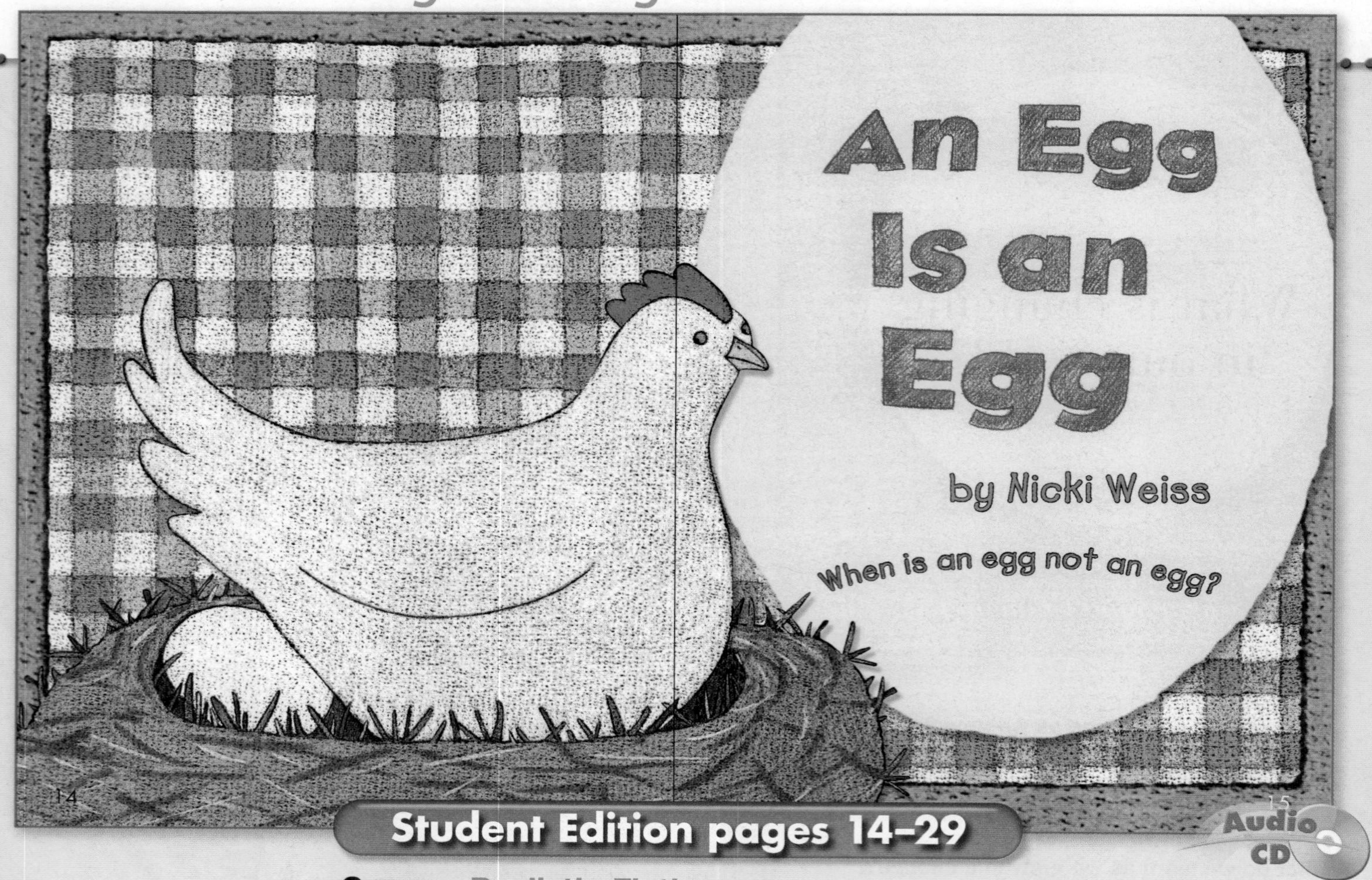

Student Edition pages 14–29

Audio CD

Genre	Realistic Fiction
Phonics	Vowel Sounds of *y* and Long Vowels (CV)
Comprehension Skill	Compare and Contrast
Comprehension Strategy	Predict

Science

Paired Selection

Reading Across Texts
Comparing Changes

Genre
Fiction

Text Features
Illustrations

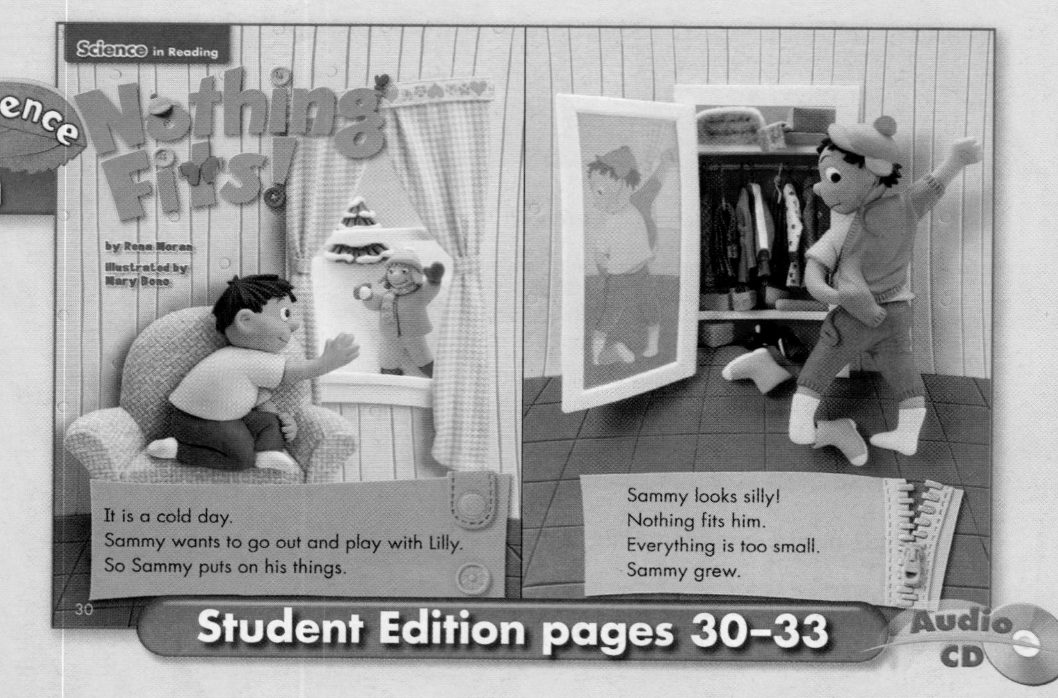

Student Edition pages 30–33

Audio CD

- Student Edition
- Leveled Readers
- Decodable Readers

Leveled Readers

Skill Compare and Contrast

Strategy Predict

Lesson Vocabulary

ELL Reader

- Concept Vocabulary
- Text Support
- Language Enrichment

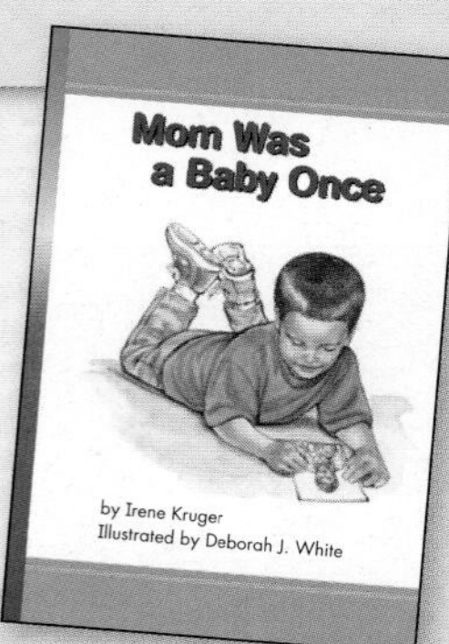

Decodable Readers

Apply Phonics

- *Will They Get Here?*
- *The Picnic*

TIME FOR Science

Integrate Science Standards

- Living Things
- Growth
- Change

An Egg Is an Egg, pp. 14–29

"Nothing Fits!," pp. 30–33

Leveled Readers

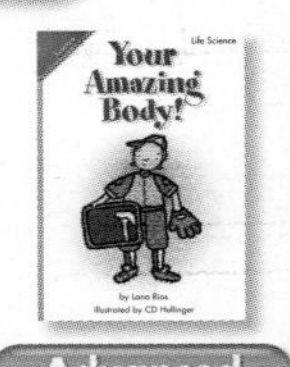

- Below-Level
  - Support Concepts
- On-Level
  - Develop Concepts
- Advanced
  - Extend Concepts
  - Science Extension Activity

ELL Reader

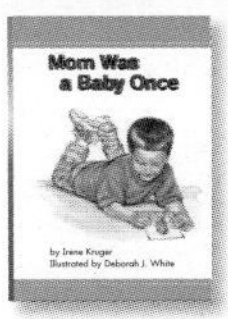

Build **Concept Vocabulary**
Growing and Changing, pp. 10r–11

Teach **Science Concepts**
Day/Night Sky, p. 22–23
Living Things, p. 30–31

Explore **Science Center**
Make Comparisons, p. 10k

Weekly Plan

READING

90–120 minutes

TARGET SKILLS OF THE WEEK

- **Phonics**
  Vowel Sounds of *y* and Long Vowel Patterns (CV)
- **Comprehension Skill**
  Compare and Contrast
- **Comprehension Strategy**
  Predict

DAY 1 PAGES 10l–11d

Oral Language

QUESTION OF THE WEEK, 10l
How do we change as we grow?

Oral Vocabulary/Share Literature, 10m
Sing with Me Big Book, Song 13
Amazing Words *adult, healthy, measurement*

Word Work

Phonemic Awareness, 10m
Segment Phonemes

Phonics, 10n–10o
Introduce Vowel Sounds of *y* **T**

Spelling, 10p
Pretest

Comprehension/Vocabulary/Fluency

Read Decodable Reader 25

Grouping Options 10f–10g

Review High-Frequency Words
Check Comprehension
Reread for Fluency

Build Background, 10r–11
Growing and Changing

Listening Comprehension, 11a–11b
Compare and Contrast **T**

DAY 2 PAGES 12a–13c

Oral Language

QUESTION OF THE DAY, 12a
Do you think people still grow and change when they are old?

Oral Vocabulary/Share Literature, 12b
Big Book *Mr. George Baker*
Amazing Words *shuffle, teeter*

Word Work

Phonemic Awareness, 12b
Substitute Phonemes

Phonics, 12c–12d
Introduce Long Vowels (CV) **T**

Spelling, 12e
Dictation

Comprehension/Vocabulary/Fluency

Read Decodable Reader 26

Grouping Options 10f–10g

Review High-Frequency Words
Check Comprehension
Reread for Fluency

High-Frequency Words, 12–13
Introduce *always, become, day, everything, nothing, stays, things* **T**

LANGUAGE ARTS

20–30 minutes

Trait of the Week

Conventions

Day 1

Shared Writing, 11c
Steps

Grammar, 11d
Introduce Action Verbs **T**

Day 2

Interactive Writing, 13a
Journal Entry

Grammar, 13b
Practice Action Verbs **T**

Speaking and Listening, 13c
Follow Directions

DAILY JOURNAL WRITING

Day 1 *Write about something you can do in first grade that you couldn't do in kindergarten.*

Day 2 *List ways you have changed.*

DAILY SCIENCE CONNECTIONS

Day 1 Baby/Now T-Chart, 10r–11

Day 2 Baby/Now T-Chart, 13c

DAILY SUCCESS PREDICTORS
for Adequate Yearly Progress

Monitor Progress and Corrective Feedback

	Day 1	Day 2
Phonics	Check Word Reading, *10o* Spiral REVIEW Phonics	Check Word Reading, *12d* Spiral REVIEW Phonics

RESOURCES FOR THE WEEK

- Practice Book 1.2, *pp. 1–10*
- Phonics and Spelling Practice Book, *pp. 49–52*
- Grammar and Writing Practice Book, *pp. 49–52*
- Selection Test, *pp. 25–28*
- Fresh Reads for Differentiated Test Practice, *pp. 73–78*
- Phonics Songs and Rhymes Chart 13
- The Grammar and Writing Book, *pp. 122–127*

Grouping Options for Differentiated Instruction

Turn the page for the small group lesson plan.

DAY 3 PAGES 14a–29d

Oral Language

QUESTION OF THE DAY, 14a
Can you think of anything that can't change?

Oral Vocabulary/Share Literature, 14b
Big Book *Mr. George Baker*
Amazing Word *crooked*

Word Work

Phonemic Awareness, 14b
Segment and Blend Phonemes

Phonics, 14c–14d
◎ Vowel Sounds of *y* and Long Vowels (CV) **T**

Spelling, 14d
Practice

Comprehension/Vocabulary/Fluency

Read *An Egg Is an Egg,* 14e–29

Grouping Options 10f–10g

Introduce Selection Words
boy, grew, night, sunset, tower

Review High-Frequency Words
always, become, day, everything, nothing, stays, things **T**

◎ Compare and Contrast **T**
◎ Predict
REVIEW Author's Purpose **T**

Fluency, 29a
Read with Accuracy and Appropriate Rate

Vocabulary, 29b
Antonyms

Trait of the Week, 29c
Introduce Conventions

Grammar, 29d
Write with Action Verbs **T**

Day 3 *Write about something you'll be able to do when you are an adult.*

Day 3 Time for Science: Day/Night Sky, 22–23

DAY 4 PAGES 30a–33c

Oral Language

QUESTION OF THE DAY, 30a
What happens to your clothes when you get bigger?

Oral Vocabulary/Share Literature, 30b
Read Aloud Anthology "'Wait for Me!' Said Maggie McGee"
Amazing Words *bounce, handsome*

Word Work

Phonemic Awareness, 30b
Segment and Count Phonemes

High-Frequency Words, 30c
Practice *always, become, day, everything, nothing, stays, things* **T**

Phonics, 30c–30d
REVIEW Long *e: e, ee* and Syllables VCCV **T**
REVIEW Word Reading **T**

Spelling, 30e
Partner Review

Comprehension/Vocabulary/Fluency

Read "Nothing Fits!" 30–33
Leveled Readers

Grouping Options 10f–10g

Antonyms
Reading Across Texts

Fluency, 33a
Read with Accuracy and Appropriate Rate

Writing Across the Curriculum, 33b
Math Story

Grammar, 33c
Review Action Verbs **T**

Day 4 *Write how you are like the boy in the story and how you are different.*

Day 4 Time for Science: Living Things, 30–31

DAY 5 PAGES 34a–35b

Oral Language

QUESTION OF THE DAY, 34a
How can you take a measurement of how much you are growing?

Oral Vocabulary/Share Literature, 34b
Read Aloud Anthology "'Wait for Me!' Said Maggie McGee"
Amazing Words Review

Word Work

Phonics, 34c
◎ Review Vowel Sounds of *y* and Long Vowels (CV) **T**

High-Frequency Words, 34c
Review *always, become, day, everything, nothing, stays, things* **T**

Spelling, 34d
Test

Comprehension/Vocabulary/Fluency

Read Leveled Readers

Grouping Options 10f–10g

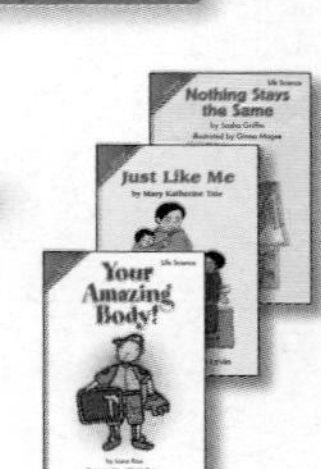

Monitor Progress, 34e–34g
Read the Sentences
Read the Story

Writing and Grammar, 34-35
Develop Conventions
Use Action Verbs **T**

Research/Study Skills, 35a
Alphabetical Order

Day 5 *Write about something you have outgrown.*

Day 5 Revisit the Baby/Now T-Chart, 35b

KEY ◎ = Target Skill **T** = Tested Skill

Fluency and Comprehension
Check High-Frequency Words, *14f*
Check Retelling, *28a*
Spiral REVIEW High-Frequency Words

Fluency
Check Fluency WCPM, *33a*
Spiral REVIEW Phonics, High-Frequency Words

Oral Vocabulary
Check Oral Vocabulary, *34b*
Assess Phonics, High-Frequency Words, Fluency, Comprehension, *34e*

SUCCESS PREDICTOR

Small Group Plan *for Differentiated Instruction*

Daily Plan AT A GLANCE

Reading

Whole Group
- Oral Language
- Word Work
- Comprehension/Vocabulary

Group Time

Meet with small groups to provide:
- Skill Support
- Reading Support
- Fluency Practice

This week's lessons for daily group time can be found behind the Differentiated Instruction (DI) tab on pp. DI·16–DI·25.

Whole Group
- Comprehension/Vocabulary
- Fluency

Language Arts
- Writing
- Grammar
- Speaking/Listening/Viewing
- Research/Study Skills

Use *My Sidewalks on Reading Street* for Tier III intensive reading intervention.

DAY 1

On-Level	Strategic Intervention	Advanced
Teacher-Led *Page 10q*	Teacher-Led *Page DI·16*	Teacher-Led *Page DI·17*
• **Read** Decodable Reader 25 • **Reread** for Fluency	• Blend and Build Words with *y*: /ē/, /ī/ • **Read** Decodable Reader 25 • **Reread** for Fluency	• Extend Word Reading • **Read** Advanced Selection 13 • Introduce Concept Inquiry

Independent Activities

While you meet with small groups, have the rest of the class...

- Reread for fluency
- Write in their journals
- Complete Practice Book 1.2, p. 3
- Visit the Word Work Center

DAY 2

On-Level	Strategic Intervention	Advanced
Teacher-Led *Page 12f*	Teacher-Led *Page DI·18*	Teacher-Led *Page DI·19*
• **Read** Decodable Reader 26 • **Reread** for Fluency	• Blend and Build Words with Long Vowel Pattern CV • **Read** Decodable Reader 26 • **Reread** for Fluency	• Extend Word Reading • **Read** *Mr. George Baker* • Continue Concept Inquiry

Independent Activities

While you meet with small groups, have the rest of the class...

- Reread for fluency
- Write in their journals
- Complete Practice Book 1.2, pp. 4–6
- Visit the Word Work Center
- Work on inquiry projects

DAY 3

On-Level	Strategic Intervention	Advanced
Teacher-Led *Pages 14–29*	Teacher-Led *Page DI·20*	Teacher-Led *Page DI·21*
• **Read** *An Egg Is an Egg*	• Blend and Read Words with *y*: /ē/, /ī/; Long Vowels CV • **Read** SI Decodable Reader 13 • **Read** or Listen to *An Egg Is an Egg*	• **Read** *An Egg Is an Egg* • Continue Concept Inquiry

Independent Activities

While you meet with small groups, have the rest of the class...

- Read self-selected reading
- Write in their journals
- Complete Practice Book 1.2, p. 7
- Visit the Listening and Writing Centers
- Work on inquiry projects

① Begin with whole class skill and strategy instruction.

② Meet with small groups to provide differentiated instruction.

③ Gather the whole class back together for fluency and language arts.

DAY 4

On-Level

Teacher-Led
Pages 30–33, LR4–LR6

- **Read** "Nothing Fits!"
- Practice with On-Level Reader *Just Like Me*

Strategic Intervention

Teacher-Led
Pages DI • 22, LR1–LR3

- Blend and Read Words
- **Reread** SI Decodable Reader 12
- **Read** or Listen to "Nothing Fits!"
- Practice with Below-Level Reader *Nothing Stays the Same*

Advanced

Teacher-Led
Pages DI • 23, LR7–LR9

- **Read** "Nothing Fits!"
- Expand Vocabulary
- Continue Concept Inquiry
- Practice with Advanced Reader *Your Amazing Body!*

i Independent Activities

While you meet with small groups, have the rest of the class...

- Reread for fluency
- Write in their journals
- Read self-selected reading
- Complete Practice Book 1.2, pp. 8–9
- Visit the Listening and Science Centers
- Work on inquiry projects

DAY 5

On-Level

Teacher-Led
Pages 34e–34g, LR4–LR6

- Sentence Reading, Set B
- Monitor Comprehension
- Practice with On-Level Reader *Just Like Me*

Strategic Intervention

Teacher-Led
Pages DI • 24, LR1–LR3

- Practice Word Reading
- Sentence Reading, Set A
- Monitor Comprehension
- Practice with Below-Level Reader *Nothing Stays the Same*

Advanced

Teacher-Led
Pages DI • 25, LR7–LR9

- Sentence Reading, Set C
- Monitor Fluency and Comprehension
- Share Concept Inquiry
- Practice with Advanced Reader *Your Amazing Body!*

i Independent Activities

While you meet with small groups, have the rest of the class...

- Reread for fluency
- Write in their journals
- Read self-selected reading
- Complete Practice Book 1.2, p. 10
- Visit the Technology Center

Grouping Place English language learners in the groups that correspond to their reading abilities in English.

Use the appropriate Leveled Reader or other text at children's instructional level.

TIP Send home the appropriate Multilingual Summary of the main selection on Day 1.

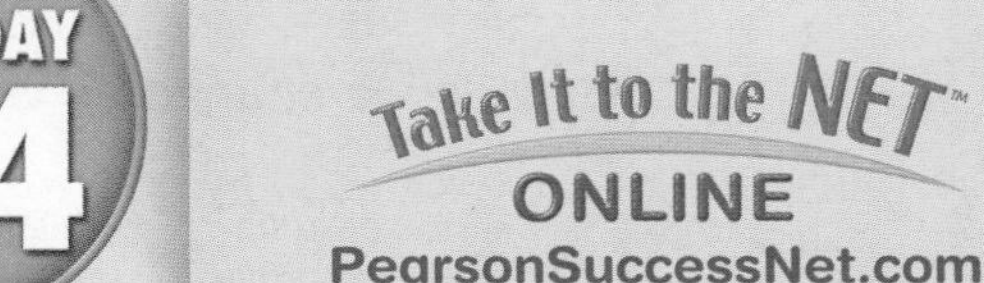

PearsonSuccessNet.com

Sharon Vaughn
For ideas on grouping for intervention and ELL students, see the article "Reading Instruction Grouping for Students with Reading Difficulties" by Scott Foresman author Sharon Vaughn and others.

TEACHER TALK

Shared writing is writing in which children contribute what will be written, and the teacher acts as scribe.

Looking Ahead

Be sure to schedule time for children to work on the unit inquiry project "Take a Closer Look." This week children should choose two objects to observe and interview others for ways to best observe them.

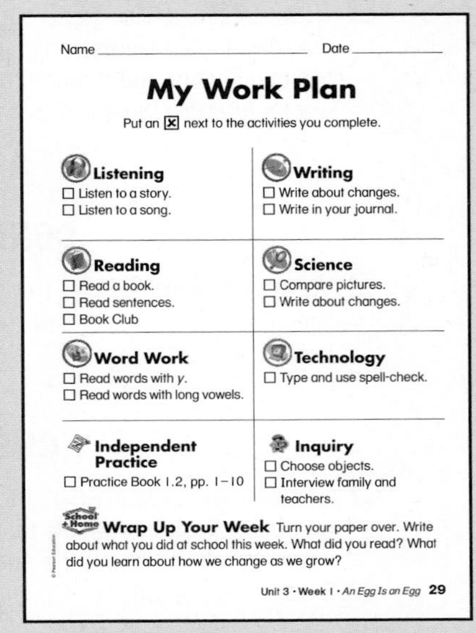

Name ______ Date ______

My Work Plan

Put an ☒ next to the activities you complete.

Listening
☐ Listen to a story.
☐ Listen to a song.

Writing
☐ Write about changes.
☐ Write in your journal.

Reading
☐ Read a book.
☐ Read sentences.
☐ Book Club

Science
☐ Compare pictures.
☐ Write about changes.

Word Work
☐ Read words with *y*.
☐ Read words with long vowels.

Technology
☐ Type and use spell-check.

Independent Practice
☐ Practice Book 1.2, pp. 1–10

Inquiry
☐ Choose objects.
☐ Interview family and teachers.

School + Home **Wrap Up Your Week** Turn your paper over. Write about what you did at school this week. What did you read? What did you learn about how we change as we grow?

Unit 3 • Week 1 • *An Egg Is an Egg* 29

▲ **Group-Time Survival Guide** p. 29, Weekly Contract

Customize Your Plan by Strand

ORAL LANGUAGE

Concept Development

How do we change as we grow?

adult *healthy* *measurement*
shuffle *teeter* *crooked*
bounce *handsome*

BUILD

- ❑ **Question of the Week** Use the Morning Warm-Up! to introduce and discuss the question of the week. This week children will talk, sing, read, and write about growing and changing. DAY 1 *10l*
- ❑ **Sing with Me Big Book** Sing a song about growing and changing. Ask children to listen for the concept-related Amazing Words *adult, healthy, measurement.* DAY 1 *10m*

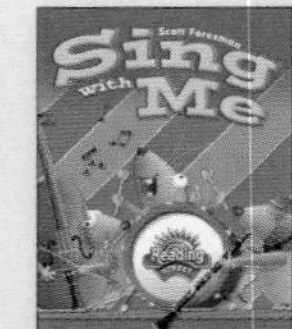

Sing with Me Big Book

- ❑ **Let's Talk About Growing and Changing** Use the Let's Talk About It lesson in the Student Edition to build background, vocabulary, and concepts. Then create a concept chart for children to add to throughout the week. DAY 1 *10r–11*

Let's Talk About It

DEVELOP

- ❑ **Question of the Day** Use the questions in the Morning Warm-Ups! to discuss lesson concepts and how they relate to the unit theme, Changes. DAY 2 *12a*, DAY 3 *14a*, DAY 4 *30a*, DAY 5 *34a*
- ❑ **Share Literature** Read big books and read aloud selections that develop concepts, language, and vocabulary related to the lesson concept and the unit theme. Continue to develop this week's Amazing Words. DAY 2 *12b*, DAY 3 *14b*, DAY 4 *30b*, DAY 5 *34b*

CONNECT

- ❑ **Wrap Up Your Week!** Revisit the Question of the Week. Then connect concepts and vocabulary to next week's lesson. DAY 5 *35b*

CHECK

- ❑ **Check Oral Vocabulary** To informally assess children's oral vocabulary, ask individuals to use some of this week's Amazing Words to tell you about the photographs and illustration on Student Edition pp. 10–11. DAY 5 *34b*

PHONEMIC AWARENESS AND PHONICS

VOWEL SOUNDS OF Y When *y* is at the end of a word, it stands for either the long *i* sound or the long *e* sound.

LONG VOWELS (CV) When a word or a syllable ends with a single vowel, the vowel sound is usually long.

TEACH

- ❑ **Segment Phonemes** Practice segmenting words with one, two, or three phonemes. DAY 1 *10m*
- ❑ **Vowel Sounds of *y*** Introduce the blending strategy for words with vowel sounds of *y*. Have children blend and sort words. DAY 1 *10n–10o*
- ❑ **Substitute Phonemes** Distinguish initial, medial, and final sounds in words. Substitute phonemes and practice segmenting. DAY 2 *12b*
- ❑ **Long Vowels (CV)** Introduce the blending strategy for words with long vowels (CV). Then have children blend and sort words. DAY 2 *12c–12d*
- ❑ **Fluent Word Reading** Use the Fluent Word Reading Routine to develop children's word reading fluency. Use the Phonics Songs and Rhymes Chart for additional word reading practice. DAY 3 *14c–14d*

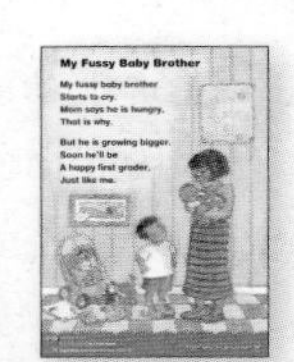

Phonics Songs and Rhymes Chart 13

PRACTICE/APPLY

- ❑ **Decodable Reader 25** Practice reading words with vowel sounds of *y* in context. DAY 1 *10q*
- ❑ **Decodable Reader 26** Practice reading words with long vowels (CV) in context. DAY 2 *12f*

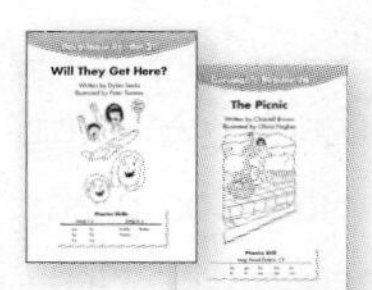

Decodable Readers 25 and 26

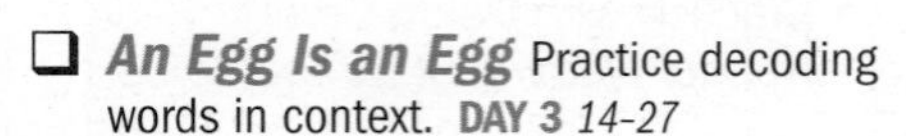

- ❑ ***An Egg Is an Egg*** Practice decoding words in context. DAY 3 *14–27*
- ❑ **Homework** Practice Book 1.2 pp. 3, 5. DAY 1 *10o*, DAY 2 *12d*

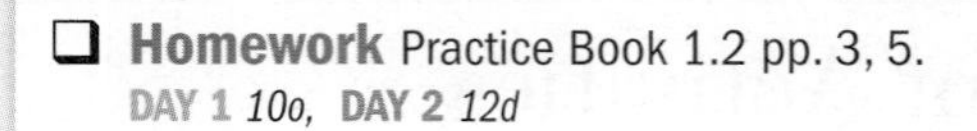

- ❑ **Word Work Center** Practice vowel sounds of *y* and long vowels (CV). ANY DAY *10j*

Main Selection—Fiction

RETEACH/REVIEW

- ❑ **Review** Review words with this week's phonics skills. DAY 5 *34c*
- ❑ **Reteach Lessons** If necessary, reteach vowel sounds of *y* and long vowels (CV). DAY 5 *DI·76*
- ❑ **Spiral REVIEW** Review previously taught phonics skills. DAY 1 *10o*, DAY 2 *12d*, DAY 4 *30c–30d*

ASSESS

- ❑ **Sentence Reading** Assess children's ability to read words with vowel sounds of *y*, long vowels CV. DAY 5 *34e–34f*

1 Use assessment data to determine your instructional focus.

2 Preview this week's instruction by strand.

3 Choose instructional activities that meet the needs of your classroom.

SPELLING

VOWEL SOUNDS OF Y When *y* is at the end of a word, it stands for either the long *i* sound or the long *e* sound. When *y* ends a word of two or more syllables, it usually has the long *e* sound.

TEACH

- ❑ **Pretest** Before administering the pretest, model how to segment words with vowel sounds of *y* to spell them. Dictate the spelling words, segmenting them if necessary. Then have children check their pretests and correct misspelled words. **DAY 1** *10p*

PRACTICE/APPLY

- ❑ **Dictation** Have children write dictation sentences to practice spelling words. **DAY 2** *12e*
- ❑ **Write Words** Have children practice writing the spelling words on cards and sort them into categories. **DAY 3** *14d*
- ❑ **Homework** Phonics and Spelling Practice Book pp. 49–52. **DAY 1** *10p*, **DAY 2** *12e*, **DAY 3** *14d*, **DAY 4** *30e*

RETEACH/REVIEW

- ❑ **Partner Review** Have pairs work together to read and write the spelling words. **DAY 4** *30e*

ASSESS

- ❑ **Posttest** Use dictation sentences to give the posttest for words with vowel sounds of *y*. **DAY 5** *34d*

Spelling Words

Long e and Long *i*: y

1. my*	6. fly
2. by	7. cry
3. try	8. lucky
4. any	9. silly
5. body	10. puppy

High-Frequency Words

11. things*	12. always*

* Words from the Selection

HIGH-FREQUENCY WORDS

WORDS TO READ

always	*become*	*day*	*everything*
nothing	*stays*	*things*	

TEACH

- ❑ **Words to Read** Introduce this week's high-frequency words and add them to the Word Wall. **DAY 2** *12-13*

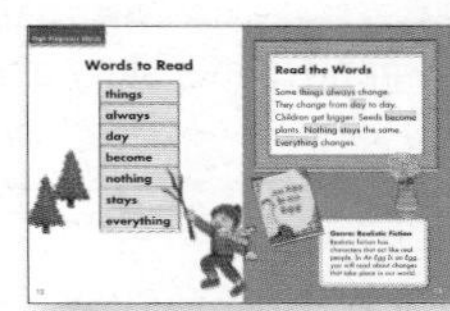
High-Frequency Words

PRACTICE/APPLY

- ❑ **Vocabulary Transparency 13** Review this week's high-frequency words, or Words to Read, before reading *An Egg Is an Egg*. **DAY 3** *14f*
- ❑ **Words in Context** Read high-frequency words in the context of *An Egg Is an Egg*. **DAY 3** *14-27*

Main Selection—Fiction

- ❑ **Word Wall** Use the Word Wall to review and practice high-frequency words throughout the week. **DAY 4** *30c*, **DAY 5** *34c*
- ❑ **Leveled Text** Practice this week's high-frequency words in the context of leveled text. **DAY 4** *LR1-LR9*, **DAY 5** *LR1-LR9*
- ❑ **Homework** Practice Book 1.2 pp. 6–7. **DAY 2** *12-13*, **DAY 3** *14e*

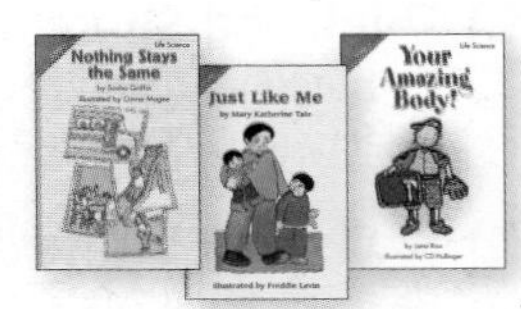

Leveled Readers

RETEACH/REVIEW

- ❑ **Spiral REVIEW** Review previously taught high-frequency words. **DAY 3** *14f*, **DAY 4** *30d*

ASSESS

- ❑ **Sentence Reading** Assess children's ability to read this week's high-frequency words. **DAY 5** *34e-34f*

VOCABULARY

TEACH

- ❑ **Vocabulary Transparency 13** Use Vocabulary Transparency 13 to introduce the selection words from *An Egg Is an Egg*. Children will read these words but will not be tested on them. **DAY 3** *14f*
- ❑ **Antonyms** Discuss antonyms. **DAY 3** *29b*

Customize Your Plan *by Strand*

COMPREHENSION

SKILL COMPARE AND CONTRAST To compare is to describe how two ideas or things are alike. To contrast is to describe how two ideas or things are different.

STRATEGY PREDICT To predict means to tell what you think will happen in a story and why it will happen.

TEACH

- ❑ **Listening Comprehension** Read "I Want to Be Six Forever!" and model *compare and contrast.* DAY 1 *11a-11b*
- ❑ **Skill/Strategy Lesson** Review *compare and contrast.* Then introduce this week's strategy, *predict.* DAY 3 *14g*

PRACTICE/APPLY

- ❑ **Skills and Strategies in Context** Read *An Egg Is an Egg,* using the Guiding Comprehension questions to apply *compare and contrast* and *predict.* DAY 3 *14-27*
- ❑ **Think and Share** Use the questions on Student Edition p. 28 to discuss the selection. DAY 3 *28a-29*
- ❑ **Skills and Strategies in Context** Read "Nothing Fits!," guiding children as they apply skills and strategies. After reading have children make connections across texts. DAY 4 *30-33*
- ❑ **Leveled Text** Apply *compare and contrast* and *predict* to read leveled text. DAY 4 *LR1-LR9,* DAY 5 *LR1-LR9*
- ❑ **Homework** Practice Book 1.2 p. 4. DAY 1 *11a*

Main Selection—Fiction

Paired Selection—Poetry

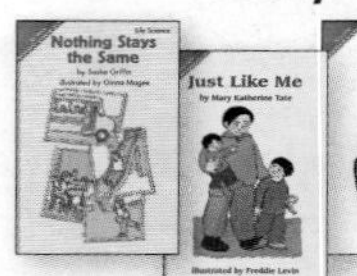

Leveled Readers

ASSESS

- ❑ **Selection Test** Determine children's understanding of the main selection and assess their ability to identify *compare and contrast.* DAY 3
- ❑ **Story Reading** Have children read the passage "Happy Trips." Have them compare and contrast things in the story and retell the story. DAY 5 *34e, 34g*

RETEACH/REVIEW

- ❑ **Reteach Lesson** If necessary, reteach *compare and contrast.* DAY 5 *DI·77*

FLUENCY

SKILL READ WITH ACCURACY AND APPROPRIATE RATE When you read, try to read all the words in a sentence with no mistakes and at a speed that sounds as if you are speaking.

REREAD FOR FLUENCY

- ❑ **Oral Rereading** Have children read orally from Decodable Reader 25 or another text at their independent reading level. Listen to children read and provide corrective feedback regarding their oral reading and their use of the blending strategy DAY 1 *10q*
- ❑ **Paired Reading** Have pairs of children take turns reading orally from Decodable Reader 26 or another text at their independent reading level. Listen to children read and provide corrective feedback regarding their oral reading and their use of the blending strategy DAY 2 *12f*

TEACH

- ❑ **Model** Use passages from *An Egg Is an Egg* to model reading with accuracy and appropriate rate. DAY 3 *29a,* DAY 4 *33a*

PRACTICE/APPLY

- ❑ **Choral Reading** Choral read passages from *An Egg Is an Egg.* Monitor progress and provide feedback regarding children's reading with accuracy and appropriate rate. DAY 3 *29a,* DAY 4 *33a*
- ❑ **Listening Center** Have children follow along with the AudioText for this week's selections. ANY DAY *10j*
- ❑ **Reading/Library Center** Have children build fluency by rereading Leveled Readers, Decodable Readers, or other text at their independent level. ANY DAY *10j*
- ❑ **Fluency Coach** Have children use Fluency Coach to listen to fluent reading or to practice reading on their own. ANY DAY

ASSESS

- ❑ **Story Reading** Take a one-minute timed sample of children's oral reading. Use the passage "Happy Trips." DAY 5 *34e, 34g*

1. Use assessment data to determine your instructional focus.
2. Preview this week's instruction by strand.
3. Choose instructional activities that meet the needs of your classroom.

WRITING

Trait of the Week

CONVENTIONS Conventions are rules for writing. Good writers check to make sure words are spelled correctly.

TEACH

- ❑ **Write Together** Engage children in writing activities that develop language, grammar, and writing skills. Include independent writing as an extension of group writing activities.
  - **Shared Writing** DAY 1 *11c*
  - **Interactive Writing** DAY 2 *13a*
  - **Writing Across the Curriculum** DAY 4 *33b*
- ❑ **Trait of the Week** Introduce and model the Trait of the Week, *conventions*. DAY 3 *29c*

PRACTICE/APPLY

- ❑ **Write Now** Examine the model on Student Edition pp. 34–35. Then have children write Steps. DAY 5 *34-35*

  Prompt *An Egg Is an Egg* shows that almost everything changes. Think about how an egg changes to become a chicken. Now write steps that tell what happens. Put the steps in order.

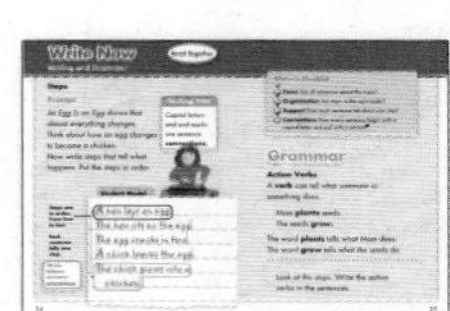

Write Now

- ❑ **Daily Journal Writing** Have children write about concepts and literature in their journals. EVERY DAY *10d-10e*
- ❑ **Writing Center** Have children write about changes they have observed. ANY DAY *10k*

ASSESS

- ❑ **Scoring Rubric** Use a rubric to evaluate steps. DAY 5 *34-35*

RETEACH/REVIEW

- ❑ **The Grammar and Writing Book** Use pp. 122–127 of The Grammar and Writing Book to extend instruction. ANY DAY

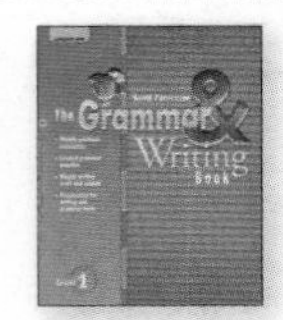

The Grammar and Writing Book

SPEAKING AND LISTENING

TEACH

- ❑ **Follow Directions** Model how to follow directions. Then have children brainstorm a list of steps they follow. DAY 2 *13c*

GRAMMAR

SKILL ACTION VERBS A verb tells what someone or something does.

TEACH

- ❑ **Grammar Transparency 13** Use Grammar Transparency 13 to teach action verbs. DAY 1 *11d*

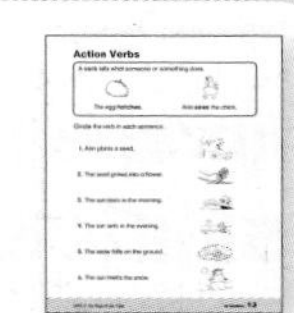

Grammar Transparency 13

PRACTICE/APPLY

- ❑ **Develop the Concept** Review the concept of *action verbs* and provide guided practice. DAY 2 *13b*
- ❑ **Apply to Writing** Have children use action verbs in writing. DAY 3 *29d*
- ❑ **Define/Practice** Review the definition of *action verbs*. Then have children demonstrate action verbs. DAY 4 *33c*
- ❑ **Write Now** Discuss the grammar lesson on Student Edition p. 35. Have children use action verbs in their own steps of how an egg becomes a chicken. DAY 5 *34-35*

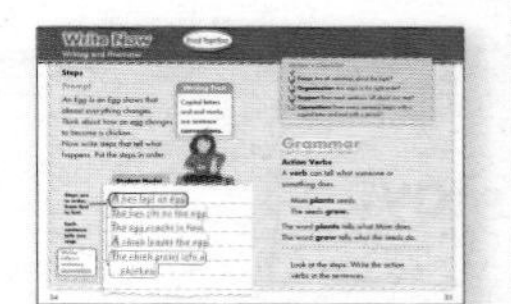

Write Now

- ❑ **Daily Fix-It** Have children find and correct errors in grammar, spelling, and punctuation. DAY 1 *11d*, DAY 2 *13b*, DAY 3 *29d*, DAY 4 *33c*, DAY 5 *34-35*
- ❑ **Homework** Grammar and Writing Practice Book pp. 49–52. DAY 2 *13b*, DAY 3 *29d*, DAY 4 *33c*, DAY 5 *34-35*

RETEACH/REVIEW

- ❑ **The Grammar and Writing Book** Use pp. 122–125 of The Grammar and Writing Book to extend instruction. ANY DAY

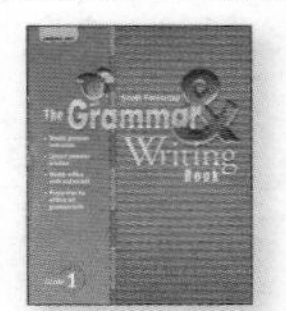

The Grammar and Writing Book

RESEARCH/INQUIRY

TEACH

- ❑ **Use Alphabetical Order** Model alphabetical order with a dictionary. Then have children practice by alphabetizing a list of words. DAY 5 *35a*
- ❑ **Unit Inquiry Project** Allow time for children to choose two objects to observe, and interview others for ways to best observe them. ANY DAY *9*

Resources for

Differentiated Instruction

LEVELED READERS

- **Comprehension**
  - **Skill** Compare and Contrast
  - **Strategy** Predict
- **Lesson Vocabulary**

  High-Frequency Words

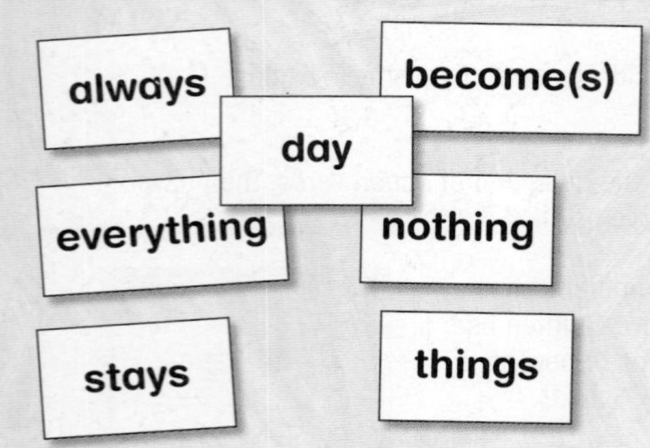

- **Science Standards**
  - Living Things
  - Growth
  - Change

PearsonSuccessNet.com

Use the Online Database of over 600 books to

- Download and print additional copies of this week's leveled readers
- Listen to the readers being read online
- Search for more titles focused on this week's skills, topic, and content

On-Level

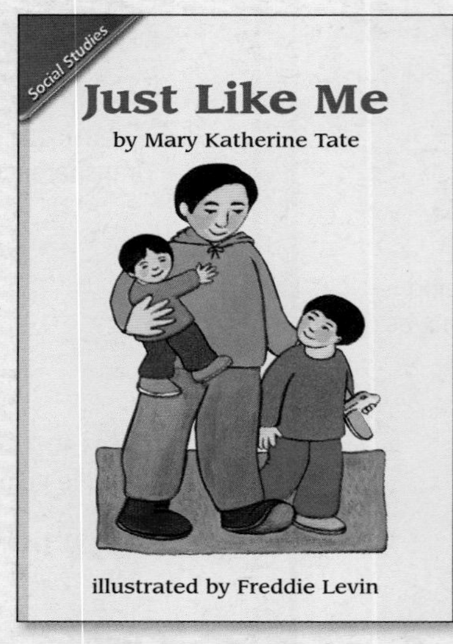

On-Level Reader

Compare and Contrast

Look at the pictures in the book. Compare the boy and his father. Tell how they are the same and how they are different.

Possible responses given.

Same	Different
1. Both have black hair.	4. The boy has on a red shirt.
2. Both hold the baby.	5. The boy is smaller.
3. Both have rosy cheeks.	6. The father is wearing gray pants.

On-Level Practice TE p. LR5

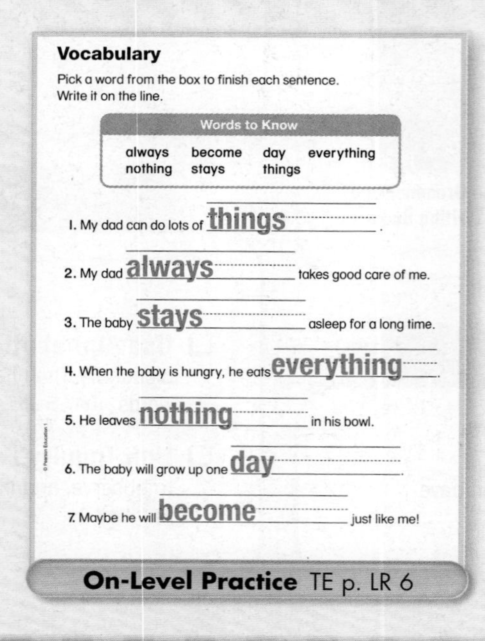

Vocabulary

Pick a word from the box to finish each sentence. Write it on the line.

Words to Know: always, become, day, everything, nothing, stays, things

1. My dad can do lots of things.
2. My dad always takes good care of me.
3. The baby stays asleep for a long time.
4. When the baby is hungry, he eats everything.
5. He leaves nothing in his bowl.
6. The baby will grow up one day.
7. Maybe he will become just like me!

On-Level Practice TE p. LR 6

Strategic Intervention

Below-Level Reader

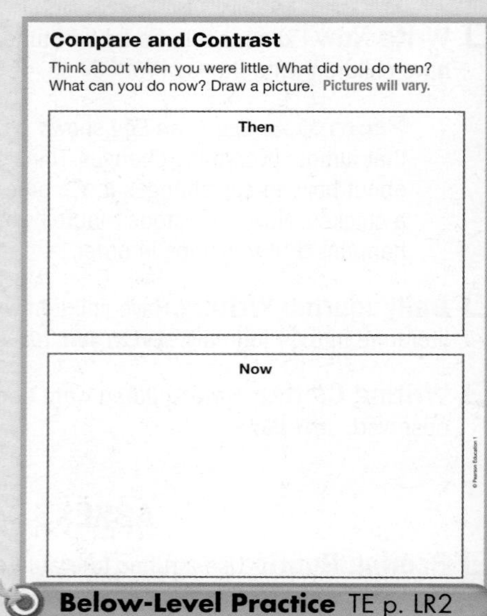

Compare and Contrast

Think about when you were little. What did you do then? What can you do now? Draw a picture. Pictures will vary.

Then

Now

Below-Level Practice TE p. LR2

Vocabulary

Read the words in the box. Write each word on the line.

Words to Know: always, become, day, everything, nothing, stays, things

1. day
2. nothing
3. become
4. things
5. always
6. everything
7. stays

Below-Level Practice TE p. LR3

Advanced

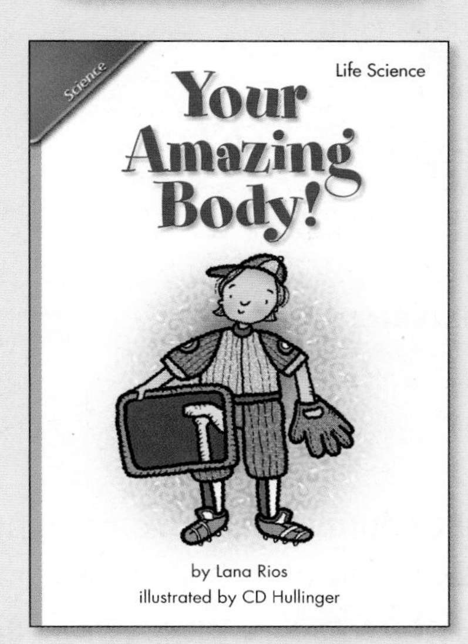

Advanced Reader

Compare and Contrast

Look at one of your hands. Compare it to a grown-up's hand. What is the same? What is different?

Possible responses given.

Same	Different
1. We both have 5 fingers.	4. My hand is smaller.
2. We both have fingernails.	5. My hand does not have hair.
3. You can see our veins.	6. My hand is more tanned.

Advanced Practice TE p. LR8

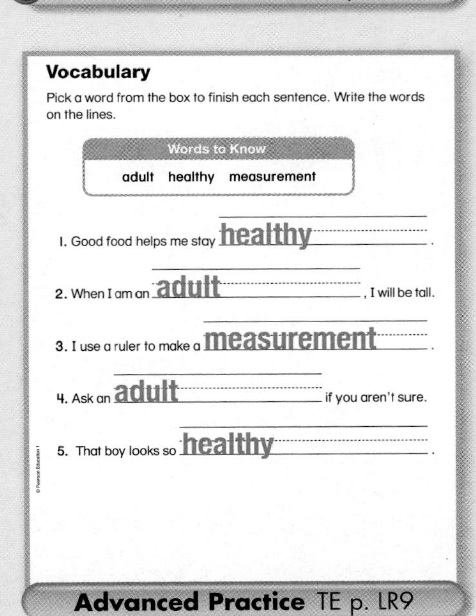

Vocabulary

Pick a word from the box to finish each sentence. Write the words on the lines.

Words to Know

adult healthy measurement

1. Good food helps me stay healthy.
2. When I am an adult, I will be tall.
3. I use a ruler to make a measurement.
4. Ask an adult if you aren't sure.
5. That boy looks so healthy.

Advanced Practice TE p. LR9

ELL

ELL Reader

ELL Poster 13

Teacher's Edition Notes

ELL notes throughout this lesson support instruction and reference additional resources at point of use.

Teaching Guide pp. 85–91, 236–237

- Multilingual summaries of the main selection
- Comprehension lesson
- Vocabulary strategies and word cards
- ELL Reader 1.3.1 lesson

ELL and Transition Handbook

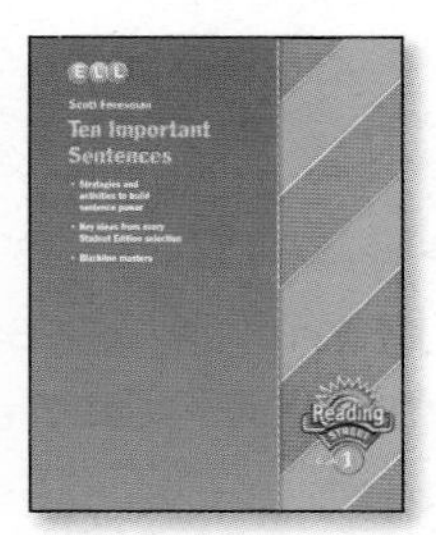

Ten Important Sentences

- Key ideas from every selection in the Student Edition
- Activities to build sentence power

More Reading

Readers' Theater Anthology

- Fluency practice
- Five scripts to build fluency
- Poetry for oral interpretation

Leveled Trade Books

Below-Level

On-Level

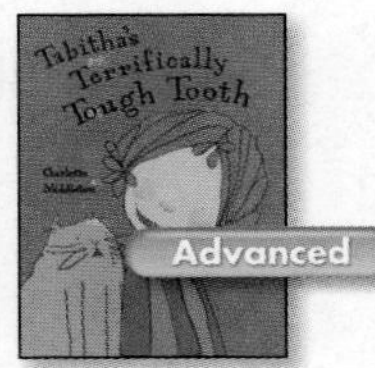

Advanced

- Extend reading tied to the unit concept
- Lessons in Trade Book Library Teaching Guide

Big Book of Poems

- Fluency practice
- Poetry for Choral Reading

Homework

- Family Times Newsletter
- ELL Multilingual Selection Summaries

Take-Home Books

- Decodable Readers
- Leveled Readers

Literacy Centers

Listening

Let's Read Along

MATERIALS
CD player, headphones, print copies of recorded pieces

SINGLES

LISTEN TO LITERATURE As children listen to the following recordings, have them follow along or read along in the print version.

AudioText
An Egg Is an Egg
"Nothing Fits!"

Sing with Me/Background Building Audio
"Oh My"

Phonics Songs and Rhymes Audio
"My Fussy Baby Brother"

Audio CD **Phonics Songs and Rhymes Chart 13**

Reading/Library

Read It Again!

MATERIALS
collection of books for self-selected reading, reading logs

SINGLES PAIRS GROUPS

REREAD BOOKS Have children select previously read books from the appropriate book box and record titles of books they read in their logs. Use these previously read books:

- Decodable Readers
- Leveled Readers
- ELL Readers
- Stories written by classmates
- Books from the library

TEN IMPORTANT SENTENCES Have children read the Ten Important Sentences for *An Egg Is an Egg* and locate the sentences in the Student Edition.

BOOK CLUB Use p. 29 of the Student Edition to set up an "Author Study" of Nicki Weiss. Encourage a group to read the other Weiss books listed and then share favorites.

Word Work

Egg Sort

MATERIALS
2 baskets, 20 paper egg shapes

PAIRS

VOWEL SOUNDS OF *y* Have pairs of children play a sorting game.

1. Label the first basket *long i* and the second basket *long e.*
2. Write words with the long *e* and long *i* sounds on egg-shaped word cards. Mix the eggs up and place them facedown in a pile.
3. Children take turns picking up an egg, reading the word, and placing the egg in the correct basket.
4. Play continues until all words have been sorted.

LONG VOWEL PATTERN CV Label the baskets *long* and *short.* Make word cards with long vowel CV words, and short vowel CVC words. Have children play the game.

This interactive CD provides additional practice.

Scott Foresman Reading Street Centers Survival Kit

Use the ***An Egg Is an Egg*** materials from the Reading Street Centers Survival Kit to organize this week's centers.

Writing

Before and After

MATERIALS
paper, pencils, crayons

SINGLES

WRITE A DESCRIPTION Recall the changes from *An Egg Is an Egg.*

1. **Ask children to think about changes they have observed.**
2. **Have them use the pattern "A _____ is a _______ until it ________. And then it is a _______." to write about changes.**
3. **Encourage children to draw before and after pictures to accompany their writing.**

LEVELED WRITING Encourage children to write at their own ability level. Some may only complete part of the frame. Others will be able to complete the frame with some attention to mechanics and spelling. Your best writers may use the frame to write about more than one change.

Science

All About Me

MATERIALS
baby pictures and current photos or drawings, paper

SINGLES

MAKE COMPARISONS Ask each child to bring in or draw a baby picture and a current picture of themselves.

1. **Have children study their pictures to identify ways they have grown.**
2. **Have them write 2–3 sentences describing the changes.**
3. **Gather the photos and writing into a class book.**
4. **Children can share their pages and make predictions about how they will continue to change as they grow.**

I am taller now. I have hair.
I have teeth.

Technology

Spelling Check

MATERIALS
computer, list of spelling words

PAIRS

TYPE A LIST Pairs of children type and spell-check lesson spelling words.

1. **Have children turn on the computer and open a word processing program.**
2. **Provide pairs with a list of lesson spelling words: *my, by, try, any, body, fly, cry, lucky, silly, puppy.* Misspell some of the words to read *luckie, trry,* and *puppi.***
3. **Children type the list and run a spell-check. They then correct incorrect words.**

ALL CENTERS

Day 1

AT A GLANCE

Oral Vocabulary
"Oh My" 13

Phonemic Awareness
Segment Phonemes

Phonics and Spelling
Vowel sounds of *y*
Spelling Pretest: Words with long *e*, long *i*: *y*

Read Apply Phonics Word Wall

Group Time < Differentiated Instruction

Build Background
Let's Talk About Growing and Changing

Listening Comprehension
Skill Compare and Contrast

Shared Writing
Steps

Grammar
Action Verbs

Materials

- *Sing with Me Big Book*
- Sound-Spelling Cards 10, 16
- Letter Tiles
- Decodable Reader 25
- Tested Word Cards
- Student Edition 10–11
- Graphic Organizer Flip Chart 4

Take It to the NET™ ONLINE

Professional Development
To learn more about think-alouds, go to PearsonSuccessNet.com and read "Think Aloud" by B. Davey.

Morning Warm-Up!

Everything changes.
Once you were a new baby.
What are some things babies do?
Now you can do other things.
How do we change as we grow?

QUESTION OF THE WEEK Tell children they will talk, sing, read, and write about Growing and Changing. Write the message and track the print as you read it. Discuss the questions.

CONNECT CONCEPTS Ask questions to connect to other selections.

- How were the baby dinosaurs in *The Big Circle* different from the adults?
- How do you think the baby dinosaurs will change as they grow?

REVIEW HIGH-FREQUENCY WORDS

- Circle the high-frequency words *new, some,* and *other* in the message.
- Have children say and spell each word as they write it in the air.

Build Background Use the Day 1 instruction on ELL Poster 13 to assess knowledge and develop concepts.

ELL Poster 13

Oral Vocabulary

SHARE LITERATURE Display p. 13 of the *Sing with Me Big Book.* Tell children that they can join you in singing a song about growing and changing. Read the title. Ask children to listen for the Amazing Words **adult, healthy,** and **measurement** as you sing. Then sing the song again and ask children to sing with you. Have children discuss what they see the people doing in the picture, demonstrating their understanding of *adult, healthy,* and *measurement.*

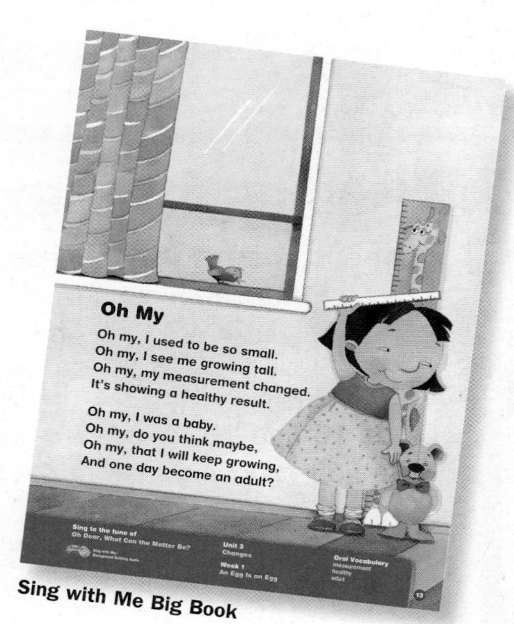

Sing with Me Big Book

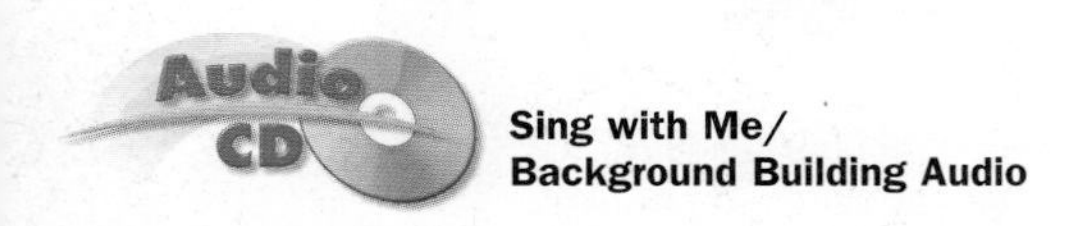

Sing with Me/
Background Building Audio

Phonemic Awareness

SEGMENT PHONEMES

- We just sang "Oh My." Listen to the sounds in *my.*
- Model saying each sound, /m/ /ī/. Have children say the sounds with you and then say the sounds by themselves.
- Now say each sound as you write the letter that goes with it. Say /m/ /ī/ as you write *m, y.*
- Have children say the sounds with you as you point to the letters. (/m/ /ī/)
- When children grow, they're happy. Listen to the sounds in *happy.*
- Model saying each sound, /h/ /a/ /p/ /ē/. Have children say the sounds with you and then say the sounds by themselves.
- Now say each sound as you write the letter that goes with it. Say /h/ /a/ /p/ /ē/ as you write *h, a, pp, y.*
- Have children say the sounds with you as you point to the letters. (/h/ /a/ /p/ /ē/)

Continue the activity with these examples.

fly **penny** **why** **sunny** **try** **sloppy**

OBJECTIVES

- Build oral vocabulary.
- Segment phonemes.

to build oral vocabulary

	MONITOR PROGRESS
adult **healthy** **measurement** **shuffle** **teeter** **crooked** **bounce** **handsome**	**If...** children lack oral vocabulary experiences about the concept Growing and Changing, **then...** use the Oral Vocabulary Routine below to teach *adult.*

Oral Vocabulary ROUTINE

1. **Introduce the Word** Relate the word *adult* to the song. Supply a child-friendly definition. Have children say the word. Example: An *adult* is a grown-up.
2. **Demonstrate** Provide an example to show meaning. Some children can't wait to be *adults.*
3. **Apply** Have children demonstrate their understanding. How do you think your responsibilities will change when you're an *adult?*
4. **Display the Word/Letter-Sounds** Write the word on a card. Display it. Have children identify *d*/d/ and *lt*/lt/. See p. DI·3 to teach *healthy* and *measurement.*

ELL

Build Oral Vocabulary Prompt children to show how they are *growing* from *small* to *tall.* You are small. Bend down low. Stand up just a little. Stand up a little more. Stand up all the way. You are tall. You will keep growing.

OBJECTIVES

- Associate the vowel sounds /ī/ and /ē/ with *y.*
- Blend, read, and sort words with the vowel sounds of *y.*

Skills Trace

Vowel Sounds of *y*

Introduce/Teach	**TE: 1.3 10n–o, 14c–d**
Practice	TE: 1.3 10q; PB: 1.2 3; DR25
Reteach/Review	TE: 1.3 34c, 64c–d, DI•76; PB: 1.2 18
Assess/Test	TE: 1.3 34e–g Benchmark Test, Unit 3

Generalization

When *y* is at the end of a word, it stands for either the long *i* sound or the long *e* sound. When *y* ends a word of two or more syllables, it usually has the long *e* sound.

Strategic Intervention

Use **Monitor Progress,** p. 10o during Group Time after children have had more practice with the vowel sounds of *y.*

Advanced

Use **Monitor Progress,** p. 10o as a preassessment to determine whether or not this group of children would benefit from this instruction in the vowel sounds of *y.*

Support Phonics In Spanish, the letter *y* is pronounced like the long *e* in English, so the long *e* sound of *y* in words, such as *funny* and *happy,* may be familiar to Spanish speakers. However, Spanish speakers may need additional practice with words that have the long *i* sound of *y,* such as *my, dry,* and *fly.*

See the Phonics Transition Lessons in the ELL and Transition Handbook.

Vowel Sounds of *y*

TEACH/MODEL

Blending Strategy

ROUTINE

1 Connect Write *hide* and *these.* You studied words like these already. What vowel sounds do you hear in these words? (/ī/ and /ē/) Today we'll learn about another letter that can stand for /ī/ and /ē/.

2 Use Sound-Spelling Cards Display Cards 16 and 10. This is *ice cream.* What sound do you hear at the beginning of *ice?* (/ī/) Say it with me: /ī/. This is *easel.* What sound is at the beginning of *easel?* (/ē/) Say it with me: /ē/.

Sound-Spelling Card 16

Sound-Spelling Card 10

3 Model Write *cry.* In this word the letter *y* stands for /ī/. Segment and blend *cry;* then have children blend with you: /k/ /r/ /ī/, *cry.*

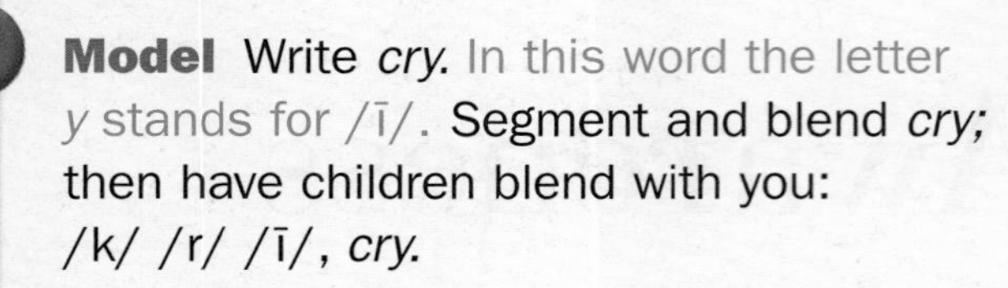

Write *bunny.* Segment and blend *bunny;* have children blend with you: /b/ /u/ /n/ /ē/, *bunny.* When the letter *y* is at the end of a word, it stands for either the long *i* sound or the long *e* sound. In this word the letter *y* stands for /ē/. When *y* ends a word that has two or more syllables, the *y* usually stands for the vowel sound /ē/.

Point out the single syllable in *cry* and the two syllables in *bunny.*

4 Group Practice Let's blend these words together. Think about whether the *y* has the sound /ī/ or /ē/. Continue with *muddy, fry, puppy, shy,* and *nanny.*

5 Review What do you know about reading these words? The letter *y* at the end of a word can stand for either long *i* or long *e.* When *y* ends a word with two or more syllables, the *y* usually stands for /ē/.

BLEND WORDS

INDIVIDUALS BLEND WORDS WITH VOWEL SOUNDS OF *y* Call on individuals to blend the words *by, candy, sky, jelly, dry,* and *tummy.* Have them tell what they know about each word before reading it. (The *y* at the end has the vowel sound /ī/ or /ē/. If the word has two or more syllables, the *y* usually stands for /ē/.) For feedback, refer to step five of the Blending Strategy Routine.

SORT WORDS

INDIVIDUALS SORT WORDS WITH THE VOWEL SOUNDS OF y Write *Long i* and *Long e* as headings of a two-column chart. Remind children that the letter *y* at the end of a word can stand for either the long *i* sound or the long *e* sound. Have children write *i* and *e* on separate cards. When I say a word, hold up the *i* card if you hear /ī/. Hold up the *e* card, if you hear /ē/: *my, sunny, why, fly, sandy, try, choppy, pretty.* Write each word in the appropriate column. Have the completed lists read.

Look at the words in the first column. How many syllables do the words have? (one) What sound does *y* stand for? (long *i*) How many syllables do the words in the second column have? (two) What sound does *y* stand for? (long *e*)

Long *i*	Long e
my	sunny
why	sandy
fly	choppy
try	pretty

Vocabulary TiP

You may wish to explain the meanings of these words.

pry lift by force
shy bashful
sly tricky

fry baby

Circle the word for each picture.

1. puppy put
2. flop fly
3. lock lucky
4. bunny ball
5. crib cry
6. sit city
7. sky skate
8. had happy

Find the word that has the same **y** sound as [fly]. **Mark** the ⊂⊃ to show your answer.

9. mommy / messy / my
10. tummy / try / twenty

Home Activity Your child practiced reading words with the vowel sounds of *y* heard in *fry* or *baby*. Work with your child to put the above answers into two word lists—one of words in which *y* represents the long e sound (baby) and one in which it represents the long i sound (fry).

▲ **Practice Book 1.2** p. 3, Vowel Sounds of *y*

Monitor Progress — Check Word Reading Vowel sounds of *y*

Write the following words and have individuals read them.

by	**dry**	**sky**	**cry**	**shy**
buddy	**happy**	**ugly**	**daddy**	**funny**
yell	**yummy**	**bumpy**	**yuck**	**sly**

If... children cannot blend words with vowel sounds of *y* at this point,

then... continue to monitor their progress using other instructional opportunities during the week so that they can be successful with the Day 5 Assessment. See the Skills Trace on p. 10n.

▶ **Day 1** Check Word Reading · **Day 2** Check Word Reading · **Day 3** Check High-Frequency Words/Retelling · **Day 4** Check Fluency · **Day 5** Assess Progress

Spiral REVIEW

- Row 3 contrasts vowel sounds of *y* with *y*/y/.

Word Reading SUCCESS PREDICTOR

OBJECTIVES

- Segment sounds to spell words.
- Spell words with the vowel sounds of *y.*

Spelling Words

Long *e* and Long *i*: *y*

1. **my***
2. **by**
3. **try**
4. **any**
5. **body**
6. **fly**
7. **cry**
8. **lucky**
9. **silly**
10. **puppy**

High-Frequency Words

11. **things***
12. **always***

* Words from the Selection

Long *e* and Long *i*: *y*

Look at the word. Say it. Listen for the long *e* or long *i* sound.

	Write the word.	Check it.
1. my	my	my
2. by	by	by
3. try	try	try
4. any	any	any
5. body	body	body
6. fly	fly	fly
7. cry	cry	cry
8. lucky	lucky	lucky
9. silly	silly	silly
10. puppy	puppy	puppy

High-Frequency Words

11. things **things** 12. always **always**

School + Home **Home Activity** Your child is learning to spell words in which the long *e* or long *i* sound is spelled *y*. To practice at home, have your child look at the word, say it, spell it, and then spell it with eyes closed.

▲ **Spelling Practice Book** p. 49

Spelling

PRETEST Vowel Sounds of *y*

MODEL WRITING FOR SOUNDS Each spelling word ends with a vowel sound of *y.* Before administering the spelling pretest, model how to segment the words to spell them.

- What sounds do you hear in *sky?* (/s/ /k/ /ī/)
- What is the letter for /s/? Write *s.* Continue with *k*/k/ and *y* /ī/.
- In *sky,* the long *i* sound is spelled with *y.*
- What sounds do you hear in *funny?* (/f/ /u/ /n/ /ē/)
- What is the letter for /f/? Write *f.* Continue with *u*/u/ *nn*/n/ *y*/ē/.
- In *funny*, the long *e* sound is spelled with *y.*
- Repeat with *dry* and *fifty.*

PRETEST Dictate the spelling words. Segment the words for children if necessary. Have children check their pretests and correct misspelled words.

HOMEWORK Spelling Practice Book, p. 49.

An Egg Is an Egg

Carlos Gets a Puppy

On Carlos's seventh birthday, he asked for a puppy. "Maybe we should get an adult dog," suggested his mother. "An adult dog is already trained so it won't be so messy and won't be such a big responsibility." But Carlos wanted a puppy.

A week later, when Carlos got home from school, he found his mother in the kitchen holding a tiny little animal. "What's that?" he asked.

"It's a puppy," said his mother. Carlos looked carefully at the tiny animal, which looked more like a mouse or a squirrel.

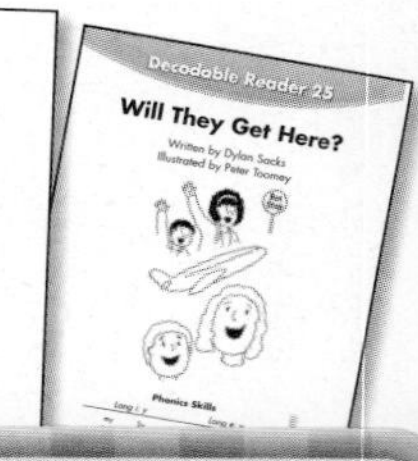

Group Time

DAY 1

On-Level	Strategic Intervention	Advanced
Read Decodable Reader 25.	**Read** Decodable Reader 25.	**Read** Advanced Selection 13.
• Use p. 10q.	• Use the **Routine** on p. DI·16.	• Use the **Routine** on p. DI·17.

Place English language learners in the groups that correspond to their reading abilities in English.

i Independent Activities

Fluency Reading Pair children to reread Leveled Readers or the ELL Reader from the previous week or other text at children's independent level.

Journal Writing Write about something you can do in first grade that you couldn't do in Kindergarten. Share writing.

Independent Reading See p. 10j for Reading/Library activities and suggestions.

Literacy Centers To practice vowel sounds of *y,* you may use Word Work, p. 10j.

Practice Book 1.2 Vowel Sounds of *y,* p. 3

Break into small groups after Spelling and before Build Background.

ELL

Support Spelling Before giving the spelling pretest, clarify the meaning of each spelling word with examples, such as pantomiming *cry* and showing children a photo of a *puppy.*

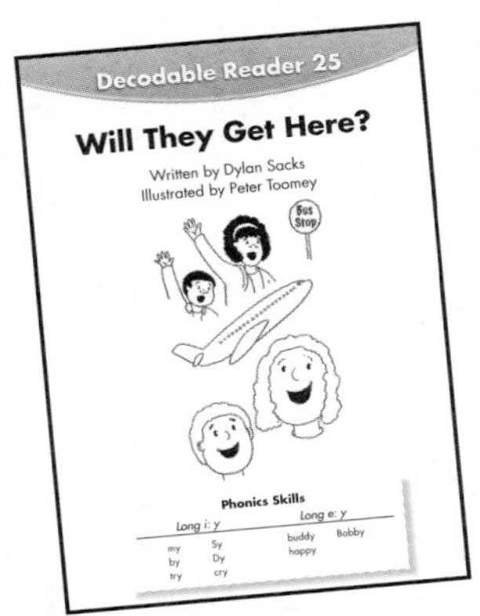

Apply Phonics

PRACTICE Vowel Sounds of *y*

HIGH-FREQUENCY WORDS Review *are, find, of, they, to,* and *you* on the Word Wall. If necessary, have children practice in pairs with word cards. Word Wall

TEXT FEATURE Point to the thought bubble on p. 5 and remind children that it shows what a character is thinking. Have children watch for thought bubbles in this story.

READ DECODABLE READER 25

- Pages 2–3 Read aloud quietly with the group.
- Pages 4–6 Have the group read aloud without you.
- Pages 5–8 Select individuals to read aloud.

CHECK COMPREHENSION AND DECODING Have children retell the story to include characters, setting, and plot. Then have children locate the words in the story that have the long *e* or long *i* sound of *y*. Help children recall that when *y* ends a word of two or more syllables, it usually has the long *e* sound. Have children sort the words according to their vowel sounds.

Long *i*		Long e
Sy	Dy	buddy
my	try	Bobby
by	cry	happy

HOMEWORK Take-Home Decodable Reader 25

REREAD FOR FLUENCY

Oral Rereading

ROUTINE

1. **Read** Have children read the entire book orally.
2. **Reread** To achieve optimal fluency, children should reread the text three or four times.
3. **Provide Feedback** Listen as children read and provide feedback regarding their oral reading and their use of the blending strategy.

OBJECTIVES

- Apply knowledge of letter-sounds and word parts to decode unknown words when reading.
- Use context with letter-sounds to confirm the identification of unknown words.
- Practice fluency with oral rereading.

Monitor Progress

Decoding

If...	then...
If... children have difficulty decoding a word,	**then...** prompt them to blend the word. • What is the new word? • Is the new word a word you know? • Does it make sense in the story?
If... children have difficulty decoding the two-syllable words *buddy, Bobby,* and *happy,*	**then...** divide the words into syllables, have them blend each syllable, and read the word.

ELL

Access Content

Beginning On pp. 5–6, point out the thought bubbles and help children make the connection that Bobby is telling Sy why he was late as he pictures it in his mind.

Intermediate Preview *Will They Get Here?* and use the illustrations to explain that *Bobby* is *Sy's buddy* or friend.

Advanced Before reading *Will They Get Here?* have children describe times when they or someone they know was late.

1

OBJECTIVES

- Build background and oral vocabulary.
- Speak clearly.

Strategic Intervention

Have children draw a picture of themselves doing something they could not do as a baby.

Advanced

Have children bring in a baby picture and a current picture, putting their names on the backs. Working with a partner's pictures, have them write how they can tell that the pictures show the same person.

Activate Prior Knowledge
Invite children to say their age in their home language and in English.

Build Background

LET'S TALK ABOUT Growing and Changing

DEVELOP ORAL LANGUAGE Read the title and have children view the photographs. Ask them to tell you what they see. Allow ample time for children to respond. Remind children to speak clearly. If they do not speak clearly, model by giving examples of clear speech and unclear speech. Then use open-ended prompts to encourage conversation. For example:

Tell me about what you see here. Yes, that's right, some children are enjoying themselves at a birthday party. How old do you think the birthday girl is? Look at the photograph on the top of p. 11. What can you tell me about these girls' teeth? Are the girls finished growing? Now tell me about the girl in the bottom photograph. How will she change and grow?

BUILD ORAL VOCABULARY As you continue the discussion, encourage children to use today's Amazing Words, *adult, healthy,* and *measurement.*

- Look at the girl in the yellow dress. How is the nurse checking her measurement?
- Use the word *healthy* to talk about the photograph of the three girls.
- Are there any adults in the photograph on p. 10? How can you tell?

DEVELOP CONCEPTS

CONCEPT CHART Remind children of the question of the week.

- How do we change as we grow?

Display Graphic Organizer 4 or draw a T-chart. Label the chart "Baby" and "Now." Discuss things babies do and list them on the "Baby" side of the chart. For each suggestion, ask, "How have you changed?" Add children's responses to the "Now" section of the chart. Display the chart for use throughout the week.

- Do very young babies have teeth? (no)
- How have some of your teeth changed? (We lose baby teeth and get permanent teeth.)

CONNECT TO READING Point out the illustration on the bottom corner of Student Edition p. 11. Ask children what the boy is doing. (looking at a picture of a baby) Explain that this week children will read a story about different things in this boy's life. Tell children that they will learn about how these things change and grow.

Oral Vocabulary

Let's Talk About Growing and Changing

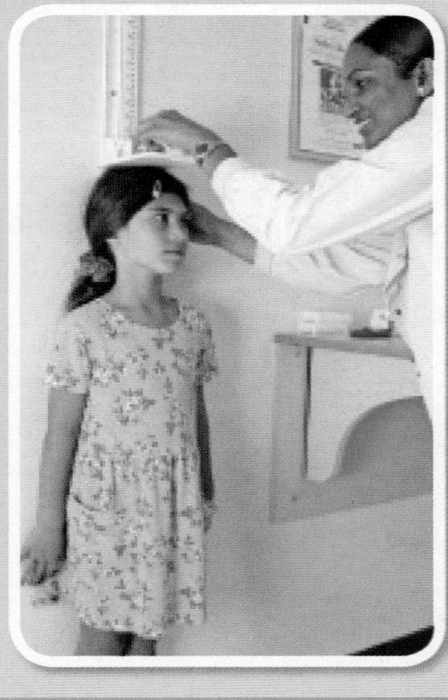

10 11

Baby	Now
no teeth	lose baby teeth and grow permanent teeth
crawl	can walk and run
have to be fed	can eat by myself
have to be dressed	can dress myself

▲ **Graphic Organizer Flip Chart 4**

Tech Files ONLINE

For a Web site that explores one of the ways children grow and change—losing their baby teeth—do an Internet search using the keywords *healthy teeth.*

Access Content To prepare children for reading *An Egg Is an Egg*, send home the story summary in English and/or the home language. See the ELL Teaching Guide, pp. 89–91.

OBJECTIVE

Compare and contrast.

Skills Trace

Compare and Contrast	
Introduce/Teach	**TE: 1.2 139a–b, 142g; 1.3 11a–b, 14g; 1.5 77a–b, 80g**
Practice	TE: 1.2 150–151; 1.3 22–23; 1.5 90–91; PB: 1.1 114; 1.2 4, 144
Reteach/Review	TE: 1.2 DI·84; 1.3 104–105, 154–155; DI·77; 1.5 128–129, DI·80
Test	Selection Test: 1.2 23–24; 1.3 25–28; 1.5 81–84 Benchmark Test: Units 3, 5

Look at the picture.
Circle the answer to each question.
Hint: One question will have two answers.

1. Who has a dress?	(Kate)	Amy
2. Who has pants?	Kate	(Amy)
3. Who has a cat?	Kate	(Amy)
4. Who has no pet?	(Kate)	Amy
5. Who has a pen?	(Kate)	(Amy)

6. **Draw** two cats that are the same.
Children's artwork should show two identical cats.

7. **Draw** two cats that are different.
Children's artwork should show two cats that differ in some way.

School + Home **Home Activity** Your child identified the ways in which two characters were alike and different. Have your child describe two of his or her relatives. Have your child tell how they are alike and different.

▲ **Practice Book 1.2** p. 4, Compare and Contrast

Access Content For a Picture It! lesson on compare and contrast, see the ELL Teaching Guide, p. 86.

Listening Comprehension

TEACH/MODEL Compare and Contrast

DEFINE COMPARE AND CONTRAST

- Things that are alike are the same or almost the same.
- Things that are different are not the same.
- Good readers look for clues that tell how things are alike and different.

READ ALOUD Read the first three paragraphs of "I Want to Be Six Forever" and model how to compare and contrast.

MODEL When I read, I think about things that are alike and different. Amy's feet have changed because they grew bigger. That means that they are different than they used to be. Her sneakers are the same size as they have always been, so they are the same. Thinking about how things are alike and different helps me understand what is going on in the story.

PRACTICE

CLUES TO COMPARE AND CONTRAST Read the rest of the story and ask children to compare and contrast other things in the story. How is Amy different now from the way she was last year? (Now she can ride a bicycle, swim, and tie her shoes. Last year she could only ride a tricycle, and she couldn't swim or tie her shoes.) How are puppies, kittens, and children alike? (They are all young and they all grow into older things, like dogs, cats, and adults.) How will Amy's new sneakers be the same as the old ones? (They will be the same kind and the same color.) How will they be different? (They will be newer and a larger size.)

RECOGNIZE COMPARE AND CONTRAST Have children recall the selection *Life in the Forest.*

- How are all the animals in the selection alike? (They all live in the forest.)
- How are woodpeckers and hummingbirds alike? (They both eat insects and fly.) How are they different? (Woodpeckers have short, fat beaks that they use to peck trees; hummingbirds have long, skinny beaks that they use to sip food and water from plants.)

CONNECT TO READING Tell children that when they read any story or selection, thinking about how things are alike and different can help them understand what they read.

I Want to Be Six Forever!

Amy tried to put on her favorite purple sneakers, but her feet would not fit into them.

"Oh, no!" Amy cried to her mother. "My shoes shrank! They are too small!"

Amy's mom smiled and said, "Your shoes didn't shrink. Your feet grew because you are getting bigger."

"But I like these shoes," Amy said, frowning. "I don't want to grow up. I want to be six forever!"

"Are you sure you don't want to grow up?" Amy's mom asked. "Remember last year when you could only ride a tricycle? Now you can ride a bicycle. And last year you didn't know how to swim or how to tie your shoes. You can do both those things now!"

"I like doing all those things," Amy agreed.

"Everything changes," Amy's mom explained. "A puppy becomes a dog, a kitten becomes a cat, and a child like you becomes an adult."

"I understand," Amy said. "But I wish my shoes could change and grow bigger with me!"

"Tomorrow we'll go to the shoe store," Amy's mom said. "The salesperson will take a measurement of your foot to see how much it has grown. Then you can pick out some new shoes. You can even get the same kind of sneakers you have now."

Amy thought for a moment and answered, "A bigger pair of shoes wouldn't be so bad if they are the same kind and the same color." Then she added, "I think I like growing up."

Read ALOUD

OBJECTIVE

- Write steps.

DAILY FIX-IT

1. i am lucki.
I am lucky.

2. Alwas try your best
Always try your best.

This week's practice sentences appear on Daily Fix-It Transparency 13.

Strategic Intervention

Children who are not able to write independently may illustrate a chicken's life cycle and then label the pictures *egg* and *chicken*.

Advanced

Have children write the steps of another animal's life cycle. Consider writing the life cycle steps of a frog or a butterfly.

Support Writing Before writing the steps of how an egg becomes a chicken, have children look through a chicken life cycle book for ideas. Have children work with a partner to write the steps involved in an egg becoming a chicken.

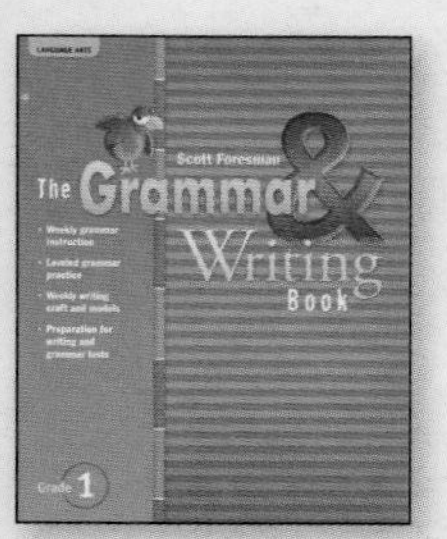

▲ **The Grammar and Writing Book**
For more instruction and practice, use pp. 122–127.

Shared Writing

WRITE Steps

GENERATE IDEAS Ask children to tell how an egg becomes a chicken. Encourage them to name the steps in order. Write their ideas on the board.

WRITE STEPS Explain that the class will write the steps by which an egg becomes a chicken.

COMPREHENSION SKILL Have children compare and contrast an egg and a chicken as they write the steps of how an egg becomes a chicken.

- Display Writing Transparency 13 and read the title.
- Ask children if there are any similarities between an egg and a chicken.
- Discuss how an egg and chicken are different.
- As children describe how an egg becomes a chicken, record their responses.

HANDWRITING While writing, model the letter forms as shown on pp. TR12–15.

READ THE STEPS Have children read the completed steps aloud as you track the print.

Egg to Chicken

1. A hen lays an egg.

Possible answers:

2. The hen sits on the egg.
3. The egg cracks.
4. A chick comes out of the egg.
5. The chick grows up to be a chicken.

Unit 3 An Egg Is an Egg — Writing Model 13

▲ **Writing Transparency 13**

INDEPENDENT WRITING

WRITE STEPS Have children write their own steps of how an egg becomes a chicken. Encourage them to use words from the Word Wall and the Amazing Words board. Let children illustrate their writing. You may gather children's work into a class book for self-selected reading.

Grammar

TEACH/MODEL Action Verbs

IDENTIFY ACTION VERBS Display Grammar Transparency 13. Read the definition aloud. Then model with item 1.

- A verb tells what someone or something does. *Ann plants a seed. Plants* is the action verb. It tells what Ann does.

Continue modeling with items 2–6.

PRACTICE

SUGGEST ACTION VERBS Have children name things they do. List each action verb on the board and ask the child to demonstrate that action.

- Name something you do.
- Is this an action word?
- Show us that action.

ADDITIONAL PRACTICE For additional practice use pp. 122–127 in the Grammar and Writing Book.

OBJECTIVE

- Identify action verbs.

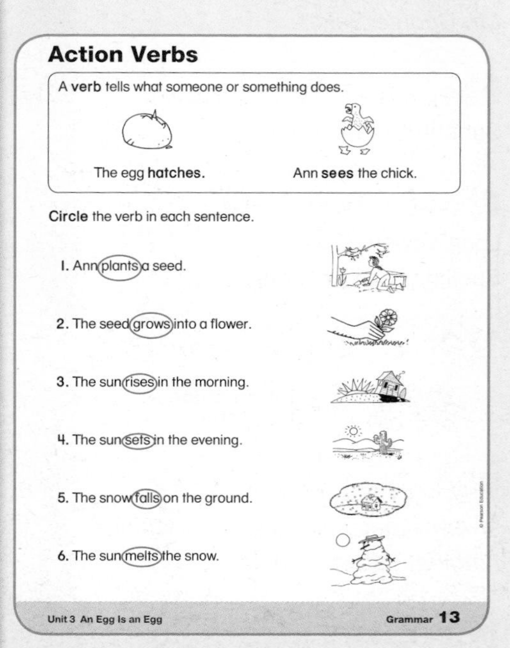
Action Verbs

A **verb** tells what someone or something does.

The egg **hatches.** Ann **sees** the chick.

Circle the verb in each sentence.

1. Ann plants a seed.
2. The seed grows into a flower.
3. The sun rises in the morning.
4. The sun sets in the evening.
5. The snow falls on the ground.
6. The sun melts the snow.

Unit 3 An Egg Is an Egg Grammar 13

▲ **Grammar Transparency 13**

Wrap Up Your Day!

VOWEL SOUNDS OF *y* Write *happy* and ask children what sound the *y* in *baby* has. (long *e*, /ē/) Continue with *my, y,* /ī/. Have children name other words that have long *e* or long *i* spelled *y*.

SPELLING LONG *e* AND LONG *i*: *y* Have children name the letters for each sound in *silly.* Have children write the word on a piece of paper. Continue with *try* and *puppy.*

COMPARE AND CONTRAST Recall "I Want to Be Six Forever" and model how to compare and contrast. I think about things that are alike and different. Amy's feet grew bigger. That means that they are different than they used to be. Her sneakers are the size they have always been, so they are the same.

LET'S TALK ABOUT IT Recall in "I Want to Be Six Forever" that Amy could not swim last year and this year she can swim. Review the Baby/Now T-chart. Where would you write *swim* on this chart?

HOMEWORK Send home this week's Family Times newsletter.

PREVIEW Day 2

Tell children that tomorrow the class will read about a 100-year-old man.

Day 2
AT A GLANCE

Share Literature
Mr. George Baker

Phonemic Awareness
Substitute Phonemes

Phonics and Spelling
Long Vowels (CV)
Spelling: Long *e*, Long *i: y*

Read Apply Phonics Word Wall

< Differentiated Instruction

High-Frequency Words
always become day everything nothing stays things

Interactive Writing
Journal Entry

Grammar
Action Words

Speaking and Listening
Follow Directions

Materials

- *Sing with Me Big Book*
- Big Book *Mr. George Baker*
- Letter Tiles
- Decodable Reader 26
- Student Edition 12–13
- Tested Word Cards

Morning Warm-Up!

Today we will read about a young boy and an old man. They are special friends. Do you think people still grow and change when they are old?

QUESTION OF THE DAY Encourage children to sing "Oh My" from the *Sing with Me Big Book* as you gather. Write and read the message and discuss the question.

REVIEW ANTONYMS

- Read the message and have children find words that have opposite meanings. *(young, old)*
- Circle each word and read each with children.
- Encourage children to suggest other words that are antonyms.

ELL

Build Background Use the Day 2 instruction on ELL Poster 13 to preview high-frequency words.

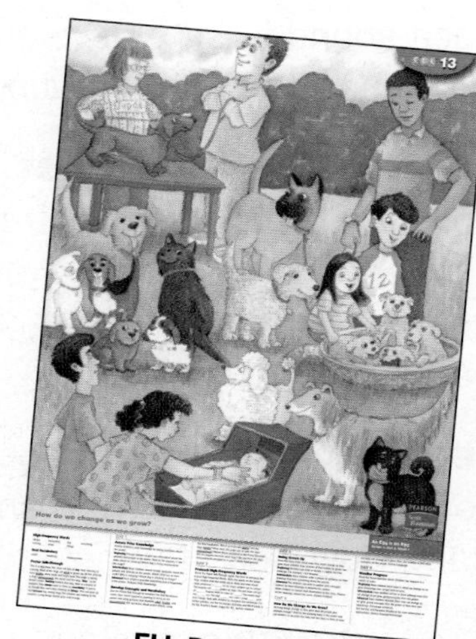
ELL Poster 13

Share Literature

BUILD CONCEPTS

TEXT FEATURES Display p. 3 of the Big Book and point to the word *hundred.* Tell children that this word is set in a special slanted type called italics. Then explain that the author probably used italics for the word *hundred* because she wanted readers to understand that a hundred years old is *very* old.

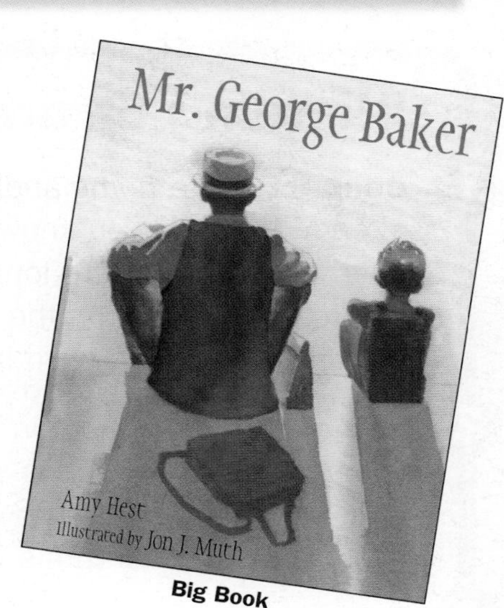

Big Book

BUILD ORAL VOCABULARY Ask children to describe how an old person moves. A person who is a hundred years old might **shuffle**, or drag, his or her feet while walking. Perhaps he or she **teeters,** or wobbles, a bit too. Ask children to listen to find out some ways that George Baker moves.

- How do George Baker and the boy walk to the bus? (shuffle)
- How do you know George's wife moves unsteadily? (She teeters out to the porch.)
- What is George learning to do at school? (read)

Phonemic Awareness

SUBSTITUTE PHONEMES

- Mr. George Baker waits. He waits for Harry. Listen to the sounds in *he*.
- Model saying each sound, /h/ /ē/. Have children say the sounds with you and then say the sounds by themselves.
- Now say each sound as you write the letter that goes with it. (Say /h/ /ē/ as you write *h, e.)*
- Have children say the sounds as you point to the letters (/h/ /ē/) and blend the sounds to say the word *(he).*
- Now listen as I change the /ē/, the last sound in *he,* to /ī/. First, I take off the /ē/. Erase *e*. Then I add /ī/. Add the letter *i: hi.* Have children say the sounds with you. (/h/ /ī/)

Continue the activity with these examples.

Change the /ī/ in *by* to /ē/. *(be)*

Change the /ē/ in *me* to /ī/ *(my)*

OBJECTIVES

- Recognize the purpose of special typefaces.
- Set purpose for listening.
- Build oral vocabulary.
- Substitute phonemes.

to build oral vocabulary

	MONITOR PROGRESS
adult **healthy** **measurement** **shuffle** **teeter** **crooked** **bounce** **handsome**	**If...** children lack oral vocabulary experiences about the concept Growing and Changing, **then...** use the Oral Vocabulary Routine. See p. DI·3 to teach *shuffle* and *teeter.*

Build Concepts Use math counters or other small objects to help children understand the concept of one hundred. Count out one hundred objects. Then have each child count out their age with the same objects. Compare the two sets, explaining that one set represents the child's age and the other set represents Mr. George Baker's age.

OBJECTIVES

- Associate the CV spelling pattern with the long vowel sounds.
- Blend, read, and sort CV words.

Skills Trace

Long Vowels (CV)

Introduce/Teach	**TE: 1.3 12c-d, 14c-d**
Practice	TE: 1.3 12f; PB: 1.2 5; DR26
Reteach/Review	TE: 1.3 34c, 64c-d, DI·76; PB: 1.2 19
Assess/Test	TE: 1.3 34e-g Benchmark Test, Unit 3

Generalization

CV When a word or a syllable ends with a single vowel, the vowel sound is usually long.

Strategic Intervention

Use **Monitor Progress,** p. 12d during Group Time after children have had more practice with long vowels (CV).

Advanced

Use **Monitor Progress,** p. 12d as a preassessment to determine whether or not this group of children would benefit from this instruction with long vowels (CV).

Support Phonics Some long vowel sounds in English are similar to the sounds made by different vowels in Spanish. As a result, Spanish speakers may spell long *e* words with *i (bi* for *be)* or long *i* words with *ai (hai* for *hi)*. Have children practice English spelling conventions for long vowels.

See the Phonics Transition Lessons in the ELL and Transition Handbook.

Long Vowels (CV)

TEACH/MODEL

Blending Strategy

ROUTINE

1 Connect Write *home* and *hide.* You studied words like these already. What do you know about the vowel sounds in these words? (The vowel sounds are long.) How can you tell the vowel sounds are long? (There is a silent *e* on the end of both words.) Today we'll learn another way you can tell when a word has a long vowel sound.

2 Model Write *go.* The *o* in this word says its name. When a word or a syllable ends with one vowel, the vowel sound is usually long. This is how I blend this word. Segment and blend *go.* Let's blend this word together: /g/ /ō/, *go.*

3 Group Practice Let's blend these words together. Continue with *me, hi, no, be, she, hello.*

4 Review What do you know about reading these words? When a word or a syllable ends with one vowel, the vowel sound is usually long.

BLEND WORDS

INDIVIDUALS BLEND CV WORDS Call on individual children to blend the words *we, so, he, she, ago, also, Jo, Mo.* Have them tell what they know about each word before reading it. (The vowel at the end of the word or the syllable usually means the vowel stands for the long vowel sound.) For feedback, refer to step four of the Blending Strategy Routine.

SORT WORDS

INDIVIDUALS SORT CV WORDS Distribute word cards for CV words. Write *Long e, Long i, Long o* as headings. Have children read their words and place their word card under the appropriate heading. Have the lists read.

Long *e*	Long *i*	Long *o*
me	hi	go
we		no
be		so
he		Jo
she		hello

Vocabulary TiP

You may wish to explain the meanings of these words.

pro in favor of something

globe a sphere with a map of the Earth on it

Circle a word to finish each sentence. **Write** it on the line.

no

1. He (Hi) "Hi," Luke said.
2. Hi (He) He is little.
3. (No) Nod No one can see him.
4. She is (so) see so big.
5. He will grow to bed (be) be big too.

Home Activity Your child practiced reading words with the long vowel pattern heard in me, hi, and go. Work with your child to make a list of words with the long e sound spelled e and the long o sound spelled o.

▲ **Practice Book 1.2** p. 5, Long Vowels (CV)

Monitor Progress

Check Word Reading Long Vowels (CV)

Write the following words and have individuals read them.

no	**me**	**hi**	**she**	**go**
we	**dive**	**so**	**my**	**these**
pet	**he**	**globe**	**pro**	**got**

If... children cannot blend words with long vowel pattern CV at this point,

then... continue to monitor their progress using other instructional opportunities during the week so that they can be successful with the Day 5 Assessment. See the Skills Trace on p. 12c.

SUCCESS PREDICTOR

Day 1 Check Word Reading | ▶ **Day 2 Check Word Reading** | Day 3 Check High-Frequency Words/Retelling | Day 4 Check Fluency | Day 5 Assess Progress

Spiral REVIEW

- Row 2 contrasts CV and CVCe patterns.
- Row 3 contrasts CV, CVCe, and CVC patterns.

OBJECTIVE

- Spell words with the vowel sounds of *y*.

Spelling Words

Long *e* and Long *i*: *y*

1. **my***
2. **by**
3. **try**
4. **any**
5. **body**
6. **fly**
7. **cry**
8. **lucky**
9. **silly**
10. **puppy**

High-Frequency Words

11. **things***
12. **always***

* Words from the Selection

Long *e* and Long *i*: *y*

Spelling Words				
my	by	try	any	body
fly	cry	lucky	silly	puppy

Write five list words that rhyme with **why**.

1. my 2. by 3. try
4. fly 5. cry

Write the missing word.

any silly lucky body puppy

6. I have a puppy named Spot.
7. He has a soft, furry body.
8. My pup acts silly.
9. Do you see any dog toys?
10. I am lucky to have a pup.

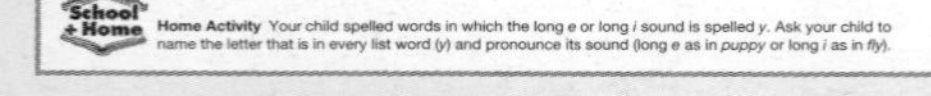

▲ **Spelling Practice Book** p. 50

Spelling

PRACTICE Vowel Sounds of *y*

WRITE DICTATION SENTENCES Have children write these sentences. Repeat words slowly, allowing children to hear each sound. Children may use the Word Wall to help with spelling high-frequency words. Word Wall

That silly puppy takes my things.

I always cry when I'm sad.

Jo will try to fly this kite.

HOMEWORK Spelling Practice Book, p. 50

Group Time

On-Level

Read Decodable Reader 26.

- Use p. 12f.

Strategic Intervention

Read Decodable Reader 26.

- Use the **Routine** on p. DI·18.

Advanced

Read *Mr. George Baker.*

- Use the **Routine** on p. DI·19.

ELL Place English language learners in the groups that correspond to their reading abilities in English.

Independent Activities

Fluency Reading Pair children to reread Decodable Reader 25, this week's Leveled Readers, the ELL Reader from the previous week, or other text at children's independent level.

Journal Writing List ways you have changed since you were a baby. Share writing.

Independent Reading See p. 10j for Reading/Library activities and suggestions.

Literacy Centers To practice long vowels (CV), you may use Word Work, p. 10j.

Practice Book 1.2 Sequence, p. 4
Long Vowels (CV), p. 5;
High-Frequency Words, p. 6

Break into small groups after Spelling and before High-Frequency Words.

Apply Phonics

PRACTICE Long Vowels (CV)

HIGH-FREQUENCY WORDS Review *come, down, now, want, said, saw, they* and *to* on the Word Wall. If necessary, have children practice in pairs with word cards. **Word Wall**

READ DECODABLE READER 26

- Pages 10–11 Read aloud quietly with the group.
- Page 12 Have the group read aloud without you.
- Pages 13–16 Select individuals to read aloud.

CHECK COMPREHENSION AND DECODING

- Why do you think the girl thought a picnic wouldn't be fun? (Answers will vary.)
- How did the girl have fun at the park? (She raced around with her friends.)
- Point to a word in the story that has only one vowel and the vowel comes at the end of the word. What is the word? List words that are named. Children may supply *no, go, Mo, he, Jo, hi, be, she,* and *we.* Children may also respond with *my* and *try,* recalling that *y* can stand for the vowel sound /ī/.
- How do you know that these words have a long vowel sound? (They all have only one vowel and it comes at the end.)

HOMEWORK Take-Home Decodable Reader 26

REREAD FOR FLUENCY

Paired Reading

ROUTINE

1. **Reader 1 Begins** Children read the entire book, switching readers at the end of each page.
2. **Reader 2 Begins** Have partners reread; now the other partner begins.
3. **Reread** For optimal fluency, children should reread three or four times.
4. **Provide Feedback** Listen to children read and provide corrective feedback regarding their oral reading and their use of the blending strategy.

OBJECTIVES

- Apply knowledge of letter-sounds and word parts to decode unknown words when reading.
- Use context with letter-sounds to confirm the identification of unknown words.
- Practice fluency with paired rereading.

Monitor Progress

Decoding

If... children have difficulty decoding a word,	**then...** prompt them to blend the word. • What is the new word? • Is the new word a word you know? • Does it make sense in the story?
If... children have difficulty decoding the two-syllable words *picnic* and *happy,*	**then...** divide the words into syllables, have them blend each syllable, and read the word.

Access Content

Beginning Use the illustrations in *The Picnic* to help children understand how the girl's feelings about going on a picnic change from the beginning of the story to the end.

Intermediate Talk about exclamation marks. Model first and then have children track and read these story phrases in the appropriate voice: No! I will not go! Hi!

Advanced Discuss homophones for story words *hi (high)* and *no (know).*

Words to Read

things
always
day
become
nothing
stays
everything

Read the Words

Some things always change. They change from day to day. Children get bigger. Seeds become plants. Nothing stays the same. Everything changes.

Genre: Realistic Fiction
Realistic fiction has characters that act like real people. In *An Egg Is an Egg,* you will read about changes that take place in our world.

OBJECTIVE

- Recognize high-frequency words.

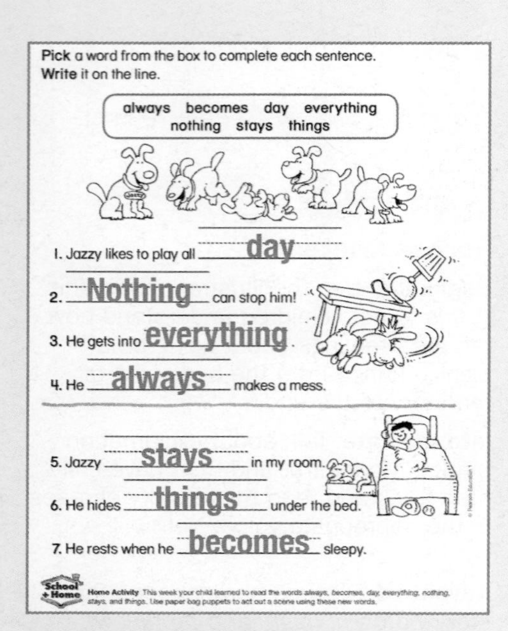
Pick a word from the box to complete each sentence. Write it on the line.

always becomes day everything nothing stays things

1. Jazzy likes to play all day.
2. Nothing can stop him!
3. He gets into everything.
4. He always makes a mess.
5. Jazzy stays in my room.
6. He hides things under the bed.
7. He rests when he becomes sleepy.

▲ **Practice Book 1.2** p. 6, High-Frequency Words

High-Frequency Words

Nondecodable Words

ROUTINE

1. **Say and Spell** Look at the words on p. 12. You cannot yet blend the sounds in these words. We will spell the words and use letter-sounds we know to learn them. Point to the first word. This word is *things, t-h-i-n-g-s, things.* What is this word? What are the letters in this word?
2. **Identify Familiar Letter-Sounds** Point to the first two letters in *things.* What are these letters? These two letters together stand for their own sound. What is the sound for these letters? (*th*/th/)
3. **Demonstrate Meaning** Tell me a sentence using this word.

Repeat the routine with the other Words to Read. Have children identify these familiar letter-sounds and word parts: *always* (*l*/l/, *w*/w/), *day* (*d*/d/), *become* (small word *be*), *nothing* (*n*/n/, *th*/th/), *stays* (*st*/st/), *everything* (*v*/v/, *th*/th/).

Have children read aloud the sentences on p. 13 and point to the Words to Read. Add the words to the Word Wall. **Word Wall**

Interactive Writing

WRITE Journal Entry

BRAINSTORM Use the Read Aloud "I Want to Be Six Forever!" on p. 11b to encourage a discussion about how we change as we grow. Identify ways children have changed in the last year or since school began.

SHARE THE PEN Have children participate in writing a journal entry. Tell children to pretend it is their birthday. They will write a journal entry that describes how they have grown and changed in the past year. To begin, write *Today is my birthday.* Have the class repeat it. Invite individuals to write familiar letter-sounds, word parts, and high-frequency words. Guide writing the journal entry by asking questions such as:

- What will I write at the beginning of each sentence? (a capital letter)
- What kind of letters are all the others? (lowercase letters)
- What is at the end of each sentence? (ending mark)
- What do I need to leave between the words in the sentence? (space)

Continue to have individuals make contributions. Frequently reread what has been written while tracking the print.

READ THE JOURNAL ENTRY Read the completed journal entry aloud, having children echo you.

Today is my birthday.
I have changed since last year.
I lost two more teeth.
I can ride my bike to school.
I am learning to read.
What a great year!

INDEPENDENT WRITING

WRITE A JOURNAL ENTRY Have children write their own journal entry about how they have grown and changed in the last year. Encourage children to illustrate their writing.

OBJECTIVE

- Write a journal entry.

Strategic Intervention

Have children copy the class generated journal entry and illustrate their writing.

Advanced

Have children who are able to write complete sentences independently pretend they are a famous athlete or celebrity and write what they think their birthday journal entry might look like.

Support Writing Before writing, reread the class journal entry and point out key words that children may want to incorporate in their own writing.

Beginning Provide a writing framework with the first and last lines the same as the class journal entry. Leave two blank lines for the child to fill in how they have changed.

Intermediate Discuss how each child has changed in the past year. Create a web of words that the child may use as they write their journal entry.

Advanced Encourage children to do a "think-aloud" with a partner to discuss what they are planning to write. Then have children write, illustrate, and share their journal entry.

Grammar

OBJECTIVE

- Identify action verbs.

DEVELOP THE CONCEPT Action Verbs

IDENTIFY ACTION VERBS Write *The dog* and *eats* on the board. Point to each word as you read it. Ask children to identify what is being done in this sentence. What is the action? (*eats*) Who is doing this action? *(the dog)*

A verb tells what someone or something does. Many verbs are action words. What do we call those verbs? (action verbs)

DAILY FIX-IT

3. take good care of your puppe.
Take good care of your puppy.

4. Those things Are sily.
Those things are silly.

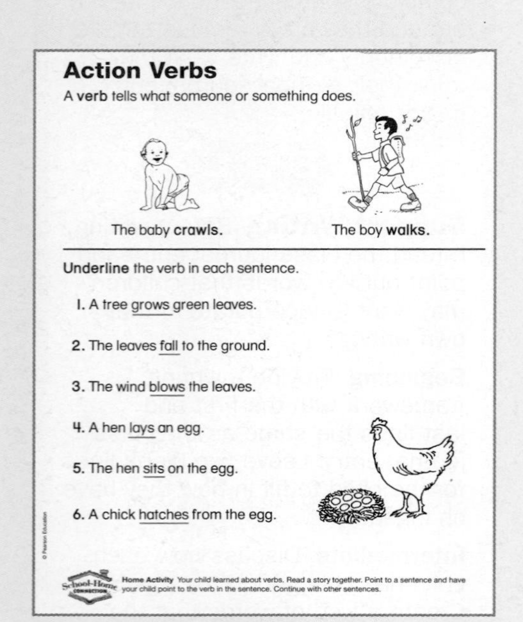

Action Verbs

A **verb** tells what someone or something does.

The baby **crawls**. The boy **walks**.

Underline the verb in each sentence.

1. A tree grows green leaves.
2. The leaves fall to the ground.
3. The wind blows the leaves.
4. A hen lays an egg.
5. The hen sits on the egg.
6. A chick hatches from the egg.

Home Activity Your child learned about verbs. Read a story together. Point to a sentence and have your child point to the verb in the sentence. Continue with other sentences.

▲ **Grammar and Writing Practice Book** p. 49

PRACTICE

IDENTIFY ACTIONS Gather several pictures of people and animals performing an action. Display a picture. Model identifying the action in the picture, for example:

MODEL This is a dog. Write *The dog.* The dog is jumping over the fence. Write *jumps over the fence.* *Jumps* is the action verb in this sentence. *Jumps* tells me what the dog is doing. *The dog jumps over the fence.*

Have children suggest sentences for the other pictures and identify the action for each sentence. Write the sentences children provide and underline the action verbs.

Support Grammar Write action verbs on index cards. Have children choose a card and act out the verb for the class. Classmates guess the action verb. See the Grammar Transition lessons in the ELL and Transition Handbook.

Speaking and Listening

FOLLOW DIRECTIONS

DEMONSTRATE SPEAKING AND LISTENING Remind children of the importance of listening to and following directions. Ask them to think about good listening behaviors as you discuss following directions when getting ready to leave school. If children have trouble following directions, have them ask questions to clarify.

Speakers	Listeners
• Make directions specific. • Give directions in the correct order. • Speak clearly. • Use visual aids, such as pictures and objects.	• Restate directions. • Remember all the steps. • Follow the directions in order.

FOLLOW DIRECTIONS Ask children the steps they follow before they go home from school every day. Create a numbered list of the activities. If possible, at the end of the school day, ask children to restate and follow the steps in the list they created.

Title: Getting Ready to Go Home

1. **Get backpack.**
2. **Put papers and lunch box in backpack.**
3. **Put on coat.**
4. **Leave the building.**

OBJECTIVES

- Speak to communicate information.
- Listen to follow directions.

Wrap Up Your Day!

HIGH-FREQUENCY WORDS Write this sentence: *The other day a family moved into that new house.* Ask children to read the sentence and identify the high-frequency words *other, family, new.*

LONG VOWELS (CV) Write *she, he, go,* and *hi.* Have children identify the vowel sounds. (long vowels)

LET'S TALK ABOUT IT Display the Baby/Now T-chart from Day 1. Recall the Big Book *Mr. George Baker.* Ask: What is one thing that George Baker can do now that he couldn't do when he was a baby? (Answers may vary but may include play drums, dance, wink.)

PREVIEW Day 3

Tell children that tomorrow they will read a story about many different objects that change.

Day 3

AT A GLANCE

Share Literature
Mr. George Baker

Phonemic Awareness
Segment and Blend Phonemes

Phonics and Spelling
Vowel Sounds of *y* and Long Vowels (CV)

Spelling: Long *e* and Long *i: y*

Build Background
Growing Up

Vocabulary
Selection Words

boy grew night sunset tower

High-Frequency Words

always become day everything nothing stays things

Comprehension
Skill Compare and Contrast

Strategy Predict

Read
Group Time < Differentiated Instruction

An Egg Is an Egg

Vocabulary
Antonyms

Fluency
Accuracy/Appropriate Rate

Writing Trait
Conventions

Grammar
Action Verbs

Materials
- *Sing with Me Big Book*
- Big Book *Mr. George Baker*
- Phonics Songs/Rhymes Chart 13
- Letter Tiles
- Background Building Audio
- Graphic Organizer Flip Chart 4
- Vocabulary Transparency 13
- Student Edition 14–29

Morning Warm~Up!

Today we will read about things that change. We'll see that just about everything can change. Can you think of anything that can't change?

QUESTION OF THE DAY Encourage children to sing "Oh My" from the *Sing with Me Big Book* as you gather. Write the message and track the print as you read it. Discuss the question.

REVIEW CONTRACTIONS

- Point to *We'll* and *can't* in the message. Ask children what these words are called. (contractions)
- Have children tell what two words are put together in each contraction. *(we will, can not)*

Build Background Use the Day 3 instruction on ELL Poster 13 to support children's use of English to communicate about lesson concepts.

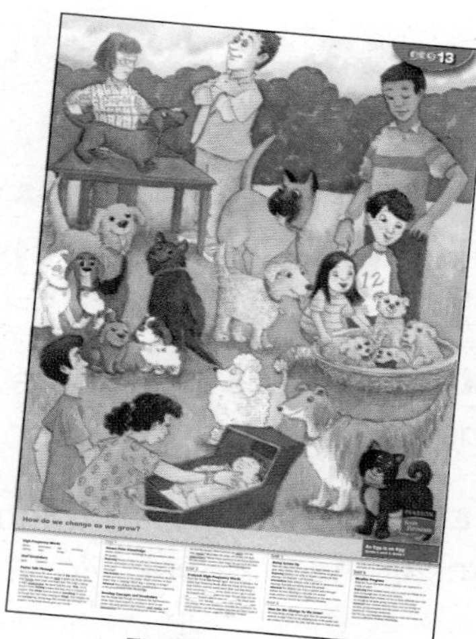

ELL Poster 13

Share Literature

LISTEN AND RESPOND

FICTION Recall what *Mr. George Baker* is about. Ask if the book is fiction or nonfiction. Explain that a made-up story is fiction, even if it tells about people who could be real.

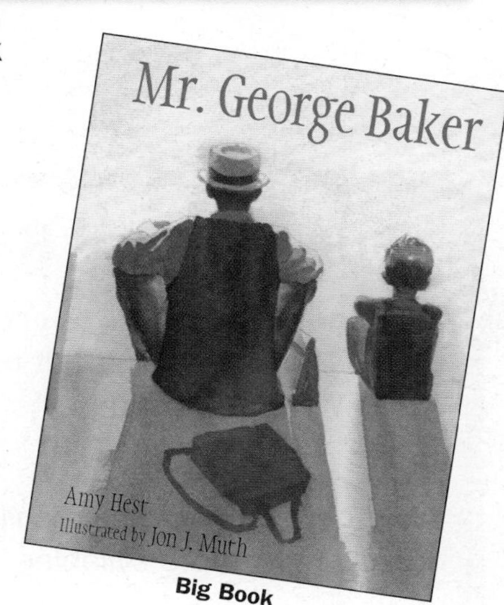

Big Book

BUILD ORAL VOCABULARY Review that yesterday the class read the book to find out how Mr. George Baker moves. We learned that older people may shuffle or teeter. Explain that an older person may stand up a bit **crooked,** or bent. Even so, they can still do many things younger people can do. Ask that children listen today to find out how you can tell that Harry and Mr. George Baker are special friends.

MONITOR LISTENING COMPREHENSION

- What things do Harry and Mr. George Baker share? (They share candy; they ride together; they are both learning to read.)
- How can you tell that Harry and Mr. George Baker are special friends? (They meet every morning; Mr. Baker ties Harry's shoes; Harry tells all the things he likes about Mr. Baker; Mr. Baker always sits with Harry.)
- How can you tell that Mr. Baker felt all twisted up when he got up to dance with Mrs. Baker? (He got up all crookedly and slow.)

Phonemic Awareness

SEGMENT AND BLEND PHONEMES

- In the morning, Mr. George Baker was snappy and happy. Listen to the sounds in *happy.*
- Model saying each sound, /h/ /a/ /p/ /ē/. Have children say the sounds with you and then say the sounds by themselves.
- Now say each sound as you write the letter that goes with it. (Say /h/ /a/ /p/ /ē/ as you write *h, a, pp, y.*)
- Have children say the sounds as you point to the letters (/h/ /a/ /p/ /ē/) and blend the sounds to say the word (*happy*).

Continue the activity with these examples.

why **we** **hi** **go** **candy** **sleepy**

OBJECTIVES

- Identify fiction.
- Set purpose for listening.
- Build oral vocabulary.
- Segment and blend phonemes.

adult
healthy
measurement
shuffle
teeter
crooked
bounce
handsome

MONITOR PROGRESS

If... children lack oral vocabulary experiences about the concept Growing and Changing,

then... use the Oral Vocabulary Routine. See p. DI·3 to teach *crooked.*

Listen and Respond Revisit page 3 and tell children that the word hundred is in special type because it is special to be a hundred years old. Explain that the slang term, *no kidding,* means "it is really the truth." Have children draw a picture of the oldest person they know. Have them share the picture and tell what this person likes to do for fun.

OBJECTIVES

- Review vowel sounds of *y* and long vowels (CV).
- Blend words with the vowel sound of *y* and long vowels (CV).
- Preview words before reading them.
- Spell words with the vowel sounds of *y*.

Strategic Intervention

Use **Strategic Intervention Decodable Reader 13** for more practice with vowel sounds of *y* and the CV pattern.

Support Phonics Give children a baby doll and have them act out "My Fussy Baby Brother." Encourage them to share the words for *baby* and *brother* in their home languages.

See the Phonics Transition Lessons in the ELL and Transition Handbook.

Vowel Sounds of *y* and Long Vowels (CV)

TEACH/MODEL

Fluent Word Reading

ROUTINE

1. **Connect** Write *sky.* You can read this word because you know that when *y* ends a word that has only one syllable, it usually stands for /ī/. What sound does the *y* in this word stand for? (/ī/, the long *i* sound) What's the word? (*sky*)

   Write *penny,* reminding children that the letter *y* at the end of a word that has two or more syllables usually stands for the sound /ē/.

   Write *so.* You can read this word because you know that when a word ends with one vowel, the vowel sound is long. What sound does the *o* in this word stand for? (/ō/) What's the word? (*so*)

2. **Model** When you come to a new word, look at all the letters in the word and think about its vowel sounds. Say the sounds in the word to yourself and then read the word. Model reading *sky, penny,* and *so* in this way. When you come to a new word, what are you going to do?

3. **Group Practice** Write *why, me, sunny, fly, go,* and *hi.* Let's read these words. Look at all the letters, think about the vowel sound, and say the sounds to yourself. When I point to the word, let's read it together. Allow 2–3 seconds previewing time for each word.

WORD READING

PHONICS SONGS AND RHYMES CHART 13 Frame each of the following words on Phonics Songs and Rhymes Chart 13. Call on individuals to read them. Guide children in previewing.

fussy he my be why me happy

Sing "My Fussy Baby Brother" to the tune of "I'm a Little Teapot," or play the CD. Have children follow along on the chart as they sing. Then have individuals take turns circling CV words and words with the vowel sounds of *y.* Identify *baby* and *hungry;* have children name the sound *y* stands for.

Phonics Songs and Rhymes Audio

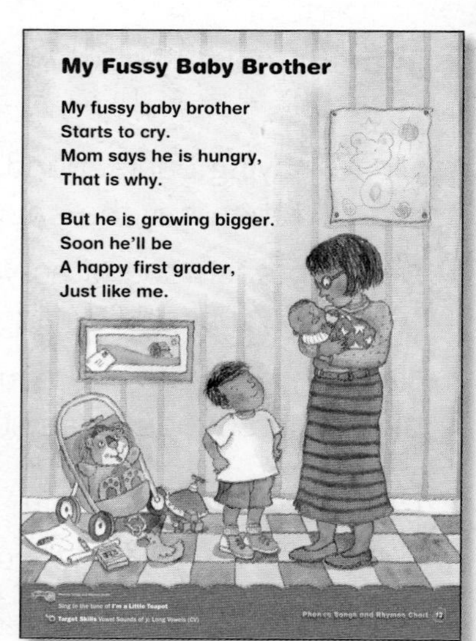

Phonics Songs and Rhymes Chart 13

SORT WORDS

INDIVIDUALS SORT WORDS Write Long *e* and Long *i* as headings in a two-column chart. Then write these words: *my, buddy, me, cry, sleepy, hi, shy, candy.* Have children read them and tell which column to write them in.

Monitor children's work and provide feedback. Complete the activity by having the lists read.

Long e	Long i
buddy	my
me	cry
sleepy	hi
candy	shy

- Words that follow the CV pattern but do not have the long vowel sound *(to, do, who)* may be pointed out as exceptions.

Spelling

PRACTICE Vowel Sounds of *y*

SORT SPELLING WORDS Have children write each spelling word on a separate card. Have partners sort the words into pairs or groups. Ask children to explain their categories. For example:

- *Silly* and *lucky* describe things or people.
- *Any* and *always* begin with the letter *a.*
- *My, by, try, fly, cry* have the letter *y* that stands for long *i.*
- *Puppy* and *fly* are living things.

HOMEWORK Spelling Practice Book, p. 51

Spelling Words

Long *e* and Long *i*: *y*

1. my*
2. by
3. try
4. any
5. body
6. fly
7. cry
8. lucky
9. silly
10. puppy

High-Frequency Words

11. things*
12. always*

* Words from the Selection

Long *e* and Long *i*: *y*

Spelling Words				
my	by	try	any	body
fly	cry	lucky	silly	puppy

Fill in the circle. **Write** the word.

1. Look at ○ fly ● my ○ body bike. — my
2. I did not eat ● any ○ try ○ by cake. — any
3. Did you ○ silly ○ puppy ● cry? — cry
4. The song is ○ any ● silly ○ my. — silly
5. She was ● lucky ○ my ○ fly. — lucky
6. I ● try ○ lucky ○ any very hard. — try
7. Bats can ○ silly ● fly ○ my. — fly
8. Do you have a ● puppy ○ cry ○ lucky? — puppy
9. His ○ any ○ by ● body is strong. — body
10. Put it ○ my ○ fly ● by the box. — by

School + Home **Home Activity** Your child wrote spelling words to complete sentences. Read a sentence from this page. Ask your child to spell the list word.

▲ **Spelling Practice Book** p. 51

OBJECTIVES

- Build background.
- Learn selection words.
- Recognize high-frequency words.

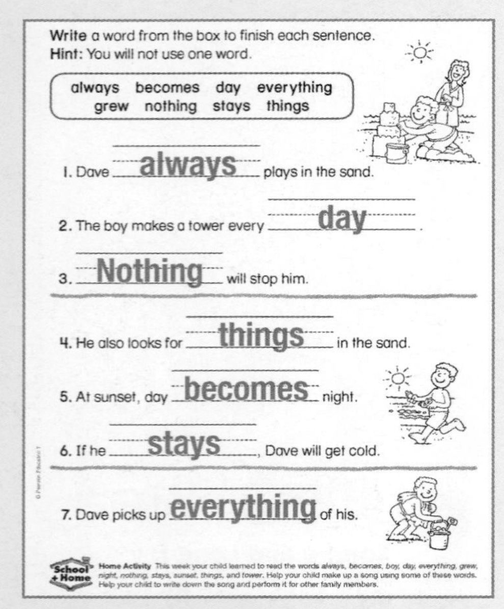
Write a word from the box to finish each sentence.
Hint: You will not use one word.

always becomes day everything
grew nothing stays things

1. Dave **always** plays in the sand.
2. The boy makes a tower every **day**.
3. **Nothing** will stop him.
4. He also looks for **things** in the sand.
5. At sunset, day **becomes** night.
6. If he **stays**, Dave will get cold.
7. Dave picks up **everything** of his.

School + Home **Home Activity** This week your child learned to read the words *always, becomes, boy, day, everything, grew, night, nothing, stays, sunset, things,* and *tower.* Help your child make up a song using some of these words. Help your child to write down the song and perform it for other family members.

▲ **Practice Book 1.2** p. 7, High-Frequency and Selection Words

Activate Prior Knowledge Display or draw a picture of an egg and say the word with children. Then draw a crack in the egg and discuss what will come out. Draw a chick and explain that the egg has changed. Have children give the words for *hatch* and *change* in their home languages.

Build Background

DISCUSS HOW CHILDREN CHANGE Display a picture of a baby, a toddler, and an 8-year-old girl. Initiate discussion by asking children what they know about how children change at different ages.

- Have you changed from the time when you were a baby?
- What kind of changes happened?

BACKGROUND-BUILDING AUDIO Have children listen to the CD and share the new information they learned about children changing over the years.

Sing with Me/ Background Building Audio

COMPLETE A T-CHART Draw a T-chart or display Graphic Organizer 4. Write *How Children Change Over Time* at the top of the left column and write *How Children Stay the Same* at the top of the right column. Ask children to suggest ideas for each column and write their responses on the chart.

How Children Change Over Time	How Children Stay the Same
bodies grow	love their family
can do more things on own	look at the world around them
learn to speak	need food and water to live
learn to eat different foods	
develop interests and hobbies	

▲ **Graphic Organizer 4**

CONNECT TO SELECTION Connect background information to *An Egg Is an Egg.*

We think we know an egg when we see one. Eggs are oval, smooth, and have a shell. But can an egg change? What can it become? In the story we are about to read, we'll find out how many things change over time.

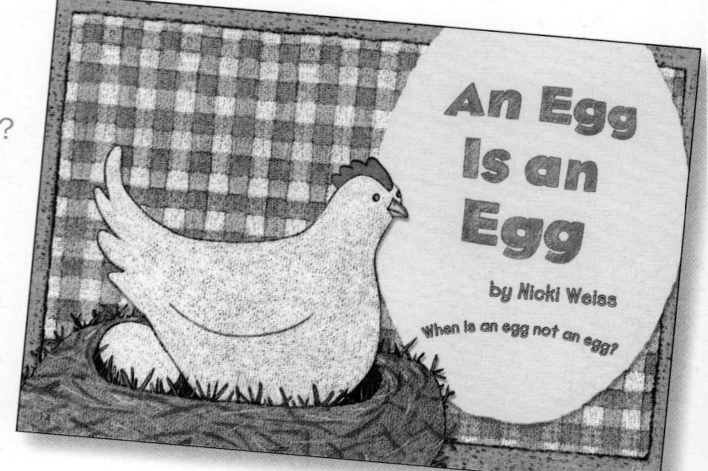

Vocabulary

SELECTION WORDS

Use Vocabulary Transparency 13 to introduce the selection words.

- Read each sentence as you track the print.
- Frame each underlined word. Explain the word's meaning.

  boy a male child
  tower a tall building or part of a building
  grew got bigger
  sunset the time when the sun is last seen in the evening
  night the time between evening and morning
- Ask children to identify familiar letter-sounds and word parts: *boy* (*b*/b/), *tower* (*t*/t/, *r*/r/), *grew* (*gr*/gr/), *sunset* (*sun* and *set*), *night* (*n*/n/, *t*/t/).
- Have children read each sentence aloud with you.
- To encourage discussion using the selection words, ask children to tell about things that might happen at night.

HIGH-FREQUENCY WORDS

Use Vocabulary Transparency 13 to review this week's words.

- Point to a word. Say and spell it.
- Have children say and spell the word.
- Ask children to identify familiar letter-sounds.

Selection Words

A Tower of Blocks

1. This boy is Scott.
2. He made a tower with his blocks.
3. The tower grew and grew.
4. At sunset he put his blocks in a box.
5. "Good night," Scott said.

High-Frequency Words

Words to Read

always	become	day	everything
nothing	stays	things	

Unit 3 An Egg Is an Egg — Vocabulary 13

▲ **Vocabulary Transparency 13**

Access Content Use the vocabulary strategies and word cards in the ELL Teaching Guide, pp. 87–88.

Monitor Progress — **Check High-Frequency Words**

Point to the following words on the Word Wall and have individuals read them.

many	**things**	**day**	**water**	**are**	**you**	**become**	
some	**always**	**now**	**there**	**they**	**stays**	**everything**	**nothing**

If... children cannot read these words,

then... have them find each word on the Word Wall, chant its spelling, and then write it. Monitor their fluency with these words during reading, and provide additional practice opportunities before the Day 5 Assessment.

Day 1 Check Word Reading · **Day 2** Check Word Reading · ▶ **Day 3 Check High-Frequency Words/Retelling** · **Day 4** Check Fluency · **Day 5** Assess Progress

Spiral REVIEW

- Reviews previously taught high-frequency words.

High-Frequency Words

SUCCESS PREDICTOR

OBJECTIVES

- Compare and contrast
- Make predictions.

Comprehension

SKILL Compare and Contrast

RECOGNIZE COMPARE AND CONTRAST Review that things that are alike are the same, and things that are different are not the same. Guide children in identifying ways the dinosaurs in *The Big Circle* were alike and different.

CONNECT TO READING

- As you read, think about how things are alike and how they are different.

STRATEGY Predict

INTRODUCE THE STRATEGY Remind children that good readers use the text and pictures to make predictions about what will happen next.

MODEL When I read, I ask myself what I think will happen and why. Then I check to see if I was right. Sometimes I read new information that makes me change my mind about what I think will happen.

CONNECT TO READING Encourage children to ask themselves these questions as they read *An Egg Is an Egg*.

- What do I think will happen and why?
- Is this what I thought would happen?
- Have I read any new information that changes what I think will happen?

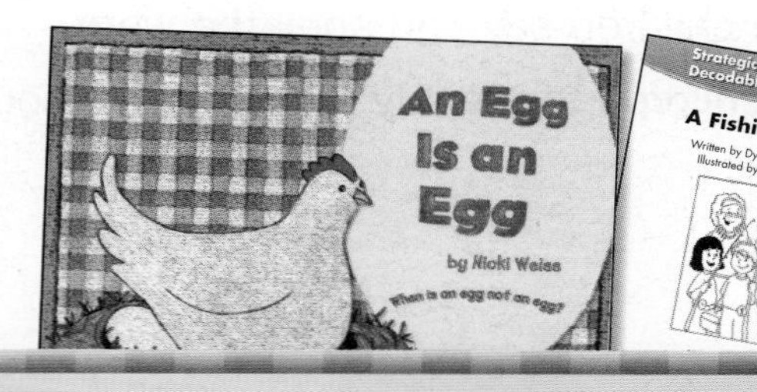

Group Time

DAY 3

On-Level	Strategic Intervention	Advanced
Read *An Egg Is an Egg.*	**Read** SI Decodable Reader 13.	**Read** *An Egg Is an Egg.*
• Use pp. 14–29.	• Read or listen to *An Egg Is an Egg.* • Use the **Routine** on p. DI·20.	• Use the **Routine** on p. DI·21.

Place English language learners in the groups that correspond to their reading abilities in English.

Independent Activities

Independent Reading See p. 10j for Reading/Library activities and suggestions.

Journal Writing Write about something you'll be able to do when you are an adult. Share writing.

Literacy Centers Use the Listening and Writing Centers for *An Egg Is an Egg* on pp. 10j and 10k.

Practice Book 1.2 High-Frequency Words and Selection Words, p. 7

Break into small groups after Comprehension and before Fluency.

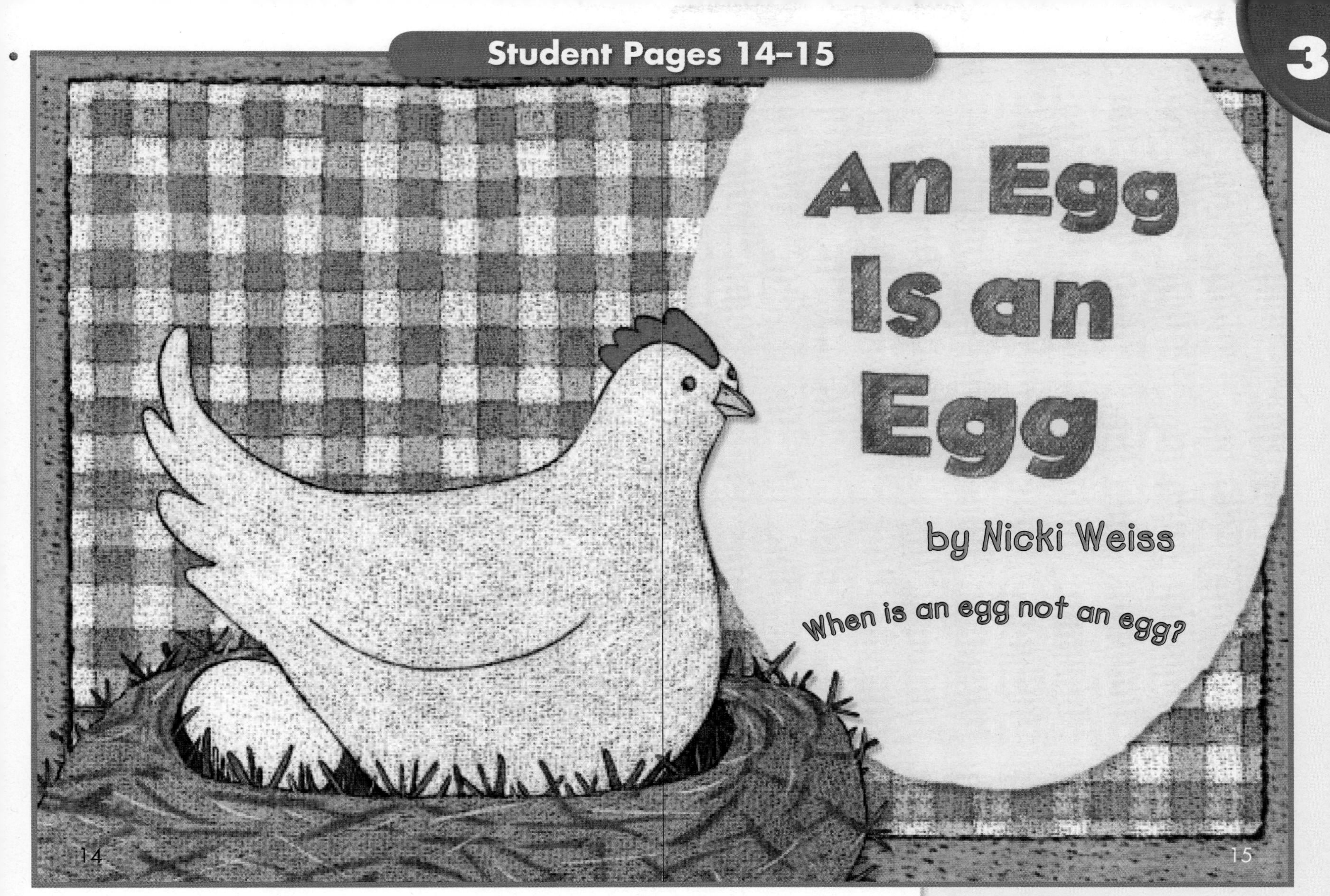

Read

Prereading Strategies

PREVIEW AND PREDICT Have children read the title of the story. Read aloud the author's name. Preview pp. 14–17 and have children predict ways an egg might change.

DISCUSS REALISTIC FICTION Discuss whether children think this will be a fantasy or a story about real things. Make sure children understand that this is a made-up story that could really happen. Reread the definition of realistic fiction on p. 13 of the Student Edition.

SET PURPOSE Read the question on p. 15. Discuss what children want to find out about how things change as they read this story.

AudioText

ELL

Access Content Before reading, review the story summary in English and/or the home language. See the ELL Teaching Guide, pp. 89–91.

An egg is an egg until it hatches.
And then it is a chick.

A branch is a branch until it breaks.
And then it is a stick.

16

Nothing stays the same.
Everything can change.

17

▲ **Pages 16–17**
Have children read to find out what happens to the egg.

Guiding Comprehension

Plot • Inferential

- **How did the egg change?**
  It opened and a chick hatched.

Details • Literal

- **What else changed on p. 16?**
  A branch broke off a tree and became a stick.

Literary Devices • Inferential

- **What is special about the words *chick* and *stick* on p. 16?**
  The words rhyme.

Compare and Contrast • Inferential

- **How are the branch and the stick alike? How are they different?**
  The branch and the stick are alike because they are both made of wood. They are different because the branch is part of a tree and the stick is not.

Monitor Progress

Decoding

If...	then... remind them to blend the word:
children come to a word they don't know,	1. Look at each letter. 2. Think of the sound for each letter. 3. Blend the sounds. 4. Read the word.

____ vowel sounds of *y* and long vowels CV   high-frequency/tested vocabulary

A seed is a seed until it is sown.
And then it is a flower.

A block is a block until there are many.
And then they become a tower.

18

Nothing stays the same.
Everything can change.

19

Strategies in Context

PREDICT

- **What do you think the next two pages will tell you about?**
  Children should predict that the next two pages will tell them about more things that change.

Monitor Progress	Predict
If... children have difficulty answering the question,	**then...** model how to make a prediction.

MODEL First I read about how an egg and a branch change. Then I read about how a seed and some blocks change. I notice that the author keeps repeating the sentences "Nothing stays the same. Everything can change." I can use what I know about this pattern to predict what will happen next.

ASSESS Have children predict what people they will see on the next page. (They should predict that they will see the mother and the little boy.)

▲ **Pages 18–19**
Ask children to read to find information to help them make a prediction.

Monitor Progress

High-Frequency Words

If... children have a problem reading a new high-frequency word,	**then...** use the High-Frequency Routine on pp. 12–13 to reteach the problematic word.

Access Content The structure of the sentences may be difficult for children acquiring English. If necessary, help them re-word the sentences in a more familiar form, such as "When a seed is sown, it becomes a flower."

Water is water until it is brewed.
And then it becomes tea.

You are you until I come.
And then you become "we."

20

Nothing stays the same.
Everything can change.

21

▲ **Pages 20–21**
Have children read to learn what happens next.

Strategy Self-Check

Have children ask themselves these questions to check their reading.

Decoding Words

- Do I blend all the sounds in a word to read it?
- Do I reread to be sure the new word makes sense in the story?

Predict

- Do I ask myself what I think will happen and why?
- Do I ask myself if this is what I thought would happen?
- Do I look for new information that changes what I think will happen?

Guiding Comprehension

Confirm Predictions • Inferential

- **Do these pages tell you about what you thought they would?**
  Children's responses will vary.

Monitor and Fix Up • Critical

- **How do the illustrations help you understand how *you* becomes *we?***
  The first illustration only shows one person. The second illustration shows two people. "We" is used to name two or more people.

Draw Conclusions • Critical

- ***Question the Author* What does the author mean when she says "Nothing stays the same. Everything can change"?**
  Possible response: Everything the story is talking about can change from one thing to another.

Summarize • Inferential

- **What has happened so far?**
  The boy and his mom watched a chick hatch and made changes by breaking a stick, planting seeds, building a tower, brewing tea, and playing together.

____ vowel sounds of *y* and long vowels CV   ☐ high-frequency/tested vocabulary

The yard is green until it snows.
And then it becomes white.

Day is day until sunset.
And then it is the night.

22

Nothing stays the same.
Everything can change.

23

▲ **Pages 22–23**
Ask children to read to find out how the yard changes.

Skills in Context

COMPARE AND CONTRAST

- **How has the yard changed at the top of page 22? How is it the same?** The yard has changed from green to white because it has snow on it. The yard is the same because the house and the trees and the sidewalk are all still there.

Monitor Progress	Compare and Contrast
If... children have difficulty answering the question,	**then...** model how to compare and contrast.

MODEL When things change they become different. The text says that the yard changes from green to white when it snows. I can tell from the pictures that the house, the trees, and the sidewalk are the same.

ASSESS Draw a T-chart or display Graphic Organizer 4. Have children tell how things are the same and how they are different at the bottom of p. 22. Record their answers. (Same: snow, snowman, trees; Different: boy, time)

Day/Night Sky

Look at the two pictures at the bottom of p. 22. Talk about the sunlight in the first picture and the stars in the sky in the second picture. Help children name and discuss other objects found in the day sky and the night sky, such as the Sun, the Moon, and planets.

Student Pages 24–25

This baby was a baby until he grew.
And now he is a boy.

24

But you can always be a baby.
You will always be my baby. . . .

25

▲ **Pages 24–25**
Have children read to find out how the boy has changed.

EXTEND SKILLS

Text Features

For instruction in ellipses, discuss the following:

- What do you see at the end of the last sentence on p. 25?
- How is this punctuation different from a period?
- These extra three dots after the period mean that the thought continues on.

Assess Have children identify ellipses in other text, such as the Big Book *A Frog in the Bog.*

Skills in Context

REVIEW AUTHOR'S PURPOSE

- **Why do you think Nicki Weiss wrote *An Egg Is an Egg?* Did she have more than one reason for writing it?**
  She wrote this story to help readers understand how things change and to entertain readers.

Monitor Progress	Author's Purpose
If... children are unable to describe an author's reasons for writing	**then...** model how to determine author's purpose.

MODEL The author tells me about different things that change. I think she wrote this story to help readers understand how things change. I also think the author wanted this story to be fun to read because it rhymes and follows a pattern.

ASSESS Have children discuss the information they learned from this story. (Children should list different things they read about that change.)

___ vowel sounds of *y* and long vowels CV   ▭ high-frequency/tested vocabulary

Some things stay the same.
Some things never change.

26

27

Guiding Comprehension

Author's Purpose • Critical

- ***Question the Author*** **How are the sentences on p. 26 different from the sentences on pp. 17, 19, 21, and 23? Why do you think the author wrote the ending this way?**
  In the rest of the story, the sentences said, "Nothing stays the same. Everything can change." Now these last two sentences say, "Some things stay the same. Some things never change." The author wanted to show that most, but not all, things change.

Draw Conclusions • Inferential

- **What stays the same and never changes?**
  The boy will always be his mother's baby. She will always love him. That won't ever change.

Make Judgments • Critical

- ***Text to World*** **Do you think an egg and a branch are good examples of things that change? Why? What other examples can you think of?**
  Possible response: Yes, because they change all the time. Puppies can change into adult dogs, and apples can change into apple pies.

▲ **Pages 26–27**
Have children read to find out how the story ends.

EXTEND SKILLS

Repetition

For instruction in how authors use repetition, discuss the following:

- The author repeats some words to make a pattern that each part of the story follows. What words are the same on p. 22?
- Write a sentence frame: _____ is _____ until _____. And then it _____.
- What words on p. 22 go in the blanks? How are these words alike? What does each set of sentences talk about?

Assess Have children discuss the pattern that repeats on each right-hand page.

Think and Share

TALK ABOUT IT Model a response. My favorite change is when the yard turns white with snow. I like when it snows outside.

1. **RETELL** Have children use the retelling strip in the Student Edition to retell the story.

Monitor Progress | **Check Retelling** 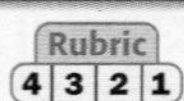

If... children have difficulty retelling the story,

then... use the Retelling Cards and the Scoring Rubric for Retelling on pp. 28–29 to help them move toward fluent retelling.

Day 1 Check Word Reading	**Day 2** Check Word Reading	▶ **Day 3 Check High-Frequency Words/Retelling**	**Day 4** Check Fluency	**Day 5** Assess Progress

2. **COMPARE AND CONTRAST** Possible response: The pictures on the bottom of p. 18 are alike because they both show the boy and at least one block. They are different because one only shows one block and the other shows the mother and a block tower.

3. **PREDICT** Possible response: Yes, I predicted the yard would turn white with snow. I knew that the yard would change because the author said everything changes.

LOOK BACK AND WRITE Read the writing prompt on p. 28 and model your thinking. I'll look back on p. 25 and read that part of the story again. I'll look for one thing that does not change. Then I'll write my response. Have children write their responses in an interactive or an independent writing activity.

Scoring Rubric | **Look Back and Write**

Top-Score Response A top-score response uses details from p. 25 of the selection to tell about one thing that does not change.

Example of a Top-Score Response

One thing that does not change is the little boy.
He will always be his mother's baby.

For additional rubrics, see p. WA10.

Retelling Plan

- ☑ **This week assess Strategic Intervention students.**
- ☐ Week 2 assess Advanced students.
- ☐ Week 3 assess Strategic Intervention students.
- ☐ Week 4 assess On-Level students.
- ☐ Week 5 assess Strategic Intervention students.
- ☐ Week 6 assess any students you have not yet checked during this unit.

Look Back and Write
For informal assessment, see the Scoring Rubric below.

Assessment Let beginning ELL children listen to other retellings before attempting to retell the selection on their own. For more ideas on assessing comprehension, see the ELL and Transition Handbook.

Reader Response

Read Together

Think and Share

Talk About It Which change in *An Egg Is an Egg* is your favorite? Tell about it.

1. Use the pictures below to retell the story. Retell
2. Choose a pair of pictures from the story. How are they alike and different? Compare/Contrast
3. Did you predict how the yard would change? What helped you? Predict

Look Back and Write Look back at page 25. Write about one thing that does not change.

Meet the Author and Illustrator

Nicki Weiss

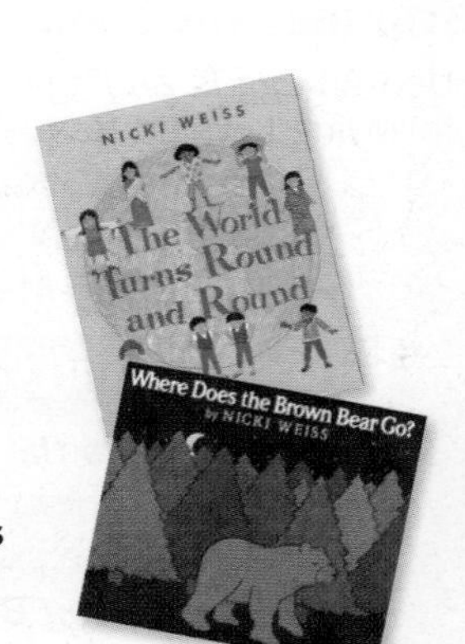

Nicki Weiss is an artist, a writer, and a teacher. Her books are about friends, family love, and changes in life.

Ms. Weiss lives in New York City. She wrote lots of books. Then she decided to become a schoolteacher. Now she teaches reading and art. She still writes books when she has the time.

Read more books by Nicki Weiss.

The World Turns Round and Round

Where Does the Brown Bear Go?

28 29

Scoring Rubric Narrative Retelling

Rubric 4 3 2 1	4	3	2	1
Connections	Makes connections and generalizes beyond the text	Makes connections to other events, stories, or experiences	Makes a limited connection to another event, story, or experience	Makes no connection to another event, story, or experience
Author's Purpose	Elaborates on author's purpose	Tells author's purpose with some clarity	Makes some connection to author's purpose	Makes no connection to author's purpose
Characters	Describes the main character(s) and any character development	Identifies the main character(s) and gives some information about them	Inaccurately identifies some characters or gives little information about them	Inaccurately identifies the characters or gives no information about them
Setting	Describes the time and location	Identifies the time and location	Omits details of time or location	Is unable to identify time or location
Plot	Describes the events in sequence using rich detail	Tells the plot with some errors in sequence that do not affect meaning	Tells parts of plot with gaps that affect meaning	Retelling has no sense of story

Use the Retelling Chart on p. TR18 to record retelling.

Selection Test To assess with *An Egg Is an Egg*, use Selection Tests, pp. 25–28.

Fresh Reads for Differentiated Test Practice For weekly leveled practice, use pp. 73–78.

Retelling SUCCESS PREDICTOR

3

OBJECTIVE

- Read aloud fluently with accuracy and at an appropriate rate.

Options for Choral Reading

Use *An Egg Is an Egg* or one of the following Leveled Readers.

On-Level

Just Like Me

Strategic Intervention

Nothing Stays the Same

Advanced

Your Amazing Body

Model reading pp. 18–22 of *An Egg Is an Egg* at an appropriate rate of speed. Have English language learners reread the passage several times at the same rate of speed.

Fluency

READ WITH ACCURACY AND APPROPRIATE RATE

MODEL READING WITH ACCURACY AND APPROPRIATE RATE

Use *An Egg Is an Egg.*

- Have children turn to pp. 16–17. I'm going to read these pages. I will read as if I am speaking, and I will try not to make any mistakes.
- Ask children to follow along as you read the pages with expression while attending to accuracy and appropriate rate.
- Have children read the pages after you. Encourage them to read without missing any words. Continue in the same way with pp. 18–19.

REREAD FOR FLUENCY

Choral Reading

ROUTINE

1. **Select a Passage** For *An Egg Is an Egg,* use pp. 20–24.
2. **Divide into Groups** Assign each group a part to read. For this story, have each group read a page.
3. **Model** Have children track the print as you read.
4. **Read Together** Have children read along with you.
5. **Independent Readings** Have the groups read aloud without you. Monitor progress and provide feedback. For optimal fluency, children should reread three to four times.

Monitor Progress	Fluency
If... children have difficulty reading accurately and at an appropriate rate,	**then...** prompt: • Read as if you are speaking to a friend. • Does each word make sense? • Look at all the letters in the word to be sure you have all the sounds correct.
If... the class cannot read fluently without you,	**then...** continue to have them read along with you.

Vocabulary

ANTONYMS

DISCUSS ANTONYMS Write the following story sentences on the chalkboard and have children read them with you. Ask children to identify the words that have opposite meanings. Remind them that words like *nothing* and *everything* that have opposite meanings are called antonyms.

Nothing stays the same.

Everything can change.

EXPAND VOCABULARY Read each of the following sentences. Have children use an antonym for a word in the sentence to give a new sentence that has an opposite meaning.

We read an old story. (We read a new story.)
Todd's bike is very slow. (Todd's bike is very fast.)
This lunchbox is empty. (This lunchbox is full.)
That backpack is too big. (That backpack is too little.)
Mary lost her mittens. (Mary found her mittens.)

OBJECTIVES

- Discuss meanings of antonyms.
- Use antonyms in sentences.

Strategic Intervention

Make two sets of word cards, one for words *go, play, small, day, soft* and another for *stop, work, large, night, hard*. Place one set in a pile facedown, and display the cards from the second set. Have children take turns selecting a card from the pile and finding the card with the word's antonym.

Advanced

Have children write a sentence about one of the pictures in *An Egg Is an Egg*, and then write a second sentence with an opposite meaning.

Extend Language Using the word cards from Strategic Intervention, have children choose a pair of opposites and say the words in English and in the home language.

OBJECTIVE

- Recognize and use conventions in writing.

DAILY FIX-IT

5. Mi pupy is white.
My puppy is white.

6. try not to cri.
Try not to cry.

Connect to Unit Writing

Writing Trait

Have children use strategies for developing **conventions** when they write a description in the Unit Writing Workshop, pp. WA2–WA9.

ELL

Conventions Identify a particular grammar convention that presents difficulty for a child or a small group. Explicitly teach the English convention using an appropriate lesson in the ELL and Transition Handbook.

Writing Trait of the Week

INTRODUCE Conventions

TALK ABOUT CONVENTIONS Explain to children that conventions are rules good writers follow. Good writers spell words a certain way. They begin sentences with capital letters. They finish sentences with end marks. Ask children to think about whether the author of *An Egg Is an Egg* follows conventions. Then model your thinking.

MODEL I'll look at the first sentence on p. 16. The sentence has a beginning capital letter and an end mark. The words in the sentence are spelled correctly. Yes, the author follows conventions. Let's look at more sentences in the selection.

Assign pairs of children one of the sentences on pp. 16–18. Ask pairs to check their sentences to see whether the author uses conventions. Have them answer these questions about their sentences: *Does this sentence begin with a capital letter? Does this sentence have an end mark? Is every word spelled correctly?* Let pairs share what they find out about their sentences.

STRATEGY FOR DEVELOPING CONVENTIONS On the board, write sentences, such as those below on the left. Work with children to decide whether each sentence is written correctly or not. Together rewrite the incorrect sentences to make them correct.

A seed grows into a flower *(A seed grows into a flower.)*
white snow covers the grass. *(White snow covers the grass.)*
A chick hatches from an eg. *(A chick hatches from an egg.)*
do babies grow up *(Do babies grow up?)*

PRACTICE

APPLY THE STRATEGY

- Ask children to look at the two pictures at the top of p. 18. Have them offer sentences about what the mother and the boy are doing. Write the sentences on the board without initial capital letters or end punctuation. Let children add both to the sentences.
- Discuss with children how a seed becomes a flower. Have them write steps that tell what happens. *(A seed is in the ground. A tiny plant grows out of the seed. The plant becomes bigger. The big plant grows flowers.)* Remind children to put the steps in order and to follow conventions when they write their sentences.

Grammar

APPLY TO WRITING Action Verbs

IMPROVE WRITING WITH ACTION VERBS Review with children that even though each of us changes as we grow, we will always be someone's baby. *Grows* and *changes* are action verbs. A verb tells what someone or something does. Writing with action verbs makes sentences interesting. Remind children to use action verbs in their own writing.

Write the following sentence frames. Have children supply action verbs for each sentence.

The baby ______.

Now the baby ______.

PRACTICE

WRITE WITH ACTION VERBS Call on individuals to supply additional action verbs that could be used in these sentences. Continue until three or four action verbs have been suggested for each sentence.

OBJECTIVE

- Use action verbs in writing.

Action Verbs

Write about things you do every day.
Use action verbs from the box or your own words.

eat	go	read
sleep	play	talk

Possible answer: I get up. I eat breakfast. Next I go to school. After school I call my mom. Then I play with my friends.

Home Activity Your child learned how to use verbs in writing. Take turns with your child telling about things that you do every day. Have your child identify any action verbs either of you uses in your sentences.

▲ **Grammar and Writing Practice Book** p. 50

Wrap Up Your Day!

COMPARE AND CONTRAST Have children compare the main characters from *Mr. George Baker.* Name two ways Harry and Mr. George Baker are similar. (They both go to school. They both ride the bus)

PREDICT Help children predict what they think will happen next in *Mr. George Baker.*

LET'S TALK ABOUT IT Display the Baby/Now T-chart from Day 1. Recall in *Mr. George Baker* that both Mr. Baker and Harry were learning how to read. Where would you write *learn how to read* on this chart—Baby or Now? (Now)

Tell children that tomorrow they will listen to a story about a boy who is growing so much that he has outgrown his clothes.

Day 4

AT A GLANCE

Share Literature
"Wait for Me!" said Maggie McGee

Phonemic Awareness
Segment and Count Phonemes

High-Frequency Words
Word Wall

always *become* *day* *everything* *nothing* *stays* *things*

Phonics and Spelling
REVIEW Long *e: e, ee;* Syllables VCCV

REVIEW Word Reading Spelling: Long *e*, Long *i: y*

Read

< Differentiated Instruction

"Nothing Fits"

Fluency
Accuracy/Appropriate Rate

Writing Across the Curriculum
Math Story

Grammar
Action Verbs

Materials
- *Sing with Me Big Book*
- Read Aloud Anthology
- Tested Word Cards
- Student Edition 30–33

Morning Warm-Up!

Today we will read about a boy who grows. Now he needs a new coat and new boots. What happens to your clothes when you get bigger?

QUESTION OF THE DAY Encourage children to sing "Oh My" from the *Sing with Me Big Book* as you gather. Write and read the message and discuss the question.

REVIEW ONE AND MORE THAN ONE

- Ask children to find words that mean one person or thing. (*boy, coat*)
- Have them find words that mean more than one thing. (*boots, clothes*)
- Discuss how they can tell which words tell about more than one. (the words end with *s*)

Extend Language Use the Day 4 instruction on ELL Poster 13 to extend and enrich language.

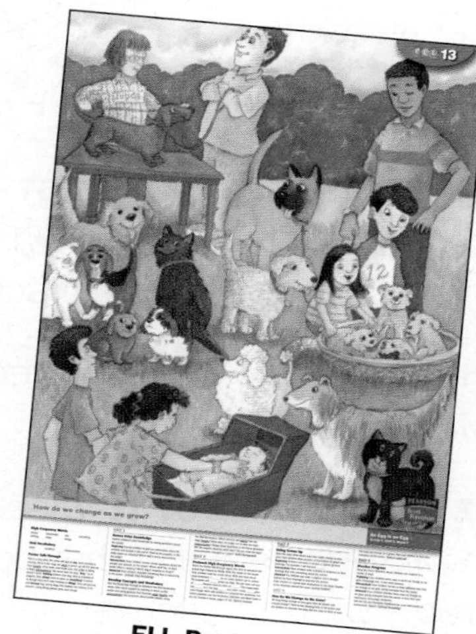

ELL Poster 13

Share Literature

CONNECT CONCEPTS

ACTIVATE PRIOR KNOWLEDGE Help children recall that the boy in *An Egg Is an Egg* used to be a baby. Explain that you will read a story about a child who can't wait to grow—"'Wait for Me,' Said Maggie McGee" by Jean Van Leeuwen.

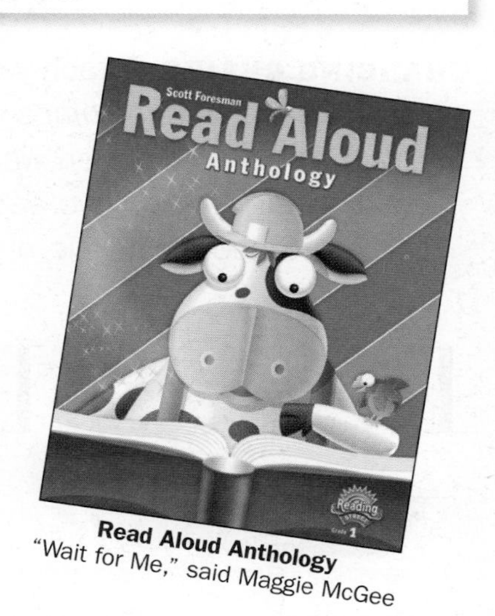

Read Aloud Anthology
"Wait for Me," said Maggie McGee

BUILD ORAL VOCABULARY Read the first four paragraphs. Ask what was Maggie's problem. (She was too little to do the things her brothers and sisters could do.) Say, When I was little I tried to reach things by **bouncing** up and down. Do you think Maggie might try that? I'll bet Maggie has to wear the clothes her brothers and sisters have outgrown. I wonder if she gets to have **handsome** new clothes of her own. Ask children to listen to find out whether Maggie grows bigger.

REVIEW ORAL VOCABULARY After reading, review all the Amazing Words for the week. Have children take turns using them in sentences that tell about the concept for the week. Then talk about the Amazing Words they learned in other weeks and connect them to the concept as well. For example, ask:

- Name some things a **cuddly** baby **requires** in order to grow.
- What would happen if a mouse grew bigger than its **enemy,** a **creeping** cat?

Phonemic Awareness

SEGMENT AND COUNT PHONEMES

- We just read how making announcements to the whole school made Maggie feel good. Listen to the word *feel.* How many sounds are in *feel?*
- Model saying the sounds as you count them on your fingers. (Say /f/ /ē/ /l/, 3.)
- Have children say the sounds as they count them on their fingers. (/f/ /ē/ /l/, 3)

Continue the activity with these examples.

sweets (5) **screech (5)** **tablet (6)** **he (2)**

If you wish to have children practice with nonsense words, continue the activity with these examples.

vilk (4) **spreep (5)** **flurk (4)** **sweems (5)**

OBJECTIVES

- Set purpose for listening.
- Build oral vocabulary.
- Segment and count phonemes.

adult
healthy
measurement
shuffle
teeter
crooked
bounce
handsome

MONITOR PROGRESS

If... children lack oral vocabulary experiences about the concept Growing and Changing,

then... use the Oral Vocabulary Routine. See p. DI•3 to teach *bounce* and *handsome.*

ELL

Connect Concepts To help children understand how Maggie's feelings change throughout the story, have children point to Maggie in the illustrations. How is Maggie feeling? Show me. Help children understand that this story takes place over several years.

OBJECTIVES

- Recognize high-frequency words.
- Review long *e: e, ee* and syllables VCCV.
- Apply decoding strategies: blend, preview words.

Circle a word to finish each sentence.
Write it on the line.

tree

1. Shelly planted a seed. (seed / sad)
2. Shelly and Lee got the weeds out. (weds / weeds)
3. "I see a big beet!" he said. (he / hi)
4. Lee said, "I need help." (nod / need)
5. Mom will peel the beet so we can eat! (peel / pal)

Home Activity Your child practiced reading words with long *e* as heard in *me* and *bee*. Work with your child to make a list of words that rhyme with *deep* and a list that rhymes with *me*.

▲ **Practice Book 1.2** p. 8, Long *e: e, ee*

Pick letters from the box to finish each word.
Write the letters on the lines.

button

dd ll pp sk

1. The man rakes the fallen leaves.
2. Plants are in a basket.
3. A bee gets the pollen.
4. A kitten is hidden.
5. What will happen when he wants the plants?

Home Activity Your child completed words with two syllables that have two consonants in the middle. Name some plants and flowers that grow in your community. Ask your child to identify the middle consonant sounds in the words.

▲ **Practice Book 1.2** p. 9, Syllables VCCV

High-Frequency Words

PRACTICE

CHANGING CHAIRS Attach word cards for *always, become, day, everything, nothing, stays,* and *things* to seven chairs in a circle. Play lively music as a group of seven children walk around the chairs. Stop the music and have the children sit down. Have each child read the card on his or her chair and use it in a sentence. Continue until everyone has had a chance to play.

Review Phonics

REVIEW LONG *e: e, ee* AND SYLLABLES VCCV

READ LONG *e: e, ee* WORDS Write *she.* Look at this word. You can read this word because you know that when a word ends with one vowel, the vowel sound is usually long. What sound does this *e* stand for? (/ē/, the long *e* sound) What's the word? *(she)* Write *sheet.* You can read this word because you know that two *e*'s together usually stand for the long *e* sound. What's the word? *(sheet)*

READ WORDS WITH SYLLABLES CVVC Write *basket.* You can read this word because you know that if a word has two consonants in the middle, you can divide the word between the consonants, read the two, and blend the syllables together to say the word. What are the two syllables of this word? (*bas, ket*) What's the word? *(basket)*

SORT WORDS Write *One Syllable* and *Two Syllables* as headings. When I say a word, hold one hand up if it has one syllable or hold two hands up if it has two syllables: *hen, pencil, problem, sweep, cheese, insect, be, traffic, teeth, mitten.* Write each word in the appropriate column. Have children identify words with long *e* (*sweep, cheese, be, teeth)* and have the lists read.

One Syllable	Two Syllables
hen	pencil
sweep	problem
cheese	insect
be	traffic
teeth	mitten

WORD READING

READ DECODABLE AND HIGH-FREQUENCY WORDS Write these words. Encourage children to preview each word before reading it.

peeping	**met**	**good**	**Pete**	**these**
kitten	**there**	**Reed**	**paper**	**some**
Ned	**meet**	**family**	**be**	**down**
other	**new**	**me**	**also**	**picnic**

Monitor Progress	Word Reading
If... children have difficulty previewing and reading whole words,	**then...** have them use sound-by-sound blending.
If... children can't read the words fluently at a rate of one to two seconds per word,	**then...** have pairs practice the list.

READ WORDS IN CONTEXT Write these sentences. Call on individuals to read a sentence. Then randomly point to the review words and have them read. To help you monitor word reading, high-frequency words are underlined and decodable words are circled.

There are these other chicks peeping also.

My family met some new people at the picnic.

Pete will meet me down by the paper bin.

Ned and Reed will be good and help the kitten.

Monitor Progress	Word Reading
If... children are unable to read an underlined word,	**then...** read the word for them and spell it, having them echo you.
If... children have difficulty reading a circled word,	**then...** have them use sound-by-sound blending.

Spiral REVIEW

- Reviews high-frequency words *also, down, family, good, new, other, paper, some,* and *there.*
- Reviews long *e (e, ee,* CVCe); syllables VCCV; and short *e* (CVC).

Support Phonics For additional review, see the phonics activities in the ELL and Transition Handbook.

OBJECTIVE

- Spell words with the vowel sounds of *y*.

Spelling Words

Long *e* and Long *i*: *y*

1.	**my***	6.	**fly**
2.	**by**	7.	**cry**
3.	**try**	8.	**lucky**
4.	**any**	9.	**silly**
5.	**body**	10.	**puppy**

High-Frequency Words

11.	**things***	12.	**always***

* Words from the Selection

Long *e* and Long *i*: *y*

Write the letter y. Then write the word.

1. fl y	fly	Spelling Words: my, by, try, any, body
2. pupp y	puppy	
3. cr y	cry	fly, cry, lucky, silly, puppy
4. bod y	body	
5. an y	any	
6. sill y	silly	
7. luck y	lucky	

Circle the words that rhyme with **fly**. Write the words.

any (try) body silly (by) (my)

8. try 9. by 10. my

School + Home Home Activity Your child has been learning to spell words in which the long e or long i sound is spelled y. Have your child underline list words with a long i sound and circle list words with a long e sound.

▲ **Spelling Practice Book** p. 52

Spelling

PARTNER REVIEW Vowel Sounds of *y*

READ AND WRITE Supply pairs of children with index cards on which the spelling words have been written. Have one child read a word while the other writes it. Then have children switch roles. Have them use the cards to check their spelling.

HOMEWORK Spelling Practice Book, p. 52

Group Time

DAY 4

On-Level	Strategic Intervention	Advanced
Read "Nothing Fits."	**Read** SI Decodable Reader 12.	**Read** "Nothing Fits."
• Use pp. 30–33.	• Read or listen to "Nothing Fits." • Use the **Routine** on p. DI·22.	• Use the **Routine** on p. DI·23.

Place English language learners in the groups that correspond to their reading abilities in English.

Independent Activities

Fluency Reading Pair children to reread *An Egg Is an Egg.*

Journal Writing Write how you are like the boy in the story. Write how you are different. Share writing.

Independent Reading See p. 10j for Reading/Library activities and suggestions.

Literacy Centers To provide listening opportunities, you may use the Listening Center on p. 10j. To extend science concepts, you may use the Science Center on p. 10k.

Practice Book 1.2 Long *e: e, ee,* p. 8
Syllables VCCV, p. 9

Break into small groups after Spelling and before Fluency.

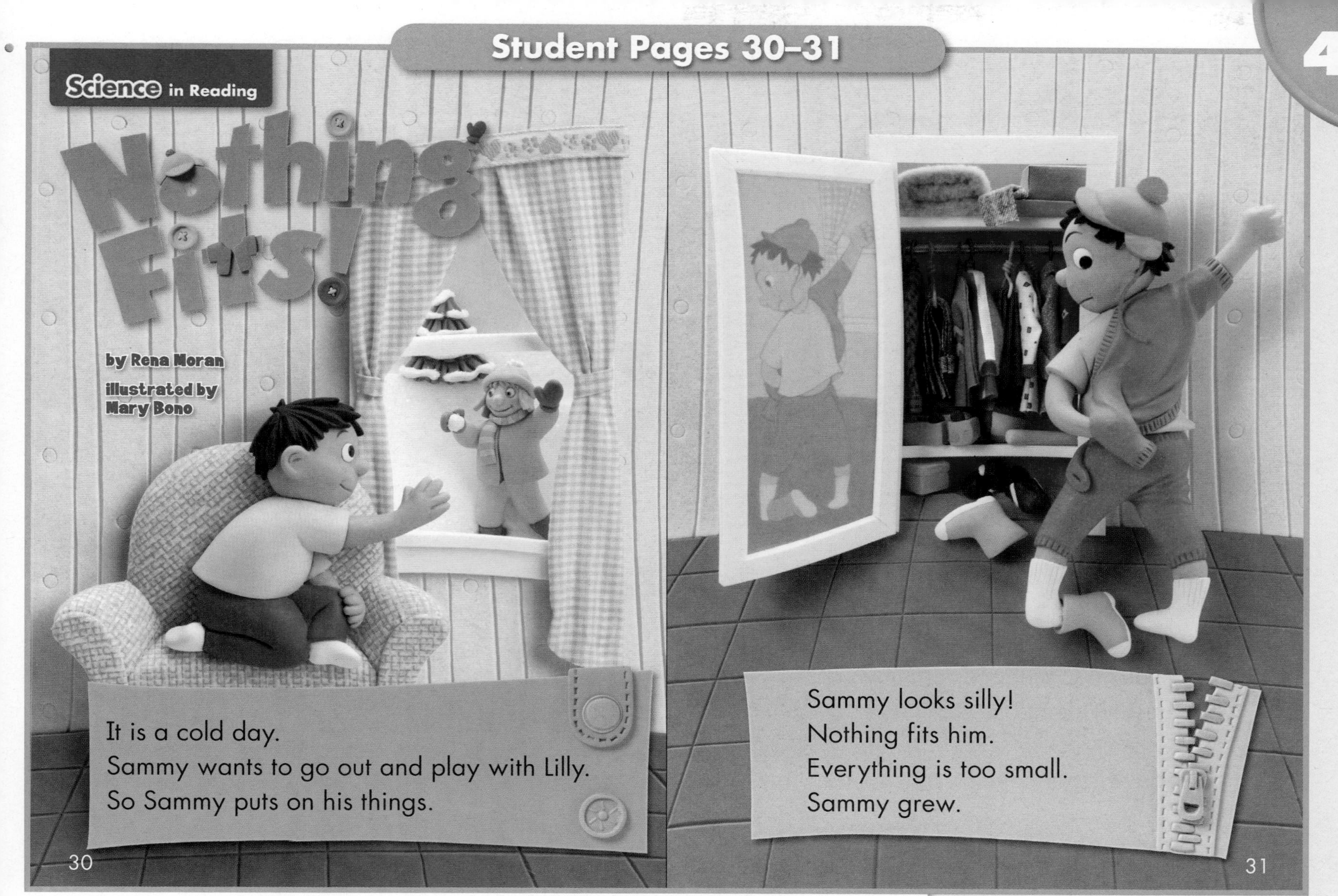

Read

Science in Reading

PREVIEW AND PREDICT Read the title and author's name. Tell children that the boy in the picture on p. 30 is named Sammy. Ask them to look at the pictures and tell what they think is happening. (Sammy wants to go play outside in the snow.) Then ask them to predict whether "Nothing Fits" tells a true story or a made-up one. Have children read to learn what has happened to Sammy.

REALISTIC FICTION Remind children that made-up stories about things that could really happen are called realistic fiction. Point out that the children in the pictures are doing things real children might do. Therefore, this story tells about something that might really happen.

VOCABULARY/ANTONYMS Review antonyms. Ask children to reread pp. 30–33 and suggest antonyms for the following words: *cold, with, nothing, small, new, inside, always.* (hot, without, everything, big, old, outside, never)

AudioText

OBJECTIVE

- Respond to a realistic story.

TIME FOR Science

Living Things

All living things grow and change. Think about some of the ways you have changed in the last year. Have you grown taller? Have you lost any teeth?

Student Pages 32–33

BUILD CONCEPTS

Predict • Inferential

- **What do you think will happen as Sammy keeps growing?**
  Sammy will keep outgrowing his clothes and needing new ones.

Compare and Contrast • Inferential

- **How are Sammy's new clothes like his old clothes? How are they different?**
  Children's responses should include that Sammy's new clothes are the same pieces (hat, coat, mittens, boots) as his old clothes, and they will keep him warm outside, just as his old clothes did. They are different because they are different styles and colors, and they are bigger than his old clothes.

CONNECT TEXT TO TEXT

What will not change about the boy in *An Egg Is an Egg*? How is that like Sammy?

The boy will always be his mother's baby, no matter how much he grows. Sammy will always be Sammy, no matter how big he grows.

ELL

Activate Prior Knowledge Ask: What do you need to do when your clothes get too small? If children need help with English words for articles of clothing, have them point to the article.

Fluency

READ WITH ACCURACY AND APPROPRIATE RATE

MODEL READING WITH ACCURACY AND APPROPRIATE RATE Use *An Egg Is an Egg.*

- Have children turn to p. 18. Listen while I read the page. I will try to read without making any mistakes. I want to read smoothly so the story makes sense and sounds as if I'm telling a story.
- Ask children to follow along as you read the page with expression, accuracy, and at an appropriate rate.
- Have children read the page after you. Encourage them to try to read smoothly without mistakes. Continue in the same way with p. 19.

REREAD FOR FLUENCY

Choral Reading

ROUTINE

1. **Select a Passage** For *An Egg Is and Egg,* use pp. 22–26.
2. **Divide into Groups** Assign each group a part to read. For this story, assign a page to each of four groups.
3. **Model** Have children track the print as you read.
4. **Read Together** Have children read along with you.
5. **Independent Readings** Have the groups read aloud without you. Monitor progress and provide feedback. For optimal fluency, children should reread three to four times.

Monitor Progress — Check Fluency WCPM

As children reread, monitor their progress toward their individual fluency goals. Current Goal: 20–30 words correct per minute. End-of-Year Goal: 60 words correct per minute.

If... children cannot read fluently at a rate of 20–30 words per minute,

then... make sure children practice with text at their independent level. Provide additional fluency practice, pairing nonfluent readers with fluent readers.

If... children already read at 60 words per minute,

then... they do not need to reread three to four times.

SUCCESS PREDICTOR

Day 1 Check Word Reading	Day 2 Check Word Reading	Day 3 Check High-Frequency Words/Retelling	▶ **Day 4 Check Fluency**	Day 5 Assess Progress

OBJECTIVE

- Read aloud fluently with accuracy and at an appropriate rate.

Options for Oral Reading

Use *Nothing Fits!* or one of the following Leveled Readers.

On-Level
Just Like Me

Strategic Intervention
Nothing Stays the Same

Advanced
Your Amazing Body!

Provide opportunities for children to read one-on-one with an aide or parent volunteer, if possible. The adult models by reading first, and the child reads and rereads the same text, with adult guidance. Allow extra repetitions for English language learners, to improve their fluency.

Words Correct Per Minute
SUCCESS PREDICTOR

OBJECTIVE

- Create a math story.

Advanced

Encourage children to choose other numbers of people and create additional illustrated math stories.

Support Writing If children suggest phrases or sentences that do not reflect conventional English, respond positively and restate the sentence without the errors. Record the phrase as it is restated.

Writing Across the Curriculum

WRITE Math Story

BRAINSTORM Have children look at p. 10 of the Student Edition and discuss inviting people to a birthday party.

SHARE THE PEN Have children participate in creating a math story. To begin, write this addition number sentence: $5 + 4 =$ ____. Explain that a math story is a way to show information using a drawing and words. Tell children 5 boys and 4 girls have been invited to a party. Have children suggest sentences for a math story using those numbers. Invite individuals to help write sentences by discussing punctuation. Ask questions, such as the following:

- What begins the first word in a sentence? (capital letter)
- What punctuation is at the end of a statement? (period)
- What punctuation is at end of a question? (question mark)
- How many sentences will be in our math story? (We will have three sentences—two telling sentences and one question.)

Have a volunteer write the first sentence: *5 boys came to my party.* Continue having individuals contribute to writing the math story. Reread the story frequently. When the story is finished, have children copy it onto a sheet of paper and add illustrations. Call on a volunteer to solve the problem.

5 boys came to my party.

4 girls came to my party too.

How many kids came to my party?

Grammar

REVIEW Action Verbs

DEFINE ACTION VERBS

- What tells what someone or something does? (a verb)
- What is a verb that describes an action? (an action verb)

PRACTICE

DEMONSTRATE ACTION VERBS Have children look through a story they have read or listened to and look for action words. Create a list of action words on the board. Have volunteers demonstrate the actions.

eating	**sleeps**	**singing**	**thinking**
kicks	**rides**	**grows**	**laughs**

OBJECTIVE

- Identify action verbs.

DAILY FIX-IT

7. The puppie ran by the door
The puppy ran by the door.

8. i am alwais late.
I am always late.

Action Verbs

Mark the sentence that has a line under the verb.

1. ○ Ann plants a seed.
⊗ Ann plants a seed.
○ Ann plants a seed.

2. ○ She pushes it into the ground.
○ She pushes it into the ground.
⊗ She pushes it into the ground.

3. ⊗ Rain falls on the ground.
○ Rain falls on the ground.
○ Rain falls on the ground.

4. ○ The sun shines on the ground.
○ The sun shines on the ground.
⊗ The sun shines on the ground.

5. ⊗ The seed grows into a plant.
○ The seed grows into a plant.
○ The seed grows into a plant.

6. ○ A flower blooms on the plant.
⊗ A flower blooms on the plant.
○ A flower blooms on the plant.

Home Activity Your child prepared for taking tests on verbs. Together read a short, simple newspaper or magazine article. Have your child circle as many action verbs as he or she can find.

▲ **Grammar and Writing Practice Book** p. 51

Wrap Up Your Day!

FLUENCY Write *Sammy will not have to stay inside.* Remind children that good readers read without mistakes at an appropriate rate. Set a good pace—not too fast and not too slow. Call on individuals to read the sentence with accuracy and at an appropriate rate.

LET'S TALK ABOUT IT Display the Baby and Now T-chart from Day 1. Help children recall the story "Nothing Fits." Discuss how Sammy has changed. Add any additional activities discussed to the chart.

PREVIEW Day 5

Remind children that they heard a story about a girl who thought she was never big enough. Tell them that tomorrow they will hear about Maggie McGee again.

Day 5

AT A GLANCE

Share Literature

"Wait for Me!" Said Maggie McGee"

Phonics and Spelling

Review Vowel Sounds of y and Long Vowels (CV)

High-Frequency Words

always *become* *day* *everything* *nothing* *stays* *things*

Word Wall

Monitor Progress

Spelling Test: Words with Long *e* and Long *i: y*

< Differentiated Assessment

Writing and Grammar

Trait: Conventions

Action Verbs

Materials

- *Sing with Me Big Book*
- Read Aloud Anthology
- Reproducible Pages TE 34f–34g
- Student Edition 34–35

Morning Warm-Up!

This week we read about ways children change as they grow to be healthy adults. What are some ways you can take a measurement of how much you are growing?

QUESTION OF THE DAY Encourage children to sing "Oh My" from the *Sing with Me Big Book* as you gather. Write and read the message, tracking the print. Discuss the question.

REVIEW ORAL VOCABULARY Have children find words in the message that

- name a fully grown person *(adult)*
- tell what you might use such tools as a ruler or a scale for *(measurement)*
- tell that a person is well and not sick *(healthy)*

Assess Vocabulary Use the Day 5 instruction on ELL Poster 13 to monitor children's progress with oral vocabulary.

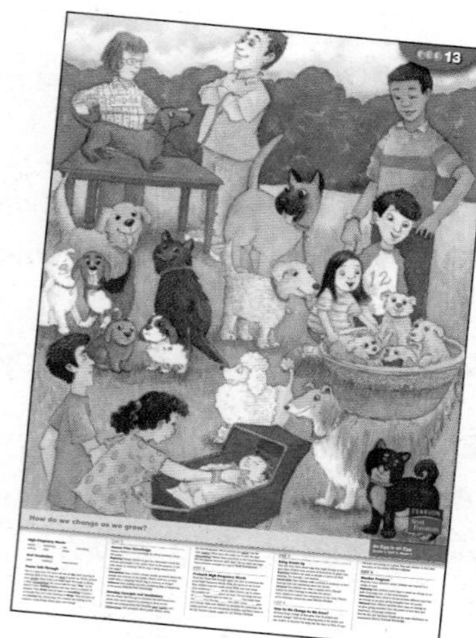

ELL Poster 13

Share Literature

LISTEN AND RESPOND

USE PRIOR KNOWLEDGE Review that yesterday the class listened to find out whether Maggie grew bigger. Suggest that today the class listen to find out what Maggie's third wish was.

Read Aloud Anthology
"Wait for Me!"
Said Maggie McGee

MONITOR LISTENING COMPREHENSION

- What is Maggie's third wish? (to be taller than all her brothers and sisters)
- How is Maggie able to help her brother, even though she is small? (She knows the lines he should say in the play; she has a shoe to use in the play.)
- What things does Maggie do when she gets to do whatever she wants? (She gives the announcements at school; her brother holds her up to play basketball.)

BUILD ORAL VOCABULARY

GENERATE DISCUSSION Recall the changes that happen to Maggie as she grows. Invite children to talk about ways they have grown. Ask, for example, if they can remember when they couldn't reach the pedals of their bicycle. Have children use some of this week's Amazing Words as they describe some of the things they can do now that they're bigger.

Monitor Progress — Check Oral Vocabulary

Display pp. 10–11 in the Student Edition and remind children of the concept for this week—Growing and Changing. Ask them to tell you about the photographs using some of this week's Amazing Words, *adult, healthy, measurement, shuffle, teeter, crooked, bounce,* and *handsome.*

If... children have difficulty using the Amazing Words,

then... ask questions about the photographs using the Amazing Words. Note which questions children can respond to. Reteach unknown words using the Oral Vocabulary Routine.

Day 1 Check Word Reading	Day 2 Check Word Reading	Day 3 Check High-Frequency Words/Retelling	Day 4 Check Fluency	▶ **Day 5 Check Oral Vocabulary/ Assess Progress**

OBJECTIVES

- Set purpose for listening.
- Build oral vocabulary.

adult	**teeter**
healthy	**crooked**
measurement	**bounce**
shuffle	**handsome**

ELL

Extend Language Work with children to use hand and body movement to demonstrate the meaning of action words from the story such as *reach, stretching, bouncing,* and *climbed.*

Oral Vocabulary
SUCCESS PREDICTOR

OBJECTIVES

- Review vowel sounds of *y* and long vowels (CV).
- Review high-frequency words.

Vowel Sounds of *y* and Long Vowels (CV)

REVIEW

IDENTIFY WORDS WITH THE VOWEL SOUNDS OF *y* AND THE CV PATTERN Write these sentences. Have children read each one aloud as you track the print. Call on individuals to name and underline the words with vowel sounds of *y* and words with the CV vowel pattern.

Danny gave me fifty cents.

Why did Di try to go?

This jelly is so messy!

No, my fussy kitty will not eat cat food.

High-Frequency Words

REVIEW

SAY AND SPELL WORDS Read the clues. Ask children to answer each clue with a word from p. 12. Have children say, spell, and locate the word on the Word Wall. Word Wall

- I'm the opposite of *never.* I have six letters. (always)
- Seven of me make a week. I rhyme with *hay.* (day)
- I start with /b/. I rhyme with *some.* (become)
- I have ten letters. I'm the opposite of *nothing.* (everything)
- I start with /n/. I'm the opposite of *something.* (nothing)
- I'm the opposite of *goes.* I have five letters. (stays)
- I start with /th/. I rhyme with *brings.* (things)

Access Content For additional practice with the high-frequency words, use the vocabulary strategies and word cards in the ELL Teaching Guide, pp. 87–88.

SPELLING TEST Vowel Sounds of *y*

DICTATION SENTENCES Use these sentences to assess this week's spelling words.

1. My puppy can do funny tricks.
2. Jo keeps a lucky stone in her desk.
3. Jimmy has a thin body.
4. My dressy pants just fit me.
5. Do you have any ripe plums?
6. Try to work together.
7. What makes you cry?
8. Andy likes to run by the lake.
9. See the kites fly up in the sky.
10. Dad tells silly jokes.

HIGH-FREQUENCY WORDS

11. Put these things on the top shelf.
12. Betty is always late for class.

ASSESS

- Spell words with Vowel Sounds of *y.*

Spelling Words

Long *e* and Long *i*: *y*

1. **my***	6. **fly**
2. **by**	7. **cry**
3. **try**	8. **lucky**
4. **any**	9. **silly**
5. **body**	10. **puppy**

High-Frequency Words

11. **things*** 12. **always***

* Words from the Selection

Group Time

On-Level

Read Set B Sentences.

- Use pp. 34e–34g.

Strategic Intervention

Read Set A Sentences.

- Use pp. 34e–34g.
- Use the **Routine** on p. DI·24.

Advanced

Read Set C Sentences and the Story.

- Use pp. 34e–34g.
- Use the **Routine** on p. DI·25.

DAY 5

ELL Place English language learners in the groups that correspond to their reading abilities in English.

Independent Activities

Fluency Reading Children reread selections at their independent level.

Journal Writing Write about something you have grown out of. Share writing.

Independent Reading See p. 10j for Reading/Library activities and suggestions.

Literacy Centers You may use the Technology Center on p. 10k to support this week's concepts and reading.

Practice Book 1.2 Alphabetical Order, p. 10

Break into small groups after Spelling and before Grammar and Writing.

ASSESS

- Decode vowel sounds of *y* and long vowels (CV).
- Read high-frequency words.
- Read aloud with appropriate speed and accuracy.
- Compare and contrast.
- Retell a story.

Differentiated Assessment

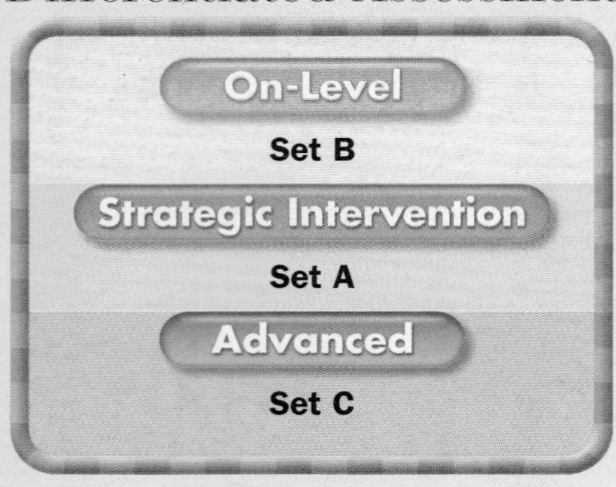

Fluency Assessment Plan

- ☑ **This week assess Advanced students.**
- ☐ Week 2 assess Strategic Intervention students.
- ☐ Week 3 assess On-Level students.
- ☐ Week 4 assess Strategic Intervention students.
- ☐ Week 5 assess any students you have not yet checked during this unit.
- ☐ Week 6 assess Strategic Intervention students.

Set individual fluency goals for children to enable them to reach the end-of-year goal.

- Current Goal: 20–30 wcpm
- End-of-Year Goal: 60 wcpm
- ELL An informal method of assessing oral reading fluency is to simply listen to a child reading orally and judge how clear the reading is.

Monitor Progress

SENTENCE READING

ASSESS VOWEL SOUNDS OF *y*, LONG VOWELS (CV), AND HIGH-FREQUENCY WORDS Use one of the reproducible lists on p. 34f to assess children's ability to read words with vowel sounds of *y*, long vowels (CV), and high-frequency words. Call on individuals to read two sentences aloud. Have each child in the group read different sentences. Start over with sentence one if necessary.

RECORD SCORES Use the Sentence Reading Chart for this unit on p. WA19.

Monitor Progress	Vowel Sounds of *y* and Long Vowels (CV)
If... children have trouble reading vowel sounds of *y* and long vowels (CV),	**then...** use the Reteach Lessons on p. DI • 76.
	High-Frequency Words
If... children cannot read a high-frequency word,	**then...** mark the missed words on a high-frequency word list and send the list home for additional word reading practice or have the child practice with a fluent reader.

FLUENCY AND COMPREHENSION

ASSESS FLUENCY Take a one-minute sample of children's oral reading. See Monitoring Fluency, pp. WA17–WA18. Have children read "Happy Trips," the on-level fluency passage on p. 34g.

RECORD SCORES Record the number of words read correctly in a minute on the child's Fluency Progress Chart.

ASSESS COMPREHENSION Have the child read to the end of the passage. (If the child had difficulty with the passage, you may read it aloud.) Ask the child to compare and contrast things in the story and have the child retell the passage. Use the Retelling Rubric on p. 28–29 to evaluate the child's retelling.

Monitor Progress	Fluency
If... a child does not achieve the fluency goal on the timed reading,	**then...** copy the passage and send it home with the child for additional fluency practice or have the child practice with a fluent reader.
	Compare and Contrast
If... a child cannot compare and contrast things in the story,	**then...** use the Reteach Lesson on p. DI • 77.

READ THE SENTENCES

Set A

1. He is always happy.
2. We wish for a sunny day.
3. Pam saw nothing go by.
4. She hopes her hat stays dry.
5. Sad things make me cry.
6. Everything becomes so messy.

Set B

1. She tells jokes that are always so funny.
2. No planes will fly on that day next week.
3. We will try to stack things on the shelf.
4. The puppy will be fine if it stays here.
5. She said nothing becomes lost in my house.
6. He made everything in the shop muddy.

Set C

1. He knows it is windy, but nothing should blow away.
2. Things in the house become dusty when we leave the door open.
3. The shy girl always says hi to me in school.
4. We go to a fish fry one day a week.
5. The bunny eats everything she feeds him and still wants more.
6. The sly fox stays so far away that I can't take its picture.

REPRODUCIBLE PAGE • See also *Assessment Handbook*, p. 259

Happy Trips

Do you like to go on trips? Do you drive or fly? 12

Trips can be the same in some ways. They will 22
get you where you want to go. You can take a pet 34
like a puppy. If you get sleepy, you can take a nap. 46
The rides can be bumpy too. It can be windy on 57
your trip. The wind can shake you. 64

Flying is a quick way to get where you want to go. 76
You fly in the sky. That is so much fun! 86
You will be on a street when you drive. 95
That is also fun for me. You always 103
see many trucks going fast on the street. 111

See also *Assessment Handbook*, p. 260 • REPRODUCIBLE PAGE

Write Now

Read Together

Writing and Grammar

Steps

Prompt

An Egg Is an Egg shows that almost everything changes. Think about how an egg changes to become a chicken. Now write steps that tell what happens. Put the steps in order.

Writing Trait

Capital letters and end marks are sentence **conventions.**

Student Model

Steps are in order, from first to last.

Each sentence tells one step.

Writer follows sentence conventions.

A hen lays an egg.
The hen sits on the egg.
The egg cracks in two.
A chick leaves the egg.
The chick grows into a chicken.

Writer's Checklist

- **Focus** Are all sentences about the topic?
- **Organization** Are steps in the right order?
- **Support** Does each sentence tell about one step?
- **Conventions** Does every sentence begin with a capital letter and end with a period?

Grammar

Action Verbs

A **verb** can tell what someone or something does.

Mom **plants** seeds.
The seeds **grow.**

The word **plants** tells what Mom does.
The word **grow** tells what the seeds do.

Look at the steps. Write the action verbs in the sentences.

34 35

Writing and Grammar

LOOK AT THE PROMPT Read p. 34 aloud. Have children select and discuss key words or phrases in the prompt. *(how an egg changes to become a chicken, steps that tell what happens, put the steps in order)*

STRATEGIES TO DEVELOP CONVENTIONS Have children

- look at sentences in the selection and identify the initial capital letter and the end mark.
- add initial capital letters and end punctuation to "sentences" you write on the board or chart paper.
- write sentences using correctly spelled vocabulary and spelling words.

See Scoring Rubric on p. WA11. Rubric 4 3 2 1

HINTS FOR BETTER WRITING Read p. 35 aloud. Use the checklist to help children revise their steps. Discuss the grammar lesson. (Answers: *lays, sits, cracks, leaves, grows*) Have children use action verbs correctly in their steps.

DAILY FIX-IT

9. mom loks at the trees. (Mom; looks)

10. the bear drinks from the lak. (The; lake.)

Action Verbs

Circle the verb in each sentence.

1. The baby (cries) in its crib.
2. The puppy (runs) to its mother.
3. The kitten (plays) with a string.

Circle the correct verb in ( ) to complete each sentence. **Write** the verb on the line.

4. The boy calls to his friend. (bakes, calls)
5. The dog barks at the man. (barks, talks)
6. The cat eats a fish. (sings, eats)

Home Activity Your child reviewed verbs. Write this sentence frame on paper: *The child ___.* Take turns with your child completing the sentence with an action verb, for example, *The child runs. The child walks. The child laughs.*

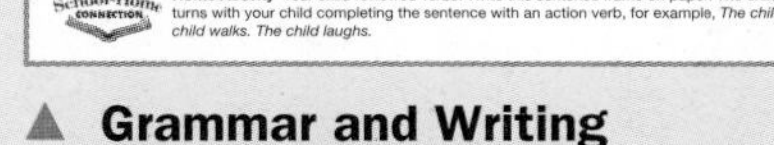

▲ **Grammar and Writing Practice Book** p. 52

OBJECTIVE

- Arrange a list of words in alphabetical order.

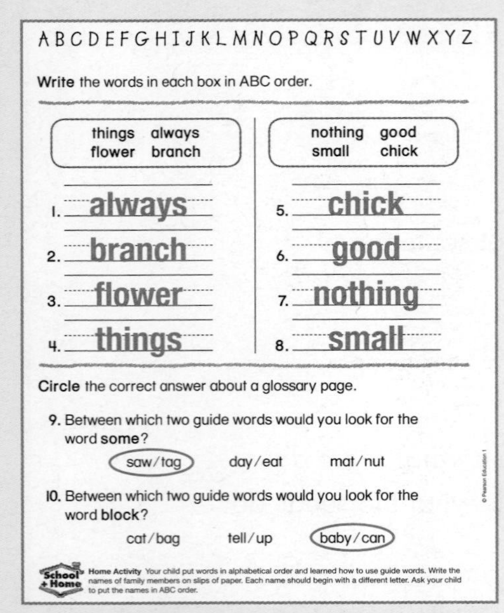

A B C D E F G H I J K L M N O P Q R S T U V W X Y Z

Write the words in each box in ABC order.

things always flower branch	nothing good small chick
1. always	5. chick
2. branch	6. good
3. flower	7. nothing
4. things	8. small

Circle the correct answer about a glossary page.

9. Between which two guide words would you look for the word **some**?
   (saw/tag) day/eat mat/nut

10. Between which two guide words would you look for the word **block**?
   cat/bag tell/up (baby/can)

School + Home **Home Activity** Your child put words in alphabetical order and learned how to use guide words. Write the names of family members on slips of paper. Each name should begin with a different letter. Ask your child to put the names in ABC order.

▲ **Practice Book 1.2** p. 10

Research/Study Skills

TEACH/MODEL Use Alphabetical Order

MODEL ALPHABETICAL ORDER Show children a dictionary and point out that thousands of words appear in this reference source. Ask what would happen if the words were not organized in alphabetical order. Guide children to see that it would be almost impossible to find words in the dictionary if they were not in alphabetical order.

Model how to use alphabetical order to find the word *egg*.

MODEL When I look up a word in the dictionary, I think about the letters in the alphabet. What is the first letter in the word *egg?* It is an *e.* I say the alphabet *a, b, c, d, e.* . . . I know that *e* comes after *d.* I look through the pages, and skip to the *e* words.

ALPHABETIZE WORDS Write several pairs of words on the board. Call on individuals to tell which one comes first in alphabetical order. Use word pairs such as tree/bush, branch/leaf, plant/grow, and garden/flower.

PRACTICE

ALPHABETIZE SELECTION WORDS Write these words from the selection on the board: *tea, flower, blocks, water, seed, egg.* Have children write the words in alphabetical order.

Access Content As you model alphabetical order, provide ample time for children to practice reciting the alphabet. You might say a letter, such as *f,* and have them say the rest of the alphabet starting with that letter.

Wrap Up Your Week!

LET'S TALK ABOUT Growing and Changing

QUESTION OF THE WEEK Recall this week's question.

- How do we change as we grow?

Display the Baby/Now chart. Discuss things the children can do now that they couldn't do as a baby. Have them make pictures to illustrate their own activities then and now.

Baby	Now
no teeth	lose baby teeth and grow permanent teeth
crawl	can walk and run
have to be fed	can eat by myself
have to be dressed	can dress myself
can't read	can read
have to be pushed in a stroller	can ride a bike

CONNECT Use questions such as these to prompt a discussion.

- What are some things you can do for yourself now to stay healthy?
- Did you grow all at once? Why do adults sometimes take your measurement?
- Why do adults tell you to wait when you want to do things they think you are too little to do?

Build Background Use ELL Poster 14 to support the Preview activity.

You've learned

this week!

You've learned

so far this year!

PREVIEW Tell children that next week they will read about things people and animals learn as they grow and change.

PREVIEW Next Week

5

Assessment Checkpoints *for the Week*

Selection Assessment

Use pp. 25–28 of Selection Tests to check:

 **Selection Understanding**

 **Comprehension Skill** *Compare and Contrast*

 **High-Frequency Words**

always	*nothing*
become	*stays*
day	*things*
everything	

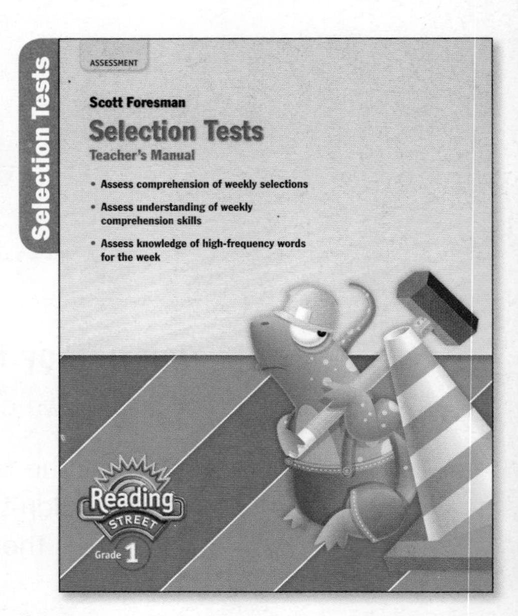

Leveled Assessment

On-Level

Strategic Intervention

Advanced

Use pp. 73–78 of Fresh Reads for Differentiated Test Practice to check:

 **Comprehension Skill** *Compare and Contrast*

 REVIEW **Comprehension Skill** *Author's Purpose*

 **Fluency** *Words Correct Per Minute*

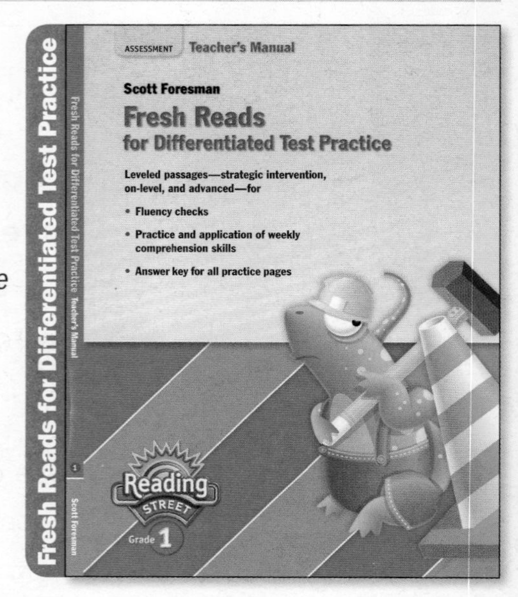

Managing Assessment

Use Assessment Handbook for:

 **Weekly Assessment Blackline Masters for Monitoring Progress**

 **Observation Checklists**

 **Record-Keeping Forms**

 **Portfolio Assessment**

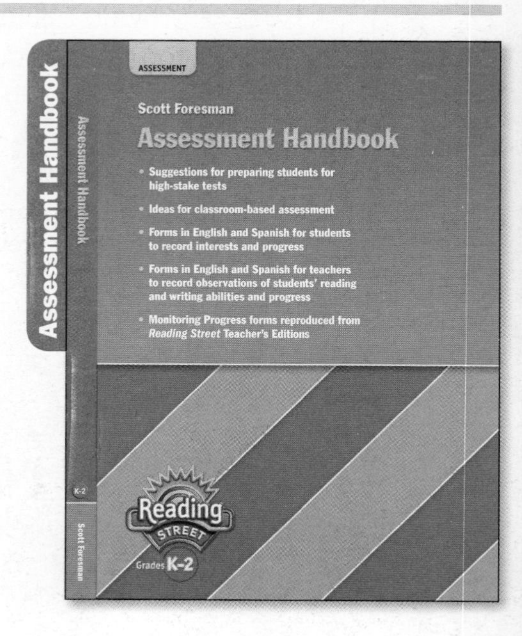

Ruby in Her
Own Time

Ruby in Her Own Time

Unit 3

Changes

CONCEPT QUESTION

What is changing in our world?

Growing and Changing

Week 1

How do we change as we grow?

Week 2

What do we learn as we grow and change?

Week 3

Why are changes exciting?

Changes in Nature

Week 4

What changes happen in a garden?

Week 5

What changes can we observe in nature?

Week 6

How does nature change during the year?

Week 2

EXPAND THE CONCEPT

What do we learn as we grow and change?

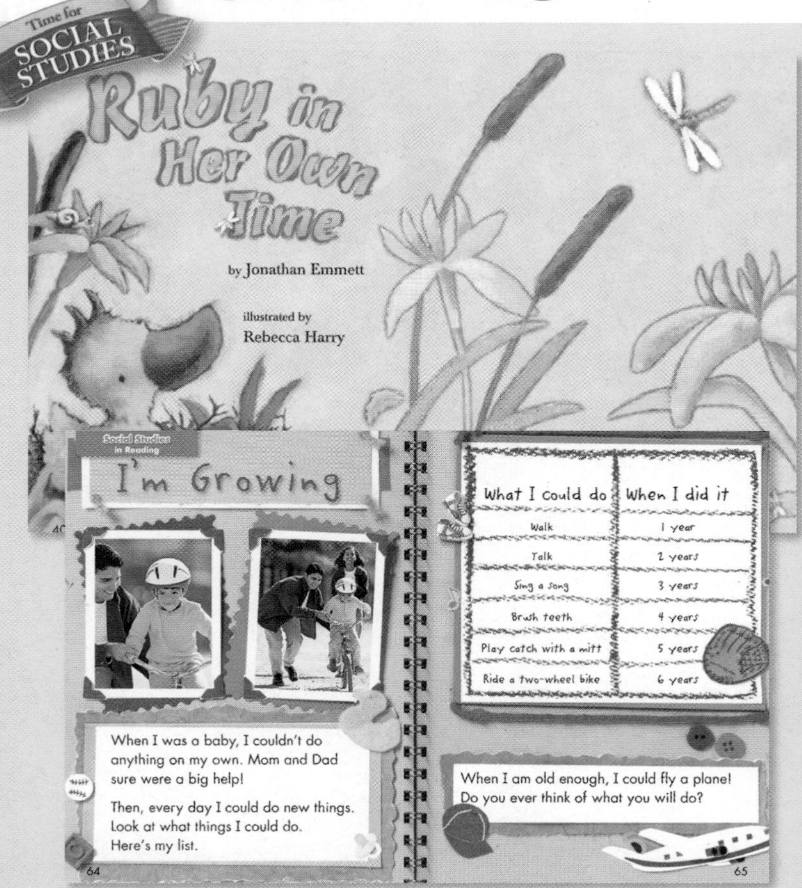

CONNECT THE CONCEPT

▶ **Build Background**

attempt *event* *lovely*
awkward *famous* *time line*
correct *flatter*

▶ **Social Studies Content**

Changes over Time, Respecting Differences, Time Lines

▶ **Writing**

List

Preview Your Week

What do we learn as we grow and change?

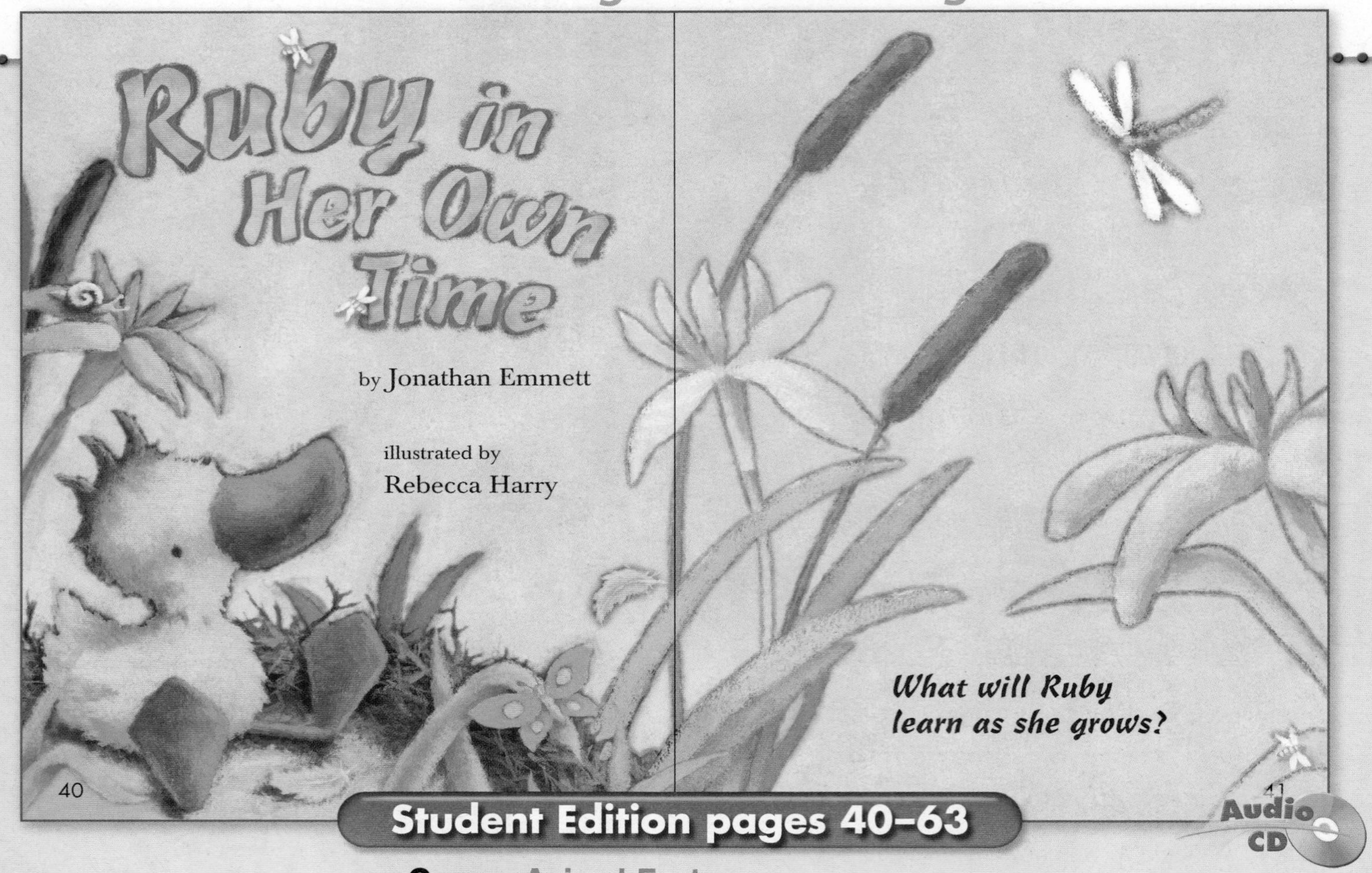

Student Edition pages 40–63

Audio CD

Genre	Animal Fantasy
Phonics	Final *ng, nk* and Compound Words
Comprehension Skill	Plot
Comprehension Strategy	Summarize

Time for SOCIAL STUDIES

Paired Selection

Reading Across Texts
Compare Change

Genre
Narrative Nonfiction

Text Features
Photographs, Chart

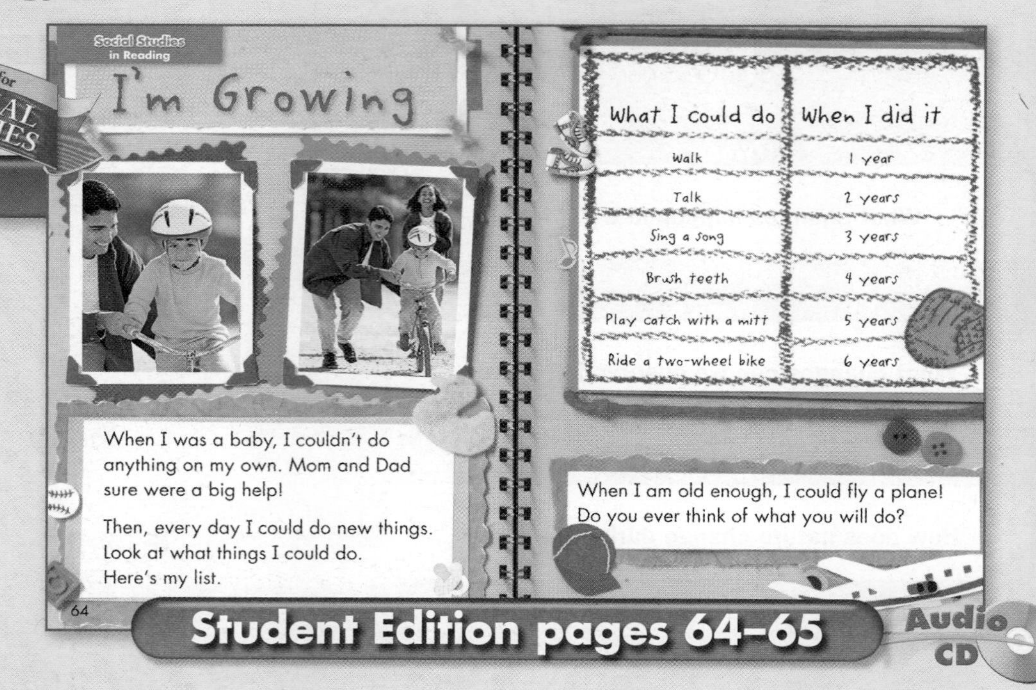

Student Edition pages 64–65

Audio CD

- Student Edition
- Leveled Readers
- Decodable Readers

Leveled Readers

Strategy Plot

Skill Summarize

Lesson Vocabulary

ELL Reader

- Concept Vocabulary
- Text Support
- Language Enrichment

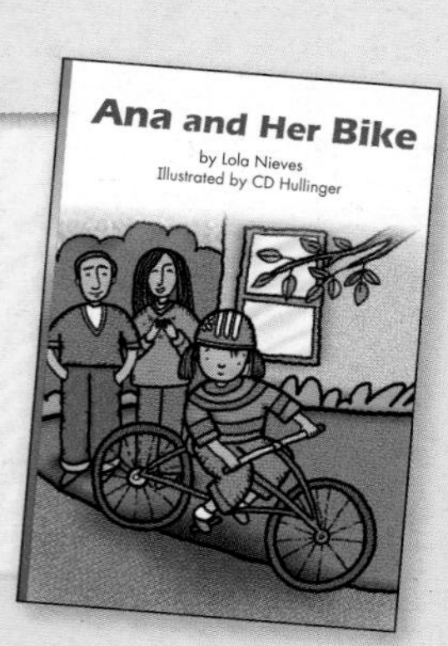

Decodable Readers

Apply Phonics

- *The Family Picnic*
- *Inside and Outside*

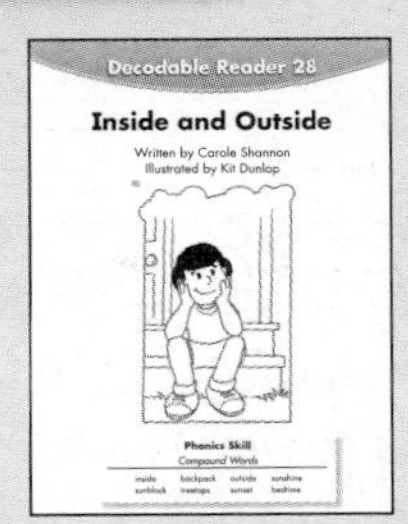

Time for SOCIAL STUDIES

Integrate Social Studies Standards

- Time Lines
- Changes Over Time
- Respecting Differences

Ruby in Her Own Time, pp. 40–63

"I'm Growing," pp. 64–65

Leveled Readers

Below-Level
- Support Concepts

On-Level
- Develop Concepts

Advanced
- Extend Concepts
- Social Studies Extension Activity

ELL Reader

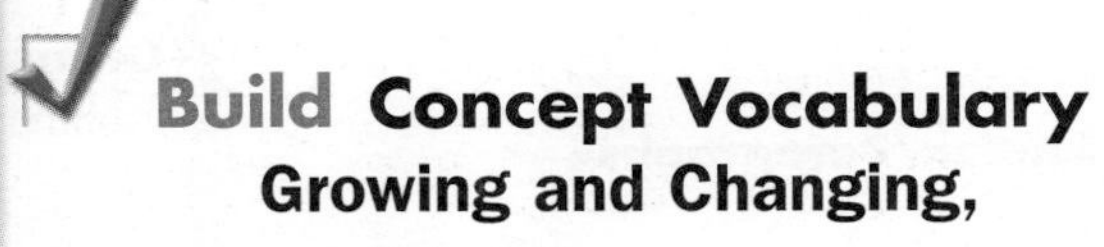

Build **Concept Vocabulary**
Growing and Changing, pp. 36r–37

Teach **Social Studies Concepts**
Respecting Differences, p. 56–57
Time Lines, p. 64–65

Explore **Social Studies Center**
Identify Personal Changes, p. 36k

Weekly Plan

READING

90–120 minutes

TARGET SKILLS OF THE WEEK

- **Phonics**
  Final *ng*, *nk* and Compound Words
- **Comprehension Skill**
  Plot
- **Comprehension Strategy**
  Summarize

DAY 1 PAGES 36l–37d

Oral Language

QUESTION OF THE WEEK, 36l
What do we learn as we grow and change?

Oral Vocabulary/Share Literature, 36m
Sing with Me Big Book, Song 14
Amazing Words *attempt, event, time line*

Word Work

Phonemic Awareness, 36m
Blend and Segment Onset/Rime

Phonics, 36n–36o
Introduce Final *ng, nk* **T**

Spelling, 36p
Pretest

Comprehension/Vocabulary/Fluency

Read Decodable Reader 27

Grouping Options 36f–36g

Review High-Frequency Words
Check Comprehension
Reread for Fluency

Build Background, 36r–37
Growing and Changing

Listening Comprehension, 37a–37b
Plot **T**

DAY 2 PAGES 38a–39c

Oral Language

QUESTION OF THE DAY, 38a
Why do you think it's important to always keep learning?

Oral Vocabulary/Share Literature, 38b
Big Book *Mr. George Baker*
Amazing Words *famous, flatter*

Word Work

Phonemic Awareness, 38b
Blend and Segment Syllables

Phonics, 38c–38d
Introduce Compound Words **T**

Spelling, 38e
Dictation

Comprehension/Vocabulary/Fluency

Read Decodable Reader 28

Grouping Options 36f–36g

Review High-Frequency Words
Check Comprehension
Reread for Fluency

High-Frequency Words, 38–39
Introduce *any, enough, ever, every, own, sure, were* **T**

LANGUAGE ARTS

20–30 minutes

Trait of the Week

Organization/Paragraphs

Day 1

Shared Writing, 37c
List

Grammar, 37d
Introduce Verbs That Add -*s* **T**

Day 2

Interactive Writing, 39a
Poem

Grammar, 39b
Practice Verbs That Add -*s* **T**

Speaking and Listening, 39c
Give Directions

	Day 1	Day 2
DAILY JOURNAL WRITING	*Write to tell how you learned to ride a bike.*	*Make a time line about your life.*
DAILY SOCIAL STUDIES CONNECTIONS	What We Can Do/What We Can't Do Chart, 36r–37	What We Can Do/What We Can't Do Chart, 39c

DAILY SUCCESS PREDICTORS for Adequate Yearly Progress

Monitor Progress and Corrective Feedback

	Day 1	Day 2
Phonics	Check Word Reading, *36o* Spiral REVIEW Phonics	Check Word Reading, *38d* Spiral REVIEW Phonics

RESOURCES FOR THE WEEK

- Practice Book 1.2, *pp. 11–20*
- Phonics and Spelling Practice Book, *pp. 53–56*
- Grammar and Writing Practice Book, *pp. 53–56*
- Selection Test, *pp. 29–32*
- Fresh Reads for Differentiated Test Practice, *pp. 79–84*
- Phonics Songs and Rhymes Chart 14
- The Grammar and Writing Book, *pp. 128–133*

Grouping Options for Differentiated Instruction

Turn the page for the small group lesson plan.

DAY 3 PAGES 40a–63d

Oral Language

QUESTION OF THE DAY, 40a
How do you learn in your own way?

Oral Vocabulary/Share Literature, 40b
Big Book *Mr. George Baker*
Amazing Word *correct*

Word Work

Phonemic Awareness, 40b
Blend and Segment Onset/Rime

Phonics, 40c–40d
◎ Final *ng, nk* and Compound Words **T**

Spelling, 40d
Practice

Comprehension/Vocabulary/Fluency

Read *Ruby in Her Own Time,* 40e–63

Grouping Options 36f–36g

Introduce Selection Words
beautiful, father, feather, flew, mother, precious

Review High-Frequency Words
any, enough, ever, every, own, sure, were **T**

◎ Plot **T**
◎ Summarize
REVIEW Sequence **T**

Fluency, 63a
Attend to Punctuation

Vocabulary, 63b
Synonyms

Trait of the Week, 63c
Introduce Organization/Paragraphs

Grammar, 63d
Write with Verbs That Add *-s* **T**

Day 3 *Write about something new you tried to do this year.*

Day 3 Time for Social Studies: Respecting Differences, 56–57

DAY 4 PAGES 64a–65d

Oral Language

QUESTION OF THE DAY, 64a
What do you want to do when you are a grown-up?

Oral Vocabulary/Share Literature, 64b
Read Aloud Anthology "The Ugly Duckling"
Amazing Words *awkward, lovely*

Word Work

Phonemic Awareness, 64b
Segment and Count Phonemes

High-Frequency Words, 64c
Practice *any, enough, ever, every, own, sure, were* **T**

Phonics, 64c–64d
REVIEW Vowel Sounds of *y* and Long Vowels (CV) **T**
REVIEW Word Reading **T**

Spelling, 64e
Partner Review

Comprehension/Vocabulary/Fluency

Read "I'm Growing," 64–65
Leveled Readers

Grouping Options 36f–36g

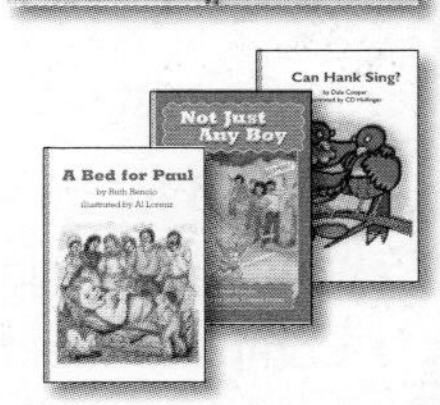

Synonyms
Reading Across Texts

Fluency, 65b
Attend to Punctuation

Writing Across the Curriculum, 65c
Time Line

Grammar, 65d
Review Verbs That Add *-s* **T**

Day 4 *Write a name that Ruby might choose for her baby and why.*

Day 4 Time for Social Studies: Time Lines, 64–65

DAY 5 PAGES 66a–67b

Oral Language

QUESTION OF THE DAY, 66a
What would you say to someone who is learning something new?

Oral Vocabulary/Share Literature, 66b
Read Aloud Anthology "The Ugly Duckling"
Amazing Words Review

Word Work

Phonics, 66c
◎ Review Final *ng, nk* and Compound Words **T**

High-Frequency Words, 66c
Review *any, enough, ever, every, own, sure, were* **T**

Spelling, 66d
Test

Comprehension/Vocabulary/Fluency

Read Leveled Readers

Grouping Options 36f–36g

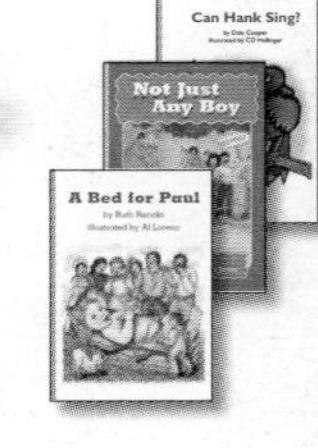

Monitor Progress, 66e–66g
Read the Sentences
Read the Story

Writing and Grammar, 66-67
Develop Organization/Paragraphs
Use Verbs That Add *-s* **T**

Research/Study Skills, 67a
Glossary

Day 5 *Write about a change you noticed.*

Day 5 Revisit the What We Can Do/What We Can't Do Chart, 67b

KEY ◎ = Target Skill **T** = Tested Skill

Fluency and Comprehension
Check High-Frequency Words, *40f*
Check Retelling, *62a*
Spiral REVIEW High-Frequency Words

Fluency
Check Fluency WCPM, *65b*
Spiral REVIEW Phonics, High-Frequency Words

Oral Vocabulary
Check Oral Vocabulary, *66b*
Assess Phonics, High-Frequency Words, Fluency, Comprehension, *66e*

SUCCESS PREDICTOR

Small Group Plan *for Differentiated Instruction*

Daily Plan AT A GLANCE

Reading

Whole Group
- Oral Language
- Word Work
- Comprehension/Vocabulary

Group Time

Meet with small groups to provide:
- Skill Support
- Reading Support
- Fluency Practice

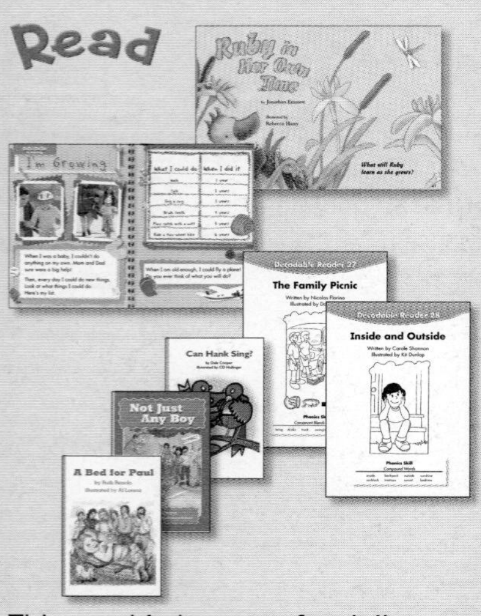

This week's lessons for daily group time can be found behind the Differentiated Instruction (DI) tab on pp. DI • 26–DI • 35.

Whole Group
- Comprehension/Vocabulary
- Fluency

Language Arts
- Writing
- Grammar
- Speaking/Listening/Viewing
- Research/Study Skills

Use *My Sidewalks on Reading Street* for Tier III intensive reading intervention.

DAY 1

On-Level	Strategic Intervention	Advanced
Teacher-Led *Page 36q* • **Read** Decodable Reader 27 • **Reread** for Fluency	**Teacher-Led** *Page DI • 26* • Blend and Build Words with Final *ng* and *nk* • **Read** Decodable Reader 27 • **Reread** for Fluency	**Teacher-Led** *Page DI • 27* • Extend Word Reading • **Read** Advanced Selection 14 • Introduce Concept Inquiry

Independent Activities

While you meet with small groups, have the rest of the class...

- Reread for fluency
- Write in their journals
- Complete Practice Book 1.2, p. 13
- Visit the Word Work Center

DAY 2

On-Level	Strategic Intervention	Advanced
Teacher-Led *Page 38f* • **Read** Decodable Reader 28 • **Reread** for Fluency	**Teacher-Led** *Page DI • 28* • Blend and Build Compound Words • **Read** Decodable Reader 28 • **Reread** for Fluency	**Teacher-Led** *Page DI • 29* • Extend Word Reading • **Read** Self-Selected Reading • Continue Concept Inquiry

Independent Activities

While you meet with small groups, have the rest of the class...

- Reread for fluency
- Write in their journals
- Complete Practice Book 1.2, pp. 14–16
- Visit the Word Work Center
- Work on inquiry projects

DAY 3

On-Level	Strategic Intervention	Advanced
Teacher-Led *Pages 40–63* • **Read** *Ruby in Her Own Time*	**Teacher-Led** *Page DI • 30* • Blend and Read Words with Final *ng, nk*; Compound Words • **Read** SI Decodable Reader 14 • **Read** or Listen to *Ruby in Her Own Time*	**Teacher-Led** *Page DI • 31* • **Read** *Ruby in Her Own Time* • Continue Concept Inquiry

Independent Activities

While you meet with small groups, have the rest of the class...

- Read self-selected reading
- Write in their journals
- Complete Practice Book 1.2, p. 17
- Visit the Listening and Writing Centers
- Work on inquiry projects

① Begin with whole class skill and strategy instruction.

② Meet with small groups to provide differentiated instruction.

③ Gather the whole class back together for fluency and language arts.

DAY 4

On-Level

Teacher-Led
Pages 64–65, LR13–LR15

- **Read** "I'm Growing"
- Practice with On-Level Reader *Not Just Any Boy*

Strategic Intervention

Teacher-Led
Pages DI • 32, LR10–LR12

- Blend and Read Words
- **Reread** SI Decodable Reader 13
- **Read** or Listen to "I'm Growing"
- Practice with Below-Level Reader *Can Hank Sing?*

Advanced

Teacher-Led
Pages DI • 33, LR16–LR18

- **Read** "I'm Growing"
- Expand Vocabulary
- Continue Concept Inquiry
- Practice with Advanced Reader *A Bed for Paul*

i Independent Activities

While you meet with small groups, have the rest of the class...

- Reread for fluency
- Write in their journals
- Read self-selected reading
- Complete Practice Book 1.2, pp. 18–19
- Visit the Listening and Social Studies Centers
- Work on inquiry projects

DAY 5

On-Level

Teacher-Led
Pages 66e–66g, LR13–LR15

- Sentence Reading, Set B
- Monitor Comprehension
- Practice with On-Level Reader *Not Just Any Boy*

Strategic Intervention

Teacher-Led
Pages DI • 34, LR10–LR12

- Practice Word Reading
- Sentence Reading, Set A
- Monitor Fluency and Comprehension
- Practice with Below-Level Reader *Can Hank Sing?*

Advanced

Teacher-Led
Pages DI • 35, LR16–LR18

- Sentence Reading, Set C
- Monitor Comprehension
- Share Concept Inquiry
- Practice with Advanced Reader *A Bed for Paul*

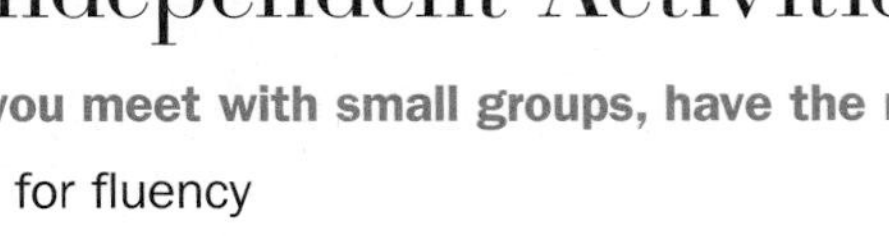

i Independent Activities

While you meet with small groups, have the rest of the class...

- Reread for fluency
- Write in their journals
- Read self-selected reading
- Complete Practice Book 1.2, p. 20
- Visit the Technology Center

Grouping Place English language learners in the groups that correspond to their reading abilities in English.

Use the appropriate Leveled Reader or other text at children's instructional level.

TIP Send home the appropriate Multilingual Summary of the main selection on Day 1.

Take It to the NET™ ONLINE
PearsonSuccessNet.com

P. David Pearson
For ideas on effective reading instruction, see the article "Effective Schools/Accomplished Teachers" by B. Taylor, Scott Foresman author P. D. Pearson, and others.

TEACHER TALK

Chunking is a strategy for finding familiar parts in unknown words. The parts may be phonograms, affixes, and so on.

Looking Ahead

Be sure to schedule time for children to work on the unit inquiry project "Take a Closer Look." This week children should begin their journals making notes and pictures about the objects they are observing.

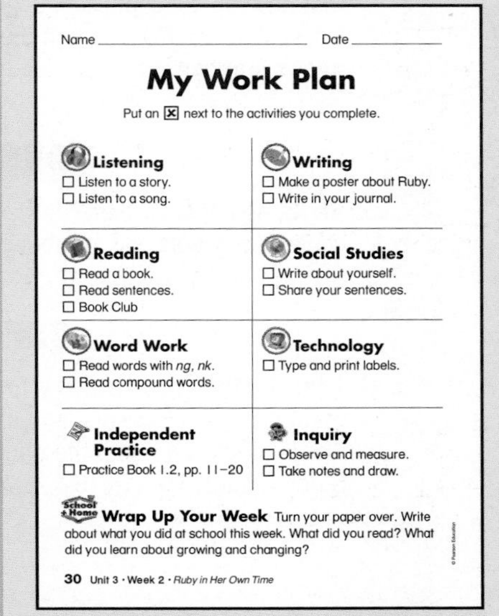

Name ______ Date ______

My Work Plan

Put an ☒ next to the activities you complete.

Listening
☐ Listen to a story.
☐ Listen to a song.

Writing
☐ Make a poster about Ruby.
☐ Write in your journal.

Reading
☐ Read a book.
☐ Read sentences.
☐ Book Club

Social Studies
☐ Write about yourself.
☐ Share your sentences.

Word Work
☐ Read words with *ng, nk.*
☐ Read compound words.

Technology
☐ Type and print labels.

Independent Practice
☐ Practice Book 1.2, pp. 11–20

Inquiry
☐ Observe and measure.
☐ Take notes and draw.

Wrap Up Your Week Turn your paper over. Write about what you did at school this week. What did you read? What did you learn about growing and changing?

30 Unit 3 • Week 2 • *Ruby in Her Own Time*

▲ **Group-Time Survival Guide** p. 30, Weekly Contract

Customize Your Plan *by Strand*

ORAL LANGUAGE

Concept Development

What do we learn as we grow and change?

attempt *event* *time line*
famous *flatter* *correct*
lovely *awkward*

BUILD

- ❑ **Question of the Week** Use the Morning Warm-Up! to introduce and discuss the question of the week. This week children will talk, sing, read, and write about growing and changing. DAY 1 *36l*

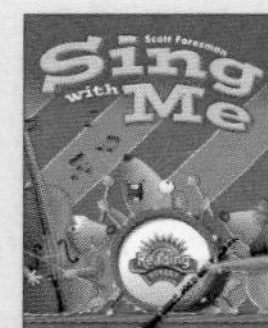

Sing with Me Big Book

- ❑ **Sing with Me Big Book** Sing a song about learning new things. Ask children to listen for the concept-related Amazing Words *attempt, event, time line*. DAY 1 *36m*

Let's Talk About It

- ❑ **Let's Talk About Growing and Changing** Use the Let's Talk About It lesson in the Student Edition to build background, vocabulary, and concepts. Then create a concept chart for children to add to throughout the week. DAY 1 *36r–37*

DEVELOP

- ❑ **Question of the Day** Use the questions in the Morning Warm-Ups! to discuss lesson concepts and how they relate to the unit theme, Changes. DAY 2 *38a*, DAY 3 *40a*, DAY 4 *64a*, DAY 5 *66a*
- ❑ **Share Literature** Read big books and read aloud selections that develop concepts, language, and vocabulary related to the lesson concept and the unit theme. Continue to develop this week's Amazing Words. DAY 2 *38b*, DAY 3 *40b*, DAY 4 *64b*, DAY 5 *66b*

CONNECT

- ❑ **Wrap Up Your Week!** Revisit the Question of the Week. Then connect concepts and vocabulary to next week's lesson. DAY 5 *67b*

CHECK

- ❑ **Check Oral Vocabulary** To informally assess children's oral vocabulary, ask individuals to use some of this week's Amazing Words to tell you about the photographs and illustration on Student Edition pp. 36–37. DAY 5 *66b*

PHONEMIC AWARENESS AND PHONICS

FINAL *NG, NK* Consonant digraphs consist of two unlike consonants that stand for a single sound that is different from either consonant alone.

COMPOUND WORDS A compound word is made up of two or more shorter words.

TEACH

- ❑ **Blend and Segment Onset/Rime** Practice saying and blending onset and rime. DAY 1 *36m*, DAY 3 *40b*
- ❑ **Final *ng, nk*** Introduce the blending strategy for words with final *ng, nk*. Then have children blend and build words. DAY 1 *36n–36o*
- ❑ **Blend and Segment Syllables** Practice blending the syllables in compound words. DAY 2 *38b*
- ❑ **Compound Words** Introduce the blending strategy for compound words. Then have children blend and sort compound words. DAY 2 *38c–38d*
- ❑ **Fluent Word Reading** Use the Fluent Word Reading Routine to develop children's word reading fluency. Use the Phonics Songs and Rhymes Chart for additional word reading practice. DAY 3 *40c–40d*

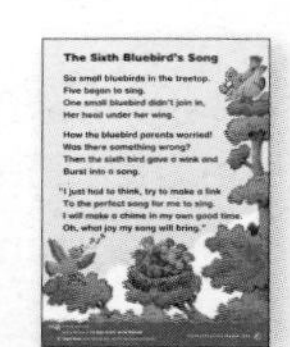

Phonics Songs and Rhymes Chart 14

PRACTICE/APPLY

- ❑ **Decodable Reader 27** Practice reading words with final *ng, nk* in context. DAY 1 *36q*
- ❑ **Decodable Reader 28** Practice reading compound words in context. DAY 2 *38f*

Decodable Readers 27 and 28

- ❑ ***Ruby in Her Own Time*** Practice decoding words in context. DAY 3 *40–61*
- ❑ **Homework** Practice Book 1.2 pp. 13, 15. DAY 1 *36o*, DAY 2 *38d*
- ❑ **Word Work Center** Practice final *ng, nk* and compound words. ANY DAY *36j*

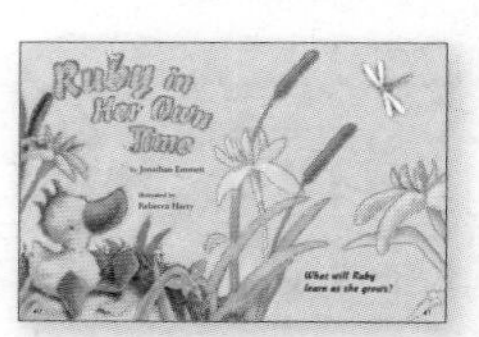

Main Selection—Fiction

RETEACH/REVIEW

- ❑ **Review** Review words with this week's phonics skills. DAY 5 *66c*
- ❑ **Reteach Lessons** If necessary, reteach final *ng, nk* and compound words. DAY 5 *DI·77–DI·78*
- ❑ **Spiral REVIEW** Review previously taught phonics skills. DAY 1 *36o*, DAY 2 *38d*, DAY 4 *64c–64d*

ASSESS

- ❑ **Sentence Reading** Assess children's ability to read words with final *ng, nk* and compound words. DAY 5 *66e–66f*

1. Use assessment data to determine your instructional focus.
2. Preview this week's instruction by strand.
3. Choose instructional activities that meet the needs of your classroom.

SPELLING

FINAL *NG, NK* Consonant digraphs consist of two unlike consonants that stand for a single sound that is different from either consonant alone.

TEACH

- ❑ **Pretest** Before administering the pretest, model how to segment words with final *ng, nk* to spell them. Dictate the spelling words, segmenting them if necessary. Then have children check their pretests and correct misspelled words. DAY 1 *36p*

PRACTICE/APPLY

- ❑ **Dictation** Have children write dictation sentences to practice spelling words. DAY 2 *38e*
- ❑ **Write Words** Have children practice writing the spelling words and adding the words under appropriate headings. DAY 3 *40d*
- ❑ **Homework** Phonics and Spelling Practice Book pp. 53-56. DAY 1 *36p*, DAY 2 *38e*, DAY 3 *40d*, DAY 4 *64e*

RETEACH/REVIEW

- ❑ **Partner Review** Have pairs work together to read and write the spelling words. DAY 4 *64e*

ASSESS

- ❑ **Posttest** Use dictation sentences to give the posttest for words with final *ng, nk*. DAY 5 *66d*

Spelling Words

Words with *ng* and *nk*

1. bring	6. wing*
2. trunk	7. rink
3. pink	8. blank
4. bank	9. rang
5. sang	10. sunk

High-Frequency Words

11. every*	12. sure*

* Words from the Selection

HIGH-FREQUENCY WORDS

WORDS TO READ

any *enough* *ever* *every*
own *sure* *were*

TEACH

- ❑ **Words to Read** Introduce this week's high-frequency words and add them to the Word Wall. DAY 2 *38-39*

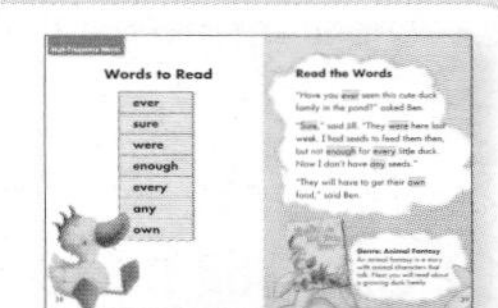
High-Frequency Words

PRACTICE/APPLY

- ❑ **Vocabulary Transparency 14** Review this week's high-frequency words, or Words to Read, before reading *Ruby in Her Own Time.* DAY 3 *40f*
- ❑ **Words in Context** Read high-frequency words in the context of *Ruby in Her Own Time.* DAY 3 *40-61*

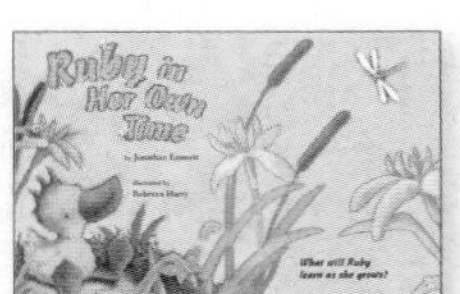
Main Selection—Fiction

- ❑ **Word Wall** Use the Word Wall to review and practice high-frequency words throughout the week. DAY 4 *64c*, DAY 5 *66c*
- ❑ **Leveled Text** Practice this week's high-frequency words in the context of leveled text. DAY 4 *LR10–LR18*, DAY 5 *LR10–LR18*

Leveled Readers

- ❑ **Homework** Practice Book 1.2 pp. 16, 17. DAY 2 38–39, DAY 3 40e

RETEACH/REVIEW

- ❑ **Spiral REVIEW** Review previously taught high-frequency words. DAY 3 *40f*, DAY 4 *64d*

ASSESS

- ❑ **Sentence Reading** Assess children's ability to read this week's high-frequency words. DAY 5 *66e-66f*

VOCABULARY

TEACH

- ❑ **Vocabulary Transparency 14** Use Vocabulary Transparency 14 to introduce the selection words from *Ruby in Her Own Time.* Children will read these words but will not be tested on them. DAY 3 *40f*
- ❑ **Synonyms** Discuss synonyms. DAY 3 *63b*

Customize Your Plan *by Strand*

COMPREHENSION

SKILL PLOT A plot is made up of what happens in the beginning, middle, and end of a story.

STRATEGY SUMMARIZE To summarize means to tell the most important parts of the story in a short way.

TEACH

- ❑ **Listening Comprehension** Read "Something Else to Do" and model *plot*. DAY 1 *37a–37b*
- ❑ **Skill/Strategy Lesson** Review *plot*. Then introduce this week's strategy, *summarize*. DAY 3 *40g*

PRACTICE/APPLY

- ❑ **Skills and Strategies in Context** Read *Ruby in Her Own Time*, using the Guiding Comprehension questions to apply *plot* and *summarize*. DAY 3 *40-61*

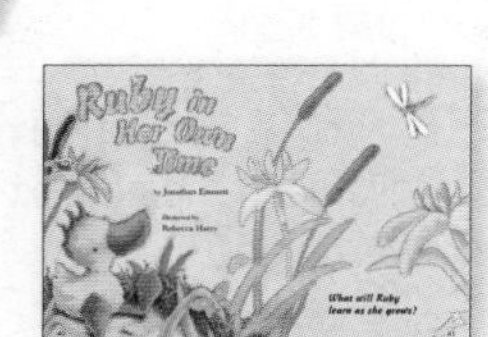

Main Selection—Fiction

- ❑ **Think and Share** Use the questions on Student Edition p. 62 to discuss the selection. DAY 3 *62a-63*
- ❑ **Skills and Strategies in Context** Read "I'm Growing," guiding children as they apply skills and strategies. After reading have children make connections across texts. DAY 4 *64-65a*

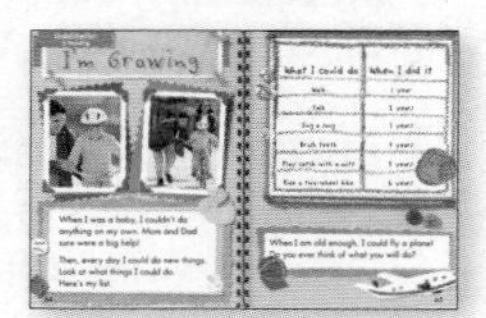

Paired Selection—Nonfiction

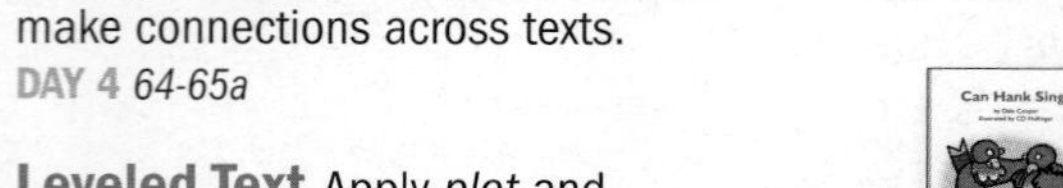

- ❑ **Leveled Text** Apply *plot* and *summarize* to read leveled text. DAY 4 *LR10–LR18*, DAY 5 *LR10–LR18*

Leveled Readers

- ❑ **Homework** Practice Book 1.2 p. 14. DAY 1 *37a*

ASSESS

- ❑ **Selection Test** Determine children's understanding of the main selection and assess their ability to identify *plot*. DAY 3
- ❑ **Story Reading** Have children read the passage "A Bath for Cupcake." Ask what the plot of the story is and have them retell the story. DAY 5 66e, 66g

RETEACH/REVIEW

- ❑ **Reteach Lesson** If necessary, reteach *plot*. DAY 5 *DI·78*

FLUENCY

SKILL ATTEND TO PUNCTUATION When you read, try to read with expression and attention to punctuation. If a sentence ends in a question mark, read it as if you are asking a question.

REREAD FOR FLUENCY

- ❑ **Oral Reading** Have children read orally from Decodable Reader 27, or another text at their independent reading level. Listen to children read and provide corrective feedback regarding their oral reading and their use of the blending strategy. DAY 1 *36q*
- ❑ **Paired Reading** Have pairs of children take turns reading orally from Decodable Reader 28, or another text at their independent reading level. Listen to children read and provide corrective feedback regarding their oral reading and their use of the blending strategy. DAY 2 38f

TEACH

- ❑ **Model** Use passages from *Ruby in Her Own Time* to model attention to punctuation. DAY 3 *63a*, DAY 4 *65b*

PRACTICE/APPLY

- ❑ **Choral Reading** Choral read passages from *Ruby in Her Own Time*. Monitor progress and provide feedback regarding children's attention to punctuation. DAY 3 *63a*, DAY 4 *65b*
- ❑ **Listening Center** Have children follow along with the AudioText for this week's selections. ANY DAY *36j*
- ❑ **Reading/Library Center** Have children build fluency by rereading Leveled Readers, Decodable Readers, or other text at their independent level. ANY DAY *36j*
- ❑ **Fluency Coach** Have children use Fluency Coach to listen to fluent reading or to practice reading on their own. ANY DAY

ASSESS

- ❑ **Story Reading** Take a one-minute timed sample of children's oral reading. Use the passage "A Bath for Cupcake." DAY 5 *66e, 66g*

1. Use assessment data to determine your instructional focus.
2. Preview this week's instruction by strand.
3. Choose instructional activities that meet the needs of your classroom.

WRITING

Trait of the Week

ORGANIZATION/PARAGRAPHS Tell what happens in the right order so your paragraphs make sense.

TEACH

- ❑ **Write Together** Engage children in writing activities that develop language, grammar, and writing skills. Include independent writing as an extension of group writing activities.
  - **Shared Writing** DAY 1 *37c*
  - **Interactive Writing** DAY 2 *39a*
  - **Writing Across the Curriculum** DAY 4 *65c*
- ❑ **Trait of the Week** Introduce and model the Trait of the Week, *organization/paragraphs.* DAY 3 *63c*

PRACTICE/APPLY

- ❑ **Write Now** Examine the model on Student Edition pp. 66-67. Then have children write a list. DAY 5 *66-67*

  Prompt In *Ruby in Her Own Time,* a baby duck grows up. Think about things Ruby does as she grows up. Now write a list of these things using numbered sentences.

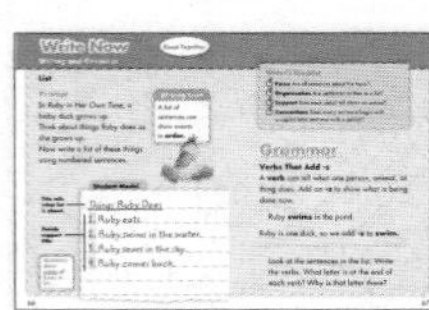

Write Now

- ❑ **Daily Journal Writing** Have children write about concepts and literature in their journals. EVERY DAY *36d-36e*
- ❑ **Writing Center** Create a poster showing what Ruby did as she grew up. ANY DAY *36k*

ASSESS

- ❑ **Scoring Rubric** Use a rubric to evaluate children's lists. DAY 5 *66-67*

RETEACH/REVIEW

- ❑ **The Grammar and Writing Book** Use pp. 128-133 of The Grammar and Writing Book to extend instruction. ANY DAY

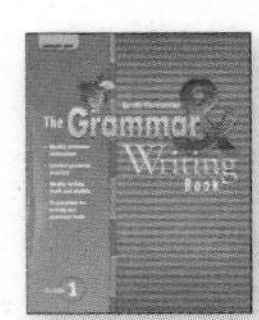

The Grammar and Writing Book

SPEAKING AND LISTENING

TEACH

- ❑ **Give Directions** Model giving directions. Have children work with a partner to practice giving and following directions. DAY 2 *39c*

GRAMMAR

SKILL VERBS THAT ADD -*S* A verb can tell what one person, animal, or thing does. Add *-s* to show what is being done now.

TEACH

- ❑ **Grammar Transparency 14** Use Grammar Transparency 14 to teach *verbs that add -s.* DAY 1 *37d*

Grammar Transparency 14

PRACTICE/APPLY

- ❑ **Develop the Concept** Review the concept of *verbs that add -s* and provide guided practice. DAY 2 *39b*
- ❑ **Apply to Writing** Have children use *verbs that add -s* in writing. DAY 3 *63d*
- ❑ **Define/Practice** Review the definition of *verbs that add -s.* Then have children add *-s* to verbs. DAY 4 *65d*
- ❑ **Write Now** Discuss the grammar lesson on Student Edition p. 67. Have children use verbs that add *-s* correctly in their own list of what Ruby does. DAY 5 *66-67*

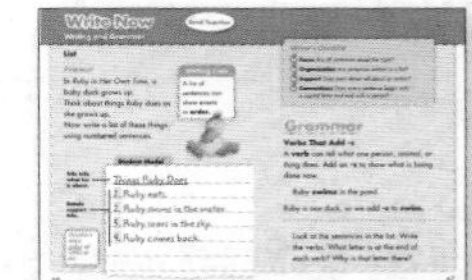

Write Now

- ❑ **Daily Fix-It** Have children find and correct errors in grammar, spelling, and punctuation. DAY 1 *37d,* DAY 2 *39b,* DAY 3 *63d,* DAY 4 *65d,* DAY 5 *66-67*
- ❑ **Homework** Grammar and Writing Practice Book pp. 53-56. DAY 2 *39b,* DAY 3 *63d,* DAY 4 *65d,* DAY 5 *66-67*

RETEACH/REVIEW

- ❑ **The Grammar and Writing Book** Use pp. 128-131 of The Grammar and Writing Book to extend instruction. ANY DAY

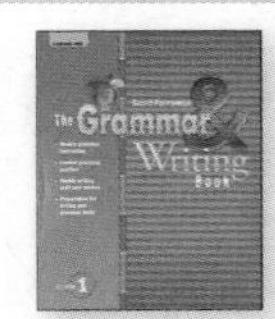

The Grammar and Writing Book

RESEARCH/INQUIRY

TEACH

- ❑ **Glossary** Model using a glossary. Have children use the glossary in their reading books to find words from the story. DAY 5 *67a*
- ❑ **Unit Inquiry Project** Allow time for children to begin their journals, making notes and pictures about the objects they are observing. ANY DAY *9*

Resources for

Differentiated Instruction

LEVELED READERS

- **Comprehension**
  - **Skill** Plot
  - **Strategy** Summarize
- **Lesson Vocabulary**

  High-Frequency Words

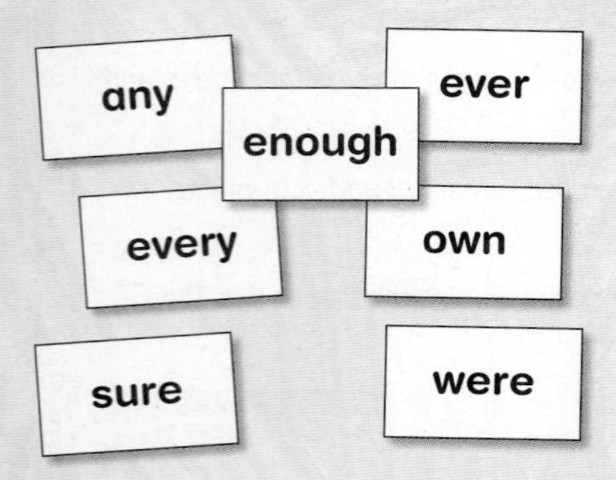

- **Social Studies Standards**
  - Time Lines
  - Changes Over Time
  - Respecting Differences

PearsonSuccessNet.com

Use the Online Database of over 600 books to

- Download and print additional copies of this week's leveled readers
- Listen to the readers being read online
- Search for more titles focused on this week's skills, topic, and content

On-Level

On-Level Reader

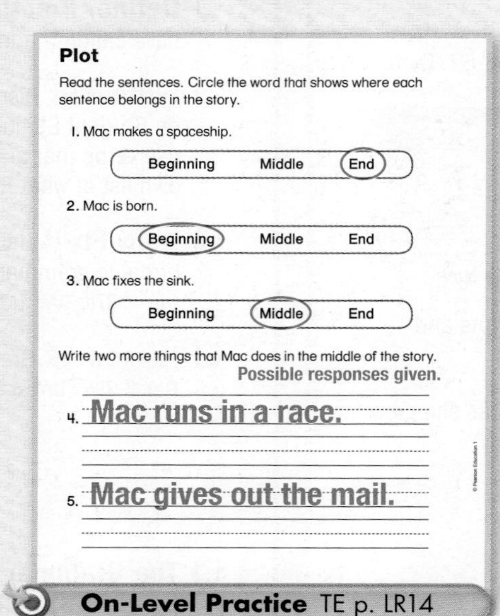

Plot

Read the sentences. Circle the word that shows where each sentence belongs in the story.

1. Mac makes a spaceship.
   Beginning Middle (End)
2. Mac is born.
   (Beginning) Middle End
3. Mac fixes the sink.
   Beginning (Middle) End

Write two more things that Mac does in the middle of the story.
Possible responses given.

4. Mac runs in a race.
5. Mac gives out the mail.

On-Level Practice TE p. LR14

Vocabulary

Find these words in the puzzle. Circle them.
Words may be across or down.

Words to Know: any enough ever every own sure were

e	v	e	r	r	a	g
y	w	r	e	e	y	y
s	e	y	e	n	r	n
u	o	y	w	w	e	r
r	w	e	r	e	e	a
e	n	o	u	g	h	n
e	v	e	r	y	w	y

On-Level Practice TE p. LR 15

Strategic Intervention

Below-Level Reader

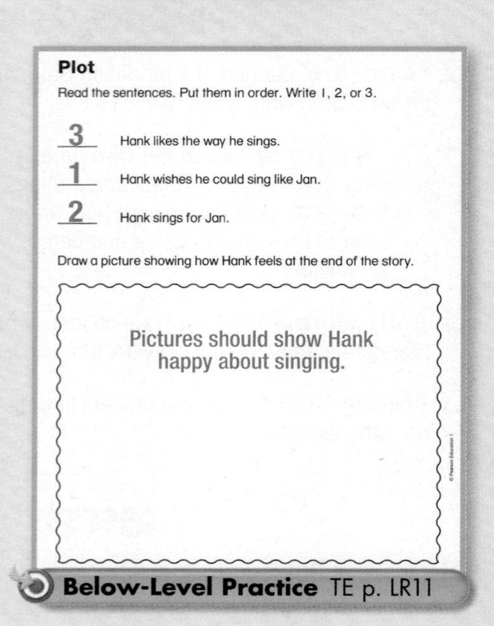

Plot

Read the sentences. Put them in order. Write 1, 2, or 3.

3 Hank likes the way he sings.
1 Hank wishes he could sing like Jan.
2 Hank sings for Jan.

Draw a picture showing how Hank feels at the end of the story.

Pictures should show Hank happy about singing.

Below-Level Practice TE p. LR11

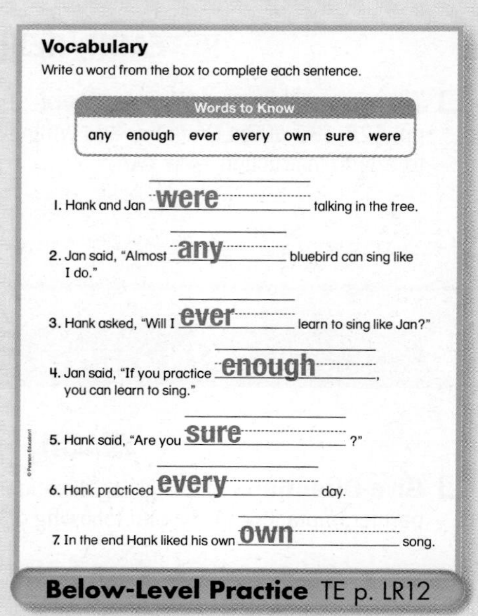

Vocabulary

Write a word from the box to complete each sentence.

Words to Know: any enough ever every own sure were

1. Hank and Jan were talking in the tree.
2. Jan said, "Almost any bluebird can sing like I do."
3. Hank asked, "Will I ever learn to sing like Jan?"
4. Jan said, "If you practice enough, you can learn to sing."
5. Hank said, "Are you sure?"
6. Hank practiced every day.
7. In the end Hank liked his own song.

Below-Level Practice TE p. LR12

Advanced

A Bed for Paul
by Ruth Renolo
illustrated by Al Lorenz

Advanced Reader

Plot

Circle the word that shows where each sentence belongs in the story.

1. Paul built the biggest log cabin and the biggest bed in all the land.
   Beginning Middle (End)
2. Paul broke his ship bed.
   Beginning (Middle) End
3. The rowboat made a fine bed for Paul.
   (Beginning) Middle End
4. Paul packed a sack and headed for the deep woods and wide country.
   Beginning Middle (End)

Advanced Practice TE p. LR17

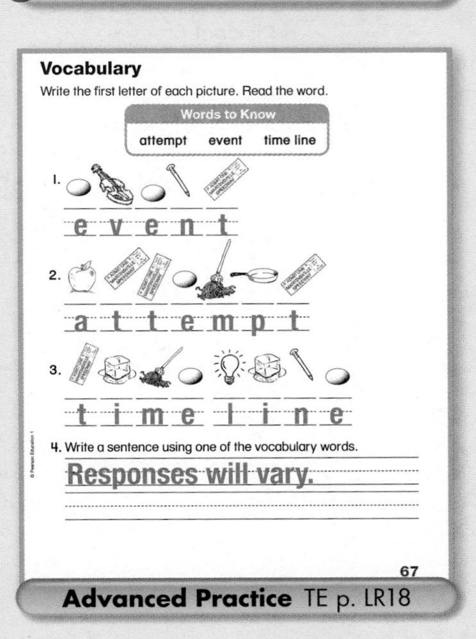
Vocabulary

Write the first letter of each picture. Read the word.

Words to Know: attempt event time line

1. event
2. attempt
3. time line
4. Write a sentence using one of the vocabulary words.
   Responses will vary.

67

Advanced Practice TE p. LR18

ELL

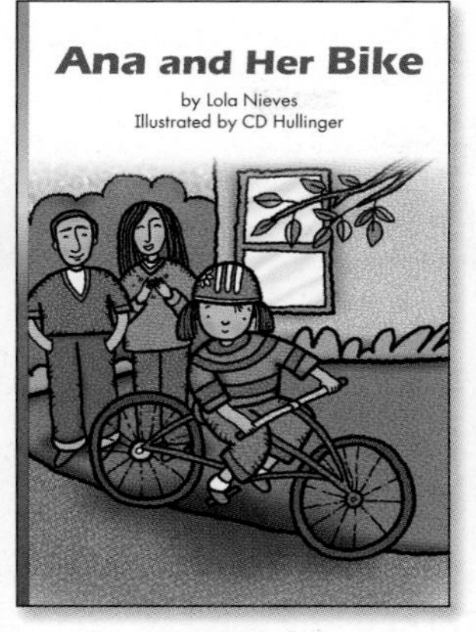

ELL Reader

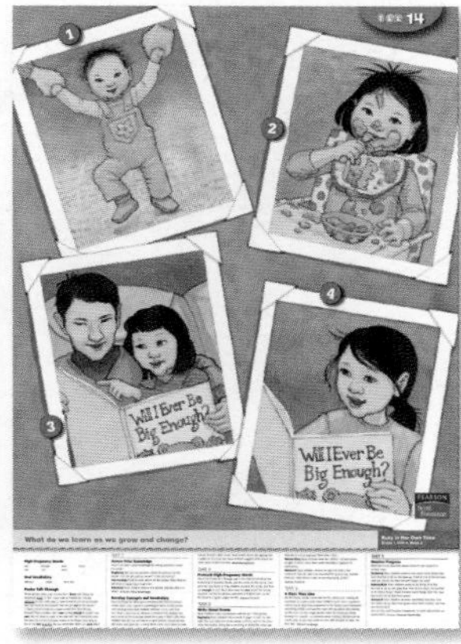

ELL Poster 14

Teacher's Edition Notes

ELL notes throughout this lesson support instruction and reference additional resources at point of use.

Teaching Guide pp. 92–98, 238–239

- Multilingual summaries of the main selection
- Comprehension lesson
- Vocabulary strategies and word cards
- ELL Reader 1.3.2 lesson

ELL and Transition Handbook

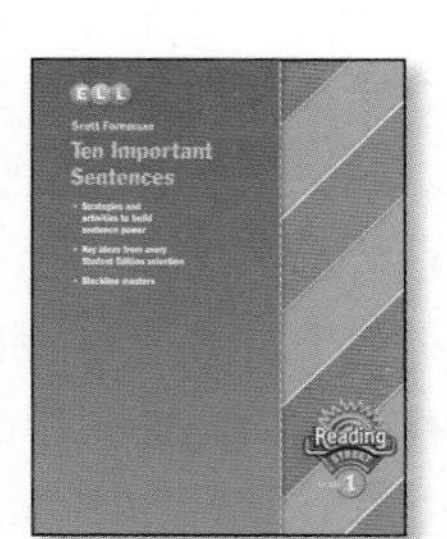

Ten Important Sentences

- Key ideas from every selection in the Student Edition
- Activities to build sentence power

More Reading

Readers' Theater Anthology

- Fluency practice
- Five scripts to build fluency
- Poetry for oral interpretation

Leveled Trade Books

Below-Level

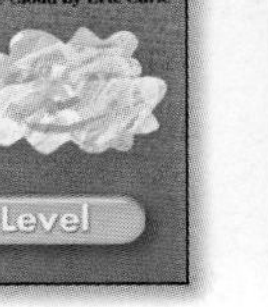

On-Level

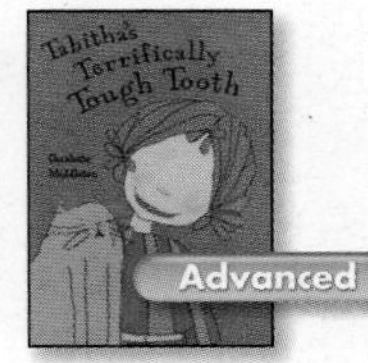

Advanced

- Extend reading tied to the unit concept
- Lessons in Trade Book Library Teaching Guide

Big Book of Poems

- Fluency practice
- Poetry for Choral Reading

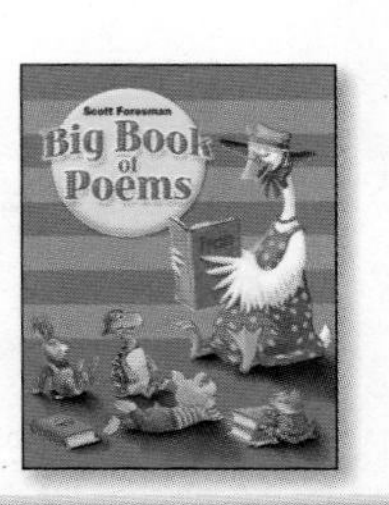

School + Home

Homework

- Family Times Newsletter
- ELL Multilingual Selection Summaries

Take-Home Books

- Decodable Readers
- Leveled Readers

Literacy Centers

Listening

Let's Read Along

MATERIALS
CD player, headphones, print copies of recorded pieces

SINGLES

LISTEN TO LITERATURE As children listen to the following recordings, have them follow along or read along in the print version.

AudioText
Ruby in Her Own Time
"I'm Growing"

Sing with Me/Background Building Audio
"On Our Own Time Line"

Phonics Songs and Rhymes Audio
"The Sixth Bluebird's Song"

The Sixth Bluebird's Song

Six small bluebirds in the treetop.
Five began to sing.
One small bluebird didn't join in,
Her head under her wing.

How the bluebird parents worried!
Was there something wrong?
Then the sixth bird gave a wink and
Burst into a song.

"I just had to think, try to make a link
To the perfect song for me to sing.
I will make a chime in my own good time.
Oh, what joy my song will bring."

Audio CD **Phonics Songs and Rhymes Chart 14**

Reading/Library

Read It Again!

MATERIALS
collection of books for self-selected reading, reading logs

SINGLES
PAIRS
GROUPS

REREAD BOOKS Have children select previously read books from the appropriate book box and record titles of books they read in their logs. Use these previously read books:

- **Decodable Readers**
- **Leveled Readers**
- **ELL Readers**
- **Stories written by classmates**
- **Books from the library**

TEN IMPORTANT SENTENCES Have children read the Ten Important Sentences for *Ruby in Her Own Time* and locate the sentences in the Student Edition.

BOOK CLUB Use p. 63 of the Student Edition to set up an "Author Study" of Jonathan Emmett. Encourage a group to read the other Emmett books listed and then share favorites.

Word Work

Mix and Match

MATERIALS
10 index cards

PAIRS

WORD FAMILIES *-ng, -nk* Have pairs of children play a word match game using *-ng* and *-nk* words.

1. **Write a word with *-ng* or *-nk* on each index card. Cut the cards in half, separating the onset consonant from the rime.**
2. **Mix the cards and place them face up on the table.**
3. **Children take turns taking two cards, putting them together, and reading the word.**
4. **Play continues until all possible matches have been created.**

COMPOUND WORDS Make a set of cards with compound words. Cut the cards, separating the two words. Have children play the game.

This interactive CD provides additional practice.

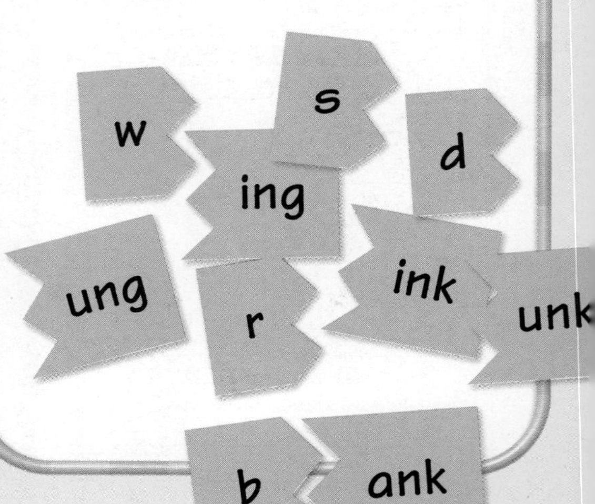

Scott Foresman Reading Street Centers Survival Kit

Use the *Ruby in Her Own Time* materials from the Reading Street Centers Survival Kit to organize this week's centers.

Writing

Growing Up

MATERIALS
posterboard, pencils, crayons, markers

PAIRS

CREATE A POSTER Recall the new things Ruby did as she grew up.

1. **Have pairs discuss the things Ruby did, such as hatching or swimming.**
2. **Ask pairs to write sentences about the things Ruby did on their posterboard. Encourage them to write the things in the order in which they happened.**
3. **Have children draw pictures to accompany their writing.**
4. **Display posters in the classroom.**

LEVELED WRITING Encourage children to write at their own ability level. Some may write only phrases. Others will be able to write simple sentences about one or two things Ruby did. Your best writers will write several sentences with greater detail and more attention to mechanics and spelling.

Social Studies

Look at Me Now

MATERIALS
writing paper, pencils, chart paper

SINGLES

IDENTIFY PERSONAL CHANGES Make a chart with these prompts: *When I was two___. When I was four ___. Now I am ___ and I can ___.* Discuss with children things they could do at different ages.

1. **Have children use the prompts on the chart to write about events they have experienced at different ages.**
2. **Children can share and discuss their sentences.**

When I was two I learned to talk.

When I was four I made a new friend.

Now I am six and I can roller blade.

Technology

How Ruby Grew

MATERIALS
computer, printer, scissors, tape

SINGLES

PRINT LABELS Have individuals type and print labels for the things that Ruby did.

1. **Ask children to turn on the computer and open a word processing program.**
2. **Ask them to type things that Ruby did.**
3. **Children then print their lists.**
4. **If children have made posters of Ruby's activities, they can cut out their labels and attach them to their posters.**

ALL CENTERS 

Day 1
AT A GLANCE

Oral Vocabulary
"On Our Own Time Line" 14

Phonemic Awareness
Blend and Segment Onset/Rime

Phonics and Spelling
Final *ng, nk*

Spelling Pretest: Words with *ng, nk*

Read Apply Phonics Word Wall

< Differentiated Instruction

Build Background
Let's Talk About Growing and Changing

Listening Comprehension
Skill Plot

Shared Writing
Poem

Grammar
Verbs That Add *-s*

Materials
- *Sing with Me Big Book*
- Sound-Spelling Cards 21, 22
- Letter Tiles
- Decodable Reader 27
- Tested Word Cards
- Student Edition 36–37
- Graphic Organizer Flip Chart 5

Take It to the NET™ ONLINE
Professional Development
To learn about reading and school success, go to PearsonSuccessNet.com and read "What Reading Does for the Mind" by A. E. Cunningham and K. Stanovich.

Morning Warm-Up!

**Nothing stays the same.
We are always learning new things.
What do we learn as we grow and change?**

QUESTION OF THE WEEK Tell children they will talk, sing, read, and write about Growing and Changing. Write the message and track the print as you read it. Discuss the question.

CONNECT CONCEPTS Ask questions to connect to other selections.
- What are some things you think the boy in *An Egg Is an Egg* learned as he grew?
- What do you think Sammy in *Nothing Fits* can do now that he couldn't do when he was little?

REVIEW HIGH-FREQUENCY WORDS
- Circle the high-frequency words *nothing, stays, always,* and *things* in the message.
- Have children say and spell each word as they write it in the air.

Build Background Use the Day 1 instruction on ELL Poster 14 to assess knowledge and develop concepts.

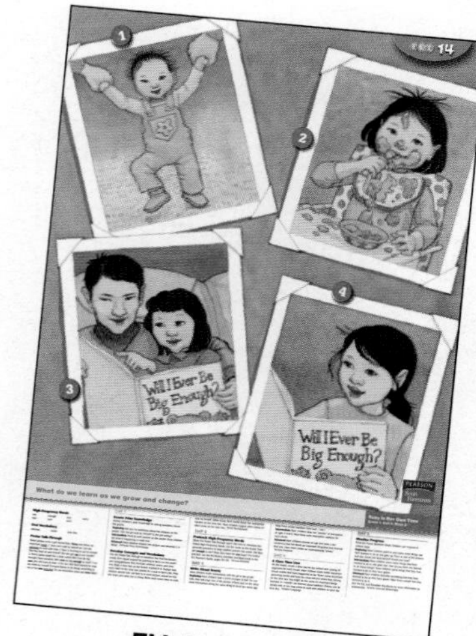

ELL Poster 14

Oral Vocabulary

SHARE LITERATURE Display p. 14 of the *Sing with Me Big Book.* Tell children that they will sing a song about learning new things. Read the title. Ask children to listen for the Amazing Words **time line, event,** and **attempt** as you sing. Then sing the song again and ask children to sing with you. Have children demonstrate their understanding of *time line, event,* and *attempt* as they tell how this song is like your classroom.

Sing with Me Big Book

Sing with Me/ Background Building Audio

Phonemic Awareness

BLEND AND SEGMENT ONSET/RIME

- We just sang about trying to learn a new thing.
- Model saying the onset and rime, /th/ /ing/. Have children say the sounds with you, /th/ /ing/ and then say the sounds by themselves.
- Now say the sound for the onset *th* and rime *ing* as you write the letters that go with each part. Say /th/ /ing/ as you write *th, ing.* When I put the sounds /th/ /ing/ together, I have the word *thing.*
- Have children say the sounds with you as you point to the letters and blend the sounds to say the word (/th/ /ing/), *(thing).*

Continue the activity by saying the onset and rime for each word and having children blend the sounds to say a word.

p/ink **s/ung** **d/unk** **st/ing** **b/ank** **h/ang**

OBJECTIVES

- Build oral vocabulary.
- Blend and segment onset/rime.

to build oral vocabulary

attempt
event
time line
famous
flatter
correct
awkward
lovely

MONITOR PROGRESS

If... children lack oral vocabulary experiences about the concept Growing and Changing,

then... use the Oral Vocabulary Routine below to teach *attempt.*

Oral Vocabulary ROUTINE

1. **Introduce the Word** Relate the word *attempt* to the song. Supply a child-friendly definition. Have children say the word. Example: When you *attempt* something, you try to do it.
2. **Demonstrate** Provide an example to show meaning. The baby will *attempt* to walk.
3. **Apply** Have children demonstrate their understanding. Have you ever *attempted* to read a chapter book?
4. **Display the Word/Letter-Sounds** Write the word on a card. Display it. Children can blend *tempt.* See p. DI•4 to teach *event* and *time line.*

ELL

Build Oral Vocabulary Model first and have children pantomime reading, writing, and riding a bike.

OBJECTIVES

- Associate the sound /ng/ with *ng* and /ngk/ with *nk*.
- Blend, read, and build words with *ng* and *nk*.

Skills Trace

Final *ng, nk*

Introduce/Teach	**TE: 1.3 36n–o, 40c–d**
Practice	TE: 1.3 36q PB: 1.2 13; DR27
Reteach/Review	TE: 1.3 66c, 88c–d; DI·77; PB: 1.2 28
Assess/Test	TE: 1.3 66e–g Benchmark Test, Unit 3

Generalization

Consonant digraphs consist of two unlike consonants that stand for a single sound that is different from either consonant alone.

Strategic Intervention

Use **Monitor Progress,** p. 36o during Group Time after children have had more practice with final *-ng, -nk.*

Advanced

Use **Monitor Progress,** p. 36o as a preassessment to determine whether or not this group of children would benefit from this instruction for final *ng, nk.*

Support Phonics Speakers of Cantonese, Khmer, and Korean will be familiar with the sound of *ng*. Other English language learners may need to practice pronouncing words, such as *rang, king,* and *sung.*

See the Phonics Transition Lessons in the ELL and Transition Handbook.

Final *ng, nk*

TEACH/MODEL

Blending Strategy

ROUTINE

1. **Connect** Write *mixing.* You know the sounds at the end of *mixing* because you know the ending *-ing.* What are the sounds? (/ing/) Today we will learn about the letters *ng and nk at the end of words.*
2. **Use Sound-Spelling Cards** Display Cards 21 and 22. This is *swing.* The sound you hear at the end of *swing* is /ng/. Say it with me: /ng/. This is *skunk.* The sounds you hear at the end of *skunk* are /ngk/. Say it with me: /ngk/.
3. **Model** Write *sing.* The two letters *ng* stand for one sound: /ng/. This is how I blend this word. Segment and blend *sing.* Let's blend this word together: /s/ /i/ /ng/, *sing.* Continue modeling with *junk.* Point out that the two letters *nk* stand for the sounds, /ngk/.
4. **Group Practice** Say the sounds of the letters and blend the words together. Point out that *ng* and *nk* never come at the beginning of words, only at the end or in the middle. Continue with *bang, blank, wing, sung,* and *stink.*
5. **Review** What do you know about reading these words? The letters *ng* stand for /ng/. The letters *nk* stand for /ngk/.

-ng

Sound/Spelling Card 21

-nk

Sound/Spelling Card 22

s i n g

j u n k

BLEND WORDS

INDIVIDUALS BLEND WORDS Call on individual children to blend the words *bunk, rang, bring, blink, drank, stung.* Have them tell what they know about each word before reading it. (The *ng* stands for /ng/ and the *nk* stands for /ngk/.) For feedback, refer to step five of the Blending Strategy Routine.

BUILD WORDS

INDIVIDUALS MAKE WORDS WITH *ng* AND *nk* Write *hang* and have the class blend it. Have children spell *hang* with letter tiles. Monitor work and provide feedback.

- Change the *h* to *s*. What is the new word?

- Change the *a* to *i*. What is the new word?

- Change the *ng* to *nk*. What is the new word?

- Change the *s* to *th*. What is the new word?

MODEL BLENDING WORD FAMILIES Write the word *king*. Model blending /k/-*ing*, *king*. Continue with *sing, ring,* and *sting*. Ask children what is the same about the words. (They end with the same letters; they rhyme.) Have children segment and blend each word using onset and rime. Do the same with words for the *-ank, -unk,* and *-ink* word families. Have the lists reread.

Have children create lists of rhming words. You may wish to set up a Word Family Wall to help children move from individual letter-sounds to recognizing common vowel patterns in words. Then have children read the rhyming words.

-ing	*-ank*	*-unk*	*-ink*
king	bank	junk	link
sing	tank	dunk	pink
sting	blank	trunk	think

Monitor Progress

Check Word Reading Final *ng, nk*

Write the following words and have individuals read them.

king	**hunk**	**rang**	**junk**	**wink**
trunk	**blank**	**drink**	**stung**	**swing**
thank	**thing**	**chunk**	**drank**	**think**

If... children cannot blend words with final *ng, nk* at this point,

then... continue to monitor their progress using other instructional opportunities during the week so that they can be successful with the Day 5 Assessment. See the Skills Trace on p. 36n.

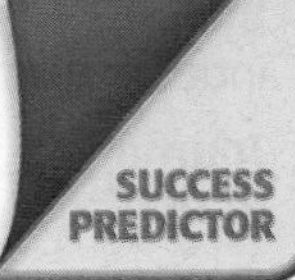

▶ **Day 1 Check Word Reading** · Day 2 Check Word Reading · Day 3 Check High-Frequency Words/Retelling · Day 4 Check Fluency · Day 5 Assess Progress

Vocabulary TiP

You may wish to explain the meanings of these words.

chunk thick piece or lump of something

trunk main stem of a tree

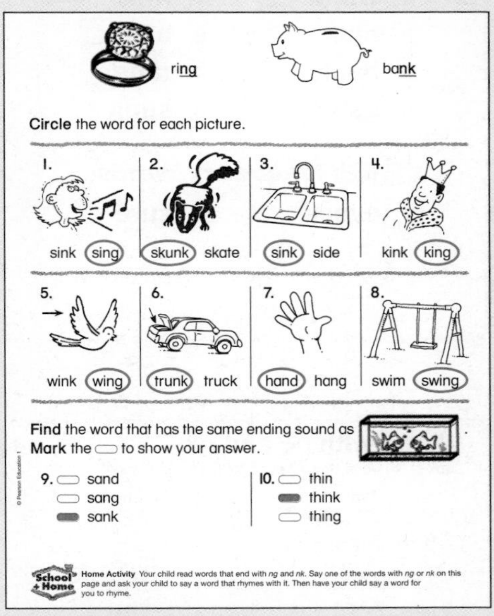
ring bank

Circle the word for each picture.

1. sink (sing) 2. (skunk) skate 3. (sink) side 4. kink (king)
5. wink (wing) 6. (trunk) truck 7. (hand) hang 8. swim (swing)

Find the word that has the same ending sound as [picture]. Mark the ⬭ to show your answer.

9. sand, sang, sank 10. thin, think, thing

▲ **Practice Book 1.2** p. 13, Final *ng* and *nk*.

Spiral REVIEW

- Row 2 reviews short vowels and initial consonant blends.
- Row 3 reviews short vowels and initial digraphs.

OBJECTIVES

- Segment sounds to spell words.
- Spell words with *ng* and *nk*.

Spelling Words

Words with *ng* and *nk*

1.	**bring**	6.	**wing***
2.	**trunk**	7.	**rink**
3.	**pink**	8.	**blank**
4.	**bank**	9.	**rang**
5.	**sang**	10.	**sunk**

High-Frequency Words

11.	**every***	12.	**sure***

* Words from the Selection

Words with *ng* and *nk*

Look at the word. Say it. Listen for the *ng* or *nk* sound.

	Write the word.	Check it.
1. bring	bring	bring
2. trunk	trunk	trunk
3. pink	pink	pink
4. bank	bank	bank
5. sang	sang	sang
6. wing	wing	wing
7. rink	rink	rink
8. blank	blank	blank
9. rang	rang	rang
10. sunk	sunk	sunk

High-Frequency Words

11. every every 12. sure sure

School + Home Home Activity Your child is learning to spell words with *ng* and *nk*. To practice at home, have your child spell each word. Then cover the word and ask them to spell it again.

▲ **Spelling Practice Book** p. 53

Spelling

PRETEST Final *ng, nk*

MODEL WRITING FOR SOUNDS Each spelling word has *ng* or *nk*. Before administering the spelling pretest, model how to segment words with *ng* and *nk* to spell them.

- What sounds do you hear in *tank?* (/t/ /a/ /ngk/)
- What is the letter for /t/? Write *t*. Continue with the *a*/a/ and *nk*/ngk/.
- In *tank*, the letters *nk* stand for /ngk/.
- Repeat with *hang*.

PRETEST Dictate the spelling words. Segment the words for children if necessary. Have children check their pretests and correct misspelled words.

HOMEWORK Spelling Practice Book, p. 53.

Grandpa's Trunk

The Family Picnic

Group Time

DAY 1

On-Level

Read Decodable Reader 27.

- Use p. 36q.

Strategic Intervention

Read Decodable Reader 27.

- Use the **Routine** on p. DI•26.

Advanced

Read Advanced Selection 14.

- Use the **Routine** on p. DI•27.

Place English language learners in the groups that correspond to their reading abilities in English.

Independent Activities

Fluency Reading Pair children to reread Leveled Readers or the ELL Reader from the previous week or other text at children's independent level.

Journal Writing Write to tell how you learned to ride a bike. Share writing.

Independent Reading See p. 36j for Reading/Library activities and suggestions.

Literacy Centers To practice word families with *-ng* and *-nk*, you may use Word Work, p. 36j.

Practice Book 1.2 Final *ng, nk*, p. 13

Break into small groups after Spelling and before Build Background.

ELL

Support Spelling Before giving the spelling pretest, clarify the meaning of each spelling word with examples, such as pointing to photos of a tree *trunk*, a packing *trunk*, and an elephant's *trunk* or saying after singing a song together: We *sang* a song.

Apply Phonics

PRACTICE Final *ng, nk*

HIGH-FREQUENCY WORDS Review *are, day, do, food, her, of, to* and *what* on the Word Wall. If necessary, have children practice in pairs with word cards. Word Wall

READ DECODABLE READER 27

- Pages 18–19 Read aloud quietly with the group.
- Page 20 Have the group read aloud without you.
- Pages 21–24 Select individuals to read aloud.

CHECK COMPREHENSION AND DECODING Have children retell the story to include characters, setting, and plot. Then have children locate words with *-ng* and *-nk* in the story. Tell children that some story words with these letters have the ending *s*. Sort words according to their spelling.

-ng	-nk
bring	drinks
sing(s)	trunk
songs	
swing(s)	

HOMEWORK Take-Home Decodable Reader 27

Oral Rereading

ROUTINE

1. **Read** Have children read the entire book orally.
2. **Reread** To achieve optimal fluency, children should reread the text three or four times.
3. **Provide Feedback** Listen as children read and provide feedback regarding their oral reading and their use of the blending strategy.

OBJECTIVES

- Apply knowledge of letter-sounds and word parts to decode unknown words when reading.
- Use context with letter-sounds to confirm the identification of unknown words.
- Practice fluency with oral rereading.

Monitor Progress

Decoding

If...	then...
children have difficulty decoding a word,	prompt them to blend the word. • What is the new word? • Is the new word a word you know? • Does it make sense in the story?

Access Content

Beginning Model first and then have children pantomime and repeat words and phrases from *The Family Picnic: bring drinks, rest by a tree trunk, swing, sing songs.*

Intermediate During reading, ask questions to involve children: Point to the drinks. Do you like to go on the swing or on the slide? Do you like to sing? What is your favorite song?

Advanced Give children sentence examples of how the story words *drinks, swing,* and *race* can be used as both nouns and verbs. Have children tell how each word is used in *The Family Picnic.*

OBJECTIVES

- Build background and oral vocabulary.
- Speak at an appropriate volume.

Strategic Intervention

Have children make their own time lines showing preschool, kindergarten, and first grade. Have them illustrate and write about something they learned at each time.

Advanced

Have children illustrate and write about something they had to try many times before they learned to do it.

Activate Prior Knowledge
Invite children to name the events in the pictures in their home language and in English.

Build Background

LET'S TALK ABOUT Growing and Changing

DEVELOP ORAL LANGUAGE Read the title and have children view the photographs. Ask them to tell you what they see. Allow ample time for children to respond. Remind children to speak loudly enough to be heard. If they do not speak at an appropriate volume, model by giving examples of speaking loudly enough and speaking too quietly. Then use open-ended prompts to encourage conversation. For example:

Tell me about what you see here. Yes, that's right, there is a row of photographs of children at different ages. Which child is the youngest? How can you tell? Look at the young boy in the middle picture on p. 36. Why do you think he needs an adult to help him walk? Which child is the one closest to your age? What changes have all these children gone through?

BUILD ORAL VOCABULARY As you continue the discussion, encourage children to use today's Amazing Words, *attempt, event,* and *time line.*

- What is the boy on p. 37 attempting to do? Do you think he will succeed?
- What do the photographs show? Use the words *time line* in your answer.
- Do you think it is an event when a baby learns to crawl? Why or why not?

DEVELOP CONCEPTS

CONCEPT CHART Remind children of the question of the week.

- What do we learn as we grow and change?

Display Graphic Organizer 5 or draw a three-column chart. Tell children they can help you make a chart that shows some skills and who can do them. Label the columns "Skill," "Can Do," "Can't Do." Discuss what the five- and six-year-old children are doing in the pictures and list each skill on the chart. Add other skills children would find difficult. Use the completed chart to discuss the different ways people learn. Point out that not everyone learns the same things at the same time.

- How many of you can tie your shoes? (Make tally marks in "Can Do" column.)
- How many are still learning to tie? (Make tally marks in "Can't Do" column.)

CONNECT TO READING Point out the illustration on the top corner of Student Edition p. 37. Ask children what they see. (a duck) Explain that this week children will read a story about this duck and her family. Tell children that they will learn about how the duck grows and changes.

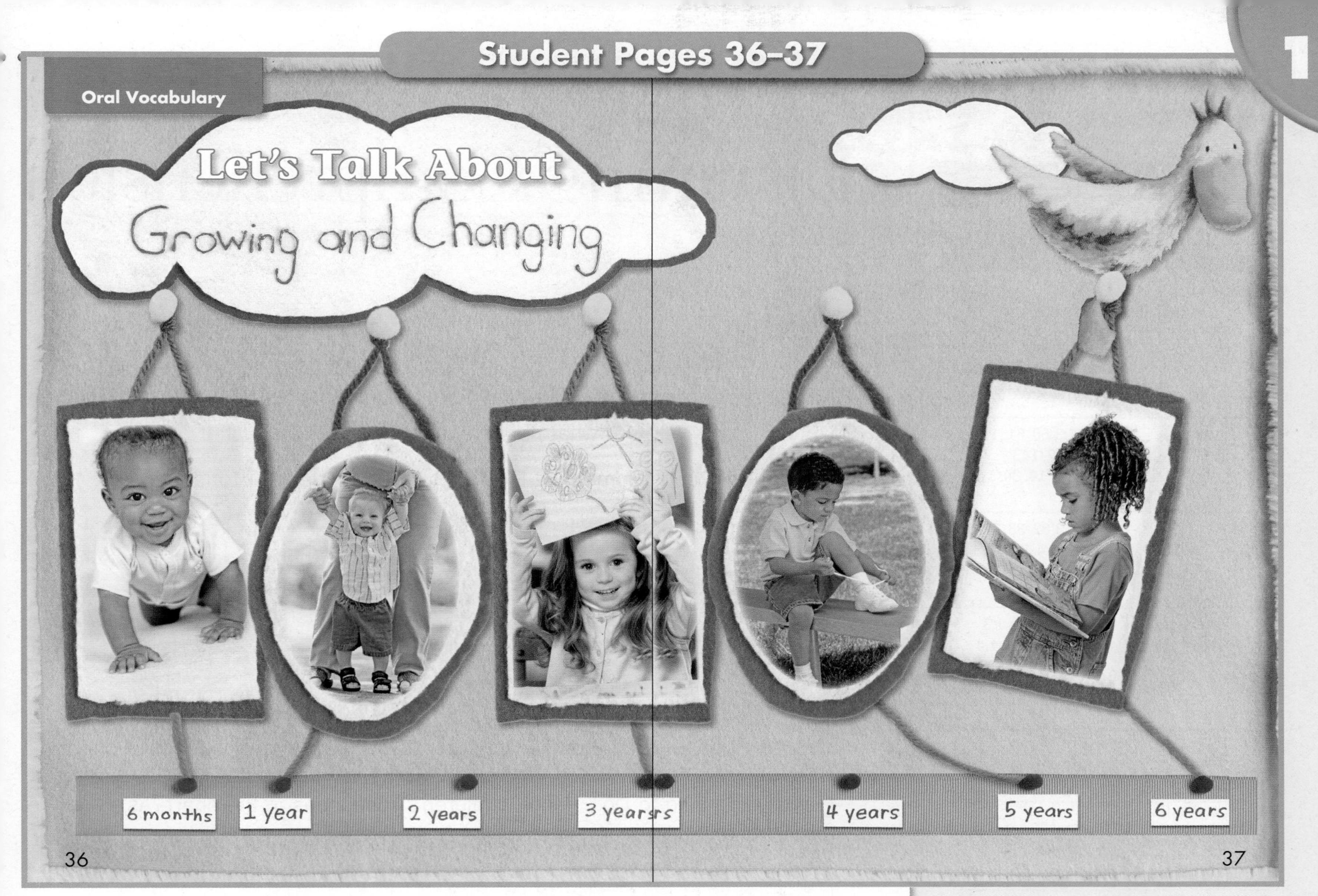

Skill	Can Do	Can't Do
tie shoes	卌 卌 卌 III	卌 I
read a story	卌 卌 卌 卌 IIII	
jump rope	卌 III	卌 卌 I
drive a car		卌 卌 卌 卌 IIII

▲ **Graphic Organizer Flip Chart 5**

Tech Files ONLINE

For a Web site that explores one of the things children learn as they grow up—how to tie their shoes—do an Internet search using the keywords *tying shoes*.

Access Content To prepare children for reading *Ruby in Her Own Time*, send home the story summary in English and/or the home language. See the ELL Teaching Guide, pp. 96–98.

OBJECTIVE

Identify plot.

Skills Trace	
Plot	
Introduce/Teach	**TE: 1.3 37a–b, 40g; 93a–b, 96g; 1.4 127a–b, 130g, 1.5 11a–b, 14g**
Practice	TE: 1.3 60–61, 111a; 1.4 142–143 PB: 1.2 14, 34, 104, 124
Reteach/Review	TE: 1.3 82–83, DI·78, DI·81; 1.4 170–171 DI·83; 1.5 98–99 190–191, DI·77
Test	Selection Test: 1.3 29–32, 37–40; 1.4 65–48; 1.5 73–76 Benchmark Test: Units 3, 4, 5

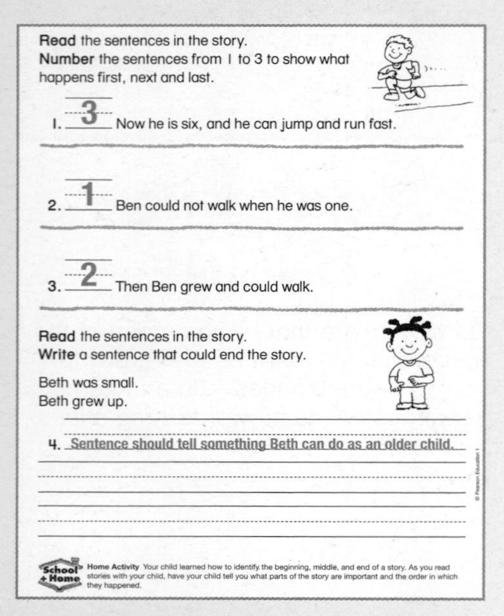
Read the sentences in the story.
Number the sentences from 1 to 3 to show what happens first, next and last.

1. 3 Now he is six, and he can jump and run fast.
2. 1 Ben could not walk when he was one.
3. 2 Then Ben grew and could walk.

Read the sentences in the story.
Write a sentence that could end the story.

Beth was small.
Beth grew up.

4. Sentence should tell something Beth can do as an older child.

Home Activity Your child learned how to identify the beginning, middle, and end of a story. As you read stories with your child, have your child tell you what parts of the story are important and the order in which they happened.

© Pearson Education 1

▲ **Practice Book 1.2** p. 14, Plot

Access Content For a Picture It! lesson on plot, see the ELL Teaching Guide, pp. 93–94.

Listening Comprehension

TEACH/MODEL Plot

DEFINE PLOT

- Stories have a beginning, a middle, and an end.
- What happens in the beginning, middle, and end makes up the plot of a story.
- Good readers listen to what happens and the order in which it happens.

READ ALOUD Read "Something Else to Do" and model how to identify plot.

MODEL When I read, I think about what happens in the beginning, middle, and end of the story. This story begins with Cheep hatching and deciding that she doesn't want to be a chicken. She tries to be a duck and a cat. In the end, she decides that being a chicken isn't so bad after all.

PRACTICE

CLUES TO PLOT Display Graphic Organizer 22 or draw a story sequence chart. Have children identify what happens in the beginning, middle, and end of "Something Else to Do." Record children's responses in the chart. As they retell, have them use descriptive words.

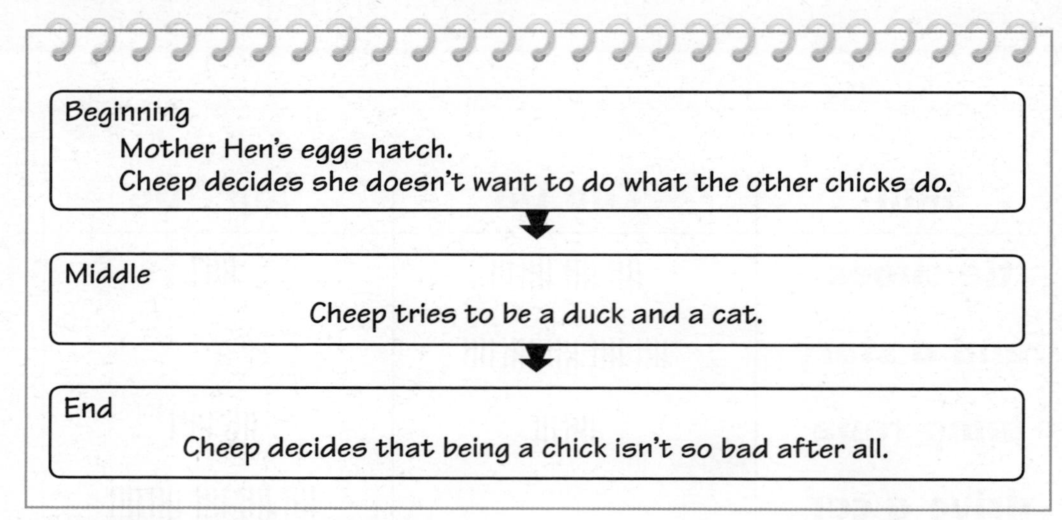

▲ **Graphic Organizer Flip Chart 22**

RECOGNIZE PLOT Have children recall the story *The Big Circle.*

- What happens in the beginning of the story? (Big T. Rex sees a triceratops baby and wants to eat it.)
- What happens in the middle of the story? (The older and bigger triceratops make a circle around the baby triceratops to protect him from Big T Rex.)
- How does the story end? (The T. Rex leaves the triceratops to look for food somewhere else.)

CONNECT TO READING Tell children that when they read, they should identify what happens in the beginning, middle, and end of a story.

Something Else to Do

Mother Hen was very proud when her eggs hatched. It was quite a happy event. She kissed each one of her darling little chicks and told them all about how to live on the farm.

"You can find the most tasty bugs in the dirt over here," she said. "And the straw in the back of the barn is the best place for naps."

The littlest chick, Cheep, didn't think this sounded like much fun.

"I don't want to eat bugs and sleep in the barn," she said. "I'll find something else to do!"

And so she trotted around the farm until she came to the pond. There the ducks were quacking happily as they flew through the air and splashed into the water.

"I can do that too!" Cheep cried and jumped into the water. She sank and sank until a duck fished her out.

"Little chicks shouldn't attempt to swim," the duck said kindly, putting Cheep down on the ground.

"Okay," Cheep said. "I'll find something else to do!"

And so she trotted around the farm until she came to a field. There the cats were purring happily as they ran over the grass and chased the field mice.

"I can do that too!" Cheep cried and ran into the field. She ran and ran after the mice until she realized that the cats were chasing her! Just as a cat was about to catch her, a mouse pulled her behind a rock to hide.

"Little chicks shouldn't attempt to chase mice," the mouse whispered kindly, pointing out the way back to the farmyard.

"Okay," Cheep said. "I'll find something else to do!"

And so she trotted back to the farm. There the chickens were pecking at the dirt for bugs.

"I can do that too!" Cheep cried, and she ate and ate.

"Hmm," she said once she was full. "I guess being a little chick isn't so bad after all." And she trotted off to the barn to take a nap.

OBJECTIVE

- Write a list.

DAILY FIX-IT

1. i sang on the way to the rinc.
   I sang on the way to the rink.
2. Put the blanck book in the trunk
   Put the blank book in the trunk.

This week's practice sentences appear on Daily Fix-It Transparency 14.

Strategic Intervention

Children who are not able to write independently may copy one or more sentences from the generated idea list and illustrate other things they can do now that they could not do as babies.

Advanced

Have children extend their list with three sentences of things they hope to be able to do as third graders that they cannot do now as first graders.

Support Writing Before writing about things they can do now, have children work in pairs and tell each other what they plan to write about.

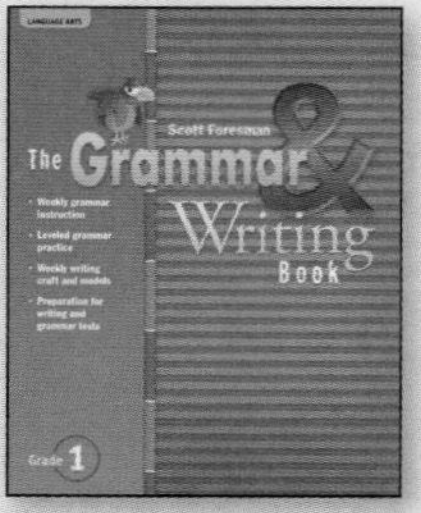

▲ **The Grammar and Writing Book**
For more instruction and practice, use pp. 128–133.

Shared Writing

WRITE List

GENERATE IDEAS Ask children to name things they can do now that they could not do when they were babies. Write their ideas on the board.

WRITE A LIST Explain that the class will write a list of things they can do now as first graders that they could not do when they were babies.

COMPREHENSION SKILL Tell children that stories generally have a beginning, a middle, and an end. Have children think of the beginning of their life. Consider what they could do when they were babies and what they can do now.

- Display Writing Transparency 14 and read the title.
- Ask children to think of the beginning of their life—their story. What could they do then?
- Encourage children to think of things they can do now that they could not do as babies.
- As children describe the activities they can do now, record their responses in list form.

HANDWRITING While writing, model the letter forms as shown on TR12–15.

READ THE LIST Have children read the completed list aloud as you track the print.

What We Can Do Now

- We can ride our bikes.

Possible answers:

- We can write our names.
- We can read a book.
- We can skip rope.
- We can make our beds.

Unit 3 Ruby in Her Own Time — Writing Model 14

▲ **Writing Transparency 14**

INDEPENDENT WRITING

WRITE LIST Have children write their own list. Encourage them to use words from the Word Wall and the Amazing Words board. Let children illustrate their writing. You may gather children's work to save in their portfolios.

ADDITIONAL PRACTICE For additional practice use pp. 128–133 in The Grammar and Writing Book.

Grammar

TEACH/MODEL Verbs That Add *-s*

REVIEW VERBS Remind children that a verb tells what someone or something does.

IDENTIFY VERBS THAT ADD *-s* Display Grammar Transparency 14. Read the definition aloud. Then model with item 1.

- Look at the picture. A baby is crawling across the floor. The action word or verb is *crawl*. Should we say *crawls* or *crawled?*
- The action is being done by one person now, so the verb should have an *-s* at the end. We should underline the word *crawls*.

Continue modeling with items 2–6.

OBJECTIVE

- Identify verbs that add *-s*.

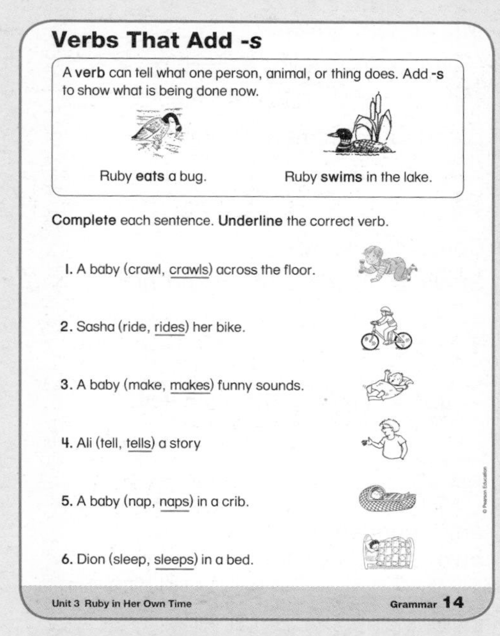
Verbs That Add -s

A **verb** can tell what one person, animal, or thing does. Add **-s** to show what is being done now.

Ruby **eats** a bug. Ruby **swims** in the lake.

Complete each sentence. **Underline** the correct verb.

1. A baby (crawl, crawls) across the floor.
2. Sasha (ride, rides) her bike.
3. A baby (make, makes) funny sounds.
4. Ali (tell, tells) a story
5. A baby (nap, naps) in a crib.
6. Dion (sleep, sleeps) in a bed.

Unit 3 Ruby in Her Own Time — Grammar 14

▲ **Grammar Transparency 14**

PRACTICE

MAKE NEW WORDS Have children name action words.

- Name an action you do at school.
- Let's pretend you are doing it right now.
- We need to add an *-s* to the end of the verb if one person does it now.

Wrap Up Your Day!

FINAL *ng* AND *nk* Write *wing* and ask a volunteer to point to the *ng* on the end of the word. Have children name other words that end with *ng*. Continue with *bank, nk*.

SPELLING WORDS WITH *ng* AND *nk* Have children classify this week's spelling words into two lists. Write words that end with *ng* in one column and words that end with *nk* in the other column.

PLOT To help children recognize plot, ask: What happens in the beginning, middle and end of "Something Else to Do"? (In the beginning Cheep doesn't want to be a chicken. She tries to be a duck and a cat. In the end, she decides that being a chicken isn't so bad after all.)

LET'S TALK ABOUT IT Display the "Skill," "Can Do," "Can't Do" chart. Discuss the activities Cheep tried to do that she couldn't do in "Something Else to Do." Add other skills children find difficult to do to the chart.

HOMEWORK Send home this week's Family Times newsletter.

PREVIEW Day 2

Tell children that tomorrow the class will read about someone who has changed and continues to change over a long period of time.

Day 2

AT A GLANCE

Share Literature
Mr. George Baker

Phonemic Awareness
Blend and Segment Syllables

Phonics and Spelling
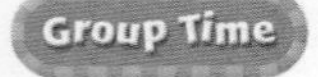
Compound Words
Spelling: Words with *ng* and *nk*

Read Apply Phonics
Word Wall

Group Time < Differentiated Instruction

High-Frequency Words
any enough ever every own sure were
Word Wall

Interactive Writing
Poem

Grammar
Verbs That Add *-s*

Speaking and Listening
Give Directions

Materials
- *Sing with Me Big Book*
- Big Book *Mr. George Baker*
- Letter Tiles
- Decodable Reader 28
- Student Edition 38–39
- Tested Word Card

Morning Warm-Up!

Today we'll read about Harry and Mr. George Baker again. George goes to school because he wants to learn. Why do you think it is important to always keep learning?

QUESTION OF THE DAY Encourage children to sing "On Our Own Time Line" from the *Sing with Me Big Book* as you gather. Write and read the message and discuss the question.

REVIEW SPECIAL TITLES

- Read the message and have children find the name of the old man. (*Mr. George Baker*)
- Point out the special title *Mr.*
- Discuss why Harry always calls his friend *Mr. George Baker.* (Because his friend is an adult. Calling him mister is polite and shows respect.)
- How do we begin words that are special titles? (with capital letters)

Build Background Use the Day 2 instruction on ELL Poster 14 to preview high-frequency words.

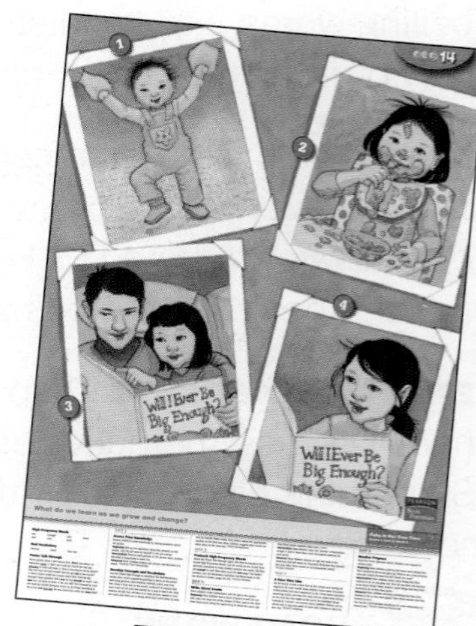

ELL Poster 14

Share Literature

BUILD CONCEPTS

REALISTIC FICTION Help children read the title and the author's name. Point out that this story is about a boy who could be a real boy and a man who could be a real person. The characters do things real people might do. When people in a made-up story act like real people, we say the story is realistic fiction.

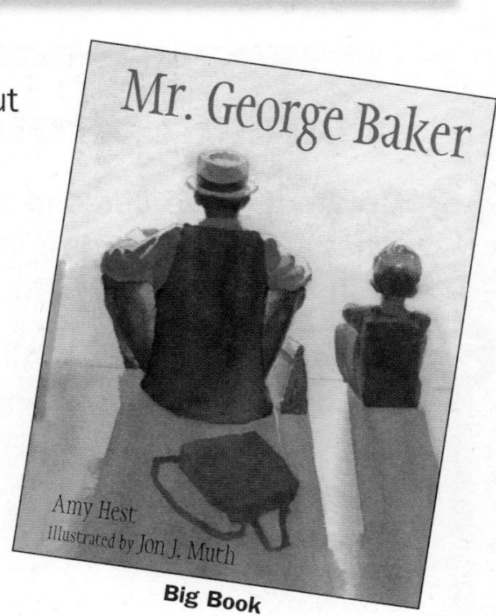

Big Book

BUILD ORAL VOCABULARY Explain that a **famous** person is one that many people have heard about. People may **flatter,** or praise someone too much, for being **famous**. Ask children to listen to find out why Mr. George Baker is famous.

- Why is Mr. George Baker famous? (He is a drummer.)
- How can you tell Mr. George Baker is famous with the children on the bus? (They all want to sit with him.)
- How does Mrs. Baker flatter Mr. Baker in the story? (Mrs. Baker tells him she loves him.)

Phonemic Awareness

BLEND AND SEGMENT SYLLABLES

- Mr. George Baker and Harry may have reading homework. Listen to the syllables in *homework.*
- Model saying each syllable, *home, work.* Have children say the syllables with you and then say the syllables by themselves.
- Now say each syllable as you write the word part that goes with it. (Say *home, work* as you write *homework.)*
- Have children say each word part as you point to the syllables and blend the syllables to say the word *(homework).* Repeat with *treetop, sandbox, classmate,* and *weekend.*

OBJECTIVES

- Discuss realistic fiction.
- Set purpose for listening.
- Build oral vocabulary.
- Blend and segment syllables.

	MONITOR PROGRESS
attempt **event** **time line** **famous** **flatter** **correct** **awkward** **lovely**	**If...** children lack oral vocabulary experiences about the concept Growing and Changing, **then...** use the Oral Vocabulary Routine. See p. DI·4 to teach *famous* and *flatter.*

Build Concepts Display examples of things people read, such as books, newspapers, magazines, letters, and recipes. Use simple sentences to discuss why Mr. George Baker might need or want to read each item. Mr. George Baker wants to read a recipe. He wants to know how to make soup. Mr. George Baker needs to read the newspaper. He needs to know what time the movie starts.

Compound Words

OBJECTIVES

- Use structural cues to decode compound words.
- Blend, read, and sort compound words.

Skills Trace

Compound Words

Introduce/Teach	**TE: 1.3 38c–d, 40c–d; 1.4 126n–o**
Practice	TE: 1.3 38f; PB: 1.2 15, 103, DR28
Reteach/Review	TE: 1.3 66c, 88c–d; 1.4 182c–d, DI·78; PB: 1.2 29, 118
Assess/Test	TE: 1.3 66e–g; 1.4 154e–g; Benchmark Test: Units 3, 4

Generalization

Compound Words A compound is a word made up of two or more shorter words.

Strategic Intervention

Use **Monitor Progress,** p. 38d during Group Time after children have had more practice with compound words.

Advanced

Use **Monitor Progress,** p. 38d as a preassessment to determine whether or not this group of children would benefit from instruction with compound words.

Support Phonics Children who speak languages where words consist of one syllable, such as Cantonese, Hmong, and Vietnamese, may need extra practice with the concept of compound words.

See the Phonics Transition Lessons in the ELL and Transition Handbook.

TEACH/MODEL

Blending Strategy

ROUTINE

1. **Connect** Write *bed* and *time.* You studied words like these already. What are these words? Today we'll learn about combining two words, such as *bed* and *time*, to make a compound word.
2. **Model** Write *bedtime.* A compound word is made up of two shorter words. The meaning of the compound word is often made up of the meanings of the two shorter words. What two words do you hear in *bedtime? (bed* and *time)* What does *bedtime* mean? (the time to go to bed)

   To read compound words, first I read the two words and then blend them into one word. Segment and blend *bedtime.* Let's blend this word together: /bed/ /tīm/, *bedtime*

   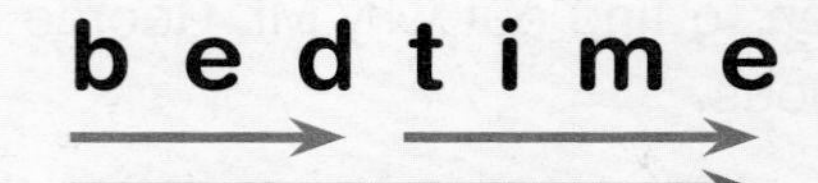

3. **Group Practice** First, look for the two smaller words that make the compound word. Read the two smaller words, and then blend them into one word. Continue with *pancake, windmill, sunrise, somewhere,* and *sandbox.* Discuss the word meanings and point out that compound words can also be made with words from the Word Wall.
4. **Review** What do you know about reading compound words? Read the two smaller words and blend them into one compound word.

BLEND WORDS

INDIVIDUALS BLEND COMPOUND WORDS Call on individuals to blend *sidewalk, backpack, baseball, hopscotch, lipstick, driveway,* and *someone.* Have them tell what they know about each word before they read it. (A compound word is made up of two or more shorter words.) For feedback, refer to step four of the Blending Strategy Routine.

SORT WORDS

READ LONGER WORDS Write the words below. Call on children to read the compound words, identify the two shorter words, and frame each shorter word. If children have difficulty reading a compound word, have them cover one shorter word and blend the other one. Discuss the meanings of the words. Have children identify the compound word with /ng/. *(something)*

Then work with children to list the compound words and the two shorter words that make up each compound word.

something	**flagpole**	**classmate**	**bathtub**
sandbox	**anthill**	**sunshine**	**weekend**

Vocabulary TiP

You may wish to explain the meanings of these words.

blueprint drawing of a building plan, using white lines on blue paper

quicksand loose sand that causes things to sink quickly

paperback book that has a paper cover

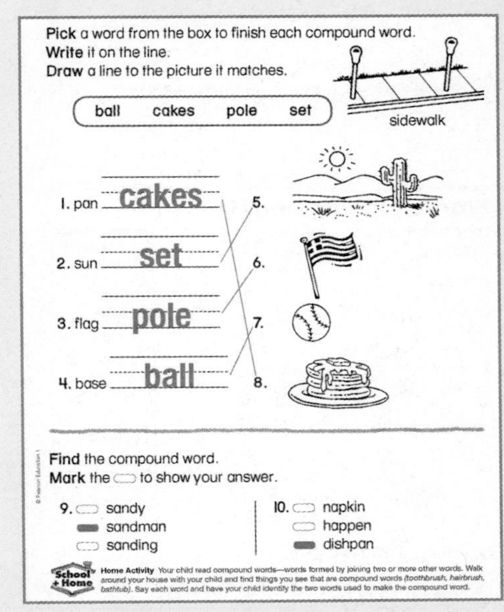
Pick a word from the box to finish each compound word.
Write it on the line.
Draw a line to the picture it matches.

ball cakes pole set

sidewalk

1. pan cakes
2. sun set
3. flag pole
4. base ball

Find the compound word.
Mark the ⊂⊃ to show your answer.

9. sandy / sandman / sanding
10. napkin / happen / dishpan

▲ **Practice Book 1.2** p. 15, Compound Words

Monitor Progress

Check Word Reading Compound Words

Write the following words and have individuals read them.

pigpen	**quicksand**	**inside**	**treetops**	**gumball**
runway	**blueprint**	**sunset**	**outside**	**newscast**
basketball	**paperback**	**nickname**	**jellyfish**	**understand**

If... children cannot blend compound words at this point,

then... continue to monitor their progress using other instructional opportunities during the week so that they can be successful with the Day 5 Assessment. See the Skills Trace on p. 38c.

Day 1 Check Word Reading · ▶ **Day 2 Check Word Reading** · Day 3 Check High-Frequency Words/Retelling · Day 4 Check Fluency · Day 5 Assess Progress

Spiral REVIEW

- Row 2 reviews high-frequency and selection words.
- Row 3 reviews two-syllable words as part of compounds.

Word Reading
SUCCESS PREDICTOR

2

OBJECTIVE

- Spell words with *ng* and *nk*.

Words with *ng* and *nk*

1.	**bring**	6.	**wing***
2.	**trunk**	7.	**rink**
3.	**pink**	8.	**blank**
4.	**bank**	9.	**rang**
5.	**sang**	10.	**sunk**

High-Frequency Words

11. **every*** 12. **sure***

* Words from the Selection

Words with *ng* and *nk*

Look at each picture.
Write two list words that rhyme.

Spelling Words
bring
trunk
pink
bank
sang
wing
rink
blank
rang
sunk

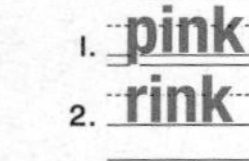

1. pink
2. rink

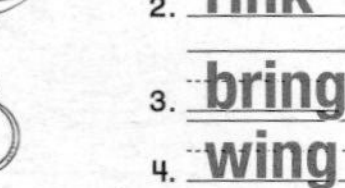

3. bring
4. wing

5. trunk
6. sunk

Read the clue. **Write** the word.

7. You keep money in it. 7. bank
8. You did it to a bell. 8. rang
9. You did it to a song. 9. sang
10. You can write a word to fill it. 10. blank

School + Home **Home Activity** Your child spelled words ending in *ng* and *nk*. Have your child identify and spell each list word that ends with *nk*.

▲ **Spelling Practice Book** p. 54

Spelling

PRACTICE Final *ng, nk*

WRITE DICTATION SENTENCES Have children write these sentences. Repeat words slowly, allowing children to hear each sound. Children may use the Word Wall to help with spelling high-frequency words. Word Wall

Make sure you bring cash to the bank.

He rang every bell.

Put the pink dress in the trunk.

We sang at the ice rink.

HOMEWORK Spelling Practice Book, p. 54

Group Time

DAY 2

On-Level	Strategic Intervention	Advanced
Read Decodable Reader 28.	**Read** Decodable Reader 28.	**Read** Self-Selected Reading.
• Use p. 38f.	• Use the **Routine** on p. DI•28.	• Use the **Routine** on p. DI•29.

Place English language learners in the groups that correspond to their reading abilities in English.

Independent Activities

Fluency Reading Pair children to reread Decodable Reader 27, this week's Leveled Readers, the ELL Reader from the previous week, or other text at children's independent level.

Journal Writing Make a list of events you could add to a time line about you. Share writing.

Independent Reading See p. 36j for Reading/Library activities and suggestions.

Literacy Centers To practice compound words, you may use Word Work, p. 36j.

Practice Book 1.2 Plot, p. 14
Compound Words, p. 15
High-Frequency Words, p. 16

Break into small groups after Spelling and before High-Frequency Words.

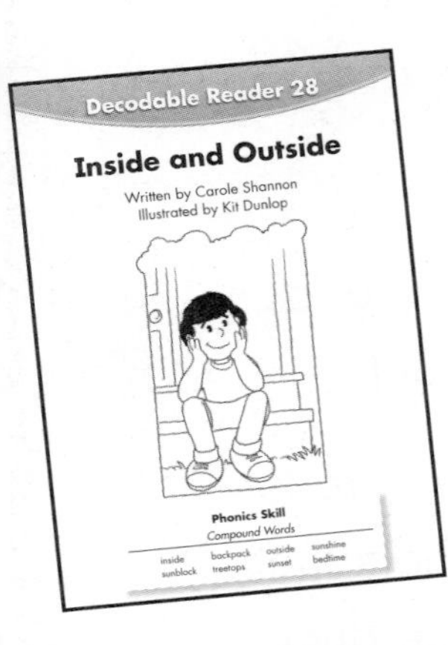

Apply Phonics

PRACTICE Compound Words

HIGH-FREQUENCY WORDS Review *day, do, eats, for, out* and *to* on the Word Wall. If necessary, have children practice in pairs with word cards. **Word Wall**

READ DECODABLE READER 28

- Pages 26–27 Read aloud quietly with the group.
- Page 28 Have the group read aloud without you.
- Pages 29–32 Select individuals to read aloud.

CHECK COMPREHENSION AND DECODING

- What does Pete do inside? (Pete feeds his fish, fills his backpack, eats lunch, takes a nap, and goes to bed.)
- What does Pete do outside? (Pete jumps rope, swims, and flies a kite.)
- Point to a compound word in the story. What is the word? List words that are named. Children may supply *backpack, bedtime, inside, sunblock, sunset, sunshine, treetops,* and *outside.*
- How do you know that these are compound words? (They are all words made up of two shorter words.)
- Discuss the meaning of the compound words.

HOMEWORK Take-Home Decodable Reader 28

Paired Reading

ROUTINE

1. **Reader 1 Begins** Children read the entire book, switching readers at the end of each page.
2. **Reader 2 Begins** Have partners reread; now the other partner begins.
3. **Reread** For optimal fluency, children should reread three or four times.
4. **Provide Feedback** Listen to children read and provide corrective feedback regarding their oral reading and their use of the blending strategy.

OBJECTIVES

- Apply knowledge of letter-sounds and word parts to decode unknown words when reading.
- Use context with letter-sounds to confirm the identification of unknown words.
- Practice fluency with paired rereading.

Monitor Progress

Decoding

If... children have difficulty decoding a word,	**then...** prompt them to blend the word. • What is the new word? • Is the new word a word you know? • Does it make sense in the story?

ELL

Access Content

Beginning Before reading, point to pictures of the backpack and treetops and explain compound words: A backpack is a pack you wear on your back. Treetops are the tops of the trees.

Intermediate Preview *Inside and Outside.* Have children point to an illustration and say *Pete is inside,* or *Pete is outside.*

Advanced Before reading, have children use a red pencil to write *back, bed, in, sun,* and *tree* on cards. Have them use black pencil to write *pack, time, side, set,* and *tops* on cards. Have partners take turns matching red and black words to form compound words. Have them use each compound word in a sentence.

Words to Read

ever
sure
were
enough
every
any
own

38

Read the Words

"Have you ever seen this cute duck family in the pond?" asked Ben.

"Sure," said Jill. "They were here last week. I had seeds to feed them then, but not enough for every little duck. Now I don't have any seeds."

"They will have to get their own food," said Ben.

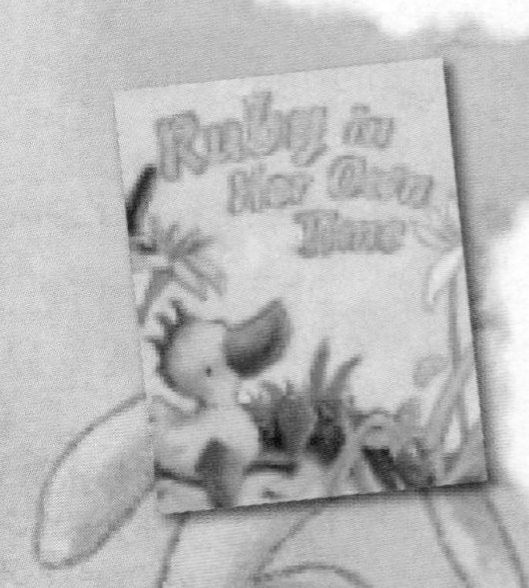

Genre: Animal Fantasy
An animal fantasy is a story with animal characters that talk. Next you will read about a growing duck family.

39

OBJECTIVE

- Recognize high-frequency words.

Write a word from the box to finish each sentence.

any enough ever
every own sure were

1. Do we have e n o u g h food?
2. Yes, I am s u r e we do.
3. Is e v e r y place set?
4. Yes, they w e r e set last night.
5. Do you need a n y flowers?
6. No, I have my o w n.
7. This will be the best day e v e r!

School + Home **Home Activity** This week your child learned to read the words *any, enough, ever, every, own, sure,* and *were*. Help your child make up a short story using some of these words. Then help your child to write down the sentences and draw a picture to go with his or her story.

▲ **Practice Book 1.2** p. 16, High-Frequency Words

High-Frequency Words

Nondecodable Words

ROUTINE

1. **Say and Spell** Look at the words on p. 38. You cannot blend the sounds in these words. We will spell the words and use letter-sounds we know to learn them. Point to the first word. This word is *ever, e-v-e-r, ever.* What is this word? What are the letters in this word?
2. **Identify Familiar Letter-Sounds** Point to the *v* in *ever.* What is this letter? What is the sound for this letter? (/v/)
3. **Demonstrate Meaning** Tell me a sentence using this word.

Repeat the routine with the other Words to Read. Have children identify these familiar letter-sounds: *sure* (r/r/), *were* (w/w/), *enough* (e/ē/, n/n/), *every* (v/v/, r/r/, y/ē/), *any* (n/n/, y/ē/), *own* (n/n/).

Have children read aloud the sentences on p. 39 and point to the Words to Read. Discuss what the quotation marks tell about these sentences. Add the words to the Word Wall. **Word Wall**

Interactive Writing

WRITE Poem

BRAINSTORM Use pp. 36–37 to encourage a discussion about what we learn as we grow. Ask children to identify things they have learned and how they have changed since they were born.

SHARE THE PEN Have children participate in writing a poem about how they grow and change. Explain that the poem will be a two-line rhyme. To begin, have children offer several first lines about what they were like as a baby. Remind them that the ending word of the first line will have a rhyming word in the next line. Guide children to end their first line with *day* or *grow*. Choose a first line and write it, inviting individuals to suggest familiar letter-sounds, word parts, and high-frequency words. Ask questions such as:

- What is the ending sound in the word *day?* (/ā/)
- What other words have this same ending sound? (*play, hay, may, pay, say, okay, ray, stay, stray, way*)
- Which of these words sound good in our poem? (Answers will vary.)

Write a two-line rhyme and have individuals help with the spelling. Frequently reread what has been written while tracking the print.

READ THE POEM Read the completed poem aloud, having children echo you.

When I was a baby, I slept all day.
Now I skip and run and play.

INDEPENDENT WRITING

WRITE A POEM Have children write their own two-line poem about growing and changing. Let children illustrate their writing.

OBJECTIVE

- Write a poem.

Strategic Intervention

Give children the first line of a poem and the beginning of the second line. Have children identify and write the rhyming word at the end.

Advanced

Have children who are able to write complete sentences independently write their own 4–6 line poem about growing and changing.

Support Writing Before writing, children might share ideas in their home languages.

Beginning Pair children with more proficient English speakers. A more proficient speaker can help the partner write a two-line poem.

Intermediate Help children identify lists of rhyming words orally prior to writing their poem.

Advanced Encourage children to write and read aloud their poems.

OBJECTIVE

- Identify verbs that add -s.

DAILY FIX-IT

3. The bird's wing Is pink
The bird's wing is pink.

4. bring your skates to the rinck.
Bring your skates to the rink.

Verbs That Add -s

A **verb** can tell what one person, animal, or thing does. Add **-s** to show what is being done now.

Ruby **grows** bigger. Ruby **spreads** her wings.

Complete each sentence.
Write the correct word on the line.

1. Pam reads a book. (reads, read)
2. Ned bakes a cake. (bake, bakes)
3. José rides a bike. (rides, ride)
4. Tina ties her shoes. (tie, ties)

Home Activity Your child learned about verbs that add -s. Write the words swim, run, walk, jump, and dance on paper. Have your child add an -s to each word and then act out the word.

▲ **Grammar and Writing Practice Book** p. 53

ELL

Support Grammar Children of various language backgrounds may add -*s* to both the nouns and verbs in sentences: *The dogs runs.* Point out that in English, verbs add -*s* for singular nouns, not plural nouns. See the Grammar Transition lessons in the ELL and Transition Handbook.

Grammar

DEVELOP THE CONCEPT Verbs That Add -*s*

IDENTIFY VERBS THAT ADD -*s* Write *Karin sing* on the board. Point to each word as you read it. Ask children to identify the verb in this sentence, the action. (*sing*) Tell children that one person is singing now, so an -*s* needs to be added to the end of the verb *sing*. (Karin sings.)

For this sentence to sound right, I need to add -*s* to the action word. When is this action happening? (now) How many people are singing? (one)

PRACTICE

MAKE NEW WORDS Gather several pictures of individual people or animals in action. Display a picture. Model writing the action verb shown in the picture and then adding an -*s* to the end of the verb to show that it is being done now by one person or thing, for example:

MODEL Write *This girl _____ the flowers.* What is this girl doing? She is watering the flowers. The action in this picture is water. Write *water* on the line and reread the sentence frame. This one girl is watering the flowers now. I need to add -*s* to *water.* Add -*s,* making *waters* and read the completed sentence frame: *This girl waters the flowers.*

Have children suggest action verbs for the other pictures and write the words on the board. Tell children these actions by one person or animal are happening now. Ask what ending will be added to each action verb. (-*s*) Invite volunteers to add -*s* to each word. Then have them use the new word in a sentence.

Speaking and Listening

GIVE DIRECTIONS

OBJECTIVES

- Speak to give clear directions.
- Listen to follow directions in the order they were given.

DEMONSTRATE GIVING DIRECTIONS Tell children that they will be listening to directions. Remind children that directions tell how to do or make something. Encourage children to focus on these behaviors as you give this three-step direction: Clap your hands, touch your nose, and then pat your head.

Speakers	Listeners
• Give directions in the correct order. • Clearly explain each step. • Speak loudly enough to be heard.	• Listen carefully. • Remember the steps and their order. • Follow the directions in the order they were given.

GIVE DIRECTIONS Have children work with a partner. One partner gives two- and three-step directions for the other partner to follow. Encourage children to describe the steps of something they can do well. Possible directions may include tying a shoe, adding two numbers, or jumping rope.

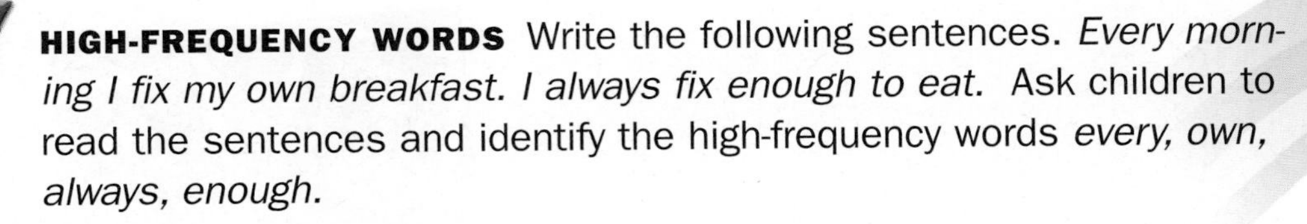

HIGH-FREQUENCY WORDS Write the following sentences. *Every morning I fix my own breakfast. I always fix enough to eat.* Ask children to read the sentences and identify the high-frequency words *every, own, always, enough.*

COMPOUND WORDS Write *everything* and ask children what two words make up this compound word. (*every* and *thing*) Follow the same procedure for *flagpole* and *inside*.

LET'S TALK ABOUT IT Recall the Big Book *Mr. George Baker*. Ask: Did George Baker learn to read when he was young? (no) Remind children that not everyone learns the same things at the same time. Discuss different ways people learn, and encourage children to add new ideas to the three-column "skill" chart.

PREVIEW Day 3

Tell children that tomorrow they will read about a family of ducks. One of the ducks takes her time to learn new things.

Day 3

AT A GLANCE

Share Literature
Mr. George Baker

Phonemic Awareness
Blend and Segment Onset/Rime

Phonics and Spelling
Final *ng*, *nk* and Compound Words

Spelling: Words with *ng* and *nk*

Build Background
Life Cycle of a Duck

Vocabulary
Selection Words

beautiful father feather flew mother precious

High-Frequency Words

any enough ever every own sure were

Comprehension
Skill Plot

Strategy Summarize

Read
Group Time < Differentiated Instruction

Ruby in Her Own Time

Vocabulary
Synonyms

Fluency
Attend to Punctuation

Writing Trait
Organization/Paragraphs

Grammar
Verbs That Add *-s*

Materials
- *Sing with Me Big Book*
- Big Book *Mr. George Baker*
- Phonics Songs/Rhymes Chart 14
- Letter Tiles
- Background Building Audio
- Graphic Organizer 21
- Vocabulary Transparency 14
- Student Edition 40–63

Morning Warm-Up!

Today we will read about Ruby—a duck that learns and grows in her own time. How do you learn in your own way?

QUESTION OF THE DAY Encourage children to sing "On Our Own Time Line" from the *Sing with Me Big Book* as you gather. Write the message and track the print as you read it. Discuss the question.

REVIEW PROPER NOUNS

- Circle the word *Ruby* in the message. Explain that *Ruby* is a proper noun.
- Have children tell how to begin proper nouns. (with capital letters)

Build Background Use the Day 3 instruction on ELL Poster 14 to support children's use of English to communicate about lesson concepts.

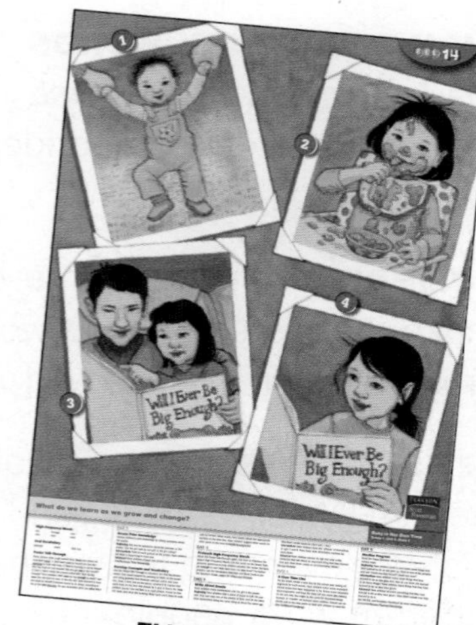

ELL Poster 14

Share Literature

LISTEN AND RESPOND

TITLE PAGE Point out the title page of *Mr. George Baker*. Explain that this page contains information for the reader, such as the author and the illustrator. The illustration, which shows someone dancing, may give readers a clue about the character in the story.

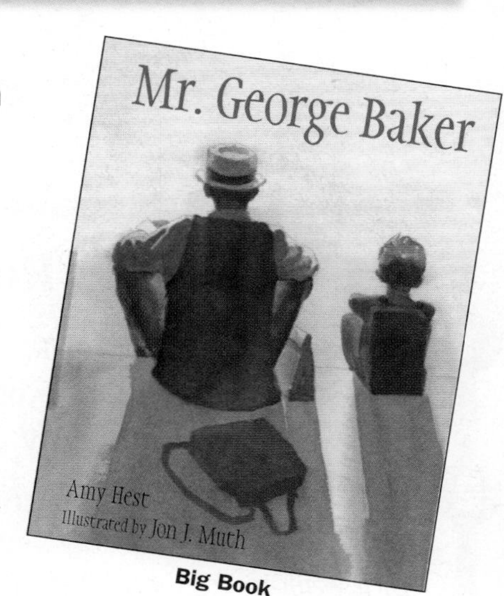

Big Book

BUILD ORAL VOCABULARY Review that yesterday the class read the book to find out why Mr. George Baker is famous. Even though Mr. George Baker is a famous drummer, he feels that something else about his life needs to be **corrected,** or fixed. Ask that children listen today to find out why Harry and Mr. George Baker meet each morning.

MONITOR LISTENING COMPREHENSION

- What does Mr. George Baker want to fix? (He can't read, and he thinks that needs to be corrected.)
- Why do Harry and Mr. George Baker meet each morning? (They are waiting for the school bus.)
- How can you tell that Mr. George Baker thinks reading is important? (He wants to go to school every day to learn; it's hard, but he keeps working.)

Phonemic Awareness

BLEND AND SEGMENT ONSET/RIME

- Mrs. Baker gave a wave and a wink. Listen to these word parts in *wink.*
- Say /w/-*ink.* Then tell children you are going to blend the two parts to say the word: /w/-*ink, wink.* Have children say the word parts with you and then by themselves.
- Write *ink.* Then write the letter *w* in front of *ink,* leaving a space between w and *ink.* Show children how to blend the onset and rime /w/-*ink, wink.* Help children do the same.
- Replace the *w* with *s.* Blend /s/ with *-ink* to read *sink.* Continue with /p/-*ink,* /dr/-*ink,* and /th/-*ink.*

Continue the activity with these word families.

s/ang	**br/ing**	**s/ank**
b/ang	**st/ing**	**bl/ank**

OBJECTIVES

- Identify the title page.
- Set purpose for listening.
- Build oral vocabulary.
- Blend and segment onset and rime.

attempt
event
time line
famous
flatter
correct
awkward
lovely

MONITOR PROGRESS

If... children lack oral vocabulary experiences about the concept Growing and Changing,

then... use the Oral Vocabulary Routine. See p. DI·4 to teach *correct.*

ELL

Listen and Respond Have children tap their fingers across their knees like Mr. George Baker, the drummer man, when you read the "Tappidy-boom" refrain on p. 19. Repeat several times and have children join in when they are ready.

OBJECTIVES

- Review final *-ng* and *-nk* and compound words.
- Read and sort compound words.
- Preview words before reading them.
- Spell words with *-ng* and *-nk.*

Strategic Intervention

Use **Strategic Intervention Decodable Reader 14** for more practice with final *-ng* and *-nk* and compound words.

Support Phonics For Spanish speakers, offer examples of compound words in Spanish, such as *cumpleanos (birthday), patio trasero (backyard),* and *alguien (someone).*

See the Phonics Transition Lessons in the ELL and Transition Handbook.

Final *ng, nk* and Compound Words

TEACH/MODEL

Fluent Word Reading

ROUTINE

1. **Connect** Write *sidewalk.* You can read this word because you know how to read compound words. What two shorter words are in the word *sidewalk? (side* and *walk)*
2. **Model** When you come to a compound word, look for the two smaller words. Read them and then read the compound word. Model reading *sidewalk* in this way. When you come to a new compound word, what are you going to do?
3. **Group Practice** Write *bathtub, snowball, sandpaper, homework, anything, bankbook.* Read these words. Look at the two shorter words; say the words to yourself, and then read the word aloud. Allow 2–3 seconds previewing time.

WORD READING

PHONICS SONGS AND RHYMES CHART 14 Frame each of the following words on Phonics Songs and Rhymes Chart 14. Call on individuals to read them. Guide children in previewing.

treetop	**sing**	**wing**	**something**
think	**link**	**bring**	

Sing "The Sixth Bluebird's Song" to the tune of "I've Been Workin' on the Railroad," or play the CD. Have children follow along on the chart as they sing. Then have individuals take turns locating /ng/ and /ngk/ words and compound words on the chart. Identify *bluebird(s)* and have children name the two words that make up the compound word. Point out *wrong* and have children identify the letters that stand for /ng/.

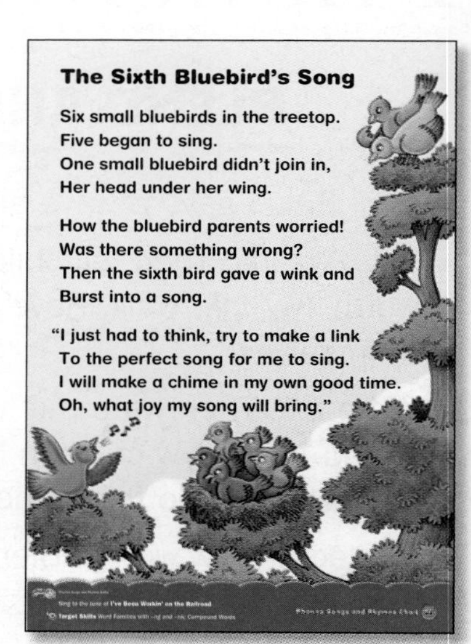

Phonics Songs and Rhymes Chart 14

Phonics Songs and Rhymes Audio

SORT WORDS

INDIVIDUALS SORT WORDS Write *compound word, first word,* and *second word* as headings. Write compound words under the first heading. Discuss the meaning of each compound. Then have children complete the activity on paper by writing the two words that form each compound. Monitor children's work and provide feedback. Ask individuals to read the words. Then have the rows read. To conclude, have children underline the letters that stand for /ng/ in *thing.*

compound word	first word	second word
flagpole	flag	pole
treetop	tree	top
weekend	week	end
everything	every	thing

Spelling

PRACTICE Final *ng, nk*

WHO'S IN THE FAMILY? Write headings *-ang, -ing, -ank, -ink,* and *-unk.* Have children write the spelling words on cards. Have them choose a card, read the word, and add it to the appropriate column. Have children use the word in a sentence.

After all the words have been sorted, ask children to read the two cards that are left over. *(every, sure)* Have them use these words in sentences. Have children read the words in each word family and then add other words.

-ang	-ing	-ank	-ink	-unk
sang	wing	bank	pink	sunk
rang	bring	blank	rink	trunk

HOMEWORK Spelling Practice Book, p. 55

Spelling Words

Words with *ng* and *nk*

1. bring
2. trunk
3. pink
4. bank
5. sang
6. wing*
7. rink
8. blank
9. rang
10. sunk

Challenge Words

11. every*
12. sure*

* Words from the Selection

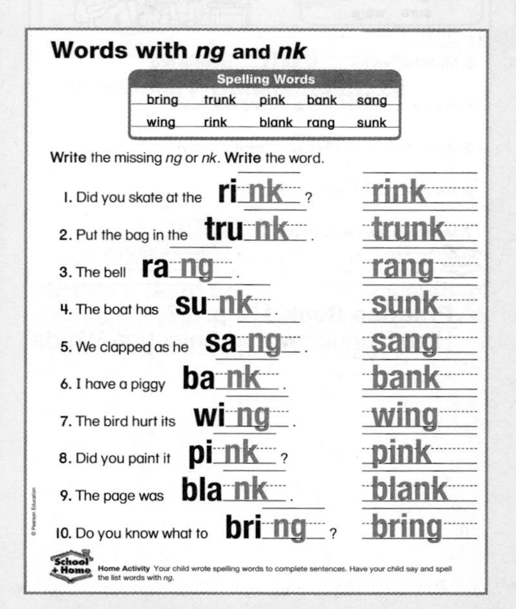
Words with *ng* and *nk*

Spelling Words				
bring	trunk	pink	bank	sang
wing	rink	blank	rang	sunk

Write the missing *ng* or *nk*. Write the word.

1. Did you skate at the ri**nk**? — rink
2. Put the bag in the tru**nk**. — trunk
3. The bell ra**ng**. — rang
4. The boat has su**nk**. — sunk
5. We clapped as he sa**ng**. — sang
6. I have a piggy ba**nk**. — bank
7. The bird hurt its wi**ng**. — wing
8. Did you paint it pi**nk**? — pink
9. The page was bla**nk**. — blank
10. Do you know what to bri**ng**? — bring

School + Home Home Activity Your child wrote spelling words to complete sentences. Have your child say and spell the list words with *ng*.

▲ **Spelling Practice Book** p. 55

3

OBJECTIVES

- Recognize plot.
- Summarize the events in a story.

Comprehension

SKILL Plot

RECOGNIZE PLOT Review that every story has a beginning, a middle, and an end. Recall the plots of previously read stories like *A Big Fish for Max.*

CONNECT TO READING

- As you read, ask yourself, "What was the first thing that happened? What happened in the middle? What happened at the end?"

STRATEGY Summarize

INTRODUCE THE STRATEGY Explain that when readers want to understand or remember what they read, they think about how to tell the most important parts of the story in a short way. Recall *The Farmer in the Hat.*

MODEL When I read I ask myself who the story is about, where it takes place, and what happens. Then I use my answers to tell about the story. For example, *The Farmer in the Hat* was about a group of children getting ready for a play at school. They made masks, and a cat ended up wearing the farmer's hat.

CONNECT TO READING Encourage children to ask themselves these questions as they read *Ruby in Her Own Time.*

- Who is this story about?
- Where does this story take place?
- What are the most important things that happen?

Group Time

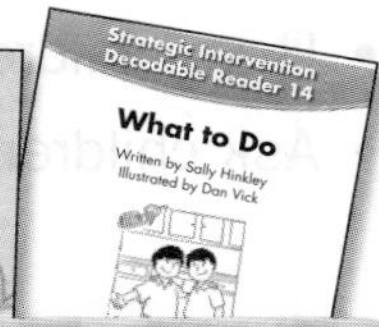

DAY 3

On-Level	Strategic Intervention	Advanced
Read *Ruby in Her Own Time.* • Use pp. 40–63.	**Read** SI Decodable Reader 14. • Read or listen to *Ruby in Her Own Time.* • Use the **Routine** on p. DI·30.	**Read** *Ruby in Her Own Time.* • Use the **Routine** on p. DI·31.

Place English language learners in the groups that correspond to their reading abilities in English.

Independent Activities

Independent Reading See p. 36j for Reading/Library activities and suggestions.

Journal Writing Write about something new you tried to do this year that you never tried to do before. Share writing.

Literacy Centers Use the Listening and Writing Centers for *Ruby in Her Own Time* on pp. 36j and 36k.

Practice Book 1.2 High-Frequency Words and Selection Words, p. 17

Break into small groups after Comprehension and before Fluency.

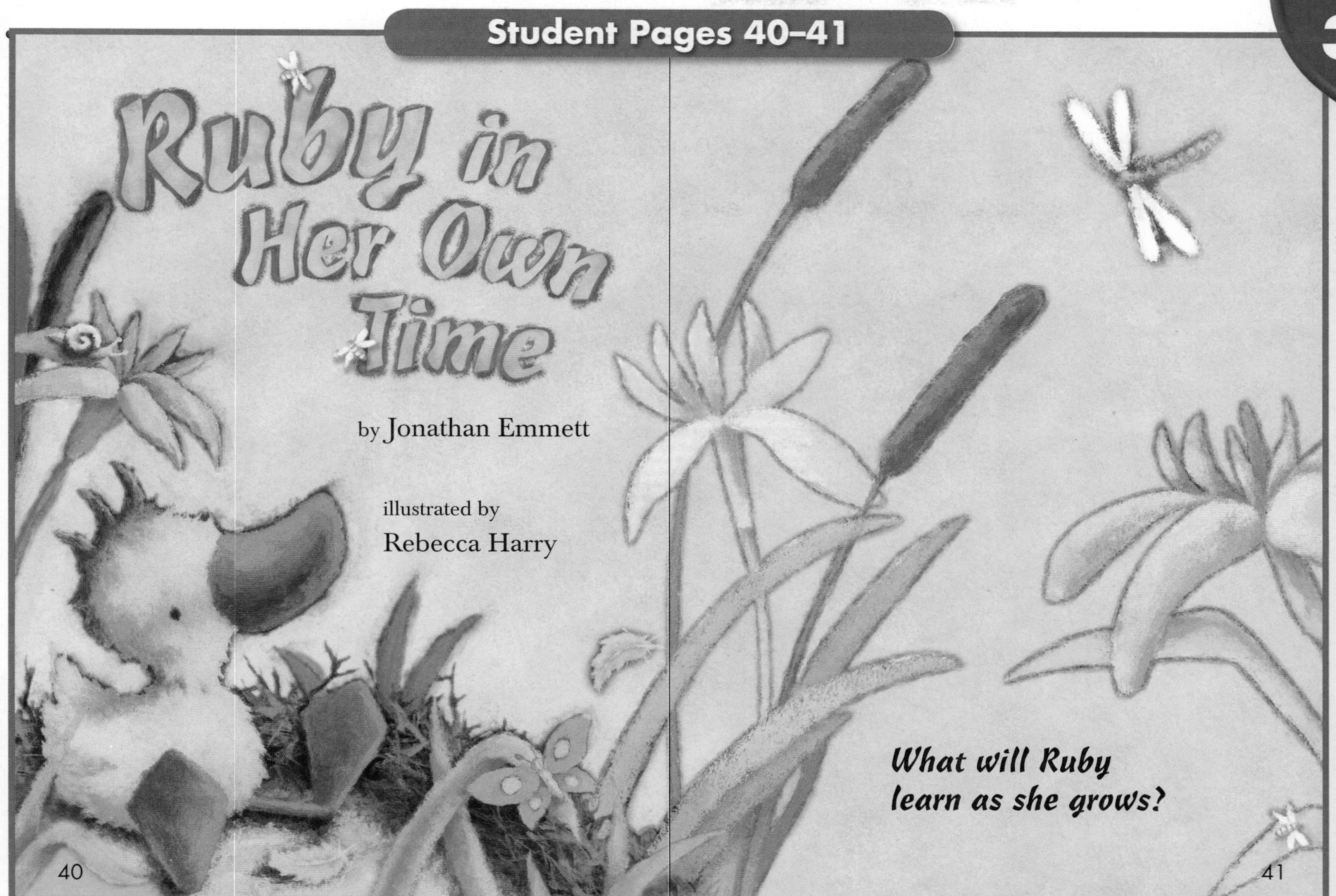

Read

Prereading Strategies

PREVIEW AND PREDICT Have children read the title of the story. Read aloud the names of the author and illustrator. Identify Ruby as the duckling in the picture. Have children preview pp. 40–53 and ask them to predict some things Ruby might need to learn as she grows up.

DISCUSS ANIMAL FANTASY Tell children that in this story, the ducks will talk. Remind them that a story about animals that do things real animals could not do is called a fantasy. Reread the definition of animal fantasy on p. 39 of the Student Edition.

SET PURPOSE Read the question on page 41. Discuss what children would like to find out about ducks as they read this story.

AudioText

ELL

Access Content Before reading, review the story summary in English and/or the home language. See the ELL Teaching Guide, pp. 96–98.

Once upon a time upon a nest beside a lake, there lived two ducks–a mother duck and a father duck.

42

There were five eggs in the nest. Mother Duck sat upon the nest, all day and all night . . .

through howling wind and driving rain, looking after the eggs–all five of them.

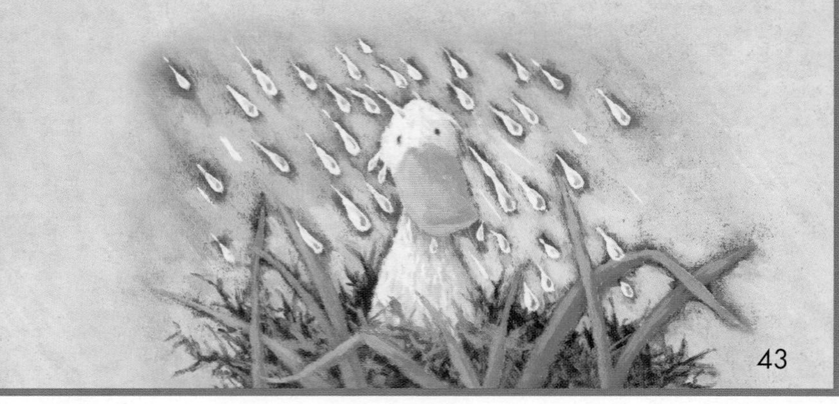

43

▲ **Pages 42–43**
Have children read to find out who the characters in the story are.

EXTEND SKILLS

Vocabulary

For instruction in using context clues to determine meaning, use the following:

- Find the words *driving rain*. What do you usually think of when you hear the word *drive*?
- Is the rain driving a car here? What do you think *driving rain* could mean?
- How does the story and the picture help you understand what the words *driving rain* mean?

Assess Have children discuss multiple meanings of the word *duck* and how they know which meaning is used in this story.

Guiding Comprehension

Character • Literal

- **Who are the characters in this story so far?**
  The characters are the mother and the father duck.

Details • Literal

- **How many eggs are in the nest?**
  There are five eggs in the nest.

Make Judgments • Critical

- **Do you think this duck will be a good mother? Why?**
  Children will probably say that she will be a good mother because she takes very good care of her eggs.

___ final *ng*, *nk* and compound words   high-frequency/tested vocabulary

Then, one bright morning, the eggs began to hatch.

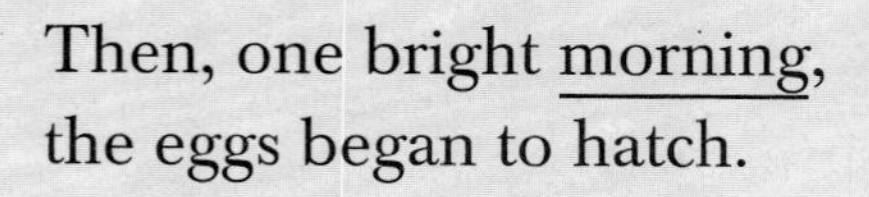

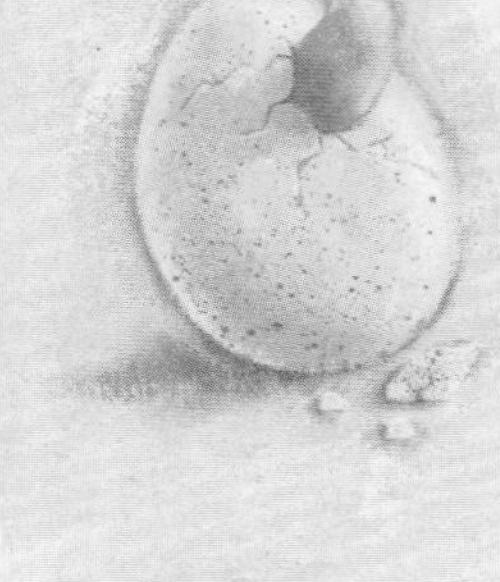

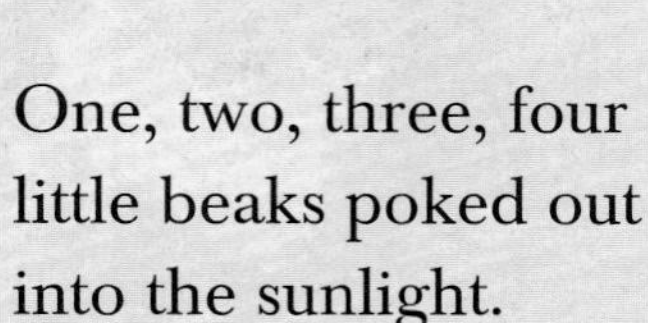

One, two, three, four little beaks poked out into the sunlight.

44

One, two, three, four little ducklings shook their feathers in the breeze.

"We'll call them Rufus, Rory, Rosie, and Rebecca," said Father Duck. And Mother Duck agreed.

45

Skills in Context

REVIEW SEQUENCE

- **What happened first, next, and last as the eggs hatched?**
  First, the ducklings' beaks poked out, then the ducklings came out of the eggs and shook their feathers, and last Father Duck named the ducklings.

Monitor Progress	Sequence
If... children have difficulty answering the question,	**then...** model how to identify sequence.

MODEL I know events in a story happen in a certain order. These pages tell about the baby ducklings hatching. First, the story says that their beaks poked out of the shells. Then it says they shook their feathers in the breeze, and I can see that from the picture that they are out of their shells. Last, the story says Father Duck named the ducklings.

ASSESS Ask children whether the parents named the ducklings before or after they shook their feathers. (They named them after.)

▲ **Pages 44–45**
Have children read to find out how the eggs hatched.

Monitor Progress

Decoding

If...	then...
If... children come to a word they don't know,	**then...** remind them to blend the word: 1. Look at each letter. 2. Think of the sound for each letter. 3. Blend the sounds. 4. Read the word.

But the fifth egg did nothing.
"Will it ever hatch?" said Father Duck.

"It will," said Mother Duck,
"in its own time."

46

And–
sure enough–
it did.

"She's very small," said Father Duck.
"What shall we call her?"

"We'll call her Ruby," said Mother Duck,
"because she's small and precious."

47

▲ **Pages 46–47**
Ask children to read to discover what happened to the fifth egg.

ELL

Access Content Point out that the word *precious* is very close to the Spanish word *precioso*, which has the same meaning, "very valuable." The name *Ruby* has the same meaning as the Spanish word for *ruby*, *Rubio*.

Monitor Progress

High-Frequency Words

If... children have a problem reading a new high-frequency word,	**then...** use the High-Frequency Routine on pp. 38–39 to reteach the problematic word.

Guiding Comprehension

Plot • Literal

- **What happened to the fifth egg?**
  It hatched later than the other eggs, and Ruby came out of it.

Draw Conclusions • Critical

- **What do you think "in her own time" means?**
  Children may suggest that it means "when she is ready" or "when the time is right."

Compare and Contrast • Inferential

- **How is Ruby like the other ducklings? How is she different?**
  Children's responses may include that Ruby is like the others because she hatched from an egg and she has a name that begins with *R*. She is different from the others because she hatched at a different time, and she is smaller than the other ducklings are.

____ final *ng*, *nk* and compound words   high-frequency/tested vocabulary

Rufus, Rory, Rosie, and Rebecca
ate whatever they were given.
They ate anything and everything.

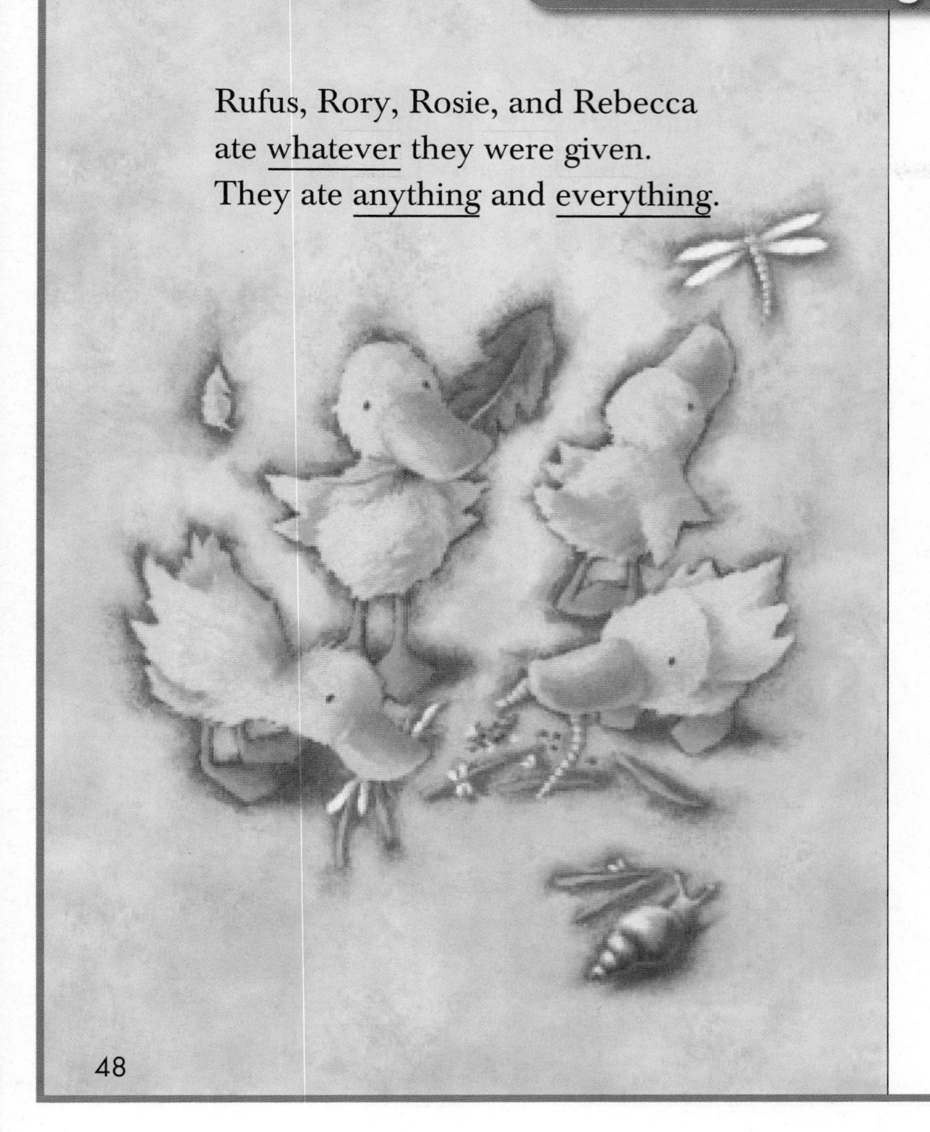

48

But Ruby ate nothing.

"Will she ever eat?" said Father Duck.

"She will," said Mother
Duck, "in her own time."

49

Strategies in Context

SUMMARIZE

- **What has happened so far in this story?**
  Mother and Father Duck had a nest beside a lake. Five eggs were in the nest. The first four eggs hatched, but the fifth hatched later. The first four ducklings ate everything, but the last duck ate nothing.

Monitor Progress	Summarize
If... children have difficulty summarizing,	**then...** model how to identify character, setting, and important events.

MODEL If I want to tell what happened in a story in a shorter way, I think about who the story is about, where it takes place, and what important events happen. The characters are Mother and Father Duck. They live in a nest. They had five eggs, and four hatched. The fifth hatched later, in its own time.

ASSESS Have children summarize just what happens on pp. 48–49. (Four ducks ate everything, but Ruby wouldn't eat.)

▲ **Pages 48–49**
Ask children to think about what has happened and to read to find out what happens next.

Strategy Self-Check

Have children ask themselves these questions to check their reading.

Decoding Words
- Do I look at all the parts of a word before I try to blend it?
- Do I look for two words that are put together to make a new word?
- Do I put the new word in the sentence to be sure it makes sense?

Summarize
- Who is this story about?
- Where does this story take place?
- What are the most important things that happen?

And–
sure enough–
she did.

Rufus, Rory, Rosie, and
Rebecca swam off whenever
they were able.

They swam anywhere
and everywhere.

50

51

▲ **Pages 50–51**
Ask children to read to see what else Ruby needs to learn.

Guiding Comprehension

Character • Critical

- **Why do you think Ruby took so long to eat?**
  Possible response: She likes to do things slowly. Maybe she learns how to do things slowly.

Hypothesize • Critical

- **The story says that the ducks swim anywhere and everywhere. Where do you think the ducks swim?**
  Possible response: In the lake or a nearby pond.

Predict • Inferential

- **What do you think will happen next?**
  Children will probably predict that Ruby will learn to swim in her own time.

EXTEND SKILLS

Alliteration

For instruction in alliteration, discuss the following:

- Say the names of the baby ducks with me. What letter does each name start with? Is it a consonant or a vowel?
- Why do you think the author used names for the ducks that all start with the same sound? (The author wanted us to think of the ducks as a family.)

Assess Have children suggest alliterative names for Mother and Father Duck.

____ final *ng*, *nk* and compound words   high-frequency/tested vocabulary

But Ruby swam nowhere.

"Will she ever swim?" said Father Duck.

"She will," said Mother Duck,
"in her own time."

And–
sure enough–
she did.

52

Rufus, Rory, Rosie, and
Rebecca grew bigger.

And Ruby grew bigger too.
Her feathers grew out, and her
wings grew broad and beautiful.

53

Guiding Comprehension

Compare and Contrast • Inferential

- **What did Ruby do that was different from her brothers and sisters? What did she do that was like them?**
  She hatched, ate, and swam in her own time, but she grew bigger at the same time that they did.

Predict • Inferential

- **What do you think Ruby will attempt now that her wings are bigger?**
  Children will probably predict that she will fly.

▲ **Pages 52–53**
Ask children to read to see how Ruby is like her brothers and sisters and how she is different.

▲ **Pages 54–55**
Have children read to find out where the ducks fly.

Guiding Comprehension

Confirm Predictions • Literal

- **Does Ruby fly with the others? Is this what you predicted?**
  Yes, Ruby does. Most children will probably say they predicted this, but some may have predicted that she would fly later, in her own time.

Author's Purpose • Inferential

- ***Question the Author*** **How does the author show that it is an exciting event when Ruby starts to fly?**
  The author puts an exclamation mark after the words *Ruby flew too.*

Sequence • Literal

- **Name in order the places where the ducks flew.**
  They flew far and wide, out across the water, and up among the trees.

___ final *ng, nk* and compound words   high-frequency/tested vocabulary

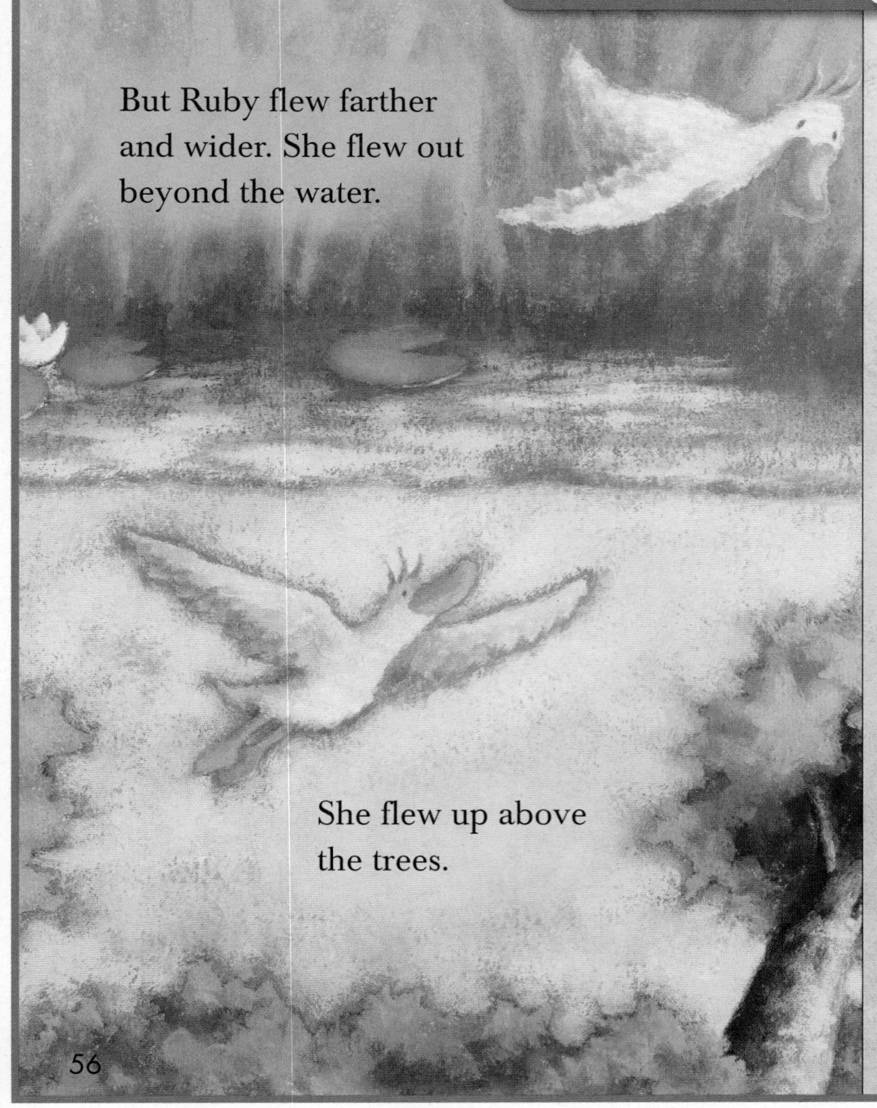

She flew anywhere and everywhere.
She stretched out her beautiful wings
and soared high among the clouds.

57

Guiding Comprehension

Character • Critical

- **How do you think Ruby feels?**
  Possible response: She feels excited to be among the clouds for the first time.

Predict • Inferential

- **What do you think Ruby will attempt next?**
  Possible response: Ruby will keep flying.

Compare and Contrast • Critical

- ***Text to Self*** **What is something you learned to do in your own time, like Ruby?**
  Children's responses will vary.

Pages 56–57
As children read, ask them to think about how Ruby has changed.

Respecting Differences

Tell children that everyone learns at different speeds. Some people learn to do things before other people do. Ask them to tell how Ruby is different from her brothers and sisters. Discuss how she does things "in her own time." Talk about how it isn't good or bad when people do things earlier or later than other people. It's just different.

Mother Duck and Father Duck watched Ruby flying off into the distance.

"Will she ever come back?" said Mother Duck.

"She will," said Father Duck, "in her own time."

▲ **Pages 58–59**
Have children read to find out what Ruby does now that she can fly.

Guiding Comprehension

Character • Critical

- **How do you think Mother and Father Duck feel? How do you know?**
  Possible response: They're proud of Ruby because she is flying. Mother Duck is worried too, because she asks if Ruby will come back.

Confirm Predictions • Inferential

- **Is this what you thought Ruby would do?**
  Children's responses will vary according to the predictions they made.

Draw Conclusions • Inferential

- **Is Ruby a baby duck anymore?**
  No, she is grown up—an adult duck.

Access Content Explain that the phrase *into the distance* means "far away."

___ final *ng, nk* and compound words

high-frequency/tested vocabulary

And–
sure enough–
she did.

60 61

▲ **Pages 60–61**
Have children read to find out how the story ends.

Skills in Context

PLOT

- **Use descriptive words to tell what happened to Ruby in the beginning, middle, and end of the story.**
  In the beginning, Ruby's egg was the last to hatch. In the middle, she did everything in her own time. When she grew up and learned to fly, she flew off on her own. In the end, she came back with her own family.

Monitor Progress	Plot
If... children have difficulty answering the question,	**then...** model how to identify the beginning, middle, and end of a story.

MODEL As I read, I think about what happens at the beginning, middle, and end of the story. First Ruby hatched. Then she followed her own time line and did everything in her own time until she flew away. In the end, she came back with her own family.

ASSESS Have children list the story events. Record their responses in Graphic Organizer 22. (Children should identify the beginning, middle, and end.)

EXTEND SKILLS

Illustrator's Craft

For instruction in using illustrations to understand the story, discuss the following:

- Illustrators can sometimes show parts of the story in the pictures that the author does not tell in words.
- What does this illustration tell you about what happened to Ruby when she came back?

Assess Ask children to look carefully at the picture. Discuss whether or not Ruby has a duckling that is different from the rest and why they think as they do. (One duckling is riding on her back instead of sitting in the water.)

Retelling Plan

- ☑ Week 1 assess Strategic Intervention Students.
- ☑ **This week assess Advanced students.**
- ☐ Week 3 assess Strategic Intervention Students.
- ☐ Week 4 assess On-Level students.
- ☐ Week 5 assess Strategic Intervention Students.
- ☐ Week 6 assess any students you have not yet checked during this unit.

Look Back and Write
For informal assessment, see the Scoring Rubric below.

Assessment Focus on comprehension and whether each child can provide good information about the selection, rather than mistakes in English. For more ideas on assessing comprehension, see the ELL and Transition Handbook.

Think and Share

TALK ABOUT IT Model a response. I was surprised Ruby flew so far that she flew away. I didn't think she would fly as far as her brothers and sisters.

1. **RETELL** Have children use the retelling strip in the Studen Edition to retell the story.

Monitor Progress **Check Retelling** 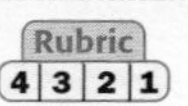

If... children have difficulty retelling the story,

then... use the Retelling Cards and the Scoring Rubric for Retelling on pp. 62–63 to help them move toward fluent retelling.

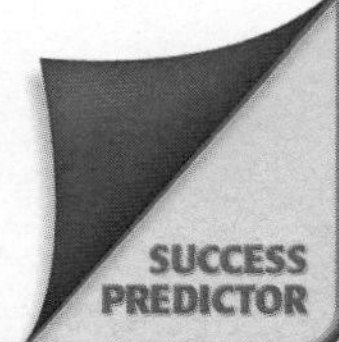

Day 1 Check Word Reading	Day 2 Check Word Reading	▶ **Day 3 Check High-Frequency Words/Retelling**	Day 4 Check Fluency	Day 5 Assess Progress

2. **PLOT** Possible response: The most exciting part was when Ruby flew away.

3. **SUMMARIZE** First Ruby learned to eat and swim. Then her wings grew bigger and she learned to fly.

LOOK BACK AND WRITE Read the writing prompt on p. 62 and model your thinking. I'll look back on p. 47 and read that part of the story again. I'll look for the reason Mother Duck named her baby duck Ruby. Then I'll write my response. Have children write their responses in an interactive or an independent writing activity.

Scoring Rubric **Look Back and Write**

Top-Score Response A top-score response uses details from p. 47 of the story to tell why Mother Duck names her baby duck Ruby.
Example of a Top-Score Response
Mother Duck names her baby duck Ruby because Ruby is small and precious.

For additional rubrics, see p. WA10.

Reader Response

Read Together

Think and Share

Talk About It What surprised you at the end of the story? Tell about it.

1. Use the pictures below to retell the order in which things happen in this story. Retell
2. What do you think was the most exciting part of this story? Plot
3. Sum up how Ruby grew and changed. Summarize

Look Back and Write Look back at page 47. Why did Mother Duck name her baby duck *Ruby*? Write about it.

Meet the Author

Jonathan Emmett

Jonathan Emmett got the idea for this story while jogging around a lake one morning. He saw a swan's nest, and the words "Once upon a time, upon a nest" popped into his head. He changed the swans to ducks, "and the story grew from there."

Mr. Emmett lives in England with his wife and two children.

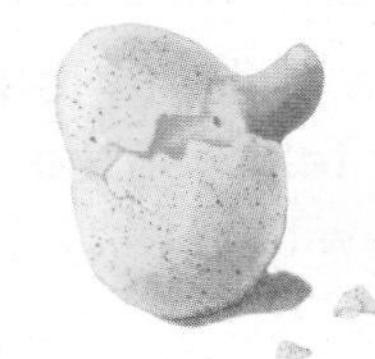

Read more books by Jonathan Emmett.

Retelling Strip

Scoring Rubric Narrative Retelling

Rubric 4 3 2 1	4	3	2	1
Connections	Makes connections and generalizes beyond the text	Makes connections to other events, stories, or experiences	Makes a limited connection to another event, story, or experience	Makes no connection to another event, story, or experience
Author's Purpose	Elaborates on author's purpose	Tells author's purpose with some clarity	Makes some connection to author's purpose	Makes no connection to author's purpose
Characters	Describes the main character(s) and any character development	Identifies the main character(s) and gives some information about them	Inaccurately identifies some characters or gives little information about them	Inaccurately identifies the characters or gives no information about them
Setting	Describes the time and location	Identifies the time and location	Omits details of time or location	Is unable to identify time or location
Plot	Describes the events in sequence using rich detail	Tells the plot with some errors in sequence that do not affect meaning	Tells parts of plot with gaps that affect meaning	Retelling has no sense of story

Use the Retelling Chart on p. TR18 to record retelling.

Selection Test To assess with *Ruby in Her Own Time,* use Selection Tests, pp. 29–32.

Fresh Reads for Differentiated Test Practice For weekly leveled practice, use pp. 79–84.

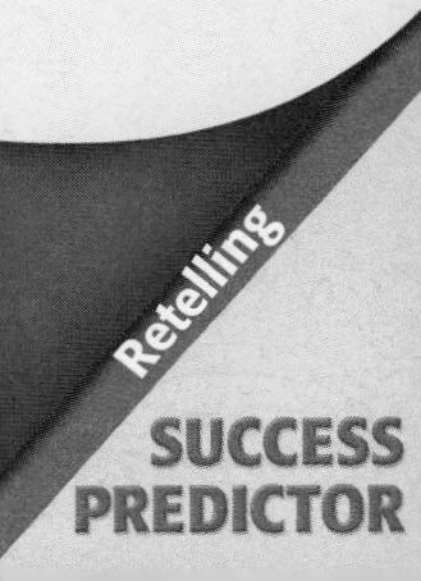

OBJECTIVE

- Read aloud fluently, attending to question marks.

Options for Choral Reading

Use *Ruby in Her Own Time* or one of the following Leveled Readers.

On-Level

Not Just Any Boy

Strategic Intervention

Can Hank Sing?

Advanced

A Bed for Paul

Reread *Ruby in Her Own Time* with children and have them track print as you read. Cue them to read aloud the text *And—sure enough—she did* together as a group when it is encountered. Discuss the phrase *sure enough* and ask children to try to find a way to express the idea in their home languages.

Fluency

ATTEND TO PUNCTUATION

MODEL READING WHILE ATTENDING TO QUESTION MARKS

Use *Ruby in Her Own Time.*

- Point to the question mark on p. 46. This mark is a question mark. It tells me that I should read this sentence as if I am asking a question. Listen as I read this page.
- Ask children to follow along as you read the page with expression and attention to punctuation.
- Have children read the page after you. Encourage them to watch for end marks that tell that the sentence should be read as a question. Continue in the same way with p. 47.

REREAD FOR FLUENCY

Choral Reading

ROUTINE

1. **Select a Passage** For *Ruby in Her Own Time,* use pp. 48–54.
2. **Divide into Groups** Assign each group a part to read. For this story, have each group read a page.
3. **Model** Have children track the print as you read.
4. **Read Together** Have children read along with you.
5. **Independent Readings** Have the groups read aloud without you. Monitor progress and provide feedback. For optimal fluency, children should reread three to four times.

Monitor Progress	Fluency
If... children have difficulty attending to punctuation at the end of lines,	**then...** prompt: • Do you look at the end marks? • How should your voice sound when you read a sentence that ends with a question mark? • Read the sentence as if you are asking a friend a question.
If... the class cannot read fluently without you,	**then...** continue to have them read along with you.

Vocabulary

SYNONYMS

DISCUSS SYNONYMS Have children recall that Mother duck sat on her eggs in the wind and the rain. Write the following phrases on the board and tell children that both phrases mean nearly the same thing. Have them discuss which phrase better helps them understand how bad the wind and rain were. Explain that when words have nearly the same meaning, they are called synonyms. Authors often use synonyms to make their stories more interesting.

through strong wind and hard rain

through howling wind and driving rain

EXPAND SELECTION VOCABULARY Discuss with children the meaning of each word listed below. Then have children look at the suggested page in *Ruby in Her Own Time* to find a synonym for the word. Have them give a sentence using the synonym.

soft wind (p. 45)	wind that blows gently	breeze
valuable (p. 47)	something that is worth a lot	precious
wide (p. 53)	large from side to side	broad
flew (p. 57)	moved through the air	soared

OBJECTIVES

- Discuss meanings of synonyms.
- Use synonyms in sentences.

Strategic Intervention

Give children a word, such as *good*, *pretty*, or *big* and have them work together to list synonyms they might use to make their own writing more interesting.

Advanced

Have children write a sentence about their classroom. Then have them use a dictionary or a thesaurus to find synonyms for words in the sentence and use them to write a new sentence.

Extend Language Help children understand that often more than one English word can have the same meaning. Discuss any words they know in their home language that have the same meaning.

Writing Trait of the Week

INTRODUCE Organization/Paragraphs

TALK ABOUT ORGANIZATION/PARAGRAPHS Explain to children that good writers organize the ideas in their writing. They put their ideas in an order that makes sense. Ask children to think about how the author organizes his ideas in *Ruby in Her Own Time.* Then model your thinking.

MODEL When I look back at the selection, I see that the author tells what happens first, second, third, and so on. This is one way writers organize their ideas. I'll write what happens in the selection.

On the board, write selection events out of order, as shown below. Read the events aloud to children.

The eggs begin to hatch. *(2)*
Mother Duck sits on the nest. *(1)*
All the young ducks fly away. *(3)*

Did I write the selection events in the right order? Does this order of the events make sense? Why or why not?

Make sure children understand that Mother Duck must sit on the nest before eggs hatch and that eggs must hatch before the young ducks grow and fly away. Ask a volunteer to write the events in the correct order. Read aloud the sentences in the new order.

STRATEGY FOR DEVELOPING ORGANIZATION/PARAGRAPHS On the board, write sentences out of order, such as those below. Work with children to rewrite the sentences in an order that makes sense.

Little ducklings hatch from the eggs. *(3)*
The mother duck lays eggs in the nest. *(2)*
Two ducks build a nest by a lake. *(1)*

PRACTICE

APPLY THE STRATEGY

- Ask children to name things they do at certain times each school day. Offer an example or two: *We eat lunch. We go to recess.* Write children's responses in no particular order in a list on the board.
- Have children write four of the actions in the order they happen. Then have them number the events and give their list a title.

OBJECTIVE

- Recognize and use organization in writing.

DAILY FIX-IT

5. I have a pinc piggy bank
I have a pink piggy bank.

6. are you shure you want to bring that?
Are you sure you want to bring that?

Connect to Unit Writing

Writing Trait

Have children use strategies for developing **organization/paragraphs** when they write a description in the Unit Writing Workshop, pp. WA2–WA9.

Organization/Paragraphs Explain that items in a list can be written with numbers to show the order. Write events that occur every year, such as holidays, on index cards, one event on each card. Help language learners first put the events in the correct order and then write the events on the board in a numbered list.

Grammar

APPLY TO WRITING Verbs

IMPROVE WRITING WITH VERBS Have children recall that a verb can tell what one person, animal, or thing does. Remind them to add an *-s* to show what is being done now. Write *She kick.* For this sentence to sound right, I need to add -s to the action word. Add the letter *-s* and then read the completed sentence *She kicks.* Remind children to use verbs in their own writing. Write the following action verbs, and have children complete the sentence stems.

She ________.		He ________.	
sing	pick	smile	run
dance	swim	walk	shop

PRACTICE

WRITE SENTENCES Call on individuals to supply more action verbs to be added to the list. Select a verb, add *-s* and write a sentence using that verb. Read the sentence with the class.

OBJECTIVE

- Use verbs in writing.

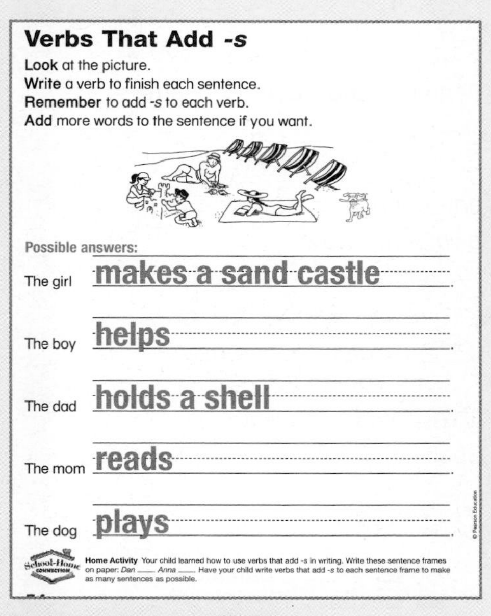

Verbs That Add -s

Look at the picture.
Write a verb to finish each sentence.
Remember to add -s to each verb.
Add more words to the sentence if you want.

Possible answers:

The girl makes a sand castle

The boy helps

The dad holds a shell

The mom reads

The dog plays

Home Activity Your child learned how to use verbs that add -s in writing. Write these sentence frames on paper: Dan ____. Anna ____. Have your child write verbs that add -s to each sentence frame to make as many sentences as possible.

▲ **Grammar and Writing Practice Book** p. 54

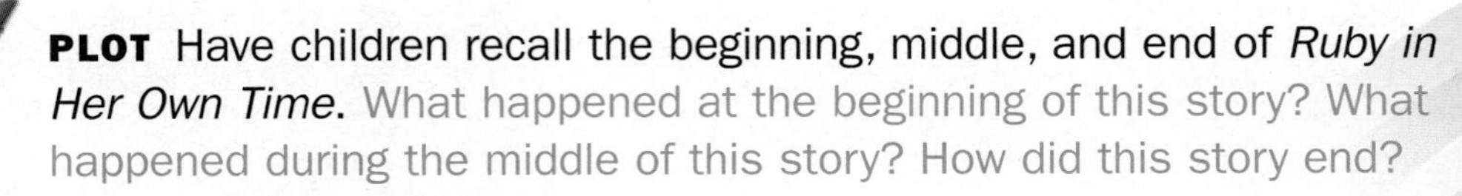

PLOT Have children recall the beginning, middle, and end of *Ruby in Her Own Time.* What happened at the beginning of this story? What happened during the middle of this story? How did this story end?

SUMMARIZE Have children summarize *Ruby in Her Own Time.* Retell the events of the story in the correct sequence. Encourage children to include answers to *who what,* and *where* questions in their summary.

LET'S TALK ABOUT IT Display the three-column chart "Skill," "Can Do," "Can't Do" from Day 1. Recall the events of *Ruby in Her Own Time.* Discuss the activities Ruby did after her brothers and sisters. (hatched, learned to eat, swim) Encourage children to add skills to the chart.

PREVIEW Day 4

Tell children that tomorrow they will listen to a story about a special duckling. The duckling grows and changes and feels lonely.

Day 4

AT A GLANCE

Share Literature
"The Ugly Duckling"

Phonemic Awareness
Segment and Count Phonemes

High-Frequency Words
any, enough, ever, every, own, sure, were 

Phonics and Spelling
 Vowel Sounds of *y*
Long Vowels (CV)
REVIEW Word Reading
Spelling: Words with *ng, nk*

Read
Group Time < Differentiated Instruction
"I'm Growing"

Fluency
Attend to Punctuation

Writing Across the Curriculum
Time Line

Grammar
Verbs that Add *-s*

Materials

- *Sing with Me Big Book*
- Read Aloud Anthology
- Tested Word Cards
- Student Edition 64–65

Morning Warm-Up!

Today we will read about things we learn to do as we get bigger. What is something you could not do when you were little? What do you want to do when you are a grown-up?

QUESTION OF THE DAY Encourage children to sing "On Our Own Time Line" from the *Sing with Me Big Book* as you gather. Write the message and track the print as you read it. Discuss the questions.

REVIEW COMPOUND WORDS

- Ask children to find a compound word in the message. *(something)*
- Discuss how a compound word is different from a contraction. (A compound word is made of two whole words. In a contraction, some of the letters in one of the words are dropped.)

Extend Language Use the Day 4 instruction on ELL Poster 14 to extend and enrich language.

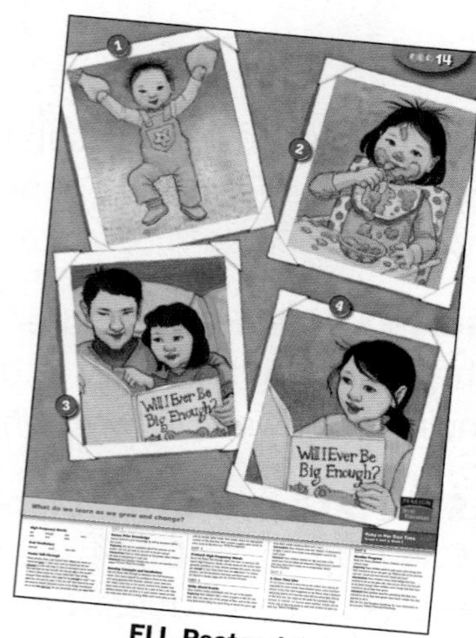

ELL Poster 14

Share Literature

CONNECT CONCEPTS

ACTIVATE PRIOR KNOWLEDGE Help children recall that Ruby was not like her brothers and sisters because she did things in her own time, but her family loved her anyway. Explain that you will read a story about another duck that is different from its brothers and sisters—"The Ugly Duckling."

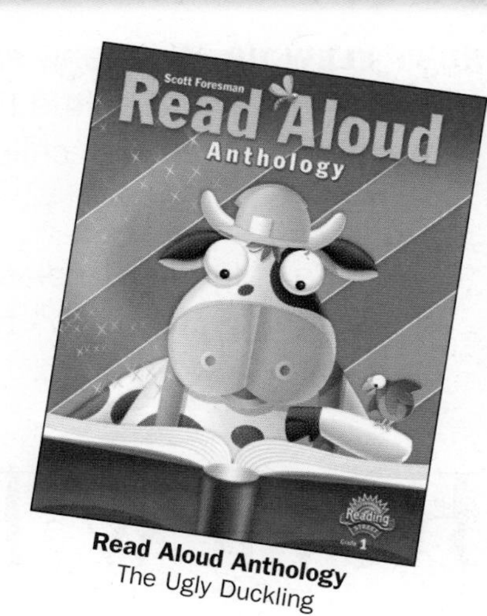

Read Aloud Anthology
The Ugly Duckling

BUILD ORAL VOCABULARY Read the first five paragraphs. Ask what was different about the new duckling. (It had a big head and big feet, its neck was long and silly looking.) This duckling was not like the mother's other, **lovely** ducklings. She thinks his long neck makes him look **awkward**, or clumsy. Ask children to listen to find out how his brothers and sisters treat the duckling that is different.

REVIEW ORAL VOCABULARY After reading, review all the Amazing Words for the week. Have children take turns using them in sentences that tell about the concept for the week. Then talk about the Amazing Words they learned in other weeks and connect them to the concept as well. For example, ask:

- Are babies **industrious** as they grow? Why or why not?
- How old were you when you learned that **medicine** can sometimes help you get **healthy**?
- Does each **individual** member of our class learn in the same way? Explain.

Phonemic Awareness

SEGMENT AND COUNT PHONEMES

- We just read a story about a duckling. When the duckling hatched from the big egg, he looked silly.
- Listen to the word *silly*. How many sounds are in *silly?* Model by saying the sounds as you count them on your fingers: /s/ /i/ /l/ /ē/, 4.
- Have children say the sounds as they count them on their fingers. (/s/ /i/ /l/ /ē/, 4)

Continue the activity with these examples.

me (2) **sandy** (5) **try** (3) **no** (2) **why** (2) **sloppy** (5)

OBJECTIVES

- Set purpose for listening.
- Build oral vocabulary.
- Segment and count phonemes.

attempt
event
time line
famous
flatter
correct
awkward
lovely

MONITOR PROGRESS

If... children lack oral vocabulary experiences about the concept Growing and Changing,

then... use the Oral Vocabulary Routine. See p. DI•4 to teach *awkward* and *lovely.*

ELL

Connect Concepts To show their understanding of how the duckling's feelings change, model first and then have children use facial expressions to show how the duckling feels throughout the story. Help children describe the feelings: The duckling feels sad. The duckling feels lonely. The duckling feels happy.

OBJECTIVES

- Recognize high-frequency words.
- Review vowel sounds of *y* and long vowels CV.
- Apply decoding strategies: blend, preview words.

Write a word from the box to match each picture.
Circle the word if it ends like **baby**.
Underline the word if it ends like **cry**.

bunny city fly
fry puppy silly

The baby will cry.

1. city 2. puppy 3. bunny
4. fly 5. silly 6. fry

Draw a picture of each word.

7. candy — Children's artwork should show candy.
8. sky — Children's artwork should show the sky.

School + Home: Home Activity Your child reviewed reading and writing words with the vowel sounds of *y* heard in *baby* or *cry*. Have your child list words that rhyme with *my*. Then list words that rhyme with *berry*.

▲ **Practice Book 1.2** p. 18, Vowel Sounds of *y*

Pick a word from the box to finish each sentence.
Write it on the line.
Remember to begin a sentence with a capital letter.

be go hi she so

me

1. She is five.
2. She will be six one day.
3. She will go into a tent.
4. That man is so funny.
5. He said hi to me.

School + Home: Home Activity Your child reviewed reading words with the long vowel pattern heard in *me*, *hi*, and *go*. Read one of the words from the box and have your child use it in a new sentence.

▲ **Practice Book 1.2** p. 19, Long Vowels (CV)

High-Frequency Words

PRACTICE

RUBY FLEW UP Write *any, enough, ever, every, own, sure,* and *were* on the board, writing each word a little higher than the other, but with the last word being in reach of children. Tell children they can pretend to be Ruby as she flew above the trees.

Call on a volunteer to place a finger on the first word, read it and use the word in a sentence, then "fly" to the next word. Continue having other children "fly" from word to word.

Review Phonics

REVIEW VOWEL SOUNDS OF *y* AND LONG VOWELS

READ WORDS WITH THE VOWEL SOUNDS OF *y* Write *fly.* Look at this word. You can read this word because you know that when *y* is at the end of a word, it stands for either /ī/ or /ē/. What sound does this *y* stand for? (/ī/) What's the word? *(fly)* Write *fluffy.* How many syllables does this word have? (two) What sound does this *y* stand for? (/ē/). What's the word? *(fluffy)*

READ WORDS WITH LONG VOWELS CV Write *go.* You can read this word because you know that when a word or syllable ends with one vowel, the vowel is usually long. What sound does *o* stand for in this word? (/ō/) What's the word? *(go)*

SORT WORDS Write *One Syllable* and *Two Syllables* as headings. When I say a word, hold one hand up if it has one syllable or two hands if it has two syllables: *by, smelly, cry, me, candy, sloppy, hi, fussy, silly, no.* Write each word in the appropriate column. Have children identify words with *y* as a vowel and identify the sound of *y.* Have them identify the words that end with a vowel. Have the lists read.

One Syllable	Two Syllables
by	smelly
cry	candy
me	sloppy
hi	fussy
no	silly

WORD READING

READ DECODABLE AND HIGH-FREQUENCY WORDS Write these words. Encourage children to preview each word before reading it.

always	**day**	**food**	**everything**	**me**
stays	**my**	**by**	**grow**	**nothing**
around	**Jimmy**	**become**	**horse**	**go**
happy	**try**	**we**	**stall**	**sky**

Monitor Progress	Word Reading
If... children have difficulty previewing and reading whole words,	**then...** have them use sound-by-sound blending.
If... children can't read the words fluently at a rate of one to two seconds per word,	**then...** have pairs practice the list.

READ WORDS IN CONTEXT Write these sentences. Call on individuals to read a sentence. Then randomly point to the review words and have them read. To help you monitor word reading, high-frequency words are underlined and decodable words are circled.

My happy horse always has food around his stall.

Everything will grow day by day and become big.

Jimmy stays with me, and we try to make things.

Nothing can go up in the sky now.

Monitor Progress	Word Reading
If... children are unable to read an underlined word,	**then...** read the word for them and spell it, having them echo you.
If... children have difficulty reading a circled word,	**then...** have them use sound-by-sound blending.

Spiral REVIEW

- Reviews high-frequency words *always, around, become, day, everything, food, grow, horse, nothing, stays.*
- Reviews vowel sounds of *y*, long vowels (CV), and initial consonant blends.

Support Phonics For additional review, see the phonics activities in the ELL and Transition Handbook.

Spelling

PARTNER REVIEW Final *ng, nk*

READ AND WRITE Supply pairs of children with index cards on which the spelling words have been written. Have one child read a word while the other writes it. Then have children switch roles. Have them use the cards to check their spelling.

HOMEWORK Spelling Practice Book, p. 56

OBJECTIVE

- Spell words with *-ng* and *-nk.*

Spelling Words

Words with *ng* and *nk*

1. **bring**
2. **trunk**
3. **pink**
4. **bank**
5. **sang**
6. **wing***
7. **rink**
8. **blank**
9. **rang**
10. **sunk**

High-Frequency Words

11. **every***
12. **sure***

* **Words from the Selection**

Words with *ng* and *nk*

Unscramble the letters to make a list word. **Write** the word.

		Spelling Words
1. k i n p	1. pink	bring
2. r n g a	2. rang	trunk
3. g n i w	3. wing	pink
4. n r i k	4. rink	bank
5. r t n k u	5. trunk	sang
		wing
		rink
		blank
		rang
		sunk

Write three list words that begin like (ball).

6. bring 7. bank 8. blank

Write two list words that begin like (sun).

9. sang 10. sunk

School + Home **Home Activity** Your child has been learning to spell words with *ng* or *nk.* Have your child spell a list word and use it in a sentence.

▲ **Spelling Practice Book** p. 56

Group Time

On-Level

Read "I'm Growing."

- Use pp. 64–65.

Strategic Intervention

Read SI Decodable Reader 13.

- Read or listen to "I'm Growing."
- Use the **Routine** on p. DI·32.

Advanced

Read "I'm Growing."

- Use the **Routine** on p. DI·33.

ELL Place English language learners in the groups that correspond to their reading abilities in English.

i Independent Activities

Fluency Reading Pair children to reread *Ruby in Her Own Time.*

Journal Writing Write a name that Ruby might choose for her baby and why. Share writing.

Independent Reading See p. 36j for Reading/Library activities and suggestions.

Literacy Centers To provide listening opportunities, you may use the Listening Center on p. 36j. To extend social studies concepts, you may use the Social Studies Center on p. 36k.

Practice Book 1.2 Vowel Sounds of *y*, p. 18 Long Vowels (CV), p. 19

Break into small groups after Spelling and before Fluency.

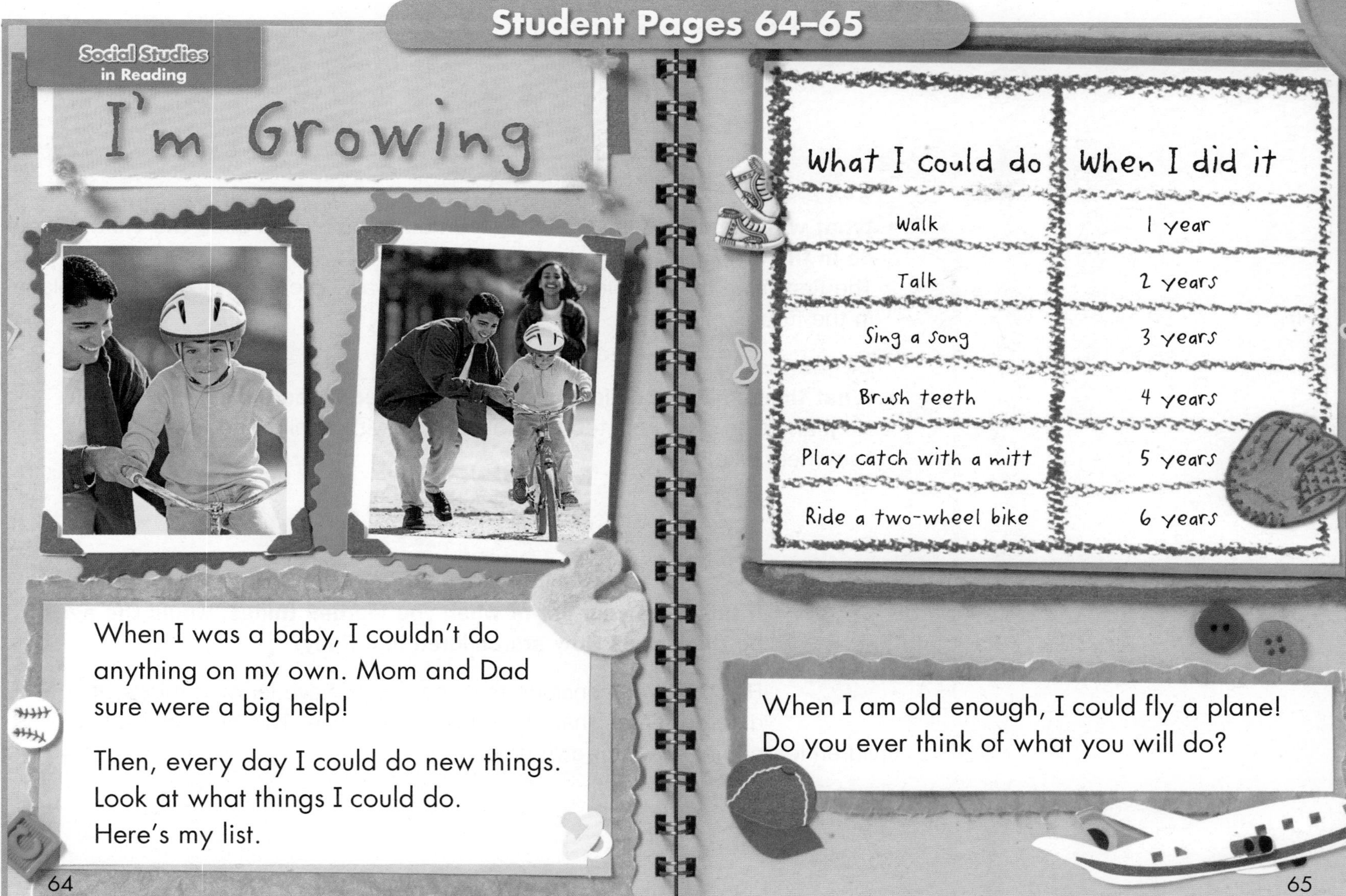

Read

Social Studies in Reading

PREVIEW AND PREDICT Have children look at the page and tell what kind of book this page looks like. (a scrap book or a photo album) Read the title and have children tell who is probably the narrator, or the person who says, "I'm growing." Have children read to learn about the things the child has learned to do.

INFORMATIONAL TEXT Review that selections about real people doing real things are called nonfiction. Point out that the photographs and the text in this article give information about a real family.

VOCABULARY/SYNONYMS Review synonyms. Ask children to reread the first paragraph on p. 64. Then ask which word in that paragraph means the same as *infant*. (baby) Ask children to tell synonyms for *talk*. (speak, tell)

AudioText

OBJECTIVE

- Recognize text structure: nonfiction.

Time for SOCIAL STUDIES

Time Lines

A time line is a chart that shows the order in which things happen. What does the chart on p. 65 show about the boy in the photos? (It shows what he learned to do and when he learned to do it.) What might you list on a time line about your week at school?

BUILD CONCEPTS

Sequence • Literal

- **What was the first thing the child learned to do? What does the child plan to do in the future?**
  The first thing the child learned was how to walk. The child plans to fly a plane in the future.

Sequence • Literal

- **What things did the child learn after he turned 3 years old?**
  He learned to brush his teeth, to play catch with a mitt, and to ride a two-wheel bike.

CONNECT TEXT TO TEXT

READING ACROSS TEXTS

If this were your list of when you learned things, would the ages be the same? How are children like Ruby?

Help children conclude that they might have learned things at different times than the child on the page. This child and other children learn things in their own time.

Activate Prior Knowledge Ask: How old were you when you learned to talk? In languages other than English, age is often expressed as the number of years a person has. Have children practice asking "How old are you?" and answering the question.

Fluency

ATTEND TO PUNCTUATION

MODEL READING WITH ATTENTION TO PUNCTUATION Use *Ruby in Her Own Time.*

- Have children turn to p. 49. Listen while I read these pages. I want to sound like the characters are speaking to each other. I will watch the end punctuation marks so I know how to use my voice with each sentence. When I see a question mark, I know my voice goes up at the end of the sentence.
- Ask children to follow along as you read the page with expression and attention to punctuation.
- Have children read the page after you. Encourage them to pay attention to the marks at the ends of the sentences. Continue in the same way with pp. 50–51.

REREAD FOR FLUENCY

Choral Reading

ROUTINE

1. **Select a Passage** For *Ruby in Her Own Time* use pp. 52–57.
2. **Divide into Groups** Assign each group a part to read. For this story, assign a page to each of four groups.
3. **Model** Have children track the print as you read.
4. **Read Together** Have children read along with you.
5. **Independent Readings** Have the groups read aloud without you. Monitor progress and provide feedback. For optimal fluency, children should reread three to four times.

Monitor Progress — Check Fluency WCPM

As children reread, monitor their progress toward their individual fluency goals. Current Goal: 20–30 words correct per minute. End-of-Year Goal: 60 words correct per minute.

If... children cannot read fluently at a rate of 20–30 words per minute,
then... make sure children practice with text at their independent level. Provide additional fluency practice, pairing nonfluent readers with fluent readers.

If... children already read at 60 words per minute,
then... they do not need to reread three to four times.

SUCCESS PREDICTOR

Day 1 Check Word Reading	Day 2 Check Word Reading	Day 3 Check High-Frequency Words/Retelling	▶ **Day 4 Check Fluency**	Day 5 Assess Progress

OBJECTIVE
- Read aloud fluently, attending to question marks.

Options for Oral Reading

Use *Ruby in Her Own Time* or one of the following Leveled Readers.

On-Level
Not Just Any Boy

Strategic Intervention
Can Hank Sing?

Advanced
A Bed for Paul

Ana and Her Bike or *Ruby in Her Own Time.* Read interesting sentences aloud to English language learners frequently, adding think-aloud comments to explain how cues such as letter patterns in words, phrases or other "chunks" of words, and punctuation can help you understand and read fluently.

Words Correct Per Minute
SUCCESS PREDICTOR

OBJECTIVE

- Create a time line.

Advanced

Encourage children to make a time line of family events. Share time lines with the class.

Support Writing Create a web of words that describe school events. Have children use these words to discuss class activities and label the events on the time line.

Writing Across the Curriculum

WRITE Time Line

BRAINSTORM Have children look at pp. 36–37 of the Student Edition and name the dates shown on this time line. Encourage them to use oral vocabulary, such as *time line* and *event.*

SHARE THE PEN Have children participate in creating a time line. To begin, draw a simple time line. Explain that the class will work together to write events for the time line. Remind children that a time line is a way to show a sequence of events. Call on an individual to name an activity the class did at the very beginning of the school year. Write this event on the far left side of the time line. Have volunteers help spell the event by writing familiar letter-sounds. Ask questions, such as the following:

- What is the first sound you hear in the word *first?* (/f/)
- What letter stands for that sound? *(f)* Have a volunteer write *f.*
- What is the last sound you hear in the word *first?* (/t/)
- What letter stands for that sound? *(t)* Have a volunteer write *t.*

Continue having individuals contribute to writing events. Frequently reread the events.

Events Time Line

Grammar

REVIEW Verbs That Add -*s*

DEFINE VERBS THAT ADD -*s*

- What tells what someone or something does? (a verb)
- When do I add an -*s* to a verb? (if one person is doing the action and is doing it now)

PRACTICE

ADD -*s* TO VERBS Have children write these words on a piece of paper. Ask them to add an -*s* to the end of each verb to let people know that one person is doing the action and it is happening now.

play	**listen**	**think**
kick	**read**	**jump**

OBJECTIVE

- Identify verbs that add -*s*.

DAILY FIX-IT

7. Are you sur the phone rangg?
   Are you sure the phone rang?
8. Take this chek to the banc.
   Take this check to the bank.

Verbs That Add -*s*

Mark the sentence that is correct.

1. ⊗ Amy plays a song.
   ○ Amys plays a song.
   ○ Amy plays a songs.
2. ○ Johns writes his name.
   ⊗ John writes his name.
   ○ John writes hiss name.
3. ○ Rosa makes one big pizzas.
   ○ Rosa makes one bigs pizza.
   ⊗ Rosa makes one big pizza.
4. ○ Daves runs a long race.
   ⊗ Dave runs a long race.
   ○ Dave runs a longs race.
5. ⊗ Kate learns a new game.
   ○ Kates learns a new game.
   ○ Kate learns a new games.
6. ○ Sam spells a hards word.
   ○ Sam spells a hard words.
   ⊗ Sam spells a hard word.

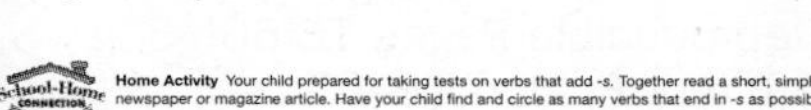

Home Activity Your child prepared for taking tests on verbs that add -*s*. Together read a short, simple newspaper or magazine article. Have your child find and circle as many verbs that end in -*s* as possible.

▲ **Grammar and Writing Practice Book** p. 55

Wrap Up Your Day!

FLUENCY Write *What can you do that's new?* Point out the question mark. What does my voice do when I come to a question mark? (It rises.) Call on individuals to read the sentence.

LET'S TALK ABOUT IT Display the three-column chart for Skill, Can Do, Can't Do. Recall *I'm Growing.* Discuss the activities listed on the chart in the story. Encourage children to add any of these skills to the chart they created on Day 1.

PREVIEW Day 5

Remind children that they heard a story about a lonely and awkward duckling. Tell them that tomorrow they will hear more about this ugly duckling.

Day 5
AT A GLANCE

Share Literature
"The Ugly Duckling"

Phonics and Spelling
Review Final *ng, nk*, and Compound Words

High-Frequency Words
any enough ever every own sure were Word Wall

Monitor Progress
Spelling Test: Words with *ng, nk*

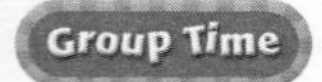

< Differentiated Assessment

Writing and Grammar
Trait: Organization/Paragraphs
Verbs that Add *-s*

Materials
- *Sing with Me Big Book*
- Read Aloud Anthology
- Reproducible Pages TE 66f–66g
- Student Edition 66–67

Morning Warm-Up!

This week we read about how everyone learns things at different times. What would you say to someone who is learning something new?

REVIEW COMPOUND WORDS

- Have children identify the compound words in the message and tell the two words that make up the compound. *(every, one—everyone; some, one—someone; some, thing—something)*
- Challenge children to use the compound words in sentences of their own.

ELL

Assess Vocabulary Use the Day 5 instruction on ELL Poster 14 to monitor children's progress with oral vocabulary.

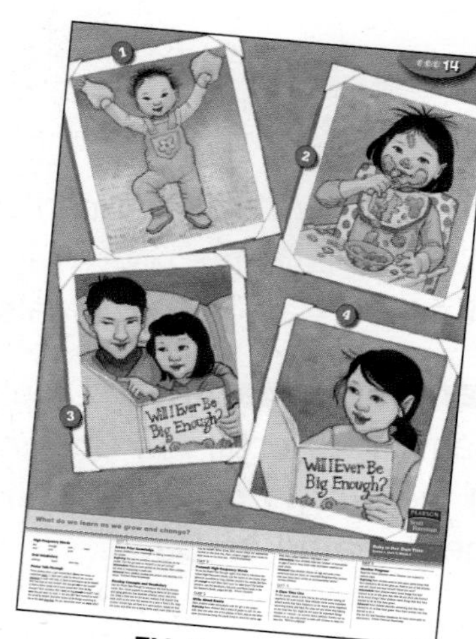

ELL Poster 14

Share Literature

LISTEN AND RESPOND

USE PRIOR KNOWLEDGE Review that yesterday the class listened to find out how the Ugly Duckling was treated by his brothers and sisters. Suggest that today the class listen to find out how the duckling changed as it grew.

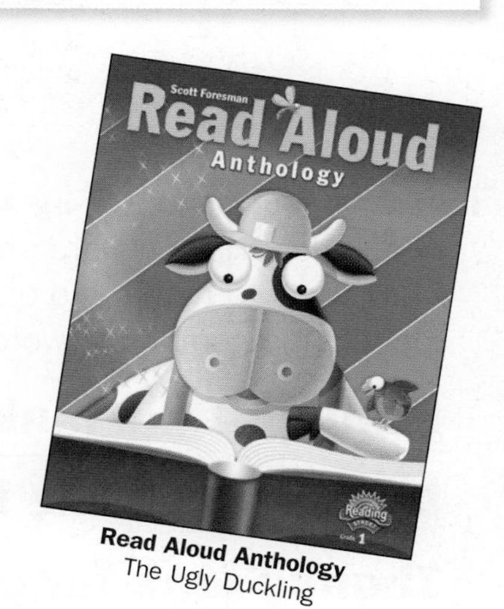

Read Aloud Anthology
The Ugly Duckling

MONITOR LISTENING COMPREHENSION

- How did the duckling change as it grew? (It grew to be a beautiful swan.)
- Why did the duckling run away from the farm? (The children on the farm kept chasing him.)
- Why did the duckling hang its head down when it saw the other swans? (Children may respond that it was ashamed of being ugly and it felt shy.)

BUILD ORAL VOCABULARY

GENERATE DISCUSSION Recall how slowly the Ugly Duckling changes. Invite children to share skills that took them longer than others to master. Then have them share skills that took a shorter time to master. Have children use some of this week's Amazing Words as they describe the pace of their time lines.

Monitor Progress | **Check Oral Vocabulary**

Display pp. 36–37 in the Student Edition and remind children of the concept for this week—Growing and Changing. Ask them to tell you about the photographs using some of this week's Amazing Words: *attempt, event, time line, famous, flatter, correct, awkward,* and *lovely.*

If... children have difficulty using the Amazing Words,

then... ask questions about the photographs using the Amazing Words. Note which questions children can respond to. Reteach unknown words using the Oral Vocabulary Routine.

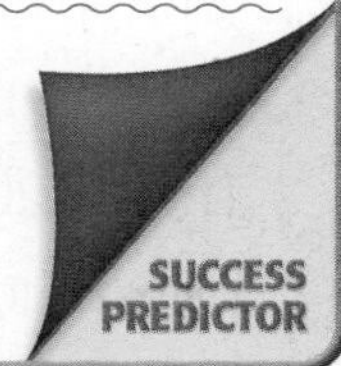

Day 1 Check Word Reading	Day 2 Check Word Reading	Day 3 Check High-Frequency Words/Retelling	Day 4 Check Fluency	▶ **Day 5 Check Oral Vocabulary/ Assess Progress**

OBJECTIVES

- Set purpose for listening.
- Build oral vocabulary.

attempt	**flatter**
event	**correct**
time line	**awkward**
famous	**lovely**

ELL

Extend Language Explain that some English words can have nearly the same meanings. Challenge children to think of words in their home language that have nearly the same meaning, such as words for *big* or *small.*

Oral Vocabulary
SUCCESS PREDICTOR

OBJECTIVES

- Review final *-ng*, *-nk* and compound words.
- Review high-frequency words.

Final *ng*, *nk* and Compound Words

REVIEW

IDENTIFY WORDS WITH *-ng* AND *-nk* AND COMPOUND WORDS Write these sentences. Have children read each one aloud as you track the print. Call on individuals to name and underline the words with /ng/ and /ngk/ and to identify the compound words.

Hank put the junk outside on the driveway.

Do you think the king can sing?

Thank Frank for bringing the homemade cupcakes.

Mom put on pink lipstick.

High-Frequency Words

REVIEW

SAY AND SPELL WORDS Read the rhymes. Ask children to use the letter clues to complete each line with one of the review words from p. 38. Have children say, spell, and locate the word on the Word Wall. Then reread the complete rhymes. Word Wall

A _ y ducky can swim. (any)
E _ _ _ y ducky can fly. (every)
But ducks never, e _ _r eat _ _ ough, (ever, enough)
No matter how they try!
When Ruby came back,
Her o _ n parents w _ re there. (own, were)
Then Ruby was _ ure, (sure)
How much they really did care!

Vocabulary For additional practice with the high-frequency words, use the vocabulary strategies and word cards in the ELL Teaching Guide, pp. 94–95.

SPELLING TEST Final *ng, nk*

DICTATION S ENTENCES Use these sentences to assess this week's spelling words.

1. Fill the blank sheet of paper.
2. The stone sunk in the lake.
3. Look out at the wing of the plane.
4. I have a pink backpack.
5. Bring the cat inside.
6. We'll go to the ice rink on the weekend.
7. Shut the lid of the trunk.
8. The bells rang.
9. Go to the bank with your check.
10. We sang at the baseball game.

HIGH-FREQUENCY WORDS

11. Every man at the desk had a laptop.
12. Are you sure you can sing?

ASSESS

- Spell words with *-ng* and *-nk.*

Spelling Words

Words with *ng* and *nk*

1.	**bring**	6.	**wing***
2.	**trunk**	7.	**rink**
3.	**pink**	8.	**blank**
4.	**bank**	9.	**rang**
5.	**sang**	10.	**sunk**

High-Frequency Words

11. **every*** 12. **sure***

* **Words from the Selection**

Group Time

On-Level

Read Set B Sentences.

- Use pp. 66e–66g.

Strategic Intervention

Read Set A Sentences and the Story.

- Use pp. 66e–66g.
- Use the **Routine** on p. DI·34.

Advanced

Read Set C Sentences.

- Use pp. 66e–66g.
- Use the **Routine** on p. DI·35.

DAY 5

ELL Place English language learners in the groups that correspond to their reading abilities in English.

Independent Activities

Fluency Reading Children reread selections at their independent level.

Journal Writing Write about a change you noticed. Share writing.

Independent Reading See p. 36j for Reading/ Library activities and suggestions.

Literacy Centers You may use the Technology Center on p. 36k to support this week's concepts and reading.

Practice Book 1.2 Glossary, p. 20

Break into small groups after Spelling and before Grammar and Writing.

ASSESS

- Decode final *ng, nk* and compound words.
- Read high-frequency words.
- Read aloud with appropriate speed and accuracy.
- Recognize story plot.
- Retell a story.

Differentiated Assessment

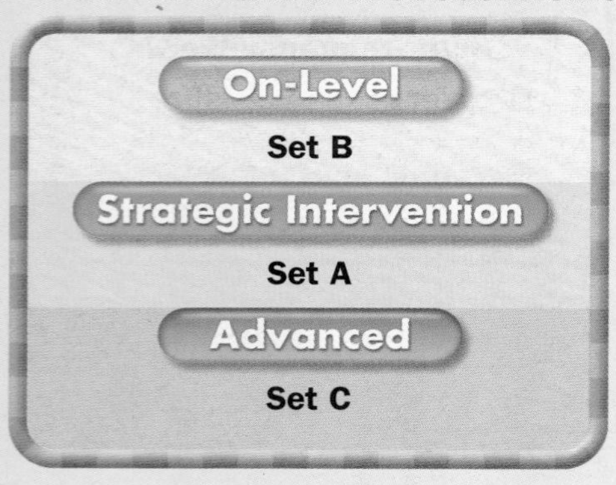

Fluency Assessment Plan

☑ Week 1 assess Advanced students.

☑ **This week assess Strategic Intervention students.**

☐ Week 3 assess On-Level students.

☐ Week 4 assess Strategic Intervention students.

☐ Week 5 assess any students you have not yet checked during this unit.

Set individual fluency goals for children to enable them to reach the end-of-year goal.

- Current Goal: 20–30 wcpm
- End-of-Year Goal: 60 wcpm
- ELL Measuring a child's oral reading speed—words per minute—provides a low-stress informal assessment of fluency. Such an assessment should not take the place of more formal measures of words correct per minute.

Monitor Progress

SENTENCE READING

ASSESS FINAL *ng, nk,* COMPOUND WORDS, AND HIGH-FREQUENCY WORDS Use one of the reproducible lists on p. 66f to assess children's ability to read words with final *ng, nk,* compound words, and high-frequency words. Call on individuals to read two sentences aloud. Have each child in the group read different sentences. Start over with sentence one if necessary.

RECORD SCORES Use the Sentence Reading Chart for this unit on p. WA19.

Monitor Progress	Final *ng, nk* and Compound Words
If... children have trouble reading final *ng, nk* and compound words,	**then...** use the Reteach Lessons on pp. DI • 77–DI • 78.
	High-Frequency Words
If... children cannot read a high-frequency word,	**then...** mark the missed words on a high-frequency word list and send the list home for additional word reading practice or have the child practice with a fluent reader.

FLUENCY AND COMPREHENSION

ASSESS FLUENCY Take a one-minute sample of children's oral reading. See Monitoring Fluency, pp. WA17–WA18. Have children read "A Bath for Cupcake," the on-level fluency passage on p. 66g.

RECORD SCORES Record the number of words read correctly in a minute on the child's Fluency Progress Chart.

ASSESS COMPREHENSION Have the child read to the end of the passage. (If the child had difficulty with the passage, you may read it aloud.) Ask questions about the plot of the story and have the child retell the passage. Use the Retelling Rubric on p. 62–63 to evaluate the child's retelling.

Monitor Progress	Fluency
If... a child does not achieve the fluency goal on the timed reading,	**then...** copy the passage and send it home with the child for additional fluency practice or have the child practice with a fluent reader.
	Plot
If... a child cannot recognize the plot of the story,	**then...** use the Reteach Lesson on p. DI • 78.

READ THE SENTENCES

Set A

1. Are there enough pancakes for Hank?
2. Can you bring your own backpack?
3. Make sure every cupcake is pink.
4. Any boy can sing by himself.
5. Did you ever skate at an outside rink?
6. The tunes were sung in the daytime.

Set B

1. We were sure the mailbox was by the bank.
2. Frank made his own treehouse in the big tree.
3. I think I put enough sand in the sandbox.
4. They put a jack inside every car trunk.
5. Did you ever see a beehive hang from a tree?
6. Are there any pinecones by the swing?

Set C

1. Make sure you don't ever yank on the little bulldog's leash.
2. Where were the flags that should have hung on the flagpoles?
3. We sang a song before bedtime every night.
4. Did everyone drink enough milk at dinner tonight?
5. She used her own money to buy a ring for herself.
6. Did you see a skunk near any of the houses this weekend?

A Bath for Cupcake

Last weekend, Frank gave his dog Cupcake a 8
bath. He could not use the bathtub. And the sink in 19
the shed was too small. 24

Frank got an old pink sandbox. It did not have 34
sand inside. Frank put the sandbox outside on the 43
grass. He filled it with water. Then he picked up 53
Cupcake. He put her into the sandbox. Plunk! She 62
flung water all around. Then she yanked herself 70
from Frank's hands and jumped out. 76

How could Frank get Cupcake to stay in the 85
sandbox? He had to think of something. He gave 94
her a bone. If Cupcake had the bone, she did not 105
jump out of the sandbox. So, everything was fine. 114
Cupcake got her bath. 118

See also *Assessment Handbook*, p. 262 • REPRODUCIBLE PAGE

Write Now

Read Together

Writing and Grammar

List

Prompt

In *Ruby in Her Own Time,* a baby duck grows up.
Think about things Ruby does as she grows up.
Now write a list of these things using numbered sentences.

Writing Trait

A list of sentences can show events in **order.**

Student Model

Title tells what list is about. → Things Ruby Does

1. Ruby eats.
2. Ruby swims in the water.
3. Ruby soars in the sky.
4. Ruby comes back.

Details support title.

Numbers show order of items in list.

66

Writer's Checklist

- **Focus** Are all sentences about the topic?
- **Organization** Are sentences written in a list?
- **Support** Does each detail tell about an action?
- **Conventions** Does every sentence begin with a capital letter and end with a period?

Grammar

Verbs That Add -s

A **verb** can tell what one person, animal, or thing does. Add an **-s** to show what is being done now.

Ruby **swims** in the pond.

Ruby is one duck, so we add **-s** to **swim.**

Look at the sentences in the list. Write the verbs. What letter is at the end of each verb? Why is that letter there?

67

Writing and Grammar

LOOK AT THE PROMPT Read p. 66 aloud. Have children select and discuss key words or phrases in the prompt. *(things Ruby does as she grows up, list, using numbered sentences)*

STRATEGIES TO DEVELOP ORDER Have children

- offer a sentence that tells what happens next after you read aloud a pair of sentences such as these: *Omar knocked on the door. Cara opened the door.*
- listen as you read aloud the two sentences on p. 44 and the first sentence on p. 45 in the selection in a scrambled order. Then put the sentences in the right order.
- work together to tell the order of events in a familiar story.

See Scoring Rubric on p. WA11. Rubric 4 3 2 1

HINTS FOR BETTER WRITING Read p. 67 aloud. Use the checklist to help children revise their lists. Discuss the grammar lesson. (Answer: *eats, swims, soars, comes; The letter s is at the end of these verbs because they tell what one animal—Ruby—does.*) Have children use verbs that add -s correctly in their lists.

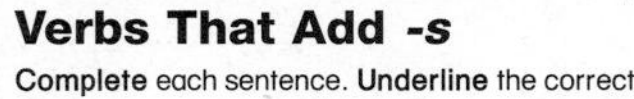

9. I am shure the dogs swims.
(sure; dog)

10. The cat cin jumps.
(can; jump)

Verbs That Add *-s*

Complete each sentence. **Underline** the correct verb.

1. The baby (needs, need) milk.
2. The boy (walk, walks) to school.
3. The man (works, work) at a store.

Add -s to the verb in ( ) to complete each sentence.
Write the verb on the line.

4. The puppy sleeps in the box. (sleep)
5. The dog jumps through a hoop. (jump)
6. Spot picks up the paper. (pick)

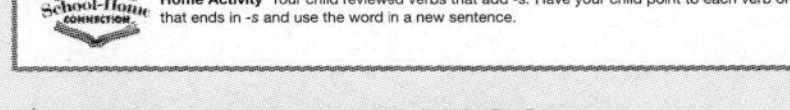
Home Activity Your child reviewed verbs that add -s. Have your child point to each verb on this page that ends in -s and use the word in a new sentence.

▲ **Grammar and Writing Practice Book** p. 56

OBJECTIVES

- Locate words and their meanings in a glossary.
- Identify parts of a glossary entry.

Access Content As you show children how to use a glossary, point out the parts. For example: This is an entry word. The definition tells the meaning of the entry word.

Find these words in the Glossary of your student book.
Draw a picture to show what each word means.

1. feather Children's drawings should illustrate the meaning of the word *feather*.	2. mother Children's drawings should illustrate the meaning of the word *mother*.
3. night Children's drawings should illustrate the meaning of the word *night*.	4. rain Children's drawings should illustrate the meaning of the word *rain*.
5. father Children's drawings should illustrate the meaning of the word *father*.	6. flew Children's drawings should illustrate the meaning of the word *flew*.

School + Home **Home Activity** Your child learned how to use a glossary to look up the meaning of words. Find a glossary in a book at home or at the library and work with your child to look up other words.

▲ **Practice Book 1.2** p. 20

Research/Study Skills

TEACH/MODEL Glossary

MODEL USING A GLOSSARY Have children refer to one of their textbooks (reading, math, science, or social studies). Point out that most textbooks have a section in the back called a glossary which tells the meaning of important words found in the book.

Model how to use a glossary to find a word meaning.

MODEL Sometimes when I read a textbook, I find words that are unfamiliar. If I want to find the meaning, I look in the glossary in the back of the book. I use alphabetical order to find the correct entry word. Next I read the definition and look at the picture if there is one. Now I can figure out what the word means.

FIND WORDS FROM THE SELECTION Have children use the glossary in their reading books to find words from the selection *Ruby in Her Own Time*. Call on individuals to find and tell the meaning of the words *precious* and *beautiful*. Invite others to name words that might be described using these words.

PRACTICE

FIND OTHER WORD MEANINGS Ask children to find the meaning of *breeze* in the glossary. Have them suggest another word that has a similar meaning.

Wrap Up Your Week!

LET'S TALK ABOUT Growing and Changing

QUESTION OF THE WEEK Recall this week's question.

- What do we learn as we grow and change?

Display the What We Can Do/What We Can't Do Chart. Discuss things some children can do and others they have not learned yet. Emphasize that we all learn things in our own time.

Skill	Can	Can't
tie shoes	卌 卌 卌 𝍷𝍷𝍷	卌 𝍷
read a story	卌 卌 卌 卌 𝍷𝍷𝍷𝍷	
jump rope	卌 𝍷𝍷𝍷	卌 卌 卌 𝍷
drive a car		卌 卌 卌 卌 𝍷𝍷𝍷𝍷
fix a snack	卌 卌 卌 卌 𝍷𝍷𝍷𝍷	
ice skate	𝍷𝍷𝍷	卌 卌 卌 卌 𝍷

CONNECT Use questions such as these to prompt a discussion.

- What did you learn on your own time line?
- What did you attempt to do when you were little? What seemed like a special event when you finally learned to do it?
- Is there anything you learned to do after a sibling corrected you?

Build Background Use ELL Poster 15 to support the Preview activity.

You've learned 008 Amazing Words this week!

You've learned 113 Amazing Words so far this year!

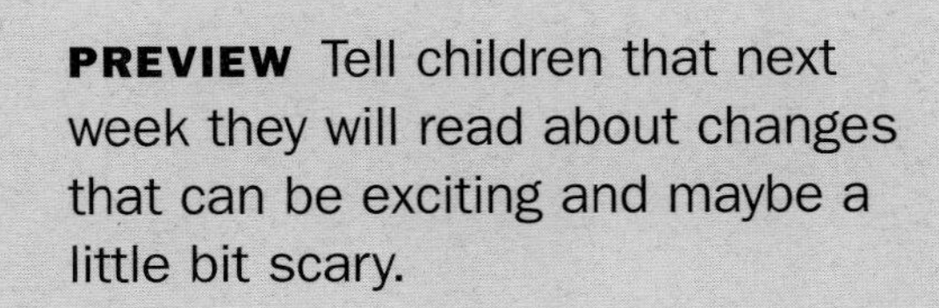

PREVIEW Tell children that next week they will read about changes that can be exciting and maybe a little bit scary.

5

Assessment Checkpoints *for the Week*

Selection Assessment

Use pp. 29–32 of Selection Tests to check:

 **Selection Understanding**

 **Comprehension Skill** *Plot*

 **High-Frequency Words**

any	*own*
enough	*sure*
ever	*were*
every	

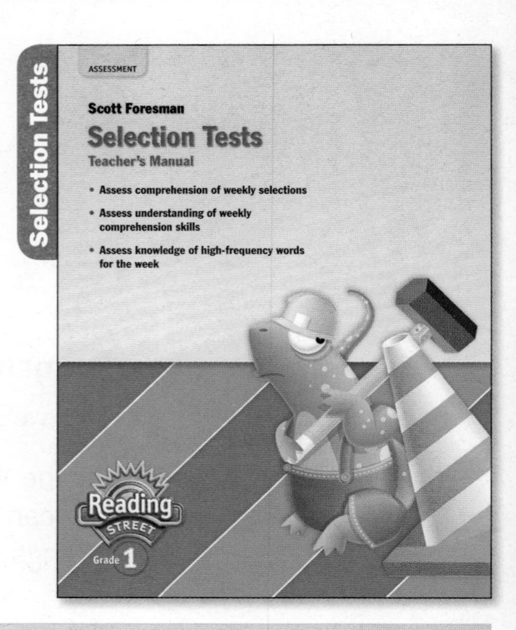

Leveled Assessment

On-Level

Strategic Intervention

Advanced

Use pp. 79–84 of Fresh Reads for Differentiated Test Practice to check:

 **Comprehension Skill** *Plot*

 REVIEW **Comprehension Skill** *Sequence*

 **Fluency** *Words Correct Per Minute*

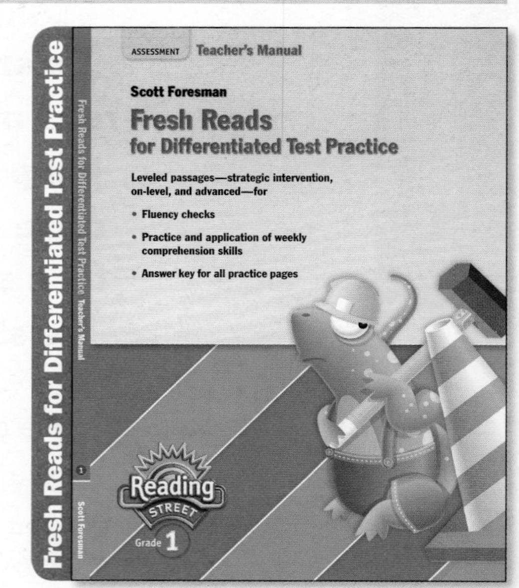

Managing Assessment

Use Assessment Handbook for:

 **Weekly Assessment Blackline Masters for Monitoring Progress**

 **Observation Checklists**

 **Record-Keeping Forms**

 **Portfolio Assessment**

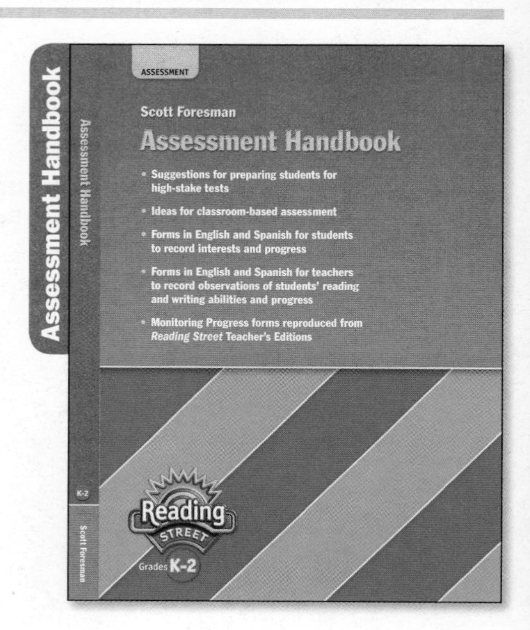

Jan's New Home

Jan's New Home

Unit 3
Changes

CONCEPT QUESTION
What is changing in our world?

Growing and Changing

Week 1
How do we change as we grow?

Week 2
What do we learn as we grow and change?

Week 3
Why are changes exciting?

Changes in Nature

Week 4
What changes happen in a garden?

Week 5
What changes can we observe in nature?

Week 6
How does nature change during the year?

Week 3

EXPAND THE CONCEPT
Why are changes exciting?

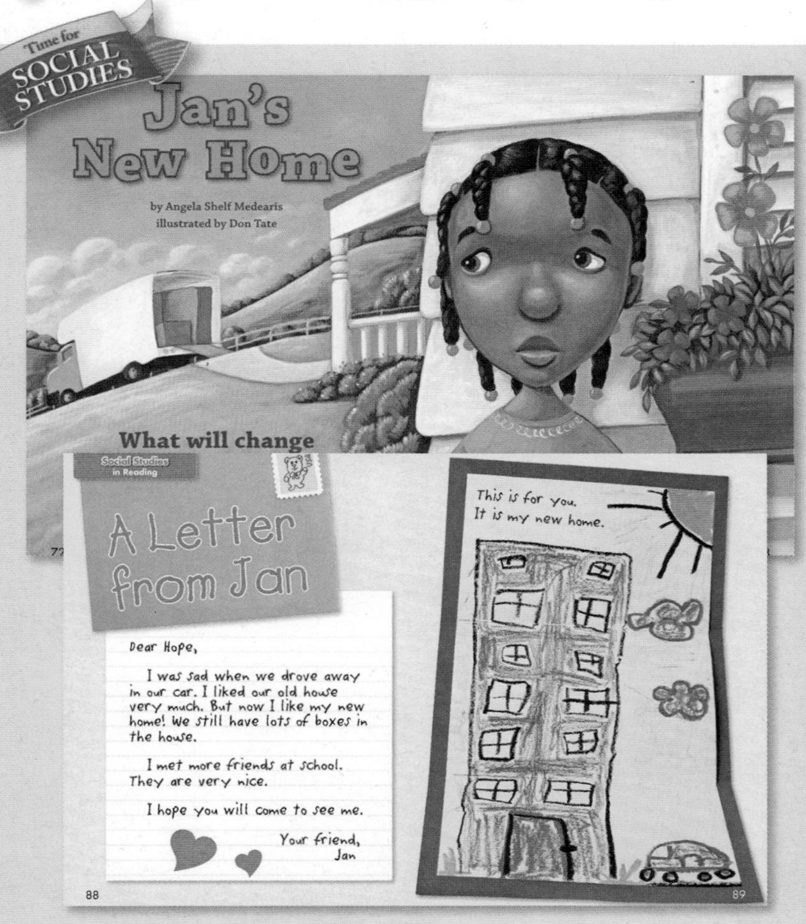

CONNECT THE CONCEPT

▶ **Build Background**

arrive *crumple* *depart* *location* *route* *stampede* *swoop* *tumble*

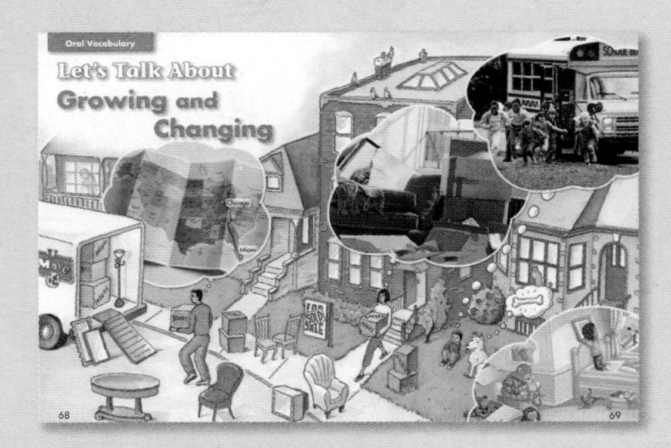

▶ **Social Studies Content**
Geography, Place, Movement

▶ **Writing**
Greeting Card

Preview Your Week

Why are changes exciting?

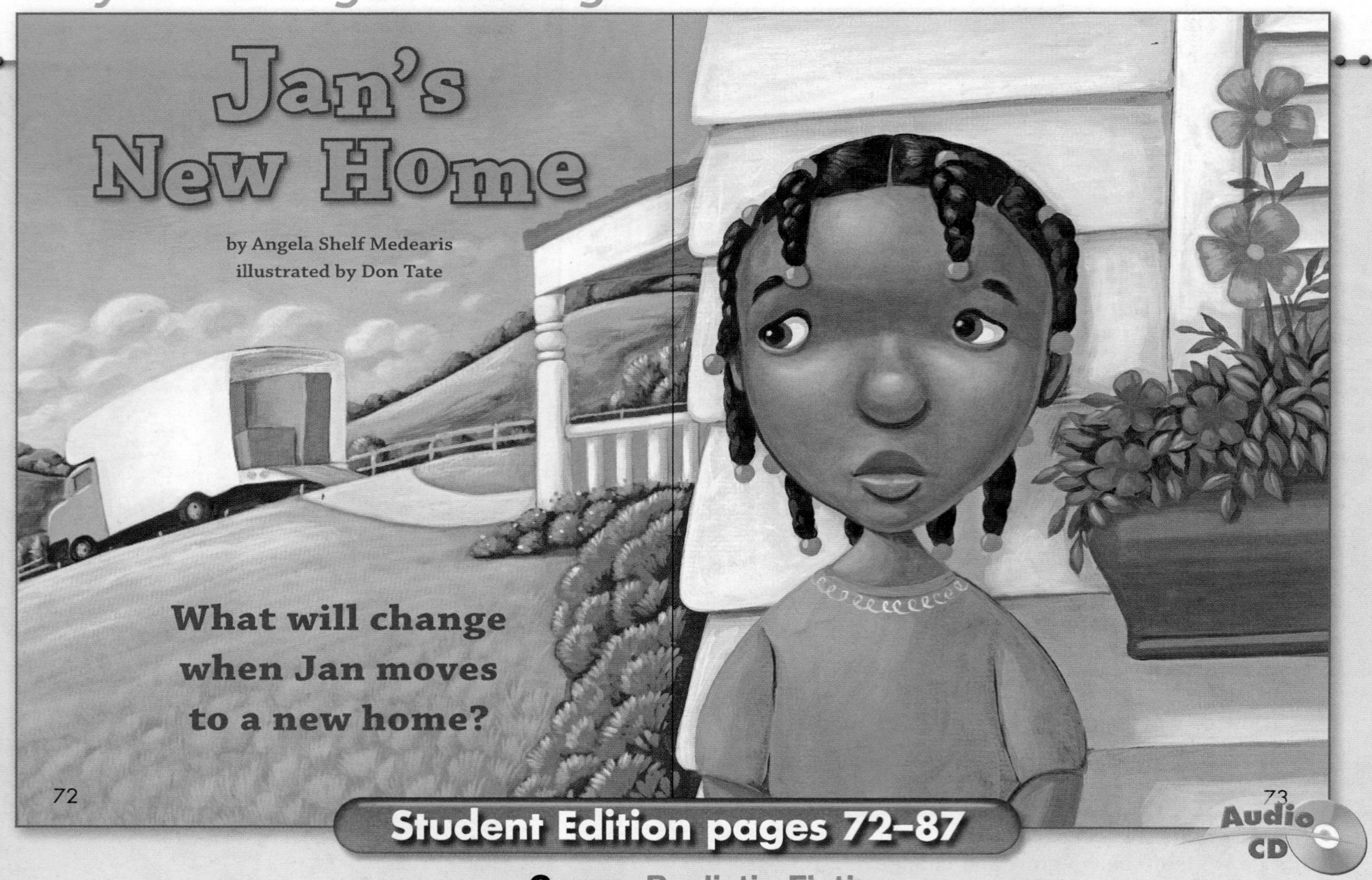

Student Edition pages 72–87

Audio CD

Genre Realistic Fiction

Phonics Ending *-es*, Plural *-es*, and *r*-Controlled *or, ore*

Comprehension Skill Theme

Comprehension Strategy Monitor and Fix Up

Time for SOCIAL STUDIES

Paired Selection

Reading Across Texts
New Places

Genre
Letter

Text Features
Letter Format

Student Edition pages 88–89

Audio CD

- Student Edition
- Leveled Readers
- Decodable Readers

Leveled Readers

Skill Theme

Strategy Monitor and Fix Up

Lesson Vocabulary

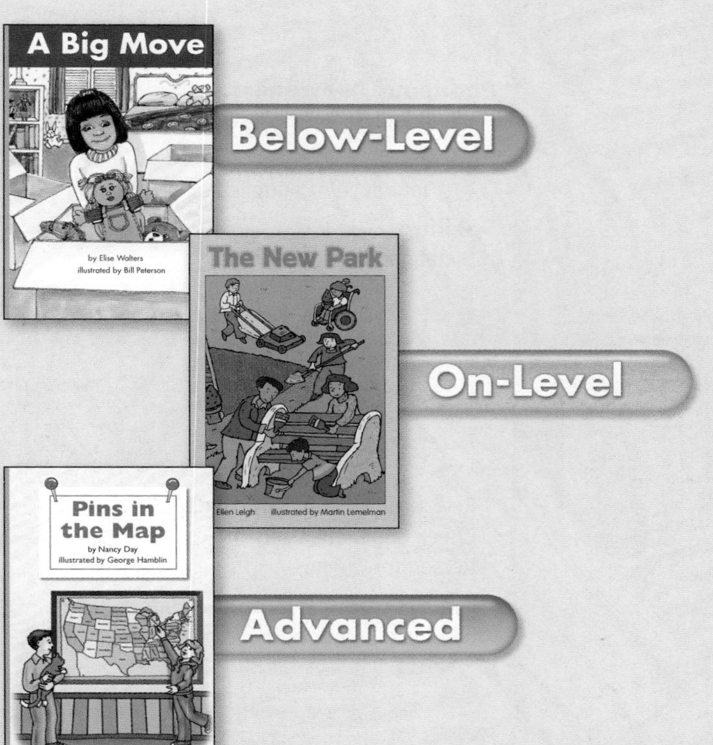

ELL Reader

- Concept Vocabulary
- Text Support
- Language Enrichment

Decodable Readers

Apply Phonics

- *We See Pets*
- *The Family Trip*

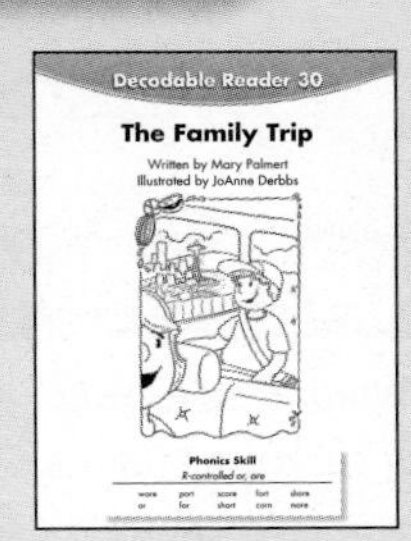

Time for SOCIAL STUDIES

Integrate Social Studies Standards

- Geography
- Place
- Movement

✓ Read

Jan's New Home, pp. 72–87

"A Letter from Jan," pp. 88–89

✓ Read

Below-Level
- Support Concepts

On-Level
- Develop Concepts

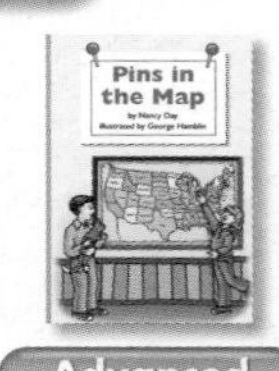

Advanced
- Extend Concepts
- Social Studies Extension Activity

✓ Read

ELL Reader

✓ Build **Concept Vocabulary**
Growing and Changing, pp. 68r–69

✓ Teach **Social Studies Concepts**
Movement, p. 74–75
Places, p. 88–89

✓ Explore **Social Studies Center**
Explore New Places, p. 68k

Weekly Plan

READING

90–120 minutes

TARGET SKILLS OF THE WEEK

- **Phonics**
  Ending -*es*; Plural -*es*; and *r*-Controlled *or, ore*
- **Comprehension Skill**
  Theme
- **Comprehension Strategy**
  Monitor and Fix Up

LANGUAGE ARTS

20–30 minutes

Trait of the Week

Voice

DAY 1 PAGES 68l–69d

Oral Language

QUESTION OF THE WEEK, 68l
Why are changes exciting?

Oral Vocabulary/Share Literature, 68m
Sing with Me Big Book, Song 15
Amazing Words *arrive, depart, location, route*

Word Work

Phonemic Awareness, 68m
Add Phonemes /əz/

Phonics, 68n–68o
Introduce Ending -*es;* Plural -*es* **T**

Spelling, 68p
Pretest

Comprehension/Vocabulary/Fluency

Read Decodable Reader 29

Grouping Options 68f–68g

Review High-Frequency Words
Check Comprehension
Reread for Fluency

Build Background, 68r–69
Growing and Changing

Listening Comprehension, 69a–69b
Theme **T**

Language Arts

Shared Writing, 69c
Greeting Card

Grammar, 69d
Introduce Verbs That Do Not Add -*s* **T**

DAILY JOURNAL WRITING — Day 1 *Write sentences about a place where you would like to live.*

DAILY SOCIAL STUDIES CONNECTIONS — Day 1 Change/Stay the Same T-Chart, 68r–69

DAY 2 PAGES 70a–71c

Oral Language

QUESTION OF THE DAY, 70a
Why do you get excited about going to school?

Oral Vocabulary/Share Literature, 70b
Big Book *Mr. George Baker*
Amazing Words *swoop, tumble*

Word Work

Phonemic Awareness, 70b
Blend and Segment Onset/Rime

Phonics, 70c–70d
Introduce *r*-Controlled *or, ore* **T**

Spelling, 70e
Dictation

Comprehension/Vocabulary/Fluency

Read Decodable Reader 30

Grouping Options 68f–68g

Review High-Frequency Words
Check Comprehension
Reread for Fluency

High-Frequency Words, 70–71
Introduce *away, car, friends, house, our, school, very* **T**

Language Arts

Interactive Writing, 71a
Letter

Grammar, 71b
Practice Verbs That Do Not Add -*s* **T**

Speaking and Listening, 71c
Make Introductions

DAILY JOURNAL WRITING — Day 2 *Write about an exciting change.*

DAILY SOCIAL STUDIES CONNECTIONS — Day 2 Change/Stay the Same T-Chart, 71c

DAILY SUCCESS PREDICTORS for Adequate Yearly Progress

Monitor Progress and Corrective Feedback

	Day 1	Day 2
Phonics	Check Word Reading, *68o* Spiral REVIEW Phonics	Check Word Reading, *70d* Spiral REVIEW Phonics

RESOURCES FOR THE WEEK

- Practice Book 1.2, *pp. 21–30*
- Phonics and Spelling Practice Book, *pp. 57–60*
- Grammar and Writing Practice Book, *pp. 57–60*
- Selection Test, *pp. 33–36*
- Fresh Reads for Differentiated Test Practice, *pp. 85–89*
- Phonics Songs and Rhymes Chart 15
- The Grammar and Writing Book, *pp. 134–139*

Grouping Options for Differentiated Instruction

Turn the page for the small group lesson plan.

DAY 3 PAGES 72a–87d

Oral Language

QUESTION OF THE DAY, 72a
What kinds of changes are fun?

Oral Vocabulary/Share Literature, 72b
Big Book *Mr. George Baker*
Amazing Word *crumple*

Word Work

Phonemic Awareness, 72b
Blend and Segment Onset/Rime

Phonics, 72c–72d
Ending *-es;* Plural *-es;* and *r*-Controlled *or, ore* T

Spelling, 72d
Practice

Comprehension/Vocabulary/Fluency

Read *Jan's New Home,* 72e–87

Grouping Options 68f–68g

Introduce Selection Words
move, toys, window

Review High-Frequency Words
away, car, friends, house, our, school, very T

Theme T
Monitor and Fix Up
REVIEW Plot T

Fluency, 87a
Attend to Punctuation

Vocabulary, 87b
Descriptive Words

Trait of the Week, 87c
Introduce Voice

Grammar, 87d
Write with Verbs That Do Not Add -s T

Day 3 *Write about a time you moved to or visited a new place.*

Day 3 Time for Social Studies: Movement, 74–75

DAY 4 PAGES 88a–89d

Oral Language

QUESTION OF THE DAY, 88a
What changes would you tell about in a letter?

Oral Vocabulary/Share Literature, 88b
Read Aloud Anthology "Gila Monsters Meet You at the Airport"
Amazing Word *stampede*

Word Work

Phonemic Awareness, 88b
Segment and Count Syllables

High-Frequency Words, 88c
Practice *away, car, friends, house, our, school, very* T

Phonics, 88c–88d
REVIEW Final *ng, nk* and Compound Words T
REVIEW Word Reading T

Spelling, 88e
Partner Review

Comprehension/Vocabulary/Fluency

Read "A Letter from Jan," 88–89
Leveled Readers

Grouping Options 68f–68g

Descriptive Words
Reading Across Texts

Fluency, 89b
Attend to Punctuation

Writing Across the Curriculum, 89c
Signs

Grammar, 89d
Review Verbs That Do Not Add -s T

Day 4 *Write what happens to Jan on her birthday at her new school.*

Day 4 Time for Social Studies: Places, 88–89

DAY 5 PAGES 90a–91b

Oral Language

QUESTION OF THE DAY, 90a
Would you be excited about moving to a new place?

Oral Vocabulary/Share Literature, 90b
Read Aloud Anthology "Gila Monsters Meet You at the Airport"
Amazing Words Review

Word Work

Phonics, 90c
Review Endings *-es;* Plurals *-es;* and *r*-Controlled *or, ore* T

High-Frequency Words, 90c
Review *away, car, friends, house, our, school, very* T

Spelling, 90d
Test

Comprehension/Vocabulary/Fluency

Read Leveled Readers

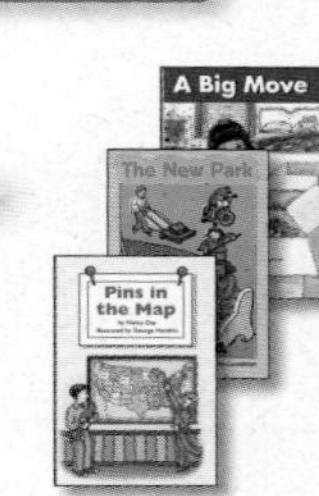

Grouping Options 68f–68g

Monitor Progress, 90e–90g
Read the Sentences
Read the Story

Writing and Grammar, 90–91
Develop Voice
Use Verbs That Do Not Add -s T

Research/Study Skills, 91a
Maps

Day 5 *Write a letter to a friend who moved away.*

Day 5 Revisit the Change/Stay the Same T-Chart, 91b

KEY ◎ = Target Skill T = Tested Skill

Fluency and Comprehension
Check High-Frequency Words, *72f*
Check Retelling, *86a*
Spiral REVIEW High-Frequency Words

Fluency
Check Fluency WCPM, *89b*
Spiral REVIEW Phonics, High-Frequency Words

Oral Vocabulary
Check Oral Vocabulary, *90b*
Assess Phonics, High-Frequency Words, Fluency, Comprehension, *90e*

SUCCESS PREDICTOR

Small Group Plan *for Differentiated Instruction*

Daily Plan AT A GLANCE

Reading

Whole Group
- Oral Language
- Word Work
- Comprehension/Vocabulary

Group Time

Meet with small groups to provide:
- Skill Support
- Reading Support
- Fluency Practice

This week's lessons for daily group time can be found behind the Differentiated Instruction (DI) tab on pp. DI • 36–DI • 45.

Whole Group
- Comprehension/Vocabulary
- Fluency

Language Arts
- Writing
- Grammar
- Speaking/Listening/Viewing
- Research/Study Skills

Use *My Sidewalks on Reading Street* for Tier III intensive reading intervention.

DAY 1

On-Level	Strategic Intervention	Advanced
Teacher-Led *Page 68q*	**Teacher-Led** *Page DI • 36*	**Teacher-Led** *Page DI • 37*
• **Read** Decodable Reader 29 • **Reread** for Fluency	• Blend and Build Words with Ending -es, Plural -es • **Read** Decodable Reader 29 • **Reread** for Fluency	• Extend Word Reading • **Read** Advanced Selection 15 • Introduce Concept Inquiry

i Independent Activities

While you meet with small groups, have the rest of the class...

- Reread for fluency
- Write in their journals
- Complete Practice Book 1.2, p. 23
- Visit the Word Work Center

DAY 2

On-Level	Strategic Intervention	Advanced
Teacher-Led *Page 70f*	**Teacher-Led** *Page DI • 38*	**Teacher-Led** *Page DI • 39*
• **Read** Decodable Reader 30 • **Reread** for Fluency	• Blend and Build Words with *r*-Controlled *or, ore* • **Read** Decodable Reader 30 • **Reread** for Fluency	• Extend Word Reading • **Read** Self-Selected Reading • Continue Concept Inquiry

i Independent Activities

While you meet with small groups, have the rest of the class...

- Reread for fluency
- Write in their journals
- Complete Practice Book 1.2, pp. 24–26
- Visit the Word Work Center
- Work on inquiry projects

DAY 3

On-Level	Strategic Intervention	Advanced
Teacher-Led *Pages 72–87*	**Teacher-Led** *Page DI • 40*	**Teacher-Led** *Page DI • 41*
• **Read** *Jan's New Home*	• Blend and Read Words with -*es*; *r*-Controlled *or, ore* • **Read** SI Decodable Reader 15 • **Read** or Listen to *Jan's New Home*	• **Read** *Jan's New Home* • Continue Concept Inquiry

i Independent Activities

While you meet with small groups, have the rest of the class...

- Read self-selected reading
- Write in their journals
- Complete Practice Book 1.2, p. 27
- Visit the Listening and Writing Centers
- Work on inquiry projects

① Begin with whole class skill and strategy instruction.

② Meet with small groups to provide differentiated instruction.

③ Gather the whole class back together for fluency and language arts.

On-Level

Teacher-Led
Pages 88–89, LR22–LR24

- **Read** "A Letter from Jan"
- Practice with On-Level Reader *The New Park*

Strategic Intervention

Teacher-Led
Pages DI • 42, LR19–LR21

- Blend and Read Words
- **Reread** SI Decodable Reader 14
- **Read** or Listen to "A Letter from Jan"
- Practice with Below-Level Reader *A Big Move*

Advanced

Teacher-Led
Pages DI • 43, LR25–LR27

- **Read** "A Letter from Jan"
- Expand Vocabulary
- Continue Concept Inquiry
- Practice with Advanced Reader *Pins in the Map*

i Independent Activities

While you meet with small groups, have the rest of the class...

- Reread for fluency
- Write in their journals
- Read self-selected reading
- Complete Practice Book 1.2, pp. 28–29
- Visit the Listening and Social Studies Centers
- Work on inquiry projects

DAY 5

On-Level

Teacher-Led
Pages 90e–90g, LR22–LR24

- Sentence Reading, Set B
- Monitor Fluency and Comprehension
- Practice with On-Level Reader *The New Park*

Strategic Intervention

Teacher-Led
Pages DI • 44, LR19–LR21

- Practice Word Reading
- Sentence Reading, Set A
- Monitor Comprehension
- Practice with Below-Level Reader *A Big Move*

Advanced

Teacher-Led
Pages DI • 45, LR25–LR27

- Sentence Reading, Set C
- Monitor Comprehension
- Share Concept Inquiry
- Practice with Advanced Reader *Pins in the Map*

i Independent Activities

While you meet with small groups, have the rest of the class...

- Reread for fluency
- Write in their journals
- Read self-selected reading
- Complete Practice Book 1.2, p. 30
- Visit the Technology Center

Grouping Place English language learners in the groups that correspond to their reading abilities in English.

Use the appropriate Leveled Reader or other text at children's instructional level.

TIP Send home the appropriate Multilingual Summary of the main selection on Day 1.

Take It to the NET
ONLINE
PearsonSuccessNet.com

Karen Wixson
For ideas on teaching reading strategies, see the article "Becoming a Strategic Reader" by S. G. Paris, M. Y. Lipson, and Scott Foresman author Karen Wixson.

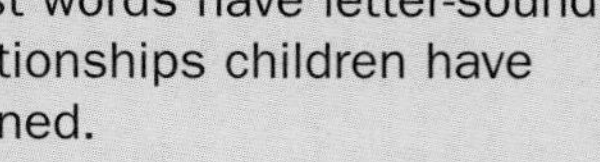

Decodable text is text in which most words have letter-sound relationships children have learned.

Looking Ahead

Be sure to schedule time for children to work on the unit inquiry project "Take a Closer Look." This week children should continue their journals by observing and measuring the objects and adding notes and pictures in an organized manner.

Name ______ Date ______

My Work Plan

Put an ☒ next to the activities you complete.

Listening
☐ Listen to a story.
☐ Listen to a song.

Writing
☐ Write about a trip.
☐ Write in your journal.

Reading
☐ Read a book.
☐ Read sentences.
☐ Book Club

Social Studies
☐ Find a picture.
☐ List reasons.

Word Work
☐ Read words with *-es*.
☐ Read words with *or* and *ore*.

Technology
☐ Type a journal entry.

Independent Practice
☐ Practice Book 1.2, pp. 21–30

Inquiry
☐ Organize information.

Wrap Up Your Week Turn your paper over. Write about what you did at school this week. What did you read? What did you learn about exciting changes?

Unit 3 • Week 3 • *Jan's New Home* **31**

▲ **Group-Time Survival Guide**
p. 31, Weekly Contract

 Customize Your Plan by Strand

ORAL LANGUAGE

Concept Development

Why are changes exciting?

arrive	*depart*	*location*
route	*swoop*	*tumble*
crumple	*stampede*	

BUILD

- ❑ **Question of the Week** Use the Morning Warm-Up! to introduce and discuss the question of the week. This week children will talk, sing, read, and write about growing and changing. DAY 1 *68l*

- ❑ **Sing with Me Big Book** Sing a song about an exciting change—moving to a new place. Ask children to listen for the concept-related Amazing Words *arrive, depart, location, route.* DAY 1 *68m*

Sing with Me Big Book

- ❑ **Let's Talk About Growing and Changing** Use the Let's Talk About It lesson in the Student Edition to build background, vocabulary, and concepts. Then create a concept chart for children to add to throughout the week. DAY 1 *68r–69*

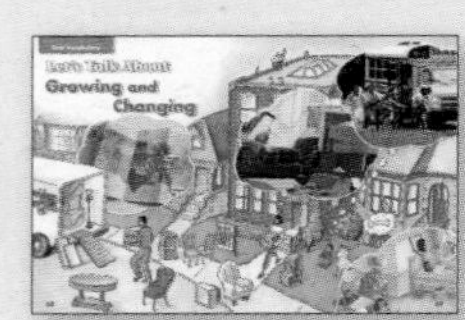

Let's Talk About It

DEVELOP

- ❑ **Question of the Day** Use the questions in the Morning Warm-Ups! to discuss lesson concepts and how they relate to the unit theme, Changes. DAY 2 *70a*, DAY 3 *72a*, DAY 4 *88a*, DAY 5 *90a*

- ❑ **Share Literature** Read big books and read aloud selections that develop concepts, language, and vocabulary related to the lesson concept and the unit theme. Continue to develop this week's Amazing Words. DAY 2 *70b*, DAY 3 *72b*, DAY 4 *88b*, DAY 5 *90b*

CONNECT

- ❑ **Wrap Up Your Week!** Revisit the Question of the Week. Then connect concepts and vocabulary to next week's lesson. DAY 5 *91b*

CHECK

- ❑ **Check Oral Vocabulary** To informally assess children's oral vocabulary, ask individuals to use some of this week's Amazing Words to tell you about the illustration on Student Edition pp. 68–69. DAY 5 *90b*

PHONEMIC AWARENESS AND PHONICS

ENDING *-ES*, PLURAL *-ES* Some words consist of a base word and the ending *-es*. Sometimes the ending *-es* means "more than one."

R*-CONTROLLED *OR, ORE A single vowel followed by the letter *r* has a sound that is neither short nor long, but *r*-controlled.

TEACH

- ❑ **Add Phonemes** Practice blending and adding /əz/ to base words. DAY 1 *68m*

- ❑ **Ending *-es*, Plural *-es*** Introduce the blending strategy for words with ending *-es* and plurals formed with *-es*. Then have children blend and sort ending *-es* and plural *-es* words. DAY 1 *68n–68o*

- ❑ **Blend and Segment** Practice blending and segmenting onset and rime in words containing *r*-controlled *ore, ore.* DAY 2 *70b*, DAY 3 *72b*

- ❑ ***r*-Controlled *or, ore*** Introduce the blending strategy for words with *r*-controlled *or, ore.* Then have children blend and build *r*-controlled *or, ore* words. DAY 2 *70c–70d*

- ❑ **Fluent Word Reading** Use the Fluent Word Reading Routine to develop children's word reading fluency. Use the Phonics Songs and Rhymes Chart for additional word reading practice. DAY 3 *72c–72d*

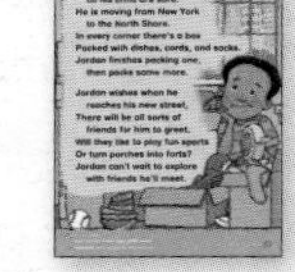

Phonics Songs and Rhymes Chart 15

PRACTICE/APPLY

- ❑ **Decodable Reader 29** Practice reading words with ending *-es*, plural *-es* in context. DAY 1 *68q*

- ❑ **Decodable Reader 30** Practice reading words with *r*-controlled *or, ore* in context. DAY 2 *70f*

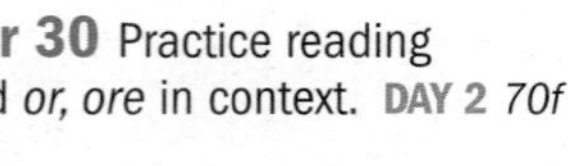

Decodable Readers 29 and 30

- ❑ ***Jan's New Home*** Practice decoding words in context. DAY 3 *72–85*

- ❑ **Homework** Practice Book 1.2, pp. 23, 25. DAY 1 *68o*, DAY 2 *70d*

- ❑ **Word Work Center** Practice ending *-es;* plural *-es;* and *r*-controlled *or, ore.* ANY DAY *68j*

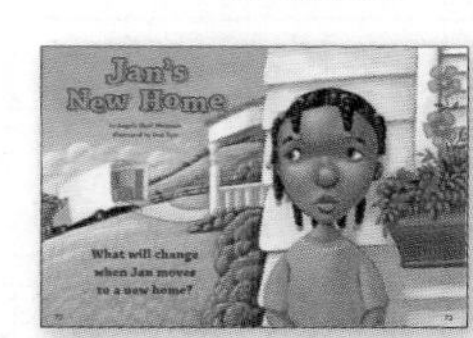

Main Selection—Fiction

RETEACH/REVIEW

- ❑ **Review** Review words with this week's phonics skills. DAY 5 *90c*

- ❑ **Reteach Lessons** If necessary, reteach ending *-es;* plural *-es;* and *r*-controlled *or, ore.* DAY 5 *DI·79*

- ❑ **Spiral REVIEW** Review previously taught phonics skills. DAY 1 *68o*, DAY 2 *70d*, DAY 4 *88c–88d*

ASSESS

- ❑ **Sentence Reading** Assess children's ability to read words with ending *-es;* plural *-es;* and *r*-controlled *or, ore.* DAY 5 *90e–90f*

1. Use assessment data to determine your instructional focus.
2. Preview this week's instruction by strand.
3. Choose instructional activities that meet the needs of your classroom.

SPELLING

ENDING *-ES*, PLURAL *-ES* Some words consist of a base word and the ending -es. Sometimes the ending -es means "more than one."

TEACH

- ❑ **Pretest** Before administering the pretest, model how to segment ending -es and plural -es words to spell them. Dictate the spelling words, segmenting them if necessary. Then have children check their pretests and correct misspelled words. DAY 1 *68p*

PRACTICE/APPLY

- ❑ **Dictation** Have children write dictation sentences to practice spelling words. DAY 2 *70e*
- ❑ **Write Words** Have children practice writing the spelling words by playing a game of "Match It." DAY 3 *72d*
- ❑ **Homework** Phonics and Spelling Practice Book pp. 57–60. DAY 1 *68p*, DAY 2 *70e* , DAY 3 *72d*, DAY 4 *88e*

RETEACH/REVIEW

- ❑ **Partner Review** Have pairs work together to read and write the spelling words. DAY 4 *88e*

ASSESS

- ❑ **Posttest** Use dictation sentences to give the posttest for words with ending -es, plural -es. DAY 5 *90d*

Spelling Words

Adding -es

1. fix	6. wishes*
2. fixes	7. kiss
3. class	8. kisses
4. classes	9. bus
5. wish	10. buses*

High-Frequency Words

11. friends* 12. very*

* Words from the Selection

HIGH-FREQUENCY WORDS

WORDS TO READ

away	*car*	*friends*	*house*
our	*school*	*very*	

TEACH

- ❑ **Words to Read** Introduce this week's high-frequency words and add them to the Word Wall. DAY 2 *70–71*

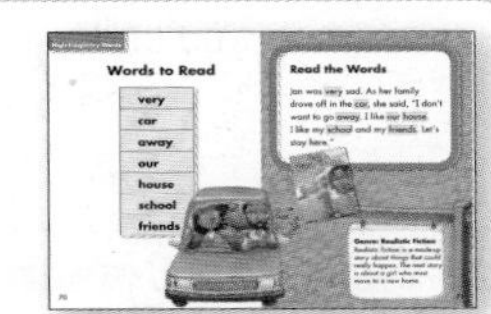
High-Frequency Words

PRACTICE/APPLY

- ❑ **Vocabulary Transparency 15** Review this week's high-frequency words, or Words to Read, before reading *Jan's New Home.* DAY 3 *72f*
- ❑ **Words in Context** Read high-frequency words in the context of *Jan's New Home.* DAY 3 *72–85*

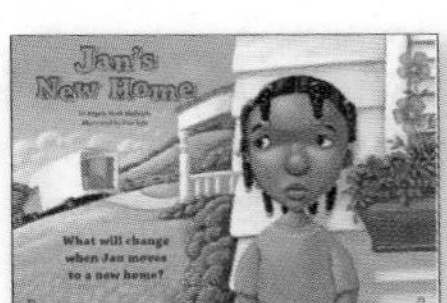

Main Selection—Fiction

- ❑ **Word Wall** Use the Word Wall to review and practice high-frequency words throughout the week. DAY 4 *88c*, DAY 5 *90c*
- ❑ **Leveled Text** Practice this week's high-frequency words in the context of leveled text. DAY 4 *LR19–LR27*, DAY 5 *LR19–LR27*

Leveled Readers

- ❑ **Homework** Practice Book 1.2 pp. 26, 27. DAY 2 *70–71*, DAY 3 *72e*

RETEACH/REVIEW

- ❑ **Spiral REVIEW** Review previously taught high-frequency words. DAY 3 *72f*, DAY 4 *88d*

ASSESS

- ❑ **Sentence Reading** Assess children's ability to read this week's high-frequency words. DAY 5 *90e–90f*

VOCABULARY

TEACH

- ❑ **Vocabulary Transparency 15** Use Vocabulary Transparency 15 to introduce the selection words from *Jan's New Home.* Children will read these words but will not be tested on them. DAY 3 *72f*
- ❑ **Descriptive Words** Discuss and use words that describe feelings. DAY 3 *87b*

Customize Your Plan *by Strand*

COMPREHENSION

SKILL THEME Theme is the big idea of a story.

STRATEGY MONITOR AND FIX UP When you read, you should stop and make sure you understand. Going back and thinking about details can help you understand what you read.

TEACH

- ❑ **Listening Comprehension** Read "The First Ride" and model how to identify *theme.* DAY 1 *69a–69b*
- ❑ **Skill/Strategy Lesson** Review how to identify *theme.* Then introduce this week's strategy, *monitor and fix up.* DAY 3 *72g*

PRACTICE/APPLY

Main Selection—Fiction

Paired Selection–Friendly Letter

Leveled Readers

- ❑ **Skills and Strategies in Context** Read *Jan's New Home,* using the Guiding Comprehension questions to apply *theme* and *monitor and fix up.* DAY 3 *72–85*
- ❑ **Think and Share** Use the questions on Student Edition p. 86 to discuss the selection. DAY 3 *86–87*
- ❑ **Skills and Strategies in Context** Read "A Letter from Jan," guiding children as they apply skills and strategies. After reading have children make connections across texts. DAY 4 *88–89a*
- ❑ **Leveled Text** Apply *theme* and *monitor and fix up* to read leveled text. DAY 4 *LR19–LR27,* Day 5 *LR19–LR27*
- ❑ **Homework** Practice Book 1.2 p. 24. DAY 1 *69a*

ASSESS

- ❑ **Selection Test** Determine children's understanding of the main selection and assess their ability to identify *theme.* DAY 3
- ❑ **Story Reading** Have children read the passage "Morning Chores." Ask what the theme of the story is and have them retell the story. DAY 5 *90e–90g*

RETEACH/REVIEW

- ❑ **Reteach Lesson** If necessary, reteach *theme.* DAY 5 *DI·80*

FLUENCY

SKILL ATTEND TO PUNCTUATION When you read, you should watch for the marks at the end of sentences. These marks tell you how your voice should sound.

REREAD FOR FLUENCY

- ❑ **Oral Reading** Have children read orally from Decodable Reader 29, or another text at their independent reading level. Listen as children read and provide corrective feedback regarding their oral reading and their use of the blending strategy. DAY 1 *68q*
- ❑ **Paired Reading** Have pairs of children read orally from Decodable Reader 30, or another text at their independent reading level. Listen as children read and provide corrective feedback regarding their oral reading and their use of the blending strategy. DAY 2 *70f*

TEACH

- ❑ **Model** Use passages from *Jan's New Home* to model reading aloud while attending to punctuation. DAY 3 *87a,* DAY 4 *89b*

PRACTICE/APPLY

- ❑ **Choral Reading** Choral read passages from *Jan's New Home.* Monitor progress and provide feedback regarding children's attention to punctuation. DAY 3 *87a,* DAY 4 *89b*
- ❑ **Listening Center** Have children follow along with the AudioText for this week's selections. ANY DAY *68j*
- ❑ **Reading/Library Center** Have children build fluency by rereading Leveled Readers, Decodable Readers, or other text at their independent level. ANY DAY *68j*
- ❑ **Fluency Coach** Have children use Fluency Coach to listen to fluent reading or to practice reading on their own. ANY DAY

ASSESS

- ❑ **Story Reading** Take a one-minute timed sample of children's oral reading. Use the passage "Morning Chores." DAY 5 *90e, 90g*

1. Use assessment data to determine your instructional focus.
2. Preview this week's instruction by strand.
3. Choose instructional activities that meet the needs of your classroom.

WRITING

Trait of the Week

VOICE Voice is the way a writer feels about a topic.

TEACH

- ❑ **Write Together** Engage children in writing activities that develop language, grammar, and writing skills. Include independent writing as an extension of group writing activities.

  Shared Writing DAY 1 *69c*
  Interactive Writing DAY 2 *71a*
  Writing Across the Curriculum DAY 4 *89c*

- ❑ **Trait of the Week** Introduce and model the Trait of the Week, *voice.* DAY 3 *87c*

PRACTICE/APPLY

- ❑ **Write Now** Examine the model on Student Edition pp. 90–91. Then have children write greeting cards. DAY 5 *90-91*

  Prompt In *Jan's New Home,* Jan moves to a new city. Think about how you would welcome Jan to your class. Now write a greeting card telling Jan about your class.

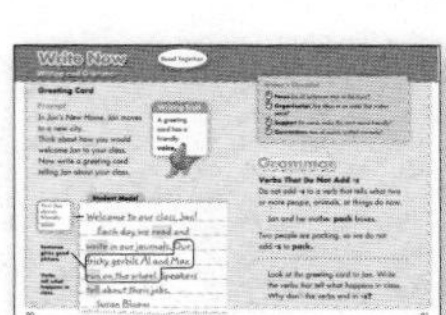

Write Now

- ❑ **Daily Journal Writing** Have children write about concepts and literature in their journals. EVERY DAY *68d-68e*
- ❑ **Writing Center** Have children write travel journals. ANY DAY *68k*

ASSESS

- ❑ **Scoring Rubric** Use a rubric to evaluate greeting cards. DAY 5 *90-91*

RETEACH/REVIEW

- ❑ **The Grammar and Writing Book** Use pp. 134–139 of The Grammar and Writing Book to extend instruction. ANY DAY

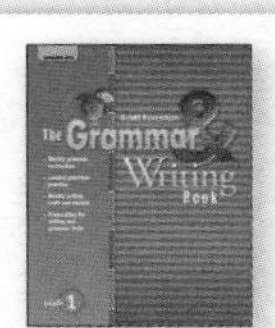

The Grammar and Writing Book

SPEAKING AND LISTENING

TEACH

- ❑ **Make Introductions** Model how to introduce someone you know to someone new. Then have children make introductions. DAY 3 *71c*

GRAMMAR

SKILL VERBS THAT DO NOT ADD -S Do not add -s to a verb that tells what two or more people, animals, or things do now.

TEACH

- ❑ **Grammar Transparency 15** Use Grammar Transparency 15 to teach *verbs that do not add -s.* DAY 1 *69d*

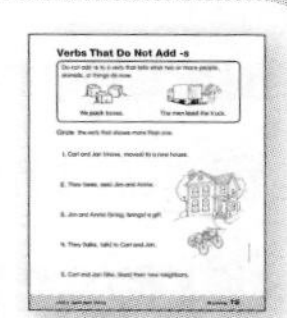

Grammar Transparency 15

PRACTICE/APPLY

- ❑ **Develop the Concept** Review the concept of *verbs that do not add -s* and provide guided practice. DAY 2 *71b*
- ❑ **Apply to Writing** Have children use verbs in writing. DAY 3 *87d*
- ❑ **Define/Practice** Review the definition of *verbs that do not add -s.* Then have children classify verbs. DAY 4 *89d*
- ❑ **Write Now** Discuss the grammar lesson on Student Edition p. 91. Have children use correct verbs in their own greeting cards. DAY 5 *90-91*

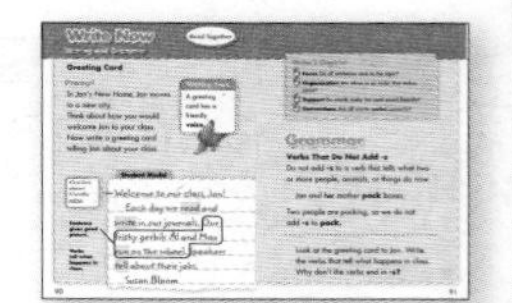

Write Now

- ❑ **Daily Fix-It** Have children find and correct errors in grammar, spelling, and punctuation. DAY 1 *69d*, DAY 2 *71b*, DAY 3 *87d*, DAY 4 *89d*, DAY 5 *90-91*
- ❑ **Homework** Grammar and Writing Practice Book pp. 57–60. DAY 2 *71b*, DAY 3 *87d*, DAY 4 *89d*, DAY 5 *90-91*

RETEACH/REVIEW

- ❑ **The Grammar and Writing Book** Use pp. 134–137 of The Grammar and Writing Book to extend instruction. ANY DAY

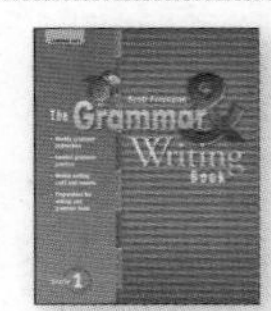

The Grammar and Writing Book

RESEARCH/INQUIRY

TEACH

- ❑ **Maps** Model using a map. Then have children draw their own maps and demonstrate how to use them. DAY 5 *91a*
- ❑ **Unit Inquiry Project** Allow time for children to observe and measure the objects they have been watching. Have them document findings in their journals, adding new notes and pictures. ANY DAY *9*

Resources for

Differentiated Instruction

LEVELED READERS

▶ **Comprehension**

Skill Theme

Strategy Monitor and Fix Up

▶ **Lesson Vocabulary**

High-Frequency Words

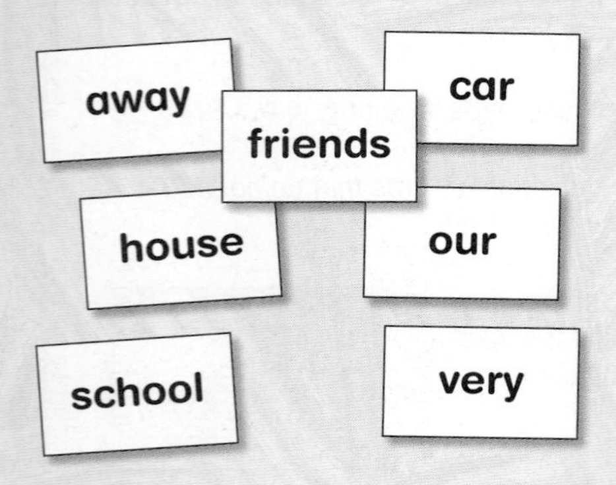

▶ **Social Studies Standards**

- Geographic
- Place
- Movement

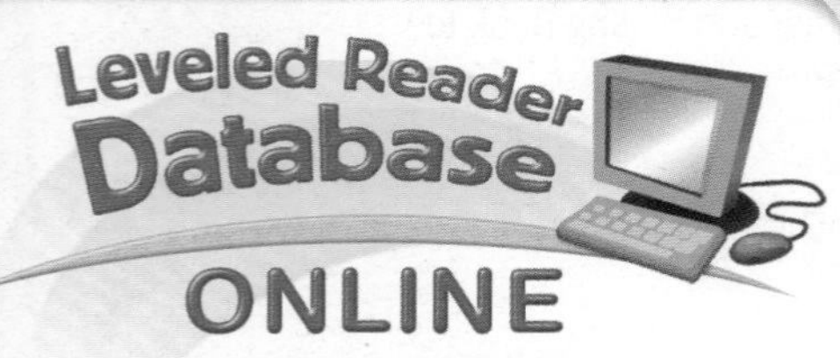

PearsonSuccessNet.com

Use the Online Database of over 600 books to

- Download and print additional copies of this week's leveled readers
- Listen to the readers being read online
- Search for more titles focused on this week's skills, topics and content

On-Level

On-Level Reader

Theme

Look at the picture below. Read the words that tell about it.

Everyone helped build the park. Some people cut away weeds and thorns. Some people planted seeds and trees. Some people made paths. Some people made a place for sports.

At last the park was done. There were paths. There were benches and trees. There was a place for sports. There was a pond for ducks.

"Now our neighborhood has everything we need!" Norm said.

Possible response given.

What "big idea," or theme, do you get from the picture and words?

People can work together to make something great. Neighborhoods need parks.

On-Level Practice TE p. LR23

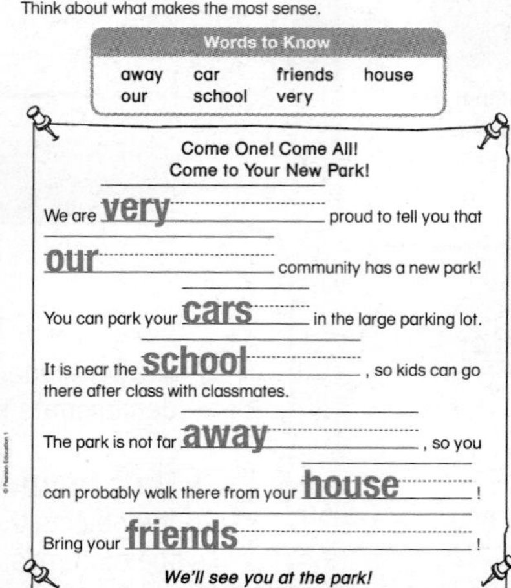

Vocabulary

Complete the poster with words from the box.
Think about what makes the most sense.

Words to Know			
away	car	friends	house
our	school	very	

Come One! Come All!
Come to Your New Park!

We are **very** proud to tell you that **our** community has a new park!

You can park your **cars** in the large parking lot.

It is near the **school**, so kids can go there after class with classmates.

The park is not far **away**, so you can probably walk there from your **house**!

Bring your **friends**!

We'll see you at the park!

On-Level Practice TE p. LR24

Strategic Intervention

Below-Level Reader

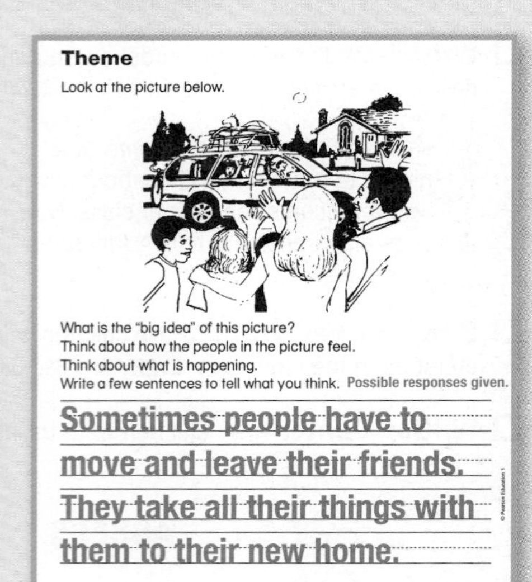

Theme

Look at the picture below.

What is the "big idea" of this picture?
Think about how the people in the picture feel.
Think about what is happening.
Write a few sentences to tell what you think. Possible responses given.

Sometimes people have to move and leave their friends. They take all their things with them to their new home.

Below-Level Practice TE p. LR20

Vocabulary

Complete the letter with words from the box.
Some words have pictures to help you.

Words to Know						
away	car	friends	house	our	school	very

Dear Carlos,

We are moving! I am **very** happy.

We are not moving too far **away**.

I can still go to the same **school**.

I can still see my **friends**.

We will put all **our** things in the **car**.

We will then go to the new **house**.

I will tell you more after we move!

Your friend,
Mira

Below-Level Practice TE p. LR21

Advanced

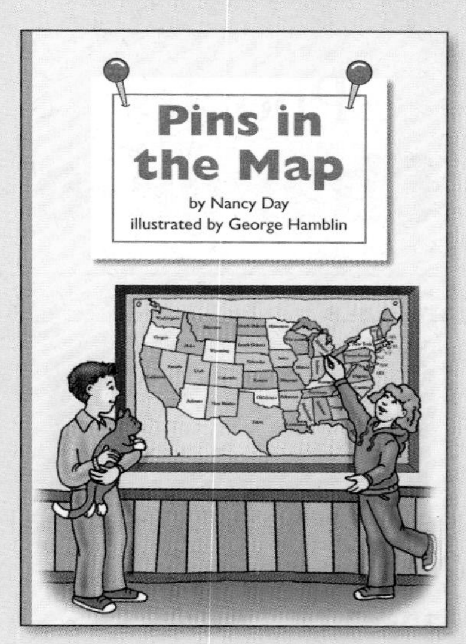

Advanced Reader

Theme

Read the story below.

"Do you like living in this town?" Sam asked, his voice a little unsure.

"I do!" said Katie. "Everyone knows everybody else. People are nice and friendly."

"Like you," Sam said.

Katie smiled. "It's fun meeting new people at the motel."

"I didn't want to move away from my friends and the mountains," Sam said.

"But now I think I'm going to like living here."

What is the "big idea," or theme, of these words? Write your ideas below. Possible responses given.

People will make new friends when they move. Moving does not need to be scary. Many people move from one place to another.

Advanced Practice TE p. LR26

Vocabulary

Draw a line to match each word on the left with a word or words on the right that have a similar meaning.

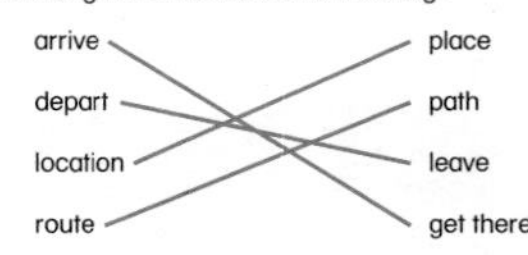

arrive	place
depart	path
location	leave
route	get there

Now use each word on the left in a sentence of your own.

1. arrive Sentences will vary, but the vocabulary words
2. depart should be used correctly.
3. location
4. route

Advanced Practice TE p. LR27

ELL

ELL Reader

ELL Poster 15

Teacher's Edition Notes

ELL notes throughout this lesson support instruction and reference additional resources at point of use.

Teaching Guide pp. 99–105, 240–241

- Multilingual summaries of the main selection
- Comprehension lesson
- Vocabulary strategies and word cards
- ELL Reader 1.3.3 lesson

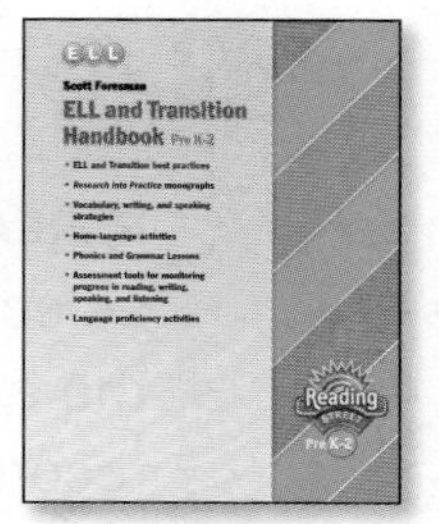

ELL and Transition Handbook

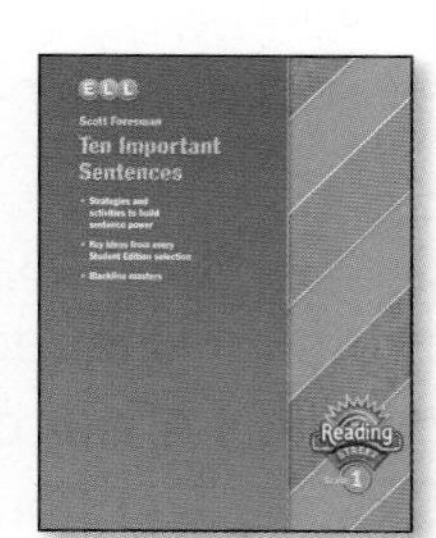

Ten Important Sentences

- Key ideas from every selection in the Student Edition
- Activities to build sentence power

More Reading

Readers' Theater Anthology

- Fluency practice
- Five scripts to build fluency
- Poetry for oral interpretation

Leveled Trade Books

Below-Level

On-Level

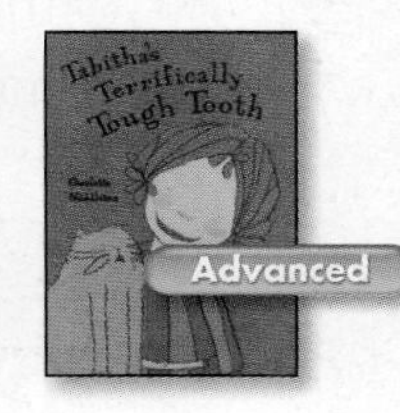

Advanced

- Extend reading tied to the unit concept
- Lessons in Trade Book Library Teaching Guide

Big Book of Poems

- Fluency practice
- Poetry for Choral Reading

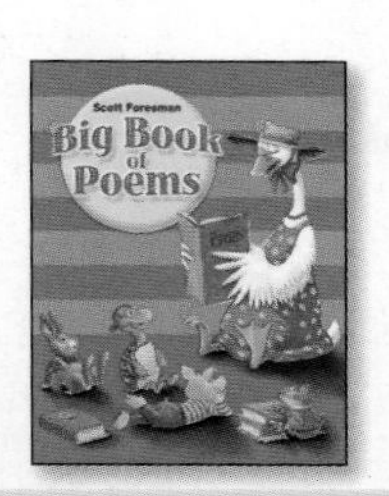

School + Home

Homework

- Family Times Newsletter
- ELL Multilingual Selection Summaries

Take-Home Books

- Decodable Readers
- Leveled Readers

Literacy Centers

Listening

Let's Read Along

MATERIALS
CD player, headphones, print copies of recorded pieces

SINGLES

LISTEN TO LITERATURE As children listen to the following recordings, have them follow along or read along in the print version.

AudioText
Jan's New Home
"A Letter from Jan"

Sing with Me/Background Building Audio
"New Location"

Phonics Songs and Rhymes
"Moving from New York"

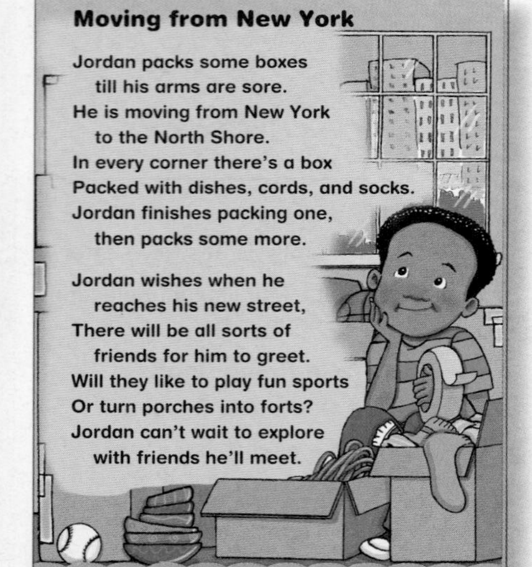

Audio CD **Phonics Songs and Rhymes Chart 15**

Reading/Library

Read It Again!

MATERIALS
collection of books for self-selected reading, reading logs

SINGLES
PAIRS
GROUPS

REREAD BOOKS Have children select previously read books from the appropriate book box and record titles of books they read in their logs. Use these previously read books:

- **Decodable Readers**
- **Leveled Readers**
- **ELL Readers**
- **Stories written by classmates**
- **Books from the library**

TEN IMPORTANT SENTENCES Have children read the Ten Important Sentences for *Jan's New Home* and locate the sentences in the Student Edition.

BOOK CLUB Encourage groups to discuss *Jan's New Home.* Ask children to discuss how Jan felt about moving and how they think they would feel if they had to move.

Word Work

Phonics Change-o

MATERIALS
16 index cards

PAIRS
GROUPS

ENDING *-es*, PLURAL *-es* Have pairs or groups of children play a game of Change-o.

1. **Write verbs with *-es,* such as *fixes* and *dashes,* or plural words with *-es,* such as *boxes* and *dishes,* on 14 index cards. Write *change* on 2 cards. Shuffle and stack facedown.**
2. **One child begins turning over cards and reading the words. When a card with the word *change* appears, the next child begins his or her turn.**
3. **When all cards have been turned over, the pile is reshuffled. Play continues until all children have found the word *change* two times.**

r*-CONTROLLED *or, ore Make a set of cards with words containing *r*-controlled *or, ore*. Have children play the game.

This interactive CD provides additional practice.

Scott Foresman Reading Street Centers Survival Kit

Use the *Jan's New Home* materials from the Reading Street Centers Survival Kit to organize this week's centers.

Writing

Travel Journal

MATERIALS
paper, pencils

SINGLES

WRITE A JOURNAL ENTRY Recall the things Jan sees during the trip to her new home.

1. **Ask children to write a journal entry about a trip they have taken.**
2. **Have them write about what they saw on the trip and how they felt.**
3. **Remind children to begin their entry with the date. Encourage them to illustrate their entries.**

LEVELED WRITING Encourage children to write at their own ability level. Some may write only phrases. Others will write some complete sentences. Your best writers will write complete and varied sentences with many details.

Social Studies

The Place for Me

MATERIALS
travel magazines, paper, maps

SINGLES
GROUPS

EXPLORE NEW PLACES Have children write about other places they might like to live.

1. **Have children look through magazines and cut out a picture of a place they might want to live.**
2. **Ask children to glue the picture on a sheet of paper, write the name of the place, and list two or three reasons they might want to live there.**
3. **Children can present their work by reading their writing. Some children may want to find the place they have chosen on a map.**

Technology

Travel Tales

MATERIALS
computer

SINGLES

TYPE A JOURNAL ENTRY Individuals type and save their journal entries from the Writing Center.

1. **Have children turn the computer on and open a word processing program.**
2. **If children have completed their travel journal entries, they should type them. Otherwise, they should type a sentence describing a trip they took.**
3. **Children then save their files.**

Day 1

AT A GLANCE

Oral Vocabulary
"New Location" 15

Phonemic Awareness
Add Phonemes /əz/

Phonics and Spelling
Ending *-es;* Plural *-es*
Spelling Pretest: Adding *-es*

Read **Apply Phonics** Word Wall

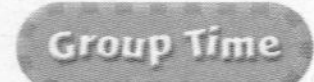

< Differentiated Instruction

Build Background
Let's Talk About Growing and Changing

Listening Comprehension
Skill Theme

Shared Writing
Greeting Card

Grammar
Verbs that Do Not Add *-s*

Materials

- *Sing with Me Big Book*
- Letter Tiles
- Decodable Reader 29
- Student Edition 68–69
- Graphic Organizer Flip Chart 4

Take It to the NET™ ONLINE

Professional Development
To learn more about text for beginning readers, go to PearsonSuccessNet.com and read "Text Matters in Learning to Read" by E. H. Hiebert.

Morning Warm-Up!

Have you ever gone to a new place?
Were you sure you would like it?
Maybe you were a little bit scared too.
Why are changes exciting?

QUESTION OF THE WEEK Tell children they will talk, sing, read, and write about Growing and Changing. Write the message and track the print as you read it. Discuss the questions.

CONNECT CONCEPTS Ask questions to connect to other selections.

- What changes do you think were exciting to Ruby in *Ruby in Her Own Time?*
- How do you think Ruby's parents felt when she left? Was it a good change for them?

REVIEW HIGH-FREQUENCY WORDS

- Circle the high-frequency words *ever, were,* and *sure* in the message.
- Have children say and spell each word as they write it in the air.

Build Background Use the Day 1 instruction on ELL Poster 15 to assess knowledge and develop concepts.

ELL Poster 15

Oral Vocabulary

SHARE LITERATURE Display p. 15 of the *Sing with Me Big Book.* Tell children that they will sing a song about moving to a new place. Read the title. Ask children to listen for the Amazing Words **location, route, arrive,** and **depart** as you sing. Then sing the song again and ask children to sing with you. Have children demonstrate their understanding of *location, route, arrive,* and *depart* as they tell how this song is like something they may have done.

Sing with Me/
Background Building Audio

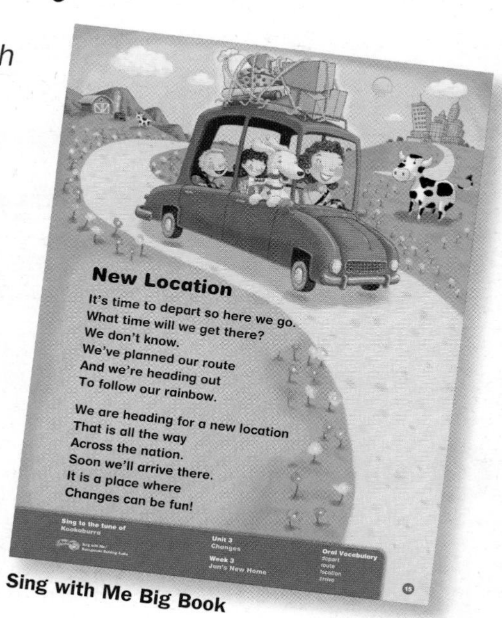

Sing with Me Big Book

Phonemic Awareness

ADD PHONEMES /əz/

- We just sang about a family who wants to rush to their new home. Listen to the sounds in *rush.*
- Model saying each sound, /r/ /u/ /sh/. Have children say the sounds with you and then say the sounds by themselves.
- Now say each sound as you write the letter that goes with it. (Say /r/ /u/ /sh/ as you write *r, u, sh.*)
- Have children say the sounds as you point to the letters (/r/ /u/ /sh/) and blend the sounds to say the word *(rush).*
- Add *es* to *rush.* Listen as I add /əz/ *to rush: rush, es, rushes.* Have children blend the word with you. *(rush, es, rushes)*

Continue the activity by adding *es*/əz/ *to flash, match, mix, kiss, toss,* and *dress.*

OBJECTIVES

- Build oral vocabulary.
- Add phonemes /əz/.

to build oral vocabulary

arrive
depart
location
route
swoop
tumble
crumple
stampede

MONITOR PROGRESS

If... children lack oral vocabulary experiences about the concept Growing and Changing,

then... use the Oral Vocabulary Routine below to teach *arrive.*

Oral Vocabulary ROUTINE

1. **Introduce the Word** Relate the word *arrive* to the song. Supply a child-friendly definition. Have children say the word. Example: When you *arrive* somewhere, you get there.
2. **Demonstrate** Provide an example to show meaning. It will be late when we *arrive* in Chicago.
3. **Apply** Have children demonstrate their understanding. What time do you *arrive* at school?
4. **Display the Word/Letter-Sounds** Write the word on a card. Display it. Have children identify *rr*/r/ and *v*/v/. See p. DI·5 to teach *depart, location,* and *route.*

ELL

Build Oral Vocabulary Help children understand the language in the song "New Location" by rephrasing "To follow our rainbow," as The family is happy to go. Then display a map of the United States and demonstrate the meaning of "Across the nation."

Ending *-es*; Plural *-es*

OBJECTIVES

- Use structural cues to decode words with ending *-es* and plurals formed with *-es*.
- Blend, read, and sort ending *-es* words and plural *-es* words.

Skills Trace

Ending *-es*; Plural *-es*

Introduce/Teach	**TE: 1.3 68n–o; 72c–d**
Practice	TE: 1.3 68g; PB 1.2 23; DR 29
Reteach/Review	TE: 1.3 90c, 114c–d DI·79; PB: 1.2 38
Assess/Test	TE: 1.3 90e–g; Benchmark Test, Unit 3

Strategic Intervention

Use **Monitor Progress,** p.68o during Group Time after children have had more practice with ending *-es* and plural *-es.*

Advanced

Use **Monitor Progress,** p. 68o as a preassessment to determine whether or not this group of children would benefit from this instruction in ending *-es* and plural *-es.*

Support Phonics In Spanish, plurals are formed by adding *-s* to words ending in a vowel *(madre/ madres)* and *-es* to words ending in a consonant *(árbol, árboles).* Because of this, Spanish speakers may add *-es* to any words ending in a consonant (/ragez/ *rages* instead of *rags*). Give children additional practice writing plural endings for words ending in consonants other than *s, ss, sh, ch,* or *z.*

See the Phonics Transition Lessons in the ELL and Transition Handbook.

TEACH/MODEL

Blending Strategy

ROUTINE

1. **Connect** Write *runs* and *rags.* You studied words like these already. What do you know about reading these words? (The words end in *-s.* The base words are *run* and *rag,* and the ending is *-s.* The *-s* on *rags* means "more than one.") Today we will learn about words with the ending *-es* and words with *-es.*

2. **Model** Write *fixes.* The word *fix* has an ending. If I cover up the ending *-es,* I see the base word is *fix.* This is how I blend this word. Segment and blend the base word /f/ /i/ /ks/, *fix.* Uncover and read the ending *-es.* Blend the two parts. Let's blend this word together: *fix, es, fixes.* Write *buses.* This is how I blend this word. Segment and blend *buses.* Let's blend this word together: bus, es, *buses.* Adding *-es* to the end of *bus* makes the word mean "more than one bus."

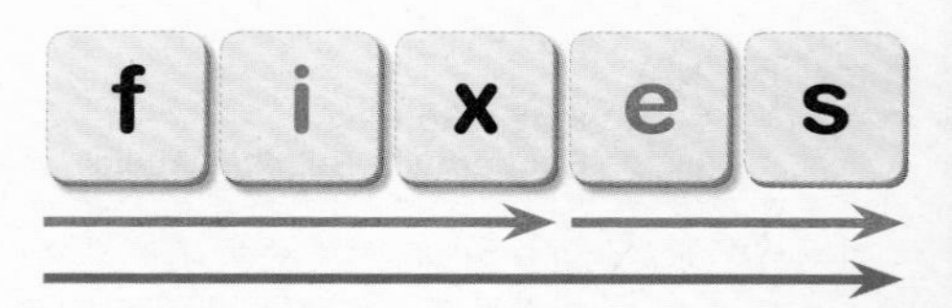

3. **Group Practice** First, see if the word has the ending *-es.* Blend the sound of each letter in the base word; read the ending; then blend the two parts together. Continue with *rushes, boxes, dresses, wishes,* and *brushes.*

4. **Review** What do you know about reading these words? When a word has the ending *-es,* blend the sounds in the base word, read the ending, and then blend the parts. Sometimes the ending *-es* means "more than one."

BLEND WORDS

INDIVIDUALS BLEND WORDS Call on individual children to blend the words *catches, mixes, crosses.* Have them tell what they know about each word before reading it. (The words have a base word and an *-es* ending.) Do the same for *glasses, foxes, classes.* (The words have *-es* at the end and mean "more than one.") For feedback, refer to step four of the Blending Strategy Routine.

SORT WORDS

SORT WORDS Write the heads *Words With -es* and *Words Without -es.* Write *mixes* and *lands.* Call on children to read the words, identify the endings, and write them below the heads. Write the words from the chart in random order. Call on children to read words, identify the ending, frame the base word and add the word to the chart. If children have difficulty reading a base word, have them cover the ending and blend the base word. Have the lists reread when they are complete.

Words With *-es*	Words Without *-es*
mixes	lands
wishes	hops
dresses	desks
boxes	mops
buses	bags

Vocabulary TiP

You may wish to explain the meaning of this word.

bosses people in charge

Greg fixes the benches.

Add the ending.
Write the new word on the line.

Word	Ending	New Word
1. mix	+ -es	mixes
2. brush	+ -es	brushes
3. glass	+ -es	glasses
4. catch	+ -es	catches
5. dress	+ -es	dresses
6. bus	+ -es	buses
7. dish	+ -es	dishes
8. fox	+ -es	foxes
9. nut	+ -s	nuts
10. patch	+ -es	patches

School + Home

Home Activity Your child added -es to verbs and nouns. Have your child use each new word in a sentence.

▲ **Practice Book 1.2** p. 23, Ending *-es;* Plural *-es*

Monitor Progress

Check Word Reading Ending *-es;* Plural *-es*

Write the following words and have individuals read them.

foxes	**rushes**	**pushes**	**classes**	**kisses**
dishes	**mops**	**glasses**	**rocks**	**bosses**
catches	**kicks**	**mixes**	**yelling**	**rested**

If… children cannot blend words with ending -es and plural -es at this point,

then… continue to monitor their progress using other instructional opportunities during the week so that they can be successful with the Day 5 Assessment. See the Skills Trace on p. 68n.

▶ **Day 1 Check Word Reading** · Day 2 Check Word Reading · Day 3 Check High-Frequency Words/Retelling · Day 4 Check Fluency · Day 5 Assess Progress

Spiral REVIEW

- Row 2 contrasts plural *-es* with *-s* plurals.
- Row 3 contrasts ending *-es* with inflected ending *-ed, ing,* and *-s* (no spelling change).

Word Reading SUCCESS PREDICTOR

OBJECTIVES

- Segment sounds to spell words.
- Spell words with ending *-es*; plural *-es*.

Spelling Words

Adding -es

1.	**fix**	6.	**wishes***
2.	**fixes**	7.	**kiss**
3.	**class**	8.	**kisses**
4.	**classes**	9.	**bus**
5.	**wish**	10.	**buses***

High-Frequency Words

11.	**friends***	12.	**very***

* Words from the Selection

Adding -es

Look at the word. Say it. Listen for the ending.

Word	Write the word.	Check it.
1. fix	fix	fix
2. fixes	fixes	fixes
3. class	class	class
4. classes	classes	classes
5. wish	wish	wish
6. wishes	wishes	wishes
7. kiss	kiss	kiss
8. kisses	kisses	kisses
9. bus	bus	bus
10. buses	buses	buses

High-Frequency Words

11. friends friends 12. very very

Home Activity Your child is learning to spell words that end with -es. To practice at home, have your child say each word. Help your child think of more words ending in -es.

▲ **Spelling Practice Book** p. 57

Spelling

PRETEST Ending *-es;* Plural *-es*

MODEL WRITING FOR SOUNDS The spelling words are base words with and without ending *-es* or plural *-es*. Before administering the spelling pretest, model how to segment ending *-es* and plural *-es* words to spell them.

- What sounds do you hear in *wax?* (/w/ /a/ /ks/)
- What is the letter for /w/? Write *w*. Continue with the *a*/a/ and *x*/ks/.
- What letters do we add to *wax* to make *waxes?* *(es)* Add *es*.
- Repeat with *patch* and *patches.*

PRETEST Dictate the spelling words. Segment the words for children if necessary. Have children check their pretests and correct misspelled words.

HOMEWORK Spelling Practice Book, p. 57

Group Time

DAY 1

On-Level	Strategic Intervention	Advanced
Read Decodable Reader 29.	**Read** Decodable Reader 29.	**Read** Advanced Selection 15.
• Use pp. 68q.	• Use the **Routine** on p. DI·36.	• Use the **Routine** on p. DI·37

Place English language learners in the groups that correspond to their reading abilities in English.

Independent Activities

Fluency Reading Pair children to reread Leveled Readers or the ELL Reader from the previous week or other text at children's independent level.

Journal Writing Write sentences about a place where you would like to live. Share writing.

Independent Reading See p. 68j for Reading/Library activities and suggestions.

Literacy Centers To practice Ending *-es;* Plural *-es,* you may use Word Work, p. 68j.

Practice Book 1.2 Ending*-es;* Plural *-es*, p. 23

Break into small groups after Spelling and before Build Background.

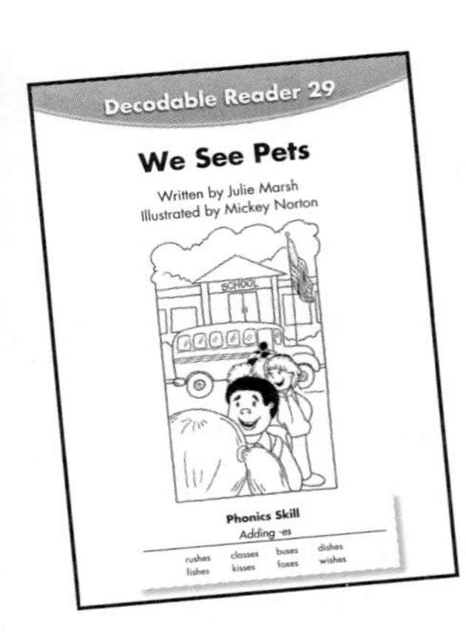

Apply Phonics

PRACTICE Ending -es; Plural -es

HIGH-FREQUENCY WORDS Review *are, down, one, said,* and *to* on the Word Wall. Word Wall

READ DECODABLE READER 29

- Pages 34–35 Read aloud quietly with the group.
- Page 36 Have the group read aloud without you.
- Pages 37–40 Select individuals to read aloud.

CHECK COMPREHENSION AND DECODING

- Where does this story happen? (at a pet store)
- What pets do the children see? (a rabbit, frogs, fishes, a snake, a puppy, a kitten)
- Point to a word in the story that has an *-es* ending. What is the word? List words that are named. Children may supply *rushes, classes, buses, dishes, fishes, kisses, foxes,* and *wishes.* Have children frame the base word and identify the ending on the words they mention. Point out that the *-es* on the end of *classes, buses, dishes, fishes,* and *foxes* means "more than one." Explain that the words *rushes, kisses,* and *wishes* are action words with the ending *-es.*

HOMEWORK Take-Home Decodable Reader 29

REREAD FOR FLUENCY

Oral Rereading

ROUTINE

1. **Read** Have children read the entire book orally.
2. **Reread** To achieve optimal fluency, children should reread the text three or four times.
3. **Provide Feedback** Listen as children read and provide corrective feedback regarding their oral reading and their use of the blending strategy.

OBJECTIVES

- Apply knowledge of letter-sounds and word parts to decode unknown words when reading.
- Use context with letter-sounds and word parts to confirm the identification of unknown words.
- Practice fluency with oral rereading.

Monitor Progress

Decoding

If...	then...
children have difficulty decoding a word,	prompt them to blend the word. • What is the new word? • Is the new word a word you know? • Does it make sense in the story?

Access Content

Beginning Lead children on a "more than one" walk through *We See Pets,* identifying *classes, buses, dishes,* and *fishes* in the pictures and print.

Intermediate Preview *We See Pets,* explaining "Buses line up" on p. 35 and "Meg makes a fish face" on p. 37.

Advanced Use pictures from *We See Pets* and pantomime to demonstrate how the words *dishes* and *fishes* can be both plural nouns with *-es* and action words with the *-es* ending.

OBJECTIVES

- Build background and oral vocabulary.
- Speak in complete sentences.

Strategic Intervention

Have children make a list of the things they would pack to put in a new bedroom.

Advanced

Have children visit the U.S. Postal Service Web site to find a list of recommended things to do when a family moves to a new home. Ask them to print out the list.

Activate Prior Knowledge
Invite children to name objects in the pictures in their home language and in English.

Build Background

LET'S TALK ABOUT Growing and Changing

DEVELOP ORAL LANGUAGE Read the title and have children view the illustration and photograph. Ask them to tell you what they see. Allow ample time for children to respond. Remind them to speak in complete sentences and to add details that explain their ideas. If children are reluctant to talk, use open-ended prompts to model language use and to encourage conversation. For example:

Tell me about what you see here. Yes, that's right, the people in the illustration are taking everything from their home and putting it into a large van. Why do you think they are doing that? Yes, it looks like the family is moving to a new home. Why might a family move to a new home?

BUILD ORAL VOCABULARY As you continue the discussion, encourage children to use today's Amazing Words, *arrive, depart, location,* and *route.*

- Tell me what might happen when the family arrives at their new home.
- Use the word *route* to tell me how the family will get to their new home.
- Is the location of the new home near or far away? How can you tell? Use the word *location* in your answer.

DEVELOP CONCEPTS

CONCEPT CHART Remind children of the question of the week.

- Why are changes exciting?

Display Graphic Organizer 4 or draw a two-column chart. Label the columns "Change," "Stay the Same." Discuss what will be the same and what things will change when the family moves to its new house. Discuss why new things are sometimes exciting and sometimes scary.

- What things will change at the new house? (Children may mention the house itself, the neighborhood, school, friends.)
- What will stay the same? (Children may mention their family, furniture, toys, pets.)

CONNECT TO READING Point out the illustration on the bottom corner of Student Edition p. 69. Ask children what the little girl is doing. (packing) Explain that this week children will read a story about this little girl and her family. Tell children that they will learn how things change when this girl moves to a new home.

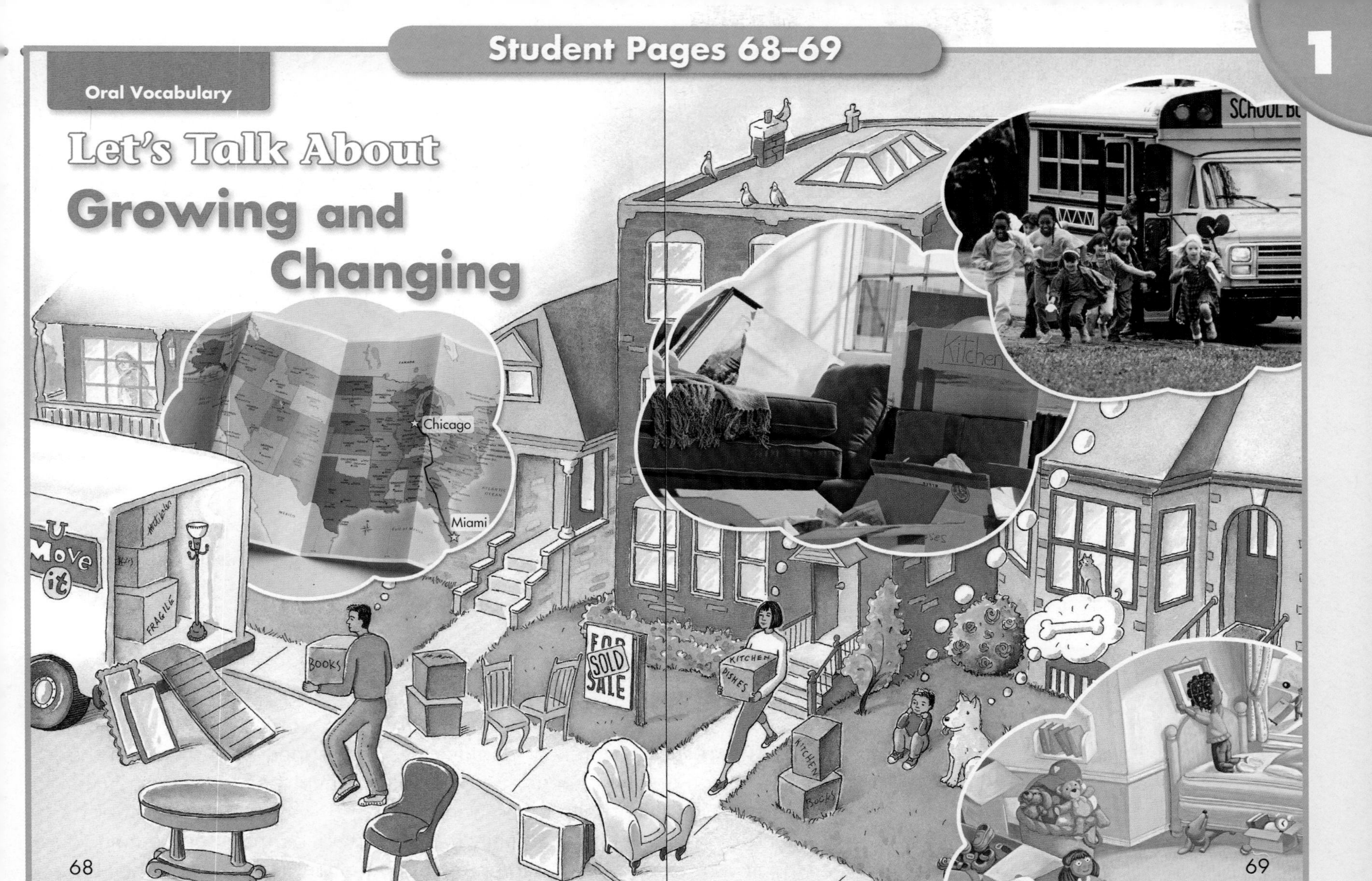

Change	Stay the Same
house	furniture
neighborhood	family members
school	toys
friends	pets

▲ **Graphic Organizer Flip Chart 4**

Tech Files ONLINE

For a Web site that explores a change children are likely to experience—changing schools—do an Internet search using the keywords *going to a new school.*

ELL

Access Content To prepare children for reading *Jan's New Home*, send home the story summary in English and/or the home language. See the ELL Teaching Guide, pp. 103–105.

1

OBJECTIVE

Identify the theme of a story.

Skills Trace	
Theme	
Introduce/Teach	**TE: 1.3 69a–b, 72g; 1.4 45a–b, 48g; 1.5 171a–b, 174g**
Practice	TE: 1.3 72g, 84–85; 1.4 48g, 64-65. 1.5 174g, 192–193 PB: 1.2 24, 74, 174
Reteach/Review	TE: 1.3 DI•80; 1.4 117a, 149a, DI•78; 1.5 30–31, DI•84
Test	TE: 1.3 33–36; 1.4 53–56; 1.5 89–92; Benchmark Test, Unit 4

Read the story.
Draw a picture of the big idea of the story.

Max and Sam

Max had a new puppy.
Sam was sad. He had no pet.
Max said, "Play with us!"
Max and Sam played with the puppy. Sam was happy.
Max was happy too.

1. Children's artwork should show two boys playing together with a puppy.

2. **Circle** the big idea of the story.

People like animals.

People feel happy when they do a good thing.

Think about the last time you did a good thing for a pal.
Draw a picture that shows what you did.

3. Children's artwork should show themselves playing with a friend or doing something good for a friend.

School + Home Home Activity Your child learned about the theme, or the big idea, in a story. Tell your child a story about a childhood event of yours. Then discuss the big idea of the story. Invite your child to tell you about a similar experience of his or hers.

▲ **Practice Book 1.2** p. 24, Theme

Access Content For a Picture It! lesson on theme, see the ELL Teaching Guide, pp. 100–101.

Listening Comprehension

TEACH/MODEL Theme

DEFINE THEME

- Every story has one big idea.
- You can use things that have happened in your own life to help you understand the big idea of a story.

READ ALOUD Read "The First Ride" and model how to identify theme.

MODEL When I read a story, I look for a big idea, or a lesson I can learn. In this story, Erik tries something new and discovers he likes it. I think the big idea of this story is that sometimes you have to try new things even though you might be scared.

PRACTICE

CLUES TO THEME Ask children to identify clues that support the theme of the story. How does Erik feel about riding the bike without training wheels? (He is scared that he might fall, but he wants to try.) How does Erik feel after he rides the bike alone? (He feels really happy.) How does this story remind you of something you felt before? (Children should tell about a time when they have pushed aside their fear to do something new.)

RECOGNIZE THEME Have children recall the story *Ruby in Her Own Time.*

- When the other ducklings hatch, eat, and swim, what does Ruby do? (She always does things later.)
- What do Mother and Father Duck always say about Ruby? (She will do things in her own time.)
- What is the big idea of this story? (It's okay to do things in your own time.)

CONNECT TO READING Tell children that when they read, they should think about the big idea of the story.

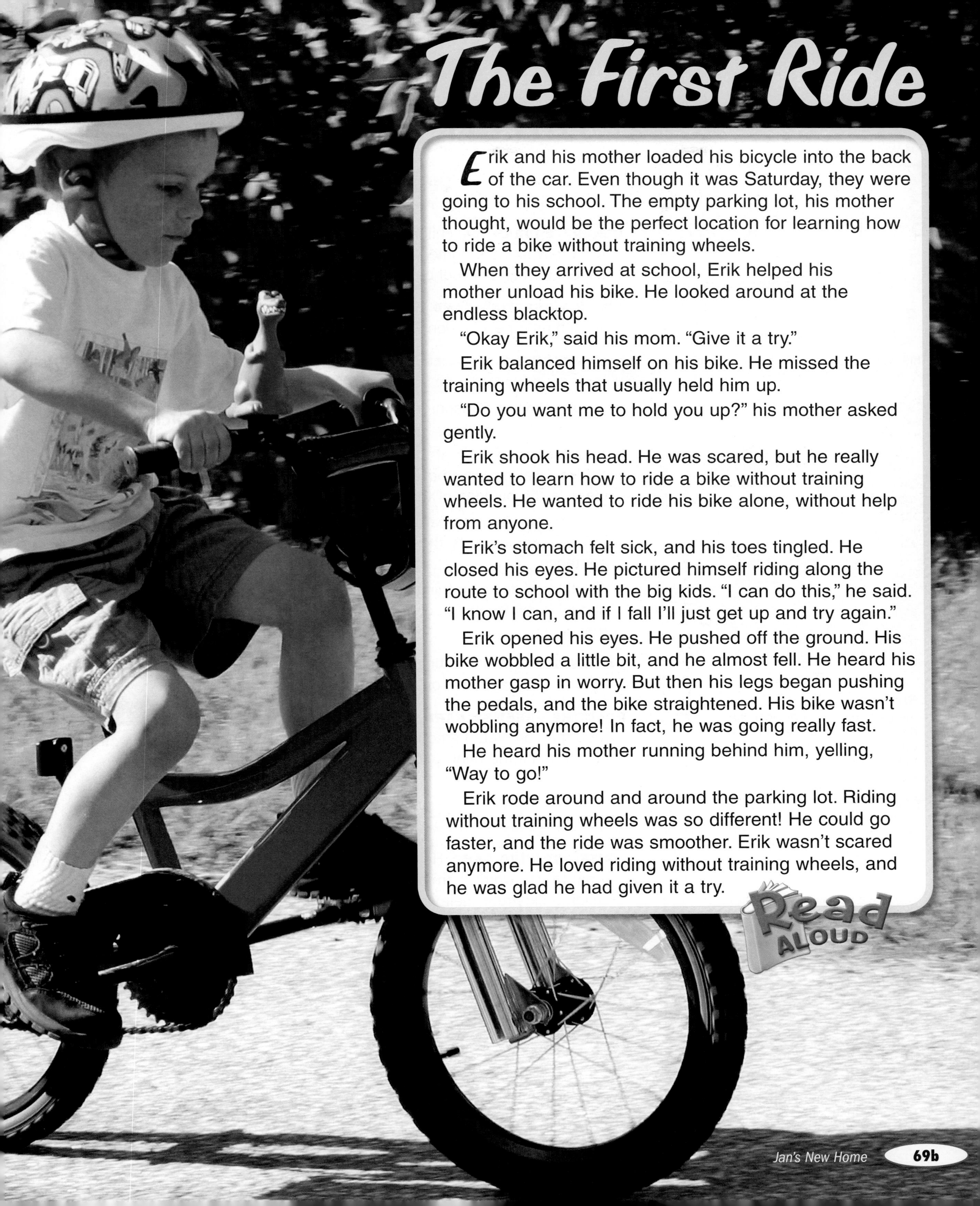

The First Ride

Erik and his mother loaded his bicycle into the back of the car. Even though it was Saturday, they were going to his school. The empty parking lot, his mother thought, would be the perfect location for learning how to ride a bike without training wheels.

When they arrived at school, Erik helped his mother unload his bike. He looked around at the endless blacktop.

"Okay Erik," said his mom. "Give it a try."

Erik balanced himself on his bike. He missed the training wheels that usually held him up.

"Do you want me to hold you up?" his mother asked gently.

Erik shook his head. He was scared, but he really wanted to learn how to ride a bike without training wheels. He wanted to ride his bike alone, without help from anyone.

Erik's stomach felt sick, and his toes tingled. He closed his eyes. He pictured himself riding along the route to school with the big kids. "I can do this," he said. "I know I can, and if I fall I'll just get up and try again."

Erik opened his eyes. He pushed off the ground. His bike wobbled a little bit, and he almost fell. He heard his mother gasp in worry. But then his legs began pushing the pedals, and the bike straightened. His bike wasn't wobbling anymore! In fact, he was going really fast.

He heard his mother running behind him, yelling, "Way to go!"

Erik rode around and around the parking lot. Riding without training wheels was so different! He could go faster, and the ride was smoother. Erik wasn't scared anymore. He loved riding without training wheels, and he was glad he had given it a try.

Read ALOUD

OBJECTIVE

- Write a greeting card.

DAILY FIX-IT

1. My dad fickses buss.
My dad fixes buses.

2. i have a vere friendly class.
I have a very friendly class.

This week's practice sentences appear on Daily Fix-It Transparency 15.

Strategic Intervention

Children who are not able to write independently may illustrate a greeting card and copy a simple label such as *Thank You* or *Happy Birthday* on the front of the card.

Advanced

Have children create a computer-generated greeting card. Children design, then print and fold the card as shown on the program.

Support Writing Before writing the greeting card, have children discuss with a partner whom they will write to and what they plan to share with that person in their greeting card.

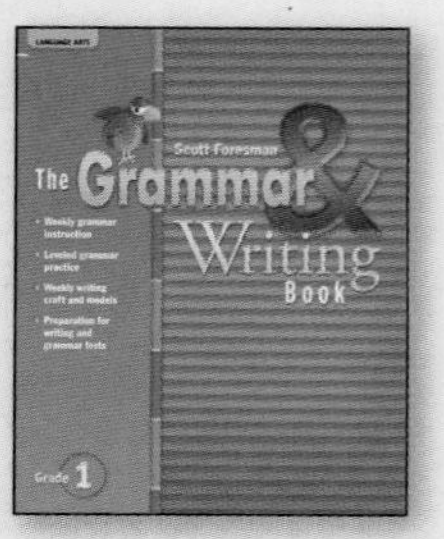

The Grammar and Writing Book
For more instruction and practice, use pp. 134–139.

Shared Writing

WRITE Greeting Card

GENERATE IDEAS Ask children to imagine that they are making a welcome card for a new student named Jan. What can they tell Jan about their classroom and school to help her feel better about the changes in her life?

WRITE A GREETING CARD Explain that the class will create a greeting card that welcomes a new student.

COMPREHENSION SKILL Have children develop the theme—the big idea—for their greeting card.

- Display Writing Transparency 15 and read the title.
- Ask children to think of the greeting card theme—welcoming a new student to their class is the big idea of the greeting card.
- Read the front of the card. Ask children for ideas to complete the *Welcome to* sentence.
- As children describe things they think Jan should know for the card, record their responses.

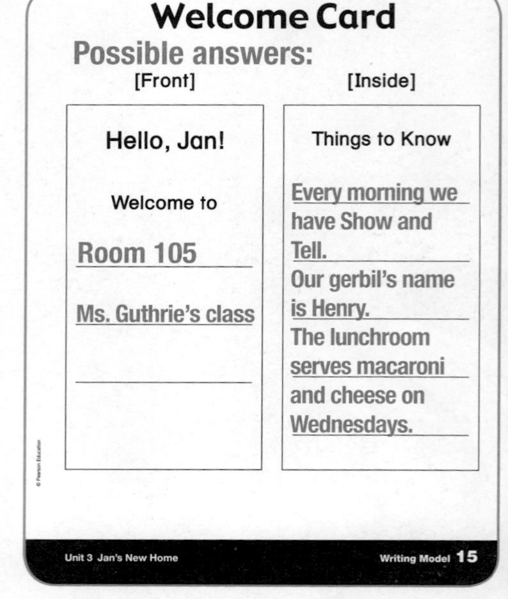

Welcome Card
Possible answers:

[Front]
Hello, Jan!
Welcome to
Room 105
Ms. Guthrie's class

[Inside]
Things to Know
Every morning we have Show and Tell.
Our gerbil's name is Henry.
The lunchroom serves macaroni and cheese on Wednesdays.

Unit 3 Jan's New Home — Writing Model 15

▲ **Writing Transparency 15**

HANDWRITING While writing, model the letter forms as shown on TR12–15.

READ THE GREETING CARD Have children read the completed greeting card aloud as you track the print.

INDEPENDENT WRITING

WRITE GREETING CARD Have children write their own greeting card. Encourage them to use words from the Word Wall and the Amazing Words board. Let children illustrate their writing. You may gather children's work to display on a Greetings bulletin board. Then allow those children who wish to send their cards to do so.

Grammar

TEACH/MODEL Verbs That Do Not Add *-s*

REVIEW VERBS Remind children that a verb tells what someone or something does.

IDENTIFY VERBS THAT DO NOT ADD *-s* Display Grammar Transparency 15. Read the definition aloud. Then model with item 1.

- The naming part is more than one, so I will not add *–s* to the action word.
- I do not add *–s* to a verb if the sentence is about two or more people. *Carl and Jan move to a new house.* Circle *move*.

Continue modeling with items 2–5.

PRACTICE

CIRCLE VERBS Write three sentences with plural subjects on the board. Have children identify the correct verb.

- Look at the naming part of the sentence.
- Does this sentence tell about two or more people, animals, or things?

ADDITIONAL PRACTICE For additional practice use pp. 134–139 in the Grammar and Writing book.

OBJECTIVE

- Identify verbs that do not add *-s*.

Verbs That Do Not Add *-s*

Do not add **-s** to a verb that tells what two or more people, animals, or things do now.

We **pack** boxes. The men **load** the truck.

Circle the verb that shows more than one.

1. Carl and Jan (move, moves) to a new house.
2. They (sees, see) Jim and Annie.
3. Jim and Annie (bring, brings) a gift.
4. They (talks, talk) to Carl and Jan.
5. Carl and Jan (like, likes) their new neighbors.

Unit 3 Jan's New Home Grammar **15**

▲ **Grammar Transparency 15**

Wrap Up Your Day!

ENDING *-es* Write *wish* and ask children to read the word. Add *-es* to create *wishes* and ask children to read this new word. Follow a similar procedure with *kiss* adding *-es* to the word.

SPELLING ADDING *-es* Have children name the letters for each sound in *class* as they write the word on a piece of paper. Now have children add the letters *-es* to the end of the word to create a new word, *classes*. Continue this spelling practice with *fix* and *bus*.

THEME To help children identify theme, ask: What is the big idea in "The First Ride"? What lesson can be learned from this story? (Sometimes you have to try new things even though you might be scared.)

LET'S TALK ABOUT IT Discuss how Erik felt in "The First Ride." Remind children that change can be both exciting and scary. How did Erik feel once he knew how to ride his bike without training wheels? (not scared, he loved riding without training wheels, glad he tried it)

HOMEWORK Send home this week's Family Times newsletter.

PREVIEW Day 2

Tell children that tomorrow the class will read about an exciting change that is happening.

Day 2

AT A GLANCE

Share Literature
Mr. George Baker

Phonemic Awareness
Blend and Segment Onset/Rime

Phonics and Spelling
r-Controlled *or, ore*
Spelling: Adding *-es*

Read Apply Phonics Word Wall

Group Time < Differentiated Instruction

High-Frequency Words
away car friends house
our school very

Interactive Writing
Letter

Grammar
Verbs That Do Not Add *-s*

Speaking and Listening
Make Introductions

Materials
- *Sing with Me Big Book*
- Big Book *Mr. George Baker*
- Sound-Spelling Card 25
- Letter Tiles
- Decodable Reader 30
- Student Edition 70–71
- Tested Word Cards

Morning Warm-Up!

Mr. George Baker goes to school to try to read. It's very hard work. But he is always excited and happy. Why do you get excited about going to school?

QUESTION OF THE DAY Encourage children to sing "New Location" from the *Sing with Me Big Book* as you gather. Write and read the message and discuss the question.

REVIEW SOUNDS OF *y*

- Read the message and ask children to find words that have the long *e* sound of *y*. (*very, happy*)
- Ask them to find words that have the long *i* sound of *y*. (*try, why*)

ELL

Build Background Use the Day 2 instruction on ELL Poster 15 to preview high-frequency words.

ELL Poster 15

Share Literature

BUILD CONCEPTS

REPETITION Ask what job Mr. George Baker once had. (drummer) Read the words the author uses to illustrate drumming: *Tappidy-boom. Tapidy-boom. Tappidy-boom-boom-tap.* Discuss how these words represent the sound of drum beats. The words repeat to show the rhythm of a drum.

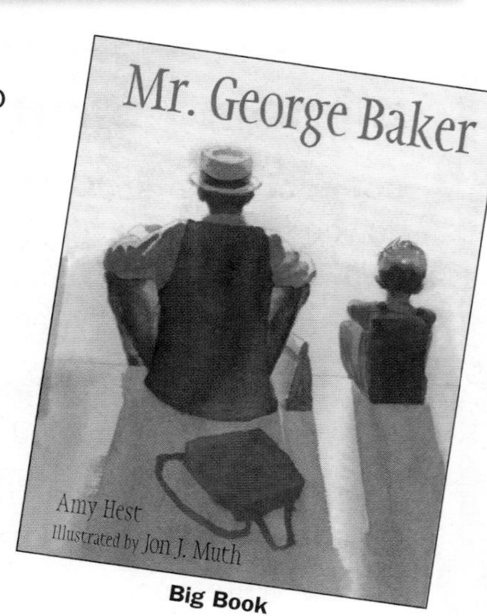

Big Book

BUILD ORAL VOCABULARY Harry and Mr. Baker spend a lot of time together waiting for the bus. They notice the falling leaves that **swoop** and **tumble.** Ask children to listen to find out what else they do while they wait.

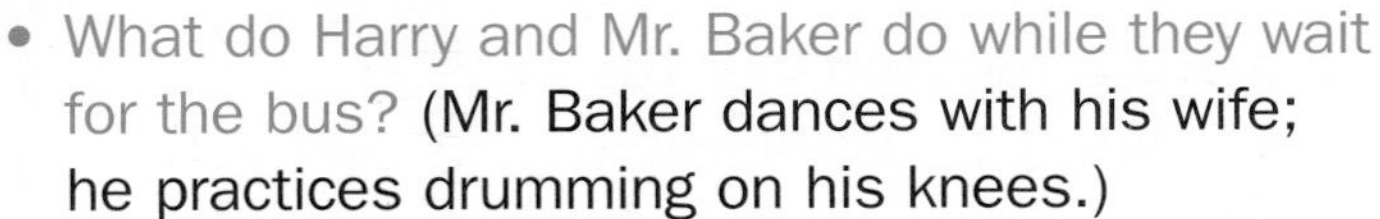

- What do Harry and Mr. Baker do while they wait for the bus? (Mr. Baker dances with his wife; he practices drumming on his knees.)

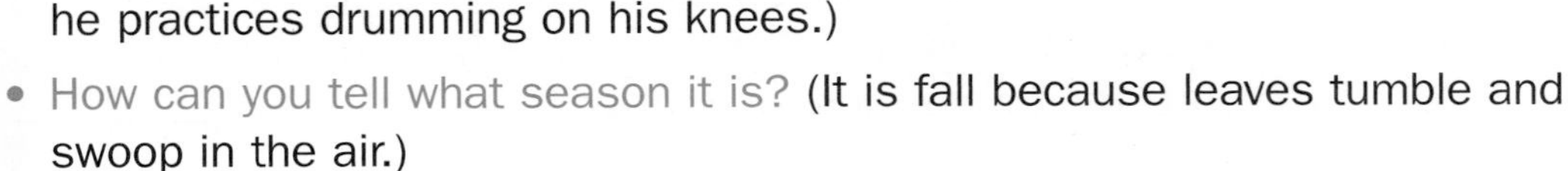

- How can you tell what season it is? (It is fall because leaves tumble and swoop in the air.)

Phonemic Awareness

BLEND AND SEGMENT ONSET/RIME

- Mr. George Baker is not short. Listen to these word parts in *short.*
- Model saying the onset and rime, /sh/-*ort.* Have children say the sounds with you, /sh/-*ort,* and then say the sounds by themselves.
- Now say each sound as you write the onset and rime that goes with it. (Say /sh/-*ort* as you write *sh, ort.*)
- Have children say the sounds as you point to the word parts (/sh/-*ort*) and blend the sounds to say the word, *short.*
- Erase *sh* and add *s* in front of *ort.* Listen as I add the /s/ sound in front of -*ort:* /s/-*ort,* *sort.* Have children say the sounds with you.

Continue the activity with these examples.

b/orn	**c/ork**	**m/ore**
h/orn	**f/ork**	**ch/ore**
th/orn	**st/ork**	**st/ore**

OBJECTIVES

- Discuss repetition.
- Set purpose for listening.
- Build oral vocabulary.
- Blend and segment onset/rime.

to build oral vocabulary

arrive
depart
location
route
swoop
tumble
crumple
stampede

MONITOR PROGRESS

If... children lack oral vocabulary experiences about the concept Growing and Changing,

then... use the Oral Vocabulary Routine. See p. DI·5 to teach *swoop* and *tumble.*

Build Concepts Revisit p. 23 and paraphrase: Harry thinks learning to read is hard. Mr. George Baker thinks learning to read is hard too. Encourage children to comment on their own experiences with learning to read. Then turn to p. 24: Mr. George Baker says, "We can do it." Mr. George Baker and Harry can learn to read. Point out children's successes with reading that show why they can do it too.

r-Controlled *or, ore*

TEACH/MODEL

Blending Strategy

ROUTINE

1. **Connect** Write *spot.* You studied words like this already. What do you know about reading this word? (The *o* in *spot* has the short *o* vowel sound: /o/.) Today we'll learn about a sound of *o* when it is followed by the letter *r*.
2. **Use Sound-Spelling Card** Display Card 25. This is *orchestra.* The sound you hear at the beginning of *orchestra* is /ôr/. /ôr/ is the *r*-controlled sound of *o*. Say it with me: /ôr/.

or, ore

Sound-Spelling Card 25

3. **Model** Write *sport.* When the letter *o* is followed by *r*, the *o* has the *r*-controlled sound. This is how I blend this word. Segment and blend *sport.* Let's blend this word together: /s/ /p/ /ôr/ /t/, *sport.* Then write *more* and follow the same modeling routine.
4. **Group Practice** Blend these words together. Continue with *for, corn, sore, porch,* and *store.*

5. **Review** What do you know about reading these words? The letters *or* and *ore* stand for /ôr/.

BLEND WORDS

INDIVIDUALS BLEND *or* AND *ore* WORDS Call on individual children to blend the words *cork, sort, snore, born, score, north,* and *forget.* Have them tell what they know about each word before reading it. (The *or* and *ore* stand for /ôr/.) For feedback, refer to step five of the Blending Strategy Routine.

OBJECTIVES

- Associate the sound /ôr/ with *or, ore.*
- Blend, read, and build *r*-controlled *or, ore* words.

Skills Trace	
r-Controlled *or, ore*	
Introduce/Teach	**TE: 1.3 70c–d, 72c–d**
Practice	TE: 1.3 70f; PB: 1.2 25; DR 30
Reteach/Review	TE: 1.3 90c; 114c–d DI·79; PB: 1.2 35
Assess/Test	TE: 1.3 90e–g Benchmark Test, Unit 3

Generalization

A single vowel followed by the letter *r* has a sound that is neither short nor long, but *r*-controlled.

Strategic Intervention

Use **Monitor Progress,** p. 70d during Group Time after children have had more practice with *r*-controlled *or, ore.*

Advanced

Use **Monitor Progress,** p. 70d as a preassessment to determine whether or not this group of children would benefit from this instruction with *r*-controlled *or, ore* words.

Support Phonics Although the *r* is pronounced differently in Spanish, there are similarities in the way some words with *or* are pronounced in English and Spanish. Point out the similarities in words such as *orden/order* and *forma/form.*

See the Phonics Transition Lessons in the ELL and Transition Handbook.

BUILD WORDS

INDIVIDUALS MAKE *or* AND *ore* WORDS Write *horn* and have the class blend it. Have children spell *horn* with letter tiles. Monitor work and provide feedback.

- Change the *h* in *horn* to *w*. What is the new word?

- Change the *n* to *e*. What is the new word?

- Change the *w* to *m*. What is the new word?

- Change the *m* to *sh*. What is the new word?

MODEL BLENDING WORD FAMILIES Write *short.* Remind children that they can also blend by looking at bigger chunks of a word. I can blend by saying the sound before the vowel, /sh/, and then saying the rest of the sound together, *-ort.* Then I blend both parts together: /sh/ *-ort, short.* Have children use onset and rime to blend these words.

-ork	***-orn***	***-ore***
cork	**born**	**tore**
fork	**corn**	**store**
stork	**thorn**	**chore**

s h o r t

Monitor Progress

Check Word Reading *r*-Controlled *or, ore*

Write the following words and have individuals read them.

torn	**chore**	**fork**	**port**	**storm**
chop	**porch**	**rock**	**corn**	**store**
fort	**hole**	**score**	**choke**	**thorn**

If... children cannot blend r-controlled *or, ore* words at this point,

then... continue to monitor their progress using other instructional opportunities during the week so that they can be successful with the Day 5 Assessment. See the Skills Trace on p. 70c.

Day 1 Check Word Reading	▶ **Day 2 Check Word Reading**	**Day 3** Check High-Frequency Words/Retelling	**Day 4** Check Fluency	**Day 5** Assess Progress

Vocabulary TiP

You may wish to explain the meanings of these words.

fort	a strong building that can easily be defended
port	harbor, place where ships load and unload
thorn	a sharp point on a stem or branch of a tree or plant

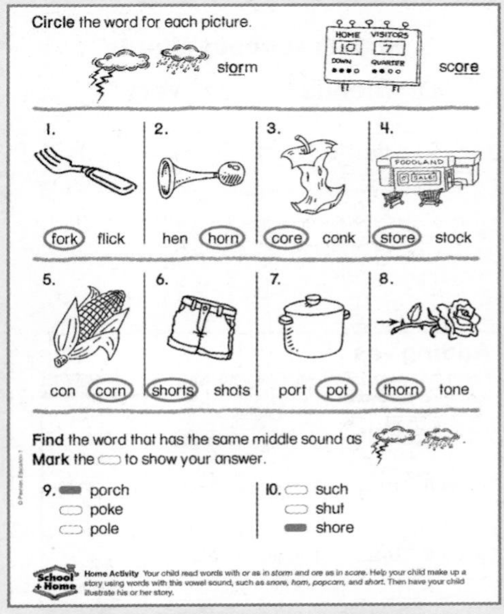
Circle the word for each picture.

storm score

1. fork flick
2. hen horn
3. core conk
4. store stock
5. con corn
6. shorts shots
7. port pot
8. thorn tone

Find the word that has the same middle sound as [storm]. **Mark** the ⊂⊃ to show your answer.

9. porch / poke / pole
10. such / shut / shore

▲ **Practice Book 1.2** p. 25, *r*-Controlled *or, ore*

Spiral REVIEW

- Row 2 contrasts *r*-controlled *or, ore* words with short vowel *o* words.
- Row 3 contrasts *r*-controlled *or, ore* words with long vowel *o* words.

Word Reading
SUCCESS PREDICTOR

2

OBJECTIVE

- Spell words with ending *-es*; plural *-es*.

Spelling Words

Adding -es

1.	**fix**	6.	**wishes***
2.	**fixes**	7.	**kiss**
3.	**class**	8.	**kisses**
4.	**classes**	9.	**bus**
5.	**wish**	10.	**buses**

High-Frequency Words

11.	**friends***	12.	**very***

* Words from the Selection

Adding -es

Finish the list word. Then write the word that means more than one.

Spelling Words: fix, fixes, class, classes, wish, wishes, kiss, kisses, bus, buses

1. one b us
2. three buses
3. one k iss
4. three kisses
5. one w ish
6. three wishes

Write the missing word.

classes, fix, fixes, class

7. My class has ten boys.
8. Sam fixes clocks.
9. Do the music classes meet here?
10. Can you fix my bike?

School + Home: Home Activity Your child spelled words that end with -es. Say a list word that does not end with -es. Ask your child to add -es and spell the new word.

▲ **Spelling Practice Book** p. 58

Spelling

PRACTICE Ending *-es;* Plural *-es*

WRITE DICTATION SENTENCES Have children write these sentences. Repeat words slowly, allowing children to hear each sound. Children may use the Word Wall to help with spelling high-frequency words. **Word Wall**

The bus ride was very bumpy.
Ford has friends in his math classes.
Dad wishes he could fix the porch.
Who fixes the yellow buses?

HOMEWORK Spelling Practice Book, p. 58

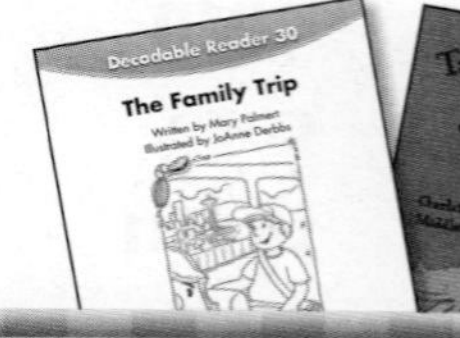

Group Time

DAY 2

On-Level	Strategic Intervention	Advanced
Read Decodable Reader 30.	**Read** Decodable Reader 30.	**Read** Self-Selected Reading.
• Use p. 70f.	• Use the **Routine** on p. DI·38.	• Use the **Routine** on p. DI·39.

Place English language learners in the groups that correspond to their reading abilities in English.

i Independent Activities

Fluency Reading Pair children to reread Decodable Reader 29, this week's Leveled Readers, the ELL Reader from the previous week, or other text at children's independent level.

Journal Writing Write about an exciting change you have experienced. Share writing.

Independent Reading See p. 68j for Reading/Library activities and suggestions.

Literacy Centers To practice ending *-es* and plural *-es*, you may use Word Work, p. 68j.

Practice Book 1.2 Theme, p. 24
r-Controlled *or, ore,* p. 25
High-Frequency Words, p. 26

Break into small groups after Spelling and before Fluency.

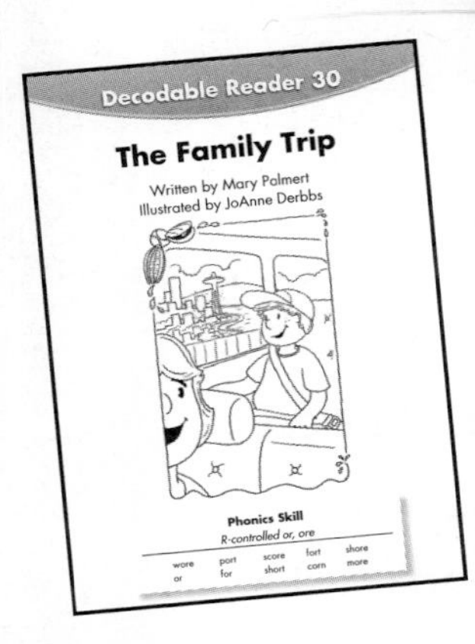

Apply Phonics

PRACTICE *r*-Controlled *or, ore*

HIGH-FREQUENCY WORDS Review *are, eat, to,* and *water* on the Word Wall. Word Wall

READ DECODABLE READER 30

- Pages 42–43 Read aloud quietly with the group.
- Page 44 Have the group read aloud without you.
- Pages 45–48 Select individuals to read aloud.

CHECK COMPREHENSION AND DECODING

- Name the places the family visits on their trip. (a port, a ballgame, a fort, the shore, and a restaurant)
- How do you know that the family likes to go places? (Answers will vary, but children may say the family seems to have fun seeing and doing a lot of different things.)
- Point to a word in the story that has the sound /ôr/. What is the word? List words that are named. Children may supply *wore, port, score, fort, shore, or, for, short, corn, more.*
- How do you know that these words have the sound /ôr/? (They have the letters *or* and *ore.*)

HOMEWORK Take-Home Decodable Reader 30

REREAD FOR FLUENCY

Paired Reading

ROUTINE

1. **Reader 1 Begins** Children read the entire book, switching readers at the end of each page.
2. **Reader 2 Begins** Have partners reread; now the other partner begins.
3. **Reread** For optimal fluency, children should reread three or four times.
4. **Provide Feedback** Listen to children read and provide corrective feedback regarding their oral reading and their use of the blending strategy.

OBJECTIVES

- Apply knowledge of letter-sounds to decode unknown words when reading.
- Use context with letter-sounds to confirm the identification of unknown words.
- Practice fluency in paired reading.

Monitor Progress

Decoding

If... children have difficulty decoding a word,	**then...** prompt them to blend the word. • What is the new word? • Is the new word a word you know? • Does it make sense in the story?

ELL

Access Content

Beginning Lead children on a picture walk through *The Family Trip.* Help them pantomime and describe actions: swimming at the shore, jumping in the waves, eating clams and corn.

Intermediate Preview *The Family Trip,* using the illustrations to explain /ôr/ words such as *port, fort,* and *corn.*

Advanced Before reading *The Family Trip,* explain the meaning of "the score is six to five" and "we go for a short walk."

Student Pages 70–71

Words to Read

very
car
away
our
house
school
friends

70

Read the Words

Jan was very sad. As her family drove off in the car, she said, "I don't want to go away. I like our house. I like my school and my friends. Let's stay here."

Jan's New Home

Genre: Realistic Fiction
Realistic fiction is a made-up story about things that could really happen. The next story is about a girl who must move to a new home.

71

OBJECTIVE

- Recognize high-frequency words.

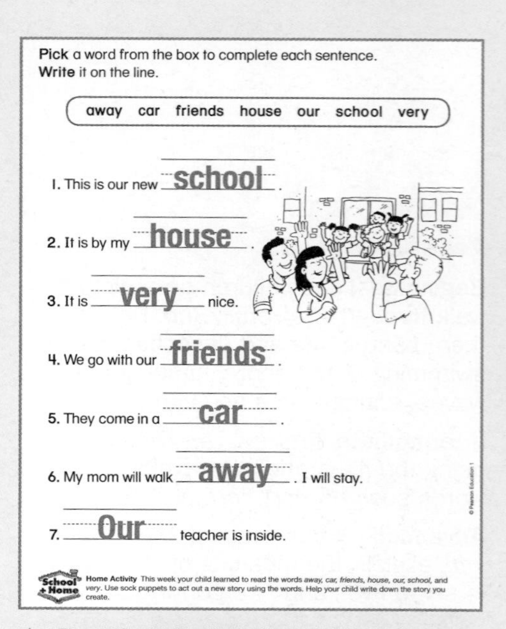

Pick a word from the box to complete each sentence.
Write it on the line.

away car friends house our school very

1. This is our new school.
2. It is by my house.
3. It is very nice.
4. We go with our friends.
5. They come in a car.
6. My mom will walk away. I will stay.
7. Our teacher is inside.

School + Home **Home Activity** This week your child learned to read the words *away, car, friends, house, our, school,* and *very*. Use sock puppets to act out a new story using the words. Help your child write down the story you create.

▲ **Practice Book 1.2** p. 26, High-Frequency Words

High-Frequency Words

Nondecodable Words

ROUTINE

1. **Say and Spell** Look at the words on p. 70. You cannot blend the sounds in these words. We will spell the words and use letter-sounds we know to learn them. Point to the first word. This word is *very, v-e-r-y, very.* What is this word? What are the letters in this word?
2. **Identify Familiar Letter-Sounds** Point to the first letter in *very.* What is this letter? What is the sound for this letter? (*v*/v/)
3. **Demonstrate Meaning** Tell me a sentence using this word.

Repeat the routine with the other Words to Read. Have children identify these familiar letter-sounds: *car* (*c*/k/), *away* (*w*/w/), *our* (*r*/r/), *house* (*h*/h/, *s*/s/), *school* (*s*/s/, *l*/l/), *friends* (*fr*/fr/, *nd*/nd/).

Have children read aloud the sentences on p. 71 and point to the Words to Read. Discuss what the quotation marks tell about these sentences. Ask who is speaking. Add the words to the Word Wall. Word Wall

Interactive Writing

WRITE Letter

BRAINSTORM Use pp. 68–69 of the Student Edition to encourage a discussion about moving. Picture walk through the pages and ask children to identify what each person is thinking about. Discuss ways people can keep in touch with one another after they move. Ask children if they have a friend who lives far away or a relative they don't see often.

SHARE THE PEN Have children participate in writing a letter to a friend. Tell children that a letter generally has five parts: date, greeting, body, closing, and a signature. To begin, have children tell you today's date. Write the date at the top of your letter. Next, decide to whom you will write and write the greeting. Then, decide the purpose of your letter. Why are you writing a letter? Do you have news to share? Have volunteers write familiar word parts and high-frequency words. Ask questions such as:

- What do I write in the greeting? (*Dear* and then the name of the person I'm writing to.)
- How do I begin each sentence? (with a capital letter)
- Which part of my letter will have the most writing? (body)
- After I write the closing, what do I do? (sign my name)

Continue to have individuals make contributions to the letter. Frequently reread what has been written while tracking the print.

READ THE LETTER Read the completed letter aloud, having children echo you.

March 4, 20__

Dear Sam,

Ms. Evans took us to the park yesterday. We looked at rocks. We brought some back with us. We will use them in science. We miss you on our field trips. Write soon.

Your friends,
Children in Room 22

INDEPENDENT WRITING

WRITE A LETTER Have children write their own letter to a friend. Let children illustrate their writing. Demonstrate how to address an envelope. Provide envelopes and have children address them and then send their letters to their friends.

OBJECTIVE

- Write a letter.

Strategic Intervention

Have children use a letter-writing framework with greeting, closing, and date line provided. Create sentence stems where children can fill in missing words and phrases.

Advanced

Have children who are able to write complete sentences independently write a letter to a former teacher. Encourage them to thank the teacher and share what they learned while in their class.

Writing Support Before writing, reread the class letter and highlight key words that children may want to use in their own letters.

Beginning Create a letter-writing framework with sentence stems where children can fill in missing words and phrases.

Intermediate Have children share orally what they will write while a teacher takes notes. Children may use these notes as they write the letter.

Advanced Review children's letter and show where more details can be added to give more information or to make the writing more interesting.

2

OBJECTIVES

- Identify verbs.
- Determine if the verb is for two or more.

DAILY FIX-IT

3. I kis my mom before I catch the buss.
I kiss my mom before I catch the bus.

4. My fiends meet at the bus sop.
My friends meet at the bus stop.

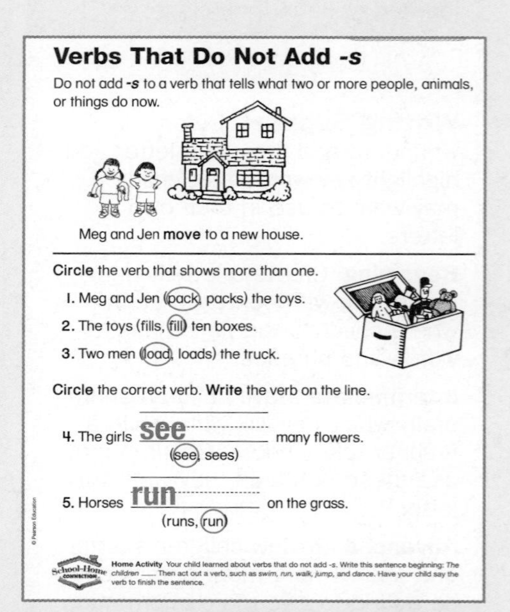

Verbs That Do Not Add *-s*

Do not add **-s** to a verb that tells what two or more people, animals, or things do now.

Meg and Jen **move** to a new house.

Circle the verb that shows more than one.

1. Meg and Jen (pack, packs) the toys.
2. The toys (fills, fill) ten boxes.
3. Two men (load, loads) the truck.

Circle the correct verb. **Write** the verb on the line.

4. The girls see many flowers. (see, sees)
5. Horses run on the grass. (runs, run)

© Pearson Education

School-Home Connection **Home Activity** Your child learned about verbs that do not add -s. Write this sentence beginning: *The children* ___. Then act out a verb, such as *swim, run, walk, jump,* and *dance*. Have your child say the verb to finish the sentence.

▲ **Grammar and Writing Practice Book** p. 57

ELL

Support Grammar Give children several examples to show that English does not add *-s* to the verb if the sentence is about more than one person. Use singular and plural subjects with the same verb to demonstrate adding *-s*. See the Grammar Transition lessons in the ELL and Transition Handbook.

Grammar

DEVELOP THE CONCEPT Verbs

IDENTIFY VERBS Write these two sentences on the board. *Erik rides his bike. Erik and his mother ride to the school.* Ask children to identify which sentence is talking about more than one person. Identify the verbs in each sentence. Point out that the verb is *ride* in both sentences. When the sentence is only talking about one person, an *-s* is added to *ride*. In the sentence about more than one person, there is no *-s* at the end of *ride*.

Verbs may tell what two or more people, animals, or things do. What is not found at the end of these verbs? (*-s*)

PRACTICE

IDENTIFY VERBS Show pictures of children doing different activities at home or school. Tell what two or more children are doing, for example:

MODEL Two boys are drawing. Write *The boys draw.* Because two boys are doing this action, I do not add an *-s* to *draw*. Two children are working on the computer. Write *They work on the computer.*

Have children suggest other sentences for the picture and identify the verb in each sentence.

2

Speaking and Listening

MAKE INTRODUCTIONS

OBJECTIVES

- Speak to make introductions.
- Listen to learn the name of person being introduced.

DEMONSTRATE MAKING INTRODUCTIONS Explain that when two people have not met, someone who knows both people can introduce them. Ask volunteers to act out making an introduction. As you dramatize this, point out these speaking and listening behaviors.

Speakers	Listeners
• Include the names of the two people being introduced. • Tell something the two have in common. • Speak clearly.	• Look at the person speaking. • Smile and shake hands. • Listen for connections.

MAKE INTRODUCTIONS Place children in groups of three. Have two children pretend they are on the playground. The third child joins them. One of the children playing introduces the other two children to each other. Then have children switch roles and repeat the activity.

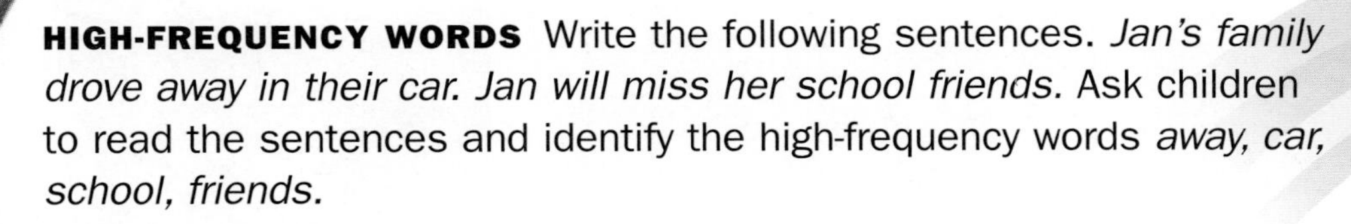

HIGH-FREQUENCY WORDS Write the following sentences. *Jan's family drove away in their car. Jan will miss her school friends.* Ask children to read the sentences and identify the high-frequency words *away, car, school, friends.*

r*-CONTROLLED *or, ore Write the sentence *She sees horses.* Ask children what sound they hear in the middle of *horses.* (/ôr/) Create a list of other words that have this /ôr/ sound.

LET'S TALK ABOUT IT Display the three-column chart "Skill," "Can Do," "Can't Do." Review the Big Book *Mr. George Baker.* Ask: What does George do with his wife in this story? (dance) Encourage children to add dance to the chart.

PREVIEW Day 3

Tell children that tomorrow they will read about a girl named Jan who is experiencing a big change in her life.

Day 3
AT A GLANCE

Share Literature
Mr. George Baker

Phonemic Awareness
Blend and Segment Onset/Rime

Phonics and Spelling
Ending *-es*, Plural *-es*, and *r*-Controlled *or, ore*
Spelling: Adding *-es*

Build Background
Moving to a New Home

Vocabulary
Selection Words
move toys window
High-Frequency Words
away car friends house our school very

Comprehension
Skill Theme
Strategy Monitor and Fix Up

Read

< Differentiated Instruction
Jan's New Home

Vocabulary
Descriptive Words

Fluency
Attend to Punctuation

Writing Trait
Voice

Grammar
Verbs That Do Not Add *-s*

Materials
- *Sing with Me Big Book*
- Big Book *Mr. George Baker*
- Phonics Songs/Rhymes Chart 15
- Letter Tiles
- Background Building Audio
- Graphic Organizer Flip Chart 33
- Vocabulary Transparency 15
- Student Edition 72–87

Morning Warm-Up!

Today we will read about a family that moves to a new house. Wow! That sounds exciting! How do you think they feel? What kind of changes are fun?

QUESTION OF THE DAY Encourage children to sing "New Location" from the *Sing with Me Big Book* as you gather. Write the message and track the print as you read it. Discuss the questions.

REVIEW END PUNCTUATION

- Read each sentence and ask children to name the end mark.
- Discuss what each end mark means.
- Reread the sentences with expression.

ELL

Build Background Use the Day 3 instruction on ELL Poster 15 to support children's use of English to communicate about lesson concepts.

ELL Poster 15

Share Literature

LISTEN AND RESPOND

BUILD ORAL VOCABULARY Review that yesterday the class read the book to find out what Harry and Mr. Baker do while they wait for the bus. Ask that children listen today to find out whether Mr. George Baker is excited about going to school.

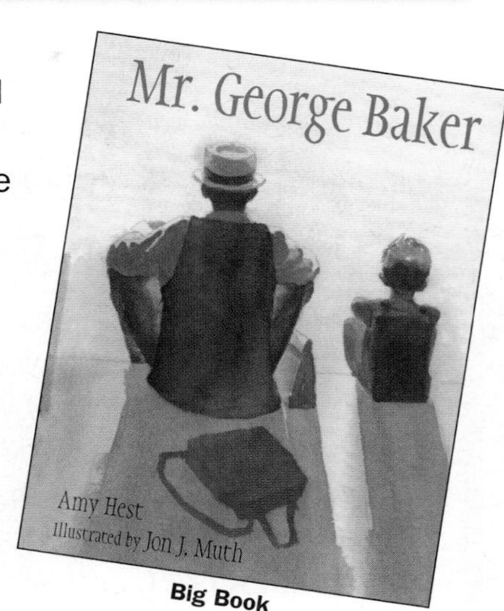

Big Book

MONITOR LISTENING COMPREHENSION

- Do you think Mr. George Baker is excited about going to school? How can you tell? (Yes, because he is always happy waiting for the bus. He dances with Mrs. Baker.)
- How do Mr. Baker's clothes look? (His hat is **crumpled,** or smashed; his pants are baggy; his shoes are crumpled; his sweater hangs.)

Phonemic Awareness

BLEND AND SEGMENT ONSET/RIME

- Mr. George Baker sits on his porch. Listen to the word parts in *porch.*
- Model saying the onset and rime, /p/-*orch.* Have children say the sounds with you, /p/-*orch,* and then say the sounds by themselves.
- Now say the onset and rime as you write the word part that goes with it. Say /p/-*orch* as you write *p, orch* and then blend the parts to say *porch.*
- Have children say the sounds as you point to the letters /p/-*orch* and blend the sounds to say the word, *porch.*
- Erase *p* and add *t* to -*orch.* Listen as I change the /p/ sound at the beginning of *porch* to the /t/ sound: /t/-*orch, torch.* Repeat with /sc/-*orch, scorch.* Have children say the sounds with you, /sc/-*orch, scorch.*

Continue the activity with these examples.

sh/ore	**f/ort**	**f/orm**
sn/ore	**sp/ort**	**st/orm**

OBJECTIVES

- Set purpose for listening.
- Build oral vocabulary.
- Blend and segment onset/rime.

arrive
depart
location
route
swoop
tumble
crumple
stampede

MONITOR PROGRESS

If... children lack oral vocabulary experiences about the concept Growing and Changing,

then... use the Oral Vocabulary Routine. See p. DI•5 to teach *crumple.*

Listen and Respond Display the Big Book *Mr. George Baker.* Go over the names. Then have children draw a picture of Mr. George Baker reading something. As children share their drawings, help them explain what he is reading and why.

OBJECTIVES

- Review ending *-es;* plural *-es* words.
- Sort words with ending *-es;* plural *es* and *r*-controlled *or, -ore* words.
- Preview words before reading them.
- Spell words with ending *-es;* plural *-es.*

Strategic Intervention

Use **Strategic Intervention Decodable Reader 15** for more practice with ending *-es;* plural *-es,* and *r*-controlled *or, ore* words.

Support Phonics Speakers of other languages may have difficulty pronouncing words with the *-es* ending and may spell them with *z.* Provide additional practice with these words.

See the Phonics Transition Lessons in the ELL and Transition Handbook.

Ending *-es*; Plural *-es*, *r*-Controlled *or, ore*

TEACH/MODEL

Fluent Word Reading

ROUTINE

1. **Connect** Write *crashes.* You can read this word because you know how to read words with endings. What is the base word? *(crash)* What is the ending? *(es)* What is the word? *(crashes)* Write *glass* and *glasses.* What's the word? *(glasses)* How does the *-es* change the meaning. (*Glasses* means "more than one glass.") Write *pork.* You can read this word because you know how to read words with *or.* What sound does *or* in this word stand for? (/ôr/) What is the word? *(pork)* Continue with *shore.*
2. **Model** When you come to a new word, look to see if it has an ending. Say the sounds in the base word to yourself and read the ending. Then blend the base word and ending to read the word. Model reading *crashes, glasses, pork,* and *shore* in this way. When you come to a new word, what are you going to do?
3. **Group Practice** Write *buses, store, sport.* Let's read these words. Look at all the letters, think about their sounds, and say the sounds to yourself. When I point to the word, let's read it together. Allow 2–3 seconds previewing time for each word. Which word means "more than one"? *(buses)* Then follow this routine to have children blend the base word and ending to read *rushes.*

WORD READING

PHONICS SONGS AND RHYMES CHART 15 Frame each of the following words on Phonics Songs and Rhymes Chart 15: *Jordan, sore, York, North, Shore, corner, cords, more, sorts, for, sports, or, porches, forts, explore, wishes, boxes, porches, dishes.* Call on individuals to read them. Guide children in previewing.

Sing "Moving to New York" to the tune of "If You're Happy and You Know It" or play the CD. Have children follow along on the chart as they sing. Then have individuals take turns locating ending *-es;* plural *-es* and *r*-controlled *or, ore* words on the chart.

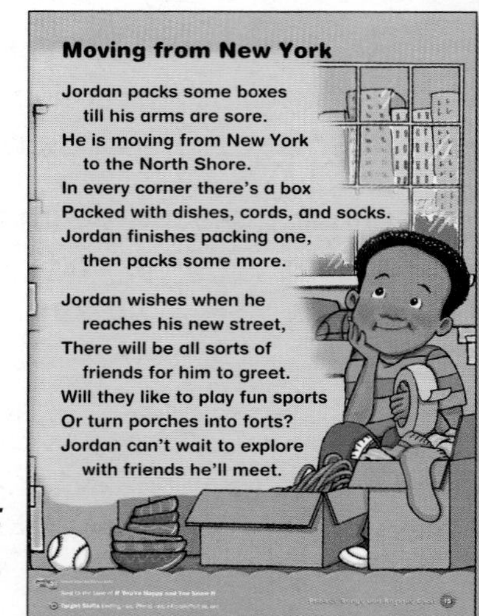

Phonics Songs and Rhymes Chart 15

Phonics Songs and Rhymes Audio

SORT WORDS

SORT WORDS Display words with ending *-es* and plural *-es* in one column and words with the sound of /ôr/ in another column. Ask children to tell how the letters in the words in each column are alike. (The words in column one all have the letters *es* at the end. The words in column two all have the letters *or* and *ore*.) Have children suggest a heading for each column. (Words with *-es;* Words with *or* and *ore)* Call on children to read the words in each column. Have them point out the endings and frame the base word in *dashes* and *rushes.* Then have children identify the words with *es* that mean "more than one." *(foxes, classes)* Have the lists read.

Words with *-es*	Words with *or* and *ore*
foxes	born
dashes	chore
classes	for
rushes	core

Spelling

PRACTICE ENDING *-es*; PLURAL *-es*

MATCH IT Have children write spelling words 1–10 on cards.

- Have partners mix the cards and put them facedown.
- Have children play "Match It," turning over two cards at a time.
- If the two cards show a base word and the same base word with the ending *-es* or a word that means "one" and the same word that means "more than one," have the child keep the pair. For example: *fix/fixes* or *bus/buses.*
- If the cards do not match, the player returns the cards to the pile.
- When the pairs are matched, have partners take turns using the words in sentences.

HOMEWORK Spelling Practice Book, p. 59

Spelling Words

Ending -es; Plural -es

1. fix
2. fixes
3. class
4. classes
5. wish
6. wishes*
7. kiss
8. kisses
9. bus
10. buses*

High-Frequency Words

11. friends*
12. very*

* Words from the Selection

Adding -es

Spelling Words: fix, fixes, class, classes, wish, wishes, kiss, kisses, bus, buses

Read about a wish. **Write** the missing list words.

1. I wish I could visit my aunt.
2. I would go by bus.
3. I might need to ride on two or three buses.
4. My aunt fixes hair in her shop.
5. She would fix my hair.
6. She teaches art classes, too.
7. I could go to a class.
8. I would give my aunt a big kiss.
9. She would give me lots of kisses.
10. I hope my wishes come true!

Home Activity Your child wrote spelling words to complete a story. Ask your child to write about a wish, using some of the list words.

▲ **Spelling Practice Book** p. 59

Build Background

OBJECTIVES
- Build background.
- Learn selection words.
- Recognize high-frequency words.

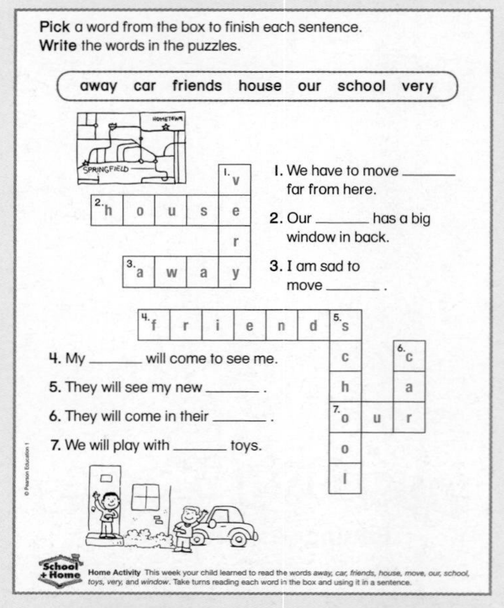
Pick a word from the box to finish each sentence.
Write the words in the puzzles.

away car friends house our school very

1. We have to move _____ far from here.
2. Our _____ has a big window in back.
3. I am sad to move _____.
4. My _____ will come to see me.
5. They will see my new _____.
6. They will come in their _____.
7. We will play with _____ toys.

Home Activity This week your child learned to read the words away, car, friends, house, move, our, school, toys, very, and window. Take turns reading each word in the box and using it in a sentence.

▲ **Practice Book 1.2** p. 27, High-Frequency and Selection Words

DISCUSS MOVING TO A NEW HOME Initiate discussion by asking children what they know about moving to a new home.

- Have you ever moved to a new place? How did you feel?
- What would change if you moved?

BACKGROUND-BUILDING AUDIO Have children listen to the CD and share the new information they learned about moving.

Sing with Me/ Background Building Audio

COMPLETE A LETTER Draw a letter or display Graphic Organizer 33. Ask children to imagine that they are moving to a new home. Ask them what they might write to a friend that describes how they feel and what they are experiencing. After the discussion, write a letter together.

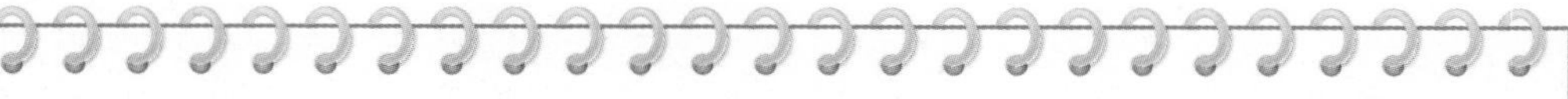

June 3, 2006

Dear Mary,

We moved to a new house. I was sad at first. I still miss my old friends. I like my new house. There is a big garden in the backyard. I also have my own room. My new school is big. I am in the art club. Will you come to visit this summer?

Your friend,

Jane

▲ **Graphic Organizer Flip Chart 33**

CONNECT TO SELECTION Connect background information to *Jan's New Home.*

Sometimes people are excited about moving to a new place. Sometimes they are afraid. Jan is a character in the story we are about to read. We'll find out what will change when Jan moves to a new home.

Activate Prior Knowledge Children whose first language is not English may have moved to this country, or their family may have moved here before they were born. Discuss with them what it was like moving to a new country and what new things they have learned.

Vocabulary

SELECTION WORDS

Use Vocabulary Transparency 15 to introduce the selection words.

- Read each sentence as you track the print.
- Frame each underlined word. Explain the word's meaning.

  window an opening in a wall or room that lets in fresh air and light
  toys things to play with
  move to change the place where you live

- Ask children to identify familiar letter-sounds and word parts: *window* (identify the word *wind*), *toys* (/t/t/, ending *-s* for "more than one"), *move* (/m/m/, /v/v/).
- Have children read each sentence aloud with you.
- To encourage discussion using the selection words, ask children to tell about what they think would be the best bedroom ever.

HIGH-FREQUENCY WORDS

Use Vocabulary Transparency 15 to review this week's words.

- Point to a word. Say and spell it.
- Have children say and spell the word.
- Ask children to identify familiar letter-sounds.

Selection Words

Moving Day

1. Dan looks out the window.
2. He sees his toys go into the truck.
3. The men will move his toys to a new house.

High-Frequency Words

Words to Read

away	car	friends	house
our	school	very	

© Pearson Education 1

Unit 3 Jan's New Home — Vocabulary 15

▲ **Vocabulary Transparency 15**

ELL

Access Content Use the vocabulary strategies and word cards in the ELL Teaching Guide, pp. 101–102.

Monitor Progress — **Check High-Frequency Words**

Point to the following words on the Word Wall and have individuals read them.

things	**school**	**very**	**house**	**away**	**could**	**friends**
our	**family**	**stay**	**down**	**car**	**home**	**everything**

If... children cannot read these words,

then... have them practice in pairs with word cards before reading the selection. Monitor their fluency with these words during reading, and provide additional practice opportunities before the Day 5 Assessment.

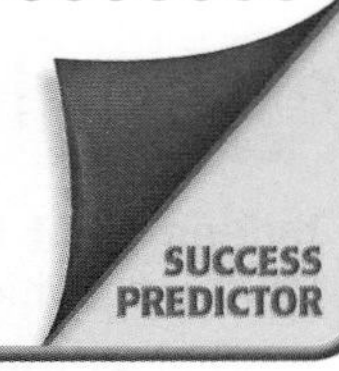

SUCCESS PREDICTOR

Day 1 Check Word Reading | **Day 2** Check Word Reading | ▶**Day 3 Check High-Frequency Words/Retelling** | **Day 4** Check Fluency | **Day 5** Assess Progress

Spiral REVIEW

- Reviews previously taught high-frequency words.

High-Frequency Words SUCCESS PREDICTOR

Comprehension

OBJECTIVES

- Identify the theme of a story.
- Summarize details in text to monitor and fix up.

THEME

RECOGNIZE THEME Remind children that all stories have a big idea. Recall previously read stories. Guide children in identifying the big idea.

CONNECT TO READING

- As you read, ask yourself what the author wants you to learn or know.
- Ask yourself if the characters learn a lesson.
- Think about things that have happened in your own life that can help you understand the big idea of the story.

MONITOR AND FIX UP

INTRODUCE THE STRATEGY Remind children that authors often give details, or small pieces of information, about what is happening in a story.

MODEL When I don't understand what I am reading, I pause and think about the details the author included. Thinking about the details helps me understand what is happening in the story.

CONNECT TO READING Encourage children to ask themselves these questions as they read *Jan's New Home*.

- Why did the author include these details?
- What do these details tell about?
- What picture can I make in my mind with these details?

Group Time

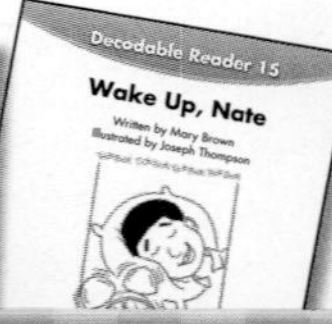

DAY 3

On-Level	Strategic Intervention	Advanced
Read *Jan's New Home.*	**Read** Decodable Reader 15.	**Read** *Jan's New Home.*
• Use pp. 72–87.	• Read or listen to *Jan's New Home.*	• Use the **Routine** on p. DI·41.
	• Use the **Routine** on p. DI·40.	

Place English language learners in the groups that correspond to their reading abilities in English.

Independent Activities

Independent Reading See p. 68j for Reading/Library activities and suggestions.

Journal Writing Write about a time you moved to or visited a new place. Share Writing.

Literacy Centers Use the Listening and Writing Centers for *Jan's New Home* on pp. 68j and 68k.

Practice Book 1.2 High-Frequency Words and Selection Words, p. 27.

Break into small groups after Comprehension and before Fluency.

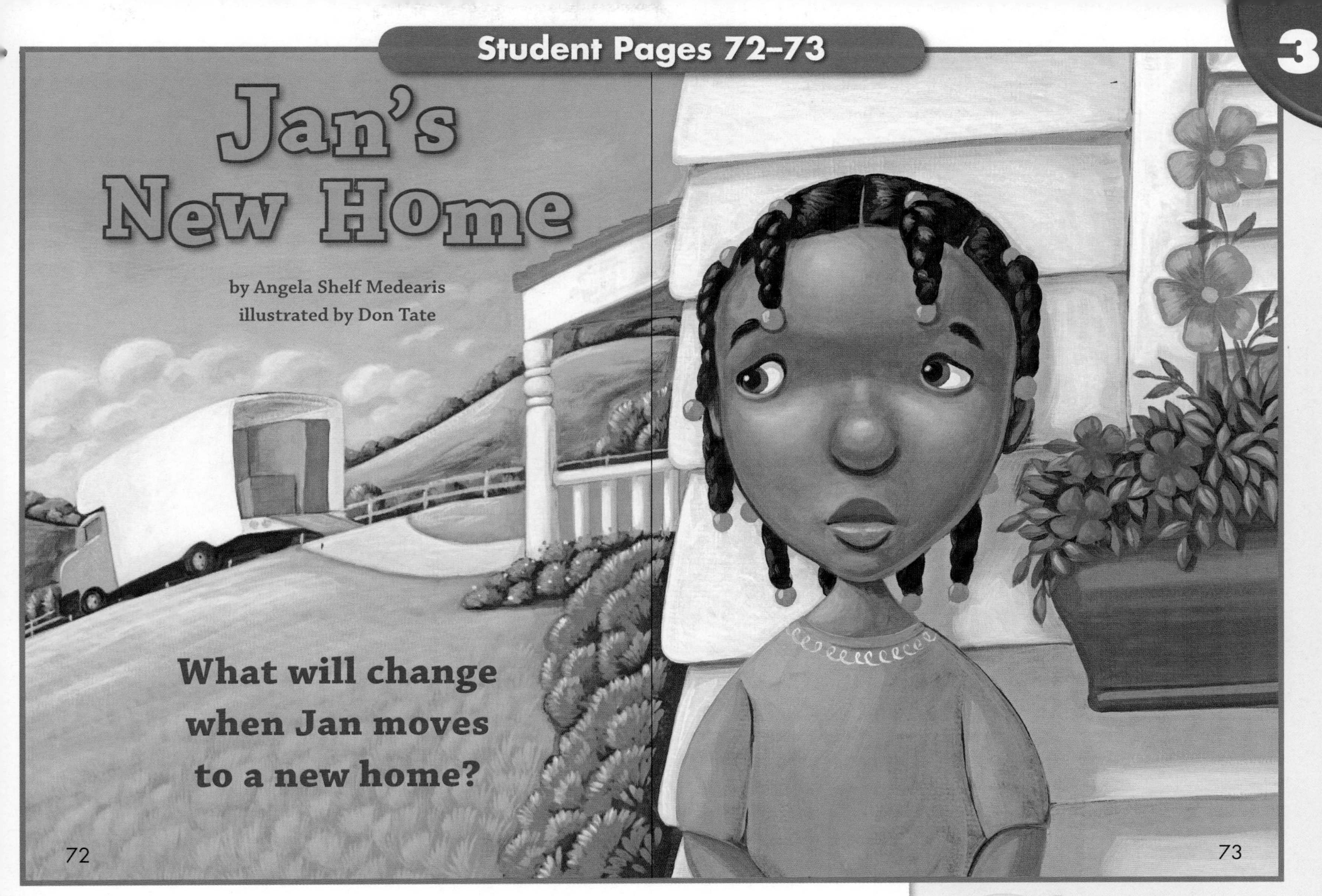

Read

Prereading Strategies

PREVIEW AND PREDICT Have children read the title of the story. Read aloud the names of the author and the illustrator. Ask children where they think Jan is in the picture and what they think is happening. Have them tell where they think the car is going.

DISCUSS REALISTIC FICTION Direct attention to the pictures on pp. 72–73. Discuss whether children think this could be a story about real people. Remind them that sometimes a made-up story tells about people that could be real or things that could really happen. Reread the definition of realistic fiction on p. 71 of the Student Edition.

SET PURPOSE Read the question on p. 72. Discuss what children would like to find out about Jan as they read this story. Then have children set a purpose for reading.

AudioText

Access Content Before reading, review the story summary in English and/or the home language. See the ELL Teaching Guide, pp. 103–105.

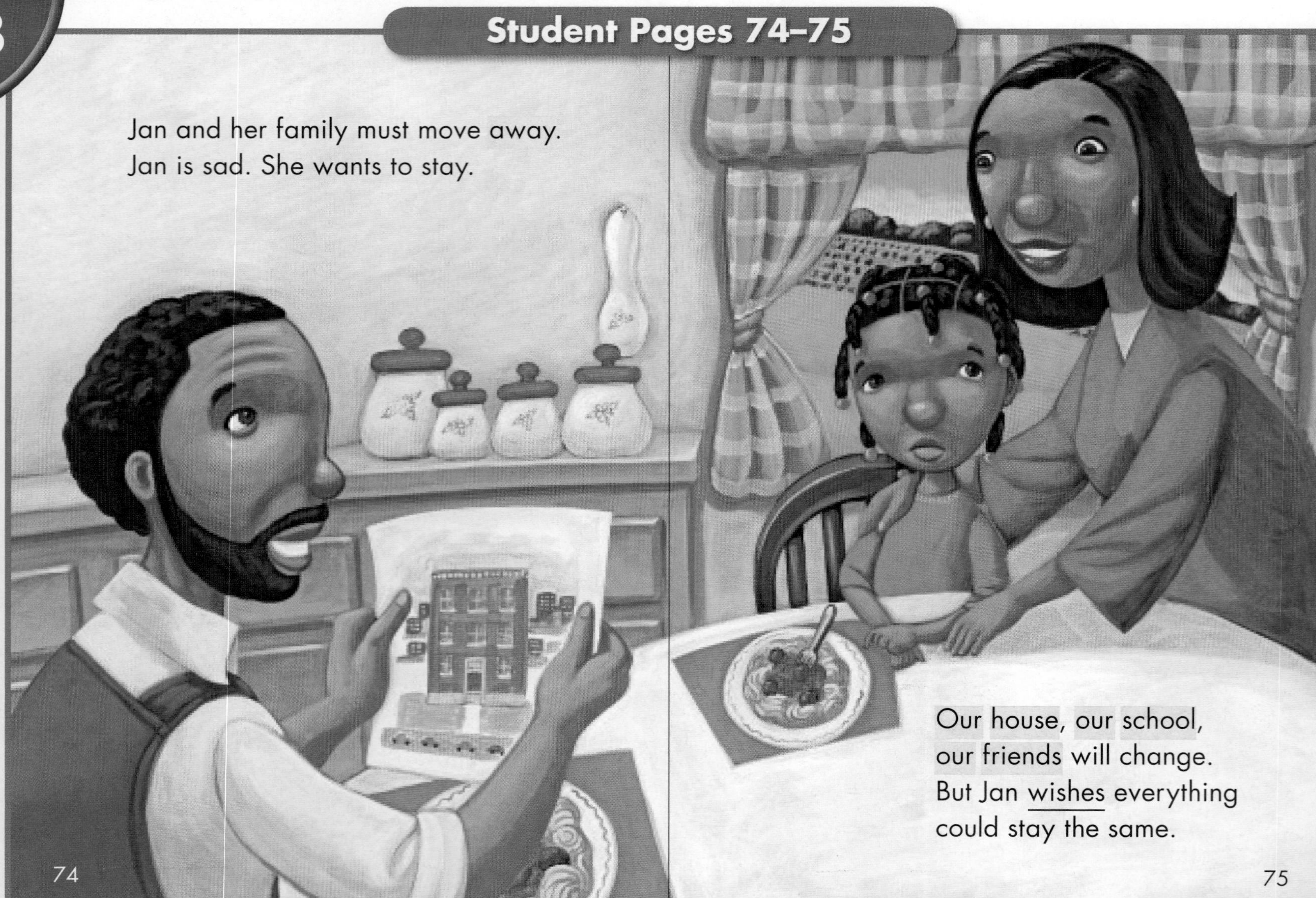

▲ **Pages 74–75**
Have children read to find out how this story begins.

Movement (Time for Social Studies)

Jan and her family must move away. This means that they can't stay where they are, even though they might want to. There are many reasons why a family might need to move to a new place. Perhaps a parent has a new job, or maybe they need to be close to other family members. Sometimes a family needs a bigger house or a smaller one. Invite children who have experienced a move to share their stories.

Guiding Comprehension

Plot • Inferential

- **What is happening at the beginning of this story?**
  Jan and her family are getting ready to move.

Draw Conclusions • Inferential

- **How do you think Jan feels about moving to a new location? How can you tell?**
  Children will probably say that she feels sad about moving because the text says she wishes things could stay the same. Also, the picture shows her looking sad.

Make Judgments • Critical

- ***Text to Self*** **Why would you want things to stay the same if you were Jan?**
  Children's answers will vary, but they may say that they do not want to give up the things they have, or that they are nervous or afraid about new places and meeting new people.

____ ending/plural *-es* and *r*-controlled *or, ore* ▭ high-frequency/tested vocabulary

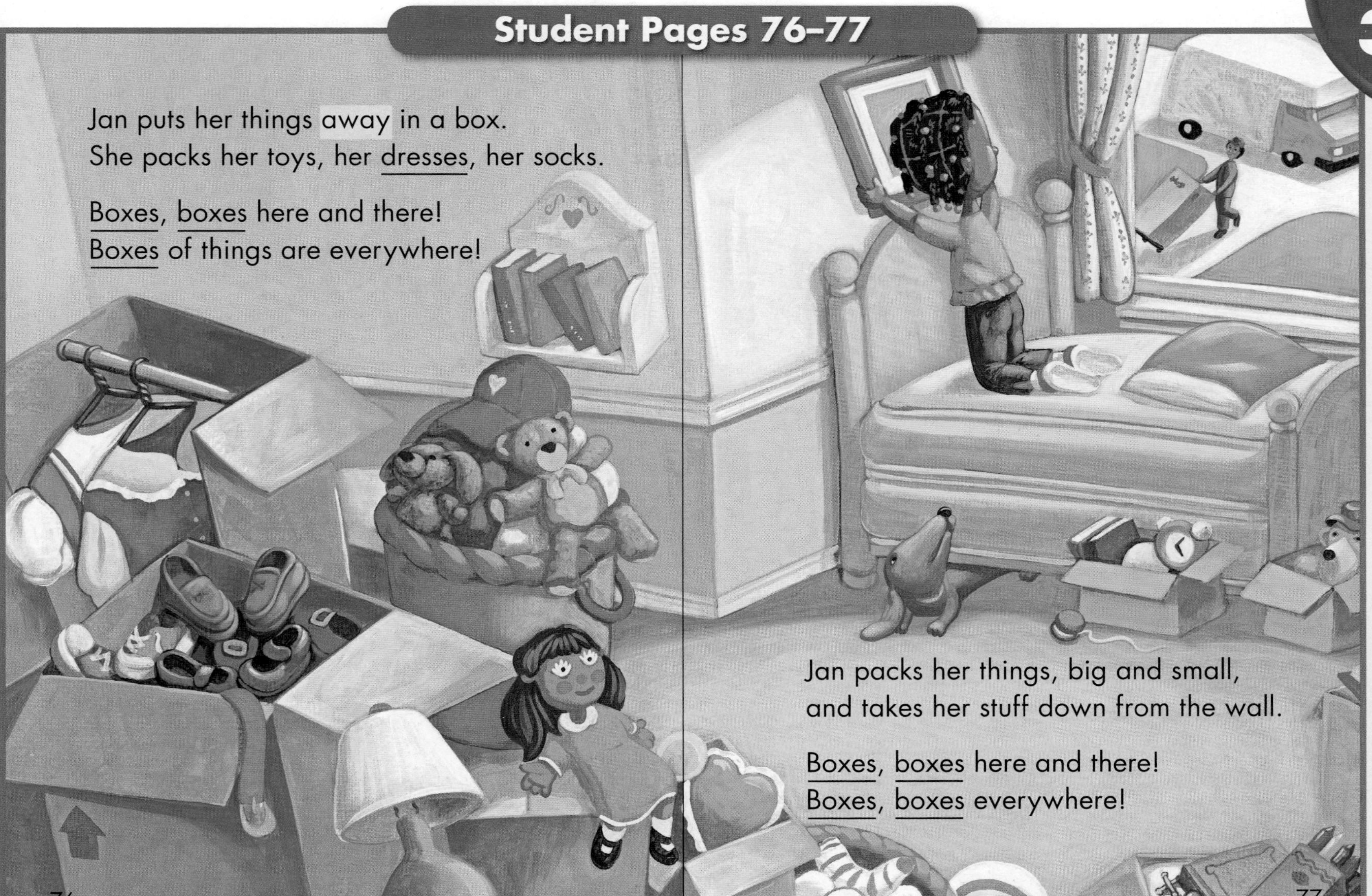

▲ **Pages 76–77**
Ask children to read to find out what Jan needs to pack.

Strategies in Context

MONITOR AND FIX UP

- **What does Jan take with her when she moves? How do you know?**
  She packs her toys, her clothes, the things on her wall, and all her stuff. I know because the author includes all these details.

Monitor Progress	Summarize Details
If... children have difficulty answering the question,	**then...** model how to summarize details to clarify and organize ideas.

MODEL I can look for details about what Jan takes with her when she moves. The story says that Jan packs her toys, dresses, and socks. I can see from the pictures that Jan packs all of her things big and small. I think Jan will take all of her things with her.

ASSESS Have children talk about how the author uses details to show why Jan does not want to move. (Possible response: The author said, "Jan wishes everything could stay the same.")

Monitor Progress	
Decoding	
If... children come to a word they don't know,	**then...** remind them to blend the word: 1. Look at each letter. 2. Think of the sound for each letter. 3. Blend the sounds. 4. Read the word.

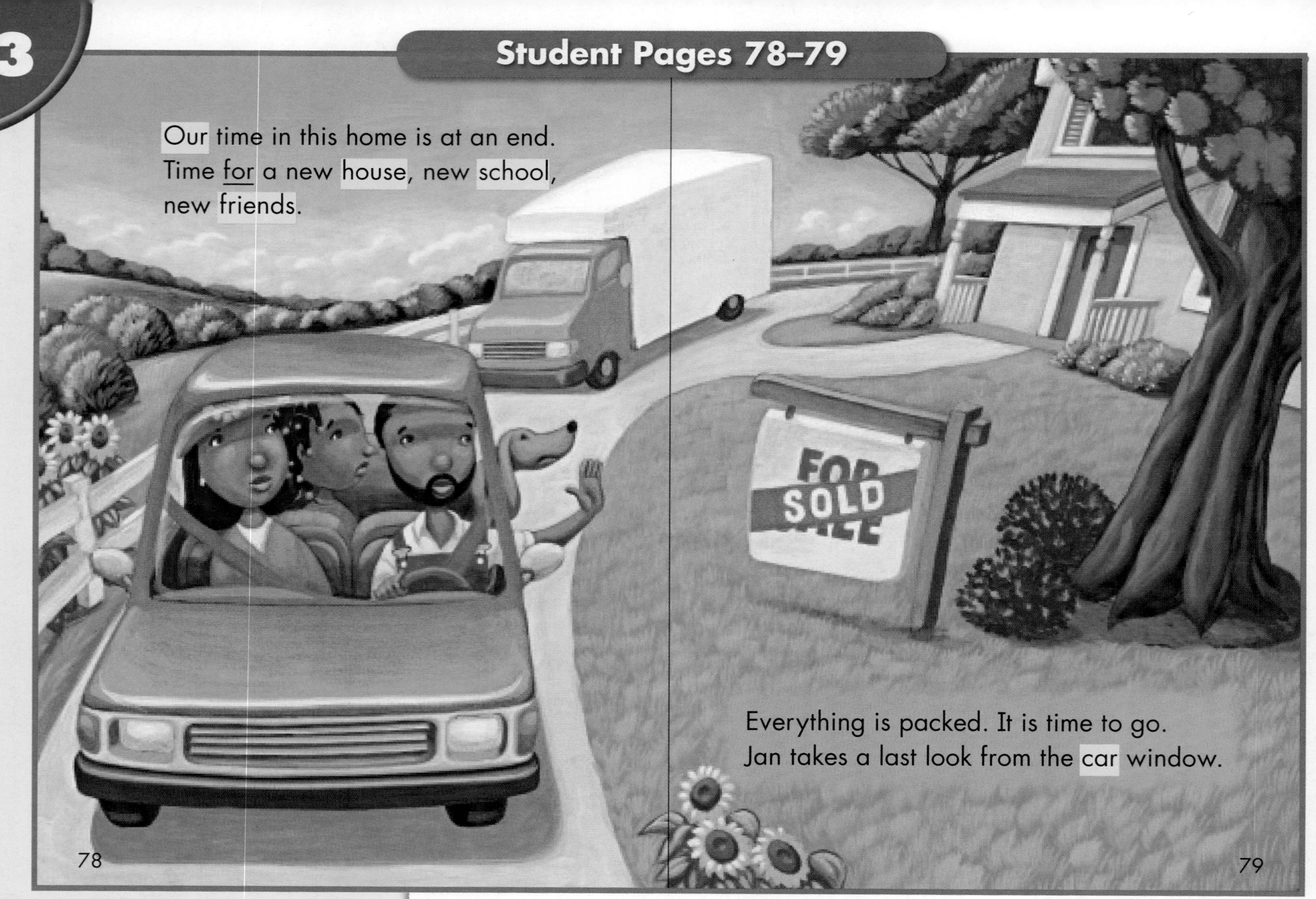

▲ **Pages 78–79**
Have children read to learn what happens next.

Monitor Progress

High-Frequency Words

If...	**then...**
children have a problem reading a new high frequency word,	use the High-Frequency Routine on pp. 70–71 to reteach the problematic word.

Guiding Comprehension

Retell • Inferential

- **What is Jan's family doing?**
  They are leaving their old house and neighborhood.

Draw Conclusions • Inferential

- **Do you think Jan's parents feel the same way she does as they all depart? How can you tell?**
  Children will probably say no because her father is smiling in the picture and Jan feels sad.

Compare and Contrast • Critical

- ***Text to Self*** **How would you feel if you, like Jan, had to move to a new place?**
  Possible response: I would be sad to leave, worried that I would never see my house again, and scared of the move.

____ ending/plural *-es* and *r*-controlled *or, ore* high-frequency/tested vocabulary

Guiding Comprehension

Setting • Inferential

- **Where are Jan and her family?**
  Children will probably say that they are in the country or near a farm because they see horses and sheep. In the picture, they are having a picnic in an area with no houses.

Draw Conclusions • Critical

- **Why do you think Jan's feelings are changing?**
  Possible response: She is excited about seeing new things along the way, so she might be excited about her new home.

Summarize • Inferential

- **What has happened in the story so far?**
  Jan is sad because she and her parents have to move to a new home. They pack up everything and leave their old house. They drive through the country and stop to have a picnic. Jan has fun playing outside.

▲ **Pages 80–81**
Ask children to read to find out about Jan's trip to her new home.

Strategy Self-Check

Have children ask themselves these questions to check their reading.

Decoding Words

- Do I look for word parts I can read?
- Do I blend all the sounds in a word?
- Do I reread to be sure the new word makes sense in the story?

Monitor and Fix Up
Summarize Details

- Do I look for details that help me understand what is happening?
- Why did the author include these details?
- What do the details tell about?

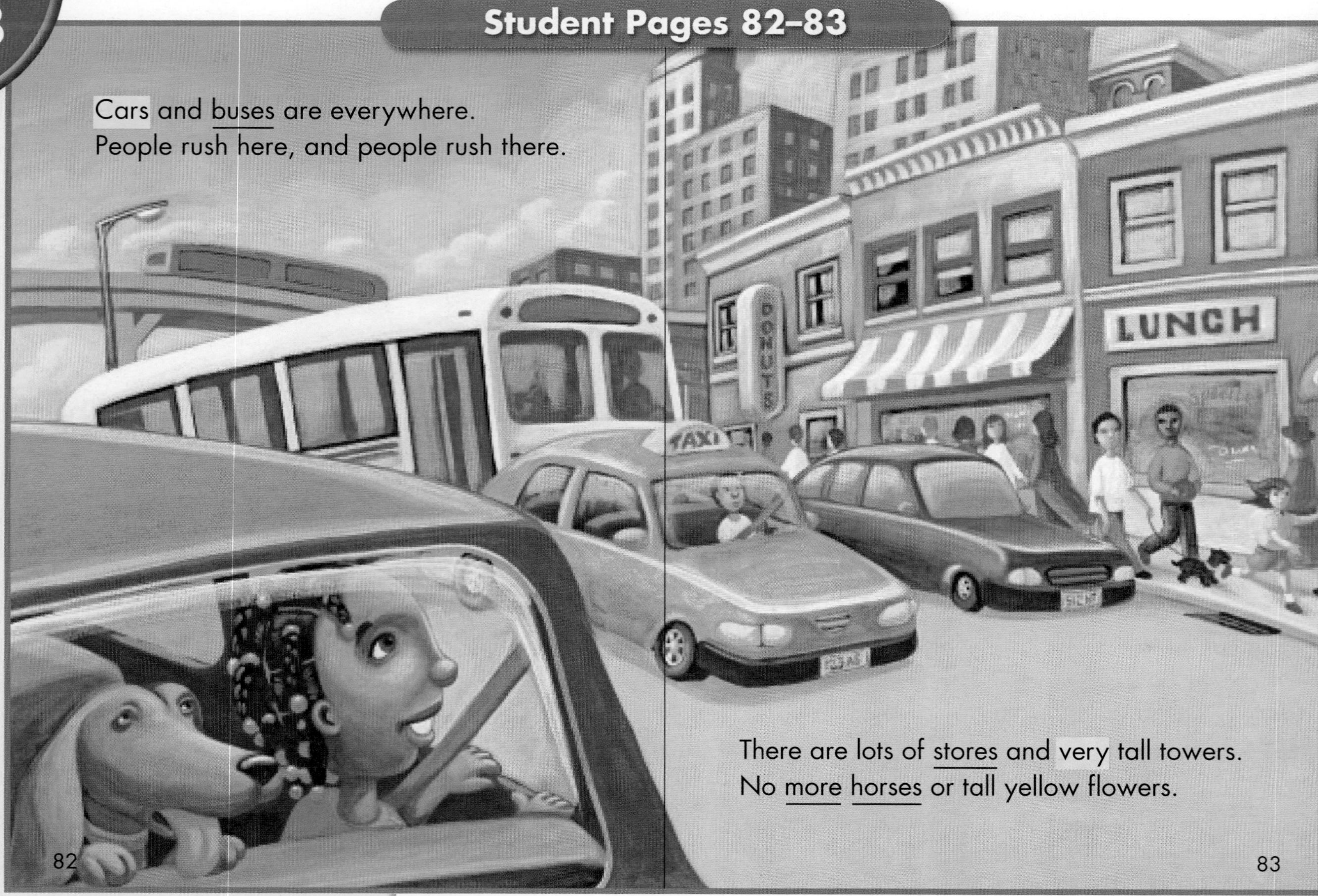

▲ **Pages 82–83**
Have children read to find out what Jan sees next.

EXTEND SKILLS

Rhyme

For instruction in how authors use rhyme, discuss the following:

- What words in this story sound the same?
- Why do you think the author used these words?
- How do the rhyming words make this story seem like a song or a poem?

Assess Have children discuss the pattern that repeats on each pair of pages.

Skills in Context

REVIEW PLOT

- **Look back through the story. What does Jan see on the route to her new house?**
  Jan sees horses, sheep, trees, flowers, and bees. In the city, Jan sees cars, buses, stores, towers, and people everywhere.

Monitor Progress	REVIEW Plot
If... children have difficulty answering the question,	**then...** model how to identify the plot of a story.

MODEL Jan first sees things during their picnic. She sees horses, sheep, trees, flowers and bees. Then I see that Jan has arrived in the city. She sees things like cars, buses, stores, towers, and people.

ASSESS Have children tell how Jan feels in the beginning of the story, in the middle, and now. (Possible response: Jan didn't want to move at the beginning. In the middle, she had fun on her picnic. Now she is excited.)

____ ending/plural *-es* and *r*-controlled *or, ore* ▭ high-frequency/tested vocabulary

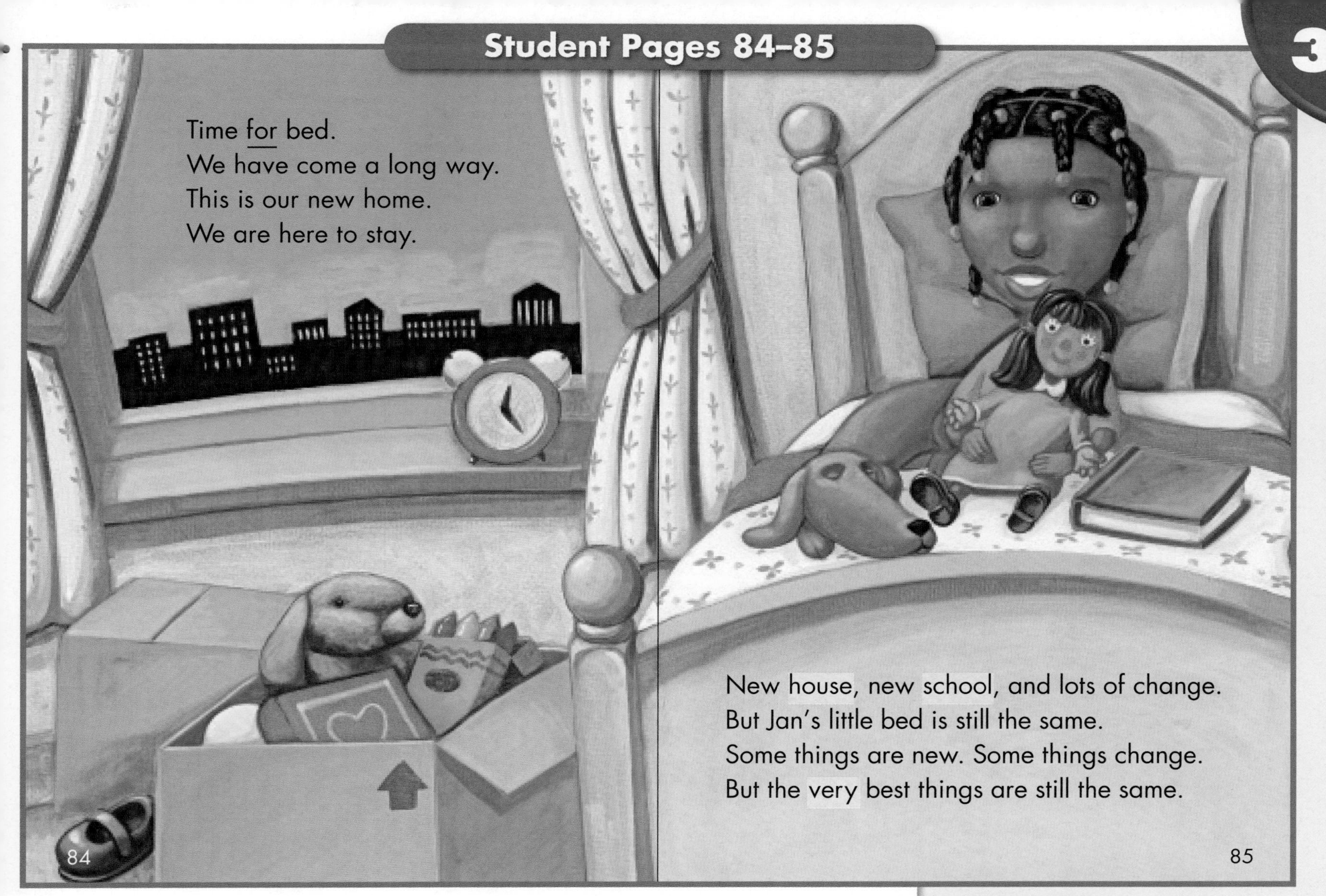

Skills in Context

THEME

- **What does Jan learn about her new home?**
  She learns that although some things are different, the most important things stay the same.

Monitor Progress	Theme
If... children have difficulty answering the question,	**then...** model how to identify the theme of a story.

MODEL Jan is worried about moving because she wants things to stay the same. I think most people feel the same way Jan does; they are a little bit afraid of new places. When Jan arrives at her new home she finds out that some of the best things are still the same. I think the author wanted me to learn that no matter how things change, some things will always be the same.

ASSESS Have children tell what they think the author wanted to tell them about making changes.

▲ **Pages 84–85**
Ask children to read to find out what Jan has learned.

EXTEND SKILLS

Story Structure
For instruction in story structure, discuss the following:

- When you want to tell someone about a story, you usually tell the most important parts of the story in the order they happen.
- Who are the characters in the story? What is the most important thing that happens at the beginning?
- What important things happened after that?

Assess Have children tell how remembering the events in the order they happened helped them to understand the story.

Retelling Plan

- ☑ Week 1 assess Strategic Intervention students.
- ☑ Week 2 assess Advanced students.
- ☑ **This week assess Strategic Intervention students.**
- ☐ Week 4 assess On-Level students.
- ☐ Week 5 assess Strategic Intervention students.
- ☐ Week 6 assess any students you have not yet checked during this unit.

Look Back and Write For informal assessment, see the Scoring Rubric below.

ELL

Check Retelling Let beginning ELL children listen to other retellings before attempting to retell the selection on their own. For more ideas on assessing comprehension, see the ELL and Transition Handbook.

Think and Share

TALK ABOUT IT Model a response. I would miss my room and the swing set in the backyard. I would miss my friends who live next door.

1. RETELL Have children use the retelling strip in the Student Edition to retell the story.

Monitor Progress | **Check Retelling**

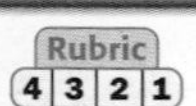

If... children have difficulty retelling the story,

then... use the Retelling Cards and the Scoring Rubric for Retelling on pp. 86–87 to help them move toward fluent retelling.

Day 1 Check Word Reading	Day 2 Check Word Reading	▶ Day 3 Check High-Frequency Words/Retelling	Day 4 Check Fluency	Day 5 Assess Progress

2. THEME Possible response: Jan learned that moving to a new home can be scary but exciting.

3. MONITOR AND FIX UP Possible response: I wasn't sure where Jan was moving, so I reread p. 82 looking for details. The author tells me there are cars and buses and lots of people. These details help me understand that Jan's new home is in the city.

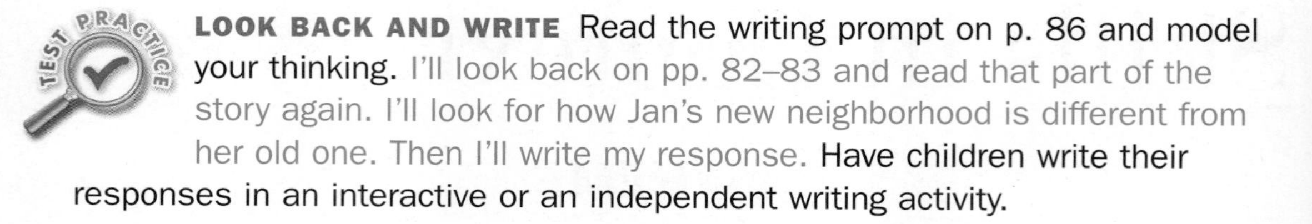

LOOK BACK AND WRITE Read the writing prompt on p. 86 and model your thinking. I'll look back on pp. 82–83 and read that part of the story again. I'll look for how Jan's new neighborhood is different from her old one. Then I'll write my response. Have children write their responses in an interactive or an independent writing activity.

Scoring Rubric | Look Back and Write

Top-Score Response A top-score response uses details from pp. 82–83 of the story to tell how Jan's new neighborhood in the city is different from her old neighborhood in the country.

Example of a Top-Score Response

Jan's new neighborhood has cars, buses, people, stores, and very tall towers. Her new neighborhood does not have horses or tall yellow flowers.

For additional rubrics, see p. WA10.

Reader Response

Read Together

Think and Share

Talk About It What would you miss most if you were to move away from your home?

1. Use the pictures below to retell the story. Retell
2. What big lesson did Jan learn about change? Theme
3. Did anything confuse you as you read? What did you do about it? How did that help? Monitor/Fix Up

Look Back and Write Look back at pages 82–83. How is Jan's new neighborhood different from her old one?

Meet the Author

Angela Shelf Medearis

Angela Medearis has moved to a new home many times. She says, "My father was in the Air Force. We moved almost every year!"

Ms. Medearis says to get better at reading, read as much as you can. "Put a book in the car. Keep a book in your backpack so you will always have something fun to do!"

Read more books by Angela Shelf Medearis.

Retelling Strip

Scoring Rubric Narrative Retelling

Rubric 4 3 2 1	4	3	2	1
Connections	Makes connections and generalizes beyond the text	Makes connections to other events, stories, or experiences	Makes a limited connection to another event, story, or experience	Makes no connection to another event, story, or experience
Author's Purpose	Elaborates on author's purpose	Tells author's purpose with some clarity	Makes some connection to author's purpose	Makes no connection to author's purpose
Characters	Describes the main character(s) and any character development	Identifies the main character(s) and gives some information about them	Inaccurately identifies some characters or gives little information about them	Inaccurately identifies the characters or gives no information about them
Setting	Describes the time and location	Identifies the time and location	Omits details of time or location	Is unable to identify time or location
Plot	Describes the events in sequence using rich detail	Tells the plot with some errors in sequence that do not affect meaning	Tells parts of plot with gaps that affect meaning	Retelling has no sense of story

Use the Retelling Chart on p. TR18 to record retelling.

Selection Test To assess with *Jan's New Home*, use Selection Tests, pp. 33–36.

Fresh Reads for Differentiated Test Practice For weekly leveled practice, use pp. 85–90.

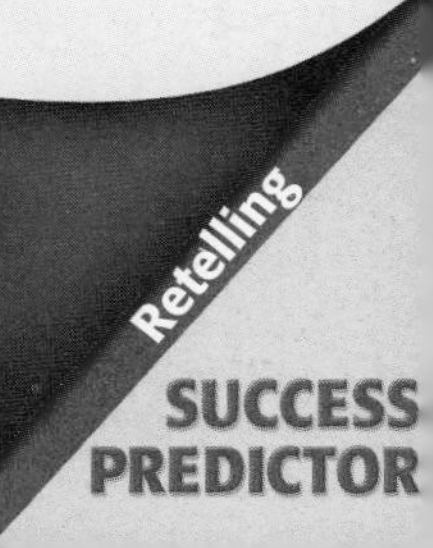

OBJECTIVE

- Read aloud fluently, attending to periods and exclamation marks.

Options for Choral Reading

Use *Jan's New Home* or one of the following Leveled Readers.

On-Level

The New Park

Strategic Intervention

A Big Move

Advanced

Pins in the Map

Reread pp. 76–77 of *Jan's New Home.* Point out the word *stuff* and ask them to say a word in their home languages with the same meaning. Ask children to name some *stuff* hanging on their bedroom walls or displayed on their shelves or dressers in English and their home languages.

Fluency

ATTEND TO PUNCTUATION

MODEL READING WHILE ATTENDING TO PUNCTUATION Use *Jan's New Home.*

- Point to the periods and exclamation marks on p. 76. A period tells me to stop. An exclamation mark tells me that my voice should show surprise or excitement. I want to watch for the marks at the ends of the sentences. These will tell me how my voice should sound.
- Ask children to follow along as you read the page with expression and attention to punctuation.
- Have children read the page after you. Encourage them to watch for the marks at the ends of sentences as they read. Continue in the same way with pp. 77–78.

REREAD FOR FLUENCY

Choral Reading

ROUTINE

1. **Select a Passage** For *Jan's New Home,* use pp. 78–81.
2. **Divide into Groups** Assign each group a part to read. For this story, have each group read two lines.
3. **Model** Have children track the print as you read.
4. **Read Together** Have children read along with you.
5. **Independent Readings** Have the groups read aloud without you. Monitor progress and provide feedback. For optimal fluency, children should reread three to four times.

Monitor Progress	Fluency
If... children have difficulty attending to periods or exclamation marks as punctuation,	**then...** prompt: • Look at the end of each sentence. What does the end mark tell you about the way each sentence should sound? • What does the mark at the end tell you about how your voice should sound?
If... the class cannot read fluently without you,	**then...** continue to have them read along with you.

Vocabulary

DESCRIPTIVE WORDS

DISCUSS WORDS THAT DESCRIBE FEELINGS Have children tell how Jan felt at the beginning of the story. Write what they say on the board. Discuss which word tells about Jan's feelings and draw a line under it. Explain that we can use words to describe our feelings.

Jan felt sad to leave her home.

EXPAND SELECTION VOCABULARY Discuss what happened in the story that made Jan feel sad, and what happened that made her feel good. Ask children to show on their faces how Jan may have looked when she was sad, and when she felt good. Then have children give other words that describe feelings. List their words on the board. Have children give a sentence that demonstrates the meaning of each word.

happy	tired	unhappy
crabby	lonely	scared
angry	proud	

OBJECTIVES

- Discuss words that describe feelings.
- Use words that describe feelings in sentences.

Strategic Intervention

Have children select a word from the list and draw a picture to illustrate it.

Advanced

Have children look through books for pictures that show how people feel. Ask them to write a sentence telling about each picture.

Extend Language Say a word that describes a feeling. Have children repeat the word and pantomime it.

Writing Trait of the Week

INTRODUCE Voice

TALK ABOUT VOICE Explain to children that voice is the way a writer feels about a topic. Ask them to think about how Jan feels when she gets to her new home. Then model your thinking.

MODEL Jan was sad at first when she found out her family was moving. When I look back at page 85, though, I see that Jan doesn't look sad anymore. Let me read these sentences Jan might have written.

My new home is in a city. The city is big. It has shops.

These sentences don't tell me how Jan feels about her new home. I think Jan is excited. How could she show her feelings in her sentences? Let's think of words and phrases that Jan might use to show how she feels about the city. Children might suggest words such as the following: *busy city, interesting, exciting, hurry, explore, colorful crowds.*

Here are some new sentences that show Jan's voice.
Read the sentences and talk about how they show voice.

My new home is on a busy street. Colorful crowds of people hurry past interesting shops. I can't wait to explore this exciting neighborhood.

STRATEGY FOR DEVELOPING VOICE On the board, write sentences with a weak voice, such as those on the left below. Then work with children to rewrite the sentences to show the writer's feelings.

I got a kitten.	**I love my soft kitten.**
I ate pizza.	**I gobbled up the tasty pizza.**

PRACTICE

APPLY THE STRATEGY

- Have children imagine that they are visiting their favorite place. Have them list words that show why they like this place *(warm, cozy, quite, private.)*
- Then have children dictate sentences to you that show their feelings about this place. If children need more support, have them complete the following: My favorite place is ___ because ___.

OBJECTIVE

- Recognize and use voice in writing.

DAILY FIX-IT

5. I wich Kim was in my klass.
I wish Kim was in my class.

6. My best freinds ride the bus
My best friends ride the bus.

Connect to Unit Writing

Writing Trait

Have children use strategies for developing **voice** when they write a description in the Unit Writing Workshop, pp. WA2–WA9.

Voice To help children add voice to their writing, work with them to develop topical word webs that include descriptive adjectives. Encourage them to use a picture dictionary, if available, to find new words to express voice.

Grammar

APPLY TO WRITING Verbs

IMPROVE WRITING WITH VERBS Review that verbs may tell what two or more people, animals, or things do. Remind children that you do not add *-s* to these verbs. Remind children to use verbs their own writing.

Write *The girls ______basketball. They ______ in the choir. The babies ______.* Have children supply a verb for each sentence. Ask if any of these verbs will end with *-s*.

The girls ______ basketball.
They _______ in the choir.
The babies _______.

PRACTICE

IDENTIFY VERBS Have children work with a partner to write sentences of their own. Ask children to write sentences about more than one person. Provide sentence stems for those students who need help. Have children circle the verbs and share sentences with the class.

OBJECTIVE

- Use verbs in writing.

Verbs That Do Not Add *-s*

Pretend you see two new girls at school.
Write about what you do.
Write about what they do.
Begin your sentences with we and they.

Possible answer: We tell the girls our names. We show them their room. They thank us.

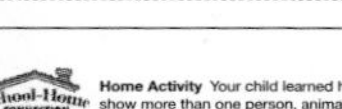

Home Activity Your child learned how to use verbs that do not add -s in writing. Point to pictures that show more than one person, animal, or thing. Ask: *What do the (children, birds, etc.) do?* Have your child write the answer to the question.

▲ **Grammar and Writing Practice Book** p. 58

Wrap Up Your Day!

THEME Have children recall the story *Mr. George Baker.* What is the big idea of this story? What is the lesson learned? (You are never too old to learn something.)

MONITOR AND FIX UP Review and reread the page in *Mr. George Baker* where Harry admires George's sweater and they hug their knees. They watch the leaves blow off trees. Discuss what time of year it must be. How can you tell? What details support this?

LET'S TALK ABOUT IT Recall the Big Book *Mr. George Baker*. Discuss what will be the same and what things will change when George Baker learns to read. Discuss why learning new things can be both exciting and scary.

PREVIEW Day 4

Tell children that tomorrow they will listen to a story about a family that moves, and the exciting changes they face.

Day 4
AT A GLANCE

Share Literature
"Gila Monsters Meet You at the Airport"

Phonemic Awareness
Segment and Count Syllables

High-Frequency Words
away *car* *friends* Word Wall
house *our* *school*
very

Phonics and Spelling
REVIEW Compound Words and Final *ng, nk*

REVIEW Word Reading

Spelling: Words That Add *-es*

Read
 < Differentiated Instruction

"A Letter From Jan"

Fluency
Attend to Punctuation

Writing Across the Curriculum
Signs

Grammar
Verbs That Do Not Add *-s*

Materials
- *Sing with Me Big Book*
- Read Aloud Anthology
- Tested Word Cards
- Student Edition 88–89

Morning Warm-Up!

Jan is going to a new school. She is meeting new friends. Today she is sending a letter to an old friend. How do you think Jan is feeling now? What changes would you tell about in a letter?

QUESTION OF THE DAY Encourage children to sing "New Location" from the *Sing with Me Big Book* as you gather. Write and read the message and discuss the questions.

REVIEW INFLECTED ENDING *-ing*

- Ask children to find words that end with *-ing*. (*going, meeting, sending, feeling*)
- Circle each word and have children frame the base word, identify the ending, and read the word.

Extend Language Use the Day 4 instruction on ELL Poster 15 to extend and enrich language.

ELL Poster 15

Share Literature

CONNECT CONCEPTS

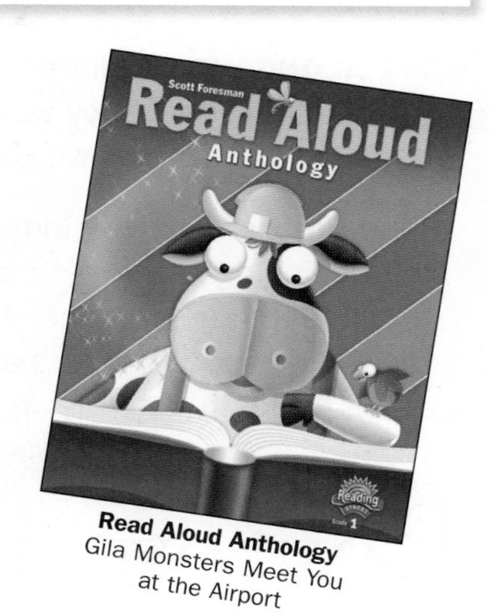

Read Aloud Anthology
Gila Monsters Meet You at the Airport

ACTIVATE PRIOR KNOWLEDGE Help children recall that Jan moved to the city from the country. Explain that you will read a story about a boy who is moving from the East to the West, and he isn't sure he wants to go—"Gila Monsters Meet You at the Airport" by Marjorie Weinman Sharmat.

BUILD ORAL VOCABULARY Read the first six sentences. Ask: What is the boy's problem? (He doesn't want to move out West.) Explain that one reason the boy does not want to move out West is because he thinks buffalo will **stampede.** Ask children to listen to find out what else the boy thinks will happen out West.

REVIEW ORAL VOCABULARY After reading, review all the Amazing Words for the week. Have children take turns using them in sentences that tell about the concept for the week. Then talk about the Amazing Words they learned in other weeks and connect them to the concept as well. For example, ask:

- If you moved from the country to the city, what kinds of **transportation** might you use in your new **community**?
- If you moved from the city to the country, what **creatures** might you **observe** that are new to you?

Phonemic Awareness

SEGMENT AND COUNT SYLLABLES

- The boy is happy to see kids playing baseball. Listen to the syllables in *baseball.*
- Segment and clap out the syllables in *baseball: base, ball.* There are two syllables in *baseball.*
- Have children say and clap out the syllables in *baseball.* How many syllables do you hear in *baseball?* (two)
- Continue the activity with these examples.

sunset (2) **bedtime** (2) **sidewalk** (2) **weekend** (2) **wastebasket** (3)

OBJECTIVES

- Set purpose for listening.
- Build oral vocabulary.
- Segment and count syllables.

arrive
depart
location
route
tumble
swoop
crumple
stampede

MONITOR PROGRESS

If... children lack oral vocabulary experiences about the concept Growing and Changing,

then... use the Oral Vocabulary Routine. See p. DI•5 to teach *stampede.*

ELL

Connect Concepts If children have moved to a new home, then relate their own experiences to the experiences of the boy in "Gila Monsters Meet You at the Airport." How did you feel about moving? Were you happy or sad? What did you imagine your new home would be like? What do you like about your new home?

OBJECTIVES

- Recognize high-frequency words.
- Review word with final *ng* and *nk* and compound words.
- Apply decoding strategies: blend, preview words.

Pick a word from the box to match each clue.
Write the words in the puzzles.

ring bank

bank	fang	king	skunk	tank

1. bank
2. king
3. tank
4. skunk
5. fang

Home Activity Your child solved two puzzles with words that end with *ng* and *nk*. Have your child use each word in a sentence.

▲ **Practice Book 1.2** p. 28, Final *ng* and *nk*

Circle the compound word in each sentence.

greenhouse

1. This weekend Jim will be in his new house.
2. He will miss his classmates.
3. His mom made homemade candy.
4. Ms. Hill made popcorn.
5. Jim gave a cupcake to Ms. Hill.
6. Jim pulled the map from his backpack.
7. He will live by the shoreline.
8. Jim will take his bulldog with him.

GOOD-BYE, JIM

Find the compound word.
Mark the ⊂⊃ to show your answer.

9. shortstop / shorten / shore
10. weedy / weeks / weekend

Home Activity Your child reviewed compound words—words formed by joining two or more words. Write words such as *out, side, in, any, thing, base, ball, some, where,* and *one* on separate slips of paper. Have your child form compound words.

▲ **Practice Book 1.2** p. 29, Compound Words

High-Frequency Words

PRACTICE

MOVE ALONG Have children use construction paper and markers to make signs with the high-frequency words: *away, car, friends, house, our, school,* and *very*, one word per sign. Have them use the Word Wall as a guide. Word Wall

Tape the signs to the floor in a path to the Word Wall. Have one child start at the beginning of the path and toss a beanbag, read the word on which it lands, and use it in a sentence. Then have another child pick up the beanbag and toss it farther along the path and do the same. Have children keep moving along the path until they reach the Word Wall.

Review Phonics

REVIEW FINAL *ng, nk* AND COMPOUND WORDS

READ *ng* AND *nk* WORDS Write *hang*. Look at this word. You can read this word because you know *ng* stands for one sound. What sound does *ng* stand for? (/ng/) What's the word? *(hang)* Continue with *link, nk*/nk/.

READ COMPOUND WORDS Write *cupcake.* You can read this compound word because you can read the two smaller words. What are the two smaller words? (*cup* and *cake*) What is the compound word? (*cupcake*)

SORT COMPOUND WORDS Write *compound word, first word,* and *second word* as headings. Write compound words under the first heading. Have children read the compound words and discuss the meaning of each compound. Then have children name the two words that form each compound. Write them in the appropriate column. Have the words read. Then have children identify the words with /ng/ and /ngk/.

Compound Word	First Word	Second Word
hangout	hang	out
kingfish	king	fish
sinkhole	sink	hole
stingray	sting	ray

WORD READING

READ DECODABLE AND HIGH-FREQUENCY WORDS Write these words. Encourage children to preview each word before reading it.

ring	ever	own	grow	sandbox
plant	new	they	live	big
sunshine	were	king	Frank	home
every	any	sure	brand	enough

Monitor Progress	Word Reading
If... children have difficulty previewing and reading whole words,	**then...** have them use sound-by-sound blending.
If... children can't read the words fluently at a rate of one to two seconds per word,	**then...** have pairs practice the list.

READ WORDS IN CONTEXT Write these sentences. Call on individuals to read a sentence. Then randomly point to the review words and have them read. To help you monitor word reading, high-frequency words are underlined and decodable words are circled.

Are you sure that the king will own every big ring?

They were in the sandbox by the porch.

Frank, did you ever live in a brand new home?

Any plant will grow with enough sunshine.

Monitor Progress	Word Reading
If... children are unable to read an underlined word,	**then...** read the word for them and spell it, having them echo you.
If... children have difficulty reading a circled word,	**then...** have them use sound-by-sound blending.

Spiral REVIEW

- Reviews high-frequency words *any, enough, ever, every, grow, live, new, own, sure,* and *were.*
- Reviews final *ng* and *nk,* short and long vowels, digraphs, and blends.

Support Phonics For additional review, see the phonics activities in the ELL and Transition Handbook.

OBJECTIVE

- Spell words with ending *-es;* plural *-es.*

Spelling Words

Adding -es

1.	**fix**	6.	**wishes***
2.	**fixes**	7.	**kiss**
3.	**class**	8.	**kisses**
4.	**classes**	9.	**bus**
5.	**wish**	10.	**buses***

High-Frequency Words

11.	**friends***	12.	**very***

* Words from the Selection

Adding -es

Read the clues. **Write** the list words.

1. It rhymes with Gus. bus
2. It rhymes with glass. class
3. It rhymes with fishes. wishes
4. It rhymes with dish. wish
5. It rhymes with mix. fix
6. It rhymes with miss. kiss

Spelling Words: fix, fixes, class, classes, wish, wishes, kiss, kisses, bus, buses

Add -es. **Write** the new word in the puzzle.

Down
7. bus
8. fix

Across
9. kiss
10. class

7 Down: buses; 8 Down: fixes; 9 Across: kisses; 10 Across: classes

School + Home **Home Activity** Your child has been learning to add -es to words. Have your child write a list word that ends with -es. Then have your child cross out -es to make a different list word.

▲ **Spelling Practice Book** p. 60

Spelling

PARTNER REVIEW Ending *-es;* Plural *-es*

READ AND WRITE Supply pairs of children with index cards on which the spelling words have been written. Have one child read a word while the other writes it. Then have children switch roles. Have them use the cards to check their spelling.

HOMEWORK Spelling Practice Book, p. 60

Group Time

On-Level

Read "A Letter from Jan."

- Use pp. 88–89.

Strategic Intervention

Read SI Decodable Reader 14.

- Read or listen to "A Letter from Jan."
- Use the **Routine** on p. DI·42.

Advanced

Read "A Letter from Jan."

- Use the **Routine** on p. DI·43.

ELL Place English language learners in the groups that correspond to their reading abilities in English.

Independent Activities

Fluency Reading Pair children to reread *Jan's New Home.*

Journal Writing Write what happens to Jan on her first day at her new school. Share writing.

Independent Reading See p. 68j for Reading/Library activities and suggestions.

Literacy Centers To provide listening opportunities, you may use the Listening Center on p. 68j. To extend social studies concepts, you may use the Social Studies Center on p. 68k.

Practice Book 1.2 Final *ng, nk,* p. 28
Compound Words, p. 29

Break into small groups after Spelling and before Fluency.

Social Studies in Reading

A Letter from Jan

Dear Hope,

I was sad when we drove away in our car. I liked our old house very much. But now I like my new home! We still have lots of boxes in the house.

I met more friends at school. They are very nice.

I hope you will come to see me.

Your friend,
Jan

88

89

Read

Social Studies in Reading

PREVIEW AND PREDICT Read the title. Have children tell what a letter is. (It is something you write to tell another person about something.) Then ask them to tell who Jan might write to. Have children read to learn what Jan wants to tell her friend.

LETTER Discuss with children the format of a letter, including the greeting, the body, and the closing. Point out the envelope and explain that this is used to carry a letter from one place to another. People write the address of the person who is to receive the letter on the envelope. The stamp is the way people pay the post office to deliver the letter.

VOCABULARY/DESCRIPTIVE WORDS Review that some words tell about feelings. They describe the way a person feels. Have children identify words Jan uses to tell how she felt about the move and words that show how she feels now. *(She felt sad, but now she likes her new house, and her new friends are nice.)*

AudioText

OBJECTIVE

- Recognize text structure: letter.

Time for SOCIAL STUDIES

Places

Jan's new home is in the city. How is the city different from where she used to live? Look at the pictures and tell ways the city is different from the country. What are some ways the city and the country are alike?

BUILD CONCEPTS

Theme • Inferential

- **What is Jan's letter about?**
  Her letter tells her friend that she is beginning to like her new home.

Summarize • Inferential

- **What information does Jan give that lets you know she is happy in her new home?**
  She says she likes her new home, she says she likes her new friends at school, she invites her friend to come see her, and she draws her new home as a happy place.

CONNECT TEXT TO TEXT

Reading Across Texts

What are some other things Jan might have told her friend in this letter?

Children might mention the picnic Jan and her family shared, or they might mention information about the city and how it is different from the country.

Access Content If children have relatives in another country, discuss who they write to and what they say in their letters.

Fluency

ATTEND TO PUNCTUATION

MODEL READING WITH ATTENTION TO PUNCTUATION Use *Jan's New Home.*

- Have children turn to p. 81. Listen as I read the page. I want to sound like I am speaking. I will watch the end punctuation marks so I know how to use my voice. When I see a period, my voice goes down at the end of the sentence. When I see an exclamation mark, I read the sentence in an excited way.
- Ask children to follow along as you read the page with expression and attention to punctuation.
- Have children read the page after you. Encourage them to pay attention to the marks at the ends of the sentences. Continue in the same way with pp. 82–83.

REREAD FOR FLUENCY

Choral Reading

ROUTINE

1. **Select a Passage** For *Jan's New Home* use pp. 77–80.
2. **Divide into Groups** Assign each group a part to read. For this story, assign a page to each of four groups.
3. **Model** Have children track the print as you read.
4. **Read Together** Have children read along with you.
5. **Independent Readings** Have the groups read aloud without you. Monitor progress and provide feedback. For optimal fluency, children should reread three to four times.

Monitor Progress — Check Fluency WCPM

As children reread, monitor their progress toward their individual fluency goals. Current Goal: 20–30 words correct per minute. End-of-Year Goal: 60 words correct per minute.

If... children cannot read fluently at a rate of 20–30 words per minute,

then... make sure children practice with text at their independent level. Provide additional fluency practice, pairing nonfluent readers with fluent readers.

If... children already read at 60 words per minute,

then... they do not need to reread three to four times.

SUCCESS PREDICTOR

Day 1 Check Word Reading	Day 2 Check Word Reading	Day 3 Check High-Frequency Words/Retelling	▶ **Day 4 Check Fluency**	Day 5 Assess Progress

OBJECTIVE

- Read aloud fluently, attending to periods and exclamation marks.

Options for Oral Reading

Use *Jan's New Home* or one of the following Leveled Readers.

On-Level

The New Park

Strategic Intervention

A Big Move

Advanced

Pins in the Map

Use *Mamá* or *Jan's New Home*. English learners benefit from assisted reading, with modeling by the teacher or by a skilled classmate. When the English learner reads the passage aloud, the more proficient reader assists by providing feedback and encouragement.

Words Correct Per Minute

SUCCESS PREDICTOR

OBJECTIVE

- Create a sign.

Advanced

Encourage children to choose another business and make a sign for it.

Support Writing Generate a word list and discus words that children may have seen on signs. Children may refer to this list when writing the sign.

Writing Across the Curriculum

WRITE Signs

BRAINSTORM Have children look at pp. 82–83 and name several things Jan sees in her new town. Encourage them to use oral vocabulary, such as *location* and *route.* Discuss billboards and signs that children have seen. Discuss traffic signs and why some signs have symbols and no words.

SHARE THE PEN Have children participate in creating traffic and highway signs. To begin, draw a simple picture of a highway billboard and explain that the class will work together to write information for this sign. Explain that a sign provides people with information. Highway signs often tell where something is located, how far away it is, and in which direction it is located. Tell children that the class sign you will write will give information about a restaurant. The restaurant's name is Kate's Kitchen. Ask children what information needs to be on the sign. Call on volunteers to suggest hours of business, directions to get there, and special foods that might be served. Write the sign, inviting individuals to help spell familiar words. Ask questions, such as the following:

- What is the first sound you hear in the words *Kate's Kitchen?* (/k/)
- What letter stands for that sound? *(K)* Have a volunteer write *K.*
- What is the second sound you hear in the word *Kate's?* (/ā/)
- What letter stands for that sound? *(a)* Have a volunteer write *a.*

Continue having individuals contribute to writing. Frequently reread the sign.

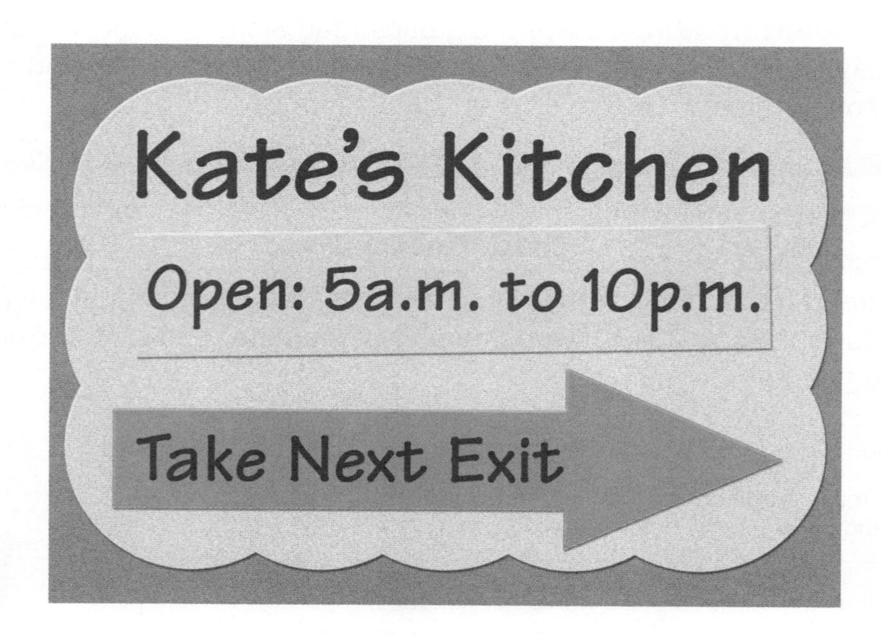

Grammar

REVIEW Verbs That Do Not Add *-s*

DEFINE VERBS THAT DO NOT ADD *-s*

- What tells what two or more people, animals, or things do? (verb)
- What is sometimes added to the end of the verb if the sentence is about only one person, animal, or thing? (an *s*)

PRACTICE

CLASSIFY VERBS Write *one person* and *more than one person* as heads in a two column chart. Have volunteers name action verbs for each column.

one person (he)	more than one person (they)
rides	ride
reads	read
sleeps	sleep

OBJECTIVE

- Identify verbs that do not add *-s*.

DAILY FIX-IT

7. I wich I could ride the bus
I wish I could ride the bus.

8. the buses were lat.
The buses were late.

Verbs That Do Not Add *-s*

Mark the sentence that is correct.

1. ○ Ann and Pat walks to a new school.
○ Ann walk to a new school.
⊗ Ann and Pat walk to a new school.

2. ⊗ The girls like their old school.
○ The girls likes their old school.
○ The girl like their old school.

3. ○ Their friend live in another town.
⊗ Their friends live in another town.
○ Their friends lives in another town.

4. ⊗ Ben and Vic talk to the girls.
○ Ben talk to the girls.
○ Ben and Vic talks to the girls.

5. ○ The boy tell about the new school.
⊗ The boys tell about the new school.
○ The boys tells about the new school.

6. ○ Pat feel better.
○ Ann and Pat feels better.
⊗ Ann and Pat feel better.

School-Home Connection **Home Activity** Your child prepared for taking tests on verbs that do not add -*s*. Together read a paragraph from a newspaper or magazine article. Have your child find and circle verbs that do not end in -*s*.

▲ **Grammar and Writing Practice Book** p. 59

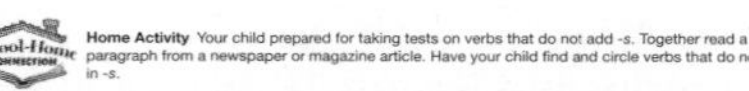

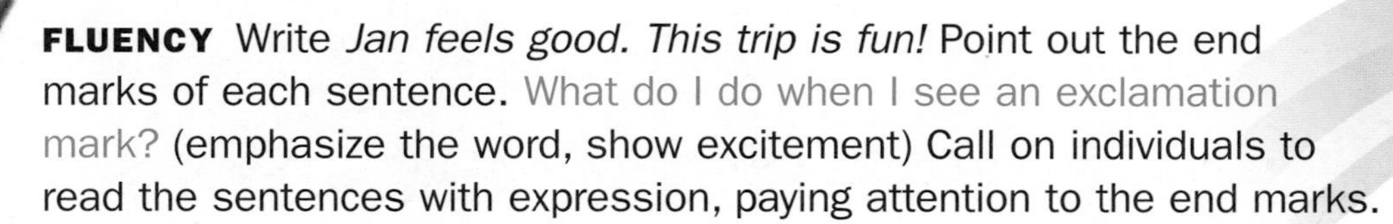

FLUENCY Write *Jan feels good. This trip is fun!* Point out the end marks of each sentence. What do I do when I see an exclamation mark? (emphasize the word, show excitement) Call on individuals to read the sentences with expression, paying attention to the end marks.

LET'S TALK ABOUT IT Recall "A Letter from Jan." Display the Change/No Change chart from Day 1. Review why experiencing new things can be both exciting and scary. Discuss how Jan's feelings have changed now that she has lived at her new house for a while.

Remind children that they read a letter about how Jan feels about her new home. Tell them that tomorrow they will read about how a little boy feels about his big move.

Day 5
AT A GLANCE

Share Literature
"Gila Monsters Meet You at the Airport"

Phonics and Spelling
Review Ending *-es*, Plural *-es*, and *r*-Controlled *or, ore*

High-Frequency Words
away	*car*	*friends*
house	*our*	*school*
very		

Word Wall

Monitor Progress
Spelling Test: Words that Add *-es*

< Differentiated Assessment

Writing and Grammar
Trait: Voice

Verbs That Do Not Add *-s*

Materials
- *Sing with Me Big Book*
- Read Aloud Anthology
- Reproducible Pages TE 90f–90g
- Student Edition 90–91

Morning Warm-Up!

It can be sad to depart from a place you know. But it can also be exciting to travel a new route and arrive at a new location. Would you be excited about moving to a new place?

QUESTION OF THE DAY Encourage children to sing "New Location" from the *Sing with Me Big Book* as you gather. Write and read the message, tracking the print. Discuss the question.

REVIEW ORAL VOCABULARY Have children find words in the message that

- are opposites (depart, arrive)
- describe how you might travel (a new route)
- describe where you arrive (new location)

Assess Vocabulary Use the Day 5 instruction on ELL Poster 15 to monitor children's progress with oral vocabulary.

ELL Poster 15

Share Literature

LISTEN AND RESPOND

USE PRIOR KNOWLEDGE Review that yesterday the class listened to find out what the boy thought would happen out West. Suggest that today the class listen to find out how the boy felt about his new location.

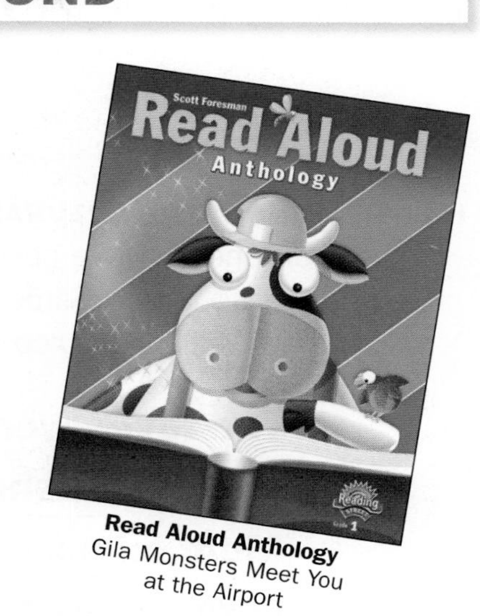

Read Aloud Anthology
Gila Monsters Meet You at the Airport

MONITOR LISTENING COMPREHENSION

- How did the boy feel about his new location? Why did he change his mind? (He starts to like it; he sees a restaurant like one in the East; he sees children playing baseball; he decides he'd like a horse.)
- How do you think he felt about the things the other boy said about the East? (He knew they weren't true; he saw that this boy was afraid of a new place, just like he was.)

BUILD ORAL VOCABULARY

GENERATE DISCUSSION Recall how the boy from the story feels about moving from one location to another. Invite children who have experienced a move to share how they felt; ask other children to predict how they would feel if they had to move to a new place. Have children use some of this week's Amazing Words as they describe what it would be like to move.

Monitor Progress — Check Oral Vocabulary

Display pp. 68–69 in the Student Edition and remind children of the concept for this week—Growing and Changing. Ask them to tell you about the illustration using some of this week's Amazing Words, *arrive, depart, location, route, swoop, tumble, crumple,* and *stampede.*

If... children have difficulty using the Amazing Words,

then... ask questions about the illustration using the Amazing Words. Note which questions children can respond to. Reteach unknown words using the Oral Vocabulary Routine.

Day 1 Check	Day 2 Check	Day 3 Check	Day 4 Check	▶ Day 5 Check
Word Reading	Word Reading	High-Frequency Words/Retelling	Fluency	Oral Vocabulary/ Assess Progress

OBJECTIVES

- Set purpose for listening.
- Build oral vocabulary.

arrive	**swoop**
depart	**tumble**
location	**crumple**
route	**stampede**

ELL

Extend Language Have children give sentences telling how they feel. Invite them to use their home language. If feelings are expressed incorrectly (*I have tired*), explain that English uses the verb *am.*

Oral Vocabulary
SUCCESS PREDICTOR

OBJECTIVES

- Review words with ending *-es*; plural *-es* and *r*-controlled *or, ore*.
- Review high-frequency words.

Ending *-es*; Plural *-es* and *r*-Controlled *or, ore*

REVIEW

IDENTIFY ENDING *-es*; PLURAL *-es* AND *r*-CONTROLLED *or, ore* WORDS Write these sentences. Have children read each one aloud as you track the print. Call on individuals to name and underline the words with ending *-es*; plurals with *-es* as well as the *r*-controlled *or, ore* words.

The foxes were born in a den.
A wave crashes on the shore.
Mom mixes the corn with a big fork.
Ford tosses the ball and Hank catches it.

High-Frequency Words

REVIEW

SAY AND SPELL WORDS Write the rhyme. Ask children to use letter clues to complete the rhyme with Words to Read from p. 70. Have children say, spell, and locate the word on the Word Wall. Then reread the rhyme. Word Wall

O __ r f __ __ __ __ __ __ drove a __ __ y in a c __ r. (Our, friends, away, car)
But our friends didn't go v __ __ y far. (very)
They went to the pool. They drove by the s __ __ __ __ l. (school)
Then ended up back at their h __ __ __ e! (house)

Vocabulary For additional practice with the high-frequency words, use the vocabulary strategies and word cards in the ELL Teaching Guide, pp. 101–102.

SPELLING TEST Ending *-es;* Plural *-es*

DICTATION SENTENCES Use these sentences to assess this week's spelling words.

1. Our class has spelling every day.
2. Fix that rip with a pin.
3. The bus will stop for me.
4. Six classes went on a trip.
5. I kiss my cat.
6. I see five buses in line.
7. You can make many wishes.
8. Jan kisses her puppy on his nose.
9. Mom fixes the car.
10. Peggy got her one wish.

HIGH-FREQUENCY WORDS

11. We have a very shy kitten.
12. My friends are going with us.

ASSESS

- Spell words with ending *-es;* plural *-es.*

Spelling Words

Adding *-es*

1. **fix**	6. **wishes***
2. **fixes**	7. **kiss**
3. **class**	8. **kisses**
4. **classes**	9. **bus**
5. **wish**	10. **buses***

High-Frequency Words

11. **friends***	12. **very***

* **Words from the Selection**

Group Time

On-Level

Read Set B Sentences and the Story.

- Use pp. 90e–90g.

Strategic Intervention

Read Set A Sentences.

- Use pp. 90e–90g.
- Use the **Routine** on p. DI·44.

Advanced

Read Set C Sentences.

- Use pp. 90e–90g.
- Use the **Routine** on p. DI·45.

DAY 5

Place English language learners in the groups that correspond to their reading abilities in English.

Independent Activities

Fluency Reading Children reread selections at their independent level.

Journal Writing Write a letter to a friend who moved away. Share writing.

Independent Reading See p. 68j for Reading/Library activities and suggestions.

Literacy Centers You may use the Technology Center on p. 68k to support this week's concepts and reading.

Practice Book 1.2 Maps, p. 30

Break into small groups after Spelling and before Grammar Writing.

Monitor Progress

ASSESS

- Decode ending *-es*, plural *-es*, and *r*-controlled *or, ore.*
- Read high-frequency words.
- Read aloud with appropriate speed and accuracy.
- Recognize story theme.
- Retell a story.

Differentiated Assessment

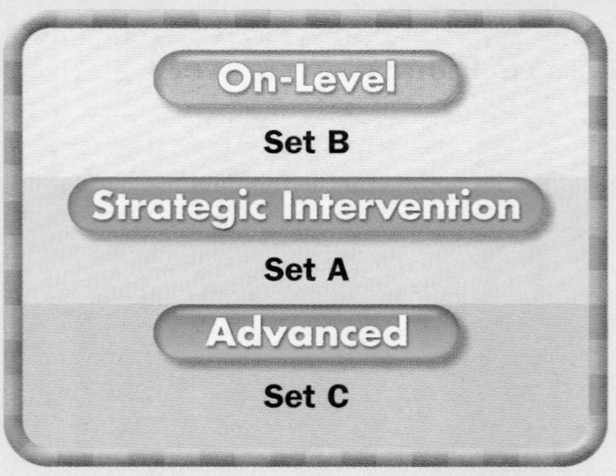

Fluency Assessment Plan

- ☑ Week 1 assess Advanced students.
- ☑ Week 2 assess Strategic Intervention students.
- ☑ **This week assess On-Level students.**
- ☐ Week 4 assess Strategic Intervention students.
- ☐ Week 5 assess any students you have not yet checked during this unit.
- ☐ Week 6 assess Strategic Intervention students.

Set individual fluency goals for children to enable them to reach the end-of-year goal.

- Current Goal: 20–30 wcpm
- End-of-Year Goal: 60 wcpm
- ELL Oral fluency depends not only on reading without halting but also on word recognition. After children read passages aloud for assessment help them recognize unfamiliar English words and their meanings. Focus on each child's progress.

SENTENCE READING

ASSESS ENDING *-es*, PLURAL *-es*, r-CONTROLLED *or, ore*, AND HIGH-FREQUENCY WORDS Use one of the reproducible lists on p. 90f to assess children's ability to read words with ending *-es*, plural *-es*, *r*-controlled *or, ore,* and high-frequency words. Call on individuals to read two sentences aloud. Have each child in the group read different sentences. Start over with sentence one if necessary.

RECORD SCORES Use the Sentence Reading Chart for this unit on p. WA19.

Monitor Progress	Ending *-es*, Plural *-es*, and *r*-Controlled *or, ore*
If... children have trouble reading ending *-es*, plural *-es*, and *r*-controlled *or, ore,*	**then...** use the Reteach Lessons on p. DI • 79.
	High-Frequency Words
If... children cannot read a high-frequency word,	**then...** mark the missed words on a high-frequency word list and send the list home for additional word reading practice or have the child practice with a fluent reader.

FLUENCY AND COMPREHENSION

ASSESS FLUENCY Take a one-minute sample of children's oral reading. See Monitoring Fluency, pp. WA17–WA18. Have children read "Morning Chores," the on-level fluency passage on p. 90.

RECORD SCORES Record the number of words read correctly in a minute on the child's Fluency Progress Chart.

ASSESS COMPREHENSION Have the child read to the end of the passage. (If the child had difficulty with the passage, you may read it aloud.) Ask what the theme of the story is and have the child retell the passage. Use the Retelling Rubric on p. 86–87 to evaluate the child's retelling.

Monitor Progress	Fluency
If... a child does not achieve the fluency goal on the timed reading,	**then...** copy the passage and send it home with the child for additional fluency practice or have the child practice with a fluent reader.
	Theme
If... a child cannot recognize the story theme,	**then...** use the Reteach Lesson on p. DI • 80.

READ THE SENTENCES

Set A

1. Jan fixes very good pork.
2. Ben waxes our sports car.
3. Put the glasses and forks away.
4. More buses came to the school.
5. His house has two benches on the porch.
6. Her friends put corn on the dishes.

Set B

1. Sam fishes in the water away from the shore.
2. The old car passes the store on the way home.
3. Dave made a fort with boxes in his house.
4. Our friends wore hats with blue patches on them.
5. A very bad storm made the red foxes hide.
6. Liz watches Ann sort the math papers at school.

Set C

1. Our school has reading classes in the morning and math classes in the afternoon.
2. Dad paid taxes on the car he got in New York.
3. The branches that fell on the house tore a hole in the roof.
4. Mom wishes she could buy a very big boat that is docked at the port.
5. Our friends work at ranches that raise many different kinds of horses.
6. Mack rushes away from the forest when it begins to rain.

REPRODUCIBLE PAGE • See also *Assessment Handbook*, p. 263

Morning Chores

Cole and Jess met on Vic's porch one morning. 9
"Can you play ball with us?" asked Cole. 17

"I have chores to do this morning," said Vic. "I 27
have to pick corn. I have to sort my toys. I also 39
have dishes to dry. Next, I have to stack boxes. 49
Then I must pick up branches." 55

"We can help you," said Jess. "We can do all 65
the jobs with you. Then we can play ball. 74

Vic's mother watches the boys as she fixes 82
lunch for them. "How lucky Vic is to have such 92
good friends," she thinks. 96

In no time at all, no more jobs were left. Now 107
they could play ball. 111

See also *Assessment Handbook*, p. 264 • REPRODUCIBLE PAGE

Write Now

Read Together

Writing and Grammar

Greeting Card

Prompt

In *Jan's New Home,* Jan moves to a new city.
Think about how you would welcome Jan to your class.
Now write a greeting card telling Jan about your class.

Writing Trait

A greeting card has a friendly **voice.**

Student Model

Welcome to our class, Jan!
Each day we read and write in our journals. Our frisky gerbils Al and Max run on the wheel. Speakers tell about their jobs.
Susan Bloom

First line shows friendly voice.

Sentence gives good picture.

Verbs tell what happens in class.

90

Writer's Checklist

- **Focus** Do all sentences stick to the topic?
- **Organization** Are ideas in an order that makes sense?
- **Support** Do words make the card sound friendly?
- **Conventions** Are all words spelled correctly?

Grammar

Verbs That Do Not Add -s

Do not add **-s** to a verb that tells what two or more people, animals, or things do now.

Jan and her mother **pack** boxes.

Two people are packing, so we do not add **-s** to **pack.**

Look at the greeting card to Jan. Write the verbs that tell what happens in class. Why don't the verbs end in **-s?**

91

Writing and Grammar

LOOK AT THE PROMPT Read p. 90 aloud. Have children select and discuss key words or phrases in the prompt. *(welcome Jan to your class, greeting card telling Jan about your class)*

STRATEGIES TO DEVELOP VOICE Have children

- talk about class activities they enjoy and tell how those activities make them feel.
- listen as you read aloud paragraphs from a humorous story and a social studies text and talk about how the voices are different.
- show how they would say sentences such as these: *Jane is my best friend. My dog ran away. I don't want to dance on stage!*

See Scoring Rubric on p. WA11. Rubric 4 3 2 1

HINTS FOR BETTER WRITING Read p. 91 aloud. Use the checklist to help children revise their greeting cards. Discuss the grammar lesson. (Answers: *read, write, run, tell. The verbs do not have* -s *because they tell what two people do now.)* Have children use verbs that do not add -*s* correctly in their greeting cards.

DAILY FIX-IT

9. Dad say good-by.
(says; good-bye)

10. Jan iz on her way?
(is; way.)

Verbs That Do Not Add -s

Circle the verb that shows more than one.

1. Jan and her parents (moves, move) to the city.
2. Her parents (drive, drives) the car.
3. They (sees, see) horses and sheep.

Circle the correct verb. **Write** the verb on the line.

4. Cars fill the road. (fills, fill)
5. Trucks roar by. (roar, roars)
6. The men wave at Jan. (waves, wave)

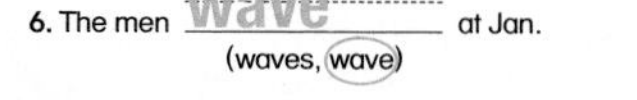

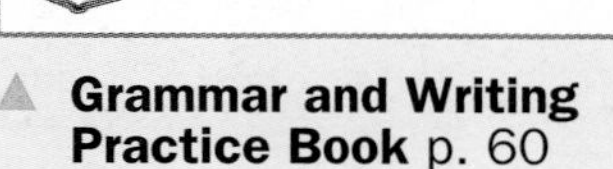

Home Activity Your child reviewed verbs that do not add -s. Have your child point to each verb on this page that does not end in -s and use the word in a new sentence.

Grammar and Writing Practice Book p. 60

OBJECTIVE

- Locate places on a map.

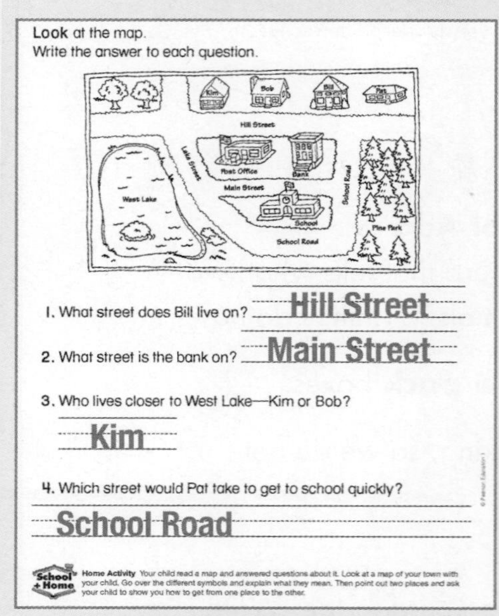

Look at the map.
Write the answer to each question.

1. What street does Bill live on? Hill Street
2. What street is the bank on? Main Street
3. Who lives closer to West Lake—Kim or Bob? Kim
4. Which street would Pat take to get to school quickly? School Road

School + Home **Home Activity** Your child read a map and answered questions about it. Look at a map of your town with your child. Go over the different symbols and explain what they mean. Then point out two places and ask your child to show you how to get from one place to the other.

▲ **Practice Book 1.2** p. 30

ELL

Access Content As you draw and label the map, identify each item. For example: This is a bus stop. The legend tells that a triangle stands for a bus stop. There are 4 bus stops on the map.

Research/Study Skills

TEACH/MODEL Maps

MODEL USING A MAP Draw an imaginary map on the board of Jan's new city neighborhood. Include three horizontal and three vertical streets. Have children suggest street names and label the map appropriately. Use rectangles to show and label a café and donut shop. Make a legend for the map. Draw a triangle and label it *Bus Stop*. Show four triangles on the map. Use a tall rectangle to represent an apartment building and label it *Jan's House*. Show other places on the map as you wish.

Jan's house
Bells Lane
Donut Shop
Hill Street
Pine Street
School
Park Steet
Café

Model how to use the map.

MODEL I can use the map to locate different places. The legend shows that a triangle stands for a bus stop. Each triangle on the map is a different bus stop. I can also use the map to find a route from place to place. First I find one bus stop. Next I find a second bus stop. I follow the roads to see how to get from the first to the second bus stop.

DESCRIBE ROUTES Call on individuals to describe routes to get from one place to another on the map: Jan's house to a bus stop, a bus stop to the café, the donut shop to Jan's house.

PRACTICE

DEMONSTRATE USING A MAP Have partners make their own map of an imaginary city. Have one child describe a walk around the city while the other traces the route on the map. Then have children switch roles.

Wrap Up Your Week!

LET'S TALK ABOUT Growing and Changing

QUESTION OF THE WEEK Recall this week's question.

- Why are changes exciting?

Display the Change/Stay the Same Chart. Discuss what things might make children feel excited about moving and what might make them feel sad. Have them draw a picture of something they might take to a new place that would make them feel comfortable.

Change	Stay the Same
house	furniture
neighborhood	family members
school	toys
friends	pets
kind of house	things you like to do
yard	

CONNECT Use questions such as these to prompt a discussion.

- What is the first thing you do when you arrive home every day?
- What would you miss if you had to depart from this school?
- What exciting location would you visit if you could swoop away in an airplane?
- What route do you take to school?

Build Background Use ELL Poster 16 to support the Preview activity.

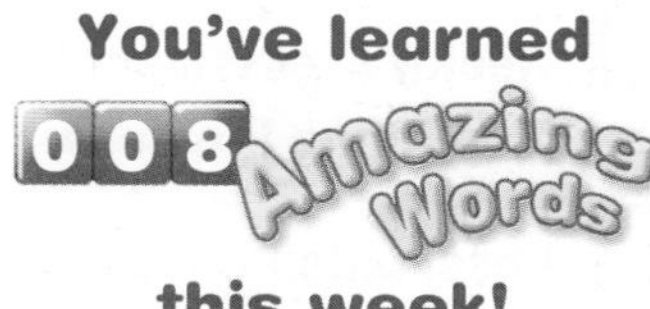

You've learned 121 Amazing Words so far this year!

PREVIEW Tell children that next week they will read about a garden and how the gardener tries to make changes happen.

Assessment Checkpoints *for the Week*

Selection Assessment

Use pp. 33–36 of Selection Tests to check:

 **Selection Understanding**

 **Comprehension Skill** *Theme*

 **High-Frequency Words**

away	*our*
car	*school*
friends	*very*
house	

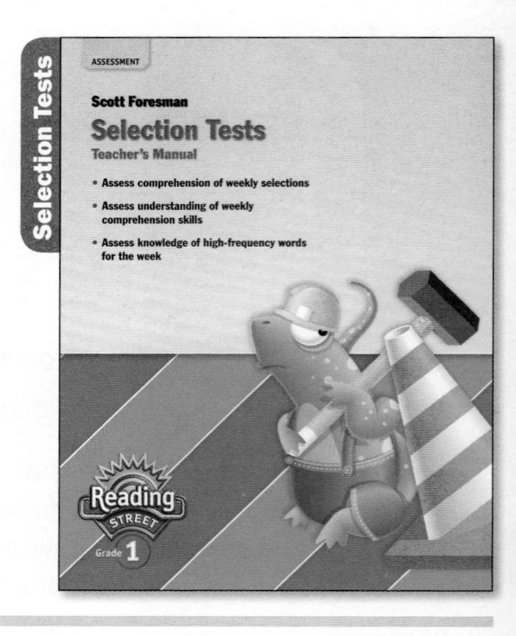

Leveled Assessment

On-Level

Strategic Intervention

Advanced

Use pp. 85–90 of Fresh Reads for Differentiated Test Practice to check:

 **Comprehension Skill** *Theme*

 REVIEW **Comprehension Skill** *Plot*

 **Fluency** *Words Correct Per Minute*

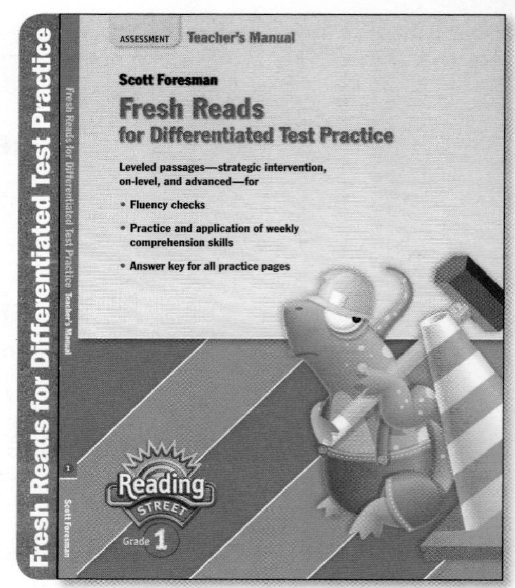

Managing Assessment

Use Assessment Handbook for:

 **Weekly Assessment Blackline Masters for Monitoring Progress**

 **Observation Checklists**

 **Record-Keeping Forms**

 **Portfolio Assessment**

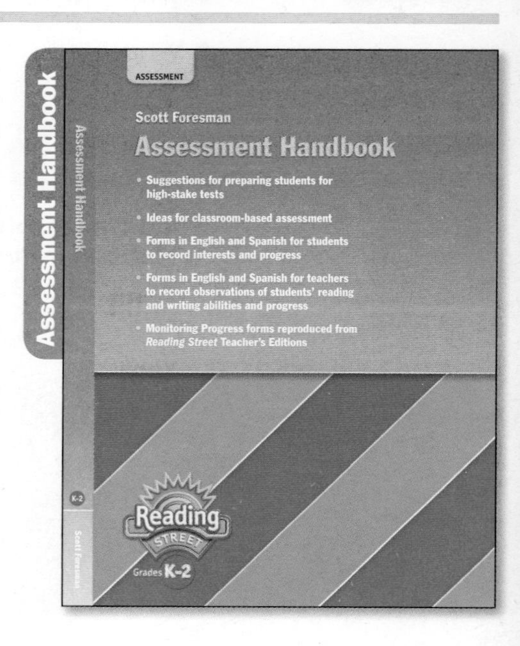

Unit 3
Changes

CONCEPT QUESTION
What is changing in our world?

Growing and Changing

Week 1
How do we change as we grow?

Week 2
What do we learn as we grow and change?

Week 3
Why are changes exciting?

Changes in Nature

Week 4
What changes happen in a garden?

Week 5
What changes can we observe in nature?

Week 6
How does nature change during the year?

Week 4

EXPAND THE CONCEPT
What changes happen in a garden?

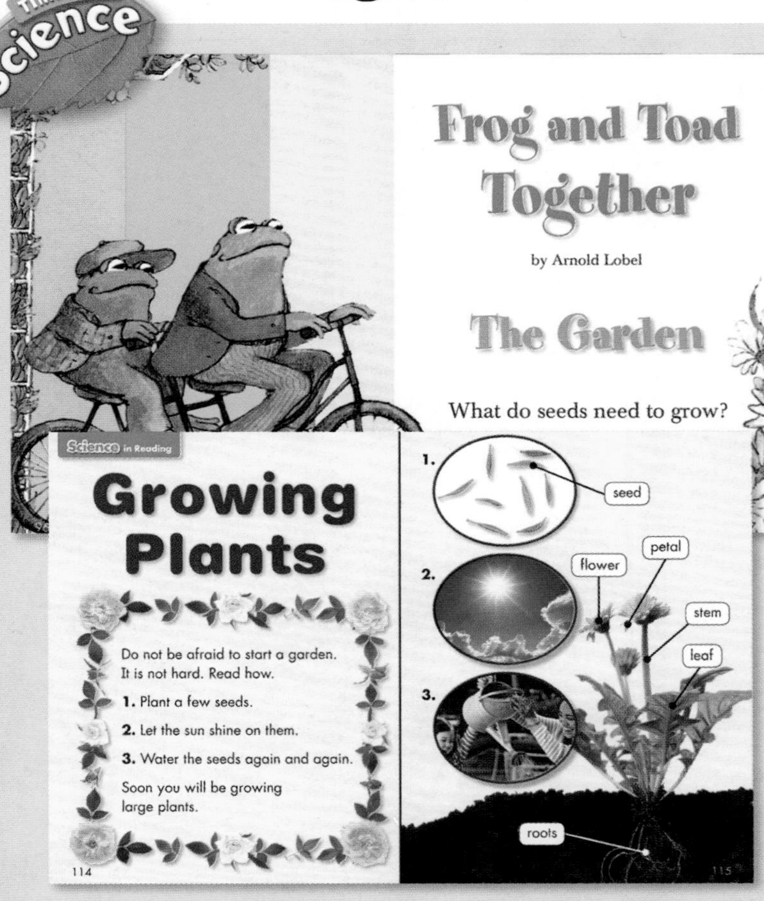

CONNECT THE CONCEPT

▶ **Build Background**

blossom *destroy* *dim* *gardener* *humongous* *nature* *shade* *sprout*

▶ **Science Content**
Plant Needs, Parts of Plants, Life Cycle of a Plant

▶ **Writing**
Poem

Preview Your Week

What changes happen in a garden?

Student Edition pages 96–113

Audio CD

Genre Animal Fantasy

Phonics Inflected Endings *-ed, -ing* and *r*-Controlled *ar*

Comprehension Skill Plot

Comprehension Strategy Visualize

Science

Paired Selection

Reading Across Texts
How to Make Plants Grow

Genre
Nonfiction

Text Features
Diagram

Science in Reading

Growing Plants

Do not be afraid to start a garden. It is not hard. Read how.

1. Plant a few seeds.
2. Let the sun shine on them.
3. Water the seeds again and again.

Soon you will be growing large plants.

1. seed
2. flower, petal, stem, leaf
3. roots

114

Student Edition pages 114–115

Audio CD

- Student Edition
- Leveled Readers
- Decodable Readers

Leveled Readers

Skill Plot
Strategy Visualize
Lesson Vocabulary

Below-Level

On-Level

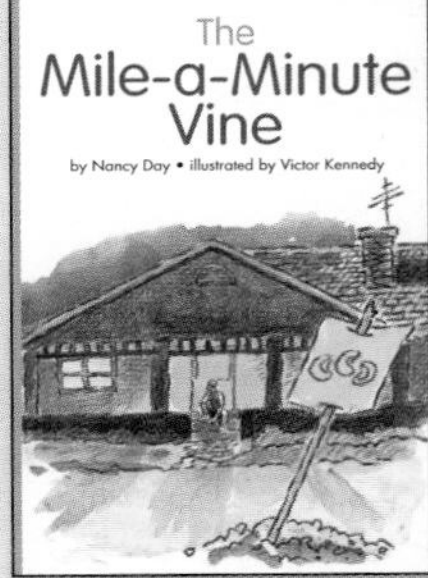

Advanced

ELL Reader
- Concept Vocabulary
- Text Support
- Language Enrichment

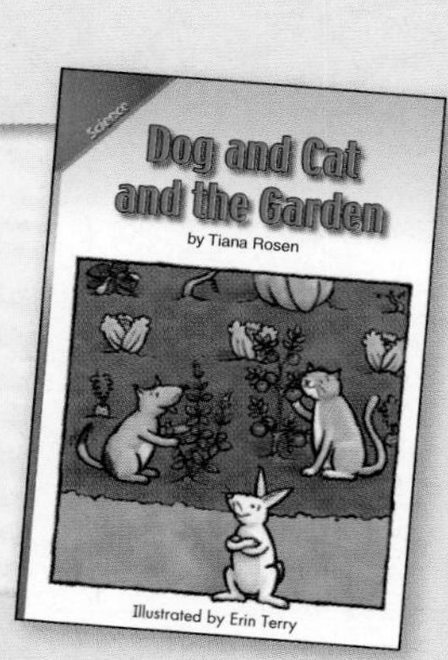

Decodable Readers

Apply Phonics
- *Mom Races*
- *Day at the Farm*

TIME FOR Science

Integrate Science Standards
- Plant Needs
- Parts of Plants
- Life Cycle of a Plant

Frog and Toad Together, pp. 96–113

"Growing Plants," pp. 114–115

Leveled Readers

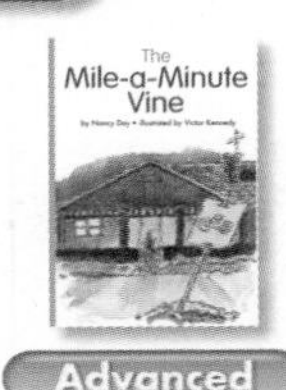

Below-Level	On-Level	Advanced
• Support Concepts	• Develop Concepts	• Extend Concepts • Science Extension Activity

ELL Reader

Build **Concept Vocabulary**
Changes in Nature, pp. 92r–93

Teach **Science Concepts**
Life Cycles, p. 108–109
Plant Needs, p. 110–111
Plants, p. 114–115

Explore **Science Center**
Record Observations, p. 92k

Weekly Plan

PearsonSuccessNet.com

READING

90–120 minutes

TARGET SKILLS OF THE WEEK

- **Phonics**
  Inflected Endings *-ed, -ing* and *r*-Controlled *ar*
- **Comprehension Skill**
  Plot
- **Comprehension Strategy**
  Visualize

LANGUAGE ARTS

20–30 minutes

Trait of the Week

Word Choice

DAY 1 PAGES 92l–93d

Oral Language

QUESTION OF THE WEEK, 92l
What changes happen in a garden?

Oral Vocabulary/Share Literature, 92m
Sing with Me Big Book, Song 16
Amazing Words *gardener, nature, sprout*

Word Work

Phonemic Awareness, 92m
Blend and Segment Syllables

Phonics, 92n–92o
Introduce Inflected Endings *-ed, -ing* **T**

Spelling, 92p
Pretest

Comprehension/Vocabulary/Fluency

Read Decodable Reader 31

Grouping Options 92f–92g

Review High-Frequency Words
Check Comprehension
Reread for Fluency

Build Background, 92r–93
Changes in Nature

Listening Comprehension, 93a–93b
Plot **T**

Language Arts

Shared Writing, 93c
Poem

Grammar, 93d
Introduce Verbs for Now and the Past **T**

DAILY JOURNAL WRITING — **Day 1** *List plants you would grow in your garden.*

DAILY SCIENCE CONNECTIONS — **Day 1** Seed to Plant Chart, 92r–93

DAY 2 PAGES 94a–95c

Oral Language

QUESTION OF THE DAY, 94a
Why do you think the seasons change?

Oral Vocabulary/Share Literature, 94b
Big Book *What Makes the Seasons?*
Amazing Words *dim, shade*

Word Work

Phonemic Awareness, 94b
Substitute Phonemes

Phonics, 94c–94d
Introduce *r*-Controlled *ar* **T**

Spelling, 94e
Dictation

Comprehension/Vocabulary/Fluency

Read Decodable Reader 32

Grouping Options 92f–92g

Review High-Frequency Words
Check Comprehension
Reread for Fluency

High-Frequency Words, 94–95
Introduce *afraid, again, few, how, read, soon* **T**

Language Arts

Interactive Writing, 95a
List

Grammar, 95b
Practice Verbs for Now and the Past **T**

Speaking and Listening, 95c
Retell a Story

DAILY JOURNAL WRITING — **Day 2** *Write about planting a seed.*

DAILY SCIENCE CONNECTIONS — **Day 2** Seed to Plant Chart, 95c

DAILY SUCCESS PREDICTORS

for Adequate Yearly Progress

Monitor Progress and Corrective Feedback

	Day 1	Day 2
Phonics	Check Word Reading, *92o* Spiral REVIEW Phonics	Check Word Reading, *94d* Spiral REVIEW Phonics

RESOURCES FOR THE WEEK

- Practice Book 1.2, *pp. 31–40*
- Phonics and Spelling Practice Book, *pp. 61–64*
- Grammar and Writing Practice Book, *pp. 61–64*
- Selection Test, *pp. 37–46*
- Fresh Reads for Differentiated Test Practice, *pp. 91–96*
- Phonics Songs and Rhymes Chart 16
- The Grammar and Writing Book, *pp. 140–145*

Grouping Options for Differentiated Instruction

Turn the page for the small group lesson plan.

DAY 3 PAGES 96a–113d

Oral Language

QUESTION OF THE DAY, 96a
What does a real garden need to grow?

Oral Vocabulary/Share Literature, 96b
Big Book *What Makes the Seasons?*
Amazing Word *blossom*

Word Work

Phonemic Awareness, 96b
Blend and Segment Phonemes

Phonics, 96c–96d
◎ Inflected Endings *-ed, -ing* and *r*-Controlled *ar* **T**

Spelling, 96d
Practice

Comprehension/Vocabulary/Fluency

Read *Frog and Toad Together,* 96e–113

Grouping Options 92f–92g

Introduce Selection Words
ground, head, rain, shouted, shouting

Review High-Frequency Words
afraid, again, few, how, read, soon **T**

◎ Plot **T**
◎ Visualize
REVIEW Compare and Contrast **T**

Fluency, 113a
Read with Expression

Vocabulary, 113b
Use Endings to Determine Meaning

Trait of the Week, 113c
Introduce Word Choice

Grammar, 113d
Write with Verbs for Now and the Past **T**

Day 3 *Write about your favorite flower, plant, or tree.*

Day 3 Time for Science: Life Cycles, 108–109; Plant Needs, 110–111

DAY 4 PAGES 114a–115d

Oral Language

QUESTION OF THE DAY, 114a
What would you plant in a garden?

Oral Vocabulary/Share Literature, 114b
Read Aloud Anthology "Jack and the Beanstalk"
Amazing Words *destroy, humongous*

Word Work

Phonemic Awareness, 114b
Add Initial and Final Phonemes

High-Frequency Words, 114c
Practice *afraid, again, few, how, read, soon* **T**

Phonics, 114c–114d
REVIEW Ending *-es;* Plural *-es; r*-Controlled *or, ore* **T**
REVIEW Word Reading **T**

Spelling, 114e
Partner Review

Comprehension/Vocabulary/Fluency

Read "Growing Plants," 114–115
Leveled Readers

Grouping Options 92f–92g

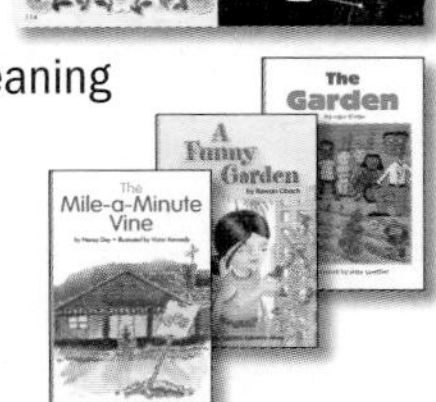

Use Endings to Determine Meaning
Reading Across Texts

Fluency, 115b
Read with Expression

Writing Across the Curriculum, 115c
List

Grammar, 115d
Review Verbs for Now and the Past **T**

Day 4 *Write to tell what Toad's garden looks like after the plants grow tall.*

Day 4 Time for Science: Plants, 114–115

DAY 5 PAGES 116a–117b

Oral Language

QUESTION OF THE DAY, 116a
What can a gardener do to grow big flowers?

Oral Vocabulary/Share Literature, 116b
Read Aloud Anthology "Jack and the Beanstalk"
Amazing Words Review

Word Work

Phonics, 116c
◎ Review Inflected Endings *-ed, -ing* and *r*-Controlled *ar* **T**

High-Frequency Words, 116c
Review *afraid, again, few, how, read, soon* **T**

Spelling, 116d
Test

Comprehension/Vocabulary/Fluency

Read Leveled Readers

Grouping Options 92f–92g

Monitor Progress, 116e–116g
Read the Sentences
Read the Story

Writing and Grammar, 116–117
Develop Word Choice
Use Verbs for Now and the Past **T**

Research/Study Skills, 117a
Diagram

Day 5 *Write about how to start a garden.*

Day 5 Revisit the Seed to Plant Chart, 117b

KEY ◎ = Target Skill **T** = Tested Skill

Fluency and Comprehension
Check High-Frequency Words, *96f*
Check Retelling, *112a*
Spiral REVIEW High-Frequency Words

Fluency
Check Fluency WCPM, *115b*
Spiral REVIEW Phonics, High-Frequency Words

Oral Vocabulary
Check Oral Vocabulary, *116b*
Assess Phonics, High-Frequency Words, Fluency, Comprehension, *116e*

SUCCESS PREDICTOR

Small Group Plan *for Differentiated Instruction*

Daily Plan AT A GLANCE

Reading

Whole Group
- Oral Language
- Word Work
- Comprehension/Vocabulary

Group Time

Meet with small groups to provide:
- Skill Support
- Reading Support
- Fluency Practice

This week's lessons for daily group time can be found behind the Differentiated Instruction (DI) tab on pp. DI • 46–DI • 55.

Whole Group
- Comprehension/Vocabulary
- Fluency

Language Arts
- Writing
- Grammar
- Speaking/Listening/Viewing
- Research/Study Skills

Use *My Sidewalks on Reading Street* for Tier III intensive reading intervention.

DAY 1

On-Level	Strategic Intervention	Advanced
Teacher-Led *Page 92q*	Teacher-Led *Page DI • 46*	Teacher-Led *Page DI • 47*
• **Read** Decodable Reader 31 • **Reread** for Fluency	• Blend and Build Words with Inflected Endings *-ed, -ing* • **Read** Decodable Reader 31 • **Reread** for Fluency	• Extend Word Reading • **Read** Advanced Selection 16 • Introduce Concept Inquiry

Independent Activities

While you meet with small groups, have the rest of the class...

- Reread for fluency
- Write in their journals
- Complete Practice Book 1.2, p. 33
- Visit the Word Work Center

DAY 2

On-Level	Strategic Intervention	Advanced
Teacher-Led *Page 94f*	Teacher-Led *Page DI • 48*	Teacher-Led *Page DI • 49*
• **Read** Decodable Reader 32 • **Reread** for Fluency	• Blend and Build Words with *r*-Controlled *ar* • **Read** Decodable Reader 32 • **Reread** for Fluency	• Extend Word Reading • **Read** *What Makes the Seasons?* • Continue Concept Inquiry

Independent Activities

While you meet with small groups, have the rest of the class...

- Reread for fluency
- Write in their journals
- Complete Practice Book 1.2, pp. 34–36
- Visit the Word Work Center
- Work on inquiry projects

DAY 3

On-Level	Strategic Intervention	Advanced
Teacher-Led *Pages 96–113*	Teacher-Led *Page DI • 50*	Teacher-Led *Page DI • 51*
• **Read** *Frog and Toad Together*	• Blend and Read Words with *-ed, -ing; r*-Controlled *ar* • **Read** SI Decodable Reader 16 • **Read** or Listen to *Frog and Toad Together*	• **Read** *Frog and Toad Together* • Continue Concept Inquiry

Independent Activities

While you meet with small groups, have the rest of the class...

- Read self-selected reading
- Write in their journals
- Complete Practice Book 1.2, p. 37
- Visit the Listening and Writing Centers
- Work on inquiry projects

① Begin with whole class skill and strategy instruction.

② Meet with small groups to provide differentiated instruction.

③ Gather the whole class back together for fluency and language arts.

DAY 4

On-Level

Teacher-Led

Pages 114–115, LR31–LR33

- **Read** "Growing Plants"
- Practice with On-Level Reader *A Funny Garden*

Strategic Intervention

Teacher-Led

Pages DI · 52, LR28–LR30

- Blend and Read Words
- **Reread** SI Decodable Reader 15
- **Read** or Listen to "Growing Plants"
- Practice with Below-Level Reader *The Garden*

Advanced

Teacher-Led

Pages DI · 53, LR34–LR36

- **Read** "Growing Plants"
- Expand Vocabulary
- Continue Concept Inquiry
- Practice with Advanced Reader *The Mile-a-Minute Vine*

i Independent Activities

While you meet with small groups, have the rest of the class...

- Reread for fluency
- Write in their journals
- Read self-selected reading
- Complete Practice Book 1.2, pp. 38–39
- Visit the Listening and Science Centers
- Work on inquiry projects

DAY 5

On-Level

Teacher-Led

Pages 116e–116g, LR31–LR33

- Sentence Reading, Set B
- Monitor Comprehension
- Practice with On-Level Reader *A Funny Garden*

Strategic Intervention

Teacher-Led

Pages DI · 54, LR28–LR30

- Practice Word Reading
- Sentence Reading, Set A
- Monitor Fluency and Comprehension
- Practice with Below-Level Reader *The Garden*

Advanced

Teacher-Led

Pages DI · 55, LR34–LR36

- Sentence Reading, Set C
- Monitor Comprehension
- Share Concept Inquiry
- Practice with Advanced Reader *The Mile-a-Minute Vine*

i Independent Activities

While you meet with small groups, have the rest of the class...

- Reread for fluency
- Write in their journals
- Read self-selected reading
- Complete Practice Book 1.2, p. 40
- Visit the Technology Center

ELL

Grouping Place English language learners in the groups that correspond to their reading abilities in English.

Use the appropriate Leveled Reader or other text at children's instructional level.

TIP Send home the appropriate Multilingual Summary of the main selection on Day 1.

PearsonSuccessNet.com

Peter Afflerbach
For research on prediction strategies, see the article "The Influence of Prior Knowledge and Text Genre on . . . Prediction Strategies" by Scott Foresman author Peter Afflerbach.

TEACHER TALK

Progress monitoring is a system for frequent assessment of student progress in a skill area. Teachers can use this information to identify students at risk and to modify the pace of instruction.

Looking Ahead

Be sure to schedule time for children to work on the unit inquiry project "Take a Closer Look." This week children should continue to observe, measure, and record their observations. Children can chart the growth of objects they are measuring.

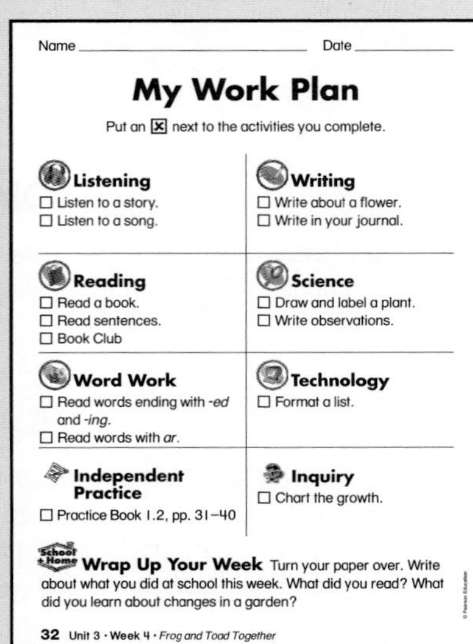

Name ____________ Date ________

My Work Plan

Put an ☒ next to the activities you complete.

Listening
☐ Listen to a story.
☐ Listen to a song.

Writing
☐ Write about a flower.
☐ Write in your journal.

Reading
☐ Read a book.
☐ Read sentences.
☐ Book Club

Science
☐ Draw and label a plant.
☐ Write observations.

Word Work
☐ Read words ending with -*ed* and -*ing*.
☐ Read words with *ar*.

Technology
☐ Format a list.

Independent Practice
☐ Practice Book 1.2, pp. 31–40

Inquiry
☐ Chart the growth.

Wrap Up Your Week Turn your paper over. Write about what you did at school this week. What did you read? What did you learn about changes in a garden?

32 Unit 3 • Week 4 • *Frog and Toad Together*

▲ **Group-Time Survival Guide**
p. 32, Weekly Contract

Customize Your Plan *by Strand*

ORAL LANGUAGE

Concept Development

What changes happen in a garden?

gardener, *dim*, *destroy*, *nature*, *shade*, *humongous*, *sprout*, *blossom*

BUILD

❑ **Question of the Week** Use the Morning Warm-Up! to introduce and discuss the question of the week. This week children will talk, sing, read, and write about changes in nature. DAY 1 *92l*

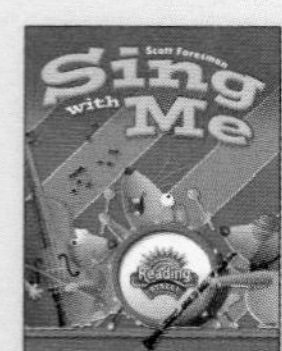

Sing with Me Big Book

❑ **Sing with Me Big Book** Sing a song about growing a garden. Ask children to listen for the concept-related Amazing Words *gardener, nature, sprout.* DAY 1 *92m*

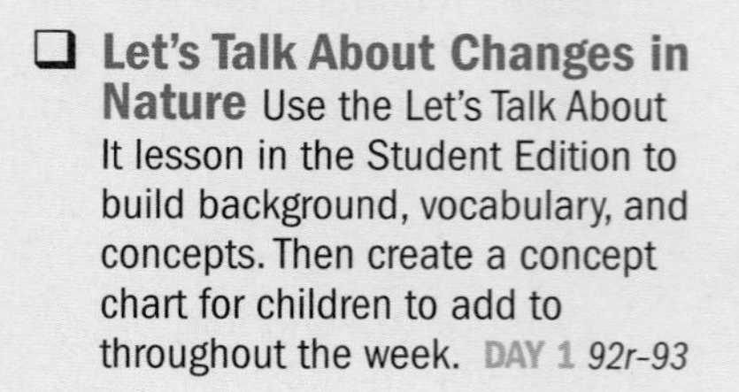

❑ **Let's Talk About Changes in Nature** Use the Let's Talk About It lesson in the Student Edition to build background, vocabulary, and concepts. Then create a concept chart for children to add to throughout the week. DAY 1 *92r-93*

Let's Talk About It

DEVELOP

❑ **Question of the Day** Use the questions in the Morning Warm-Ups! to discuss lesson concepts and how they relate to the unit theme, Changes. DAY 2 *94a*, DAY 3 *96a*, DAY 4 *114a*, DAY 5 *116a*

❑ **Share Literature** Read big books and read aloud selections that develop concepts, language, and vocabulary related to the lesson concept and the unit theme. Continue to develop this week's Amazing Words. DAY 2 *94b*, DAY 3 *96b*, DAY 4 *114b*, DAY 5 *116b*

CONNECT

❑ **Wrap Up Your Week!** Revisit the Question of the Week. Then connect concepts and vocabulary to next week's lesson. DAY 5 *117b*

CHECK

❑ **Check Oral Vocabulary** To informally assess children's oral vocabulary, ask individuals to use some of this week's Amazing Words to tell you about the photographs and illustration on Student Edition pp. 92-93. DAY 5 *116b*

PHONEMIC AWARENESS AND PHONICS

INFLECTED ENDINGS *-ED, -ING* For many words that end in CVC, the last consonant is doubled before an ending is added.

R*-CONTROLLED *AR A single vowel followed by the letter *r* has a sound that is neither short nor long, but *r*-controlled.

TEACH

❑ **Blend and Segment** Practice segmenting and blending syllables and phonemes. DAY 1 *92m*, DAY 3 *96b*

❑ **Inflected Endings *-ed, -ing*** Introduce the blending strategy for words with inflected endings *-ed, -ing*. Then have children blend and sort words with inflected endings *-ed, -ing*. DAY 1 *92n-92o*

❑ **Substitute Phonemes** Practice substituting the long *a* sound in words with the *r*-controlled phoneme. DAY 2 *94b*

❑ ***r*-Controlled *ar*** Introduce the blending strategy for words with *r*-controlled *ar*. Then have children blend and build /är/ words. DAY 2 *94c-94d*

❑ **Fluent Word Reading** Use the Fluent Word Reading Routine to develop children's word reading fluency. Use the Phonics Songs and Rhymes Chart for additional word reading practice. DAY 3 *96c-96d*

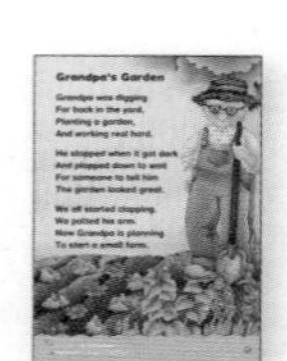

Phonics Songs and Rhymes Chart 16

PRACTICE/APPLY

❑ **Decodable Reader 31** Practice reading words with inflected endings *-ed, -ing* in context. DAY 1 *92q*

❑ **Decodable Reader 32** Practice reading words with *r*-controlled *ar* in context. DAY 2 *94f*

Decodable Readers 31 and 32

❑ ***Frog and Toad Together*** Practice decoding words in context. DAY 3 *96-111*

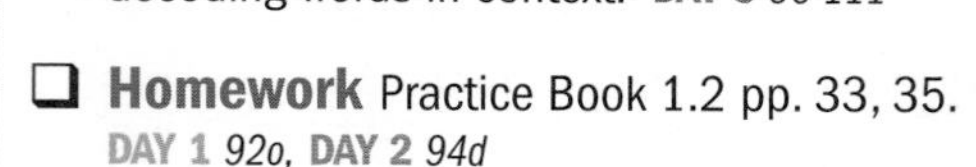

❑ **Homework** Practice Book 1.2 pp. 33, 35. DAY 1 *92o*, DAY 2 *94d*

❑ **Word Work Center** Practice inflected endings *-ed, -ing* and *r*-controlled *ar*. ANY DAY *92j*

Main Selection—Fiction

RETEACH/REVIEW

❑ **Review** Review words with this week's phonics skills. DAY 5 *116c*

❑ **Reteach Lessons** If necessary, reteach inflected endings *-ed, -ing* and *r*-controlled *ar*. DAY 5 *DI•80-DI•81*

❑ **Spiral REVIEW** Review previously taught phonics skills. DAY 1 *92o*, DAY 2 *94d*, DAY 4 *114c-114d*

ASSESS

❑ **Sentence Reading** Assess children's ability to read words with inflected endings *-ed, -ing* and *r*-controlled *ar*. DAY 5 *116e-116f*

1. Use assessment data to determine your instructional focus.
2. Preview this week's instruction by strand.
3. Choose instructional activities that meet the needs of your classroom.

SPELLING

INFLECTED ENDING *-ED* For many words that end in consonant-vowel-consonant, the last consonant is doubled before an ending is added.

TEACH

- ❑ **Pretest** Before administering the pretest, model how to segment inflected ending *-ed* words to spell them. Dictate the spelling words, segmenting them if necessary. Then have children check their pretests and correct misspelled words. DAY 1 *92p*

PRACTICE/APPLY

- ❑ **Dictation** Have children write dictation sentences to practice spelling words. DAY 2 *94e*
- ❑ **Write Words** Have children practice writing the spelling words by writing an action sentence. DAY 3 *96d*
- ❑ **Homework** Phonics and Spelling Practice Book pp. 61-64. DAY 1 *92p*, DAY 2 *94e*, DAY 3 *96d*, DAY 4 *114e*

RETEACH/REVIEW

- ❑ **Partner Review** Have pairs work together to read and write the spelling words. DAY 4 *114e*

ASSESS

- ❑ **Posttest** Use dictation sentences to give the posttest for words with inflected ending *-ed*. DAY 5 *116d*

Spelling Words

Adding *-ed*

1. ask	6. helped
2. asked*	7. jog
3. plan	8. jogged
4. planned	9. call
5. help*	10. called

High-Frequency Words

11. again*	12. soon*

* Words from the Selection

HIGH-FREQUENCY WORDS

WORDS TO READ

afraid *again* *few* *how*
read *soon*

TEACH

- ❑ **Words to Read** Introduce this week's high-frequency words and add them to the Word Wall. DAY 2 *94-95*

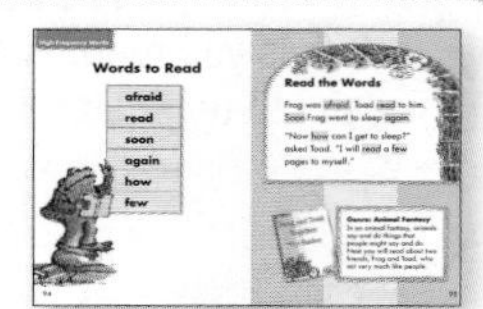
High-Frequency Words

PRACTICE/APPLY

- ❑ **Vocabulary Transparency 16** Review this week's high-frequency words, or Words to Read, before reading *Frog and Toad Together.* DAY 3 *96f*
- ❑ **Words in Context** Read high-frequency words in the context of *Frog and Toad Together.* DAY 3 *96-111*

Main Selection—Fiction

- ❑ **Word Wall** Use the Word Wall to review and practice high-frequency words throughout the week. DAY 4 *114c*, DAY 5 *116c*
- ❑ **Leveled Text** Practice this week's high-frequency words in the context of leveled text. DAY 4 *LR28–LR36*, DAY 5 *LR28–LR36*

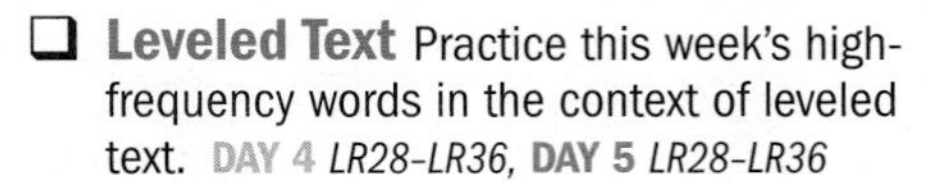

Leveled Readers

- ❑ **Homework** Practice Book 1.2 pp. 36, 37. DAY 2 *94-95*, DAY 3 *96e*

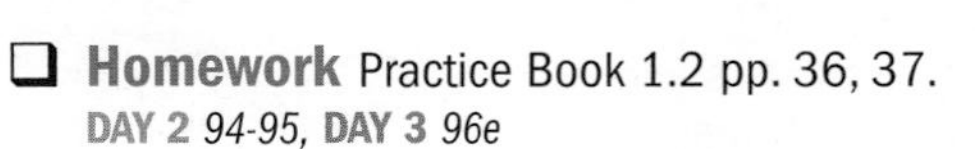

RETEACH/REVIEW

- ❑ **Spiral REVIEW** Review previously taught high-frequency words. DAY 3 *96f*, DAY 4 *114d*

ASSESS

- ❑ **Sentence Reading** Assess children's ability to read this week's high-frequency words. DAY 5 *116e-116f*

VOCABULARY

TEACH

- ❑ **Vocabulary Transparency 16** Use Vocabulary Transparency 16 to introduce the selection words from *Frog and Toad Together*. Children will read these words but will not be tested on them. DAY 3 *96f*
- ❑ **Use Endings to Determine Meaning** Discuss and use words with inflected endings. DAY 3 *113b*

Customize Your Plan *by Strand*

COMPREHENSION

SKILL PLOT A plot is made up of what happens in the beginning, middle, and end of a story.

STRATEGY VISUALIZE Visualize means you make pictures in your mind as you read. Picturing the characters, setting, and events makes it easier to understand a story.

TEACH

- ❑ **Listening Comprehension** Read "Carlee's Garden" and model how to identify *plot*. DAY 1 *93a-93b*
- ❑ **Skill/Strategy Lesson** Review how to identify *plot*. Then introduce this week's strategy, *visualize*. DAY 3 *96g*

PRACTICE/APPLY

- ❑ **Skills and Strategies in Context** Read *Frog and Toad Together*, using the Guiding Comprehension questions to apply *plot* and *visualize*. DAY 3 *96-111a*

Main Selection—Fiction

- ❑ **Think and Share** Use the questions on Student Edition p. 112 to discuss the selection. DAY 3 *112a-113*
- ❑ **Skills and Strategies in Context** Read "Growing Plants," guiding children as they apply skills and strategies. After reading have children make connections across texts. DAY 4 *114-115a*

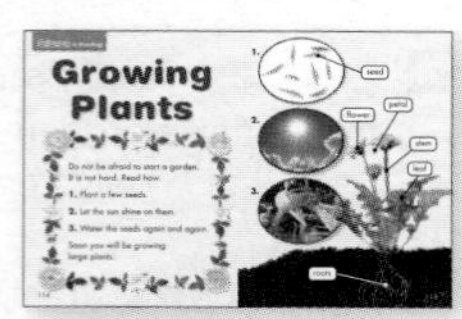

Paired Selection—Nonfiction

- ❑ **Leveled Text** Apply *plot* and *visualize* to read leveled text. DAY 4 *LR28-LR36*, DAY 5 *LR28-LR36*

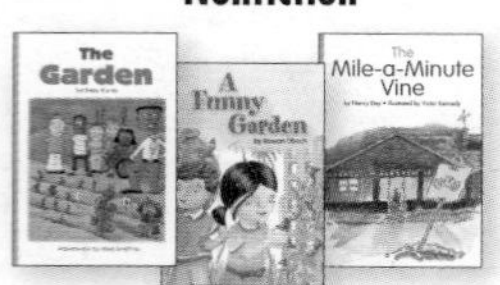

Leveled Readers

- ❑ **Homework** Practice Book 1.2 p. 34. DAY 1 *93a*

ASSESS

- ❑ **Selection Test** Determine children's understanding of the main selection and assess their ability to identify *plot*. DAY 3
- ❑ **Story Reading** Have children read the passage "Clark and Star." Ask what the *plot* of the story is and have them retell the story. DAY 5 *116e, 116g*

RETEACH/REVIEW

- ❑ **Reteach Lesson** If necessary, reteach *plot*. DAY 5 *DI·81*

FLUENCY

SKILL READ WITH EXPRESSION When you read, try to read with expression, reading the part in quotation marks the way the character would say it.

REREAD FOR FLUENCY

- ❑ **Oral Reading** Have children read orally from Decodable Readers 31 and 32, or another text at their independent reading level. Listen to children read and provide corrective feedback regarding their oral reading and their use of the blending strategy. DAY 1 *92q*, DAY 2 *94f*

TEACH

- ❑ **Model** Use passages from *Frog and Toad Together* to model expression. DAY 3 *113a*, DAY 4 *115b*

PRACTICE/APPLY

- ❑ **Choral Reading** Choral read passages from *Frog and Toad Together*. Monitor progress and provide feedback regarding children's reading with expression. DAY 3 *113a*, DAY 4 *115b*
- ❑ **Listening Center** Have children follow along with the AudioText for this week's selections. ANY DAY *92j*
- ❑ **Reading/Library Center** Have children build fluency by rereading Leveled Readers, Decodable Readers, or other text at their independent level. ANY DAY *92j*
- ❑ **Fluency Coach** Have children use Fluency Coach to listen to fluent reading or to practice reading on their own. ANY DAY

ASSESS

- ❑ **Story Reading** Take a one-minute timed sample of children's oral reading. Use the passage "Clark and Star." DAY 5 *116e, 116g*

1 Use assessment data to determine your instructional focus.

2 Preview this week's instruction by strand.

3 Choose instructional activities that meet the needs of your classroom.

WRITING

Trait of the Week

WORD CHOICE Good word choice makes your writing more interesting. Words help readers see what you are saying.

TEACH

- ❑ **Write Together** Engage children in writing activities that develop language, grammar, and writing skills. Include independent writing as an extension of group writing activities.
  - **Shared Writing** DAY 1 *93c*
  - **Interactive Writing** DAY 2 *95a*
  - **Writing Across the Curriculum** DAY 4 *115c*
- ❑ **Trait of the Week** Introduce and model the Trait of the Week, *word choice.* DAY 3 *113c*

PRACTICE/APPLY

- ❑ **Write Now** Examine the model on Student Edition pp. 116-117. Then have children write a poem. DAY 5 *116-117*

  Prompt *Frog and Toad Together* tells about planting seeds to grow flowers in gardens. Think about things that grow—seeds, flowers, or gardens. Now write a poem about one of these things.

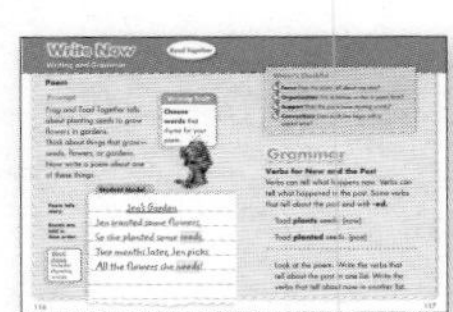

Write Now

- ❑ **Daily Journal Writing** Have children write about concepts and literature in their journals. EVERY DAY *92d-92e*
- ❑ **Writing Center** Have children write about how to grow a flower from a seed. ANY DAY *92k*

ASSESS

- ❑ **Scoring Rubric** Use a rubric to evaluate children's poems. DAY 5 *116-117*

RETEACH/REVIEW

- ❑ **The Grammar and Writing Book** Use pp. 140-145 of The Grammar and Writing Book to extend instruction. ANY DAY

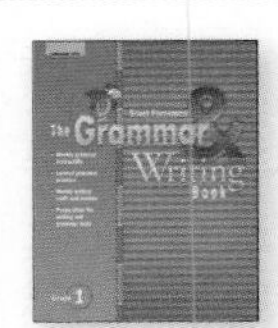

The Grammar and Writing Book

SPEAKING AND LISTENING

TEACH

- ❑ **Retell a Story** Discuss how to retell a story. Then have children retell a familiar story in proper order. DAY 2 *95c*

GRAMMAR

SKILL VERBS FOR NOW AND THE PAST Verbs can tell what happens now. Verbs can tell what happened in the past. Some verbs that tell about the past end with *-ed.*

TEACH

- ❑ **Grammar Transparency 16** Use Grammar Transparency 16 to teach *verbs for now and the past.* DAY 1 *93d*

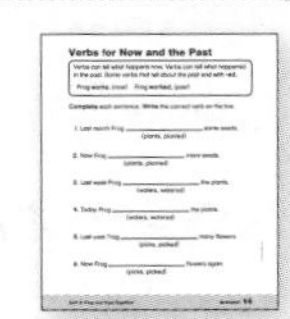

Grammar Transparency 16

PRACTICE/APPLY

- ❑ **Develop the Concept** Review the concept of *verbs for now and the past* and provide guided practice. DAY 2 *95b*
- ❑ **Apply to Writing** Have children use *verbs for now and the past* in writing. DAY 3 *113d*
- ❑ **Define/Practice** Review the definition of *verbs for now and the past.* Then have children classify verbs. DAY 4 *115d*
- ❑ **Write Now** Discuss the grammar lesson on Student Edition p. 117. Have children use *verbs for now and the past* correctly in their own poem about things that grow. DAY 5 *116-117*

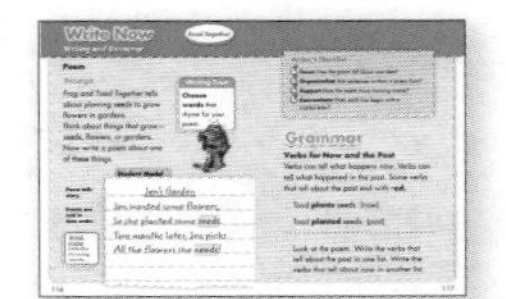

Write Now

- ❑ **Daily Fix-It** Have children find and correct errors in grammar, spelling, and punctuation. DAY 1 *93d,* DAY 2 *95b,* DAY 3 *113d,* DAY 4 *115d,* DAY 5 *116-117*
- ❑ **Homework** Grammar and Writing Practice Book pp. 61-64. DAY 2 *95b,* DAY 3 *113d,* DAY 4 *115d,* DAY 5 *116-117*

RETEACH/REVIEW

- ❑ **The Grammar and Writing Book** Use pp. 140-143 of The Grammar and Writing Book to extend instruction. ANY DAY

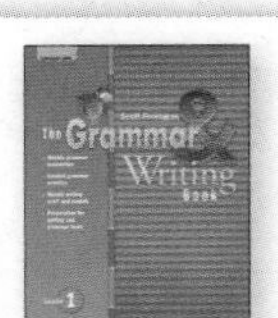

The Grammar and Writing Book

RESEARCH/INQUIRY

TEACH

- ❑ **Diagram** Model interpreting a diagram. Have children identify the purpose of diagrams in other textbooks and explain what the labels show. DAY 5 *117a*
- ❑ **Unit Inquiry Project** Allow time for children to observe, measure, and record their observations. Children can chart the growth of objects they are measuring. ANY DAY *9*

Resources for

Differentiated Instruction

LEVELED READERS

- **Comprehension**
  - **Skill** Plot
  - **Strategy** Visualize
- **Lesson Vocabulary**

  High-Frequency Words

  afraid | again | few | how | read | soon

- **Science Standards**
  - Plant Needs
  - Parts of Plants
  - Life Cycle of a Plant

PearsonSuccessNet.com

Use the Online Database of over 600 books to

- Download and print additional copies of this week's leveled readers
- Listen to the readers being read online
- Search for more titles focused on this week's skills, topic, and content

On-Level

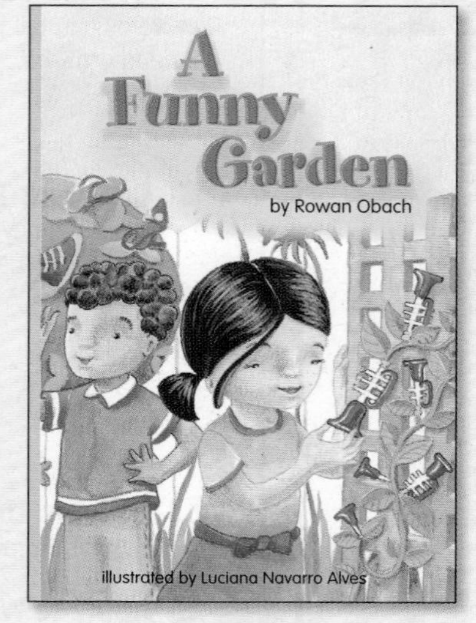

On-Level Reader

Plot

Read the story.
Then draw a picture in each box to show the plot.

One day Miss Jones read a book about plants and gardens to her class.

"Can we plant a silly garden?" asked Tom.

"Yes!" said Miss Jones. "We can!"

Soon the class was busy. They dug holes in the yard and planted a zebra, a trumpet, some bells, and some shoes.

In a few weeks, Miss Jones looked out the window. "Come and see the funny garden!" she said.

1. Beginning — Drawings will vary.
2. Middle
3. End

On-Level Practice TE p. LR32

Vocabulary

Fill in the blank with the word that best fits each sentence.

Words to Know: afraid again few how read soon

1. Read these steps and learn about gardens.
2. First you plant a few seeds.
3. Soon you will have a beautiful garden.
4. You can learn how to grow seeds.
5. If you garden doesn't grow, try again.
6. Don't be afraid to try your plan.

On-Level Practice TE p. LR33

Strategic Intervention

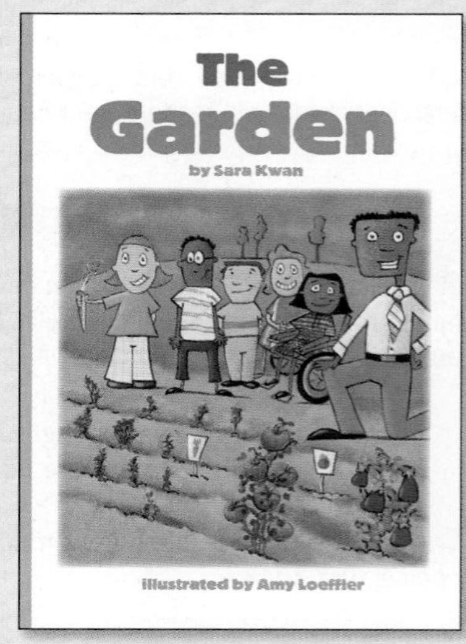

Below-Level Reader

Plot

Think about what you read in *The Garden*.

1. Draw what happened in the beginning of the story. — Drawings will vary.
2. Draw what happened in the middle of the story. — Drawings will vary.
3. Draw what happened at the end of the story. — Drawings will vary.
4. Now use your pictures to talk about the story.

Below-Level Practice TE p. LR29

Vocabulary

Some of the following sentences use the wrong word from the box.
Put an X before any sentence that doesn't make sense.
Then, cross out the wrong word.
Write the right word at the end of the sentence.

Words to Know: afraid again few how read soon

X 1. I am ~~soon~~ the plants won't grow. afraid
no X 2. I like to read books about plants.
no X 3. How can we grow food for others?
X 4. There are very ~~again~~ seeds left. few
no X 5. Soon the plants will grow.
X 6. They had to use water ~~afraid~~. again

Below-Level Practice TE p. LR30

Advanced

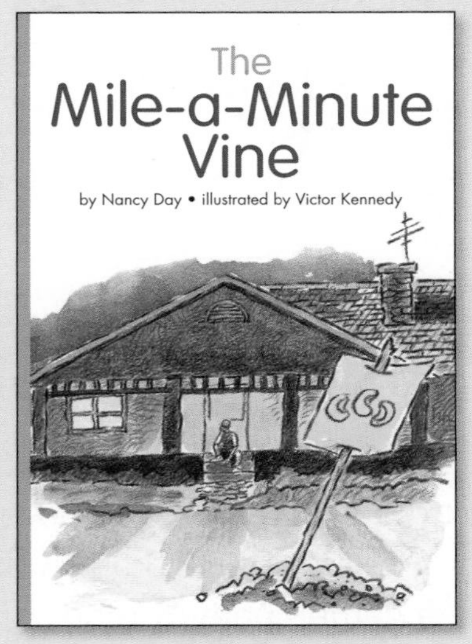

Advanced Reader

Plot

Put an X by the events that did not happen in *The Mile-a-Minute Vine*.

_____ 1. Jake's peanut crop dried up.

_____ 2. Jake bought beans from an old man.

_____ 3. Jake planted the beans.

__X__ 4. Cows would not eat the vine.

__X__ 5. Everybody saw Jake and the vine on television.

_____ 6. Jake used the vine to make things like baskets, jelly, and tea.

_____ 7. In the end, Jake and his mother were able to make money by selling things made from the vine.

__X__ 8. The vine dried up and never came back to life.

Advanced Practice TE p. LR35

Vocabulary

Use the correct word from the box to complete each sentence below.

Words to Know
gardener nature sprout

1. The gardener likes to grow roses and other flowers.
2. Soon a sprout pushed up through the ground.
3. Our class likes to take long nature walks to learn more about trees.

4-5. Write your own sentence using *gardener* and *sprout*.

Possible response:
The gardener carefully
watered the sprout.

Advanced Practice TE p. LR36

ELL

ELL Reader

ELL Poster 16

Teacher's Edition Notes

ELL notes throughout this lesson support instruction and reference additional resources at point of use.

Teaching Guide pp. 106–112, 242–243

- Multilingual summaries of the main selection
- Comprehension lesson
- Vocabulary strategies and word cards
- ELL Reader 1.3.4 lesson

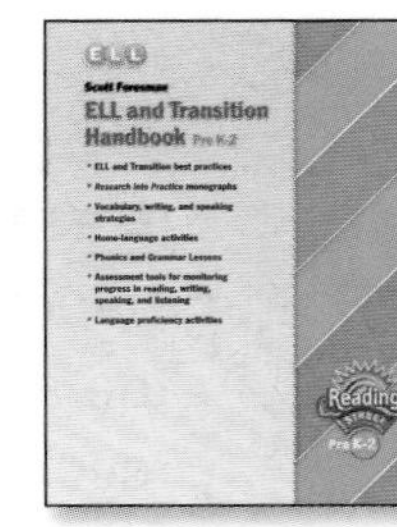

ELL and Transition Handbook

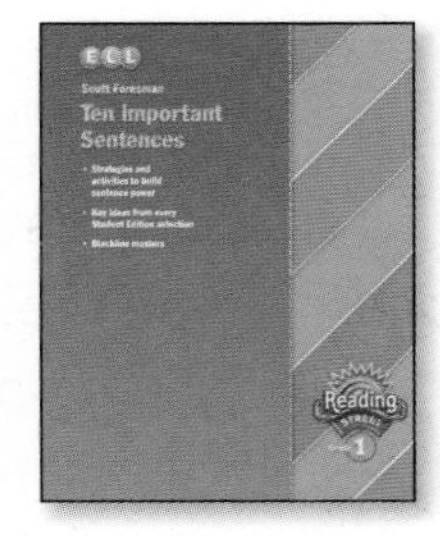

Ten Important Sentences

- Key ideas from every selection in the Student Edition
- Activities to build sentence power

More Reading

Readers' Theater Anthology

- Fluency practice
- Five scripts to build fluency
- Poetry for oral interpretation

Leveled Trade Books

Below-Level

On-Level

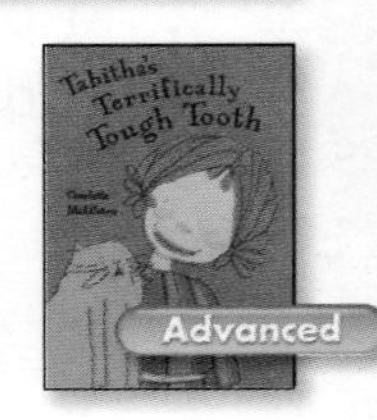

Advanced

- Extend reading tied to the unit concept
- Lessons in Trade Book Library Teaching Guide

Big Book of Poems

- Fluency practice
- Poetry for Choral Reading

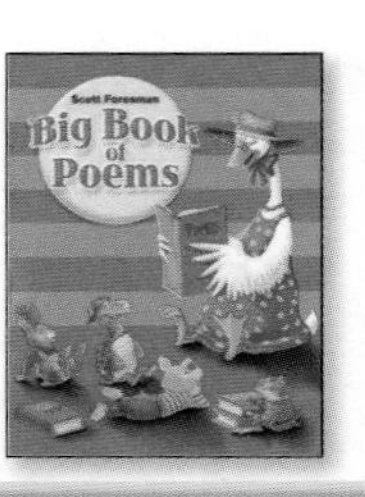

School + Home

Homework

- Family Times Newsletter
- ELL Multilingual Selection Summaries

Take-Home Books

- Decodable Readers
- Leveled Readers

Literacy Centers

Listening

Let's Read Along

MATERIALS
CD player, headphones, print copies of recorded pieces

SINGLES

LISTEN TO LITERATURE As children listen to the following recordings, have them follow along or read along in the print version.

AudioText
Frog and Toad Together
"Growing Plants"

Sing with Me/Background Building Audio
"Sprout! It's a Garden"

Phonics Songs and Rhymes Audio
"Grandpa's Garden"

Reading/Library

Read It Again!

MATERIALS
collection of books for self-selected reading, reading logs

SINGLES
PAIRS
GROUPS

REREAD BOOKS Have children select previously read books from the appropriate book box and record titles of books they read in their logs. Use these previously read books:

- Decodable Readers
- Leveled Readers
- ELL Readers
- Stories written by classmates
- Books from the library

TEN IMPORTANT SENTENCES Have children read the Ten Important Sentences for *Frog and Toad Together* and locate the sentences in the Student Edition.

BOOK CLUB Use p. 113 of the Student Edition to set up an "Illustrator Study" of Arnold Lobel. Encourage a group to read the other Lobel books listed and then discuss the pictures.

Word Work

Phonics Garden Path

MATERIALS
16 index cards, 2 erasers or small place markers

SINGLES
PAIRS
GROUPS

INFLECTED ENDINGS *-ed, -ing* Have pairs or groups of children "walk" along a garden path by reading words with inflected *-ed* and *-ing*.

1. **Write a word with an *-ed* or *-ing* ending on 12 index cards. Write words without inflected endings on 4 cards. Place the cards on a tabletop to form a winding path.**
2. **Children move their marker from card to card reading the words. When a child reaches a word without an ending, play passes to the other child.**
3. **Play continues until both children reach the end of the path.**

r*-CONTROLLED *ar Make a set of *r*-controlled *ar* cards. Have children play the game.

This interactive CD provides additional practice.

hopping grabbed jump stepped running

Scott Foresman Reading Street Centers Survival Kit

Use the *Frog and Toad Together* materials from the Reading Street Centers Survival Kit to organize this week's centers.

Writing

Grow a Garden

MATERIALS
paper, pencils, crayons

SINGLES

WRITE DIRECTIONS Recall the things that Toad did to make his seeds grow.

1. **Ask children to think about what seeds need to grow.**
2. **Have them write about how to grow a flower. Suggest that they number the steps they would follow.**
3. **Have children draw a picture or pictures to accompany the steps.**

LEVELED WRITING Encourage children to write at their own ability level. Some may write only one or two steps. Others will be able to write, order, and number a few steps correctly. Your best writers will write, order, and number several detailed steps.

Science

Observe Plants

MATERIALS
paper, crayons or markers, houseplants, rulers, magnifying glasses

SINGLES
GROUPS

RECORD OBSERVATIONS Place several houseplants in the Science Center. Discuss the parts of a plant—leaves, flowers, and stem.

1. **Ask children to draw one of the plants and label its parts.**
2. **Have them write about what they observe, such as the plant's color and size.**
3. **Children can share and discuss their observations.**

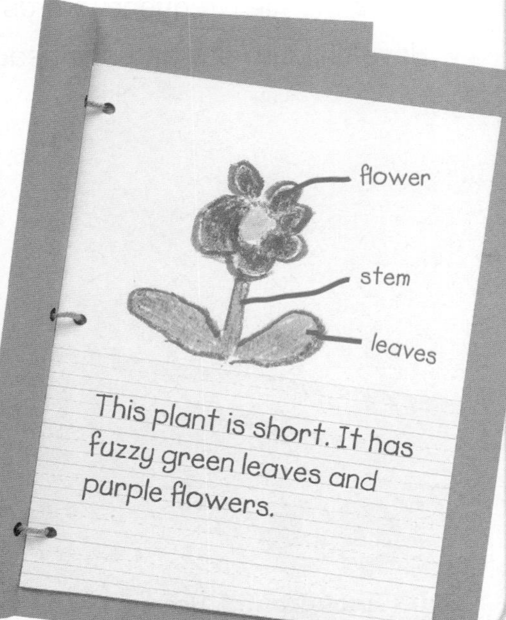

Technology

Format Fun

MATERIALS
computer

SINGLES

TYPE A LIST Individuals type a list and format it in different ways.

1. **Ask children to turn on the computer and open a word processing program.**
2. **If children have completed a list of steps for the Writing Center, they may type their steps. Otherwise, they should write a short description of a flower.**
3. **Children should practice formatting the text in the following manners: align center, align right, boldface, italic, and underline.**

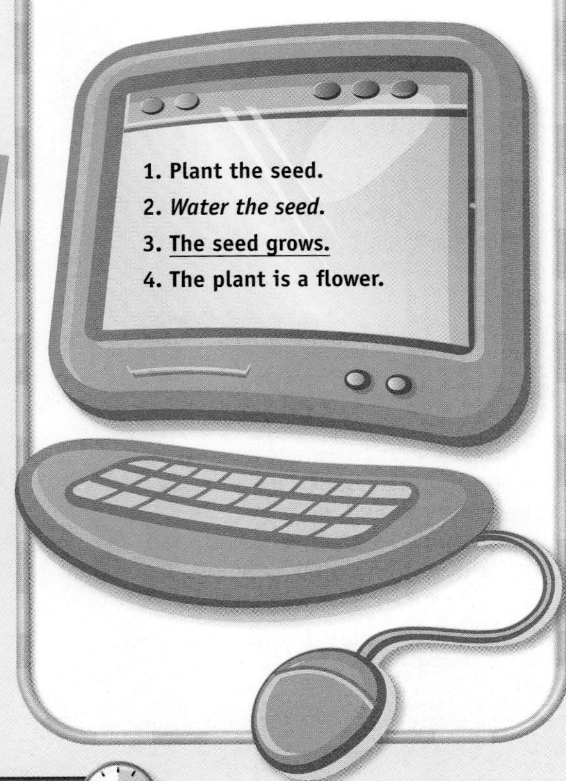

ALL CENTERS

Day 1
AT A GLANCE

Oral Vocabulary
"Sprout! It's a Garden" 16

Phonemic Awareness
Blend and Segment Syllables

Phonics and Spelling
Inflected Endings *-ed, -ing*
Spelling Pretest: Adding *-ed*

Read Apply Phonics 

 < Differentiated Instruction

Build Background
Let's Talk About Changes in Nature

Listening Comprehension
Skill Plot

Shared Writing
Poem

Grammar
Verbs for Now and the Past

Materials

- *Sing with Me Big Book*
- Letter Tiles
- Decodable Reader 31
- Student Edition 92–93
- Graphic Organizer Flip Chart 31

Take It to the NET™ ONLINE

Professional Development
To learn more about repeated reading, go to PearsonSuccessNet.com and read the article "Repeated Reading" by S. L. Dowhower.

Morning Warm-Up!

In winter, flowers go away.
In spring, flowers start to grow in gardens.
Do we have a garden near our school?
What changes happen in a garden?

QUESTION OF THE WEEK Tell children they will talk, sing, read, and write about Changes in Nature. Write the message and track the print as you read it. Discuss the questions.

CONNECT CONCEPTS Ask questions to connect to other selections.

- How did trees and plants change in *An Egg Is an Egg?*
- When Jan moved to her new house in *Jan's New Home,* how did the plants around her change?

REVIEW HIGH-FREQUENCY WORDS

- Circle the high-frequency words *away, our,* and *school* in the message.
- Have children say and spell each word as they write it in the air.

Build Background Use the Day 1 instruction on ELL Poster 16 to assess knowledge and develop concepts.

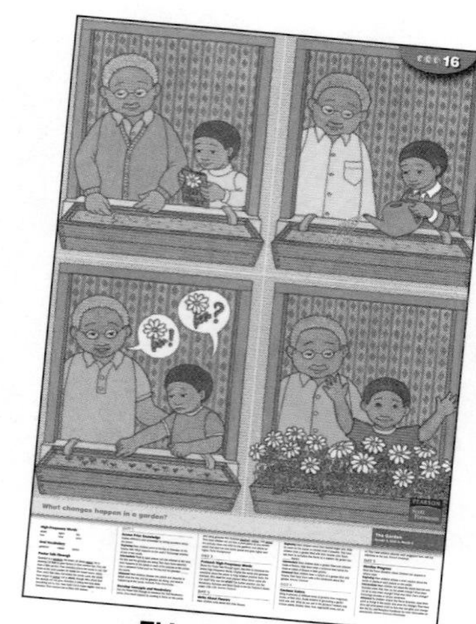
ELL Poster 16

Oral Vocabulary

SHARE LITERATURE Display p. 16 of the *Sing With Me Big Book.* Tell children that they will sing a song about growing a garden. Read the title. Ask children to listen for the Amazing Words **gardener, nature,** and **sprout** as you sing. Then sing the song again and ask children to sing with you. Have children demonstrate their understanding of *gardener, nature,* and *sprout* as they tell how the plants in this song are like plants they know.

Sing with Me/
Background Building Audio

Sing with Me Big Book

OBJECTIVES

- Build oral vocabulary.
- Blend and segment syllables.

to build oral vocabulary

gardener
nature
sprout
dim
shade
blossom
destroy
humongous

MONITOR PROGRESS

If... children lack oral vocabulary experiences about the concept of Changes in Nature,

then... use the Oral Vocabulary Routine below to teach *gardener.*

Oral Vocabulary ROUTINE

1. **Introduce the Word** Relate the word *gardener* to the song. Supply a child-friendly definition. Have children say the word. Example: A *gardener* is someone who grows plants.
2. **Demonstrate** Provide an example to show meaning. *Gardeners* decide what they will plant long before spring.
3. **Apply** Have children demonstrate their understanding. Tell me some things a good *gardener* knows.
4. **Display the Word/Letter-Sounds** Write the word on a card. Display it. Children can identify *g*/g/ and *n*/n/. See p. DI·6 to teach *nature* and *sprout.*

Phonemic Awareness

BLEND AND SEGMENT SYLLABLES

- We just sang about a gardener who planted seeds. Listen to the syllables in *planted.*
- Say *plant, ed* and then blend the syllables to say the word, *planted.*
- Have children segment and blend the syllables with you. *(plant, ed, planted)*

Continue the activity with these examples.

wagging **rested** **grinning** **dusted** **happening**

ELL

Build Oral Vocabulary Work with children to create a hand-play for "Sprout! It's a Garden," including motions for "sunshine golden," "rain falls down," and "Sprout!"

OBJECTIVES

- Use structural cues to decode words with inflected endings *-ed, -ing* (spelling change: double final consonant).
- Blend, read, and sort words with the inflected endings *-ed, -ing.*

Skills Trace

Inflected Endings, *-ed, -ing*

Introduce/Teach	**TE: 1.1 76c–d; 1.3 92n–o, 96c–d**
Practice	TE: 1.1 76f; PB: 1.1 35; 1.2 33; DR·31
Reteach/Review	TE: 1.1 110c–d; 1.3 116c, 140c–d; DI·80; PB: 1.1 49; 1.2 48
Assess/Test	TE: 1.3 116e–g; Benchmark Test, Units 1, 3

Generalization

For many words that end in consonant-vowel-consonant, the last consonant is doubled before an ending is added.

Strategic Intervention

Use **Monitor Progress,** p. 92o during Group Time after children have had more practice with inflected endings *-ed, -ing.*

Advanced

Use **Monitor Progress,** p. 92o as a preassessment to determine whether or not this group of children would benefit from this inflected ending *-ed, -ing* instruction.

Support Phonics Children of various language backgrounds may not hear the difference between *-ing* and *-in,* so they may say *hoppin* and *diggin* instead of *hopping* and *digging.* Help children practice saying words that end with *-ing: rip/ripping; pet/petting; swim/swimming.*

See the Phonics Transition Lessons in the ELL and Transition Handbook.

Inflected Endings

TEACH/MODEL

Blending Strategy

ROUTINE

1. **Connect** Write *melted* and *melting.* What do you know about reading these words? (The words both have a base word and an ending. Read the base word; read the ending; then blend the two parts.) Today we will learn about words whose spellings change before an ending is added.

2. **Model** Write *pet, petted, petting.* The last consonant in *pet, t,* was doubled before the endings were added. This happens in short vowel words that end in just one consonant. This is how I blend these words. Cover the added consonant and ending to read the base word; uncover and read the ending. Blend the two parts. Let's blend these words together: *pet, ted, petted; pet, ting, petting.*

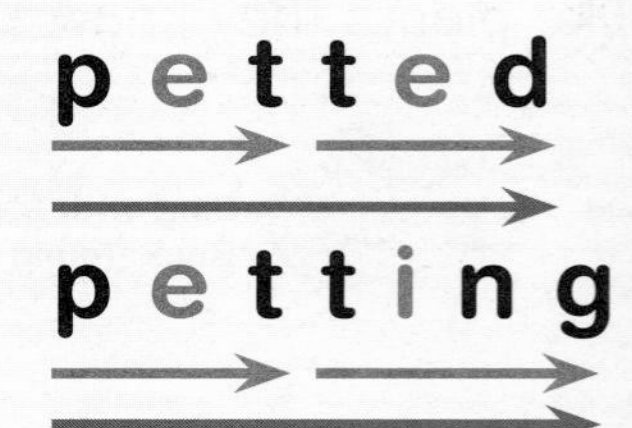

3. **Group Practice** First see if the last consonant in the base word was doubled. Read the base word, read the ending, and then blend the two parts. Continue with *batting, ripped, hopping, stepped, shutting.*

4. **Review** What do you know about reading words with endings? See if the base word has a doubled consonant. Read the base word, read the ending, and then blend the parts.

BLEND WORDS

INDIVIDUALS BLEND WORDS Call on individual children to blend the words *tagged, digging, begging, slipped, chopped, swimming, stopping.* Have them tell what they know about each word before reading it. (The last consonant was doubled before the ending was added.) For feedback, refer to step four of the Blending Strategy Routine.

SORT WORDS

INDIVIDUALS SORT WORDS WITH INFLECTED ENDINGS *-ed, -ing* Write *planned* and *letting.* Call on children to read the words. Point out that *planned* has the ending *-ed* and *letting* has the ending *-ing.* Write the words below. Call on children to read the words, identify the ending, and frame the base word. If children have difficulty reading a base word, have them cover the ending *-ed* or *-ing* and blend the base word. Then have children work independently to list the words in which the last consonant was doubled before an ending was added.

Ending -ed	Ending -ing
planned	letting
rested	jumping
tripped	landing
thanked	hugging

Monitor Progress

Check Word Reading Inflected Endings *-ed, -ing*

Write the following words and have individuals read them.

tapping	**sipped**	**jogging**	**running**	**pinned**
flipped	**ringing**	**clapping**	**hummed**	**asked**
fixes	**getting**	**yelled**	**wishes**	**zipped**

If... children cannot blend words with endings *-ed, -ing* at this point,

then... continue to monitor their progress using other instructional opportunities during the week so that they can be successful with the Day 5 Assessment. See the Skills Trace on p. 92n.

▶ **Day 1 Check Word Reading** · **Day 2** Check Word Reading · **Day 3** Check High-Frequency Words/Retelling · **Day 4** Check Fluency · **Day 5** Assess Progress

Vocabulary TiP

You may wish to explain the meanings of these words.

jogging running at a slow, steady pace

sipped drank slowly in small amounts

Dan is mopping up the mess.
The mess is mopped up.

Add -ed and -ing to each word.
Write the new words on the line.

	Add -ed	Add -ing
1. nap	napped	napping
2. pat	patted	patting
3. nod	nodded	nodding
4. jog	jogged	jogging
5. wag	wagged	wagging
6. stop	stopped	stopping
7. pet	petted	petting
8. drop	dropped	dropping
9. clap	clapped	clapping
10. plan	planned	planning

School + Home **Home Activity** Your child practiced writing words that end in -ed and -ing. Together with your child make up a story using the words above.

▲ **Practice Book 1.2** p. 33, Inflected Endings *-ed, -ing*

Spiral REVIEW

- Row 2 contrasts inflected endings *-ed, -ing* with and without spelling changes.
- Row 3 reviews inflected endings *-ed, -ing* with or without spelling changes and inflected ending *-es.*

Word Reading
SUCCESS PREDICTOR

OBJECTIVES

- Segment sounds to spell words.
- Spell words with inflected ending *-ed*.

Spelling Words

Adding *-ed*

1.	**ask**	6.	**helped**
2.	**asked***	7.	**jog**
3.	**plan**	8.	**jogged**
4.	**planned**	9.	**call**
5.	**help***	10.	**called**

High-Frequency Words

11.	**again***	12.	**soon***

* Words from the Selection

Adding *-ed*
Look at the word. Say it. Listen for the ending.

	Write the word.	Check it.
1. ask	ask	ask
2. asked	asked	asked
3. plan	plan	plan
4. planned	planned	planned
5. help	help	help
6. helped	helped	helped
7. jog	jog	jog
8. jogged	jogged	jogged
9. call	call	call
10. called	called	called

High-Frequency Words

11. again again 12. soon soon

School + Home **Home Activity** Your child is learning to spell words that end with -ed. To practice at home, have your child look at the word, say it, spell it, and then write the word. Help your child see how the word changes when adding -ed.

▲ **Spelling Practice Book** p. 61

Support Spelling Before giving the spelling pretest, clarify the meaning of each spelling word with examples, such as acting out *jog* and using a cell phone to illustrate one meaning of *call.*

Spelling

PRETEST Inflected Ending *-ed*

MODEL WRITING FOR SOUNDS The spelling words are words with and without ending *-ed*. In some base words, the final consonant is doubled before the ending *-ed* is added. Before administering the spelling pretest, model how to segment ending *-ed* words to spell them.

- What sounds do you hear in *rub?* (/r/ /u/ /b/)
- What is the letter for /r/? Write *r.* Continue with the *u*/u/ and *b*/b/.
- What letter do we add to the end of the *rub* before adding the ending *-ed?* *(b)* Add *b.* Add *-ed.*
- In *rub,* there is a consonant-vowel-consonant at the end, so the last consonant, *b,* is doubled before the ending *-ed* is added.
- Repeat with *shop* and *shopped.*

PRETEST Dictate the spelling words. Segment the words for children if necessary. Have children check their pretests and correct misspelled words.

HOMEWORK Spelling Practice Book, p. 61

Bean Sprouts

A bean is a kind of seed. Gardeners plant beans to grow more bean plants to eat. These beans sprout, or begin to grow, in the dirt. This is how they usually grow in nature, but some beans will also sprout in water. You can make your own bean sprouts to eat

Frog and Toad Together

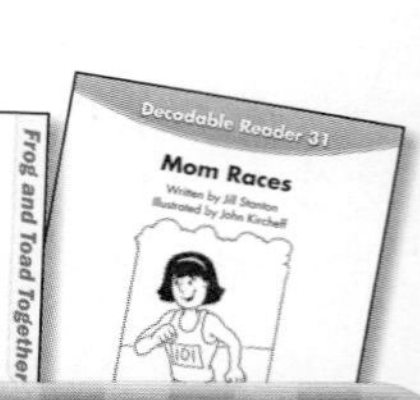

Group Time

DAY 1

On-Level	Strategic Intervention	Advanced
Read Decodable Reader 31. • Use p. 92q.	**Read** Decodable Reader 31. • Use the **Routine** on p. DI·46.	**Read** Advanced Selection 16. • Use the **Routine** on p. DI·47.

Place English language learners in the groups that correspond to their reading abilities in English.

Independent Activities

Fluency Reading Pair children to reread Leveled Readers or the ELL Reader from the previous week or other text at children's independent level.

Journal Writing List plants you would grow in your garden. Share writing.

Independent Reading See p. 92j for Reading/Library activities and suggestions.

Literacy Centers To practice inflected endings *-ed, -ing,* you may use Word Work, p. 92j.

Practice Book 1.2 Inflected endings *-ed, -ing,* p. 33.

Break into small groups after Spelling and before Build Background.

Apply Phonics

PRACTICE Inflected Endings *-ed, -ing*

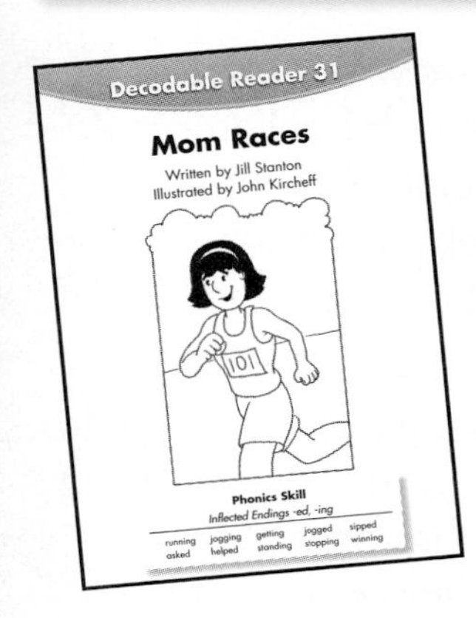

HIGH-FREQUENCY WORDS Review *comes, her, said, to,* and *water* on the Word Wall. Word Wall

READ DECODABLE READER 31

- Pages 50–52 Read aloud quietly with the group.
- Page 53 Have the group read aloud without you.
- Pages 54–56 Select individuals to read aloud.

CHECK COMPREHENSION AND DECODING Have children retell the story to include characters, setting, and plot. Then have children locate and read words with *-ed* ending in the story. List the words they mention. *(jogged, sipped, asked, helped)* Have children identify the words on the list in which the last consonant was doubled before *-ed* ending was added. Repeat the routine for words with *-ing* ending. *(running, jogging, getting, stopping, winning, standing)*

HOMEWORK Take-Home Decodable Reader 31

REREAD FOR FLUENCY

Oral Rereading

ROUTINE

1. **Read** Have children read the entire book orally.
2. **Reread** For optimal fluency, have children reread three or four times.
3. **Provide Feedback** Listen as children read and provide feedback regarding their oral reading and their use of the blending strategy.

OBJECTIVES

- Apply knowledge of letter-sounds and word parts to decode unknown words when reading.
- Use context with letter-sounds and word parts to confirm the identification of unknown words.
- Practice fluency with oral rereading.

Monitor Progress

Decoding

If...	then...
children have difficulty decoding a word,	prompt them to blend the word. • What is the new word? • Is the new word a word you know? • Does it make sense in the story?

Access Content

Beginning As you read *Mom Races* together, have children pantomime words with *-ed* and *-ing* endings, such as *running, jogged, sipped,* and *stopping.*

Intermediate Reread p. 55 of *Mom Races,* and have children echo, "Is she winning?" Have children turn to p. 56. Mom didn't win the race. How does Mom feel now? Show me.

Advanced Point out that action words with *-ed* mean that something already happened. Have children reread p. 51 of *Mom Races.* Have them identify and read the words with *-ed* endings. When did Mom jog? When did Mom sip water? (She jogged last week. She sipped water last week.)

OBJECTIVES

- Build background and oral vocabulary.
- Listen quietly as others speak.

Strategic Intervention

Have children list three things they can do to help flowers grow.

Advanced

Have children draw three pictures of a flower as it grows. Ask them to write a sentence about each picture that tells how it is different from the one before.

Activate Prior Knowledge
Invite children to tell about what they see in the pictures in their home language and in English.

Build Background

LET'S TALK ABOUT Changes in Nature

DEVELOP ORAL LANGUAGE Read the title and have children view the photographs. Ask them to tell you what they see. Allow ample time for children to respond and remind them to listen quietly as others speak. If children do not listen quietly, model good speaking and listening behavior. Then use open-ended prompts to model to encourage conversation.
For example:

Tell me about what you see here. Yes, that's right, some people are taking care of plants. These people are all inside a greenhouse. What is the woman doing that will help the flowers grow? What do you think the man in the big photograph is doing? Tell me about the colors you see. What changes are taking place here?

BUILD ORAL VOCABULARY As you continue the discussion, encourage children to use today's Amazing Words, *gardener, nature,* and *sprout.*

- How is the gardener in the top picture taking care of plants?
- Do you think this woman likes nature?
- Look at the reddish plant the man is holding. Using the word *sprout,* tell me about how this plant grew from a seed.

DEVELOP CONCEPTS

CONCEPT CHART Remind children of the question of the week.

- What changes happen in a garden?

Display Graphic Organizer 31 or draw three boxes labeled Step 1, Step 2, and Step 3. Discuss what happens when seeds are planted. Have children refer to the pictures to tell about plants as they grow.

- How do seeds look when you first plant them? (Seeds are small and usually hard.)
- What happens next? (A baby plant starts to grow. It gets leaves.)
- What happens last? (The plant gets big and the flower blooms.)

CONNECT TO READING Point out the illustration on the bottom corner of Student Edition p. 93. Ask children what the frog is doing. (kneeling down and looking at the ground) Explain that this week children will read a story about this frog and his friend, a toad. Tell children that they will learn what changes happen in a garden.

Oral Vocabulary

Let's Talk About Changes in Nature

92

93

Seed to Plant

Step 1
Plant little seeds and cover them with soil.

Step 2
A baby plant starts to grow. It gets leaves.

Step 3
Flowers bloom.

▲ **Graphic Organizer Flip Chart 31**

Tech Files ONLINE

For a Web site that explores the changes that happen in a garden, do an Internet search using the keywords *plants* or *gardening*.

ELL

Access Content To prepare children for reading *Frog and Toad Together,* send home the story summary in English and/or the home language. See the ELL Teaching Guide, pp. 110–112.

OBJECTIVE

- Identify the plot of a story.

Skills Trace

Plot

Introduce/Teach	**TE: 1.3 37a–b, 40g; 93a–b, 96g; 1.4 127a–b, 130g; 1.5 11a–b, 14g, 16–17**
Practice	PB: 1.2 82–83, 34, 104, 124
Reteach/Review	TE: 1.3 82–83, DI·78, DI·81; 1.4 170–171, DI·83; 1.5 98–99, 190–191, DI·77
Test	TE: 1.3 66e–66g; 1.4 154e–154g; 1.5 42e–42g; Selection Test: 1.3 30–31, 38–40; 1.4 66–68; 1.5 74–76 Benchmark Test, Units 3,5

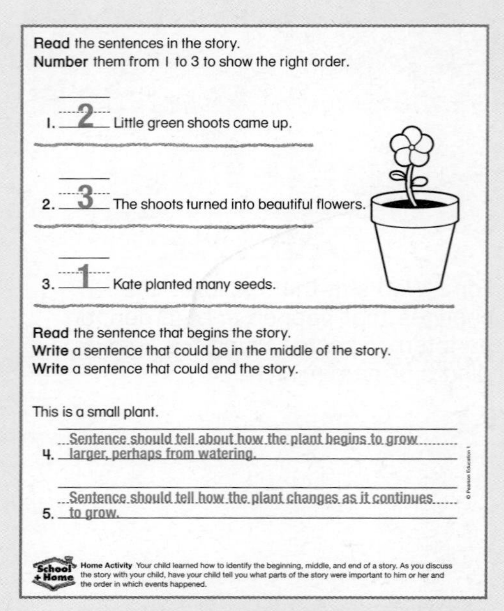
Read the sentences in the story.
Number them from 1 to 3 to show the right order.

1. 2 Little green shoots came up.
2. 3 The shoots turned into beautiful flowers.
3. 1 Kate planted many seeds.

Read the sentence that begins the story.
Write a sentence that could be in the middle of the story.
Write a sentence that could end the story.

This is a small plant.

4. Sentence should tell about how the plant begins to grow larger, perhaps from watering.
5. Sentence should tell how the plant changes as it continues to grow.

Home Activity Your child learned how to identify the beginning, middle, and end of a story. As you discuss the story with your child, have your child tell you what parts of the story were important to him or her and the order in which events happened.

▲ **Practice Book 1.2** p. 34, Plot

Access Content For a Picture It! lesson on plot, see the ELL Teaching Guide, pp. 107–108.

Listening Comprehension

TEACH/MODEL Plot

DEFINE PLOT

- A story's plot is what happens in the beginning, middle, and end of the story.
- Good readers pay attention to what happens and the order in which it happens.

READ ALOUD Read "Carlee's Garden" and model how to identify plot.

MODEL When I read, I think about what happens in the beginning, middle and end of the story. This story begins with Carlee and her dad planting a garden. It's hard work, but they keep at it. Next the plants grow and rabbits come and eat some of them. In the end, Carlee and her dad figure out how to keep their plants safe from the rabbits.

PRACTICE

CLUES TO PLOT Ask children to discuss the problem Carlee and her dad have. What problem do Carlee and her dad have? (Rabbits are eating the plants in their garden.) How do they solve this problem? (They build a fence that keeps the rabbits out of the garden.)

IDENTIFY PLOT Have children recall the story *Jan's New Home*.

- What happens in the beginning of the story? (Jan doesn't want to move. She wants everything to stay the same.)
- What happens in the middle of the story? (Jan's family moves to the city. She has fun on the trip there.)
- How does the story end? (Even though Jan is in a new place, her bed is the same.)

CONNECT TO READING Tell children that thinking about what happens in the beginning, middle, and end of a story helps them better understand what they read.

Carlee's Garden

"This garden is hard work," Carlee told her dad. They had been digging and planting all morning, and Carlee was hot and tired.

"It will be worth it," her father said. "If we are good gardeners, then we will grow many plants to eat!"

"All I see is dirt and seeds," Carlee grumbled. But she kept working, and soon the garden had been planted.

For the next few weeks, Carlee and her dad watered the garden every day. It was in a wonderful, sunny location, and soon sprouts began popping up all over. Carlee felt very hungry thinking about the tasty meal they would have once the plants were ready to be picked.

Then one morning Carlee went out to check on the garden. She was surprised to see nibble marks on lettuce, peas, and beets.

"Dad!" she called. "Something has been nibbling on my plants!"

"Uh-oh," Carlee's dad said. "We must have rabbits living nearby. They love to sneak into gardens and eat plants."

"What will we do?" Carlee asked. "If the rabbits eat all our plants, there won't be any left for us!"

"Don't worry," Carlee's dad answered. "We'll put up a fence."

Carlee and her dad went to the store and bought some chicken wire and wooden posts. Then Carlee's dad built a fence around their garden, burying the bottom part of the chicken wire under the ground so the rabbits couldn't dig their way in.

"I hope this works," Carlee said as they went inside for the night.

The next morning Carlee ran outside to check on their garden. Nothing new had been eaten.

"You were right, Dad," Carlee said. "The fence kept the rabbits out and our plants safe! I hope the rabbits can find other food, though."

"They can find food in nature," her dad told her. "And we'll find food right here in our garden. Come on! It's time to pick our dinner!"

Shared Writing

WRITE Poem

OBJECTIVE

- Write a poem.

DAILY FIX-IT

1. Dan helpped me plant my seeds
Dan helped me plant my seeds.

2. They will be litle plants son.
They will be little plants soon.

This week's practice sentences appear on Daily Fix-It Transparency 16.

GENERATE IDEAS Ask children to share their knowledge about what seeds need to grow into plants and how they change as they grow. Write children's ideas on the board.

WRITE A POEM Explain that the class will write a poem about the things that seeds need. Remind children that a poem may or may not rhyme.

COMPREHENSION SKILL Have children think about plot—the beginning, middle, and end—for their poem about what seeds need.

- Display Writing Transparency 16 and read the title.
- Ask children to think about the first thing a seed needs (to be put in soil), as well as what happens next and what happens last.
- Read the prompts.
- As children brainstorm what seeds need, record their responses.

HANDWRITING While writing, model the letter forms as shown on pp. TR12–15.

READ THE POEM Have children read the completed poem aloud as you track the print.

Poem About Seeds

What Seeds Need

Possible answers:

Seeds need water.

Seeds need sun.

Seeds need time

to grow into plants.

Here they come!

Unit 3 Frog and Toad Together Writing Model 16

▲ Writing Transparency 16

Strategic Intervention

Children who are not able to write independently may copy one or more of the sentences about what seeds need to grow and add an illustration.

Advanced

Have children write a poem about a plant's life with information about the beginning, middle, and end—for example, a seed is planted, a seedling sprouts, the plant grows big and strong.

Support Writing Before writing about what seeds need, have children work in pairs to tell each other what they are planning to write about.

INDEPENDENT WRITING

WRITE POEM Have children write their own poem of what seeds need. Encourage them to use words from the Word Wall and the Amazing Words board. Let children illustrate their writing. You may display children's work in the classroom.

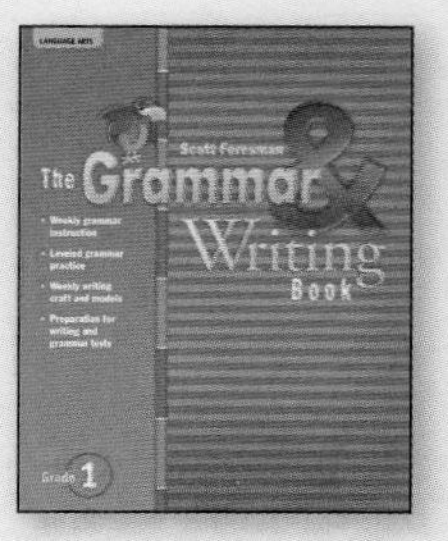

▲ **The Grammar and Writing Book**
For more instruction and practice, use pp. 140–145.

Grammar

TEACH/MODEL Verbs for Now and the Past

IDENTIFY VERBS FOR NOW AND THE PAST Display Grammar Transparency 16. Read the definition aloud. Then model with item 1.

- *Last month* is a time in the past.
- Some verbs that tell about the past end with *-ed.*

Continue modeling with items 2–6.

PRACTICE

SUGGEST VERBS Have children name other verbs for now and the past. Write the verbs.

- Name an action that a person or animal we have read about might do now.
- Use that same action word to name what the person or animal might have done in the past.

ADDITIONAL PRACTICE For additional practice, use pp. 140–145 in the Grammar and Writing Book.

OBJECTIVE

- Identify verbs for now and the past.

Verbs for Now and the Past

Verbs can tell what happens now. Verbs can tell what happened in the past. Some verbs that tell about the past end with **-ed.**

Frog **works.** (now) Frog **worked.** (past)

Complete each sentence. **Write** the correct verb on the line.

1. Last month Frog planted some seeds. (plants, planted)
2. Now Frog plants more seeds. (plants, planted)
3. Last week Frog watered the plants. (waters, watered)
4. Today Frog waters the plants. (waters, watered)
5. Last year Frog picked many flowers. (picks, picked)
6. Now Frog picks flowers again. (picks, picked)

Unit 3 Frog and Toad Together Grammar 16

▲ Grammar Transparency 16

Wrap Up Your Day!

ENDINGS *-ed* Write *work* and ask children what it would be if it was used to describe something in the past. (worked) Have children name other verbs that end in *-ed.*

SPELLING ADDING *-ed* Write a CVCC word such as *work* and remind children that the spelling of *work* does not change when *-ed* is added. Write a CVC word such as *plan* and remind children that the consonant is doubled before adding *-ed.* List *help, call,* and *jog.* Have children add *-ed* to each word and use it in a sentence.

PLOT To help children recognize the importance of plot, ask: Would the story "Carlee's Garden" make sense if either the beginning, middle, or ending was missing? Why not?

LET'S TALK ABOUT IT Display the Seed to Plant chart and use it to discuss the changes in Carlee's garden. What did Carlee do to grow the garden? (She dug and planted. Then she watered the garden. Soon sprouts grew.)

HOMEWORK Send home this week's Family Times newsletter.

PREVIEW Day 2

Tell children that tomorrow the class will read about changing seasons.

Day 2

AT A GLANCE

Share Literature
What Makes the Seasons?

Phonemic Awareness
Substitute Phonemes

Phonics and Spelling
r-controlled *ar*
Spelling: Adding *-ed*

Read **Apply Phonics** Word Wall

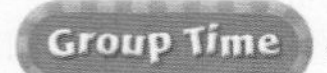
< Differentiated Instruction

High-Frequency Words
afraid again few
how read soon

Interactive Writing
List

Grammar
Verbs for Now and the Past

Speaking and Listening
Retell a Story

Materials

- *Sing with Me Big Book*
- Big Book *What Makes the Seasons?*
- Sound-Spelling Card 3
- Letter Tiles
- Decodable Reader 32
- Student Edition 94–95
- Tested Word Cards

Morning Warm-Up!

We will read about the four seasons.
Many things change with each season.
Why do you think the seasons change?

QUESTION OF THE DAY Encourage children to sing "Sprout! It's a Garden" from the *Sing with Me Big Book* as you gather. Write and read the message and discuss the question.

REVIEW VOWEL SOUNDS OF *y*

- Reread the message.
- Ask children to find words that end in *y*. Have them identify the words with the long *i* sound, *(why)* and the words with the long *e* sound *(many)*.

Build Background Use the Day 2 instruction on ELL Poster 16 to preview high-frequency words.

ELL Poster 16

Share Literature

BUILD CONCEPTS

NONFICTION Have children read the title. Identify the author. Review that books about real events are nonfiction. Authors often write nonfiction books because they want to teach us something. Discuss what children think the author wanted readers to learn by reading this book.

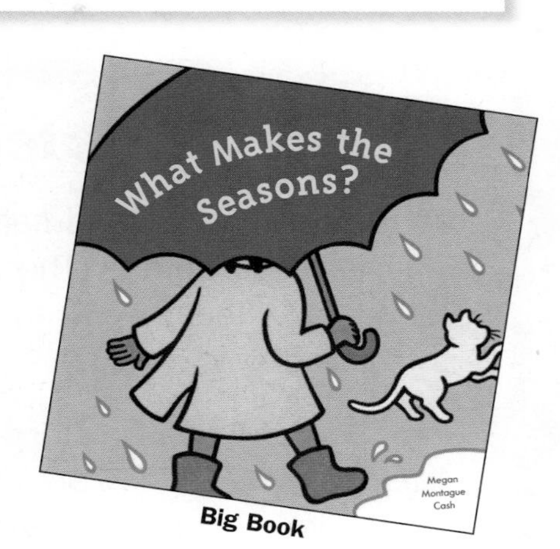

Big Book

BUILD ORAL VOCABULARY Discuss the four seasons and how they affect nature. Explain that many plants do not grow when light is **dim.** Most plants grow better when they are not in the **shade.** Suggest children listen while you read to find out how the seasons can change a garden.

- Which season would you expect to have the most flowers? (Possible response: Spring or summer because that's when the sun shines the most.)
- What happens in the shade or when light is dim? (Possible response: The plants don't grow as well in the shade because they don't get enough sunlight.)

Phonemic Awareness

SUBSTITUTE PHONEMES

- We just read about what makes the seasons. Listen to the sounds in *make.*
- Model saying each sound, /m/ /ā/ /k/. Have children say the sounds with you and then say the sounds by themselves.
- Now say each sound as you write the letter that goes with it. Say /m/ /ā/ /k/ as you write *m, a, k, e.* Have children say the sounds with you.
- Listen as I change the /ā/ sound in the middle of make to /är/: /m/ /är/ /k/, *mark.*
- Model saying each sound, /m/ /är/ /k/. Have children say the sounds with you and then say the sounds by themselves.
- Now say each sound as you write the letter(s) that go with it. Have children say the sounds with you.

Continue the activity with these examples.

bake—bark **lake—lark** **date—dart** **shake—shark**

OBJECTIVES

- Discuss characteristics of nonfiction.
- Set purpose for listening.
- Build oral vocabulary.
- Substitute phonemes.

	MONITOR PROGRESS
gardener **nature** **sprout** **dim** **shade** **blossom** **destroy** **humongous**	**If...** children lack oral vocabulary experiences about the concept Changes in Nature, **then...** use the Oral Vocabulary Routine. See p. DI•6 to teach *dim* and *shade.*

ELL

Build Concepts To help children understand the concept of change through the seasons, display pictures in *What Makes the Seasons?* as they act out planting seeds in the spring, watering tall plants in summer, jumping in leaves in autumn, and playing in snow in the winter.

OBJECTIVE

- Associate the sound /är/ with *ar*.
- Blend, read, and build regular /är/ words.

Skills Trace	
r-Controlled *ar*	
Introduce/Teach	**TE: 1.3 94c–d, 96c–d**
Practice	TE: 1.3 94f; PB: 1.2 35
Reteach/Review	TE: 1.3 140c; PB: 1.2 49
Assess/Test	TE: 1.3 116e-g; Benchmark Test, Unit 3

Strategic Intervention

Use **Monitor Progress,** p. 94d during Group Time after children have had more practice with *r*-controlled *ar*.

Advanced

Use **Monitor Progress,** p. 94d as a preassessment to determine whether or not this group of children would benefit from this *r*- controlled *ar* instruction.

Support Phonics Although the *r* is pronounced differently in Spanish, there are similarities in the way some words with *ar* are pronounced in English and Spanish. Point out the similarities with pairs such as *arte/art* and *parte/part.*

See the Phonics Transition Lessons in the ELL and Transition Handbook.

r-Controlled *ar*

TEACH/MODEL

Blending Strategy

ROUTINE

1. **Connect** Write *cat* and *had.* What do you know about reading these words? (The words both have the short vowel sound /a/.) Today we'll learn about the sound of *a* when it is followed by *r.*
2. **Use Sound-Spelling Card** Display Card 3. This is *artist. Artist* has the sound /är/ at the beginning. /är/ is the *r*-controlled sound of *a.* Say it with me: /är/.
3. **Model** Write *hard.* When the letter *a* is followed by *r,* the *a* has an *r*-controlled sound. Listen as I blend this word. Segment and blend *hard.* Let's blend this word together: /h/ /är/ /d/, *hard.*
4. **Group Practice** Say the sound of each letter and blend the word together. Continue with *far, card, barn, smart, march.*
5. **Review** What do you know about reading these words? The letters *ar* stand for /är/.

Sound-Spelling Card 3

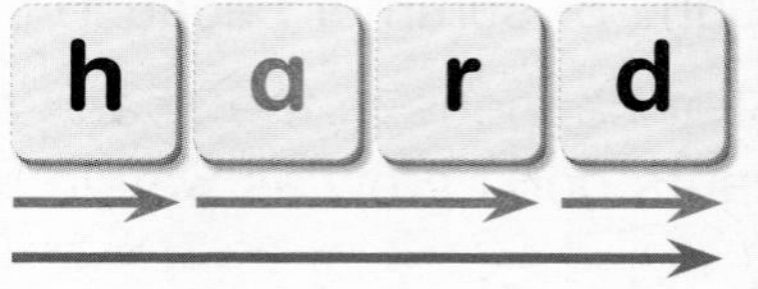

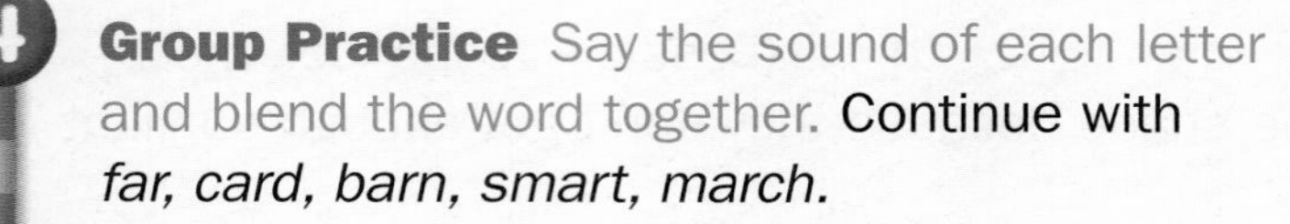

BLEND WORDS

INDIVIDUALS BLEND *ar* WORDS Call on individual children to blend the words *car, mark, yarn, harp, star, chart, large.* Have them tell what they know about each word before reading it. (The *ar* has the sound /är/.) For feedback, refer to step five of the Blending Strategy Routine.

BUILD WORDS

INDIVIDUALS MAKE *ar* WORDS Write *art* and have the class blend it. Have children spell *art* with letter tiles. Monitor work and provide feedback.

- Add *c* to the beginning of *art*. What is the new word?

- Change the *c* to *p*. What is the new word?

- Change the *t* to *k*. What is the new word?

p a r k

- Change the *p* to *sp*. What is the new word?

s p a r k

- Change the *sp* to *sh*. What is the new word?

sh a r k

MODEL BLENDING WORD FAMILIES Write *bark.* Model blending /b/—*ark, bark.* Have children blend *bark* with you. Then have them blend these words using onset and rime: *dark, mark, card, yard, hard, farm, harm, charm, cart, start, smart.*

Monitor Progress — Check Word Reading r-Controlled *ar*

Write the following words and have individuals read them.

jar	**yard**	**dark**	**hard**	**sharp**
sort	**more**	**scarf**	**porch**	**start**
cat	**cart**	**ham**	**harm**	**bark**

If... children cannot blend *ar* words at this point,

then... continue to monitor their progress using other instructional opportunities during the week so that they can be successful with the Day 5 Assessment. See the Skills Trace on p. 94c.

SUCCESS PREDICTOR

Day 1 Check Word Reading · ▶ **Day 2 Check Word Reading** · **Day 3** Check High-Frequency Words/Retelling · **Day 4** Check Fluency · **Day 5** Assess Progress

Vocabulary TIP

You may wish to explain the meanings of these words.

bark sound a dog makes
harm hurt
porch a platform with a roof along the outside of a house

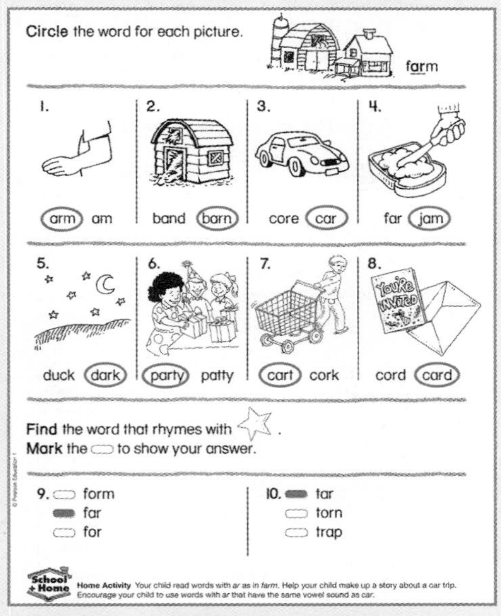
Circle the word for each picture. farm

1. arm am 2. band barn 3. core car 4. far jam
5. duck dark 6. party patty 7. cart cork 8. cord card

Find the word that rhymes with ☆. Mark the ⊂⊃ to show your answer.

9. form / far / for
10. tar / torn / trap

▲ **Practice Book 1.2** p. 35, r-Controlled *ar*

Spiral REVIEW

- Row 2 contrasts *r*-controlled *ar* with *r*-controlled *or, ore.*
- Row 3 contrasts *r*-controlled *ar* with short *a.*

Word Reading SUCCESS PREDICTOR

2

OBJECTIVE

- Spell words with inflected ending *-ed*.

Spelling Words

Adding *-ed*

1. ask	6. helped
2. asked*	7. jog
3. plan	8. jogged
4. planned	9. call
5. help*	10. called

High-Frequency Words

11. again*	12. soon*

* Words from the Selection

Adding *-ed*

Write the list word to finish the chart.

	Base Word	*-ed* Word
1.	ask	asked
2.	jog	jogged
3.	help	helped
4.	plan	planned

Spelling Words: ask, asked, plan, planned, help, helped, jog, jogged, call, called

Read the clues. Write the list word.

It rhymes with [picture] It starts with pl. 5. plan
It rhymes with [picture] It starts with c. 6. call
It rhymes with [picture] It starts with j. 7. jog

Write the list word that tells what happened in the past.

8. We can ask for paper. We asked for paper.
9. I will call my friends. I called my friends.
10. He can help. He helped.

School + Home — Home Activity Your child spelled words that do and do not end with -ed. Say a list word that does not end with -ed. Have your child say and spell the corresponding -ed word.

▲ **Spelling Practice Book** p. 62

Spelling

PRACTICE Inflected Ending *-ed*

WRITE DICTATION SENTENCES Have children write these sentences. Repeat words slowly, allowing children to hear each sound. Children may use the Word Wall to help with spelling high-frequency words. Word Wall

We planned to jog again soon.

Mom called Clark so he could help her.

Dad asked us to plan a trip to the farm.

HOMEWORK Spelling Practice Book, p. 62

Group Time

Bean Sprouts

A bean is a kind of seed. Gardeners plant beans to grow more bean plants to eat. These beans sprout, or begin to grow, in the dirt. This is how they usually grow in nature, but some beans will also sprout in water. You can make your own bean sprouts to eat.

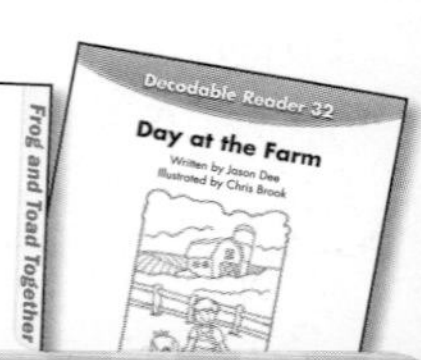

DAY 2

On-Level	Strategic Intervention	Advanced
Read Decodable Reader 32.	**Read** Decodable Reader 32.	**Read** Self-Selected Reading.
• Use p. 94f.	• Use the **Routine** on p. DI · 48.	• Use the **Routine** on p. DI · 49.

Place English language learners in the groups that correspond to their reading abilities in English.

i Independent Activities

Fluency Reading Pair children to reread Decodable Reader 31, this week's Leveled Readers, the ELL Reader from the previous week, or other text at children's independent level.

Journal Writing Write about a time when you or someone you know planted a seed. Share writing.

Independent Reading See p. 92j for Reading/Library activities and suggestions.

Literacy Centers To practice *r*-controlled *ar*, you may use Word Work, p. 92j.

Practice Book 1.2 Plot, p. 34 *r*-Controlled *ar*, p. 35 High-Frequency Words, p. 36.

Break into small groups after Spelling and before High-Frequency Words.

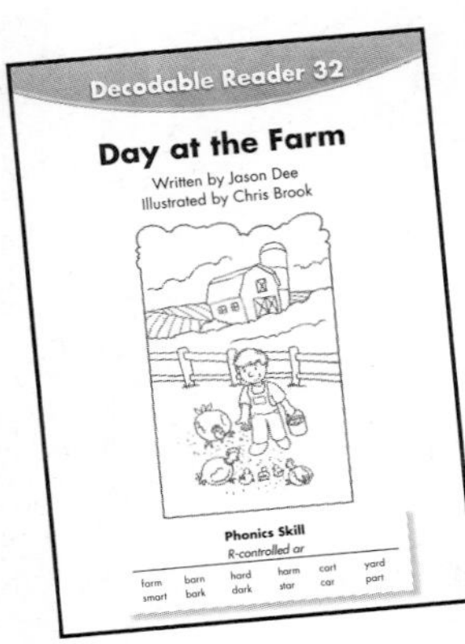

Apply Phonics

PRACTICE *r*-Controlled *ar*

HIGH-FREQUENCY WORDS Review *could, every, from, live, look, they,* and *very* on the Word Wall. If necessary, have children practice in pairs with word cards. Word Wall

COMMAS Point out the comma on p. 59 and explain that commas mean to pause briefly. Model reading a sentence with a comma. Have children watch for commas.

READ DECODABLE READER 32

- Pages 58–59 Read aloud quietly with the group.
- Page 60–61 Have the group read aloud without you.
- Pages 62–64 Select individuals to read aloud.

CHECK COMPREHENSION AND DECODING

- Why does Cass gently pet the kittens? (If Cass pets them too hard, she could harm the kittens.)
- Why do you think the best part of the farm for Cass is seeing Kate and Mike? (Answers will vary, but may include that seeing good friends and having fun with them is best no matter where you are.)
- Point to a word in the story that has the /är/ sound. What is the word? List words that are named. Children may supply *farm, barn, hard, harm, cart, yard, smart, bark, dark, star, car, part.*
- How do you know that these words have the /är/ sound? (They all have the letter *a* followed by the letter *r*.)

HOMEWORK Take-Home Decodable Reader 32

REREAD FOR FLUENCY

Oral Rereading

ROUTINE

1. **Read** Have children read the entire book orally.
2. **Reread** For optimal fluency, have children reread three or four times.
3. **Provide Feedback** Listen as children read and provide feedback regarding their oral reading and their use of the blending strategy.

OBJECTIVES

- Apply knowledge of letter-sounds to decode unknown words when reading.
- Use context with letter-sounds to confirm the identification of unknown words.
- Practice fluency with oral rereading.

Monitor Progress

Decoding

If...	then...
children have difficulty decoding a word,	prompt them to blend the word. • What is the new word? • Is the new word a word you know? • Does it make sense in the story?
children have difficulty decoding words with *-ing* endings *going* and *seeing,*	have them cover the ending and blend the base word; read the ending *-ing;* then blend the two parts.

Access Content

Beginning Lead children on a character walk through *Day at the Farm,* identifying Cass, Kate, and Mike in the pictures. On p. 63, explain that *Mom honks the car horn* because Mom wants Cass to know it is time to get in the car. Mom wants Cass to know it is time to go home.

Intermediate Preview *Day at the Farm,* pointing out /är/ words, such as *farm, barn, cart, yard, dark,* and *car* in the pictures and print.

Advanced Discuss the multiple meanings for /är/ story words *hard, yard, smart,* and *bark.*

Words to Read

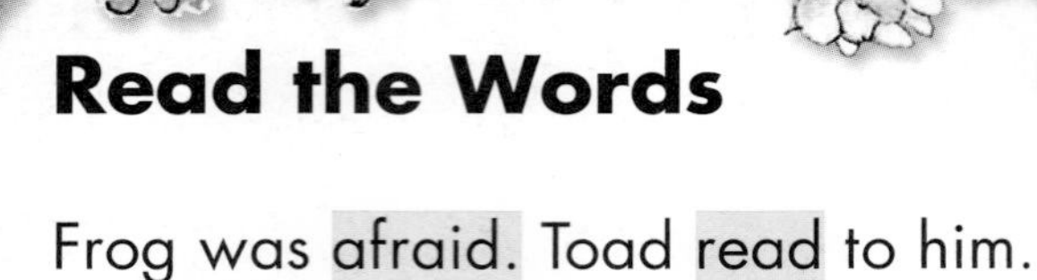

Read the Words

Frog was afraid. Toad read to him. Soon Frog went to sleep again.

"Now how can I get to sleep?" asked Toad. "I will read a few pages to myself."

Genre: Animal Fantasy
In an animal fantasy, animals say and do things that people might say and do. Next you will read about two friends, Frog and Toad, who act very much like people.

OBJECTIVE

- Recognize high-frequency words.

Circle a word to finish each sentence.
Write it on the line.

1. We have a few to take back. (how / few)
2. We read them all and came for new ones. (afraid / read)
3. Can we get some again? (again / few)
4. We can read how to plant flowers. (soon / how)
5. I am afraid this is not the best one. (afraid / few)
6. My mom will be here soon. (afraid / soon)

School + Home: Home Activity This week your child learned to read the words afraid, again, few, how, read, and soon. Make some flash cards and have your child practice reading the words.

▲ **Practice Book 1.2** p. 36, High-Frequency Words

High-Frequency Words

Nondecodable Words

ROUTINE

1. **Say and Spell** Look at the words on p. 94. You cannot yet blend the sounds in these words. We will spell the words and use letter-sounds we know to learn them. Point to the first word. This word is *afraid, a-f-r-a-i-d, afraid.* What is this word? What are the letters in this word?
2. **Identify Familiar Letter-Sounds** Point to the *fr* in *afraid.* What are these letters? What is the sound of these letters? (/fr/)
3. **Demonstrate Meaning** Tell me a sentence using this word.

Repeat the routine with the other Words to Read. Have children identify these familiar letter-sounds: *read* (r/r/, d/d/; explain that *read* can be pronounced with a long *e* sound, /r/ /ē/ /d/ and with a short *e* sound, /r/ /e/ /d/), *soon* (s/s/, n/n/), *again* (g/g/, n/n/), *how* (h/h/), *few* (f/f/).

Have children read aloud the sentences on p. 95 and point to the Words to Read. Discuss the question in the fourth sentence and whether Toad's plan will work. Add the words to the Word Wall. **Word Wall**

Interactive Writing

WRITE List

BRAINSTORM Use the Big Book *What Makes the Seasons?* to encourage a discussion about what the seasons are like. Picture walk through the book and ask children to identify characteristics of the different seasons.

SHARE THE PEN Have children participate in writing a list of characteristics of the seasons. To begin, have a child name a season and say a sentence about some of the things that happen during that season. Have the class repeat the sentence. Write the sentence, reminding individuals to use the rules they've learned about sentences. Ask questions such as:

- What does the sentence start with? (capital letter)
- Does the sentence tell something or ask something? (tell)
- What does the sentence end with? (period)

Continue to have individuals make contributions. Frequently reread what has been written while tracking the print.

READ THE LIST Read the completed list aloud, having children echo you.

Seasons

Spring	**It is warm and things start to grow.**
Summer	**It is hot and sunny.**
Fall	**The leaves change color and fall from the trees.**
Winter	**It is cold and sometimes it snows.**

INDEPENDENT WRITING

WRITE A LIST Have children write their own list of season characteristics. Let children illustrate their writing.

OBJECTIVE

- Write a list.

Strategic Intervention

Have children make a list of the seasons and illustrate their writing.

Advanced

Have children who are able to write complete sentences independently write their own list of their favorite things about their favorite season.

Writing Support Before writing, children might share ideas in their home languages.

Beginning Let children look at the Big Book for visual support as they write.

Intermediate Have children work in small groups to discuss what they will write. One child takes notes. Children can use these notes when they write.

Advanced Help children create a word list to use in the assignment.

OBJECTIVE

- Identify verbs for now and the past.

DAILY FIX-IT

3. I plantted seeds last spring
   I planted seeds last spring.
4. next year I will do it agan.
   Next year I will do it again.

Verbs for Now and the Past

Verbs can tell what happens now. Verbs can tell what happened in the past. Some verbs that tell about the past end with **-ed**.

Toad **walks**. (now) Toad **walked**. (past)

Read each word in the box. **Write** the word under *Now* if it tells about now. **Write** the word under *The Past* if it tells about the past.

wants	liked	jumped
helped	shouts	asks

Now	The Past
1. wants	4. helped
2. shouts	5. liked
3. asks	6. jumped

School-Home Connection **Home Activity** Your child learned about verbs for now and the past. Write the verbs *talk*, *laugh*, and *yell* on paper. Have your child add *-s* and *-ed* to each word and tell whether each new word tells about now or the past.

▲ **Grammar and Writing Practice Book** p. 61

Support Grammar In Romance languages such as Spanish, French, and Portuguese, verb endings show the tense of the verb. In Chinese, Hmong, and Vietnamese, verbs do not change to show the tense. Instead, adverbs or expressions of time indicate when an action has taken place. See the Grammar and Transition lessons in the ELL and Transition Handbook.

Grammar

DEVELOP THE CONCEPT
Verbs for Now and the Past

IDENTIFY VERBS FOR NOW AND THE PAST Write *turns* and *turned* on the board. Point to each word as you read it. Ask children to identify the verb that tells what happens now. (*turns*) Ask children to identify the verb that tells what happened in the past. (*turned*)

Verbs can tell what happens now and what happened in the past. Some verbs that tell about the past end with *-ed*. What is an example of a verb that tells about the past that ends in *-ed?* (*jumped*)

PRACTICE

IDENTIFY VERBS FOR NOW AND THE PAST Gather several pictures of people and animals involved in some sort of action. Display a picture. Model using a verb for now and a verb for the same action in the past, for example:

Think Aloud **MODEL** This is a girl. She is jumping. If she is jumping now, I can say "The girl jumps now." If the action takes place in the past, I can say "The girl jumped yesterday." Write *jumps* and *jumped*.

Have children suggest verbs for now and verbs for the past for the other pictures. Write the verbs children provide.

Speaking and Listening

RETELL A STORY

DEMONSTRATE SPEAKING AND LISTENING Remind children of appropriate listening and speaking behaviors for a discussion, such as speaking clearly and listening quietly. Then discuss how to retell a story.

- When you retell a story you have heard, you start at the beginning. Tell what happened first.
- Then you tell the middle of the story, or what happened next.
- Finally, you tell what happened last. This is the end of the story.
- Model how to retell using a familiar story.

TELL A STORY Ask children to retell a story they have heard in proper order. Allow children the opportunity to complete a Story Sequence Graphic Organizer before taking their turn speaking to the class.

OBJECTIVES

- Speak to retell a story in sequence.
- Listen to understand a story.

Wrap Up Your Day!

HIGH-FREQUENCY WORDS Write and read the following sentences. *Bob could only read a few words. His mom told him not to be afraid. He would soon learn how to read.* Ask children to identify the high-frequency words *afraid, few, how, read, soon.*

INFLECTED ENDINGS *-ed, -ing* Point to the word *hopped* and ask children what the base word is. (*hop*) List other words with *-ed* and *-ing* endings. Remind children that for a CVC word such as *jog* the consonant is doubled before adding *-ed* or *-ing.*

LET'S TALK ABOUT IT Recall the Big Book *What Makes the Seasons?* Ask: What changes happen in a garden during different seasons? (Seeds are planted in spring. Plants bloom in spring or summer. The plants drop their seeds in fall. They die in winter.) Display the Seed to Plant chart from Day 1. Encourage children to add new ideas. Then have them tell about a time when they did some kind of gardening.

PREVIEW Day 3

Tell children that tomorrow they will read about a toad's work in a garden and the changes that he sees.

Day 3

AT A GLANCE

Share Literature
What Makes the Seasons?

Phonemic Awareness
Blend and Segment Phonemes

Phonics and Spelling
Inflected Endings *-ed, -ing* and *r*-controlled *ar*
Spelling: Adding *-ed*

Build Background
Gardens

Vocabulary
Selection Words
ground head rain
shouted shouting
High-Frequency Words
afraid again few
how read soon

Comprehension
Skill Plot
Strategy Visualize

Read

< Differentiated Instruction

Frog and Toad Together

Vocabulary
Use Word Structure

Fluency
Read with Expression

Writing Trait
Word Choice

Grammar
Verbs for Now and the Past

Materials

- *Sing with Me Big Book*
- *What Makes the Seasons?*
- Phonics Songs/Rhymes Chart 16
- Letter Tiles
- Background Building Audio
- Graphic Organizer Flip Chart 17
- Vocabulary Transparency 16
- Student Edition 96–113

Morning Warm-Up!

Today we will read about Toad.
Toad plants seeds in a garden.
He reads and sings and shouts at his seeds.
What does a real garden need to grow?

QUESTION OF THE DAY Encourage children to sing "Sprout! It's a Garden" from the *Sing with Me Big Book* as you gather. Write the message and track the print as you read it. Discuss the question.

REVIEW ACTION VERBS

- Point to *plants, reads, sings,* and *shouts* in the message. Ask children what these words are called. (action verbs)
- Point out that every sentence has a verb, and many of them are action verbs. Ask children to suggest other action verbs for the words in the sentences.

Build Background Use the Day 3 instruction on ELL Poster 16 to support children's use of English to communicate about lesson concepts.

ELL Poster 16

Share Literature

LISTEN AND RESPOND

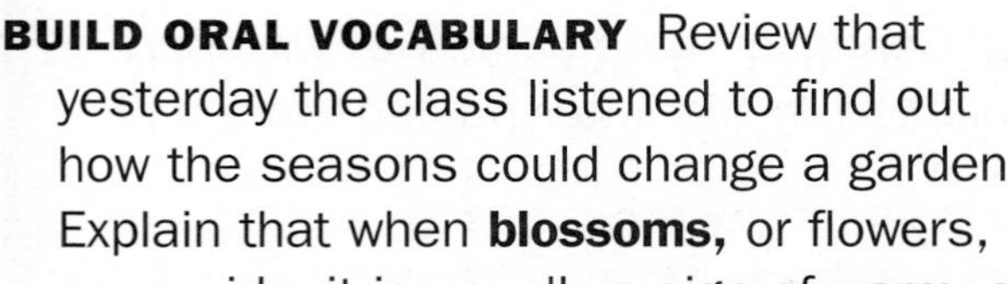

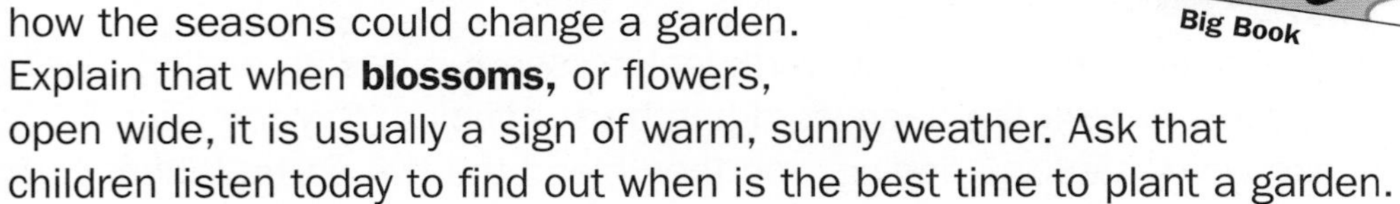

Big Book

FICTION/NONFICTION Review the pictures and information in *What Makes the Seasons?* Ask whether this looks like a fiction or a nonfiction book. (Children will probably respond that it looks like a fiction book because of the art.) Is the information in this book true or made up? (true) Remind children that this book is nonfiction because the information is true.

BUILD ORAL VOCABULARY Review that yesterday the class listened to find out how the seasons could change a garden. Explain that when **blossoms,** or flowers, open wide, it is usually a sign of warm, sunny weather. Ask that children listen today to find out when is the best time to plant a garden.

MONITOR LISTENING COMPREHENSION

- When is the best time to plant a garden? Why? (In the spring because the ground is warm and the rain helps the plants sprout and grow.)
- If we plant flowers in the spring, when will the blossoms appear? (The blossoms will appear in the summer.)
- Do flowers grow quickly or slowly? How can you tell? (Children will probably say slowly because you have to wait from spring to summer.)

Phonemic Awareness

BLEND AND SEGMENT PHONEMES

- We just read that in the spring, rain tapped at the windowpane. Listen to the sounds in *tapped.*
- Model saying each sound, /t/ /a/ /p/ /t/. Have children say the sounds with you and then say the sounds by themselves.
- Now say each sound as you write the letter that goes with it. (Say /t/ /a/ /p/ /t/ as you write *t, a, pp, ed.*)
- Have children say the sounds as you point to the letters (/t/ /a/ /p/ /t/) and blend the sounds to say the word (*tapped*).

Continue the activity with these examples.

hopped **jar** **pinned** **park** **charge** **hugged**

OBJECTIVES

- Identify fiction/nonfiction.
- Set purpose for listening.
- Build oral vocabulary.
- Blend and segment phonemes.

gardener
nature
sprout
dim
shade
blossom
destroy
humongous

MONITOR PROGRESS

If... children lack oral vocabulary experiences about the concept Changes in Nature,

then... use the Oral Vocabulary Routine. See p. DI•6 to teach *blossom.*

Listen and Respond Display seasonal-related clothing shown in *What Makes the Seasons?,* such as a slicker, umbrella, sunglasses, straw hat, sweater, mittens, and knit scarf. Think aloud as you choose an item: I will go outside today. I need sunglasses. It is summer. The trees will have green leaves. Have children take turns choosing an item and using the language you modeled.

OBJECTIVES

- Review words with inflected endings *-ed, -ing* (spelling change: double final consonant) and *ar* words.
- Build, read, and sort words with inflected endings *-ed, -ing* and *ar* words.
- Preview words before reading them.
- Spell words with *-ed* ending.

Strategic Intervention

Use **Strategic Intervention Decodable Reader 16** for more practice with inflected endings *-ed, -ing* and *r*-controlled *ar* words.

Support Phonics Languages such as Chinese, Hmong, and Vietnamese do not use inflected endings to form verb tenses. Review with children that adding *-ed* to an action word shows that the action happened in the past.

Inflected Endings and *r*-Controlled *ar*

TEACH/MODEL

Fluent Word Reading

ROUTINE

1. **Connect** Write *clapping.* You can read this word because you know how to read words with endings. Which consonant in the base word has been doubled? *(p)* What is the base word? *(clap)* What is the ending? *(-ing)* What's the word? *(clapping)* Continue in the same way with *part*, reminding children that the letter *a* followed by the letter *r* stands for /är/.
2. **Model** When you come to a new word, look to see if it has an ending; see if the last consonant in the base word has been doubled. Say the sounds in the base word, read the ending, and then blend the two parts. When you come to a new word without an ending, look at all the letters in the word and think about their sounds. Say the sounds in the word to yourself and then read the word. Model reading *clapping* and *part* in this way. When you come to a new word, what are you going to do?
3. **Group Practice** Write *thanked, smart, flipping, large.* Let's read these words. Look at all the letters, think about their sounds, and say the sounds to yourself. When I point to the word, let's read it together. Allow 2–3 seconds previewing time for each word.

WORD READING

PHONICS SONGS AND RHYMES CHART 16

Frame each of the following words on Phonics Songs and Rhymes Chart 16. Call on individuals to read them. Guide children in previewing.

garden	**far**	**stopped**	**yard**	**plopped**
dark	**patted**	**hard**	**started**	**digging**
start	**arm**	**clapping**	**farm**	**planning**

Sing "Grandpa's Garden" to the tune of "On Top of Old Smokey," or play the CD. Have children follow along on the chart as they sing. Then have individuals take turns locating words with *-ed, -ing* endings and *ar* words on the chart.

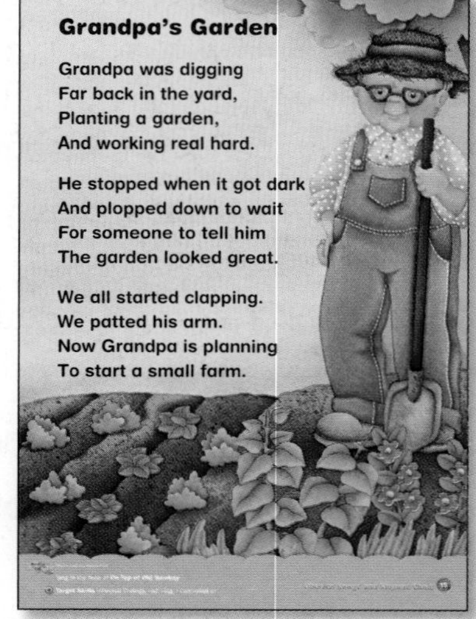

Phonics Songs and Rhymes Chart 16

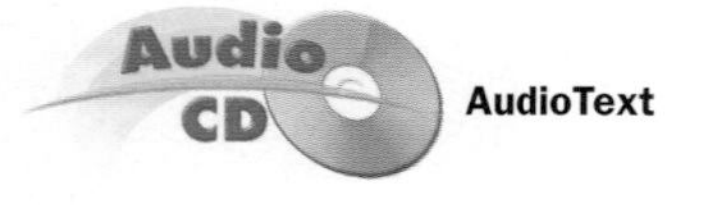

AudioText

SORT WORDS

INDIVIDUALS SORT WORDS Display words with inflected endings *-ed* and *-ing* in two columns. Ask children to tell how the words in each column are alike. (The words in column one have ending *-ed*. The words in column two have ending *-ing*.) Have children suggest a title for each column. (Ending *-ed*; Ending *-ing*) Call on children to read the words in each column. Have them point out the endings and frame the base words. Ask children to tell if the last consonant in the base word has been doubled. Then have children identify words with /är/. Monitor children's work and provide feedback. Ask individuals to read the words. Then have the rows read.

Ending *-ed*	Ending *-ing*
barked	digging
stepped	parking
started	swimming
hummed	marching

Spelling

PRACTICE Inflected Ending *-ed*

GARDEN ACTION Have children write an action sentence about what might happen in a garden for each of the spelling words, such as:

I ask for some seeds.

I plan to dig a little hole.

Have partners trade their sentences and underline and check each other's spelling words.

HOMEWORK Spelling Practice Book, p. 63

Spelling Words

Adding *-ed*

1.	ask	6.	helped
2.	asked*	7.	jog
3.	plan	8.	jogged
4.	planned	9.	call
5.	help*	10.	called

High-Frequency Words

11.	again*	12.	soon*

* Words from the Selection

Adding *-ed*

Spelling Words				
ask	asked	plan	planned	help
helped	jog	jogged	call	called

Write the missing list words.

1. He asked if I could come.
2. We have not planned a trip.
3. She jogged on the path.
4. Has your mom called you back home?
5. Jack helped clean.
6. Did you call your dog?
7. I will ask for more.
8. Tom likes to jog and run.
9. Liz will help plan.
10. All can help us.

School + Home **Home Activity** Your child wrote words that end with -ed and their base words. Ask your child to find two words in which the final consonant was doubled before adding -ed (plan/planned, jog/jogged).

▲ **Spelling Practice Book** p. 63

Build Background

OBJECTIVES

- Build background.
- Learn selection words.
- Recognize high-frequency words.

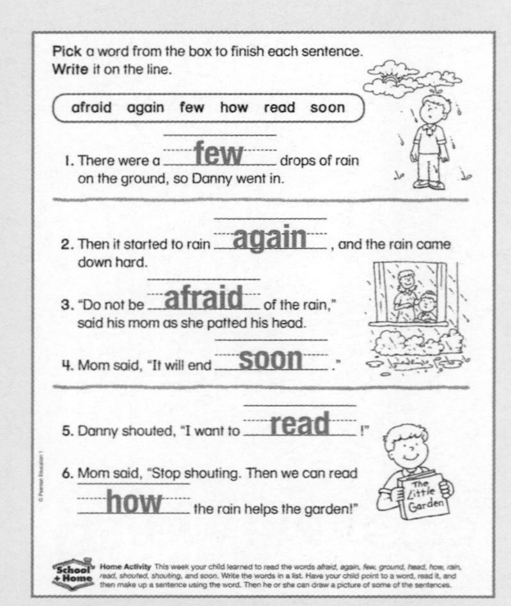
Pick a word from the box to finish each sentence.
Write it on the line.

afraid again few how read soon

1. There were a **few** drops of rain on the ground, so Danny went in.
2. Then it started to rain **again**, and the rain came down hard.
3. "Do not be **afraid** of the rain," said his mom as she patted his head.
4. Mom said, "It will end **soon**."
5. Danny shouted, "I want to **read**!"
6. Mom said, "Stop shouting. Then we can read **how** the rain helps the garden!"

School + Home Home Activity This week your child learned to read the words afraid, again, few, ground, head, how, rain, read, shouted, shouting, and soon. Write the words in a list. Have your child point to a word, read it, and then make up a sentence using the word. Then he or she can draw a picture of some of the sentences.

▲ **Practice Book 1.2** p. 37, High-Frequency and Selection Words

DISCUSS GARDENING Display pictures of different vegetables or gardens or have children turn to pp. 92–93 of the Student Edition. Initiate discussion by asking children what they know about growing a garden.

- What kinds of plants can grow in gardens?
- What do you put in the ground to make a garden?
- What do gardeners do to take care of their gardens?

BACKGROUND-BUILDING AUDIO Have children listen to the CD and share the new information they learned about gardens.

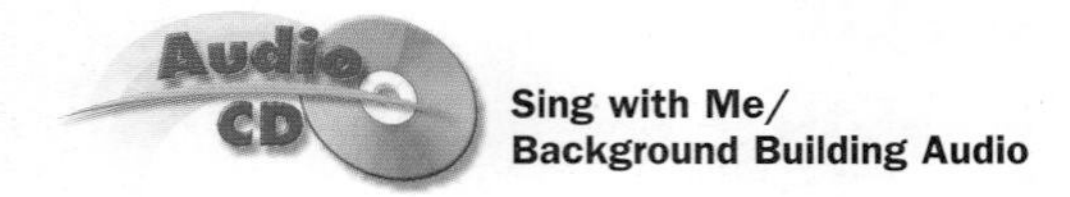

Sing with Me/ Background Building Audio

COMPLETE A WEB Draw a web or display Graphic Organizer 17. Write *gardens* in the center. Ask children to suggest things they know about gardens. Add their responses to the web.

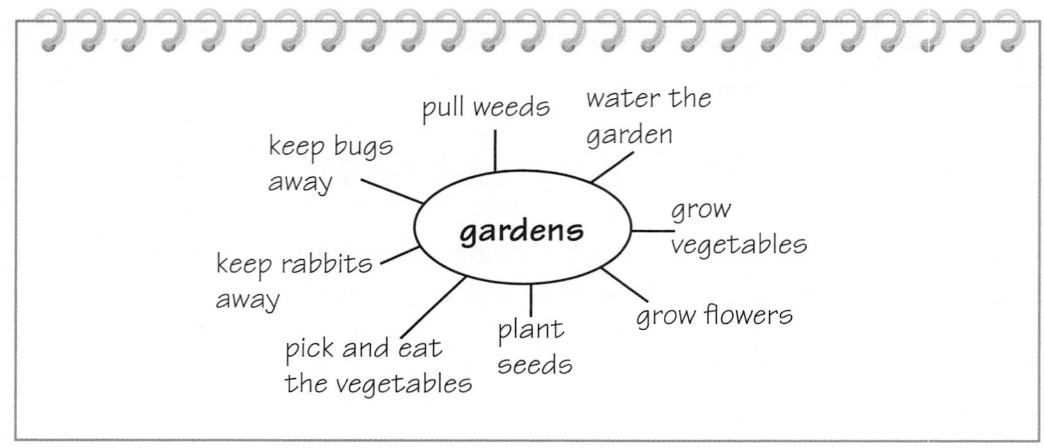

▲ **Graphic Organizer Flip Chart 17**

CONNECT TO SELECTION Connect background information to "The Garden" from *Frog and Toad Together.*

Sometimes people try different things to keep the plants in their garden growing. Toad is a character in the story we are about to read. His garden is not growing the way he thinks it should. We'll find out what advice Frog gives Toad and if anything ever grows in the garden.

Activate Prior Knowledge Display or draw a picture of several flowers growing in the ground. Tell children that we call this a garden. Have them give the word for garden in their home languages. Discuss what children know about taking care of plants.

Vocabulary

SELECTION WORDS

Use Vocabulary Transparency 16 to introduce the selection words.

- Read each sentence as you track the print.
- Frame each underlined word. Explain the word's meaning.

  rain water that falls in drops from the clouds
  ground the soil or dirt on the surface of the Earth
  head the top part of your body or the front part of most animals' bodies
  shouted called out or yelled loudly
  shouting calling or yelling

- Ask children to identify familiar letter-sounds and word parts: *rain* (*r*/r/, *n*/n/), *ground* (consonant blends *gr, nd*), *head* (*h*/h/, *d*/d/), *shouted* (digraph *sh*, small word *out*, ending *-ed*), *shouting* (digraph *sh*, small word *out*, ending *-ing,* note similarity to *shouted*).
- Have children read each sentence aloud with you.
- To encourage discussion using the selection words, ask children to tell about how they would take care of their own gardens.

HIGH-FREQUENCY WORDS

Use Vocabulary Transparency 16 to review this week's words.

- Point to a word. Say and spell it.
- Have children say and spell the word.
- Ask children to identify familiar letter-sounds.

Monitor Progress | **Check High-Frequency Words**

Point to the following words on the Word Wall and have individuals read them.

work	**again**	**few**	**were**	**read**	**soon**	
very	**grow**	**day**	**how**	**afraid**	**home**	**together**

If... children cannot read these words,

then ... have them find each word on the Word Wall, chant its spelling, and then write it. Monitor their fluency with these words during reading, and provide additional practice opportunities before the Day 5 Assessment.

SUCCESS PREDICTOR

Day 1 Check Word Reading | **Day 2** Check Word Reading | ▶**Day 3 Check High-Frequency Words/Retelling** | **Day 4** Check Fluency | **Day 5** Assess Progress

Selection Words

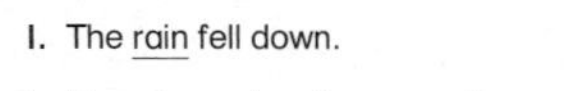

Rain Go Away

1. The rain fell down.
2. It made mud on the ground.
3. It fell on Anna's head.
4. "Stop raining!" she shouted.
5. Why is she shouting at the rain?

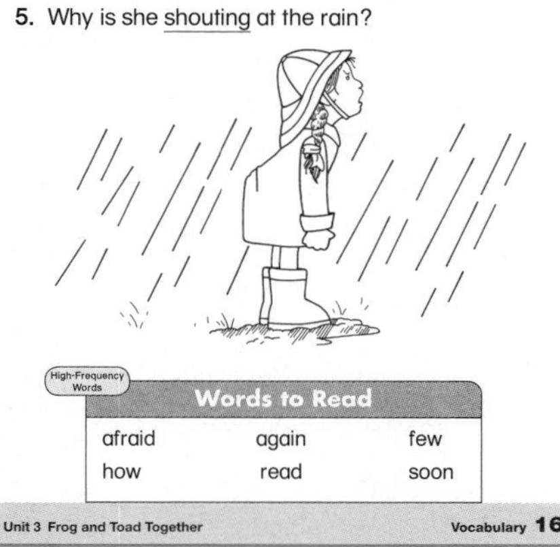

High-Frequency Words

Words to Read

afraid	again	few
how	read	soon

Unit 3 Frog and Toad Together — Vocabulary 16

▲ **Vocabulary Transparency 16**

Access Content Use the vocabulary strategies and word cards in the ELL Teaching Guide, pp. 108–109.

Spiral REVIEW

- Reviews previously taught high-frequency words.

High-Frequency Words SUCCESS PREDICTOR

3

OBJECTIVES

- Recognize plot.
- Visualize characters, settings, and events.

Comprehension

PLOT

RECOGNIZE PLOT Remind children that all stories have a plot—a beginning, a middle, and an end. Explain that the events of a story often tell about how a character's problem is solved. Recall previously read stories and their plots.

CONNECT TO READING

- Ask yourself, "What happens at the beginning, middle, and end of the story?"
- Think about the characters and how their problems get solved.

VISUALIZE

INTRODUCE THE STRATEGY Explain that good readers often make pictures in their minds to help them imagine what they read about. Picturing the characters, setting, and events makes it easier to understand a story.

MODEL When I read a story, I picture the characters and what they do in my mind. I also picture where the story takes place. Sometimes the author gives information that helps me picture what is going to happen.

CONNECT TO READING Encourage children to ask themselves these questions as they read *Frog and Toad Together.*

- How do the characters look? Can I picture them in my mind?
- What are the characters doing? Can I close my eyes and picture what is happening?

Group Time

DAY 3

On-Level	Strategic Intervention	Advanced
Read *Frog and Toad Together.* • Use pp. 96–113.	**Read** SI Decodable Reader 16. • Read or listen to *Frog and Toad Together.* • Use the **Routine** on p. DI·50.	**Read** *Frog and Toad Together.* • Use the **Routine** on p. DI·51.

Place English language learners in the groups that correspond to their reading abilities in English.

i Independent Activities

Independent Reading See p. 92j for Reading/Library activities and suggestions.

Journal Writing Write about your favorite flower, plant, or tree. Share writing.

Literacy Centers Use the Listening and Writing Centers for *Frog and Toad Together* on pp. 92j and 92k.

Practice Book 1.2 High-Frequency Words and Selection Words, p. 37

Break into small groups after Comprehension and before Fluency.

Frog and Toad Together

by Arnold Lobel

The Garden

What do seeds need to grow?

96 97

Read

Prereading Strategies

PREVIEW AND PREDICT Identify and read the title and the name author-illustrator. Ask children to look at the pictures and tell what they might already know about Frog and Toad.

DISCUSS ANIMAL FANTASY Direct attention to the pictures on pages 96–97. Discuss whether children think this will be a made-up story or a story about real animals. Remind them that a fantasy is a story about animals or people that do things real animals and people cannot do. Reread the definition of animal fantasy on p. 95 of the Student Edition.

SET PURPOSE Read the question on page 97. Discuss what children want to learn as they read this story. Have them set a purpose for reading.

AudioText

ELL

Access Content Before reading, review the story summary in English and/or the home language. See the ELL Teaching Guide, pp. 110–112.

Frog was in his garden.
Toad came walking by.

"What a fine garden you have, Frog,"
he said.

"Yes," said Frog. "It is very nice,
but it was hard work."

98

"I wish I had a garden," said Toad.

"Here are some flower seeds.
Plant them in the ground," said Frog,
"and soon you will have a garden."

99

▲ **Pages 98–99**
Have children to read to find out what Toad wants.

Monitor Progress

High-Frequency Words

If... children have a problem reading a new high frequency word,	**then...** use the High-Frequency Routine on pp.94–95 to reteach the problematic word.

Access Content Point out that the word *hard* has two meanings in English. It can mean "firm and solid," as a hard stone; it can also mean "difficult" as in a job that is hard to do.

Guiding Comprehension

Draw Conclusions • Critical

- **What does Toad want? Why do you think he wants it?**
  Toad wants to have a garden. Children will probably say he wants it because Frog has one or because he thinks Frog's garden looks nice.

Prior Knowledge • Critical

- **What kind of hard work do you think Frog had to do for his garden?**
  Children will probably say that Frog had to water the plants, pull weeds, and keep insects away.

Predict • Inferential

- **Do you think Toad will work hard for his garden? Why?**
  Children may predict that he will because Frog warns him about working hard. Others will say that he won't because he might just want a garden without working hard to get it.

____ inflected endings *-ed, -ing* and *r*-controlled *ar*   high-frequency/tested vocabulary

"How soon?" asked Toad.

"Quite soon," said Frog.

Toad ran home.
He planted the flower seeds.

"Now seeds," said Toad, "start growing."

Toad walked up and down a few times.
The seeds did not start to grow.

100

Toad put his head close to the ground and said loudly,

"Now seeds, start growing!"

101

Guiding Comprehension

Plot • Inferential

- **What problem does Toad have?**
  His seeds will not grow.

Confirm Predictions • Inferential

- **What work does Toad do in his garden?**
  Toad plants the seeds. Then he shouts at them to grow.

Character • Inferential

- **A person who is impatient is in a hurry for things to happen. How does the author show us that Toad is an impatient gardener?**
  Toad walks up and down and starts telling his seeds to grow.

Compare and Contrast • Critical

- ***Text to Self*** **Are you ever impatient like Toad is? What have you learned about trying to hurry things up?**
  Possible response: I always want my birthday to be here sooner. I've learned that I can't make it get here any faster.

▲ **Pages 100–101**
Have children read to find out how Toad starts his garden.

Monitor Progress

Decoding

If... children come to a word they don't know,	**then...** remind them to blend the word: 1. Look at each letter. 2. Think of the sound for each letter. 3. Blend the sounds. 4. Read the word.

Toad looked at the ground again.
The seeds did not start to grow.

Toad put his head very close
to the ground and shouted,

"NOW SEEDS,
START GROWING!"

102

Frog came running up the path.
"What is all this noise?" he asked.

"My seeds will not grow," said Toad.

"You are shouting too much," said Frog.
"These poor seeds are afraid to grow."

103

▲ **Pages 102–103**
Have children read to discover how Toad tries to make his seeds grow.

EXTEND SKILLS

Text Features
For instruction in interpreting the purpose of different kinds of text, use the following:

- How do Toad's words "NOW SEEDS, START GROWING!" look different from the rest of the page?
- How do the size of the letters tell you about how Toad was talking?

Assess Have children look back at the previous pages to find other text that is different. Discuss why. (On p. 101 the words are in big type to show that Toad is speaking loudly to the seeds.)

Strategies in Context

VISUALIZE

- **What is Toad doing to try to make his seeds grow?**
  Toad is bent down to the ground and shouting at his seeds to grow.

Monitor Progress	**Visualize**
If... children have difficulty answering the question,	**then...** model how to make a mental picture of the text.

Think Aloud **MODEL** When I read Toad's words and look at the picture, I can see in my mind just what he is doing. I can close my eyes and see a picture of him leaning down to talk right to his seeds. I can see him shouting because he thinks the seeds can't hear him. I think he looks pretty funny.

ASSESS Have children tell about the picture they make in their minds when they think about what Frog does and what he says to Toad. Invite them to pantomime Frog as they read his words.

____ inflected endings *-ed, -ing* and *r*-controlled *ar*   high-frequency/tested vocabulary

"My seeds are afraid to grow?"
asked Toad.

"Of course," said Frog.
"Leave them alone for a few days.
Let the sun shine on them,
let the rain fall on them.
Soon your seeds will start to grow."

104

That night Toad looked out of his window.

"Drat!" said Toad. "My seeds have not started to grow. They must be afraid of the dark." Toad went out to his garden with some candles.

105

▲ **Pages 104–105**
Have children look at the picture and think about how Frog and Toad are different.

Skills in Context

REVIEW COMPARE AND CONTRAST

- **How is Frog different from Toad?**
  Frog is bigger than Toad; Frog knows how to grow a garden; Frog is patient and wants to help Toad.

Monitor Progress	Compare and Contrast
If... children have difficulty answering the question,	**then...** model how to compare and contrast the characters.

MODEL I remember that Toad was impatient and he shouted at his seeds to grow. Here Frog tells Toad to wait. Frog is patient. When I look at the picture I see that Frog and Toad look alike except that Frog is bigger.

ASSESS Draw a T-chart or display Graphic Organizer 4. Have children contribute to the chart by telling how Frog and Toad are alike and different.

EXTEND SKILLS

Author's Craft
For instruction in how authors use language to identify characters, discuss the following:

- How do the things Toad says and the things Frog says show you who knows a lot about gardens?
- What does Frog say that shows he is patient?

Assess Have children point out what words show that Toad does not know much about seeds. (He talks to the seeds a few times. Then on p. 105 he says that they are "afraid of the dark.")

▲ **Pages 106–107**
Have children read to find out how Toad took care of his seeds.

Strategy Self-Check

Have children ask themselves these questions to check their reading.

Decoding Words

- Do I look for word parts I can read?
- Do I blend all of the sounds in a word to read it?
- Do I reread to make sure the word make sense in the story?

Visualize

- Do I think about how the characters look and what they are doing?
- Do I make a picture in my mind of what is happening?

Guiding Comprehension

Summarize • Inferential

- **What has happened in the story so far?**
First, Toad wants a garden, so Frog gives him seeds. Then Toad plants the seeds and shouts at them to grow. Next Toad takes care of his seeds by reading to them, singing to them, and playing them music.

Draw Conclusions • Critical

- **Why do you think Toad thinks singing and reading to his seeds will make them less afraid?**
Possible response: Those are things that make people happy, so maybe Toad thinks they will make the seeds happy.

Predict • Inferential

- **What do you think will happen next?**
Children may predict that Toad will give up, or that his seeds will eventually sprout.

___ inflected endings *-ed, -ing* and *r*-controlled *ar*   ☐ high-frequency/tested vocabulary

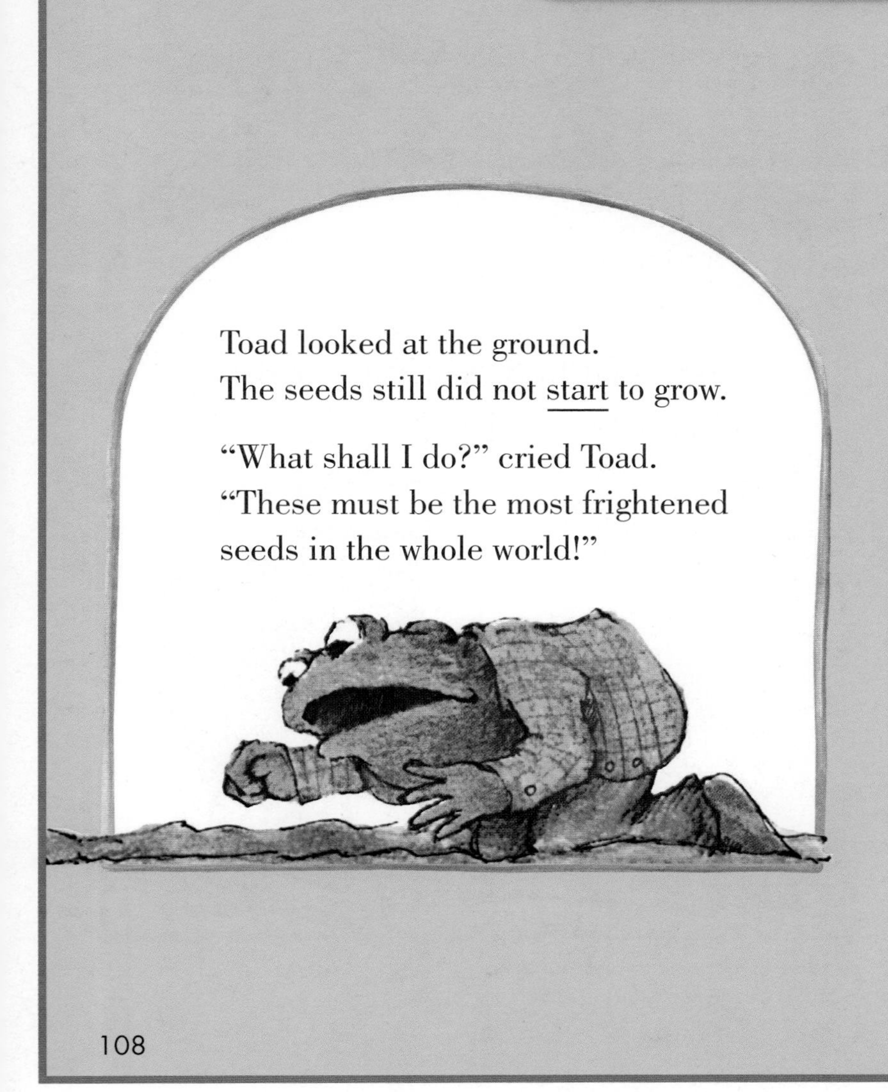
Toad looked at the ground.
The seeds still did not start to grow.

"What shall I do?" cried Toad.
"These must be the most frightened
seeds in the whole world!"

108

Then Toad felt very tired, and he fell asleep.

"Toad, Toad, wake up," said Frog.
"Look at your garden!"

Toad looked at his garden.

109

Guiding Comprehension

Draw Conclusions • Inferential

- **Why does Toad think his seeds are the most frightened seeds in the world?**
  He thinks his seeds are afraid to grow. All the things he has done haven't helped, so he thinks the seeds are still frightened.

Make Judgments • Critical

- **Do you think Toad has worked hard in his garden?**
  Children will probably say that Toad has worked hard because he has done a lot to make his seeds grow.

Compare and Contrast • Inferential

- ***Text to Text*** **How are Toad's seeds like Ruby in *Ruby in Her Own Time?***
  Toad's seeds will grow when they are ready just like Ruby did things when she was ready.

▲ **Pages 108–109**
Ask children to read to see if the seeds grow.

TIME FOR Science

Life Cycles

When you plant a seed and give it water, it starts to grow. As plants get bigger, they form leaves and flowers. Then plants produce seeds that fall off and become new plants. Then the new plants grow, flower, and make seeds. This cycle happens again and again.

Student Pages 110–111

Little green plants were coming up out of the ground.

"At last," shouted Toad, "my seeds have stopped being afraid to grow!"

110

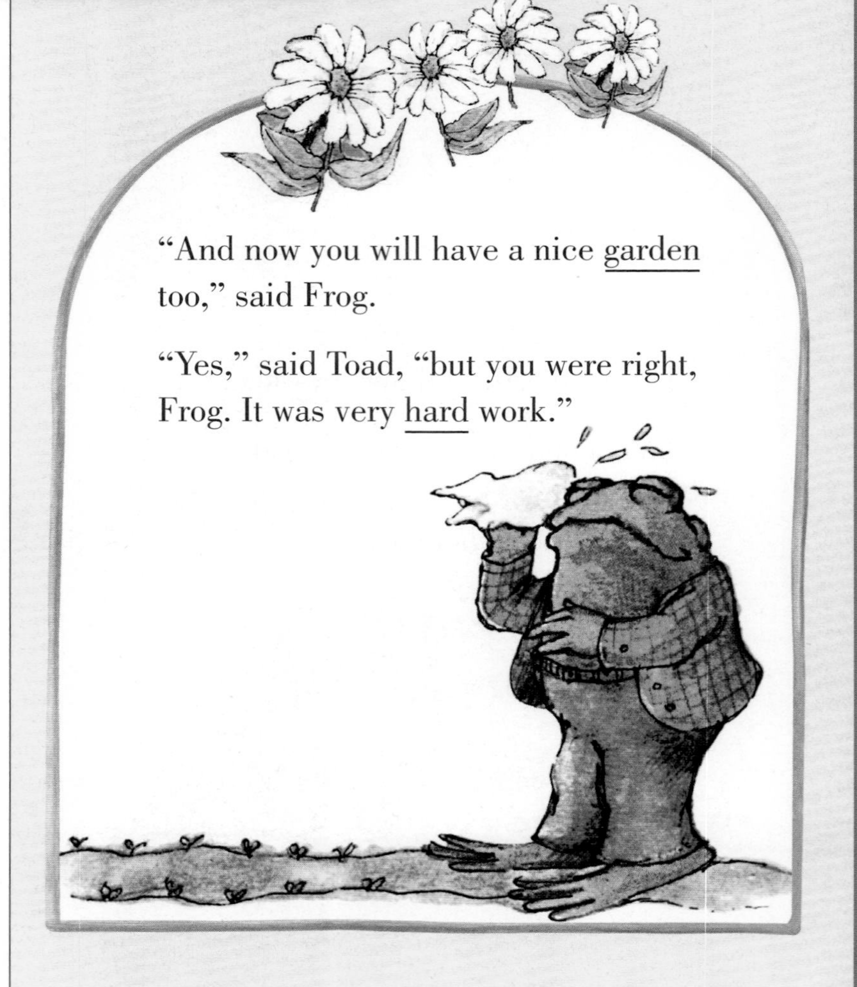

"And now you will have a nice garden too," said Frog.

"Yes," said Toad, "but you were right, Frog. It was very hard work."

111

▲ **Pages 110–111**
Ask children to read to find out how the story ends.

TIME FOR Science

Plant Needs

All living things need certain things to survive. Help children identify the things plants need: water, light, air, food from soil, and space to grow. Discuss how a gardener might make sure plants have these things.

____ inflected endings *-ed, -ing* and *r*-controlled *ar* ▭ high-frequency/tested vocabulary

Skills in Context

PLOT

- **How does the story end?**
  Toad's seeds grow on their own.

Monitor Progress	Plot
If... children have difficulty answering the question,	**then...** model how to identify plot.

Think Aloud

MODEL In the beginning of the story Toad had a problem because he wanted his seeds to grow. In the middle, he tried to make his seeds grow by shouting at them, reading to them, singing to them, and playing them music. Finally, when he fell asleep, his seeds sprouted on their own.

ASSESS Have children compare Toad's problem to Ruby's problem in *Ruby in Her Own Time.* (Possible response: Everyone had to wait for Ruby until she was ready to fly. Toad had to wait until the seeds were ready to grow.)

Retelling Plan

- ☑ Week 1 assess Strategic Intervention students.
- ☑ Week 2 assess Advanced students.
- ☑ Week 3 assess Strategic Intervention students.
- ☑ **This week assess On-Level students.**
- ☐ Week 5 assess Strategic Intervention students.
- ☐ Week 6 assess any students you have not yet checked during this unit.

Look Back and Write For informal assessment, see the Scoring Rubric below.

ELL

Check Retelling Model how to retell by talking about the first picture. For more ideas on assessing comprehension, see the ELL and Transition Handbook.

Think and Share

TALK ABOUT IT Model a response. I think the funniest thing that Toad did was yell at the seeds. The story says, "Toad put his head close to the ground and said loudly, 'Now seeds, start growing!'"

1. RETELL Have children use the retelling strip in the Student Edition to retell the story.

Monitor Progress **Check Retelling** Rubric 4 3 2 1

If... children have difficulty retelling the story,

then... use the Retelling Cards and the Scoring Rubric for Retelling on pp. 112–113 to help them move toward fluent retelling.

Day 1 Check Word Reading	**Day 2** Check Word Reading	▶ **Day 3 Check High-Frequency Words/Retelling**	**Day 4** Check Fluency	**Day 5** Assess Progress

2. PLOT Possible response: I liked the story's ending because Toad learned that it takes time for seeds to grow.

3. VISUALIZE Possible response: I pictured Toad playing his violin for the seeds. That helped me think about how silly Toad was being.

LOOK BACK AND WRITE Read the writing prompt on p. 112 and model your thinking. I'll look back on p. 104 and read that part of the story again. I'll look for advice Frog gives to Toad. Then I'll write my response. Have children write their responses in an interactive or an independent writing activity.

Scoring Rubric **Look Back and Write**

Top-Score Response A top-score response uses details from p. 104 of the story to tell about the advice Frog gives to Toad.

Example of a Top-Score Response

Frog tells Toad to leave the seeds alone for a few days.
Frog says the seeds will grow after they get sun and rain.

For additional rubrics, see p. WA10.

Reader Response

Read Together

Think and Share

Talk About It What was the funniest thing Toad did to get his seeds to grow? Read that part out loud.

1. Use the pictures below to retell the story. Retell
2. What did you think about the story's ending? Tell about it. Plot
3. What picture came to your mind when you read about Toad playing music for his plants? How did that help you? Visualize

Look Back and Write Look back at page 104. What advice does Frog give to Toad?

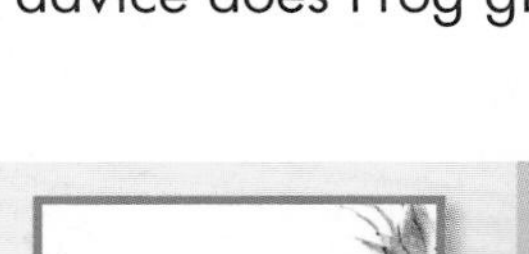

Meet the Author and Illustrator

Arnold Lobel

When Arnold Lobel first wrote about Frog and Toad, there were not many books for beginning readers that were fun to read. Mr. Lobel used easy words, and children love those good friends Frog and Toad!

As a boy, Mr. Lobel liked to draw silly animal pictures for his friends. When he grew up, he wrote and illustrated almost 100 books!

Read more stories about Frog and Toad.

Retelling Strip

Scoring Rubric Narrative Retelling

Rubric 4 3 2 1	4	3	2	1
Connections	Makes connections and generalizes beyond the text	Makes connections to other events, stories, or experiences	Makes a limited connection to another event, story, or experience	Makes no connection to another event, story, or experience
Author's Purpose	Elaborates on author's purpose	Tells author's purpose with some clarity	Makes some connection to author's purpose	Makes no connection to author's purpose
Characters	Describes the main character(s) and any character development	Identifies the main character(s) and gives some information about them	Inaccurately identifies some characters or gives little information about them	Inaccurately identifies the characters or gives no information about them
Setting	Describes the time and location	Identifies the time and location	Omits details of time or location	Is unable to identify time or location
Plot	Describes the events in sequence using rich detail	Tells the plot with some errors in sequence that do not affect meaning	Tells parts of plot with gaps that affect meaning	Retelling has no sense of story

Use the Retelling Chart on p. TR18 to record retelling.

Selection Test To assess with *Frog and Toad Together*, use Selection Tests, pp. 37–40.

Fresh Reads for Differentiated Test Practice For weekly leveled practice, use pp. 91–96.

OBJECTIVE

- Read aloud fluently with expression.

Options for Oral Reading

Use *Frog and Toad Together* or one of the following Leveled Readers.

On-Level

A Funny Garden

Strategic Intervention

The Garden

Advanced

The Mile-A-Minute Vine

Read aloud pp. 99–102 of *Frog and Toad Together* with expression to support comprehension for beginning English language learners. Increase the emphasis of words and phrases such as *Now seeds, start growing!* shown in larger type and with an exclamation mark. Have children practice rereading the same pages with expression.

Fluency

READ WITH EXPRESSION

MODEL READING WITH DIALOGUE Use *Frog and Toad Together.*

- Point to the quotation marks on p. 98. Quotation marks show that someone is talking. I try to read the part in quotation marks the way the character would say it.
- Ask children to follow along as you read the pages with expression.
- Have children read the pages after you. Encourage them to try to read the way Frog and Toad would speak. Continue in the same way with p. 99.

REREAD FOR FLUENCY

Choral Reading

ROUTINE

1. **Select a Passage** For *Frog and Toad Together,* use pp. 100–102.
2. **Divide into Groups** Assign each group a part to read. For this story, have a group read the narrator's part, a group read Frog's part, and a group read Toad's part.
3. **Model** Have children track the print as you read.
4. **Read Together** Have children read along with you.
5. **Independent Readings** Have the groups read aloud without you. Monitor progress and provide feedback. For optimal fluency, children should reread three to four times.

Monitor Progress	Fluency
If... children have difficulty reading the dialogue,	**then...** prompt: • Find the marks that tell someone is speaking. • Who is speaking? How does he feel? How should he sound?
If... the class cannot read fluently without you,	**then...** continue to have them read along with you.

Vocabulary

USE ENDINGS TO DETERMINE MEANING

DISCUSS WORDS WITH INFLECTED ENDINGS Have children recall what Toad first did to make his seeds grow. Write the following sentences on the board and discuss that the *-s* at the end of *shouts* tells about now, the *-ed* at the end of *shouted* tells about the past, and the *-ing* at the end of *shouting* tells that it has been going on and will continue.

Toad shouts at his seeds.

Toad shouted at his seeds.

Toad is shouting at his seeds.

EXPAND SELECTION VOCABULARY Display Graphic Organizer 5 or draw a three-column chart. Have children help you write the inflected forms of these words from the story: *start, plant, walk, look, play.* Have children use each word in a sentence that demonstrates its meaning.

-s	*-ed*	*-ing*
starts	started	starting
plants	planted	planting
walks	walked	walking
looks	looked	looking
plays	played	playing

▲ Graphic Organizer 5

OBJECTIVES

- Discuss meanings of words with inflected endings.
- Use words with inflected endings in sentences.

Strategic Intervention

Make two sets of cards, one with endings *-s, -ed, -ing,* and a second set with these words: *play, jump, work, help.* Have children choose a word and an ending and then write the word with the ending.

Advanced

Have children write at least three sentences telling about Toad and his seeds. Have them use words with inflected endings in their sentences.

Extend Language Help children practice saying sentences that tell about something that happens now and that happened yesterday, using the *-s* and *-ed* inflected ending.

OBJECTIVE

- Recognize and use word choice in writing.

DAILY FIX-IT

5. I put thre seeds in one pot?
I put three seeds in one pot.

6. then I gave them watter.
Then I gave them water.

Connect to Unit Writing

Writing Trait

Have children use strategies for developing **word choice** when they write a description in the Unit Writing Workshop, pp. WA2–WA9.

Word Choice Work with children to use vivid words that appeal to readers' senses. A bilingual dictionary, picture dictionary, or thesaurus, as well as other home-language speakers, may help provide words that create pictures for readers.

Writing Trait of the Week

INTRODUCE Word Choice

TALK ABOUT WORD CHOICE Explain to children that writers choose exact, strong words to make word pictures for readers. Read aloud pp. 106–107 of *Frog and Toad Together.* Ask children to think about the words the author chooses. Then model your thinking.

MODEL When I look at the words on pp. 106–107, I see that the author chooses words to tell what Toad does. We learn exactly what he does to make his seeds grow. Now I am going to write a different sentence about Toad's actions.

Write this sentence on the board and read it aloud.

Toad did stuff to his seeds.

This sentence doesn't give us a clear picture of what Toad is doing. What words can we use instead of the underlined words?

As children offer words to replace the underlined words *(read poems, read stories, sang songs, played music [for]),* rewrite the sentence using their suggestions. Talk about how the new sentences give much clearer, more interesting pictures of Toad's actions.

STRATEGY FOR DEVELOPING WORD CHOICE On the board, write sentences that need strong verbs. Work with children to replace the underlined weak verbs with strong verbs so that the sentences give clearer word pictures.

First get some seeds, tiny and brown. *(choose, find)*
Then put them deep into the ground. *(press, plant)*
The rain comes, and the sun shines down. *(falls, pours)*
Up go the flowers, large and round. *(pop, spring)*

PRACTICE

APPLY THE STRATEGY

- Ask pairs of children to complete these sentences with strong verbs.
  We ____ to the store. (raced, jogged, biked)
  On warm days, I like to ___. (swim, sunbathe, skate)
- Have children write a poem about friends, like Frog and Toad. Remind children to use clear, exact words. Suggest that they use verbs from the previous exercises in this lesson as well as rhyming words.

Grammar

APPLY TO WRITING Verbs for Now and the Past

IMPROVE WRITING WITH VERBS FOR NOW AND THE PAST Explain to children that writing with verbs for now and the past lets readers know when things happen. Remind children to use verbs for now and the past in their own writing.

Write *walks, hopes, picks.* Have children identify whether these are verbs for now or for the past (now). Then have children make them verbs for the past and use them in sentences.

Frog walked home.
He hoped Toad was there.
He picked a flower.

PRACTICE

CHANGE VERBS FOR THE PAST TO VERBS FOR NOW Write *called, jumped, liked, talked, cared* on the board. Have children identify whether these are verbs for now or for the past (past). Call on individuals to make them verbs for now. Have children write sentences using each verb.

OBJECTIVE

- Use verbs for now and the past in writing.

Verbs for Now and the Past

In the past you were a baby.
Tell about things you did then.

Possible answer: I crawled. I stayed in a crib. I played with baby toys.

Now you are in first grade.
Tell about things you do now.

Possible answer: I walk. I talk with friends. I play baseball.

Home Activity Your child learned how to use verbs for now and the past in writing. With your child, look through a family photo album. Talk about what you were doing then using verbs for the past. Talk about what you are doing now using verbs for now.

▲ **Grammar and Writing Practice Book** p. 62

Wrap Up Your Day!

PLOT Have children recall what happens first, next, and at the end of "The Garden" from *Frog and Toad Together.* (First, Frog gives Toad some seeds. Next, Toad yells at the seeds but they do not grow. Finally, the seeds get water and sunlight and they begin to grow.) Could the events in the story take place in a different order? Why not?

VISUALIZE Help children visualize the characters and their actions in "The Garden" from *Frog and Toad Together.* (Frog is green. He hands some seeds to Toad. Toad is brown. He yells loudly at the seeds.)

LET'S TALK ABOUT IT Toad plants some seeds. What changes happen in his garden? (The seeds sprout.)

PREVIEW Day 4

Tell children that tomorrow they will listen to a story about a boy who plants some magic beans.

Day 4
AT A GLANCE

Share Literature
"Jack and the Beanstalk"

Phonemic Awareness
Add Initial and Final Phonemes

High-Frequency Words
afraid *again* *few*
how *read* *soon*

Phonics and Spelling
REVIEW Ending *-es*, Plural *-es*; *r*-Controlled *or, ore,*
REVIEW Word Reading
Spelling: Adding *-ed*

Read

< Differentiated Instruction

"Growing Plants"

Fluency
Read with Expression

Writing Across the Curriculum
List

Grammar
Verbs for Now and the Past

Materials
- *Sing with Me Big Book*
- Read Aloud Anthology
- Tested Word Cards
- Student Edition 114–115

Toad tried to make his seeds sprout.

Today we will read about what flowers really need to grow.

What would you plant in a garden?

QUESTION OF THE DAY Encourage children to sing "Sprout! It's a Garden" from the Sing with Me Big Book as you gather. Write the message and track the print as you read it. Discuss the question.

REVIEW CONSONANT BLENDS

- Ask children to find words that begin with consonant blends (*tried, sprout, flowers, grow, plant*).
- Circle each word and have children read it.

Extend Language Use the Day 4 instruction on ELL Poster 16 to extend and enrich language.

ELL Poster 16

Share Literature

CONNECT CONCEPTS

ACTIVATE PRIOR KNOWLEDGE Help children recall that Toad waited a long time for his plants to sprout. Today you will read about an amazing plant that grows overnight in "Jack and the Beanstalk."

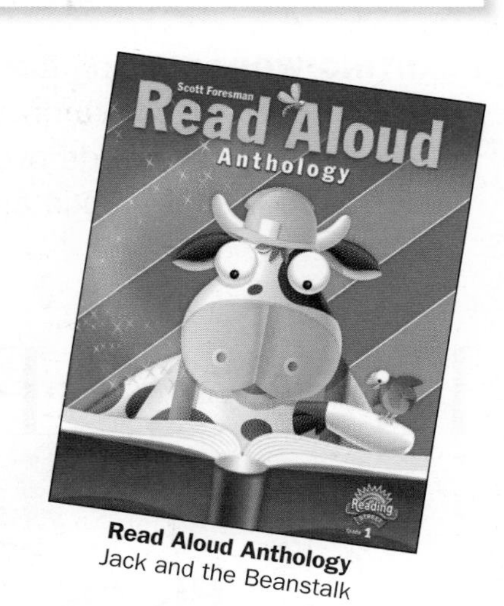

Read Aloud Anthology
Jack and the Beanstalk

BUILD ORAL VOCABULARY Read the first four paragraphs. Discuss what **humongous** plant has grown overnight. Observe that Jack had better be careful. It might be difficult to **destroy**, or kill, a huge plant like this. Ask children to listen to find out what the boy does when he finds the plant.

REVIEW ORAL VOCABULARY After reading, review all the Amazing Words for the week. Have children take turns using them in sentences that tell about the concept for the week. Then talk about the Amazing Words they learned in other weeks and connect them to the concept as well. For example, ask:

- What **tools** would you need to do garden **chores**?
- If you **holler** at the ground, will seeds start to sprout? Explain.
- Do you think flowers grow in moon **craters**? Why or why not?

Phonemic Awareness

ADD INITIAL AND FINAL PHONEMES

- We read a story about a giant beanstalk. Jack cut the beanstalk and tore it down. Listen to the sounds in *tore*.
- Model saying each sound, /t/ /ôr/. Have children say the sounds with you and then say the sounds by themselves.
- Now say each sound as you write the letter that goes with it. Say /t/ /ôr/ as you write *tore.*
- Have children say the sounds as you point to the letters (/t/ /ôr/) and blend the sounds to say the word (*tore).*
- Add *s* to the beginning of *tore.* Listen as I add /s/ to the beginning of *tore*, /s/ /t/ /ôr/, *store.* Have children say the sounds with you. (/s/ /t/ /ôr/)

Continue the activity with these examples.

Listen as I add /k/ to the end of *for.* (*fork*)

Listen as I add /s/ to the beginning of *port.* (*sport*)

OBJECTIVES

- Set purpose for listening.
- Build oral vocabulary.
- Add initial and final phonemes.

	MONITOR PROGRESS
gardener **nature** **sprout** **dim** **shade** **blossom** **destroy** **humongous**	**If...** children lack oral vocabulary experiences about the concept Changes in Nature, **then...** use the Oral Vocabulary Routine. See p. DI•6 to teach *destroy* and *humongous.*

Connect Concepts So that children have a sense of setting, describe the place as they pantomime Jack climbing up and down the beanstalk. Jack is at the giant's castle. Jack is at home.

OBJECTIVES

- Recognize high-frequency words.
- Review ending *-es;* plural *-es* and *r*-controlled *or, -ore.*
- Apply decoding strategies: blend, preview words.

Add -s or **-es** to each verb.
Write the new verb on the line.

1. fix — fixes
2. kiss — kisses
3. run — runs
4. wish — wishes
5. help — helps
6. catch — catches

Add -es to each word.
Write the new word on the line.
Draw a picture of the word.

7. box — boxes
8. Children's artwork should show more than one box.
9. glass — glasses
10. Children's artwork should show more than one drinking glass or eyeglass pair.

School + Home **Home Activity** Your child added -s and -es to verbs and nouns. Look through a catalog or magazine with your child. Take turns naming pictures that show more than one item. Then have your child use the plural word in a sentence.

▲ **Practice Book 1.2** p. 38, Ending *-es;* Plural *-es*

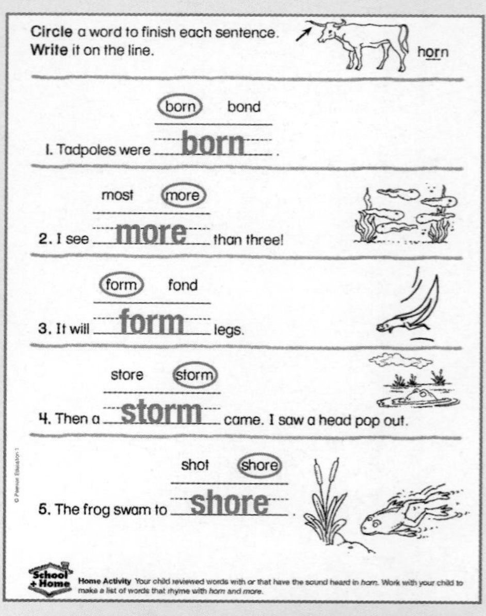
Circle a word to finish each sentence.
Write it on the line.

horn

(born) bond
1. Tadpoles were born.

most (more)
2. I see more than three!

(form) fond
3. It will form legs.

store (storm)
4. Then a storm came. I saw a head pop out.

shot (shore)
5. The frog swam to shore.

School + Home **Home Activity** Your child reviewed words with or that have the sound heard in horn. Work with your child to make a list of words that rhyme with horn and more.

▲ **Practice Book 1.2** p. 39, *r*-Controlled *or, ore*

High-Frequency Words

PRACTICE

PLANTING WORDS Using the Word Wall as a guide, have children use a glue stick to write each high-frequency word on a separate sheet of construction paper. Have them place seeds over the word. Then have children read, spell, and use each word in a sentence as they trace over the seed letters with their fingers. Word Wall

Review Phonics

REVIEW Ending *-es;* Plural *-es; r*-controlled *or, ore*

READ ENDING -es and PLURAL -es WORDS Write *fixes.* Look at this word. You can read this word because you know how to blend the base word and the *-es* ending together. Blend the base word. What is the base word? *(fix)* Blend the base word and the *-es* ending. What's the word? *(fixes)* Write *fox.* Add *-es* to *fox.* Remind children that adding *-es* to a word that names an animal or thing makes it mean "more than one." You can read this word because you know that *-es* stands for the sound /əz/. What sound does this *-es* stand for? (/əz/) What is the word? *(foxes)* What does the word *foxes* mean? (more than one fox)

READ *or, ore* WORDS Write *corn.* You can read this word because you know that the letter *o* followed by *r* stands for the *r*-controlled sound. What's the sound? (/ôr/) What's the word? *(corn)* Do the same for *chore.*

SORT WORDS Write *Words With or, ore* and *Words Without or, ore* as headings. Imagine you have a horn. When I say a word, blow your horn if you hear /ôr/: *torches, mixes, born, rushes, shore, buzzes, sport, tosses.* Write each word in the appropriate column. Have the lists read. Have children identify words with ending *-es* and the plural *-es* word.

Words With *or, ore*	Words Without *or, ore*
torches	mixes
born	rushes
shore	buzzes
sport	tosses

WORD READING

READ DECODABLE AND HIGH-FREQUENCY WORDS Write these words. Encourage children to preview each word before reading it.

school	**their**	**some**	**fixes**	**house**
old	**Mort**	**away**	**our**	**store**
sorts	**very**	**shore**	**Ford**	**drums**
porches	**other**	**horns**	**people**	**friends**

Monitor Progress | **Word Reading**

If... children have difficulty previewing and reading whole words,	**then...** have them use sound-by-sound blending.
If... children can't read the words fluently at a rate of one to two seconds per word,	**then...** have pairs practice the list.

READ WORDS IN CONTEXT Write these sentences. Call on individuals to read a sentence. Then randomly point to the review words and have them read. To help you monitor word reading, high-frequency words are underlined and decodable words are circled.

Ford fixes and sorts the horns and drums.

Their very old house has two porches.

Our friends shopped at the school store.

Mort went away to the shore with some other people.

Monitor Progress | **Word Reading**

If... children are unable to read an underlined word,	**then...** read the word for them and spell it, having them echo you.
If... children have difficulty reading a circled word,	**then...** have them use sound-by-sound blending.

Spiral REVIEW

- Reviews high-frequency words *away, friends, house, old, other, our, people, school, some, their* and *very*.
- Reviews ending *-es;* plural *-es; r*-controlled *or, ore;* and *-s* plurals.

Support Phonics For additional review, see the phonics activities in the ELL and Transition Handbook.

Spelling

PARTNER REVIEW Inflected Ending -*ed*

READ AND WRITE Supply pairs of children with index cards on which the spelling words have been written. Have one child read a word while the other writes it. Then have children switch roles. Have them use the cards to check their spelling.

HOMEWORK Spelling Practice Book, p. 64

OBJECTIVE

- Spell words with inflected ending-*ed*.

Spelling Words

Adding -*ed*

1.	**ask**	6.	**helped**
2.	**asked***	7.	**jog**
3.	**plan**	8.	**jogged**
4.	**planned**	9.	**call**
5.	**help***	10.	**called**

High-Frequency Words

11.	**again***	12.	**soon***

* **Words from the Selection**

Adding -*ed*

Read the base word. **Write** the -*ed* word in the puzzle.

Across
2. help 4. call
5. jog

Down
1. ask
3. plan

Answers: 1. asked 2. helped 3. planned 4. called 5. jogged

Spelling Words: ask, asked, plan, planned, help, helped, jog, jogged, call, called

Circle the word that is spelled correctly.

6. (plan) plann 7. asc (ask)
8. cal (call) 9. (help) halp
10. (jog) joj

School + Home: **Home Activity** Your child has been learning to add -*ed* to base words. Have your child write a list word that ends with -*ed*. Then have your child cross out the ending (-*ed* or consonant + -*ed*) to find the base word.

▲ **Spelling Practice Book** p. 64

Group Time

DAY 4

On-Level	Strategic Intervention	Advanced
Read "Growing Plants."	**Read** SI Decodable Reader 15.	**Read** "Growing Plants."
• Use pp. 114–115.	• Read or listen to "Growing Plants." • Use the **Routine** on p. DI·52.	• Use the **Routine** on p. DI·53.

Place English language learners in the groups that correspond to their reading abilities in English.

Independent Activities

Fluency Reading Pair children to reread *Frog and Toad Together.*

Journal Writing Write to tell what Toad's garden looks like after the plants grow tall. Share writing.

Independent Reading See p. 92j for Reading/Library activities and suggestions

Literacy Centers To provide listening opportunities, you may use the Listening Center on p. 92j. To extend science concepts, you may use the Science Center on p. 92k.

Practice Book 1.2 Ending -*es;* Plural -*es* p. 38 *r*-Controlled *or, ore* p. 39

Break into small groups after Spelling and before Fluency.

Science in Reading

Growing Plants

Do not be afraid to start a garden.
It is not hard. Read how.

1. Plant a few seeds.

2. Let the sun shine on them.

3. Water the seeds again and again.

Soon you will be growing large plants.

114

115

AudioText

Read

Science in Reading

PREVIEW AND PREDICT Read the title. Have children look at the numbered sentences and tell what they think the list will teach them to do. Have children read the directions to learn about how to grow plants. If possible, provide materials and have children follow the directions.

INFORMATIONAL TEXT Review that selections that give information are called non-fiction. Point out that this selection gives information about how to grow plants.

VOCABULARY/USING INFLECTED ENDINGS TO DETERMINE MEANING Review using inflected endings. Ask children to read the first item in the list and tell which word is a verb. (plant) Write *plant* on the board and ask children how to make this verb mean that it happened yesterday. (add *-ed)* Perform this same exercise with *water* from the last item on the list.

OBJECTIVE

- Recognize text structure: nonfiction.

TIME FOR Science

Plants

Plants have different parts. Some of these parts are roots, stems, and flowers. The roots keep the plant in the ground and draw food and water from the soil into the plant. The stems are tall and carry the food and water to the rest of the plant. Many plants also have leaves, flowers, or both.

EXTEND SKILLS

Graphic Sources: Diagram

To help children understand using a diagram, discuss the following:

- How do the pictures numbered *1, 2,* and *3* go with the words on p. 114?
- What do the words on p. 115 tell you? (the names of the parts of the plant)
- How does the picture help you understand the meaning of each word?

Access Content Have children say the names of the parts of a flower in English and in their home language.

BUILD CONCEPTS

Visualize: • Inferential

- **Think about what Step 1 says to do. Now make a picture in your mind of what you would do to plant seeds. Tell us about your picture.**
  Responses will vary, but children should include that they can see digging a hole in the ground or in a pot of soil, dropping seeds in the hole, and covering them with dirt.

Compare and Contrast • Literal

- **How are these instructions like the ones Frog gave Toad?**
  Frog told Toad to plant some seeds in the ground.

CONNECT TEXT TO TEXT

Did Toad follow these steps to grow his garden? What else did Toad do to make his seeds grow?

Yes. Toad lit candles to give light to his seeds, read them a story, sang songs to them, read poems to them, and played music for them.

Fluency

READ WITH EXPRESSION

MODEL READING WITH EXPRESSION Use *Frog and Toad Together.*

- Point out the quotation marks on p. 103. Quotation marks show that a character is talking. I try to read the part in quotation marks the way the character would say it.
- Ask children to follow along as you read the page with expression.
- Have children read the page after you. Encourage them to try to read the way they think Toad would speak. Continue in the same way with p. 104.

REREAD FOR FLUENCY

Choral Reading

ROUTINE

1. **Select a Passage** For "The Garden" from *Frog and Toad Together,* use pp. 105–109.
2. **Divide into Groups** Assign each group a part to read. For this story, assign a page to each of four groups.
3. **Model** Have children track the print as you read.
4. **Read Together** Have children read along with you.
5. **Independent Readings** Have the groups read aloud without you. Monitor progress and provide feedback. For optimal fluency, children should reread three to four times.

Monitor Progress — Check Fluency WCPM

As children reread, monitor their progress toward their individual fluency goals. Current Goal: 25–35 words correct per minute. End-of-Year Goal: 60 words correct per minute.

If... children cannot read fluently at a rate of 25–35 words per minute,

then... make sure children practice with text at their independent level. Provide additional fluency practice, pairing nonfluent readers with fluent readers.

If... children already read at 60 words per minute,

then... they do not need to reread three to four times.

SUCCESS PREDICTOR

Day 1 Check Word Reading	Day 2 Check Word Reading	Day 3 Check High-Frequency Words/Retelling	▶ **Day 4 Check Fluency**	Day 5 Assess Progress

OBJECTIVE

- Read aloud fluently with expression.

Options for Oral Reading

Use *Frog and Toad Together* or one of the following Leveled Readers.

On-Level

A Funny Garden

Strategic Intervention

The Garden

Advanced

The Mile-a-Minute Vine

Use *Dog and Cat and Garden* or *Frog and Toad Together.* Provide opportunities for children to echo read, repeating a passage phrase-by-phrase as each phrase is read by the teacher, aide, or another skilled reader such as a proficient student.

Words Correct Per Minute

SUCCESS PREDICTOR

OBJECTIVE

- Create a list.

Advanced

Encourage children to write a list of plants they might find in a garden.

Home Language Connection
Invite children to find out the names for what a plant needs in order to grow in their home languages. List the names on a multilingual diagram. Resources for home-language words may include parents, bilingual staff members, or bilingual dictionaries.

Writing Across the Curriculum

WRITE List

BRAINSTORM Have children think about how plants grow. What must happen first? What do plants need to grow? Encourage children to use oral vocabulary, such as *sprout, seed,* and *gardener.*

SHARE THE PEN Have children participate in creating a list. To begin, write a vertical list of numbers (1-3) on the board or display Graphic Organizer 34. Explain that the class will work together to write words, phrases, or sentences that tell what must happen before a plant will grow. Have the children copy the list on their own paper. Call on an individual to name the first thing that must happen and have the class repeat it. (A seed must be planted in dirt.) Write the statement, inviting individuals to help spell the words by writing familiar letter-sounds. Ask questions, such as the following

- What is the base word in the word *planted?* *(plant)*
- What is the ending for the word *planted?* (*-ed*)
- What is the final sound you hear in the word *planted?* (/d/)
- What letter stands for that sound? *(d)* Have a volunteer write *d.*

Continue having individuals contribute to the list. Frequently reread the list.

Have children write a sentence at the bottom of their list, answering the question "What does a plant need in order to grow?"

What Does a Plant Need in Order to Grow?
1) A seed must be planted in dirt.
2) A seed needs sunshine or other light.
3) A seed needs rain or other water.

▲ **Graphic Organizer Flip Chart 34**

Grammar

REVIEW Verbs for Now and the Past

DEFINE VERBS FOR NOW AND THE PAST

- How do verbs for now usually end? (*-s*)
- How do verbs for the past usually end? (*-ed*)

PRACTICE

CLASSIFY VERBS FOR NOW AND THE PAST Write *Now* on one end of the board and *Past* on the other end. Provide a stack of index cards, each one with a verb for now or a verb for the past written on it. Have individuals draw cards and then place them under the correct category.

Now	Past
plays	wanted
looks	winked
helps	fixed

OBJECTIVE

- Identify verbs for now and the past.

DAILY FIX-IT

7. They ned sunn.
They need sun.

8. I am hapy when they gro.
I am happy when they grow.

Verbs for Now and the Past

Mark the sentence that is correct.

1. ○ Last year Joe tends a garden.
○ Last year Joe tend a garden.
⊗ Last year Joe tended a garden.

2. ⊗ Now Jan wants a garden.
○ Now Jan wanted a garden.
○ Now Jan want a garden.

3. ○ Last week Beth works in the garden.
⊗ Last week Beth worked in the garden.
○ Last week Beth work in the garden.

4. ⊗ Today Sam helps Beth.
○ Today Sam helped Beth.
○ Today Sam help Beth.

5. ○ Last month Ali pick red roses.
⊗ Last month Ali picked red roses.
○ Last month Ali picks red roses.

6. ○ Now Dan looked for white tulips.
○ Now Dan look for white tulips.
⊗ Now Dan looks for white tulips.

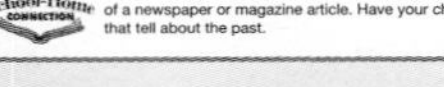

School-Home Connection **Home Activity** Your child prepared for taking tests on verbs for now and the past. Together read part of a newspaper or magazine article. Have your child circle verbs that tell about now and underline verbs that tell about the past.

▲ **Grammar and Writing Practice Book** p. 63

Wrap Up Your Day!

FLUENCY Write *"Drat!" said Toad. "My seeds have not started to grow."* Point out the quotation marks. What do quotation marks mean? (Someone is talking.) Call on individuals to read the sentence with expression, the way that Toad would say it.

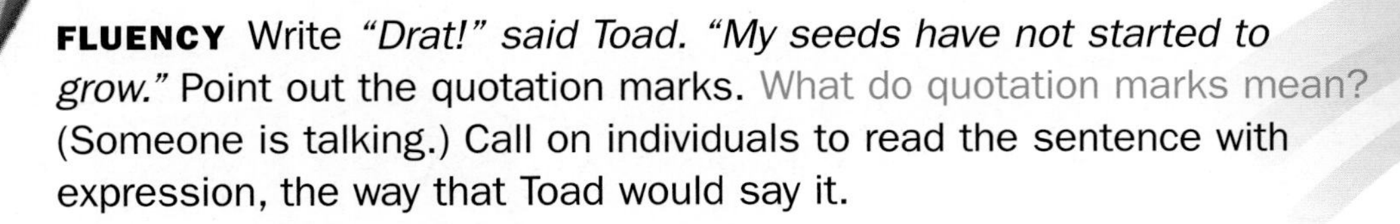

LET'S TALK ABOUT IT After Jack from "Jack and the Beanstalk" plants his seeds, they sprout and grow all the way into the clouds overnight. Do plants really grow this fast? What would real seeds need in order to grow?

PREVIEW Day 5

Remind children that they heard a story about a boy who plants some magic beans. Tell them that tomorrow they will hear about the boy and his magic beans again.

Day 5
AT A GLANCE

Share Literature
"Jack and the Beanstalk"

Phonics and Spelling
Inflected Endings *-ed, -ing,*
r-Controlled *ar*

High-Frequency Words
afraid again few how
read soon

Monitor Progress
Spelling Test: Adding *-ed*

< Differentiated Assessment

Writing and Grammar
Trait: Word Choice
Verbs for Now and the Past

Materials
- *Sing with Me Big Book*
- Read Aloud Anthology
- Reproducible Pages TE 116f–116g
- Student Edition 116–117

Morning Warm-Up!

We have learned how blossoms sprout from seeds. We know that dim light can destroy some plants. What can a gardener do to grow big flowers?

QUESTION OF THE DAY Encourage children to sing "Sprout! It's a Garden" from the *Sing with Me Big Book* as you gather. Write and read the message, tracking the print. Discuss the question.

REVIEW ORAL VOCABULARY Have children find words in the message that

- have meanings that are nearly the same (*blossoms, flowers; grow, sprout*)
- have nearly the same meaning as *huge* and *enormous* (*big*)
- tell what would happen to a garden if it never had any rain (*destroy*)

ELL

Assess Vocabulary Use the Day 5 instruction on ELL Poster 16 to monitor children's progress with oral vocabulary.

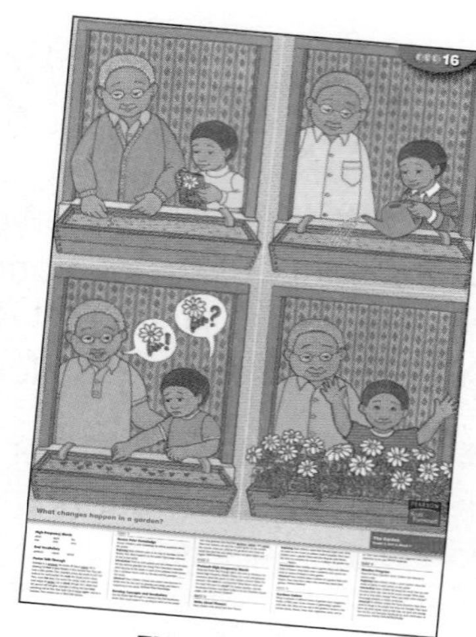
ELL Poster 16

Share Literature

LISTEN AND RESPOND

USE PRIOR KNOWLEDGE Review that yesterday the class listened to find out what Jack did when he found the plant. Suggest that today the class listen to find out what things Jack took from the giant.

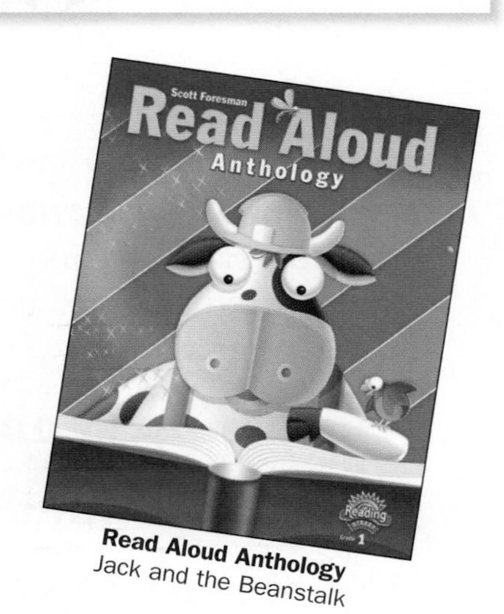

Read Aloud Anthology
Jack and the Beanstalk

MONITOR LISTENING COMPREHENSION

- What did Jack take from the giant? (a goose that laid golden eggs, a bag of gold, and a magic harp)
- Why did Jack take these things? (He found out that the giant had taken them from his family.)
- Why did Jack destroy the beanstalk? (The giant was chasing him.)

BUILD ORAL VOCABULARY

GENERATE DISCUSSION Recall the beans Jack plants. Invite children to share what they know about gardening, being sure to ask if what happened to Jack could ever really happen. Have children use some of this week's Amazing Words as they compare realistic gardening with fantasy gardening.

Monitor Progress Check Oral Vocabulary

Display pp. 92–93 in the Student Edition and remind children of the concept for this week—Changes in Nature. Ask them to tell you about the photographs using some of this week's Amazing Words, *gardener, nature, sprout, dim, shade, blossom, humongous,* and *destroy.*

If... children have difficulty using the Amazing Words,

then... ask questions about the photographs using the Amazing Words. Note which questions children can respond to. Reteach unknown words using the Oral Vocabulary Routine.

Day 1 Check Word Reading	Day 2 Check Word Reading	Day 3 Check High-Frequency Words/Retelling	Day 4 Check Fluency	▶ **Day 5 Check Oral Vocabulary/ Assess Progress**

OBJECTIVES

- Set purpose for listening.
- Build oral vocabulary.

gardener	**shade**
nature	**blossom**
sprout	**destroy**
dim	**humongous**

ELL

Extend Language Have children suggest sentences that tell about something they like to do, using the words *now* and *yesterday.* Point out the use of inflected endings in their examples.

Oral Vocabulary
SUCCESS PREDICTOR

OBJECTIVES

- Review words with inflected endings *-ed, -ing* and *r*-controlled *ar* words.
- Review high-frequency words.

Inflected Endings and *r*-Controlled *ar*

REVIEW

IDENTIFY WORDS WITH ENDINGS *-ed, -ing* AND *ar* WORDS Write these sentences. Have children read each one aloud as you track the print. Call on individuals to name and underline the words with inflected endings *-ed, -ing* and the words with /är/.

Clark tripped on a sharp rock in the yard.

Running around a large park is fun.

We stopped to look at the stars in the dark sky.

The sharks are swimming in deep water.

High-Frequency Words

REVIEW

SAY AND SPELL WORDS Read each rhyme. Ask children to complete each line with one of the Words to Read from p. 94. Have children say, spell, and locate the word on the Word Wall. Then reread the rhymes. Word Wall

_____ lots of books about Frog and Toad. (Read)

Read many, not a _____. (few)

Read them over and over _____. (again)

Each time will seem brand new!

Don't be _____ to plant a seed. (afraid)

_____ will it grow? You know. (How)

Rain, sun, and time, and _____ a plant (soon)

Will start to grow and grow!

Vocabulary For additional practice with the high-frequency words, use the vocabulary strategies and word cards in the ELL and Transition Handbook.

SPELLING TEST Inflected Ending *-ed*

DICTATION SENTENCES Use these sentences to assess this week's spelling words.

1. Gram helped me plant a seed.
2. Call me to come home.
3. Can I ask for a drink?
4. We planned to go last week.
5. I jog with my friends.
6. Pete called his mom.
7. Will you help me with this homework?
8. We jogged to the farm.
9. Who will plan the trip?
10. Jane asked for two new dresses.

HIGH-FREQUENCY WORDS

11. Can we march again?
12. We'll eat soon.

ASSESS

- Spell words with inflected ending *-ed*.

Spelling Words

Adding *-ed*

1. **ask**
2. **asked***
3. **plan**
4. **planned**
5. **help***
6. **helped**
7. **jog**
8. **jogged**
9. **call**
10. **called**

High-Frequency Words

11. **again***
12. **soon***

* **Words from the Selection**

Group Time

On-Level

Read Set B Sentences.

- Use pp. 116e–116g.

Strategic Intervention

Read Set A Sentences and the Story.

- Use pp. 116e–116g.
- Use the **Routine** on p. DI•54.

Advanced

Read Set C Sentences.

- Use pp. 116e–116g.
- Use the **Routine** on p. DI•55.

DAY 5

Place English language learners in the groups that correspond to their reading abilities in English.

Independent Activities

Fluency Reading Children reread selections at their independent level.

Journal Writing Write about how to start a garden. Share writing.

Independent Reading See p. 92j for Reading/Library activities and suggestions.

Literacy Centers You may use the Technology Center on p. 92k to support this week's concepts and reading.

Practice Book 1.2 Diagram, p. 40

Break into small groups after Spelling and before Grammar and Writing.

ASSESS

- Decode inflected endings *-ed, -ing* and *r*-controlled *ar.*
- Read high-frequency words.
- Read aloud with appropriate speed and accuracy.
- Recognize story plot.
- Retell a story.

Differentiated Assessment

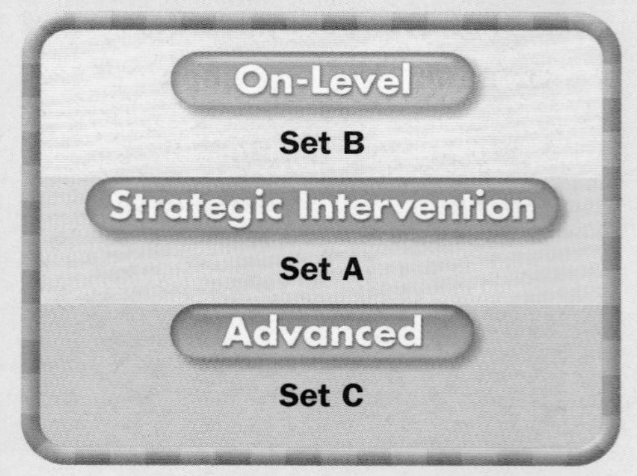

Fluency Assessment Plan

- ☑ Week 1 assess Advanced students.
- ☑ Week 2 assess Strategic Intervention students.
- ☑ Week 3 assess On-Level students.
- ☑ **This week assess Strategic Intervention students.**
- ☐ Week 5 assess any students you have not yet checked during this unit.
- ☐ Week 6 assess Strategic Intervention students.

Set individual fluency goals for children to enable them to reach the end-of-year goal.

- Current Goal: 25–35 wcpm
- End-of-Year Goal: 60 wcpm
- ELL Fluency, particularly for English learners reading texts in English, develops gradually and through much practice. Focus on each child's improvement rather than solely monitoring the number of words correct per minute.

SENTENCE READING

ASSESS INFLECTED ENDINGS *-ed, -ing, r*-CONTROLLED *ar*, AND HIGH-FREQUENCY WORDS Use one of the reproducible lists on p. 116f to assess children's ability to read words with inflected endings *-ed, -ing,* words with *r*-controlled *ar,* and high-frequency words. Call on individuals to read two sentences aloud. Have each child in the group read different sentences. Start over with sentence one if necessary.

RECORD SCORES Use the Sentence Reading Chart for this unit on p. WA19.

Monitor Progress	Inflected Endings *-ed, -ing* and *r*-Controlled *ar*
If... children have trouble reading inflected endings *-ed, -ing* and *r*-controlled *ar,*	**then...** use the Reteach Lessons on pp. DI•80–DI•81.
High-Frequency Words	
If... children cannot read a high-frequency word,	**then...** mark the missed words on a high-frequency word list and send the list home for additional word reading practice or have the child practice with a fluent reader.

FLUENCY AND COMPREHENSION

ASSESS FLUENCY Take a one-minute sample of children's oral reading. See Monitoring Fluency, pp. WA17–WA18. Have children read "Clark and Star," the on-level fluency passage on pp. 116g.

RECORD SCORES Record the number of words read correctly in a minute on the child's Fluency Progress Chart.

ASSESS COMPREHENSION Have the child read to the end of the passage. (If the child had difficulty with the passage, you may read it aloud.) Ask questions about the plot of the story and have the child retell the passage. Use the Retelling Rubric on p. 112–113 to evaluate the child's retelling.

Monitor Progress	Fluency
If... a child does not achieve the fluency goal on the timed reading,	**then...** copy the passage and send it home with the child for additional fluency practice or have the child practice with a fluent reader.
Plot	
If... a child cannot recognize the plot of the story,	**then...** use the Reteach Lesson on p. DI•81.

READ THE SENTENCES

Set A

1. You dropped a few cards.
2. Soon Bill jogged to the barn.
3. How far did Rob get when he stopped?
4. The dog is running in the park again.
5. Meg was getting to be afraid of the dark.
6. It is hard to read sitting in the car.

Set B

1. We soon skipped on the path to the farm.
2. Luke napped as Jack read the paper in the yard.
3. Kim planned to see more than a few stars.
4. Gabe was afraid the glass jar was tipping.
5. How well is Mark hitting the ball when you play?
6. I went shopping for yarn again at the mall.

Set C

1. Clark begged his teacher to read the story again the next day.
2. Soon the dog wagged its tail and started to play with us.
3. Faith grabbed some darts again and began playing another game with Jason.
4. The other fish were afraid of the sharks swimming near them.
5. Mom was knitting, and Mary was playing a few songs on her harp.
6. How long has Maria been clipping charms onto the silver chain?

Clark and Star

Clark had a horse named Star. Clark wanted Star to jump. But Star was afraid. Star liked running but not jumping. 8 17 21

Every day Clark jogged to the barn. He rode Star all morning. Star trotted around the farm. But he did not jump. Clark patted Star's neck and said, "Good boy. Soon you will jump." 30 39 49 55

One day Clark was humming as he ate figs. "Figs! That is it!" he said. 64 70

Clark grabbed a bunch of figs. He went to the barn. Clark put the figs on the other side of a rail. Star was a smart horse. To get the figs, he had to jump. So, up he went. Star got the figs. Clark was happy that Star now jumps. 79 90 101 112 120

See also *Assessment Handbook*, p. 266 • REPRODUCIBLE PAGE

5

Write Now

Read Together

Writing and Grammar

Poem

Prompt

Frog and Toad Together tells about planting seeds to grow flowers in gardens.
Think about things that grow—seeds, flowers, or gardens.
Now write a poem about one of these things.

Writing Trait

Choose words that rhyme for your poem.

Student Model

Poem tells story.

Events are told in time order.

Word choice includes rhyming words.

Jen's Garden

Jen wanted some flowers,
So she planted some seeds.
Two months later, Jen picks
All the flowers she needs!

116

Writer's Checklist

- **Focus** Does the poem tell about one idea?
- **Organization** Are sentences written in poem form?
- **Support** Does the poem have rhyming words?
- **Conventions** Does each line begin with a capital letter?

Grammar

Verbs for Now and the Past

Verbs can tell what happens now. Verbs can tell what happened in the past. Some verbs that tell about the past end with **-ed.**

Toad **plants** seeds. (now)

Toad **planted** seeds. (past)

Look at the poem. Write the verbs that tell about the past in one list. Write the verbs that tell about now in another list.

117

Writing and Grammar

LOOK AT THE PROMPT Read p. 116 aloud. Have children select and discuss key words or phrases in the prompt. *(seeds, flowers, gardens, poem about one of these things)*

STRATEGIES TO DEVELOP WORD CHOICE Have children

- describe pictures of flowers and gardens that you show them using as many exact, vivid words as they can.
- add descriptive words to plain sentences such as these: *The horse ran. The balloon went up.*
- look for places in their poems where they can change vague words to clearer ones *(wiggle* instead of *move).*

See Scoring Rubric on p. WA11. Rubric 4 3 2 1

HINTS FOR BETTER WRITING Read p. 117 aloud. Use the checklist to help children revise their poems. Discuss the grammar lesson. (Answers: *List 1, Past: wanted, planted; List 2, Now: picks, needs*) Have children use verbs for now and the past correctly in their poems.

DAILY FIX-IT

9. he planted the seds. (He; seeds)

10. Jan and I waters the garden (water; garden.)

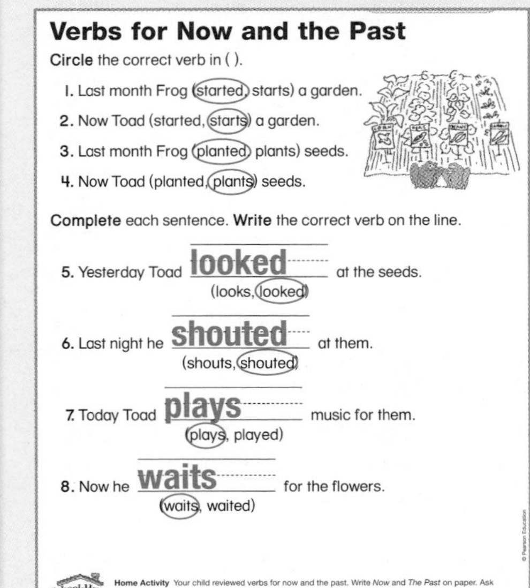

Verbs for Now and the Past

Circle the correct verb in ( ).

1. Last month Frog (started, starts) a garden.
2. Now Toad (started, starts) a garden.
3. Last month Frog (planted, plants) seeds.
4. Now Toad (planted, plants) seeds.

Complete each sentence. Write the correct verb on the line.

5. Yesterday Toad looked at the seeds. (looks, looked)
6. Last night he shouted at them. (shouts, shouted)
7. Today Toad plays music for them. (plays, played)
8. Now he waits for the flowers. (waits, waited)

▲ **Grammar and Writing Practice Book** p. 64

OBJECTIVE

- Answer questions about a diagram or scale drawing.

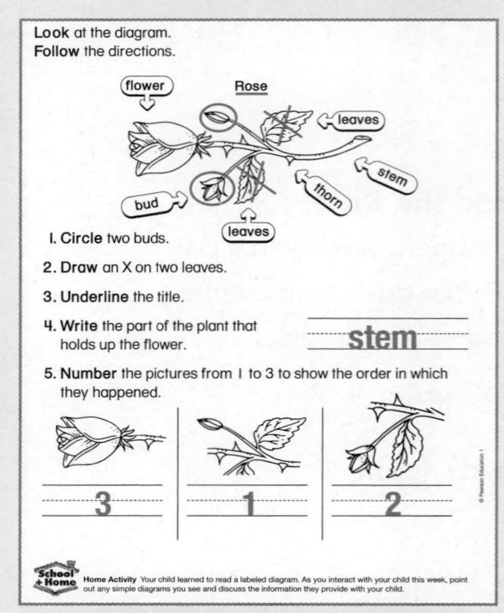
Look at the diagram.
Follow the directions.

1. **Circle** two buds.
2. **Draw** an X on two leaves.
3. **Underline** the title.
4. **Write** the part of the plant that holds up the flower. stem
5. **Number** the pictures from 1 to 3 to show the order in which they happened.

3 | 1 | 2

© Pearson Education 1

School + Home **Home Activity** Your child learned to read a labeled diagram. As you interact with your child this week, point out any simple diagrams you see and discuss the information they provide with your child.

▲ **Practice Book 1.2** p. 40, Diagram

Research/Study Skills

TEACH/MODEL Diagram

MODEL INTERPRETING A DIAGRAM Have children refer to the plant diagram on p. 115 of the Student Edition. Explain that diagrams can show how something is put together. They can also show how an object's parts relate to one another or show how something works. Point out that diagrams often use text, labels, and arrows along with pictures to demonstrate an idea or identify the parts of the object.

MODEL Sometimes diagrams are the best way to show information. It is easy for me to look at this diagram and see what the parts of a plant are. It would be hard for me to understand all of these parts without a picture. I can look at a label, such as the label for the petal, and see just where the petal is located. Now when I look at a real flower, I know what the petal is.

USE A DIAGRAM Ask children questions about the plant diagram on p. 115. Ask volunteers to find different parts of the plant and tell where they are located. For example, identify a petal as part of the flower.

PRACTICE

INTERPRET DIAGRAMS Find examples of diagrams in other textbooks. Ask children to identify the purpose of the diagrams and explain what the labels show.

Access Content As you discuss the plant diagram with children, show how to interpret the labels. For example: This part of the plant is the roots. The diagram shows that the roots are under the ground.

Wrap Up Your Week!

LET'S TALK ABOUT Changes in Nature

QUESTION OF THE WEEK Recall this week's question.

- What changes happen in a garden?

Display and review the Seed to Plant Chart from Day 1. Then discuss what changes children observe in a plant after it begins to grow. Little buds appear; the buds open into flowers; the petals fall off; the plant makes seeds.

Step 1
Plant little seeds and cover them with soil.

↓

Step 2
A baby plant starts to grow. It gets leaves.

↓

Step 3
Flowers bloom.

CONNECT Use questions such as these to prompt a discussion.

- What comes after a seed: a sprout, or a blossom?
- Would a gardener plant a garden in the shade? Why not?
- How do you like to spend time in nature?

ELL

Build Background Use ELL Poster 17 to support the Preview activity.

You've learned

this week!

You've learned

so far this year!

PREVIEW Tell children that next week they will read about changes that happen to insects.

PREVIEW Next Week

Assessment Checkpoints for the Week

Selection Assessment

Use pp. 37–40 of Selection Tests to check:

 **Selection Understanding**

 **Comprehension Skill** *Plot*

 **High-Frequency Words**

afraid *read*
again *soon*
few
how

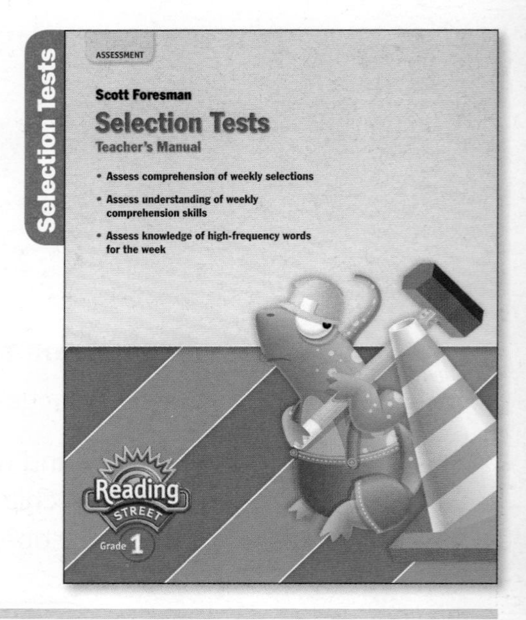

Leveled Assessment

On-Level
Strategic Intervention
Advanced

Use pp. 91–96 of Fresh Reads for Differentiated Test Practice to check:

 **Comprehension Skill** *Plot*

 REVIEW **Comprehension Skill** *Compare and Contrast*

 **Fluency** *Words Correct Per Minute*

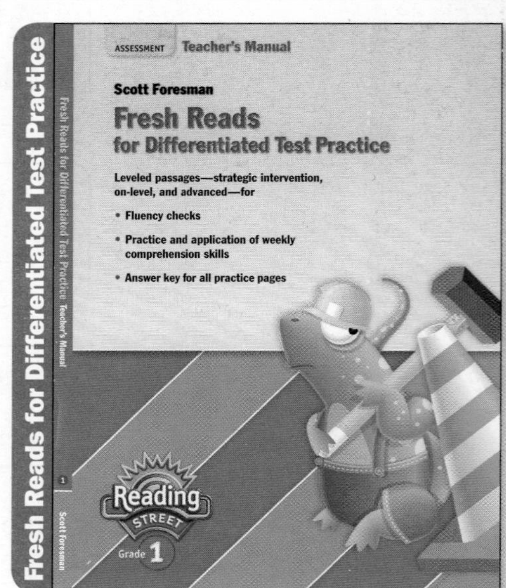

Managing Assessment

Use Assessment Handbook for:

 **Weekly Assessment Blackline Masters for Monitoring Progress**

 **Observation Checklists**

 **Record-Keeping Forms**

 **Portfolio Assessment**

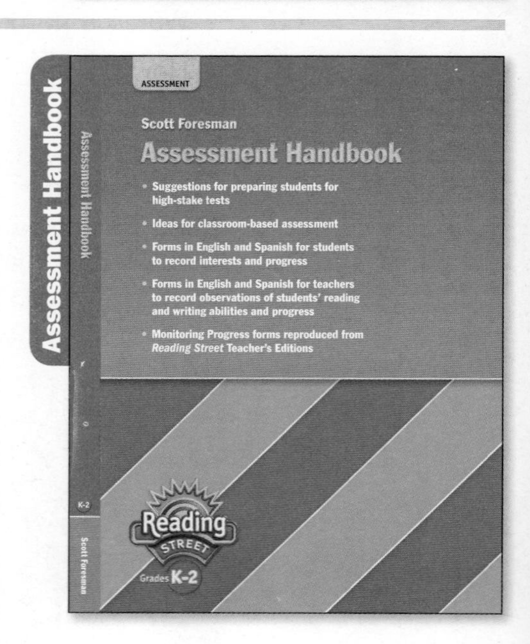

I'm a Caterpillar

I'm a Caterpillar

Unit 3
Changes

CONCEPT QUESTION
What is changing in our world?

Growing and Changing

Week 1
How do we change as we grow?

Week 2
What do we learn as we grow and change?

Week 3
Why are changes exciting?

Changes in Nature

Week 4
What changes happen in a garden?

Week 5
What changes can we observe in nature?

Week 6
How does nature change during the year?

Week 5

EXPAND THE CONCEPT
What changes can we observe in nature?

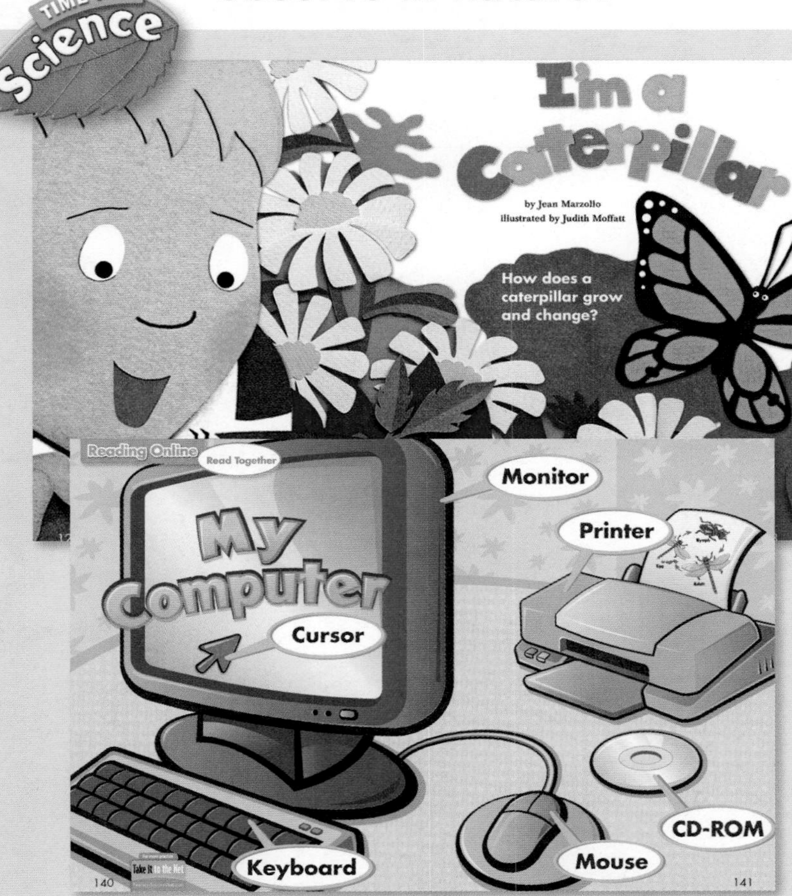

CONNECT THE CONCEPT

▶ **Build Background**

cycle	*fragile*	*vessel*
develop	*insect*	*yearly*
emerge	*rearrange*	

▶ **Social Studies Content**
Life Cycles, Adaptations

▶ **Writing**
Facts

Preview Your Week

What changes can we observe in nature?

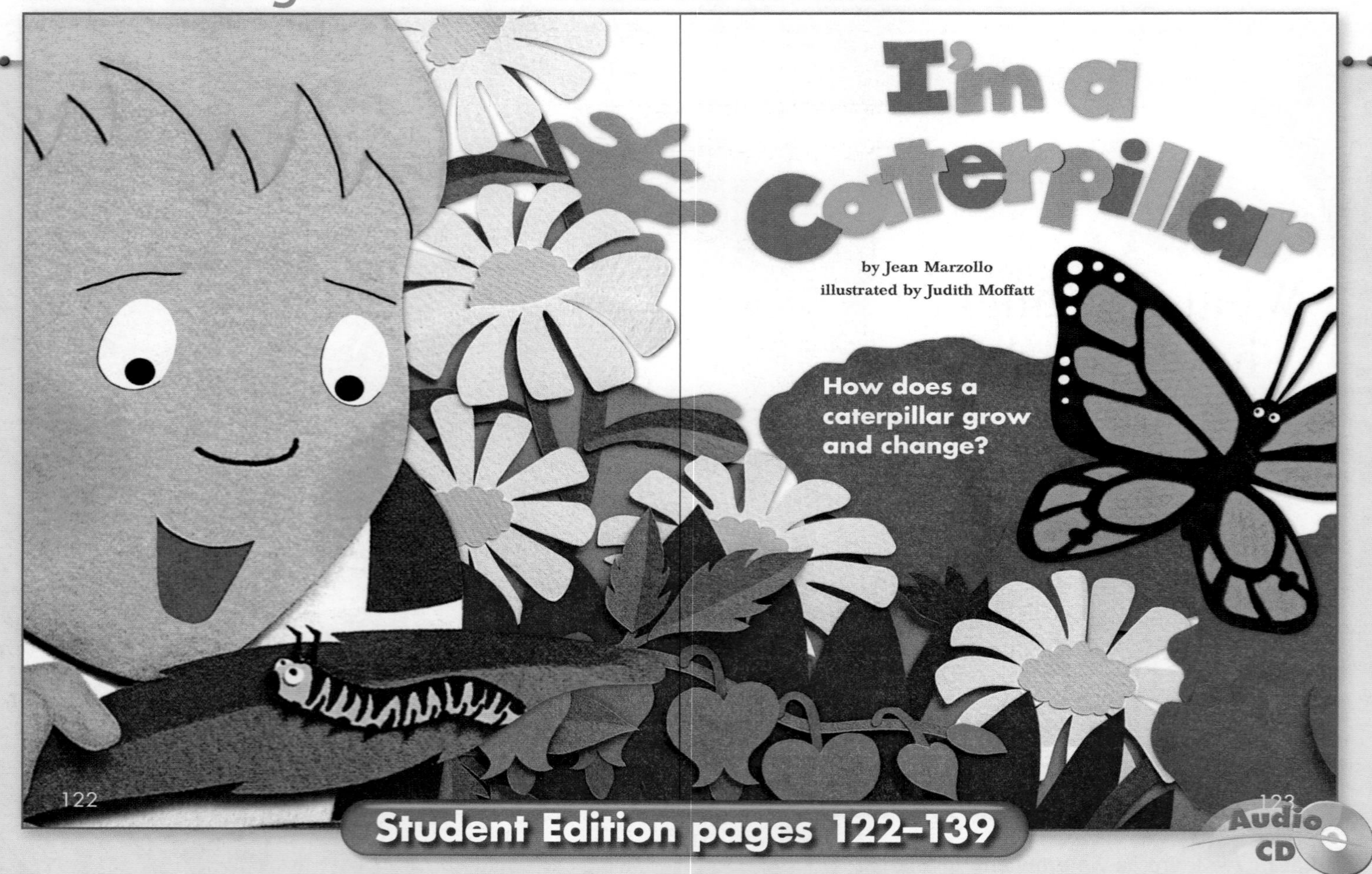

Genre Narrative Nonfiction

Phonics *r*-Controlled *er, ir, ur* and Contractions *'s, 've, 're*

Comprehension Skill Draw Conclusions

Comprehension Strategy Text Structure

Paired Selection

Reading Across Texts
Learning About Butterflies

Genre
Reading Online

Text Features
Captions

- Student Edition
- Leveled Readers
- Decodable Readers

Leveled Readers

Skill Draw Conclusions

Strategy Text Structure

Lesson Vocabulary

Below-Level

On-Level

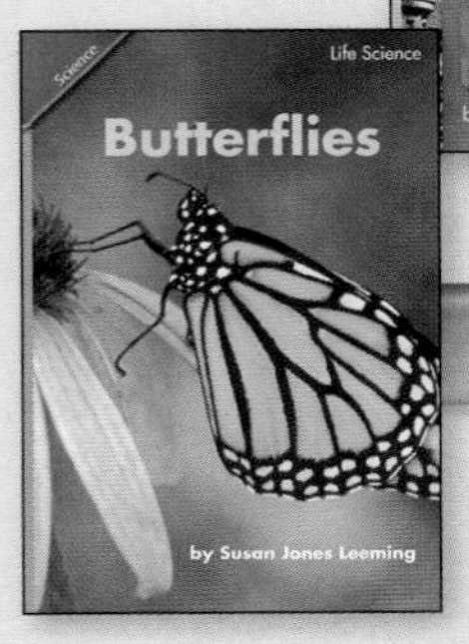

Advanced

ELL Reader

- Concept Vocabulary
- Text Support
- Language Enrichment

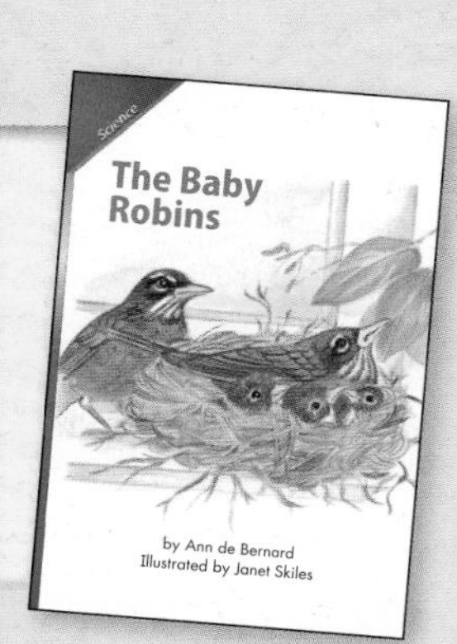

Decodable Readers

Apply Phonics

- *A Big Day for Mom*
- *Sam Can Fly!*

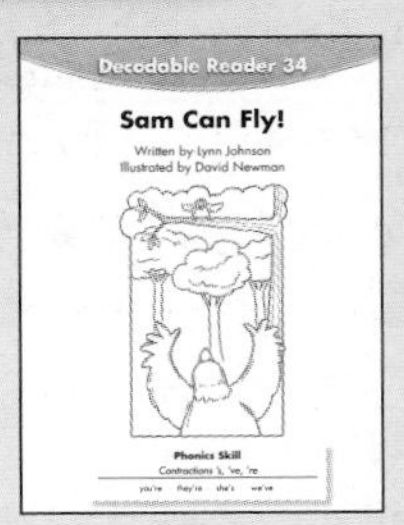

TIME FOR Science

Integrate Science Standards

- Life Cycles
- Adaptations

I'm a Caterpillar, pp. 122–139

"My Computer," pp. 140–141

Leveled Readers

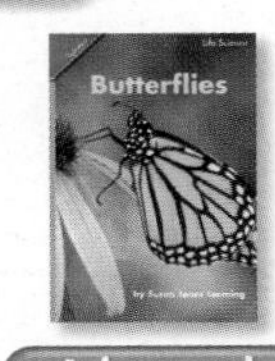

Below-Level	On-Level	Advanced
• Support Concepts	• Develop Concepts	• Extend Concepts • Science Extension Activity

ELL Reader

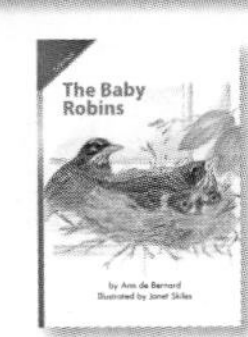

Build **Concept Vocabulary**
Changes in Nature, pp. 118r–119

Teach **Science Concepts**
Adaptations, p. 134–135
Life Cycles, p. 136–137

Explore **Science Center**
Identify Sequence, p. 118k

Weekly Plan

READING

90–120 minutes

TARGET SKILLS OF THE WEEK

Phonics
r-Controlled *er, ir, ur* and Contractions *'s, 've, 're*

Comprehension Skill
Draw Conclusions

Comprehension Strategy
Text Structure

LANGUAGE ARTS

20–30 minutes

Trait of the Week

Focus/Ideas

DAILY JOURNAL WRITING

DAILY SCIENCE CONNECTIONS

DAY 1 PAGES 118l–119d

Oral Language

QUESTION OF THE WEEK, 118l
What changes can we observe in nature?

Oral Vocabulary/Share Literature, 118m
Sing with Me Big Book, Song 17
Amazing Words *cycle, develop, insect*

Word Work

Phonemic Awareness, 118m
Blend and Segment Onset/Rime

Phonics, 118n–118o
Introduce *r*-Controlled *er, ir, ur* **T**

Spelling, 118p
Pretest

Comprehension/Vocabulary/Fluency

Read Decodable Reader 33

Grouping Options 118f–118g

Review High-Frequency Words
Check Comprehension
Reread for Fluency

Build Background, 118r–119
Changes in Nature

Listening Comprehension, 119a–119b
Draw Conclusions **T**

Shared Writing, 119c
Facts

Grammar, 119d
Introduce *Am, Is, Are, Was,* and *Were* **T**

Day 1 *Write to tell how a pet you know changed as it grew.*

Day 1 Cycle Chart, 118r–119

DAY 2 PAGES 120a–121c

Oral Language

QUESTION OF THE DAY, 120a
What season are we in?

Oral Vocabulary/Share Literature, 120b
Big Book *What Makes the Seasons?*
Amazing Words *rearrange, yearly*

Word Work

Phonemic Awareness, 120b
Delete Final Phonemes

Phonics, 120c–120d
Introduce Contractions *'s, 've, 're* **T**

Spelling, 120e
Dictation

Comprehension/Vocabulary/Fluency

Read Decodable Reader 34

Grouping Options 118f–118g

Review High-Frequency Words
Check Comprehension
Reread for Fluency

High-Frequency Words, 120–121
Introduce *done, know, push, visit, wait* **T**

Interactive Writing, 121a
Description

Grammar, 121b
Practice *Am, Is, Are, Was,* and *Were* **T**

Speaking and Listening, 121c
Summarize Information

Day 2 *Write about how an egg changes.*

Day 2 Cycle Chart, 121c

DAILY SUCCESS PREDICTORS for Adequate Yearly Progress

Monitor Progress and Corrective Feedback

Phonics — Check Word Reading, *118o*
Spiral **REVIEW** Phonics

Phonics — Check Word Reading, *120d*
Spiral **REVIEW** Phonics

RESOURCES FOR THE WEEK

- Practice Book 1.2, *pp. 41–50*
- Phonics and Spelling Practice Book, *pp. 65–68*
- Grammar and Writing Practice Book, *pp. 65–68*
- Selection Test, *pp. 41–44*
- Fresh Reads for Differentiated Test Practice, *pp. 97–102*
- Phonics Songs and Rhymes Chart 17
- The Grammar and Writing Book, *pp. 146–151*

Grouping Options for Differentiated Instruction

Turn the page for the small group lesson plan.

DAY 3 PAGES 122a–139d

Oral Language

QUESTION OF THE DAY, 122a
What changes might a caterpillar make?

Oral Vocabulary/Share Literature, 122b
Big Book *What Makes the Seasons?*
Amazing Words *rearrange, yearly*

Word Work

Phonemic Awareness, 122b
Blend and Segment Onset/Rime

Phonics, 122c–122d
r-Controlled *er, ir, ur* and Contractions *'s, 've, 're* **T**

Spelling, 122d
Practice

Comprehension/Vocabulary/Fluency

Read *I'm a Caterpillar,* 122e–139

Grouping Options 118f–118g

Introduce Selection Words
caterpillar, chrysalis, crawl, pupa, shiver

Review High-Frequency Words
done, know, push, visit, wait **T**

Draw Conclusions **T**
Text Structure
REVIEW Sequence **T**

Fluency, 139a
Attend to End Punctuation

Vocabulary, 139b
Use Reference Sources

Trait of the Week, 139c
Introduce Focus/Ideas

Grammar, 139d
Write with *Am, Is, Are, Was,* and *Were* **T**

Day 3 *Make a list of the things you would like to know about a butterfly.*

Day 3 Time for Science: Adaptations, 134–135; Life Cycles, 136–137

DAY 4 PAGES 140a–141d

Oral Language

QUESTION OF THE DAY, 140a
How can a computer help us learn?

Oral Vocabulary/Share Literature, 140b
Read Aloud Anthology "Song of the Cicada"
Amazing Words *emerge, fragile, vessel*

Word Work

Phonemic Awareness, 140b
Substitute Phonemes

High-Frequency Words, 140c
Practice *done, know, push, visit, wait* **T**

Phonics, 140c–140d
REVIEW Inflected Endings *-ed, -ing; r*-Controlled *ar* **T**
REVIEW Word Reading **T**

Spelling, 140e
Partner Review

Comprehension/Vocabulary/Fluency

Read "My Computer," 140–141
Leveled Readers

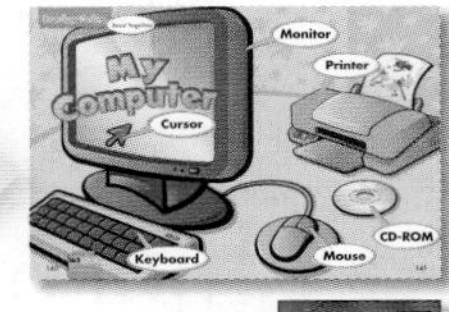

Grouping Options 118f–118g

Use Reference Sources
Reading Across Texts

Fluency, 141b
Attend to End Punctuation

Writing Across the Curriculum, 141c
Cycle Chart

Grammar, 141d
Review *Am, Is, Are, Was,* and *Were* **T**

Day 4 *Write another title for* I'm a Caterpillar.

Day 4 Science Center: Watch Me Grow, 118k

DAY 5 PAGES 142a–143b

Oral Language

QUESTION OF THE DAY, 142a
How do insects change and grow?

Oral Vocabulary/Share Literature, 142b
Read Aloud Anthology "Song of the Cicada"
Amazing Words Review

Word Work

Phonics, 142c
Review *r*-Controlled *er, ir, ur* and Contractions *'s, 've, 're* **T**

High-Frequency Words, 142c
Review *done, know, push, visit, wait* **T**

Spelling, 142d
Test

Comprehension/Vocabulary/Fluency

Read Leveled Readers

Grouping Options 118f–118g

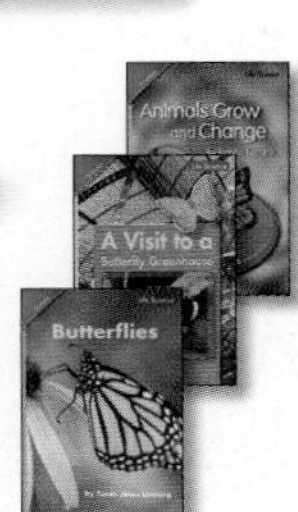

Monitor Progress, 142e–142g
Read the Sentences
Read the Story

Writing and Grammar, 142-143
Develop Focus/Ideas
Use *Am, Is, Are, Was,* and *Were* **T**

Research/Study Skills, 143a
Technology: My Computer

Day 5 *List ways you use a computer.*

Day 5 Revisit the Cycle Chart, 143b

KEY ◎ = Target Skill **T** = Tested Skill

SUCCESS PREDICTOR

Fluency and Comprehension
Check High-Frequency Words, *122f*
Check Retelling, *138a*
Spiral **REVIEW** High-Frequency Words

Fluency
Check Fluency WCPM, *141b*
Spiral **REVIEW** Phonics, High-Frequency Words

Oral Vocabulary
Check Oral Vocabulary, *142b*
Assess Phonics, High-Frequency Words, Fluency, Comprehension, *142e*

Small Group Plan *for Differentiated Instruction*

Daily Plan AT A GLANCE

Reading

Whole Group
- Oral Language
- Word Work
- Comprehension/Vocabulary

Group Time

Meet with small groups to provide:
- Skill Support
- Reading Support
- Fluency Practice

Read

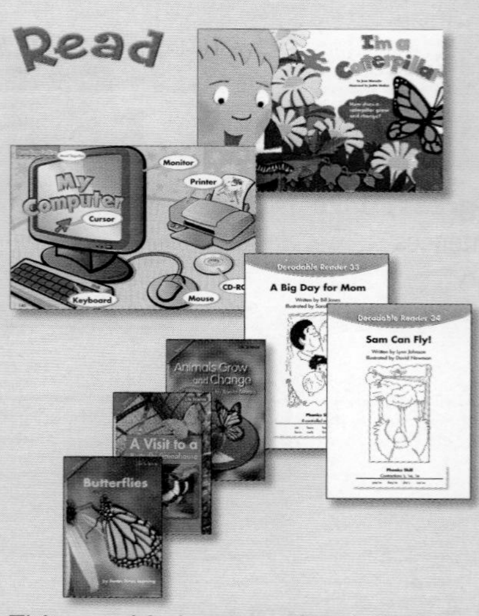

This week's lessons for daily group time can be found behind the Differentiated Instruction (DI) tab on pp. DI·56–DI·65.

Whole Group
- Comprehension/Vocabulary
- Fluency

Language Arts
- Writing
- Grammar
- Speaking/Listening/Viewing
- Research/Study Skills

Use *My Sidewalks on Reading Street* for Tier III intensive reading intervention.

DAY 1

On-Level	Strategic Intervention	Advanced
Teacher-Led *Page 118q*	Teacher-Led *Page DI·56*	Teacher-Led *Page DI·57*
• **Read** Decodable Reader 33 • **Reread** for Fluency	• Blend and Build Words with *r*-controlled *er, ir, ur* • **Read** Decodable Reader 33 • **Reread** for Fluency	• Extend Word Reading • **Read** Advanced Selection 17 • Introduce Concept Inquiry

Independent Activities

While you meet with small groups, have the rest of the class...

- Reread for fluency
- Write in their journals
- Complete Practice Book 1.2, p. 43
- Visit the Word Work Center

DAY 2

On-Level	Strategic Intervention	Advanced
Teacher-Led *Page 120f*	Teacher-Led *Page DI·58*	Teacher-Led *Page DI·59*
• **Read** Decodable Reader 34 • **Reread** for Fluency	• Blend and Build Words with Contractions *'s, 've, 're* • **Read** Decodable Reader 34 • **Reread** for Fluency	• Extend Word Reading • **Read** Self-Selected Reading • Continue Concept Inquiry

Independent Activities

While you meet with small groups, have the rest of the class...

- Reread for fluency
- Write in their journals
- Complete Practice Book 1.2, pp. 44–46
- Visit the Word Work Center
- Work on inquiry projects

DAY 3

On-Level	Strategic Intervention	Advanced
Teacher-Led *Pages 122–139*	Teacher-Led *Page DI·60*	Teacher-Led *Page DI·61*
• **Read** *I'm a Caterpillar*	• Blend and Read Words with *r*-controlled *er, ir, ur; 's, 've, 're* • **Read** SI Decodable Reader 17 • **Read** or Listen to *I'm a Caterpillar*	• **Read** *I'm a Caterpillar* • Continue Concept Inquiry

Independent Activities

While you meet with small groups, have the rest of the class...

- Read self-selected reading
- Write in their journals
- Complete Practice Book 1.2, p. 47
- Visit the Listening and Writing Centers
- Work on inquiry projects

① Begin with whole class skill and strategy instruction.

② Meet with small groups to provide differentiated instruction.

③ Gather the whole class back together for fluency and language arts.

DAY 4

On-Level	Strategic Intervention	Advanced
Teacher-Led *Pages 140–141, LR40–LR42*	**Teacher-Led** *Pages DI • 62, LR37–LR39*	**Teacher-Led** *Pages DI • 63, LR43–LR45*
• **Read** "My Computer" • Practice with On-Level Reader *A Visit to a Butterfly Greenhouse*	• Blend and Read Words • **Reread** SI Decodable Reader 16 • **Read** or Listen to "My Computer" • Practice with Below-Level Reader *Animals Grow and Change*	• **Read** "My Computer" • Expand Vocabulary • Continue Concept Inquiry • Practice with Advanced Reader *Butterflies*

ⓘ Independent Activities

While you meet with small groups, have the rest of the class...

- Reread for fluency
- Write in their journals
- Read self-selected reading
- Complete Practice Book 1.2, pp. 48–49
- Visit the Listening and Science Centers
- Work on inquiry projects

DAY 5

On-Level	Strategic Intervention	Advanced
Teacher-Led *Pages 142e–142g, LR40–LR42*	**Teacher-Led** *Pages DI • 64, LR37–LR39*	**Teacher-Led** *Pages DI • 65, LR43–LR45*
• Sentence Reading, Set B • Monitor Fluency and Comprehension • Practice with On-Level Reader *A Visit to a Butterfly Greenhouse*	• Practice Word Reading • Sentence Reading, Set A • Monitor Fluency and Comprehension • Practice with Below-Level Reader *Animals Grow and Change*	• Sentence Reading, Set C • Monitor Fluency and Comprehension • Share Concept Inquiry • Practice with Advanced Reader *Butterflies*

ⓘ Independent Activities

While you meet with small groups, have the rest of the class...

- Reread for fluency
- Write in their journals
- Read self-selected reading
- Complete Practice Book 1.2, p. 50
- Visit the Technology Center

ELL

Grouping Place English language learners in the groups that correspond to their reading abilities in English.

Use the appropriate Leveled Reader or other text at children's instructional level.

TIP Send home the appropriate Multilingual Summary of the main selection on Day 1.

Take It to the NET™ ONLINE
PearsonSuccessNet.com

Connie Juel
For ideas on phonics for strategic intervention, see the article "Learning to Read Words" by Scott Foresman author C. Juel and C. Minden-Cupp.

TEACHER TALK

Choral reading is reading aloud together as a group. **Echo reading** is reading aloud phrase-by-phrase slightly after a live or taped model.

Looking Ahead

Be sure to schedule time for children to work on the unit inquiry project "Take a Closer Look." This week children should observe, measure, and record their observations for the last time. Children comment in their journals on the changes they have observed.

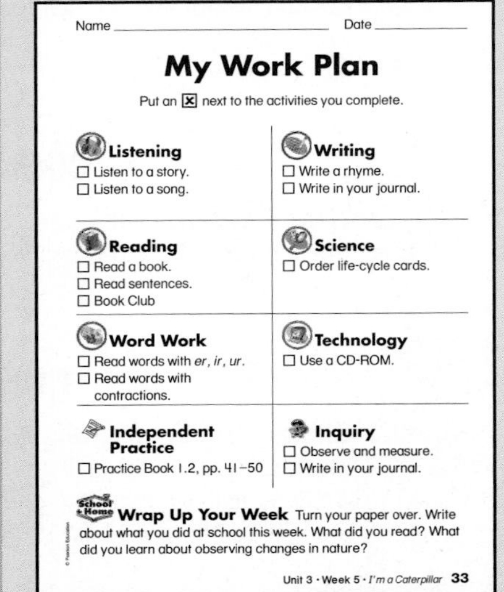

Name ______________ Date ________

My Work Plan

Put an ☒ next to the activities you complete.

Listening ☐ Listen to a story. ☐ Listen to a song.	**Writing** ☐ Write a rhyme. ☐ Write in your journal.
Reading ☐ Read a book. ☐ Read sentences. ☐ Book Club	**Science** ☐ Order life-cycle cards.
Word Work ☐ Read words with *er, ir, ur*. ☐ Read words with contractions.	**Technology** ☐ Use a CD-ROM.
Independent Practice ☐ Practice Book 1.2, pp. 41–50	**Inquiry** ☐ Observe and measure. ☐ Write in your journal.

Wrap Up Your Week Turn your paper over. Write about what you did at school this week. What did you read? What did you learn about observing changes in nature?

Unit 3 • Week 5 • *I'm a Caterpillar* 33

▲ **Group-Time Survival Guide** p. 33, Weekly Contract

Customize Your Plan *by Strand*

ORAL LANGUAGE

Concept Development

What changes can we observe in nature?

cycle	*develop*	*insect*
rearrange	*yearly*	*fragile*
emerge	*vessel*	

BUILD

❑ **Question of the Week** Use the Morning Warm-Up! to introduce and discuss the question of the week. This week children will talk, sing, read, and write about changes in nature. DAY 1 *118l*

❑ **Sing with Me Big Book** Sing a song about a caterpillar. Ask children to listen for the concept-related Amazing Words *cycle, develop, insect.* DAY 1 *118m*

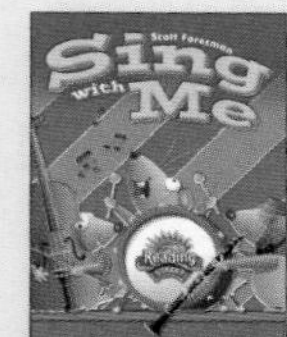

Sing with Me Big Book

❑ **Let's Talk About Changes in Nature** Use the Let's Talk About It lesson in the Student Edition to build background, vocabulary, and concepts. Then create a concept chart for children to add to throughout the week. DAY 1 *118r-119*

Let's Talk About It

DEVELOP

❑ **Question of the Day** Use the questions in the Morning Warm-Ups! to discuss lesson concepts and how they relate to the unit theme, Changes. DAY 2 *120a*, DAY 3 *122a*, DAY 4 *140a*, DAY 5 *142a*

❑ **Share Literature** Read big books and read aloud selections that develop concepts, language, and vocabulary related to the lesson concept and the unit theme. Continue to develop this week's Amazing Words. DAY 2 *120b*, DAY 3 *122b*, DAY 4 *140b*, DAY 5 *142b*

CONNECT

❑ **Wrap Up Your Week!** Revisit the Question of the Week. Then connect concepts and vocabulary to next week's lesson. DAY 5 *143b*

CHECK

❑ **Check Oral Vocabulary** To informally assess children's oral vocabulary, ask individuals to use some of this week's Amazing Words to tell you about the photographs and illustration on Student Edition pp. 118-119. DAY 5 *142b*

PHONEMIC AWARENESS AND PHONICS

R-CONTROLLED *ER, IR, UR* A single vowel followed by the letter *r* has a sound that is neither short nor long, but *r*-controlled.

CONTRACTIONS *'S, 'VE, 'RE* A contraction is a shortened form of two words. An apostrophe appears where letters have been dropped.

TEACH

❑ **Blend and Segment Onset/Rime** Practice segmenting and blending phonemes. DAY 1 *118m*

❑ ***r*-Controlled *er, ir, ur*** Introduce the blending strategy for words with *r*-controlled *er, ir, ur*. Have children blend and sort words. DAY 1 *118n-118o*

❑ **Delete Final Phonemes** Practice deleting the final phoneme in one-syllable words. DAY 2 *120b*

❑ **Contractions *'s, 've, 're*** Introduce the blending strategy for words with contractions *'s, 've, 're*. Then have children blend and sort contractions. DAY 2 *120c-120d*

❑ **Fluent Word Reading** Use the Fluent Word Reading Routine to develop children's word reading fluency. Use the Phonics Songs and Rhymes Chart for additional word reading practice. DAY 3 *122c-122d*

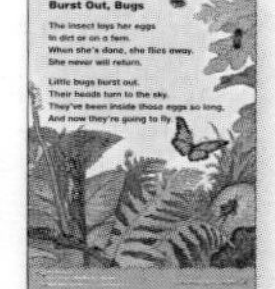
Phonics Songs and Rhymes Chart 17

PRACTICE/APPLY

❑ **Decodable Reader 33** Practice reading words with *r*-controlled *er, ir, ur* in context. DAY 1 *118q*

❑ **Decodable Reader 34** Practice reading words with contractions *'s, 've, 're* in context. DAY 2 *120f*

Decodable Readers 33 and 34

❑ ***I'm a Caterpillar*** Practice decoding words in context. DAY 3 *122-137*

❑ **Homework** Practice Book 1.2 pp. 43, 45. DAY 1 *118o*, DAY 2 *120d*

❑ **Word Work Center** Practice *r*-controlled *er, ir, ur* and contractions *'s, 've, 're*. ANY DAY *118j*

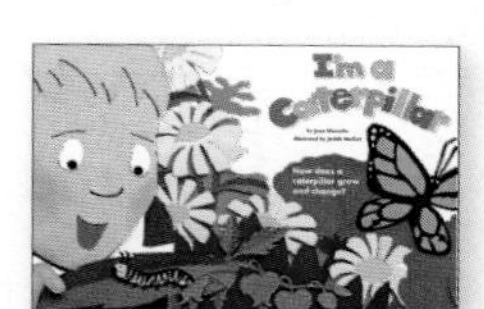

Main Selection—Nonfiction

RETEACH/REVIEW

❑ **Review** Review words with this week's phonics skills. DAY 5 *142c*

❑ **Reteach Lessons** If necessary, reteach *r*-controlled *er, ir, ur* and contractions *'s, 've, 're*. DAY 5 *DI-82*

❑ **Spiral REVIEW** Review previously taught phonics skills. DAY 1 *118o*, DAY 2 *120d*, DAY 4 *140c-140d*

ASSESS

❑ **Sentence Reading** Assess children's ability to read words with *r*-controlled *er, ir, ur* and contractions *'s, 've, 're*. DAY 5 *142e-142f*

1 Use assessment data to determine your instructional focus.

2 Preview this week's instruction by strand.

3 Choose instructional activities that meet the needs of your classroom.

SPELLING

R*-CONTROLLED *ER, IR, UR A single vowel followed by the letter *r* has a sound that is neither short nor long, but *r*-controlled.

TEACH

- ❑ **Pretest** Before administering the pretest, model how to segment words with *r*-controlled *er, ir,* and *ur* to spell them. Dictate the spelling words, segmenting them if necessary. Then have children check their pretests and correct misspelled words. DAY 1 *118p*

PRACTICE/APPLY

- ❑ **Dictation** Have children write dictation sentences to practice spelling words. DAY 2 *120e*
- ❑ **Write Words** Have children practice writing the spelling words by using self-stick notes to cover *er, ir,* and *ur* in the words. DAY 3 *122d*
- ❑ **Homework** Phonics and Spelling Practice Book pp. 65-68. DAY 1 *118p,* DAY 2 *120e,* DAY 3 *122d,* DAY 4 *140e*

RETEACH/REVIEW

- ❑ **Partner Review** Have pairs work together to read and write the spelling words. DAY 4 *140e*

ASSESS

- ❑ **Posttest** Use dictation sentences to give the posttest for words with *r*-controlled *er, ir, ur.* DAY 5 *142d*

Spelling Words

Words with *er, ir, ur*

1. her	6. were
2. first	7. shirt
3. bird*	8. fur
4. girl	9. hurt
5. burn	10. sir

High-Frequency Words

11. visit*	12. done*

* Words from the Selection

HIGH-FREQUENCY WORDS

WORDS TO READ
done *know* *push* *visit* *wait*

TEACH

- ❑ **Words to Read** Introduce this week's high-frequency words and add them to the Word Wall. DAY 2 *120-121*

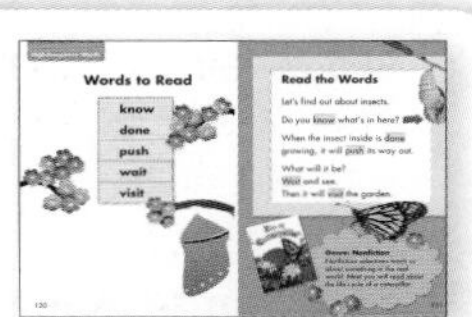
High-Frequency Words

PRACTICE/APPLY

- ❑ **Vocabulary Transparency 17** Review this week's high-frequency words, or Words to Read, before reading *I'm a Caterpillar.* DAY 3 *122f*
- ❑ **Words in Context** Read high-frequency words in the context of *I'm a Caterpillar.* DAY 3 *122-137*

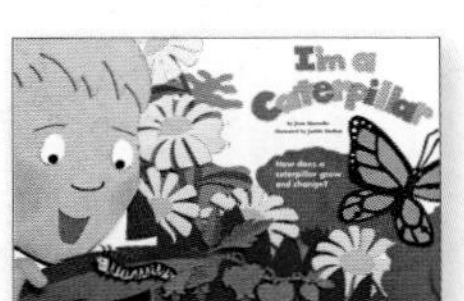
Main Selection—Nonfiction

- ❑ **Word Wall** Use the Word Wall to review and practice high-frequency words throughout the week. DAY 4 *140c,* DAY 5 *142c*

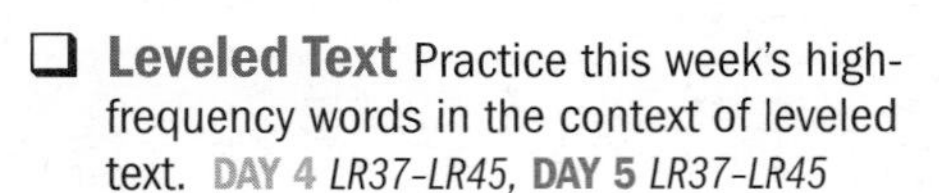

- ❑ **Leveled Text** Practice this week's high-frequency words in the context of leveled text. DAY 4 *LR37–LR45,* DAY 5 *LR37–LR45*

Leveled Readers

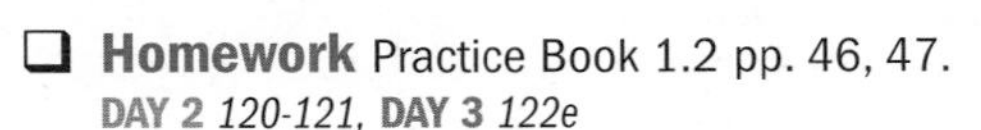

- ❑ **Homework** Practice Book 1.2 pp. 46, 47. DAY 2 *120-121,* DAY 3 *122e*

RETEACH/REVIEW

- ❑ **Spiral REVIEW** Review previously taught high-frequency words. DAY 3 *122f,* DAY 4 *140d*

ASSESS

- ❑ **Sentence Reading** Assess children's ability to read this week's high-frequency words. DAY 5 *142e–142f*

VOCABULARY

TEACH

- ❑ **Vocabulary Transparency 17** Use Vocabulary Transparency 17 to introduce the selection words from *I'm a Caterpillar.* Children will read these words but will not be tested on them. DAY 3 *122f*
- ❑ **Use Reference Sources** Discuss using a dictionary to find the meanings of words. DAY 3 *139b*

Customize Your Plan *by Strand*

COMPREHENSION

SKILL DRAW CONCLUSIONS To draw conclusions, use clues in the words and pictures to figure out something that is not written in a story.

STRATEGY TEXT STRUCTURE Text structure puts things that happen in a certain order, called sequence.

TEACH

- ❑ **Listening Comprehension** Read "The Nest on Josh's Back Porch" and model how to *draw conclusions*. DAY 1 *119a–119b*
- ❑ **Skill/Strategy Lesson** Review draw conclusions. Then introduce this week's strategy, *text structure*. DAY 3 *122g*

PRACTICE/APPLY

- ❑ **Skills and Strategies in Context** Read *I'm a Caterpillar*, using the Guiding Comprehension questions to apply *draw conclusions* and *text structure*. DAY 3 *122-137a*
- ❑ **Think and Share** Use the questions on Student Edition p. 138 to discuss the selection. DAY 3 *138a-139*
- ❑ **Skills and Strategies in Context** Read "My Computer," guiding children as they apply skills and strategies. After reading have children make connections across texts. DAY 4 *140-141a*
- ❑ **Leveled Text** Apply *draw conclusions* and *text structure* to read leveled text. DAY 4 *LR37–LR45*, DAY 5 *LR37–LR45*
- ❑ **Homework** Practice Book 1.2 p. 44. DAY 1 *119a*

Main Selection—Nonfiction

Paired Selection—Nonfiction

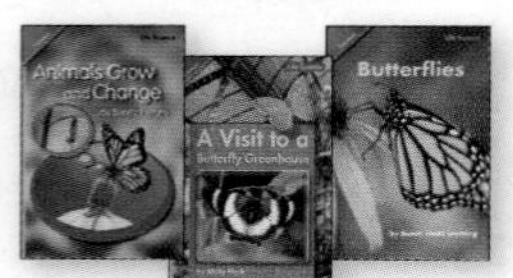

Leveled Readers

ASSESS

- ❑ **Selection Test** Determine children's understanding of the main selection and assess their ability to *draw conclusions*. DAY 3
- ❑ **Story Reading** Have children read the passage "Who's Talking?" Ask them to *draw conclusions* about the story and have them retell the story. DAY 5 142e, 142g

RETEACH/REVIEW

- ❑ **Reteach Lesson** If necessary, reteach *draw conclusions*. DAY 5 *DI·82*

FLUENCY

SKILL ATTEND TO END PUNCTUATION When you read, look for end marks that tell you to stop, to read in an excited way, or to read as if you are asking a question.

REREAD FOR FLUENCY

- ❑ **Paired Reading** Have pairs of children read orally from Decodable Reader 33, or another text at their independent reading level. Listen to children read and provide corrective feedback regarding their oral reading and their use of the blending strategy. DAY 1 *118q*
- ❑ **Oral Rereading** Have children read orally from Decodable Reader 34, or another text at their independent reading level. Listen to children read and provide corrective feedback regarding their oral reading and their use of the blending strategy. DAY 2 *120f*

TEACH

- ❑ **Model** Use passages from *I'm a Caterpillar* to model attending to end punctuation. DAY 3 *139a*, DAY 4 *141b*

PRACTICE/APPLY

- ❑ **Choral Reading** Choral read passages from *I'm a Caterpillar*. Monitor progress and provide feedback regarding children's attention to end punctuation. DAY 3 *139a*, DAY 4 *141b*
- ❑ **Listening Center** Have children follow along with the AudioText for this week's selections. ANY DAY *118j*
- ❑ **Reading/Library Center** Have children build fluency by rereading Leveled Readers, Decodable Readers, or other text at their independent level. ANY DAY *118j*
- ❑ **Fluency Coach** Have children use Fluency Coach to listen to fluent reading or to practice reading on their own. ANY DAY

ASSESS

- ❑ **Story Reading** Take a one-minute timed sample of children's oral reading. Use the passage "Who's Talking?" DAY 5 *142e, 142g*

1. Use assessment data to determine your instructional focus.
2. Preview this week's instruction by strand.
3. Choose instructional activities that meet the needs of your classroom.

WRITING

Trait of the Week

FOCUS/IDEAS All sentences should focus on a main idea. Keep the purpose of your writing in mind, such as teaching something.

TEACH

- ❑ **Write Together** Engage children in writing activities that develop language, grammar, and writing skills. Include independent writing as an extension of group writing activities.
  - **Shared Writing** DAY 1 *119c*
  - **Interactive Writing** DAY 2 *121a*
  - **Writing Across the Curriculum** DAY 4 *141c*
- ❑ **Trait of the Week** Introduce and model the Trait of the Week, *focus ideas.* DAY 3 *139c*

PRACTICE/APPLY

- ❑ **Write Now** Examine the model on Student Edition pp. 142-143. Then have children write facts about a caterpillar or butterfly. DAY 5 *142-143*

  Prompt In *I'm a Caterpillar,* a caterpillar changes into a butterfly. Think about these two insects. Now write facts about how the caterpillar looked before and how the butterfly looks now.

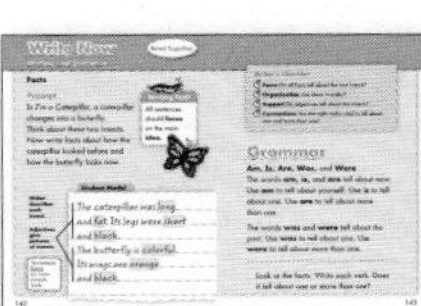
Write Now

- ❑ **Daily Journal Writing** Have children write about concepts and literature in their journals. EVERY DAY *118d-118e*
- ❑ **Writing Center** Have children write a rhyme. ANY DAY *118k*

ASSESS

- ❑ **Scoring Rubric** Use a rubric to evaluate facts. DAY 5 *142-143*

RETEACH/REVIEW

- ❑ **The Grammar and Writing Book** Use pp. 146-151 of The Grammar and Writing Book to extend instruction. ANY DAY

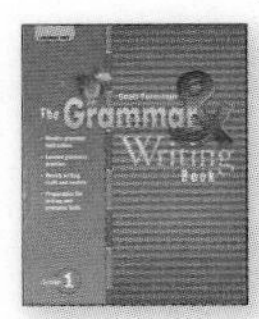

The Grammar and Writing Book

SPEAKING AND LISTENING

TEACH

- ❑ **Summarize Information** Discuss summarizing. Have children tell important parts of a nonfiction story. DAY 2 *121c*

GRAMMAR

SKILL *AM, IS, ARE, WAS,* AND *WERE* The words *am, is,* and *are* tell about now. Use *am* or *is* to tell about one. The words *was* and *were* tell about the past. Use *was* to tell about one.

TEACH

- ❑ **Grammar Transparency 17** Use Grammar Transparency 17 to teach *am, is, are, was,* and *were.* DAY 1 *119d*

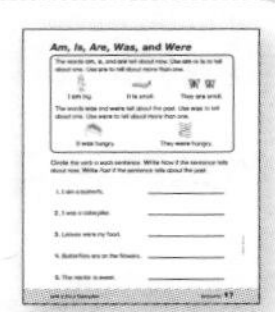
Grammar Transparency 17

PRACTICE/APPLY

- ❑ **Develop the Concept** Review the concept of *am, is, are, was, and were* and provide guided practice. DAY 2 *121b*
- ❑ **Apply to Writing** Have children use *am, is, are, was,* and *were* in writing. DAY 3 *139d*
- ❑ **Define/Practice** Review the definition of *am, is, are, was and were.* Then have children use them in sentences. DAY 4 *141d*
- ❑ **Write Now** Discuss the grammar lesson on Student Edition p. 143. Have children use correct verbs in their own fact sentences about a caterpillar and butterfly. DAY 5 *142-143*

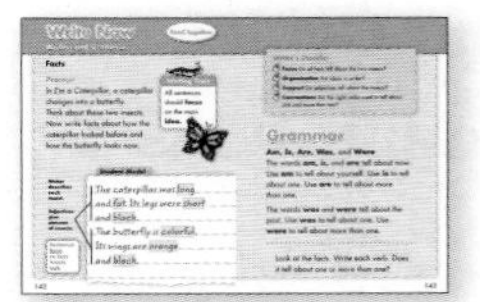
Write Now

- ❑ **Daily Fix-It** Have children find and correct errors in grammar, spelling, and punctuation. DAY 1 *119d,* DAY 2 *121b,* DAY 3 *139d,* DAY 4 *141d,* DAY 5 *142-143*
- ❑ **Homework** Grammar and Writing Practice Book pp. 65-68. DAY 2 *121b,* DAY 3 *139d,* DAY 4 *141d,* DAY 5 *142-143*

RETEACH/REVIEW

- ❑ **The Grammar and Writing Book** Use pp. 146-149 of The Grammar and Writing Book to extend instruction. ANY DAY

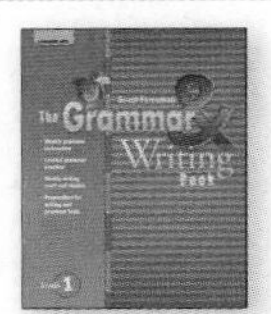

The Grammar and Writing Book

RESEARCH/INQUIRY

TEACH

- ❑ **Technology: My Computer** Model using a computer. Have children create their own documents that include two or three facts they have learned about caterpillars. DAY 5 *143a*
- ❑ **Unit Inquiry Project** Allow time for children to observe, measure, and record their observations for the last time. Have children comment in their journals on the changes they have observed. ANY DAY *9*

Resources for

Differentiated Instruction

LEVELED READERS

- **Comprehension**
  - **Skill** Draw Conclusions
  - **Strategy** Text Structure
- **Lesson Vocabulary**
  High-Frequency Words

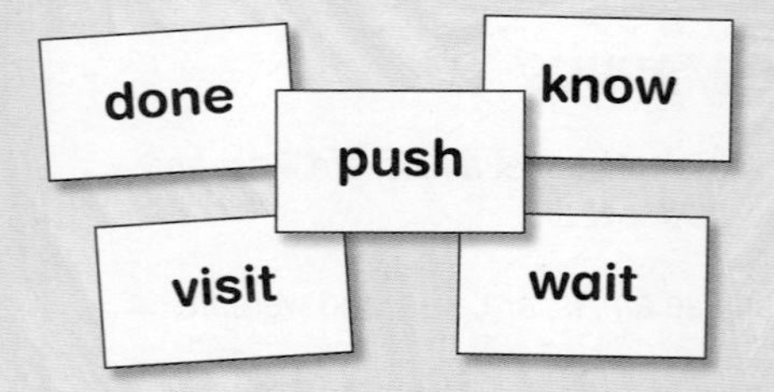

- **Science Standards**
  - Life Cycles
  - Adaptations

PearsonSuccessNet.com

Use the Online Database of over 600 books to

- Download and print additional copies of this week's leveled readers
- Listen to the readers being read online
- Search for more titles focused on this week's skills, topic, and content

On-Level

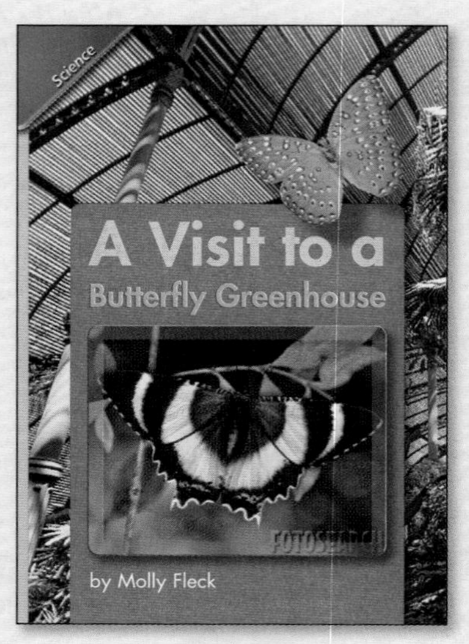

On-Level Reader

Draw Conclusions
Write conclusions based on the information from the book *A Visit to a Butterfly Greenouse.*

1. A butterfly greenhouse has flowers. A butterfly drinks nectar from flowers.
   Conclusion:
   A butterfly can get its food in the greenhouse.
2. People can learn a lot at a butterfly greenhouse. You can watch a butterfly come out of its chrysalis there.
   Conclusion:
   A butterfly greenhouse is an interesting place to visit.

On-Level Practice TE p. LR41

Vocabulary
Find each of the following vocabulary words in *A Visit to a Butterfly Greenhouse.* Write the page number on which you found the word. Then write your own sentence using a vocabulary word.

1. done: page 8
2. know: page 3, 4, 5, 6, 7, 8, 11, or 12
3. push: page 6
4. visit: page 4
5. wait: page 10
6. Responses will vary.

On-Level Practice TE p. LR42

Strategic Intervention

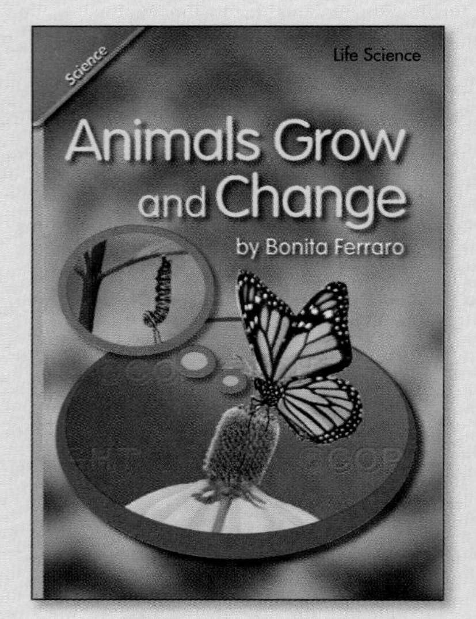

Below-Level Reader

Draw Conclusions
Draw a line from each set of facts to the correct conclusion. Use *Animals Grow and Change* to help you.

A kitten has fur, whiskers, and a tiny cat body. It will grow larger to become a grown-up cat. — Some baby animals look like small grown-ups when they are young.

A caterpillar crawls at first. It becomes a pupa. It turns into a butterfly. — Some animals change shape when they grow.

Below-Level Practice TE p. LR38

Vocabulary
Circle the word that best completes each sentence. Write the word in the blank.

one wait (know)
1. Do you know what a butterfly is?

visit crawl (done)
2. You are not done growing yet.

push (wait) know
3. If you wait long enough, it will get bigger.

one (visit) know
4. Children visit their friends after school.

crawl done (push)
5. Friends can push you on the swing to go higher.

Below-Level Practice TE p. LR39

Advanced

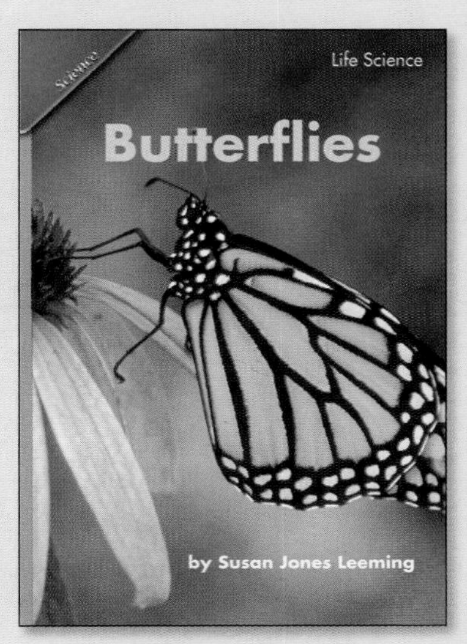

Advanced Reader

Draw Conclusions
Write conclusions based on information from the book *Butterflies*.

1. The caterpillar eats and eats and eats. Soon it grows large.
   Conclusion: The caterpillar eats so that it can grow.
2. The butterfly shivers because its wings are wet. It rests in the sun and waits for its wings to dry.
   Conclusion: The sun dries the butterfly's wings.
3. Camouflage makes a butterfly hard to see. Camouflage helps a butterfly hide from danger.
   Conclusion: The butterfly will be safe from its enemies.

Advanced Practice TE p. LR44

Vocabulary
Use the words in the box to help you complete each sentence.

Words to Know		
cycle	develop	insect

1. A butterfly is a type of insect.
2. The butterfly life cycle begins with an egg.
3. The caterpillar will develop into a butterfly inside the chrysalis.

4-5. Write two sentences about facts you learned from *Butterflies*. Use the three words from the box in your sentences.
Responses will vary.

Advanced Practice TE p. LR45

ELL

ELL Reader

ELL Poster 17

Teacher's Edition Notes

ELL notes throughout this lesson support instruction and reference additional resources at point of use.

Teaching Guide pp. 113–119, 244–245

- Multilingual summaries of the main selection
- Comprehension lesson
- Vocabulary strategies and word cards
- ELL Reader 1.3.5 lesson

ELL and Transition Handbook

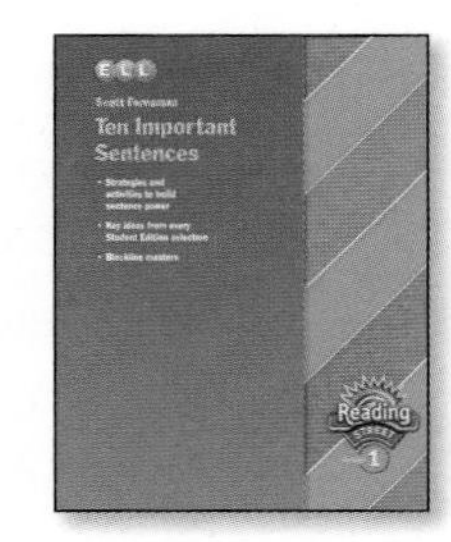

Ten Important Sentences

- Key ideas from every selection in the Student Edition
- Activities to build sentence power

More Reading

Readers' Theater Anthology

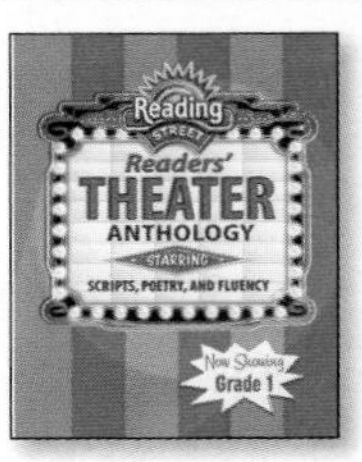

- Fluency practice
- Five scripts to build fluency
- Poetry for oral interpretation

Leveled Trade Books

Below-Level

On-Level

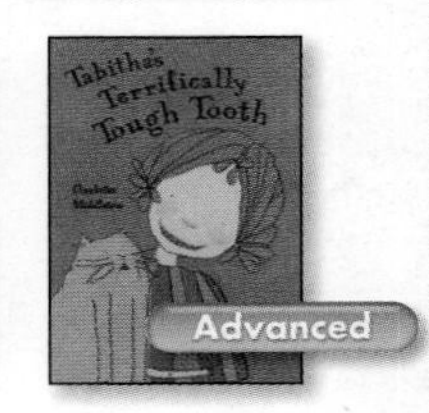

Advanced

- Extend reading tied to the unit concept
- Lessons in Trade Book Library Teaching Guide

Big Book of Poems

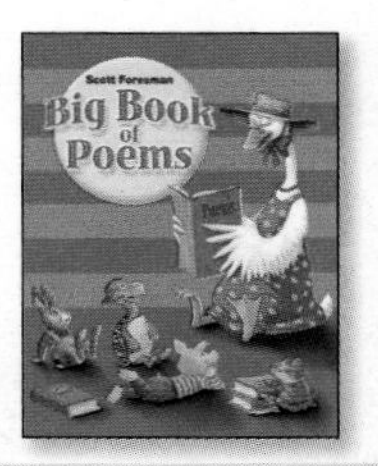

- Fluency practice
- Poetry for Choral Reading

Homework

- Family Times Newsletter
- ELL Multilingual Selection Summaries

Take-Home Books

- Decodable Readers
- Leveled Readers

Literacy Centers

Listening

Let's Read Along

MATERIALS
CD player, headphones, print copies of recorded pieces

SINGLES

LISTEN TO LITERATURE As children listen to the following recordings, have them follow along or read along in the print version.

AudioText
I'm a Caterpillar
"My Computer"

Sing with Me/Background Building Audio
"Life Cycle"

Phonics Songs and Rhymes Audio
"Burst Out, Bugs"

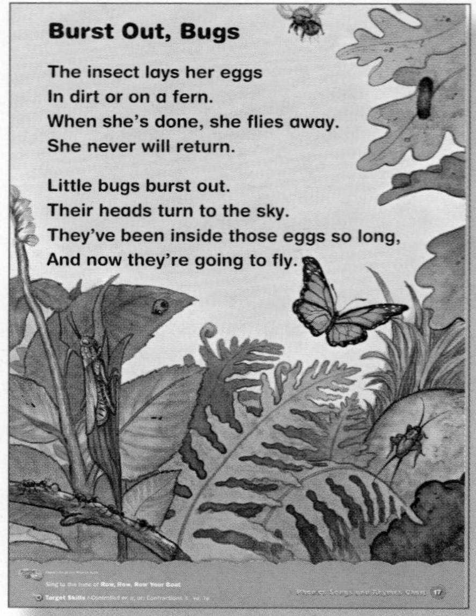

Audio CD **Phonics Songs and Rhymes Chart 17**

Reading/Library

Read It Again!

MATERIALS
collection of books for self-selected reading, reading logs

SINGLES PAIRS GROUPS

REREAD BOOKS Have children select previously read books from the appropriate book box and record titles of books they read in their logs. Use these previous ly read books:

- Decodable Readers
- Leveled Readers
- ELL Readers
- Stories written by classmates
- Books from the library

TEN IMPORTANT SENTENCES Have children read the Ten Important Sentences for *I'm a Caterpillar* and locate the sentences in the Student Edition.

BOOK CLUB Read p. 139 of the Student Edition with children. Have them write three questions they would like to ask Marzollo and share their questions with groups.

Word Work

Phonics Drop a Word

MATERIALS
12 index cards

PAIRS GROUPS

r*-CONTROLLED *er, ir, ur Have pairs or small groups of children play Drop a Word using words with *r*-controlled *er, ir,* and *ur.*

1. **Write a different word with *r*-controlled *er, ir,* or *ur* on each index card. Place the cards in a pile.**
2. **Children take turns choosing a card and dropping it on the table. If the word lands face up, the child reads the word and repeats with another card. If the blank side of the card lands face up, play moves to the next child.**
3. **Play continues until each child has had three turns.**

CONTRACTIONS *'s, 've, 're* Make a set of cards with words with contractions *'s, 've,* and *'re* and have children play the game.

This interactive CD provides additional practice.

girl
herd
turn

Use the ***I'm a Caterpillar*** materials from the Reading Street Centers Survival Kit to organize this week's centers.

Writing

Rhyme TIME

MATERIALS
paper, pencils, crayons

SINGLES
GROUPS

WRITE A RHYME Recall that the author of *I'm a Caterpillar* used the words *crunch* and *munch* to tell how the caterpillar ate leaves.

1. **Ask groups to use the selection to help them find rhyming words they could use to tell about butterflies and caterpillars. For example *fly, sky; crawl, small; wing, sing.***
2. **Then have each child write a rhyme about a caterpillar or a butterfly.**
3. **Encourage them to draw a picture to accompany their writing.**

LEVELED WRITING Encourage children to write at their own ability level. Some may write only two words that rhyme. Others will be able to write simple rhyming sentences. Your best writers will write rhyming sentences with attention to mechanics and spelling.

Science

Watch Me Grow

MATERIALS
pictures of the butterfly life cycle, paper, pencils, crayons

SINGLES
GROUPS

IDENTIFY SEQUENCE OF EVENTS Have children identify the stages in the life cycle of a butterfly.

1. **Create picture cards depicting butterfly eggs, a caterpillar, a chrysalis, and a butterfly. Label each card.**
2. **Mix up the cards and place them in the Science Center.**
3. **Have children put the cards in order to demonstrate the life cycle of a butterfly.**
4. **Ask children to use *I'm a Caterpillar* to make sure they have placed the cards in the correct order.**
5. **If time allows, encourage each child to choose a card and tell what happens at that stage.**

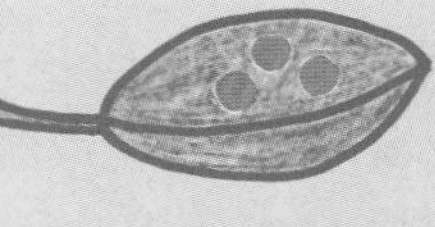

Technology

Focus on Phonics

MATERIALS
computer, Phonics Activities CD-ROM

PAIRS

USE A CD-ROM Have pairs of children use a CD-ROM.

1. **Have children turn on the computer and open the Phonics Activities CD-ROM.**
2. **Pairs of children complete one of the CD-ROM activities.**

ALL CENTERS

Day 1

AT A GLANCE

Oral Vocabulary
"Life Cycle" 17

Phonemic Awareness
Blend and Segment Onset/Rime

Phonics and Spelling
r-Controlled *er, ir, ur*
Spelling Pretest:
Words with *er, ir, ur*

Read Apply Phonics
Word Wall

Group Time < Differentiated Instruction

Build Background
Let's Talk About Changes in Nature

Listening Comprehension
Skill Draw Conclusions

Shared Writing
Facts

Grammar
Verbs *Am, Is, Are, Was, Were*

Materials
- *Sing with Me Big Book*
- Sound-Spelling Card 11
- Letter Tiles
- Decodable Reader 33
- Student Edition 118–119
- Graphic Organizer Flip Chart 30

Take It to the NET™ ONLINE
Professional Development
To learn more about informational text, go to PearsonSuccessNet.com and read the article "The Scarcity of Informational Texts. . ." by N. Duke.

Morning Warm-Up!

What changes can we observe in nature? Let's take a closer look. We learned about how some plants change. Soon we'll read about a few ways animals change.

QUESTION OF THE WEEK Tell children they will talk, sing, read, and write about Changes in Nature. Write the message and track the print as you read it. Discuss the question.

CONNECT CONCEPTS Ask questions to connect to other selections.

- What changes did Toad try to make happen in his garden?
- Look carefully at *An Egg Is an Egg*. What changes can you see?

REVIEW HIGH-FREQUENCY WORDS

- Circle the words *how, read, soon,* and *few* in the message.
- Have children say and spell each word as they write it in the air.
- Help children use context to determine if *read* should be pronounced with a long *e* or a short *e*. (long *e*)

Build Background Use the Day 1 instruction on ELL Poster 17 to assess knowledge and develop concepts.

ELL Poster 17

Oral Vocabulary

SHARE LITERATURE Display p. 17 of the *Sing With Me Big Book.* Tell children that they will sing a song about a caterpillar. Read the title. Ask children to listen for the Amazing Words **cycle, develop,** and **insect** as you sing. Then sing the song again and ask children to sing with you. Have children demonstrate their understanding of *cycle, develop,* and *insect* as they discuss the caterpillar's changes.

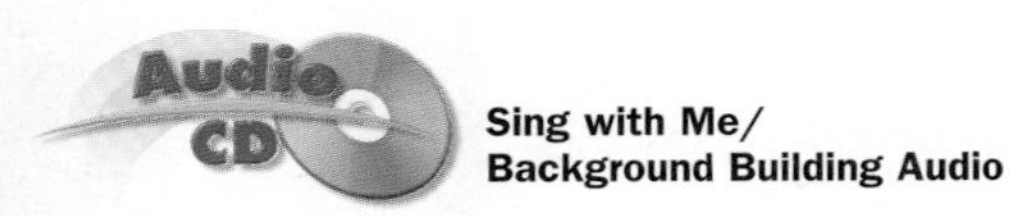

Sing with Me/
Background Building Audio

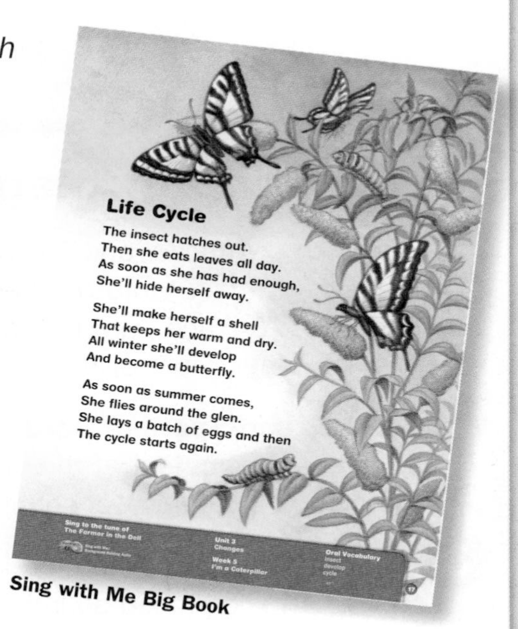

Sing with Me Big Book

Phonemic Awareness

BLEND AND SEGMENT ONSET/RIME

- We just sang about a butterfly. The butterfly will whirl around the glen.
- Model saying the onset and rime, /hw/ /ėrl/. Have children say the sounds with you, /hw/ /ėrl/, and then say the sounds by themselves.
- Now say the onset and rime as you write the letters that go with each part. Say /hw/ /ėrl/ as you write *wh, irl.* When I put the sounds /hw/ /ėrl/ together, I have the word *whirl.*
- Have children say the sounds as you point to the letters and blend the sounds to say the word (/hw/, /ėrl/, *whirl.*)

Continue the activity by saying the onset and rime for each word and having children blend the sounds to say a word.

n/erve	**t/urn**	**d/irt**
sw/erve	**ch/urn**	**sh/irt**

OBJECTIVES

- Build oral vocabulary.
- Blend and segment onset/rime.

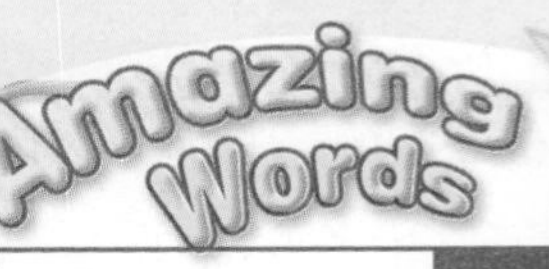

to build oral vocabulary

cycle
develop
insect
rearrange
yearly
emerge
fragile
vessel

MONITOR PROGRESS

If... children lack oral vocabulary experiences about the concept of Changes in Nature,

then... use the Oral Vocabulary Routine below to teach *cycle.*

Oral Vocabulary ROUTINE

1. **Introduce the Word** Relate the word *cycle* to the song. Supply a child-friendly definition. Have children say the word. Example: A *cycle* is a series of events that always happens in the same order.
2. **Demonstrate** Provide an example to show meaning. The class studied the life *cycle* of the frog.
3. **Apply** Have children demonstrate their understanding. In the *cycle* of nature, which season comes after winter?
4. **Display the Word/Letter-Sounds** Write the word on a card. Display it. Identify the letter-sounds for *c*/s/ and *c*/k/.
See p. DI·7 to teach *develop* and *insect.*

ELL

Build Oral Vocabulary To help children understand the pronoun *she* in "Life Cycle," have them cut out a caterpillar, a chrysalis, and a butterfly, using photos as models. Have children hold up the matching prop as they sing each verse.

OBJECTIVES

- Associate the sound /ėr/ with *er, ir, ur.*
- Blend, read, and build /ėr/ words.

Skills Trace

r-Controlled *er, ir, ur*

Introduce/Teach	**TE: 1.3 118n–o; 122c–d**
Practice	TE: 1.3 118q; PB: 1.2 43; DR33
Reteach/Review	TE: 1.3 142c, 168c-d, DI•82; PB: 1.2 58
Assess/Test	TE: 1.3 142e-g; Benchmark Test, Unit 3

Generalization

A single vowel followed by the letter *r* has a sound that is neither short nor long, but *r*-controlled.

Strategic Intervention

Use **Monitor Progress,** p. 118o during Group Time after children have had more practice with *r*-controlled *er, ir, ur.*

Advanced

Use **Monitor Progress,** p. 118o as a preassessment to determine whether or not this group of children would benefit from this *r*-controlled *er, ir, ur* instruction.

Support Phonics Spanish does not have a sound that is equivalent to /ėr/, so Spanish speakers may pronounce *dirt* as *deert.* Have children practice saying and writing words such as *her, bird,* and *turn.*

See the Phonics Transition Lessons in the ELL and Transition Handbook.

r-Controlled *er, ir, ur*

TEACH/MODEL

Blending Strategy

ROUTINE

1. **Connect** Write *for* and *far.* What do you know about the vowel sounds in these words? (The words both have *r*-controlled vowel sounds, /ôr/ and /är/.) Today we will learn about words with another *r*-controlled vowel sound.
2. **Use Sound-Spelling Card** Display Card 11. This is *Earth.* The sound you hear at the beginning of *Earth* is /ėr/. /ėr/ is an *r*-controlled vowel sound. Say it with me: /ėr/.
3. **Model** Write *her.* When the letter *e* is followed by *r,* the *e* has an *r*-controlled sound, /ėr/. This is how I blend this word. Segment and blend *her.* Let's blend this word together: /h/ /ėr/, *her.* Continue modeling with *bird.* Point out that *i* followed by *r* has an *r*-controlled sound, /ėr/. Then model with *turn,* explaining that the letters *ur* also stand for /ėr/.
4. **Group Practice** Say the sounds of the letters and blend the words together. Continue with *verb, sir, curl, verse, thirst.*
5. **Review** What do you know about reading these words? The letters *er, ir,* and *ur* stand for /ėr/.

er, ir, ur

Sound-Spelling Card 11

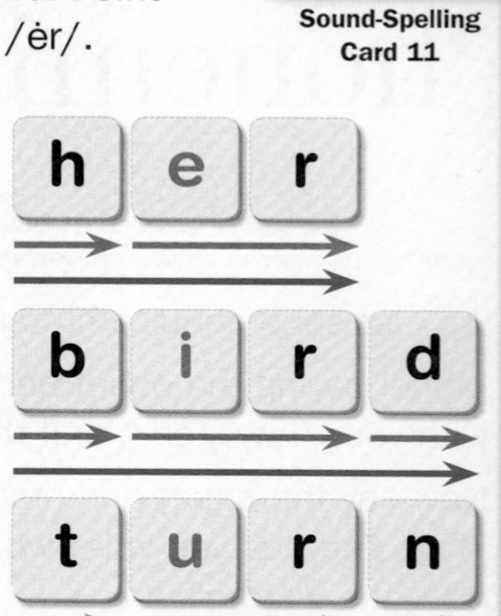

BLEND WORDS

INDIVIDUALS BLEND *er, ir, ur* WORDS Call on individuals to blend the words *perch, stir, surf, twirl, church, swerve, third.* Have them tell what they know about each word before reading it. (The *er, ir,* and *ur* stand for /ėr/.) For feedback, refer to step five of the Blending Strategy Routine.

SORT WORDS

INDIVIDUALS READ AND SORT *er, ir, ur* WORDS Write the heads *er, ir, ur;* write *germ, dirt,* and *fur.* Have children read the words *germ, dirt,* and *fur* and point out which letters stand for /ėr/ in each word. Repeat with *clerk, girl, hurt* and then *serve, first, burst.* Complete the activity by having the lists read.

er	*ir*	*ur*
germ	dirt	fur
clerk	girl	hurt
serve	first	burst

Monitor Progress — Check Word Reading *r*-Controlled *er, ir, ur*

Write the following words and have individuals read them.

ferns	**swirl**	**curb**	**chirp**	**nurse**
smart	**turn**	**shore**	**thirty**	**fork**
chicken	**jerk**	**curve**	**skirt**	**spun**

If… children cannot blend *er, ir, ur* words at this point,

then… continue to monitor their progress using other instructional opportunities during the week so that they can be successful with the Day 5 Assessment. See the Skills Trace on p. 118n.

▶ **Day 1 Check Word Reading** | Day 2 Check Word Reading | Day 3 Check High-Frequency Words/Retelling | Day 4 Check Fluency | Day 5 Assess Progress

Vocabulary TiP

You may wish to explain the meanings of these words.

chirp sound made by a bird
curb edge of a sidewalk next to the street
ferns plants with feathery leaves

her bird surf

Circle the word for each picture.

1. short shirt
2. clerk click
3. curl chill
4. barn burn
5. fern fan
6. skirt skit
7. fist first
8. stir store

Find the word that has the same vowel sound as [picture]. Mark the ⬭ to show your answer.

9. hard / hut / hurt
10. torn / turn / tune

School + Home **Home Activity** Your child read words spelled with *er, ir,* and *ur* that have the same vowel sound as *bird.* Help your child make up rhymes using words with this vowel sound spelled *er, ir, ur.* For example, *You can't wear that shirt. It is covered in dirt!*

▲ **Practice Book 1.2** p. 43, *r*-Controlled *er, ir, ur*

Spiral REVIEW

- Row 2 contrasts *or, ore, ar* with *er, ir, ur.*
- Row 3 contrasts short vowels *e, i, u* with *er, ir, ur.*

Word Reading
SUCCESS PREDICTOR

OBJECTIVES

- Segment sounds to spell words.
- Spell words with *er, ir, ur*.

Spelling Words

Words with *er, ir, ur*

1.	**her**	6.	**were**
2.	**first**	7.	**shirt**
3.	**bird***	8.	**fur**
4.	**girl**	9.	**hurt**
5.	**burn**	10.	**sir**

High-Frequency Words

11.	**visit***	12.	**done***

* **Words from the Selection**

Words with *er, ir, ur*

Look at the word. **Say** it. **Look** for the vowel spelling.

	Write the word.	Check it.
1. her	her	her
2. first	first	first
3. bird	bird	bird
4. girl	girl	girl
5. burn	burn	burn
6. were	were	were
7. shirt	shirt	shirt
8. fur	fur	fur
9. hurt	hurt	hurt
10. sir	sir	sir

High-Frequency Words

11. visit	visit	12. done	done

School + Home **Home Activity** Your child is learning to spell words with *er, ir,* and *ur*. To practice at home, have your child say each word and point to the vowel spelling.

▲ **Spelling Practice Book** p. 65

Spelling

PRETEST *r*-Controlled *er, ir, ur*

MODEL WRITING FOR SOUNDS Each spelling word has *er, ir,* or *ur*. Before administering the spelling pretest, explain that since *er, ir,* and *ur* all have the same sound, children will have to remember the correct vowel for each spelling word.

- What sounds do you hear in *jerk?* (/j/ /ėr/ /k/)
- What is the letter for /j/? Write *j*. Continue with the *er*/ėr/ and *k*/k/.
- Do you remember what the letters stand for /ėr/ in *jerk?* *(er)* Continue with *k*/k/.
- Repeat with *shirt: ir*/ėr/ and *purse: ur*/ėr/
- What letter must follow *e, i,* or *u* to make the /ėr/ sound? *(r)*

PRETEST Dictate the spelling words. Segment the words for children if necessary. Have children check their pretests and correct misspelled words.

HOMEWORK Spelling Practice Book, p. 65

I'm a Caterpillar

The Caterpillar and the Fawn

Once upon a time, two young animals lived in a forest. One was an insect—a little caterpillar. The other was a fawn—a baby deer. Even though they were very different animals, they were good friends.

One day, Caterpillar was too tired to play. She climbed up into a tree, made herself a cozy place to rest, and fell into a deep sleep.

Fawn lay at the base of the tree. She waited and waited, but Caterpillar did not come down. Time passed, and

Group Time

DAY 1

On-Level	Strategic Intervention	Advanced
Read Decodable Reader 33.	**Read** Decodable Reader 33.	**Read** Advanced Selection 17.
• Use p. 118q.	• Use the **Routine** on p. DI·56.	• Use the **Routine** on p. DI·57.

Place English language learners in the groups that correspond to their reading abilities in English.

Independent Activities

Fluency Reading Pair children to reread Leveled Readers or the ELL Reader from the previous week or other text at children's independent level.

Journal Writing Write to tell how a pet you know changed as it grew. Share writing.

Independent Reading See p. 118j for Reading/Library activities and suggestions.

Literacy Centers To practice *r*-Controlled *er, ir, ur,* you may use Word Work, p. 118j.

Practice Book 1.2 *r*-Controlled *er, ir, ur,* p. 43

Break into small groups after Spelling and before Build Background.

ELL

Support Spelling Before giving the spelling pretest, clarify the meaning of each spelling word with examples, such as by pointing out a *girl* and a *shirt* and by putting a few children in a line and pointing to the *first* child.

Apply Phonics

PRACTICE *r*-Controlled *er, ir, ur*

HIGH-FREQUENCY WORDS Review *afraid, grow, have, lives, many, new, put, soon,* and *they* on the Word Wall. If necessary, have children practice in pairs with word cards. Word Wall

READ DECODABLE READER 33

- Pages 66–67 Read aloud quietly with the group.
- Pages 68–69 Have the group read aloud without you.
- Pages 70–72 Select individuals to read aloud.

CHECK COMPREHENSION AND DECODING Have children retell the story to include characters, setting, and plot. Then have children locate /ėr/ words in the story. Review /ėr/ spelling patterns: *er, ir, ur.* Sort words according to their spelling patterns.

er	*ir*	*ur*
ferns	bird	burn
her	chirp	curb
	dirt	
	stir	

HOMEWORK Take-Home Decodable Reader 33

REREAD FOR FLUENCY

Paired Reading

ROUTINE

1. **Reader 1 Begins** Children read the entire book, switching readers at the end of each page.
2. **Reader 2 Begins** Have partners reread; now the other partner begins.
3. **Reread** For optimal fluency, children should reread three or four times.
4. **Provide Feedback** Listen to children read and provide corrective feedback regarding their oral reading and their use of the blending strategy.

OBJECTIVES

- Apply knowledge of letter-sounds to decode unknown words when reading.
- Use context with letter-sounds to confirm the identification of unknown words.
- Practice fluency in paired reading.

Monitor Progress

Decoding

If... children have difficulty decoding a word,	**then...** prompt them to blend the word. • What is the new word? • Is the new word a word you know? • Does it make sense in the story?
If... children have difficulty decoding *wishes,*	**then...** prompt them to cover the *es* ending, blend the base word, *wish;* blend the base word and ending together.

ELL

Access Content

Beginning As you read *A Big Day for Mom,* ask questions: Where is the black dirt? Point to it. Does the girl have ferns or flowers for Mom? Is the bird small and yellow? Does Mom smile?

Intermediate Have children act out scenes from *A Big Day for Mom.* Ask them to stir a cake, dig in dirt, put pots on the curb, and chirp like a bird.

Advanced Have children write these /ėr/ words from *A Big Day for Mom* on separate cards: *bird, burn, chirp, curb, dirt, ferns, stir.* Have them read each word and sort them into two piles: naming words and action words. Have children use the words in sentences.

OBJECTIVES

- Build background and oral vocabulary.
- Stay on topic when speaking.

Strategic Intervention

Have children draw or cut out pictures of baby animals. Ask them to write what each baby is called, such as a pup, kitten, cub, and so on.

Advanced

Have children use a CD-ROM encyclopedia to research an animal they know. Have them write sentences that tell the name of the animal, where it lives, and what its babies are called.

Activate Prior Knowledge
Invite children to tell about the changes they see in the pictures in their home language and in English.

Build Background

LET'S TALK ABOUT Changes in Nature

DEVELOP ORAL LANGUAGE Read the title and have children view the photographs. Ask them to tell you what they see. Allow ample time for children to respond and remind them to stay on topic while speaking. If children do not stay on topic, model doing so by giving an example of a statement that is on topic and one that is not. Say, "The eggshell is beginning to crack" is on topic. "I had eggs for breakfast today" is not on topic. Then use open-ended prompts to model to encourage conversation. For example:

Tell me about what you see here. Yes, that's right, a chick is hatching from an egg. This shows the life cycle of a chicken. Why do you think the chick is wet? What will the chick grow up to be? Look at the life cycle of the frog. What is the small round thing? Yes, it is a frog egg. How is a frog egg different from a chicken egg? What will come out of the frog egg?

BUILD ORAL VOCABULARY As you continue the discussion, encourage children to use today's Amazing Words, *cycle, develop,* and *insect.*

- In which part of the frog's life cycle do you see the most change?
- How long do you think it might take for an egg to develop into a chick?
- Frogs eat insects. Do you think tadpoles eat insects too?

DEVELOP CONCEPTS

CONCEPT CHART Remind children of the question of the week.

- What changes can we observe in nature?

Display Graphic Organizer 30 or draw a series of circles in a cycle. Have children discuss animals they have seen grow. Select one cycle on the page and have children help you write about the changes.

- What happens first? (The egg hatches.)
- What happens next? (A baby chick comes out of the egg. Its feathers are wet.)
- What happens after that? (The chick gets bigger. Its feathers are soft and fluffy.)
- What happens after that? (The baby chick grows into an adult.)
- Then what can happen? (The grown-up chicken can lay an egg.)

CONNECT TO READING Point out the illustration on the bottom corner of Student Edition p. 119. Ask children what they see. (a butterfly) Explain that this week children will read a selection about the life cycle of a butterfly. Tell children that they will learn what changes we can observe in nature.

Oral Vocabulary

Let's Talk About Changes in Nature

118 119

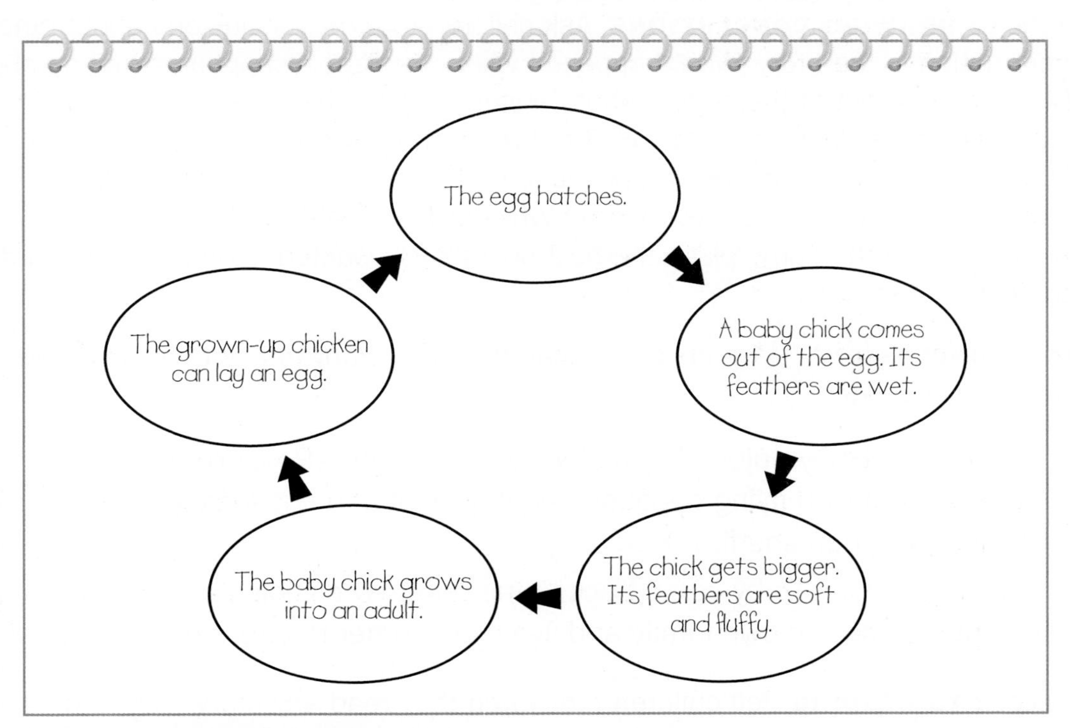

▲ **Graphic Organizer Flip Chart 30**

Tech Files ONLINE

For a Web site that explores animals and how they grow and change, do an Internet search using the keywords *animals* or *life cycles.*

Access Content To prepare children for reading *I'm a Caterpillar*, send home the story summary in English and/or the home language. See the ELL Teaching Guide, pp. 117–119.

OBJECTIVE

Draw conclusions about the characters and events in a story.

Skills Trace

Draw Conclusions

Introduce/Teach	**TE: 1.3 119a–b, 122g; 1.4 11a–b, 14g; 1.5 141a–b, 144g**
Practice	TE: 1.3 124–125; 1.4 16–17; 1.5 152–153; PB: 1.2 44, 64, 164
Reteach/Review	TE: 1.1 82–83, 1.3 DI•83 1.4 54–55, 80–81, DI•77; 1.5 DI•83
Test	TE: 1.3 41–44; 1.4 49–52; 1.5 89–92; Benchmark Test, Unit 4

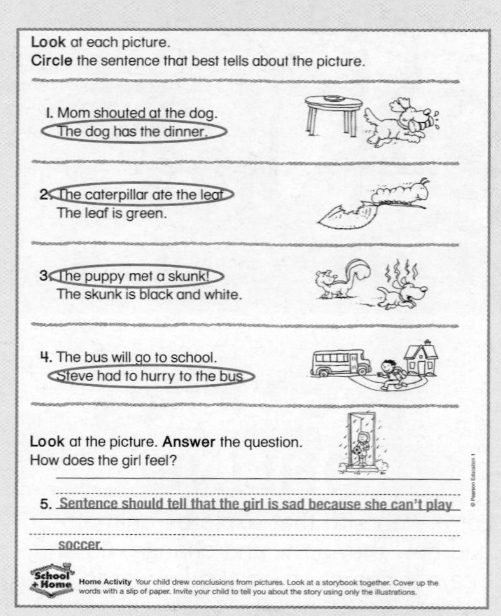

Look at each picture.
Circle the sentence that best tells about the picture.

1. Mom shouted at the dog.
The dog has the dinner.

2. The caterpillar ate the leaf.
The leaf is green.

3. The puppy met a skunk!
The skunk is black and white.

4. The bus will go to school.
Steve had to hurry to the bus.

Look at the picture. **Answer** the question.
How does the girl feel?

5. Sentence should tell that the girl is sad because she can't play soccer.

School + Home **Home Activity** Your child drew conclusions from pictures. Look at a storybook together. Cover up the words with a slip of paper. Invite your child to tell you about the story using only the illustrations.

▲ **Practice Book 1.2** p. 44, Draw Conclusions

Access Content For a Picture It! lesson on drawing conclusions, see the ELL Teaching Guide, pp. 114–115.

Listening Comprehension

TEACH/MODEL Draw Conclusions

DEFINE DRAW CONCLUSIONS

- Sometimes clues in the words and pictures can help a reader figure out something that is not written in a story or article.
- Good readers use what they read and what they know about real life to figure out more about the characters and what happens in a selection.

READ ALOUD Read "The Nest on Our Back Porch" and model how to draw conclusions.

MODEL When I read this story, I thought about why the mother bird chose to build her nest in the hanging basket. The story tells me that being under the roof kept the nest dry when it rained and that hanging high above the yard kept the nest safe from cats. I think the mother bird built her nest in the hanging basket to keep her eggs dry and safe.

PRACTICE

CLUES TO DRAWING CONCLUSIONS Ask children to draw conclusions about other information in the story. What happened when the eggs disappeared? (The baby birds hatched out of the eggs.) What happened when the birds disappeared? (The baby birds grew up and flew off to live on their own.) Why was Josh sad? How do you know? (He was sad because he liked watching the birds. I know because he watched them every day.) Why did Josh make sure the hanging basket was in the same place the next spring? (He wanted another mother bird to build a nest in it.)

DRAW CONCLUSIONS Have children recall the story *Ruby in Her Own Time* and draw conclusions.

- Do you think Ruby enjoyed flying? Why or why not? (Possible response: Yes, Ruby enjoyed flying because she flew a lot and she looked happy in the pictures when she flew.)
- Why do you think Ruby came back to the pond? (Possible response: So she could raise her own family and live close to her mother and father.)

CONNECT TO READING Tell children that when they read any story, they should think about what they know and what they have read to figure out more about the characters and what happens to them.

The Nest on Josh's Back Porch

Read ALOUD

One spring morning something exciting happened on Josh's back porch. A bird made a nest in his mother's hanging flower basket!

Josh watched the bird sitting in the basket hanging under the roof. He waited for the bird to fly off to look for insects. Then he carefully looked inside the nest. There were three small pink eggs inside!

Every day Josh went outside to check on the nest. Some days it rained, but the mother bird and her eggs were dry in the basket under the roof. Sometimes cats walked through Josh's yard looking for something to eat, but the mother bird and her eggs were safe in the basket hanging high above.

One day the eggs were gone. In their place were three small baby birds! Josh watched the birds develop and grow bigger and bigger until they were as big as their mother.

Weeks later, Josh woke up to find that the mother bird and her babies were gone. He looked all over the yard and all over the neighborhood, but he couldn't find them anywhere. Josh was sad, but then he had a great idea. He and his mother made a bird feeder to hang on the back porch. Now they could watch birds all summer long!

The next spring, Josh made sure that the hanging basket was in the same place on the porch. Then he sat inside by the window and waited. He was very excited to see what would happen next.

OBJECTIVE

- Write facts.

DAILY FIX-IT

1. The gurl saw a bug
The girl saw a bug.

2. it was on hur shirt.
It was on her shirt.

This week's practice sentences appear on Daily Fix-It Transparency 17.

Strategic Intervention

Children who are not able to write independently can look at illustrations in nonfiction books about caterpillars and butterflies. Have them describe what is happening in the photos.

Advanced

Have children find facts about another animal that changes dramatically as it grows. For example, tadpoles turn into frogs.

Support Writing Let children look at the photographs and drawings in nonfiction books about caterpillars and butterflies for visual support as they write.

▲ **The Grammar and Writing Book**
For more instruction and practice, use pp. 146–151.

Shared Writing

WRITE Facts

GENERATE IDEAS Have children share what they know about butterflies and caterpillars. Ask: What do the insects look like? How do they move? What do they eat? Then ask children whether butterflies change into caterpillars or caterpillars change into butterflies.

WRITE FACTS Explain that the class will write facts about butterflies and caterpillars and tell how the two kinds of insects are connected.

COMPREHENSION SKILL Have children draw conclusions—decide something about the facts—about butterflies and caterpillars.

- Display Writing Transparency 17 and read the title.
- Read the first sentences and the prompts.
- Have children suggest facts about butterflies and caterpillars to add to the list.
- Point out that the last sentence on the page is an example of drawing a conclusion. Guide children to complete the conclusion.

HANDWRITING While writing, model the letter forms as shown on pp. TR12–TR15.

READ THE FACTS Have children read the completed facts aloud as you track the print.

Two Bugs

Facts About Butterflies
Butterflies have wings.
Butterflies fly. Possible answers:
Butterflies are colorful.
Butterflies drink nectar from flowers.

Facts About Caterpillars
Caterpillars have legs.
Caterpillars crawl.
Caterpillars are long and fat.
Caterpillars eat leaves.

Caterpillars change into butterflies.

Unit 3 I'm a Caterpillar — Writing Model 17

▲ **Writing Transparency 17**

INDEPENDENT WRITING

WRITE FACTS Have children write their own facts about butterflies and caterpillars. Encourage them to use words from the Word Wall and the Amazing Words board. Let children illustrate their writing. You may gather children's work into a class book for self-selected reading.

Grammar

TEACH/MODEL *Am, Is, Are, Was,* and *Were*

IDENTIFY *Am, Is, Are, Was,* AND *Were* Display Grammar Transparency 17. Read the definition aloud. Then model with item 1.

- *Am* is the verb in sentence one.
- *Am* tells about now, so I will write the word *now* on the line.

Continue modeling with items 2–5.

PRACTICE

USE *Am, Is, Are, Was,* AND *Were* Write the following sentences on the board: *The dog are cute. The cats was soft. We is happy.* Have children write the sentences correctly on their paper.

ADDITIONAL PRACTICE For additional practice use pp. 146–151 in the Grammar and Writing Book.

OBJECTIVE

- Identify *am, is, are, was,* and *were.*

Am, Is, Are, Was, and Were

The words **am, is,** and **are** tell about now. Use **am** or **is** to tell about one. Use **are** to tell about more than one.

I **am** big. It **is** small. They **are** small.

The words **was** and **were** tell about the past. Use **was** to tell about one. Use **were** to tell about more than one.

It **was** hungry. They **were** hungry.

Circle the verb in each sentence. **Write** *Now* if the sentence tells about now. **Write** *Past* if the sentence tells about the past.

1. I (am) a butterfly. Now
2. I (was) a caterpillar. Past
3. Leaves (were) my food. Past
4. Butterflies (are) on the flowers. Now
5. The nectar (is) sweet. Now

Unit 3 I'm a Caterpillar Grammar 17

▲ Grammar Transparency 17

Wrap Up Your Day!

r-CONTROLLED *er, ir, ur* Write *her* and ask children what sound stands for the spelling *er* in *her.* (/ėr/). Repeat with *bird* and *fur.*

SPELLING WORDS WITH *er, ir, ur* Have children name and write the letters for each sound in *her.* Continue with *bird* and *fur.*

DRAW CONCLUSIONS To help children draw a conclusion, ask: In the story "The Nest on Josh's Back Porch," what did Josh probably think about birds? (Possible response: They are interesting and fun to watch.)

LET'S TALK ABOUT IT Use the cycle chart about hatching eggs to talk about the birds on Josh's back porch. What changes did Josh see with the baby birds? (They hatched out of their eggs, grew big, and flew away.)

HOMEWORK Send home this week's Family Times newsletter.

PREVIEW Day 2

Tell children that tomorrow the class will read more about the changes that happen during the seasons.

Day 2

AT A GLANCE

Share Literature
What Makes the Seasons?

Phonemic Awareness
Delete Final Phonemes

Phonics and Spelling
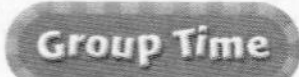
Contractions *'s, 've, 're*
Spelling: Words with *er, ir, ur*

Read **Apply Phonics** Word Wall

Group Time < Differentiated Instruction

High-Frequency Words
done *know* *push*
visit *wait*

Interactive Writing
Description

Grammar
Verbs *Am, Is, Are, Was, Were*

Speaking and Listening
Summarize Information

Materials

- *Sing with Me Big Book*
- Big Book *What Makes the Seasons?*
- Letter Tiles
- Decodable Reader 34
- Student Edition 120–121
- Tested Word Cards

Morning Warm-Up!

Summer, winter, spring, and fall.
I can name the seasons all.
Autumn is another name.
Fall and autumn are the same.
What season are we in?

QUESTION OF THE DAY Encourage children to sing "Life Cycle" from the *Sing with Me Big Book* as you gather. Write and read the message and discuss the question.

REVIEW THE SOUNDS OF *a*

- Read the sentences of the message.
- Have children find words that have long *a (name, same)*, short *a, (and, can)*, and *a* as in *ball (fall, all)*.

Build Background Use the Day 2 instruction on ELL Poster 17 to preview high-frequency words.

ELL Poster 17

Share Literature

BUILD CONCEPTS

NONFICTION Have children read the title. Identify the author. Review that nonfiction books give information that is true. Explain that this nonfiction book is written like a poem with sentences that rhyme.

Big Book

BUILD ORAL VOCABULARY Discuss the four seasons and how the **yearly** changes affect the weather. As you read, ask children to listen for ways the sun is different in each season.

- Some changes are yearly; they take place every year. What changes are yearly? (Possible answer: The weather changes from warm to hot to cool to cold as the seasons go from spring to summer to fall to winter.)
- What plans might you have to **rearrange** if the weather changes from day to day? (Possible answer: If it rains or snows you might have to stay inside instead of playing outside.)

Phonemic Awareness

DELETE FINAL PHONEMES

- We just read that in the summer plants grow quickly or have a growth spurt. Listen to the sounds in *spurt.*
- Model saying each sound, /s/ /p/ /ėr/ /t/. Have children say the sounds with you and then say the sounds by themselves.
- Now say each sound as you write the letter that goes with it. (Say /s/ /p/ /ėr/ /t/ as you write *s, p, ur, t.)*
- Have children say the sounds as you point to the letters, /s/ /p/ /ėr/ /t/ and blend the sounds to say the word *spurt.*
- Erase the *t* at the end of *spurt.* Listen as I take off the /t/ sound at the end of *spurt*: /s/ /p/ /ė/ /r/, *spur.*
- Have children say the sounds with you. (/s/ /p/ /ėr/)

Continue the activity with these examples.

herd—her **whirl—whir** **firm—fir** **blurt—blur**

OBJECTIVES

- Discuss characteristics of nonfiction.
- Set purpose for listening.
- Build oral vocabulary.
- Delete final phonemes.

cycle
develop
insect
rearrange
yearly
emerge
fragile
vessel

MONITOR PROGRESS

If... children lack oral vocabulary experiences about the concept Changes in Nature,

then... use the Oral Vocabulary Routine. See p. DI·7 to teach *rearrange* and *yearly.*

Build Concepts Plants and trees changing through the seasons is a main theme in *What Makes the Seasons?* Have children demonstrate their understanding by drawing pictures of a tree in the spring, summer, winter, and fall.

OBJECTIVES

- Use structural cues to recognize contractions with *'s, 've* and *'re.*
- Read and sort contractions *'s, 've, 're.*

Skills Trace	
Contractions	
Introduce/Teach	**TE: 1.3 120c-d; 122c-d**
Practice	TE: 1.3 120f; PB: 1.2 45, DR 34
Reteach/Review	TE: 1.3; PB: 1.2 59, 142c, 168c-d, DI·82
Assess/Test	TE: 1.3 142e-g; Benchmark Test, Unit 3

Generalization

A contraction is a shortened form of two words. An apostrophe appears where letters have been dropped from the original words.

Strategic Intervention

Use **Monitor Progress,** p. 120d during Group Time after children have had more practice with contractions *'s, 've, 're.*

Advanced

Use **Monitor Progress,** p. 120d as a preassessment to determine whether or not this group of children would benefit from this contraction *'s, 've, 're* instruction.

Support Phonics Some languages such as Romance languages include contractions. If possible, provide some examples of contractions in the home language. In Spanish, *de + el = del*; in Portuguese, *por + os = pelos.* Tell children that in English, contractions use an apostrophe to replace the missing letters.

See the Phonics Transition Lessons in the ELL and Transition Handbook.

Contractions

TEACH/MODEL

Blending Strategy

ROUTINE

1. **Connect** Write *aren't* and *she'll.* You studied words like these already. What are these words? (They are contractions.) Today we will learn how to make other contractions.

2. **Model** Write *she's. She's* is a contraction. Remember that a contraction is a short way of writing two words as one. Beneath, write *she* and *is* on the board. *She* and *is* make up the contraction *she's. She's* is a short way of writing *she is.* This is how I blend this word: *She, s—She's.*

Write *you've* beneath *you have.* The contraction *you've* is made from the words *you* and *have.* An apostrophe takes the place of the letters *ha* in contractions with *have.*

Write *we're* beneath *we are.* The contraction *we're* is made from the words *we* and *are.* An apostrophe takes the place of the letter *a* in contractions with *are.*

3. **Group Practice** Together read contractions *what's, I've, you're* and identify the words that form them: *what is, I have, you are.*

4. **Review** What do you know about reading contractions? When you see a contraction, you know that it is a short way of writing two words. The apostrophe takes the place of letters that are left out.

BLEND WORDS

INDIVIDUALS READ CONTRACTIONS Call on individuals to read these contractions: *it's, we've, they're, let's,* and *they've.* Have them tell what they know about each word before reading it. (The contraction is a short way of writing two words. The apostrophe takes the place of letters that are left out.) For feedback, refer to step four of the Blending Strategy Routine. After reading each word, have children identify the two words that make up each contraction.

SORT WORDS

INDIVIDUALS SORT CONTRACTIONS Distribute word cards with contractions formed with *is, have,* and *are.* Write *is, have,* and *are* as headings in a three-column chart. Have children read their contractions and place their card under the appropriate heading. Then have them name the two words that make up the contraction.

is	*have*	*are*
he's	you've	you're
she's	they've	they're
it's	we've	we're
who's	I've	

Vocabulary TiP

You may wish to explain the meanings of this word.

let's let us

Pick a word from the box that means the same as each pair of words. Write it on the line.

She is tall.
She's tall.

he's	it's	I've	that's	they're
they've	we're	we've	you're	you've

1. I + have — I've
2. we + are — we're
3. it + is — it's
4. that + is — that's
5. you + have — you've
6. they + have — they've
7. we + have — we've
8. he + is — he's
9. they + are — they're
10. you + are — you're

School + Home **Home Activity** Your child practiced making contractions with 's, 've, and 're. Read each contraction on this page aloud. Challenge your child to use each one in a sentence. Then work together to write each sentence.

▲ **Practice Book 1.2** p. 45, Contractions

Monitor Progress — Check Word Reading Contractions

Write the following words and have individuals read them.

he's	**you've**	**it's**	**I've**	**we're**
isn't	**they're**	**I'm**	**they'll**	**what's**
you'll	**she's**	**didn't**	**we've**	**wasn't**

If... children cannot read contractions at this point,

then... continue to monitor their progress using other instructional opportunities during the week so that they can be successful with the Day 5 Assessment. See the Skills Trace on p. 120c.

Day 1 Check Word Reading
▶ **Day 2 Check Word Reading**
Day 3 Check High-Frequency Words/Retelling
Day 4 Check Fluency
Day 5 Assess Progress

Spiral REVIEW

- Rows 2 and 3 review contractions with *n't, 'm, 'll.*

Word Reading SUCCESS PREDICTOR

OBJECTIVE

- Spell words with *er, ir, ur.*

Spelling Words

Words with *er, ir, ur*

1. her	6. were
2. first	7. shirt
3. bird*	8. fur
4. girl	9. hurt
5. burn	10. sir

High-Frequency Words

11. visit*	12. done*

* Words from the Selection

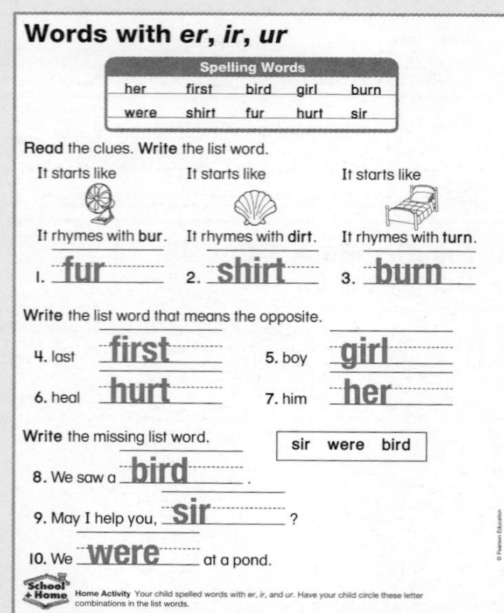

Words with *er*, *ir*, *ur*

Spelling Words				
her	first	bird	girl	burn
were	shirt	fur	hurt	sir

Read the clues. Write the list word.

It starts like | It starts like | It starts like

It rhymes with **bur**. | It rhymes with **dirt**. | It rhymes with **turn**.

1. fur 2. shirt 3. burn

Write the list word that means the opposite.

4. last first 5. boy girl
6. heal hurt 7. him her

Write the missing list word. sir were bird

8. We saw a bird.
9. May I help you, sir?
10. We were at a pond.

School + Home Home Activity Your child spelled words with er, ir, and ur. Have your child circle these letter combinations in the list words.

▲ **Spelling Practice Book** p. 66

Spelling

PRACTICE *r*-Controlled *er, ir, ur*

WRITE DICTATION SENTENCES Have children write these sentences. Repeat words slowly, allowing children to hear each sound. Children may use the Word Wall to help with spelling high-frequency words. **Word Wall**

The first girl hurt her hand.
Let's visit Gram and feed her bird.
We were glad to be done with our jobs.

HOMEWORK Spelling Practice Book, p. 66

Group Time

On-Level

Read Decodable Reader 34.

- Use p. 120f.

Strategic Intervention

Read Decodable Reader 34.

- Use the **Routine** on p. DI·58.

Advanced

Read Self-Selected Reading.

- Use the **Routine** on p. DI·59.

ELL Place English language learners in the groups that correspond to their reading abilities in English.

Independent Activities

Fluency Reading Pair children to reread Decodable Reader 33, this week's Leveled Readers, the ELL Reader from the previous week, or other text at children's independent level.

Journal Writing Write about how a chicken egg or a frog egg changes. Share writing.

Independent Reading See p. 118j for Reading/Library activities and suggestions.

Literacy Centers To practice contractions *'s, 've, 're,* you may use Word Work, p. 118j.

Practice Book 1.2 Draw Conclusions, p. 44
Contractions, p. 45
High-Frequency Words, p. 46

Break into small groups after Spelling and before High-Frequency Words.

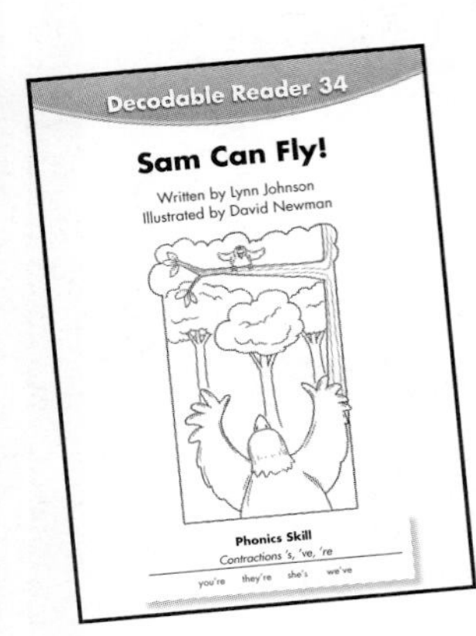

Apply Phonics

PRACTICE Contractions

HIGH-FREQUENCY WORDS Review *day, one, said, to,* and *you* on the Word Wall. If necessary, have children practice in pairs with word cards. Word Wall

QUOTATION MARKS Point out the quotation marks on p. 75 and explain they show that someone is talking. Have children watch for quotation marks.

READ DECODABLE READER 34

- Pages 74–75 Read aloud quietly with the group.
- Pages 76–77 Have the group read aloud without you.
- Pages 78–80 Select individuals to read aloud.

CHECK COMPREHENSION AND DECODING

- Why does Sam feel small and sad? (Sam cannot fly.)
- How do you know that Dad and Mom care about Sam? (They helped Sam to learn to fly.)
- How do you think Dad and Mom feel about Sam trying hard? (They feel happy and proud.)
- Point to a contraction in the story. What is the contraction? List words that are named. Children may supply *she's, they're, you're, we've.*
- Have children name the two words that make up each contraction in the story. List the word pair next to the matching contraction.

HOMEWORK Take-Home Decodable Reader 34

REREAD FOR FLUENCY

Oral Rereading

ROUTINE

1. **Read** Have children read the entire book orally.
2. **Reread** To achieve optimal fluency, children should reread the text three or four times.
3. **Provide Feedback** Listen as children read and provide corrective feedback regarding their oral reading and their use of the blending strategy.

OBJECTIVES

- Apply knowledge of letter-sounds and word parts to decode unknown words when reading.
- Use context with letter-sounds and word parts to confirm the identification of unknown words.
- Practice fluency in oral rereading.

Monitor Progress

Decoding

If...	then...
If... children have difficulty decoding a word,	**then...** prompt them to blend the word. • What is the new word? • Is the new word a word you know? • Does it make sense in the story?
If... children have difficulty decoding *padded* and *hopped,*	**then...** prompt them to cover the added consonant and the *-ed* ending to read the base word; uncover the ending and blend the base word and ending to read the word.

ELL

Access Content

Beginning Point to the pictures and paraphrase *Sam Can Fly!* For example, on p. 74: Sam is sad. Sam cannot fly.

Intermediate Read the sentences that include contractions. Use the pictures to show to whom or to what each refers. For example, on p. 78: They're so strong. Point to Sam's feet. Sam's feet are so strong.

Advanced Have children read sentences that include contractions. Have them reread each sentence with the two words that make up the contraction.

Words to Read

- know
- done
- push
- wait
- visit

120

Read the Words

Let's find out about insects.

Do you know what's in here?

When the insect inside is done growing, it will push its way out.

What will it be?
Wait and see.
Then it will visit the garden.

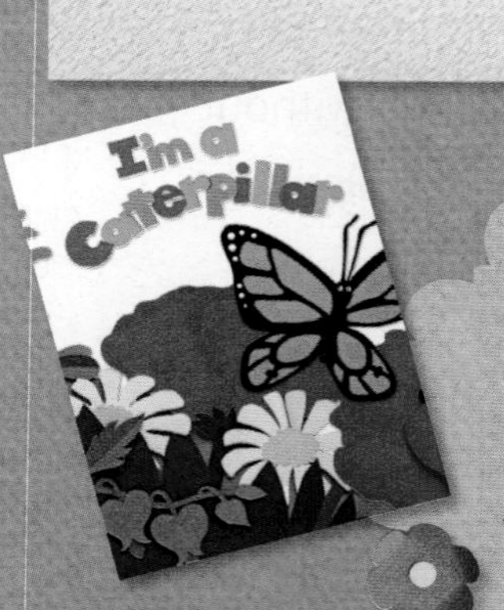

Genre: Nonfiction
Nonfiction selections teach us about something in the real world. Next you will read about the life cycle of a caterpillar.

121

OBJECTIVE

- Recognize high-frequency words.

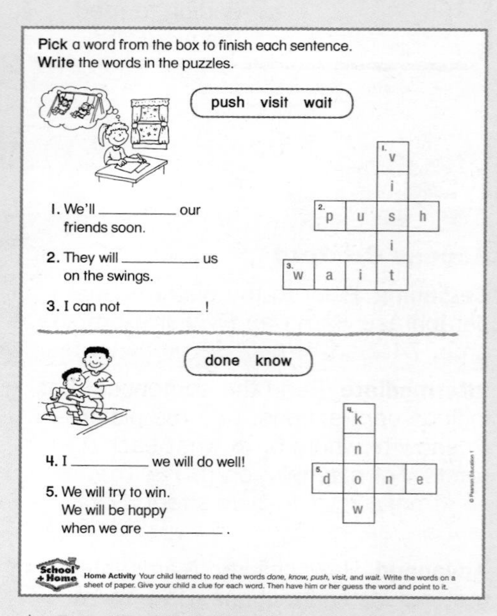

Pick a word from the box to finish each sentence.
Write the words in the puzzles.

push visit wait

1. We'll ________ our friends soon.
2. They will ________ us on the swings.
3. I can not ________!

done know

4. I ________ we will do well!
5. We will try to win. We will be happy when we are ________.

Home Activity Your child learned to read the words done, know, push, visit, and wait. Write the words on a sheet of paper. Give your child a clue for each word. Then have him or her guess the word and point to it.

▲ **Practice Book 1.2** p. 46, High-Frequency Words

High-Frequency Words

Nondecodable Words

ROUTINE

1. **Say and Spell** Look at the words on p. 120. You cannot yet blend the sounds in these words. We will spell the words and use letter-sounds we know to learn them. Point to the first word. This word is *know* as in "I know we are in school." *K-n-o-w, know.* What is this word? What are the letters in this word?
2. **Identify Familiar Letter-Sounds** Point to the second letter in *know.* What is this letter? What is its sound? (*n*/n/) Point out that the *k* is silent.
3. **Demonstrate Meaning** Tell me a sentence using this word.

Repeat the routine with the other Words to Read. Have children identify these familiar letter-sounds: *done* (*d*/d/, *n*/n/), *push* (*p*/p/, *sh*/sh/), *wait* (*w*/w/, *t*/t/), *visit* (*v*/v/, *s*/z/, *t*/t/).

Have children read aloud the sentences on p. 121, point to the Words to Read, and discuss the questions in sentences 2 and 4. Add the words to the Word Wall. **Word Wall**

Interactive Writing

WRITE Description

BRAINSTORM Use the Big Book *What Makes the Seasons?* to encourage a discussion. Picture walk through the book and ask children to identify what makes the seasons change.

SHARE THE PEN Have children participate in writing a description of what makes the seasons change and how the seasons are different. To begin, have a child describe what the Earth does each year (The Earth moves around the sun every year). Write the sentence, inviting individuals to write familiar letter-sounds, word parts, and high-frequency words. Ask questions such as:

- What is the first sound you hear in the word *sun?* (/s/)
- What letter stands for that sound? *(s)* Have a volunteer write *s.*
- What is the last sound you hear in the word *sun?* (/n/)
- What letter stands for that sound? *(n)* Have a volunteer write *n.*

Continue to have individuals make contributions. Frequently reread what has been written while tracking the print.

READ THE DESCRIPTION Read the completed description aloud, having children echo you.

Changing Seasons

The Earth moves around the sun every year. Spring is warm. The days are long and hot in summer. Fall is cool. The days are short and cold in winter.

INDEPENDENT WRITING

WRITE A DESCRIPTION Have children write their own description about changing seasons. Let children illustrate their writing.

OBJECTIVE

- Write a description.

Strategic Intervention

Have children look at pictures of the different seasons discussed throughout the book. As they look at the pictures, have them give a short description of what is happening.

Advanced

Have children who are able to write complete sentences independently write their own description of their favorite season.

Writing Support Before writing, explain how the Earth moves around the sun each year.

Beginning Provide a writing framework that children can copy, filling in missing words.

Intermediate Have children talk with you about their ideas about writing. Clarify one of their main ideas in conventional English to guide their writing.

Advanced Have children do a "think-aloud" with a partner to discuss what they are planning to write.

2

OBJECTIVE

- Identify *am, is, are, was,* and *were.*

DAILY FIX-IT

3. She did not want to hert it?
She did not want to hurt it.

4. she pickked it up.
She picked it up.

Am, Is, Are, Was, and *Were*

The words **am, is,** and **are** tell about now. Use **am** or **is** to tell about one. Use **are** to tell about more than one.

I **am** big. It **is** little. They **are** tiny.

The words **was** and **were** tell about the past. Use **was** to tell about one. Use **were** to tell about more than one.

It **was** hungry. They **were** hungry.

Circle the verb in each sentence. **Write** *Now* if the sentence tells about now. **Write** *Past* if the sentence tells about the past.

1. I (was) an egg. Past
2. I (am) a caterpillar. Now
3. They (are) caterpillars. Now
4. They (were) eggs. Past
5. The change (is) amazing. Now

School-Home Connection **Home Activity** Your child learned about *am, is, are, was,* and *were*. Read a story with your child. Have your child point out the verbs *am, is, are, was,* and *were* in the story and tell whether the sentence tells about now or the past.

▲ **Grammar and Writing Practice Book** p. 65

Support Grammar In some languages including Chinese, Hmong, and Haitian Creole, the verb *to be* can be left out of a sentence. If children say *I happy* instead of *I am happy,* provide extra practice with forms of the verb *to be.* See the Grammar Transition lessons in the ELL and Transition Handbook.

Grammar

DEVELOP THE CONCEPT
Am, Is, Are, Was, and Were

IDENTIFY *Am, Is, Are, Was,* AND *Were* Write *am* and *was* on the board. Point to each word as you read it. Ask children to identify the word that tells about now and the word that tells about the past. (*Am* tells about now*; was* tells about the past.) Continue with *are* and *were.*

Am, is, and *are* tell about now. *Was* and *were* tell about the past. Which of these words tell about one? *(am, is, was)* Which words tell about more than one? *(are, were)*

PRACTICE

USE *Am, Is, Are, Was,* AND *Were IN SENTENCES* Write a list containing *am, is, are, was,* and *were* on the board. Then write the sentences listed below. Model completing the sentence.

MODEL Last night is in the past. *He* tells about one. I need a word that tells about the past and that tells about one. *Was* tells about the past, and it tells about one. Write *was. Last night he was hungry.*

Have children identify the correct words for the other sentences. Write the words children provide in the blank spaces.

am	is	are	was	were

Last night he ___ hungry. *(was)*
Today she ___ happy. *(is)*
Yesterday the dogs ___ tired. *(were)*
Now I ___ six years old. *(am)*
Today the kittens ___ quiet. *(are)*

Speaking and Listening

SUMMARIZE INFORMATION

OBJECTIVES

- Speak to summarize information.
- Listen to understand information.

MODEL SPEAKING AND LISTENING Remind children of appropriate speaking and listening behaviors. Then discuss how to summarize information.

- A summary is always shorter than the original story.
- First, you find the most important parts of the story.
- Then you tell the main idea of the story in your own words.

Model how to summarize information using the Big Book *What Makes the Seasons?*

SUMMARIZE NONFICTION Ask children to summarize information by telling the most important parts of a nonfiction story they have read or had read to them. Encourage children to think about the main idea of the story and its most important parts before taking their turn speaking to the class. Tell children that it is important to stay on topic when speaking.

Wrap Up Your Day!

HIGH-FREQUENCY WORDS Write the following sentences. *We had to wait to visit our friend. I know how it is done. They do not like for us to push past the gate.* Ask children to read the sentences and identify the high-frequency words *done, know, push, visit, wait.*

r*-CONTROLLED *er, ir, ur Write *her* and ask children what sound the *er* in *her* has. (/ėr/). Repeat with *bird* and *fur.*

LET'S TALK ABOUT IT Recall the Big Book *What Makes the Seasons?* Ask: What changes can we observe in nature? (Possible response: the seasons change. We can see seeds sprout, plants grow, and days get longer.) Then display the cycle chart from Day 1. Have children suggest what a cycle chart for a plant might include.

PREVIEW Day 3

Tell children that tomorrow they will read about a caterpillar that grows and changes.

Day 3

AT A GLANCE

Oral Vocabulary
What Makes the Seasons?

Phonemic Awareness
Blend and Segment Onset/Rime

Phonics and Spelling
r-controlled *er, ir, ur,* and Contractions *'s, 've, 're*

Spelling: Words with *er, ir, ur*

Build Background
Caterpillars and Butterflies

Vocabulary
Selection Words

caterpillar chrysalis crawl pupa shiver

High-Frequency Words

done know push visit wait

Comprehension
Skill Draw Conclusions

Strategy Text Structure

Read
Group Time < Differentiated Instruction

I'm a Caterpillar

Vocabulary
Use Reference Sources

Fluency
Attend to End Punctuation

Writing Trait
Focus/Ideas

Grammar
Am, Is, Are, Was, Were

Materials
- *Sing with Me Big Book*
- *What Makes the Seasons?*
- Phonics Songs/Rhymes Chart 17
- Background Building Audio
- Graphic Organizer Flip Chart 19
- Vocabulary Transparency 17
- Student Edition 122–139

Morning Warm-Up!

Have you ever seen a large caterpillar inch across the schoolyard? Today we'll read about how this insect makes an amazing change. What changes might a caterpillar make?

QUESTION OF THE DAY Encourage children to sing "Life Cycle" from the *Sing with Me Big Book* as you gather. Write the message and track the print as you read it. Discuss the questions.

REVIEW R-CONTROLLED ar

- Ask children to find words that have the /är/ sound. *(large, schoolyard)*
- Circle each word and have children identify the letters that stand for the /är/ sound. *(ar)*

ELL

Build Background Use the Day 3 instruction on ELL Poster 17 to support children's use of English to communicate about lesson concepts.

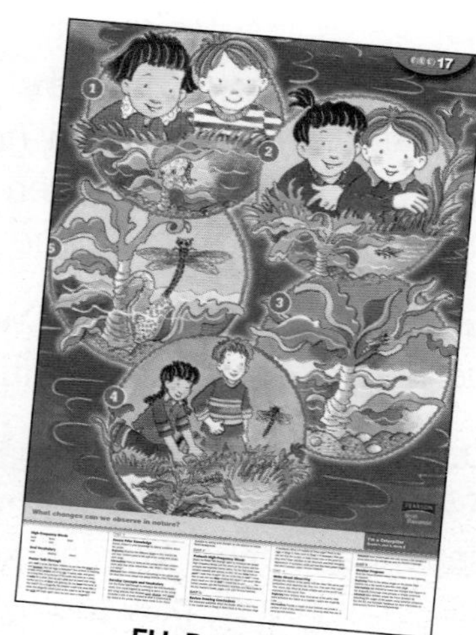

ELL Poster 17

Share Literature

LISTEN AND RESPOND

BUILD ORAL VOCABULARY Review that yesterday the class listened to find out how the sun is different in each season. Explain that sometimes we may need to **rearrange** our outdoor plans because of weather conditions. Ask that children listen today to find out how our lives may change with the seasons each year.

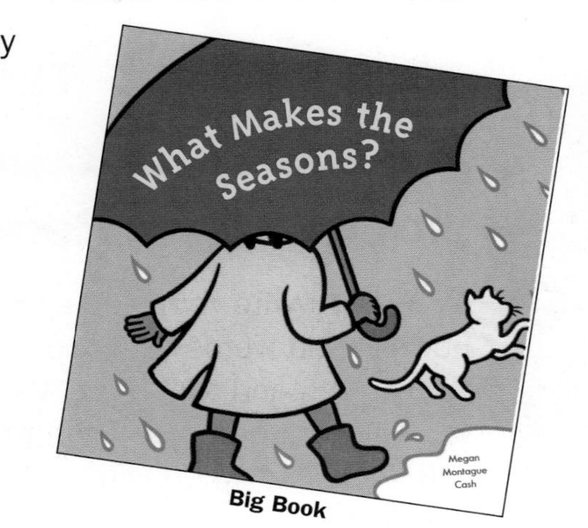

Big Book

MONITOR LISTENING COMPREHENSION

- How might we change our lives as the seasons change **yearly**? (Possible response: We change our activities.)
- What plans might you have to change, or rearrange, when the weather changes? (We might have to rearrange outdoor activities, such as camping, swimming, or picnics if it rains. We might have to rearrange winter plans if it snows too hard to go out.)

Phonemic Awareness

BLEND AND SEGMENT ONSET/RIME

- We just read that some animals sleep or hibernate in winter. The animals that do not hibernate must have thick fur. Listen to the word parts in *fur.*
- Model saying the onset and rime, /f/ /ėr/. Have children say the sounds /f/ /ėr/ and then say the sounds by themselves.
- Now say the onset and rime as you write the letter that goes with it. Say /f/ /ėr/ as you write *f, ur.* Have children say the sounds as you point to the letters /f/ *-ur* and blend the sounds to say the word *(fur).*
- Change the *f* to *bl.* Listen as I change the sound at the beginning of *fur* to the /bl/ sound: *blur.* Have children say the sounds with you. (/bl/*-ur*) and blend the sounds to say the word *(blur).* Repeat with /sp/, *ur, spur.*

Continue with these samples:

st/ir	**f/ern**	**c/url**
wh/ir	**st/ern**	**h/url**

OBJECTIVES

- Set purpose for listening.
- Build oral vocabulary.
- Blend and segment onset and rime.

to build oral vocabulary

cycle
develop
insect
rearrange
yearly
emerge
fragile
vessel

MONITOR PROGRESS

If... children lack oral vocabulary experiences about the concept Changes in Nature,

then... use the Oral Vocabulary Routine. See p. DI•7 to review *rearrange* and *yearly.*

ELL

Listen and Respond Have children act out these words in dark print in the selection *What Makes the Seasons?: tall* (p. 11), *cold* (p. 14), *dance* (p. 16), and *hibernate* (p. 23).

OBJECTIVES

- Review *r*-controlled *er, ir, ur* words and contractions *'s, 've, 're.*
- Build, read, and sort regular *r*-controlled *er, ir, ur* words and contractions *'s, 've, 're.*
- Preview words before reading them.
- Spell words with *er, ir, ur.*

Strategic Intervention

Use **Strategic Intervention Decodable Reader 17** for more practice with *r*-controlled *er, ir, ur* and contractions *'s, 've, 're.*

Support Phonics Haitian Creole does not include contractions. Haitian Creole speakers may need extra practice reading and writing contractions and including the apostrophe. You may want to have them use letter tiles and a piece of elbow macaroni as the apostrophe to build and read contractions.

r-Controlled *er, ir, ur* and Contractions

TEACH/MODEL

Fluent Word Reading

ROUTINE

1. **Connect** Write *fern.* You can read this word because you know how to read words with *r*-controlled vowels. What sounds does *er* in this word stand for? (/ėr/) What's the word? *(fern)* Continue in the same way with *dirt* and *curl.* Then write *he's.* You can read this word because you know that when you see an apostrophe, the word may be a contraction that is made up of two words. What is the first word? *(he)* What is the contraction? *(he's)*
2. **Model** When you come to a new word, look at all the letters in the word and think about their sounds. Say the sounds in the word to yourself and then read the word. Model reading *fern, dirt,* and curl this way. When you come to a new word or a contraction, what will you do?
3. **Group Practice** Write *jerk, you've, sir, you're, purse.* Let's read these words. Look at all the letters, think about their sounds, and say the sounds to yourself. Also, notice if the word is a contraction. When I point to the word, let's read it together. Allow 2–3 seconds previewing time for each word.

WORD READING

PHONICS SONGS AND RHYMES CHART 17 Frame each of the following words on Phonics Songs and Rhymes Chart 17. Call on individuals to read them. Guide children in previewing.

her	**dirt**	**fern**	**burst**
she's	**they're**	**they've**	**turn**

Sing "Burst Out Bugs" to the tune of "Row, Row, Row Your Boat," or play the CD. Have children follow along on the chart as they sing. Then have individuals take turns locating /ėr/ words and contractions. Identify the word *return* and have children name the letters that stand for /ėr/.

Phonics Songs and Rhymes Audio

Phonics Songs and Rhymes Chart 17

SORT WORDS

INDIVIDUALS SORT *er, ir, ur* WORDS AND CONTRACTIONS Have children list the /ėr/ words from Phonics Songs and Rhymes Chart 17 and sort them according to their vowel spellings.

her	**dirt**	**burst**
fern		**turn**
		return

Then write the contractions from Chart 17 and have children name the two words that make up the contraction.

she's	**she is**
they're	**they are**
they've	**they have**

Spelling

PRACTICE *r*-Controlled *er, ir, ur*

TURN THE CARDS Have children write the *er, ir, ur* spelling words on cards, one word per card. Have them use tiny self-stick notes to cover *er, ir,* and *ur* in the words.

- Have partners place their cards face down on a table or desk.
- Have one child choose a card, remove the note, and spell the word. Have this child replace the note, spell the word from memory, and use it in a sentence. Then have partners switch roles.
- To conclude, have partners write the high-frequency words on cards and take turns spelling the words and using the words in sentences.

HOMEWORK Spelling Practice Book, p. 67

Spelling Words

Words with *er, ir, ur*

1. her	6. were
2. first	7. shirt
3. bird*	8. fur
4. girl	9. hurt
5. burn	10. sir

High-Frequency Words

11. visit*	12. done*

* Words from the Selection

Words with *er, ir, ur*

Circle the word that is spelled correctly. Write it.

1. I like your ___. sherl (shirt) shurt — shirt
2. I knew where you ___. (were) wir wure — were
3. Meet the new ___. gerl (girl) gurl — girl
4. Let the candle ___. bern birn (burn) — burn
5. Judy said, "Yes, ___." ser (sir) sur — sir
6. Look at the ___. berd (bird) burd — bird
7. Can I be ___? ferst (first) furst — first
8. His dog has black ___. fer fure (fur) — fur
9. Did you get ___? hert hirt (hurt) — hurt
10. I played a game with ___. (her) hir hur — her

Spelling Words: her, first, bird, girl, burn, were, shirt, fur, hurt, sir

School + Home — Home Activity Your child used spelling words in sentences. Help your child make up a new sentence for each spelling word.

▲ **Spelling Practice Book** p. 67

Build Background

DISCUSS CATERPILLARS AND BUTTERFLIES Display pictures of caterpillars and butterflies. Initiate discussion by asking children what they already know about caterpillars and butterflies.

- How can you tell a caterpillar from another insect?
- What do caterpillars eat?
- How does a caterpillar change?

BACKGROUND-BUILDING AUDIO Have children listen to the CD and share the new information they learned about caterpillars and butterflies.

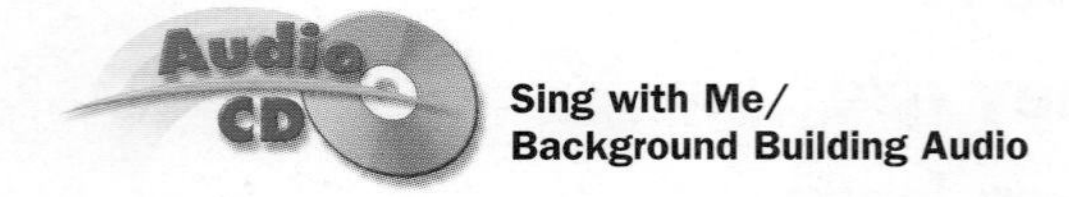

**Sing with Me/
Background Building Audio**

COMPLETE A VENN DIAGRAM Draw two large overlapping circles. Write *Caterpillars* above the left-hand circle and *Butterflies* above the right-hand circle. The overlapping parts of each circle will include similarities between the two. Ask children to suggest things they already know about caterpillars and butterflies. After each response ask if it applies to only one or both of them. Write their responses in the appropriate portion of the circles.

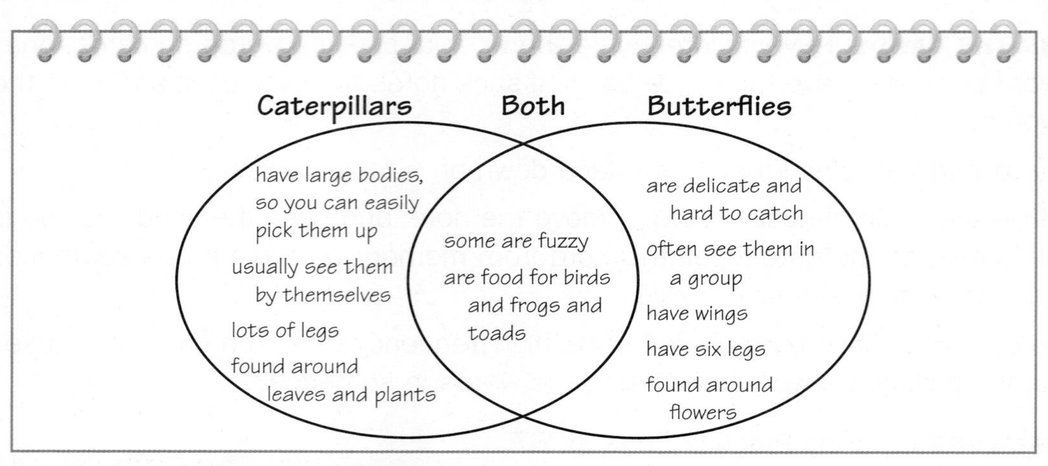

▲ **Graphic Organizer Flip Chart 28**

CONNECT TO SELECTION Connect background information to *I'm a Caterpillar.*

Caterpillars like to eat and eat and eat. The caterpillar in the selection we are going to read likes to eat too. When it's impossible for him to eat anything more, some things begin to change. We'll find out what changes.

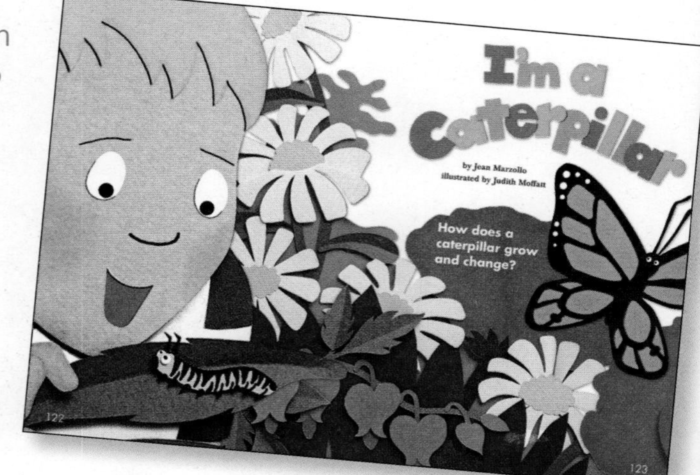

OBJECTIVES

- Build background.
- Learn selection words.
- Recognize high-frequency words.

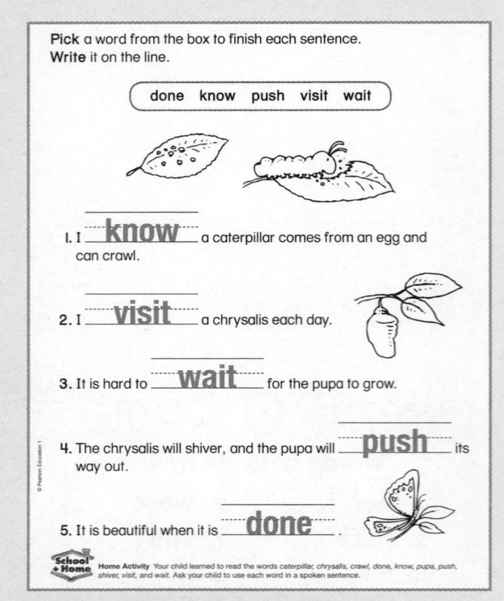

Pick a word from the box to finish each sentence.
Write it on the line.

done know push visit wait

1. I **know** a caterpillar comes from an egg and can crawl.
2. I **visit** a chrysalis each day.
3. It is hard to **wait** for the pupa to grow.
4. The chrysalis will shiver, and the pupa will **push** its way out.
5. It is beautiful when it is **done**.

Home Activity Your child learned to read the words caterpillar, chrysalis, crawl, done, know, pupa, push, shiver, visit, and wait. Ask your child to use each word in a spoken sentence.

▲ **Practice Book 1.2** p. 47, High-Frequency and Selection Words

Activate Prior Knowledge Display or draw a picture of a caterpillar and say the word with children. Explain that a caterpillar is an insect that eats plants. Have them give the word for caterpillar in their home languages. Discuss what children know about caterpillars.

Vocabulary

SELECTION WORDS

Use Vocabulary Transparency 17 to introduce the selection words.

- Read each sentence as you track the print.
- Frame each underlined word. Explain the word's meaning.

  caterpillar an insect that changes into a moth or butterfly
  crawl move on your hands and knees or with your body close to the ground
  chrysalis forms from the body of a caterpillar and has a hard shell that protects the caterpillar as it changes into a butterfly
  pupa the form of an insect while it is changing from a wormlike larva into an adult
  shiver to shake

- Ask children to identify familiar letter-sounds and word parts: *caterpillar* (small words *cat* and *pill*), *crawl* (*cr*/kr/, *l*/l/), *chrysalis* (*s*/s/), *pupa* (*p*/p/), *shiver* (*sh*/sh/, *v*/v/, *r*/r/).
- Have children read each sentence aloud with you.
- To encourage discussion using the story vocabulary, ask children to tell what they know about caterpillars.

HIGH-FREQUENCY WORDS

Use Vocabulary Transparency 17 to review this week's words.

- Point to a word. Say and spell it.
- Have children say and spell the word.
- Ask children to identify familiar letter-sounds.

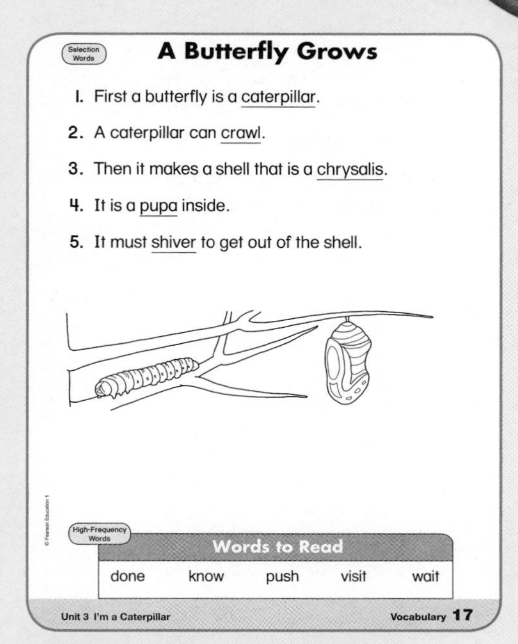
Selection Words

A Butterfly Grows

1. First a butterfly is a caterpillar.
2. A caterpillar can crawl.
3. Then it makes a shell that is a chrysalis.
4. It is a pupa inside.
5. It must shiver to get out of the shell.

High-Frequency Words

Words to Read				
done	know	push	visit	wait

Unit 3 I'm a Caterpillar Vocabulary 17

▲ **Vocabulary Transparency 17**

Access Content Use the vocabulary strategies and word cards in the ELL Teaching Guide, pp. 115–116.

Monitor Progress **Check High-Frequency Words**

Point to the following words on the Word Wall and have individuals read them.

done	**now**	**know**	**push**	**food**
afraid	**visit**	**wait**	**away**	**soon**

If ... children cannot read these words,

then ... have them practice in pairs with word cards before reading the selection. Monitor their fluency with these words during reading, and provide additional practice opportunities before the Day 5 Assessment.

Day 1 Check Word Reading · Day 2 Check Word Reading · ▶ **Day 3 Check High-Frequency Words/Retelling** · Day 4 Check Fluency · Day 5 Assess Progress

Spiral REVIEW

- Reviews previously taught high-frequency words.

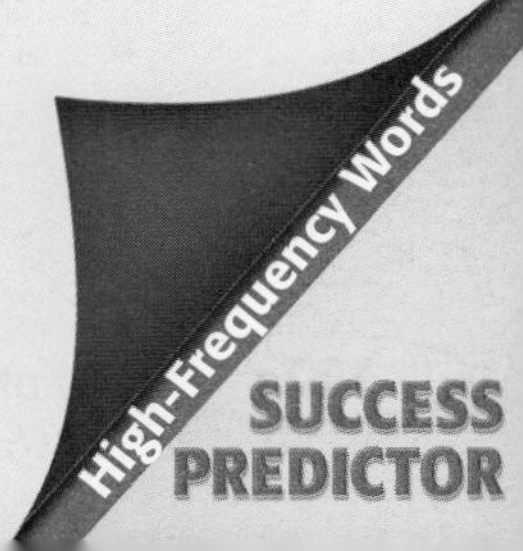

OBJECTIVES

- Draw conclusions.
- Recognize chronological/ sequential text structure.

Comprehension

DRAW CONCLUSIONS

RECOGNIZE DRAWING CONCLUSIONS Remind children that authors don't always tell readers exactly what happens in a story or article and that they may have to use clues in the words and pictures to figure out information on their own. Guide children to draw conclusions about previously read stories.

CONNECT TO READING

- Look for clues in the words and pictures that help you understand.
- Use what you read and what you know about real life to help you understand.

TEXT STRUCTURE

INTRODUCE THE STRATEGY Things often happen in a certain order. When an author tells things in sequence, he or she tells them in the order in which they happen.

MODEL When I read a nonfiction selection, I ask myself if the author tells things in the order in which they happen.

CONNECT TO READING Encourage children to ask themselves these questions as they read *I'm a Caterpillar.*

- Does the author tell things in the order in which they happen?
- What happens first? Next?

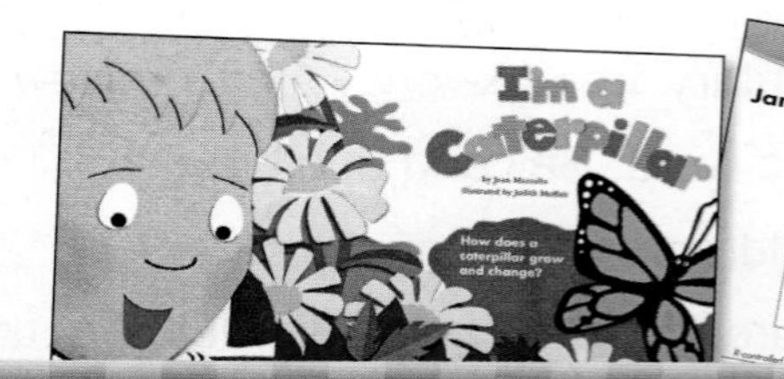

Group Time

DAY 3

On-Level	Strategic Intervention	Advanced
Read *I'm a Caterpillar.*	**Read** *I'm a Caterpillar.*	**Read** *I'm a Caterpillar.*
• Use pp. 122–139.	• Use pp. 122–139. • Use the **Routine** on p. DI·60.	• Use the **Routine** on p. DI·61.

ELL Place English language learners in the groups that correspond to their reading abilities in English.

Independent Activities

Independent Reading See p. 118j for Reading/Library activities and suggestions.

Journal Writing Make a list of the things you would like to know about a butterfly. Share writing.

Literacy Centers Use the Listening and Writing Centers from *I'm a Caterpillar* on pp. 118j and 118k.

Practice Book 1.2 High-Frequency Words and Selection Words, p. 47

Break into small groups after Comprehension and before Fluency.

I'm a Caterpillar

by Jean Marzollo
illustrated by Judith Moffatt

How does a caterpillar grow and change?

122 123

Prereading Strategies

PREVIEW AND PREDICT Read the title and identify the author and illustrator. Reread the title and ask who children think is saying, "I'm a caterpillar." Tell children to listen to find out who or what the narrator is throughout the selection.

DISCUSS NONFICTION Direct attention to the pictures on pp. 122–123. Discuss whether children think this selection will be about real things. Remind them that even if the pictures are made by an artist, a selection can give real information. Reread the definition of nonfiction on p. 121 of the Student Edition.

SET PURPOSE Read the question on p. 123 and have children set a purpose for reading.

AudioText

ELL

Access Content Before reading, review the story summary in English and/or the home language. See the ELL Teaching Guide, pp. 117–119.

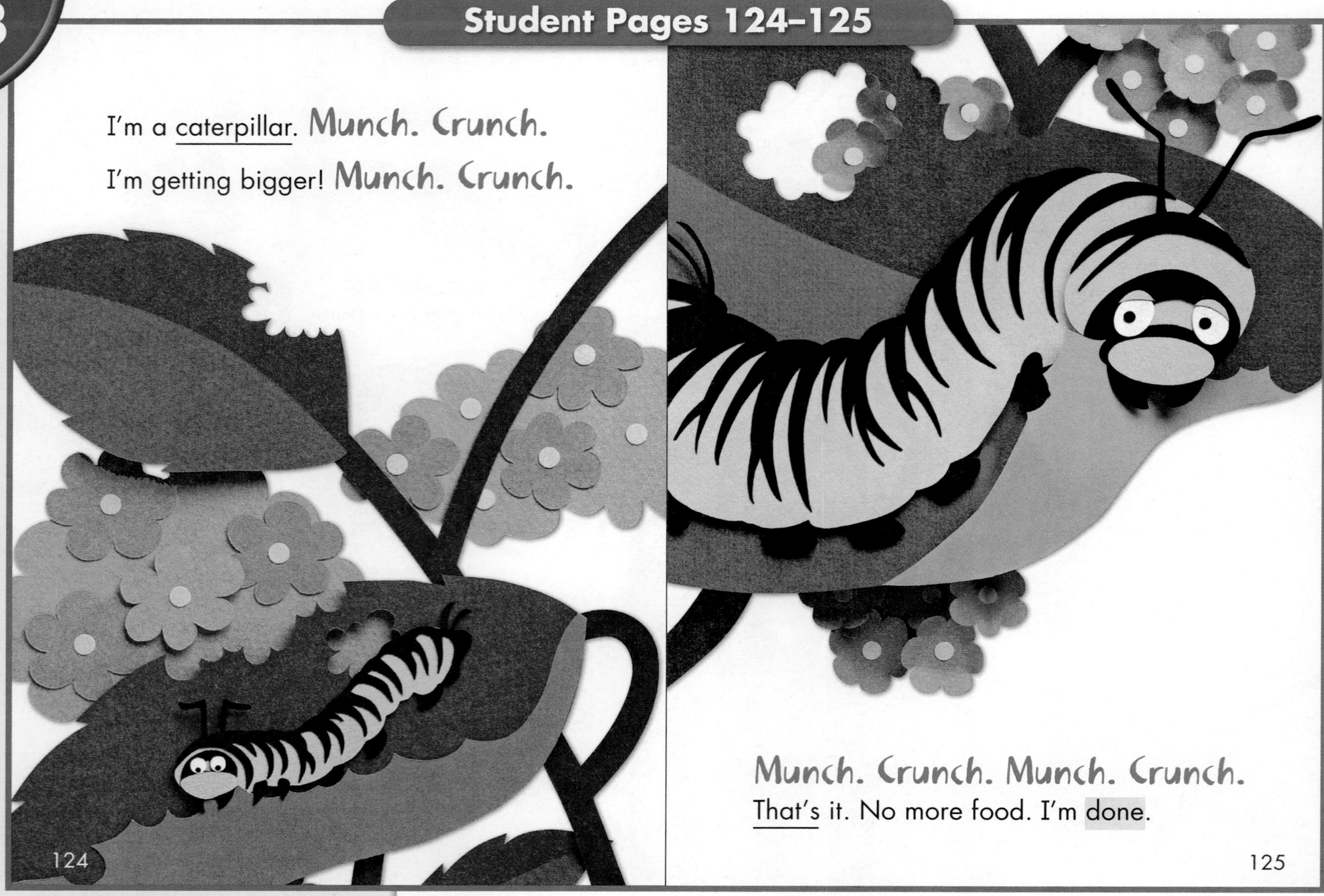

▲ **Pages 124–125**
Have children read to find out what the caterpillar is doing.

Monitor Progress	
Decoding	
If... children come to a word they don't know,	**then...** remind them to blend the word: 1. Look at each letter. 2. Think of the sound for each letter. 3. Blend the sounds. 4. Read the word.

Skills in Context

DRAW CONCLUSIONS

- **Why do you think the caterpillar is finished eating?**
  The caterpillar is finished growing.

Monitor Progress	Draw Conclusions
If... children have difficulty answering the question,	**then...** model how to draw conclusions and make inferences from the text.

MODEL When I read the last line, where the caterpillar says, "I'm done," I ask myself, "Done with what?" I know that the caterpillar was eating and growing. Then it says it needs no more food. I think that means that it has eaten all it needs because it has grown all it needs to grow.

ASSESS Have children tell what the caterpillar eats and how they can tell. (It eats leaves because the pictures show the caterpillar taking bites out of the leaf it is sitting on.)

___ *r*-controlled *er, ir, ur* and contractions *'s, 've, 're* high-frequency/tested vocabulary

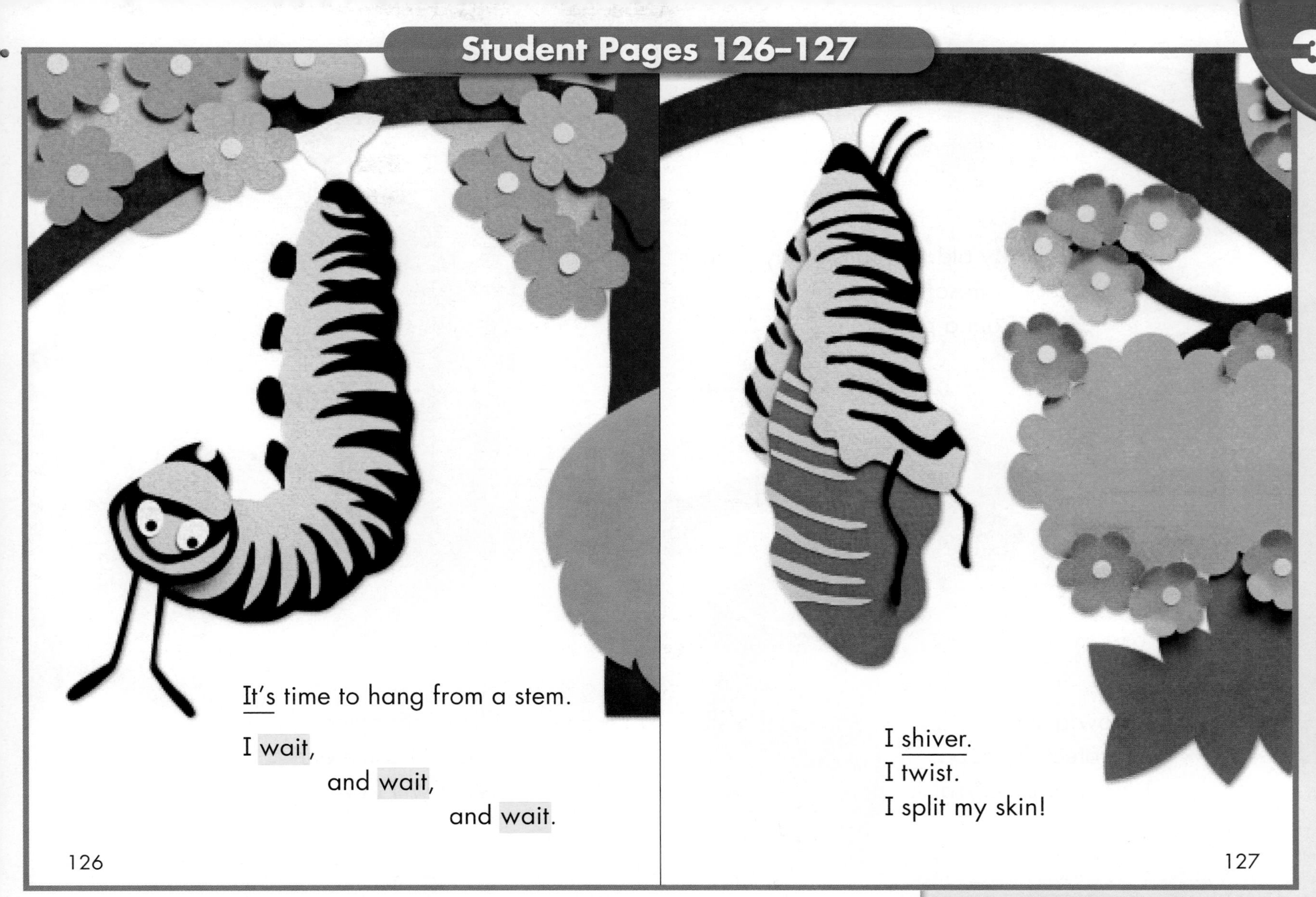

Guiding Comprehension

Compare and Contrast • Critical

- ***Text to World*** **What animals have you seen or read about that are similar to the caterpillar?**
  Possible response: I've seen worms in the garden. They're long and skinny like the caterpillar.

Text Structure • Inferential

- **How does the caterpillar change? Tell about the changes in the order that they happen.**
  First the caterpillar eats and grows, next it hangs from a stem, and then it splits out of its skin.

Use Illustrations • Inferential

- **How has the caterpillar changed on page 127?**
  Children will probably say it doesn't look like a caterpillar anymore because you can't see its head or its legs.

▲ **Pages 126–127**
Have children read to find out what the caterpillar does.

Access Content Help children understand the actions of the caterpillar by explaining the words *shiver, twist,* and *split*. Ask children to pantomime the actions of the caterpillar with you.

Monitor Progress

High-Frequency Words

If...	then...
If... children have a problem reading a new high frequency word,	**then...** use the High-Frequency Routine on pp. 120–121 to reteach the problematic word.

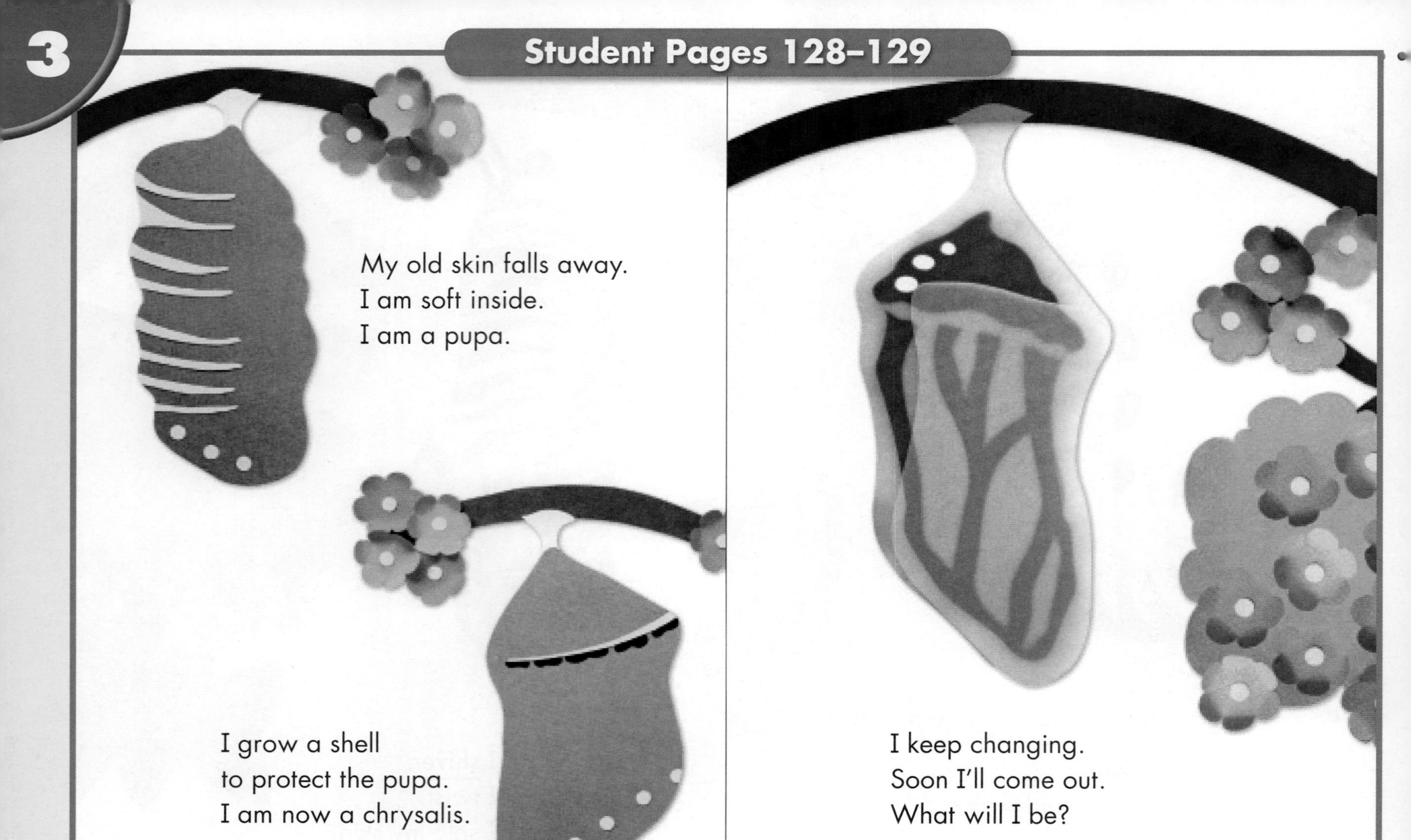

▲ **Pages 128–129**
Have children read to find out what happens next.

Strategies in Context

TEXT STRUCTURE

- **What happens to the caterpillar next?**
  Its skin falls away, and it is a soft pupa. Then it grows, or develops, a shell to protect the pupa. It keeps changing inside the shell.

Monitor Progress	Text Structure
If... children have difficulty answering the question,	**then...** model how to identify sequential text order.

Think Aloud **MODEL** Authors often tell us about true events in the order that they happen. The author begins with the first thing that happens—the caterpillar's skin falls away. Then she tells what happens next—it grows a shell. Then she tells what happens after that—it keeps changing.

ASSESS Have children tell about the things that have happened so far to the caterpillar, from the beginning to now.

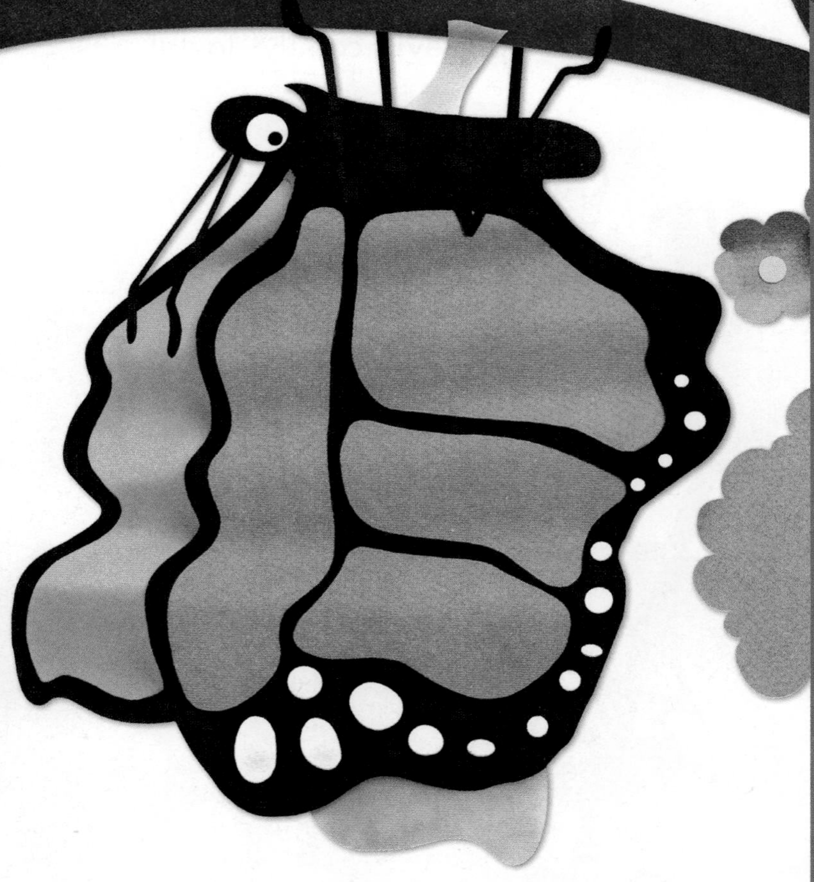

Guiding Comprehension

Draw Conclusions • Inferential

- **What happened while the caterpillar was in the chrysalis?**
  The caterpillar developed into a butterfly while it was in the chrysalis.

Draw Conclusions • Critical

- **Why doesn't the butterfly fly right away when it comes out of the chrysalis?**
  Children will probably say it can't fly right away because its wings are wet and need to unfold.

Summarize • Inferential

- **What has happened so far?**
  The caterpillar ate and grew. Then it became a chrysalis. When the chrysalis opened, a butterfly came out.

▲ **Pages 130–131**
Have children read to find out how the caterpillar changed.

Strategy Self-Check

Have children ask themselves these questions to check their reading.

Decoding Words

- Do I look for word parts I can read?
- Do I blend all the sounds in a word to read it?
- Do I reread to make sure the word makes sense in the story?

Text Structure/Chronological Sequence

- Does the author tell things in order?
- Do I know what happened first, next, and last?

Flap. Flap. Hey! I can fly! Ta-da!

132

I visit flowers. I drink nectar. Yum!

My mouth is like a straw.

Sip. Sip. Sip.

133

▲ **Pages 132–133**
Have children read to see what the butterfly does.

EXTEND SKILLS

Text Features

For instruction in how authors use different type sizes and formats, discuss the following:

- Why do you think the author used special type for the words *sip, sip, sip*? (Because *sip* is an action word like *munch* and *crunch*.)
- What do you think an author might do if he wanted to show words that are whispered? (Use a small type.)

Assess Have children look back at page 130 and discuss why they think the author used big letters for the word *butterfly*.

Skills in Context

REVIEW SEQUENCE

- **What does the butterfly do after it starts to fly?**
  It visits flowers and drinks nectar.

Monitor Progress	Sequence
If... children have difficulty answering the question,	**then...** model how to recognize the sequence of events.

MODEL When I read, I pay attention to what happens and I try to remember the order in which things happen. The butterfly waits for its wings to dry off and unfold. Then it starts to fly. Once it can fly, it visits flowers and drinks nectar.

ASSESS Have children tell about what happened to the caterpillar after it finished eating. (It hung from a stem and lost its skin.)

___ *r*-controlled *er, ir, ur* and contractions *'s, 've, 're* ☐ high-frequency/tested vocabulary

▲ **Pages 134–135**
Have children read to learn about butterflies.

Guiding Comprehension

Details and Facts • Literal

- **Why aren't these butterflies afraid of birds?**
  The birds know the butterflies taste awful.

Draw Conclusions • Critical

- ***Text to World*** **Why is it important for some animals to taste bad?**
  Possible response: Other animals won't eat animals that taste bad.

Predict • Inferential

- **What do you think might happen next? How will the cycle continue?**
  Children will probably predict that the butterfly will lay her eggs and hatch little butterflies.

TIME FOR Science

Adaptations

Many animals have special body parts that help them eat or protect them from enemies. We call these adaptations. For example, anteaters have long, skinny tongues that can reach down into anthills to eat ants. Discuss how a butterfly is adapted for drinking nectar from flowers. Then have children tell what adaptation keeps birds from eating the butterfly in *I'm a Caterpillar?*

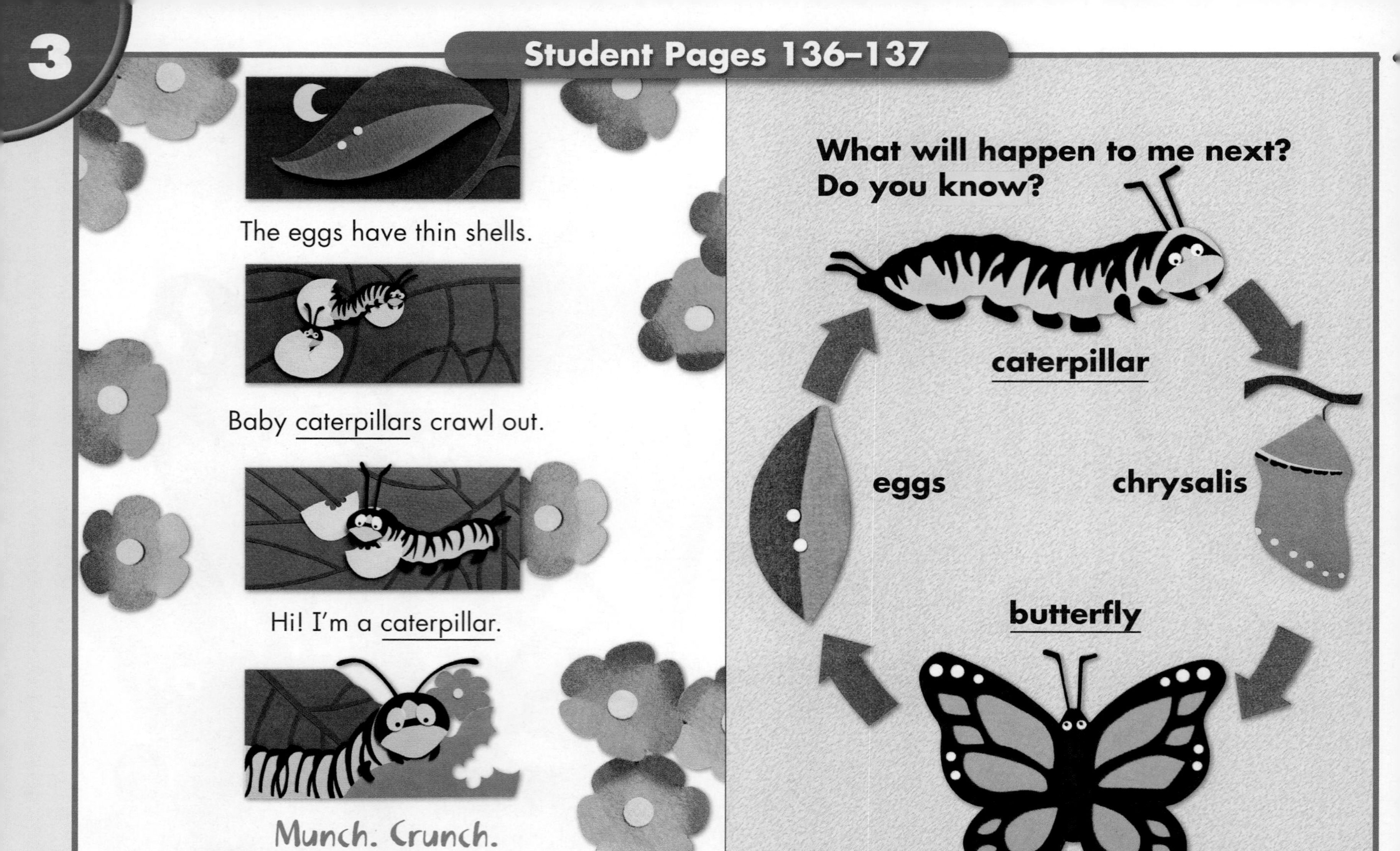

▲ **Pages 136–137**
Ask children to read to review what happens in a butterfly's life.

TIME FOR Science

Life Cycles

The illustration on this page shows the life cycle of the butterfly and how it grows and changes through its life. Think about the life cycle of a plant from *Frog and Toad Together*. How do plants grow and change? What other living things do you know that grow and change throughout their lives?

____ *r*-controlled *er, ir, ur* and contractions *'s, 've, 're* high-frequency/tested vocabulary

Guiding Comprehension

Confirm Predictions • Literal

- **What hatches from a butterfly's eggs?**
  Caterpillars hatch from the eggs.

Text Features • Critical

- **How does the diagram on p. 137 help you understand what happens in a butterfly's life cycle?**
  Children may say that the diagram helps them understand a butterfly's life cycle because it shows the steps and the order in which they happen. It also shows that the steps occur over and over again.

Compare and Contrast • Critical

- ***Text to Text*** **Think about what you learned in *Honey Bees* in Unit 2. How are butterflies like bees? How are these insects different?**
  Children may say bees and butterflies are alike because they are both insects, they both fly, and they both drink nectar from flowers. They are different because bees live and work together, bees take care of each other, bees do not change from caterpillars into bees, butterflies have bigger and more colorful wings, butterflies do not sting, and butterflies can't make honey. You may wish to record children's responses in a T-Chart.

EXTEND SKILLS

Text Features

For instruction in using diagrams, discuss the following:

- What are the labels on this diagram? (eggs, caterpillar, chrysalis, butterfly)
- What does this diagram tell about? (the life cycle of a butterfly)

Assess Have children suggest a title for the diagram. Then have them say or write four sentences describing the information presented in the diagram.

Retelling Plan

- ☑ Week 1 assess Strategic Intervention students.
- ☑ Week 2 assess Advanced students.
- ☑ Week 3 assess Strategic Intervention students.
- ☑ Week 4 assess On-Level students.
- ☑ **This week assess Strategic Intervention students.**
- ☐ Week 6 assess any students you have not yet checked during this unit.

Look Back and Write For informal assessment, see the Scoring Rubric below.

ELL

Check Retelling Focus on comprehension and whether each child can provide good information about the selection, rather than mistakes in English. For more ideas on assessing comprehension, see the ELL and Transition Handbook.

Think and Share

TALK ABOUT IT Model a response. I learned that caterpillars eat leaves. The caterpillars at the beginning and end of the selection are both munching on leaves.

1. **RETELL** Have children use the retelling strip in the Student Edition to retell the selection.

Monitor Progress **Check Retelling** 

If... children have difficulty retelling the selection,

then... use the Retelling Cards and The Scoring Rubric for Retelling on pp. 138–139 to help them move toward fluent retelling.

Day 1 Check Word Reading	Day 2 Check Word Reading	▶ **Day 3 Check High-Frequency Words/Retelling**	Day 4 Check Fluency	Day 5 Assess Progress

2. **DRAW CONCLUSIONS** Possible response: Caterpillars have to eat a lot because they need lots of energy to change into butterflies.

3. **TEXT STRUCTURE** Possible response: Reading about the events in order helped me learn about the life cycle of a butterfly.

LOOK BACK AND WRITE Read the writing prompt on p. 138 and model your thinking. I'll look back on p. 134 and read that part of the selection again. I'll look for the reason these butterflies are not afraid of birds. Then I'll write my response. Have children write their responses in an interactive or an independent writing activity.

Scoring Rubric **Look Back and Write**

Top-Score Response A top-score response uses details from p. 134 of the selection to tell why butterflies aren't afraid of birds.

Example of a Top-Score Response

These butterflies are not afraid of birds because birds will not eat these butterflies.
The birds know that these butterflies taste bad.

For additional rubrics, see p. WA10.

Reader Response

Read Together

Think and Share

Talk About It What is one thing you learned about caterpillars? Tell about it.

1. Use the pictures below to summarize what you learned. Retell
2. Why do caterpillars eat so much? Draw Conclusions
3. The writer tells about caterpillars from little to big or from caterpillar to butterfly. How did that order help you read and understand the story? Text Structure

Look Back and Write Look back at page 134. Why aren't butterflies afraid of birds?

Meet the Author

Jean Marzollo

Jean Marzollo was a high school teacher and a magazine editor. Now she has written more than 100 books for children! She writes about science, and she writes poetry, made-up stories, and *I Spy* books.

Ms. Marzollo likes to sew and work in her garden. She says writing is creative in the same way. It is hard and fun.

Read other books by Jean Marzollo.

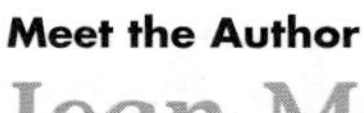

Retelling Strip

Scoring Rubric Expository Retelling

Rubric 4 3 2 1	4	3	2	1
Connections	Makes connections and generalizes beyond the text	Makes connections to other events, texts, or experiences	Makes a limited connection to another event, text, or experience	Makes no connection to another event, text, or experience
Author's Purpose	Elaborates on author's purpose	Tells author's purpose with some clarity	Makes some connection to author's purpose	Makes no connection to author's purpose
Topic	Describes the main topic	Identifies the main topic with some details early in retelling	Identifies the main topic	Retelling has no sense of topic
Important Ideas	Gives accurate information about ideas using key vocabulary	Gives accurate information about ideas with some key vocabulary	Gives limited or inaccurate information about ideas	Gives no information about ideas
Conclusions	Draws conclusions and makes inferences to generalize beyond the text	Draws conclusions about the text	Is able to tell some learnings about the text	Is unable to draw conclusions or make inferences about the text

Use the Retelling Chart on p. TR19 to record retelling.

Selection Test To assess with *I'm a Caterpillar*, use Selection Tests, pp. 41–44.

Fresh Reads for Differentiated Test Practice For weekly leveled practice, use pp. 97–102.

Retelling

SUCCESS PREDICTOR

3

OBJECTIVE

- Read aloud fluently, attending to end punctuation.

Options for Choral Reading

Use *I'm a Caterpillar* or one of the following Leveled Readers.

On-Level

A Visit to a Butterfly Greenhouse

Strategic Intervention

Animals Grow and Change

Advanced

Butterflies

Reread pp. 129–133 of *I'm a Caterpillar*. Model correct intonation for English language learners by letting your voice go up at the end of questions and down at the end of statements. End sentences that end with exclamation marks in an excited way. Have children echo what you say using the same intonation.

Fluency

ATTEND TO END PUNCTUATION

MODEL READING WHILE ATTENDING TO PUNCTUATION Use *I'm a Caterpillar.*

- Have children identify the various end marks on pp. 129–130. Discuss what each end mark means. I am going to read these pages. I will look for end marks that tell me to stop, to read in an excited way, or to read as if I'm asking a question.
- Ask children to follow along as you read the pages with expression and attention to punctuation.
- Have children read the pages after you. Encourage them to watch for the marks at the ends of sentences as they read. Continue in the same way with pp. 132–133.

REREAD FOR FLUENCY

Choral Reading

ROUTINE

1. **Select a Passage** For *I'm a Caterpillar,* use pp. 124–130.
2. **Divide into Groups** Assign each group a part to read. For this story, have each group read one page.
3. **Model** Have children track the print as you read.
4. **Read Together** Have children read along with you.
5. **Independent Readings** Have the groups read aloud without you. Monitor progress and provide feedback. For optimal fluency, children should reread three to four times.

Monitor Progress	Fluency
If... children have difficulty attending to the end marks,	**then...** prompt: • What do the punctuation marks tell you about the way each sentence should be read? • Try to make your voice sound like the caterpillar is speaking.
If... the class cannot read fluently without you,	**then...** continue to have them read along with you.

Vocabulary

USE REFERENCE SOURCES

DISCUSS USING A DICTIONARY Ask what the caterpillar became while waiting to change into a butterfly. (a chrysalis) Hold up a dictionary and tell children that this is a special kind of book that tells the meanings of words. If the story did not tell you what a chrysalis was, you could look up the word *chrysalis* in the dictionary to find out. Explain that all the words are listed in alphabetical order, or in order according to their first letters. If a word begins with *a* it will be at the front of the dictionary, and if a word begins with *w* it will be near the end of the dictionary. Look up the word *chrysalis* and read its definition.

You may also wish to tell children that a dictionary can be used to check word spelling. If children are not sure a word they wrote is spelled correctly, they can use a dictionary to verify spelling.

EXPAND MEANING List the following words on the chalkboard. Have children help you put them in alphabetical order: *butterfly, ant, deer, caterpillar.* Then have groups of children work together to look up the meaning of each word in a children's dictionary.

ant
butterfly
caterpillar
deer

OBJECTIVES

- Discuss using a dictionary.
- Use a dictionary to find word meanings.

Strategic Intervention

Make word cards for the following words and have children put them in alphabetical order: *afraid, done, push, visit, wait.* Have them pick one word, find it in a dictionary, and read aloud its definition.

Advanced

Have children use a dictionary to explain the difference between a chrysalis and a cocoon.

Extend Language Help children practice using a dictionary by looking up some words from the selection. If possible, use a dictionary with the home language and English for finding word meanings.

Writing Trait of the Week

INTRODUCE Focus/Ideas

TALK ABOUT FOCUS/IDEAS Explain to children that good writers focus on an idea. All their sentences tell about this idea. Ask children to think about the idea the author focuses on in *I'm a Caterpillar.* Then model your thinking.

MODEL When I look back at the selection, I see that every page tells about how *a caterpillar grows and changes into a butterfly.* So I think that is the idea the author is focusing on. I can check this. I'll reread p. 124. The page tells about a caterpillar eating and getting bigger. Does that tell about the author's idea? Yes, because it tells about how a caterpillar grows.

Write the main idea.

A caterpillar grows and changes into a butterfly.

Illustrate the main idea with other pages from the selection. First have a volunteer read a page aloud. Ask after each page is read: What does the page tell about a caterpillar growing and changing into a butterfly?

STRATEGY FOR DEVELOPING FOCUS/IDEAS On the board, write a set of sentences in which all but one tells about the same idea. Work with children to identify and cross out the sentence that does not focus on the idea.

Nectar is a sweet liquid in flowers.
Flowers are many colors. *(Cross out.)*
Butterflies eat nectar.
Bees make honey from nectar.

PRACTICE

APPLY THE STRATEGY

- Ask children to look at the illustration on p. 133. Discuss what the illustration shows. Then work together to write a sentence that tells about the illustration. (Possible answer: *The butterfly sips nectar from the flowers.)*
- Have children write at least three facts about caterpillars, butterflies, or another kind of insect they know. *(Bees live in hives. The queen bee lays eggs. Worker bees take care of the eggs.)* Remind children that their fact sentences should focus on one idea: telling about the insect they chose.

OBJECTIVE

- Recognize and use focus/ideas in writing.

DAILY FIX-IT

5. The bug yelow wings had.
The bug had yellow wings.

6. what kind of bug was it.
What kind of bug was it?

Connect to Unit Writing

Writing Trait

Have children use strategies for developing **focus/ideas** when they write a description in the Unit Writing Workshop, pp. WA2–WA9.

Focus/Ideas Talk with English learners about what they plan to write. Record their ideas and help them generate words to use. Check to see that their details support their ideas. See more writing support in the ELL and Transition Handbook.

Grammar

APPLY TO WRITING *Am, Is, Are, Was, and Were*

IMPROVE WRITING WITH *Am, Is, Are, Was,* AND *Were* Explain to children that when talking about one thing or person, *am, is,* or *was* can be used. Explain that when talking about more than one thing or person, *are* or *were* can be used. Point out that *am, is,* and *are* tell about now, while *was* and *were* tell about the past. Remind children to use *am, is, are, was,* and *were* in their own writing.

Write the following sentences. Have children supply the proper verbs after looking at who or what the sentence is about.

She ___ funny. (*is* or *was*)
My mom ___ kind. (*is* or *was*)
I __ tired. (*am* or *was*)
The children ___ silly. (*are* or *were*)

PRACTICE

WRITE SENTENCES WITH *Am, Is, Are, Was,* AND *Were* Write *am, is, are, was, and were* on the chalkboard. Have children write sentences on their paper using each word. Call on individuals to share their sentences.

OBJECTIVE

- Use *am, is, are, was,* and *were* in writing.

Am, Is, Are, Was, and Were

Look at the picture.
Tell about what you see.
Use *am, is, are, was,* or *were.*

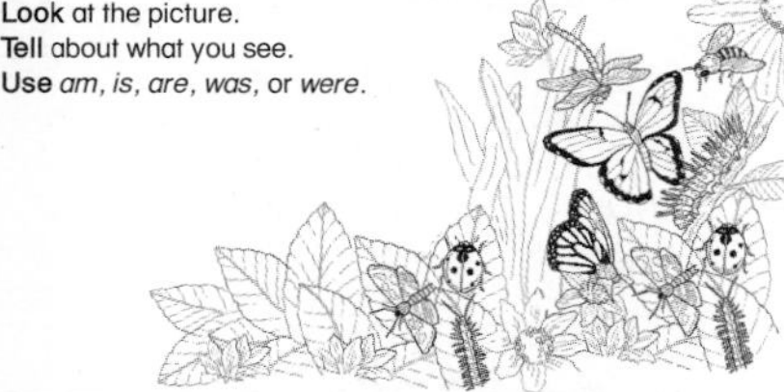

Possible answer: I am looking at a picture. Some butterflies are flying. One butterfly is on a flower. The butterfly was a caterpillar. The caterpillars were hungry.

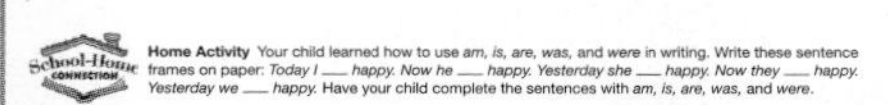

Home Activity Your child learned how to use *am, is, are, was,* and *were* in writing. Write these sentence frames on paper: *Today I ___ happy. Now he ___ happy. Yesterday she ___ happy. Now they ___ happy. Yesterday we ___ happy.* Have your child complete the sentences with *am, is, are, was,* and *were.*

▲ **Grammar and Writing Practice Book** p. 66

Wrap Up Your Day!

DRAW CONCLUSIONS Have children draw conclusions about *I'm a Caterpillar.* What do caterpillars turn into? (butterflies) Why does the new butterfly wait a while before flying?

TEXT STRUCTURE Help children list the sequence of events in *I'm a Caterpillar.* (A caterpillar becomes a chrysalis. The chrysalis becomes a butterfly. The butterfly lays eggs. The eggs contain baby caterpillars.)

LET'S TALK ABOUT IT What are the changes in nature that take place in *I'm a Caterpillar?* Do you know of any other animals that change from one thing to another? (Tadpoles become frogs.)

Tell children that tomorrow they will listen to a story about an insect called a cicada.

Day 4

AT A GLANCE

Share Literature
"Song of the Cicada"

Phonemic Awareness
Substitute Phonemes

High-Frequency Words
done *know* *push* *visit* *wait* Word Wall

Phonics and Spelling
REVIEW *r*-controlled *ar* and Inflected Endings *-ed, -ing*

REVIEW Word Reading

Spelling: Words with *er, ir, ur*

Read

Group Time < Differentiated Instruction

"My Computer"

Fluency
Attend to Punctuation

Writing Across the Curriculum
Cycle Chart

Grammar
Review *Am, Is, Are, Was, Were*

Materials
- *Sing with Me Big Book*
- Read Aloud Anthology
- Tested Word Cards
- Student Edition 140–141

Morning Warm-Up!

Today we'll learn how to use computers.
A computer can be a huge help.
How can a computer help us learn?

QUESTION OF THE DAY Encourage children to sing "Life Cycle" from the *Sing with Me Big Book* as you gather. Write and read the message and discuss the question.

REVIEW LONG *u*

- Ask children to find words that have the long sound of *u* spelled *u*–consonant–*e*. (*use* and *huge*) You may wish to point out the long *u* sound in *computer.*
- Circle each word and have children read it.

Extend Language Use the Day 4 instruction on ELL Poster 17 to extend and enrich language.

ELL Poster 17

Share Literature

CONNECT CONCEPTS

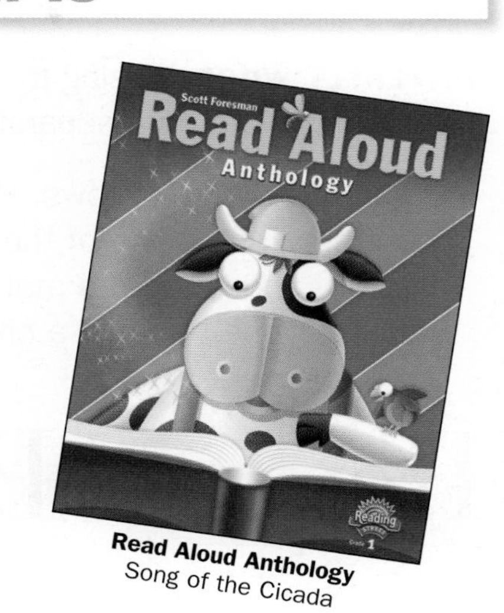

Read Aloud Anthology
Song of the Cicada

ACTIVATE PRIOR KNOWLEDGE Help children recall that when the chrysalis opened, a butterfly came out. Explain that you will read a story about another kind of insect—"Song of the Cicada" by Tristin Toohill.

BUILD ORAL VOCABULARY Read the first two paragraphs. Ask why the cicadas left their shells. (They grew bigger.) Something that is **fragile** is easily broken. How would you have to touch a fragile insect shell? (carefully) **Emerging** means "to come out." What do you think would be emerging from a cicada shell? (a cicada) **Vessels** are tiny tubes. Ask children to listen to find out what the girl learns as she observes a cicada.

REVIEW ORAL VOCABULARY After reading, review all the Amazing Words for the week. Have children take turns using them in sentences that tell about the concept for the week. Then talk about the Amazing Words they learned in other weeks and connect them to the concept as well. For example, ask:

- Why are a butterfly's wings **crumpled** when it comes out of its **snug** chrysalis?
- If you **respect nature,** how can you **protect** the **environment**?

Phonemic Awareness

SUBSTITUTE PHONEMES

- Addy had cicada shells in her yard. Listen to the sounds in *had.*
- Model saying each sound, /h/ /a/ /d/. Have children say the sounds with you and then say the sounds by themselves.
- Now say each sound as you write the letter that goes with it. Say /h/ /a/ /d/ as you write *h, a, d.*
- Change the *a* in *had* to *ar.* Listen as I change the /a/ sound in the middle of *had* to the /är/ sound: /h/ /är/ /d/, *hard.*
- Have children say the sounds as you point to the letters (/h/ /är/ /d/) and blend the word *(hard).*

Continue the activity with these examples.

ship—sharp **ham—harm** **bat—Bart** **chat—chart**

OBJECTIVES

- Set purpose for listening.
- Build oral vocabulary.
- Substitute phonemes.

	MONITOR PROGRESS
cycle **develop** **insect** **rearrange** **yearly** **emerge** **fragile** **vessel**	**If...** children lack oral vocabulary experiences about the concept Changes in Nature, **then...** use the Oral Vocabulary Routine. See p. DI·7 to teach *emerge, fragile,* and *vessel.*

Connect Concepts Have children act out how a cicada emerges from its shell. Then ask: How is a cicada like a butterfly? How is it different?

OBJECTIVES

- Recognize high-frequency words.
- Review inflected endings *-ed, -ing* and *r*-controlled *ar.*
- Apply decoding strategies: blend, preview words.

Add -ing to each word.
Write the new word on the line.

1. sit sitting
2. nap napping

Add -ed to each word.
Write the new word on the line.

3. dot dotted
4. hop hopped

Use the words you wrote to finish the sentences.
Write the words on the lines.

5. The caterpillar is napping.
6. The butterfly has dotted wings.
7. The butterfly hopped to a rock.
8. It is sitting on a plant.

School + Home Home Activity Your child reviewed words that end with -ed and -ing. Read a storybook with your child and look for words that end in -ed. Have your child use each word you find in a new sentence. Repeat with words that end in -ing.

▲ **Practice Book 1.2** p. 48, Inflected endings *-ed, -ing*

Circle a word to finish each sentence.
Write it on the line.

garden

1. What is that in the yard? (yard / yak)
2. Look on the tree bark! (base / bark)
3. It will not harm you. (harm / ham)
4. It is eating the large leaf. (large / lung)
5. One day it will fly to a park. (pork / park)

School + Home Home Activity Your child reviewed words with ar that have the sound heard in garden. Work with your child to make a list of words that rhyme with bark and yard.

▲ **Practice Book 1.2** p. 49, *r*-Controlled *ar*

High-Frequency Words

PRACTICE

BUTTERFLY WORDS Using the Word Wall as a guide, have children write each high-frequency word on a separate card: *done, know, push, visit, wait.* Word Wall

Organize children in rows. Have the first child in each row say a sentence about a butterfly, using one of the words. Ask the other children in the row to listen carefully and hold up a matching word card when they hear the word. Continue until everyone has had a chance to say a sentence.

Review Phonics

REVIEW INFLECTED ENDINGS; *r*-CONTROLLED *ar*

READ WORDS WITH INFLECTED ENDINGS Write *patted.* You can read this word because you know how to blend base words and endings when the final consonant is doubled. Blend the sounds in the base word. What is the base word? *(pat)* Now blend the base word, *pat,* with the ending *-ed.* What is the word? *(patted)* Repeat for *patting.*

READ WORDS WITH *ar* Write *park.* You can read this word because you know how to read *r*-controlled vowels. What's the sound of *ar?* (/är/) What's the word? *(park)*

SORT WORDS Write the headings *-ed* and *-ing.* Then add the words to the chart one at a time. Call on children to read each word, identify the ending, and frame the base word. Have them note if the final consonant was doubled before the ending was added. Have the completed lists read. Then have children identify and read words with /är/.

-ed	*-ing*
flipped	marking
barked	jogging
harmed	marching
dropped	stepping

WORD READING

READ DECODABLE AND HIGH-FREQUENCY WORDS Write these words. Encourage children to preview each word before reading it.

jar	**shark**	**want**	**large**	**hugged**
park	**there**	**who**	**how**	**read**
few	**hopping**	**Clark**	**soon**	**again**
dark	**afraid**	**water**	**kissed**	**swimming**

Monitor Progress	Word Reading
If... children have difficulty previewing and reading whole words,	**then...** have them use sound-by-sound blending.
If... children can't read the words fluently at a rate of one to two seconds per word,	**then...** have pairs practice the list.

READ WORDS IN CONTEXT Write these sentences. Call on individuals to read a sentence. Then randomly point to the review words and have them read. To help you monitor word reading, high-frequency words are underlined and decodable words are circled.

Who has a few large bugs hopping in a jar?

How is Clark the dark shark swimming in the water?

Clark was afraid to go so he kissed and hugged Mom again.

She'll want to read the park map to get there soon.

Monitor Progress	Word Reading
If... children are unable to read an underlined word,	**then...** read the word for them and spell it, having them echo you.
If... children have difficulty reading a circled word,	**then...** have them use sound-by-sound blending.

Spiral REVIEW

- Reviews high-frequency words *afraid, again, few, how, read, soon, there, want, water, who.*
- Reviews inflected endings *-ed, -ing* (with and without spelling change); *r*-controlled *ar.*

ELL

Support Phonics For additional review, see the phonics activities in the ELL and Transition Handbook.

OBJECTIVE

- Spell words with *er, ir, ur.*

Spelling Words

Words with *er, ir, un*

1.	**her**	6.	**were**
2.	**first**	7.	**shirt**
3.	**bird***	8.	**fur**
4.	**girl**	9.	**hurt**
5.	**burn**	10.	**sir**

High-Frequency Words

11.	**visit***	12.	**done***

* Words from the Selection

Words with *er, ir, ur*

Spelling Words				
her	first	bird	girl	burn
were	shirt	fur	hurt	sir

Use this code. **Write** the words.

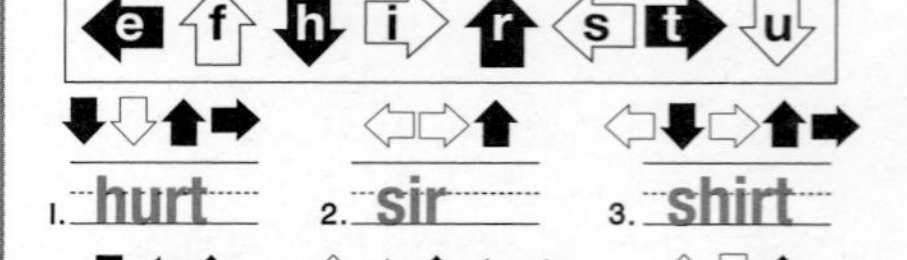

1. hurt 2. sir 3. shirt

4. her 5. first 6. fur

Draw a line through the word that does not match.
Then **write** the word that matches.

7. were ~~where~~ were — were
8. bird bird ~~bid~~ — bird
9. ~~grill~~ girl girl — girl
10. burn ~~turn~~ burn — burn

School + Home **Home Activity** Your child has been learning to spell words with *er, ir,* and *ur.* Write a list word, but replace the letter before *r* with a blank (b_rd). Ask your child to correctly fill in the blank.

▲ **Spelling Practice Book** p. 68

Spelling

PARTNER REVIEW *r*-Controlled *er, ir, ur*

READ AND WRITE Supply pairs of children with index cards on which the spelling words have been written. Have one child read a word while the other writes it. Then have children switch roles. Have them use the cards to check their spelling.

HOMEWORK Spelling Practice Book, p. 68

Group Time

DAY 4

On-Level

Read "My Computer."

- Use pp. 140–141.

Strategic Intervention

Read SI Decodable Reader 16.

- Read or listen to "My Computer."
- Use the **Routine** on p. DI·62.

Advanced

Read "My Computer."

- Use the **Routine** on p. DI·63.

Place English language learners in the groups that correspond to their reading abilities in English.

Independent Activities

Fluency Reading Pair children to reread *I'm a Caterpillar.*

Journal Writing Write another title for *I'm a Caterpillar*. Share writing.

Independent Reading See p. 118j for Reading/Library activities and suggestions.

Literacy Centers To provide listening opportunities, you may use the Listening Center on p. 118j. To extend science concepts, you may use the Science Center on p. 118k.

Practice Book 1.2 Inflected Endings *-ed, -ing,* p. 48; *r*-Controlled *ar,* p. 49

Break into small groups after Spelling and before Fluency.

Reading Online

Read Together

My Computer

Monitor

Printer

Nymph

Egg

Adult

Cursor

CD-ROM

Mouse

Keyboard

For more practice
Take It to the Net
PearsonSuccessNet.com

140 141

Reading Online

PREVIEW AND PREDICT Read the title. Have children look at the pictures and the labels on the page. Tell children that they can use this page to discuss using a computer.

ILLUSTRATIONS WITH CAPTIONS Review that selections that give information are called nonfiction. This page gives information through illustrations. The words name objects in the pictures and are called captions.

VOCABULARY/USE REFERENCE SOURCES Review dictionary skills. Write the following definition on the board: *a device that is used to listen to or watch something.* Ask children to tell which item pictured on p. 141 fits this definition. (monitor) Read aloud the following definitions for *mouse:* a small animal with soft fur and a long, thin tail; a tool used with a computer. Ask children to tell which meaning of mouse relates to the illustration.

AudioText

OBJECTIVE

- Recognize text structure: nonfiction illustrations with captions.

EXTEND SKILLS

Text Features

To help children understand using captions, discuss the following:

- What do the words on these pages tell? (the names of the computer parts)
- How did the artist help you know exactly what each word names? (Each word has an arrow pointing to what it names.)

ELL

Access Content Have children say the names of the parts of a computer in English and in their home language.

BUILD CONCEPTS

Prior Knowledge • Inferential

- **How can you use a CD-ROM to learn about something?**
Responses will vary, but children should include that they can get information such as dictionary definitions and encyclopedia entries from a CD-ROM.

Compare and Contrast • Inferential

- **How is a computer like a book? How is it different?**
You can get information and read it on the screen like you would read a book. A computer is different because it doesn't have pages, and you can get many different kinds of information on the same computer.

CONNECT TEXT TO TEXT

How might you use the information we discussed on this page to learn more about butterflies?

Possible answer: We can go online to look for information about butterflies.

Fluency

READ WITH EXPRESSION

MODEL READING WHILE ATTENDING TO END PUNCTUATION Use *I'm a Caterpillar.*

- Have children identify the various end marks on pp. 130–131. Discuss what each end mark means. I am going to read these pages. I will look for end marks that tell me to stop, to read in an excited way, or to read as if I'm asking a question.
- Ask children to follow along as you read the page with expression and attention to punctuation.
- Have children read the page after you. Encourage them to use the end marks to tell them how to read each sentence. Continue with pp. 132–133.

REREAD FOR FLUENCY

Choral Reading

ROUTINE

1. **Select a Passage** For *I'm a Caterpillar* use pp. 126–129.
2. **Divide into Groups** Assign each group a part to read. For this story, assign a page to each of four groups.
3. **Model** Have children track the print as you read.
4. **Read Together** Have children read along with you.
5. **Independent Readings** Have the groups read aloud without you. Monitor progress and provide feedback. For optimal fluency, children should reread three to four times.

Monitor Progress — Check Fluency WCPM

As children reread, monitor their progress toward their individual fluency goals. Current Goal: 25–35 words correct per minute. End-of-Year Goal: 60 words correct per minute.

If... children cannot read fluently at a rate of 25–35 words per minute,

then... make sure children practice with text at their independent level. Provide additional fluency practice, pairing nonfluent readers with fluent readers.

If... children already read at 60 words per minute,

then... they do not need to reread three to four times.

SUCCESS PREDICTOR

Day 1 Check Word Reading | **Day 2** Check Word Reading | **Day 3** Check High-Frequency Words/Retelling | ▶ **Day 4 Check Fluency** | **Day 5** Assess Progress

OBJECTIVE

- Read aloud fluently, attending to end punctuation.

Options for Oral Reading

Use *I'm a Caterpillar* or one of the following Leveled Readers.

On-Level

A Visit to a Butterfly Greenhouse

Strategic Intervention

Animals Grow and Change

Advanced

Butterflies

Use *The Baby Robins* or *I'm a Caterpillar.* Encourage children to repeatedly read aloud texts that they already understand. This extra practice reinforces and improves fluency.

Words Correct Per Minute
SUCCESS PREDICTOR

OBJECTIVE

- Create a cycle chart.

Advanced

Encourage children to choose another living thing, such as a plant, and make a cycle chart of its life stages.

ELL

Support Writing Since the writing product contains content-area words that children may not know, generate a word list to discuss the terms orally before children write together.

Writing Across the Curriculum

WRITE Cycle Chart

BRAINSTORM Have children think about the different stages in the life of a butterfly. Encourage them to use oral vocabulary, such as *develop, insect,* and *cycle.*

SHARE THE PEN Have children participate in creating a cycle chart. To begin, draw a cycle chart or display Graphic Organizer 30. Explain that the class will work together to complete the chart. Explain that a cycle chart is a way to show each stage of the insect's life. Call on an individual to name a stage in the insect's life and have the class repeat it. Fill in the appropriate square, inviting individuals to help spell the word by writing familiar letter-sounds. Ask questions, such as the following:

- What is the first sound you hear in the word *egg?* (/e/)
- What letter stands for that sound? *(e)* Have a volunteer write *e.*
- What is the final sound you hear in the word *egg?* (/g/)
- What letter stands for that sound? *(g)* Have a volunteer write *g.*

Continue having individuals contribute to the chart. Frequently reread the words in each stage of the insect's life.

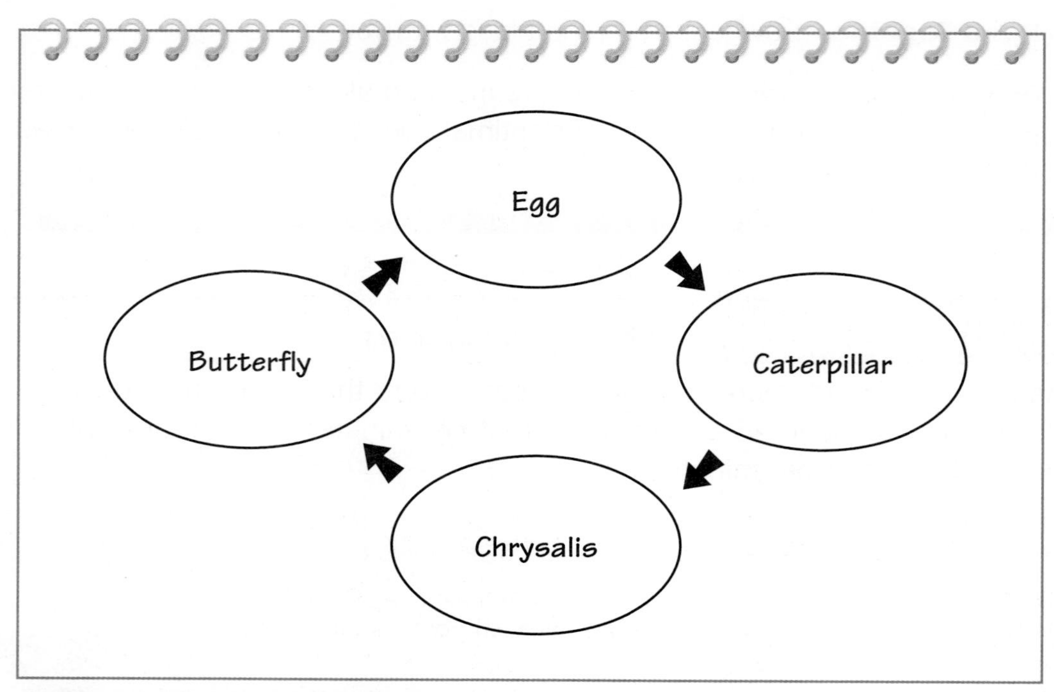

▲ **Graphic Organizer Flip Chart 30**

Grammar

REVIEW *Am, Is, Are, Was,* and *Were*

DEFINE *Am, Is, Are, Was,* AND *Were*

- Do the words *am, is,* and *are* tell about now or the past? (now)
- Do the words *was* and *were* tell about now or the past? (past)

PRACTICE

CREATE SENTENCES USING *Am, Is, Are, Was,* AND *Were* Write pronouns such as *I, you, we, he, she, it,* and *they* on one set of index cards. Write adjectives such as *nice, funny, happy, tall, short, old,* and *tired* on another set of index cards. Have individuals take turns picking a card from each pile and then completing a sentence by using the proper verb (*am, is, are, was,* and *were*).

I __ tall.
You __ funny.
It __ old.

OBJECTIVE

- Identify *am, is, are, was,* and *were*.

DAILY FIX-IT

7. It can fli veree high.
It can fly very high.

8. She saw it fly awae?
She saw it fly away.

Am, Is, Are, Was, and Were

Mark the sentence that is correct.

1. ⊗ Raj is in the garden.
   ○ Raj am in the garden.
   ○ Raj are in the garden.

2. ○ Butterflies is on the flowers.
   ○ Butterflies was on the flowers.
   ⊗ Butterflies are on the flowers.

3. ○ One butterfly were yellow.
   ⊗ One butterfly was yellow.
   ○ One butterfly are yellow.

4. ○ Those flowers am white.
   ○ Those flowers was white.
   ⊗ Those flowers were white.

5. ⊗ I am next to Raj.
   ○ I are next to Raj.
   ○ I is next to Raj.

6. ○ We am happy in the garden.
   ⊗ We are happy in the garden.
   ○ We was happy in the garden.

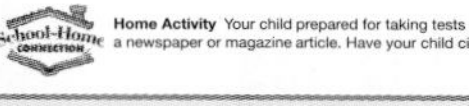

Home Activity Your child prepared for taking tests on *am, is, are, was,* and *were*. Together read part of a newspaper or magazine article. Have your child circle the verbs *am, is, are, was,* and *were*.

▲ **Grammar and Writing Practice Book** p. 67

Wrap Up Your Day!

FLUENCY Write *"Just as Addy reached for one of the shells, it began to walk! The cicada was still inside."* Point out the end marks. What does an exclamation point mean? (Something is exciting or surprising.) What do you do when you come to a period? (Pause briefly.) Call on individuals to read the sentence while attending to punctuation.

LET'S TALK ABOUT IT How do the cicadas change? What happens after they come out of their shells?

PREVIEW Day 5

Remind children that they heard a story about an insect called a cicada. Tell them that tomorrow they will hear about the cicada again.

Day 5
AT A GLANCE

Share Literature
Song of the Cicada

Phonics and Spelling
Review *r*-Controlled *er, ir, ur* and Contractions *'s, 've, 're*

High-Frequency Words
done *know* *push* *visit* *wait* Word Wall

Monitor Progress
Spelling Test: Words with *er, ir, ur*

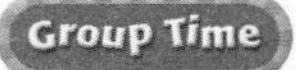
< Differentiated Assessment

Writing and Grammar
Trait: Focus/Ideas

Am, Is, Are, Was, Were

Materials
- *Sing with Me Big Book*
- Read Aloud Anthology
- Reproducible Pages TE 142f–142g
- Student Edition 142–143

Morning Warm-Up!

Butterflies are very pretty,
but once that was not so.
How do insects change and grow?

QUESTION OF THE DAY Encourage children to sing "Life Cycle" from the *Sing with Me Big Book* as you gather. Write and read the message, tracking the print. Discuss the question.

REVIEW ORAL VOCABULARY Have children find words in the message that
- mean almost the same as "bug" *(insect)*
- mean almost the same as "develop" *(grow)*

Assess Vocabulary Use the Day 5 instruction on ELL Poster 17 to monitor children's progress with oral vocabulary.

ELL Poster 17

Share Literature

LISTEN AND RESPOND

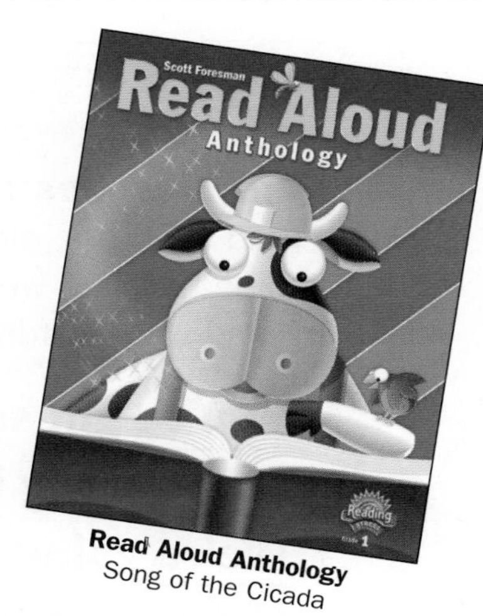

Read Aloud Anthology
Song of the Cicada

USE PRIOR KNOWLEDGE Review that yesterday the class listened to find out what the girl learned by observing the cicada. Suggest that today the class listen to find out what happened to the cicada.

MONITOR LISTENING COMPREHENSION

- What do you think happened to the cicada? (Children will probably respond that it flew off into the trees and is singing with all the other cicadas.)
- Would you like to be a scientist that observes nature? Why or why not? (Possible responses: Yes, because it would be interesting to learn about plants and animals; no, because they would have to sit still too long.)

BUILD ORAL VOCABULARY

GENERATE DISCUSSION Recall the cicada shell that Addy observes. Invite children to share any experiences they may have had with observing changes in nature; have others talk about which animal's life cycle they find the most interesting. Have children use some of this week's Amazing Words as they describe what can be learned by observing changes in nature.

Monitor Progress | **Check Oral Vocabulary**

Display pp. 118–119 in the Student Edition and remind children of the concept for this week—Changes in Nature. Ask them to tell you about the photographs using some of this week's Amazing Words, *cycle, develop, insect, rearrange, yearly, emerge, fragile,* and *vessel.*

If... children have difficulty using the Amazing Words,

then... ask questions about the photographs using the Amazing Words. Note which questions children can respond to. Reteach unknown words using the Oral Vocabulary Routine.

Day 1 Check Word Reading	Day 2 Check Word Reading	Day 3 Check High-Frequency Words/Retelling	Day 4 Check Fluency	▶ **Day 5 Check Oral Vocabulary/ Assess Progress**

OBJECTIVES

- Set purpose for listening.
- Build oral vocabulary.

cycle	**yearly**
develop	**emerge**
insect	**fragile**
rearrange	**vessel**

ELL

Extend Language If possible use a bilingual dictionary to show children how to look up words in their home language to find the English word. Compare this to a dictionary that gives word meanings.

Oral Vocabulary
SUCCESS PREDICTOR

OBJECTIVES

- Review *r*-controlled *er, ir, ur* words and contractions.
- Review high-frequency words.

Vocabulary For additional practice with the high-frequency words, use the vocabulary strategies and word cards in the ELL Teaching Guide, pp. 115–116.

r-Controlled *er, ir, ur* and Contractions

REVIEW

IDENTIFY *er, ir, ur* WORDS AND CONTRACTIONS Write these sentences. Have children read each one aloud as you track the print. Call on individuals to name and underline the /ėr/ words and the contractions. Have them tell what letters spell /ėr/ and what words make each contraction.

You've got some dirt on your shirt.
That's a big bird on a small perch.
We're going to surf in the deep water.
She's a clerk in the garden store.

High-Frequency Words

REVIEW

SAY AND SPELL WORDS Read the rhyme. Ask children to complete each line with one of the Words to Read from p. 120. Have children say, spell, and locate the word on the Word Wall. Then reread the rhyme. Word Wall

When chores are _____, (done)

I _____ and see (wait)

If ants can _____ things up their hill. (push)

Butterflies will _____ (visit)

When they _____ that I am still. (know)

SPELLING TEST *r*-Controlled *er, ir, ur*

DICTATION SENTENCES Use these sentences to assess this week's spelling words.

1. His shirt got wet in the sink.
2. Do not hurt the cat!
3. The bird will sip the water.
4. That girl has a small purse.
5. Burn the trash in a safe place.
6. You're in first grade.
7. Sir, can I go now?
8. The kitten has soft fur.
9. We were sitting with our friends.
10. She put on her spotted skirt.

HIGH-FREQUENCY WORDS

11. Bert came for a visit.
12. Have you done your homework?

ASSESS

- Spell words with *er, ir, ur.*

Spelling Words

Words with *er, ir, un*

1.	**her**	6.	**were**
2.	**first**	7.	**shirt**
3.	**bird***	8.	**fur**
4.	**girl**	9.	**hurt**
5.	**burn**	10.	**sir**

High-Frequency Words

11.	**visit***	12.	**done***

* Words from the Selection

Group Time

On-Level

Read Set B Sentences and the Story.

- Use pp. 142e–142g.

Strategic Intervention

Read Set A Sentences and the Story.

- Use pp. 142e–142g.
- Use the **Routine** on p. DI·64.

Advanced

Read Set C Sentences and the Story.

- Use pp. 142e–142g.
- Use the **Routine** on p. DI·65.

DAY 5

Place English language learners in the groups that correspond to their reading abilities in English.

Independent Activities

Fluency Reading Children reread selections at their independent level.

Journal Writing List ways you use a computer. Share writing.

Independent Reading See p. 118j for Reading/Library activities and suggestions.

Literacy Centers You may use the Technology Center on p. 118k to support this week's concepts and reading.

Practice Book 1.2 Technology, p. 50

Break into small groups after Spelling and before Grammar and Writing.

Monitor Progress

ASSESS

- Decode *r*-controlled *er, ir, ur* and contractions *'s, 've, 're*.
- Read high-frequency words.
- Read aloud with appropriate speed and accuracy.
- Draw conclusions.
- Retell a story.

Differentiated Assessment

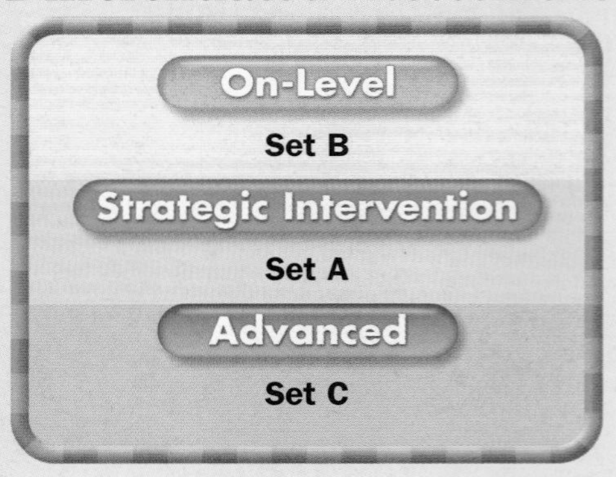

Fluency Assessment Plan

- ☑ Week 1 assess Advanced students.
- ☑ Week 2 assess Strategic Intervention students.
- ☑ Week 3 assess On-Level students.
- ☑ Week 4 assess Strategic Intervention students.
- ☑ **This week assess any students you have not yet checked during this unit.**
- ☐ Week 6 assess Strategic Intervention students.

Set individual fluency goals for children to enable them to reach the end-of-year goal.

- Current Goal: 20–30 wcpm
- End-of-Year Goal: 60 wcpm
- ELL Encourage children to repeatedly read aloud texts that they already understand. This extra practice reinforces and improves fluency.

SENTENCE READING

ASSESS *r*-CONTROLLED *er, ir, ur*, CONTRACTIONS *'s, 've, 're*, AND HIGH-FREQUENCY WORDS Use one of the reproducible lists on p. 142f to assess children's ability to read words with *r*-controlled *er, ir, ur,* words with contractions *'s, 've, 're,* and high-frequency words. Call on individuals to read two sentences aloud. Have each child in the group read different sentences. Start over with sentence one if necessary.

RECORD SCORES Use the Sentence Reading Chart for this unit on p. WA19.

Monitor Progress	*r*-Controlled *er, ir, ur* and Contractions *'s, 've, 're*
If... children have trouble reading *r*-controlled *er, ir, ur* and contractions *'s, 've, 're,*	**then...** use the Reteach Lessons on p. DI•82.
High-Frequency Words	
If... children cannot read a high-frequency word,	**then...** mark the missed words on a high-frequency word list and send the list home for additional word reading practice or have the child practice with a fluent reader.

FLUENCY AND COMPREHENSION

ASSESS FLUENCY Take a one-minute sample of children's oral reading. See Monitoring Fluency, pp. WA17–WA18. Have children read "Who's Talking?", the on-level fluency passage on p. 142g.

RECORD SCORES Record the number of words read correctly in a minute on the child's Fluency Progress Chart.

ASSESS COMPREHENSION Have the child read to the end of the passage. (If the child had difficulty with the passage, you may read it aloud.) Ask the child to draw conclusions about the story and have the child retell the passage. Use the Retelling Rubric on p. 112–113 to evaluate the child's retelling.

Monitor Progress	Fluency
If... a child does not achieve the fluency goal on the timed reading,	**then...** copy the passage and send it home with the child for additional fluency practice or have the child practice with a fluent reader.
Draw Conclusions	
If... a child cannot draw conclusions,	**then...** use the Reteach Lesson on p. DI•83.

READ THE SENTENCES

Set A

1. He's done singing his third song.
2. You've got to wait for the clerk.
3. Let's visit the girl at home.
4. They've got to push the herd into the barn.
5. The nurse will know we're here.
6. They're going to visit the shore to surf.

Set B

1. You're first in line to visit the new park.
2. I've got to wait at the birch tree for my friend.
3. She's done with the last term at school.
4. I know there's more perch to catch.
5. We've got to push the car up and turn it around.
6. They know that's the furry bunny they saw in the backyard.

Set C

1. You've got to wait far behind the curb for your ride to school.
2. They're going to wait by the curb for us, and then we will all go to the mall.
3. He's done washing the stain out of his new shirt.
4. Do you know who's going to wear the purple hat at the party?
5. We're going to push her on the swings first.
6. I know it's almost time for the circus to begin.

REPRODUCIBLE PAGE • See also *Assessment Handbook*, p. 267

Who's Talking?

Vern had a cat of her own. But she also wanted a bird. 11 13
"Let's go to the pet store," said Mom. 21
The clerk said, "Here's a bird that can talk." 30
"I've got to have that bird," said Vern. 38
"Sir, we will take the bird on that perch," said Mom. 48 48
"You're a lucky girl," said the clerk. Vern was happy. 58 59
"Let's play a trick on Dad," said Vern. 67
When Dad got home, the bird said, "Hi, Dad." Dad turned to look around. 76 81
"Who's talking?" asked Dad. 85
"That's the cat," said Vern. The cat purred. 93
Then Dad saw a blur fly by. "What's that?" 102
Dad looked at Vern. He said, "You've played a trick on me!" Vern just grinned. 111 117

See also *Assessment Handbook*, p. 268 • REPRODUCIBLE PAGE

Write Now

Read Together

Writing and Grammar

Facts

Prompt

In *I'm a Caterpillar,* a caterpillar changes into a butterfly. Think about these two insects. Now write facts about how the caterpillar looked before and how the butterfly looks now.

Writing Trait

All sentences should **focus** on the main **idea.**

Student Model

Writer describes each insect.

Adjectives give pictures of insects.

Sentences focus on how insects look.

The caterpillar was long and fat. Its legs were short and black.
The butterfly is colorful. Its wings are orange and black.

142

Writer's Checklist

- **Focus** Do all facts tell about the two insects?
- **Organization** Are ideas in order?
- **Support** Do adjectives tell about the insects?
- **Conventions** Are the right verbs used to tell about one and more than one?

Grammar

Am, Is, Are, Was, and **Were**

The words **am, is,** and **are** tell about now. Use **am** to tell about yourself. Use **is** to tell about one. Use **are** to tell about more than one.

The words **was** and **were** tell about the past. Use **was** to tell about one. Use **were** to tell about more than one.

Look at the facts. Write each verb. Does it tell about one or more than one?

143

Writing and Grammar

LOOK AT THE PROMPT Read p. 142 aloud. Have children select and discuss key words or phrases in the prompt. *(facts about how the caterpillar looked before, how the butterfly looks now)*

STRATEGIES TO DEVELOP FOCUS/IDEAS Have children

- write sentences that tell the main ideas of pictures in the selection.
- suggest sentences that tell about an idea you write on the board or chart paper.
- read a set of three sentences and identify the sentence that is not about the same topic as the other two sentences.

See Scoring Rubric on p. WA12. Rubric 4 3 2 1

HINTS FOR BETTER WRITING Read p. 143 aloud. Use the checklist to help children revise their facts. Discuss the grammar lesson. (Answers: *was, one; were, more than one; is, one; are, more than one*) Have children use the verbs *am, is, are, was,* and *were* correctly in their facts.

DAILY FIX-IT

9. ann watch butterflies.
(Ann; watches or watched)

10. Its your turn to bat
(It's; bat.)

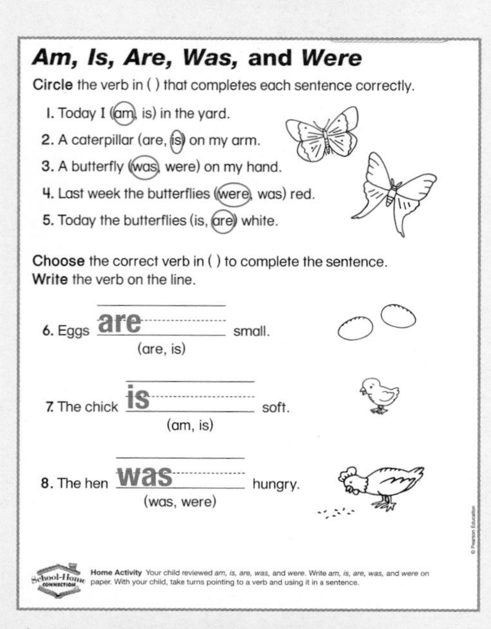

Am, Is, Are, Was, and Were

Circle the verb in ( ) that completes each sentence correctly.

1. Today I (am, is) in the yard.
2. A caterpillar (are, is) on my arm.
3. A butterfly (was, were) on my hand.
4. Last week the butterflies (were, was) red.
5. Today the butterflies (is, are) white.

Choose the correct verb in ( ) to complete the sentence. Write the verb on the line.

6. Eggs are small. (are, is)
7. The chick is soft. (am, is)
8. The hen was hungry. (was, were)

Home Activity Your child reviewed am, is, are, was, and were. Write am, is, are, was, and were on paper. With your child, take turns pointing to a verb and using it in a sentence.

▲ **Grammar and Writing Practice Book** p. 68

OBJECTIVE

- Create a word processing document.

ELL

Access Content As you discuss the computer components with children, point to and name each one. For example: This is the keyboard. You use it to type letters, numbers, and symbols.

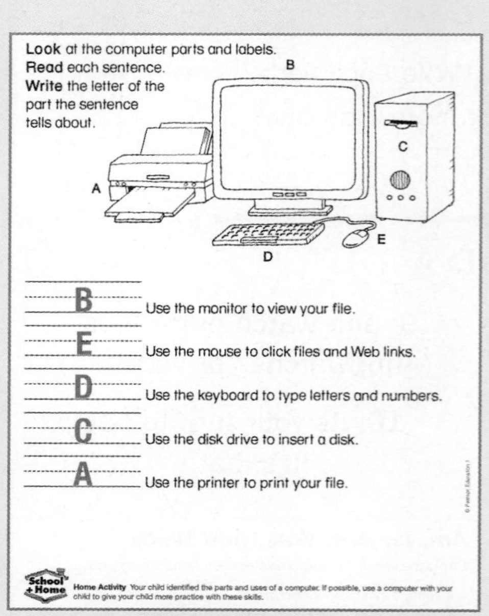

Look at the computer parts and labels.
Read each sentence.
Write the letter of the part the sentence tells about.

B Use the monitor to view your file.
E Use the mouse to click files and Web links.
D Use the keyboard to type letters and numbers.
C Use the disk drive to insert a disk.
A Use the printer to print your file.

School + Home **Home Activity** Your child identified the parts and uses of a computer. If possible, use a computer with your child to give your child more practice with these skills.

▲ **Practice Book 1.2** p. 50, Technology

Research/Study Skills

TEACH/MODEL Technology: My Computer

MODEL USING A COMPUTER Display a computer, or a picture of a computer. Explain that a computer runs programs that allow you to do many different things. Programs are used to create text documents, make calculations with numbers, and even play games.

MODEL I look at the monitor to see what the computer is doing. I use the keyboard to input words and numbers. I can point at and select objects on the monitor with the mouse. I use the mouse and keyboard together to run the computer. When I look at the monitor, I see a blinking mark on the screen. It is called a cursor, and it shows where I am typing in a document.

CREATE A TEXT DOCUMENT Give children directions on how to create a word processing document. Have them use a computer as you introduce these terms and ideas. Modify the actions as necessary to work with the word processing program you use in school.

- Tell children to open the word processing program and create a new document. They can use the keyboard to input some words or numbers.
- Next, children save the document by giving it a name. Explain that they can open the document later to do more work with it.
- Have children do a spell check to find errors in the document. Finally, they close the document when they are done working on it. Make sure to save it.

PRACTICE

CREATE A DOCUMENT ABOUT CATERPILLARS Have children create their own documents and print them out if a printer is available. The document should include two or three facts they have learned about caterpillars.

Wrap Up Your Week!

LET'S TALK ABOUT Changes in Nature

QUESTION OF THE WEEK Recall this week's question.

- What changes can we observe in nature?

Display the Cycle Chart. Add the butterfly's life cycle to the chart. Have children pretend to be caterpillars all scrunched up in a chrysalis. Then have them break out of the chrysalis and dry their butterfly wings. Finally, have them gently flap their butterfly wings.

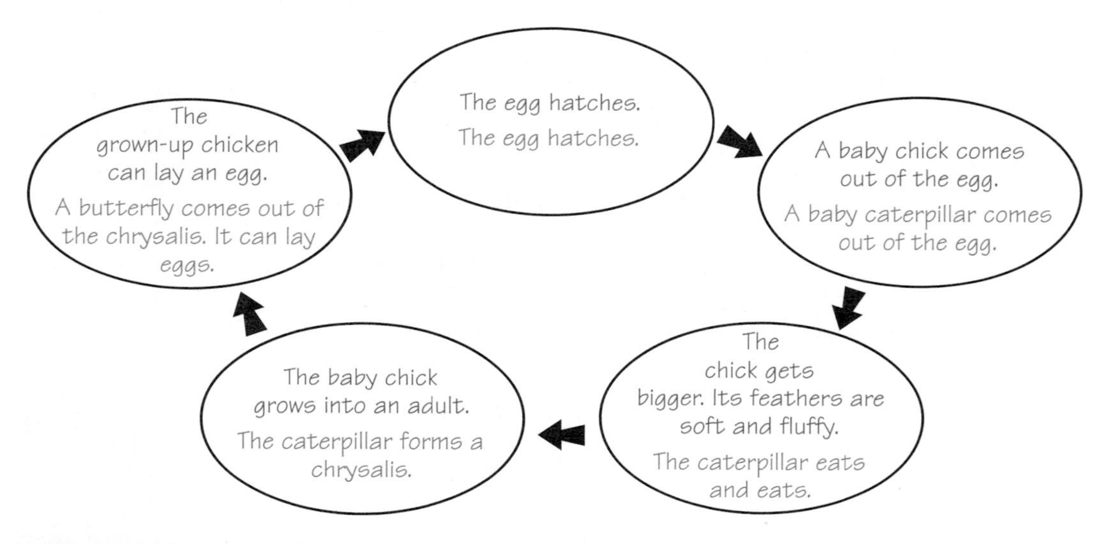

CONNECT Use questions such as these to prompt a discussion.

- What insect changes completely in its yearly cycle?
- Why are a butterfly's wings fragile when it is emerging from a chrysalis?
- What animals do you know that develop from eggs?

Build Background Use ELL Poster 18 to support the Preview activity.

You've learned

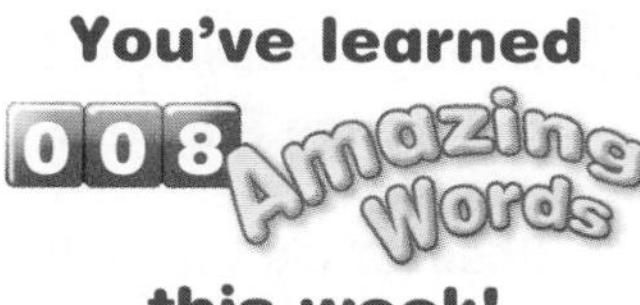

this week!

You've learned 137 Amazing Words so far this year!

PREVIEW Tell children that next week they will read about changes that animals make when the seasons change.

5

Assessment Checkpoints *for the Week*

Selection Assessment

Use pp. 41–44 of Selection Tests to check:

 **Selection Understanding**

 **Comprehension Skill** *Draw Conclusions*

 **High-Frequency Words**

done
know
push
visit
wait

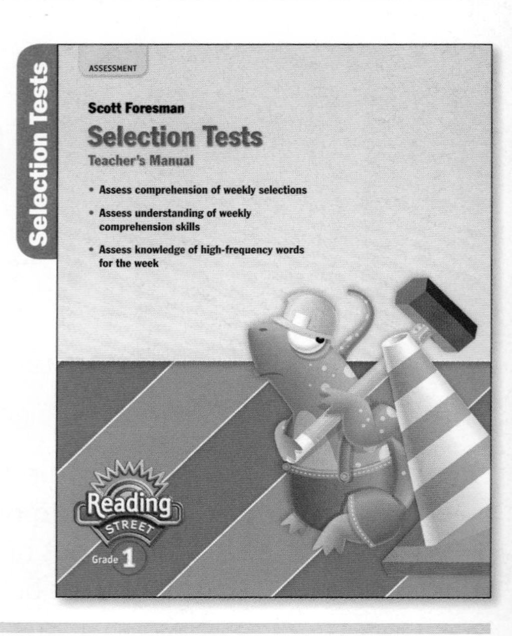

Leveled Assessment

On-Level

Strategic Intervention

Advanced

Use pp. 97–102 of Fresh Reads for Differentiated Test Practice to check:

 **Comprehension Skill** *Draw Conclusions*

 REVIEW **Comprehension Skill** *Sequence*

 **Fluency** *Words Correct Per Minute*

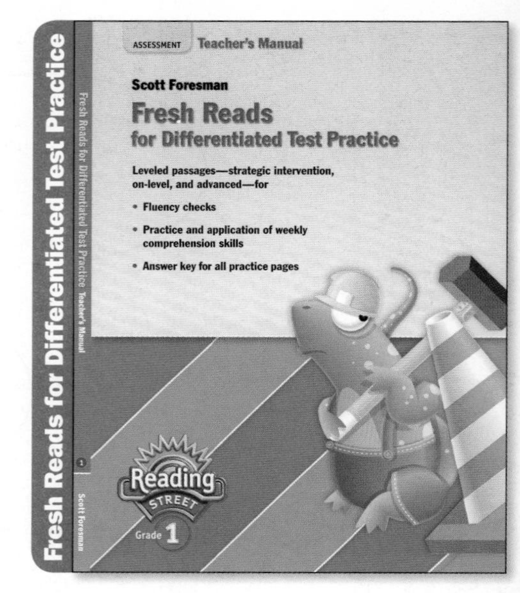

Managing Assessment

Use Assessment Handbook for:

 **Weekly Assessment Blackline Masters for Monitoring Progress**

 **Observation Checklists**

 **Record-Keeping Forms**

 **Portfolio Assessment**

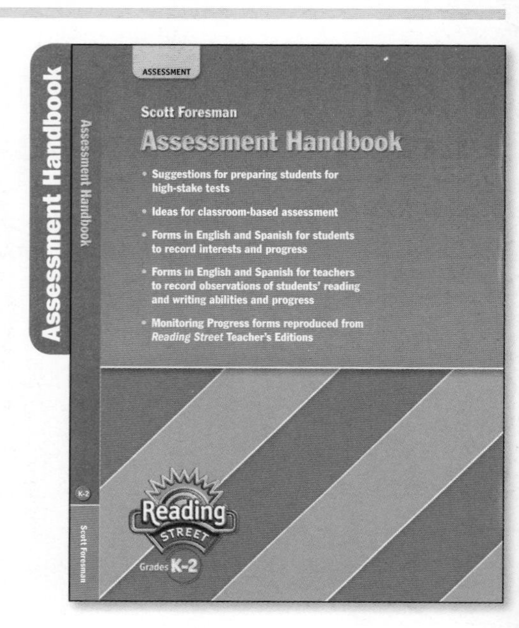

Where Are My Animal Friends?

Where Are My Animal Friends?

Unit 3

Changes

CONCEPT QUESTION

What is changing in our world?

Growing and Changing

Week 1

How do we change as we grow?

Week 2

What do we learn as we grow and change?

Week 3

Why are changes exciting?

Changes in Nature

Week 4

What changes happen in a garden?

Week 5

What changes can we observe in nature?

Week 6

How does nature change during the year?

Week 6

EXPAND THE CONCEPT

How does nature change during the year?

TIME FOR Science

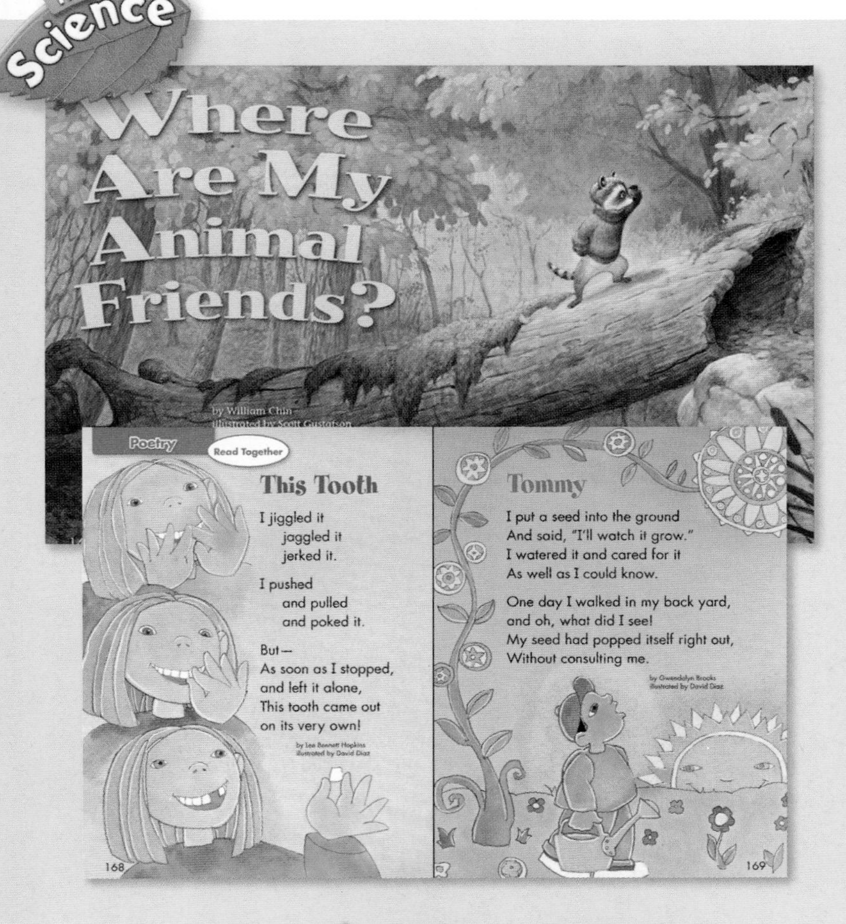

CONNECT THE CONCEPT

▶ Build Background

autumn *bitterly* *freeze* *hibernate* *migrate* *season* *temperature* *weary*

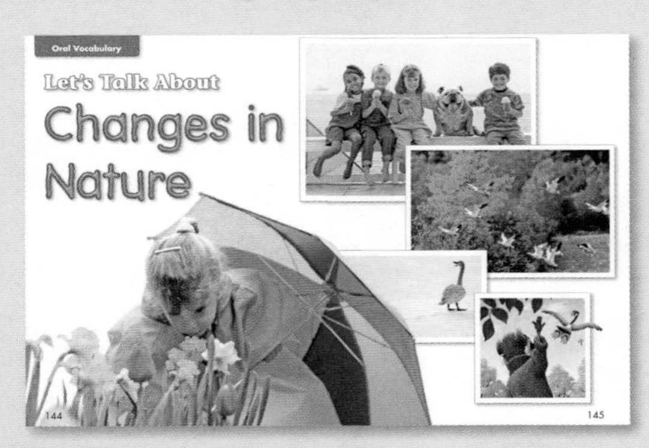

▶ Science Content

Seasonal Changes, Animal Behavior, Weather

▶ Writing

Song

Preview Your Week

How does nature change during the year?

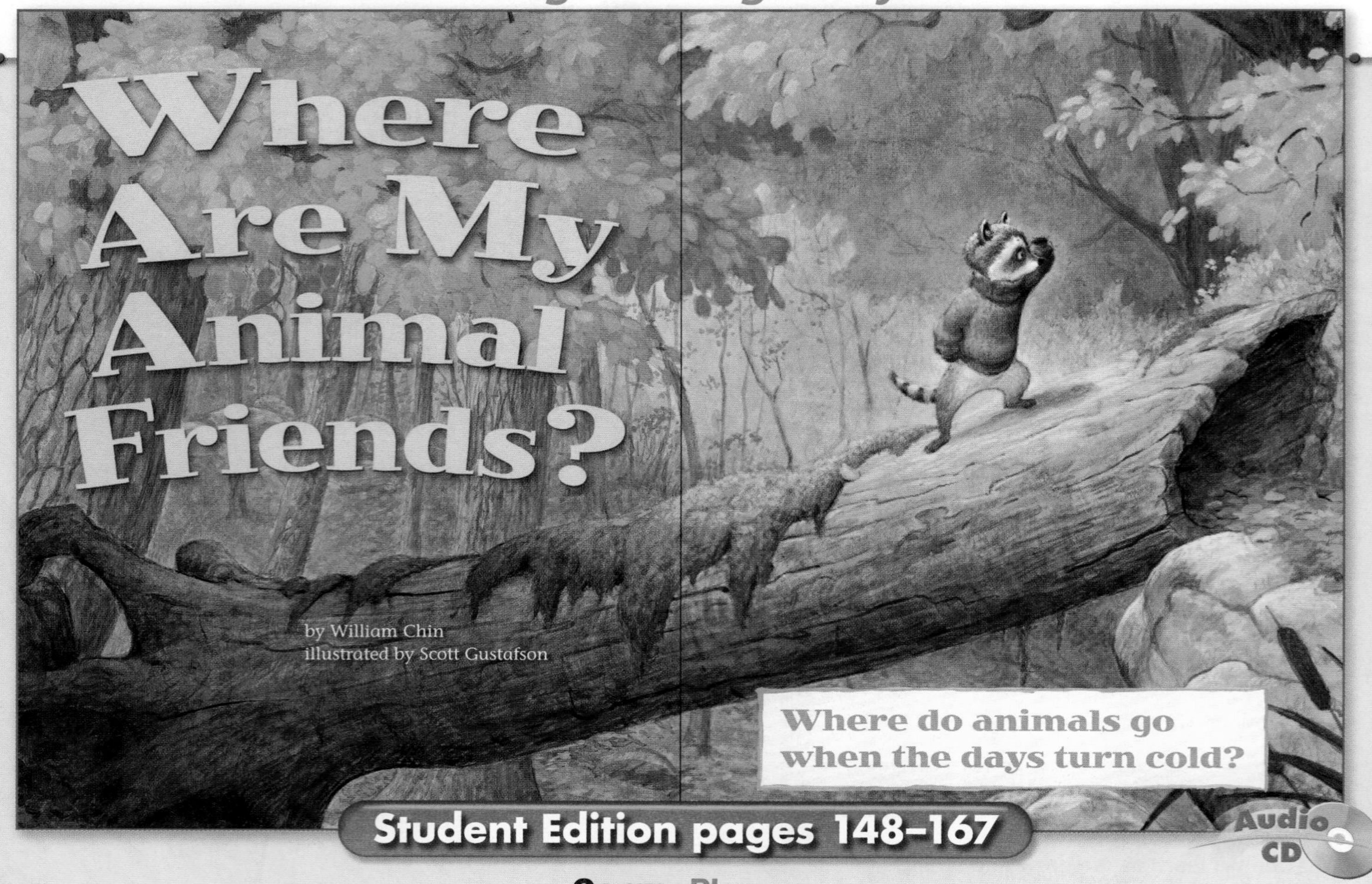

Student Edition pages 148–167

Audio CD

Genre Play

Phonics Comparative Endings *-er, -est* and *dge*/j/

Comprehension Skill Sequence

Comprehension Strategy Prior Knowledge

Science

Paired Selection

Reading Across Texts
Seasonal Changes

Genre
Poetry

Text Features
Rhyme and Rhythm

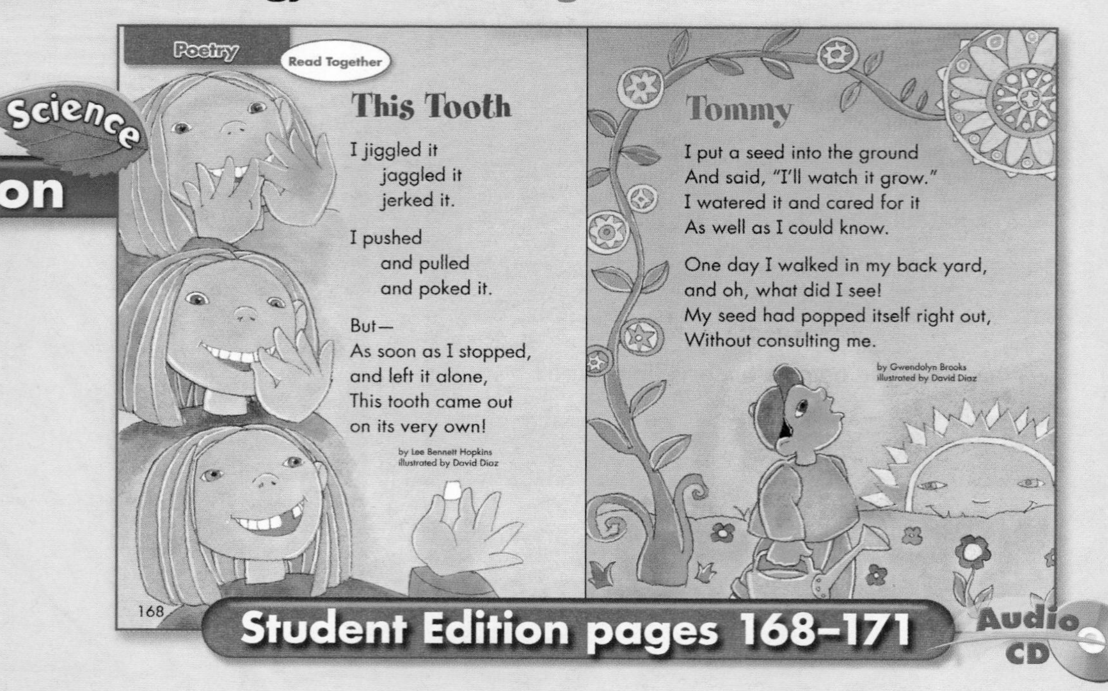

Student Edition pages 168–171

Audio CD

- Student Edition
- Leveled Readers
- Decodable Readers

Leveled Readers

Skill Sequence

Strategy Prior Knowledge

Lesson Vocabulary

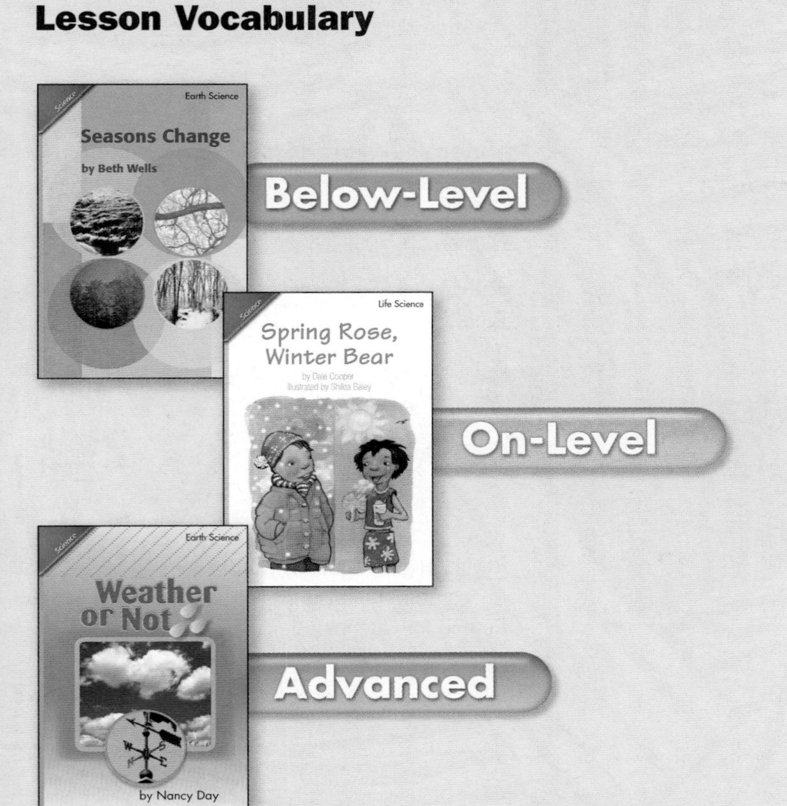

ELL Reader

- Concept Vocabulary
- Text Support
- Language Enrichment

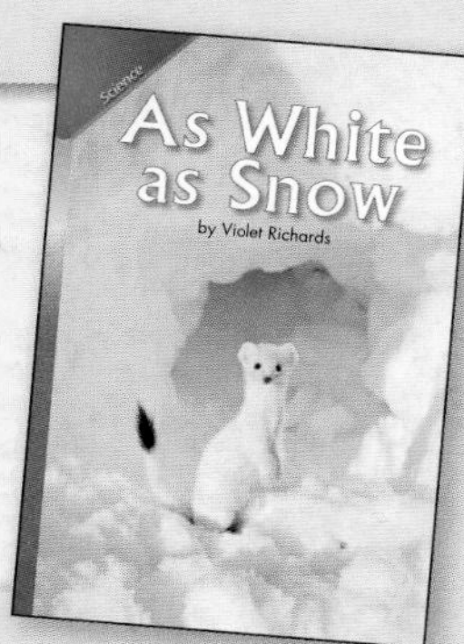

Decodable Readers

Apply Phonics

- *The Big Race*
- *Where Is My Badge?*

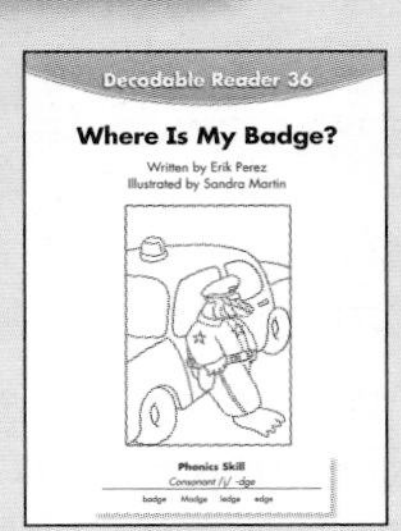

TIME FOR Science

Integrate Science Standards

- Seasonal Changes
- Animal Behavior
- Weather

Where Are My Animal Friends?, pp. 148–167

"This Tooth," "Tommy," and "Where Do Fish Go in Winter?", pp. 168–171

Below-Level	On-Level	Advanced
• Support Concepts	• Develop Concepts	• Extend Concepts • Science Extension Activity

Build **Concept Vocabulary**
Changes in Nature, pp. 144r–145

Teach **Science Concepts**
Seasons, p. 158–159
Animal Behavior, p. 160–161

Explore **Science Center**
Weather Graph, p. 144k

Weekly Plan

	DAY 1 PAGES 144l–145d	DAY 2 PAGES 146a–147c
READING *90–120 minutes* **TARGET SKILLS OF THE WEEK** **Phonics** Comparative Endings and *dge*/j/ **Comprehension Skill** Sequence **Comprehension Strategy** Prior Knowledge	**Oral Language** QUESTION OF THE WEEK, 144l *How does nature change during the year?* **Oral Vocabulary/Share Literature,** 144m Sing with Me Big Book, Song 18 Amazing Words *hibernate, migrate, season, temperature* **Word Work** **Phonemic Awareness,** 144m Add Phonemes /er/, /est/ **Phonics,** 144n–144o Introduce Comparative Endings **T** **Spelling,** 144p Pretest **Comprehension/Vocabulary/Fluency** Read Decodable Reader 35 **Grouping Options** 144f–144g Review High-Frequency Words Check Comprehension Reread for Fluency **Build Background,** 144r–145 Changes in Nature **Listening Comprehension,** 145a–145b Sequence **T**	**Oral Language** QUESTION OF THE DAY, 146a *How do our clothes change each season?* **Oral Vocabulary/Share Literature,** 146b Big Book *What Makes the Seasons?* Amazing Word *autumn* **Word Work** **Phonemic Awareness,** 146b Segment Phonemes **Phonics,** 146c–146d Introduce *dge*/j/ **T** **Spelling,** 146e Dictation **Comprehension/Vocabulary/Fluency** Read Decodable Reader 36 **Grouping Options** 144f–144g Review High-Frequency Words Check Comprehension Reread for Fluency **High-Frequency Words,** 146-147 Introduce *before, does, good-bye, oh, right, won't* **T**
LANGUAGE ARTS *20–30 minutes* **Trait of the Week** **Sentences**	**Shared Writing,** 145c Song **Grammar,** 145d Introduce Contractions with *Not* **T**	**Interactive Writing,** 147a Journal Entry **Grammar,** 147b Practice Contractions with *Not* **T** **Speaking and Viewing,** 147c Nonverbal Communication
DAILY JOURNAL WRITING	**Day 1** *Write to tell what bears and geese do when winter is coming.*	**Day 2** *Write a fact from* What Makes the Seasons?
DAILY SCIENCE CONNECTIONS	**Day 1** Seasons Sorting Boxes Concept Chart, 144r–145	**Day 2** Seasons Sorting Boxes Concept Chart, 147c
DAILY SUCCESS PREDICTORS for Adequate Yearly Progress **Monitor Progress and Corrective Feedback**	Phonics Check Word Reading, *144o* Spiral REVIEW Phonics	Phonics Check Word Reading, *146d* Spiral REVIEW Phonics

RESOURCES FOR THE WEEK

- Practice Book 1.2, *pp. 51–60*
- Phonics and Spelling Practice Book, *pp. 69–72*
- Grammar and Writing Practice Book, *pp. 69–72*
- Selection Test, *pp. 45–48*
- Fresh Reads for Differentiated Test Practice, *pp. 103–108*
- Phonics Songs and Rhymes Chart 18
- The Grammar and Writing Book, *pp. 152–157*

Grouping Options for Differentiated Instruction

Turn the page for the small group lesson plan.

DAY 3 PAGES 148a–167d

Oral Language

QUESTION OF THE DAY, 148a
What's something you get ready for each year?

Oral Vocabulary/Share Literature, 148b
Big Book *What Makes the Seasons?*
Amazing Word *freeze*

Word Work

Phonemic Awareness, 148b
Blend and Segment Phonemes

Phonics, 148c–148d
Comparative Endings and *dge*/j/ **T**

Spelling, 148d
Practice

Comprehension/Vocabulary/Fluency

Read *Where Are My Animal Friends?,* 148e–167

Grouping Options 144f–144g

Introduce Selection Words
goose, raccoon, spring, warm

Review High-Frequency Words
before, does, good-bye, oh, right, won't **T**

Sequence **T**
Prior Knowledge
REVIEW Compare and Contrast **T**

Fluency, 167a
Read with Expression and Intonation

Vocabulary, 167b
Multiple-Meaning Words

Trait of the Week, 167c
Introduce Sentences

Grammar, 167d
Write with Contractions with *Not* **T**

Day 3 *Write about an animal you might like to be and what you would do in winter.*

Day 3 Time for Science: Seasons, 158–159; Animal Behavior, 160–161

DAY 4 PAGES 168a–171c

Oral Language

QUESTION OF THE DAY, 168a
What changes might be funny?

Oral Vocabulary/Share Literature, 168b
Read Aloud Anthology "Busy Busy Moose"
Amazing Words *bitterly, weary*

Word Work

Phonemic Awareness, 168b
Blend and Segment Onset/Rime

High-Frequency Words, 168c
Practice *before, does, good-bye, oh, right, won't* **T**

Phonics, 168c–168d
REVIEW *r*-Controlled *er, ir, ur* and Contractions *'s, 've, 're* **T**
REVIEW Word Reading **T**

Spelling, 168e
Partner Review

Comprehension/Vocabulary/Fluency

Read Poetry Collection, 168–171
Leveled Readers

Grouping Options 144f–144g

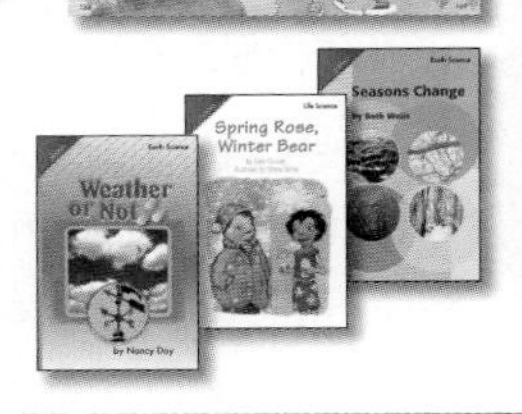

Unfamiliar Words
Reading Across Texts

Fluency, 171a
Read with Expression and Intonation

Writing Across the Curriculum, 171b
Math Story

Grammar, 171c
Review Contractions with *Not* **T**

Day 4 *Write what Raccoon and the other animal friends do next spring.*

Day 4 Science Center: Our Weather Chart, 144k

DAY 5 PAGES 172a–173b

Oral Language

QUESTION OF THE DAY, 172a
What other changes do animals make during the year?

Oral Vocabulary/Share Literature, 172b
Read Aloud Anthology "Busy Busy Moose"
Amazing Words Review

Word Work

Phonics, 172c
Review Comparative Endings and *dge*/j/ **T**

High-Frequency Words, 172c
Review *before, does, good-bye, oh, right, won't* **T**

Spelling, 172d
Test

Comprehension/Vocabulary/Fluency

Read Leveled Readers

Grouping Options 144f–144g

Monitor Progress, 172e–172g
Read the Sentences
Read the Story

Writing and Grammar, 172–173
Develop Sentences
Use Contractions with *Not* **T**

Research/Study Skills, 173a
Bar Graph

Day 5 *Write to tell what animals do in the winter.*

Day 5 Revisit the Seasons Sorting Boxes Concept Chart, 173b

KEY (target icon) = Target Skill **T** = Tested Skill

Fluency and Comprehension
Check High-Frequency Words, *148f*
Check Retelling, *166a*
Spiral REVIEW High-Frequency Words

Fluency
Check Fluency WCPM, *171a*
Spiral REVIEW Phonics, High-Frequency Words

Oral Vocabulary
Check Oral Vocabulary, *172b*
Assess Phonics, High-Frequency Words, Fluency, Comprehension, *172e*

SUCCESS PREDICTOR

Small Group Plan *for Differentiated Instruction*

Daily Plan AT A GLANCE

Reading

Whole Group
- Oral Language
- Word Work
- Comprehension/Vocabulary

Group Time

Meet with small groups to provide:
- Skill Support
- Reading Support
- Fluency Practice

This week's lessons for daily group time can be found behind the Differentiated Instruction (DI) tab on pp. DI · 66–DI · 75.

Whole Group
- Comprehension/Vocabulary
- Fluency

Language Arts
- Writing
- Grammar
- Speaking/Listening/Viewing
- Research/Study Skills

Use *My Sidewalks on Reading Street* for Tier III intensive reading intervention.

DAY 1

On-Level
Teacher-Led
Page 144q
- **Read** Decodable Reader 35
- **Reread** for Fluency

Strategic Intervention
Teacher-Led
Page DI · 66
- Blend and Build Words with Comparative Endings *-er, -est*
- **Read** Decodable Reader 35
- **Reread** for Fluency

Advanced
Teacher-Led
Page DI · 67
- Extend Word Reading
- **Read** Advanced Selection 18
- Introduce Concept Inquiry

Independent Activities
While you meet with small groups, have the rest of the class...
- Reread for fluency
- Write in their journals
- Complete Practice Book 1.2, p. 53
- Visit the Word Work Center

DAY 2

On-Level
Teacher-Led
Page 146f
- **Read** Decodable Reader 36
- **Reread** for Fluency

Strategic Intervention
Teacher-Led
Page DI · 68
- Blend and Build Words with *dge/j/*
- **Read** Decodable Reader 36
- **Reread** for Fluency

Advanced
Teacher-Led
Page DI · 69
- Extend Word Reading
- **Read** Self-Selected Reading
- Continue Concept Inquiry

Independent Activities
While you meet with small groups, have the rest of the class...
- Reread for fluency
- Write in their journals
- Complete Practice Book 1.2, pp. 54–56
- Visit the Word Work Center
- Work on inquiry projects

DAY 3

On-Level
Teacher-Led
Pages 148–167
- **Read** *Where Are My Animal Friends?*

Strategic Intervention
Teacher-Led
Page DI · 70
- Blend and Read Words with dge/j/; Endings *-er, -est*
- **Read** SI Decodable Reader 18
- **Read** or Listen to *Where Are My Animal Friends?*

Advanced
Teacher-Led
Page DI · 71
- **Read** *Where Are My Animal Friends?*
- Continue Concept Inquiry

Independent Activities
While you meet with small groups, have the rest of the class...
- Read self-selected reading
- Write in their journals
- Complete Practice Book 1.2, p. 57
- Visit the Listening and Writing Centers
- Work on inquiry projects

① Begin with whole class skill and strategy instruction.

② Meet with small groups to provide differentiated instruction.

③ Gather the whole class back together for fluency and language arts.

DAY 4

On-Level

Teacher-Led
Pages 168–171, LR49–LR51

- **Read** Poetry Collection
- Practice with On-Level Reader *Spring Rose, Winter Bear*

Strategic Intervention

Teacher-Led
Pages DI • 72, LR46–LR48

- Blend and Read Words
- **Reread** SI Decodable Reader 17
- **Read** or Listen to Poetry Collection
- Practice with Below-Level Reader *Seasons Change*

Advanced

Teacher-Led
Pages DI • 73, LR52–LR54

- **Read** Poetry Collection
- Expand Vocabulary
- Continue Concept Inquiry
- Practice with Advanced Reader *Weather or Not*

i Independent Activities

While you meet with small groups, have the rest of the class...

- Reread for fluency
- Write in their journals
- Read self-selected reading
- Complete Practice Book 1.2, pp. 58–59
- Visit the Listening and Science Centers
- Work on inquiry projects

DAY 5

On-Level

Teacher-Led
Pages 172e–172g, LR49–LR51

- Sentence Reading, Set B
- Monitor Comprehension
- Practice with On-Level Reader *Spring Rose, Winter Bear*

Strategic Intervention

Teacher-Led
Pages DI • 74, LR46–LR48

- Practice Word Reading
- Sentence Reading, Set A
- Monitor Fluency and Comprehension
- Practice with Below-Level Reader *Seasons Change*

Advanced

Teacher-Led
Pages DI • 75, LR52–LR54

- Sentence Reading, Set C
- Monitor Comprehension
- Share Concept Inquiry
- Practice with Advanced Reader *Weather or Not*

i Independent Activities

While you meet with small groups, have the rest of the class...

- Reread for fluency
- Write in their journals
- Read self-selected reading
- Complete Practice Book 1.2, p. 60
- Visit the Technology Center

ELL

Grouping Place English language learners in the groups that correspond to their reading abilities in English.

Use the appropriate Leveled Reader or other text at children's instructional level.

TIP Send home the appropriate Multilingual Summary of the main selection on Day 1.

Take It to the NET™ ONLINE
PearsonSuccessNet.com

P. David Pearson
For ideas on teaching comprehension strategies, see the article "Developing Expertise in Reading Comprehension" by Scott Foresman author P. D. Pearson and others.

TEACHER TALK

A **base word** is a word that can stand alone or take endings and affixes, such as *walk*.

Be sure to schedule time for children to work on the unit inquiry project "Take a Closer Look." This week children should publish the information in their journals by sharing them in a conference with you.

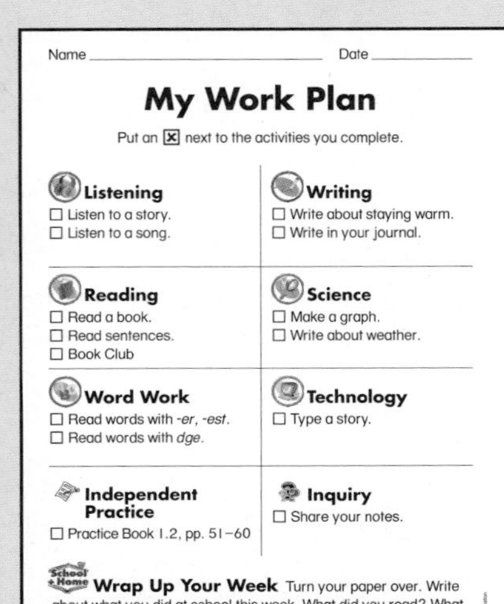

Name ______________ Date ______

My Work Plan

Put an ☒ next to the activities you complete.

Listening
☐ Listen to a story.
☐ Listen to a song.

Writing
☐ Write about staying warm.
☐ Write in your journal.

Reading
☐ Read a book.
☐ Read sentences.
☐ Book Club

Science
☐ Make a graph.
☐ Write about weather.

Word Work
☐ Read words with *-er*, *-est*.
☐ Read words with *dge*.

Technology
☐ Type a story.

Independent Practice
☐ Practice Book 1.2, pp. 51–60

Inquiry
☐ Share your notes.

Wrap Up Your Week Turn your paper over. Write about what you did at school this week. What did you read? What did you learn about how nature changes over the year?

34 Unit 3 • Week 6 • *Where Are My Animal Friends?*

▲ **Group-Time Survival Guide**
p. 34, Weekly Contract

Customize Your Plan *by Strand*

ORAL LANGUAGE

Concept Development

How does nature change during the year?

hibernate *migrate* *season*
temperature *autumn* *freeze*
bitterly *weary*

BUILD

- ❑ **Question of the Week** Use the Morning Warm-Up! to introduce and discuss the question of the week. This week children will talk, sing, read, and write about changes in nature. DAY 1 *144l*

- ❑ **Sing with Me Big Book** Sing a song about animals in winter. Ask children to listen for the concept-related Amazing Words *hibernate, migrate, season, temperature.* DAY 1 *144m*

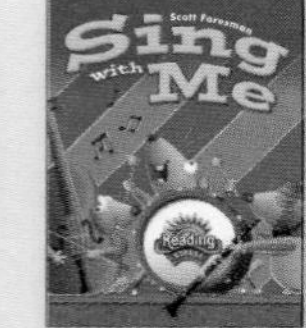

Sing with Me Big Book

- ❑ **Let's Talk About Changes in Nature** Use the Let's Talk About It lesson in the Student Edition to build background, vocabulary, and concepts. Then create a concept chart for children to add to throughout the week. DAY 1 *144r–145*

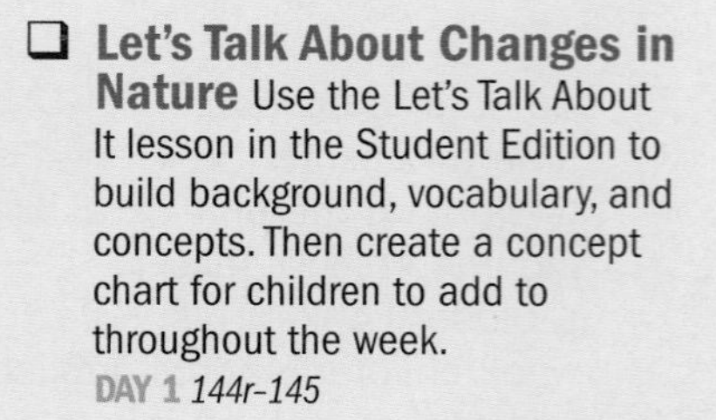

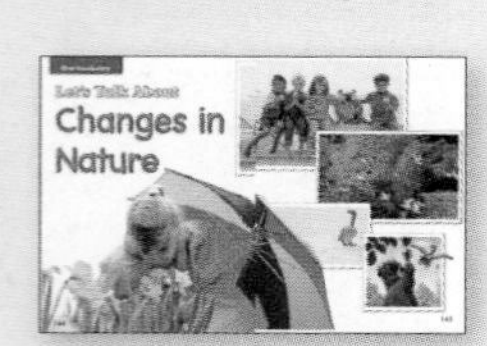

Let's Talk About It

DEVELOP

- ❑ **Question of the Day** Use the questions in the Morning Warm-Ups! to discuss lesson concepts and how they relate to the unit theme, Changes. DAY 2 *146a*, DAY 3 *148a*, DAY 4 *168a*, DAY 5 *172a*

- ❑ **Share Literature** Read big books and read aloud selections that develop concepts, language, and vocabulary related to the lesson concept and the unit theme. Continue to develop this week's Amazing Words. DAY 2 *146b*, DAY 3 *148b*, DAY 4 *168b*, DAY 5 *172b*

CONNECT

- ❑ **Wrap Up Your Week!** Revisit the Question of the Week. Then connect concepts and vocabulary to next week's lesson. DAY 5 *173b*

CHECK

- ❑ **Check Oral Vocabulary** To informally assess children's oral vocabulary, ask individuals to use some of this week's Amazing Words to tell you about the photographs and illustration on Student Edition pp. 144-145. DAY 5 *172b*

PHONEMIC AWARENESS AND PHONICS

COMPARATIVE ENDINGS Add the ending *-er* to some base words to compare two things and add *-est* to compare three or more things.

DGE/J/ The letters *dge* stand for /j/.

TEACH

- ❑ **Add Phonemes** Practice saying a base word and blending it with the endings *-er* and *-est*. DAY 1 *144m*

- ❑ **Comparative Endings** Introduce the blending strategy for words with endings. Have children blend and build words. DAY 1 *144n–144o*

- ❑ **Segment Phonemes** Practice saying and blending the sounds for each word. DAY 2 *146b*, DAY 3 *148b*

- ❑ ***dge*/j/** Introduce the blending strategy for words with *dge*/j/. Then have children blend and build *dge* words. DAY 2 *146c–146d*

- ❑ **Fluent Word Reading** Use the Fluent Word Reading Routine to develop children's word reading fluency. Use the Phonics Songs and Rhymes Chart for additional word reading practice. DAY 3 *148c–148d*

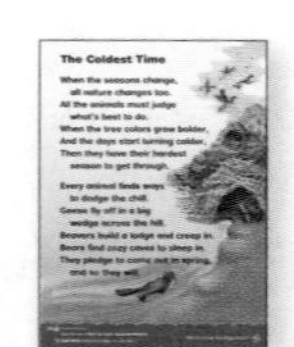

Phonics Songs and Rhymes Chart 18

PRACTICE/APPLY

- ❑ **Decodable Reader 35** Practice reading words with comparative endings in context. DAY 1 *144g*

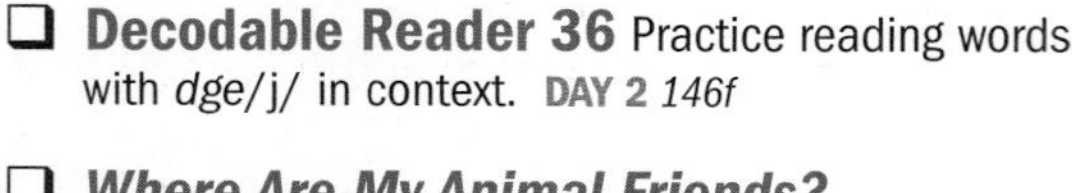

- ❑ **Decodable Reader 36** Practice reading words with *dge*/j/ in context. DAY 2 *146f*

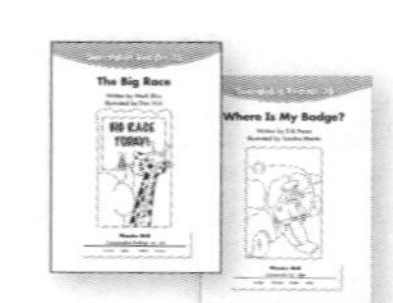

Decodable Readers 35 and 36

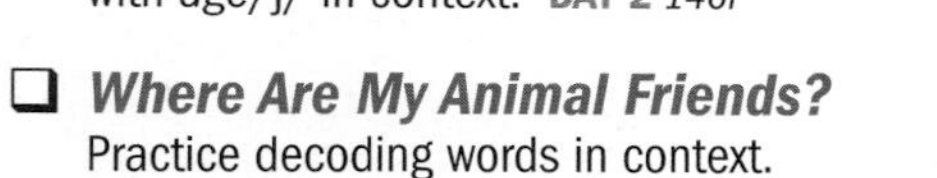

- ❑ ***Where Are My Animal Friends?*** Practice decoding words in context. DAY 3 *148-163*

- ❑ **Homework** Practice Book 1.2 pp. 53, 55. DAY 1 *144o*, DAY 2 *146d*

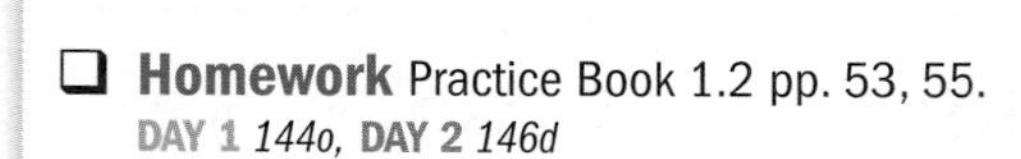

- ❑ **Word Work Center** Practice comparative endings, /dge/j/. ANY DAY *144j*

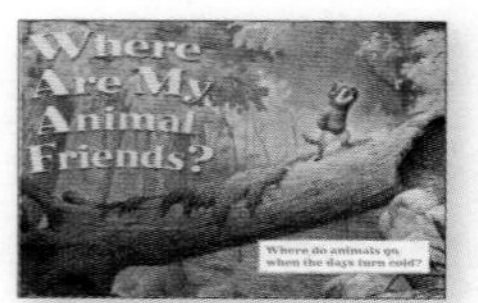

Main Selection—Fiction

RETEACH/REVIEW

- ❑ **Review** Review words with this week's phonics skills. DAY 5 *172c*

- ❑ **Reteach Lessons** If necessary, reteach comparative endings and *dge*/j/. DAY 5 *DI·83-DI·84*

- ❑ **Spiral REVIEW** Review previously taught phonics skills. DAY 1 *144o*, DAY 2 *146d*, DAY 4 *168c-168d*

ASSESS

- ❑ **Sentence Reading** Assess children's ability to read words with comparative endings and *dge*/j/. DAY 5 *172e–172f*

❶ Use assessment data to determine your instructional focus.

❷ Preview this week's instruction by strand.

❸ Choose instructional activities that meet the needs of your classroom.

SPELLING

COMPARATIVE ENDINGS Some words consist of a base word and the ending *-er* or *-est*. Add the ending *-er* to words to compare two things and add *-est* to compare three or more things.

TEACH

❑ **Pretest** Before administering the pretest, model how to segment words with comparative endings to spell them. Dictate the spelling words, segmenting them if necessary. Then have children check their pretests and correct misspelled words. DAY 1 *144p*

PRACTICE/APPLY

❑ **Dictation** Have children write dictation sentences to practice spelling words. DAY 2 *146e*

❑ **Spelling Words** Have children practice their spelling words by making foldout books, adding comparative endings *-er* and *-est* to base words, and illustrating with pictures. DAY 3 *148d*

❑ **Homework** Phonics and Spelling Practice Book pp. 69-72. DAY 1 *144p*, DAY 2 *146e*, DAY 3 *148d*, DAY 4 *168e*

RETEACH/REVIEW

❑ **Partner Review** Have pairs work together to read and write the spelling words. DAY 4 *168e*

ASSESS

❑ **Posttest** Use dictation sentences to give the posttest for words with comparative endings *-er, -est*. DAY 5 *172d*

Spelling Words

Adding *-er* and *-est*

1. bigger	6. slowest
2. biggest	7. shorter*
3. faster	8. shortest
4. fastest	9. sadder
5. slower	10. saddest*

High-Frequency Words

11. good-bye*	12. before*

* Words from the Selection

HIGH-FREQUENCY WORDS

WORDS TO READ

before *does* *good-bye* *oh*
right *won't*

TEACH

❑ **Words to Read** Introduce this week's high-frequency words and add them to the Word Wall. DAY 2 *146-147*

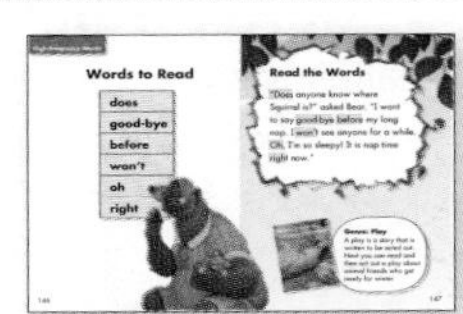

High-Frequency Words

PRACTICE/APPLY

❑ **Vocabulary Transparency 18** Review this week's high-frequency words, or Words to Read, before reading *Where Are My Animal Friends?* DAY 3 *148f*

❑ **Words in Context** Read high-frequency words in the context of *Where Are My Animal Friends?* DAY 3 *148-165*

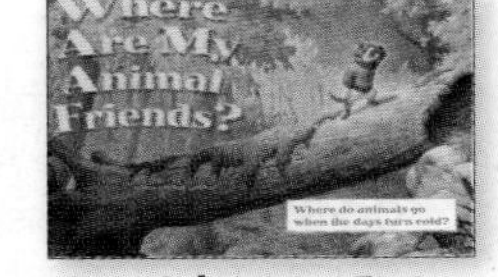

Main Selection—Fiction

❑ **Word Wall** Use the Word Wall to review and practice high-frequency words throughout the week. DAY 4 *168c*, DAY 5 *172c*

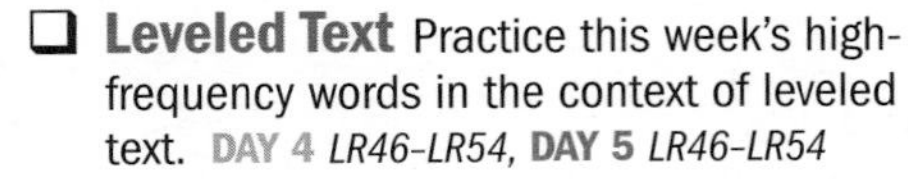

❑ **Leveled Text** Practice this week's high-frequency words in the context of leveled text. DAY 4 *LR46–LR54*, DAY 5 *LR46–LR54*

Leveled Readers

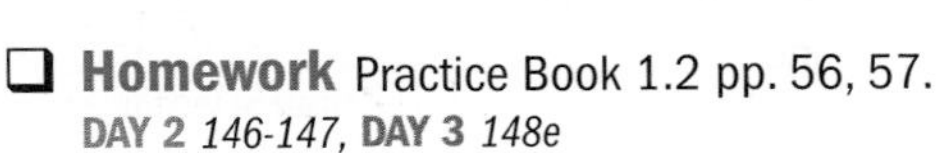

❑ **Homework** Practice Book 1.2 pp. 56, 57. DAY 2 *146-147*, DAY 3 *148e*

RETEACH/REVIEW

❑ **Spiral REVIEW** Review previously taught high-frequency words. DAY 3 *148f*, DAY 4 *168d*

ASSESS

❑ **Sentence Reading** Assess children's ability to read this week's high-frequency words. DAY 5 *172e-172f*

VOCABULARY

TEACH

❑ **Vocabulary Transparency 18** Use Vocabulary Transparency 18 to introduce the selection words from *Where Are My Animal Friends?* Children will read the words but will not be tested on them. DAY 3 *148f*

❑ **Multiple Meaning Words** Discuss words that have more than one meaning, provide examples, and have partners write sentences for each meaning. DAY 3 *167b*

Customize Your Plan *by Strand*

COMPREHENSION

SKILL SEQUENCE Sequence means events in a story happen in a certain order. Words such as *first, next,* and *last* help readers figure out the order of events.

STRATEGY PRIOR KNOWLEDGE Prior knowledge is what you already know about a topic.

TEACH

- ❑ **Listening Comprehension** Read "Back and Forth" and model how to identify *sequence.* DAY 1 *145a-145b*
- ❑ **Skill/Strategy Lesson** Review *sequence.* Then introduce this week's strategy, *prior knowledge.* DAY 3 *148g*

PRACTICE/APPLY

- ❑ **Skills and Strategies in Context** Read *Where Are My Animal Friends?* using the Guiding Comprehension questions to apply *sequence* and *prior knowledge.* DAY 3 *148-167*

Main Selection—Play

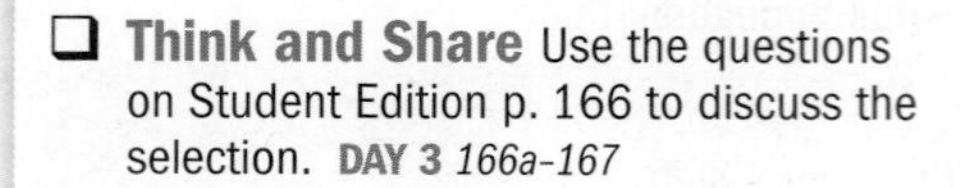

- ❑ **Think and Share** Use the questions on Student Edition p. 166 to discuss the selection. DAY 3 *166a-167*

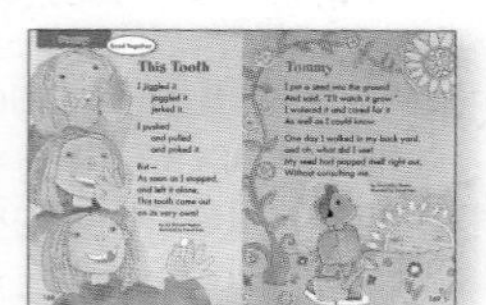
Paired Selection — Poetry

- ❑ **Skills and Strategies in Context** Read the poems, guiding children as they apply skills and strategies. After reading have children make connections across texts. DAY 4 *168-171*

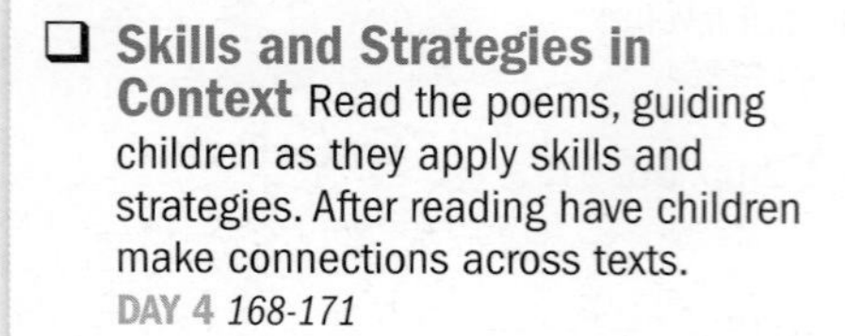

- ❑ **Leveled Text** Apply *sequence* and *prior knowledge* to read leveled text. DAY 4 *LR46-LR54,* DAY 5 *LR46-LR54*

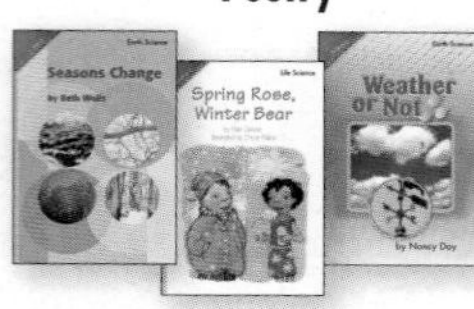

Leveled Readers

- ❑ **Homework** Practice Book 1.2 p. 54. DAY 1 *145a*

ASSESS

- ❑ **Selection Test** Determine children's understanding of the main selection and assess their ability to identify *sequence.* DAY 3
- ❑ **Story Reading** Have children read the passage "The Sweetest Yard." Ask what the *sequence* of the story is and have them retell the story. DAY 5 *172e, 172g*

RETEACH/REVIEW

- ❑ **Reteach Lesson** If necessary, reteach *sequence.* DAY 5 *DI·84*

FLUENCY

SKILL READ WITH EXPRESSION AND INTONATION When you read, use your voice to sound like each of the different characters.

REREAD FOR FLUENCY

- ❑ **Oral Reading** Have children read orally from Decodable Readers 35 and 36, or another text at their independent reading level. Listen to children read and provide corrective feedback regarding their oral reading and their use of the blending strategy. DAY 1 *144q,* DAY 2 *146f*

TEACH

- ❑ **Model** Use passages from *Where Are My Animal Friends?* to model reading aloud with expression and intonation. DAY 3 *167a,* DAY 4 *171a*

PRACTICE/APPLY

- ❑ **Choral Reading** Choral read passages from *Where Are My Animal Friends?* Monitor progress and provide feedback regarding children's reading with expression and intonation. DAY 3 *167a,* DAY 4 *171a*
- ❑ **Listening Center** Have children follow along with the AudioText for this week's selections. ANY DAY *144j*
- ❑ **Reading/Library Center** Have children build fluency by rereading Leveled Readers, Decodable Readers, or other text at their independent level. ANY DAY *144j*
- ❑ **Fluency Coach** Have children use Fluency Coach to listen to fluent reading or to practice reading on their own. ANY DAY

ASSESS

- ❑ **Story Reading** Take a one-minute timed sample of children's oral reading. Use the passage "The Sweetest Yard." DAY 5 *172e, 172g*

1 Use assessment data to determine your instructional focus.

2 Preview this week's instruction by strand.

3 Choose instructional activities that meet the needs of your classroom.

WRITING

Trait of the Week

SENTENCES Sentences should make sense. Words should be in the right order. A mix of short and long sentences gives writing rhythm.

TEACH

- ❑ **Write Together** Engage children in writing activities that develop language, grammar, and writing skills. Include independent writing as an extension of group writing activities.
  - **Shared Writing** DAY 1 *145c*
  - **Interactive Writing** DAY 2 *147a*
  - **Writing Across the Curriculum** DAY 4 *171c*
- ❑ **Trait of the Week** Introduce and model the Trait of the Week, *sentences*. DAY 3 *167c*

PRACTICE/APPLY

- ❑ **Write Now** Examine the model on Student Edition pp. 172–173. Then have children write songs. DAY 5 *172-173*

  Prompt In *Where Are My Animal Friends?*, animals get ready for winter in different ways. Think about what the animals do. Now write a song that tells what the animals don't do.

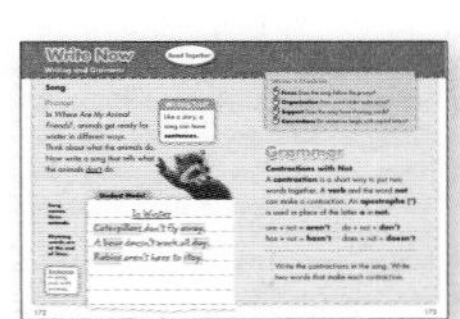
Write Now

- ❑ **Daily Journal Writing** Have children write about concepts and literature in their journals. EVERY DAY *144d-144e*
- ❑ **Writing Center** Have children write a description. ANY DAY *144k*

ASSESS

- ❑ **Scoring Rubric** Use a rubric to evaluate songs. DAY 5 *172-173*

RETEACH/REVIEW

- ❑ **The Grammar and Writing Book** Use pp. 152-157 of The Grammar and Writing Book to extend instruction. ANY DAY

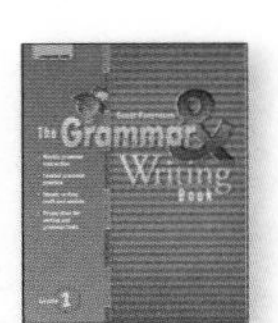
The Grammar and Writing Book

SPEAKING AND VIEWING

TEACH

- ❑ **Nonverbal Communication** Discuss nonverbal communication. Have children speak, using gestures, eye contact, and so on. DAY 2 *147c*

GRAMMAR

SKILL CONTRACTIONS WITH *NOT* A contraction is a shortened way to put two words together. A verb and the word *not* can be put together to make a contraction. An apostrophe (') is used in place of the letter *o*.

- ❑ **Grammar Transparency 18** Use Grammar Transparency 18 to teach *contractions with not*. DAY 1 *145d*

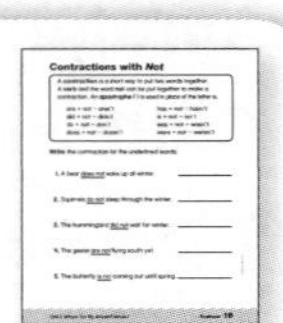
Grammar Transparency 18

PRACTICE/APPLY

- ❑ **Develop the Concept** Review the concept of *contractions with not* and provide guided practice. DAY 2 *147b*
- ❑ **Apply to Writing** Have children use *contractions with not* in writing. DAY 3 *167d*
- ❑ **Define/Practice** Review the definition of *contractions with not*. Then have children write sentence pairs and classify *contractions with not*. DAY 4 *171d*
- ❑ **Write Now** Discuss the grammar lesson on Student Edition p. 173. Have children use the contraction *don't* in their own song about what animals don't do. DAY 5 *172-173*

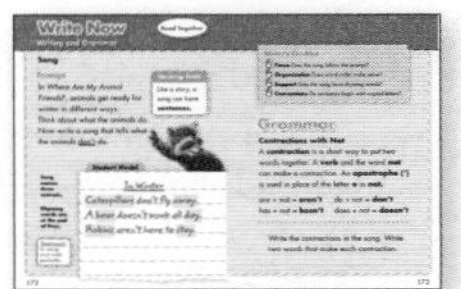
Write Now

- ❑ **Daily Fix-It** Have children find and correct errors in grammar, spelling, and punctuation. DAY 1 *145d*, DAY 2 *147b*, DAY 3 *167d*, DAY 4 *171d*, DAY 5 *172-173*
- ❑ **Homework** Grammar and Writing Practice Book pp. 69-72. DAY 2 *145b*, DAY 3 *147d*, DAY 4 *167d*, DAY 5 *171c*, *172-173*

RETEACH/REVIEW

- ❑ **The Grammar and Writing Book** Use pp. 152-155 of The Grammar and Writing Book to extend instruction. ANY DAY

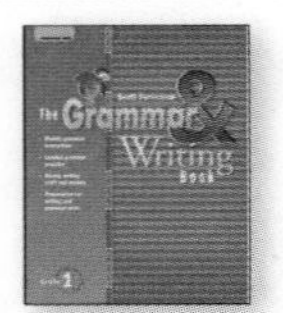
The Grammar and Writing Book

RESEARCH/INQUIRY

TEACH

- ❑ **Graphs: Bar Graph** Model reading a bar graph. Have children work in groups to analyze the information in the graph. DAY 5 *173a*
- ❑ **Unit Inquiry Project** Allow time for children to publish the information in their journals by sharing them in a conference with you. ANY DAY *9*

Resources for

Differentiated Instruction

LEVELED READERS

- **Comprehension**
  - **Skill** Sequence
  - **Strategy** Prior Knowledge
- **Lesson Vocabulary**

  High-Frequency Words

before | does | good-bye | oh | right | won't

- **Science Standards**
  - Seasonal Changes
  - Animal Behavior
  - Weather

PearsonSuccessNet.com

Use the Online Database of over 600 books to

- Download and print additional copies of this week's leveled readers
- Listen to the readers being read online
- Search for more titles focused on this week's skills, topic and content

On-Level

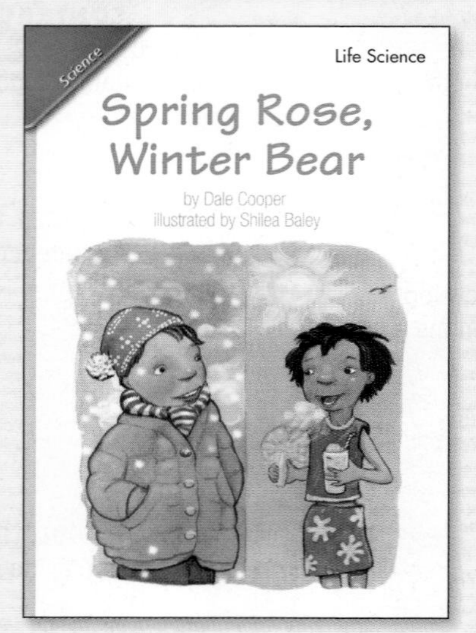

On-Level Reader

Sequence

In the spring, leaves grow on the trees. In the summer the trees are green. In the fall the leaves change color and fall off the trees. In the winter the trees are bare.

First 1. leaves grow on the trees

Next 2. trees are green

Then 3. leaves change color and fall off the trees

Last 4. trees are bare

On-Level Practice TE p. LR50

Vocabulary

Write the word from the box that best fits in each sentence.

Words to Know		
before	does	good-bye
oh	right	won't

1. Before the winter comes, a bear must eat and eat.
2. The bear does this to become fat.
3. If it doesn't eat, the bear won't sleep.
4. The bear waits until the time is right.
5. Then it is time to say good-bye until spring.
6. Oh, hello, bear! It is spring again!

On-Level Practice TE p. LR51

Strategic Intervention

Below-Level Reader

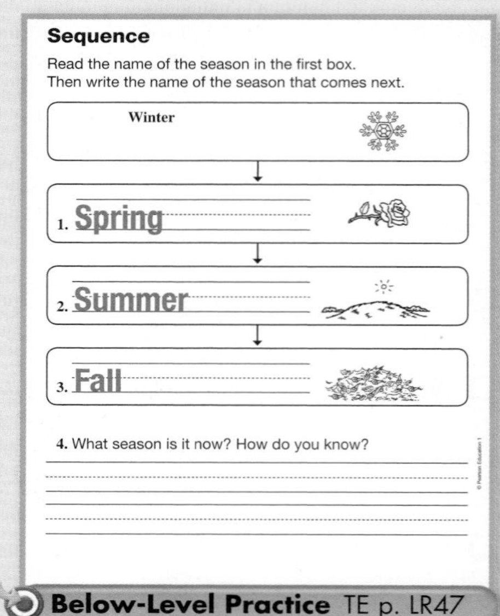

Sequence

Read the name of the season in the first box.
Then write the name of the season that comes next.

Winter

1. Spring
2. Summer
3. Fall
4. What season is it now? How do you know?

Below-Level Practice TE p. LR47

Vocabulary

Read the poem below, or listen as someone reads it to you. Look for the words from the box in the poem. Then circle the vocabulary words that you find in the poem.

Words to Know		
before	does	good-bye
oh	right	won't

How does it feel?
Let's go outside.
Oh! It is spring!
Let's wave good-bye—

To winter—won't
you miss the cold?
It will come back,
Or so I'm told.

You are right!
Before you know it,
Winter is back,
And it is snowing.

Below-Level Practice TE p. LR48

Advanced

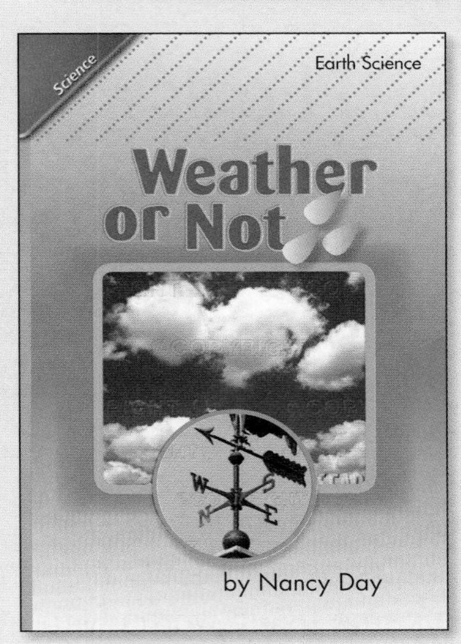

Advanced Reader

Sequence

Read the paragraph. Think about what happens first, next, and last. Complete the chart below.

Tree leaves grow with their shiny side facing the sun. The wind that comes before a storm blows them so you can see their lighter-green backs. Then it starts to rain.

First
1. Leaves grow with shiny side up facing the sun.

Next
2. Wind blows the leaves so you can see the other side.

Last
3. It starts to rain.

Advanced Practice TE p. LR53

Vocabulary

Read the definitions.
Write the word from the box under its definition.

Words to Know
hibernate migrate season temperature

1. Definition: to spend the winter sleeping or resting
Word: hibernate

2. Definition: how hot or cold something is
Word: temperature

3. Definition: one of the four times of the year
Word: season

4. Definition: to move from one place to another
Word: migrate

Advanced Practice TE p. LR54

ELL

ELL Reader

ELL Poster 18

Teacher's Edition Notes

ELL notes throughout this lesson support instruction and reference additional resources at point of use.

Teaching Guide pp. 120–126, 246–247

- Multilingual summaries of the main selection
- Comprehension lesson
- Vocabulary strategies and word cards
- ELL Reader 1.3.6 lesson

ELL and Transition Handbook

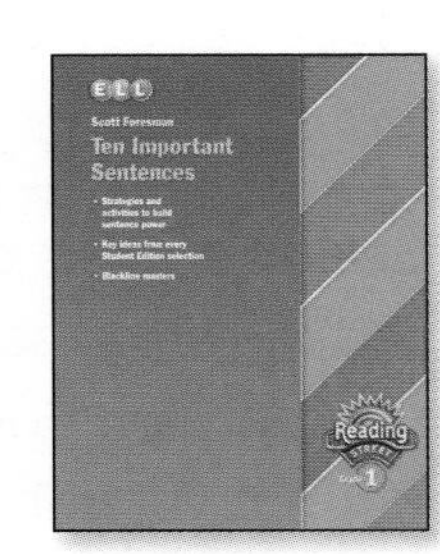

Ten Important Sentences

- Key ideas from every selection in the Student Edition
- Activities to build sentence power

More Reading

Readers' Theater Anthology

- Fluency practice
- Five scripts to build fluency
- Poetry for oral interpretation

Leveled Trade Books

Below-Level

On-Level

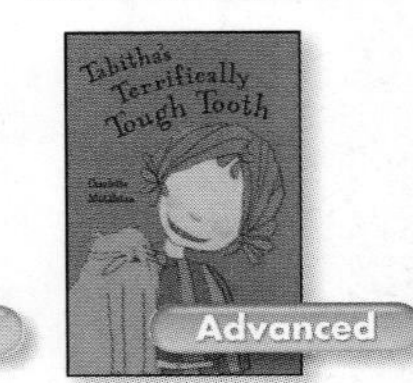

Advanced

- Extend reading tied to the unit concept
- Lessons in Trade Book Library Teaching Guide

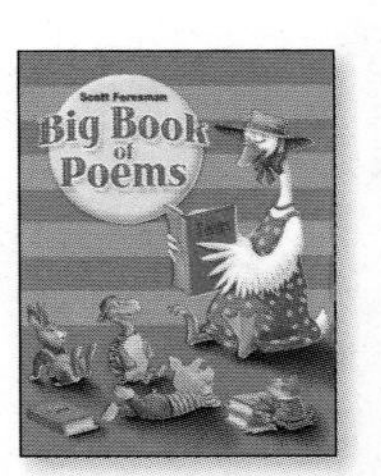

Big Book of Poems

- Fluency practice
- Poetry for Choral Reading

Homework

- Family Times Newsletter
- ELL Multilingual Selection Summaries

Take-Home Books

- Decodable Readers
- Leveled Readers

Literacy Centers

Listening

Let's Read Along

MATERIALS
CD player, headphones, print copies of recorded pieces

SINGLES

LISTEN TO LITERATURE As children listen to the following recordings, have them follow along or read along in the print version.

AudioText
Where Are My Animal Friends?
Poetry

Sing with Me/Background Building Audio
"Change of Season"

Phonics Songs and Rhymes Audio
"The Coldest Time"

The Coldest Time

When the seasons change,
all nature changes too.
All the animals must judge
what's best to do.
When the tree colors grow bolder,
And the days start turning colder,
Then they have their hardest
season to get through.

Every animal finds ways
to dodge the chill.
Geese fly off in a big
wedge across the hill.
Beavers build a lodge and creep in.
Bears find cozy caves to sleep in.
They pledge to come out in spring,
and so they will.

Audio CD **Phonics Songs and Rhymes Chart 18**

Reading/Library

Read It Again!

MATERIALS
collection of books for self-selected reading, reading logs

SINGLES PAIRS GROUPS

REREAD BOOKS Have children select previously read books from the appropriate book box and record titles of books they read in their logs. Use these previously read books:

- Decodable Readers
- Leveled Readers
- ELL Readers
- Stories written by classmates
- Books from the library

TEN IMPORTANT SENTENCES Have children read the Ten Important Sentences for *Where Are My Animal Friends?* and locate the sentences in the Student Edition.

BOOK CLUB Have children discuss *Where Are My Animal Friends?* Have them say what they liked and did not like about the play.

Word Work

Phonics Pick A Bunch

MATERIALS
16 index cards, number cube, container

PAIRS GROUPS

COMPARATIVE ENDINGS *-er, -est*
Have pairs or groups of children play a game using words with comparative endings.

1. **Write a word with the comparative endings *-er* or *-est* on each index card. Place the cards in a container.**
2. **Children take turns tossing the number cube, selecting the number of cards indicated on the cube, and reading the words.**
3. **Children return the cards to the container, and play continues until each child has had four turns.**

-dge/j/ Make a set of cards with words with the /j/ sound spelled *-dge* and have children play the game.

This interactive CD provides additional practice.

Use the *Where Are My Animal Friends?* materials from the Reading Street Centers Survival Kit to organize this week's centers.

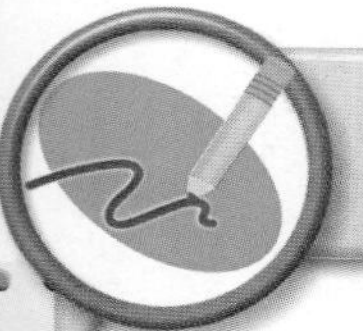

Writing

Staying Warm

MATERIALS
paper, pencils, crayons

SINGLES

WRITE A DESCRIPTION Recall that *Where Are My Animal Friends?* told about what animals do in the winter.

1. **Ask children to think about ways they can keep warm in cool weather.**
2. **Ask them to write about what they might do to stay warm when it is cold out.**
3. **Then have them draw a picture to accompany their writing.**

LEVELED WRITING Encourage children to write at their own ability level. Some may only label their pictures with words or phrases. Others will be able to write simple sentences with some attention to mechanics and spelling. Your best writers will write sentences with greater detail and more attention to mechanics and spelling.

Science

Our Weather Chart

MATERIALS
weather chart, writing paper, pencils

SINGLES

GROUPS

MAKE A WEATHER GRAPH Create a graph showing different types of weather and place it in the Science Center.

1. **Have children choose their favorite type of weather and write their name next to it on the graph.**
2. **Then ask children to write about their favorite type of weather. Encourage them to tell about activities they like to do during their favorite weather.**
3. **After all children have visited the center, you may tally the results to determine the class favorite.**

Technology

Seasonal Story

MATERIALS
computer, printer

GROUPS

WRITE A GROUP STORY Children add on to a group story about seasons.

1. **Set up a file containing a few sentences that begin a story set in a specific season.**
2. **Ask children to turn on the computer and open the word processing file you created.**
3. **Children take turns typing additions to the story.**
4. **After everyone has added to the story, have children print it out and take turns reading it aloud.**

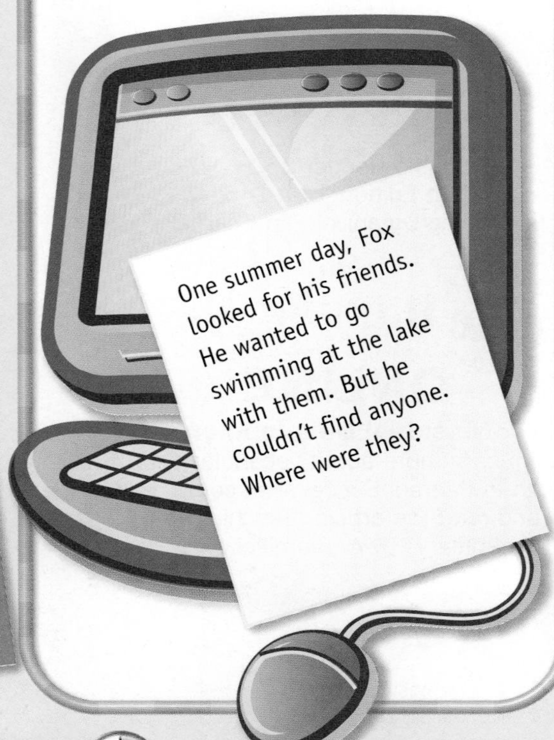

ALL CENTERS

Day 1
AT A GLANCE

Oral Vocabulary
"Change of Season" 18

Phonemic Awareness
Add Phonemes

Phonics and Spelling
Comparative Endings *-er, -est*
Spelling Pretest: Adding *-er, -est*

Read Apply Phonics Word Wall

 < Differentiated Instruction

Build Background
Let's Talk About Changes in Nature

Listening Comprehension
Skill Sequence

Shared Writing
Song

Grammar
Contractions with *Not*

Materials

- *Sing with Me Big Book*
- Letter Tiles
- Decodable Reader 35
- Student Edition 144–145
- Graphic Organizer Flip Chart 8

Take It to the NET™ ONLINE

Professional Development
To learn more about vocabulary, go to PearsonSuccessNet.com and read the article "Teaching Vocabulary" by A. Biemiller.

Morning Warm-Up!

When summer is done,
We know winter will soon be here.
How does nature change
during the year?

QUESTION OF THE WEEK Tell children they will talk, sing, read, and write about Changes in Nature. Write the message and track the print as you read it. Discuss the question.

CONNECT CONCEPTS Ask questions to connect to other selections.

- What season changes did you see in *Ruby in Her Own Time?*
- What winter changes can you see in *An Egg Is an Egg?*

REVIEW HIGH-FREQUENCY WORDS

- Circle the high-frequency words *done* and *know* in the message.
- Have children say and spell each word as they write it in the air.

Build Background Use the Day 1 instruction on ELL Poster 18 to assess knowledge and develop concepts.

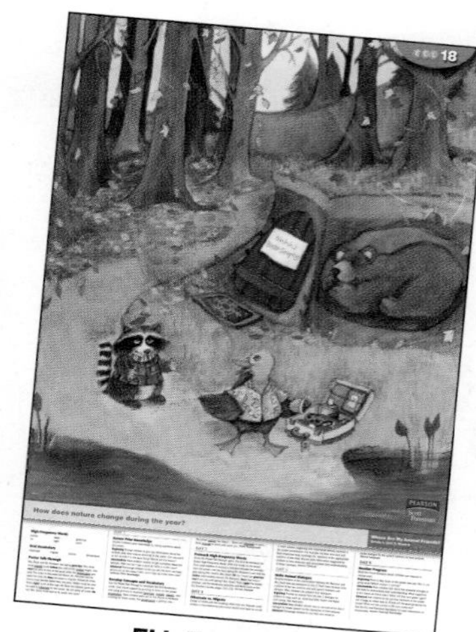

ELL Poster 18

Oral Vocabulary

SHARE LITERATURE Display p. 18 of the *Sing with Me Big Book.* Tell children that they will sing a song about animals in winter. Read the title. Ask children to listen for the Amazing Words **temperature, season, hibernate,** and **migrate** as you sing. Then sing the song again and ask children to sing with you. Have children demonstrate their understanding of *temperature, season, hibernate,* and *migrate* as they discuss what they know about how animals face the cold of winter.

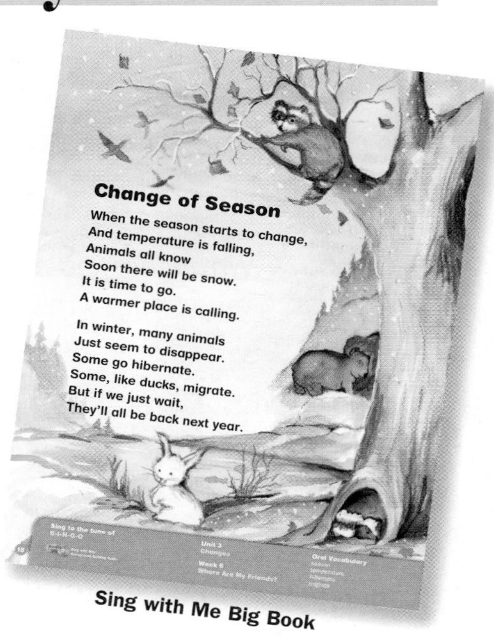

Sing with Me Big Book

Sing with Me/
Background Building Audio

Phonemic Awareness

ADD PHONEMES

- We just sang about winter coming. In winter, the animals will not eat green plants. Listen to the sounds in *green.*
- Model saying each sound, /g/ /r/ /ē/ /n/. Have children say the sounds with you and then say the sounds by themselves.
- Now say each sound as you write the letter that goes with it. Say /g/ /r/ /ē/ /n/ as you write *g, r, ee, n.*
- Have children say the sounds as you point to the letters, /g/ /r/ /ē/ /n/ and blend the sounds to say the word, *green.*
- Add /ər/ to green. Listen as I add /ər/ to *green.* Model saying the base word, *green,* and blending it with the ending, *-er,* to say the word, *greener.* Do the same with *green* and the ending *-est, greenest.*

Continue the activity with these examples.

small, smaller, smallest **hot, hotter, hottest** **flat, flatter, flattest**

OBJECTIVES

- Build oral vocabulary.
- Add phonemes.

hibernate
migrate
season
temperature
autumn
freeze
bitterly
weary

MONITOR PROGRESS

If... children lack oral vocabulary experiences about the concept Changes in Nature,

then... use the Oral Vocabulary Routine below to teach *hibernate.*

Oral Vocabulary ROUTINE

1. **Introduce the Word** Relate the word *hibernate* to the song. Supply a child-friendly definition. Have children say the word. Example: *Hibernate* means "to spend the winter sleeping."
2. **Demonstrate** Provide an example to show meaning. Bears *hibernate* in the winter.
3. **Apply** Have children demonstrate their understanding by showing what it would look like to *hibernate.*
4. **Display the Word/Letter-Sounds** Write the word on a card. Display it. Have children identify the small word *hi* and blend *nate.*

See p. DI·8 to teach *migrate, season,* and *temperature.*

Build Oral Vocabulary Use the illustrations to help children understand the meaning of phrases in the song, "Change of Season."

OBJECTIVES

- Use structural cues to decode words with comparative endings.
- Blend, read, and build words with comparative endings *-er, -est.*

Skills Trace

Comparative Endings

Introduce/Teach	**TE: 1.3 144n–o, 148c–d**
Practice	TE: 1.3 144q; PB: 1.2 53; DR35
Reteach/Review	TE: 1.3 172c, DI•83; 1.4 40c–d PB: 1.2 68
Assess/Test	TE: 1.3 172e–g; Benchmark Test, Unit 3

Strategic Intervention

Use **Monitor Progress,** p. 144o during Group Time after children have had more practice with comparative endings *-er, -est.*

Advanced

Use **Monitor Progress,** p. 144o as a preassessment to determine whether or not this group of children would benefit from this instruction on comparative endings *-er, -est.*

Support Phonics In Spanish, *er* is pronounced like *air* in English so Spanish speakers may pronounce a word like *faster* as *fas-tair.* Give children extra practice in saying words with ending *-er* such as *deeper, wetter,* and *smarter.*

See the Phonics Transition Lessons in the ELL and Transition Handbook.

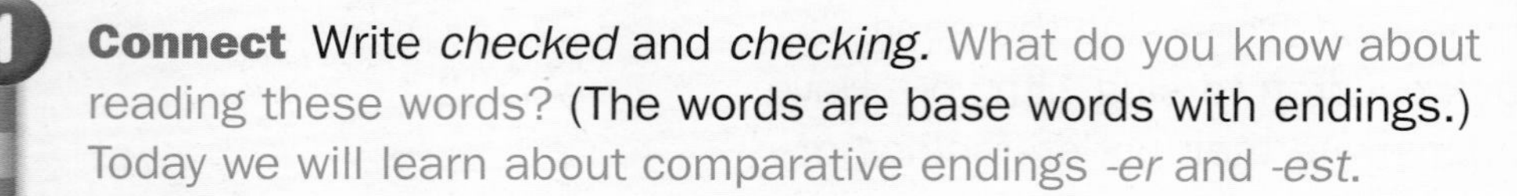

Comparative Endings

TEACH/MODEL

Blending Strategy

ROUTINE

1. **Connect** Write *checked* and *checking.* What do you know about reading these words? (The words are base words with endings.) Today we will learn about comparative endings *-er* and *-est.*

2. **Model** Write *faster.* This word is made from the base word *fast* and the ending *-er.* We add the ending *-er* to words to compare two things and *-est* to compare three or more things. I see that the base word is *fast.* You can cover the ending, read the base word, and then blend the base word and the ending to read the whole word. This is how I blend this word. Cover the ending *er* to read the base word; uncover and read the ending. Blend the two parts. Let's blend this word together: *fast, er, faster.* Repeat with *fastest.* Write *bigger* and continue as above, pointing out that the last consonant of the base word, *big,* was doubled before the ending *-er* was added. Do the same with *biggest.*

3. **Group Practice** Blend each base word and the ending to read the word. Continue with *thickest, darker, hottest, stiffer, flattest.*

4. **Review** What do you know about reading words with endings? Read the base word, read the ending, and then blend the two parts.

BLEND WORDS

INDIVIDUALS BLEND WORDS WITH COMPARATIVE ENDINGS Call on individuals to blend the words *fatter, newest, saddest, deeper, slimmest, greenest.* Have them tell what they know about each word before reading it. (The words are base words with endings *-er, -est.*) Read the base word, read the ending, and then blend the two parts.) For feedback, refer to step four of the Blending Strategy Routine.

BUILD WORDS

INDIVIDUALS MAKE WORDS WITH COMPARATIVE ENDINGS Write *base word, -er* and *-est* as heads for a three-column chart. Write the base words below in the first column. Have children add the *-er* and *-est* endings, read the new words, and tell how the spelling changed when the endings were added.

Base Word	Ending *-er*	Ending *-est*
smart	smarter	smartest
thin	thinner	thinnest
wet	wetter	wettest
quick	quicker	quickest

Vocabulary TiP

You may wish to explain the meanings of these words.

firmest the most solid or firm

slimmer thinner than another

Circle the word for each picture.

small smaller smallest

1. faster fastest
2. bigger biggest
3. taller tallest
4. sweeter sweetest
5. thicker thickest
6. thinner thinnest

Write -er or -est to finish the word in each sentence.

7. The little bird has the few est eggs.
8. The little bird has a long er tail than the big bird.

Home Activity Your child identified the comparative endings -er and -est as in smaller and smallest. Discuss the sizes, shapes, and colors of animals. Have your child compare the animals using -er when comparing two and -est when comparing more than two.

▲ **Practice Book 1.2** p. 53, Comparative Endings

Monitor Progress — Check Word Reading Comparative Endings

Write the following words and have individuals read them.

fewer	**sweeter**	**newest**	**firmest**	**shorter**
smaller	**taller**	**smallest**	**stalled**	**tallest**
bigger	**hottest**	**skipped**	**thinnest**	**trotting**

If... children cannot blend words with comparative endings *-er, -est* at this point,

then... continue to monitor their progress using other instructional opportunities during the week so that they can be successful with the Day 5 Assessment. See the Skills Trace on p. 144n.

▶**Day 1 Check Word Reading** : Day 2 Check Word Reading : Day 3 Check High-Frequency Words/Retelling : Day 4 Check Fluency : Day 5 Assess Progress

Spiral REVIEW

- Row 2 reviews the sound of *a* in *ball.*
- Row 3 reviews doubling the final consonant before endings.

OBJECTIVES

- Segment sounds and word parts to spell words.
- Spell words with comparative endings.

Spelling Words

Adding *-er* and *-est*

1.	**bigger**	6.	**slowest**
2.	**biggest**	7.	**shorter***
3.	**faster**	8.	**shortest**
4.	**fastest**	9.	**sadder**
5.	**slower**	10.	**saddest***

High-Frequency Words

11.	**good-bye***	12.	**before***

* Words from the Selection

Adding *-er* and *-est*

Look at the word. Say it. Listen for the word ending.

	Write the word.	Check it.
1. bigger	bigger	bigger
2. biggest	biggest	biggest
3. faster	faster	faster
4. fastest	fastest	fastest
5. slower	slower	slower
6. slowest	slowest	slowest
7. shorter	shorter	shorter
8. shortest	shortest	shortest
9. sadder	sadder	sadder
10. saddest	saddest	saddest

High-Frequency Words

11. good-bye good-bye 12. before before

School + Home Home Activity Your child is learning to spell words that end with -er and -est. To practice at home, have your child look at the word, say it, spell it, and then spell it with eyes closed.

▲ **Spelling Practice Book** p. 69

ELL

Support Spelling Before giving the spelling pretest, clarify the meaning of *bigger* and *biggest*. Give children three objects that illustrate big, bigger, and biggest, such as balls, boxes, or blocks and have children order them. Do the same for objects that illustrate short, *shorter*, and *shortest*, such as crayons, pencils or string.

Spelling

PRETEST Comparative Endings

MODEL WRITING FOR WORD PARTS The spelling words all have comparative endings *-er* or *-est*. Some have base words that do not change when the ending is added and others double the final consonant. Before administering the spelling pretest, model how to segment words with comparative endings *-er, -est* to spell them.

- The word *deeper* has an ending. What is the ending? *(-er)* What is the base word? *(deep)*
- What sounds do you hear in *deep?* What is the letter for /d/? Write *d.* Continue with the *ee,* /ē/, and *p*/p/.
- Now let's add the ending *-er.* Write *er.*
- Repeat with *deepest, slimmer, slimmest.*

PRETEST Dictate the spelling words. Segment the words for children if necessary. Have children check their pretests and correct misspelled words.

HOMEWORK Spelling Practice Book, p. 69

A Long Winter Sleep

The days get shorter. The temperature drops. The winter season is beginning. Some animals are getting ready for a long winter sleep. They eat as much as they can. They store fat in their bodies. They will be able to live off this fat when there is no food to find during the winter.

Bears and some other animals hibernate during the cold winter season. Hibernation is like sleeping, but it is not exactly the same. The animal is not awake or moving around.

Where Are My Friends?

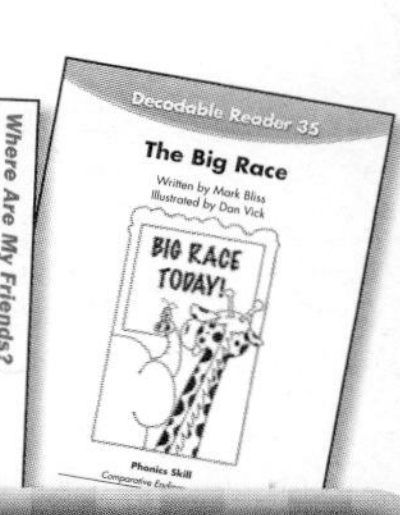

Group Time

On-Level

Read Decodable Reader 35.

- Use pp. 144q.

Strategic Intervention

Read Decodable Reader 35.

- Use the **Routine** on DI·66.

Advanced

Read Advanced Selection 18.

- Use the **Routine** on p. DI·67.

Place English language learners in the groups that correspond to their reading abilities in English.

Independent Activities

Fluency Reading Pair children to reread Leveled Readers or the ELL Reader from the previous week or other text at children's independent level.

Journal Writing Write to tell what bears and geese do when winter is coming. Share writing.

Independent Reading See p.144j for Reading/Library activities and suggestions.

Literacy Centers To practice comparative endings, you may use Word Work, p. 144j.

Practice Book 1.2 Comparative Endings, p. 53

Break into small groups after Spelling and before Build Background.

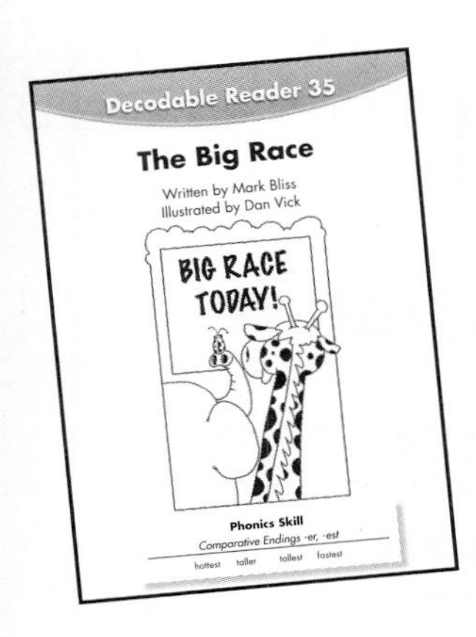

Apply Phonics

PRACTICE Comparative Endings

HIGH-FREQUENCY WORDS Review *day, done, down, friends, said, wait, who,* and *you* on the Word Wall. If necessary, have children practice in pairs with word cards. **Word Wall**

READ DECODABLE READER 35

- Pages 82–83 Read aloud quietly with the group.
- Pages 84–85 Have the group read aloud without you.
- Pages 86–88 Select individuals to read aloud.

CHECK COMPREHENSION AND DECODING

- Who is the tallest? (Slim, the giraffe)
- Who is the fastest? (Gus, the elephant and June, the ladybug)
- How do you know that the racers must be hot? (It is the hottest day.)
- Point to a word in the story that has the ending *-er* or *-est*. What is the word? List words that are named. Children may mention *fastest, hottest, taller, tallest.* Have the list read. Ask children to identify the ending and frame the base word.

HOMEWORK Take-Home Decodable Reader 35

REREAD FOR FLUENCY

Oral Rereading

ROUTINE

1. **Read** Have children read the entire book orally.
2. **Reread** To achieve optimal fluency, children should reread the text three or four times.
3. **Provide Feedback** Listen as children read and provide corrective feedback regarding their oral reading and their use of the blending strategy.

OBJECTIVES

- Apply knowledge of letter-sounds and word parts to decode unknown words when reading.
- Use context with letter-sounds and word parts to confirm the identification of unknown words.
- Practice fluency with oral rereading.

Monitor Progress

Decoding

if...	then...
children have difficulty decoding a word,	prompt them to blend the word. • What is the new word? • Is the new word a word you know? • Does it make sense in the story?

Access Content

Beginning On p. 83, have children use the illustrations to point out the animals in order: tall, taller, tallest.

Intermediate Preview *The Big Race,* explaining words with comparative endings such as *taller* and *tallest.*

Advanced After reading the first two pages together, have children retell what happens.

OBJECTIVES

- Build background and oral vocabulary.
- Use vivid words while speaking.

Strategic Intervention

Have children fold a paper into fourths. Ask them to write the name of a season in each box and to draw a picture to illustrate that season.

Advanced

Have children write sentences telling how the weather today is different from or the same as yesterday's weather.

Activate Prior Knowledge
Invite children to name the seasons in their home language and in English. Ask them to tell what they know about each season and which is their favorite.

Build Background

LET'S TALK ABOUT Changes in Nature

DEVELOP ORAL LANGUAGE Read the title and have children view the photographs. Ask them to tell you what they see. Allow ample time for children to respond and remind them to use vivid words as they speak. If children do not use vivid words, model examples of descriptions that use them and of those that do not. Then use open-ended prompts to encourage conversation. For example:

Tell me about what you see here. Yes, that's right, a little girl is smelling some flowers. During which season do you think this photograph was taken? How can you tell? Look at the picture at the top of p. 145. How do you know that this is not a winter scene? Are any of the photographs on these pages taken during the winter?

BUILD ORAL VOCABULARY As you continue the discussion, encourage children to use today's Amazing Words, *hibernate, migrate, season,* and *temperature.*

- What is the flock of birds doing? Use the word *migrate* in your answer.
- Is the girl with the umbrella going to hibernate when winter comes? How do you know?
- Tell me about the temperature in the picture that shows four children and a dog.
- Look at each photograph and tell me during which season it was taken.

DEVELOP CONCEPTS

CONCEPT CHART Remind children of the question of the week.

- How does nature change during the year?

Display Graphic Organizer 8 or draw four sorting boxes. Label the boxes with the heads *spring, summer, fall, and winter.* Have children tell what they know about the different seasons.

- What can you tell me about spring?
- What do you know about summer?
- What happens in the fall?
- How is winter different from the other seasons?

CONNECT TO READING Point out the illustration on the bottom corner of Student Edition p. 145. Ask children what they see. (an animal waving good-bye to a bird) Explain that this week children will read a play about some animal friends. Tell children that they will learn what some animals do as nature changes during the year.

Oral Vocabulary

Let's Talk About Changes in Nature

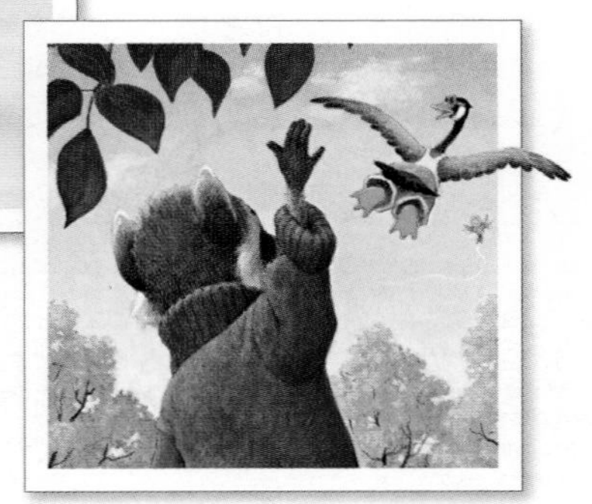

144

145

Spring	Summer
Flowers bloom in spring. It rains a lot. The weather starts to get warm.	The weather is hot. We can swim. Trees and grass are green.
Fall	**Winter**
The weather starts to get cooler. Leaves turn colors and fall.	The weather is cold. It might snow. We have to wear coats.

▲ **Graphic Organizer Flip Chart 8**

Tech Files ONLINE

For a Web site that explores seasonal changes throughout the country, do an Internet search using the keywords *seasons* or *weather.*

ELL

Access Content To prepare children for reading *Where Are My Animal Friends?*, send home the story summary in English and/or the home language. See the ELL Teaching Guide, pp. 124–126.

OBJECTIVE

Identify the sequence of events.

Skills Trace	
Sequence	
Introduce/Teach	**TE: 1.2 85a–b, 88g; 1.3 145a–b, 148g; 1.5 45a–b, 48g**
Practice	PB: 1.1 94; 1.2 54, 134
Reteach/Review	TE: 1.1 20–21; 1.2 DI·81; 1.3 44–45, 132–133, DI·84; 1.5 DI·78
Test	Selection Test: 1.2 20; 1.3 46–48; 1.5 77–80; Benchmark Test, Unit 3

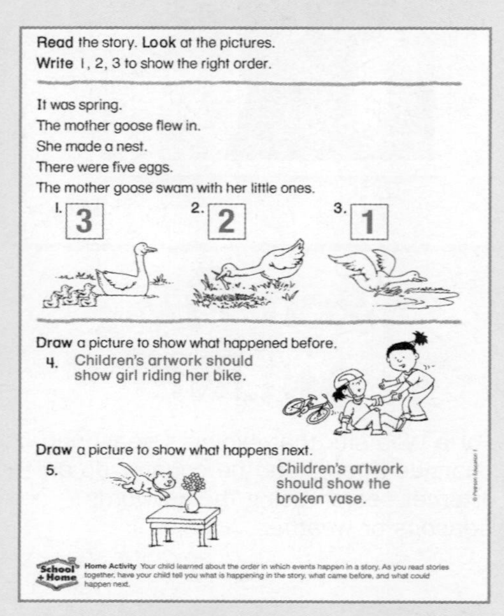
Read the story. **Look** at the pictures.
Write 1, 2, 3 to show the right order.

It was spring.
The mother goose flew in.
She made a nest.
There were five eggs.
The mother goose swam with her little ones.

1. 3
2. 2
3. 1

Draw a picture to show what happened before.
4. Children's artwork should show girl riding her bike.

Draw a picture to show what happens next.
5. Children's artwork should show the broken vase.

School + Home **Home Activity** Your child learned about the order in which events happen in a story. As you read stories together, have your child tell you what is happening in the story, what came before, and what could happen next.

▲ **Practice Book 1.2** p. 54, Sequence

Access Content For a Picture It! lesson on sequence, see the ELL Teaching Guide, pp. 121–122.

Listening Comprehension

TEACH/MODEL Sequence

DEFINE SEQUENCE

- Events in a story happen in a certain order.
- Words such as *first, then, next,* and *last* can help readers figure out the order of events.

READ ALOUD Read "Back and Forth" and model how to identify the sequence.

Think Aloud **MODEL** When I read, I look for words such as *first, then, next,* and *last* to help me pay attention to the order in which things happen. *First* Robin is happy living in the north. *Then* he notices it is getting colder and birds are flying away. *Next* it begins to snow, and Robin listens to Duck and flies south.

PRACTICE

CLUES TO SEQUENCE Ask children to tell what happens in the story after Robin and Duck fly south. What happens after Robin and Duck fly south? (Robin builds a new nest and enjoys the warmer temperature and tasty bugs.) Then what happens? (Duck comes to tell Robin that the snow is gone and it is time to go back north.) What happens last in the story? (Robin and Duck go back north to live until the next fall.)

IDENTIFY SEQUENCE Recall the story *Frog and Toad Together.*

- What does Toad do after Frog gives him the flower seeds? (He plants them.)
- What happens after Toad plants the seeds? (The seeds do not grow immediately, so Toad yells at them.)
- What happens after Frog tells Toad that all the yelling makes the seeds scared? (Toad reads the seeds a story and sings them songs.)
- What is the last thing that happens in the story? (The seeds begin to come up.)

CONNECT TO READING Tell children that when they read any story, they should think about the order in which things happen.

Back and Forth

At first, Robin was very happy living in the north. He had a nice nest and there were plenty of insects to eat. He never ever wanted to move.

Then one day Robin noticed that the temperature was getting colder. Leaves started to fall from the trees, and it was harder to find bugs to eat. Soon many of Robin's friends began to fly away.

"Where is everyone going?" Robin asked Duck.

"Everyone has decided to migrate," Duck explained. "They are flying south, where it is warmer and there are more bugs to eat. We should leave too."

"But what about my nest?" Robin asked. "I like my nest here."

"Forget that nest," Duck said. "You can build a new nest in the south."

Robin still didn't want to leave, but next it began to snow. Sadly, Robin flew south with Duck.

In the south, Robin built a new nest. He enjoyed the warmer temperature and the tasty bugs. Soon he had almost forgotten what it was like to live up north. Then one day Duck came to tell Robin it was time to fly back north.

"But what about my new nest?" Robin asked. "Now I like my nest here."

Duck said, "Leave your nest. You can build another nest in the north. It's time to go back home. The snow is gone, there are leaves on the trees, and yummy bugs are flying around everywhere."

Robin flapped his wings. "Say no more! I'm on my way!" he said.

Robin and Duck flew and flew until they were back north. Happily Robin built himself a new nest and began eating the delicious bugs flying around.

"At last, we're back home in the north," Robin said.

"And we won't have to migrate again until next fall," Duck added.

"Good," Robin said. "That gives me plenty of time to enjoy my new nest!"

OBJECTIVE

- Write a song.

DAILY FIX-IT

1. The bigest burd said good-bye first.
The biggest bird said good-bye first.

2. It was the sadest day?
It was the saddest day.

This week's practice sentences appear on Daily Fix-It Transparency 18.

Strategic Intervention

Have children find pictures that show the seasons in magazines and label them *spring, summer, fall,* or *winter.*

Advanced

Have children write a song about the seasons that focuses on not only the sequence of the seasons, but the sequence of events in each season—for example, during fall, the leaves change colors, then they fall off the trees, then it gets colder.

Support Writing Let children dictate their song to a more proficient English speaker.

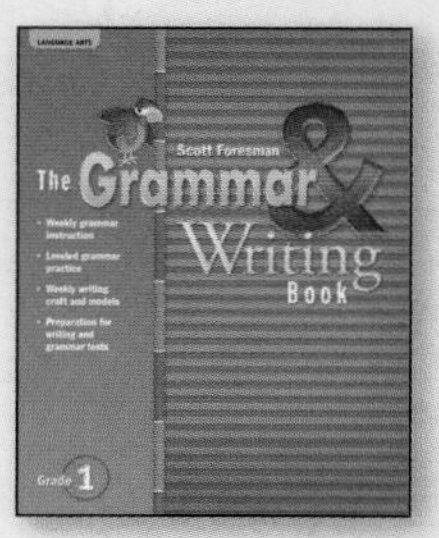

▲ **The Grammar and Writing Book** For more instruction and practice, use pp. 128–133.

Shared Writing

WRITE Song

GENERATE IDEAS Ask children to describe each of the four seasons. Ask: Is it hot or cold? Wet or snowy? What happens to the trees? Write children's answers on the board.

WRITE A SONG Explain that the class will write a song that tells about the seasons and how they change. Suggest that children use a familiar tune, such as "This Is the Way We Wash Our Clothes" or "London Bridge Is Falling Down."

COMPREHENSION SKILL Have children think about sequence of events—the order in which things happen—for the seasons.

- Display Writing Transparency 18 and read the title.
- Read the prompts.
- As children describe what each season is, record their responses.

HANDWRITING While writing, model the letter forms as shown on pp. TR12–15.

READ THE SONG Have children read the completed song aloud as you track the print.

Song of the Seasons

Possible answers:

Spring is rainy, spring is warm.
Flowers are blooming and birds sing.

Summer is sunny, summer's hot.
School's out, hurray, let's go swim.

Fall is windy, fall is cool.
Leaves turn colors, they fall down.

Winter is snowy, winter's cold.
Snow falls, wind blows, we dress warm.

Unit 3 Where Are My Animal Friends? Writing Model 18

▲ **Writing Transparency 18**

INDEPENDENT WRITING

WRITE A SONG Have children write their own song about the seasons. Encourage them to use words from the Word Wall and the Amazing Words board. Let children illustrate their writing. You may save children's work in their portfolios.

Grammar

TEACH/MODEL Contractions with *Not*

IDENTIFY CONTRACTIONS WITH *Not* Display Grammar Transparency 18. Read the definition aloud.

- *Does* and *not* can be put together to make a contraction.
- Put an apostrophe where the letter *o* used to be in *not*.

Continue modeling with items 2–5.

PRACTICE

USE CONTRACTIONS WITH *Not* Write the following on the board: *has + not = hasn't; was + not = wasn't; were + not = weren't.* Have children write sentences using the contractions.

ADDITIONAL PRACTICE For additional practice use pp. 152–157 in the Grammar and Writing Book.

OBJECTIVE

- Identify contractions with *not.*

Contractions with *Not*

A **contraction** is a short way to put two words together. A **verb** and the word **not** can be put together to make a contraction. An **apostrophe** (') is used in place of the letter **o**.

are + not = aren't	has + not = hasn't
did + not = didn't	is + not = isn't
do + not = don't	was + not = wasn't
does + not = doesn't	were + not = weren't

Write the contraction for the underlined words.

1. A bear does not wake up all winter. doesn't
2. Squirrels do not sleep through the winter. don't
3. The hummingbird did not wait for winter. didn't
4. The geese are not flying south yet. aren't
5. The butterfly is not coming out until spring. isn't

Unit 3 Where Are My Animal Friends? Grammar 18

▲ Grammar Transparency 18

Wrap Up Your Day!

COMPARATIVE ENDINGS Write *fast* and ask children to change it by adding *-er* and then *-est*. Repeat with *slow.*

SPELLING ADDING *-er, -est* Write a CVC word such as *big* and remind children that the consonant is doubled before adding *-er* or *-est* because the base word ends in one consonant after a short vowel. List *kind, hot*, and *sad*. Have children add *-er* and *-est* to each word and use it in a sentence.

SEQUENCE To help children recognize the importance of sequence, ask: Could the story "Back and Forth" have occurred in a different order—for example, could Robin have flown south during the summer and north during the winter? Why not?

LET'S TALK ABOUT IT Display the four seasons chart. Point to the season when Robin moves south. (Fall) When do you think he moved back north? (Spring)

HOMEWORK Send home this week's Family Times newsletter.

PREVIEW Day 2

Tell children that tomorrow the class will read more about the seasons of the year.

Day 2

AT A GLANCE

Share Literature
What Makes the Seasons?

Phonemic Awareness
Segment Phonemes

Phonics and Spelling
dge/j/
Spelling: Addings *-er, -est*

Read Apply Phonics Word Wall

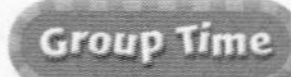
Group Time < Differentiated Instruction

High-Frequency Words
before *does* *good-bye*
oh *right* *won't*

Interactive Writing
Journal Entry

Grammar
Contractions with *Not*

Speaking and Listening
Nonverbal Communication

Materials

- *Sing with Me Big Book*
- Big Book *What Makes the Seasons?*
- Sound-Spelling Card 17
- Letter Tiles
- Decodable Reader 36
- Student Edition 146–147
- Tested Word Cards

Morning Warm-Up!

**Today we'll read more about the seasons.
Each season is part of the year.
When one season ends, another starts.
How do our clothes change
with each season?**

QUESTION OF THE DAY Encourage children to sing "Change of Season" from the *Sing with Me Big Book* as you gather. Write and read the message and discuss the question.

REVIEW *r*-CONTROLLED *ar, ore*

- Read the sentences of the message.
- Have children find words that have *r*-controlled *ar (part, starts*), and *r*-controlled *ore. (more)*

Build Background Use the Day 2 instruction on ELL Poster 18 to preview high-frequency words.

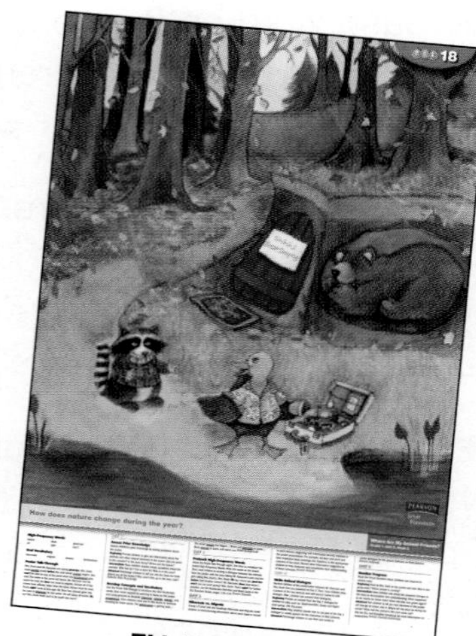

ELL Poster 18

Share Literature

BUILD CONCEPTS

NONFICTION Have children read the title. Identify the author. Remind children that this nonfiction book about the seasons is written like a poem. Ask children to listen for the rhythm as you read. Have them clap the rhythm for a few pages.

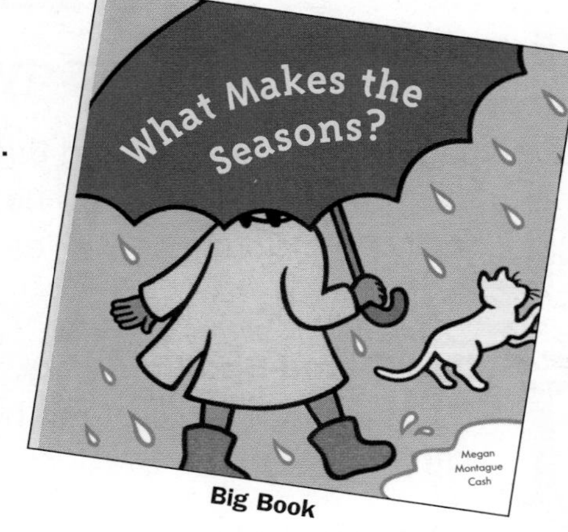

Big Book

BUILD ORAL VOCABULARY Discuss what happens as the seasons change from summer to **autumn.** As you read, ask children to listen for ways the sun is different in each season.

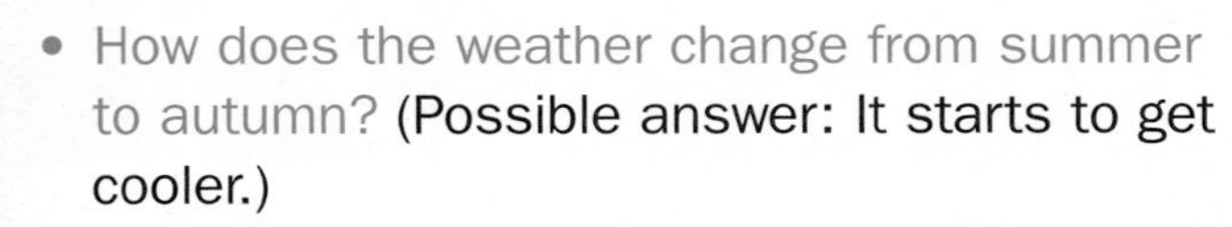

- How does the weather change from summer to autumn? (Possible answer: It starts to get cooler.)
- How does autumn help plants and animals prepare for winter? (The trees lose their leaves and seeds fall to wait for warm weather. Some animals feel the cooler weather and move to where it is warm or find warm places to hibernate.)

Phonemic Awareness

SEGMENT PHONEMES

- We just saw leaves sprout in a flower box on a ledge. Listen to the sounds in *ledge*.
- Model saying each sound, /l/ /e/ /j/. Have children say the sounds with you and then say the sounds by themselves.
- Now say each sound as you write the letter that goes with it. Say /l/ /e/ /j/ as you write *l, e, dge*.
- Have children say the sounds as you point to the letters, /l/ /e/ /j/.
- You can see that *ledge* has five letters but only three sounds.

Continue the activity with these examples.

badge (3) **ridge** (3) **lodge** (3) **edge** (2) **trudge** (4)

OBJECTIVES

- Discuss characteristics of nonfiction.
- Set purpose for listening.
- Build oral vocabulary.
- Segment phonemes.

	MONITOR PROGRESS
hibernate **migrate** **season** **temperature** **autumn** **freeze** **bitterly** **weary**	**If...** children lack oral vocabulary experiences about the concept Changes in Nature, **then...** use the Oral Vocabulary Routine. See p. DI·8 to teach *autumn*.

Build Concepts Have children help you create a cause-and-effect picture chart: spring rain—seeds sprout; summer sun—plants grow tall; autumn cold—leaves turn gold.

OBJECTIVES

- Associate the sound /j/ with *dge*.
- Blend, read, and build *dge* words.

Skills Trace

dge/j/

Introduce/Teach	**TE: 1.3 146c–d**
Practice	TE 1.3 146f, 148c–d; PB 1.2 55; DR36
Reteach/Review	TE 1.3 172c, DI•84; 1.4 40c–d; PB: 1.2 69
Assess/Test	TE 1.3 172e–g Benchmark Test, Unit 3

Generalization

The letters *dge* stand for /j/.

Strategic Intervention

Use **Monitor Progress,** p. 146d during Group Time after children have had more practice with *dge*/j/.

Advanced

Use **Monitor Progress,** p. 146d as a preassessment to determine whether or not this group of children would benefit from this *dge*/j/ instruction.

Support Phonics French, Hmong, and Spanish do not have the /j/ sound that is heard in words like *edge* and *fudge.* Provide additional practice saying and writing words with *dge,* such as *bridge, badge,* and *ledge.*

dge/j/

TEACH/MODEL

Blending Strategy

ROUTINE

1. **Connect** Write *gem* and *cage.* What do you know about reading these words? (The words both have the letter *g* that stands for the sound /j/.) Today we will learn about other letters that stand for /j/.
2. **Use Sound-Spelling Card** Display Card 17. This is *jet.* The sound you hear at the beginning of *jet* is /j/. Say it with me: /j/.
3. **Model** Write *bridge.* In this word the letters *dge* stand for the sound /j/. This is how I blend this word. Segment and blend *bridge.* Let's blend this word together: /b/ /r/ /i/ /j/, *bridge.*
4. **Group Practice** Say the sounds and blend the word together. Continue with *badge, dodge, ridge, pledge, trudge.*
5. **Review** What do you know about reading these words? The letters *dge* stand for /j/.

-dge

Sound-Spelling Card 17

b r i d g e

BLEND WORDS

INDIVIDUALS BLEND *dge* WORDS Call on individuals to blend the words *wedge, judge, Madge, edge, sludge, ledge.* Have them tell what they know about each word before reading it. (The *dge* at the end stands for /j/. They all have short vowels.) For feedback, refer to step five of the Blending Strategy Routine.

BUILD WORDS

INDIVIDUALS MAKE *dge* WORDS Write *edge* and have the class blend it. Have children spell *edge* with letter tiles. Monitor work and provide feedback.

- Add *l* to the beginning of *edge*. What is the new word? — **l e d g e**
- Change the *l* to *br*. Change the first *e* to *i*. What is the new word? — **b r i d g e**
- Take away the *b*. What is the new word? — **r i d g e**
- Change the *r* to *b*. Change the *i* to *u*. What is the new word? — **b u d g e**
- Change the *u* to *a*. What is the new word? — **b a d g e**

Vocabulary TiP

You may wish to explain the meanings of these words.

badge small sign you pin to your clothes

ledge a narrow shelf

nudge small push

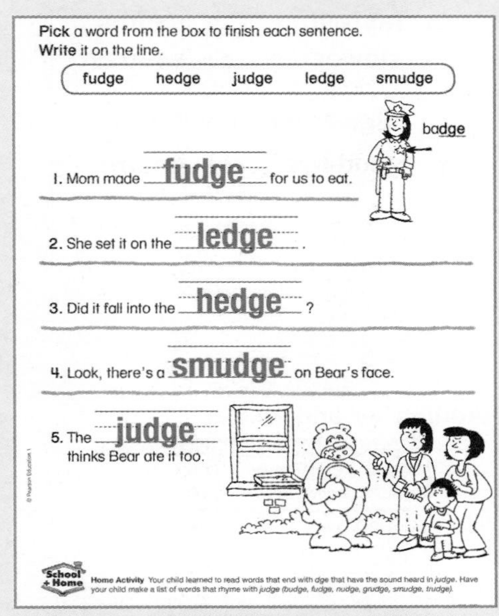
Pick a word from the box to finish each sentence.
Write it on the line.

fudge hedge judge ledge smudge

1. Mom made fudge for us to eat.
2. She set it on the ledge.
3. Did it fall into the hedge?
4. Look, there's a smudge on Bear's face.
5. The judge thinks Bear ate it too.

▲ **Practice Book 1.2** p. 55, *dge*/j/

Monitor Progress

Check Word Reading *dge*/j/

Write the following words and have individuals read them.

judge	**lodge**	**pledge**	**bridge**	**smudge**
gem	**ridge**	**page**	**nudge**	**large**
game	**fudge**	**gate**	**porridge**	**ginger**

If... children cannot blend *dge*/j/ words at this point,

then... continue to monitor their progress using other instructional opportunities during the week so that they can be successful with the Day 5 Assessment. See the Skills Trace on p. 146c.

Spiral REVIEW

- Row 2 contrasts *dge*/j/ with *g*/j/.
- Row 3 contrasts *dge*/j/ with *g*/j/ and *g*/g/.

OBJECTIVE

- Spell words with comparative endings.

Spelling Words

Adding *-er* and *-est*

1. bigger
2. biggest
3. faster
4. fastest
5. slower
6. slowest
7. shorter*
8. shortest
9. sadder
10. saddest*

High-Frequency Words

11. good-bye*
12. before*

* Words from the Selection

Adding *-er* and *-est*

Spelling Words				
bigger	biggest	faster	fastest	slower
slowest	shorter	shortest	sadder	saddest

Look at the pictures. **Write** list words that end with *-er* and *-est*.

short 1. shorter 2. shortest

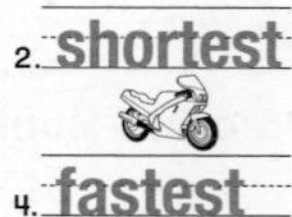

fast 3. faster 4. fastest

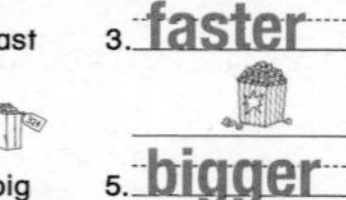

big 5. bigger 6. biggest

Write a list word that rhymes with the underlined word.

7. The mower runs slower uphill.
8. The lowest branches move slowest in the wind.
9. His face grew sadder as he put away the ladder.
10. This is the saddest and the maddest he's ever been.

School + Home **Home Activity** Your child spelled words that end with -er and -est. Say a base word, such as *big*. Ask your child to say and spell the -er and -est words (*bigger*, *biggest*).

▲ **Spelling Practice Book** p. 70

Spelling

PRACTICE Comparative Endings

WRITE DICTATION SENTENCES Have children write these sentences. Repeat words slowly, allowing children to hear each sound. Children may use the Word Wall to help with spelling high-frequency words. Word Wall

Is a bug slower or faster than a bird?
We ride the biggest but slowest bus.
What is bigger than a whale?
Midge looked sadder than Meg before she said good-bye.

HOMEWORK Spelling Practice Book, p. 70

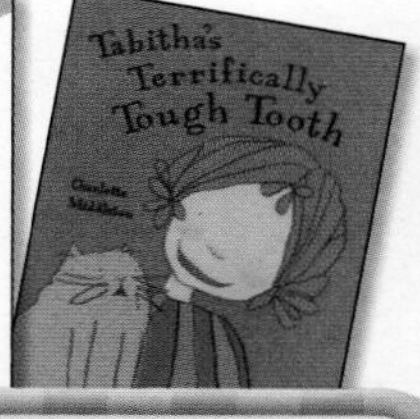

Group Time

DAY 2

On-Level	Strategic Intervention	Advanced
Read Decodable Reader 36.	**Read** Decodable Reader 36.	**Read** Self-Selected Reading.
• Use pp. 146f.	• Use the **Routine** on p. DI·68.	• Use the **Routine** on p. DI·69.

ELL Place English language learners in the groups that correspond to their reading abilities in English.

Independent Activities

Fluency Reading Pair children to reread Decodable Reader 35, this week's Leveled Readers, the ELL Reader from the previous week, or other text at children's independent level.

Journal Writing Write one fact you learned from *What Makes the Seasons?* Share writing.

Independent Reading See p. 144j for Reading/Library activities and suggestions.

Literacy Centers To practice *dge*/j/ you may use Word Work, p. 144j.

Practice Book 1.2 Sequence, p. 54 *dge*/j/, p. 55 High-Frequency Words, p. 56

Break into small groups after Spelling and before High-Frequency Words.

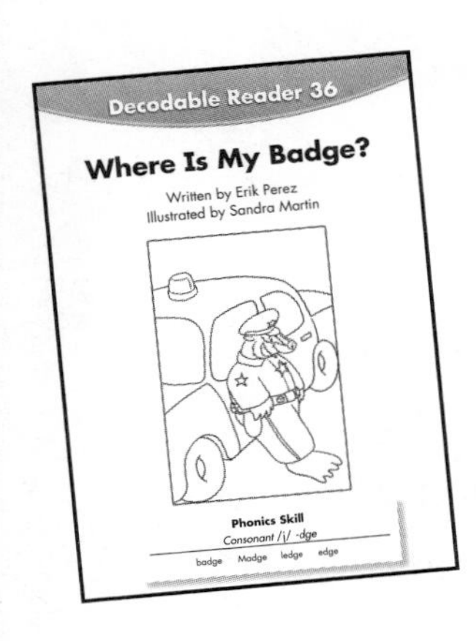

Apply Phonics

PRACTICE dge/j/

HIGH-FREQUENCY WORDS Review *find, of, said, where,* and *your* on the Word Wall. Word Wall

READ DECODABLE READER 36

- Pages 90–91 Read aloud quietly with the group.
- Pages 92–93 Have the group read aloud without you.
- Pages 94–96 Select individuals to read aloud.

CHECK COMPREHENSION AND DECODING

- What is Bucky's problem? (Bucky can't find his red badge.)
- How does Madge help Bucky solve his problem? (She finds his badge behind her hairbrush.)
- Point to a word in the story that has a /j/ sound at the end. What is the word? List words that are named. Children may supply *badge, edge, ledge,* and *Madge.*
- How do you know that these words have the /j/ sound at the end? (They all have the letters *dge* at the end.)

HOMEWORK Take-Home Decodable Reader 36

REREAD FOR FLUENCY

Oral Rereading

ROUTINE

1. **Read** Have children read the entire book orally.
2. **Reread** To achieve optimal fluency, children should reread the text three or four times.
3. **Provide Feedback** Listen as children read and provide corrective feedback regarding their oral reading and their use of the blending strategy.

OBJECTIVES

- Apply knowledge of letter-sounds to decode unknown words when reading.
- Use context with letter-sounds to confirm the identification of unknown words.
- Practice fluency with oral rereading.

Monitor Progress

Decoding

If...	then...
children have difficulty decoding a word,	prompt them to blend the word. • What is the new word? • Is the new word a word you know? • Does it make sense in the story?

ELL

Access Content

Beginning Lead children on a noun walk through *Where Is My Badge?,* identifying *badge, ledge,* and *edge* (of desk) in the pictures and print.

Intermediate Preview *Where Is My Badge?,* pointing out that a badge is often worn by a person who does a special job, such as police officer.

Advanced After reading *Where Is My Badge?,* have children use their own words to retell the story.

Words to Read

does
good-bye
before
won't
oh
right

146

Read the Words

"Does anyone know where Squirrel is?" asked Bear. "I want to say good-bye before my long nap. I won't see anyone for a while. Oh, I'm so sleepy! It is nap time right now."

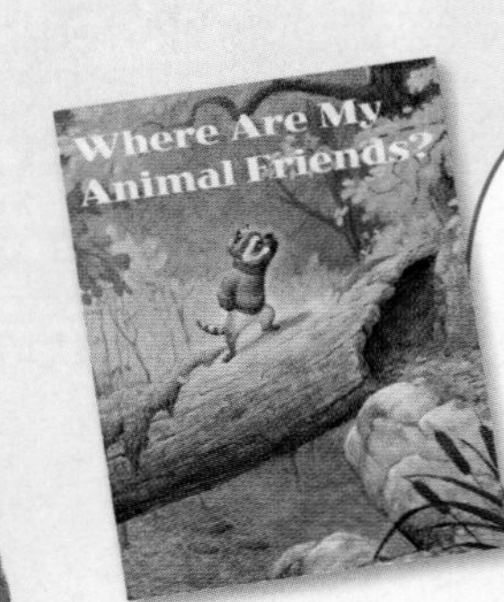

Genre: Play
A play is a story that is written to be acted out. Next you can read and then act out a play about animal friends who get ready for winter.

147

OBJECTIVE

- Recognize high-frequency words.

Pick a word from the box that is the opposite of each word below. **Write** it on the line.

before good-bye right won't

1. after ___before___
2. will ___won't___
3. hello ___good-bye___
4. wrong ___right___

Pick a word from the box to finish each sentence. **Write** it on the line. **Remember** to use capital letters.

oh does

5. ___Does___ a bear start its long sleep in the spring?
6. ___Oh___, no. It sleeps when the days start to get cold.

School + Home **Home Activity** Your child learned to read the words *before, does, good-bye, oh, right,* and *won't*. Write the opposite of these words on cards and mix them up. Have your child match the words that are opposites and then read the pairs. Then have him or her write two sentences using *does* and *oh*.

▲ **Practice Book 1.2** p. 56, High-Frequency Words

High-Frequency Words

Nondecodable Words

ROUTINE

1. **Say and Spell** Look at the words on p. 146. You cannot yet blend the sounds in these words. We will spell the words and use letter-sounds we know to learn them. Point to the first word. This word is *does, d-o-e-s, does.* What is this word? What are the letters in this word?
2. **Identify Familiar Letter Sounds** Point to the first letter in *does.* What is this letter? What is its sound? (*d*/d/)
3. **Demonstrate Meaning** Tell me a sentence using this word.

Repeat the routine with the other Words to Read. Have children identify these familiar letter-sounds and word parts: *good-bye* (*g*/g/, *d*/d/, *b*/b/), *before* blend the syllables: *be fore, won't* (*w*/w/, *n*/n/, *t*/t/; point out that this is a contraction), *oh* (*o*/ō/), *right* (*r*/r/, *t*/t/).

Have children read aloud the sentences on p. 146, and point to the Words to Read. Ask children to respond to the question in the first sentence. Add the words to the Word Wall. **Word Wall**

Interactive Writing

WRITE Journal Entry

BRAINSTORM Use the Big Book *What Makes the Seasons?* to encourage a discussion about what season it is. Picture walk through the book and ask children to identify the things that match the season they are currently experiencing.

SHARE THE PEN Have children participate in writing a journal entry about the current season. To begin, have a child say a sentence that describes some aspect of the current season. Have the class repeat it. Write the sentence, reminding individuals to use the rules they've learned about sentences. Ask questions such as:

- What does the sentence start with? (capital letter)
- Does the sentence tell something or ask something? (tell)
- What does the sentence end with? (period)

Continue to have individuals make contributions. Frequently reread what has been written while tracking the print.

READ THE JOURNAL ENTRY Read the completed journal entry aloud, having children echo you.

It is spring. It is warm and sunny.
Plants are growing.

INDEPENDENT WRITING

WRITE A JOURNAL ENTRY Have children write their own journal entries about the current season. Let children illustrate their writing.

OBJECTIVE

- Write a journal entry.

Strategic Intervention

Offer a verbal alternative to written responses. Support students by allowing them to dictate to you. Paraphrase and elaborate on their responses to help them create a journal entry about the current season.

Advanced

Have children who are able to write complete sentences independently write a journal entry about the current season, including details such as clothing, holidays, and outdoor activities.

Writing Support Before writing, children might share ideas in their home languages.

Beginning Pair children with more proficient English speakers. A more proficient speaker can help the partner write a journal entry about the current season.

Intermediate Help children create a word list to use in their writing assignment.

Advanced Review children's writing and show where details can be added to make the writing more accurate and more interesting.

OBJECTIVE

- Identify contractions with *not.*

DAILY FIX-IT

3. jay was the fasttest bird.
Jay was the fastest bird.

4. Duck were the slowest bird
Duck was the slowest bird.

Contractions with *Not*

A **contraction** is a short way to put two words together. A **verb** and the word **not** can be put together to make a contraction. An **apostrophe (')** is used in place of the letter **o** in **not**.

are + not = aren't	has + not = hasn't
did + not = didn't	is + not = isn't
do + not = don't	was + not = wasn't
does + not = doesn't	were + not = weren't

Circle the contraction in each sentence.

1. The animals (don't) have much time.
2. Caterpillar (doesn't) come out until spring.
3. Goose (isn't) staying for the winter.

Write the contraction for the underlined words.

4. The leaves are not on the trees. **aren't**
5. Raccoon was not leaving the forest. **wasn't**

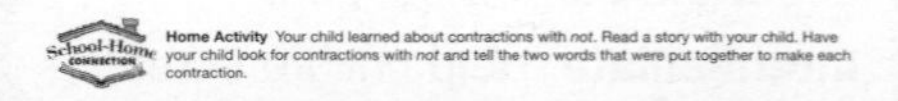

Home Activity Your child learned about contractions with *not*. Read a story with your child. Have your child look for contractions with *not* and tell the two words that were put together to make each contraction.

▲ **Grammar and Writing Practice Book** p. 69

ELL

Support Grammar Some languages such as the Romance languages include contractions. If possible, provide some examples of contractions in the home language. (In Spanish, *a* + *el* = *al;* in Portuguese, *de* + *as* = *das.)* Explain that in English, contractions use an apostrophe to replace the missing letters. See the Grammar Transition lessons in the ELL and Transition Handbook.

Grammar

DEVELOP THE CONCEPT Contractions with *Not*

IDENTIFY CONTRACTIONS WITH *Not* Write *aren't* and *hasn't* on the board. Point to each word as you read it. Ask children to identify the two words that have been made into the contraction. (*are not, has not*)

A short way to put two words together is called a contraction. What letter has been left out of the contractions above? (*o*)

PRACTICE

USE CONTRACTIONS WITH *Not* IN SENTENCES List the contractions *hasn't, weren't,* and *wasn't* on the board. Then write sentences such as those listed below. Point to the first sentence. Model completing the sentence.

Think Aloud

MODEL The contraction for *has not* is *hasn't*. I replace the *o* with an apostrophe. Write *hasn't.*

Have children identify the correct words for the other sentences. Write the words children provide in the blank spaces.

The boy has not come home. (hasn't)
My pants were not dirty. (weren't)
She was not tired. (wasn't)

Speaking and Viewing

NONVERBAL COMMUNICATION

DEMONSTRATE SPEAKING AND VIEWING Remind children of appropriate speaking and viewing behaviors. Then demonstrate these behaviors as you lead a discussion about nonverbal communication.

- If you are telling an exciting story or talking about something you love, you might want to use gestures to show how you feel. Gestures include nodding your head, shrugging your shoulders, and moving your hands.
- The way you stand, the eye contact you make with the audience, and how you move your body all can help show your thoughts and feelings.

USING NONVERBAL COMMUNICATION Ask children to present information about something of interest to them. Encourage them to use nonverbal communication, including eye contact, various facial expressions, gestures, and so on.

OBJECTIVES

- Speak to communicate information.
- View to understand nonverbal communication.

Wrap Up Your Day!

HIGH-FREQUENCY WORDS Write the following sentences. *Oh, I turned right too soon. Now I won't get there before he does. I hope I get to say good-bye.* Ask children to read the sentences and identify the high-frequency words *before, does, good-bye, oh, right, won't.*

COMPARATIVE ENDINGS *-er, -est* List *fast* and *short*. Have children add *-er* and *-est* to each word.

LET'S TALK ABOUT IT Recall the Big Book *What Makes the Seasons?* Ask: How does nature change during the year? (The seasons change. Each season has different types of weather.) Then display the sorting box chart from Day 1. Have children add information they've learned about the seasons in the appropriate box.

PREVIEW Day 3

Tell children that tomorrow they will read about animals that move when the seasons change.

Day 3 AT A GLANCE

Share Literature
What Makes the Seasons?

Phonemic Awareness
Blend and Segment Phonemes

Phonics and Spelling
Comparative Endings; *dge*/j/
Spelling: Words with *er* and *est*

Build Background
Animal Migration and Hibernation

Vocabulary
Selection Words
goose raccoon spring warm
High-Frequency Words
before does good-bye
oh right won't

Comprehension
Skill Sequence
Strategy Prior Knowledge

Read
Group Time < Differentiated Instruction
Where Are My Animal Friends?

Vocabulary
Multiple Meaning Words

Fluency
Read with Expression/Intonation

Writing Trait
Sentences

Grammar
Contractions with *Not*

Materials

- *Sing with Me Big Book*
- *What Makes the Seasons?*
- Phonics Songs/Rhymes Chart 18
- Letter Tiles
- Background Building Audio
- Graphic Organizer Flip Chart 4
- Vocabulary Transparency 18
- Student Edition 148–167

Morning Warm-Up!

Animals know when the seasons begin to change. We're going to read how animals get ready for winter. What's something you get ready for each year?

QUESTION OF THE DAY Encourage children to sing "Change of Season" from the *Sing with Me Big Book* as you gather. Write the message and track the print as you read it. Discuss the question.

REVIEW CONTRACTIONS

- Ask children to find words that are contractions. (*we're, what's*)
- Circle each word and have children identify the two words the contraction stands for. *(we are, what is)*

Build Background Use the Day 3 instruction on ELL Poster 18 to support children's use of English to communicate about lesson concepts.

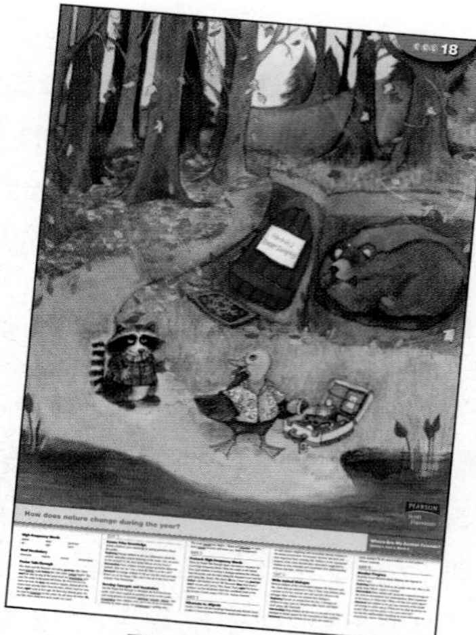

ELL Poster 18

Share Literature

LISTEN AND RESPOND

BUILD ORAL VOCABULARY Review that yesterday the class listened to find out how the sun is different in each season. Explain that as seasons change and the weather gets colder, things begin to **freeze,** or turn solid from the cold. Ask that children listen today to find out how our lives change with the seasons.

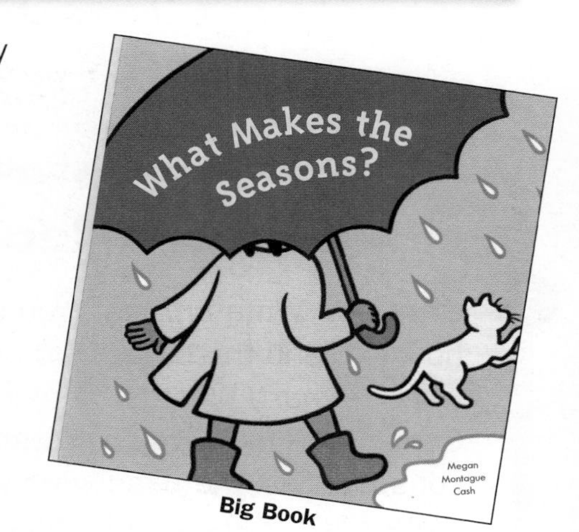

Big Book

MONITOR LISTENING COMPREHENSION

- How do we change our lives as the seasons change? (Children will probably respond that we change our activities.)
- How does autumn help plants and animals prepare for winter? (Some trees lose their leaves, and seeds fall to wait for warm weather. Some animals find seeds to store to eat in the winter; others feel the cooler weather and move to where it is warm or find warm places to hibernate.)
- Why do animals need to be ready before the weather is so cold things will freeze? (They need to store food because when things freeze, it is hard for animals to find food; they need to find a warm place before it is too cold for them to go out; they may not be able to find water to drink.)

Phonemic Awareness

BLEND AND SEGMENT PHONEMES

- We just read that some animals sleep in the winter. These animals don't move or budge. Listen to the sounds in *budge*.
- Model saying each sound, /b/ /u/ /j/. Have children say the sounds with you and then say the sounds by themselves.
- Now say each sound as you write the letter that goes with it. Say /b/ /u/ /j/ as you write *b, u, dge*.
- Have children say the sounds as you point to the letters (/b/ /u/ /j/) and blend the sounds to say the word *(budge)*.

Continue the activity with these examples.
wedge **bridge** **badge** **smudge**

OBJECTIVES

- Set purpose for listening.
- Build oral vocabulary.
- Blend and segment phonemes.

hibernate
migrate
season
temperature
autumn
freeze
bitterly
weary

MONITOR PROGRESS

If... children lack oral vocabulary experiences about the concept Changes in Nature,

then... use the Oral Vocabulary Routine. See p. DI•8 to teach *freeze.*

ELL

Listen and Respond Have children draw themselves having fun outdoors in their favorite season. Have them show plants and trees in the drawing. Encourage children to describe their pictures.

OBJECTIVES

- Review words with comparative endings and *dge*/j/ words.
- Build, read, and sort words with comparative endings and *dge*/j/ words.
- Preview words before reading them.
- Spell words with comparative endings.

Strategic Intervention

Use **Strategic Intervention Decodable Reader 18** for more practice with comparative endings and *dge*/j/ words.

Support Phonics Because Spanish words do not end with *st,* Spanish speakers may drop the *t* from words with comparative ending *-est,* saying *hardes* instead of *hardest.* Give children extra practice saying and writing words ending in *-est,* such as *thinnest, smartest,* and *hottest.*

Comparative Endings and *dge*/j/

TEACH/MODEL

Fluent Word Reading

ROUTINE

1. **Connect** Write *smarter.* You can read this word because you know how to blend the base word and ending together. What is the base word? *(smart)* What is the ending? *(-er)* What is the word? *(smarter)* Continue in the same way with *thinnest,* reminding children that the last consonant on the base word was doubled before the ending was added. Write *ridge.* You can read this word because you know that the letters *dge* stand for /j/. What sound does *dge* stand for? (/j/) What is the word? *(ridge)*
2. **Model** When you come to a new word, look for a base word and an ending, or look at all the letters in the word and think about their sounds. Say the sounds in the word to yourself and then read the word. Model reading *smarter, thinnest,* and *ridge* in this way. When you come to a new word, what are you going to do?
3. **Group Practice** Write *badge, wetter, grudge, smallest.* Let's read these words. Look at all the letters, think about their sounds, and say the sounds to yourself. When I point to the word, let's read it together. Allow 3–4 seconds previewing time for each word.

WORD READING

PHONICS SONGS AND RHYMES CHART 18 Frame each of the following words on Phonics Songs and Rhymes Chart 18. Call on individuals to read them. Guide children in previewing.

hardest judge dodge wedge lodge pledge

Sing "The Coldest Time" to the tune of "She'll Be Coming 'Round the Mountain," or play the CD. Have children follow along on the chart as they sing. Have children take turns reading the words with *dge* and words with endings *-er, -est.* Help children identify *bolder, colder,* and *coldest.*

Phonics Songs and Rhymes Audio CD

The Coldest Time

When the seasons change,
all nature changes too.
All the animals must judge
what's best to do.
When the tree colors grow bolder,
And the days start turning colder,
Then they have their hardest
season to get through.

Every animal finds ways
to dodge the chill.
Geese fly off in a big
wedge across the hill.
Beavers build a lodge and creep in.
Bears find cozy caves to sleep in.
They pledge to come out in spring,
and so they will.

Phonics Songs and Rhymes Chart 18

SORT WORDS

INDIVIDUALS READ WORDS WITH COMPARATIVE ENDINGS AND *dge*/j/ Write the words listed below in random order. Call on children to read the words, identifying the base word and ending when appropriate. Then work together to sort the words into the following categories: *Ending -er, Ending -est, No Ending.*

Complete the activity by having the lists read.

Endings *-er,*	Endings *-est,*	No Ending
stiffer	stiffest	fudge
bigger	biggest	budge
darker	dimmest	bridge
shorter	tallest	pledge

- You may want to remind children that the letter *j* at the beginning of a word also stands for /j/.

Spelling

PRACTICE Comparative Endings *-er, -est*

FOLDOUT BOOK Have children fold a sheet of paper in thirds. Have them draw and label pictures to illustrate *big, bigger, biggest,* one drawing per section. Distribute four more sheets of paper to each child. Have them continue the activity with *fast, faster, fastest; slow, slower, slowest; short, shorter, shortest; sad, sadder, saddest.* Show children how to attach the pages to make a five page foldout book. Have partners take turns reading each other's books, spelling each word, and using it in a sentence.

HOMEWORK Spelling Practice Book, p. 71

Spelling Words

Adding *-er* and *-est*

1. bigger
2. biggest
3. faster
4. fastest
5. slower
6. slowest
7. shorter*
8. shortest
9. sadder
10. saddest*

High-Frequency Words

11. good-bye*
12. before*

* Words from the Selection

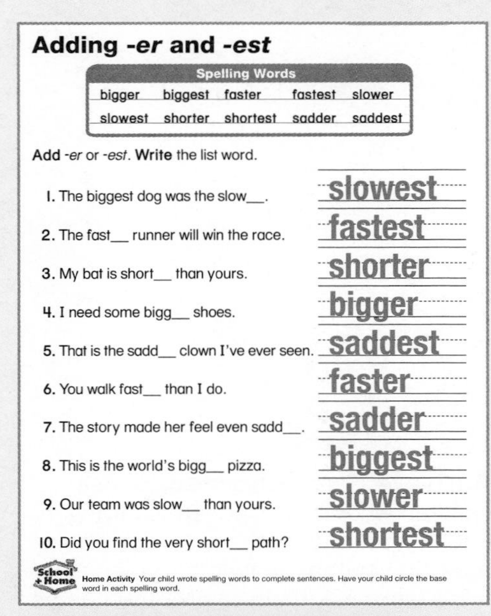

Adding *-er* and *-est*

Spelling Words				
bigger	biggest	faster	fastest	slower
slowest	shorter	shortest	sadder	saddest

Add *-er* or *-est*. **Write** the list word.

1. The biggest dog was the slow__. slowest
2. The fast__ runner will win the race. fastest
3. My bat is short__ than yours. shorter
4. I need some bigg__ shoes. bigger
5. That is the sadd__ clown I've ever seen. saddest
6. You walk fast__ than I do. faster
7. The story made her feel even sadd__. sadder
8. This is the world's bigg__ pizza. biggest
9. Our team was slow__ than yours. slower
10. Did you find the very short__ path? shortest

School + Home **Home Activity** Your child wrote spelling words to complete sentences. Have your child circle the base word in each spelling word.

▲ **Spelling Practice Book** p. 71

Build Background

OBJECTIVES

- Build background.
- Learn selection words.
- Recognize high-frequency words.

Read the words in the box.
Match a word from the box to each clue in the puzzle. **Write** it.

before does good-bye goose oh right won't

1. Winter is the ______ season for mittens.
2. When ______ it start to get warm?
3. In spring we say ______ to cold days.
4. ______! How I love to see the trees turn green.
5. Then, ______ long, the days grow warmer!
6. It ______ be long before I see a raccoon peeking out at dusk.
7. I may even see a ______ with white feathers.

▲ **Practice Book 1.2** p. 57, High-Frequency and Selection Words

DISCUSS HIBERNATION AND MIGRATION Display pictures that show animals during the summer and during the winter. Initiate discussion by asking children what they know about animal hibernation or migration during winter.

- What seasons of the year do we have?
- How do seasons affect animals?
- How do you think animals need to change in the winter?

BACKGROUND BUILDING AUDIO Have children listen to the CD and share the new information they learned about animal migration and hibernation.

Sing with Me/ Background Building Audio

COMPLETE A T-CHART Draw a T-chart or display Graphic Organizer 4. Write the heading *Animals During Summer Months* at the top of column 1. Write the heading *Animals During Winter Months* at the top of column 2. Have children suggest some ways animal behavior changes during the two seasons.

Animals During Summer Months	Animals During Winter Months
Birds are nesting.	Birds migrate to warmer climates.
Bears look for food to eat.	Bears hibernate.
Insects are active.	Insects are scarce.
Deer, raccoons, squirrels, and foxes are busy.	Some animals such as raccoons and squirrels remain throughout the winter.

▲ **Graphic Organizer Flip Chart 4**

CONNECT TO SELECTION Connect background information to *Where Are My Animal Friends?*

People can tell when the seasons change. We might wear different clothing and do different things. What do you think animals do when the seasons change? We'll find out as we read a play that tells about some changes animals go through when the weather gets very cold.

Activate Prior Knowledge Ask children who have experienced living in another country to share stories about how the weather changes from season to season. Ask them to give the names of the seasons in their home languages.

Vocabulary

SELECTION WORDS

Use Vocabulary Transparency 18 to introduce the selection words.

- Read each sentence as you track the print.
- Frame each underlined word. Explain the word's meaning.

  spring the season of the year between winter and summer, when plants begin to grow
  warm more hot than cold
  goose a large bird with a long neck
  raccoon a small animal with thick fur whose markings resemble rings on its tail and a black mask around its eyes

- Ask children to identify familiar letter-sounds and word parts: *spring* (consonant blend *spr*, ending *-ing*), *warm* (*w*/w/, *m*/m/), *goose* (*g*/g/, *s*/s/), *raccoon* (*r*/r/, *a*/a/, point out that the *oo*/ü/ sound is the same *oo* as in *goose*).
- Have children read each sentence aloud with you.
- To encourage discussion using the story vocabulary, ask children to tell what they know about animals in the spring.

HIGH-FREQUENCY WORDS

Use Vocabulary Transparency 18 to review this week's words.

- Point to a word. Say and spell it.
- Have children say and spell the word.
- Ask children to identify familiar letter-sounds.

Selection Words

Spring Time

1. It is spring in the forest.
2. The warm sun shines.
3. Mother goose sits on her nest.
4. A raccoon hunts for food.

High-Frequency Words

Words to Read

before	does	good-bye
oh	right	won't

Unit 3 Where Are My Animal Friends? Vocabulary **18**

▲ **Vocabulary Transparency 18**

Access Content Use the vocabulary strategies and word cards in the ELL Teaching Guide, pp. 122–123.

Monitor Progress | **Check High-Frequency Words**

Point to the following words on the Word Wall and have individuals read them.

small	**does**	**many**	**oh**	**right**	**friends**
every	**won't**	**good-bye**	**before**	**inside**	**away**

If... children cannot read these words,

then ... have them find each word on the Word Wall, chant its spelling, and then write it. Monitor their fluency with these words during reading, and provide additional practice opportunities before the Day 5 Assessment.

SUCCESS PREDICTOR

Day 1 Check Word Reading | **Day 2** Check Word Reading | ▶ **Day 3 Check High-Frequency Words/Retelling** | **Day 4** Check Fluency | **Day 5** Assess Progress

Spiral REVIEW

- Reviews previously taught high-frequency words.

High-Frequency Words

SUCCESS PREDICTOR

OBJECTIVES

- Recognize sequence.
- Activate and use prior knowledge.

Comprehension

SEQUENCE

RECOGNIZE SEQUENCE Remind children that the events in a story happen in a certain order. Recall previously read stories and guide children as they identify the sequence of events.

CONNECT TO READING

- As you read, pay attention to the order in which things happen.
- Look for clue words such as *first, next, then,* and *last* to help you figure out the order of events.

PRIOR KNOWLEDGE

INTRODUCE THE STRATEGY Explain that good readers think about what they read and compare it to what they already know or to other stories they have read.

MODEL When I read a story about a big storm, I think about storms I have experienced. I visualize the sights and sounds of a storm—wind, rain, lightning, and thunder—to help me understand what I read.

CONNECT TO READING Encourage children to ask themselves these questions as they read *Where Are My Animal Friends?*

- What do I know about what is happening in this story?
- Does this story remind me of something that's happened in my life?
- How is this story like others I have read?

Group Time

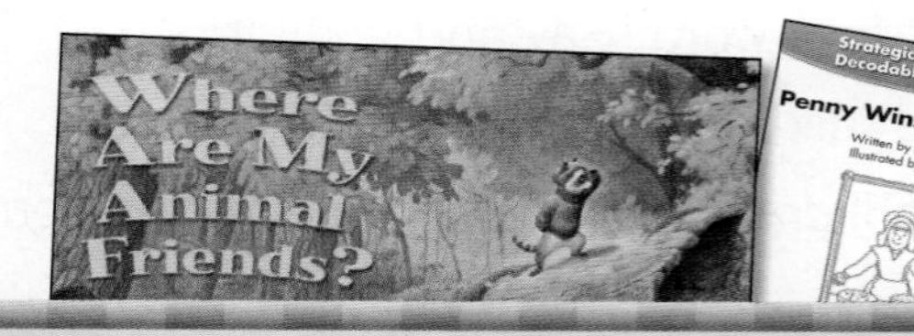

DAY 3

On-Level

Read *Where Are My Animal Friends?*

- Use pp. 148–167.

Strategic Intervention

Read Decodable Reader 18.

- Read or listen to *Where Are My Animal Friends?*
- Use the **Routine** on p. DI·70.

Advanced

Read *Where Are My Animal Friends?*

- Use the **Routine** on p. DI·71.

Place English language learners in the groups that correspond to their reading abilities in English.

Independent Activities

Independent Reading See p. 144j for Reading/Library activities and suggestions.

Journal Writing Write about an animal you might like to be and what you would do in the winter. Share writing.

Literacy Centers To provide experiences with *Where Are My Animal Friends?*, you may use the Listening and Writing Centers on pp. 144j and 144k.

Practice Book 1.2 High-Frequency Words and Selection Words, p. 57

Break into small groups after Comprehension and before Fluency.

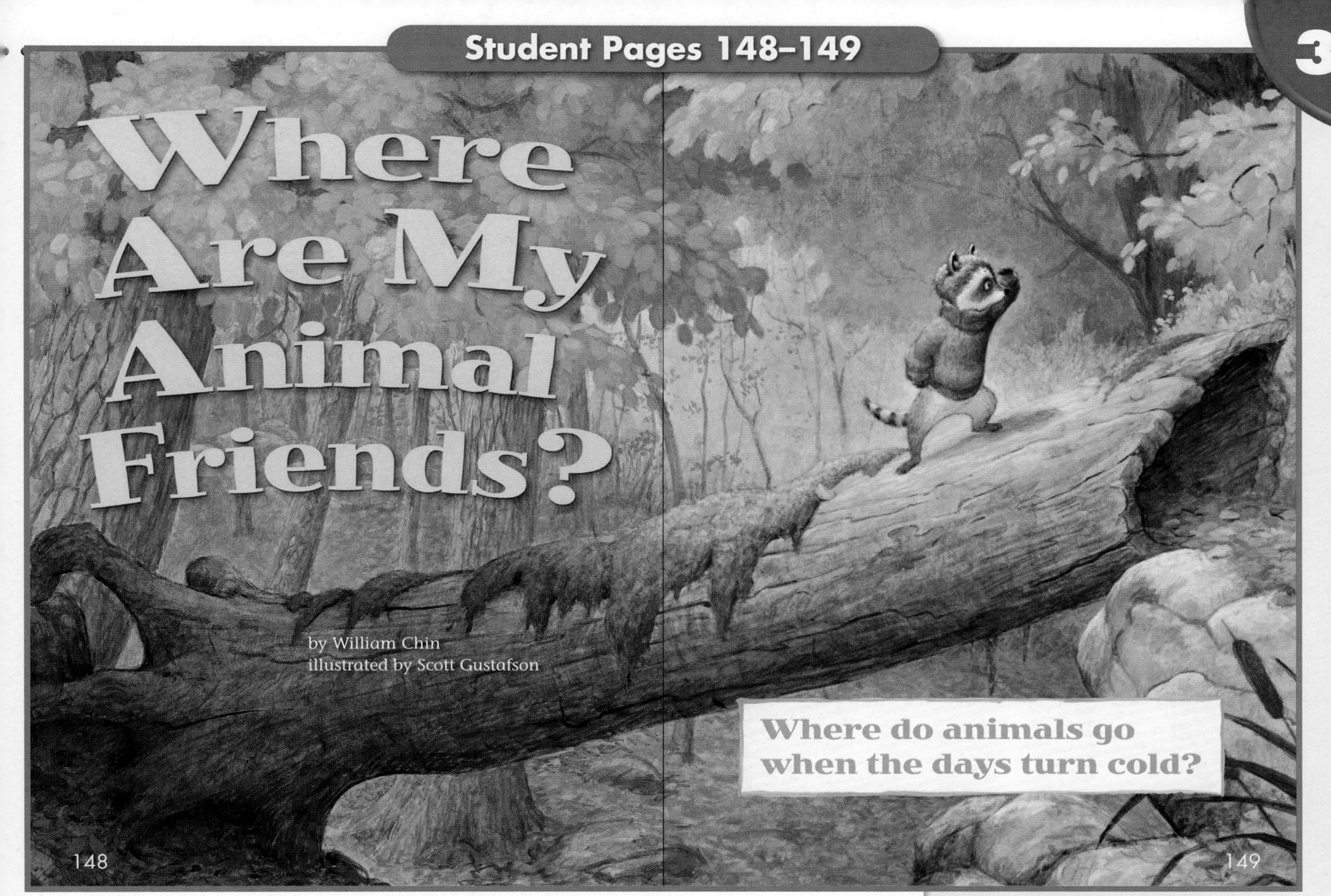

Read

Prereading Strategies

PREVIEW AND PREDICT Have children read the title. Read aloud the author's and illustrator's names. Reread the title and ask who might be looking for animal friends. Have children look through the first few pages and discuss where this selection takes place.

DISCUSS PLAYS Direct attention to the text and pictures on pp. 150–151. Then point out the list of character names on p. 150. Explain that this selection is a play that is meant to be acted out. The text has the words the different characters say. Reread the definition of plays on p. 147 of the Student Edition.

SET PURPOSE Read and discuss the question on p. 149. Have children set a purpose for reading.

AudioText

ELL

Access Content Before reading, review the story summary in English and/or the home language. See the ELL Teaching Guide, pp. 124–126.

Raccoon

Goose

Bear

Hummingbird

Squirrel

150

Hello, Goose! Why are you shivering?

The forest is chilly, Raccoon. The days are shorter now. And it's getting colder every day.

Then we don't have much time to find our friends.

You're right, Raccoon. Let's look for Caterpillar.

151

▲ **Pages 150–151**
Have children read for clues about what is changing in the forest.

Monitor Progress

Decoding

If...	then...
If... children come to a word they don't know,	**then...** remind them to blend the word: 1. Look at each letter. 2. Think of the sound for each letter. 3. Blend the sounds. 4. Read the word.

Strategies in Context

PRIOR KNOWLEDGE

- **What is changing in the forest?**
  The season is changing to winter.

Monitor Progress	Prior Knowledge
If... children have difficulty answering the question,	**then...** model how to use prior knowledge.

Think Aloud **MODEL** The words on this page give me some clues about what is happening. Goose is shivering, the days are shorter, and it's getting colder every day. I already know that when the seasons change from summer to winter, the days get shorter and the temperature gets colder. I can use what I know about seasons to understand what is happening in the play.

ASSESS Have children list other things they know about autumn.

____ comparative endings *-er, -est and -dge/j/* ▭ high-frequency/tested vocabulary

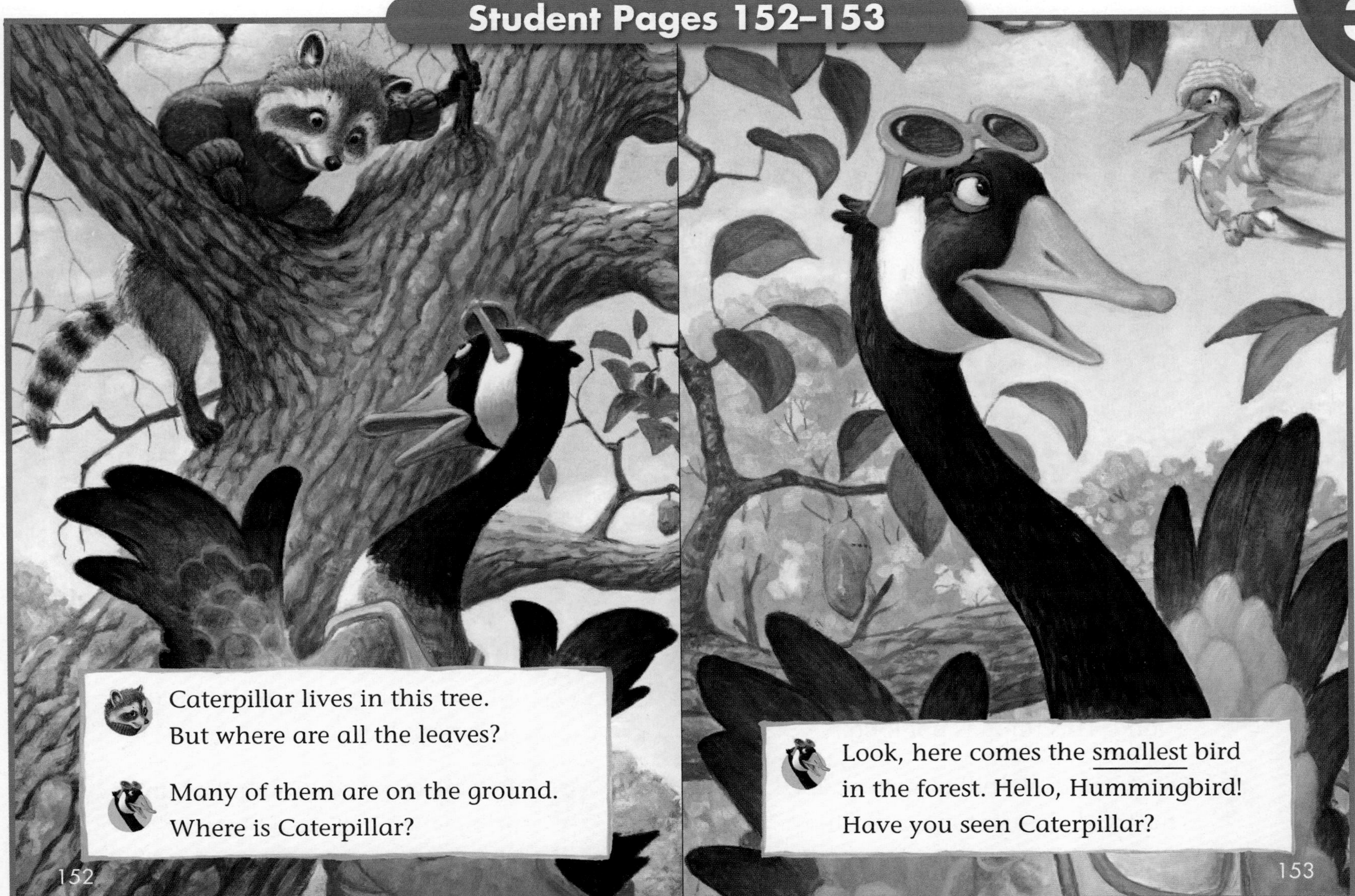

Guiding Comprehension

Draw Conclusions • Inferential

- **How has Caterpillar's tree changed? Why?**
  The leaves have fallen off because it is fall and winter is coming.

Prior Knowledge • Critical

- **What do you know about caterpillars that might help you figure out what has happened to this caterpillar?**
  Children should recall that a caterpillar becomes a chrysalis.

Prior Knowledge • Critical

- ***Text to World*** **What changes have you seen in plants and animals in different seasons?**
  Responses will vary. Children in temperate climates might have noticed fewer animals outside in the winter or trees losing leaves in the autumn. Children in warmer regions might have noticed birds arriving in the winter and leaving in the spring.

▲ **Pages 152–153**
Have children read to find out what the animals are talking about.

EXTEND SKILLS

Text Features

To help children understand the structure and features of plays, discuss the following:

- In a play, the words are to be spoken by actors who pretend to be the characters.
- The words of a play look different from the words of a story. The name of each character is followed by the words that character says. This play uses pictures of the characters, not their written names.

Assess Have children find and read the words spoken by Raccoon.

Student Pages 154–155

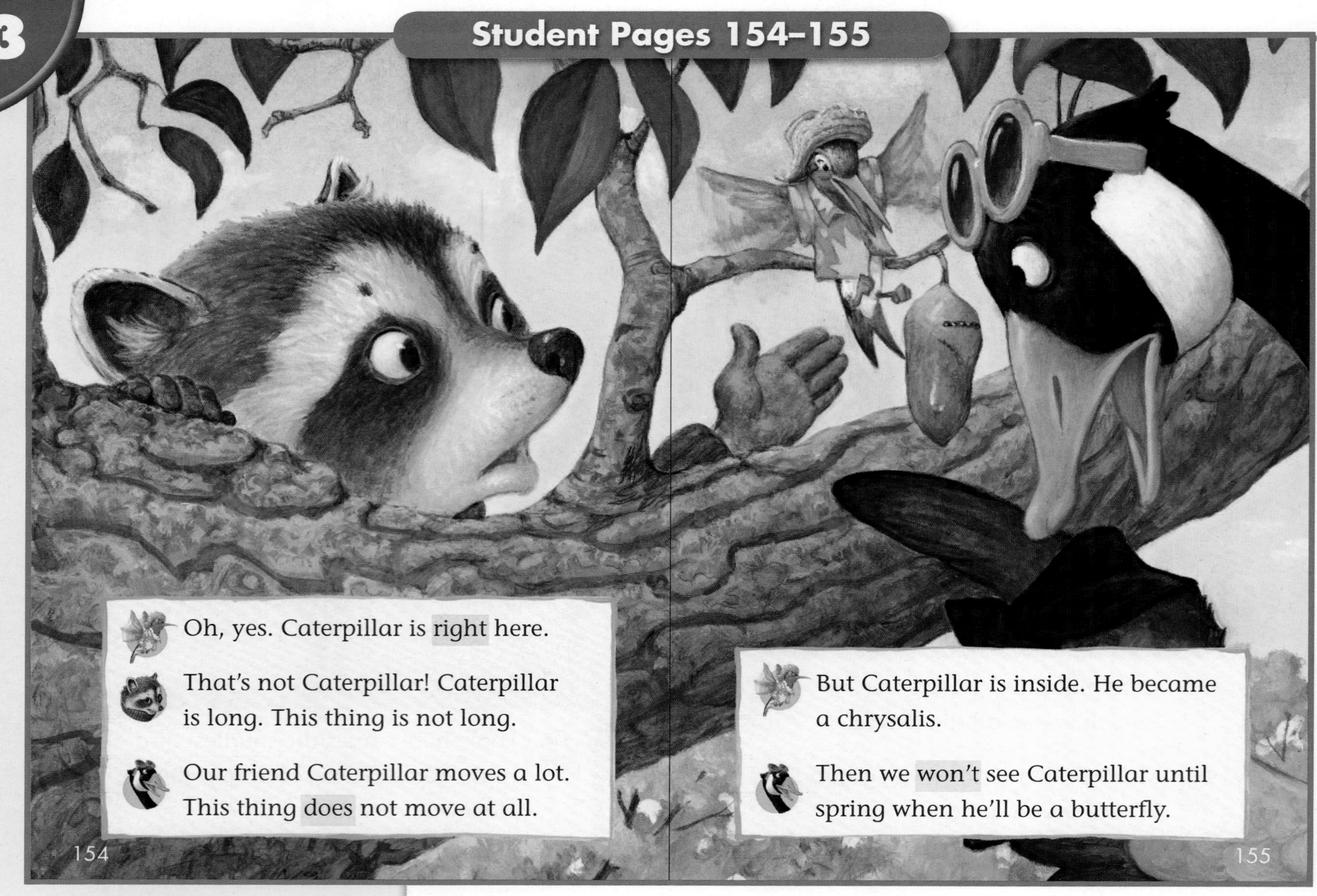

▲ **Pages 154–155**
Have children read to find out why the animals can't find caterpillar.

Monitor Progress	
High-Frequency Words	
If... children have a problem reading a new high-frequency word,	**then...** use the High-Frequency Routine on pp. 146–147 to reteach the problematic word.

Skills in Context

REVIEW COMPARE AND CONTRAST

- **How is Caterpillar different?**
  Caterpillar is a chrysalis; the chrysalis is not long and it doesn't move.

Monitor Progress	Compare and Contrast
If... children have difficulty answering the question,	**then...** model how to compare and contrast.

Think Aloud **MODEL** Raccoon notices that Caterpillar was long and the chrysalis is not long. Goose says that Caterpillar moved a lot and the chrysalis does not move. Both animals are noticing ways the chrysalis is different from Caterpillar.

ASSESS Have children tell about ways the forest is different now that winter is coming. (The forest is chilly. The trees have lost their leaves.)

____ comparative endings *-er, -est and -dge/j/*　　▭ high-frequency/tested vocabulary

Well, I'm glad you will be here for the winter.

Oh, no, Raccoon. I can't stay. I must fly away to where it is warm. Hummingbird does too.

Yes, we must go now.

156

Oh, my! I am the saddest raccoon in the forest. Will you come back?

Yes, we'll be back in the spring. Good-bye, Raccoon!

Good-bye, Goose! Good-bye, Hummingbird! I will see if Bear is at home.

157

Guiding Comprehension

Summarize • Inferential

- **What has happened so far?**
  The days are getting colder, and the leaves are falling. Winter is coming, and the animals are getting ready for it. Caterpillar has become a chrysalis for the winter. Goose and Hummingbird are going to fly to a warmer place.

Draw Conclusions • Inferential

- **Why is Raccoon sad?**
  He is sad because his friends will fly away for the winter.

Predict • Inferential

- **Do you think Raccoon will be able to play with Bear?**
  Children will probably say no, because Bear will be getting ready for winter too.

▲ **Pages 156–157**
Have children read to find out what the animals will do.

Strategy Self-Check

Have children ask themselves these questions to check their reading.

Decoding Words

- Do I look for word parts I can read?
- Do I blend all the sounds?
- Do I reread to make sure the word makes sense in the story?

Prior Knowledge

- Do I know what is happening?
- Does this story remind me of something that's happened in my life?
- Does this story remind me of others I have read?

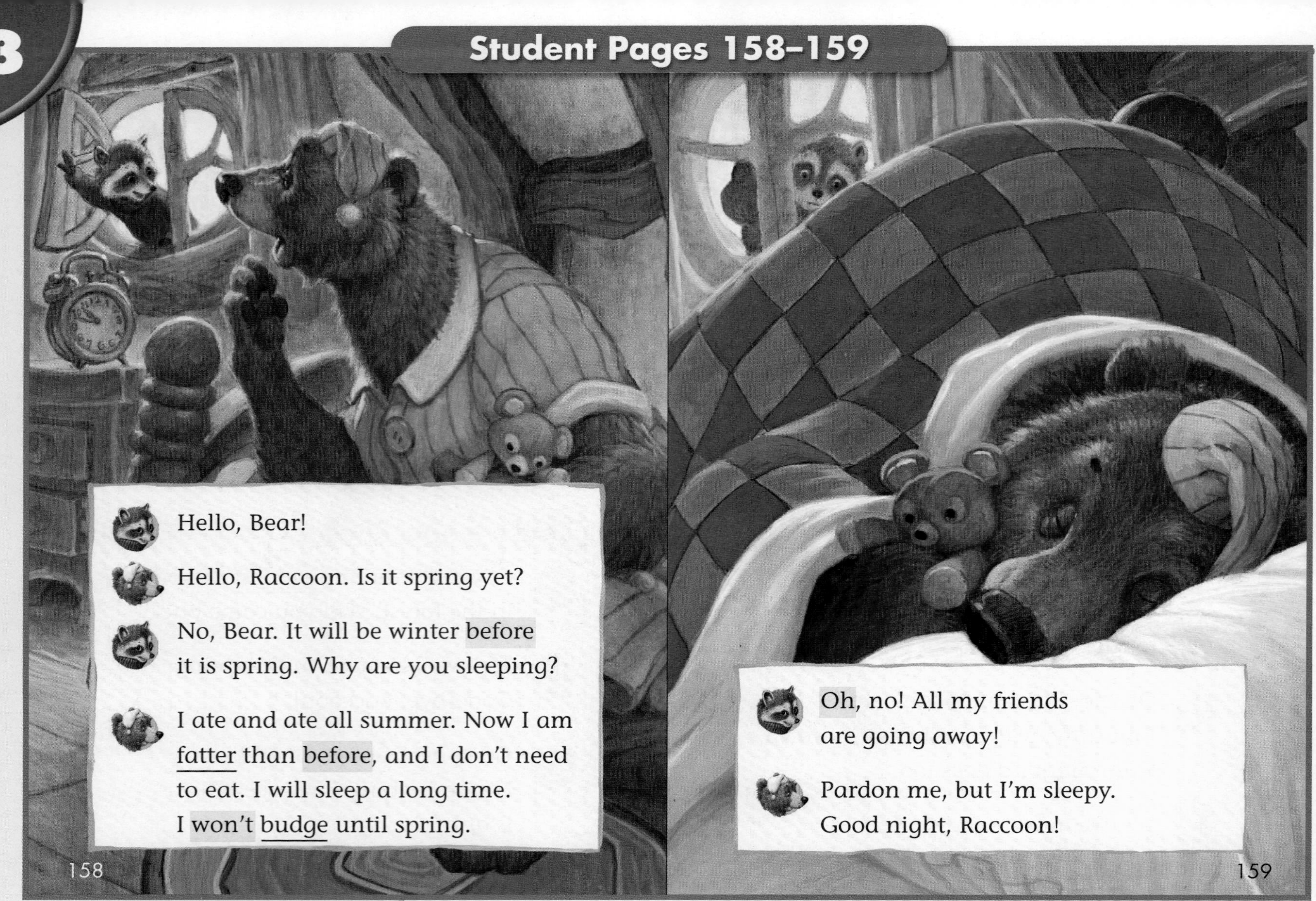

▲ **Pages 158–159**
Have children read to see what happens next.

TIME FOR Science

Seasons

Most areas experience seasonal changes of one kind or another. Some places, as in this play, have four different seasons: summer, fall, winter, and spring. In what season is this play taking place? What clues in the play help you know how the season is changing? What will the next season be?

Skills in Context

SEQUENCE

- **What does Bear do after he talks to Raccoon?**
  Bear goes to sleep for the winter.

Monitor Progress	Sequence
If... children have difficulty answering the question,	**then...** model how to recognize the sequence of events.

MODEL I see that Bear is talking to Raccoon. He is telling him that he is planning on sleeping all winter. Then Bear says, "Pardon me, but I'm sleepy. Good night, Raccoon!" That tells me that he is about to hibernate.

ASSESS Have children make a list of the things the animals do to get ready for winter and number them in order.

___ comparative endings *-er, -est and -dge/j/* high-frequency/tested vocabulary

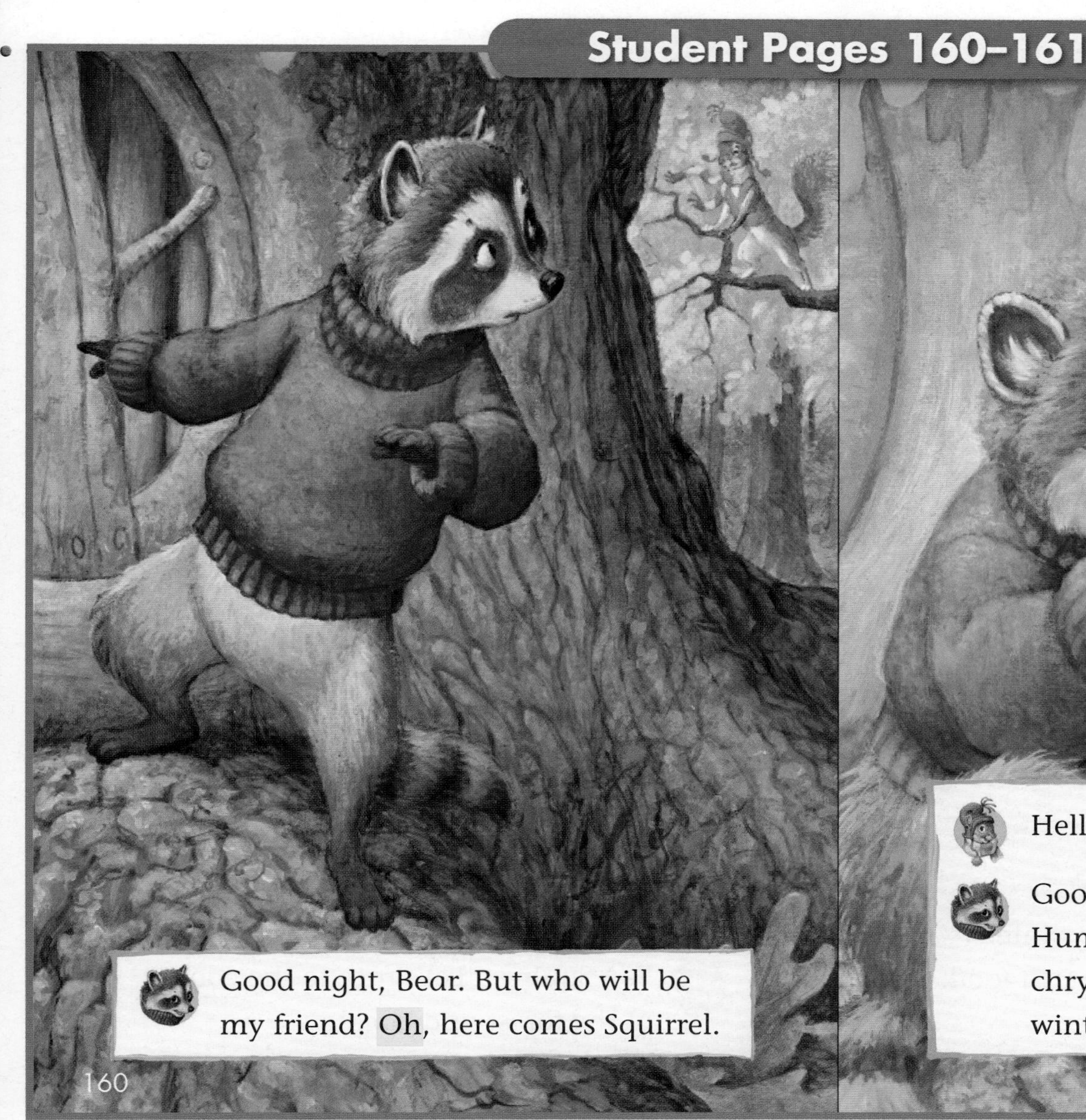

▲ **Pages 160–161**
Have children read to find out which animal Raccoon meets next.

Guiding Comprehension

Details • Literal

- **What new friend does Raccoon meet?**
  Raccoon meets Squirrel.

Draw Conclusions • Critical

- **Why does Raccoon ask Squirrel if he is going away?**
  Children will probably say he asks because all his other friends have gone somewhere for the winter.

Predict • Inferential

- **What do you think Squirrel will say? Why?**
  Predictions will vary, but children should be able to give a reason for their predictions.

Animal Behavior

The changes in weather that occur in winter make it very difficult for many animals to find food. Many birds have the ability to fly long distances. They migrate, or fly away to places where the weather is warmer. They return when the seasons change again. Other animals cannot travel such great distances. These animals find shelter in holes or deep caves and "sleep" or hibernate until the weather is warmer. Their bodies can store food as fat. These animals include bears, and bats, as well as reptiles such as frogs, turtles, and snakes.

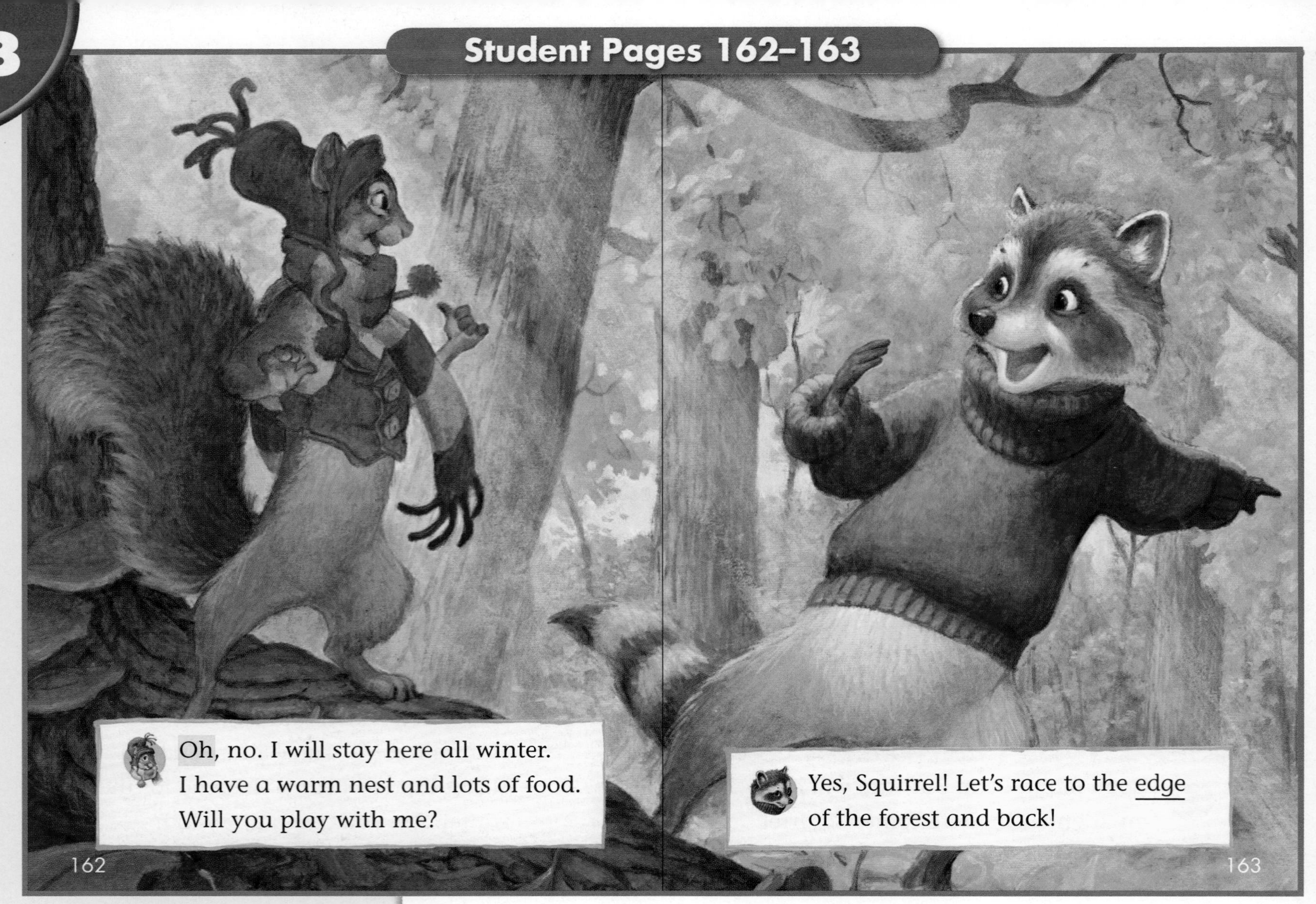

▲ **Pages 162–163**
Have children read to find out if Squirrel will stay.

Guiding Comprehension

Confirm Predictions • Literal

- **Will Squirrel migrate during the winter? Is this what you predicted?**
  Squirrel will stay for the winter. Predictions will have varied.

Draw Conclusions • Inferential

- **Why do you think Squirrel and Raccoon do not have to migrate?**
  They have a warm place to live and can find food.

Main Idea • Inferential

- **What is this play about?**
  This play tells about what the animals do in winter.

Main Idea • Critical

- ***Text to Self*** **The play tells us about ways the animals change in winter. What are some changes that we make in winter?**
  Accept all reasonable responses, such as wearing warmer clothing, heating their homes, staying inside to play more often, and eating warm foods

___ comparative endings *-er, -est and -dge/j/* high-frequency/tested vocabulary

Put on a Play!

What you will need:

Costumes

Costumes can be simple or fancy.

Props

One prop you will need for this play is a chrysalis. Will you need anything else?

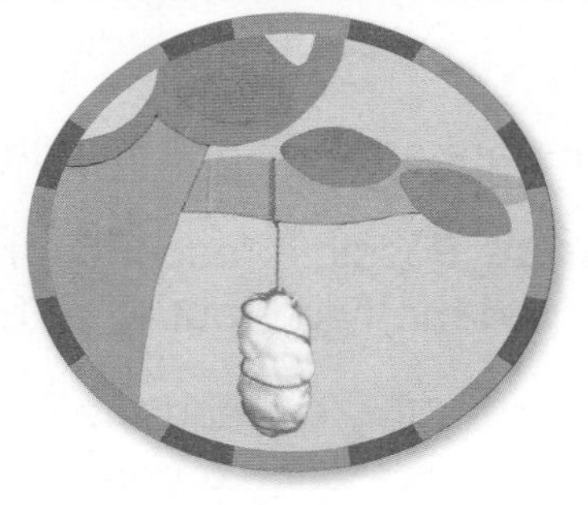

164

Scenery

Simple sets can show that the play is set in a forest in the fall.

An Audience

Practice your parts. Then ask another class to come to the play!

165

Guiding Comprehension

Author's Purpose • Critical

- **Is the information included in this selection enough to help you understand how to put on a play? What other information would you like to know about putting on a play?**
  Possible response: Yes, I think we could put on a play by using this information. I would also like information about how we could make sounds to go along with our play.

Draw Conclusions • Inferential

- **What are props?**
  Children will probably reply that props are objects that the characters use in a play.

Analyze • Inferential

- ***Text to Text* What do you think you might use from this page to put on the play *Where Are My Animal Friends?***
  Accept children's suggestions, such as what kind of costumes to make, how they might make scenery, or what they might use as props.

▲ **Pages 164–165**
Have children read to find out how to put on a play.

Access Content Help children understand the words *costumes, props, scenery,* and *audience.* Have them say the words in English and ask them to point to parts of the illustration that demonstrate each word.

Think and Share

TALK ABOUT IT Model a response. I think Raccoon and Squirrel will play in the snow. They will have a snowball fight and skate on the ice.

1. RETELL Have children use the retelling strip in the Student Edition to retell the play.

Monitor Progress **Check Retelling** 

If... children have difficulty retelling the selection,

then... use the Retelling Cards and the Scoring Rubric for Retelling on p. 166–167 to help them move toward fluent retelling.

Day 1 Check Word Reading	Day 2 Check Word Reading	▶ **Day 3 Check High-Frequency Words/Retelling**	Day 4 Check Fluency	Day 5 Assess Progress

2. SEQUENCE Bear eats a lot before he goes to sleep.

3. PRIOR KNOWLEDGE Possible response: I knew that a caterpillar turns into a chrysalis. That helped me figure out what happened to Caterpillar in the play.

LOOK BACK AND WRITE Read the writing prompt on p. 166 and model your thinking. I'll look back on pp. 151–152 and read that part of the play again. I'll look for reasons the animals know winter is coming to the forest. Then I'll write my response. Have children write their responses in an interactive or an independent writing activity.

Scoring Rubric Look Back and Write

Top-Score Response A top-score response uses details from pp. 151–152 of the play to tell how the animals know that winter is coming to the forest.

Example of a Top-Score Response

The animals know that winter is coming because the forest is chilly.
The days are shorter.
It is getting colder.
There aren't many leaves left on the trees.
The leaves have fallen on the ground.

For additional rubrics, see p. WA10.

Retelling Plan

- ☑ Week 1 assess Strategic Intervention students.
- ☑ Week 2 assess Advanced students.
- ☑ Week 3 assess Strategic Intervention students.
- ☑ Week 4 assess On-Level students.
- ☑ Week 5 assess Strategic Intervention students.
- ☑ **This week assess any students you have not yet checked during this unit.**

Look Back and Write For informal assessment, see the Scoring Rubric below.

Check Retelling Focus on comprehension and whether each child can provide good information about the selection, rather than mistakes in English. For more ideas on assessing comprehension, see the ELL and Transition Handbook.

Reader Response

Read Together

Think and Share

Talk About It Only one of Raccoon's friends will stay for the winter. What do you think they will do together all winter long?

1. Use the pictures below to retell the story. Retell
2. What does Bear do before he goes to sleep for the winter? Sequence
3. What did you know about caterpillars that helped as you read? Prior Knowledge

Look Back and Write Look back at pages 151 and 152. How do the animals know that winter is coming to the forest?

Meet the Author

William Chin

William Chin likes the winter. He lives in Chicago, where it gets cold in winter. His daughter is a figure skater. He and his wife skate too.

Mr. Chin sang in musicals in school. Now he is a choir director. He works with a children's choir. He is also a conductor for the Chicago Symphony Chorus.

Here are more books about winter.

166 167

Scoring Rubric Narrative Retelling

Rubric 4 3 2 1	4	3	2	1
Connections	Makes connections and generalizes beyond the text	Makes connections to other events, stories, or experiences	Makes a limited connection to another event, story, or experience	Makes no connection to another event, story, or experience
Author's Purpose	Elaborates on author's purpose	Tells author's purpose with some clarity	Makes some connection to author's purpose	Makes no connection to author's purpose
Characters	Describes the main character(s) and any character development	Identifies the main character(s) and gives some information about them	Inaccurately identifies some characters or gives little information about them	Inaccurately identifies the characters or gives no information about them
Setting	Describes the time and location	Identifies the time and location	Omits details of time or location	Is unable to identify time or location
Plot	Describes the events in sequence using rich detail	Tells the plot with some errors in sequence that do not affect meaning	Tells parts of plot with gaps that affect meaning	Retelling has no sense of story

Use the Retelling Chart on p. TR18 to record retelling.

Selection Test To assess with *Where Are My Animal Friends?*, use Selection Tests, pp. 45–48.

Fresh Reads for Differentiated Test Practice For weekly leveled practice, use pp. 103–108.

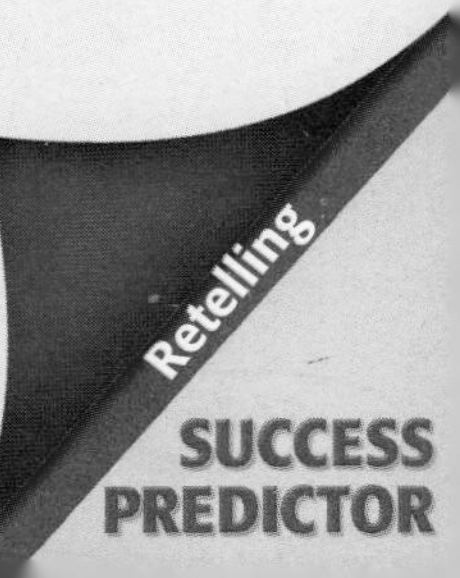

OBJECTIVE

- Read aloud fluently with expression and intonation.

Options for Oral Reading

Use *Where Are My Animal Friends?* or one of the following Leveled Readers.

On-Level

Spring Rose, Winter Bear

Strategic Intervention

Seasons Change

Advanced

Weather or Not?

Point out action words in *Where Are My Animal Friends?* Read phrases such as *ate and ate all summer* and *won't budge until spring* with expression to support comprehension for beginning English language learners. Have children practice rereading the same phrases with expression.

Fluency

READ WITH EXPRESSION AND INTONATION

MODEL READING WITH EXPRESSION AND INTONATION Use *Where Are My Animal Friends?*

- Have children turn to p. 151. I'm going to read this page. I want to sound like the different characters talking to each other. I will try to use my voice to sound the way each character might sound.
- Ask children to follow along as you read the pages with expression.
- Have children read the pages after you. Encourage them to try to read the way the characters might speak. Continue in the same way with pp. 152–153.

REREAD FOR FLUENCY

Choral Reading

ROUTINE

1. **Select a Passage** For *Where Are My Animal Friends?*, use pp. 158–160.
2. **Divide into Groups** Assign each group a part to read. For this story, have each group read one character: Bear or Raccoon.
3. **Model** Have children track the print as you read.
4. **Read Together** Have children read along with you.
5. **Independent Readings** Have the groups read aloud without you. Monitor progress and provide feedback. For optimal fluency, children should reread three to four times.

Monitor Progress	Fluency
If... children have difficulty reading with expression,	**then...** prompt: • Who is the character speaking? • How does your character feel? • How do you think your character sounds when he is saying this?
If... the class cannot read fluently without you,	**then...** continue to have them read along with you.

Vocabulary

MULTIPLE-MEANING WORDS

DISCUSS MULTIPLE-MEANING WORDS Have children recall that the animals won't see Caterpillar until spring. Remind them that *spring* can mean "a time of year" or "a small stream of water." Write these sentences on the board and have children identify the meaning of the word *spring* in each sentence.

Many flowers bloom in spring.

The animals got a drink at the spring.

EXPAND SELECTION VOCABULARY Discuss with children the two meanings of each word listed below. Provide an example for each meaning. Have children work with partners to write sentences for each meaning of each word. Invite volunteers to share their sentences.

right the side of your body opposite the left
I use my right hand to write.
to be correct
Chuck had the right answer.

back to return
We go back home after school.
opposite of front
The table is at the back of the room.

play a story acted out on stage
The class had a play about animals.
to have fun
We like to play ball.

OBJECTIVES

- Discuss meanings of multiple-meaning words.
- Use multiple-meaning words in sentences.

Strategic Intervention

Have children illustrate the two meanings of *back*. Then help them write a caption using the word *back* for each picture.

Advanced

Have children use a dictionary to list meanings for the words *tag* and *plant*. Have them write and illustrate a sentence that shows each meaning of each word.

Extend Language Help children practice telling which meaning of *spring* makes sense in each sentence by paying attention to the words around it.

Writing Trait of the Week

INTRODUCE Sentences

TALK ABOUT SENTENCES Explain that good writers make their sentences interesting to read. They do not begin all their sentences with the same word. Read aloud the sentences on p. 152. Ask children to think about the sentence beginnings. Then model your thinking.

MODEL When I look at the sentences on p. 152, I can see that the author begins each sentence with a different word—*Caterpillar, But, Many,* and *Where.* Here are some sentences that begin with the same words. Listen as I read the sentences.

This tree is bare in winter. This tree will have blossoms next spring. This tree has leaves now.

What words do all these sentences begin with? *(This tree)* Sentences with the same beginning words are not interesting to read or to listen to. Let's listen to how these sentences sound with different beginnings.

In winter this tree is bare. Next spring it will have blossoms. Now this tree has leaves.

The sentences sound better without the same beginnings. Notice that sometimes you can give sentences different beginnings by just rearranging the words.

STRATEGY FOR DEVELOPING SENTENCES On the board, write sentences that begin with the same words. Work with children to rearrange the words in the sentences so that each sentence has a different beginning.

I like to be warm in winter. *(In winter I like to be warm.)*

I really can't stay, Raccoon. *(Raccoon, I really can't stay.)*

I will come back next spring. *(Next spring I will come back.)*

PRACTICE

APPLY THE STRATEGY

- Have children offer sentences that tell what the animals in the selection do in winter. Write the sentences on the board. Help children identify whether the sentences begin with different words and revise any that do not.
- Ask children to write about one of the animals in the selection. Have them use complete sentences. When they finish, they should check that each of their sentences has a different beginning.

OBJECTIVE

- Recognize and use sentences in writing.

DAILY FIX-IT

5. It is cold last week?
It was cold last week.

6. some birds can not find fod.
Some birds can not find food.

Connect to Unit Writing

Writing Trait

Have children use strategies for developing **sentences** when they write a description in the Unit Writing Workshop, pp. WA2–WA9.

Sentences Have English language learners read their sentences aloud to check completeness and sense. Use student writing to point out how to change the beginnings of sentences by rearranging or adding words.

Grammar

APPLY TO WRITING Contractions with *Not*

IMPROVE WRITING WITH CONTRACTIONS WITH *NOT* Explain to children that a contraction is a short way to put two words together. Add that writing with contractions can make the writing seem more casual. Remind children to use contractions with *not* in their own writing.

Write *are + not, did + not, has + not,* and *were + not.* Have children supply the contractions for each word pair. Ask what is used in place of the letter *o*.

are + not	did + not	has + not	were + not
aren't	didn't	hasn't	weren't

PRACTICE

WRITE SENTENCES WITH CONTRACTIONS WITH *NOT* Write *aren't, didn't, hasn't,* and *weren't* on the chalkboard. Have children write sentences on their paper using each word. Call on individuals to share their sentences.

OBJECTIVE

- Use contractions with *not* in writing.

Contractions with *Not*

Write a sentence about each season.
Use a contraction with *not* in each sentence.

Winter Possible answers:

Winter isn't hot.

Spring

Days aren't cold in the spring.

Summer

Summer doesn't last long.

Fall

Trees don't stay green in the fall.

Home Activity Your child learned how to use contractions with *not* in writing. Write these sentences on paper: *He does not like winter. They do not like summer. She is not sad in the fall. We are not cold in the spring.* Have your child write the sentences using contractions with *not*.

▲ **Grammar and Writing Practice Book** p. 70

Wrap Up Your Day!

SEQUENCE Have children recall the sequence of events in *Where Are My Animal Friends?* (Goose and Raccoon look for their friends. Hummingbird explains that Caterpillar will be a chrysalis until spring. Then Goose and Hummingbird fly away to where it's warm. Raccoon talks to Bear, who is hibernating. Then Raccoon talks to Squirrel. Neither animal is going away for the winter. They begin to play together.)

PRIOR KNOWLEDGE Have children share what they already know about migration and hibernation. (Possible response: Birds fly to warmer climates where there is more food. Some animals sleep during parts of the winter months, such as skunks and bears.)

LET'S TALK ABOUT IT In the story, the animals are changing their routines. What is causing them to do this?

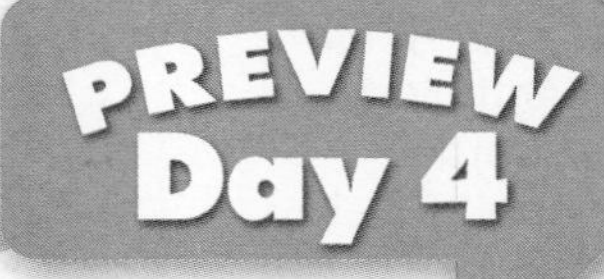

Tell children that tomorrow they will listen to a story about the things a moose does when the seasons change.

Day 4
AT A GLANCE

Share Literature
Busy Busy Moose

Phonemic Awareness
Blend and Segment Onset/Rime

High-Frequency Words
before *does* *good-bye* Word Wall
oh *right* *won't*

Phonics and Spelling
REVIEW *r*-controlled *er, ir, ur* and Contractions *'s, 've, 're*
REVIEW Word Reading
Spelling: Words with *-er, -est*

Read
Group Time < Differentiated Instruction
Poetry

Fluency
Read with Expression and Intonation

Writing Across the Curriculum
Math Story

Grammar
Contractions with Not

Materials
- *Sing with Me Big Book*
- Read Aloud Anthology
- Tested Word Cards
- Student Edition 168–171

Morning Warm-Up!

Today we are going to read some poems.
Each poem is about changes.
Some poems are funny.
What changes might be funny?

QUESTION OF THE DAY Encourage children to sing "Change of Season" from the *Sing with Me Big Book* as you gather. Write and read the message and discuss the question.

REVIEW ONE AND MORE THAN ONE
- Ask children to find a word that tells about one. *(poem)*
- Ask children to find a word that tells about more than one. *(poems)*

ELL

Extend Language Use the Day 4 instruction on ELL Poster 18 to extend and enrich language.

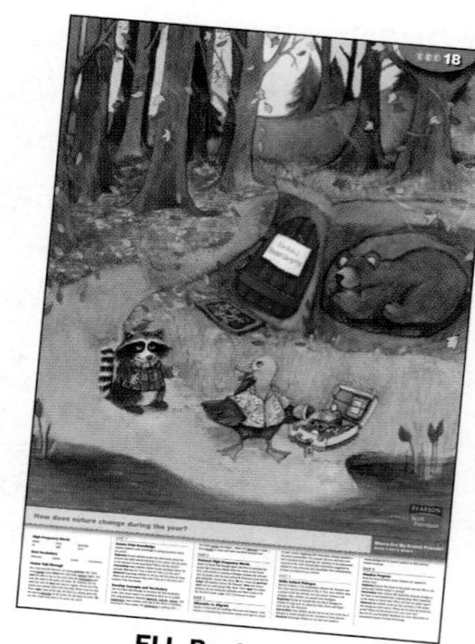
ELL Poster 18

Share Literature

CONNECT CONCEPTS

ACTIVATE PRIOR KNOWLEDGE Help children recall that the animals in *Where Are My Animal Friends?* were getting ready for winter. Explain that you will read a story about a group of animals and the things they do in each season of the year—"Busy Busy Moose" by Nancy Van Laan.

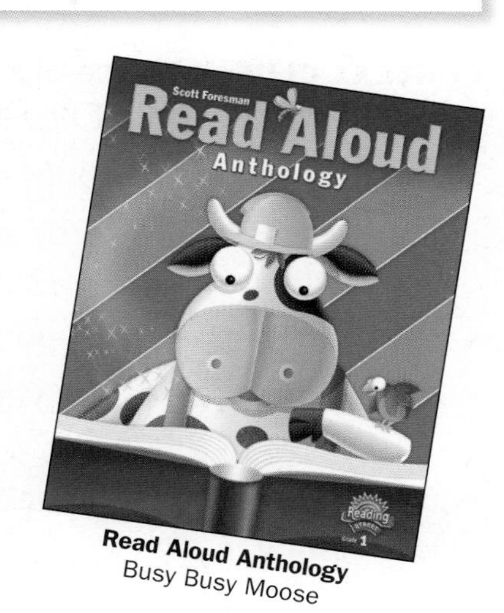

Read Aloud Anthology
Busy Busy Moose

BUILD ORAL VOCABULARY Tell children this story is about a moose, a beaver, a rabbit, and a squirrel. Explain that **weary** means to be very tired. Discuss why animals would be weary in the fall. After fall comes winter, when the weather can be **bitterly** cold. Ask children to listen to find out how Moose is busy all through the year.

REVIEW ORAL VOCABULARY After reading, review all the Amazing Words for the week. Have children take turns using them in sentences that tell about the concept for the week. Then talk about the Amazing Words they learned in other weeks and connect them to the concept as well. For example, ask:

- What do you think snakes do in the winter? Do they **slither** through the snow?
- Some places in the **world** do not have a change of seasons. Do you think a **desert** has cold winters?

Phonemic Awareness

BLEND AND SEGMENT ONSET/RIME

- We read that in fall the birds rested in Moose's antlers, but the birds didn't hurt Moose. Listen to the word parts in *hurt*.
- Model saying the onset and rime, /h/ *-urt*. Have children say the sounds with you, /h/ /ėr/ /t/, and then say the sounds by themselves.
- Now say the onset and rime as you write the letters that go with it. Say /h/ *-urt* as you write *h, urt*.
- Have children say the sounds as you point to the letters, /h/ *-urt*, and blend the parts to say the word, *hurt*.
- Have children say the sounds with you as you point to the letters.

Continue the activity with *swirl, clerk,* and *churn.*

sp/ur	**sw/irl**	**cl/erk**
sl/ur	**wh/irl**	**s/erve**
ch/urn	**tw/irl**	**sw/erve**

OBJECTIVES

- Set purpose for listening.
- Build oral vocabulary.
- Blend and segment onset and rime.

hibernate
migrate
season
temperature
autumn
freeze
bitterly
weary

MONITOR PROGRESS

If... children lack oral vocabulary experiences about the concept Changes in Nature,

then... use the Oral Vocabulary Routine. See p. DI·8 to teach *bitterly* and *weary.*

Connect Concepts After reading the chapter titled "Fall," have children use the illustrations to act out what the animals meant by " the busiest time of the year." Have them act out what Moose meant by "(he) had nothing busy to do."

OBJECTIVES

- Recognize high-frequency words.
- Review *r*-controlled *er, ir, ur* words and contractions *'s, 've, 're.*
- Apply decoding strategies: blend, preview words.

Pick the letters from the box to finish each word.
Write the letters on the line.

er ir ur

1. c ur l
2. f ir st
3. f er n
4. d ir t
5. sk ir t
6. h er
7. b ir d
8. b ur n
9. cl er k
10. h ur t

School + Home Home Activity Your child reviewed words with er, ir, and ur that have the sound heard in fern, shirt, and turtle. Make a list of er, ir, and ur words that have this vowel sound, such as fern, her, dirt, bird, curl, and burn. Ask your child to sort the words by their spelling.

▲ **Practice Book 1.2** p. 58, *r*-Controlled *er, ir, ur*

Write the contraction for each pair of words.

1. we + have = we've
2. he + is = he's
3. I + have = I've
4. they + have = they've
5. that + is = that's
6. it + is = it's
7. you + are = you're
8. you + have = you've

Here is my balloon.
Here's my balloon.

Find the contraction.
Mark the ⊂⊃ to show your answer.

9. ● she's ○ she ○ sons
10. ○ were ● we're ○ went

School + Home Home Activity Your child reviewed contractions—words made up of two words and an apostrophe. Write the words he, she, it, is, they, you, have, and are on pieces of paper. Ask your child to see how many different contractions he or she can form.

▲ **Practice Book 1.2** p. 59, Contractions *'s, 've, 're*

High-Frequency Words

PRACTICE

CONTEXT CLUES Provide clues such as the following. Have children find the word on the Word Wall that fits each clue. **Word Wall**

- The word means the opposite of *left.* (right)
- The word begins with /d/ and rhymes with *fuzz* and *buzz.* It makes sense in this sentence: Bear _____ lots of work, then he sleeps. (does)
- The word means the opposite of *after.* (before)
- The word rhymes with *go* and *so* and makes sense in this sentence: _____, look at me! (Oh)
- The word means the opposite of *hello.* (good-bye)
- This word is the contraction for *will not.* (won't)

Review Phonics

REVIEW *r*-Controlled *er, ir, ur* AND Contractions

READ *r*-CONTROLLED *er, ir, ur* WORDS Write *her.* You can read this word because you know that the letter *e* followed by *r* stands for the *r*-controlled sound. What sound does *er* stand for? (/ėr/) What's the word? *(her)* Continue with *sir, ir* /ėr/ and *fur, ur* /ėr/.

READ CONTRACTIONS WITH *'s, 've, 're* Write *it's.* You can read this word because you know that the word is a contraction. What is the first word? *(it)* What is the last sound? (/s/) What's the word? *(it's)* You know that *it's* is made up of two words. What are the two words? *(it is)*

SORT WORDS Write *er, ir, ur* and *Contractions* as headings. When I say a word, twirl your hand up high if it has /ėr/ or put your two hands together if it is a contraction: *surf, let's, herd, you've, chirp, they're, burn, she's.* Write each word in the appropriate column and have the lists read. Have children name the two words that make up each contraction.

er, ir, ur	Contractions
surf	let's
herd	you've
chirp	they're
burn	she's

WORD READING

READ DECODABLE AND HIGH-FREQUENCY WORDS Write these words. Encourage children to preview each word before reading it.

wait	**her**	**know**	**visit**	**turn**
perch	**doesn't**	**I'll**	**swirling**	**clerk**
push	**first**	**we're**	**bird**	**Fern**
we'll	**let's**	**we've**	**done**	**I'm**

Monitor Progress	Word Reading
If... children have difficulty previewing and reading whole words,	**then...** have them use sound-by-sound blending.
If... children can't read the words fluently at a rate of one to two seconds per word,	**then...** have pairs practice the list.

READ WORDS IN CONTEXT Write these sentences. Call on individuals to read a sentence. Then randomly point to the review words and have them read. To help you monitor word reading, high-frequency words are underlined and decodable words are circled.

If the clerk doesn't know which button to push, let's help her.

We've got time to wait so I'll take a turn.

When we're done with chores, we'll visit Fern first.

I'm swirling like a bird that has left its perch.

Monitor Progress	Word Reading
If... children are unable to read an underlined word,	**then...** read the word for them and spell it, having them echo you.
If... children have difficulty reading a circled word,	**then...** have them use sound-by-sound blending.

Spiral REVIEW

- Reviews high-frequency words *done, know, push, visit,* and *wait.*
- Reviews *r*-controlled *er, ir, ur;* contractions *'s, 've, 're, n't, 'm, 'll.*

ELL

Support Phonics For additional review, see the phonics activities in the ELL and Transition Handbook.

OBJECTIVE

- Spell words with comparative endings *-er, -est.*

Spelling Words

Adding *-er* and *-est*

1. bigger
2. biggest
3. faster
4. fastest
5. slower
6. slowest
7. shorter*
8. shortest
9. sadder
10. saddest*

High-Frequency Words

11. good-bye*
12. before*

* Words from the Selection

Adding *-er* and *-est*

Spelling Words				
bigger	biggest	faster	fastest	slower
slowest	shorter	shortest	sadder	saddest

Finish the list words.

1. slower
2. shorter
3. slowest
4. shortest
5. sadder
6. biggest
7. bigger
8. saddest

Write the missing words.

9. Hopper is faster than Froggy.
10. Hopper is fastest.

fastest
faster

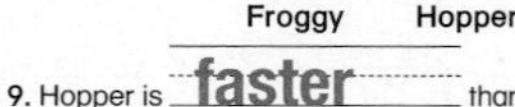

Home Activity Your child has been learning to spell words ending in -er and -est. Play a game with your child by tossing a coin onto this page. Read the list word that is closest to where the coin lands and have your child spell it. Take turns.

▲ **Spelling Practice Book** p. 72

Spelling

PARTNER REVIEW Comparative Endings

READ AND WRITE Supply pairs of children with index cards on which the spelling words have been written. Have one child read a word while the other writes it. Then have children switch roles. Have them use the cards to check their spelling.

HOMEWORK Spelling Practice Book, p. 72

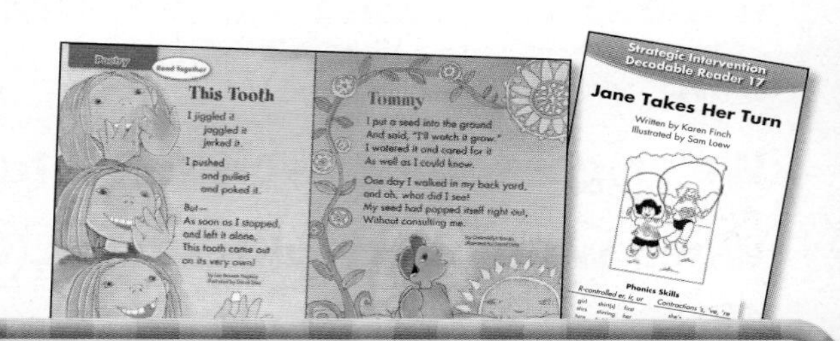

Group Time

DAY 4

On-Level	Strategic Intervention	Advanced
Read Poetry. • Use pp. 168–171.	**Read** SI Decodable Reader 17. • Read or listen to Poetry. • Use the **Routine** on p. DI·72.	**Read** Poetry. • Use the **Routine** on p. DI·73.

ELL Place English language learners in the groups that correspond to their reading abilities in English.

Independent Activities

Fluency Reading Pair children to reread *Where Are My Animal Friends?*

Journal Writing Write what Raccoon and the other animal friends do the next spring. Share writing.

Independent Reading See p. 144j for Reading/Library activities and suggestions.

Literacy Centers To provide listening opportunities, you may use the Listening Center on p. 144j. To extend science concepts, you may use the Science Center on p. 144k.

Practice Book 1.2 *r*-Controlled *er, ir, ur,* p. 58 Contractions *'s, 've, 're,* p. 59

Break into small groups after Spelling and before Fluency.

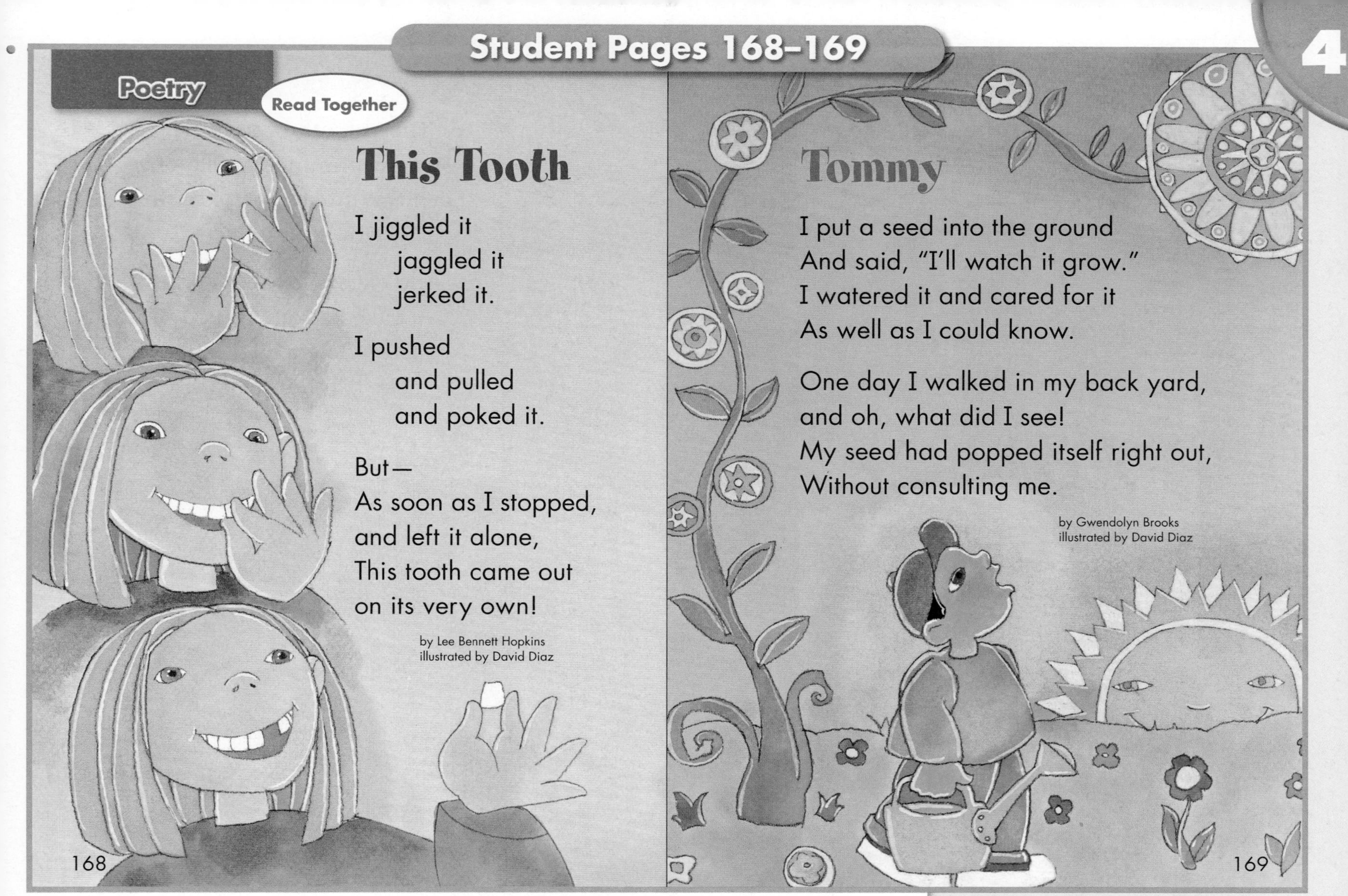

Read

Poetry

PREVIEW AND PREDICT Read the titles and poets' names. Have children look at the words and discuss how a poem looks different from a story. (The lines are short. Some lines on p. 168 make a pattern, or rhyme.) Have children read to learn which poets write about a surprise.

POETRY Review that a poem often has a rhythm when you read the words. Usually a poem will have words that rhyme.

VOCABULARY Discuss the meanings of *consult* (to seek advice from someone) and *repose* (rest; sleep). Encourage children to use these words in a discussion about the poems.

AudioText

OBJECTIVE

- Respond to poetry read aloud.

Read Together

Where Do Fish Go in Winter?

When lakes turn to ice
And are covered with snow,
What becomes of the fish
Who are living below?

It's not so exciting
Down under the ice,
But fish find it restful
And really quite nice.

It's dark and it's cold,
But the water's not frozen.
In fact, it's just perfect
For fish to repose in.

They breathe very little.
Their swimming gets slower.
Each fish makes his heart rate
Go lower and lower.

And except for occasional
Lake bottom treats,
The whole winter long
The fish hardly eats.

by Amy Goldman Koss
illustrated by Laura J. Bryant

170 171

BUILD CONCEPTS

Sequence • Literal

- **Tell what happened first, next, and last when the child lost a tooth.**
  First, the child jiggled and pushed and pulled at the tooth, and then she stopped and left the tooth alone. Finally, the tooth came out on its own.

Use Prior Knowledge • Inferential

- **What do you know about plants that helped you understand "Tommy"?**
  Children will probably respond that they know that seeds will grow into plants when they are ready. You can't make them grow by watching them.

Make Comparisons • Inferential

- **How is a fish like a bear?**
  They are alike because they both sleep in winter.

CONNECT TEXT TO TEXT

What do you think a fish might have told Racoon in *Where Are My Animal Friends?*

Responses will vary, but children should include that the fish can't play in winter because it will be resting at the bottom of the pond.

Activate Prior Knowledge Ask if any children have lost teeth. Have them pantomime how it feels to have a loose tooth.

Fluency

READ WITH EXPRESSION

MODEL READING WITH EXPRESSION AND INTONATION Use *Where Are My Animal Friends?*

- Direct children's attention to pp. 154–155. Listen while I read these pages. This is a play, and all the characters talk to each other. I want to read this the way the different characters might sound.
- Ask children to follow along as you read the pages with expression.
- Have children read the pages after you. Encourage them to try to sound the way they think the characters would sound. Continue in the same way with pp. 156–157.

REREAD FOR FLUENCY

Choral Reading

ROUTINE

1. **Select a Passage** For *Where Are My Animal Friends?* use pp. 151–155.
2. **Divide into Groups** Assign each group a part to read. For this story, assign one page to each of four groups.
3. **Model** Have children track the print as you read.
4. **Read Together** Have children read along with you.
5. **Independent Readings** Have the groups read aloud without you. Monitor progress and provide feedback. For optimal fluency, children should reread three to four times.

Monitor Progress — Check Fluency WCPM

As children reread, monitor their progress toward their individual fluency goals. Current Goal: 25–35 words correct per minute. End-of-Year Goal: 60 words correct per minute.

If... children cannot read fluently at a rate of 25–35 words per minute,

then... make sure children practice with text at their independent level. Provide additional fluency practice, pairing nonfluent readers with fluent readers.

If... children already read at 60 words per minute,

then... they do not need to reread three to four times.

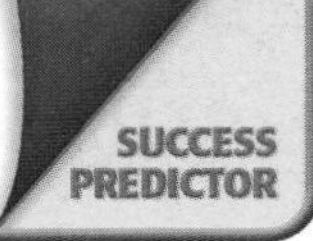

Day 1 Check Word Reading	Day 2 Check Word Reading	Day 3 Check High-Frequency Words/Retelling	▶ **Day 4 Check Fluency**	Day 5 Assess Progress

OBJECTIVE

- Read aloud fluently with expression and intonation.

Options for Oral Reading

Use *Where Are My Animal Friends?* or one of the following Leveled Readers.

On-Level

Spring Rose Winter Bear

Strategic Intervention

Seasons Change

Advanced

Weather or Not

Use *As White as Snow* or *Where Are My Animal Friends.* Build children's fluency by encouraging them to repeatedly read aloud passages from familiar and favorite selections, including books that reflect their cultures.

SUCCESS PREDICTOR — Words Correct Per Minute

Writing Across the Curriculum

OBJECTIVE

- Create a math story.

Advanced

Encourage children to create another math story using a different subject and different numbers.

Support Writing If children suggest sentences that do not reflect conventional English, respond positively and restate the sentence without the errors.

WRITE Math Story

DISCUSS Have children discuss the number of animals in the story. How many animals are there? How many animals fly away? How many animals go to sleep? Encourage them to use oral vocabulary, such as *hibernate, migrate, season,* and *temperature.*

SHARE THE PEN Have children participate in creating a math story. Ask the class to create a math story using numbers of characters or events found in the story. Call on an individual to read his or her story aloud. Write the sentences on the board, and have the class solve the problem. Ask questions, such as the following:

- What does a sentence start with? (capital letter)
- What does a sentence end with? (appropriate end punctuation, such as period, question mark, or exclamation point)
- What are two things a sentence has to have? (subject and verb)

Ask other individuals to share their stories. Continue having the class solve the math stories.

1 bug + 2 birds = ___ animals

3 animals - 2 animals = ___ animal

Grammar

REVIEW Contractions with *Not*

DEFINE CONTRACTIONS WITH *Not*

- What is a short way to put two words together called? (contraction)
- What is used in place of the letter that is left out of a contraction? (an apostrophe)

PRACTICE

CLASSIFY CONTRACTIONS WITH *Not* Write the following sentence pairs. Have individuals determine which words from the first sentence form the contraction in the second sentence.

The boys are not home.
The boys aren't home. (are not)

The water is not cold.
The water isn't cold. (is not)

The birds do not sing.
The birds don't sing. (do not)

OBJECTIVE

- Identify contractions with *not*.

DAILY FIX-IT

7. today isnt cold.
Today isn't cold.

8. Some birds havent' gon.
Some birds haven't gone.

Contractions with *Not*

Mark the sentence that spells the contraction correctly.

1. ⊗ Days aren't long in the winter.
   ○ Days arent long in the winter.
   ○ Days are'nt long in the winter.
2. ○ A raccoon does'nt sleep all winter long.
   ○ A raccoon doesnt sleep all winter long.
   ⊗ A raccoon doesn't sleep all winter long.
3. ○ The chrysalis hasnt moved at all.
   ⊗ The chrysalis hasn't moved at all.
   ○ The chrysalis has'nt moved at all.
4. ○ Bears do'nt come out until spring.
   ○ Bears dont come out until spring.
   ⊗ Bears don't come out until spring.
5. ⊗ Many birds didn't stay here.
   ○ Many birds did'nt stay here.
   ○ Many birds didnt stay here.
6. ○ The fat bear was'nt hungry.
   ⊗ The fat bear wasn't hungry.
   ○ The fat bear wasnt hungry.

Home Activity Your child prepared for taking tests on contractions with *not*. Together read part of a short newspaper or magazine article. Take turns with your child circling contractions with *not*. Ask your child what two words make up each contraction.

▲ **Grammar and Writing Practice Book** p. 71

Wrap Up Your Day!

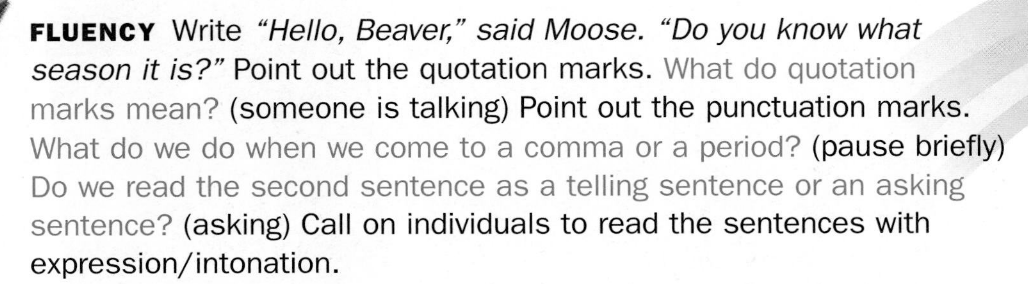

FLUENCY Write *"Hello, Beaver," said Moose. "Do you know what season it is?"* Point out the quotation marks. What do quotation marks mean? (someone is talking) Point out the punctuation marks. What do we do when we come to a comma or a period? (pause briefly) Do we read the second sentence as a telling sentence or an asking sentence? (asking) Call on individuals to read the sentences with expression/intonation.

LET'S TALK ABOUT IT The animals in the story "Busy Busy Moose" are busy with different tasks. What has changed that makes the animals in the story do different things?

PREVIEW Day 5

Remind children that they heard a story about the things a moose does when the seasons change. Tell them that tomorrow they will hear about the moose again.

Day 5

AT A GLANCE

Share Literature
Busy Busy Moose

Phonics and Spelling
Review Comparative Endings; *dge* /j/

High-Frequency Words
before *does* *good-bye* *oh* *right* *won't* Word Wall

Monitor Progress
Spelling Test: Words with *-er, -est*

< Differentiated Assessment

Writing and Grammar
Trait: Sentences

Contractions with *Not*

Materials

- *Sing with Me Big Book*
- Read Aloud Anthology
- Reproducible Pages TE 172f–172g
- Student Edition 172–173

Morning Warm-Up!

We have read how the temperature can change from season to season. In autumn, some animals get ready to sleep or to move to warm places. What other changes do animals make during the year?

QUESTION OF THE DAY Encourage children to sing "Change of Season" from the *Sing with Me Big Book* as you gather. Write and read the message, tracking the print. Discuss the question.

REVIEW ORAL VOCABULARY Have children find words in the message that

- tell what happens when animals **hibernate** (they sleep)
- tell what happens when animals **migrate** (move to warm places)
- tell what you can read on a thermometer (temperature)
- name a season (autumn)

Assess Vocabulary Use the Day 5 instruction on ELL Poster 18 to monitor children's progress with oral vocabulary.

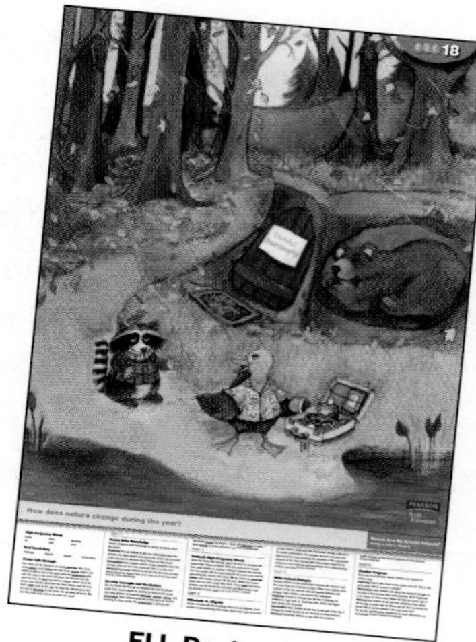

ELL Poster 18

Share Literature

LISTEN AND RESPOND

USE PRIOR KNOWLEDGE Review that yesterday the class listened to find out how Moose is busy throughout the year. Suggest that today the class listen to find out what happens when Beaver and Moose each try to do something nice for the other.

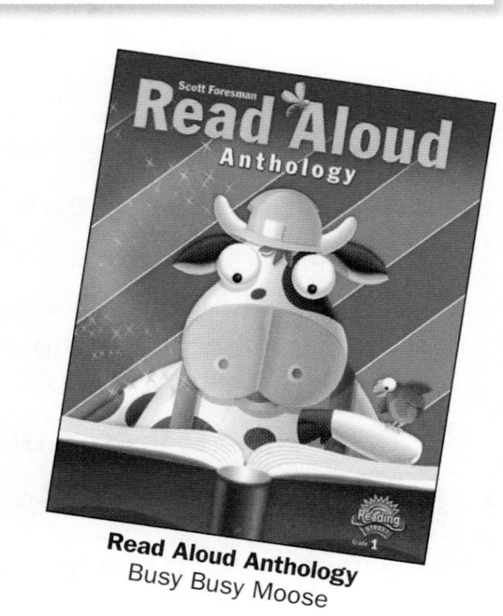

Read Aloud Anthology
Busy Busy Moose

MONITOR LISTENING COMPREHENSION

- What nice thing does Moose do for Beaver? (He builds a path of stones across the stream so Beaver's friends can visit.)
- What nice thing does Beaver do for Moose? (He builds his house on the other side of the stream so Moose would not have to bring his friends across.)
- Why did Moose go to wait in a field when fall came? (He was waiting for the birds to stop and rest on his antlers again.)
- How is this story a cycle? (It tells about how the same things repeat each season.)

BUILD ORAL VOCABULARY

GENERATE DISCUSSION Recall what Moose does to stay busy throughout the year. Invite children to share activities they do during different seasons. Have children use some of this week's Amazing Words as they describe each activity and how it keeps them busy.

Monitor Progress | **Check Oral Vocabulary**

Display pp. 144–145 in the Student Edition and remind children of the concept for this week—Changes in Nature. Ask them to tell you about the photographs using some of this week's Amazing Words, *hibernate, migrate, season, temperature, autumn, freeze, bitterly,* and *weary.*

If... children have difficulty using the Amazing Words,

then... ask questions about the photographs using the Amazing Words. Note which questions children can respond to. Reteach unknown words using the Oral Vocabulary Routine.

Day 1 Check Word Reading	Day 2 Check Word Reading	Day 3 Check High-Frequency Words/Retelling	Day 4 Check Fluency	▶ **Day 5 Check Oral Vocabulary/ Assess Progress**

OBJECTIVES

- Set purpose for listening.
- Build oral vocabulary.

hibernate	**autumn**
migrate	**freeze**
season	**bitterly**
temperature	**weary**

Extend Language Tell children that some words in English have more than one meaning. Write words from *Busy Busy Moose* on the board, and then read each word with children and help them form a sentence that demonstrates meaning. Write words such as *fall, bark, spot, rest,* and *back.*

OBJECTIVES

- Review words with comparative endings and *dge*/j/.
- Review high-frequency words.

Comparative Endings and *dge*/j/

REVIEW

IDENTIFY WORDS WITH COMPARATIVE ENDINGS *-er, -est* and *dge*/j/ Write these sentences. Have children read each one aloud as you track the print. Call on individuals to name and underline the words with endings *-er* and *-est* and words with /j/ at the end.

Midge will try to dodge the smallest ball.
That cat won't budge from the edge of the shorter ledge.
The biggest dish of porridge is the hottest too.
The greenest wedge of grass is by the park lodge.

High-Frequency Words

REVIEW

SAY AND SPELL WORDS Read the rhyme. Ask children to complete each line with one of the Words to Read from p. 146. Have children say, spell, and locate the word on the Word Wall. Then read the completed rhyme. Word Wall

Raccoon will have to say ________. (good-bye)
His friends ________ stay. (won't)
Oh, me. ________, my. (Oh)
They leave ________ the cold winds blow. (before)
________Raccoon cry? (Does)
Oh, no. Oh, no.
He runs ________ out to play in snow! (right)

Access Vocabulary For additional practice with the high-frequency words, use the vocabulary strategies and word cards in the ELL Teaching Guide, pp. 122–123.

SPELLING TEST Comparative Endings *-er, -est*

DICTATION SENTENCES Use these sentences to assess this week's spelling words.

1. My dog runs faster than her cat.
2. A bus is bigger than a car.
3. This line is shorter than that line.
4. She was saddest at the end of the day.
5. Madge is the fastest person in the class.
6. Does a duck swim slower than a fish?
7. Here is the shortest paper strip in the pack.
8. That is the biggest bird I've ever seen.
9. Jan looked sadder than Jim when we lost.
10. The third ant in line is the slowest.

HIGH-FREQUENCY WORDS

11. Good-bye for now.
12. Before you go, stop in to see me.

ASSESS

- Spell words with comparative endings.

Spelling Words

Adding *-er* and *-est*

1. **bigger**
2. **biggest**
3. **faster**
4. **fastest**
5. **slower**
6. **slowest**
7. **shorter***
8. **shortest**
9. **sadder**
10. **saddest***

High-Frequency Words

11. **good-bye***
12. **before***

* Words from the Selection

Group Time

On-Level

Read Set B Sentences.

- Use pp. 172e–172g.

Strategic Intervention

Read Set A Sentences and the Story.

- Use pp. 172e–172g.
- Use the **Routine** on p. D1•74.

Advanced

Read Set C Sentences.

- Use pp. 172e–172g.
- Use the **Routine** on p. D1•75.

DAY 5

ELL Place English language learners in the groups that correspond to their reading abilities in English.

Independent Activities

Fluency Reading Children reread selections at their independent level.

Journal Writing Choose an animal. Write to tell what it does in the winter. Share writing.

Independent Reading See p. 144j for Reading/Library activities and suggestions.

Literacy Centers You may use the Technology Center on p. 144k to support this week's concepts and reading.

Practice Book 1.2 Bar Graph, p. 60

Break into small groups after Spelling and before Grammar and Writing.

ASSESS

- Decode comparative endings *-er, -est* and *-dge* /j/.
- Read high-frequency words.
- Read aloud with appropriate speed and accuracy.
- Identify sequence of events.
- Retell a story.

Differentiated Assessment

Fluency Assessment Plan

- ☑ Week 1 assess Advanced students.
- ☑ Week 2 assess Strategic Intervention students.
- ☑ Week 3 assess On-Level students.
- ☑ Week 4 assess Strategic Intervention students.
- ☑ Week 5 assess any students you have not yet checked during this unit.
- ☑ **This week assess Strategic Intervention students.**

Set individual fluency goals for children to enable them to reach the end-of-year goal.

- Current Goal: 25–35 wcpm
- End-of-Year Goal: 60 wcpm
- ELL For English language learners, emphasize repeated readings to build fluency with enjoyable passages in English, with as much teacher guidance as feasible.

SENTENCE READING

ASSESS COMPARATIVE ENDINGS, *-dge* /j/, AND HIGH-FREQUENCY WORDS Use one of the reproducible lists on p. 172f to assess children's ability to read words with comparative endings, words with *-dge* /j/, and high-frequency words. Call on individuals to read two sentences aloud. Have each child in the group read different sentences. Start over with sentence one if necessary.

RECORD SCORES Use the Sentence Reading Chart for this unit on p. WA19.

Monitor Progress	Comparative Endings and *-dge* /j/
If... children have trouble reading comparative endings and *-dge* /j/.	**then...** use the Reteach Lessons on pp. DI•83–DI•84.
High-Frequency Words	
If... children cannot read a high-frequency word,	**then...** mark the missed words on a high-frequency word list and send the list home for additional word reading practice or have the child practice with a fluent reader.

FLUENCY AND COMPREHENSION

ASSESS FLUENCY Take a one-minute sample of children's oral reading. See Monitoring Fluency, pp. WA17–WA18j. Have children read "The Sweetest Yard," the on-level fluency passage on p. 172g.

RECORD SCORES Record the number of words read correctly in a minute on the child's Fluency Progress Chart.

ASSESS COMPREHENSION Have the child read to the end of the passage. (If the child had difficulty with the passage, you may read it aloud.) Ask about the sequence of events in the story and have the child retell the passage. Use the Retelling Rubric on p. 166–167 to evaluate the child's retelling.

Monitor Progress	Fluency
If... a child does not achieve the fluency goal on the timed reading,	**then...** copy the passage and send it home with the child for additional fluency practice or have the child practice with a fluent reader.
Sequence	
If... a child cannot identify the sequence of events in the story,	**then...** use the Reteach Lesson on p. DI•84.

READ THE SENTENCES

Set A

1. Cut the grass before you trim the thickest hedge.
2. The taller judge said good-bye to us.
3. Does Tad like the sweetest fudge?
4. Oh, the whitest wall has a smudge on it.
5. The bigger wedge of pie is on the right side.
6. You won't want to sit on the tallest ledge.

Set B

1. The larger horse won't walk on the edge of the cliff.
2. Ben and Jade said good-bye to the thinner judge.
3. He ate the freshest cheese wedge before lunch.
4. Oh, the smallest bird sits on the hedge every day.
5. Does the fudge get softer if it is in the sun?
6. Nudge Jake right before it is time for his hike up the shortest hill.

Set C

1. We said the pledge later in the day before the band started playing.
2. Oh, the judge said the skaters were much luckier this year than they were last year.
3. The hedge on the right is the greenest of them all.
4. The smudge won't be seen on the door because it is the darkest color on the house.
5. It was the saddest day of the week as we sat on the ledge and said good-bye.
6. Does this batch of fudge look flatter than the last batch?

The Sweetest Yard

Ted fixed up his yard. First, he planted a hedge. 10
This one is greener than the last one. It is also 21
taller. The hedge is on the sunny side of the 31
house. 32

Then, he planted three trees. The largest is in 41
the backyard. The smallest is on one side of the 51
house. 52

Next, he put in roses. These roses are the 61
reddest I have ever seen. They are in the yard 71
by the porch. 74

Last, he dug around the edge of the sidewalk. 83
He put in some plants that grow slower than 92
others. 93

Let's make me the judge. I say Ted's yard is 103
the finest on the block. 108

See also *Assessment Handbook*, p. 270 • REPRODUCIBLE PAGE

Write Now

Writing and Grammar

Read Together

Song

Prompt

In *Where Are My Animal Friends?*, animals get ready for winter in different ways. Think about what the animals do. Now write a song that tells what the animals don't do.

Writing Trait

Like a story, a song can have **sentences.**

Student Model

In Winter

Caterpillars don't fly away.
A bear doesn't work all day.
Robins aren't here to stay.

Song names three animals.

Rhyming words are at the end of lines.

Sentences in song end with periods.

Writer's Checklist

- **Focus** Does the song follow the prompt?
- **Organization** Does word order make sense?
- **Support** Does the song have rhyming words?
- **Conventions** Do sentences begin with capital letters?

Grammar

Contractions with Not

A **contraction** is a short way to put two words together. A **verb** and the word **not** can make a contraction. An **apostrophe (')** is used in place of the letter **o** in **not.**

are + not = **aren't**   do + not = **don't**

has + not = **hasn't**   does + not = **doesn't**

Write the contractions in the song. Write two words that make each contraction.

Writing and Grammar

LOOK AT THE PROMPT Read p. 172 aloud. Have children select and discuss key words or phrases in the prompt. *(animals get ready for winter, song, what the animals* *don't* *do)*

STRATEGIES TO DEVELOP SENTENCES Have children

- look through the selection and find examples of statements and questions.
- choose statements in the selection and rewrite them as questions.
- write statements and questions and then trade papers with a partner to check each other's capitalization and end punctuation.

See Scoring Rubric on p. WA12. Rubric 4 3 2 1

HINTS FOR BETTER WRITING Read p. 173 aloud. Use the checklist to help children revise their songs. Discuss the grammar lesson. (Answers: *don't, do not; doesn't, does not; aren't; are not*) Provide other contractions: was + not = wasn't; were not = weren't; did + not = didn't; is + not = isn't. Have children use contractions with *not* correctly in their songs.

DAILY FIX-IT

9. this animal is the bigger of all. (This; biggest)

10. yesterday some toads hop around. (Yesterday; hopped)

Contractions with *Not*

Draw a line from the words to their contraction.

1. are not	doesn't
2. did not	wasn't
3. do not	hasn't
4. does not	aren't
5. has not	weren't
6. is not	didn't
7. was not	don't
8. were not	isn't

Write the contraction for the underlined words.

9. A bear does not eat all winter. **doesn't**

10. Bears do not wake up until spring. **don't**

11. Squirrels are not going away. **aren't**

12. The squirrel was not in its nest. **wasn't**

Home Activity Your child reviewed contractions with *not*. Have your child write contractions with *not* on one side of index cards and the words for each contraction on the other side. Use the flash cards to test your child.

▲ **Grammar and Writing Practice Book** p. 72

OBJECTIVE

- Create and read a bar graph.

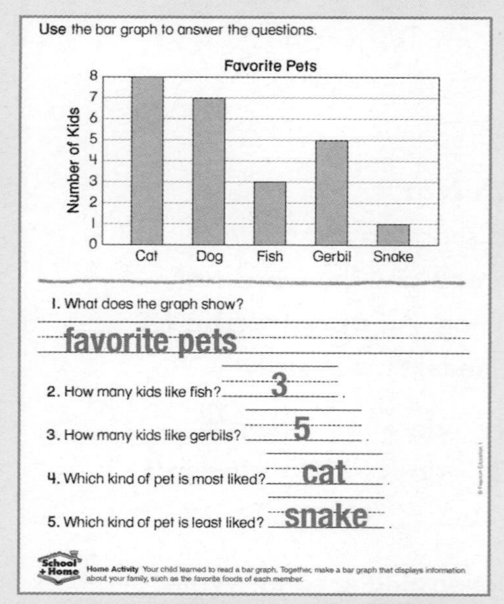
Use the bar graph to answer the questions.

1. What does the graph show? favorite pets
2. How many kids like fish? 3
3. How many kids like gerbils? 5
4. Which kind of pet is most liked? cat
5. Which kind of pet is least liked? snake

▲ **Practice Book 1.2** p. 60, Bar Graph

ELL

Access Content As you introduce the parts, show children where they are on a real bar graph. For example: These are the bars. They show numbers or amounts.

Research/Study Skills

TEACH/MODEL Graphs: Bar Graph

MODEL READING A BAR GRAPH Find an example of a bar graph in the children's math or social studies textbook. Ask all children to refer to the same graph.

Model how to read the graph.

Think Aloud **MODEL** I know that a bar graph uses bars (or lines) to compare amounts. The bars can go up and down or across the page. First I read the title to find out what the graph is about. Next I read the information that tells what the bars represent. To read the graph, I find the number that lines up with the end of a bar.

OUR FAVORITE ANIMALS GRAPH Take a class poll about favorite animals. Make a list of some animals in the story *Where Are My Animal Friends?* Include *raccoon*, *bear*, *squirrel*, *goose*, and *hummingbird*. Have children vote on their favorite animal from the list. Use tally marks to record each vote. With the class, create a bar graph that shows the results.

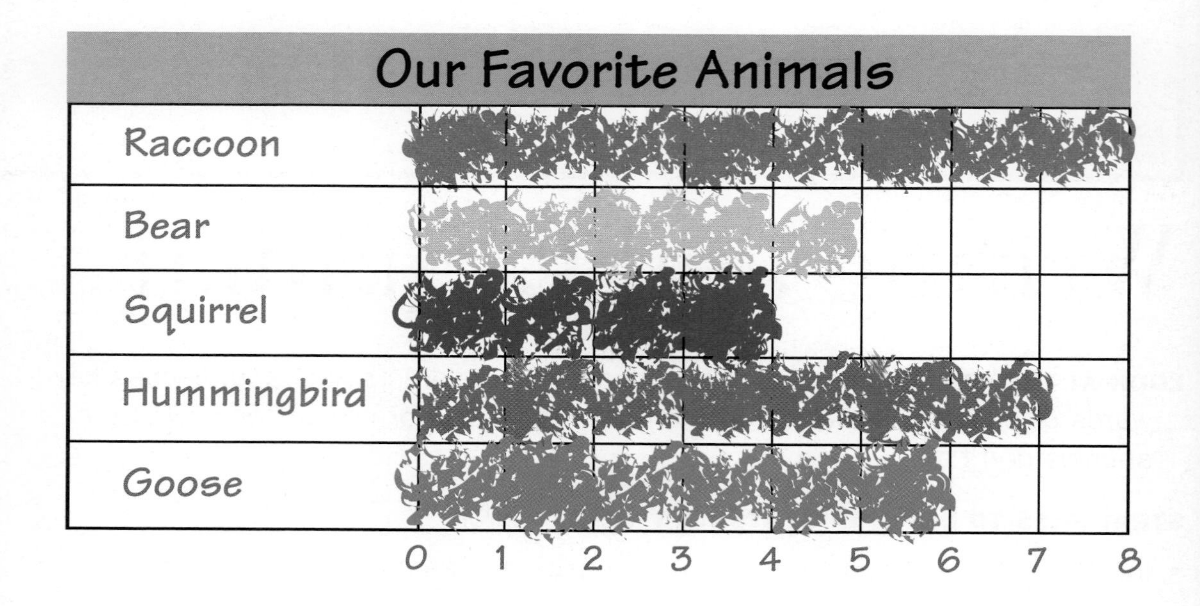

PRACTICE

ANALYZE THE GRAPH Have children work in groups to analyze the information in the graph and decide upon two or three facts that they can find using the graph. Invite groups to present their findings to the class.

Wrap Up Your Week!

LET'S TALK ABOUT Changes in Nature

QUESTION OF THE WEEK Recall this week's question.

- How does nature change during the year?

Display the Seasons sorting boxes from Day 1. Discuss ways changes in nature happen over and over. Have children draw an outdoor scene that takes place during their favorite season.

Spring	Summer
Flowers bloom in spring. It rains a lot. The weather starts to get warm. Birds build nests and baby birds hatch.	The weather is hot. We can swim. Trees and grass are green. Birds and animals live and eat.
Fall	**Winter**
The weather starts to get cooler. Leaves turn colors and fall. Some birds fly to warm places. Some animals store food for winter. Some animals get ready to hibernate.	The weather is cold. It might snow. We have to wear coats. Some animals have gone away. Some animals hibernate.

CONNECT Use questions such as these to prompt a discussion.

- How do plants and animals change in autumn?
- Can you name some animals that hibernate in the winter season?
- If the temperature is bitter, would things freeze or get hot?

ELL

Build Background Use ELL Poster 19 to support the Preview activity.

You've learned

this week!

You've learned

so far this year!

PREVIEW Tell children that next week they will read about a surprise that a boy plans for a family member.

PREVIEW Next Week

5

Assessment Checkpoints *for the Week*

Selection Assessment

Use pp. 45–48 of Selection Tests to check:

 **Selection Understanding**

 **Comprehension Skill** *Sequence*

 **High-Frequency Words**

before *right*
does *want*
good-bye
oh

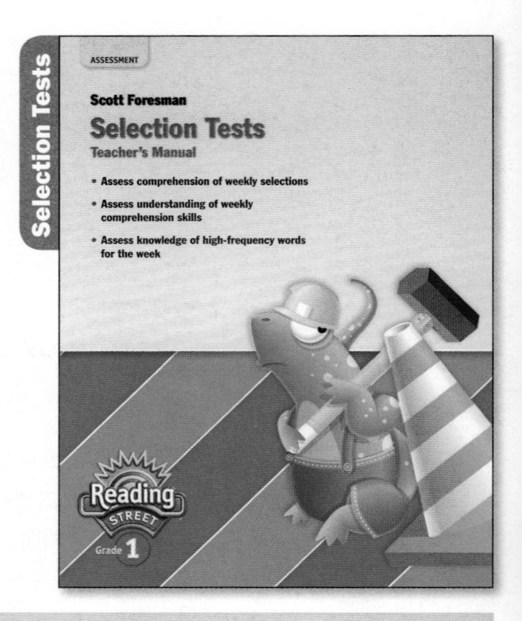

Leveled Assessment

On-Level

Strategic Intervention

Advanced

Use pp. 103–108 of Fresh Reads for Differentiated Test Practice to check:

 **Comprehension Skill** *Sequence*

 REVIEW **Comprehension Skill** *Compare and Contrast*

 **Fluency** *Words Correct Per Minute*

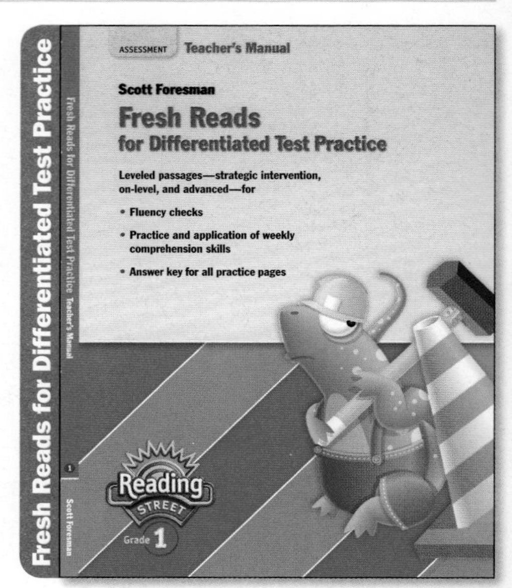

Managing Assessment

Use Assessment Handbook for:

 **Weekly Assessment Blackline Masters for Monitoring Progress**

 **Observation Checklists**

 **Record-Keeping Forms**

 **Portfolio Assessment**

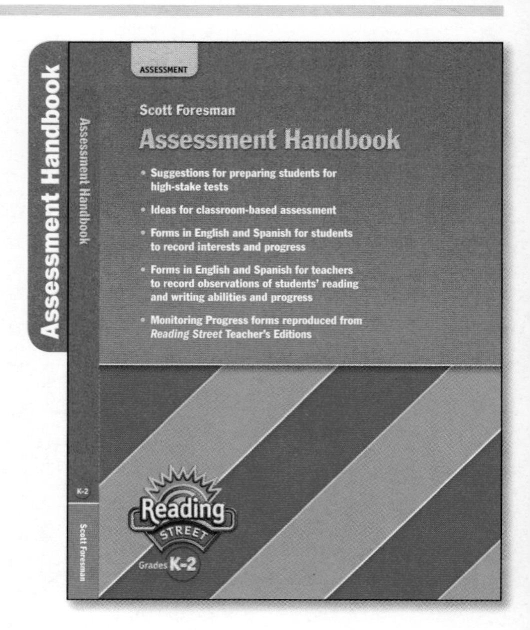

Unit 3

Concept Wrap-Up

CONCEPT QUESTION

What is changing in our world?

Children are ready to express their understanding of the unit concept question through discussion and wrap-up activities and to take the Unit 3 Benchmark Test.

Unit Wrap-Up

Use the Unit Wrap-Up on pp. 174–175 to discuss the unit theme, Changes, and to have children show their understanding of the theme through cross-curricular activities.

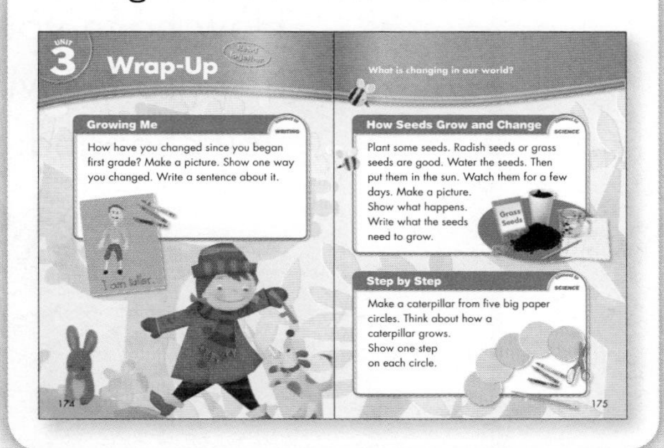

Unit Project

On p. 9, you assigned children a unit-long inquiry project, a journal that documents changes they see. Children have investigated, analyzed, and synthesized information during the course of the unit as they prepared their journals. Schedule time for children to present their projects. The project rubric can be found below.

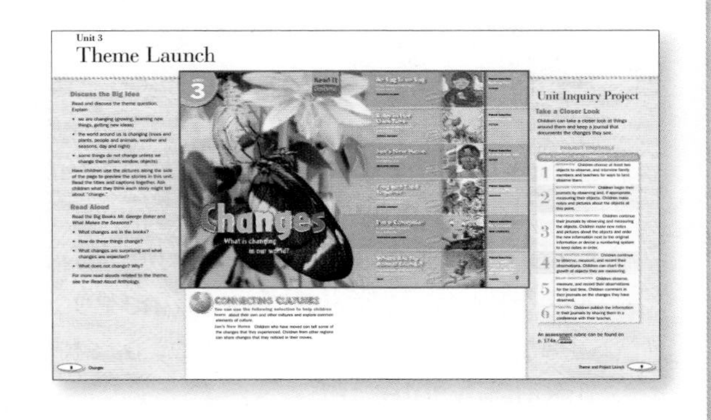

Unit Inquiry Project Rubric

4	3	2	1
• Journals are well organized with observations and measurements of the same object grouped together or ordered in some way. • Observations and measurements are accurate and highly detailed.	• Journals are organized with most observations and measurements of the same object grouped together or ordered in some way. • Observations and measurements are mostly accurate and somewhat detailed.	• Journals are organized with some observations and measurements of the same object grouped together or ordered. • Few observations and measurements are accurate and detailed.	• Journals are not organized. No observations and measurements of the same object are grouped together. • No observations or measurements are accurate or detailed.

Unit 3

Wrap-Up

OBJECTIVES

- Discuss the unit theme.
- Connect content across selections.
- Combine content and skills in meaningful activities that build literacy.
- Respond to unit selections through a variety of modalities.

CHANGES

Discuss the Big Idea

What is changing in our world?

Help children relate the theme question for this unit to the selections and their own experiences. Write the question and prompt discussion with questions such as the following. Then assign the Wrap-Up activities.

- **What changes happened in this unit?** (Possible answers: *An Egg Is an Egg* An egg, branch, seed, block, seasons, tea, people, day, and baby changed. *Ruby in Her Own Time* Ruby grew. *Jan's New Home* Jan moved to the city. *Frog and Toad Together* The seeds grew. *I'm a Caterpillar* The caterpillar became a butterfly. *Where Are My Animal Friends?* Trees and seasons changed; animals flew away or slept through winter.)
- **What did not change?** (Possible answers: *An Egg Is an Egg* The boy will always be his mother's baby. *Ruby in Her Own Time* Ruby came back. *Jan's New Home* Jan's bed is the same. *Frog and Toad Together* Frog and Toad's friendship is the same. *I'm a Caterpillar* The cycle began again. *Where Are My Animal Friends?* Raccoon and Squirrel stayed.)
- **Tell about how you changed when you were a baby. Do all babies change in the same way?** (Answers will vary.)

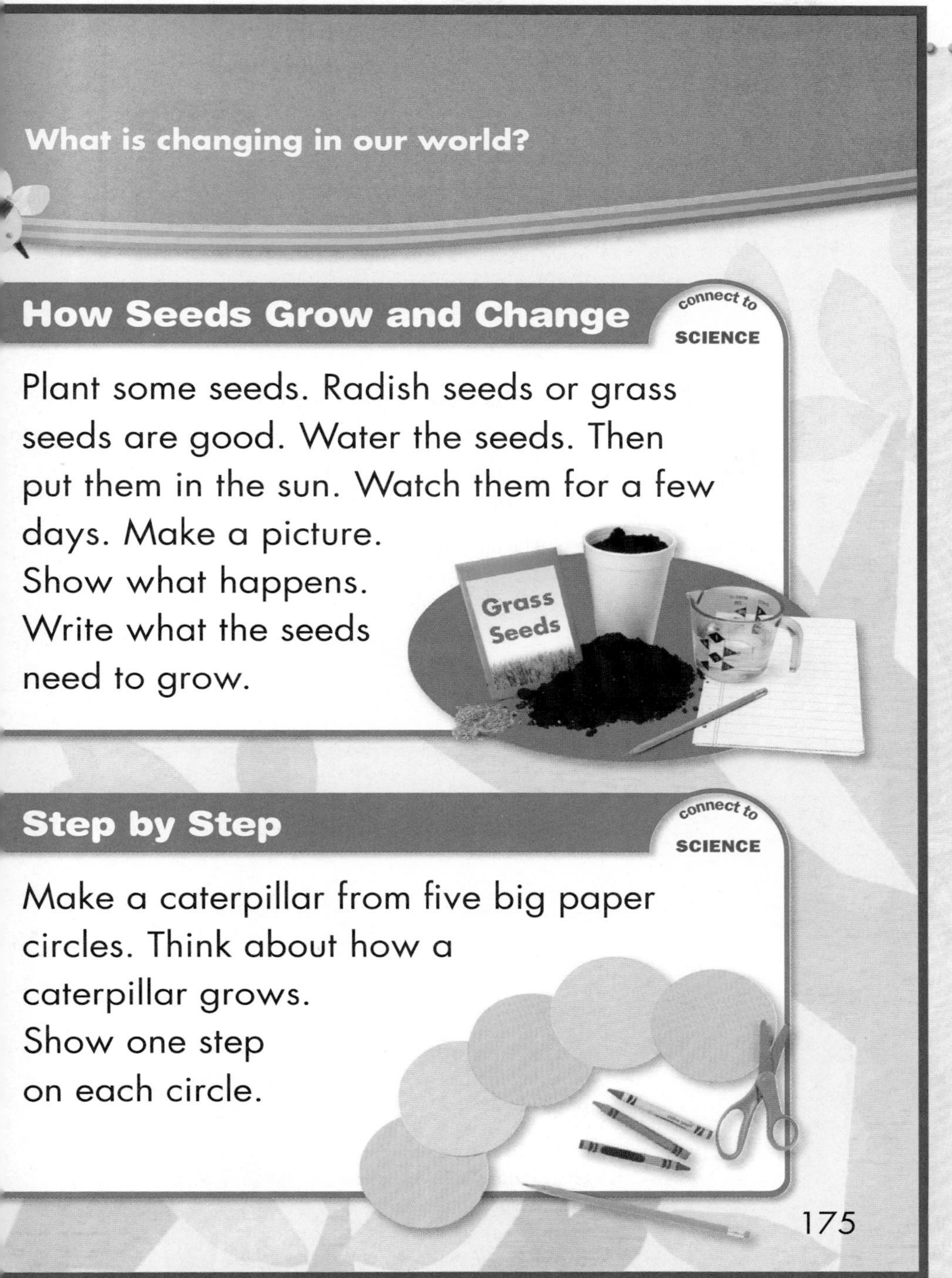
What is changing in our world?

How Seeds Grow and Change

connect to SCIENCE

Plant some seeds. Radish seeds or grass seeds are good. Water the seeds. Then put them in the sun. Watch them for a few days. Make a picture. Show what happens. Write what the seeds need to grow.

Step by Step

connect to SCIENCE

Make a caterpillar from five big paper circles. Think about how a caterpillar grows. Show one step on each circle.

175

ACTIVITIES

Growing Me

Trace Their Steps Have children stand as if taking a step on a large sheet of paper, and trace around their feet. Have children color in their footprints and write their names nearby. Post the paper in the classroom wall and title it "Step by Step, We Are Changing." Use the display to prompt a discussion about how children are changing. Then have children write and draw about a change.

How Seeds Grow and Change

Point and Tell Discuss how plants grow from seeds. Take the children on a schoolyard walk and make a class list of all the things they see that grew from seeds. Then work together to plant some seeds.

Step by Step

Act It Out Recall *I'm a Caterpillar* in which the caterpillar went through the stages to become a butterfly. Invite children to act out the stages as you recount them together. Encourage children to use the cycle diagram on Student Edition p. 137 to help them fill in the circles on their caterpillars.

Glossary

Glossary

Bb

beautiful If something is **beautiful,** it is very pretty to see or hear. After the rain stopped, it became a **beautiful,** sunny day.

boy A **boy** is a male child. A **boy** grows up to be a man.

boy

Cc

caterpillar A **caterpillar** is an insect that looks like a furry worm. **Caterpillars** turn into moths or butterflies.

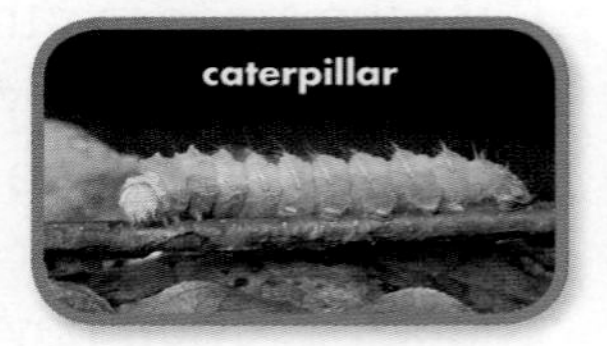

caterpillar

chrysalis A caterpillar becomes a **chrysalis** when it grows a hard shell around itself.

chrysalis

crawl When you **crawl**, you move on your hands and knees or with your body close to the ground. Worms, snakes, and lizards **crawl.**

Ff

father A **father** is a man who has a child or children.

feather A **feather** is one of the light, soft things that cover a bird's body.

feather

flew The bird **flew** away. We **flew** to New York in an airplane.

Gg

goose A **goose** is a large bird with a long neck. A **goose** looks like a duck but is larger.

goose

grew The grass **grew** very fast from all the rain.

ground The **ground** is the soil or dirt on the surface of the Earth. The **ground** was rocky.

Hh

head Your **head** is the top part of your body or the front part of most animals' bodies. Your **head** is where your eyes, ears, nose, mouth, and brain are.

head

Mm

mother A **mother** is a woman who has a child or children.

mother

move To **move** means to change the place where you live. We live in the city now, but my parents want to **move** to the country.

Nn

night **Night** is the time between evening and morning.

night

Pp

precious **Precious** means having great value. Mom's ring is very **precious** to her.

precious

pupa The **pupa** is the form of an insect while it is changing from a wormlike larva into an adult.

Rr

raccoon A **raccoon** is a small animal with thick fur. Its tail is long and has rings of a different color. **Raccoons** look for food at night.

raccoon

rain

rain **Rain** is the water that falls in drops from the clouds. The **rain** made us all wet as we walked home from school.

Ss

shiver To **shiver** is to shake.

shouted When you have **shouted,** you have called out or yelled loudly. She **shouted** for help.

shouting

shouting When you are **shouting,** you are calling or yelling.

spring **Spring** is the season of the year between winter and summer. **Spring** is the season when plants begin to grow.

sunset **Sunset** is the time when the sun is last seen in the evening.

sunset

Tt

tower

tower A **tower** is a tall building or part of a building. A **tower** may stand alone or may be a part of a church, castle, or other building.

toys **Toys** are things to play with. Dolls, blocks, and teddy bears are **toys.**

toys

Ww

warm If something is **warm,** it is more hot than cold. The water is **warm** enough to swim in. He sat in the **warm** sunshine.

window A **window** is an opening in a wall or roof. A **window** lets in light or fresh air.

window

Acknowledgments

Tested Words

An Egg Is an Egg

always
become
day
everything
nothing
stays
things

Jan's New Home

away
car
friends
house
our
school
very

Ruby in Her Own Time

any
enough
ever
every
own
sure
were

Frog and Toad Together

afraid
again
few
how
read
soon

184

185

Tested Words

I'm a Caterpillar

done
know
push
visit
wait

Where Are My Animal Friends?

before
does
good-bye
oh
right
won't

186

Acknowledgments

Text

Page 14: From *An Egg Is an Egg* by Nicki Weiss, copyright © 1990 by Monica J. Weiss. Used by permission G.P. Putnam's Sons, A Division of Penguin Young Readers Group, A Member of Penguin Group (USA) Inc., 345 Hudson Street, New York, NY 10014. All rights reserved.

Page 40: *Ruby in Her Own Time* by Jonathan Emmett, illustrated by Rebecca Horry. Text copyright © 2003 by Jonathan Emmett, illustration copyright © 2003 by Rebecca Harry. Reprinted by permission of Scholastic Inc.

Page 96: "The Garden" from *Frog and Toad Together* by Arnold Lobel. Used by permission of HarperCollins Publishers.

Page 122: From *I'm A Caterpillar* by Jean Marzollo, illustrated by Judith Moffat. A Hello Science Reader! Book published by Cartwheel Books/Scholastic Inc. Text copyright © 1997 by Jean Marzollo, illustrations copyright © 1997 by Judith Moffat. Reprinted by permission. Hello Reader and Cartwheel Books are registered trademarks of Scholastic Inc.

Page 168: "This Tooth" by Lee Bennett Hopkins. Copyright © 1970 by Lee Bennett Hopkins. First appeared in *ME!*, published by Seabury Press. Reprinted by permission of Curtis Brown, Ltd.

Page **169:** "Tommy" by Gwendolyn Brooks. Reprinted by consent of Brooks Permission.

Page 170: "Where Do Fish Go In Winter?", from *Where fish Go in Winter And Other great Mysteries* by Amy Goldman Koss, copyright © 1987, by Amy Goldman Koss, text. Illustrated by Laura J. Bryant, copyright © 2002 by Laura J. Bryant, illustrations. Used by permission of Dial Books for Young Readers, A Division of Penguin Young Readers Group, A Member of Penguin Group (USA) Inc., 345 Hudson Street, New York, NY 10014. All rights reserved.

Illustrations

Cover: Daniel Moreton

11-27, 34-35, 174-175 Julia Woolf; **30-33** Mary Bono; **68** Steven Mach; **69-85, 90-91** Don Tate; **145-163, 173** Scott Gustafson; **164-165** Courtesy David Diaz

Photographs

Every effort has been made to secure permission and provide appropriate credit for photographic material. The publisher deeply regrets any omission and pledges to correct errors called to its attention in subsequent editions.

Unless otherwise acknowledged, all photographs are the property of Scott Foresman, a division of Pearson Education.

Photo locators denoted as follows: Top (T), Center (C), Bottom (B), Left (L), Right (R), Background (Bkgd).

8 ©Michael & Patricia Fogden/Corbis, (Bkgd) ©Clay Perry/Corbis

10 ©Ariel Skelley/Corbis

11 (T) ©Kevin Dodge/Masterfile Corporation, (BL) ©Michael Newman/PhotoEdit

29 ©Nicki Weiss

36 (BC) Digital Vision, (BL) ©Jim Craigmyle/Corbis, (BR) ©Tom & Dee Ann McCarthy/Corbis

37 (BL) ©Royalty-Free/Corbis, (BR) ©Janette Beckman/Corbis

64 (CR, CL) ©Ariel Skelley/Corbis

69 (CL) Getty Images, (TR) Tom & Dee Ann McCarthy/Corbis

92 ©Frank Cruz/Index Stock Imagery

93 (TL) ©Ben Weaver/Getty Images, (CR) ©Roger Ball/Corbis

114 Dave King/©DK Images

115 (CL) ©D. Boone/Corbis, (BL) ©William Taufic/Corbis

118 (CC) ©John Isaac/Getty Images, (CL, BC, CR) ©DK Images

119 (TL, TR, CC) ©DK Images, (TC) Frank Greenaway/©DK Images

121 (TR) ©John Mason (JLMO)/Ardea, (CC) ©Richard Cummins/Corbis

144 ©Ted Horowitz/Corbis

145 (T) ©LWA-Dann Tardif/Corbis, (C) ©James L. Amos/Corbis, (B) ©Carol Fuegi/Corbis

176 (TL) Rubberball Productions, (B) Digital Vision

177 (TR) Getty Images, (BL) Hemera Technologies

178 Hemera Technologies

179 (BC) Getty Images, (TR) Rubberball Productions

180 (TR) Hemera Technologies, (CR) ©Royalty-Free/Corbis, (BL) Ghislain & Marie David de Lossy/Image Bank/Getty Images

182 (L, CC, CL) Hemera Technologies, (CR, TR) Getty Images

183 (C) Getty Images

Glossary

The contents of this glossary have been adapted from *First Dictionary*. Copyright © 2000, Pearson Education, Inc.

187

Writing

Writing Trait of the Week

Writing Workshop

Rubrics

Rubric 4 3 2 1

Assessment

Assessment

Student Tips for Making Top Scores in Writing Tests

1. **Use words such as these to connect ideas, sentences, or paragraphs.**

first	last	before	now
next	finally	after	then

2. **Write a good beginning. Make readers want to read more.**
   - I peeked in the room and screamed.
   - Never try to mess with an angry bee.
   - When I was four, I saw a purple dog.
   - Have you ever heard of a talking tree?

3. **Focus on the topic.**
   If a word or sentence is not about the topic, get rid of it.

4. **Organize your ideas.**
   Have a plan in mind before you start writing. Your plan can be a list or a web. Your writing will go faster if you spend time planning first.

5. **Support your ideas.**
   - Use examples and details to make your ideas clear.
   - Use vivid words that create pictures.
   - Try not to use dull *(get, go, say),* unclear *(thing, stuff, lots of),* or overused *(really, very)* words.
   - Use a voice that your readers will understand.

6. **Make writing conventions as error-free as possible.**
   Proofread your work carefully. Read it three times. Look for correct punctuation, then capitalization, and finally spelling.

7. **Write an ending that wraps things up. "The end" is not a good ending.**
   - That's why I don't eat grapes anymore.
   - I still think Chip is the best cat ever.
   - My bedroom was never the same again.
   - Next time I'll wear my raincoat.

Focus/Ideas
Organization/ Paragraphs
Voice
Word Choice
Sentences
Conventions

Writing Traits

- **Focus/Ideas** refers to the main purpose for writing and the details that make the subject clear and interesting. It includes development of ideas through support and elaboration.
- **Organization/Paragraphs** refers to the overall structure of a piece of writing that guides readers. Within that structure, transitions show how ideas, sentences, and paragraphs are connected.
- **Voice** shows the writer's unique personality and establishes a connection between writer and reader. Voice, which contributes to style, should be suited to the audience and the purpose for writing.
- **Word Choice** is the use of precise, vivid words to communicate effectively and naturally. It helps create style through the use of specific nouns, lively verbs and adjectives, and accurate, well-placed modifiers.
- **Sentences** covers strong, well-built sentences that vary in length and type. Skillfully written sentences have pleasing rhythms and flow fluently.
- **Conventions** refers to mechanical correctness and includes grammar, usage, spelling, punctuation, capitalization, and paragraphing.

Description

OBJECTIVES

- Develop an understanding of descriptive writing.
- Use sensory words and strong details in a description.
- Use processes and strategies that good writers use.

Key Features

Description

A good description helps readers visualize what the writer is describing.

- Creates a picture of a person, place, or thing
- Uses words that appeal to our senses
- Elaborates with strong details

Connect to Weekly Writing

Writing Transparencies 13–18

Strategic Intervention

See Differentiated Instruction p. WA8.

Advanced

See Differentiated Instruction p. WA9.

See Differentiated Instruction p. WA9.

Additional Resource for Writing
Writing Rubrics and Anchor Papers, pp. 14–17

Writing Prompt: Changes
Think of a place or a thing in nature. It might be a park, a tree, or a season. Write a paragraph that describes the place or thing. Tell how it looks, sounds, smells, tastes, or feels.
Purpose: Describe
Audience: A classmate

READ LIKE A WRITER

Ask children to look back at *Jan's New Home.* Remind them that the writer describes what Jan and her parents see in the country and in the city. Read aloud those parts of the story. Tell children that they will write a description of something in nature.

SHOW THE MODEL AND RUBRIC

GUIDED WRITING Read the model aloud. Point out the strong action verbs. (*pours, flashes, booms, hurts*)

- Read the title and the opening sentence. Point out that the writer tells readers what he will describe.
- Explain that the writer uses details that help readers see, hear, and feel the storm. Read aloud examples of these details.
- Discuss how the model reflects traits of good writing.

A Big Storm

A big storm is noisy. The rain pours down. The lightning flashes. It makes a crack in the sky. The thunder booms. The sound hurts my ears. Then the storm moves on and it is quiet again.

Unit 3 Description • PREWRITE — Writing Process 13

▲ **Writing Transparency** WP13

Traits of a Good Description

Focus/Ideas	Description sticks to topic and gives details.
Order/ Paragraphs	Writer introduces topic in title and opening sentence. Storm events are described in order.
Voice	Description is lively and interesting. Writer likes the topic.
Word Choice	Writer uses good adjectives (*noisy, quiet*) and action words (*pours, flashes, booms, hurts*).
Sentences	Sentences are complete.
Rules	Writer uses good grammar and capitalization.

Unit 3 Description • PREWRITE — Writing Process 14

▲ **Writing Transparency** WP14

IDING A TOPIC

T THROUGH MEMORIES Suggest ıat children look through photo ıbums and journals and brain-torm with friends and family ıembers about places or things ı nature that children have seen. :hildren can also draw pictures of hings in nature to generate ideas.

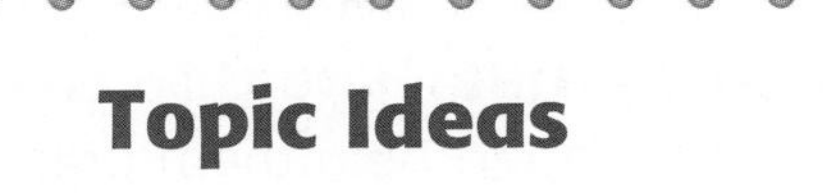

Topic Ideas

visit to natural history museum
fall leaves
hurricanes

RROW THE CHOICE Have children ısk questions about the ideas they have chosen. They might ask: What do remember about this place or thing? Do I know enough details to write a ;ood description of it?

MODEL The topic is a place or a thing in nature. The visit to the natural history museum doesn't fit the topic. I don't think I know enough about hurricanes. I couldn't describe them very well. I do know about trees in fall. I can think of many details about their leaves.

REWRITING STRATEGY

E A DETAILS WEB Use Writing Transparency WP15 to show how to organize the details for a description.

MODEL The topic that the writer chose, fall leaves, is in the center of the web. Around the center are details about fall leaves. These details show how the fall leaves look, sound, and feel. The writer will use the details to create a picture of fall leaves for readers.

REWRITING ACTIVITY Have children use the Details Web graphic organizer on Grammar and Writing Practice Book p. 159 to help them organize their details.

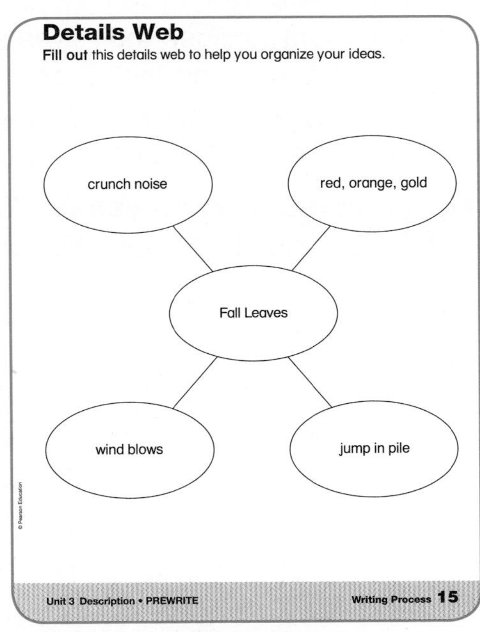

Details Web

Fill out this details web to help you organize your ideas.

Unit 3 Description • PREWRITE — Writing Process 15

▲ **Writing Transparency** WP15

Monitor Progress

Differentiated Instruction

If... children have trouble thinking of a topic,	**then...** ask them what ideas their friends and family members suggested and list the ideas on the board.

Guided Writing

Some children will need additional guidance as they plan and write their descriptions. You might give these children the option of writing a group description under your supervision or pair them with a more able writer.

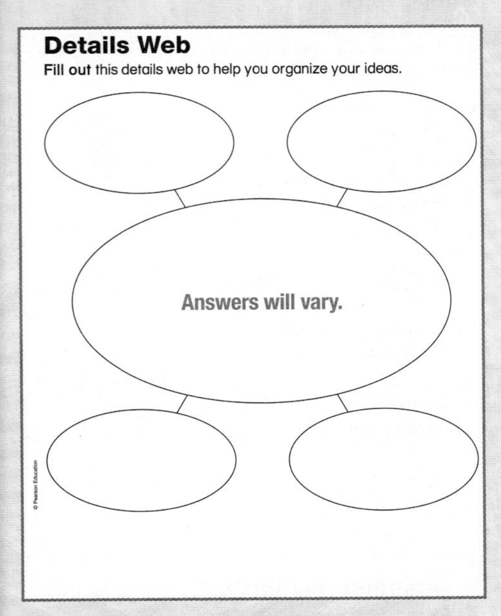

Details Web

Fill out this details web to help you organize your ideas.

▲ **Grammar and Writing Practice Book** p. 159

Think Like a Writer

Brainstorm Details Start by writing as many details about your topic as you can. Write *See, Hear, Smell, Taste,* and *Feel* as headings and write the details under the headings. Then when you can't think of any more details, look at what you have written. Choose the best details in each group to use in your description.

Support Writing Invite children to talk with you about what they plan to write. Record key words and ideas they mention and help them generate language for other key words and ideas. See the ELL and Transition Handbook for additional strategies that support the writing process.

Strong Verbs

Look at the verbs in dark type.
Which sentence in each pair has a stronger verb?
Underline the sentence.

1. The boys **race** to the park.
   The boys **go** to the park.
2. Dan **says**, "Look at me!"
   Dan **shouts**, "Look at me!"

3. She **put** flowers in the garden.
   She **planted** flowers in the garden.
4. Ann **cuts** a rose from the bush.
   Ann **gets** a rose from the bush.

5. They **make** a birdhouse.
   They **build** a birdhouse.

▲ **Grammar and Writing Practice Book** p. 160

WRITING THE FIRST DRAFT

GUIDED WRITING Have children review their Details Web to help them organize details as they write their first drafts. Remind them to do the following.

- Include details that appeal to readers' senses.
- Use strong verbs and good describing words.
- Create a picture in readers' minds.
- Introduce the topic in the title and the opening sentence.

Strong Verbs

run
walk
skip
ride
march
hurry

ELABORATING WITH STRONG VERBS List the strong verbs on the board. Explain that these verbs can be used in place of the weak verb *go.* Point out that strong verbs create a vivid picture for reader Say this sentence: *The girls go to school.* Then say the sentence replacing *go* with each strong verb. Ask children what they picture the girls doing when the hear each sentence.

DRAFTING STRATEGIES

WRITE WHAT YOU SEE Have children visualize the place or thing they have chosen. Ask them to close their eyes and to picture in their minds what they see, hear, smell, taste, and feel. In the first draft, they should get their ideas on paper quickly. They can worry about spelling and punctuation later. Once they have written their ideas, have them write a draft using complete sentences.

PRACTICE USING STRONG VERBS Have children use Grammar and Writing Practice Book p. 160 to practice using strong verbs.

VISING STRATEGIES

ED WRITING Use Writing ansparency WP16 to model how revise a description.

Think Aloud **MODEL** The title and the first sentence tell what the writer will describe. The details help eaders see, hear, and feel the leaves. he writer took out the detail that does ot tell about fall leaves. I like the trong verbs *crunch, jump,* and *blow.* he writer added another strong verb, *akes,* to replace the weak verb, *puts.* he writer also added a describing vord *(cool).* That helps readers feel the vind.

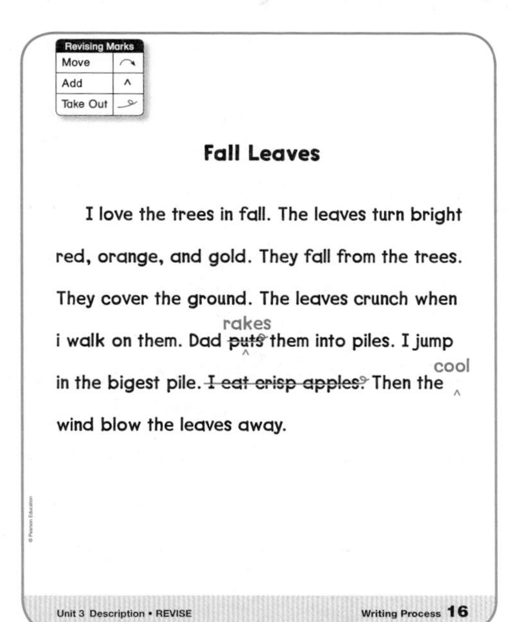

Revising Marks	
Move	⌒
Add	^
Take Out	~~e~~

Fall Leaves

I love the trees in fall. The leaves turn bright red, orange, and gold. They fall from the trees. They cover the ground. The leaves crunch when i walk on them. Dad ~~puts~~ rakes them into piles. I jump in the bigest pile. ~~I eat crisp apples.~~ Then the cool wind blow the leaves away.

Unit 3 Description • REVISE   Writing Process 16

▲ **Writing Transparency** WP16

Revising Checklist

- ✔ Does my description stay focused on my topic?
- ✔ Have I used strong verbs?
- ✔ Have I included describing words?
- ✔ Did I make a picture in readers' minds?

Extend Language To help children add strong verbs to their writing, work with them to develop word webs with a weak verb in the center and around it strong verbs that can replace it. Encourage children to use a picture dictionary, if available, to find strong verbs.

WRITER'S CRAFT Focus/Ideas

ELABORATION Remind children that when they write about a topic, all their sentences should be about that topic. Write the sentences below on the board. Ask children to explain which sentence does not belong and why it does not belong.

Which sentence does not belong?

A hen lays an egg.

~~The rooster crows loudly.~~

A chick hatches from the egg.

Writing Trait: Focus/Ideas

Which sentence in each group does NOT belong?
Draw a line through the sentence.

1. Many flowers bloom in spring.
   Flowers can be many colors.
   ~~My favorite color is blue.~~
   Some flowers bloom in summer.

2. Andy is six years old.
   ~~My name is Beth.~~
   He can ride a bike.
   He can write his name.

Finish the sentence below.
Write another sentence about this idea.

I can

Possible answers: I can make my bed. I can also tie my shoes.

▲ **Grammar and Writing Practice Book** p. 161

DDITIONAL SUPPORT Point out how taking out the sentence that was not about the topic improves the writing model on Writing Transparency WP16.

Jse Grammar and Writing Practice Book p. 161 to improve focus/ideas.

PPLY WRITER'S CRAFT Have children examine focus/ideas in their writing.

- Encourage them to take out details that do not tell about their topic.
- Write the Revising Checklist on the board or make copies to distribute. Children can use this checklist to revise their descriptions.

Monitor Progress

Differentiated Instruction

If...	**then...**
children have trouble knowing when to use *am, is, are, was,* and *were,*	review the grammar lesson on p. 119d.

EDITING STRATEGY

READ YOUR WORK ALOUD Suggest that children read their work aloud to help them find errors. Explain that sometimes it is easier to find errors when we hear them. Model this strategy using Writing Transparency WP17.

MODEL I will read this description aloud as I look for errors. I see that the word *i* should be capitalized in the fifth sentence. I also see that the word *bigest* is misspelled in the seventh sentence. It should be *biggest*. When I read the last sentence aloud, something doesn't sound right. The verb *blow* needs an *-s* at the end because it tells what one thing, the wind, does. Reading aloud helped me find that mistake.

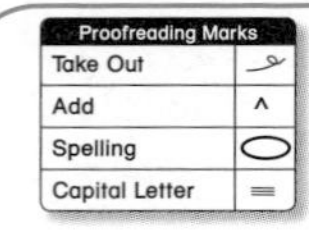

Proofreading Marks	
Take Out	⌐
Add	^
Spelling	○
Capital Letter	≡

Fall Leaves

I love the trees in fall. The leaves turn brigh red, orange, and gold. They fall from the trees They cover the ground. The leaves crunch when i walk on them. Dad ~~puts~~ rakes them into piles. I jump in the (bigest) biggest pile. ~~I eat crisp apples.~~ Then the wind blow^s the leaves away.

Unit 3 Description • EDIT Writing Process 17

▲ **Writing Transparency** WP17

Write the Editing Checklist on the board or make copies to distribute. Children can use this checklist to edit their descriptions. They can also use a dictionary to verify spelling.

Editing Checklist

- ✔Did I spell words correctly, including those with *-er* and *-est?*
- ✔Did I add *-s* to verbs that tell what one person, animal, or thing does?
- ✔Does each sentence begin with a capital letter and end with a punctuation mark?

Tech Talk ONLINE If children are using a computer to type their description, they may find these tips useful.

- When you have questions about how to do something on the computer, ask friend or use the Help menu.
- You can set margins, line lengths, borders, shading, paragraph indents for the first sentence of a paragraph, and other features using the Format menu

Support Writing When reviewing a child's draft, focus on ideas more than errors. Keep in mind that a consistent grammatical error may reflect the writing conventions of the home language. Choose one or two skills, and use the appropriate Grammar Transition lessons in the ELL and Transition Handbook to explicitly teach English conventions.

_F-EVALUATION

ɔare children to fill out a Self-
uation Guide. Display Writing
ısparency WP18 to model the self-
luation process.

Think Aloud **MODEL** My sentences all tell about the topic. I have used good action and describing vords. I would mark *Yes* for numbers ., 2, and 3. My favorite part is about he leaves crunching. If I wrote this lescription again, I would add that Aom wets some leaves and puts them ɔn the flower bed. That protects it over he winter.

sign Grammar and Writing Practice ok p. 162. Children can save ɜir Self-Evaluation Guides and their work in a portfolio to monitor their velopment as writers. Encourage them to build on their skills and note eas to improve.

Fall Leaves

I love the trees in fall. The leaves turn bright red, orange, and gold. They fall from the trees. They cover the ground. The leaves crunch when I walk on them. Dad rakes them into piles. I jump in the biggest pile. Then the cool wind blows the leaves away.

Unit 3 Description • PUBLISH Writing Process **18**

▲ **Writing Transparency** WP18

Ideas for Publishing

Writer's Circle Children can read aloud their descriptions in small groups. Classmates may ask questions about the descriptions.

Nature Display Children can draw or find pictures to go with their descriptions. Post both on a bulletin board.

Self-Evaluation Guide

Check *Yes* or *No* about focus/ideas in your description.

	Yes	No
1. All my sentences tell about my topic.		
2. I used one or more action words.		
3. I used one or more describing words.		

Answer the questions.

4. What is the best part of your description?

Answers will vary.

5. What is one thing you would change about this description if you could write it again?

▲ **Grammar and Writing Practice Book** p. 162

Scoring Rubric Description

Rubric 4 3 2 1	4	3	2	1
Focus/Ideas	Description focused on topic; many vivid details	Description mostly focused on topic; some vivid details	Description not always on topic; few vivid details	Description not focused on topic; no vivid details
Organization/ Paragraphs	Topic introduced at beginning; details in sequence	Topic introduced at beginning; details mostly in sequence	Topic not introduced at beginning; details confused	Topic not introduced; no order to details
Voice	Shows feelings about topic	Shows some feelings about topic	Shows few feelings about topic	Not involved with topic
Word Choice	Uses many sensory words and strong verbs	Uses some sensory words and strong verbs	Uses few sensory words or strong verbs	Uses no sensory words or strong verbs
Sentences	Complete, varied sentences	Complete sentences; some variety	Some incomplete or unclear sentences	Incomplete, unclear sentences
Conventions	Shows good understanding of writing conventions	Shows understanding of most writing conventions	Shows understanding of some writing conventions	Contains serious errors that detract from writing and may prevent understanding

For 6-, 5-, and 3-point Scoring Rubrics, see pp. WA13–WA16.

Description
Differentiated Instruction

WRITING PROMPT: Changes

Think of a place or a thing in nature. It might be a park, a tree, or a season. Write a paragraph that describes the place or thing. Tell how it looks, sounds, smells, tastes, or feels.

Purpose: Describe

Audience: A classmate

MODIFY INSTRUCTION

ALTERNATIVE PROMPTS

Pick One

ALTERNATIVE PROMPT: Descriptive Writing

Strategic Intervention Think about a season you like. What do you see and do in that season? Draw a picture of the things you like about the season. Then write several sentences that tell about your picture.

On-Level In a book or magazine, find a picture of a place in nature, such as a meadow, lake, or mountain. Write a description of the picture. Describe what you see. Use your imagination to describe what you might hear, smell, taste, and feel.

Advanced Write your description as dialogue, or conversation, between you and another person. Let the person ask you questions that you answer by giving descriptive details. Then with a partner read your dialogue aloud.

Strategic Intervention

MODIFY THE PROMPT

Help emerging writers by pairing them with more able writers or having them write collaboratively with a group under your supervision. The partners or group choose the topic and work together to write a description.

PREWRITING SUPPORT

- Show pictures of things in nature and have children discuss what they see and tell how they would describe the pictures.
- Display a natural object and demonstrate how you would describe the object. Tell how the object looks, sounds, smells, tastes, and feels, as appropriate.
- Let children dictate to you the details they want to use in their descriptions. Record their details and note whether these appeal to people's senses. Ask children questions that prompt them to add details.

OPTIONS

- Give children the option of writing a group description under your supervision.

CHECK PROGRESS Segment the assignment into manageable pieces. Check work at intervals, such as graphic organizers and first drafts, to make sure writing is on track.

Advanced

MODIFY THE PROMPT

Expect advanced writers to produce a description that creates a clear, vivid picture in readers' minds. They should include only details that tell about their topic and arrange these details in a logical order. Their descriptions should include sensory words and strong verbs.

APPLY SKILLS

- As children revise their work, have them consider some ways to improve it.

  Begin with a sentence that clearly states the topic of the description.

  Make sure that every sentence tells a detail about the topic.

  Look for places to substitute strong verbs for weak ones or to add describing words.

  Combine two simple sentences into a compound sentence using the word "and."

OPTIONS

- Work with children to create their own class rubrics. Follow these steps.
  1. Read examples of class descriptions and rank them 1–4, with 4 the highest.
  2. Discuss how they arrived at each rank.
  3. Isolate the six traits and make a rubric based on them.

CHECK PROGRESS Discuss children's Self-Evaluation Guides. Work with children to monitor their growth and identify their strengths and weaknesses as writers.

MODIFY THE PROMPT

Have beginning speakers name key details they want to include in their description. Help them restate the key details as complete sentences. Record the sentences and have children copy them.

BUILD BACKGROUND

- Point out that a description tells about how something looks, sounds, smells, tastes, and/or feels. Explain that a good description helps readers "see" what the writer is describing. Discuss the Key Features of a description that appear in the left column of p. WA2.

OPTIONS

- As children write their descriptions, guide them toward books, magazines, or Web sites that provide comprehension support through features such as:

  articles about nature subjects

  detailed photographs and illustrations

  strong picture/text correspondence

  text in the home-language
- For more suggestions on scaffolding the Writing Workshop, see the ELL and Transition Handbook.

CHECK PROGRESS You may need to explain certain traits and help children fill out their Self-Evaluation Guides. Downplay conventions and focus more on ideas. Recognize examples of vocabulary growth and efforts to use language in more complex ways.

Scoring Rubric Look Back and Write

2 points	The response indicates that the student has a complete understanding of the reading concept embodied in the task. The response is accurate, complete, and fulfills all the requirements of the task. Necessary support and/or examples are included, and the information given is clearly text-based.
1 point	The response indicates that the student has a partial understanding of the reading concept embodied in the task. The response includes information that is essentially correct and text-based, but the information is too general or too simplistic. Some of the support and/or examples may be incomplete or omitted.
0 points	The response indicates that the student does not demonstrate an understanding of the reading concept embodied in the task. The student has either failed to respond or has provided a response that is inaccurate or has insufficient information.

Scoring Rubric Look Back and Write

4 points	The response indicates that the student has a thorough understanding of the reading concept embodied in the task. The response is accurate, complete, and fulfills all the requirements of the task. Necessary support and/or examples are included, and the information is clearly text-based.
3 points	The response indicates that the student has an understanding of the reading concept embodied in the task. The response is accurate and fulfills all the requirements of the task, but the required support and/or details are not complete or clearly text-based.
2 points	The response indicates that the student has a partial understanding of the reading concept embodied in the task. The response that includes information is essentially correct and text-based, but the information is too general or too simplistic. Some of the support and/or examples and requirements of the task may be incomplete or omitted.
1 point	The response indicates that the student has a very limited understanding of the reading concept embodied in the task. The response is incomplete, may exhibit many flaws, and may not address all requirements of the task.
0 points	The response indicates that the student does not demonstrate an understanding of the reading concept embodied in the task. The student has either failed to respond or has provided a response that is inaccurate or has insufficient information.

Writing Trait Rubric *An Egg Is an Egg,* pp. 34–35

	4	3	2	1
entions	Excellent control of spelling, punctuation, and capitalization	Good control of spelling, punctuation, and capitalization	Some control of spelling, punctuation, and capitalization	Poor control of spelling, punctuation, and capitalization
	Few or no errors in steps	No serious errors that affect understanding of steps	Few distracting errors in steps	Many errors that prevent understanding of steps

Writing Trait Rubric *Ruby in Her Own Time,* pp. 66–67

	4	3	2	1
anization/ ragraphs	Strong structure that clearly shows how ideas are connected	Logical structure that shows how ideas are connected	Limited structure that provides some connections among ideas	Lacks identifiable structure; no connections among ideas
	Ideas in list easy to follow, in order that makes sense	Ideas in list mostly easy to follow	Order of ideas in list sometimes confusing	Ideas in list either muddled or missing

Writing Trait Rubric *Jan's New Home,* pp. 90–91

	4	3	2	1
Voice	Strong sense of writer behind words; writer well aware of audience and purpose	Clear sense of writer behind words; writer aware of audience and purpose	Some sense of writer behind words; writer somewhat involved with topic	No sense of writer behind words; writer not involved with topic
	Uses words in greeting card that clearly show feelings about topic	Uses words in greeting card that show feelings about topic	Needs to use more words in greeting card that show feelings about topic	Uses no words in greeting card that show feelings about topic

Writing Trait Rubric *Frog and Toad Together,* pp. 116–117

	4	3	2	1
Word Choice	Variety of exact nouns, strong verbs, vivid adjectives; clear, interesting word pictures	Many exact nouns, strong verbs, vivid adjectives; interesting word pictures	Needs more exact nouns, strong verbs, vivid adjectives; few word pictures	Dull or vague words; no word pictures
	Uses variety of interesting, well-chosen words in poem	Uses carefully chosen words in poem	Poem weakened by use of some dull or weak words	Poem lacking interest because of dull or incorrect words

Writing Trait Rubric *I'm a Caterpillar,* pp. 142–143

	4	3	2	1
Focus/ Ideas	Strong focus on topic; supports ideas with clear, well-chosen details	Good focus on topic; supports ideas with clear details	Attempts to keep focus on topic; ideas insufficiently supported with details	Does not focus on topic; ideas up; no supporting details
	Excellent, focused facts well elaborated with details	Good, focused facts elaborated with details	Generally focused facts; needs more supporting details	Rambling facts; lacks focus ar details

Writing Trait Rubric *Where Are My Animal Friends?,* pp. 172–173

	4	3	2	1
Sentences	Expresses complete ideas clearly in all sentences	Expresses ideas clearly in most sentences	Often does not express ideas clearly in sentences	Does not express ideas in sente
	All sentences in song complete and clear	Most sentences in song complete and clear	Many sentences in song either incomplete or unclear	Sentences in song incomplete o unclear

Scoring Rubric Narrative Writing

	6	5	4	3	2	1
/Ideas	Excellent, focused narrative; well elaborated with quality details	Good, focused narrative; elaborated with telling details	Narrative focused; adequate elaboration	Generally focused narrative; some supporting details	Sometimes unfocused narrative; needs more supporting details	Rambling narrative; lacks development and detail
zation/ graphs	Strong beginning, middle, and end; appropriate order words	Coherent beginning, middle, and end; some order words	Beginning, middle, and end easily identifiable	Recognizable beginning, middle, and end; some order words	Little direction from beginning to end; few order words	Lacks beginning, middle, end; incorrect or no order words
ice	Writer closely involved; engaging personality	Reveals personality	Pleasant but not compelling voice	Sincere voice but not fully engaged	Little writer involvement, personality	Careless writing with no feeling
Choice	Vivid, precise words that bring story to life	Clear words to bring story to life	Some specific word pictures	Language adequate but lacks color	Generally limited or redundant language	Vague, dull, or misused words
ences	Excellent variety of sentences; natural rhythm	Varied lengths, styles; generally smooth	Correct sentences with some variations in style	Correctly constructed sentences; some variety	May have simple, awkward, or wordy sentences; little variety	Choppy; many incomplete or run-on sentences
entions	Excellent control; few or no errors	No serious errors to affect understanding	General mastery of conventions but some errors	Reasonable control; few distracting errors	Weak control; enough errors to affect understanding	Many errors that prevent understanding

Scoring Rubric Narrative Writing

	5	4	3	2	1
/Ideas	Excellent, focused narrative; well elaborated with quality details	Good, focused narrative; elaborated with telling details	Generally focused narrative; some supporting details	Sometimes unfocused narrative; needs more supporting details	Rambling narrative; lacks development and detail
zation/ graphs	Strong beginning, middle, and end; appropriate order words	Coherent beginning, middle, and end; some order words	Recognizable beginning, middle, and end; some order words	Little direction from beginning to end; few order words	Lacks beginning, middle, end; incorrect or no order words
ice	Writer closely involved; engaging personality	Reveals personality	Sincere voice but not fully engaged	Little writer involvement, personality	Careless writing with no feeling
Choice	Vivid, precise words that bring story to life	Clear words to bring story to life	Language adequate but lacks color	Generally limited or redundant language	Vague, dull, or misused words
ences	Excellent variety of sentences; natural rhythm	Varied lengths, styles; generally smooth	Correctly constructed sentences; some variety	May have simple, awkward, or wordy sentences; little variety	Choppy; many incomplete or run-on sentences
entions	Excellent control; few or no errors	No serious errors to affect understanding	Reasonable control; few distracting errors	Weak control; enough errors to affect understanding	Many errors that prevent understanding

Scoring Rubric Narrative Writing

	3	2	1
/Ideas	Excellent, focused narrative; well elaborated with quality details	Generally focused narrative; some supporting details	Rambling narrative; lacks development and detail
zation/ graphs	Strong beginning, middle, and end; appropriate order words	Recognizable beginning, middle, and end; some order words	Lacks beginning, middle, end; incorrect or no order words
ice	Writer closely involved; engaging personality	Sincere voice but not fully engaged	Careless writing with no feeling
Choice	Vivid, precise words that bring story to life	Language adequate but lacks color	Vague, dull, or misused words
ences	Excellent variety of sentences; natural rhythm	Correctly constructed sentences; some variety	Choppy; many incomplete or run-on sentences
entions	Excellent control; few or no errors	Reasonable control; few distracting errors	Many errors that prevent understanding

Scoring Rubric Descriptive Writing

	6	5	4	3	2	1
Focus/Ideas	Excellent, focused description; well elaborated with quality details	Good, focused description; elaborated with telling details	Description focused; good elaboration	Generally focused description; some supporting details	Sometimes unfocused description; needs more supporting details	Rambling descript development and
Organization/ Paragraphs	Compelling ideas enhanced by order, structure, and transitions	Appealing order, structure, and transitions	Structure identifiable and suitable; transitions used	Adequate order, structure, and some transitions to guide reader	Little direction from beginning to end; few transitions	Lacks direction ar identifiable structu no transitions
Voice	Writer closely involved; engaging personality	Reveals personality	Pleasant but not compelling voice	Sincere voice but not fully engaged	Little writer involvement, personality	Careless writing w no feeling
Word Choice	Vivid, precise words that create memorable pictures	Clear, interesting words to bring description to life	Some specific word pictures	Language adequate; appeals to senses	Generally limited or redundant language	Vague, dull, or mis words
Sentences	Excellent variety of sentences; natural rhythm	Varied lengths, styles; generally smooth	Correct sentences with variations in style	Correctly constructed sentences; some variety	May have simple, awkward, or wordy sentences; little variety	Choppy; many inc run-on sentences
Conventions	Excellent control; few or no errors	No serious errors to affect understanding	General mastery of conventions but some errors	Reasonable control; few distracting errors	Weak control; enough errors to affect understanding	Many errors that understanding

Scoring Rubric Descriptive Writing

	5	4	3	2	1
Focus/Ideas	Excellent, focused description; well elaborated with quality details	Good, focused description; elaborated with telling details	Generally focused description; some supporting details	Sometimes unfocused description; needs more supporting details	Rambling description; lacks development and detail
Organization/ Paragraphs	Compelling ideas enhanced by order, structure, and transitions	Appealing order, structure, and transitions	Adequate order, structure, and some transitions to guide reader	Little direction from beginning to end; few transitions	Lacks direction and identifiable structure; no transitions
Voice	Writer closely involved; engaging personality	Reveals personality	Sincere voice but not fully engaged	Little writer involvement, personality	Careless writing with no feeling
Word Choice	Vivid, precise words that create memorable pictures	Clear, interesting words to bring description to life	Language adequate; appeals to senses	Generally limited or redundant language	Vague, dull, or misused words
Sentences	Excellent variety of sentences; natural rhythm	Varied lengths, styles; generally smooth	Correctly constructed sentences; some variety	May have simple, awkward, or wordy sentences; little variety	Choppy; many incomplete or run-on sentences
Conventions	Excellent control; few or no errors	No serious errors to affect understanding	Reasonable control; few distracting errors	Weak control; enough errors to affect understanding	Many errors that prevent understanding

Scoring Rubric Descriptive Writing

	3	2	1
Focus/Ideas	Excellent, focused description; well elaborated with quality details	Generally focused description; some supporting details	Rambling description; lacks development and detail
Organization/ Paragraphs	Compelling ideas enhanced by order, structure, and transitions	Adequate order, structure, and some transitions to guide reader	Lacks direction and identifiable structure; no transitions
Voice	Writer closely involved; engaging personality	Sincere voice but not fully engaged	Careless writing with no feeling
Word Choice	Vivid, precise words that create memorable pictures	Language adequate; appeals to senses	Vague, dull, or misused words
Sentences	Excellent variety of sentences; natural rhythm	Correctly constructed sentences; some variety	Choppy; many incomplete or run-on sentences
Conventions	Excellent control; few or no errors	Reasonable control; few distracting errors	Many errors that prevent understanding

Scoring Rubric Persuasive Writing

	6	5	4	3	2	1
s/Ideas	Persuasive argument carefully built with quality details	Persuasive argument well supported with details	Persuasive argument focused; good elaboration	Persuasive argument with one or two convincing details	Persuasive piece sometimes unfocused; needs more support	Rambling persuasive argument; lacks development and detail
nization/ agraphs	Information chosen and arranged for maximum effect	Evident progression of persuasive ideas	Progression and structure evident	Information arranged in a logical way with some lapses	Little structure or direction	No identifiable structure
/oice	Writer closely involved; persuasive but not overbearing	Maintains persuasive tone	Persuasive but not compelling voice	Sometimes uses persuasive voice	Little writer involvement, personality	Shows little conviction
d Choice	Persuasive words carefully chosen for impact	Argument supported by persuasive language	Uses some persuasive words	Occasional persuasive language	Generally limited or redundant language	Vague, dull, or misused words; no persuasive words
ntences	Excellent variety of sentences; natural rhythm	Varied lengths, styles; generally smooth	Correct sentences with variations in style	Carefully constructed sentences; some variety	Simple, awkward, or wordy sentences; little variety	Choppy; many incomplete or run-on sentences
ventions	Excellent control; few or no errors	No serious errors to affect understanding	General mastery of conventions but some errors	Reasonable control; few distracting errors	Weak control; enough errors to affect understanding	Many errors that prevent understanding

Scoring Rubric Persuasive Writing

	5	4	3	2	1
cus/Ideas	Persuasive argument carefully built with quality details	Persuasive argument well supported with details	Persuasive argument with one or two convincing details	Persuasive piece sometimes unfocused; needs more support	Rambling persuasive argument; lacks development and detail
anization/ ragraphs	Information chosen and arranged for maximum effect	Evident progression of persuasive ideas	Information arranged in a logical way with some lapses	Little structure or direction	No identifiable structure
Voice	Writer closely involved; persuasive but not overbearing	Maintains persuasive tone	Sometimes uses persuasive voice	Little writer involvement, personality	Shows little conviction
rd Choice	Persuasive words carefully chosen for impact	Argument supported by persuasive language	Occasional persuasive language	Generally limited or redundant language	Vague, dull, or misused words; no persuasive words
entences	Excellent variety of sentences; natural rhythm	Varied lengths, styles; generally smooth	Carefully constructed sentences; some variety	Simple, awkward, or wordy sentences; little variety	Choppy; many incomplete or run-on sentences
onventions	Excellent control; few or no errors	No serious errors to affect understanding	Reasonable control; few distracting errors	Weak control; enough errors to affect understanding	Many errors that prevent understanding

Scoring Rubric Persuasive Writing

	3	2	1
ocus/Ideas	Persuasive argument carefully built with quality details	Persuasive argument with one or two convincing details	Rambling persuasive argument; lacks development and detail
rganization/ aragraphs	Information chosen and arranged for maximum effect	Information arranged in a logical way with some lapses	No identifiable structure
Voice	Writer closely involved; persuasive but not overbearing	Sometimes uses persuasive voice	Shows little conviction
ord Choice	Persuasive words carefully chosen for impact	Occasional persuasive language	Vague, dull, or misused words; no persuasive words
Sentences	Excellent variety of sentences; natural rhythm	Carefully constructed sentences; some variety	Choppy; many incomplete or run-on sentences
Conventions	Excellent control; few or no errors	Reasonable control; few distracting errors	Many errors that prevent understanding

Scoring Rubric Expository Writing

	6	5	4	3	2	1
Focus/Ideas	Insightful, focused exposition; well elaborated with quality details	Informed, focused exposition; elaborated with telling details	Exposition focused, good elaboration	Generally focused exposition; some supporting details	Sometimes unfocused exposition needs more supporting details	Rambling expositi development and
Organization/ Paragraphs	Logical, consistent flow of ideas; good transitions	Logical sequencing of ideas; uses transitions	Ideas sequenced with some transitions	Sequenced ideas with some transitions	Little direction from beginning to end; few order words	Lacks structure ar transitions
Voice	Writer closely involved; informative voice well suited to topic	Reveals personality; voice suited to topic	Pleasant but not compelling voice	Sincere voice suited to topic	Little writer involvement, personality	Careless writing w no feeling
Word Choice	Vivid, precise words to express ideas	Clear words to express ideas	Words correct and adequate	Language adequate but may lack precision	Generally limited or redundant language	Vague, dull, or mis words
Sentences	Strong topic sentence; fluent, varied structures	Good topic sentence; smooth sentence structure	Correct sentences that are sometimes fluent	Topic sentence correctly constructed; some sentence variety	Topic sentence unclear or missing; wordy, awkward sentences	No topic sentence incomplete or run- sentences
Conventions	Excellent control; few or no errors	No serious errors to affect understanding	General mastery of conventions but some errors	Reasonable control; few distracting errors	Weak control; enough errors to affect understanding	Many errors that p understanding

Scoring Rubric Expository Writing

	5	4	3	2	1
Focus/Ideas	Insightful, focused exposition; well elaborated with quality details	Informed, focused exposition; elaborated with telling details	Generally focused exposition; some supporting details	Sometimes unfocused exposition needs more supporting details	Rambling exposition; lacks development and detail
Organization/ Paragraphs	Logical, consistent flow of ideas; good transitions	Logical sequencing of ideas; uses transitions	Sequenced ideas with some transitions	Little direction from beginning to end; few order words	Lacks structure and transitions
Voice	Writer closely involved; informative voice well suited to topic	Reveals personality; voice suited to topic	Sincere voice suited to topic	Little writer involvement, personality	Careless writing with no feeling
Word Choice	Vivid, precise words to express ideas	Clear words to express ideas	Language adequate but may lack precision	Generally limited or redundant language	Vague, dull, or misused words
Sentences	Strong topic sentence; fluent, varied structures	Good topic sentence; smooth sentence structure	Topic sentence correctly constructed; some sentence variety	Topic sentence unclear or missing; wordy, awkward sentences	No topic sentence; many incomplete or run-on sentences
Conventions	Excellent control; few or no errors	No serious errors to affect understanding	Reasonable control; few distracting errors	Weak control; enough errors to affect understanding	Many errors that prevent understanding

Scoring Rubric Expository Writing

	3	2	1
Focus/Ideas	Insightful, focused exposition; well elaborated with quality details	Generally focused exposition; some supporting details	Rambling exposition; lacks development and detail
Organization/ Paragraphs	Logical, consistent flow of ideas; good transitions	Sequenced ideas with some transitions	Lacks structure and transitions
Voice	Writer closely involved; informative voice well suited to topic	Sincere voice suited to topic	Careless writing with no feeling
Word Choice	Vivid, precise words to express ideas	Language adequate but may lack precision	Vague, dull, or misused words
Sentences	Strong topic sentence; fluent, varied structures	Topic sentence correctly constructed; some sentence variety	No topic sentence; many incomplete or run-on sentences
Conventions	Excellent control; few or no errors	Reasonable control; few distracting errors	Many errors that prevent understanding

Ionitoring Fluency

Ongoing assessment of a child's reading fluency is one of the most valuable measures we have of children's reading skills. One of the most effective ways to assess fluency is taking timed samples of children's oral reading and measuring the number of words correct per minute (WCPM).

How to Measure Words Correct Per Minute—WCPM

Choose a Text

Start by choosing a text for the child to read. The text should be:

- narrative
- unfamiliar
- on grade level

Make a copy of the text for yourself and have one for the child.

Timed Reading of the Text

Tell the child: As you read this aloud, I want you to do your best reading and to read as quickly as you can. That doesn't mean it's a race. Just do your best, fast reading. When I say *begin,* start reading.

As the child reads, follow along in your copy. Mark words that are read incorrectly.

Incorrect
- omissions
- substitutions
- mispronunciations
- reversals

Correct
- self-corrections within 3 seconds
- repeated words

After One Minute

At the end of one minute, draw a line after the last word that was read. Have the child finish reading but don't count any words beyond one minute. Arrive at the words correct per minute—WCPM—by counting the total number of words that the child read correctly in one minute.

Fluency Goals

Grade 1 End-of-Year Goal = 60 WCPM

Target goals by unit

Unit 2 no target goal yet

Unit 3 Weeks 1–3 20 to 30 WCPM
Weeks 4–6 25 to 35 WCPM

Unit 4 Weeks 1–3 30 to 40 WCPM
Weeks 4–6 35 to 45 WCPM

Unit 5 Weeks 1–3 40 to 50 WCPM
Weeks 4–6 45 to 55 WCPM

More Frequent Monitoring

You may want to monitor some children more frequently because they are falling far below grade-level benchmarks or they have a result that doesn't seem to align with their previous performance. Follow the same steps above, but choose 2 or 3 additional texts.

Fluency Progress Chart Copy the chart on the next page. Use it to record each child's progress across the year.

See also *Assessment Handbook*, p. 165

Fluency Progress Chart, Grade 1

Name ________________________

WCPM																														
110																														
105																														
100																														
95																														
90																														
85																														
80																														
75																														
70																														
65																														
60																														
55																														
50																														
45																														
40																														
35																														
30																														
25																														
20																														
15																														
	1	2	3	4	5	6	7	8	9	10	11	12	13	14	15	16	17	18	19	20	21	22	23	24	25	26	27	28	29	30

Timed Reading

Name

Sentence Reading Chart

Unit 3

	Phonics		High-Frequency		Reteach	Reassess: Words Correct
	Total Words	Words Correct	Total Words	Words Correct	✓	
Week 1 *An Egg Is an Egg* A B C						
Vowel Sounds of *y*	2					
Long Vowels (CV)	2					
High-Frequency Words			2			
Week 2 *Ruby in Her Own Time* A B C						
Final *ng, nk*	2					
Compound Words	2					
High-Frequency Words			2			
Week 3 *Jan's New Home* A B C						
Ending *-es;* Plural *-es*	2					
r-Controlled *or, ore*	2					
High-Frequency Words			2			
Week 4 *Frog and Toad Together* A B C						
Inflected Endings *-ed, -ing*	2					
r-Controlled *ar*	2					
High-Frequency Words			2			
Week 5 *I'm a Caterpillar* A B C						
r-Controlled *er, ir, ur*	2					
Contractions *'s, 've, 're*	2					
High-Frequency Words			2			
Week 6 *Where Are My Animal Friends?* A B C						
Comparative Endings	2					
dge/j/	2					
High-Frequency Words			2			
Unit Scores	**24**		**12**			

- **RECORD SCORES** Use this chart to record scores for the Day 5 Sentence Reading Assessment. Circle A, B, or C to record which set of sentences was used.
- **RETEACH PHONICS SKILLS** If the child is unable to read all the tested phonics words, then reteach the phonics skills using the Reteach lessons on pp. DI•76–DI•84.
- **PRACTICE HIGH-FREQUENCY WORDS** If the child is unable to read all the tested high-frequency words, then provide additional practice for the week's words. See pp. 34e, 66e, 90e, 116e, 142e, and 172e.
- **REASSESS** Use the same set of sentences or an easier set for reassessment.

See also *Assessment Handbook*, p. 271 •

Unit 3

Assess and Regroup

FYI In Grade 1 there are opportunities for regrouping every six weeks—at the end of Units 2, 3, and 4. These options offer sensitivity to each child's progress although some teachers may prefer to regroup less frequently.

Regroup for Unit 4

To make regrouping decisions at the end of Unit 3, consider children's end-of-unit scores for

- Unit 3 Sentence Reading (Day 5 Assessments)
- Fluency (WCPM)
- Unit 3 Benchmark Test

Group Time

On-Level

To continue On-Level or to move into the On-Level group, children should

- score 80% or better on their cumulative Unit Scores for Sentence Reading for phonics and high-frequency words
- meet the current benchmark for fluency (25–35 WCPM), reading On-Level text such as Student Edition selections
- score 80% or better on the Unit 3 Benchmark Test
- be capable of working in the On-Level group based on teacher judgment

Strategic Intervention

Children would benefit from Strategic Intervention if they

- score 60% or lower on their cumulative Unit Scores for Sentence Reading for phonics and high-frequency words, regardless of their fluency scores
- do not meet the current benchmark for fluency (25–35 WCPM)
- score below 80% on their cumulative Unit Scores for Sentence Reading for phonics and high-frequency words AND have fluency scores below the current benchmark of 25–35 WCPM
- score below 60% on the Unit 3 Benchmark Test
- are struggling to keep up with the On-Level group based on teacher judgment

Advanced

To move to the Advanced group, children should

- score 100% on their cumulative Unit Scores for Sentence Reading for phonics and high-frequency words
- score 95% on the Unit 3 Benchmark Test
- read above grade-level material (25–35 WCPM) with speed, accuracy, and expression. You may try them out on one of the Advanced Selections.
- use expansive vocabulary and ease of language in retelling.
- be capable of handling the problem solving and the investigative work of the Advanced group based on teacher judgment

QUESTIONS TO CONSIDER

- What types of test questions did the child miss? Are they specific to a particular skill or strategy?
- Does the child have adequate background knowledge to understand the test passages or selections for retelling?
- Has the child's performance met expectations for daily lessons and assessments with little or no reteaching?
- Is the child performing more like children in another group?
- Does the child read for enjoyment, different purposes, and with varied interests?

Unit Scores for Sentence Reading

Phonics	High-Frequency Words
100% = **24**	100% = **12**
80% = **19**	80% = **10**
60% = **14**	60% = **7**

Benchmark Fluency Scores

Current Goal: **25–35 WCPM**

End-of-Year Goal: **60 WCPM**

Leveled Readers

Table of Contents

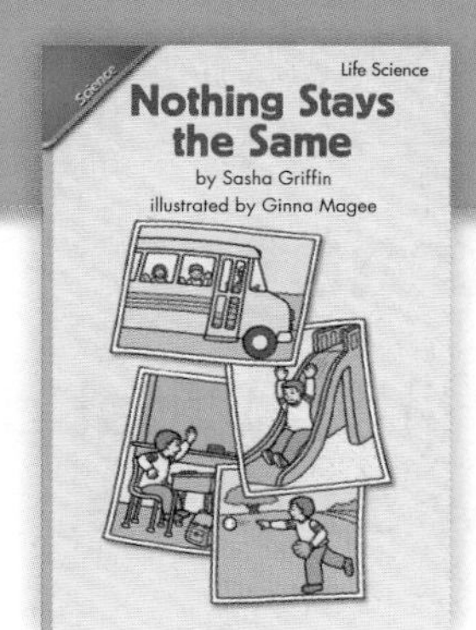

Unit 3 Week 1

/othing Stays he Same

COMPARE AND CONTRAST

PREDICT

LESSON VOCABULARY always, become(s), day, everything, nothing, stays, things

IMARY In this story, a young boy looks at his baby ım and identifies the ways he has changed over time.

RODUCE THE BOOK

.D BACKGROUND Ask children if they have ever seen ures of themselves when they were babies. Discuss ' they looked and what they did when they were very ıll.

VIEW/TAKE A PICTURE WALK Have children examine cover of the book and look inside at the illustrations. them to think about what the boy might learn in this y, based on what they know about growing up.

:H/REVIEW VOCABULARY Display the word *nothing* in ɔcket chart. Read the word together. Then ask children ırn the pages of *Nothing Stays the Same* and find word. Read aloud the sentence in which it is used. children to think of another sentence that uses this d. Repeat for the other words. Display the vocabulary ds on the word wall.

Show children a book or magazine that contains tographs of babies. Describe the babies and their vities. Focus on action words, such as *sleep, cry,* *eat.*

RGET SKILL AND STRATEGY

COMPARE AND CONTRAST Point out to children that ıy things have changed since the boy was a little y. As they read the book, suggest that children look ways the boy has changed.

PREDICT Point out to children that as they read, it good idea to think about what may happen next in story. This is called *predicting.* Turn to page 5 and "The boy will see a baby album here. There will also some pictures of the baby crying." As children read, npt them to make predictions, using what they have d and what they already know.

READ THE BOOK

Use the following questions to support comprehension.

PAGE 3 Who is the baby in the photo album? (*The boy's baby pictures are in the photo album.)*

PAGE 6 What did the boy eat when he was a baby? Does he eat the same food now? How can you tell? *(The illustration shows the baby drinking from a bottle and the boy eating an apple.)*

PAGE 8 What are some other things the boy can do now? (*Responses will vary but should relate to the illustrations.)*

TALK ABOUT THE BOOK

THINK AND SHARE

1. Responses will vary but should identify ways in which the boy is different now.
2. The boy will probably play ball.
3. *every, thing*
4. The boy looks at a photo album.

RESPONSE OPTIONS

WRITING Ask children to write about something they can do now that they couldn't do when they were little. Encourage them to imitate the *"When I was a baby, . . ."* sentence pattern from the story.

CONTENT CONNECTIONS

TIME FOR Science

SCIENCE Suggest that children find out how their favorite animals grow and learn. Provide a selection of books and magazines relating to baby animals and their development. Encourage children to look for similarities and differences between animal babies and human babies.

Name________________________________

Compare and Contrast

Think about when you were little. What did you do then? What can you do now? Draw a picture.

Now

Name______________________________

Vocabulary

Read the words in the box. Write each word on the line.

Words to Know

always **become** **day** **everything**
nothing **stays** **things**

1. day ______________________

2. nothing ______________________

3. become ______________________

4. things ______________________

5. always ______________________

6. everything ______________________

7. stays ______________________

Just Like Me
by Mary Katherine Tate
illustrated by Freddie Levin

Unit 3 Week 1

COMPARE AND CONTRAST

PREDICT

LESSON VOCABULARY always, become(s), day, everything, nothing, stays, things

Just Like Me

SUMMARY A boy notices both differences and similarities when he compares himself to his baby brother.

INTRODUCE THE BOOK

BUILD BACKGROUND Discuss siblings and how they are alike in some ways and different in others. If children have brothers and sisters at home, invite them to talk about some of their similarities and differences. Remind children of other stories they have read about brothers and sisters.

PREVIEW/TAKE A PICTURE WALK Have children examine the cover of the book and then turn the pages and look at the illustrations. Together, brainstorm a list of predictions about the story.

ELL Show children a photograph of a family. Help them notice similarities and differences among the family members.

TEACH/REVIEW VOCABULARY Print each vocabulary word on an index card. Show the cards one at a time. Ask: What is the first letter in this word? Does this word have a smaller word inside it? You may wish to highlight a smaller word within the vocabulary word. Read the words aloud as a group. Then display them on the word wall.

TARGET SKILL AND STRATEGY

COMPARE AND CONTRAST Point out to children that the brothers in the story are alike in some ways and different in others. As they read the book, suggest that children look for words that describe the two brothers.

PREDICT As children read, ask them to think about what might happen next. Have them look for clues in the story to help them make their predictions.

READ THE BOOK

Use the following questions to support comprehension.

PAGE 3 Do you think that the baby looks just like his older brother? Why or why not? *(Responses will vary but should relate to the appearance of the characters.)*

PAGE 5 When the baby grows up, will his feet still be little? Will his eyes still be blue? *(The baby's feet will grow bigger, but his eyes will probably stay blue.)*

PAGES 6–7 How is the father's shirt the same on these pages? How is it different? *(The father's shirt is green on both pages. On page 6, it has a crewneck and stitching around the cuff. On page 7, it has a hood.)*

PAGE 8 Did this story end the way you thought it would? Did you like the end of this story? *(Responses will vary.)*

TALK ABOUT THE BOOK

THINK AND SHARE

1. *Boy:* big feet, brown eyes, draws; *Baby:* small, little feet, cries a lot, blue eyes; *Both:* black hair, noses, smiles, Dad
2. He will probably be happy. At the end of the story, he says he hopes the baby always looks like him.
3. *nothing, everything, things*
4. The picture shows the boy hugging his brother and smiling, so you can tell he loves him.

RESPONSE OPTIONS

WRITING Suggest that children write a few sentences comparing themselves to a friend or family member.

CONTENT CONNECTIONS

TIME FOR Science

SCIENCE Encourage children to investigate how animals grow and change by finding pictures of baby animals and corresponding adult animals in books or on the Internet.

Name ____________________

Compare and Contrast

Look at the pictures in the book. Compare the boy and his father. Tell how they are the same and how they are different.

Same	Different
1.	4.
2.	5.
3.	6.

Name ______________________

Vocabulary

Pick a word from the box to finish each sentence.
Write it on the line.

Words to Know

always	become	day	everything
nothing	stays	things	

1. My dad can do lots of ______________ .

2. My dad ______________ takes good care of me.

3. The baby ______________ asleep for a long time.

4. When the baby is hungry, he eats ______________.

5. He leaves ______________ in his bowl.

6. The baby will grow up one ______________.

7. Maybe he will ______________ just like me!

Your Amazing Body!

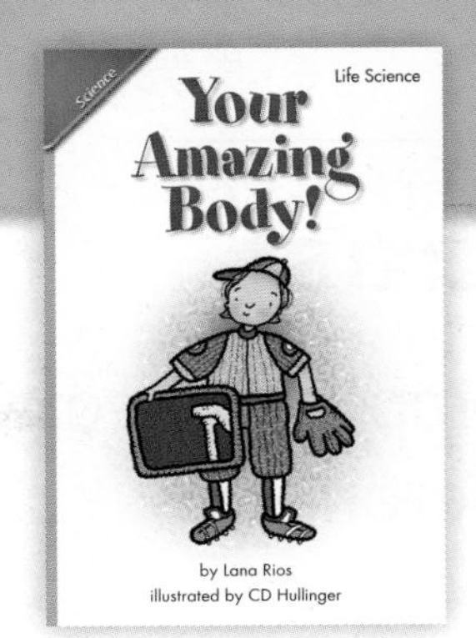

Unit 3 Week 1

COMPARE AND CONTRAST

PREDICT

LESSON VOCABULARY adult, healthy, measurement

SUMMARY Amazing facts about human growth and development are the focus of this book.

INTRODUCE THE BOOK

BUILD BACKGROUND Discuss some of the ways that bodies change as they grow. Ask children to describe how their bodies are changing as they grow older.

PREVIEW/USE TEXT FEATURES As children preview the book, have them pay close attention to the illustrations and captions. Point out that reading the captions is a quick way to see what information a book contains.

TEACH/REVIEW VOCABULARY Display the word *adult* in a pocket chart. Read the word aloud. Then have children find the word on page 5. Have them read the sentence aloud. Ask, What is another word for *adult*? Repeat for the other words on the list.

ELL Point out to Spanish-speaking children that the English word *adult* is similar to the Spanish word *adulto.*

TARGET SKILL AND STRATEGY

COMPARE AND CONTRAST Point out to children that they can notice ways in which two things are alike and different. As they read about growing bodies, prompt children to think about ways that they change as they grow and ways that they stay the same. You may wish to record their responses on a t-chart for later reference.

PREDICT Point out to children that as they read, they should think about what might come next. Readers make predictions by comparing what they are reading to what they already know. Turn to page 4 and model: "I see a skeleton here. I predict we will learn about why people have bones. What else might we learn?" As children continue to read, prompt them to predict what information they might learn next. Encourage them to give reasons for their predictions.

READ THE BOOK

Use the following questions to support comprehension.

PAGE 5 How does the number of bones of an adult compare to those of a baby? *(A baby has about 350 bones. An adult has about 206 bones.)*

PAGE 6 What kinds of food might help a child grow tall? What kinds of food would probably not help a child grow? *(Responses will vary but should relate to nutrition.)*

PAGE 8 Why are healthy teeth and gums important? What things can you do to take good care of your teeth? Think about what you already know. *(Healthy teeth and gums are needed for chewing food. Answers will vary but should relate to dental care and nutrition.)*

PAGE 9 Look at the illustration. Which heart is bigger—the heart on the poster or the boy's heart? How can you tell? *(The heart on the poster is bigger because it is larger than the boy's fist.)*

TALK ABOUT THE BOOK

THINK AND SHARE

1. *Child:* twenty teeth; *Adult:* thirty-two; *Both:* use their teeth to chew
2. Answers will vary but should relate to factors mentioned in the text, such as height of family members and diet.
3. *body, baby, many*
4. The thighbone is the longest bone in your body.

RESPONSE OPTIONS

WRITING Suggest that students write a sentence or two about why their bodies are amazing.

CONTENT CONNECTIONS

TIME FOR Science

SCIENCE Provide children with books, models, and other resources that relate to the human body. Suggest that they learn more about the body and how it works.

Name ______________________

Compare and Contrast

Look at one of your hands. Compare it to a grown-up's hand. What is the same? What is different?

Same	Different
1.	4.
2.	5.
3.	6.

Name ______________________

Vocabulary

Pick a word from the box to finish each sentence. Write the words on the lines.

Words to Know

adult healthy measurement

1. Good food helps me stay ____________ .

2. When I am an ____________ , I will be tall.

3. I use a ruler to make a ____________ .

4. Ask an ____________ if you aren't sure.

5. That boy looks so ____________ .

Can Hank Sing?
by Dale Cooper
illustrated by CD Hullinger

Unit 3 Week 2

PLOT

SUMMARIZE

LESSON VOCABULARY any, enough, ever every, own, sure, were

Can Hank Sing?

SUMMARY A bluebird named Hank is frustrated because he cannot sing like his friend Jan. With practice and encouragement, he learns to appreciate his own unique singing voice.

INTRODUCE THE BOOK

BUILD BACKGROUND Ask children to think about a time when they learned to do something new. Encourage them to recall their feelings at the beginning of the process and describe how those feelings changed as their skills developed.

PREVIEW/TAKE A PICTURE WALK As children preview the book, encourage them to look closely at the illustrations. Ask: Based on the illustrations, what do you think will happen in this story?

TEACH/REVIEW VOCABULARY Print each vocabulary word on a separate sticky note. Read the words aloud with the children and talk about the definition of each word. Then ask volunteers to match the words on the sticky notes to words in the book.

ELL Print the vocabulary words on word cards. Read the words list aloud, as a group. Then scatter the cards on the floor. Hand flashlights to one or two children. Call out a word from the list and let the children shine the flashlight on the corresponding word card.

TARGET SKILL AND STRATEGY

PLOT Point out to children that every story has a beginning, middle, and end. These events make up the story's *plot.* As children read *Can Hank Sing?* have them look for the beginning, middle, and end of the story. Suggest that they record these events on a story map.

SUMMARIZE Point out that a *summary* of a story is a short description of the characters and main events in a story. A summary answers the questions *Who?* and *What?* As children read, prompt them to ask themselves: Who are the main characters? What is happening?

READ THE BOOK

Use the following questions to support comprehension.

PAGE 3 How does Hank feel at the beginning of the story? How can you tell? *(Hank feels sad; the illustration show him frowning.)*

PAGE 5 What does the speech bubble on this page tell us? *(The speech bubble indicates that Hank is singing in a small voice like a mouse.)*

PAGE 7 What does Hank learn in this story? *(Hank learn to like the way he sings.)*

TALK ABOUT THE BOOK

THINK AND SHARE

1. Possible responses: In the beginning, Hank wishes he could sing like Jan. In the middle, he sings for Jan At the end, Hank accepts his different way of singing
2. Possible response: 1. Hank said he could not sing. 2. Jan encouraged Hank and told him that his own way of singing was fine. 3. Hank sang. 4. Hank accepted his way of singing.
3. *bluebird; blue, bird*
4. Responses will vary but should be about a trait of the reader.

RESPONSE OPTIONS

SPEAKING Ask children to summarize the story in their own words. Remind them to tell who was in the story and what happened. Encourage them to use transition words, such as *first, then,* and *finally* in their retelling.

CONTENT CONNECTIONS

TIME FOR Science

SCIENCE Help children use the Internet to locate the song of a real bluebird. Encourage them to compare the bluebird's song to those of other common birds.

Name ______________________

Plot

Read the sentences. Put them in order. Write 1, 2, or 3.

______ Hank likes the way he sings.

______ Hank wishes he could sing like Jan.

______ Hank sings for Jan.

Draw a picture showing how Hank feels at the end of the story.

Name ______________________

Vocabulary

Write a word from the box to complete each sentence.

Words to Know						
any	enough	ever	every	own	sure	were

1. Hank and Jan ______________ talking in the tree.

2. Jan said, "Almost ______________ bluebird can sing like I do."

3. Hank asked, "Will I ______________ learn to sing like Jan?"

4. Jan said, "If you practice ______________, you can learn to sing."

5. Hank said, "Are you ______________ ?"

6. Hank practiced ______________ day.

7. In the end Hank liked his own ______________ song.

Unit 3 Week 2

PLOT

SUMMARIZE

LESSON VOCABULARY any, enough, ever, every, own, sure, were

Not Just Any Boy

SUMMARY In this fantasy, newborn infant Mac learns at a super-human rate and amazes his parents and others. A time line at the end of the book summarizes Mac's incredible accomplishments.

INTRODUCE THE BOOK

BUILD BACKGROUND Discuss what children know about how babies grow. If they have experience with newborn babies, have them talk about what babies can and cannot do.

PREVIEW/TAKE A PICTURE WALK Ask children to look at the illustrations to predict what will happen in this story.

TEACH/REVIEW VOCABULARY Arrange children in pairs. Give each pair a list of vocabulary words, a highlighter, and a simple newspaper or magazine. Have the children highlight the vocabulary words they find in the material.

ELL Print each vocabulary word on two separate index cards. Invite children to play a concentration game. As they turn over the cards, have the children read the words aloud. The goal is to find two cards with the same word.

TARGET SKILL AND STRATEGY

PLOT Remind children that every story has a beginning, middle, and end. The events, or things that happen, make up the story's *plot.* As children read *Not Just Any Boy,* have them look for the beginning, middle, and end of the story. Format a story map for the students and suggest that they record these events on the map.

SUMMARIZE Point out that a *summary* of a story describes the characters and main things that happened in a story. Remind children that a summary answers the questions Who? and What happened? As children read, have them look for the main characters and the most important story events.

READ THE BOOK

Use the following questions to support comprehension.

PAGE 3 What is the first thing that happens in this story? *(Mac talks at one week old.)*

PAGE 7 How does Mac's mom feel when he fixes the sink for her? How can you tell? *(She was surprised and happy. The illustrations show her smiling.)*

PAGE 9 What does it mean when the author says, "Mac was not just any boy"? *(Mac does things that other babies cannot do.)*

TALK ABOUT THE BOOK

THINK AND SHARE

1. Possible response: In the beginning, Mac talks at five weeks old. In the middle, he fixes a sink. At the end, he flies a spaceship.
2. Responses will vary but may include: Mac talked; Mac ran a race; Mac fixed the sink; Mac delivered the mail; Mac made and flew a spaceship.
3. *mailman, mailbox, mail*
4. Responses will vary but should include personal episodes from the reader's life.

RESPONSE OPTIONS

WORD WORK Make a word-and-picture card for the compound word *mailman.* Draw mail and a man on one side and print the word *mailman* on the other side. Show the picture to the children and have them guess the word. Then invite them to make word-and-picture cards for other compound words.

CONTENT CONNECTIONS

Time for SOCIAL STUDIES

SOCIAL STUDIES Have children bring in photographs of themselves as babies for a class display. Encourage them to discuss what they did as babies and how they have learned and grown since that time.

Name ______________________________

Plot

Read the sentences. Circle the word that shows where each sentence belongs in the story.

1. Mac makes a spaceship.

Beginning Middle End

2. Mac is born.

Beginning Middle End

3. Mac fixes the sink.

Beginning Middle End

Write two more things that Mac does in the middle of the story.

4. ______________________________

5. ______________________________

Name ____________________

Vocabulary

Find these words in the puzzle. Circle them.
Words may be across or down.

Words to Know

any	enough	ever	every
own	sure	were	

e	v	e	r	r	a	g
y	w	r	e	e	y	y
s	e	y	e	n	r	n
u	o	y	w	w	e	r
r	w	e	r	e	e	a
e	n	o	u	g	h	n
e	v	e	r	y	w	y

A Bed for Paul
by Ruth Renolo
illustrated by Al Lorenz

Unit 3 Week 2

PLOT

SUMMARIZE

LESSON VOCABULARY attempt, event, time line

A Bed for Paul

SUMMARY In this tall tale, it isn't easy to find a bed big enough for the fast-growing baby, Paul Bunyan. A time line at the end of the book outlines the main plot events.

INTRODUCE THE BOOK

BUILD BACKGROUND Explain to children that they will be reading a tall tale, which is a funny story full of exaggeration, or events that "stretch the truth." Ask them to think of examples of exaggeration from stories they have been told, or have read, or even from stories of their own experiences.

PREVIEW/TAKE A PICTURE WALK As children preview the book, encourage them to examine the illustrations. Ask: Based on the illustrations, what do you think might happen in this story?

TEACH/REVIEW VOCABULARY Write the word *attempt* on the board. Ask children if they know what this word means. Model how to look up the word in a children's dictionary. Ask a volunteer to read the definition aloud. Together, brainstorm a sentence using the vocabulary word. Repeat for the other words on the list.

ELL Print the vocabulary words on word cards. Have children choose partners. Give each pair of children a word card and challenge the children to find their words somewhere in the classroom.

TARGET SKILL AND STRATEGY

PLOT Point out to children that every story has a beginning, a middle, and an end. These events make up the story's *plot.* As children read *A Bed for Paul,* have them try to identify the beginning, middle, and end of the story. Suggest that they record these events on a story map.

SUMMARIZE Point out that a *summary* of a story is a short description of the story's characters and its main events. As children read, prompt them to ask themselves, "What is happening here?"

READ THE BOOK

Use the following questions to support comprehension.

PAGE 4 The author describes Paul as "an amazing baby." What was so special about him? *(Answers will vary but should refer to Paul's size or rate of growth.)*

PAGES 8–9 What are some examples of exaggeration on these pages? *(Possible responses: Paul slept in a ship; there weren't enough blankets to cover him; he was too big to fit in a cabin.)*

PAGE 15 What did Paul need in this story? How did he get it? *(Paul needed a bed that fit him. His parents and neighbors built him a ship to use as a bed, and when he grew bigger, he built one for himself.)*

TALK ABOUT THE BOOK

THINK AND SHARE

1. Paul leaves home to find space to live.
2. Possible responses: In the beginning of the story, Pau slept in his parents' bed and a rowboat; in the middle Paul's parents and neighbors built him a ship to use as a bed; finally, he left home to find space to live.
3. A time line is a chart showing events arranged in the order that they occurred. This time line shows what happens to Paul as he grew.
4. Responses will vary but should recount a personal, specific episode.

RESPONSE OPTIONS

WRITING Invite children to make up tall tales about when they were babies.

CONTENT CONNECTIONS

SOCIAL STUDIES Have children use the Internet, books, and magazines to learn more about lumberjacks.

Name ______________________________

Plot

Circle the word that shows where each sentence belongs in the story.

1. Paul built the biggest log cabin and the biggest bed in all the land.

Beginning	Middle	End

2. Paul broke his ship bed.

Beginning	Middle	End

3. The rowboat made a fine bed for Paul.

Beginning	Middle	End

4. Paul packed a sack and headed for the deep woods and wide country.

Beginning	Middle	End

Name ________________________

Vocabulary

Write the first letter of each picture. Read the word.

Words to Know

attempt **event** **time line**

1. 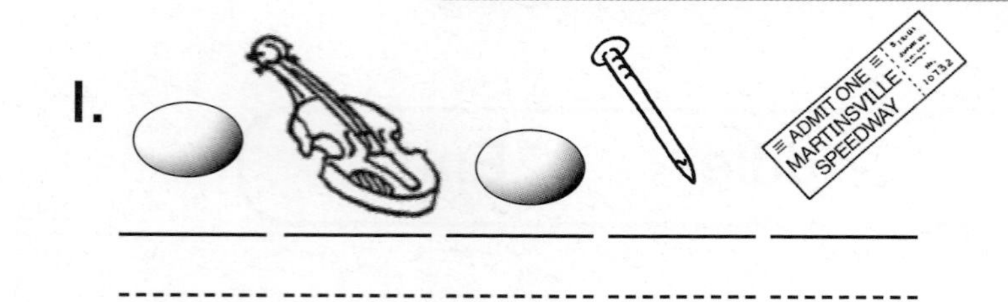

2. 

3. 

4. Write a sentence using one of the vocabulary words.

Unit 3 Week 3

A Big Move

THEME

MONITOR AND FIX UP

LESSON VOCABULARY away, car, friends, house, our, school, very

SUMMARY In this story, a girl and her mother must move when her mother takes a new job in a different place. The sequence in the family's process is emphasized.

INTRODUCE THE BOOK

BUILD BACKGROUND Share with children that sometimes families must move. Sometimes the move might be very nearby. Other times families choose to move to different states, or even different countries. Talk with children about why a family might move, for example, to start a new job or to be closer to family members.

PREVIEW/TAKE A PICTURE WALK Invite children to preview the pictures in this book. Have children identify the family consisting of a mother and a daughter. Ask children what the sign means in the picture on page 6.

ELL On the board, draw a simple picture of a house, a car, and your school building. Write the word for each item and have children say the words with you. Ask children to draw their own pictures of these places and copy the correct word beneath each.

TEACH/REVIEW VOCABULARY Write the words on the board and invite children to read them with you. Then, say sentences and have children complete each sentence with the correct word. For example: *Some people live in a ____________. Every day we go to ____________.*

TARGET SKILL AND STRATEGY

THEME Share with children that the *theme* of a story is the big idea or lesson that readers learn from the book. Have children decide what this story is mostly about. Then, to arrive at the theme, have them think about what we should learn from this story.

MONITOR AND FIX UP Mention to children that sometimes when they read, they form an idea which they may later discover was incorrect. Model for the group how to *monitor* and *fix up* by using illustrations, rereading, and seeking help from others.

READ THE BOOK

Use the following questions to support comprehension.

PAGE 3 Why do the girl and her mother have to move? *(The girl's mother has a new job.)*

PAGE 4 Why are boxes needed for moving? *(The boxes are used to take belongings to a new home.)*

PAGE 5 Do the girl and her mother have a place to live yet? Reread the text to confirm your ideas. *(No, they must look for a house.)*

TALK ABOUT THE BOOK

THINK AND SHARE

1. Possible response: Sometimes people must move from one place to another.
2. Possible responses: get boxes; pack their things in the boxes; look for a new home; say good-bye to friends
3. *boxes*
4. Children's answers will vary but might reflect feeling anxious, nervous, or excited.

RESPONSE OPTIONS

WRITING Have children write a list of three things they would need to do if they had to move. Tell children to use information from the book or other ideas they have. You might have children copy and complete this sentence starter: *To get ready to move, you must ____________.*

CONTENT CONNECTIONS

Time for SOCIAL STUDIES

SOCIAL STUDIES Discuss with children why someone might move to their community. Have children suggest places in the community where new residents might work, live, shop, go to school, and have fun.

Name ______________________

Theme

Look at the picture below.

What is the "big idea" of this picture?
Think about how the people in the picture feel.
Think about what is happening.
Write a few sentences to tell what you think.

Name ______________________

Vocabulary

Complete the letter with words from the box.
Some words have pictures to help you.

Words to Know						
away	**car**	**friends**	**house**	**our**	**school**	**very**

Dear Carlos,

We are moving! I am ______________ happy.

We are not moving too far ______________ .

I can still go to the same ______________ .

I can still see my ______________ .

We will put all ______________ things

in the ______________ .

We will then go to the new ______________ .

I will tell you more after we move!

Your friend,

Mira

Unit 3 Week 3

THEME

MONITOR AND FIX UP

LESSON VOCABULARY away, car, friends, house, our, school, very

The New Park

SUMMARY Norm and his parents' neighborhood has everything they need except a park. The community holds a meeting to discuss building a new park. Everyone agrees and works together to build one.

INTRODUCE THE BOOK

BUILD BACKGROUND Have children describe or identify places in their communities, and list their ideas on the board. Ask: Do you think your communities always looked the same way? Did they always have the same shops? the same buildings? the same streets? Share with children that communities change over time.

PREVIEW/TAKE A PICTURE WALK Prompt children to explore the illustrations in the book and become familiar with the placement of text. Ask them to describe the neighborhood in which the story characters live. Then have children turn to page 10 and speculate what the people are doing. Check children's ideas after reading.

ELL Show children four pictures: a *house,* a *car,* a *school,* and some *friends.* As you say each word, ask children to point to the correct picture.

TEACH/REVIEW VOCABULARY On sentence strips, write a sentence for each vocabulary word. Display a sentence strip, say the vocabulary word, and have a child find the word on the strip. Discuss the word's meaning.

TARGET SKILL AND STRATEGY

THEME Share with children that the *theme* of a story is the big idea or the message that readers get from the story. As they read, suggest that children think about the message they can learn from this story.

MONITOR AND FIX UP Tell children that when they read, they form ideas about the text. When they reread, however, they may find that they misunderstood some parts of it. Model how to *monitor and fix up* by using illustrations, rereading, or asking for help.

READ THE BOOK

Use the following questions to support comprehension.

PAGE 3 What might be the big idea of this book? *(Neighborhoods have lots of places that people need.)*

PAGE 4 Does the family have everything they need in their community? Reread the page to confirm your ideas. *(At first they think they do, but then Norm says they do not.)*

PAGE 6 Why does the community have a meeting? *(to talk about building a park)*

TALK ABOUT THE BOOK

THINK AND SHARE

1. Possible response: Neighborhoods are always changing.
2. Possible responses: play sports, sit under trees, walk, feed ducks
3. Possible responses: *Norm, stores, sports*
4. Responses will vary.

RESPONSE OPTIONS

WRITING Have children imagine that they are among the people who built the park. The group decides to send out invitations to the rest of the community to celebrate the park's opening day. What should the invitations say? Ask children to write invitations, inviting everyone to the park.

CONTENT CONNECTIONS

Time for SOCIAL STUDIES

SOCIAL STUDIES Try to find pictures of your community from several decades ago. (Your local library is a good place to start.) Discuss the pictures, asking: What changes do you notice? Why might these changes have been made? What other changes might you suggest to people in your community?

Name ____________________

Theme

Look at the picture below. Read the words that tell about it.

Everyone helped build the park. Some people cut away weeds and thorns. Some people planted seeds and trees. Some people made paths. Some people made a place for sports.

At last the park was done. There were paths. There were benches and trees. There was a place for sports. There was a pond for ducks.

"Now our neighborhood has everything we need!" Norm said.

What "big idea," or theme, do you get from the picture and words?

Name ______________________

Vocabulary

Complete the poster with words from the box.
Think about what makes the most sense.

Words to Know			
away	car	friends	house
our	school	very	

Come One! Come All!
Come to Your New Park!

We are ______________ proud to tell you that

______________ community has a new park!

You can park your ______________ in the large parking lot.

It is near the ______________, so kids can go there after class with classmates.

The park is not far ______________, so you

can probably walk there from your ______________!

Bring your ______________!

We'll see you at the park!

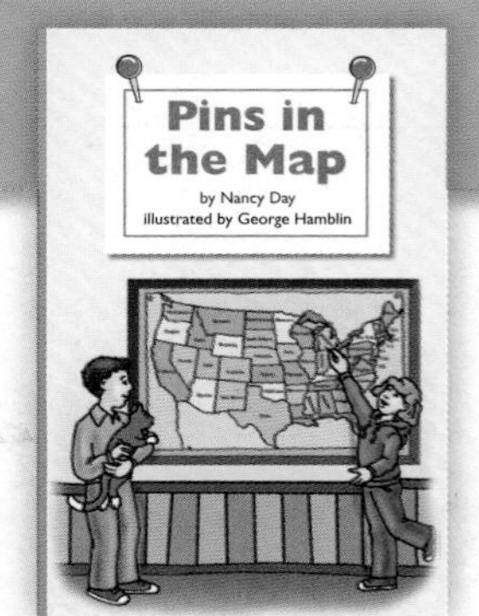

Unit 3 Week 3

- **THEME**
- **MONITOR AND FIX UP**

LESSON VOCABULARY arrive, depart, location, route

Pins in the Map

SUMMARY Katie's family runs a motel in Michigan, where she meets a boy named Sam. Sam is sad because his family has just moved. Katie tells Sam about the different places she has lived, and Sam realizes that moving does not have to be all bad.

INTRODUCE THE BOOK

BUILD BACKGROUND Have children describe their community. Then ask children if they think all communities are like theirs. Mention that some communities, such as cities, are filled with people and buildings. Other communities, such as towns, have fewer buildings and people.

PREVIEW/USE TEXT FEATURES Invite children to look through the book to become familiar with the text and the illustrations. Ask children to identify the item they see on page 5 and pages 6 and 7. *(the map)* Speculate with children why a map might be important to the story.

TEACH/REVIEW VOCABULARY Write the words on the board and read them with the class. Ask children what idea the words have in common—travel. Have children sort the words into two groups: nouns *(route, location)* and verbs *(arrive, depart).*

ELL Using a map and toy car, demonstrate for children the vocabulary words, i.e., *depart* from one area and *arrive* at another, travel along a *route* to a specific *location.* Have them practice the words with the props.

TARGET SKILL AND STRATEGY

THEME Share with children that the *theme* of a story is the big idea or the lesson that readers learn from the story. Encourage children to consider the theme of this story as they read the book.

MONITOR AND FIX UP Mention to children that sometimes when they read, they form an idea about the text that they later find to be incorrect. Demonstrate rereading to *monitor and fix up.*

READ THE BOOK

Use the following questions to support comprehension.

PAGE 1 How might the book's title relate to the story's theme? *(The theme involves living in different places, and the pins reflect those different places on the map.)*

PAGE 5 Think about where the boy lives. Reread the text to see if you are correct. *(Some children might think the boy lives in New Mexico; actually he lives at the motel.)*

PAGES 6–7 What do we learn about the pins on the map? *(The pins represent the places where Katie has lived and where people who visit the motel came from.)*

TALK ABOUT THE BOOK

THINK AND SHARE

1. Possible response: Even though communities are different, you can still find friends and enjoy life.
2. Possible response: The map shows that New York is all the way across the country from California.
3. Sentences will vary but should show that children understand that *relocate* means to move to a new location.
4. Possible responses: New York City; Pacifica, CA (suburb); Branchville, SC (rural); Grand Haven, MI (town)

RESPONSE OPTIONS

WRITING Encourage children to write letters from Sam to a friend in Santa Fe that include details from the book about his new life in Michigan.

CONTENT CONNECTIONS

Time for SOCIAL STUDIES

SOCIAL STUDIES Write the words *city, town, suburb,* and *rural* on the board, and ask children to match each with the name of a place where Katie lived. Have them recall details that helped them arrive at these conclusions.

Name ______________________________

Theme

Read the story below.

"Do you like living in this town?" Sam asked, his voice a little unsure.

"I do!" said Katie. "Everyone knows everybody else. People are nice and friendly."

"Like you," Sam said.

Katie smiled. "It's fun meeting new people at the motel."

"I didn't want to move away from my friends and the mountains," Sam said.

"But now I think I'm going to like living here."

What is the "big idea," or theme, of these words? Write your ideas below.

Name ______________________

Vocabulary

Draw a line to match each word on the left with a word or words on the right that have a similar meaning.

arrive	place
depart	path
location	leave
route	get there

Now use each word on the left in a sentence of your own.

1. arrive ______________________

2. depart ______________________

3. location ______________________

4. route ______________________

The Garden
by Sara Kwan
Illustrated by Amy Loeffler

Unit 3 Week 4

PLOT

VISUALIZE

LESSON VOCABULARY afraid, again, few, how, read, soon

The Garden

SUMMARY In this story, a first-grade class plants a garden and grows food to give to other people. It supports and extends the lesson concept that plants grow and change.

INTRODUCE THE BOOK

BUILD BACKGROUND Ask children to share what they know about planting a garden. Discuss reasons people might plant gardens: Do they want to grow pretty flowers? Do they want to grow vegetables to eat?

PREVIEW/TAKE A PICTURE WALK Have children look at the pictures in the book before reading. Where does the story take place? What do they think is going to happen in the book?

TEACH/REVIEW VOCABULARY Write each vocabulary word on the board. Then make a set of cards with the following word or words: *scared, a second time, not many, in what way, see the words, before long.* Show and read the cards to the children. Ask volunteers to say the vocabulary words that match the definitions on the cards. Use the words in sentences if children are having difficulty.

TARGET SKILL AND STRATEGY

PLOT Tell children that a story has a beginning, middle, and end. As they preview the story, ask children to point out the beginning, the middle, and the end of the story. Let children know that they will fill in a chart after reading, showing what happened in the beginning, the middle, and the end of the story.

VISUALIZE Say: "As you listen to or read a story, close your eyes and try to see pictures in your mind." Ask children to close their eyes. Read the title aloud. Then ask children to tell you what picture came to mind when they heard the title. What did they see, hear, or smell? Ask children to try and picture the whole story as they read.

READ THE BOOK

Use the following questions to support comprehension.

PAGES 4–5 What happened after Barb said that the class could plant a garden? *(The class started to plan a garden.)*

PAGES 6–7 Why do you think nothing happened after the class first planted the seeds? *(It takes time for plants to grow.)*

PAGE 7 What do you think would be in a picture that came after this one? *(Possible response: children picking vegetables from the garden)*

ELL To check understanding, have children explain to you what is happening in the illustrations.

TALK ABOUT THE BOOK

THINK AND SHARE

1. Beginning: The class planned a garden. Middle: The class planted the garden. End: The garden grew.
2. Possible response: First there was just dirt. Then tiny plants came up. The plants got bigger. Finally, vegetables grew on the plants.
3. *digging; dig* is circled
4. Possible response: They felt happy the plan worked.

RESPONSE OPTIONS

WRITING Arrange children in groups. Working together, the members of each group should decide what they would want to grow in their gardens and why. Afterward have one person from each group explain to the class the group's decisions as well as their reasoning.

CONTENT CONNECTIONS

TIME FOR Science

SCIENCE Display books that illustrate the life cycles of plants. Encourage children to look through the books. Afterward, have children imagine they were garden plants and describe how they would grow from seeds to plants ready for harvest.

Name________________________________

Plot

Think about what you read in *The Garden.*

1. Draw what happened in the beginning of the story.

2. Draw what happened in the middle of the story.

3. Draw what happened at the end of the story.

4. Now use your pictures to talk about the story.

Name________________________________

Vocabulary

Some of the following sentences use the wrong word from the box.
Put an X before any sentence that doesn't make sense.
Then, cross out the wrong word.
Write the right word at the end of the sentence.

Words to Know					
afraid	**again**	**few**	**how**	**read**	**soon**

_____ **1.** I am soon the plants won't grow. ____________

_____ **2.** I like to read books about plants. ____________

_____ **3.** How can we grow food for others? ____________

_____ **4.** There are very again seeds left. ____________

_____ **5.** Soon the plants will grow. ____________

_____ **6.** They had to use water afraid. ____________

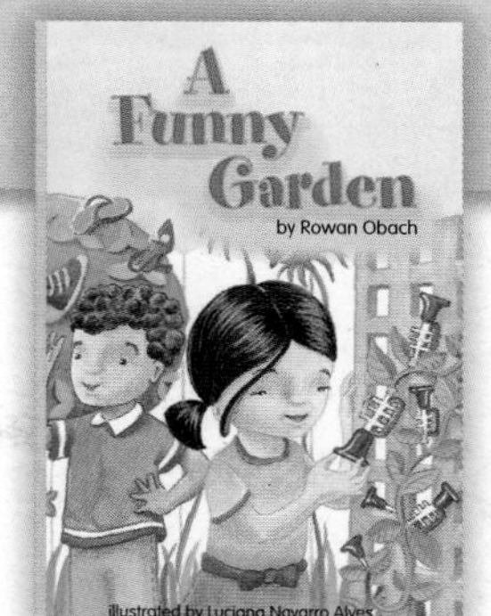

Unit 3 Week 4

PLOT

VISUALIZE

LESSON VOCABULARY afraid, again, few, how, read, soon

A Funny Garden

SUMMARY When Miss Jones reads a book about gardens to her class, they become inspired to plant their own garden with things such as toys and shoes. To their surprise, the garden grows.

INTRODUCE THE BOOK

BUILD BACKGROUND Involve children in a discussion about gardening. Ask children to brainstorm plants that grow in a garden. Together, classify the plants by type.

PREVIEW/TAKE A PICTURE WALK Turn to the title page and ask volunteers to read the title. On page 3, point out Miss Jones and her class. Point out the toy zebra and the toy trumpet on pages 4 and 5. Ask how these items might relate to a garden. On page 8, point out that the children are burying their toys in the dirt. Does that seem like a good idea? Turn to pages 10 and 11 and talk about the class's funny garden.

TEACH/REVIEW VOCABULARY Print vocabulary word cards and scatter them face up on a table. Call out a word, asking a volunteer to pick up the corresponding card and use the word in a sentence.

ELL Ask children to sort vocabulary word cards according to initial letter, final letter, or number of syllables.

TARGET SKILL AND STRATEGY

PLOT Point out to children that when they read a story, they can think about what happened first, next, and last. Understanding the *plot* of a story makes it easier to talk about the story. Review *A Funny Garden* and discuss the sequence of events. Then work with children to develop a story map.

VISUALIZE Remind children that good readers form pictures in their heads when they read a story. *Visualizing* helps readers remember a story's plot. As you read *A Funny Garden,* think aloud: "When I close my eyes, I can see the boys and girls planting their toys. I see a zebra and lots of shoes."

READ THE BOOK

Use the following questions to support comprehension.

PAGE 4 Why do you think Tom wanted to plant his stuffed zebra? *(Possible response: He wanted to grow more zebras.)*

PAGES 9–10 What happened after the children planted their garden? *(The garden grew.)*

PAGE 10 Close your eyes and picture the funny garden in your mind. What do you see? *(Responses should include vivid descriptions of the fantasy plants.)*

TALK ABOUT THE BOOK

THINK AND SHARE

1. In the beginning, Miss Jones reads a book to the class. In the middle, the class plants a garden. At the end, the garden grows.
2. Responses will vary but should relate to the story content.
3. *garden, gardens, Marc, hard, yard, started*
4. Responses will vary but may involve a play on words such as the ones in the story.

RESPONSE OPTIONS

WORD WORK Point out the word play in the names of the class's imaginary plants. Help children find pictures of the actual plants that have these names and compare the pictures to the illustrations in the books. Then invite children to name their own imaginary plants and draw pictures of them.

CONTENT CONNECTIONS

TIME FOR Science

SCIENCE Suggest that children start their own windowsill garden. Provide gardening books and other resources to help children plan what to plant and figure out how to care for the seedlings. Take photographs to monitor growth.

Name ______________________________

Plot

Read the story.
Then draw a picture in each box to show the plot.

One day Miss Jones read a book about plants and gardens to her class.

"Can we plant a silly garden? asked Tom.

"Yes!" said Miss Jones. "We can!"

Soon the class was busy. They dug holes in the yard and planted a zebra, a trumpet, some bells, and some shoes.

In a few weeks, Miss Jones looked out the window. "Come and see the funny garden!" she said.

I. Beginning

2. Middle

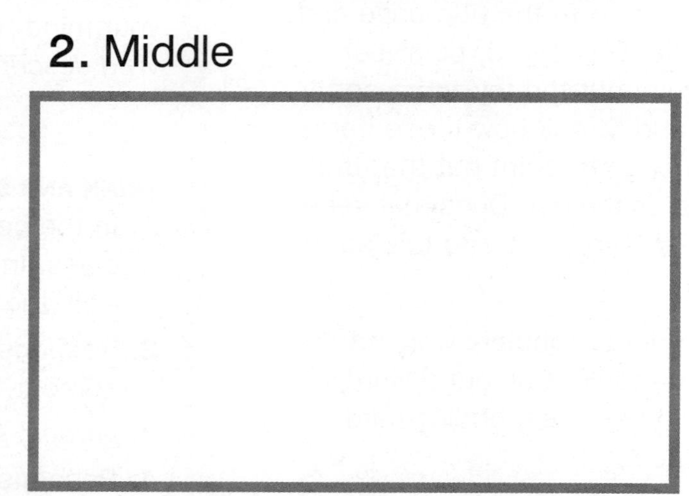

3. End

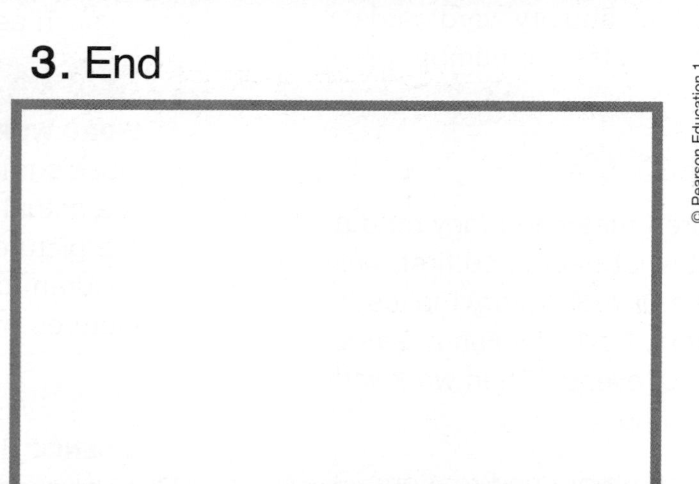

Name ______________________

Vocabulary

Fill in the blank with the word that best fits each sentence.

Words to Know
afraid again few how read soon

1. ______________ these steps and learn about gardens.

2. First you plant a ______________ seeds.

3. ______________ you will have a beautiful garden.

4. You can learn ______________ to grow seeds.

5. If you garden doesn't grow, try ______________ .

6. Don't be ______________ to try your plan.

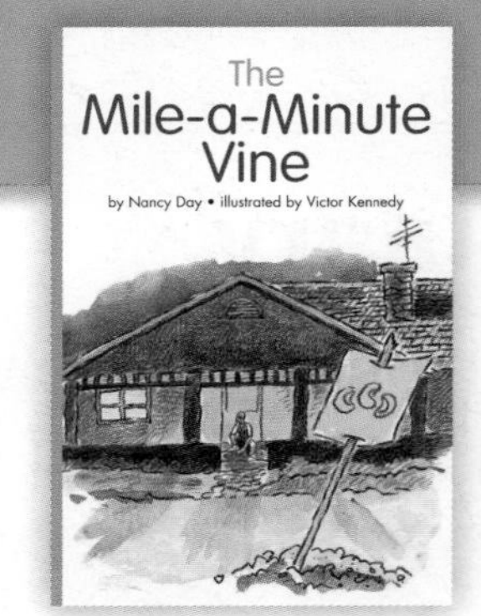

The Mile-a-Minute Vine

PLOT

VISUALIZE

LESSON VOCABULARY gardener, nature, sprout

SUMMARY In this story, a young boy plants a vine that soon grows out of control. It supports and extends the lesson concept that plants grow and change.

INTRODUCE THE BOOK

BUILD BACKGROUND Ask children to tell what they know about vines, such as grapevines. Explain how you can train vines to grow up around poles or fences, but that they can grow everywhere if their growth is not guided.

PREVIEW/TAKE A PICTURE WALK Invite children to look through the pictures in the book. Ask: Who do you think the characters in the story will be? What do you think will happen in the story?

ELL Let children know that the expression *mile-a-minute* means "really fast."

TEACH/REVIEW VOCABULARY Have children make word cards for each vocabulary word. Then have them make cards for each of these word groups: *river, trees, rocks; person, planter, picker;* and *plant, small, green.* Ask children to match each word group with the vocabulary word that goes best with that group.

TARGETED SKILL AND STRATEGY

PLOT Tell children that a story has a beginning, middle, and end. As they read, have children look for the beginning, middle, and end of this story. Ask: What happens before Jake gets the seeds? What happens when Jake plants the seeds? What happens after the vine has grown? Let children know that, after reading, they will fill in a chart to show what happened in the beginning, the middle, and the end of the story.

VISUALIZE Say: "As you hear or read a story, close your eyes sometimes and try to see pictures in your mind." Have children close their eyes. Read page 3 aloud. Ask: What picture comes to mind as I read? Is your picture like the one on the page? How does it help you understand Jake and his mother's problem? Ask children to picture story events as they read.

READ THE BOOK

Use the following questions to support comprehension.

PAGE 5 When Jake thinks of a boy who did well trading a cow for beans, who is he thinking of? *(Jack from "Jack and the Beanstalk")*

PAGES 6–7 What happened after Jake planted the beans? *(A vine sprouted and quickly grew.)*

PAGE 13 What pictures came to mind when you read that Jake made things from the vines? *(Possible response: plants cut to look like people and animals)*

TALK ABOUT THE BOOK

THINK AND SHARE

1. Possible response: Beginning: Jake trades cow for magic beans. Middle: The vine grows out of control. End: Jake makes his fortune.
2. Her mouth made a round *O.*
3. Possible responses: *dried, slammed, wrapped, rained, sighed, suggested, traded, planted, rushed, replied, tried, chewed, covered, turned*
4. Possible response: I would have used a big tractor to cut the vines.

RESPONSE OPTIONS

VIEWING Have children choose a favorite part of the story to illustrate and write about.

CONTENT CONNECTIONS

TIME FOR Science

SCIENCE Have children browse books or other materials that give facts about planting and growing different kinds of vines. Ask them to pick a vine, describe how they would plant and care for it, and what they would get out of planting the vine.

Name ______________________________

Plot

Put an X by the events that did not happen in *The Mile-a-Minute Vine*.

__________ 1. Jake's peanut crop dried up.

__________ 2. Jake bought beans from an old man.

__________ 3. Jake planted the beans.

__________ 4. Cows would not eat the vine.

__________ 5. Everybody saw Jake and the vine on television.

__________ 6. Jake used the vine to make things like baskets, jelly, and tea.

__________ 7. In the end, Jake and his mother were able to make money by selling things made from the vine.

__________ 8. The vine dried up and never came back to life.

Name ___________________________

Vocabulary

Use the correct word from the box to complete each sentence below.

Words to Know

gardener **nature** **sprout**

1. The ___________________________ likes to grow roses and other flowers.

2. Soon a ___________________________ pushed up through the ground.

3. Our class likes to take long ___________________________ walks to learn more about trees.

4-5. Write your own sentence using *gardener* and *sprout*.

____

____

____

Animals Grow and Change

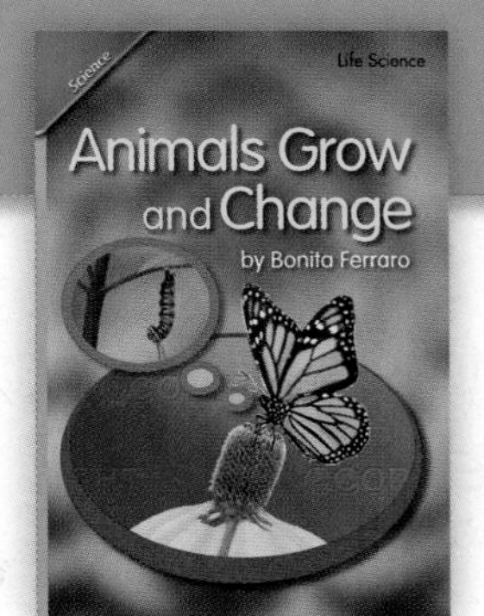

Unit 3 Week 5

DRAW CONCLUSIONS

TEXT STRUCTURE

LESSON VOCABULARY done, know, push, visit, wait

SUMMARY This informational book describes how different animals grow and change over time. It supports the lesson concept that insects and animals grow and change.

INTRODUCE THE BOOK

BUILD BACKGROUND Discuss with children how they change and grow. Ask: How are you different from when you were a baby? How will you change as you get older?

PREVIEW/USE PHOTOGRAPHS Have children preview the book. Look specifically at the photographs on pages 4 and 5 and ask the children to describe what is happening. Encourage them to explore the other photographs and make predictions about the text.

ELL Invite children to share the names of the young and adult animals in their home languages.

TEACH/REVIEW VOCABULARY Create a set of vocabulary word cards and give them to the children. Create a set of cards with the following synonyms: *finished, understand, shove, stop by, stay.* Show each synonym card and say the word or words aloud. Ask children to show the vocabulary word that has the same meaning.

TARGET SKILL AND STRATEGY

DRAW CONCLUSIONS Remind children that they can make decisions using what they read and what they know about real life to figure out more about what happens in a book. Draw their attention to the arrows between the pictures and refer to the text encouraging them to identify when each animal is younger and older.

TEXT STRUCTURE Review with children that books may explain things by describing what happens first, next, and last. Ask children to look at the text and pictures on page 8. Invite children to retell this sequence using the words *first, then,* and *last* while pointing to the photographs and arrows for support.

READ THE BOOK

Use the following questions to support comprehension.

PAGES 4–5 Where did the egg in the picture come from? *(the mother bird)*

PAGE 6 How does the gerbil change? *(It gets bigger, its eyes open, and it grows fur.)*

PAGE 8 What is the difference between how a butterfly changes over time and how people change? *(A butterfly has three different forms, but people keep the same basic form as they grow.)*

TALK ABOUT THE BOOK

THINK AND SHARE

1. They also grow and change.
2. Children's pictures should mirror the photographs on page 8.
3. *They, have*
4. It starts out as a tadpole, grows legs, and becomes a frog.

RESPONSE OPTIONS

SPEAKING Ask children to describe the stages of a butterfly life cycle in their own words. Coach them in using the words *first, then,* and *last* to organize the sequence of events.

CONTENT CONNECTIONS

Time for Science

SCIENCE Create a bulletin board. On one half, put the words *Animals Change and Grow* and invite the children to draw or help find photographs of baby and adult animals to put on the board. Label the other half of the board *We Change and Grow.* Invite the children to bring in two pictures of themselves: one current and one as a baby or younger child. Provide photographs of yourself as well. Look at the board together and discuss the differences you see between the pictures.

Name________________________

Draw Conclusions

Draw a line from each set of facts to the correct conclusion. Use *Animals Grow and Change* to help you.

A kitten has fur, whiskers, and a tiny cat body.

It will grow larger to become a grown-up cat.

Some animals change shape when they grow.

A caterpillar crawls at first.

It becomes a pupa.

It turns into a butterfly.

Some baby animals look like small grown-ups when they are young.

Name________________________

Vocabulary

Circle the word that best completes each sentence.
Write the word in the blank.

one wait know

1. Do you ________________ what a butterfly is?

visit crawl done

2. You are not ________________ growing yet.

push wait know

3. If you ________________ long enough, it will get bigger.

one visit know

4. Children ________________ their friends after school.

crawl done push

5. Friends can ________________ you on the swing to go higher.

Unit 3 Week 5

A Visit to a Butterfly . . .

DRAW CONCLUSIONS

TEXT STRUCTURE

LESSON VOCABULARY done, know, push, visit, wait

SUMMARY This nonfiction book depicts what people can see and learn at a butterfly greenhouse. It supports and extends the lesson concept that insects, like other animals, grow and change.

INTRODUCE THE BOOK

BUILD BACKGROUND Invite children to describe butterflies they may have seen (size, shape, color). Ask: Where might you see a butterfly? What do you know about butterflies?

PREVIEW/USE TEXT FEATURES Have the children preview the book, looking at the pictures. Guide them in using the labels to understand and describe what they see in the photographs. Encourage them to use this information to make predictions about the text.

TEACH/REVIEW VOCABULARY Create a set of vocabulary word cards and give them to children. Make sentence strips with the following sentences: *I am finished. I learned something. I moved the door. I went to see my friend. I stayed until the end.* Show each sentence and read it aloud. Ask children to show the vocabulary word that goes best with each sentence.

ELL Have children list unfamiliar words and write the corresponding words from their home languages.

TARGET SKILL AND STRATEGY

DRAW CONCLUSIONS Let children know that they can make decisions using what they read and what they know about real life to figure out more about what happens in a book. After children have read page 9, say: "It says that a chrysalis is like a hard shell. What other things have shells? How does the chrysalis help the caterpillar or pupa?"

TEXT STRUCTURE Remind children that the sequence in a book helps us understand the information. Model how to use a series-of-events chain. Have children draw in the stages of the butterfly life cycle as explained on pages 6–10.

READ THE BOOK

Use the following questions to support comprehension.

PAGE 5 Why does a butterfly drink nectar? *(It needs nectar to live.)*

PAGE 8 Describe what happens first, next, and last. *(First, the caterpillar crawls, eats, and grows. Then, it stops growing. Last, a big change happens.)*

PAGE 11 What do you think would be most exciting about visiting a butterfly greenhouse? Why? *(Possible response: watching a butterfly crawl out of its chrysalis)*

TALK ABOUT THE BOOK

THINK AND SHARE

1. Possible response: so they can see the butterflies grow and change
2. egg: page 6; butterfly: page 11
3. *it's/it is*
4. Children should describe the color and shape of the chrysalis.

RESPONSE OPTIONS

WRITING Ask children to write a few sentences about what they might see at a butterfly greenhouse. Guide them in using clue words to sequence their narratives.

CONTENT CONNECTIONS

TIME FOR Science

SCIENCE Provide additional resources about butterflies. Encourage the class to find out which kinds of butterflies live in the area where they live. Children can create their own diagrams of the butterfly life cycle.

Name ________________________________

Draw Conclusions

Write conclusions based on the information from the book *A Visit to a Butterfly Greenouse.*

1. A butterfly greenhouse has flowers. A butterfly drinks nectar from flowers.
   Conclusion:

2. People can learn a lot at a butterfly greenhouse. You can watch a butterfly come out of its chrysalis there.
   Conclusion:

Name ______________________________

Vocabulary

Find each of the following vocabulary words in *A Visit to a Butterfly Greenhouse.* Write the page number on which you found the word. Then write your own sentence using a vocabulary word.

1. **done:** page ______________

2. **know:** page ______________

3. **push:** page ______________

4. **visit:** page ______________

5. **wait:** page ______________

6. ____

____

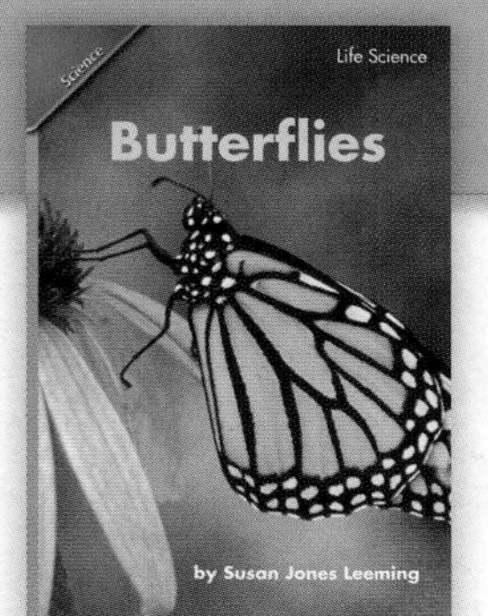

Unit 3 Week 5

DRAW CONCLUSIONS

TEXT STRUCTURE

LESSON VOCABULARY cycle, develop, insect

Butterflies

SUMMARY This informational book supports the lesson concept that insects and animals grow and change by describing the different stages and sequence of the butterfly life cycle.

INTRODUCE THE BOOK

BUILD BACKGROUND Engage children in a discussion about butterflies. Invite them to describe butterflies they have seen and share what they know about them.

PREVIEW/USE TEXT FEATURES Have children preview the book by looking at the pictures and make predictions about the text. Call their attention to the labels and captions, and explain how these features can help them better understand the information in the text.

ELL Point out the following words: page 3—*flutter,* page 6—*shivers,* page 11—*predators.* Restate the words and explain what they mean.

TEACH/REVIEW VOCABULARY Arrange children in pairs. Have one partner write a sentence for a vocabulary word replacing the word with a blank. Ask them to exchange sentences and fill in the correct words. Repeat the activity until all the words have been used at least once.

TARGET SKILL AND STRATEGY

DRAW CONCLUSIONS Remind children that they can make decisions using what they read and what they know about real life to figure out more about what happens in a book. After children have read page 8, say: "It says that the antennae, or feelers, help the butterfly know what's around it. What does it mean to *feel* something? How does the butterfly use its antennae?"

TEXT STRUCTURE Review that books may explain things by describing what happens first, next, and last. Give children a series-of-events chain to track the stages of the butterfly life cycle as they read. Include clue words such as *first, next, then,* and *last.* Ask them to write a short description of each stage.

READ THE BOOK

Use the following questions to support comprehension.

PAGE 6 Why are the butterfly's wings wet when it comes out of the chrysalis? *(The inside of the chrysalis must be wet.)*

PAGE 9 Why do you think a butterfly rests during the night and on rainy days? *(Possible responses: too dark, dangerous, might get wet)*

PAGES 10–11 How does this butterfly's camouflage make it hard to see? *(It is reddish-brown, just like the leaves.)*

TALK ABOUT THE BOOK

THINK AND SHARE

1. The flowers contain the butterflies' food.
2. First: color is camouflage; next: color signals bad taste, poison, or danger; last: fly away fast
3. there's/there is, caterpillar's/caterpillar is, what's/what is, they're/they are, don't/do not, aren't/are not
4. Answers will vary but should be supported with information from the text.

RESPONSE OPTIONS

WRITING Ask children to write a short description of a butterfly. They should use information they have learned from the book and also include some of the vocabulary words.

CONTENT CONNECTIONS

TIME FOR Science

SCIENCE Encourage children to learn more about the butterfly life cycle by using the library or the Internet. They can create and illustrate their own diagrams of the butterfly life cycle and write short descriptions of each stage.

Name ______________________________

Draw Conclusions

Write conclusions based on information from the book *Butterflies*.

1. The caterpillar eats and eats and eats. Soon it grows large.

   Conclusion:

2. The butterfly shivers because its wings are wet. It rests in the sun and waits for its wings to dry.

   Conclusion:

3. Camouflage makes a butterfly hard to see. Camouflage helps a butterfly hide from danger.

   Conclusion:

Name ______________________

Vocabulary

Use the words in the box to help you complete each sentence.

Words to Know		
cycle	develop	insect

1. A butterfly is a type of ______________________ .

2. The butterfly life ______________ begins with an egg.

3. The caterpillar will ______________________ into a butterfly inside the chrysalis.

4-5. Write two sentences about facts you learned from *Butterflies*. Use the three words from the box in your sentences.

____

____

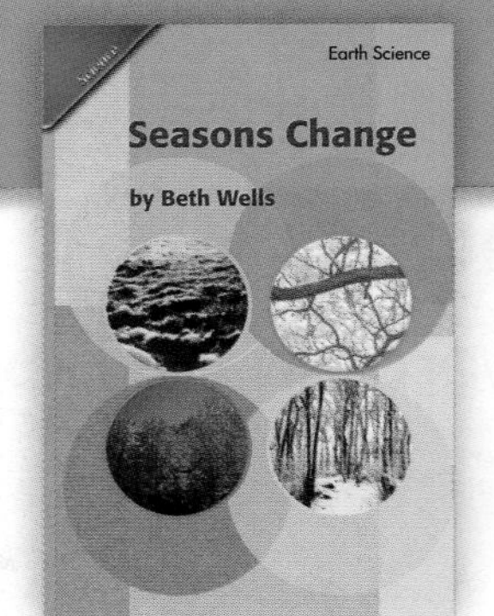

Unit 3 Week 6

SEQUENCE

PRIOR KNOWLEDGE

LESSON VOCABULARY before, does, good-bye, oh, right, won't

Seasons Change

SUMMARY One reason the weather changes is because of the seasons. The weather begins to warm in the spring, and turns hot in the summer. It begins to cool in the fall, and is the coldest in winter.

INTRODUCE THE BOOK

BUILD BACKGROUND Ask children what the words *spring, summer, fall,* and *winter* stand for. *(the seasons)* Invite them to talk about the weather where they live. Ask: How does it feel outside in the spring? in the summer? in the fall? in the winter?

PREVIEW/USE PHOTOGRAPHS Ask children if they think this book will be a story or about something real. Point out that the photographs suggest that this book will tell them about something real. Have children study a specific page, and ask them to predict which season they will read about on that page.

ELL Pretend to walk away from the group, waving. Ask children what you should say, and have them all say *good-bye* with you. Make other hand or body motions for other vocabulary words, such as nodding your head for *right* (correct) and making a surprised face for *oh.*

TEACH/REVIEW VOCABULARY Write the words on the board. Say each word in random order and have a volunteer point out the correct word. Use the words in sentences.

TARGET SKILL AND STRATEGY

SEQUENCE Remind children that *sequence* is the order in which things happen. Discuss with children the sequence of the seasons and have them notice whether the seasons appear in the same order in the book.

PRIOR KNOWLEDGE Share with children that *prior knowledge* is what they know before they begin reading. Considering what they already know can help them better understand what they read.

READ THE BOOK

Use the following questions to support comprehension.

PAGE 5 Which season follows spring? *(summer)*

PAGE 6 What do you know about fall? How do the pictures confirm what you know? *(I know that leaves change color in fall. The pictures show colorful leaves.)*

PAGE 7 How are trees in winter different from trees in fall? *(Trees in winter are bare. Trees in fall have colorful leaves.)*

TALK ABOUT THE BOOK

THINK AND SHARE

1. winter
2. Possible response: Spring is warmer than winter, but still cool. Flowers bloom in spring. Leaves begin to grow.
3. *good-bye;* 4 times
4. Possible response: It is raining, so the sky is probably cloudy and gray.

RESPONSE OPTIONS

WRITING Invite children to write about their favorite seasons. Write the following sentences on the board for children to copy to jumpstart their ideas: *How does it feel outside? It is ________. It feels ________.*

CONTENT CONNECTIONS

TIME FOR Science

SCIENCE Talk with children about the clothes they wear for the different seasons and kinds of weather. Describe the weather and have children supply what they would wear. For example: *It feels cold! I should wear ________.*

Name________________________

Sequence

Read the name of the season in the first box.
Then write the name of the season that comes next.

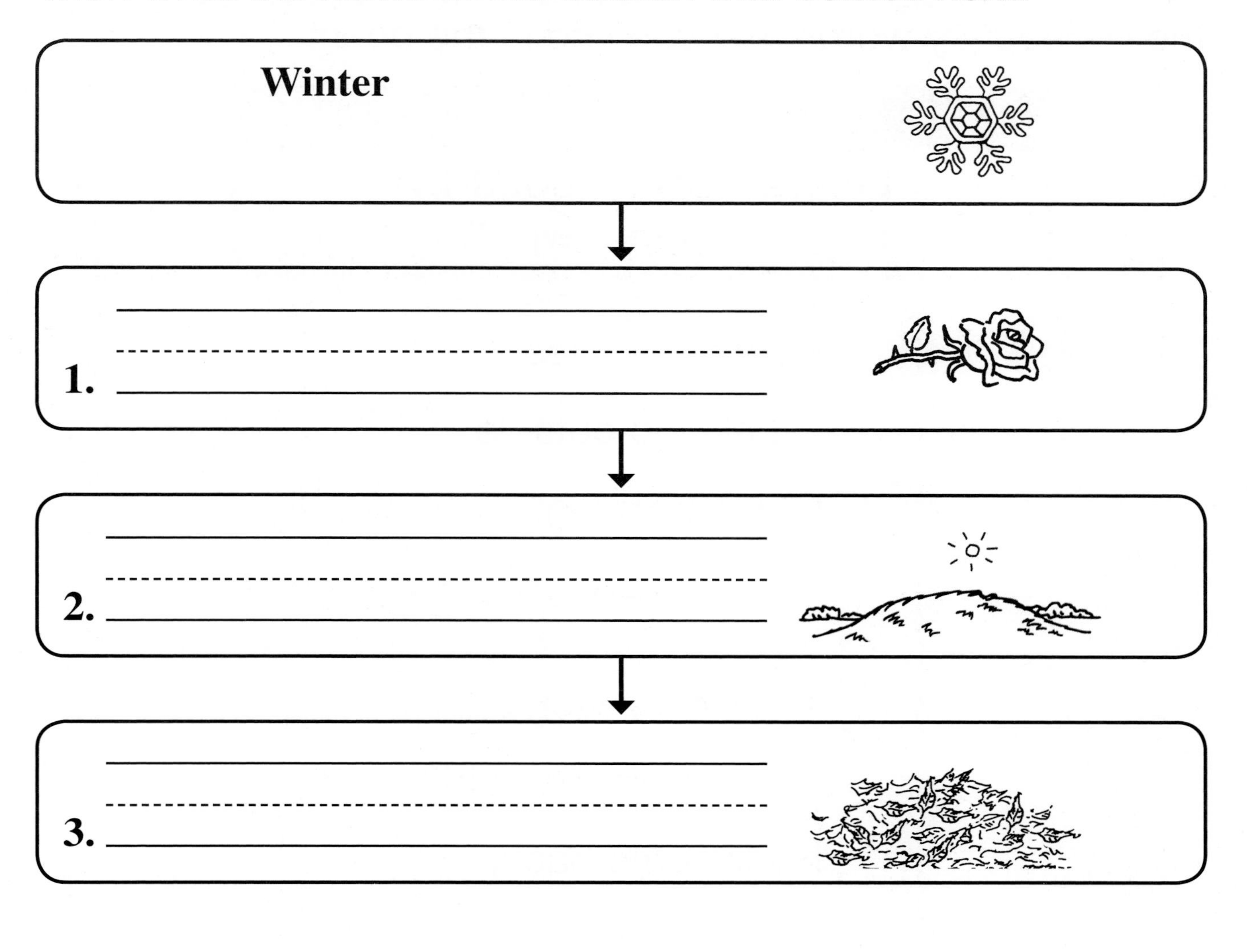

4. What season is it now? How do you know?

Name ______________________________

Vocabulary

Read the poem below, or listen as someone reads it to you. Look for the words from the box in the poem. Then circle the vocabulary words that you find in the poem.

Words to Know		
before	**does**	**good-bye**
oh	**right**	**won't**

How does it feel?
  Let's go outside.
Oh! It is spring!
  Let's wave good-bye—

To winter—won't
  you miss the cold?
It will come back,
  Or so I'm told.

You are right!
  Before you know it,
Winter is back,
  And it is snowing.

Spring Rose, Winter Bear

SEQUENCE

PRIOR KNOWLEDGE

LESSON VOCABULARY before, does, good-bye, oh, right, won't

UMMARY People, plants, and animals adjust to the veather in each season. This nonfiction book helps eaders discover these seasonal changes.

NTRODUCE THE BOOK

UILD BACKGROUND Invite children to consider how they lress differently for each season. If your area does not ave dramatic seasonal changes, you might have children peculate what clothing people might wear in various ypes of weather. Share with children that plants and nimals also make changes with the seasons.

REVIEW/USE TEXT FEATURES Prompt children to look hrough the book. Have children pause on pages 6 and 7. oint out the text below each picture. Confirm that this text s a label and that labels give information about pictures.

ELL Write each word on an index card. Hold up the ard and say it for the group. Encourage children to say with you. Make up a sentence for each word and have hildren repeat the sentences.

EACH/REVIEW VOCABULARY Write the words on the oard. Then write and say words that mean the opposite. lave children match the words to show they know the neaning. For example: *good-bye/hello; right/wrong.*

ARGET SKILL AND STRATEGY

SEQUENCE Remind children that *sequence* is the rder in which things happen. Suggest that children onsider the sequence of changes described in this ook. For example, ask: What do bears do before hey hibernate? *(eat a lot)* What do bears do after they ibernate? *(eat again)*

PRIOR KNOWLEDGE Share with children that *prior nowledge* is what they know about a topic before reading. rior knowledge helps them better understand what they ead. Invite children to share what they already know about ow plants or animals change with the seasons. Be sure o discuss the sequence of these changes.

READ THE BOOK

Use the following questions to support comprehension.

PAGE 3 Which season is so cold that people need to wear warm clothing? *(winter)*

PAGE 5 Which season will come after winter? *(spring)*

PAGE 6 Why is it important for the fox to blend in with the snow and the ground? *(Blending in helps the fox to hide from animals that might want to catch it.)*

TALK ABOUT THE BOOK

THINK AND SHARE

1. Possible response: In the spring, a tree grows flowers and leaves. In the summer, fruit may grow. In the fall, the fruit gets ripe and leaves fall from the tree. In the winter, the tree is bare.
2. Possible response: I knew that some trees in the winter have no leaves. Knowing this helped me understand the pictures on pages 10 and 11.
3. *edges, hedge*
4. winter and summer

RESPONSE OPTIONS

WRITING Speculate with children why this book is titled *Spring Rose, Winter Bear.* Have children write a sentence for each part of the title that explains how it relates to the changing seasons. Let children draw pictures for their sentences.

CONTENT CONNECTIONS

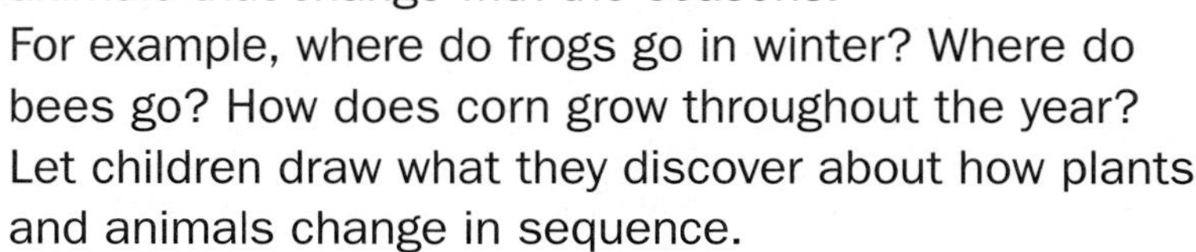

SCIENCE Help children conduct research to learn about other plants or animals that change with the seasons. For example, where do frogs go in winter? Where do bees go? How does corn grow throughout the year? Let children draw what they discover about how plants and animals change in sequence.

Name ______________________________

Sequence

In the spring, leaves grow on the trees. In the summer the trees are green. In the fall the leaves change color and fall off the trees. In the winter the trees are bare.

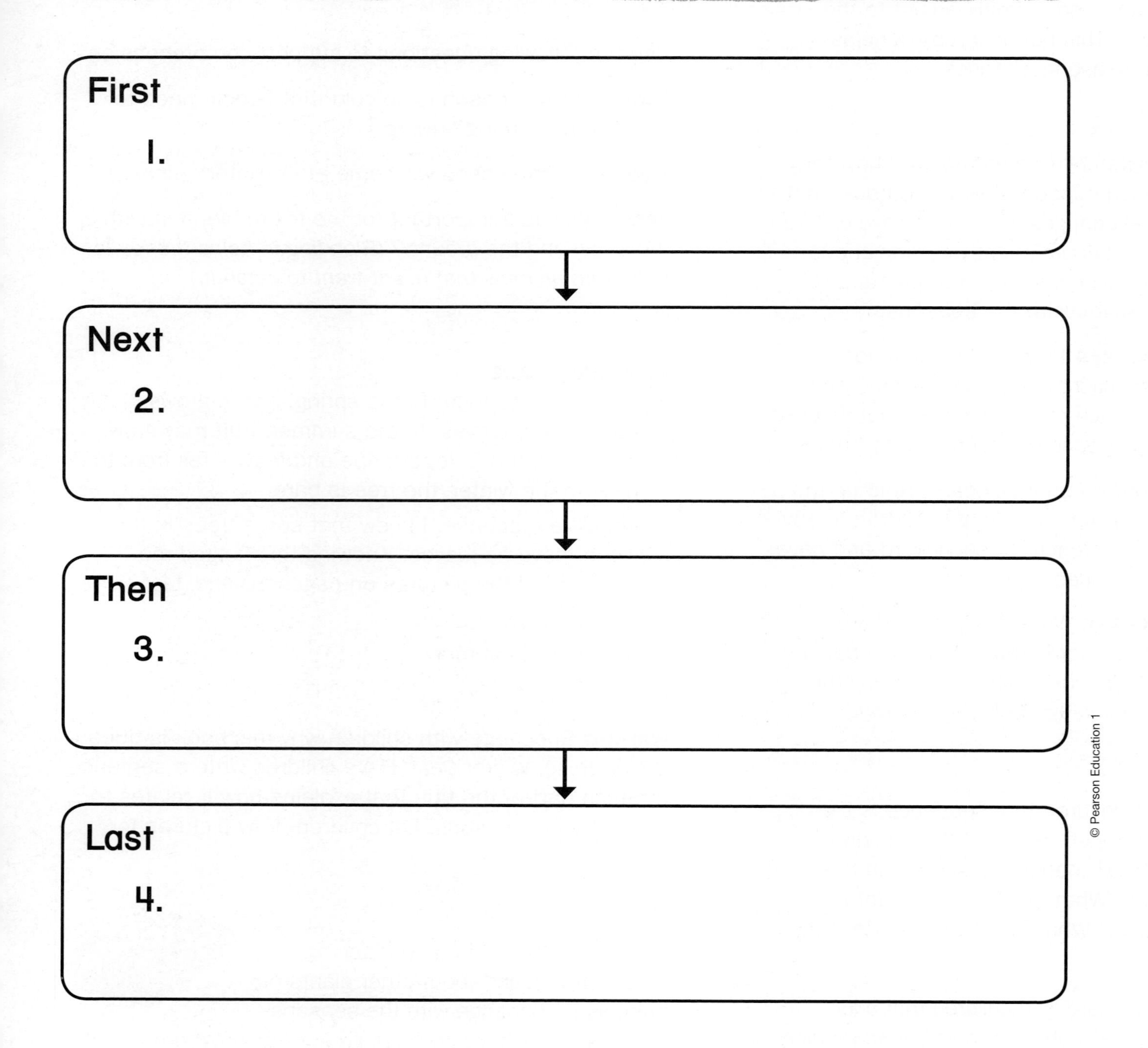

Name ______________________

Vocabulary

Write the word from the box that best fits in each sentence.

Words to Know		
before	does	good-bye
oh	right	won't

1. ______________ the winter comes, a bear must eat and eat.

2. The bear ______________ this to become fat.

3. If it doesn't eat, the bear ______________ sleep.

4. The bear waits until the time is ______________ .

5. Then it is time to say ______________ until spring.

6. ______________ , hello, bear! It is spring again!

Unit 3 Week 6

SEQUENCE

PRIOR KNOWLEDGE

LESSON VOCABULARY hibernate, migrat
season, temperature

Weather or Not

SUMMARY Today, we have scientific instruments to help us predict the weather. Long ago, however, people, relied on examining changes in the sky, plants, and animals to predict the weather. This book explores some of the folklore associated with weather prediction.

INTRODUCE THE BOOK

BUILD BACKGROUND Explain that *folklore* is what people once believed to explain what happened. Mention that people have always been fascinated with the weather and how to predict it. Long ago, people relied on folklore to figure out what the weather would be like.

PREVIEW/USE TEXT FEATURES Encourage children to flip through this book and notice features of the nonfiction text. For example, the book has photographs instead of illustrations. Also call attention to the words highlighted in yellow on page 12. Explain that these words are defined in the book's glossary.

ELL Find pictures that can help children understand these four words, *spring, summer, fall,* and *winter,* such as birds migrating, bears hibernating, a thermometer telling temperature, and a picture that shows all four seasons. Have children say each word.

TEACH/REVIEW VOCABULARY Write the word *season* on the board, and have children explain what the word refers to. Then say the words *hibernate, migrate,* and *temperature,* and talk about how these words relate to the seasons.

TARGET SKILL AND STRATEGY

SEQUENCE Remind children that *sequence* is the order in which things happen. Suggest that children consider the sequence of information in this book: first we learn about watching the sky and clouds; next about watching plants; last about watching animals.

PRIOR KNOWLEDGE Invite children to share their *prior knowledge,* what they already know, about the weather. You might discuss the sequence of a coming storm.

READ THE BOOK

Use the following questions to support comprehension.

PAGE 5 In the poem, what is the sequence of a day? *(morning, then night)*

PAGES 6–7 Look at the clouds on these pages. What is your experience with these kinds of clouds? *(White, puffy clouds mean a sunny day. Dark clouds mean rain.)*

PAGE 8 How do you know when it might rain? *(The air smells damp; the wind picks up; the sky gets dark.)*

TALK ABOUT THE BOOK

THINK AND SHARE

1. Possible responses: Flowers smell stronger. Leaves turn over. Hair gets curly. Joints hurt.
2. Possible response: People on the news make weather predictions using special tools.
3. They travel from place to place to find warm weather
4. Responses will vary. Encourage creativity.

RESPONSE OPTIONS

WRITING Invite children to pretend they are weather forecasters today, but instead of modern terminology, they use folklore to predict the weather. Have children write a weather report using examples of folklore from this book.

CONTENT CONNECTIONS

SCIENCE For one week, invite children to predict the weather, using the folklore in this book. Track how close their predictions are and discuss the results.

Name ______________________

Sequence

Read the paragraph. Think about what happens first, next, and last. Complete the chart below.

Tree leaves grow with their shiny side facing the sun. The wind that comes before a storm blows them so you can see their lighter-green backs. Then it starts to rain.

First

1.

Next

2.

Last

3.

Name ______________________

Vocabulary

Read the definitions.
Write the word from the box under its definition.

Words to Know

hibernate **migrate** **season** **temperature**

1. **Definition:** to spend the winter sleeping or resting

   Word: ______________________

2. **Definition:** how hot or cold something is

   Word: ______________________

3. **Definition:** one of the four times of the year

   Word: ______________________

4. **Definition:** to move from one place to another

   Word: ______________________

Nothing Stays the Same LR1

Compare and Contrast, LR2
Pictures will vary.

Vocabulary, LR3
1. day **2.** nothing **3.** become **4.** things **5.** always **6.** everything **7.** stays

Can Hank Sing? LR10

Plot, LR11
1 2
Pictures should show Hank happy about singing.

Vocabulary, LR12
1. were **2.** any **3.** ever **4.** enough **5.** sure **6.** every **7.** own

A Big Move LR19

Theme, LR20
Possible responses: Sometimes people have to move and leave their friends. They take all their things with them to their new home.

Vocabulary, LR21
very, away, school, friends, our, car, house

The Garden LR28

Plot, LR29
1. Drawings will vary. **2.** Drawings will vary. **3.** Drawings will vary.

Vocabulary, LR30
1. X the word *soon;* afraid **2.** no X **3.** no X **4.** X the word *again;* few
5. no X **6.** X the word *afraid;* again

Animals Grow and Change LR37

Draw Conclusions, LR38
A kitten has fur, whiskers, and a tiny cat body. It will grow larger to become a grown up cat—Some baby animals look like small grown-ups when they are young.
A caterpillar crawls at first. It becomes a pupa. It turns into a butterfly.—Some animals change shape when they grow.

Vocabulary, LR39
1. know **2.** done **3.** wait **4.** visit **5.** push

Seasons Change LR46

Sequence, LR47
1. Spring **2.** Summer **3.** Fall

Vocabulary, LR48
does, Oh!, good-bye, won't, right!, Before

Just Like Me LR4

Compare and Contrast, LR5
Possible responses given. **1.** Both have black hair. **2.** Both hold the baby. **3.** Both have rosy cheeks. **4.** The boy has on a red shirt. **5.** The boy is smaller. **6.** The father is wearing gray pants.

Vocabulary, LR6
1. things **2.** always **3.** stays **4.** everything **5.** nothing **6.** day **7.** become

Not Just Any Boy LR13

Plot, LR14
1. End **2.** Beginning **3.** Middle
Possible responses given. **4.** Mac runs in a race. **5.** Mac gives out the mail.

Vocabulary, LR15
ever, sure, own, were, enough, any, every

The New Park LR22

Theme, LR23
Possible responses given. People can work together to make something great. Neighborhoods need parks.

Vocabulary, LR24
very, our, cars, school, away, house, friends

A Funny Garden LR31

Plot, LR32
Drawings will vary.

Vocabulary, LR33
1. Read **2.** few **3.** Soon **4.** how **5.** again **6.** afraid

Answer Key for Leveled Reader Practice

A Visit to a Butterfly Greenhouse LR40

Draw Conclusions, LR41
Possible responses given. **1.** A butterfly can get its food in the greenhouse. **2.** A butterfly greenhouse is an interesting place to visit.

Vocabulary, LR42
1. 8 **2.** 3, 4, 5, 6, 7, 8, 11, or 12 Responses will vary. **3.** 6 **4.** 4 **5.** 10 **6.** Responses will vary.

Spring Rose, Winter Bear LR49

Sequence, LR50
1. leaves grow on the trees. **2.** trees are green. **3.** leaves change color and fall off the trees. **4.** trees are bare.

Vocabulary, LR51
1. Before **2.** does **3.** won't **4.** right **5.** good-bye **6.** Oh

Your Amazing Body! LR7

Compare and Contrast, LR8
Possible respones given. **1.** We both have 5 fingers. **2.** We both have fingernails. **3.** You can see our veins. **4.** My hand is smaller. **5.** My hand does not have hair. **6.** My hand is more tanned.

Vocabulary, LR9
1. healthy **2.** adult **3.** measurement **4.** adult **5.** healthy

A Bed for Paul LR16

Plot, LR17
1. End **2.** Middle **3.** Beginning **4.** End

Vocabulary, LR18
1. event **2.** attempt **3.** time line **4.** Responses will vary.

Pins in the Map LR25

Theme, LR26
Possible responses given. People will make new friends when they move. Moving does not need to be scary. Many people move from one place to another.

Vocabulary, LR27
arrive—get there, depart—leave, location—place, route—path
1–4. Sentences will vary but the vocabulary words should be used correctly.

The Mile-a-Minute Vine LR34

Plot, LR35
4. X **5.** X **8.** X

Vocabulary, LR36
1. gardener **2.** sprout **3.** nature **4–5.** Possible response: The gardener carefully watered the sprout.

Butterflies LR43

Draw Conclusions, LR44
Possible respones given. **1.** The caterpillar eats so that it can grow. **2.** The sun dries the butterfly's wings. **3.** The butterfly will be safe from its enemies.

Vocabulary, LR45
1. insect **2.** cycle **3.** develop **4–5.** Responses will vary.

Weather or Not LR52

Sequence, LR53
1. Leaves grow with shiny side up facing the sun. **2.** Wind blows the leaves so you can see the other side. **3.** It starts to rain.

Vocabulary, LR54
1. hibernate **2.** temperature **3.** season **4.** migrate

Differentiated Instruction

Amazing Words to build oral vocabulary

Table of Contents

Advanced Selections for Group Time

Daily Group Time Lessons

Continued on back of tab

Daily Group Time Lessons, continued

Let's Learn Amazing Words

TEACH/MODEL

ROUTINE

Oral Vocabulary

1. **Introduce the Word** Relate the word to the song or story in which it appears. Supply a child-friendly definition. Have children say the word. Example:
   - The girl in the song uses a *measurement* chart. A *measurement* is the size or amount of something. By using a *measurement* chart, the girl can see how much she has grown. Say the word *measurement* with me, *measurement.*

2. **Demonstrate** Provide familiar examples to demonstrate meaning. When possible, use gestures to help convey meaning. Examples:
   - When you check your height on a *measurement* chart, you should stand tall with your back to the wall. The person who *measures* you should mark the spot at the top of your head.

3. **Apply** Have children demonstrate understanding with a simple activity. Suggestions for step 3 activities appear on the next page. Example:
   - Show me how you would use a *measurement* chart. Show me how you would *measure* someone.

4. **Display the Word/Letter-Sounds** Write the word on a card and display it on a classroom Amazing Words board. Have children identify some familiar letter-sounds or word parts. Example:
   - This word is *measurement*. What consonant letter and sound is at the beginning of *measurement*? How would you blend *ment*?

Use the Oral Vocabulary Routine along with the definitions, examples, letter-sounds, and word parts that are provided on the following pages to introduce each Amazing Word.

ABOUT ORAL VOCABULARY A child's oral vocabulary development is a predictor of future reading success. Oral vocabulary development now boosts children's comprehension as they become fluent readers. Oral vocabulary is informally assessed.

ACTIVITIES

To allow children to demonstrate understanding of the Amazing Words, use activities such as these in step 3 of the Routine.

ANSWER QUESTIONS Would you prefer to have a *festive* day or an *ordinary* day? Why?

CREATE EXAMPLES What is something a good *citizen* might do?

MAKE CHOICES If any of the things I name can *hatch*, say *hatch*; if not, say nothing: a train, a chicken, a jar of jam, a snake, a tadpole, a horse.

PANTOMIME Show me how an eagle *soars*, a rocket, an airplane.

PERSONAL CONTEXT Some people are *fond* of fishing. Tell about something you are *fond* of. Use the word *fond* when you tell about it.

SYNONYMS AND ANTONYMS Name a word that means the opposite of *genuine*; name a word that means about the same as *genuine*.

Monitor Progress | Check Oral Vocabulary

To monitor understanding of concepts and vocabulary that have been explicitly taught each week:

- Display the week's Build Background pages in the Student Edition.
- Remind the child of the concept that the class has been talking about that week.
- Ask the child to tell you about the Build Background illustrations using some of the week's Amazing Words.

If... a child has difficulty using the Amazing Words,
then... ask questions about the illustration using the Amazing Words. Note which questions the child can respond to. Reteach unknown words using the Oral Vocabulary Routine.

to build oral vocabulary

Definitions, examples, and **letter-sounds** to use with the Oral Vocabulary Routine on p. DI • 1.

USE WITH

DAY 1

	ADULT	HEALTHY	MEASUREMENT
1	**ADULT** An *adult* is a grown-up.	**HEALTHY** If you are *healthy*, your body is strong and well.	**MEASUREMENT** A *measurement* is the size or amount of something.
2	**Examples:** Some children can't wait to be *adults*. You'll have more responsibility when you are an *adult*. At Thanksgiving at our house, the *adults* sit at one table and the children sit at another.	**Examples:** The woman in the TV commercial has *healthy* hair. My doctor says I am very *healthy*. To stay *healthy*, you need to eat right and get lots of exercise.	**Examples:** When you check your height on a measurement chart, you should stand tall with your back against the wall. The person who measures you should mark the spot at the top of your head.
4	**Letter-Sounds:** Have children identify *d*/d/ and *lt*/lt/.	**Letter-Sounds:** Have children identify the vowel sound of *y*. (/ē/)	**Letter-Sounds:** Have children identify *m*/m/ and blend *ment*.

DAY 2

1	**SHUFFLE** *Shuffle* means "to walk slowly and drag your feet."	**TEETER** *Teeter* means "to walk in a wobbly way as if you are about to fall."
2	**Examples:** The tired man *shuffles* his feet when he walks. Does your mom ever tell you not to *shuffle* your feet? Show me how to *shuffle* your feet.	**Examples:** The teenage girl *teeters* on her new high heels. The clown *teeters* on his stilts. Show me how you would *teeter*.
4	**Letter-Sounds:** Have children identify *sh*/sh.	**Word Parts:** Run your hand under the two word parts *tee-ter* as you read the word.

DAY 3

	CROOKED
1	**CROOKED** If something is *crooked*, it is not straight.
2	**Examples:** The road to my house is very *crooked*. My sister got braces because her teeth were *crooked*. That tree trunk is quite *crooked*.
4	**Letter-Sounds:** Have children identify the blend *cr*/cr/.

DAY 4

	BOUNCE	HANDSOME
1	**BOUNCE** *Bounce* means "spring back after hitting something."	**HANDSOME** *Handsome* means "good-looking."
2	**Examples:** How many times can you *bounce* the ball? The baby was *bouncing* up and down in her little seat. Show me how you look when you are *bouncing*.	**Examples:** The princess fell in love with the *handsome* prince. The *handsome* actor was the star of the movie. The men in my family are very *handsome*.
4	**Letter-Sounds:** Have children identify *b*/b/, *n*/n/, and *c*/s/.	**Letter-Sounds:** Children can blend *hand*.

Definitions, examples, and **letter-sounds** to use with the Oral Vocabulary Routine on p. DI•1.

to build oral vocabulary

USE WITH

DAY 1

	ATTEMPT	EVENT	TIME LINE
1	**ATTEMPT** When you *attempt* something, you try to do it.	**EVENT** An *event* is something that happens.	**TIME LINE** A *time line* is the order you follow to succeed at something.
2	**Examples:** The baby will *attempt* to walk. The soccer player *attempts* to score a goal in every game. The actor *attempts* to remember his lines.	**Examples:** Riding your bike for the first time is an exciting *event*. The talent show was the main *event* at the school carnival. The newspaper reports important *events*.	**Examples:** My brother had a *time line* for learning to play the trumpet. A *time line* can also be a chart that shows the order in which things happen. We studied a *time line* of George Washington's life.
4	**Letter-Sounds:** Children can blend *tempt*.	**Letter-Sounds:** Children can identify the letter *e* and blend *vent*.	**Letter-Sounds:** Children can decode *time line*.

DAY 2

	FAMOUS	FLATTER
1	**FAMOUS** *Famous* means "well-known."	**FLATTER** When you *flatter* someone, you say something very nice about him or her that may not be true.
2	**Examples:** The basketball star is very *famous*. The cook is *famous* for her tasty pies. I read a book about a *famous* explorer.	**Examples:** The boy tried to *flatter* his grandma so she would buy him a new toy. You can *flatter your mother by saying how beautiful she is. Do you think people will like you* better if you flatter them?
4	**Word Parts:** Run your hand under the two word parts *fa-mous* as you read the word.	**Letter-Sounds:** Children can blend *flat*.

DAY 3

	CORRECT
1	**CORRECT** *Correct* means "to change something to make it right." If something is *corrected*, it is changed.
2	**Examples:** You must *correct* the mistakes on this paper. Does your mother ever tell you to *correct* your table manners? Do you like being *corrected* when you use a wrong word?
4	**Word Parts:** Run your hand under the two word parts *cor-rect* as you read the word.

DAY 4

	AWKWARD	LOVELY
1	**AWKWARD** An *awkward* movement is a movement that is not smooth.	**LOVELY** If something is *lovely*, it is very pretty.
2	**Examples:** Babies are *awkward* when they begin to walk alone. The beginning skater looked *awkward* on the ice. Show me an *awkward* movement.	**Examples:** The flowers in the garden are very *lovely*. Mother looked *lovely* in her new dress. Grandma was wearing a *lovely* necklace.
4	**Word Parts:** Run your hand under the two word parts *awk-ward* as you read the word.	**Letter-Sounds:** Have children identify the initial /l/.

to build oral vocabulary

Definitions, examples, and **letter-sounds** to use with the Oral Vocabulary Routine on p. DI•1.

USE WITH

DAY 1

1	**ARRIVE** When you *arrive* somewhere, you get there.	**DEPART** When you *depart*, you leave.	**LOCATION** A *location* is the place where something is.	**ROUTE** A *route* is the way you go to get somewhere.
2	**Examples:** Try to *arrive* early for the concert. It will be late when we *arrive* in Chicago. Do you *arrive* for school on time each day?	**Examples:** The plane will *depart* at nine o'clock. If you aren't there on time, it will *depart* without you. We will *depart* for vacation early tomorrow morning.	**Examples:** My family likes the *location* of our house. We had trouble finding the *location* of the hotel. The new library will be in a different *location*.	**Examples:** We always take the same *route* to get to Grandma's house. The shortest *route* to school is down that street. When you go on a trip, it is important to plan the *route* you will take.
4	**Letter-Sounds:** Have children identify *rr*/r/ and *v*/v/.	**Letter-Sounds:** Children can identify *d*/d/, *p*/p/, and *t*/t/.	**Letter-Sounds:** Children can identify the letter-sounds for *L*/L/, *c*/c/ and *n*/n/.	**Letter-Sounds:** Have children identify *r*/r/ and *t*/t/.

DAY 2

1	**SWOOP** When things *swoop*, they move down suddenly.	**TUMBLE** *Tumble* means "to roll or toss about."
2	**Examples:** The owl *swoops* to catch the mouse. The eagle is waiting to *swoop* on the rabbit. Show me how you would *swoop* down to catch something.	**Examples:** We watched the leaves *tumble* in the wind. When groceries fall out of a bag, they *tumble* all over the floor. Puppies sometimes *tumble* as they are learning to get around.
4	**Letter-Sounds:** Children can identify *sw*/sw/ and *p*/p/.	**Letter-Sounds:** Children can blend *tum*.

DAY 3

1	**CRUMPLE** When you *crumple* something, you crush it into wrinkles. If something is *crumpled*, it is wrinkled.
2	**Examples:** *Crumple* the paper before you throw it away. The boy's *crumpled* shirt looked terrible. Show me how you would *crumple* something.
4	**Letter-Sounds:** Children can blend *crum*.

DAY 4

1	**STAMPEDE** A *stampede* is a wild rush of animals or people.
2	**Examples:** The loud noise scared the cattle and caused a *stampede*. There was a *stampede* to get to the front of the line. Show me what you would do if you were in the middle of a *stampede*.
4	**Letter-Sounds:** Children can decode *stampede*.

Definitions, examples, and **letter-sounds** to use with the Oral Vocabulary Routine on p. DI•1.

to build oral vocabulary

USE WITH

DAY 1

	GARDENER	NATURE	SPROUT
1	**GARDENER** A *gardener* is someone who grows plants.	**NATURE** *Nature* is everything in the world that is not made by people.	**SPROUT** *Sprout* means "to begin to grow."
2	**Examples:** *Gardeners* spend a lot of time making sure their plants grow. We have so many fresh vegetables because my mother is a *gardener*. *Gardeners* decide what they will plant long before spring.	**Examples:** Mountains are a wonder of *nature*. It is important to respect and take care of *nature*. We enjoy the beauty of *nature* when we go camping.	**Examples:** How long does it take seeds to start to *sprout*? The rain will help the corn to *sprout*. Some seeds never *sprout*.
4	**Letter-Sounds:** Children can identify the *g*/g/ and *n*/n/.	**Word Parts:** Run your hand under the two word parts *na-ture* as you read the word.	**Letter-Sounds:** Have children identify the *t*/t/.

DAY 2

	DIM	SHADE
1	**DIM** *Dim* means "not bright."	**SHADE** *Shade* is a place that is darker than the area around it because light has been blocked from the sun. *Shade* also means "the darkness or lightness of a color."
2	**Examples:** The lights in the basement are *dim*. We have a *dim* light in our garage. Because it was so cloudy, it was a very *dim* day.	**Examples:** It was so hot that the boys sat in the *shade*. That huge tree gives a lot of *shade*. The leaves were a beautiful *shade* of green.
4	**Letter-Sounds:** Children can decode *dim*.	**Letter-Sounds:** Children can decode *shade*.

DAY 3

	BLOSSOM
1	**BLOSSOM** A *blossom* is the flower of a plant. When a plant *blossoms* it has flowers.
2	**Examples:** The apple tree has beautiful pink *blossoms* in the spring. Other trees *blossom* in the spring too. I love it when the rose bush *blossoms*.
4	**Letter-Sounds:** Children can blend *blos*.

DAY 4

	DESTROY	HUMONGOUS
1	**DESTROY** When you *destroy* something, you ruin it.	**HUMONGOUS** If something is *humongous*, it is very, very big.
2	**Examples:** Fires sometimes *destroy* forests. Insects sometimes *destroy* crops. Be sure to put your shoes away or my puppy may *destroy* them.	**Examples:** Basketball players have *humongous* hands. Dinosaurs were *humongous* animals. An ocean is a *humongous* body of water.
4	**Word Parts:** Run your hand under the two word parts *de-stroy* as you read the word.	**Word Parts:** Run your hand under the three word parts *hu-mon-gous* as you read the word.

to build oral vocabulary

Definitions, examples, and **letter-sounds** to use with the Oral Vocabulary Routine on p. DI • 1.

USE WITH

DAY 1

1	**CYCLE** A *cycle* is a series of events that always happens in the same order.	**DEVELOP** *Develop* means "grow."	**INSECT** An *insect* is an animal that has six legs and usually has wings.
2	**Examples:** The class studied the life *cycle* of a frog. Nature follows certain *cycles*, such as summer comes after spring. A cocoon is part of the life *cycle* of a butterfly.	**Examples:** Baby chicks *develop* inside eggs. If you want to *develop* muscles, you should exercise. As deer get older, they sometimes *develop* antlers.	**Examples:** A grasshopper is an *insect*. A spider is not an *insect* because it has eight legs. Spiders catch *insects* for food.
4	**Letter-Sounds:** Identify the letter-sounds for c/s/ and c/k/.	**Letter-Sounds:** Have children identify d/d/ and p/p/.	**Word Parts:** Children can decode *insect*.

DAY 2

1	**REARRANGE** When you *rearrange* something, you put things in a different order.	**YEARLY** *Yearly* means "once a year."
2	**Examples:** The woman will *rearrange* the flowers in the vase. The boy asked his mother to *rearrange* the furniture in his bedroom. I'm going to change the seating chart and *rearrange* the desks.	**Examples:** Our *yearly* trip to the cabin is fun. Leaves fall off the trees *yearly*. Everyone enjoys the *yearly* field trip to the zoo.
4	**Word Parts:** Point out *arrange*. *Arrange* means "to put in a kind of order." *Re* means "to do again." So *rearrange* means "to put in another order."	**Word Parts:** Point out *year*. *Year* means "365 days." The ending *-ly* means "every." *Yearly* means "every year."

DAY 4

1	**EMERGE** *Emerge* means "to come into view."	**FRAGILE** If something is *fragile*, it can be easily broken.	**VESSEL** A *vessel* is a thin tube inside your body.
2	**Examples:** The video showed the chick *emerge* from the egg. At three o'clock, we *emerge* from our classroom. I saw the sun *emerge* from behind the cloud.	**Examples:** Those cups are *fragile*. Be sure to put lots of paper in the box when mailing *fragile* items. Show me how you would carry something that is *fragile*.	**Examples:** A *vessel* is like a straw. Blood *vessels* carry blood throughout your body. Show me a blood *vessel* in your wrist.
4	**Letter-Sounds:** Children can identify e/ē/ and blend *merge*.	**Letter-Sounds:** Have children identify the initial blend *fr*/fr/. Point out the g/j/.	**Word Parts:** Run your hand under the two parts *ves-sel* as you read the word.

Definitions, examples, and **letter-sounds** to use with the Oral Vocabulary Routine on p. DI • 1.

to build oral vocabulary

USE WITH

DAY 1

1	**HIBERNATE** *Hibernate* means "to spend the winter sleeping."	**MIGRATE** *Migrate* means "to move from one place to another."	**SEASON** A *season* is one of the four parts of the year.	**TEMPERATURE** *Temperature* is how cold or hot something is.
2	**Examples:** Bears *hibernate* in the winter. Sometimes I wish I could *hibernate* so I wouldn't have to deal with the cold weather. Show what it would be like to *hibernate*.	**Examples:** Some birds *migrate* to the south in the fall. If a bird doesn't *migrate*, it has to be able to find food in cold weather.	**Examples:** Fall is my favorite *season*. Winter is the coldest *season*. Summer is the *season* that comes after spring.	**Examples:** The *temperature* last summer was at an all-time high. The boy had to stay home from school because he had a *temperature* of 101 degrees. The weatherman warned that the *temperature* would drop.
4	**Letter-Sounds:** Have children identify the small word *hi* and blend *nate*.	**Letter-Sounds:** Have children blend *grate*.	**Letter-Sounds:** Children can blend *sea* and identify *s*/s/ and *n*/n/.	**Word Parts:** Run your hand under the four parts *tem-per-a-ture* as you read the word.

DAY 2

1. **AUTUMN** *Autumn* is one of the four seasons.

2. **Examples:** Leaves fall off the trees in *autumn*. Another word for *autumn* is "fall." I like to visit the pumpkin farm in *autumn*.

4. **Word Parts:** Run your hand under the two word parts *au-tumn* as you read the word.

DAY 3

1. **FREEZE** *Freeze* means "to turn into something hard because of the cold."

2. **Examples:** The pond will *freeze* when it gets cold enough outside. When you *freeze* water, you get ice. When rain *freezes*, it turns into snow.

4. **Letter-Sounds:** Children can decode *freeze*.

DAY 4

1	**BITTERLY** *Bitter* means "showing sadness or pain." *Bitterly* means "in a sad or painful way."	**WEARY** When you are *weary*, you are very tired.
2	**Examples:** I wore a scarf over my face because of the *bitterly* cold wind. There were many *bitterly* cold days last winter. The children were *bitterly* disappointed after the team lost the game.	**Examples:** The mountain climber was *weary* after the hard day. The doctor was *weary* after the long operation. The children were *weary* after the long test.
4	**Letter-Sounds:** Children can blend *bit*.	**Letter-Sounds:** Have children identify *w*/w/, *r*/r/, and *y*/ē/.

Grade 1

Oral Vocabulary Words

DEVELOP LANGUAGE

Unit 1: Animals, Tame & Wild

Animal Friends

cuddle
faithful
fetch
heel
needs
responsibility
shelter
tickle

---

career
comfort
exercise
scrub
search
service
sloppy
tool

---

danger
enormous
past
powerful
present
produce
serve
snuggle
transportation

Wild Animals

dangle
medicine
nape
observe
parent
poisonous
solo
wild

---

gentle
habitat
hatch
moist
nudge
perch
private
survive

---

beneath
desert
forest
native
reserve
snug
surf
world

Unit 2: Communities

People in Communities

chore
commute
cooperation
display
downtown
household
rule
subway

---

aquarium
borrow
group
lines
rehearsal
respect
share
soothe

---

branch
citizen
community
earn
headquarters
law
leader
patrol

Communities in Nature

bluff
boisterous
crater
enemy
extinct
holler
protect
swamp

---

capture
creature
environment
inhale
require
slimy
sludge
thrive

---

creep
eagerly
individual
industrious
romp
slither
special
wander

Unit 3: Changes

Growing and Changing

adult
bounce
crooked
handsome
healthy
measurement
shuffle
teeter

---

attempt
awkward
correct
event
famous
flatter
lovely
time line

---

arrive
crumple
depart
location
route
stampede
swoop
tumble

Changes in Nature

blossom
destroy
dim
gardener
humongous
nature
shade
sprout

---

cycle
develop
emerge
fragile
insect
rearrange
vessel
yearly

---

autumn
bitterly
freeze
hibernate
migrate
season
temperature
weary

Unit 4: Treasures

Surprising Treasures

celebrate
cherish
delicate
genuine
grateful
loot
rarest

---

carve
create
doodle
hobby
imagination
inspiration
masterpiece
sculptor

---

abandon
decompose
excavate
fossil
nourish
soil
splinter
sunken

Treasures to Share

delightful
errand
festive
fiesta
memory
ordinary
refreshments
symbol

---

collector
flourish
jealous
porridge
relatives
secret
seriousness
sibling

---

admire
discover
dwell
resident
sadness
substantial
tremendous
welcome

Unit 5: Great Ideas

Clever Solutions!

advice
clever
intend
plump(er)
predicament
proudly
scrawny
wise

---

dawn
fond
freedom
miserable
proper
scaly
scarcely
selfish
speckled

---

case
darling
explanation
gorgeous
rafters
riddle
suspects
wonder

Ideas That Changed

cellar
convenient
engine
equipment
furnace
gadget
pilot
steer

---

biplane
determined
inventor
sketch
speech
stable
stall
technology

---

contraption
curious
doubt
energy
glider
intelligent
(un)manned
soar

REMEMBER that oral vocabulary is informally assessed.

Carlos Gets a Puppy

On Carlos's seventh birthday, he asked for a puppy. "Maybe we should get an adult dog," suggested his mother. "An adult dog is already trained so it won't be so messy and won't be such a big responsibility." But Carlos wanted a puppy.

A week later, when Carlos got home from school, he found his mother in the kitchen holding a tiny little animal. "What's that?" he asked.

"It's a puppy," said his mother. Carlos looked carefully at the tiny animal, which looked more like a mouse or a squirrel.

"It's only three weeks old," said his mother. "The animal shelter was full, so I said I'd help take care of it. I was hoping you'd help me." Carlos helped his mother feed the tiny puppy.

When they were done feeding the puppy, Carlos asked, "Can I play with it now?"

"No," said his mother. "A puppy this little needs to eat and sleep."

Carlos was disappointed. He had wanted a puppy to play with, but it was too small to play.

In time, and with lots of rest, the puppy grew bigger and stronger. Carlos and his mother took the puppy to the vet, who said that the little dog was healthy. "What's its name?" he asked.

"We call him Tiny," said Carlos, "but if he keeps growing, he may need a new name!"

ADVANCED SELECTION 13 **VOCABULARY:** adult, healthy

Grandpa's Trunk

Greg loved visiting his grandparents. They had a lot of old stuff that he could play with. Greg always began his visit by going to the attic to find something. This time he came across a trunk that he had never noticed before. Greg opened it and found that it was full of old letters and photographs. Greg recognized his grandparents in the pictures even though they were very young in some of them.

He went through everything in the trunk. He tried to picture his grandparents' lives from what he found, but it was too confusing. The papers and photos were all jumbled together. Then he had an idea.

Greg recalled making a time line in social studies class at school. It helped him better understand when different historical events had happened. He decided to make a time line about his grandparents' lives using the things in the trunk.

Greg sorted everything from the trunk into piles. He found dates on some of the papers and photographs. Then he made his time line. When he was done, he took it down to show his grandparents.

They were very pleased with his work. The family spent the entire evening going over the time line, remembering events and telling stories about the past.

ADVANCED SELECTION 14 **VOCABULARY:** event, time line

San Francisco, California

What would it be like to live in San Francisco? What would you do? What would you see? Would you like to find out? Then hop on board! Your tour is about to depart.

You are on a cable car. Some people think cable cars are more fun than regular buses. You can ride on the outside of a cable car. But hold on tight! San Francisco is famous for its steep hills. You don't want to fall off. Riding a cable car up and down San Francisco's streets is a fun way to see the city. There are several different cable car routes. One route will take you down to the waterfront and Fisherman's Wharf.

Fisherman's Wharf has many shops and places that sell fresh fish. It also has sea lions! You can see these animals sun bathing on some of the wooden piers. This is more fun than seeing them at the zoo. Then, look out over the bay to see Alcatraz.

Alcatraz was once a jail. Now you can ride a boat out to the island. When you arrive, have a look around. Alcatraz is a fun place to visit.

After visiting Alcatraz you can check out San Francisco Exploratorium. The Exploratorium is a science museum for children. There are many hands-on games that make learning about science a lot of fun.

But don't stay too long. There is a lot more to see in San Francisco!

Bean Sprouts

A mung bean is a kind of seed. Gardeners plant beans to grow more bean plants to eat. These beans sprout, or begin to grow, in the dirt. This is how they usually grow in nature, but some beans will also sprout in water. You can make your own bean sprouts to eat.

You will need:

- mung beans
- a clean, quart-size glass jar
- cheesecloth
- a rubber band

What to do:

1. Rinse the mung beans and put them in the glass jar.
2. Cover the top of the jar with the cheesecloth. Use the rubber band to keep it on tightly. You can still pour water in and out of the jar with the cover on.
3. Fill the jar with warm water so the beans are covered. Leave the beans to soak overnight.
4. The next day, pour all the water off through the cover and rinse the beans very well in clean water at least two times.
5. Leave the jar in a warm, dark place to encourage the seeds to sprout. If you want your sprouts to turn green, you can put them in the sunlight. Leave on the cover until after the beans have sprouted and are ready to harvest.
6. Rinse the sprouts again, and they're ready to eat!

ADVANCED SELECTION 16 **VOCABULARY:** gardener, nature, sprout

The Caterpillar and the Fawn

Once upon a time, two young animals lived in a forest. One was an insect—a little caterpillar. The other was a fawn—a baby deer. Even though they were very different animals, they were good friends.

One day, Caterpillar was too tired to play. She climbed up into a tree, made herself a cozy place to rest, and fell into a deep sleep.

Fawn lay at the base of the tree. She waited and waited, but Caterpillar did not come down. Time passed, and eventually Caterpillar woke up. She wiggled out of her silky resting spot and stretched her body. She felt different, but she wasn't sure exactly how. She looked around for Fawn. She saw a large animal with antlers beginning to grow out of its head and decided to ask that animal if it had seen Fawn. "Excuse me," she said. "I am looking for my friend—"

"That's strange," the large animal interrupted. "I'm also looking for my friend, a small caterpillar."

"But that's me," said Caterpillar.

"You're not a caterpillar. Look at yourself."

Caterpillar looked at her reflection in a puddle of water. She was a moth with big, beautiful wings.

"Fawn?" said the moth. "Is that you? Your fur is different. Your spots are gone."

"I guess we have both changed," said the deer. "But we can still be friends."

A Long Winter Sleep

The days get shorter. The temperature drops. The winter season is beginning. Some animals are getting ready for a long winter sleep. They eat as much as they can. They store fat in their bodies. They will be able to live off this fat when there is no food to find during the winter.

Bears and some other animals hibernate during the cold winter season. Hibernation is like sleeping, but it is not exactly the same. The animal is not awake or moving around. The animal's body works in a different way when it is hibernating. The animal does not eat or drink for a long time. Its body temperature drops, and its breathing may slow down.

Bears know it is almost time to hibernate when it becomes harder for them to find food. Some bears dig a den or find a cave and crawl inside to hibernate.

Bears that live where winter is coldest and longest may hibernate for up to seven months, until there is food again. Bears that live where winter is not so long and cold may hibernate less. And some bears do not hibernate at all, because they can find food all year long.

Polar bears live where it is very cold, but they do not hibernate because they can hunt and fish for food all year long.

ADVANCED SELECTION 18 **VOCABULARY:** hibernate, season, temperature

Group Time

Strategic Intervention

ROUTINE

DAY 1

1 Word Work

PHONEMIC AWARENESS Reteach p. 10m. Additional practice items:

by **kitty** **cry** **choppy** **shy**

VOWEL SOUNDS OF y Reteach p. 10n. Additional words to blend:

funny **pry** **sandy** **spy** **penny**

Then have children spell *my* with letter tiles. Monitor their work.

- Change the *m* in *my* to *fr*. What is the new word? f r y
- Change the *r* in *fry* to *l*. What is the new word? f l y
- Change the *fl* in *fly* to *wh*. What is the new word? w h y

SPELLING Reteach p. 10p. Model spelling *try* and *puppy*. You may wish to give children fewer words to learn.

2 Read Decodable Reader 25

BEFORE READING Review the words with the vowel sounds of *y* and the high-frequency words on p. 10q. Then have children blend these story words: *trip, five, made, when, stops.* Be sure children understand meanings of words such as *buddy*.

DURING READING Use p. 10q.

Monitor Progress	Word and Story Reading
If... children have difficulty with any of these words,	**then...** reteach them by modeling. Have children practice the words, with feedback from you, until they can read them independently.
If...children have difficulty reading the story individually,	**then...** read a sentence aloud as children point to each word. Then have the group reread the sentence as they continue pointing. Continue reading in this way before children read individually.

3 Reread for Fluency

Use the Oral Rereading Routine, p. 10q, and text at each child's independent reading level.

MORE READING FOR

Group Time

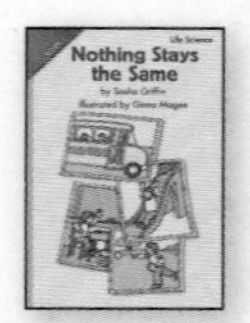

Use this Leveled Reader or other text at children's instructional level.

Below-Level

Reviews
- High-Frequency Words *always, become(s), day, everything, nothing, stays, things*
- Compare and Contrast

Check this database for additional titles.

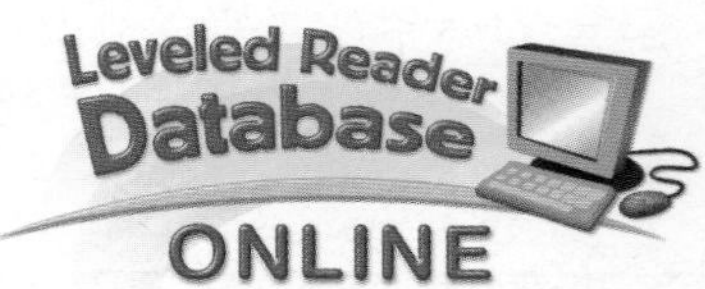

PearsonSuccessNet.com

Advanced

ROUTINE

DAY 1

1 Word Work

Vowel Sounds of *y* Practice with longer words containing *y* with a long *i* or long *e* sound. If children know the words on first read, they may need no further practice. Practice items:

heavy	**reply**	**beauty**	**money**	**cycle**
lullaby	**magnify**	**secretary**	**usually**	**family**
python	**simplify**	**anything**	**babysit**	**ladybug**

Have children write the words on cards and sort by the sound of *y*. Then have individuals choose several words to use in a sentence.

2 Read Advanced Selection 13

BEFORE READING Have children identify these story words: *adult, healthy.*

DURING READING Provide guidance as children read silently.

AFTER READING Have children recall the two most important ideas in the selection. (Taking care of a puppy is a big responsibility; with care, puppies can grow healthy.) Ask:

- Would you want a puppy or an adult dog? Why?
- Do you know a dog? Tell about it.

On the back of the selection page have children write three sentences about a pet they would like to have.

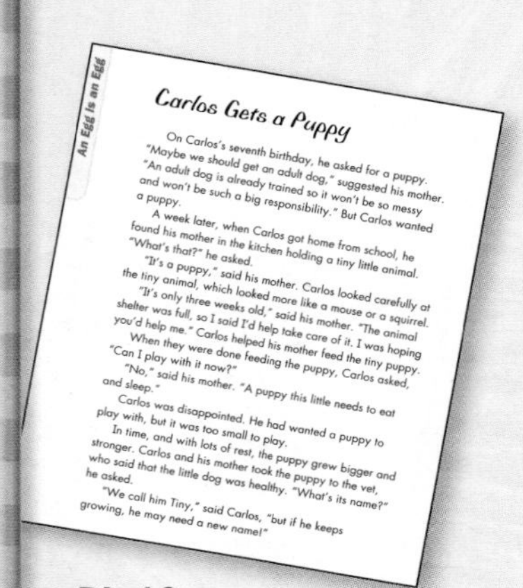
An Egg Is an Egg

Carlos Gets a Puppy

On Carlos's seventh birthday, he asked for a puppy. "Maybe we should get an adult dog," suggested his mother. "An adult dog is already trained so it won't be so messy and won't be such a big responsibility." But Carlos wanted a puppy.

A week later, when Carlos got home from school, he found his mother in the kitchen holding a tiny little animal. "What's that?" he asked.

"It's a puppy," said his mother. Carlos looked carefully at the tiny animal, which looked more like a mouse or a squirrel.

"It's only three weeks old," said his mother. "The animal shelter was full, so I said I'd help take care of it. I was hoping you'd help me." Carlos helped his mother feed the tiny puppy.

When they were done feeding the puppy, Carlos asked, "Can I play with it now?"

"No," said his mother. "A puppy this little needs to eat and sleep."

Carlos was disappointed. He had wanted a puppy to play with, but it was too small to play.

In time, and with lots of rest, the puppy grew bigger and stronger. Carlos and his mother took the puppy to the vet, who said that the little dog was healthy. "What's its name?" he asked.

"We call him Tiny," said Carlos, "but if he keeps growing, he may need a new name!"

DI•10

3 Extend Concepts Through Inquiry

IDENTIFY QUESTIONS Have children choose an African American artist and write a paragraph about him or her. Dancers such as Gregory Hines and Alvin Ailey would echo the character Mr. Baker in the Big Book. Other choices could include musicians such as Louis Armstrong and Duke Ellington, or actors such as Sidney Poitier. During the week, children should learn more about their choices from reading, studying pictures, and talking with adults or older children. On Day 5 they will share what they learned. Guide children in brainstorming possible sources of information.

- Think about your choices. What were their performances like? Did they start performing or studying to perform as children?

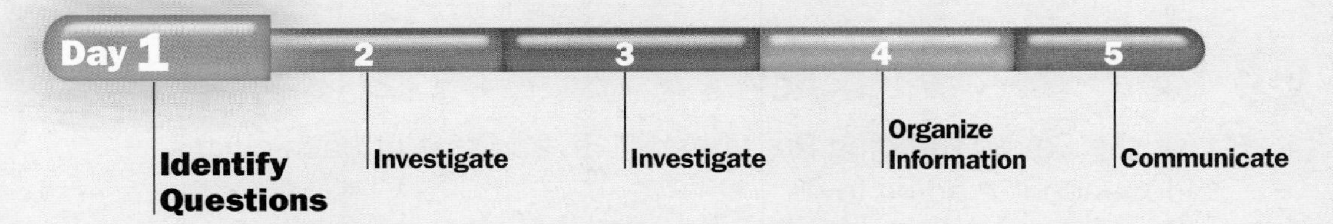

MORE READING FOR

Group Time

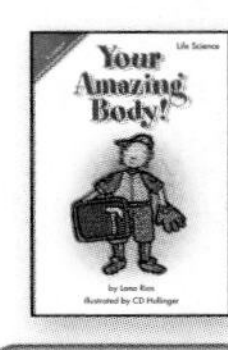

Use this Leveled Reader or other text at children's instructional level.

Advanced

Reviews

- Concept Vocabulary
- Compare and Contrast

Group Time

DAY 2

Strategic Intervention

ROUTINE

1 Word Work

PHONEMIC AWARENESS Reteach p. 12b. Additional practice items:

by—be **shy—she** **my—me**

LONG VOWELS (CV) Reteach p. 12c. Additional words to blend:

be **go** **so** **me** **hello**

Then have children spell be with letter tiles. Monitor their work.

- Change the *b* in *be* to *sh*. What is the new word? s h e
- Drop the *s* in *she*. What is the new word? h e
- Add *llo* to *he*. What is the new word? h e l l o

PRETEACH HIGH-FREQUENCY WORDS Write *always, become(s), day, everything, nothing, stays, things* and have children say each word, spell it as they point to each letter, and say it again. Have individuals practice reading the words from word cards.

Decodable Reader 26
The Picnic
Written by Chantell Brown
Illustrated by Olivia Hughes

2 Read Decodable Reader 26

BEFORE READING Review the long vowel (CV) and the high-frequency words on p. 12f. Then have children blend these other decodable story words: *picnic, bring, waved, race, safe, tired.* Be sure children understand that *Jo* and *Mo* are names of the girl and boy in the story.

DURING READING Use p. 12f.

Monitor Progress	Word and Story Reading
If... children have difficulty with any of these words,	**then...** reteach them by modeling. Have children practice the words, with feedback from you, until they can read them independently.
If... children have difficulty reading the story individually,	**then...** read a sentence aloud as children point to each word. Then have the group reread the sentence as they continue pointing. Continue reading in this way before children read individually.

3 Reread for Fluency

Use the Paired Reading Routine, p. 12f, and text at each child's independent reading level.

MORE READING FOR
Group Time

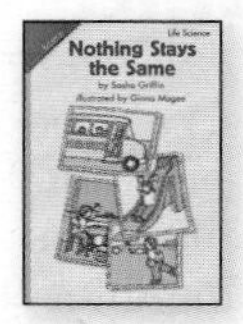

Use this Leveled Reader or other text at children's instructional level.

Below-Level

Reviews
- High-Frequency Words *always, become(s), day, everything, nothing, stays, things*
- Compare and Contrast

Advanced

ROUTINE

DAY 2

1 Word Work

Long Vowels (CV) Practice with longer words. If children know the words on first read, they may need no further practice. Practice items:

potato	**human**	**maybe**	**agent**	**zebra**
secret	**giant**	**bicycle**	**spider**	**program**
moment	**cargo**	**volcano**	**museum**	**vacation**

Have children write the words and divide between the syllables. Show children that breaking a word into syllables can help them read it. Discuss the meanings of unfamiliar words and then ask children to use each word in a sentence.

2 Read *Mr. George Baker*

DURING READING Children may read silently. Provide guidance as needed.

AFTER READING Ask:

- Why did everyone like Mr. Baker?
- Make a list of reasons why someone should learn to read.

3 Extend Concepts Through Inquiry

INVESTIGATE Guide children in choosing material at their independent reading level to explore their topic. Some books that may be appropriate are *Performing Artists (Profiles of Great Black Americans)* by Richard S. Rennert and Coretta Scott King or *African American Musicians (Black Stars)* by Eleanora E. Tate.

Help children decide how they will present their information. Children may use a Venn diagram or other graphic organizer, a written format, photographs, drawings, or models.

MORE READING FOR
Group Time

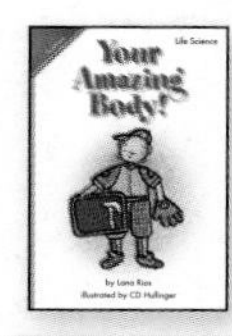

Use this Leveled Reader or other text at children's instructional level.

Advanced

Reviews
- Concept Vocabulary
- Compare and Contrast

Group Time

DAY 3

Strategic Intervention

ROUTINE

1 Word Work

PHONEMIC AWARENESS Reteach p. 14b. Additional practice items:

shy **be** **pretty** **easy** **so**

VOWEL SOUNDS OF *y* AND LONG VOWELS (CV) Reteach p. 14c. Additional words to blend:

we **hi** **smelly** **try**
no **bunny** **my** **she**

2 Read Strategic Intervention Decodable Reader 13

BEFORE READING Point out the exclamation mark on p. 7 and explain that it comes at the end of an exclamation. Tell them that an exclamation shows strong feeling.

DURING READING Read p. 2 aloud with the group. Have them read pp. 3–4 without you. Select individuals to read aloud to the end.

AFTER READING Check comprehension by having children retell the story, including the characters, setting, and plot. Have children locate words with *y* as a vowel and words with long vowels that follow the CV pattern in the story. List words children name. Have children sort the words they found below columns labeled Long *i*, Long *e*, Long *o*.

Long *i*	Long *e*	Long *o*
Ty	Jenny	Bo
my	funny	go
try	tummy	
fry	he	
hi	we	
	be	

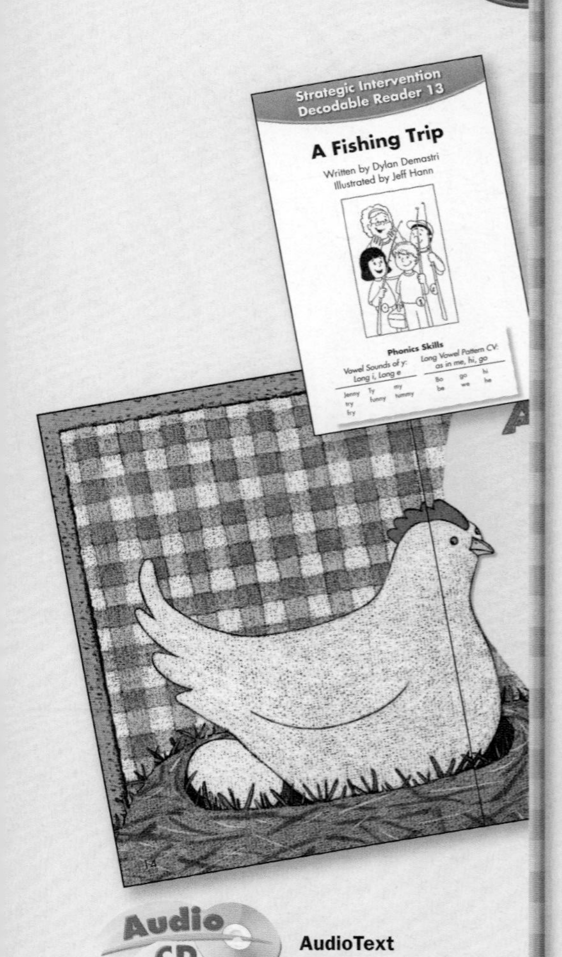

Audio CD AudioText

3 Read *An Egg Is an Egg*

BEFORE READING Have children practice the words below—first as a group and then individually. Monitor their practice and correct as needed. Then use Guiding Comprehension, pp. 14–29, to monitor understanding.

hatches **brewed** **flower** **sown** **change**
breaks **until** **tea** **yard** **baby**

Monitor Progress	Word and Story Reading
If... children have difficulty with any of these words,	**then...** coach them in blending and have them practice in pairs with word cards before reading the story.
If... children have difficulty reading the story individually,	**then...** have them follow along as they listen to the AudioText. They may also read pages of the selection aloud together, first with you and then without you, before reading individually.

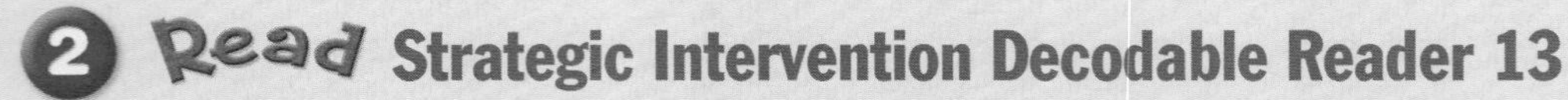

Advanced

ROUTINE

DAY 3

1 Read *An Egg Is an Egg*

DURING READING Have children read silently to p. 21. Provide guidance as needed. Ask:

- What are some of the things that change?
- What are some changes that you have seen?

Have children read silently to p. 27. Then ask:

- How do babies change?
- What is one thing that stays the same?

Compare and Contrast Have children recall some of the things that change. Discuss how those things stayed partly the same even while they changed.

- How did the things change?
- How did the things stay the same?

Predict Ask children to recall some of the changes talked about in the book. Have them write sentences predicting what the next change might be. (Day turns to night, then turns back to day.)

RESPONSE Ask children to predict what they will look like when they are adults. Have them draw their predictions and write two descriptive sentences about themselves as adults below the picture.

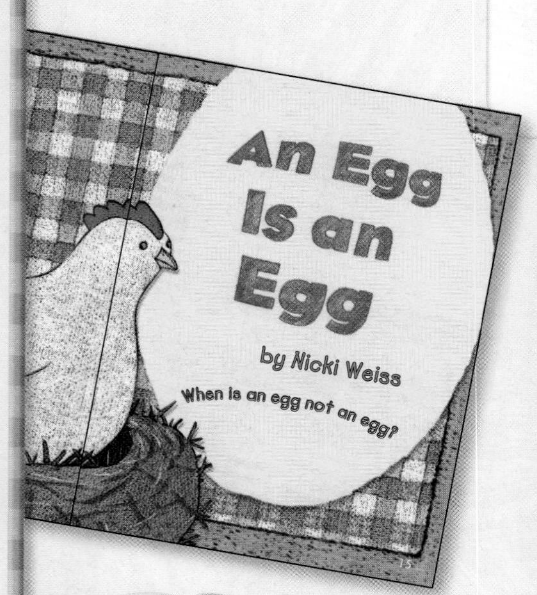

Audio CD AudioText

2 Extend Concepts Through Inquiry

INVESTIGATE Give children time to investigate the African Americans they are presenting and to begin preparing their information.

An Egg Is an Egg

Group Time

DAY 4

AudioText

MORE READING FOR
Group Time

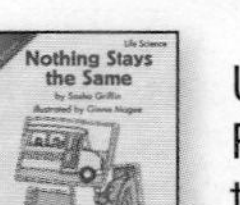

Use this Leveled Reader or other text at children's instructional level.

Below-Level

Reviews
- High-Frequency Words *always, become(s), day, everything, nothing, stays, things*
- Compare and Contrast

Strategic Intervention

ROUTINE

1 Word Work

PHONEMIC AWARENESS Reteach p. 30b. Additional practice items:

be (2)	**tennis** (5)	**need** (3)	**tree** (3)	**wheel** (3)
rabbit (5)	**sleep** (4)	**until** (5)	**speech** (4)	**we** (2)

REVIEW **LONG *e: e, ee* AND SYLLABLES VCCV** Reteach p. 30c, using these additional words. Have children sort the words into *One Syllable* and *Two Syllables* lists.

picnic	**me**	**deep**	**jacket**	**napkin**	**free**
queen	**cheek**	**tablet**	**happen**	**sheep**	**button**

REVIEW **WORD READING** Use the words and sentences on p. 30d to review decoding skills. Have children practice words in pairs until they can read one word every one or two seconds.

2 Reread Strategic Intervention Decodable Reader 12

BEFORE READING Have children review these decodable story words: *Dee, deep, green, keeps, she, feet, sweet, see, be, he, basket, rabbit, kitten.*

DURING READING Read p. 2 aloud with the group. Have them read pp. 3–4 aloud without you. Select individuals to read aloud to the end.

AFTER READING Have children retell the story. Point to words in the story with long *e: e, ee* or words with syllables VCCV and ask individuals to read them.

3 Read "Nothing Fits!"

BEFORE READING Have children practice the words below—first as a group and then individually. Monitor their practice and correct as needed. Then use Science in Reading, pp. 30–33.

cold	**puts**	**play**	**looks**	**growing**

Monitor Progress	Word and Selection Reading
If... children have difficulty with any of these words,	**then...** have them practice in pairs reading word cards before reading the selection.
If... children have difficulty reading the selection individually,	**then...** have them follow along as they listen to the AudioText. They may also read pages of the selection aloud together, first with you and then without you, before reading individually.

Advanced

ROUTINE

1 Read "Nothing Fits!"

AFTER READING Ask:

- What should you do before going outside on a cold day?
- What happens to your clothes as you grow?
- How is it that Sammy grows but is still Sammy? What about him stays the same?

2 Vocabulary

Extend vocabulary with questions such as these:

- How is an *adult* different from a child?
- What are some things you can do to stay *healthy*?
- If we took a *measurement*, about how tall would you be?

Encourage children to use the words in their writing.

3 Extend Concepts Through Inquiry

ORGANIZE INFORMATION Give children time to continue reading about the African Americans they are presenting. Remind them that tomorrow they will share their information. By now they should have begun putting the information in a presentation format.

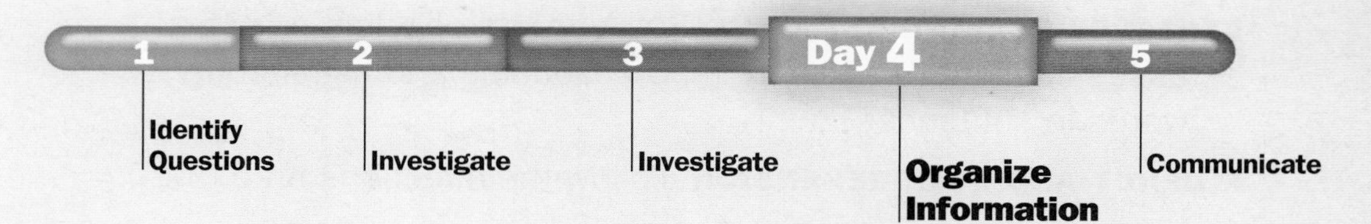

AudioText

MORE READING FOR
Group Time

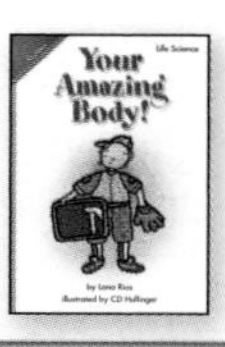

Use this Leveled Reader or other text at children's instructional level.

Advanced

Reviews
- Concept Vocabulary
- Compare and Contrast

An Egg Is an Egg

Group Time

DAY 5

Strategic Intervention

ROUTINE

1 Word Work

VOWEL SOUNDS OF *y* AND LONG VOWELS (CV) Write these sentences. Have children read aloud as you track the print. Call on individuals to blend the underlined words.

Patty will try to fly a kite.

Can he pet my fluffy bunny?

Go to a sunny place to dry it.

No, I'm not sleepy yet.

HIGH-FREQUENCY WORDS Use p. 12–13 to review *always, become(s), day, everything, nothing, stays, things.*

Monitor Progress	High-Frequency Words
If... children have difficulty with any of these words,	**then...** tell them the word and have them repeat it. Have children spell the word and tell what word they spelled. Have them practice in pairs with word cards.

2 Monitor Progress

SENTENCE READING SET A Use Set A on reproducible p. 34f to assess children's ability to read decodable and high-frequency words in sentences.

FLUENCY AND COMPREHENSION Follow the directions on p. 34e.

MORE READING FOR

Group Time

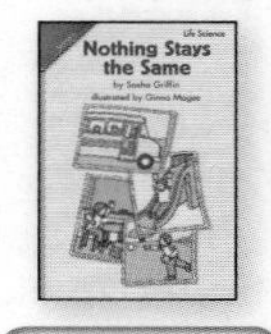

Use this Leveled Reader or other text at children's instructional level.

Below-Level

Reviews
- High-Frequency Words *always, become(s), day, everything, nothing, stays, things*
- Compare and Contrast

Advanced

ROUTINE

DAY 5

1 Monitor Progress

SENTENCE READING SET C Use Set C on reproducible page 34f to assess children's ability to read decodable and high-frequency words in sentences.

COMPREHENSION Have each child read "Happy Trips" on reproducible page 34g. Have the child choose one event in the story and predict what happens next. Then have the child retell the passage. Use the Retelling Rubric on p. 28–29 to evaluate the child's retelling.

2 Extend Concepts Through Inquiry

COMMUNICATE Have children share their paragraphs about African American artists.

MORE READING FOR
Group Time

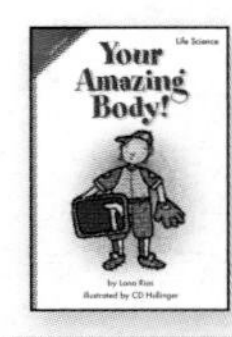

Use this Leveled Reader or other text at children's instructional level.

Advanced

Reviews
- Concept Vocabulary
- Compare and Contrast

Group Time

DAY 1

Strategic Intervention

ROUTINE

1 Word Work

PHONEMIC AWARENESS Reteach p. 36m. Additional practice items:

s-ink **h-ung** **j-unk** **w-ing** **t-ank** **r-ang**

FINAL *ng, nk* Reteach p. 36n. Additional words to blend:

hang **pink** **sing** **thank** **skunk**

Then have children spell *sank* with letter tiles. Monitor their work.

- Change the *nk* in *sank* to *ng*. What is the new word? — s a n g
- Change the s in *sang* to *b*. What is the new word? — b a n g
- Change the *ng* in *bang* to *nk*. What is the new word? — b a n k

SPELLING Reteach p. 36p. Model spelling *bring* and *sunk*. You may wish to give children fewer words to learn.

Decodable Reader 27
The Family Picnic
Written by Nicolas Florino
Illustrated by Dan Vick

2 Read Decodable Reader 27

BEFORE READING Review the final *ng, nk* words and the high-frequency words on p. 36q. Then have children blend these other decodable story words: *basket, grass, makes, place, while, yum, happy.* Be sure children understand meanings of words such as *trunk.*

DURING READING Use p. 36q.

Monitor Progress	Word and Story Reading
If... children have difficulty with any of these words,	**then...** reteach them by modeling. Have children practice the words, with feedback from you, until they can read them independently.
If... children have difficulty reading the story individually,	**then...** read a sentence aloud as children point to each word. Then have the group reread the sentence as they continue pointing. Continue reading in this way before children read individually.

3 Reread for Fluency

Use the Oral Rereading Routine, p. 36q, and text at each child's independent reading level.

MORE READING FOR
Group Time

Use this Leveled Reader or other text at children's instructional level.

Below-Level

Reviews
- High-Frequency Words *any, enough, ever, every, own, sure, were*
- Plot

Check this database for additional titles.

PearsonSuccessNet.com

Advanced

ROUTINE

DAY 1

1 Word Work

Final *ng, nk* Practice with more words with *ng* or *nk*. If children know the words on first read, they may need no further practice. Practice items:

blinker	**sprinkler**	**ankle**	**wrinkle**
angle	**thankful**	**triangle**	**anger**
bunker	**Thanksgiving**	**prankster**	**springtime**

Have children write the words on cards and sort by *nk* or *ng*. Discuss unfamiliar words. Then have individuals choose several words to use in a sentence.

2 Read Advanced Selection 14

BEFORE READING Have children identify these story words: *time line, event.*

DURING READING Children may read silently. Provide guidance as needed.

AFTER READING Have children recall the two most important ideas in the selection. (People change as they grow older; a time line helps put events in order.) Ask:

- Would you enjoy playing in an attic? Why or why not?
- Do you have a grandparent? Tell about him or her.

On the back of the selection page have children write a paragraph about something they would like to do with a grandparent or other older person.

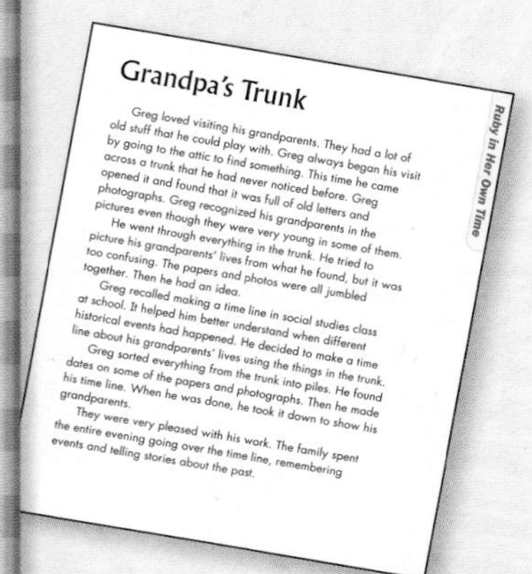

Grandpa's Trunk

Ruby in Her Own Time

Greg loved visiting his grandparents. They had a lot of old stuff that he could play with. Greg always began his visit by going to the attic to find something. This time he came across a trunk that he had never noticed before. Greg opened it and found that it was full of old letters and photographs. Greg recognized his grandparents in the pictures even though they were very young in some of them.

He went through everything in the trunk. He tried to picture his grandparents' lives from what he found, but it was too confusing. The papers and photos were all jumbled together. Then he had an idea.

Greg recalled making a time line in social studies class at school. It helped him better understand when different historical events had happened. He decided to make a time line about his grandparents' lives using the things in the trunk.

Greg sorted everything from the trunk into piles. He found dates on some of the papers and photographs. Then he made his time line. When he was done, he took it down to show his grandparents.

They were very pleased with his work. The family spent the entire evening going over the time line, remembering events and telling stories about the past.

DI•11

3 Extend Concepts Through Inquiry

IDENTIFY QUESTIONS Have children choose a story to summarize. During the week, they should learn more about their choices by reading and studying them. They might also find or illustrate pictures to go along with their summaries. On Day 5 they will share these summaries. Guide children in brainstorming possible choices.

- Think about your story. What happens first? What happens next? How does the story end?

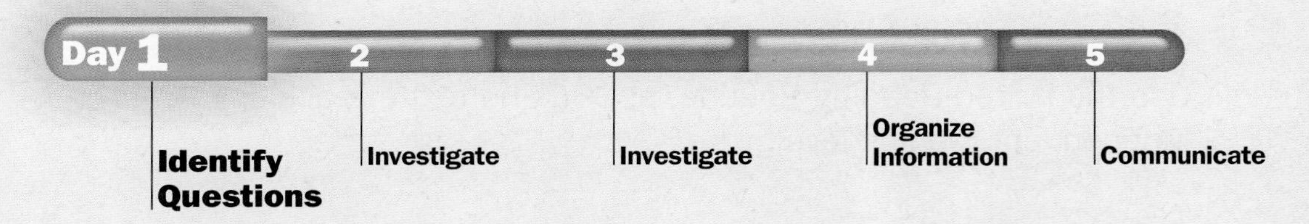

MORE READING FOR
Group Time

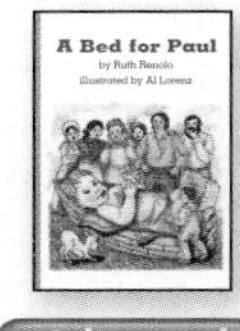

Use this Leveled Reader or other text at children's instructional level.

Advanced

Reviews
- Concept Vocabulary
- Plot

Group Time

DAY 2

Strategic Intervention

ROUTINE

1 Word Work

PHONEMIC AWARENESS Reteach p. 38b. Additional practice items:

pigpen **bedtime** **lipstick** **dishpan**

COMPOUND WORDS Reteach p. 38c. Additional words to blend:

lampshade **inland** **cupcake** **sunglasses** **homework**

Write the following words below. Have children identify the two smaller words that make up each compound. Have them blend the two smaller words and then blend the two words to read the compound word. Discuss the meanings of the compound words.

homemade **sunrise** **landslide** **bagpipe**
wishbone **catfish** **lookout** **racetrack**

PRETEACH HIGH-FREQUENCY WORDS Write *any, enough, ever, every, own, sure, were* and have children say each word, spell it as they point to each letter, and say it again. Then have them finger trace the letters in each word, naming the letters as they trace. Have individuals practice reading the words from word cards.

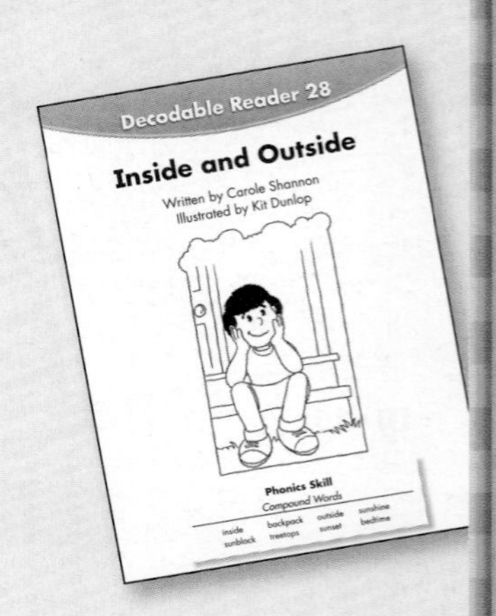

2 Read Decodable Reader 28

BEFORE READING Review the compound words and high-frequency words on p. 38f. Then have children blend these other decodable story words: *feeds, fish, home, kite, takes, while, likes, swim, nice.* Be sure children understand the meanings of words such as *backpack* and *sunset*.

DURING READING Use p. 38f.

Monitor Progress	Word and Story Reading
If... children have difficulty with any of these words,	**then...** reteach them by modeling. Have children practice the words, with feedback from you, until they can read them independently.
If... children have difficulty reading the story individually,	**then...** read a sentence aloud as children point to each word. Have the group reread the sentence as they continue pointing. Read in this way before children read individually.

3 Reread for Fluency

Use the Paired Reading Routine, p. 38f, and text at each child's independent reading level.

MORE READING FOR
Group Time

Use this Leveled Reader or other text at children's instructional level.

Below-Level

Reviews
- High-Frequency Words *any, enough, ever, every, own, sure, were*
- Plot

Advanced

ROUTINE

DAY 2

1 Word Work

Compound Words Practice with other compound words. If children know the words on first read, they may need no further practice. Practice items:

afternoon	**scarecrow**	**thunderstorm**	**understand**	**inchworm**
tablecloth	**sweatshirt**	**seashore**	**sailboat**	**peppermint**

Discuss the meanings of unfamiliar words. Point out how breaking the words apart helps to show their meaning. Show children how breaking a word into syllables can help them read it.

2 Read Self-Selected Reading

BEFORE READING Have children select a trade book or Leveled Reader to read independently. Guide children in selecting books of appropriate difficulty.

AFTER READING When they have finished, have each child select an interesting passage to read aloud to a partner.

3 Extend Concepts Through Inquiry

INVESTIGATE Guide children in choosing material to summarize at their independent reading level. Some books that may be appropriate are *Verdi* by Janell Cannon or *The Littlest Wolf* by Larry Dane Brimmer.

Help children decide how they will present their information. Children may use a Venn diagram or other graphic organizer, a written format, photographs, drawings, or models.

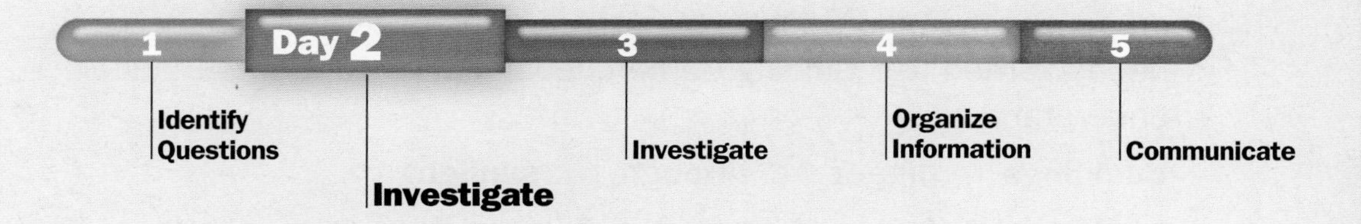

Trade Books for Self-Selected Reading

VERDI by Janell Cannon, Harcourt Brace, © 1997

THE LITTLEST WOLF by Larry Dane Brimmer, HarperCollins Children's Books, © 2002

MORE READING FOR
Group Time

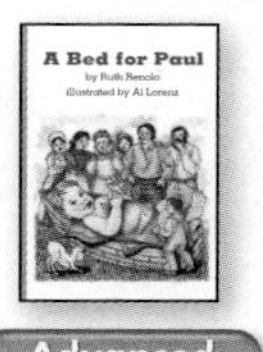

Use this Leveled Reader or other text at children's instructional level.

Advanced

Reviews
- Concept Vocabulary
- Plot

Group Time

DAY 3

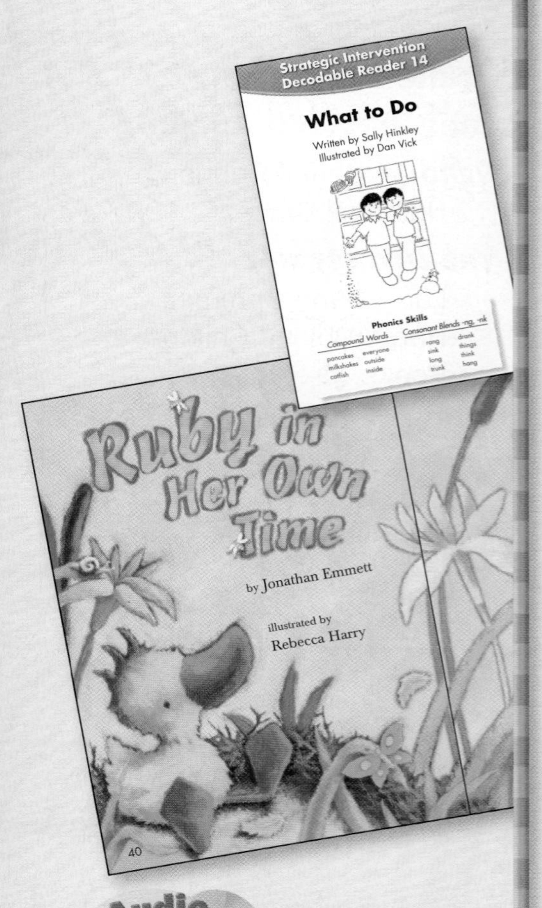

Audio CD AudioText

Strategic Intervention

ROUTINE

1 Word Work

PHONEMIC AWARENESS Reteach p. 40b. Additional practice items:

j, s, tr -unk ***th, s, br -ink*** ***t, th, dr -ank***

 **FINAL *ng, nk* AND COMPOUND WORDS** Reteach p. 40c. Additional words to practice:

gang **drink** **ring** **blank**
sunrise **anthill** **cutout** **anywhere**

2 Read Strategic Intervention Decodable Reader 14

BEFORE READING Take a picture walk through the book, stopping on p. 5 to talk about the twins looking outside at the snowy day. Have children predict what might happen next.

DURING READING Read p. 2 aloud with the group. Have them read pp. 3–4 aloud without you. Select individuals to read aloud to the end.

AFTER READING Check comprehension by having children retell the story, including the characters, setting, and plot. Have children locate words with final *ng, nk* and compound words in the story. List words children name. Children may name *pancakes, sink, rang, hang, trunk, think, milkshakes, thing, drank, everyone, catfish, inside,* and *outside.* Have children identify the compound words. Name the two words that make up the compound, and tell the meaning. Then have the list read.

3 Read *Ruby in Her Own Time*

BEFORE READING Have children practice the words below—first as a group and then individually. Monitor their practice and correct as needed. Then use Guiding Comprehension, pp. 40–63, to monitor understanding.

ducklings **bigger** **through** **sunlight**
beaks **far** **bright** **stretched**

Monitor Progress	Word and Story Reading
If... children have difficulty with any of these words,	**then...** coach them in blending and have them practice in pairs with word cards before reading the story.
If... children have difficulty reading the story individually,	**then...** have them follow along as they listen to the AudioText. They may also read pages of the selection aloud together, first with you and then without you, before reading individually.

Advanced

ROUTINE

DAY 3

1 Read *Ruby in Her Own Time*

DURING READING Have children read silently to p. 50. Provide guidance as needed. Ask:

- Why did Father worry about Ruby? Did Mother worry?
- What makes Father's worry go away?

Have children read silently to p. 61. Then ask:

- How did the ducklings change?
- How was Ruby's flying different than her brothers and sisters?

Plot Have children recall the things that happen in the story.

- What happened first in the story?
- What happened last?

Summarize Children can work with a partner to complete a story summary. Draw a chart or distribute copies of Graphic Organizer 22 (Story Sequence).

Beginning
Ruby hatches later than her brothers and sisters.

↓

Middle
Ruby does other things later than her brothers and sisters.

↓

End
Ruby flies higher and farther than her brothers and sisters.

▲ Graphic Organizer Flip Chart 22

RESPONSE Ask children to draw a different animal. Have them draw the animal as a baby, as a youth, and as an adult.

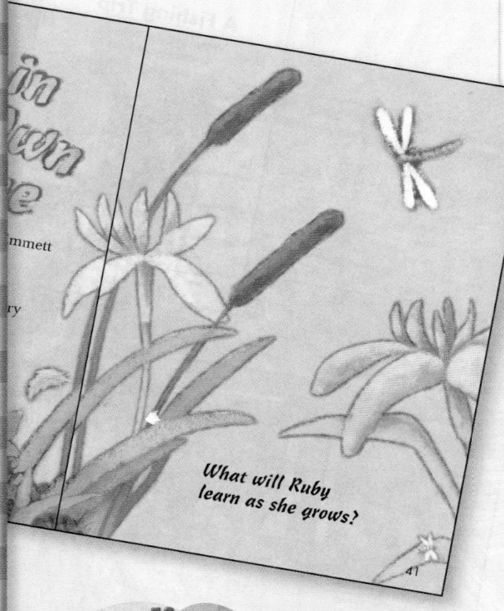

Audio CD AudioText

2 Extend Concepts Through Inquiry

INVESTIGATE Give children time to work with the stories they are summarizing.

Jan's New Home

Group Time

Strategic Intervention

ROUTINE

DAY 1

1 Word Work

PHONEMIC AWARENESS Reteach p. 68m. Additional practice items:

fix **brush** **catch** **class**

ENDING *-es*; PLURAL *-es* Reteach p. 68n. Additional words to blend:

mixes **kisses** **wishes** **patches** **buzzes**

Then write *tosses* and *foxes* below the heads *Ending -es* and *More Than One -es*. Have children read *tosses* and spell it with letter tiles. Continue with *foxes* and then *rushes, glasses, waxes,* and *matches*. If children have difficulty reading a word, have them cover *-es* and blend the base word.

Ending *-es*	More Than One *-es*
tosses	foxes
rushes	glasses
waxes	matches

SPELLING Reteach p. 68p. Model spelling *wishes* and *buses*. You may wish to give children fewer words to learn.

2 Read Decodable Reader 29

BEFORE READING Review the ending *-es* and plural *-es* words and the high-frequency words on p. 68q. Then have children blend these other decodable story words: *class, Patty, kitten, snake, steps, puppy.* Be sure children understand meanings of words such as *foxes* and *fishes.*

DURING READING Use p. 68q.

Monitor Progress	Word and Story Reading
If... children have difficulty with any of these words,	**then...** reteach them by modeling. Have children practice the words, with feedback from you, until they can read them independently.
If... children have difficulty reading the story individually,	**then...** read a sentence aloud as children point to each word. Then have the group reread the sentence as they continue pointing. Continue reading in this way before children read individually.

3 Reread for Fluency

Use the Oral Rereading Routine, p. 68q, and text at each child's independent reading level.

MORE READING FOR
Group Time

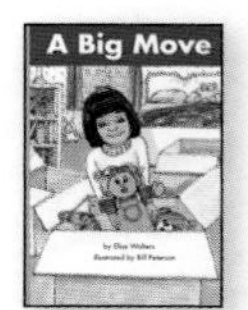

Use this Leveled Reader or other text at children's instructional level.

Below-Level

Reviews

- High-Frequency Words *away, car, friends, house, our, school, very*
- Theme

Check this database for additional titles.

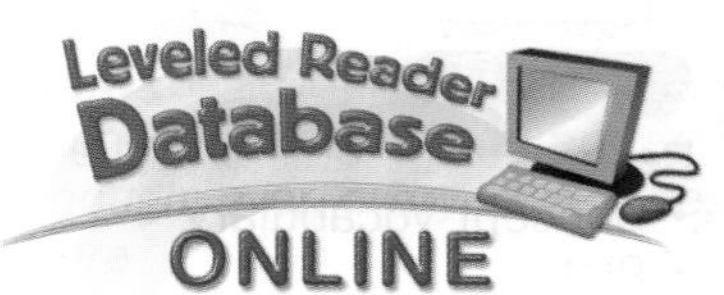

ONLINE
PearsonSuccessNet.com

Advanced

ROUTINE

DAY 1

1 Word Work

Ending *-es*, plural *-es* Practice longer words and words with spelling changes. If children know the words on first read, they may need no further practice. Practice items:

beaches	**reaches**	**teaches**	**touches**	**searches**
leashes	**marshes**	**babies**	**bunnies**	**studies**
scurries	**spies**	**strawberries**	**scarves**	**leaves**

Point out the words that change *y* to *i* or *f* to *v* before adding *-es*. Discuss unfamiliar words and then have individuals choose several words to use in a sentence.

2 Read Advanced Selection 15

BEFORE READING Have children identify these story words: *route, arrive, depart.*

DURING READING Children may read silently. Provide guidance as needed.

AFTER READING Have children recall the two most important ideas in the selection. (It would be fun to live in San Francisco; there are many interesting things to do in San Francisco.) Ask:

- Which of these activities would be the most fun for you? Why?
- Would you like to live in San Francisco? Why or why not?

On the back of the selection page have children write about something that is fun to do in their hometown. Have them add a drawing of the activity.

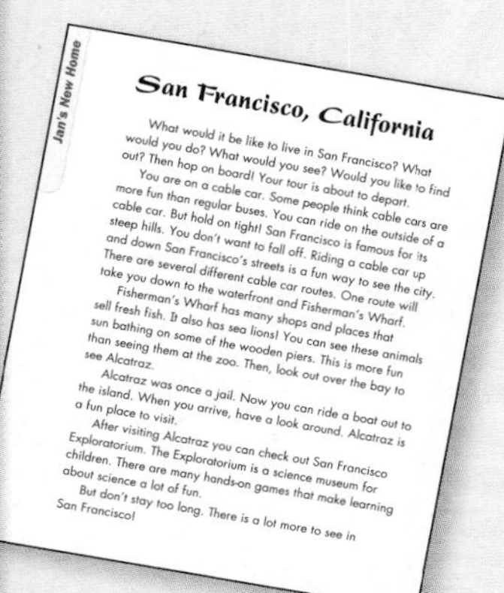
Jan's New Home

San Francisco, California

What would it be like to live in San Francisco? What would you do? What would you see? Would you like to find out? Then hop on board! Your tour is about to depart.

You are on a cable car. Some people think cable cars are more fun than regular buses. You can ride on the outside of a cable car. But hold on tight! San Francisco is famous for its steep hills. You don't want to fall off. Riding a cable car up and down San Francisco's streets is a fun way to see the city. There are several different cable car routes. One route will take you down to the waterfront and Fisherman's Wharf.

Fisherman's Wharf has many shops and places that sell fresh fish. It also has sea lions! You can see these animals sun bathing on some of the wooden piers. This is more fun than seeing them at the zoo. Then, look out over the bay to see Alcatraz.

Alcatraz was once a jail. Now you can ride a boat out to the island. When you arrive, have a look around. Alcatraz is a fun place to visit.

After visiting Alcatraz you can check out San Francisco Exploratorium. The Exploratorium is a science museum for children. There are many hands-on games that make learning about science a lot of fun.

But don't stay too long. There is a lot more to see in San Francisco!

DI•12

3 Extend Concepts Through Inquiry

IDENTIFY QUESTIONS Have children choose a city to investigate. During the week, they should learn more about their choices from reading, studying pictures, and talking with adults or older children. On Day 5 they will share what they learned. Guide children in brainstorming possible choices.

- Think about your choice. Are there fun things to do in this city? What does it look like?

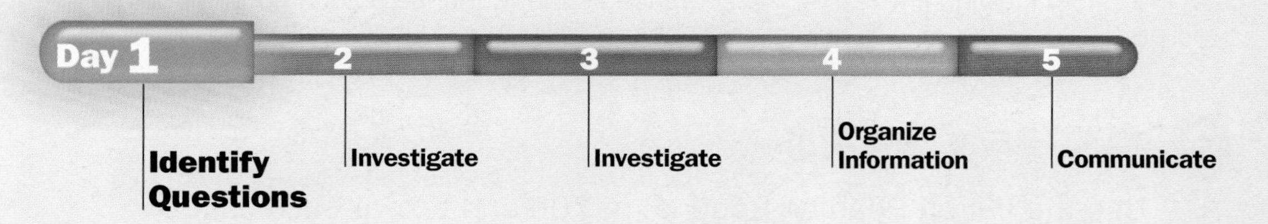

MORE READING FOR
Group Time

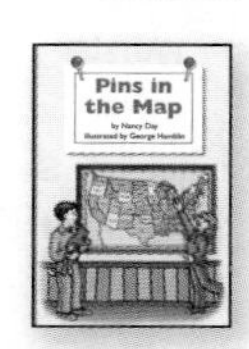

Advanced

Use this Leveled Reader or other text at children's instructional level.

Reviews
- Concept Vocabulary
- Theme

Jan's New Home

Group Time

DAY 2

Strategic Intervention

ROUTINE

1 Word Work

PHONEMIC AWARENESS Reteach p. 70b. Additional practice items:

p, f, sp –ort **p, w, sh –ore** **p, t –orch**

r-CONTROLLED *or, ore* Reteach p. 70c. Additional words to blend:

for **horn** **more** **short** **storm**

Then have children spell *born* with letter tiles. Monitor their work.

- Change the *b* in *born* to *c*. What is the new word? c o r n
- Change the *n* in *corn* to *k*. What is the new word? c o r k
- Change the *k* in *cork* to *e*. What is the new word? c o r e

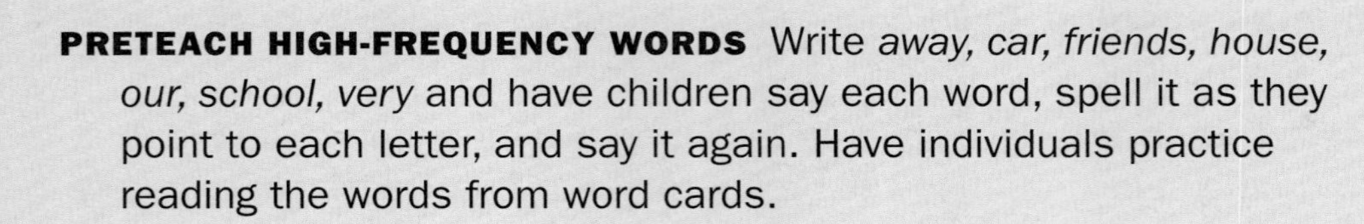

PRETEACH HIGH-FREQUENCY WORDS Write *away, car, friends, house, our, school, very* and have children say each word, spell it as they point to each letter, and say it again. Have individuals practice reading the words from word cards.

Decodable Reader 30
The Family Trip
Written by Mary Palmert
Illustrated by JoAnne Derbbs

2 Read Decodable Reader 30

BEFORE READING Review the *r*-controlled *or, ore* words and the high-frequency words on p. 70f. Then have children blend these other decodable story words: *time, swim, backpack, ships, ballgame, waves, clams.* Be sure children understand the meanings of words such as *port* and *clams*.

DURING READING Use p. 70f.

Monitor Progress	Word and Story Reading
If... children have difficulty with any of these words,	**then...** reteach them by modeling. Have children practice the words, with feedback from you, until they can read them independently.
If... children have difficulty reading the story individually,	**then...** read a sentence aloud as children point to each word. Have the group reread the sentence as they continue pointing. Read in this way before children read individually.

3 Reread for Fluency

Use the Paired Reading Routine, p. 70f, and text at each child's independent reading level.

MORE READING FOR
Group Time

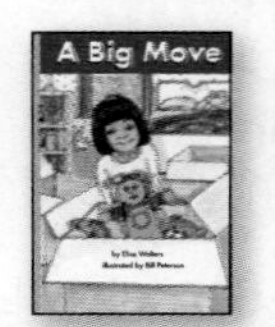

Use this Leveled Reader or other text at children's instructional level.

Below-Level

Reviews
- High-Frequency Words *away, car, friends, house, our, school, very*
- Theme

Advanced

ROUTINE

DAY 2

1 Word Work

r*-Controlled *or, ore Practice with longer words with *r*-controlled *or* and *ore*. If children know the words on first read, they may need no further practice. Practice items:

seashore	**orchestra**	**important**	**ordinary**	**before**
storefront	**auditorium**	**laboratory**	**portfolio**	**information**

Discuss the meanings of unfamiliar words. Have children write the words and circle the letters that stand for the /ôr/ sound.

2 Read Self-Selected Reading

BEFORE READING Have children select a trade book or Leveled Reader to read independently. Guide children in selecting books of appropriate difficulty.

AFTER READING When they have finished, have each child select an interesting passage to read aloud to a partner.

3 Extend Concepts Through Inquiry

INVESTIGATE Guide children in choosing material at their independent reading level to explore their topic. Some books that may be appropriate are *Material World: A Global Family Portrait* by Peter Menzel or *Ms. Frizzle's Adventures: Ancient Egypt* by Joanna Cole and Bruce Degen.

Help children decide how they will present their information. Children may use a Venn diagram or other graphic organizer, a written format, photographs, drawings, or models.

Trade Books for Self-Selected Reading

MATERIAL WORLD: A GLOBAL FAMILY PORTRAIT by Peter Menzel, Sierra Club Books, © 1995

MS. FRIZZLE'S ADVENTURES: ANCIENT EGYPT by Joanna Cole and Bruce Degen, Scholastic Books, © 2003

MORE READING FOR
Group Time

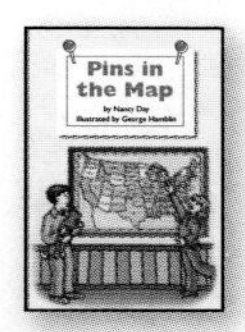

Use this Leveled Reader or other text at children's instructional level.

Advanced

Reviews
- Concept Vocabulary
- Theme

Group Time

DAY 3

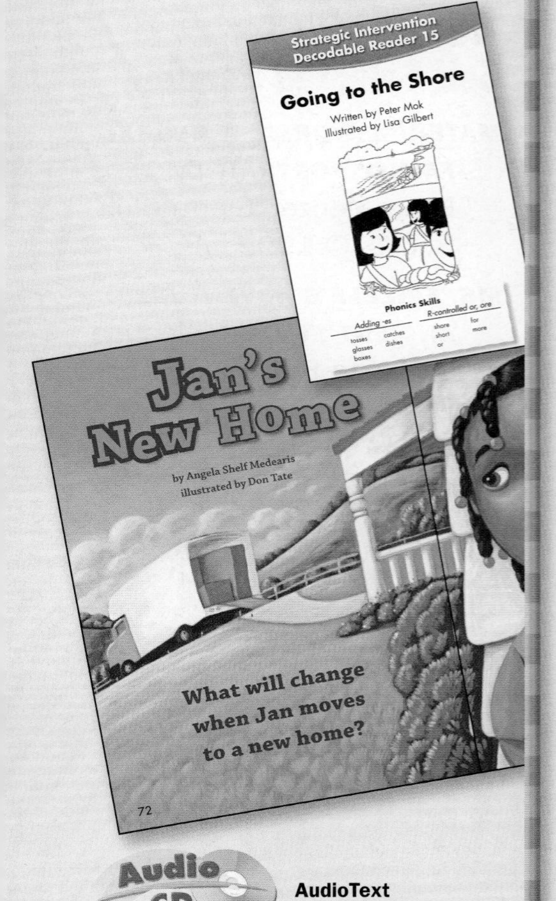

Audio CD AudioText

Strategic Intervention

ROUTINE

1 Word Work

PHONEMIC AWARENESS Reteach p. 72b. Additional practice items:

c, h, w –orn **c, f, p –ork** **st, ch, b –ore**

ENDING *-es*, PLURAL *-es* AND *r*-CONTROLLED *or, ore* Reteach p. 72c. Additional words to practice:

dresses **patches** **dishes** **flashes**
fort **born** **porch** **snore**

2 Read Strategic Intervention Decodable Reader 15

BEFORE READING Before reading, review *away, car,* and *very* on the Word Wall. Take a picture walk through the book. Have children talk about what they would pack for a trip to the shore.

DURING READING Read p. 2 aloud with the group. Have them read pp. 3–4 aloud without you. Select individuals to read aloud to the end.

AFTER READING Check comprehension by having children retell the story, including the characters, setting, and plot. Have children locate words with ending *-es,* plurals formed with *-es,* and *r*-controlled *or, ore* words in the story. List words children name. Children may name *boxes, or, for, tosses, short, more, dishes, shore, glasses,* and *catches.* Have individuals identify the words with *r*-controlled *or, ore.* Then have the list read.

3 Read *Jan's New Home*

BEFORE READING Have children practice the words below—first as a group and then individually. Monitor their practice and correct as needed. Then use Guiding Comprehension, pp. 72–87, to monitor understanding.

long **change** **everything**
rush **horses** **everywhere**

Monitor Progress	Word and Story Reading
If... children have difficulty with any of these words,	**then...** coach them in blending and have them practice in pairs with word cards before reading the story.
If... children have difficulty reading the story individually,	**then...** have them follow along as they listen to the AudioText. They may also read pages of the selection aloud together, first with you and then without you, before reading individually.

Advanced

ROUTINE

DAY 3

1 Read *Jan's New Home*

DURING READING Have children read silently to p. 78. Provide guidance as needed. Ask:
- How does Jan feel about moving?
- What are the new things in Jan's life going to be?

Have children read silently to p. 85. Then ask:
- Where was Jan's old house?
- Where is Jan's new house?

Theme Have children think about the big idea in the story. Discuss what the story teaches them.
- How do Jan's feeling change in the story?
- What does this story teach us about change?

Monitor and Fix Up Then have them work with a partner to summarize details of the story. Have children use Graphic Organizer 23 to identify story events and details.

RESPONSE Ask children to visualize their dream home—a home they would enjoy moving to. Have them draw the house.

Title Jan's New Home	
Characters Jan, her mother	**Setting** Jan's house

Events	
1. First:	Jan is sad about moving.
2. Next:	Jan packs.
3. Then:	Jan's family drives to her new house.
4. Last:	Jan arrives at her new home in the city.

▲ **Graphic Organizer Flip Chart 23**

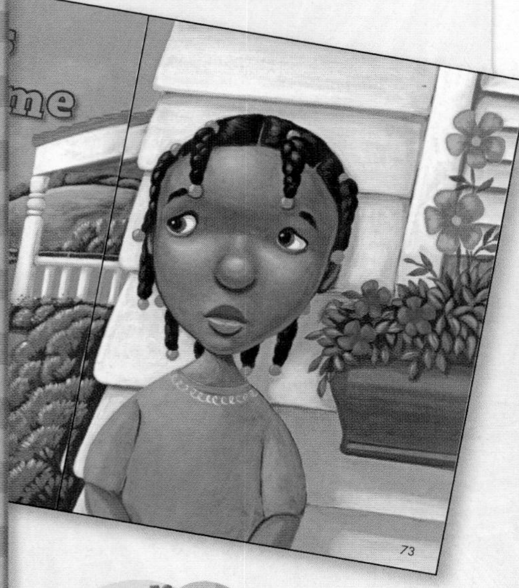

Audio CD AudioText

2 Extend Concepts Through Inquiry

INVESTIGATE Give children time to investigate the city they will report on and to begin preparing their information.

Group Time

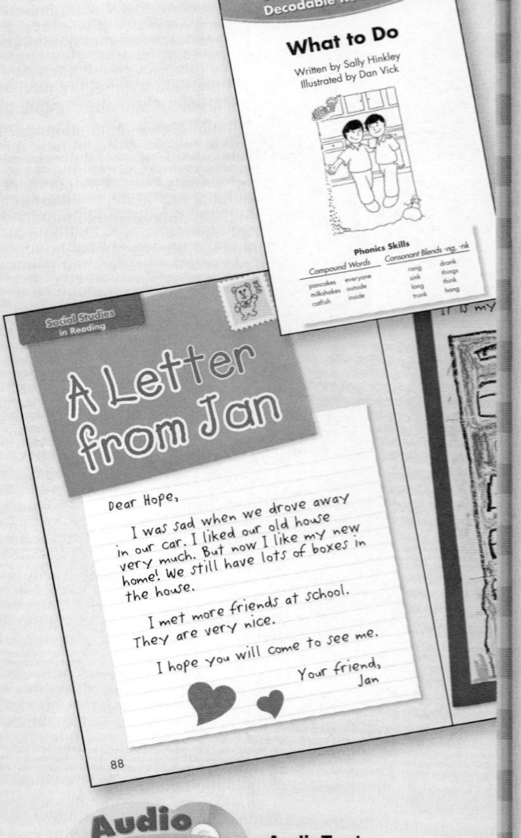

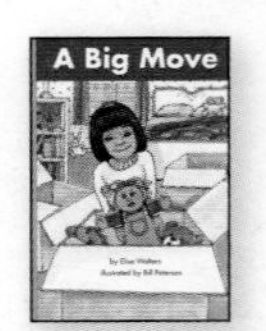

AudioText

MORE READING FOR
Group Time

A Big Move

Use this Leveled Reader or other text at children's instructional level.

Below-Level

Reviews
- High-Frequency Words *away, car, friends, house, our, school, very*
- Theme

DAY 4

Strategic Intervention

ROUTINE

1 Word Work

PHONEMIC AWARENESS Reteach p. 88b. Additional practice items:

anthill cupcake wishbone classmate jellyfish

REVIEW FINAL *ng, nk* AND COMPOUND WORDS Reteach p. 88c, using these additional words.

sang	**ring**	**bank**	**junk**	**stung**
sidewalk	**suntan**	**driveway**	**lipstick**	**basketball**

REVIEW WORD READING Use the words and sentences on p. 88d to review decoding skills. Have children practice words in pairs until they can read one word every one or two seconds.

2 Reread Strategic Intervention Decodable Reader 14

BEFORE READING Have children review these decodable story words: *thing, rang, drank, sink, think, trunk, hung, pancakes, milkshakes, outside, catfish, inside, snug, plates, walk, stove.*

DURING READING Read p. 2 aloud with the group. Have them read pp. 3–4 aloud without you. Select individuals to read aloud to the end.

AFTER READING Have children retell the story. Point to words in the story with *ng, nk* or compound words and ask individuals to read them.

3 Read "A Letter from Jan"

BEFORE READING Have children practice the words below—first as a group and then individually. Monitor their practice and correct as needed. Then use Social Studies in Reading, pp. 88–89.

our car liked

Monitor Progress	Word and Selection Reading
If... children have difficulty with any of these words,	**then...** have them practice in pairs reading word cards before reading the selection.
If... children have difficulty reading the selection individually,	**then...** have them follow along as they listen to the AudioText. They may also read pages of the selection aloud together, first with you and then without you, before reading individually.

Advanced

ROUTINE

1 Read "A Letter from Jan"

AFTER READING Ask:

- How did Jan feel about her old house?
- How does she feel about her new house?
- How do you know that Jan's family is still unpacking?

2 Vocabulary

Extend vocabulary with questions such as these:

- What is the *location* of your school?
- What *route* do you take to get to school?
- What time do you *arrive* at school?
- What time do you *depart* from your house?

Encourage children to use the words in their writing.

3 Extend Concepts Through Inquiry

ORGANIZE INFORMATION Give children time to continue reading about the cities they are reporting on. Remind them that tomorrow they will share their information. By now they should have begun putting the information in a presentation format.

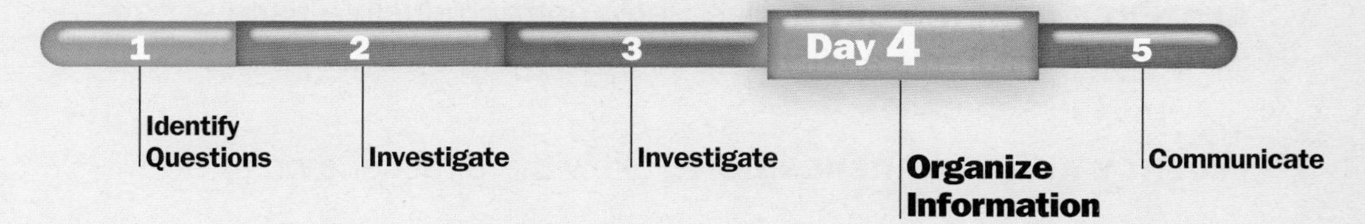

AudioText

MORE READING FOR
Group Time

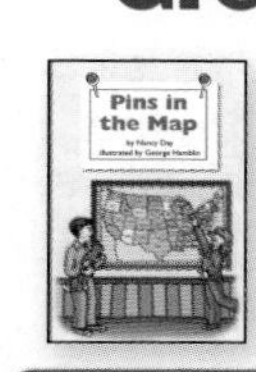

Use this Leveled Reader or other text at children's instructional level.

Advanced

Reviews
- Concept Vocabulary
- Theme

Group Time

Strategic Intervention

ROUTINE

DAY 5

1 Word Work

ENDING *-es*, PLURAL *-es* AND *r*-CONTROLLED *or, ore* Write these sentences. Have children read aloud as you track the print. Call on individuals to blend the underlined words.

Go north to get to the pet store.

We packed boxes of glasses and dishes.

Mom patches the torn dresses.

Mort will score when he tosses the ball.

HIGH-FREQUENCY WORDS Use pp. 70–71 to review *away, car, friends, house, our, school, very.*

Monitor Progress	High-Frequency Words
If... children have difficulty with any of these words,	**then...** tell them the word and have them repeat it. Have children spell the word and tell what word they spelled. Have them practice in pairs with word cards.

2 Monitor Progress

SENTENCE READING SET A Use Set A on reproducible page 90f to assess children's ability to read decodable and high-frequency words in sentences.

FLUENCY AND COMPREHENSION Follow the directions on p. 90e.

MORE READING FOR

Group Time

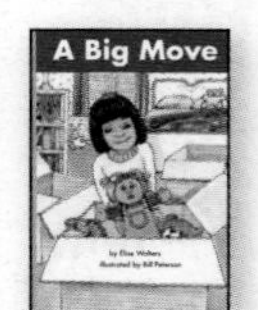

Use this Leveled Reader or other text at children's instructional level.

Below-Level

Reviews

- High-Frequency Words *away, car, friends, house, our, school, very*
- Theme

Advanced

ROUTINE

DAY 5

1 Monitor Progress

SENTENCE READING SET C Use Set C on reproducible p. 90f to assess children's ability to read decodable and high-frequency words in sentences.

COMPREHENSION Have each child read "Morning Chores" on reproducible p. 90g. Ask what is the main idea of the story (theme), and have the child retell the passage. Use the Retelling Rubric on p. 86–87 to evaluate the child's retelling.

2 Extend Concepts Through Inquiry

COMMUNICATE Have children share reports on cities.

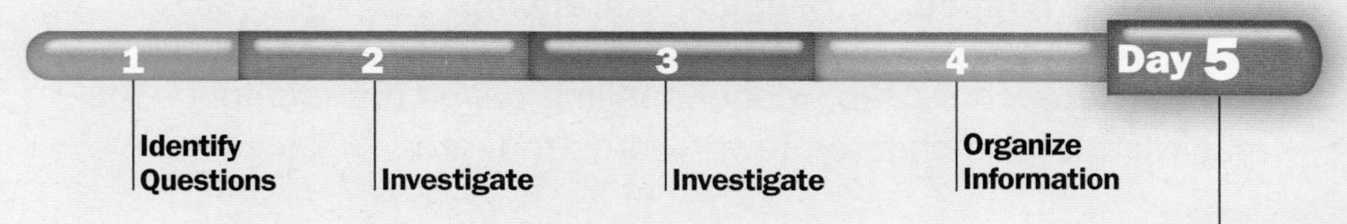

MORE READING FOR
Group Time

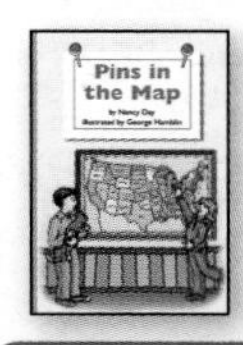

Use this Leveled Reader or other text at children's instructional level.

Advanced

Reviews
- Concept Vocabulary
- Theme

Group Time

Strategic Intervention

ROUTINE

DAY 1

1 Word Work

PHONEMIC AWARENESS Reteach p. 92m. Additional practice items:

landed **hugging** **batted** **drinking** **petted** **getting**

INFLECTED ENDINGS Reteach p. 92n. Additional words to practice:

sunning **gripped** **rubbing** **clapped** **skipping**

Write the words below. Call on children to read the words, identify the endings, and frame the base words. If children have difficulty reading a base word, have them cover the added consonant and the ending and blend the base word.

sipping **quitting** **winning** **flipped**
tapped **hopped** **begged** **stepping**

SPELLING Reteach p. 92p. Model spelling *called* and *planned*. You may wish to give children fewer words to learn.

2 Read Decodable Reader 31

BEFORE READING Review the words with inflected endings and the high-frequency words on p. 92q. Then have children blend these other decodable story words: *race, shape, week, tips, quick, line, drink, best.* Be sure children understand meanings of words such as *tips*.

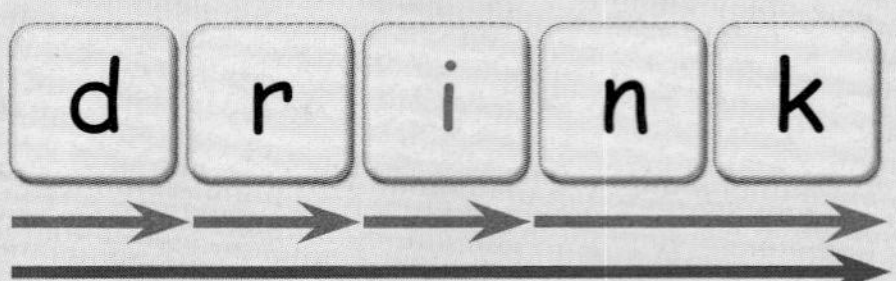

DURING READING Use p. 92q.

Monitor Progress	Word and Story Reading
If... children have difficulty with any of these words,	**then...** reteach them by modeling. Have children practice the words, with feedback from you, until they can read them independently.
If... children have difficulty reading the story individually,	**then...** read a sentence aloud as children point to each word. Then have the group reread the sentence as they continue pointing. Continue reading in this way before children read individually.

3 Reread for Fluency

Use the Oral Rereading Routine, p. 92q, and text at each child's independent reading level.

MORE READING FOR
Group Time

Use this Leveled Reader or other text at children's instructional level.

Below-Level

Reviews
- High-Frequency Words *afraid, again, few, how, read, soon*
- Plot

Check this database for additional titles.

PearsonSuccessNet.com

Advanced

ROUTINE

DAY 1

1 Word Work

Inflected Endings Practice with longer words with inflected endings *-ed* or *-ing*. If children know the words on first read, they may need no further practice. Practice items:

omitted **omitting** **occurred** **occurring** **starred** **starring**

Have children write the words and identify the base word and the ending. Then have individuals choose several words to use in a sentence.

2 Read Advanced Selection 16

BEFORE READING Have children identify these story words: *gardener, nature, sprout.*

DURING READING Children may read silently. Provide guidance as needed.

AFTER READING Have children recall the two most important ideas in the selection. (Beans are a kind of seed; soaking the beans in warm water makes them sprout.) Ask:

- Make a list of things you need to sprout some beans.
- What kinds of beans have you eaten?

On the back of the selection page have children write a four-line poem about plants.

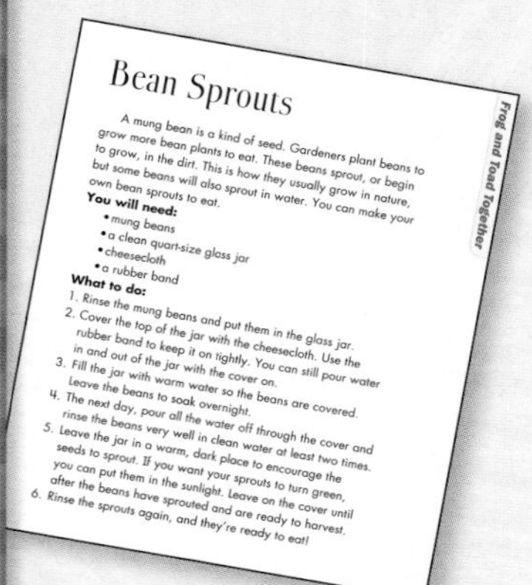

Bean Sprouts

Frog and Toad Together

A mung bean is a kind of seed. Gardeners plant beans to grow more bean plants to eat. These beans sprout, or begin to grow, in the dirt. This is how they usually grow in nature, but some beans will also sprout in water. You can make your own bean sprouts to eat.

You will need:

- mung beans
- a clean quart-size glass jar
- cheesecloth
- a rubber band

What to do:

1. Rinse the mung beans and put them in the glass jar.
2. Cover the top of the jar with the cheesecloth. Use the rubber band to keep it on tightly. You can still pour water in and out of the jar with the cover on.
3. Fill the jar with warm water so the beans are covered. Leave the beans to soak overnight.
4. The next day, pour all the water off through the cover and rinse the beans very well in clean water at least two times.
5. Leave the jar in a warm, dark place to encourage the seeds to sprout. If you want your sprouts to turn green, you can put them in the sunlight. Leave on the cover until after the beans have sprouted and are ready to harvest.
6. Rinse the sprouts again, and they're ready to eat!

DI•13

3 Extend Concepts Through Inquiry

IDENTIFY QUESTIONS Have children find a story that inspires them to visualize themselves as one of its characters. During the week, they should study the story so that they can retell the major events and think about their visualization in detail so they can tell classmates about it. On Day 5 they will share what they have prepared. Guide children in brainstorming possible choices.

- Think about your choice. How do you feel as you put yourself in the character's place? Can you think of something the character might do after the story ends?

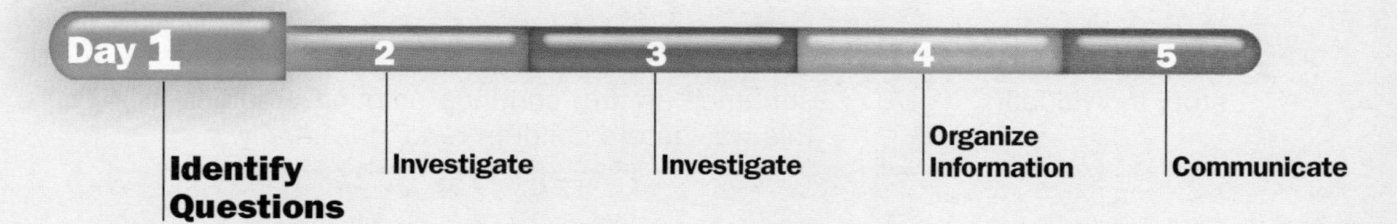

MORE READING FOR
Group Time

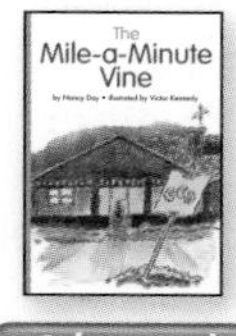

Use this Leveled Reader or other text at children's instructional level.

Advanced

Reviews

- Concept Vocabulary
- Plot

Group Time

DAY 2

Strategic Intervention

ROUTINE

1 Word Work

PHONEMIC AWARENESS Reteach p. 94b. Additional practice items:

cat—cart **had—hard** **chat—chart** **shape—sharp**

r*-CONTROLLED *ar Reteach p. 94c. Additional words to blend:

arm **charm** **harp** **farm** **start**

Then have children spell *bar* with letter tiles. Monitor their work.

- Add *n* to the end of *bar*. What is the new word? — b a r n
- Change the *n* in *barn* to *k*. What is the new word? — b a r k
- Change the *b* in *bark* to *d*. What is the new word? — d a r k

PRETEACH HIGH-FREQUENCY WORDS Write *afraid, again, few, how, read, soon* and have children say each word, spell it as they point to each letter, and say it again. Have individuals practice reading the words from word cards.

2 Read Decodable Reader 32

BEFORE READING Review the *r*-controlled *ar* words and the high-frequency words on p. 94f. Then have children blend these other decodable story words: *sees, kittens, corn, feed, chicks, sheep, shines, honks, horn, best, seeing.* Be sure children understand the meanings of words such as *honks*.

DURING READING Use p. 94f.

Monitor Progress	Word and Story Reading
If... children have difficulty with any of these words,	**then...** reteach them by modeling. Have children practice the words, with feedback from you, until they can read them independently.
If... children have difficulty reading the story individually,	**then...** read a sentence aloud as children point to each word. Have the group reread the sentence as they continue pointing. Reading in this way before children read individually.

3 Reread for Fluency

Use the Oral Rereading Routine, p. 94f, and text at each child's independent reading level.

MORE READING FOR

Group Time

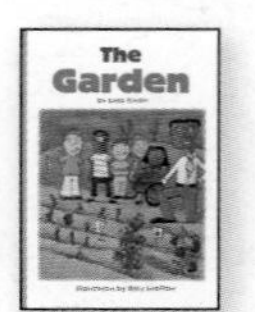

Use this Leveled Reader or other text at children's instructional level.

Below-Level

Reviews

- High-Frequency Words *afraid, again, few, how, read, soon*
- Plot

Advanced

ROUTINE

DAY 2

1 Word Work

r*-Controlled *ar Practice with longer words that have *r*-controlled *ar*. If children know the words on first read, they may need no further practice. Practice items:

target	**darkness**	**charming**	**starter**
charcoal	**sparkle**	**partner**	**marble**

Discuss the meanings of unfamiliar words. Point out the *ar* in each word. If children have difficulty, cover up all of the word except the first letter or blend and the *ar*.

2 Read *What Makes the Seasons?*

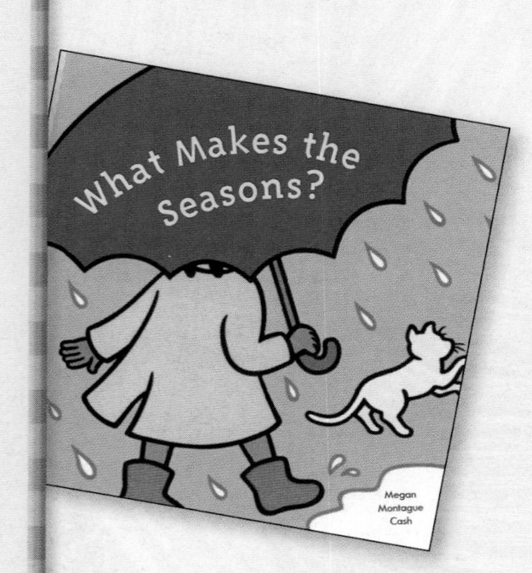

DURING READING Children may read silently. Provide guidance as needed.

AFTER READING Ask:

- What are the four seasons talked about in the selection?
- What happens to the seeds in spring?

3 Extend Concepts Through Inquiry

INVESTIGATE Guide children in choosing material at their independent reading level to explore their visualization. Some books that may be appropriate are *Beardream* by Will Hobbs or *Plantzilla* by Jerdine Nolen.

Help children decide how they will present their story and their visualization. Children may use a Venn diagram or other graphic organizer, a written format, photographs, drawings, or models.

MORE READING FOR
Group Time

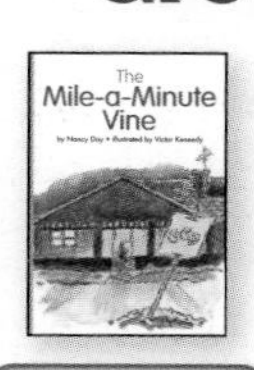

Use this Leveled Reader or other text at children's instructional level.

Advanced

Reviews

- Concept Vocabulary
- Plot

Group Time

DAY 3

Audio CD AudioText

Strategic Intervention

ROUTINE

1 Word Work

PHONEMIC AWARENESS Reteach p. 96b. Additional practice items:

tagged **card** **ripped** **mark** **stepped** **barn**

INFLECTED ENDINGS AND *r*-CONTROLLED *ar* Reteach p. 96c. Additional words to practice:

running **getting** **tapped** **flopping**
far **park** **yard** **sharp**

2 Read Strategic Intervention Decodable Reader 16

BEFORE READING Before reading, review *again* on the Word Wall. Take a picture walk through the book, pointing out the changes in setting.

DURING READING Read p. 2 aloud with the group. Have them read pp. 3–4 aloud without you. Select individuals to read aloud to the end.

AFTER READING Check comprehension by having children retell the story, including the characters, setting, and plot. Have children locate words with inflected endings and *r*-controlled *ar* words in the story. List words children name. Children may name *cars, falling, farm, stars, napping, park, jogging, stopped, jogged,* and *dark.* Have individuals identify the words with inflected endings. Then have the list read.

3 Read *Frog and Toad Together*

BEFORE READING Have children practice the words below—first as a group and then individually. Monitor their practice and correct as needed. Then use Guiding Comprehension, pp. 96–113, to monitor understanding.

noise **loudly** **leave** **candles** **story**
poems **music** **frightened** **night** **tired**

Monitor Progress	Word and Story Reading
If... children have difficulty with any of these words,	**then...** coach them in blending and have them practice in pairs with word cards before reading the story.
If... children have difficulty reading the story individually,	**then...** have them follow along as they listen to the AudioText. They may also read pages of the selection aloud together, first with you and then without you, before reading individually.

Advanced

ROUTINE

DAY 3

1 Read *Frog and Toad Together*

DURING READING Have children read silently to p. 106. Provide guidance as needed. Ask:

- What kind of seeds did Toad plant?
- Why do you think the plants did not grow when Toad wanted them to?

Have children read silently to p. 111. Then ask:

- What things did Toad do to help his seeds be less afraid?
- What was Toad doing when his seeds sprouted?

Plot Have children recall the events in the story.

- What happened first in the story?
- What happened in the middle?
- How did the story end?

Visualize Children can work with a partner to visualize themselves as Toad and Frog. Draw a web or distribute copies of Graphic Organizer 18. Children can do a web for both characters.

RESPONSE Ask children to visualize a new kind of plant. Have them draw a picture of that plant and the place in which it grows.

Audio CD AudioText

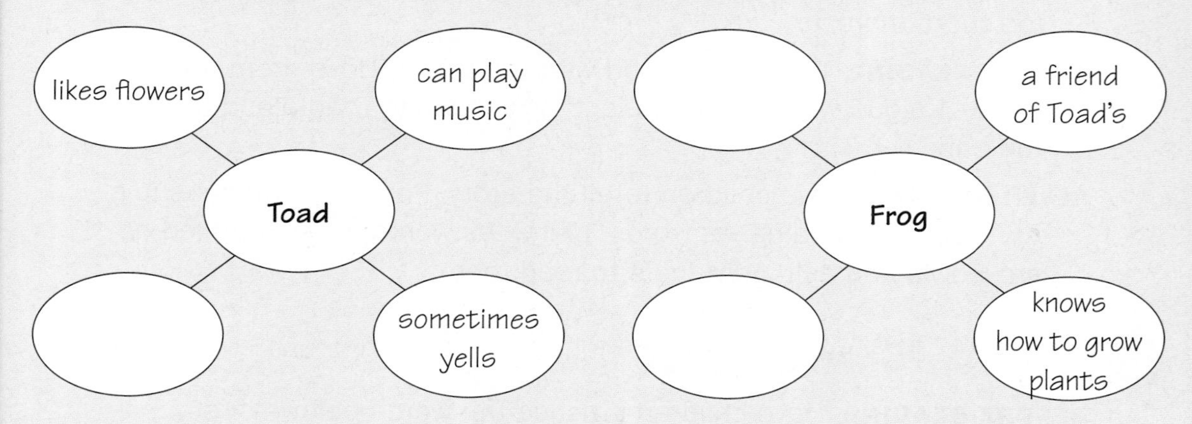

2 Extend Concepts Through Inquiry

INVESTIGATE Give children time to work with their stories and to begin preparing their presentation.

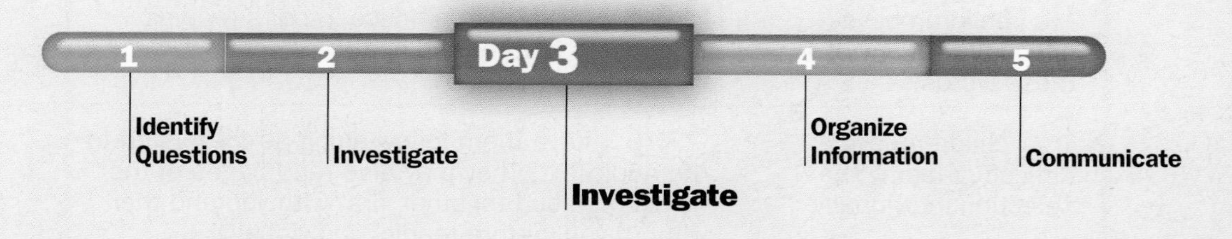

Group Time

Strategic Intervention

ROUTINE

DAY 4

1 Word Work

PHONEMIC AWARENESS Reteach p. 114b. Additional practice items:

/f/or *(for)*

/s/core *(score)*

for/t/ *(fort)*

REVIEW ENDING *-es*; PLURAL *-es* AND *r*-CONTROLLED *or, ore* Reteach p. 114c, using these additional words. Have children sort the words into *Words With or, ore* and *Words Without or, ore* lists.

wishes	**glasses**	**boxes**	**presses**	**matches**	**rashes**
more	**fork**	**torn**	**sort**	**store**	**porch**

REVIEW WORD READING Use the words and sentences on p. 114d to review decoding skills. Have children practice words in pairs until they can read one word every one or two seconds.

2 Reread Strategic Intervention Decodable Reader 15

BEFORE READING Have children review these decodable story words: *tosses, catches, fixes, glasses, dishes, boxes, close(s), grapes, shore, for, short, more, or.*

DURING READING Read p. 2 aloud with the group. Have them read pp. 3–4 aloud without you. Select individuals to read aloud to the end.

AFTER READING Have children retell the story. Point to sentences in the story with ending *-es* words, plural *-es* words, or *r*-controlled *or, ore* words and ask individuals to read them.

3 Read "Growing Plants"

BEFORE READING Have children practice the words below—first as a group and then individually. Monitor their practice and correct as needed. Then use Science in Reading, pp. 114–115.

petal **leaf** **roots**

Monitor Progress	Word and Selection Reading
If... children have difficulty with any of these words,	**then...** have them practice in pairs reading word cards before reading the selection.
If... children have difficulty reading the selection individually,	**then...** have them follow along as they listen to the AudioText. They may also read pages of the selection aloud together, first with you and then without you, before reading individually.

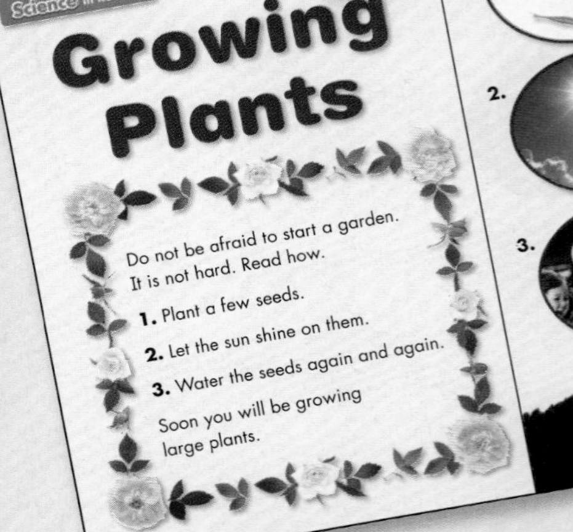

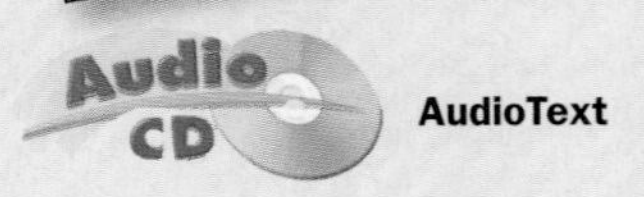

AudioText

MORE READING FOR
Group Time

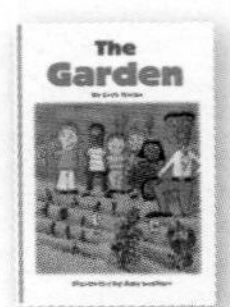

Use this Leveled Reader or other text at children's instructional level.

Below-Level

Reviews
- High-Frequency Words *afraid, again, few, how, read, soon*
- Plot

Advanced

ROUTINE

1 Read "Growing Plants"

AFTER READING Ask:

- Why should you not be afraid to start a garden?
- What is the first thing you do to start a garden of your own?
- What do you call the part of a plant that grows under the ground?

2 Vocabulary

Extend vocabulary with questions such as these:

- Have you ever smelled a cherry *blossom?* Describe the smell.
- Is it easy or difficult to read when the lights are *dim?*
- Who in your family is a *gardener?*
- Have you ever seen a seed *sprout?* Tell about it.

Encourage children to use the words in their writing.

3 Extend Concepts Through Inquiry

ORGANIZE INFORMATION Give children time to continue working with their stories. Remind them that tomorrow they will make their presentation. By now they should have begun putting their visualization in a presentation format.

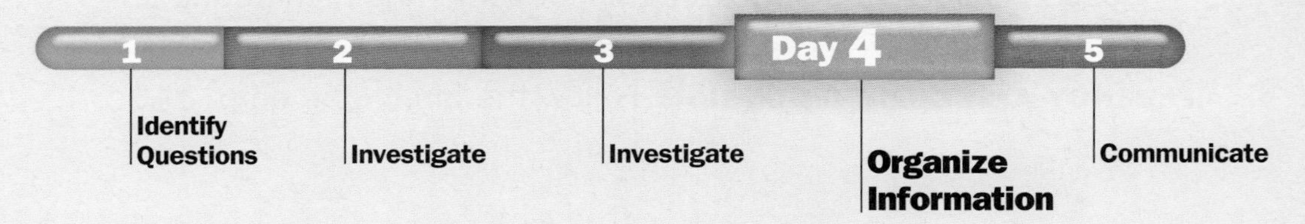

Audio CD AudioText

MORE READING FOR
Group Time

Use this Leveled Reader or other text at children's instructional level.

Advanced

Reviews
- Concept Vocabulary
- Plot

Group Time

Strategic Intervention

ROUTINE

DAY 5

1 Word Work

INFLECTED ENDINGS AND *r*-CONTROLLED *-ar* Write these sentences. Have children read aloud as you track the print. Call on individuals to blend the underlined words.

We jogged past the barn.

Dad was clapping when the band marched.

I hit my arm on a sharp stick.

The hard part was winning the game.

HIGH-FREQUENCY WORDS Use p. 94–95 to review *afraid, again, few, how, read, soon.*

Monitor Progress	High-Frequency Words
If... children have difficulty with any of these words,	**then...** tell them the word and have them repeat it. Have children spell the word and tell what word they spelled. Have them practice in pairs with word cards.

2 Monitor Progress

SENTENCE READING SET A Use Set A on reproducible p. 116f to assess children's ability to read decodable and high-frequency words in sentences.

FLUENCY AND COMPREHENSION Follow the directions on p. 116e.

MORE READING FOR

Group Time

Use this Leveled Reader or other text at children's instructional level.

Below-Level

Reviews
- High-Frequency Words *afraid, again, few, how, read, soon*
- Plot

Advanced

ROUTINE

DAY 5

1 Monitor Progress

SENTENCE READING SET C Use Set C on reproducible p. 116f to assess children's ability to read decodable and high-frequency words in sentences.

COMPREHENSION Have each child read "Clark and Star" on reproducible p. 116g. Ask: What are the events that take place in the story? Which came first? Which came last? Use the Retelling Rubric on p. 112–113 to evaluate the child's retelling.

2 Extend Concepts Through Inquiry

COMMUNICATE Have children share their stories and visualizations.

MORE READING FOR
Group Time

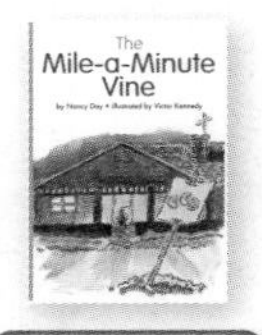

Use this Leveled Reader or other text at children's instructional level.

Advanced

Reviews
- Concept Vocabulary
- Plot

Group Time

Strategic Intervention

ROUTINE

DAY 1

1 Word Work

PHONEMIC AWARENESS Reteach p. 118m. Additional practice items:

s -ir	**h -urt**	**f -ur**
st -ir	**sp -urt**	**bl -ur**

r*-CONTROLLED *er, ir, ur Reteach p 118n. Additional words to blend:

herd **her** **dirt** **burn** **clerk**

Then have children spell *bird* with letter tiles. Monitor their work.

- Change the *b* in *bird* to *th*. What is the new word?

t h i r d

- Change the *d* in *third* to *st*. What is the new word?

t h i r s t

- Change the *th* in *thirst* to *f*. What is the new word?

f i r s t

SPELLING Reteach p. 118p. Model spelling *girl* and *hurt*. You may wish to give children fewer words to learn.

Decodable Reader 33
A Big Day for Mom
Written by Bill Jones
Illustrated by Sarah Swanson

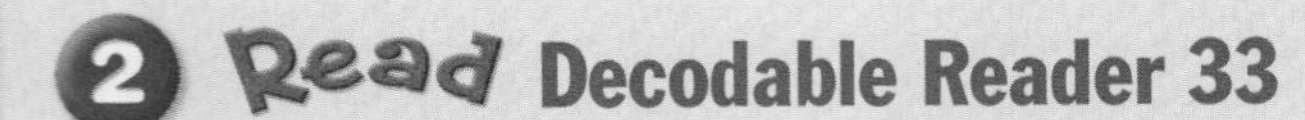

2 Read Decodable Reader 33

BEFORE READING Review the *r*-controlled *er, ir, ur* and the high-frequency words on p. 118q. Then have children blend these other decodable story words: *cage, green, grin, plants, smile, things, wishes.* Be sure children understand meanings of words such as *grin* and *ferns*.

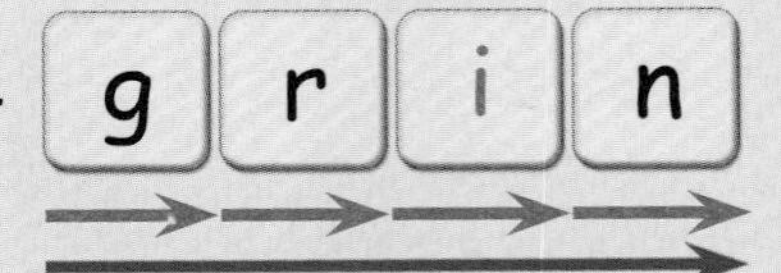

DURING READING Use p. 118q.

Monitor Progress	Word and Story Reading
If... children have difficulty with any of these words,	**then...** reteach them by modeling. Have children practice the words, with feedback from you, until they can read them independently.
If...children have difficulty reading the story individually,	**then...** read a sentence aloud as children point to each word. Then have the group reread the sentence as they continue pointing. Continue reading in this way before children read individually.

3 Reread for Fluency

Use the Paired Reading Routine, p. 118q, and text at each child's independent reading level.

MORE READING FOR
Group Time

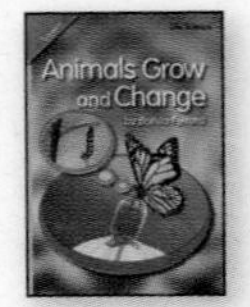

Use this Leveled Reader or other text at children's instructional level.

Below-Level

Reviews
- High-Frequency Words *done, know, push, visit, wait*
- Draw Conclusions

Check this database for additional titles.

PearsonSuccessNet.com

Advanced

ROUTINE

DAY 1

1 Word Work

r-Controlled *er, ir, ur* Practice with longer words that have *r*-controlled *er, ir, and ur.* If children know the words on first read, they may need no further practice. Practice items:

circle	**birthmark**	**gardener**	**yesterday**	**surprise**
thirsty	**turkey**	**silver**	**purpose**	**furnace**
thirteen	**verse**	**kernel**	**injury**	**furniture**

Have children write the words on cards and sort by *r*-controlled letters. Discuss unfamiliar words and then have individuals choose several words to use in a sentence.

2 Read Advanced Selection 17

BEFORE READING Have children identify this story word: *insect*.

DURING READING Children may read silently. Provide guidance as needed.

AFTER READING Have children recall the two most important ideas in the selection. (A caterpillar can change to a moth; a fawn grows up into a deer.) Ask:

- How did Caterpillar find out what she had turned into?
- Name two ways that Fawn changed.

On the back of the selection page have children write three sentences about another animal and how it changes as it grows.

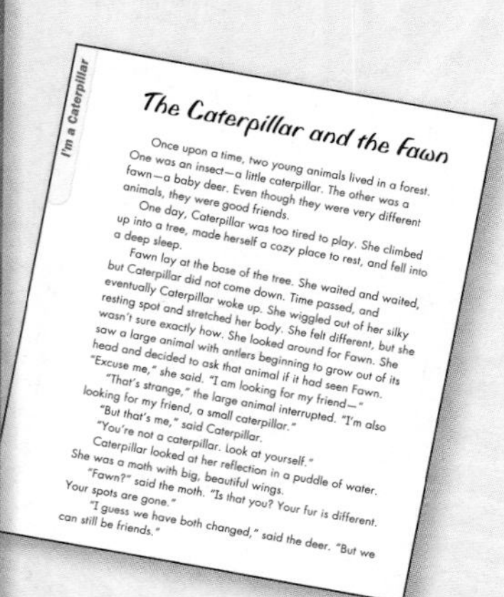
I'm a Caterpillar

The Caterpillar and the Fawn

Once upon a time, two young animals lived in a forest. One was an insect—a little caterpillar. The other was a fawn—a baby deer. Even though they were very different animals, they were good friends.

One day, Caterpillar was too tired to play. She climbed up into a tree, made herself a cozy place to rest, and fell into a deep sleep.

Fawn lay at the base of the tree. She waited and waited, but Caterpillar did not come down. Time passed, and eventually Caterpillar woke up. She wiggled out of her silky resting spot and stretched her body. She felt different, but she wasn't sure exactly how. She looked around for Fawn. She saw a large animal with antlers beginning to grow out of its head and decided to ask that animal if it had seen Fawn.

"Excuse me," she said. "I am looking for my friend—"

"That's strange," the large animal interrupted. "I'm also looking for my friend, a small caterpillar."

"But that's me," said Caterpillar.

"You're not a caterpillar. Look at yourself."

Caterpillar looked at her reflection in a puddle of water. She was a moth with big, beautiful wings.

"Fawn?" said the moth. "Is that you? Your fur is different. Your spots are gone."

"I guess we have both changed," said the deer. "But we can still be friends."

DI•14

3 Extend Concepts Through Inquiry

IDENTIFY QUESTIONS Have children prepare a short history of their lives, paying special attention to ways they have changed or changes (such as moving, a new baby in the house, a new school) that they have lived through. During the week, they should prepare by recalling, studying pictures and talking with adults or older children. On Day 5 they will share what they learned. Guide children in brainstorming possible choices.

- Think about your choices. How have you changed? How have things in your life changed?

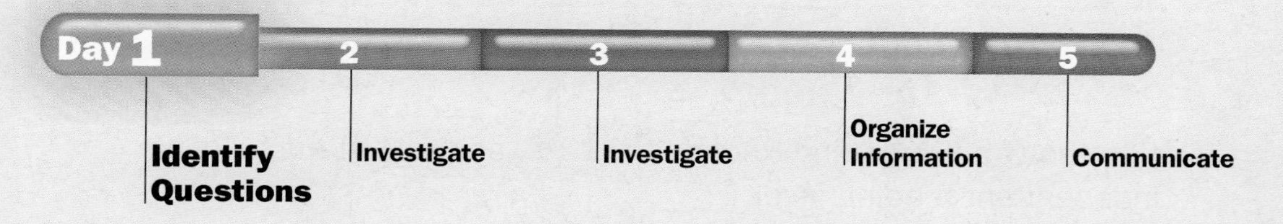

MORE READING FOR Group Time

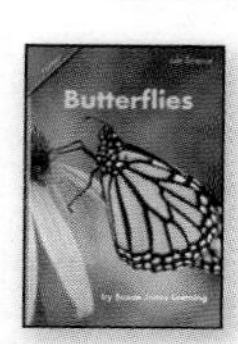

Use this Leveled Reader or other text at children's instructional level.

Advanced

Reviews

- Concept Vocabulary
- Draw Conclusions

Group Time

DAY 2

Strategic Intervention

ROUTINE

1 Word Work

PHONEMIC AWARENESS Reteach p. 120b. Additional practice items:

thirsty—thirst **slurp—slur** **blurb—blur**

CONTRACTIONS *'s, 've, 're* Reteach p. 120c. Additional words to practice:

that's **we've** **you're** **he's** **I've** **they're**

Then write these contractions. Have children read the first word and blend the sounds of the letters after the apostrophe to read the contractions. Have children name the two words that make up the contraction.

she's **they've** **we're** **you've** **it's**

PRETEACH HIGH-FREQUENCY WORDS Write *done, know, push, visit, wait* and have children say each word, spell it as they point to each letter, and say it again. Then have them finger trace the letters in each word, naming the letters as they trace. Have individuals practice reading the words from word cards.

Decodable Reader 34
Sam Can Fly!
Written by Lynn Johnson
Illustrated by David Newman

2 Read Decodable Reader 34

BEFORE READING Review the contractions *'s, 've, 're* and the high-frequency words on p. 120f. Then have children blend these other decodable story words: *bird, branch, cannot, happy, hard, hopped, lifted, patted, small, started, cry, wings, feet, strong, try.* Be sure children understand the meanings of words such as *hard, lifted,* and *patted*.

DURING READING Use p. 120f.

Monitor Progress	Word and Story Reading
If... children have difficulty with any of these words,	**then...** reteach them by modeling. Have children practice the words, with feedback from you, until they can read them independently.
If... children have difficulty reading the story individually,	**then...** read a sentence aloud as children point to each word. Have the group reread the sentence as they continue pointing. Read in this way before children read individually.

3 Reread for Fluency

Use the Oral Rereading Routine, p. 120f, and text at each child's independent reading level.

MORE READING FOR
Group Time

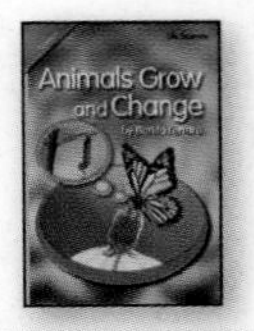

Use this Leveled Reader or other text at children's instructional level.

Below-Level

Reviews
- High-Frequency Words *done, know, push, visit, wait*
- Draw Conclusions

Advanced

ROUTINE

DAY 2

1 Word Work

Contractions *'s, 've, 're* Practice with longer words and other uses of contractions *'s, 've,* and *'re.* If children know the words on first read, they may need no further practice. Practice items:

might've	**he's**	**she's**	**we're**
could've	**Joe's**	**you're**	**they're**

Discuss the meanings of unfamiliar words. Point out that *'s* may indicate possession or stand for *is*. Show children how the meaning must be found in the context.

2 Read Self-Selected Reading

BEFORE READING Have children select a trade book or Leveled Reader to read independently. Guide children in selecting books of appropriate difficulty.

AFTER READING When they have finished, have each child select an interesting passage to read aloud to a partner.

3 Extend Concepts Through Inquiry

INVESTIGATE Guide children in choosing material at their independent reading level to aid them in preparing their histories. Some books that may be appropriate are *Look to the North: A Wolf Pup Diary* by Jean Craighead George or *Eyewitness: World War II* by Simon Adams.

Help children decide how they will present their information. Children may use a Venn diagram or other graphic organizer, a written format, photographs, drawings, or models.

Trade Books for Self-Selected Reading

LOOK TO THE NORTH: A WOLF PUP DIARY by Jean Craighead George, HarperCollins Children's Books, © 1998

EYEWITNESS: WORLD WAR II by Simon Adams, DK Publishing, © 2000

MORE READING FOR
Group Time

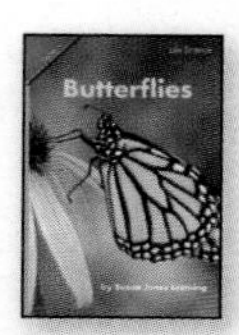

Use this Leveled Reader or other text at children's instructional level.

Advanced

Reviews
- Concept Vocabulary
- Draw Conclusions

Group Time

Audio CD AudioText

Strategic Intervention

ROUTINE

DAY 3

1 Word Work

PHONEMIC AWARENESS Reteach p. 122b. Additional practice items:

sw -irl **d -irt** **b -urn**

tw -irl **sh -irt** **t -urn**

r*-CONTROLLED *er, ir, ur* AND CONTRACTIONS *'s, 've, 're Reteach p. 122c. Additional words to practice:

her **stir** **fur** **bird**

that's **we've** **they're** **let's**

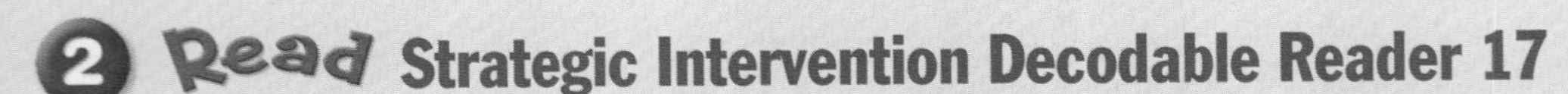

2 Read Strategic Intervention Decodable Reader 17

BEFORE READING Before reading, review *done, push, visit* and *wait* on the Word Wall. Take a picture walk through the book, stopping on p. 7 to discuss why the older girl is shaking her head "no." Have children predict what will happen next.

DURING READING Read p. 2 aloud with the group. Have them read pp. 3–4 without you. Select individuals to read aloud to the end.

AFTER READING Check comprehension by having children retell the story, including the characters, setting, and plot. Have children locate *r*-controlled *er, ir, ur* words and contractions with *'s, 've,* and *'re* in the story. List words children name. Children may name *they're, it's, first, swirls, girl, we've, she's, stirs, shirts, her, twirls,* and *turn.* Have individuals identify the words with contractions and tell what two words each contraction stands for. Then have the lists read.

3 Read *I'm a Caterpillar*

BEFORE READING Have children practice the words below—first as a group and then individually. Monitor their practice and correct as needed. Then use Guiding Comprehension, pp. 122–139, to monitor understanding.

butterfly **protect** **nectar** **changing** **mouth** **unfold**

Monitor Progress	Word and Selection Reading
If... children have difficulty with any of these words,	**then...** coach them in blending and have them practice in pairs with word cards before reading the story.
If... children have difficulty reading the selection individually,	**then...** have them follow along as they listen to the AudioText. They may also read pages of the selection aloud together, first with you and then without you, before reading individually.

Advanced

ROUTINE

DAY 3

1 Read *I'm a Caterpillar*

DURING READING Have children read silently to p. 132. Provide guidance as needed. Ask:

- What does the caterpillar do to get bigger? What does this do to the plants?
- What is a chrysalis?

Have children read silently to p. 137. Then ask:

- What do butterflies drink from the flowers? How do you think it tastes?
- What comes out of the butterfly's eggs?

Draw Conclusions Draw children's attention to the end of the story. Help them draw conclusions about the life cycle of the butterfly.

- What do caterpillars turn into?
- What will the new caterpillar do to get bigger?

Text Structure Children can work with a partner to complete a story sequence. Draw a chart or distribute copies of Graphic Organizer 21, (Sequence).

RESPONSE Have children think of a change they like to see in nature. For example, bears hibernating or chameleons that can change color. Have them draw pictures of the change.

First
The caterpillar eats and grows.

↓

Next
The caterpillar turns into a pupa inside a chrysalis.

↓

Last
A butterfly emerges and lays eggs.

▲ **Graphic Organizer Flip Chart 21**

I'm a Caterpillar
by Jean Marzollo
illustrated by Judith Moffatt
How does a caterpillar grow and change?
123

AudioText

2 Extend Concepts Through Inquiry

INVESTIGATE Give children time to investigate their histories and to begin preparing their information.

Group Time

Strategic Intervention

ROUTINE

DAY 4

1 Word Work

PHONEMIC AWARENESS Reteach p. 140b. Additional practice items:

fat—farm **cat—cart** **ban—barn** **pat—part**

REVIEW **INFLECTED ENDINGS *-ed, -ing* AND *r*-CONTROLLED *ar***
Reteach p. 140c, using these additional words. Have children sort the words into *Ending -ed* and *Ending -ing* lists.

parted	**farming**	**hugged**	**flipping**
zipped	**stepping**	**started**	**parking**

REVIEW **WORD READING** Use the words and sentences on p. 140d to review decoding skills. Have children practice words in pairs until they can read one word every one or two seconds.

2 Reread Strategic Intervention Decodable Reader 16

BEFORE READING Have children review these decodable story words: *park, farm, dark, stars, star, cars, jogging, jogged, falling, stopped, napping, race, sky, truck.*

DURING READING Read p. 2 aloud with the group. Have them read pp. 3–4 aloud without you. Select individuals to read aloud to the end.

AFTER READING Have children retell the story. Point to sentences in the story with words containing inflected endings *-ed, -ing* or words with *r*-controlled *ar.* Ask individuals to read them.

3 Read "My Computer"

BEFORE READING Have children practice the words below—first as a group and then individually. Monitor their practice and correct as needed. Then use Reading Online, pp. 140–141.

computer **cursor** **keyboard** **monitor** **mouse**

Monitor Progress	Word and Selection Reading
If... children have difficulty with any of these words,	**then...** have them practice in pairs reading word cards before reading the selection.
If... children have difficulty reading the selection individually,	**then...** have them follow along as they listen to the AudioText. They may also read pages of the selection aloud together, first with you and then without you, before reading individually.

AudioText

MORE READING FOR
Group Time

Use this Leveled Reader or other text at children's instructional level.

Below-Level

Reviews
- High-Frequency Words *done, know, push, visit, wait*
- Draw Conclusions

Advanced

ROUTINE

DAY 4

1 Read "My Computer"

AFTER READING Ask:

- Where do you type on the computer?
- Where do you find the cursor?
- How would writing be harder without the computer?

2 Vocabulary

Extend vocabulary with questions such as these:

- What are some stages in the life *cycle* of a person?
- How will you *develop* as you grow older?
- What is your favorite *insect?* Why?
- Name some things that are *fragile*.

Encourage children to use the words in their writing.

3 Extend Concepts Through Inquiry

ORGANIZE INFORMATION Give children time to continue working on their histories. Remind them that tomorrow they will share their history. By now they should have begun putting the information in a presentation format.

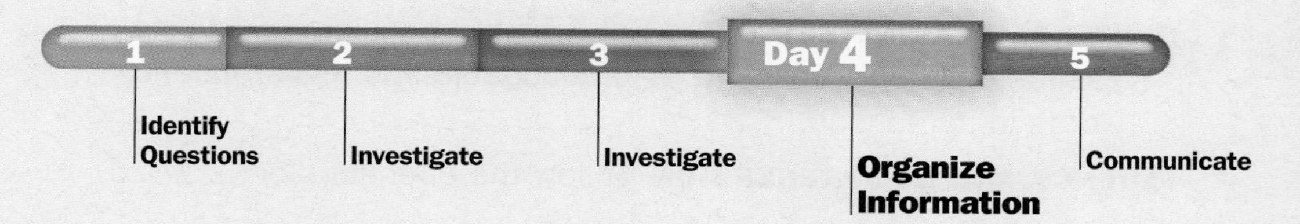

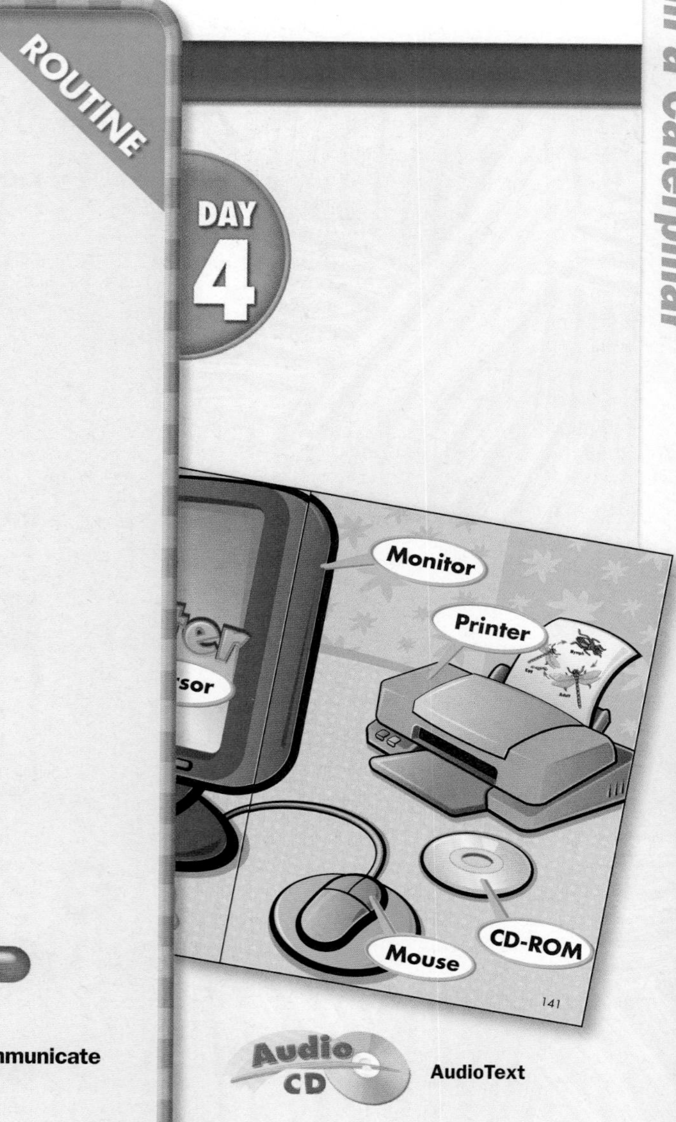

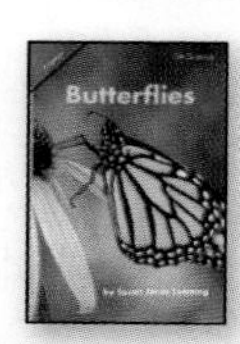

AudioText

MORE READING FOR
Group Time

Use this Leveled Reader or other text at children's instructional level.

Advanced

Reviews
- Concept Vocabulary
- Draw Conclusions

Group Time

DAY 5

Strategic Intervention

ROUTINE

1 Word Work

r*-CONTROLLED *er, ir, ur* AND CONTRACTIONS *'s, 've, 're Write these sentences. Have children read aloud as you track the print. Call on individuals to blend the underlined words.

It's your turn to stir the pot.
Birds chirp in our birch tree.
I've got dirt on my shirt.
We're going to plant a fern.

HIGH-FREQUENCY WORDS Use pp. 120–121 to review *done, know, push, visit, wait.*

Monitor Progress	High-Frequency Words
If... children have difficulty with any of these words,	**then...** tell them the word and have them repeat it. Have children spell the word and tell what word they spelled. Have them practice in pairs with word cards.

2 Monitor Progress

SENTENCE READING SET A Use Set A on reproducible p. 142f to assess children's ability to read decodable and high-frequency words in sentences.

FLUENCY AND COMPREHENSION Follow the directions on p. 142e.

MORE READING FOR
Group Time

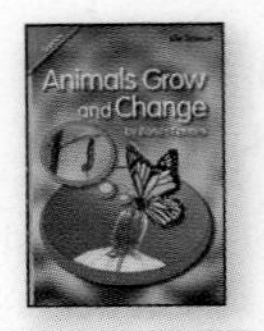

Use this Leveled Reader or other text at children's instructional level.

Below-Level

Reviews
- High-Frequency Words *done, know, push, visit, wait*
- Draw Conclusions

Advanced

ROUTINE

DAY 5

1 Monitor Progress

SENTENCE READING SET C Use Set C on reproducible page 142f to assess children's ability to read decodable and high-frequency words in sentences.

COMPREHENSION Have each child read "Who's Talking?" on reproducible page 142g. Ask children what conclusions they can draw from the story, and have the child retell the passage. Use the Retelling Rubric on p. 112–113 to evaluate the child's retelling.

2 Extend Concepts Through Inquiry

COMMUNICATE Have children share their histories.

MORE READING FOR
Group Time

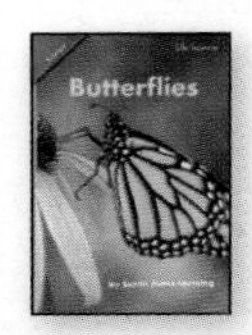

Use this Leveled Reader or other text at children's instructional level.

Advanced

Reviews
- Concept Vocabulary
- Draw Conclusions

Group Time

DAY 1

Strategic Intervention

ROUTINE

1 Word Work

PHONEMIC AWARENESS Reteach p. 144m. Additional practice items:

deep, deeper, deepest **wet, wetter, wettest**
thin, thinner, thinnest

COMPARATIVE ENDINGS Reteach p. 144n. Additional words to practice:

harder **hotter** **sickest** **fitter** **taller**

Then write the words below. Call on children to read the words, identify the endings, and frame the base words. If children have difficulty reading the base word, have them cover the ending and blend the base word. Help them note if the last consonant was doubled before the ending was added.

bigger **thickest** **hotter**
sweetest **faster** **slimmest**

SPELLING Reteach p. 144p. Model spelling *biggest* and *faster*. You may wish to give children fewer words to learn.

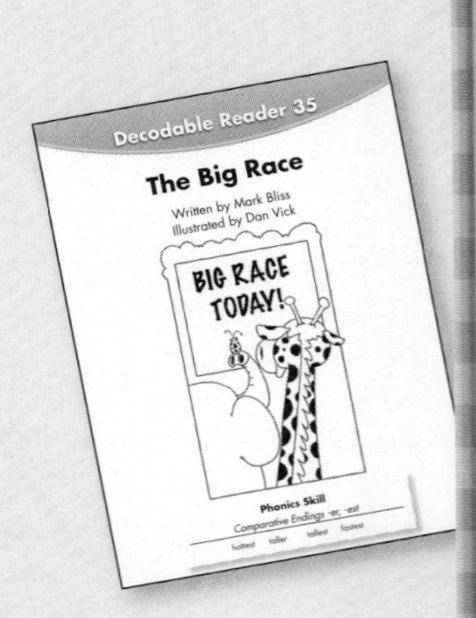

2 Read Decodable Reader 35

BEFORE READING Review the words with comparative endings and the high-frequency words on p. 144q. Then have children blend these other decodable story words: *by, go, hills, race, size, trunk, uses, yells.* Be sure children understand meanings of words such as *size* and *trunk*.

DURING READING Use p. 144q.

Monitor Progress	Word and Story Reading
If... children have difficulty with any of these words,	**then...** reteach them by modeling. Have children practice the words, with feedback from you, until they can read them independently.
If... children have difficulty reading the story individually,	**then...** read a sentence aloud as children point to each word. Then have the group reread the sentence as they continue pointing. Continue reading in this way before children read individually.

3 Reread for Fluency

Use the Oral Rereading Routine, p. 144q, and text at each child's independent reading level.

MORE READING FOR
Group Time

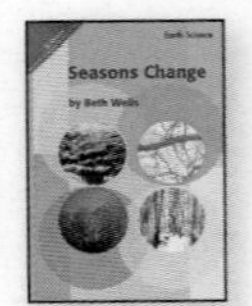

Use this Leveled Reader or other text at children's instructional level.

Below-Level

Reviews
- High-Frequency Words *before, does, good-bye, oh, right, won't*
- Sequence

Check this database for additional titles.

PearsonSuccessNet.com

Advanced

ROUTINE

DAY 1

1 Word Work

Comparative Endings Practice with more words with comparative endings *-er* and *-est*. If children know the words on first read, they may need no further practice. Practice items:

looser	**brighter**	**cleanest**	**happiest**	**bravest**
tightest	**faintest**	**plainest**	**dimmest**	**nicest**

Have children write the words on cards and circle the endings. Point out the *y* to *i* spelling change in *happiest.* Then have individuals choose several words to use in a sentence.

2 Read Advanced Selection 18

BEFORE READING Have children identify these story words: *temperature, season, hibernate.*

DURING READING Provide guidance as children read silently.

AFTER READING Have children recall the two most important ideas in the selection. (Some bears hibernate in winter; hibernating is somewhat like sleeping.) Ask:

- How do bears' bodies change when they are getting ready to hibernate?
- Why don't polar bears hibernate?

On the back of the selection page have children write a four-line poem about winter.

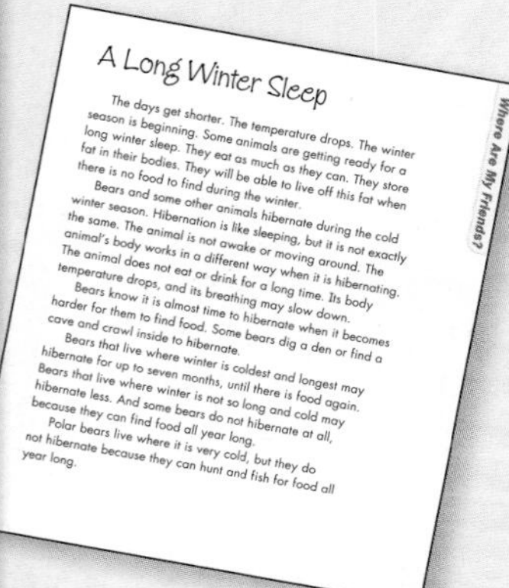
A Long Winter Sleep

The days get shorter. The temperature drops. The winter season is beginning. Some animals are getting ready for a long winter sleep. They eat as much as they can. They store fat in their bodies. They will be able to live off this fat when there is no food to find during the winter.

Bears and some other animals hibernate during the cold winter season. Hibernation is like sleeping, but it is not exactly the same. The animal is not awake or moving around. The animal's body works in a different way when it is hibernating. The animal does not eat or drink for a long time. Its body temperature drops, and its breathing may slow down.

Bears know it is almost time to hibernate when it becomes harder for them to find food. Some bears dig a den or find a cave and crawl inside to hibernate.

Bears that live where winter is coldest and longest may hibernate for up to seven months, until there is food again. Bears that live where winter is not so long and cold may hibernate less. And some bears do not hibernate at all, because they can find food all year long.

Polar bears live where it is very cold, but they do not hibernate because they can hunt and fish for food all year long.

Where Are My Friends?

DI•15

3 Extend Concepts Through Inquiry

IDENTIFY QUESTIONS Tell children about some of the people who have explored the very cold climates on Earth, such as Sir Edmund Hillary and Tenzing Norgay, Roald Amundsen, Frederick Cook, and Admiral Robert Perry. Have students choose one of these and write a paragraph about them. During the week, children should collect information by reading, studying pictures, and talking with adults or older children. On Day 5 they will share what they learned. Guide children in brainstorming places to find information.

- Think about going to a very, very cold place. What would you need? What would you want to take with you?

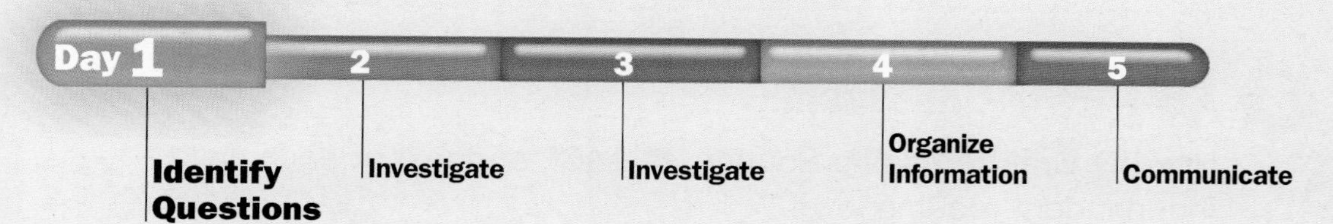

MORE READING FOR
Group Time

Use this Leveled Reader or other text at children's instructional level.

Advanced

Reviews
- Concept Vocabulary
- Sequence

Group Time

DAY 2

Strategic Intervention

ROUTINE

1 Word Work

PHONEMIC AWARENESS Reteach p. 146b. Additional practice items:

budge **judge** **Madge** **bridge** **pledge**

dge /j/ Reteach p. 146c. Additional words to blend:

fudge **badge** **hedge** **Midge** **trudge**

Then have children spell *wedge* with letter tiles. Monitor their work.

- Change the *w* in *wedge* to *l*. What is the new word?

- Change the first *e* in *ledge* to *o*. What is the new word?

l o d g e

- Change the *l* in *lodge* to *d*. What is the new word?

d o d g e

Decodable Reader 36
Where Is My Badge?
Written by Erik Perez
Illustrated by Sandra Martin

PRETEACH HIGH-FREQUENCY WORDS Write *before, does, good-bye, oh, right, won't* and have children say each word, spell it as they point to each letter, and say it again. Have individuals practice reading the words from word cards.

2 Read Decodable Reader 36

BEFORE READING Review the words with *dge/j/* and the high-frequency words on p. 146f. Then have children blend these other decodable story words: *Bucky, left, seemed, yelled, asked, brush, jumped, let's, sadder, shelf, thanks, first.* Be sure children understand the meanings of words such as *sadder* and *edge*.

DURING READING Use p. 146f.

Monitor Progress	Word and Story Reading
If... children have difficulty with any of these words,	**then...** reteach them by modeling. Have children practice the words, with feedback from you, until they can read them independently.
If... children have difficulty reading the story individually,	**then...** read a sentence aloud as children point to each word. Have the group reread the sentence as they continue pointing. Read in this way before children read individually.

3 Reread for Fluency

Use the Oral Rereading Routine, p. 146f, and text at each child's independent reading level.

MORE READING FOR
Group Time

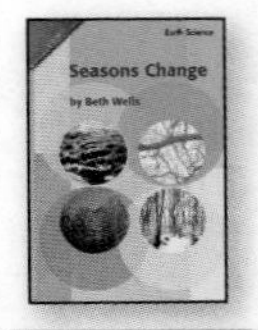

Use this Leveled Reader or other text at children's instructional level.

Below-Level

Reviews
- High-Frequency Words *before, does, good-bye, oh, right, won't*
- Sequence

Advanced

ROUTINE

DAY 2

1 Word Work

dge/j/ Practice with longer words containing the /j/ sound. If children know the words on first read, they may need no further practice. Practice items:

gadget	**fidget**	**drudgery**	**ledger**
budget	**midget**	**porridge**	**knowledge**

Discuss the meanings of unfamiliar words. Segment and blend the words.

2 Read Self-Selected Reading

BEFORE READING Have children select a trade book or Leveled Reader to read independently. Guide children in selecting books of appropriate difficulty.

AFTER READING When they have finished, have each child select an interesting passage to read aloud to a partner.

3 Extend Concepts Through Inquiry

INVESTIGATE Guide children in choosing material at their independent reading level to explore their biographies. Some books that may provide background are *Freddie's Everest Diary: The Dream of Frederick T. Bear* by Pat Falvey and Clare O'Leary or *To the Top of Everest* by Laurie Skreslet with Elizabeth MacLeod.

Help children decide how they will present their information. Children may use a graphic organizer, a written format, photographs, drawings, or models.

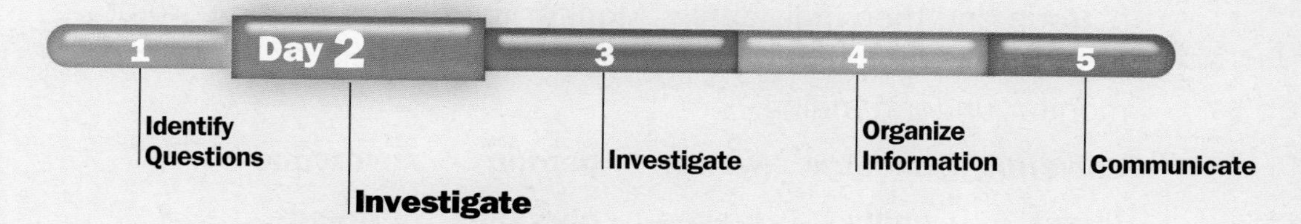

Trade Books for Self-Selected Reading

FREDDIE'S EVEREST DIARY: THE DREAM OF FREDERICK T. BEAR by Pat Falvey and Clare O'Leary, The Collins Press, © 2004

TO THE TOP OF EVEREST by Laurie Skreslet with Elizabeth MacLeod, Kids Can Press, © 2001

MORE READING FOR
Group Time

Use this Leveled Reader or other text at children's instructional level.

Advanced

Reviews
- Concept Vocabulary
- Sequence

Group Time

Strategic Intervention

ROUTINE

DAY 3

Audio CD AudioText

1 Word Work

PHONEMIC AWARENESS Reteach p. 148b. Additional practice items:

ledge **wetter** **ridge** **judge** **tallest** **dodge**

COMPARATIVE ENDINGS AND *dge*/j/ Reteach p. 148c. Additional words to practice:

deepest **smaller** **taller** **slimmest**
nudge **edge** **ridge** **sludge**

2 Read Strategic Intervention Decodable Reader 18

BEFORE READING Before reading, review *does* and *won't* on the Word Wall. Take a picture walk through the book, stopping on p. 3 to discuss why Penny is looking sadly at the cake. Have children predict what will happen next.

DURING READING Read p. 2 aloud with the group. Have them read pp. 3–4 without you. Select individuals to read aloud to the end.

AFTER READING Check comprehension by having children retell the story, including the characters, setting, and plot. Have children locate words with comparative endings and *dge*/j/ words in the story. List words children name. Have children sort the words they found below *Endings* and *-dge*.

Endings	-dge
biggest	fudge
hotter	judge
faster	
flattest	

3 Read *Where Are My Animal Friends?*

BEFORE READING Have children practice the words below—first as a group and then individually. Monitor their practice and correct as needed. Then use Guiding Comprehension, pp. 148–167, to monitor understanding.

shivering **became** **winter** **pardon** **everyone**
forest **chilly** **leaves** **chrysalis** **ground**

Monitor Progress	Word and Story Reading
If... children have difficulty with any of these words,	**then...** coach them in blending and have them practice in pairs with word cards before reading the story.
If... children have difficulty reading the play individually,	**then...** have them follow along as they listen to the AudioText. They may also read pages of the selection aloud together, first with you and then without you, before reading individually.

Advanced

ROUTINE

1 Read Where Are My Animal Friends?

DURING READING Have children read silently to p. 155. Provide guidance as needed. Ask:

- What season of the year has begun?
- What happened to Caterpillar?

Have children read silently to p. 163. Then ask:

- What do Goose and Hummingbird do?
- What animal friend will play with Raccoon during the winter?

Sequence of Events Ask children to think about the order in which things happened in the story.

- Does having Raccoon playing with Squirrel at the end of the story make a happy ending? Why or why not?

Children can work with a partner to complete a story sequence. Draw a chart or distribute copies of Graphic Organizer 23 (Story Sequence).

Title Where Are My Animal Friends?	
Characters	**Setting**
Raccoon, Goose, Hummingbird, Bear, Squirrel	the forest

Events	
First:	Goose and Hummingbird find Caterpillar and tell Raccoon they have to fly away.
Next:	Bear tells Raccoon that he will sleep until spring.
Last:	Raccoon finds Squirrel and they play.

▲ **Graphic Organizer Flip Chart 23**

Prior Knowledge Ask children to tell what else they know about animals in winter. For example, some dogs and cats get thicker fur and stay indoors more.

RESPONSE Have children suppose that they are going to stay inside a cave all winter. Have them make a list of the things they would like to have with them.

DAY 3

AudioText

2 Extend Concepts Through Inquiry

INVESTIGATE Give children time to investigate their biographies and to begin preparing their information.

Group Time

DAY 4

Strategic Intervention

ROUTINE

1 Word Work

PHONEMIC AWARENESS Reteach p. 168b. Additional practice items:

b, t -urn **j, p -erk** **d, sh, sk -irt**

REVIEW ***r*-CONTROLLED *er, ir, ur* AND CONTRACTIONS *'s, 've, 're*** Reteach p. 168c, using these additional words. Have children sort the words into *er, ir, ur* and *Contractions* lists.

fern	**bird**	**turn**	**germ**	**stir**	**hurt**
what's	**I've**	**he's**	**you're**	**that's**	**we've**

REVIEW **WORD READING** Use the words and sentences on p. 168d to review decoding skills. Have children practice words in pairs until they can read one word every one or two seconds.

2 Reread Strategic Intervention Decodable Reader 17

BEFORE READING Have children review these decodable story words: *first, girl, her, shirt, shirts, stirs, swirls, turn, twirls, it's, she's, we've, they're.*

DURING READING Read p. 2 aloud with the group. Have them read pp. 3–4 aloud without you. Select individuals to read aloud to the end.

AFTER READING Have children retell the story. Point to sentences in the story with *r*-controlled *er, ir, ur* words or contractions with *'s, 've, 're* and ask individuals to read them.

3 Read Poetry

BEFORE READING Have children practice the words below—first as a group and then individually. Monitor their practice and correct as needed. Then use Poetry, pp. 168–171.

jiggled	**pulled**	**tooth**	**frozen**	**breathe**	**heart**

Monitor Progress	Word and Selection Reading
If... children have difficulty with any of these words,	**then...** have them practice in pairs reading word cards before reading the selection.
If... children have difficulty reading the poems individually,	**then...** have them follow along as they listen to the AudioText. They may also read pages of the selection aloud together, first with you and then without you, before reading individually.

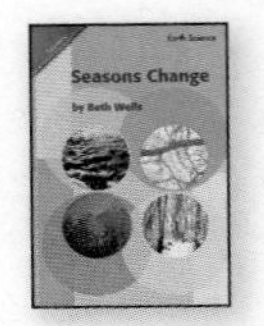

AudioText

MORE READING FOR
Group Time

Use this Leveled Reader or other text at children's instructional level.

Below-Level

Reviews
- High-Frequency Words *before, does, good-bye, oh, right, won't*
- Sequence

Advanced

ROUTINE

1 Read Poetry

AFTER READING Ask:

- Have you lost a tooth yet? Did it happen as it did in the poem?
- When do seeds usually pop out of the ground?
- What do you think *repose* means?

2 Vocabulary

Extend vocabulary with questions such as these:

- How low does the *temperature* get where you live?
- What is your favorite *season?* Why?
- Do all bears *hibernate?* Why don't people *hibernate?*
- Why do you think birds *migrate* south in the winter?

Encourage children to use the words in their writing.

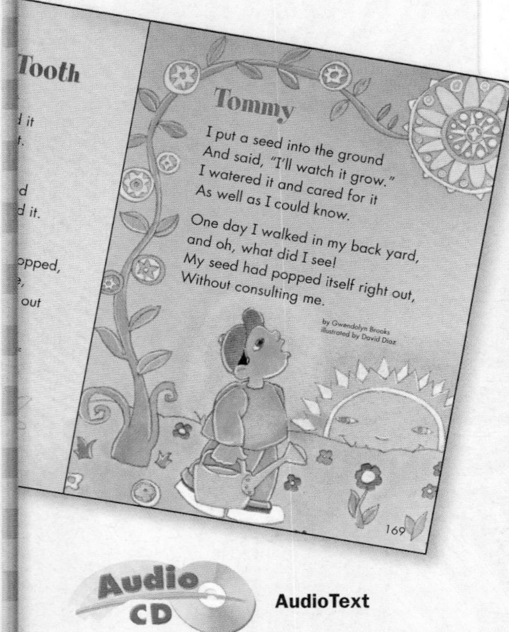

Audio CD AudioText

3 Extend Concepts Through Inquiry

ORGANIZE INFORMATION Give children time to continue reading about cold climates and those who braved them. Remind them that tomorrow they will share their information. By now they should have begun putting the information in a presentation format.

MORE READING FOR

Group Time

Use this Leveled Reader or other text at children's instructional level.

Advanced

Reviews

- Concept Vocabulary
- Sequence

Group Time

Strategic Intervention

ROUTINE

DAY 5

1 Word Work

COMPARATIVE ENDINGS AND *dge*/j/ Write these sentences. Have children read aloud as you track the print. Call on individuals to blend the underlined words.

Madge ate the biggest wedge of cheese.
Who was the quickest to cross the bridge?
This badge is thinner than a button.
We walked to the edge of the deepest lake.

HIGH-FREQUENCY WORDS Use p. 146–147 to review *before, does, good-bye, oh, right, won't.*

Monitor Progress	High-Frequency Words
If... children have difficulty with any of these words,	**then...** tell them the word and have them repeat it. Have children spell the word and tell what word they spelled. Have them practice in pairs with word cards.

2 Monitor Progress

SENTENCE READING SET A Use Set A on reproducible p. 172f to assess children's ability to read decodable and high-frequency words in sentences.

FLUENCY AND COMPREHENSION Follow the directions on p. 172e.

MORE READING FOR
Group Time

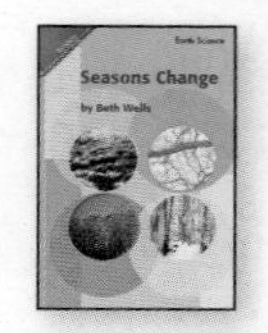

Use this Leveled Reader or other text at children's instructional level.

Below-Level

Reviews
- High-Frequency Words *before, does, good-bye, oh, right, won't*
- Sequence

Advanced

ROUTINE

DAY 5

1 Monitor Progress

SENTENCE READING SET C Use Set C on reproducible page 172f to assess children's ability to read decodable and high-frequency words in sentences.

COMPREHENSION Have each child read "The Sweetest Yard" on reproducible page 172g. Ask what happens first, next, and last, and have the child retell the passage. Use the Retelling Rubric on p. 166–167 to evaluate the child's retelling.

2 Extend Concepts Through Inquiry

COMMUNICATE Have children share their biographies with the class.

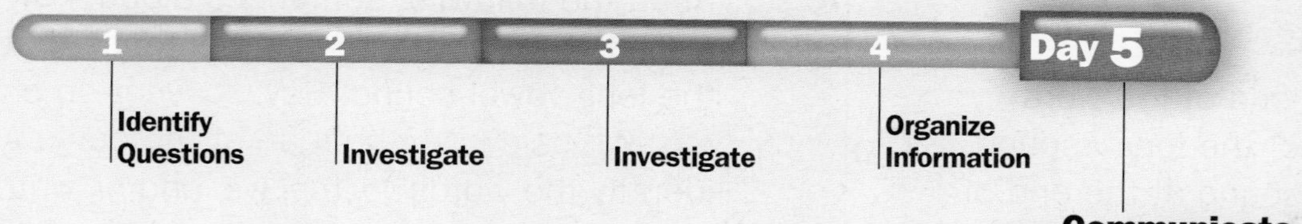

MORE READING FOR
Group Time

Use this Leveled Reader or other text at children's instructional level.

Advanced

Reviews
- Concept Vocabulary
- Sequence

An Egg Is an Egg

Vowel Sounds of *y*

1 TEACH

Write the word *lucky* on the board. Say it slowly, emphasizing the ending sound /ē/. Ask: What sound is heard at the end of *lucky*? (/ē/) What letter stands for the ending sound? *(y)*

Write the word *my* on the board. Say it slowly, emphasizing the ending sound /ī/. Ask: What sound is heard at the end of *my*? (/ī/) What letter stands for the long *i* sound? *(y)*

Explain to children that *y* at the end of the word can stand for the long *e* sound or the long *i* sound. It usually stands for the long *e* sound at the end of words that have two or more syllables.

2 PRACTICE AND ASSESS

Write the following words on the board:

cry	shy	windy	pretty
silly	sunny	by	dry

Have children read each word aloud and tell what sound the letter *y* stands for at the end of the word. Then give the following clues. Have volunteers frame and read the correct word on the board. Say:

When the wind is blowing it is... (windy)
The opposite of wet is... (dry)
A quiet person might just be... (shy)
When the sun is shining, it is... (sunny)
Babies sometimes... (cry)
Another word for goofy is... (silly)

Then make a chart and have children sort the words into those where the *y* stands for long *e* sound and those where the *y* stands for the long *i* sound.

An Egg Is an Egg

Long Vowels CV

1 TEACH

Write *these* and ask children what vowel sound they hear in the middle of the word. Remind them that the vowel followed by a consonant and the vowel *e* stands for the long vowel sound.

Write the word *she* on the board and blend the word. Underline the letter *e* and explain that when a word or syllable ends with one vowel, the vowel sound is usually long. Follow the same procedure with *hi* and *go*.

Read the following sentences aloud. Ask children to name the words in each sentence that end with the long vowel sound. Say: Jo went on a trip with me. We said hi to the man at the desk. As children identify the words *Jo, me, we,* and *hi,* write them on the board and underline the vowel in each word. Ask children what sound each vowel stands for.

2 PRACTICE AND ASSESS

Write the word *so* on the board and have children blend the sounds, emphasizing the /ō/. Tell children to clap their hands when they hear a word that ends with a long vowel sound. Say *me, lake, hi, go, no, bone, hello, no.*

Divide the class into groups and distribute the following letter tiles to each group: *b, e, g, h, i, J, m, n, o,* and *s.* Ask the groups to use the letters to make words that have a long vowel sound at the end of the word. Tell one child in each group to write the words on a sheet of paper. Have each group share their word list with the class.

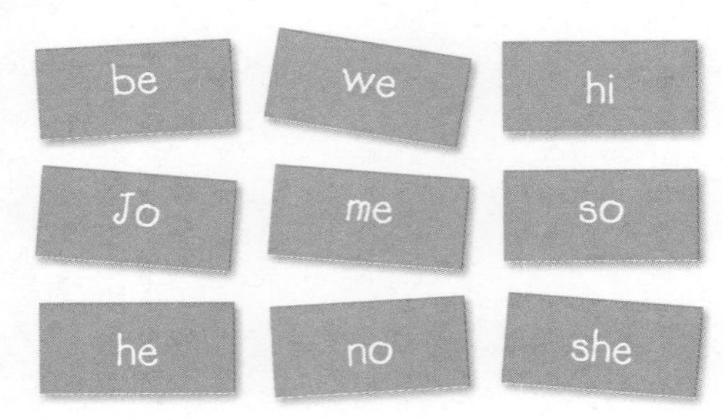

An Egg Is an Egg

Compare and Contrast

1 TEACH

Hold up two different pencils and ask children to tell how they are alike and how they are different. Remind children that another way you can learn about two things is to find how the things are alike or how they are different. Tell children you will say some sentences. They should tell you whether the sentence is showing how things are alike or how they are different. Say:

A cat and a tiger are both cats. (alike)
A cat is much smaller than a tiger. (different)
A pencil and a crayon both write. (alike)
A pencil and a crayon are made of different materials. (different)

2 PRACTICE AND ASSESS

Reread *Honey Bees* and discuss with children the ways that the queen bee and the worker bees are alike and different. Explain that when you tell how things in a story are alike or different, it helps you understand the story better.

Draw a large Venn diagram on the board and label the one circle *bike* and the other *car*. Ask volunteers to describe a bike, and jot their suggestions in that circle. Repeat the process for a car. Ask children if they notice any details that are the same. As children note similarities, erase them from the circle area and rewrite them in the center overlapped part.

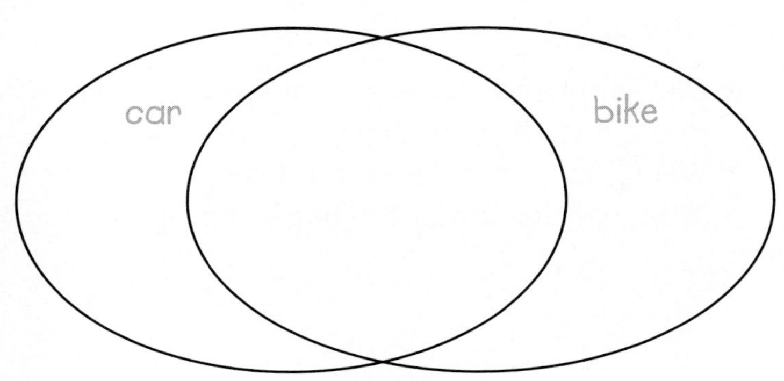

Ruby in Her Own Time

Final *ng, nk*

1 TEACH

Write the following words on the board: *sang, king, rung, bank, pink, junk.* Tell children to listen for the sound they hear at the end of each word. Point to each word as you read it, and have children repeat it. Have them identify the ending sound and circle the letters that make the sound or sounds. (For example, *ng* makes the sound /ng/ in *sang.)* Continue until each word has been read and its ending sound and letters identified.

Point out that *sang, king,* and *rung* all end with the /ng/ sound, but each word belongs to a different vowel family. Write *sang* and underline *ang*. Ask children to name other words that belong to the *ang* vowel family. Continue identifying the vowel family for the other words on the board.

2 PRACTICE AND ASSESS

Display the following word cards with double-sided tape on the back of each:

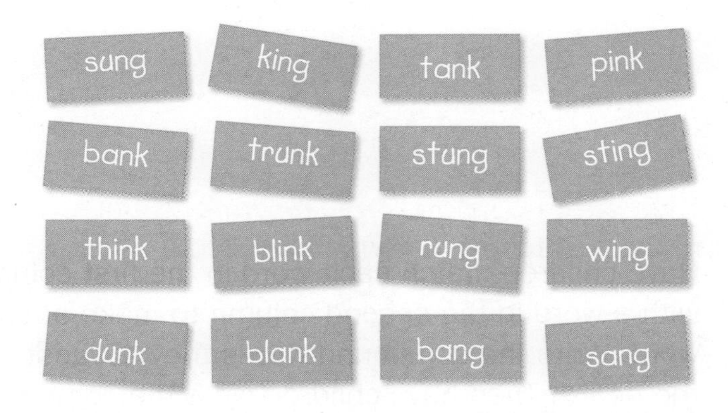

Create a chart as shown. Tell children that they will sort the words by vowel family.

-ang	-ing	-ung	-ink	-unk

Point to a word card and have a volunteer blend it. Have children repeat the word. Then have the volunteer place the card in the correct column. When all the words have been sorted, read the words in each column together.

Ruby in Her Own Time

Compound Words

1 TEACH

Write the words *some* and *thing* on the board and help children read each. Then write the word *something* on the board and read it. Explain that *something* is a compound word. It is made by putting two small words, *some* and *thing*, together to make a longer word, *something*. Point out that both whole words *some* and *thing* appear in the compound word.

2 PRACTICE AND ASSESS

Write the following words on the board: *fireplace, raincoat, treehouse.* Say *fireplace* and ask if children see two shorter words in *fireplace*. Ask what two words they see. Frame the words *fire* and *place* and have children read each. Continue with the other words, asking children to identify the two smaller words that make up the compound word.

Write the following words on columns on the board:

sun	ball
home	corn
basket	fly
butter	shine
pop	work

Have children match each word in the first column with a word in the second column to make a new word. Write the compound words they suggest on the board. Then have children write the compound words on a sheet of paper and draw a picture of each one.

Ruby in Her Own Time

Plot

1 TEACH

Tell children that all stories have a beginning, middle and an end. The beginning, middle, and end of a story all together are called the plot. Ask children to think about the story "Goldilocks and the Three Bears." Say: If I were telling the plot of the story "Goldilocks and the Three Bears," I might say "Three bears go for a walk. A little girl gets into their house and breaks things. When the bears come home, they scare her away."

Ask children if you have retold the entire story. Ask if you have only told an idea of what happened in the beginning, middle, and end of the story. Remind them that this is what a plot is.

2 PRACTICE AND ASSESS

Reread the selection *Ruby in Her Own Time*. Ask children what happened first. (Ruby hatched out of her egg.)

Ask what happened in the middle of the story. (Ruby flew farther than the others.)

Then ask how the story ended. (Ruby came home.)

To check children's understanding of plot, write this story on the board:

Sam walked to the top of the hill.
"I want to go fast," he said.
He jumped on his sled.
Down the hill he went!

Have children write a short answer to each of the following questions and then share their answers. Say:

- Did Sam jump on his sled at the beginning, in the middle, or at the end of the story?
- When did Sam go down the hill?
- What did Sam do at the beginning of the story?

Jan's New Home

r-Controlled *or, ore*

1 TEACH

Write the words *fort* and *store* on the board and blend them. Ask children what sounds they hear in the middle of *fort* and *store*. (/ôr/) Remind children that the letter *r* can change the sound of the vowel that comes before it.

Ask children to name other words in which they hear /ôr/. Write the words on the board and say them with children. Have volunteers underline the letters that stand for /ôr/ in each word. Remind children that *or* and *ore* stand for /ôr/.

2 PRACTICE AND ASSESS

Write the following words on the board:

cork sort
torch horn
chore

Have children read the words aloud. Tell them that you will point to one of these words as you read a clue. The answer to the clue will rhyme with the word you are pointing to. They should then write the answer on their paper. Say:

Rhymes with *chore*. You buy things at a ________. (store)
Rhymes with *cork*. You pick up food with a ________. (fork)
Rhymes with *sort*. It's fun to build a ________. (fort)
Rhymes with *horn*. You eat ________ off a cob. (corn)
Rhymes with *torch*. Sometimes houses have a front ________. (porch)

Have children share their answers when finished.

Jan's New Home

Ending *-es*; Plural *-es*

1 TEACH

Write this sentence on the board and have a volunteer read it:

Bill mix the paint.

Ask if the sentence sounds right. Ask why not. If children do not make suggestions, add *-es* to *mix*. Then read the sentence again. Explain that sometimes *-es* needs to be added at the end of an action word to make it sound right in a sentence.

Write the word *box* on the board. Ask children to say the word that means "more than one box." Write *boxes* on the board and read it aloud, emphasizing both syllables. Tell children that *-es* can also be added to mean more than one.

2 PRACTICE AND ASSESS

Display the following word cards:

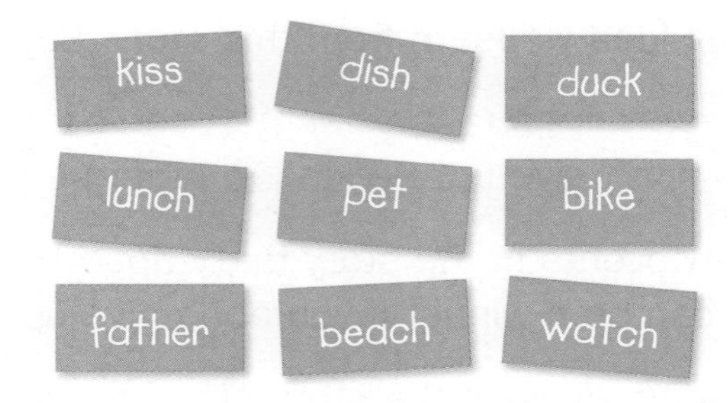

Put the cards for *-es* and *-s* facedown. Have children take turns selecting a card and then choosing a word that can have that ending. Have the child write the word with the ending on the board and read it. Ask another child to use the word with the ending in a sentence.

Ask volunteers to suggest a base word and then have another child say what ending it would get: *-es* or *-s*. Write the new words on the board.

Jan's New Home

Theme

1 TEACH

Explain to children that the author of a story often has a big idea that is the most important idea in the story. Sometimes this big idea is something the reader can learn from the story.

Help children review the events in the story "The Three Little Pigs." Guide them to understand that the first two pigs were in such a hurry to build houses that they did poor jobs. The wolf had no trouble blowing the houses down. The third pig, however, took his time building a brick house that the wolf could not blow down. Help children recognize that the big idea of the story is that it's important to take your time to do a job well.

2 PRACTICE AND ASSESS

Remind children that every story has a big idea that is the most important idea. Ask them to listen carefully as you tell the Aesop's tale "The Tortoise and the Hare." As they listen they should think about the big idea of the fable. After telling the fable, ask children which of the following ideas is the big idea we learn from this story. Say:

It's best to be a fast runner. You can be a winner if you don't give up. Be kind to other people.

Review events in the story that support the idea, "You can be a winner if you don't give up."

If needed, discuss the story "The Tale of Peter Rabbit." Ask children what they think the big idea of the story is. Guide them to understand that "listen to what your parent tells you to do or you could get into trouble" is the big idea.

Frog and Toad Together

r-Controlled *ar*

1 TEACH

Write the word *farm* on the board and say it slowly. Tell children that although *farm* has the letter *a*, you don't hear either the short sound /a/ or the long sound /ā/. Explain that the letter *r* can change the sound of the vowel that comes before it.

Have children say *farm*. Then circle the letters *ar* in *farm* and tell children these letters can stand for the /är/ sound. Write the following words on the board:

car   far   star

Have children read each word.

2 PRACTICE AND ASSESS

Have children write *car* on a sheet of paper, then follow instructions to make new words.

Put *d* at the end. What's the word? (card)
Change *d* to *t*. What's the word? (cart)
Change *c* to *p*. What's the word? (part)
Change *t* to *k*. What's the word? (park)
Change *p* to *m*. What's the word? (mark))

Display these word cards:

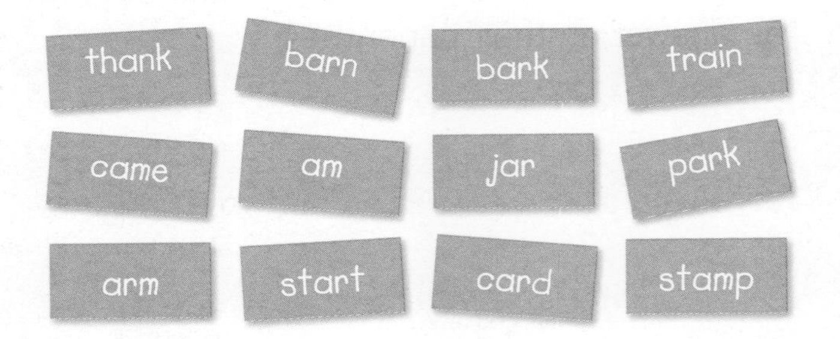

Make a chart as shown. Have volunteers select a word card, read it, and then place it in the correct column. When all the words have been placed, ask children if they can think of other words with /är/.

ar	Short *a*	Long *a*

Frog and Toad Together

Inflected Endings *-ed, -ing*

1 TEACH

Write the word *pick* on the board and have children read it. Then say: I pick up my dog. Explain that the word *pick* shows that you are doing the action now. Write the word *picked* on the board and say: I picked up my dog last night. Point out that when you add *-ed* to a word, it means that the action happened in the past.

Write *lock, locked* and *stop, stopped*. Have children identify the ending that means something has already happened. Then ask children how *stopped* is different from *stop*. Guide children to understand that in some words that end with one vowel followed by a consonant, the final consonant is written again before adding the *-ed.*

Remind children that the letters *-ing* can be added to many action words to make a new word. Write *stopping* on the board. Frame *stop* in *stopping*. Tell children that just like the final consonant is doubled before adding the *-ed,* the final consonant is also doubled before adding the *-ing*. Circle the two *p*'s in *stopping*.

2 PRACTICE AND ASSESS

Remind children that the letters *-ed* and *-ing* are added to action words. Write the following words on the board and have children read them. Have a volunteer point out which words had the final consonant doubled before *-ed* or *-ing* was added.

walked swimming dropped hearing

Write these words on the board:

skip stop wish
want chop tip

Have volunteers add the *-ed* and *-ing* to each word. They might need to double a consonant.

Frog and Toad Together

Plot

1 TEACH

Remind children that every story has a beginning, middle, and an end. Recall *Frog and Toad Together.* Ask what happened at the beginning of the story (Frog gives Toad seeds), what happened in the middle (Toad tries different things to get the seeds to grow), and what happened at the end (the seeds begin to grow).

Write the answers to the previous questions on the board. Explain that these sentences show the plot of *Frog and Toad Together.*

2 PRACTICE AND ASSESS

Write the following sentences on strips of paper and display them with double-sided tape on the back of each:

A little green robot looked out.
He quickly closed the door.
A rocket landed in the field.
Slowly, the door opened.
He said, "This is not my home."

Read the sentences with children. Have volunteers place the sentence strips in order to show the plot of a story.

Choose a selection from Unit 3 to read aloud.

When you are finished reading ask children to recall the beginning, middle, and end of the story.

I'm a Caterpillar

r-Controlled *er, ir, ur*

1 TEACH

Write the following sentence and have it read:

Jill turns her bird cage

Ask children which words have the sound /ėr/. Underline the words as they direct, and then have children circle the letters that stand for the /ėr/ sounds.

Explain that the sounds /ėr/ are heard in many words when the letters *e, i,* or *u* are followed by *r*. Remind children that the letter *r* can change the sound of the vowel when it comes before it.

2 PRACTICE AND ASSESS

Write these words:

perch	twirl	purse
skirt	clerk	fern
curb	curl	thirsty

Have each word read. Then have volunteers sort the words into three lists according to their spelling pattern, *er, ir, or ur,* and write them on the board.

Ask children to name other words that have the /ėr/ sounds. Other words that may be added are *purr, dirt, church, third,* and *germ*. List their suggestions in the appropriate column on the board. Have the three lists reread.

I'm a Caterpillar

Contractions *'s, 've, 're*

1 TEACH

Remind children that a contraction is a short way of writing two words as one. Write on the board *he is*. Have a volunteer use *he is* in a sentence. Repeat the sentence, replacing *he is* with *he's*.

Ask children how you changed the words *he is* to make *he's*. Guide them to recognize that you replaced the *i* with a mark called an apostrophe and that there is now only one word where there were two. Make sure children understand that *he's* means the same as *he is*. Repeat the process with *we have* and *we are*.

2 PRACTICE AND ASSESS

Write *that is.* Ask children how to change the two words to make the contraction *that's*. Let them erase the *i* and insert an apostrophe to make one word. Have a volunteer make up a sentence with *that is*. Repeat the procedure with these words:

that is	I have
you are	it is
you have	do not
they are	he is

Have children return to *I'm a Caterpillar* and tell them that there are five different contractions in the story. Have children work independently to find the contractions. They should cover each with a sticky note on which they have written the two words that make the contraction.

Afterwards, read together the pages on which children put their sticky notes, saying the words they wrote in place of the contractions. Ask the child if the sentence means the same thing with the two words in place of the contraction. They should realize that the meaning is the same.

I'm a Caterpillar

Draw Conclusions

1 TEACH

Ask children what they think the weather must be like if someone came into the school wearing a raincoat and carrying a wet umbrella. Ask them what clues helped them decide their answer.

Explain to children that sometimes you can use clues in what you read and what you already know to figure out something that is not actually written in a story, just as they figured out the weather question.

2 PRACTICE AND ASSESS

Write the following sentences on the board and read them aloud.

Oscar was on the sidewalk.
Many people were lined up.
Then he heard loud noises.
He saw a marching band.
He saw beautiful floats.

Ask what children think Oscar was doing. (watching a parade) Discuss what clues in the story helped them figure this out. Also have children tell what they already knew that helped them figure out their answer.

Have children recall *Frog and Toad Together* and discuss what clues they read and what they already know that helped them understand why Frog said it was hard work to grow a garden. (Seeds need care and attention, as well as sunshine and rain to grow.)

Where Are My Animal Friends?

Comparative Endings

1 TEACH

Say these sentences:

The black dog is short.
The white dog is shorter than the black dog.
The brown dog is the shortest of all.

Write the words *short, shorter,* and *shortest* on the board. Ask children how the words are different. When they identify the endings of the words, explain that *-er* is added when two things are compared and *-est* is added when three or more things are compared. Ask what two things are compared in the second sentence. (the black dog and the white dog) Then ask what three things are compared in the third sentence. (the black dog, the white dog, and the brown dog)

2 PRACTICE AND ASSESS

Display the following word and ending cards:

Read the following sentences aloud and ask volunteers to put two cards together to make the word that completes each sentence. Have them write the new word on the board. To check, restate the sentence using the new words. Say:

A bicycle is slow.
A car is ______ than a jet. (slower)
A person walking is ______ of all. (slowest)
Tara ran fast.
Terrell runs ______ than Tara. (faster)
Nat is the ______runner of all. (fastest)

Have children look around for simple objects they can compare and have them make up a comparative sentence.

Where Are My Animal Friends?

dge/j/

1 TEACH

Write *gem* and *page* on the board. Ask children what letter stands for /j/ in each word. Then write the following sentence on the board and read it:

Madge stood at the edge of the ledge.

Pronounce /j/ and have children repeat it with you. Ask them to jump when they hear a word with /j/ as you reread the sentence. Underline each word they identify. Then circle the letter pattern *dge* in each word. Explain that /j/ can be spelled *dge* at the end of words.

2 PRACTICE AND ASSESS

Write the sentences below on chart paper.

Madge got a smudge of fudge on her skirt.
The scout got a badge for learning the pledge.

Read aloud each sentence. Define each unfamiliar word. Reread the sentences with children. Have them underline each word that has /j/. Tell them to circle the letters that stand for /j/ in each word.

Have children write *fudge* on a sheet of paper. Tell children to follow your instructions to make new words.

Change *f* to *n*. What's the word? (nudge)
Change *n* to *b*. What's the word? (budge)
Change *u* to *a*. What's the word? (badge)
Change *ba* to *le*. What's the word? (ledge)
Change *l* to *w*. What's the word? (wedge)
Take away *w*. What's the word? (edge)

Where Are My Animal Friends?

Sequence

1 TEACH

Explain to children that many things they do every day must be done in a certain order. Ask children to share some activities they do on a school day and list them on the board. Read the list with children and then ask: What comes first?

Help children order the events. (See sample below.)

get on school bus
wake up and get dressed
eat breakfast

Point out that events in stories also happen in a certain order. Clue words, such as *first, next,* and *last* sometimes signal the order of events. Reread the activities on the board, using clue words to tell the sequence of events. (For example, "First you wake up and get dressed.")

2 PRACTICE AND ASSESS

Reread *I'm a Caterpillar* and have volunteers tell what comes *first, next,* and *last* in the story. Remind children to use clue words when they retell a story.

Display the following sentences on strips of paper with double-faced tape on the back of each. Read them and have children reorder them to show the sequence.

Lee watered the small plants.
Lee planted seeds.
Lee picked flowers in the garden.

Tell children to rewrite the sentences, using the words *first, next,* and *last* to show the order of events. Have children draw pictures to show the story sequence.

Providing children with reading materials they can and want to read is an important step toward developing fluent readers. A running record allows you to determine each child's instructional and independent reading level. Information on how to take a running record is provided on pp. DI•87–DI•88.

Instructional Reading Level

Only approximately 1 in 10 words will be difficult when reading a selection from the Student Edition for children who are at grade level. (A typical first-grader reads approximately 45–60 words correct per minute.)

- Children reading at grade level should read regularly from the Student Edition and On-Level Leveled Readers, with teacher support as suggested in the Teacher's Editions.
- Children reading below grade level can read the Strategic Intervention Leveled Readers and the Decodable Readers. Instructional plans can be found in the Teacher's Edition and the Leveled Reader Teaching Guide.
- Children who are reading above grade level can use the Advanced Leveled Readers and the Advanced Selection in the Teacher's Edition. Instructional plans can be found in the Teacher's Edition and the Leveled Reader Teaching Guide.

Independent Reading Level

Children should read regularly in independent-level texts in which no more than approximately 1 in 20 words is difficult for the reader. Other factors that make a book easy to read include the child's interest in the topic, the amount of text on a page, how well illustrations support meaning, and the complexity and familiarity of the concepts. Suggested books for self-selected reading are provided for each lesson on p. TR16 in this Teacher's Edition.

Guide children in learning how to self-select books at their independent reading level. As you talk about a book with children, discuss the challenging concepts in it, list new words children find in sampling the book, and ask children about their familiarity with the topic. A blackline master to help children evaluate books for independent reading is provided on p. DI•86.

Self-Selected/Independent Reading

While oral reading allows you to assess children's reading level and fluency, independent reading is of crucial importance to children's futures as readers and learners. Children need to develop their ability to read independently for increasing amounts of time.

- Schedule a regular time for sustained independent reading in your classroom. During the year, gradually increase the amount of time devoted to independent reading.
- More fluent readers may choose to read silently during independent reading time. Other children might read to a partner, to a stuffed animal, or to an adult volunteer.
- Help children track the amount of time they read independently and the number of pages they read in a given amount of time. Tracking will help motivate them to gradually increase their duration and speed. Blackline masters for tracking independent reading are provided on pp. DI•86 and TR17.

Name ______________________________

Choosing a Book to Read by Yourself

These questions can help you pick a book to read.

_____ 1. Is this book about something that I like?

_____ 2. This book may be about a real person, about facts, or a made-up story. Do I like reading this kind of book?

_____ 3. Have I read other things by this author? Do I like the author?

If you say "yes" to question 1, 2, or 3, go on.

_____ 4. Were there fewer than 5 hard words on the first page?

_____ 5. Does the number of words on a page look about right to me?

If you say "yes" to questions 4 and 5, the book is right for you.

Silent Reading

Write the date, the title of the book, and the number of minutes you read.

Date	Title	Minutes

Taking a Running Record

A running record is an assessment of a child's oral reading accuracy and oral reading fluency. Reading accuracy is based on the number of words read correctly. Reading fluency is based on the reading rate (the number of words correct per minute) and the degree to which a child reads with a "natural flow."

How to Measure Reading Accuracy

1. Choose a grade-level text of about 80 to 120 words that is unfamiliar to the child.
2. Make a copy of the text for yourself. Make a copy for the child or have the child read aloud from a book.
3. Give the child the text and have the child read aloud. (You may wish to record the child's reading for later evaluation.)
4. On your copy of the text, mark any miscues or errors the child makes while reading. See the running record sample on page DI•88, which shows how to identify and mark miscues.
5. Count the total number of words in the text and the total number of errors made by the child. Note: If a child makes the same error more than once, such as mispronouncing the same word multiple times, count it as one error. Self-corrections do not count as actual errors. Use the following formula to calculate the percentage score, or accuracy rate:

$$\frac{\text{Total Number of Words} - \text{Total Number of Errors}}{\text{Total Number of Words}} \times 100 = \text{percentage score}$$

Interpreting the Results

- A child who reads **95–100%** of the words correctly is reading at an **independent level** and may need more challenging text.
- A child who reads **90–94%** of the words correctly is reading at an **instructional level** and will likely benefit from guided instruction.
- A child who reads **89%** or fewer of the words correctly is reading at a **frustrational level** and may benefit most from targeted instruction with lower-level texts and intervention.

How to Measure Reading Rate (WCPM)

1. Follow Steps 1–3 above.
2. Note the exact times when the child begins and finishes reading.
3. Use the following formula to calculate the number of words correct per minute (WCPM):

$$\frac{\text{Total Number of Words Read Correctly}}{\text{Total Number of Seconds}} \times 60 = \text{words correct per minute}$$

Interpreting the Results

An appropriate reading rate for a first-grader is 45–60 (WCPM).

Running Record Sample

Running Record Sample

"Please pass me a hot dog," said Beth. She and her friends were eating in the park.

"Tell us about your trip to the beach," Beth said to one of her friends.

"It was great!" her friend said.

Beth's friends talked about sports teams. Later, they talked about movies. Beth was not talking. She was looking at something.

"Beth?" they called to her.

Beth did not speak. Her friends saw that she was looking at a bird. It flew over them and landed on a sign. Beth just stared. She turned her head this way and that.

—From *How Beth Feels*
On-Level Reader 1.4.2

Miscues

Omission
The student omits words or word parts.

Mispronunciation/Misreading
The student pronounces or reads a word incorrectly.

Insertion
The student inserts words or parts of words that are not in the text.

Self-Correction
The student reads a word incorrectly but then corrects the error. Do not count self-corrections as actual errors. However, noting self-corrections will help you identify words the student finds difficult.

Hesitation
The student hesitates over a word, and the teacher provides the word. Wait several seconds before telling the student what the word is.

Substitution
The student substitutes words or parts of words for the words in the text.

Running Record Results
Total Number of Words: **97**
Number of Errors: **5**

Reading Time: **128 seconds**

Reading Accuracy

$\frac{97 - 5}{97} = \frac{92}{97} = .948 = 95\%$

Accuracy Percentage Score: **95%**

Reading Rate—WCPM

$\frac{92}{128} \times 60 = 43.123 = 43$ words correct per minute

Reading Rate: **43 WCPM**

Teacher Resources

Table of Contents

Bookmarks

Fiction

- Who are the characters?
- Where does the story take place?
- When does the story take place?
- What happens . . .
  at the beginning?
  in the middle?
  at the end?

Nonfiction

- What did I learn?
- What is this mainly about?

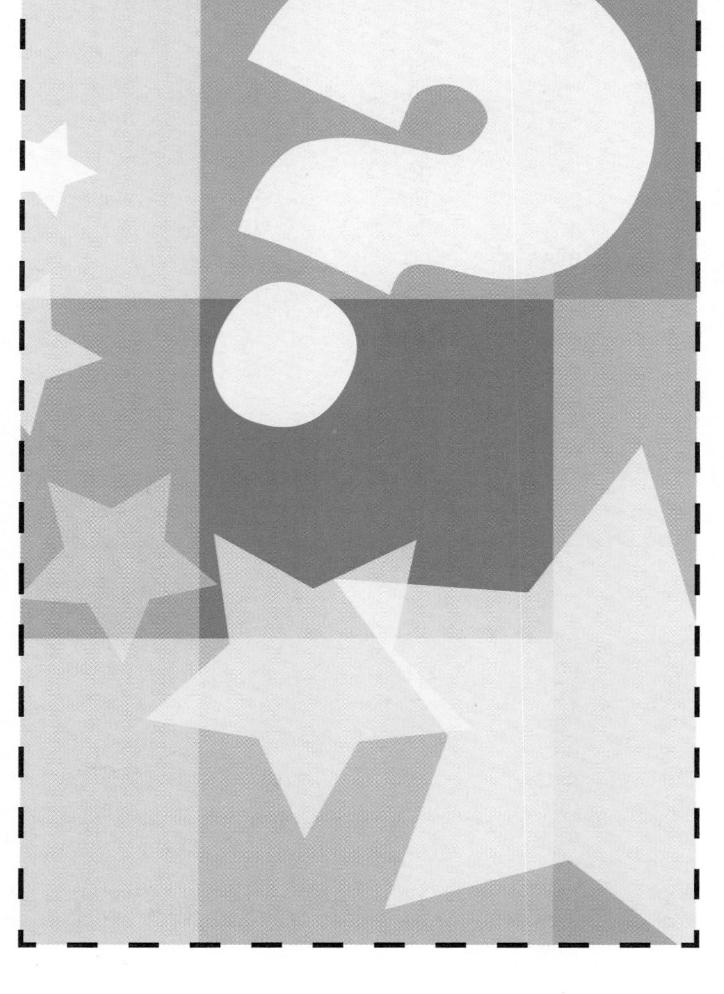

Sam, Come Back!

Short *a*

ad, am, an, at, back, bad, bag, bat, black, cab, can, cap, cat, dab, dad, fan, fat, gas, had, ham, has, jab, Jack, jam, lad, lap, Mack, mad, man, map, mat, Matt, nab, pack, pal, pass, pat, ram, ran, rat, sack, sad, sag, Sam, sat, snack, tab, tag, tan, tap, that, van, wag, yak, zap

Final *ck*

back, black, Jack, lack, Mack, pack, quack, rack, sack, sick, snack, tack, trick, Zack

Spelling Words

am, at, back, bat, can, cat, dad, mad, ran, sack

High-Frequency/ Tested Words

in, on, way

Pig in a Wig

Short *i*

bib, big, bin, bit, bits, did, dig, dip, fill, fin, fit, fix, grin, hip, hit, if, in, it, jig, kid, kiss, kit, lick, lid, lip, lit, miss, mix, nip, pick, pig, quick, rib, rid, rip, sick, sip, sit, six, thin, tick, Tim, tin, tip, wig, will, zip

Final *x*

fix, fax, flax, Max, mix, sax, six, wax

Spelling Words

did, fix, in, it, lip, mix, pin, sit, six, wig

High-Frequency/ Tested Words

and, take, up

Selection Words

play

The Big Blue Ox

Short *o*

bob, box, cobs, cots, dogs, Dot, flocks, fox, hogs, hop, hot, jobs, locks, lot, Mom, mop, not, off, on, ox, Pop, pot, pots, rob, rock, rot, top, tot, tots

-s Plurals

bats, bends, bibs, bills, bins, bumps, cabs, cans, cats, cobs, cots, dogs, fans, fins, flocks, hams, hats, hills, hogs, jams, jobs, kids, kits, lids, lips, locks, maps, mats, pans, pigs, pins, pots, racks, rags, ribs, sacks, tabs, tots, wigs

Spelling Words

got, hop, hot, lock, mom, mop, ox, pop, pot, rock

High-Frequency/ Tested Words

get, help, use

Selection Words

mud, town

A Fox and a Kit

Inflected Ending -s

bats, caps, digs, dips, fits, gabs, gets, helps, hits, hops, jabs, kicks, licks, likes, looks, naps, nips, nods, packs, picks, pins, plays, pops, quits, rips, rocks, sees, sips, sits, tacks, tags, takes, taps, wags, wins, yaps

Inflected Ending *-ing* *(without spelling changes)*

backing, doing, filling, fixing, going, helping, jumping, kicking, licking, locking, packing, passing, picking, playing, quacking, rocking, seeing, tacking, watching, waxing

Spelling Words

fit, fits, hit, hits, nap, naps, sit, sits, win, wins

High-Frequency/ Tested Words

eat, her, this, too

Selection Words

animals, dinner, watch

Get the Egg!

Short *e*

bed, beg, bell, Ben, deck, dress, egg, fed, fell, get, helping, hen, Jen, jet, leg, less, men, mess, met, nests, net, peg, pen, pet, press, red, set, sled, smell, spell, spend, step, tell, ten, web, webs, well, wet, yelling, yes, yet

Initial Consonant Blends (CCVC)

black, block, blocks, Brad, brick, bricks, clam, clap, clock, crab, crop, cross, dress, drip, flap, flip, flop, Fran, frog, glad, glass, grab, grin, grip, press, skip, sled, slick, slip, smell, snap, spell, spend, spill, spin, spot, stack, step, stiff, stop, swim, trick, trim, trip, twig

Spelling Words

bed, jet, leg, men, net, red, sled, step, ten, wet

High-Frequency/ Tested Words

saw, small, tree, your

Selection Words

bird, nest

Animal Park

Short *u*

bug, bugs, bump, bun, bus, bust, but, buzz, cubs, cuff, cup, cut, duck, ducks, dug, dusk, dust, fun, gulls, gum, Gus, hugs, hum, hump, hunt, hut, jump, luck, lump, mud, mug, must, plug, plum, Pug, pup, rub, rug, run, runs, rust, skunks, slump, snug, stuff, stump, sub, suds, sun, truck, tub, tusk, up, yum

Final Consonant Blends (CVCC)

and, band, belt, bend, bent, best, blend, bump, bust, camp, clasp, crisp, desk, drift, dusk, dust, fast, gift, held, help, hump, hunt, jump, last, lump, mask, melt, milk, must, nest, past, pond, raft, rest, rust, sand, slump, stamp, stand, stomp, stump, tent, tusk, went

Spelling Words

bump, bus, cut, jump, must, nut, rug, run, sun, up

High-Frequency/ Tested Words

home, into, many, them

Selection Words

park, zebras, hippos, elephants

A Big Fish for Max

Digraphs *sh, th*

brush, crash, crush, dish, fish, flash, fresh, rush, shack, share, shark, shed, shell, ship, shop, show, shut, trash, wish, bath, math, path, than, thank, that, them, then, there, thick, thin, think, this, thud, with

Sound of *a* in *ball, walk*

all, bald, ball, call, fall, hall, halt, mall, malt, salt, small, stalk, stall, talk, tall, walk, wall

Spelling Words

fish, rush, shell, ship, shop, shut, then, thin, trash, with

High-Frequency/ Tested Words

catch, good, no, put, want

The Farmer in the Hat

Long *a* (CVCe)

ace, age, ages, ape, ate, bake, base, brace, brake, brave, cage, cake, case, cave, caves, classmates, crate, date, Dave, face, fade, fame, gage, game, gate, gave, Grace, grape, hate, Jake, lake, late, made, make, mane, name, Nate, page, place, places, plane, plate, race, rage, rake, same, save, shade, shake, shape, skate, snake, space, stage, state, take, takes, tame, tape, trace, trade, wage, wake, wave, waves

c/s/ and *g*/j/

brace, cell, cent, face, fence, Grace, ice, lace, pace, pencil, place, places, race, rice, slice, space, trace, age, ages, cage, gage, gel, gem, gerbil, ginger, Ginger, giraffe, page, rage, stage, wage

Spelling Words

age, cage, cake, face, late, made, make, name, safe, take

High-Frequency/ Tested Words

be, could, horse, old, paper

Selection Words

farmer, gerbil, MacDonald, squeak

Who Works Here?

Long *i* (CVCe)

bike, bikes, bite, dime, dine, dive, drive, fine, fire, fires, five, glide, hide, hive, ice, kite, life, like, lime, line, mice, Mike, mile, mine, nice, nine, outside, pine, pipe, price, pride, prize, rice, ride, ripe, rise, shine, sidewalk, size, slice, slide, smile, spine, tide, tile, time, vine, while, white, wide, wife, wipe, wise

Digraphs *wh, ch, tch*

whack, whale, what, when, which, whiff, while, whim, whip, whisk, white, whiz

chalk, champ, chase, chat, check, chess, chick, children, chill, chime, chin, chip, chips, chive, chop, chores, each, inch, lunch, much, munch, ranch, rich, such, which

batch, catch, clutch, ditch, fetch, itch, latch, match, pitch, switch, watch

Spelling Words

bike, dime, hide, ice, kite, like, ride, smile, time, white

High-Frequency/ Tested Words

live, out, people, who, work

Selection Words

busy, mail, neighborhood

The Big Circle

Long *o* (CVCe)

bone
bones
broke
choke
chose
close
code
Cole
cone
doze
drove
froze
globe
home
hope
Hope
hose
joke
mope
nose
note
poke
pole
robe
rode
role
rope
rose
Rose
slope
spoke
stole
stone
stones
stove
those
vote
woke
zone

Contractions *n't, 'm, 'll*

aren't
can't
couldn't
didn't
don't
hadn't
hasn't
haven't
isn't
wasn't
won't

I'm

he'll
I'll
it'll
she'll
they'll
we'll
you'll

Spelling Words

bone
home
hope
hose
joke
rode
rose
stone
those
woke

High-Frequency/ Tested Words

down
inside
now
there
together

Selection Words

baby
circle
herd
meat
triceratops

Life in the Forest

Long *u* (CVCe); Long *e* (CVCe)

cube
cute
Duke
dune
flute
fume
fuse
huge
June
mule
mute
prune
rude
rule
tube
tubes
tune
use
uses

eve
Gene
Pete
scene
Steve
these
Zeke

Inflected Ending *-ed* *(without spelling changes)*

added
asked
blocked
brushed
called
checked
filled
grilled
handed
helped
jumped
landed
listed
looked
melted
missed
mixed
packed
pecked
pitched
planted
printed
rested
rushed
smelled
spelled
spilled
thanked
tilted
twisted
walked
wanted
wished
worked
yelled

Spelling Words

cube
cute
flute
huge
June
mule
rude
rule
tube
use

High-Frequency/ Tested Words

around
find
food
grow
under
water

Selection Words

bear
forest
hummingbirds
leaves
squirrels
woodpecker

Honey Bees

Long *e: e, ee*

be
bee
beef
bees
beet
cheese
deep
feed
feeds
feel
feet
free
green
he
heel
keep
Lee
me
meet
need
peep
peeping
queen
Reed
see
seed
she
sheep
sleep
steep
sweep
sweet
teeth
tree
we
weed
week
wheel

Syllables VCCV

attack
attic
Bandit
basket
bonnet
button
buzzy
collect
fabric
happen
happy
hidden
insects
invent
kitten
mitten
napkin
object
pencil
picnic
pollen
pretzel
problem
rabbit
rabbits
ribbon
tablet
tennis
traffic
trumpet
until

Spelling Words

be
feet
green
he
me
see
she
tree
we
week

High-Frequency/ Tested Words

also
family
new
other
some
their

Selection Words

cold
flowers
honey
nectar
worker

An Egg Is an Egg

Vowel Sounds of *y*

- by
- cry
- dry
- Dy
- fly
- fry
- my
- shy
- sky
- sly
- Sy
- try
- why

- baby
- Bobby
- buddy
- bumpy
- bunny
- candy
- choppy
- daddy
- Danny
- fifty
- fluffy
- funny
- fussy
- happy
- hungry
- jelly
- Jimmy
- kitty
- lucky
- many
- messy
- muddy
- nanny
- penny
- pretty
- puppy
- sandy
- silly
- sleepy
- sloppy
- smelly
- sunny
- tummy
- ugly
- very
- yummy

Long Vowels CV

- ago
- also
- be
- by
- cry
- Di
- Dy
- fly
- fry
- go
- he
- hello
- hi
- I
- Jo
- me
- Mo
- my
- no
- pro
- she
- shy
- sky
- sly
- so
- Sy
- try
- we
- why

Spelling Words

- any
- body
- by
- cry
- fly
- lucky
- my
- puppy
- silly
- try

High-Frequency/ Tested Words

- always
- become
- day
- everything
- nothing
- stays
- things

Selection Words

- boy
- grew
- night
- sunset
- tower

Ruby in Her Own Time

Compound Words

- anthill
- anything
- anywhere
- backpack
- bankbook
- baseball
- basketball
- bathtub
- bedtime
- blueprint
- classmate
- cupcake
- driveway
- everyone
- everything
- everywhere
- flagpole
- gumball
- homemade
- homework
- hopscotch
- inside
- jellyfish
- lipstick
- newscast
- nickname
- nowhere
- outside
- pancake
- paperback
- pigpen
- quicksand
- runway
- sandbox
- sandpaper
- sidewalk
- snowball
- someone
- something
- somewhere
- sunblock
- sunrise
- sunset
- sunshine
- treetop
- upon
- weekend
- whatever
- whenever
- windmill

Final *-ng* and *-nk*

- anything
- bang
- bring
- bringing
- ducklings
- everything
- hang
- king
- nothing
- rang
- ring
- sang
- sing
- sings
- something
- song
- songs
- sting
- stung
- sung
- swing
- thing
- wing
- wings
- wrong

- bank
- blank
- blink
- bunk
- chunk
- drank
- drink
- drinks
- dunk
- Frank
- Hank
- hunk
- junk
- link
- pink
- rink
- sink
- skunk
- stink
- sunk
- tank
- thank
- think
- trunk
- wink

Spelling Words

- bank
- blank
- bring
- pink
- rang
- rink
- sang
- sunk
- trunk
- wing

High-Frequency/ Tested Words

- any
- enough
- ever
- every
- own
- sure
- were

Selection Words

- beautiful
- father
- feather
- flew
- mother
- precious

Jan's New Home

Controlled *or, ore*

- born
- chore
- cords
- core
- cork
- corn
- corner
- explore
- for
- Ford
- forget
- fork
- form
- fort
- forts
- horn
- horns
- horses
- Jordan
- more
- Mort
- New York
- north
- North Shore
- or
- porch
- porches
- port
- scorch
- score
- shore
- short
- snore
- sore
- sort
- sorts
- sport
- sports
- store
- stores
- stork
- storm
- thorn
- torch
- torches
- torn
- wore
- worn

Ending *-es*; Plural *-es*

- bosses
- boxes
- buses
- buzzes
- catches
- classes
- crashes
- crosses
- dishes
- dresses
- finishes
- fishes
- fixes
- foxes
- glasses
- kisses
- mixes
- patches
- porches
- pushes
- reaches
- rushes
- torches
- tosses
- waxes
- wishes

Spelling Words

- bus
- buses
- class
- classes
- fix
- fixes
- kiss
- kisses
- wish
- wishes

High-Frequency/ Tested Words

- away
- car
- friends
- house
- our
- school
- very

Selection Words

- move
- toys
- window

Frog and Toad Together

Controlled *ar*

- arm
- artist
- bark
- barked
- barn
- Bart
- car
- cart
- charge
- chart
- Clark
- dark
- dart
- far
- farm
- garden
- hard
- harm
- harp
- jar
- large
- march
- marching
- mark
- park
- parking
- part
- scarf
- shark
- sharp
- smart
- spark
- star
- start
- started
- yard
- yarn

Inflected Endings *-ed, -ing (double final consonant)*

- batting
- begging
- chopped
- clapping
- digging
- dropped
- flipped
- flipping
- getting
- hopped
- hopping
- hugged
- hugging
- hummed
- jogged
- jogging
- letting
- patted
- patting
- petted
- petting
- pinned
- planned
- ripped
- running
- shopped
- shutting
- sipped
- slipped
- stepped
- stepping
- stopped
- stopping
- swimming
- tagged
- tapping
- tripped
- winning
- zipped

Spelling Words

- ask
- asked
- call
- called
- help
- helped
- jog
- jogged
- plan
- planned

High-Frequency/ Tested Words

- afraid
- again
- few
- how
- read *(both pronunciations)*
- soon

Selection Words

- ground
- head
- rain
- shouted
- shouting

I'm a Caterpillar

Controlled *er, ir, ur*

- butterfly
- clerk
- fern
- ferns
- germ
- her
- jerk
- nerve
- perch
- serve
- stern
- swerve
- verb
- verse
- bird
- birds
- chirp
- dirt
- first
- girl
- shirt
- sir
- stir
- swirl
- third
- thirst
- twirl
- whir
- blur
- burn
- burst
- church
- churn
- curb
- curl
- fur
- hurl
- hurt
- purse
- return
- slur
- spur
- surf
- turn

Contractions *'s, 've, 're*

- he's
- it's
- let's
- she's
- that's
- what's
- who's

- I've
- they've
- we've
- you've

- they're
- we're
- you're

Spelling Words

- bird
- burn
- first
- fur
- girl
- her
- hurt
- shirt
- sir
- were

High-Frequency/ Tested Words

- done
- know
- push
- visit
- wait

Selection Words

- caterpillar
- chrysalis
- crawl
- pupa
- shiver

Where Are My Animal Friends?

Comparative Endings *-er, -est*

- bigger
- biggest
- bolder
- colder
- coldest
- darker
- deeper
- deepest
- dimmest
- faster
- fastest
- fatter
- fewer
- firmest
- flattest
- greenest
- hardest
- hotter
- hottest
- kinder
- kindest
- newest
- quicker
- quickest
- sadder
- saddest
- shorter
- shortest
- slimmer
- slimmest
- slower
- slowest
- smaller
- smallest
- smarter
- smartest
- stiffer
- stiffest
- sweeter
- taller
- tallest
- thickest
- thinner
- thinnest
- wetter
- wettest

-dge/j/

- badge
- bridge
- budge
- dodge
- edge
- fudge
- grudge
- judge
- ledge
- lodge
- Madge
- Midge
- pledge
- porridge
- ridge
- smudge
- wedge

Spelling Words

- bigger
- biggest
- faster
- fastest
- sadder
- saddest
- shorter
- shortest
- slower
- slowest

High-Frequency/ Tested Words

- before
- does
- good-bye
- oh
- right
- won't

Selection Words

- goose
- raccoon
- spring
- warm

WORD LIST

Mama's Birthday Present

Long a: ai, ay

braid
brain
chain
claim
drain
fail
grain
hail
mail
main
nail
paid
pail
pain
paint
rail
rain
sail
snail
strain
tail
trails
train
wait

always
Bay
birthday
clay
day
fray
Friday
gray
hay
lay
Monday
pay
play
ray
Saturday
say
stay
stray
Sunday
sway
Thursday
today
tray
Tuesday
way
Wednesday

Possessives

Ben's
Bing's
boy's
bride's
Chuck's
Dad's
Dan's
everyone's
family's
Frank's
Gail's
Gene's
Gina's
girl's
Grandma's
Greg's
Hank's
hen's
Jane's
Jay's
Ken's
king's
Liz's
Mama's
man's
May's
Mike's
Molina's
Nan's
Perez's
Ray's
Sam's
Steve's
Sunny's
Tom's
train's

birds'
boys'
cats'
cows'
dogs'
ducks'
friends'
girls'
kittens'
people's
pigs'
rabbits'
snails'
whales'

Spelling Words

afraid
day
gray
mail
may
play
rain
tail
train
way

High-Frequency/Tested Words

about
enjoy
give
surprise
worry
would

Selection Words

buñuelos
confetti
guitar
piñata
present
tortilla
wonderful

The Dot

Long e: ea

beach
bead
beam
bean
beast
beat
bleach
clean
cream
Dean
dream
each
easel
easy
eat
feast
gleam
glean
heat
Jean
leaned
leap
leaves
meals
mean
meat
neat
peace
peach
peak
peas
reach
read
screamed
sea
seal
seat
sneak
speak
squealed
steam
streaming
tea
teach
teacher
team
tease
weave
wheat

Inflected Endings *(spelling change: y to i)*

bumpier
carries
copied
creamier
creamiest
cried
cries
dirtiest
dried
dries
easier
easiest
flies
foggier
fried
funnier
happier
happiest
hurried
hurries
jolliest
luckiest
messiest
muddier
muddiest
pennies
prettier
sillier
silliest
sleepier
sleepiest
sloppiest
sneakier
spied
stickier
studied
studies
sunnier
sunniest
tried
tries
trophies
worried
worries

Spelling Words

beach
clean
dream
each
eat
lean
please
sea
team
treat

High-Frequency/Tested Words

colors
draw
drew
great
over
show
sign

Selection Words

artist
experimenting
gold
splash
squiggle
stared
straight

Mister Bones: Dinosaur Hunter

Long o: oa, ow

boast
boat
coach
coat
coax
float
foal
goat
goats
groan
Joan
Joan's
load
loaded
loaf
moan
oak
oat
road
roamed
roast
soak
soap
throat
toast
topcoat
whoa

blow
blown
bowl
crow
elbow
flow
flown
glow
grow
grown
growth
know
low
mow
own
pillow
rainbows
row
show
slow
snow
throw
tow
yellow

Three-Letter Consonant Blends

scram
scrap
scrape
scraps
scratch
scream
screams
screen
scrub
shrimp
shrink
shrub
shrug
splash
splendid
splint
split
splotch
sprain
spray
spring
sprint
spruce
strange
strap
stray
stream
street
stretch
strict
strike
string
strip
stripe
stripes
strong
three
thrill
throat
throw

Spelling Words

blow
boat
coat
loaf
pillow
road
row
snow
soap
yellow

High-Frequency/Tested Words

found
mouth
once
took
wild

Selection Words

bandannas
cowboy
gigantic
lizard
Montana
museum
tyrant

The Lady in the Moon

Long *i: ie, igh*

cries
die
flies
lie
pie
potpie
skies
tie
tied
tried
vie

bright
delight
fight
firefighter
flight
fright
high
highway
light
lighthouse
lights
might
night
nighttime
right
sigh
sight
slight
thigh
tight

kn/n/ and *wr/r/*

knack
knee
kneecap
kneel
knelt
knife
knight
knit
knives
knob
knock
knockout
knot
knothole
knots
know
known
handwriting
shipwreck
wrap
wrapped
wrapper
wreath
wreck
wren
wrench
wring
wrist
wristwatch
write
written
wrong
wrote

Spelling Words

bright
high
lie
light
might
night
pie
right
tie
tight

High-Frequency/ Tested Words

above
eight
laugh
moon
touch

Selection Words

festival
lotus leaves
pears
poems
treasures

Peter's Chair

Vowels *ew, ue, ui*

blew
chew
crew
dew
drew
few
flew
grew
knew
new
newspaper
newt
outgrew
screw
threw
blue
bluebird
blueprint
clue
clues
due
glue
gluestick
sue
Sue
true
bruise
cruise
fruit
grapefruit
juice
suit
suitcase
sunsuit

Compound Words

anyway
anywhere
ballplayer
beanstalk
bedtime
beehive
birthday
chopsticks
daylight
doghouse
dragonfly
driveway
evergreen
everyone
firefighter
grasshopper
handwriting
highway
homework
houseboat
housefly
hummingbird
kickball
kneecap
knockout
knothole
lighthouse
necktie
nighttime
oatmeal
outsmart
pancake
popcorn
potpie
rainbow
raincoats
runway
sailboat
sandpaper
shipwreck
snowflake
snowman
sunflower
sunrise
sunset
sunshine
tugboat
weekend
wristwatch
yardstick

Spelling Words

backpack
baseball
bluebird
brainstorm
flashlight
herself
inside
lunchbox
outside
suitcase

High-Frequency/ Tested Words

picture
remember
room
stood
thought

Selection Words

biscuits
cookie
cradle
crocodile
curtain
idea

Henry and Mudge and Mrs. Hopper's House

Vowels *oo* in *moon*

afternoon
bloom
boost
boot
broom
coo
cool
coolly
droop
droopy
food
fool
gloomy
goose
hoops
hoot
loop
loose
moo
mood
noon
ooze
pooch
poodle
pool
proof
room
roost
school
smooth
snooze
snoozed
spool
spoon
spoonful
stool
too
tool
tooth
zoo
zoom
zoomed

Suffixes *-ly, -ful*

boastful
careful
cheerful
colorful
delightful
faithful
graceful
grateful
harmful
helpful
hopeful
painful
peaceful
playful
restful
roomful
shameful
spoonful
thankful
useful
wonderful

badly
bravely
brightly
carefully
completely
coolly
friendly
gladly
helpfully
hopefully
mainly
neatly
nicely
peacefully
perfectly
plainly
quickly
quietly
really
sadly
safely
sharply
slowly
smoothly
softly
suddenly
sweetly
wildly

Spelling Words

careful
gladly
nicely
painful
playful
quickly
sadly
slowly
useful
wonderful

High-Frequency/ Tested Words

across
because
dance
only
opened
shoes
told

Selection Words

gargoyle
heart
shiny
tuxedo
Valentine's Day
waltz

Tippy-Toe Chick, Go!

Diphthong *ow/ou/*

brow, brown, chow, clown, clowns, cow, crowd, crown, down, drown, flower, fowl, frown, frowned, gown, growl, growling, how, howl, now, plow, powder, prowl, scowl, shower, tower, town, wow

Syllables *C + le*

able, babble, baffle, battle, bottle, bubble, bundle, candle, cattle, crinkle, cuddle, dangle, dimple, double, giggle, huddle, hurdle, jingle, juggle, jungle, little, middle, muzzle, paddle, peddle, purple, puzzle, rattle, riddle, rumble, saddle, sample, settle, simple, startle, tattle, thimble, trouble, tumble, turtle, uncle, waddle, wriggle, wrinkle

Spelling Words

brown, clown, cow, crowd, down, frown, growl, how, now, town

High-Frequency/ Tested Words

along, behind, eyes, never, pulling, toward

Selection Words

breath, disagreed, favorite, potato bugs, tippy-toe

Mole and the Baby Bird

Diphthong *ou/ou/*

about, bounce, cloud, cloudy, couch, count, counted, doubt, found, grouch, ground, hound, houses, loud, mouse, mouth, ouch, out, outside, pouch, pound, pout, proud, round, shout, shouted, slouch, sound, south, trout, underground

Syllables VCV

baby, basin, begins, below, bonus, cozy, decent, frozen, human, humid, lazy, Mabel, moment, motel, music, opens, opened, over, pilot, pony, pupil, robot, silence, siren, sofa, taken, tiger, tulip, zebra

cabin, camel, clever, ever, dragon, finish, forest, habit, lemon, limit, limits, model, never, river, robin, salad, second, seven, shadow, talent, talents, travel, value, vanish, visit, wagon

Spelling Words

cloud, count, found, house, mouth, ouch, our, out, round, shout

High-Frequency/ Tested Words

door, loved, should, wood

Selection Words

borrowed, presently, usually

Dot & Jabber and the Great Acorn Mystery

Vowels *oo* as in *book*

book, books, brook, cook, crook, crooks, foot, good, hood, hoof, hook, look, nook, roof, shook, stood, took, wood, Woody

Inflected Endings *(drop e before -ed, -ing)*

arrived, baking, blamed, chasing, chimed, choked, closing, danced, dancing, dined, glided, hiding, hiking, hoped, hoping, joking, liked, living, loved, loving, named, placing, poked, raced, riding, rising, ruled, saved, saving, shaking, skated, skating, sliced, smiled, smiling, solved, stared, surprised, surprising, tamed, taming, tired, waved

Spelling Words

book, food, foot, good, look, moon, noon, pool, took, zoo

High-Frequency/ Tested Words

among, another, instead, none

Selection Words

detectives, hey, hurray, meadow, million, mystery, solve

Simple Machines

Diphthongs *oi, oy*

avoid
boil
broil
broiler
choice
coil
coin
foil
hoist
join
joiner
joint
moist
noise
noisy
oil
oink
oinks
pointer
points
poison
soil
spoil
toil
voice
void

annoy
boy
cowboy
enjoy
Floyd
joy
ploy
Roy
royal
soy
toy

Suffixes *-er, -or*

actor
ballplayer
beeper
broiler
buzzer
catcher
cleaners
collector
conductor
dancer
director
editor
farmer
governor
helper
inspector
inventor
joiner
leader
mower
opener
painter
player
pointer
reporter
runner
sailor
singer
speaker
starter
swimmer
teacher
visitor
winner
writer

Spelling Words

boil
boy
coin
join
oil
oink
point
soil
toy
voice

High-Frequency/ Tested Words

against
goes
heavy
kinds
today

Selection Words

axles
inclined planes
lawn
machines
pulleys
surface
vacuum

Alexander Graham Bell

Short *e: ea*

ahead
bread
breakfast
breath
dead
deaf
dealt
dread
feather
head
health
heavy
instead
leather
meant
read
ready
spread
sweat
sweater
thread
threat
tread
wealth
weather

Vowels *aw, au*

awesome
awful
awning
brawl
caw
crawl
dawn
draw
draws
fawn
flaw
hawk
jaw
law
lawn
paw
pawn
paws
raw
saw
sprawl
squawk
straw
tawny
thaw
yawn
yawns

applaud
auto
autos
cause
fault
flaunt
fraud
haul
haunt
launch
Maude
pause
sauce
saucer
taught

Spelling Words

crawl
draw
hawk
jaw
law
lawn
paw
saw
straw
yawn

High-Frequency/ Tested Words

built
early
learn
science
through

Selection Words

Boston
communicate
electricity
famous
piano
Scotland
telephone

Ben Franklin and His First Kite

Prefixes *un-, re-*

unafraid
uncap
unchain
unclean
undo
undress
unfold
unhappy
unhelpful
unkind
unlike
unload
unlock
unlucky
unmade
unmake
unmanned
unpack
unplug
unsafe
unseen
unsure
untie
untold
untrue
unwind
unzip

recheck
recycle
redraw
reheat
remade
remake
renew
repack
reprint
repaint
replace
replant
replay
reread
resend
restart
retest
rethink
retold
reuse
revisit
rewind
rewrite

Long Vowels *i, o*

host
most
post
poster

bold
cold
fold
gold
hold
mold
old
refold
scold
ten-year-old
told
unfold
behind
blind
kind
mind
rind
wind
unwinds

child
mild
wild

Spelling Words

refill
refund
reopen
repay
retell
undo
undress
unhappy
unkind
untie

High-Frequency/ Tested Words

answered
brothers
carry
different
poor

Selection Words

amazing
harbor
hasty pudding
hearth
invention

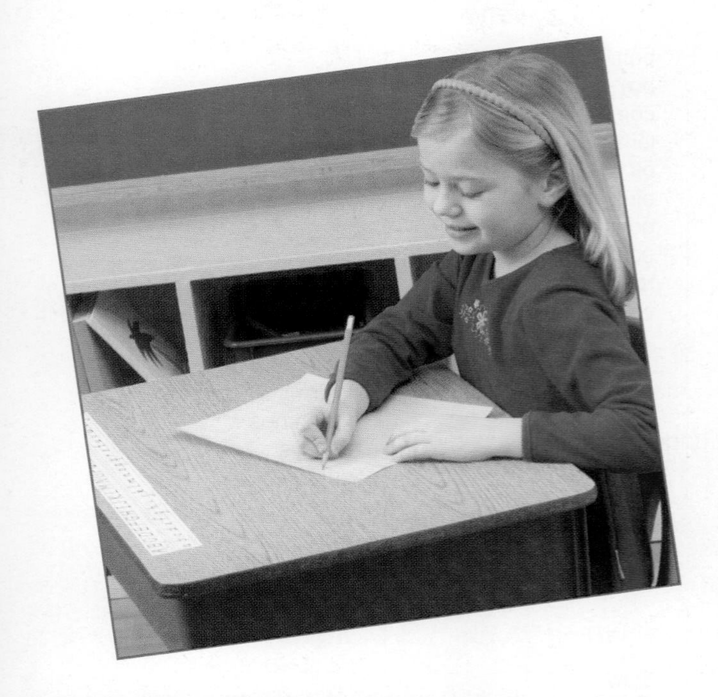

Position for Writing

Left-handed and right-handed writers slant their papers differently from one another, but they sit and hold their pencils the same way.

Body Position

- Children should sit tall, with both feet flat on the floor and arms relaxed on a table or desk.
- Children should hold their papers with their non-writing hand.

Paper Slant

- Paper should be positioned at a slant that is approximately parallel to the writing arm.
- For left-handed children, the paper should slant from the right at the top to the left at the bottom.
- Right-handed children should slant the paper from the left at the top to the right at the bottom.

Pencil Grip

- Children should grasp the pencil lightly between the thumb and index finger, usually about an inch above the pencil point.
- For a child who grasps the pencil too close to the point, a simple remedy is to wrap a rubber band around the pencil about an inch above the point. Have the child hold the pencil above the rubber band.

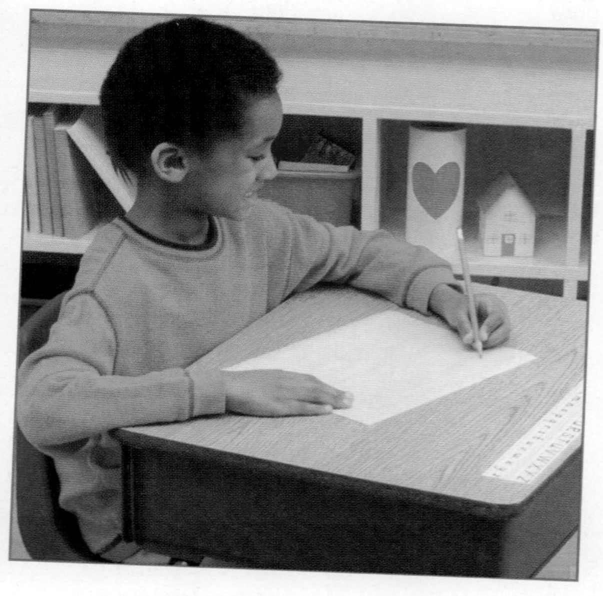

Legibility

Legibility should be the goal of handwriting instruction. Children should be praised for writing legibly, even though their writing may deviate from a perfect model. Legibility is based on flexible but standard criteria for letter form, size, and slant, and for letter and word spacing.

Letter Form

- Standards for letter form enable each letter to be distinguished clearly from other letters.
- In the letter *a*, for example, the round part of the letter must be open, and the letter must be closed at the top. The letter *a* must not be confused with *u, d,* or *o.*
- The letters *t* and *f* must be crossed; the letters *i* and *j* dotted.

Letter Size

- Small letters sit on the bottom line and touch the middle line.
- Tall letters sit on the bottom line and touch the top line.
- Letters with descenders have tails that go down under the bottom line and touch the line below.

Letter Slant

- Letter slant should be consistent.
- All letters may slant to the right, to the left, or be straight up and down.

Letter and Word Spacing

- Letters in a word should be evenly spaced. They should not be written too close together or too far apart.
- There should be more space between words in a sentence than between letters in a word. This allows each word to stand out.

Mario

Hints for Handwriting Instruction

My Name

You might want to give each child a model of his or her name, written on heavy paper or cardboard. It can be placed on the child's table for reference.

Handwriting Center

You may want to set up a handwriting center in your classroom. Include the following materials:

- many different colors and types of pencils
- many different colors and types of paper
- a picture file with a picture for each upper- and lower-case letter
- write-on/wipe-off boards
- a sandbox or container of sand in which children can finger trace letters
- a chalkboard, with chalk and an eraser

Encouraging Neatness

From the beginning, encourage children to cross out incorrect letters instead of erasing them. Young children tend to erase long and hard. This makes for messy papers that sometimes end up with holes in them. This can be upsetting for the child. By simply crossing out letters, pupils have neater papers and can learn from the mistakes they have made.

D'Nealian™ Alphabet

a b c d e f g h i
j k l m n o p q r s t
u v w x y z

A B C D E F G
H I J K L M N O
P Q R S T U V
W X Y Z . , ' ?

1 2 3 4 5 6
7 8 9 10

Manuscript Alphabet

Unit 3 *Changes*

To Read Aloud!	Below-Level	On-Level	Advanced
An Egg Is an Egg			
The Growing-Up Tree by Vera Rosenberry (Holiday House, 2003) Over the years a tree and a boy grow together in this warm, simple story that explores the idea of generations.	**That's Hard, That's Easy** by Margery Bernstein (Millbrook, 1998) A little girl notices that many of the things that were once hard to do are now easy since she's gotten older.	**Tadpoles** by Betsy James (E.P. Dutton, 1999) As Molly watches frog eggs change into tadpoles, she also notices her baby brother change and grow.	**Mama, Do You Love Me?** by Barbara M. Joosse (Scholastic, 1991) In this beautiful story, an Inuit daughter discovers her mother's love for her through time.
Ruby in Her Own Time			
Ferdinand the Bull by Munro Leaf (Puffin, 1977) A little Spanish bull would rather sit and smell the flowers than fight.	**Leo the Late Bloomer** by Robert Kraus (Harcourt, 1971) Leo isn't reading, or writing, or even speaking, and his father is concerned. But Leo's mother knows he will do all those things, and more, when he's ready.	**Borka: The Adventures of a Goose with No Feathers** by John Burningham (Dragonfly, 1994) Borka is a goose born without feathers. Rejected by her family and by other geese, she sets out to find her place in the world.	**Across the Stream** by Mirra Ginsburg (Scholastic, 1982) A hen and her chicks—with the help of a duck and her ducklings—find a way to put their bad dreams behind them!
Jan's New Home			
Alexander, Who's Not (Do You Hear Me? I Mean It!) Going to Move by Judith Viorst (Atheneum, 1995) Alexander is horrified at the prospect of moving 1,000 miles away in this raucous picture book.	**My Best Friend Moved Away** by Nancy Carlson (Viking, 2001) A girl is convinced that she will never have fun again after her best friend moves away.	**Where's Jamela?** by Niki Daly (Farrar Straus Giroux, 2004) Jamela's mom gets a new job. When she and her mom must move away, Jamela is sad to say good-bye to everything she knows.	**Leaving Morning** by Angela Johnson (Orchard Books, 1992) This is the story of what happens to two sisters whose family is moving from the neighborhood.
"The Garden" *from* Frog and Toad Together			
A Gardener's Alphabet by Mary Azarian (Houghton Mifflin, 2000) From arbor to zucchini, students can grow their vocabularies through this lovely book.	**Jack's Garden** by Henry Cole (Greenwillow, 1995) Through the cumulative text, this book presents the growth of a garden.	**Flower Garden** by Eve Bunting (Harcourt Brace, 1994) A young African American girl and her father together plant a window-box garden as a surprise for her mother.	**All About Seeds** by Susan Kuchalla (Troll, 1989) This book teaches about seeds and how they grow and change.
I'm a Caterpillar			
Where Butterflies Grow by Joanne Ryder (Puffin, 1989) This book describes what it feels like to change from a caterpillar into a butterfly and includes gardening tips to attract butterflies.	**I Like Bugs** by Margaret Wise Brown (Golden Books, 1999) This is a rhyming book about bugs.	**What Do You See?** by Rozanne Lanczak Williams (Harcourt, 1997) A caterpillar changes into a butterfly.	**Ten Little Caterpillars** by Avelyn Davidson (Rigby, 1993) This is a caterpillar-counting adventure.
Where Are My Animal Friends?			
In November by Cynthia Rylant (Harcourt, 2000) In this descriptive and poetic text, birds, animals, and people experience the cold as fall gives way to winter.	**Snow** by Manya Stojic (Alfred A. Knopf, 2002) As snow approaches and begins to fall, Moose, Bear, Fox, and other forest creatures prepare for winter.	**Every Autumn Comes the Bear** by Jim Arnosky (Putnam, 1993) Every autumn a bear shows up behind the farm and goes through a series of routines before finding a den for the winter.	**Last Leaf First Snowflake to Fall** by Leo Yerxa (Scholastic, 1994) An Indian parent and child move through the forest and over a pond, observing the changes as nature passes from fall to winter.

See also *Assessment Handbook*, p 115

Unit 3 Reading Log

Name ______________________

Dates Read	Title and Author	What is it about?	How would you rate it?	Explain your rating.
From ________ to ________			Great Awful 5 4 3 2 1	
From ________ to ________			Great Awful 5 4 3 2 1	
From ________ to ________			Great Awful 5 4 3 2 1	
From ________ to ________			Great Awful 5 4 3 2 1	
From ________ to ________			Great Awful 5 4 3 2 1	

See also *Assessment Handbook*, p 109

Unit 3 Narrative Retelling Chart

Selection Title ______________________ **Name** ______________________ **Date** __________

Retelling Criteria/Teacher Prompt	**Teacher-Aided Response**	**Student-Generated Response**	**Rubric Score** (Circle one.)
Connections Does this story remind you of anything else?			4 3 2 1
Author's Purpose Why do you think the author wrote this story? What was the author trying to tell us?			4 3 2 1
Characters What can you tell me about ________ (use character's name)?			4 3 2 1
Setting Where and when did the story happen?			4 3 2 1
Plot What happened in the story?			4 3 2 1

Summative Retelling Score 4 3 2 1

Comments ____

See also *Assessment Handbook*, p 110

Unit 3 Expository Retelling Chart

Selection Title ______________________ **Name** ______________________ **Date** __________

Retelling Criteria/Teacher Prompt	**Teacher-Aided Response**	**Student-Generated Response**	**Rubric Score** (Circle one.)
Connections Did this selection make you think about something else you have read? What did you learn about as you read this selection?			4 3 2 1
Author's Purpose Why do you think the author wrote this selection?			4 3 2 1
Topic What was the selection mostly about?			4 3 2 1
Important Ideas What is important for me to know about ________ (topic)?			4 3 2 1
Conclusions What did you learn from reading this selection?			4 3 2 1

Summative Retelling Score 4 3 2 1

Comments ____

____

____

Reading

Concepts of Print and Print Awareness	Pre-K	K	1	2	3	4	5	6
Develop awareness that print represents spoken language and conveys and preserves meaning	•	•	•					
Recognize familiar books by their covers; hold book right side up	•	•						
Identify parts of a book and their functions (front cover, title page/title, back cover, page numbers)	•	•	•					
Understand the concepts of letter, word, sentence, paragraph, and story	•	•	•					
Track print (front to back of book, top to bottom of page, left to right on line, sweep back left for next line)	•	•	•					
Match spoken to printed words	•	•	•					
Know capital and lowercase letter names and match them	•	• T	•					
Know the order of the alphabet	•	•	•					
Recognize first name in print	•	•	•					
Recognize the uses of capitalization and punctuation		•	•					
Value print as a means of gaining information	•	•	•					

Phonological and Phonemic Awareness	Pre-K	K	1	2	3	4	5	6
Phonological Awareness								
Recognize and produce rhyming words	•	•	•					
Track and count each word in a spoken sentence and each syllable in a spoken word	•	•	•					
Segment and blend syllables in spoken words			•					
Segment and blend onset and rime in one-syllable words		•	•					
Recognize and produce words beginning with the same sound	•	•	•					
Identify beginning, middle, and/or ending sounds that are the same or different	•	•	•					
Understand that spoken words are made of sequences of sounds	•	•	•					
Phonemic Awareness								
Identify the position of sounds in words		•	•					
Identify and isolate initial, final, and medial sounds in spoken words	•	•	•					
Blend sounds orally to make words or syllables		•	•					
Segment a word or syllable into sounds; count phonemes in spoken words or syllables		•	•					
Manipulate sounds in words (add, delete, and/or substitute phonemes)	•	•	•					

Phonics and Decoding	Pre-K	K	1	2	3	4	5	6
Phonics								
Understand and apply the ***alphabetic principle*** that spoken words are composed of sounds that are represented by letters	•	•	•					
Know letter-sound relationships	•	• T	• T	• T				
Blend sounds of letters to decode		•	• T	• T	• T			
Consonants, consonant blends, and consonant digraphs		•	• T	• T	• T			
Short, long, and r-controlled vowels; vowel digraphs; diphthongs; common vowel patterns			• T	• T	• T			
Phonograms/word families		•	•	•	•			
Word Structure								
Decode words with common word parts		•	• T	• T	• T	•	•	•
Base words and inflected endings			• T	• T	•	•	•	•
Contractions and compound words			• T	• T	• T	•	•	•
Suffixes and prefixes			• T	• T	• T	•	•	•
Greek and Latin roots						•	•	•
Blend syllables to decode words			• T	• T	• T	•	•	•
Decoding Strategies								
Blending strategy: Apply knowledge of letter-sound relationships to decode unfamiliar words		•	•	•	•			
Apply knowledge of word structure to decode unfamiliar words		•	•	•	•	•	•	•
Use context and syntax along with letter-sound relationships and word structure to decode		•	•	•	•	•	•	•
Self-correct			•	•	•	•	•	•

Fluency	Pre-K	K	1	2	3	4	5	6
Read aloud fluently with accuracy, comprehension, appropriate pace/rate; with expression/intonation (prosody); with attention to punctuation and appropriate phrasing			• T	• T	• T	• T	• T	• T
Practice fluency in a variety of ways, including choral reading, partner/paired reading, Readers' Theater, repeated oral reading, and tape-assisted reading		•	•	•	•	•	•	•

• instructional opportunity

T tested in standardized test form

	Pre-K	K	1	2	3	4	5	6
Work toward appropriate fluency goals by the end of each grade			• T	• T	• T	• T	• T	• T
Read regularly in independent-level material			•	•	•	•	•	•
Read silently for increasing periods of time			•	•	•	•	•	•

Vocabulary (Oral and Written)	Pre-K	K	1	2	3	4	5	6
Word Recognition								
Recognize regular and irregular high-frequency words	•	•	• T	• T				
Recognize and understand selection vocabulary		•	•	• T	•	•	•	•
Understand content-area vocabulary and specialized, technical, or topical words			•	•	•	•	•	•
Word Learning Strategies								
Develop vocabulary through direct instruction, concrete experiences, reading, listening to text read aloud	•	•	•	•	•	•	•	•
Use knowledge of word structure to figure out meanings of words			•	• T	• T	• T	• T	• T
Use context clues for meanings of unfamiliar words, multiple-meaning words, homonyms, homographs			•	• T	• T	• T	• T	• T
Use grade-appropriate reference sources to learn word meanings	•	•	•	•	• T	• T	• T	• T
Use picture clues to help determine word meanings	•	•	•	•	•			
Use new words in a variety of contexts	•	•	•	•	•	•	•	•
Examine word usage and effectiveness		•	•	•	•	•	•	•
Create and use graphic organizers to group, study, and retain vocabulary			•	•	•	•	•	•
Extend Concepts and Word Knowledge								
Academic language	•	•	•	•	•	•	•	•
Classify and categorize	•	•	•	•	•	•	•	•
Antonyms and synonyms			•	• T	• T	• T	• T	• T
Homographs, homonyms, and homophones				•	• T	• T	• T	• T
Multiple-meaning words			•	•	• T	• T	• T	• T
Related words and derivations					•	•	•	•
Analogies					•		•	
Connotation/denotation						•	•	•
Figurative language and idioms			•	•	•	•	•	•
Descriptive words (location, size, color, shape, number, ideas, feelings)	•	•	•	•	•	•	•	•
High-utility words (shapes, colors, question words, position/directional words, and so on)	•	•	•	•				
Time and order words	•	•	•	•	•	•	•	•
Transition words						•	•	•
Word origins: Etymologies/word histories; words from other languages, regions, or cultures					•	•	•	•
Shortened forms: abbreviations, acronyms, clipped words			•	•	•	•	• T	

Text Comprehension	Pre-K	K	1	2	3	4	5	6
Comprehension Strategies								
Preview the text and formulate questions	•	•	•	•	•	•	•	•
Set and monitor purpose for reading and listening	•	•	•	•	•	•	•	•
ctivate and use prior knowledge	•	•	•	•	•	•	•	•
Make predictions	•	•	•	•	•	•	•	•
Monitor comprehension and use fix-up strategies to resolve difficulties in meaning: adjust reading rate, eread and read on, seek help from reference sources and/or other people, skim and scan, summarize, se text features			•	•	•	•	•	•
Create and use graphic and semantic organizers		•	•	•	•	•	•	•
Answer questions (text explicit, text implicit, scriptal), including *who, what, when, where, why, what if, how*	•	•	•	•	•	•	•	•
Look back in text for answers			•	•	•	•	•	•
Answer test-like questions			•	•	•	•	•	•
Generate clarifying questions, including *who, what, where, when, how, why,* and *what if*	•	•	•	•	•	•	•	•
Recognize text structure: story and informational (cause/effect, chronological, compare/contrast, escription, problem/solution, propostion/support)	•	•	•	•	•	•	•	•
Summarize text		•	•	•	•	•	•	•
Recall and retell stories	•	•	•	•	•	•	•	•
Identify and retell important/main ideas (nonfiction)	•	•	•	•	•	•	•	•
Identify and retell new information			•	•	•	•	•	•
isualize; use mental imagery		•	•	•	•	•	•	•
se strategies flexibly and in combination			•	•	•	•	•	•

Comprehension Skills								
Author's purpose			• T	• T	• T	• T	• T	• T
Author's viewpoint/bias/perspective					•	•	•	• T
Categorize and classify	•	•	•	•				
Cause and effect		•	• T	• T	• T	• T	• T	• T
Compare and contrast		•	• T	• T	• T	• T	• T	• T
Details and facts		•	•	•	•	•	•	•
Draw conclusions		•	• T	• T	• T	• T	• T	• T
Fact and opinion				• T	• T	• T	• T	• T
Follow directions/steps in a process	•	•	•	•	•	•	•	•
Generalize					• T	• T	• T	• T
Graphic sources		•	•	•	•	• T	• T	• T
Main idea and supporting details		• T	• T	• T	• T	• T	• T	• T
Paraphrase			•	•	•	•	•	•
Persuasive devices and propaganda				•	•	•	•	•
Realism/fantasy		•	• T	• T	• T	•	•	•
Sequence of events		• T	• T	• T	• T	• T	• T	• T
Higher Order Thinking Skills								
Analyze				•	•	•	•	•
Describe and connect the essential ideas, arguments, and perspectives of a text			•	•	•	•	•	•
Draw inferences, conclusions, or generalizations, support them with textual evidence and prior knowledge		•	•	•	•	•	•	•
Evaluate and critique ideas and text			•	•	•	•	•	•
Hypothesize						•	•	•
Make judgments about ideas and text			•	•	•	•	•	•
Organize and synthesize ideas and information			•			•	•	•
Literary Analysis, Response, & Appreciation	**Pre-K**	**K**	**1**	**2**	**3**	**4**	**5**	**6**
Genre and Its Characteristics								
Recognize characteristics of a variety of genre	•	•	•	•	•	•	•	•
Distinguish fiction from nonfiction		•	•	•	•	•	•	•
Identify characteristics of literary texts, including drama, fantasy, traditional tales		•	•	•	•	•	•	•
Identify characteristics of nonfiction texts, including biography, interviews, newspaper articles		•	•	•	•	•	•	•
Identify characteristics of poetry and song, including nursery rhymes, limericks, blank verse	•	•	•	•	•	•	•	•
Literary Elements and Story Structure								
Character	•	• T	• T	• T	• T	• T	• T	•
Recognize and describe traits, actions, feelings, and motives of characters		•	•	•	•	•	•	•
Analyze characters' relationships, changes, and points of view		•	•	•	•	•	•	•
Analyze characters' conflicts				•		•	•	•
Plot and plot structure	•	• T	• T	• T	• T	• T	• T	•
Beginning, middle, end	•	•	•	•	•			
Goal and outcome or problem and solution/resolution		•	•	•	•	•	•	•
Rising action, climax, and falling action/denouement; setbacks						•	•	•
Setting	•	• T	• T	• T	• T	• T	•	•
Relate setting to problem/solution						•	•	•
Explain ways setting contributes to mood						•	•	•
Theme		•	• T	• T	•	•	•	•
Use Literary Elements and Story Structure	•	•	•	•	•	•	•	•
Analyze and evaluate author's use of setting, plot, character				•	•	•	•	•
Identify similarities and differences of characters, events, and settings within or across selections/cultures		•	•	•	•	•	•	•
Literary Devices								
Allusion								•
Dialect						•	•	•
Dialogue and narration	•	•	•	•	•	•	•	•
Exaggeration/hyperbole					•	•	•	•
Figurative language: idiom, jargon, metaphor, simile, slang			•	•	•	•	•	•

• instructional opportunity **T** tested in standardized test forr

Flashback						•	•	•
Foreshadowing							•	•
Formal and informal language				•	•	•	•	•
Humor					•	•	•	•
Imagery and sensory words			•	•	•	•	•	•
Mood				•	•		•	•
Personification				•	•	•	•	•
Point of view (first person, third person, omniscient)					•	•	•	•
Puns and word play				•	•	•	•	•
Sound devices and poetic elements	•	•	•	•	•	•	•	•
Alliteration, assonance, onomatopoeia	•	•	•	•	•	•	•	•
Rhyme, rhythm, repetition, and cadence	•	•	•	•	•	•	•	•
Word choice				•	•	•	•	•
Symbolism				•	•	•	•	•
Tone							•	•
Author's and Illustrator's Craft								
Distinguish the roles of author and illustrator		•	•	•				
Recognize/analyze author's and illustrator's craft or style			•	•	•	•	•	•
Literary Response								
Recollect, talk, and write about books	•	•	•	•	•	•	•	•
Reflect on reading and respond (through talk, movement, art, and so on)	•	•	•	•	•	•	•	•
Ask and answer questions about text	•	•	•	•	•	•	•	•
Write about what is read	•	•	•	•	•	•	•	•
Use evidence from the text to support opinions, interpretations, or conclusions		•	•	•	•	•	•	•
Support ideas through reference to other texts and personal knowledge				•	•	•	•	•
Locate materials on related topic, theme, or idea				•	•	•	•	•
Generate alternative endings to plots and identify the reason for, and the impact of, the alternatives	•	•	•	•	•	•	•	•
Synthesize and extend the literary experience through creative responses	•	•	•	•	•	•	•	•
Make connections: text to self, text to text, text to world	•	•	•	•	•	•	•	•
Evaluate and critique the quality of the literary experience				•	•	•	•	•
Offer observations, react, speculate in response to text				•	•	•	•	•
Literary Appreciation/Motivation								
Show an interest in books and reading; engage voluntarily in social interaction about books	•	•	•	•	•	•	•	•
Choose text by drawing on personal interests, relying on knowledge of authors and genres, estimating text difficulty, and using recommendations of others	•	•	•	•	•	•	•	•
Read a variety of grade-level appropriate narrative and expository texts		•	•	•	•	•	•	•
Read from a wide variety of genres for a variety of purposes	•	•	•	•	•	•	•	•
Read independently			•	•	•	•	•	•
Establish familiarity with a topic			•	•	•	•	•	•
Cultural Awareness								
Develop attitudes and abilities to interact with diverse groups and cultures	•	•	•	•	•	•	•	•
Connect experiences and ideas with those from a variety of languages, cultures, customs, perspectives	•	•	•	•	•	•	•	•
Understand how attitudes and values in a culture or during a period in time affect the writing from that culture or time period						•	•	•
Compare language and oral traditions (family stories) that reflect customs, regions, and cultures		•	•	•	•	•	•	•
Recognize themes that cross cultures and bind them together in their common humanness						•	•	•

Language Arts

Writing	Pre-K	K	1	2	3	4	5	6
Concepts of Print for Writing								
Develop gross and fine motor skills and hand/eye coordination	•	•	•					
Print own name and other important words	•	•	•					
Write using pictures, some letters, and transitional spelling to convey meaning	•	•	•					
Dictate messages or stories for others to write	•	•	•					

	Pre-K	K	1	2	3	4	5	6
Create own written texts for others to read; write left to right on a line and top to bottom on a page	•	•	•					
Participate in shared and interactive writing	•	•	•					
Traits of Writing								
Focus/Ideas								
Maintain focus and sharpen ideas		•	•	•	•	•	•	•
Use sensory details and concrete examples; elaborate		•	•	•	•	•	•	•
Delete extraneous information			•	•	•	•	•	•
Rearrange words and sentences to improve meaning and focus				•	•	•	•	•
Use strategies, such as tone, style, consistent point of view, to achieve a sense of completeness						•	•	•
Organization/Paragraphs								
Use graphic organizers to group ideas		•	•	•	•	•	•	•
Write coherent paragraphs that develop a central idea			•	•	•	•	•	•
Use transitions to connect sentences and paragraphs			•	•	•	•	•	•
Select an organizational structure based on purpose, audience, length						•	•	•
Organize ideas in a logical progression, such as chronological order or by order of importance		•	•	•	•	•	•	•
Write introductory, supporting, and concluding paragraphs					•	•	•	•
Write a multi-paragraph paper				•	•	•	•	•
Voice								
Develop personal, identifiable voice and an individual tone/style			•	•	•	•	•	•
Maintain consistent voice and point of view						•	•	•
Use voice appropriate to audience, message, and purpose						•	•	•
Word Choice								
Use clear, precise, appropriate language		•	•	•	•	•	•	•
Use figurative language and vivid words				•	•	•	•	•
Select effective vocabulary using word walls, dictionary, or thesaurus		•	•	•	•	•	•	•
Sentences								
Combine, elaborate, and vary sentences		•	•	•	•	•	•	•
Write topic sentence, supporting sentences with facts and details, and concluding sentence			•	•	•	•	•	•
Use correct word order				•	•	•	•	•
Use parallel structure in a sentence							•	•
Conventions								
Use correct spelling and grammar; capitalize and punctuate correctly		•	•	•	•	•	•	•
Correct sentence fragments and run-ons					•	•	•	•
Use correct paragraph indention				•	•	•	•	•
The Writing Process								
Prewrite using various strategies	•	•	•	•	•	•	•	•
Develop first drafts of single- and multiple-paragraph compositions		•	•	•	•	•	•	•
Revise drafts for varied purposes, including to clarify and to achieve purpose, sense of audience, precise word choice, vivid images, and elaboration		•	•	•	•	•	•	•
Edit and proofread for correct spelling, grammar, usage, and mechanics		•	•	•	•	•	•	•
Publish own work	•	•	•	•	•	•	•	•
Types of Writing								
Narrative writing (such as personal narratives, stories, biographies, autobiographies)	•	•	• T	• T	• T	• T	• T	• T
Expository writing (such as essays, directions, explanations, news stories, research reports, summaries)		•	• T	• T	• T	• T	• T	• T
Descriptive writing (such as labels, captions, lists, plays, poems, response logs, songs)	•	•	• T	• T	• T	• T	• T	• T
Persuasive writing (such as ads, editorials, essays, letters to the editor, opinions, posters)		•	• T	• T	• T	• T	• T	• T
Writing Habits and Practices								
Write on a daily basis	•	•	•	•	•	•	•	•
Use writing as a tool for learning and self-discovery				•	•	•	•	•
Write independently for extended periods of time			•	•	•	•	•	•

ENGLISH LANGUAGE CONVENTIONS in WRITING and SPEAKING	Pre-K	K	1	2	3	4	5	6
Grammar and Usage in Speaking and Writing								
Sentences								
Types (declarative, interrogative, exclamatory, imperative)	•	•	• T	• T	• T	• T	• T	• T
Structure (simple, compound, complex, compound-complex)	•	•	•	•	•	• T	• T	• T

• instructional opportunity T tested in standardized test for[mat]

	Pre-K	K	1	2	3	4	5	6
Parts (subjects/predicates: complete, simple, compound; phrases; clauses)				• T	•	• T	• T	• T
Fragments and run-on sentences		•	•	•	•	•	•	•
Combine sentences, elaborate			•	•	•	•	•	•
Parts of speech: nouns, verbs and verb tenses, adjectives, adverbs, pronouns and antecedents, conjunctions, prepositions, interjections		•	• T	• T	• T	• T	• T	• T
Usage								
Subject-verb agreement		•	• T	•	•	• T	• T	• T
Pronoun agreement/referents			• T	•	•	• T	• T	• T
Misplaced modifiers						•	• T	• T
Misused words					•	•	•	• T
Negatives; avoid double negatives					•	•	•	•
Mechanics in Writing								
Capitalization (first word in sentence, proper nouns and adjectives, pronoun *I*, titles, and so on)	•	•	• T	• T	• T	• T	• T	• T
Punctuation (apostrophe, comma, period, question mark, exclamation mark, quotation marks, and so on)		•	• T	• T	• T	• T	• T	• T
Spelling	**Pre-K**	**K**	**1**	**2**	**3**	**4**	**5**	**6**
Spell independently by using pre-phonetic knowledge, knowledge of letter names, sound-letter knowledge	•	•	•	•	•	•	•	•
Use sound-letter knowledge to spell	•	•	•	•	•	•	•	•
Consonants: single, double, blends, digraphs, silent letters, and unusual consonant spellings		•	•	•	•	•	•	•
Vowels: short, long, *r*-controlled, digraphs, diphthongs, less common vowel patterns, schwa		•	•	•	•	•	•	•
Use knowledge of word structure to spell			•	•	•	•	•	•
Base words and affixes (inflections, prefixes, suffixes), possessives, contractions and compound words			•	•	•	•	•	•
Greek and Latin roots, syllable patterns, multisyllabic words			•	•	•	•	•	•
Spell high-frequency, irregular words		•	•	•	•	•	•	•
Spell frequently misspelled words correctly, including homophones or homonyms			•	•	•	•	•	•
Use meaning relationships to spell					•	•	•	•
Handwriting	**Pre-K**	**K**	**1**	**2**	**3**	**4**	**5**	**6**
Gain increasing control of penmanship, including pencil grip, paper position, posture, stroke	•	•	•	•				
Write legibly, with control over letter size and form; letter slant; and letter, word, and sentence spacing		•	•	•	•	•	•	•
Write lowercase and capital letters	•	•	•	•				
Manuscript	•	•	•	•	•	•	•	•
Cursive				•	•	•	•	•
Write numerals	•	•	•					
Listening and Speaking	**Pre-K**	**K**	**1**	**2**	**3**	**4**	**5**	**6**
Listening Skills and Strategies								
Listen to a variety of presentations attentively and politely	•	•	•	•	•	•	•	•
Self-monitor comprehension while listening, using a variety of skills and strategies	•	•	•	•	•	•	•	•
Listen for a purpose								
For enjoyment and appreciation	•	•	•	•	•	•	•	•
To expand vocabulary and concepts	•	•	•	•	•	•	•	•
To obtain information and ideas	•	•	•	•	•	•	•	•
To follow oral directions	•	•	•	•	•	•	•	•
To answer questions and solve problems	•	•	•	•	•	•	•	•
To participate in group discussions	•	•	•	•	•	•	•	•
To identify and analyze the musical elements of literary language	•	•	•	•	•	•	•	•
To gain knowledge of one's own culture, the culture of others, and the common elements of cultures	•	•	•	•	•	•	•	•
Recognize formal and informal language			•	•	•	•	•	•
Listen critically to distinguish fact from opinion and to analyze and evaluate ideas, information, experiences		•		•	•	•	•	•
Evaluate a speaker's delivery				•	•	•	•	•
Interpret a speaker's purpose, perspective, persuasive techniques, verbal and nonverbal messages, and use of rhetorical devices					•	•	•	•
Speaking Skills and Strategies								
Speak clearly, accurately, and fluently, using appropriate delivery for a variety of audiences, and purposes	•	•	•	•	•	•	•	•
Use proper intonation, volume, pitch, modulation, and phrasing		•	•	•	•	•	•	•
Speak with a command of standard English conventions	•	•	•	•	•	•	•	•
Use appropriate language for formal and informal settings	•	•	•	•	•	•	•	•

Speak for a purpose								
To ask and answer questions	•	•	•	•	•	•	•	•
To give directions and instructions	•	•	•	•	•	•	•	•
To retell, paraphrase, or explain information		•	•	•	•	•	•	•
To communicate needs and share ideas and experiences	•	•	•	•	•	•	•	•
To participate in conversations and discussions	•	•	•	•	•	•	•	•
To express an opinion	•	•	•	•	•	•	•	•
To deliver dramatic recitations, interpretations, or performances	•	•	•	•	•	•	•	•
To deliver presentations or oral reports (narrative, descriptive, persuasive, and informational)	•	•	•	•	•	•	•	•
Stay on topic	•	•	•	•	•	•		•
Use appropriate verbal and nonverbal elements (such as facial expression, gestures, eye contact, posture)	•	•	•	•	•	•	•	•
Identify and/or demonstrate methods to manage or overcome communication anxiety						•	•	•

Viewing/Media	Pre-K	K	1	2	3	4	5	6
Interact with and respond to a variety of print and non-print media for a range of purposes	•	•	•	•	•	•	•	•
Compare and contrast print, visual, and electronic media					•	•	•	•
Analyze and evaluate media			•	•	•	•	•	•
Recognize purpose, bias, propaganda, and persuasive techniques in media messages			•	•	•	•	•	•

Research and Study Skills

Understand and Use Graphic Sources	Pre-K	K	1	2	3	4	5	6
Advertisement			•	•	•	•	•	•
Chart/table	•	•	•	•	•	•	•	•
Diagram/scale drawing			•	•	•	•	•	•
Graph (bar, circle, line, picture)		•	•	•	•	•	•	•
Illustration, photograph, caption, label	•	•	•	•	•	•	•	•
Map/globe	•	•	•	•	•	•	•	•
Order form/application						•	•	•
Poster/announcement	•	•	•	•	•	•	•	
Schedule						•	•	•
Sign	•	•	•	•		•		
Time line				•	•	•	•	•

Understand and Use Reference Sources	Pre-K	K	1	2	3	4	5	6
Know and use parts of a book to locate information	•	•	•	•	•	•	•	•
Use alphabetical order			•	•	•	•		
Understand purpose, structure, and organization of reference sources (print, electronic, media, Internet)	•	•	•	•	•	•	•	•
Almanac						•	•	•
Atlas		•		•	•	•	•	•
Card catalog/library database				•	•	•	•	•
Dictionary/glossary		•	•	•	• T	• T	• T	• T
Encyclopedia			•	•	•	•	•	•
Magazine/periodical				•	•	•	•	•
Newspaper and Newsletter			•	•	•	•	•	•
Readers' Guide to Periodical Literature						•	•	•
Technology (computer and non-computer electronic media)		•	•	•	•	•	•	•
Thesaurus				•	•	•	•	•

Study Skills and Strategies	Pre-K	K	1	2	3	4	5	6
Adjust reading rate			•	•	•	•	•	•
Clarify directions	•	•	•	•	•	•	•	•
Outline				•	•	•	•	•
Skim and scan			•	•	•	•	•	•
SQP3R						•	•	•
Summarize		•	•	•	•	•	•	•
Take notes, paraphrase, and synthesize			•	•	•	•	•	•
Use graphic and semantic organizers to organize information		•	•	•	•	•	•	•

• instructional opportunity

T tested in standardized test for

Test-Taking Skills and Strategies	Pre-K	K	1	2	3	4	5	6
Understand the question, the vocabulary of tests, and key words			•	•	•	•	•	•
Answer the question; use information from the text (stated or inferred)		•	•	•	•	•	•	•
Write across texts				•	•	•	•	•
Complete the sentence				•	•	•	•	•

Technology/New Literacies	Pre-K	K	1	2	3	4	5	6
Non-Computer Electronic Media								
Audio tapes/CDs, video tapes/DVDs	•	•	•	•	•	•	•	
Film, television, and radio		•	•	•	•	•	•	•
Computer Programs and Services: Basic Operations and Concepts								
Use accurate computer terminology	•	•	•	•	•	•	•	•
Create, name, locate, open, save, delete, and organize files		•	•	•	•	•	•	•
Use input and output devices (such as mouse, keyboard, monitor, printer, touch screen)	•	•	•	•	•	•	•	•
Use basic keyboarding skills		•	•	•	•	•	•	•
Responsible Use of Technology Systems and Software								
Work cooperatively and collaboratively with others; follow acceptable use policies	•	•	•	•	•	•	•	•
Recognize hazards of Internet searches			•	•	•	•	•	•
Respect intellectual property					•	•	•	•
Information and Communication Technologies: Information Acquisition								
Use electronic web (non-linear) navigation, online resources, databases, keyword searches			•	•	•	•	•	•
Use visual and non-textual features of online resources	•	•	•	•	•	•	•	•
Internet inquiry			•	•	•	•	•	•
Identify questions			•	•	•	•	•	•
Locate, select, and collect information			•	•	•	•	•	•
Analyze information			•	•	•	•	•	•
Evaluate electronic information sources for accuracy, relevance, bias				•	•	•	•	•
Understand bias/subjectivity of electronic content (about this site, author search, date created)					•	•	•	•
Synthesize information					•	•	•	•
Communicate findings				•	•	•	•	•
Use fix-up strategies (such as clicking *Back, Forward,* or *Undo;* redoing a search; trimming the URL)			•	•	•	•	•	•
Communication								
Collaborate, publish, present, and interact with others		•	•	•	•	•	•	•
Use online resources (e-mail, bulletin boards, newsgroups)			•	•	•	•	•	•
Use a variety of multimedia formats			•	•	•	•	•	•
Problem Solving								
Select the appropriate software for the task	•	•	•	•	•	•	•	•
Use technology resources for solving problems and making informed decisions			•	•	•	•	•	•
Determine when technology is useful				•	•	•	•	•

The Research Process	Pre-K	K	1	2	3	4	5	6
Choose and narrow the topic; frame and revise questions for inquiry		•	•	•	•	•	•	•
Choose and evaluate appropriate reference sources			•	•	•	•	•	•
Locate and collect information	•	•	•	•	•	•	•	•
Take notes/record findings				•	•	•	•	•
Combine and compare information				•	•	•	•	•
Evaluate, interpret, and draw conclusions about key information		•	•	•	•	•	•	•
Summarize information		•	•	•	•	•	•	•
Make an outline				•	•	•	•	•
Organize content systematically		•	•	•	•	•	•	•
Communicate information		•	•	•	•	•	•	•
Write and present a report			•	•	•	•	•	•
Include citations						•	•	•
Respect intellectual property/plagiarism						•	•	•
Select and organize visual aids		•	•	•	•	•	•	•

A

D

E

F

H

I

J

L

M

N

O

P

S

U

V

Teacher's Edition

Text
KWL Strategy: The KWL Interactive Reading Strategy was developed and is used by permission of Donna Ogle, National-Louis University, Evanston, Illinois, co-author of *Reading Today and Tomorrow*, Holt, Rinehart & Winston Publishers, 1988. (See also *The Reading Teacher*, February 1986, pp. 564–570.)

Artists
Daniel Moreton: cover, page i

Luciana Navarro Alves: page 93B

Jamie Smith: page 145B

Photographs
Every effort has been made to secure permission and provide appropriate credit for photographic material. The publisher deeply regrets any omission and pledges to correct errors called to its attention in subsequent editions.

Unless otherwise acknowledged, all photographs are the property of Scott Foresman, a division of Pearson Education.

Photo locators denoted as follows: Top (T), Center (C), Bottom (B), Left (L), Right (R), Background (Bkgd).

Page 39B: PhotoDisc

Page 68K (BCL, BCR): Getty Images

Page 69B: ©Susan Van Etten/PhotoEdit

TEACHER NOTES